S0-ADT-932

THE RYRIE STUDY BIBLE

NEW TESTAMENT

NEW AMERICAN STANDARD VERSION

With introductions, annotations, outlines, marginal references, subject index, harmony of the Gospels, maps and timeline charts

CHARLES CALDWELL RYRIE, Th.D., Ph.D.
Chairman, Department of Systematic Theology
Dallas Theological Seminary

MOODY PRESS
CHICAGO

© 1976 by
THE MOODY BIBLE INSTITUTE
OF CHICAGO

All rights reserved

The Scripture text of the New American Standard Bible and marginal references are used by permission of The Lockman Foundation, La Habra, California, © 1960, 1962, 1963, 1968, 1971, 1972, 1973, 1975. All rights reserved.

Library of Congress Cataloging in Publication Data

Bible. N. T. English. New American standard. 1976.
The Ryrie study Bible.

I. Ryrie, Charles Caldwell, 1925–
II. Title.

BS2095.N35 1976 225.5′2 76-20615
ISBN: 0-8024-7441-1

Designer: Ernst Reichl

Cover Design: Ray Lahikainen

Second Printing, 1977

Printed in the United States of America

CONTENTS

THE NAMES AND ORDER OF THE BOOKS OF THE NEW TESTAMENT

TO THE READER

The Bible is the greatest of all books; to study it is the noblest of all pursuits; to understand it, the highest of all goals. The *Ryrie Study Bible* is especially designed to help you achieve that goal.

Every time you read this Bible, whether carefully or casually, be sure to look at the notes at the bottom of the page. These are designed to illuminate and help you understand the verses you are reading. The notes provide a variety of helps: some furnish historical or archaeological background; others translate or interpret the text more clearly; some define words and doctrines; and many refer you to other passages which relate to the same subject.

When you wish to study a book of the Bible more systematically, you will want to read the Introduction to that book, which will give you information about the author, background, and contents. A unique feature of this Bible is the outline of each book printed at the end of each Introduction and also interspersed throughout the text. In this way you can readily see as you are reading through a book exactly where you are in the development of the ideas of that book by simply referring to the complete outline in the Introduction. The Introductions will help lead you into the messages of the books; the outlines will help you see the development of the messages; and the notes will help shed light on the messages.

In addition, you will find at the back of the Bible an index of the principal subjects treated in the notes. For example, if you want to study the doctrine of Christ, you will find in that index a list of references to notes where various aspects of that subject are mentioned. There is also a Harmony of the Gospels for use when you want to locate the several accounts of an event in the Gospels. Finally, the maps will enable you to see where these events took place.

Useful as helps can be, the most important thing is to read the Bible itself. This is God's Word to you. I pray that these notes will serve to make it clearer and more personally meaningful.

CHARLES CALDWELL RYRIE, Th.D., Ph.D.

Scriptural Promise

"The grass withers, the flower fades, but the word of our God stands forever." Isaiah 40:8

FOREWORD

The New American Standard Bible has been produced with the conviction that the words of Scripture as originally penned in the Hebrew and Greek were inspired by God. Since they are the eternal Word of God, the Holy Scriptures speak with fresh power to each generation, to give wisdom that leads to salvation, that men may serve Christ to the glory of God.

The Editorial Board had a twofold purpose in making this translation: to adhere as closely as possible to the original languages of the Holy Scriptures, and to make the translation in a fluent and readable style according to current English usage.

The Fourfold Aim of The Lockman Foundation

1. These publications shall be true to the original Hebrew and Greek.
2. They shall be grammatically correct.
3. They shall be understandable to the masses.
4. They shall give the Lord Jesus Christ His proper place, the place which the Word gives Him; therefore, no work will ever be personalized.

PRINCIPLES OF TRANSLATION

Greek text. Consideration was given to the latest available manuscripts with a view to determining the best Greek text. In most instances the 23rd edition of the Nestle Greek New Testament was followed.

Modern English usage. The attempt has been made to render the grammar and terminology in contemporary English. When it was felt that the word-for-word literalness was unacceptable to the modern reader, a change was made in the direction of a more current English idiom. In the instances where this has been done, the more literal rendering has been indicated in the notes.

Greek tenses.

1. A careful distinction has been made in the treatment of the Greek aorist tense (usually translated as the English past, "He did") and the Greek imperfect tense (rendered either as English past progressive, "He was doing"; or, if inceptive, as "He *began* to do" or "He started to do"); or else if customary past, as "He used to do." "Began" is italicized if it renders an imperfect tense, in order to distinguish it from the Greek verb for "begin."
2. On the other hand, not all aorists have been rendered as English pasts ("He did"), for some of them are clearly to be rendered as English perfects ("He has done"), or even as past perfects ("He had done"), judging from the context in which they occur. Such aorists have been rendered as perfects or past perfects in this translation.
3. As for the distinction between aorist and present imperatives, the translators have usually rendered these imperatives in the customary manner, rather than attempting any such fine distinction as, "Begin to do!" (for the aorist imperative), or, "Continually do!" (for the present imperative).
4. As for sequence of tenses, the translators took care to follow English rules rather than Greek in translating Greek presents, imperfects and aorists. Thus, where English says, "We knew that he was doing," Greek puts it, "We knew that he does"; similarly, "We knew that he had done," is the Greek, "We knew that he did." Likewise, the English, "When he had come, they met him," is represented in Greek by: "When he came, they met him." In all cases a consistent transfer has been made from the Greek tense in the subordinate clause to the appropriate tense in English.

5. In the rendering of negative questions introduced by the particle **mē** (which always expects the answer, "No") the wording has been altered from a mere, "Will he not do this?" to a more accurate, "He will not do this, will he?"

THE LOCKMAN FOUNDATION

EXPLANATION OF GENERAL FORMAT OF THE NEW AMERICAN STANDARD BIBLE

Cross references are placed in the outside column of the page and are listed under verse numbers to which they refer. Superior letters in the book refer to cross references. Cross references in italics indicate parallel passages.

Paragraphs are designated by boldface numbers.

Quotation marks are used in the text in accordance with modern English usage.

"Thou," "thy," and "thee" are changed to "you" except in the language of prayer when addressing Deity.

Personal pronouns are capitalized when pertaining to Deity.

Italics are used in the text to indicate words which are not found in the original Greek but are implied by it.

Small caps are used in the text to indicate Old Testament quotations.

Asterisks in the text indicate verbs that have been changed in tense. In regard to the use in Greek of the historical present, the translators recognized that in some contexts the present tense seems more unexpected and unjustified to the English reader than a past tense would have been. But Greek authors frequently used the present tense for the sake of heightened vividness, thereby transporting their readers in imagination to the actual scene at the time of occurrence. However, the translators felt that it would be wise to change these historical presents to English past tenses. Therefore verbs marked with an asterisk (*) represent historical presents in the Greek which have been translated with an English past tense in order to conform to modern usage.

The supernumerical notes usually included in the New American Standard Bible translation have been deleted in this edition, by permission of The Lockman Foundation.

ABBREVIATIONS AND SPECIAL MARKINGS

A.D.	*Anno Domini* (in the year of our Lord)
B.C.	Before Christ
cf.	*confer* (compare)
chap(s).	chapter(s)
e.g.	*exempli gratia* (for example)
f., ff.	following verse or verses
i.e.	*id est* (that is)
Lit.	A literal translation, literally
LXX	The Septuagint (Greek translation of the Old Testament)
ms., mss.	manuscript, manuscripts
N.T.	New Testament
Or	An alternate translation justified by the Greek.
O.T.	Old Testament
p., pp.	page, pages
ref(s).	reference(s)
v., vv.	verse, verses
[ ]	Brackets in the text are around words probably not in the original writings.
★	A five-pointed star preceding a verse or verses in the marginal notes indicates that this passage is treated in the footnotes.

INTRODUCTION TO THE NEW TESTAMENT

The name given to the second half of the English Bible is "the New Testament," which literally means "the New Covenant" (see Luke 22:20). The word *covenant* meant an arrangement made by one party which the other party involved could accept or reject but could not alter. The Old Testament primarily records God's dealings with Israel on the basis of the covenant given through Moses at Mt. Sinai, while the New Testament describes the new arrangement of God with men through Christ on the basis of the New Covenant (see Ex. 24:1-8; Luke 22:14-20; 2 Cor. 3:6-11). The Old Covenant revealed the holiness of God in the righteous standard of the Law and promised a coming Redeemer; the New Covenant shows the holiness of God in His righteous Son. The New Testament, then, contains those writings which reveal the content of this New Covenant.

The message of the New Testament centers around (1) the Person who gave Himself for the remission of sins (Matt. 26:28) and (2) the people (the church) who have received His salvation. Thus the central theme of the New Testament is salvation. The Gospels introduce the Savior. The book called the Acts of the Apostles describes the spread of the good news about His salvation through a large part of the Mediterranean world of the first century A.D. The Epistles give details of the blessings of that salvation, and the Revelation previews the culmination of salvation.

The Arrangement of the Books of the New Testament

The New Testament includes 27 books written by nine different authors (unless Paul wrote Hebrews, then only eight) over about 50 years' time. These books fall naturally into four divisions:

(1) The Four Gospels. These describe the life and ministry of Jesus Christ. Although they were written later than many other books of the New Testament, it was natural that, in the order of the books, a priority position should be given to these accounts of Jesus' earthly life and ministry.

(2) The book of Acts. This is the history of the beginning of the church and the spread of Christianity throughout the Greco-Roman world.

(3) The 21 letters (Romans through Jude). Since archaeological discoveries have shown that letter writing was a common means of communication in the first Christian centuries, it is not surprising to find that most of the books of the New Testament were in the form of letters. The apostle Paul, the great missionary and theologian of the early church, wrote 13 or 14 of these letters. They were addressed to churches as well as to individuals, and they teach Christian doctrine both in a formal way (as in Romans) and in application to life situations (as in 1 Corinthians and Philemon).

(4) The Revelation. This last book describes the ultimate triumph of Jesus Christ and His people in the future.

The Order of the Books of the New Testament

As already suggested, the order of the books of the New Testament is logical. First come the Gospels, which record the life of Christ; then Acts, which gives

the history of the spread of Christianity; then the letters, which show the development of the doctrines of the church along with its problems; and finally the vision of the second coming of Christ in the Revelation.

The order of the writing of the books, however, was approximately like this:

James	A.D. 45–50	Matthew	60's
Galatians	49	1 Timothy	63
1 and 2 Thessalonians	51	1 Peter	63
Mark	50's	Titus	65
1 Corinthians	56	2 Timothy	66
2 Corinthians	57	2 Peter	66
Romans	58	Hebrews	64–68
Luke	60	Jude	70–80
Colossians, Ephesians, Philippians, Philemon	61	John	85–90
Acts	61	1, 2, 3 John	90
		Revelation	90's

The Collection of the Books

After they were written, the individual books were not immediately gathered together into the canon, or collection of 27 which comprise the New Testament. Groups of books like Paul's letters and the Gospels were preserved at first by the churches or people to whom they were sent, and gradually all 27 books were collected and formally acknowledged by the church as a whole.

This process took about 350 years. In the second century the circulation of books that promoted heresy accentuated the need for distinguishing valid scripture from other Christian literature. Certain tests were developed to determine which books should be included. (1) Was the book written or approved by an apostle? (2) Were its contents of a spiritual nature? (3) Did it give evidence of being inspired by God? (4) Was it widely received by the churches?

Not all of the 27 books that were eventually recognized as canonical were accepted by all the churches in the early centuries, but this does not mean that those that were not immediately or universally accepted were spurious. Letters addressed to individuals (Philemon, 2 and 3 John) would not have been circulated as widely as those sent to churches. The books most disputed were James, Jude, 2 Peter, 2 and 3 John, and Philemon, but ultimately these were included and the canon was certified at the Council of Carthage in A.D. 397.

Although no original copy of any of the writings which comprise the New Testament has survived, there exist more than 4,500 Greek manuscripts of all or part of the texts, plus some 8,000 Latin manuscripts and at least 1,000 other versions into which the original books were translated. Careful study and comparison of these many copies has given us an accurate and trustworthy New Testament.

INTRODUCTION TO THE GOSPELS

What Are the Gospels?

Gospel means "good news." The Gospels are so called because they record the good news that a way of salvation has been opened to all mankind through the death and resurrection of Jesus Christ (Mark 1:1; 1 Cor. 15:3-4).

Biography as we know it was unknown when the Gospels were written, and they are not really biographies as we understand that literary form today. They were written that people might know who Jesus was and believe on Him (John 20:31).

Why Did the Gospels Need to Be Written?

The rapid spread of Christianity precipitated the need for written accounts of the life of Christ. Too, as major figures in the stories and eyewitnesses began to die, there was an increasing need for written accounts of what they had seen and heard. These written Gospels were used to evangelize, to catechize new converts, and probably were part of early Christian worship (Luke 1:1-4). In the Introduction to each Gospel we shall try to show its distinctive quality.

Why Four Gospels?

Although there were numerous other gospel accounts written, only four were deemed worthy to be included in the New Testament. The other gospels were written later and are of doubtful reliability. Although they contain some of the information that is in the four canonical Gospels, they also add much that is obviously fanciful and legendary (like the story of Jesus' condemning a boy to die because he had knocked Him down, as reported in an apocryphal Gnostic writing known as 1 Infancy). They also often tried to bolster heretical or sectarian viewpoints.

The early church distinguished these gospels from the true ones and regarded the apocryphal ones as of much lesser importance. One of the reasons was that the Four Gospels were written by apostles or by a close associate. Later church councils confirmed the authenticity of these books and included only the four in the canon, or collection of books recognized as inspired and authoritative.

The Gospels were written to the four general groups of people in the first century. Matthew was written for the Jews; Mark for the Romans; Luke for the other pagan Gentiles; and John for Christians.

What Are the Synoptic Gospels?

Matthew, Mark, and Luke present much similar material about the life of Christ, as even a quick examination of a harmony of His life will show. They have a more or less common view of His activities and teachings and of the chronology of events. They are therefore called the Synoptic Gospels (from *synopsis,* a viewing together). For example, all but 31 verses in Mark have parallels in either Matthew or Luke. On the other hand, much of the material in John's Gospel is unique, and it is organized according to long discourses. The differences in the four Gospels supplement each other without contradiction and the similarities complement each other. The result is a comprehensive fourfold record of the redemptive ministry of Jesus Christ.

INTRODUCTION TO THE GOSPEL ACCORDING TO MATTHEW

AUTHOR: Matthew DATE: 60's

Authorship *Matthew, who was surnamed Levi (Mark 2:14), was a Jewish tax collector (publican) for the Roman government (Matt. 9:9). Because he collaborated with the Romans, who were hated by the Jews as overlords of their country, Matthew (and all publicans) was despised by fellow Jews. Nevertheless, Matthew responded to Christ's simple call to follow Him. After the account of the banquet he gave for his colleagues so they too could meet Jesus, he is not mentioned again except in the list of the Twelve (Matt. 10:3; see also Acts 1:13). Tradition says that he preached in Palestine for a dozen years after the resurrection of Christ and then went to other lands, but there is no certainty of this.*

Distinctive Approach of Matthew *Matthew was written to Jews to answer their questions about Jesus of Nazareth who claimed to be their Messiah. Was He in fact the Messiah predicted in the Old Testament? If He was, why did He fail to establish the promised kingdom? Will it ever be established? What is God's purpose in the meantime? Thus, in this Gospel, Jesus is often spoken of as the Son of David and the One who fulfills the Old Testament prophecies of Messiah; and the kingdom of heaven is the subject of much of His recorded teaching.*

Matthew is also characterized by its inclusion of people outside of Judaism. The closing verses record the commission to go into all the world, and only in Matthew does the word church appear in the Gospels (16:18; 18:17). Jesus is also designated as the Son of Abraham (1:1), for in Abraham "all the families of the earth shall be blessed" (Gen. 12:3).

Date *Although the Gospel has sometimes been dated in the 80's or 90's, the fact that the destruction of Jerusalem in* A.D. *70 is viewed as an event yet future (24:2) seems to require an earlier date. Some feel that this was the first of the Gospels to be written (about 50), while others think it was not the first and that it was written in the 60's.*

Contents *Important sections in Matthew are the Sermon on the Mount (chapters 5-7), including the Beatitudes (5:3-12) and the Lord's Prayer (6:9-13); the parables of the kingdom (chapter 13); and the Olivet Discourse concerning future events (chapters 24-25). The theme of the book is Christ the King, and the outline reflects that theme.*

OUTLINE OF THE GOSPEL OF MATTHEW

I. The Person of the King, 1:1-4:25
- A. His Background, 1:1-17
- B. His Birth, 1:18-2:23
  1. The announcement of the birth, 1:18-25
  2. The adoration of the baby, 2:1-12
  3. The advancement of the boy, 2:13-23
- C. His Baptism, 3:1-17
- D. His Temptation, 4:1-11
- E. His Inauguration, 4:12-25

II. The Preaching of the King, 5:1-7:29
- A. The Picture of Kingdom Life, 5:1-16
- B. The Precepts for Kingdom Life, 5:17-48
  1. The law of Moses, 5:17-20
  2. The law of murder, 5:21-22
  3. The law of reconciliation, 5:23-26
  4. The law of adultery, 5:27-30
  5. The law of divorce, 5:31-32
  6. The law of oaths, 5:33-37
  7. The law of nonresistance, 5:38-42
  8. The law of love, 5:43-48
- C. The Practice of Kingdom Life, 6:1-7:12
  1. In relation to almsgiving, 6:1-4
  2. In relation to prayer, 6:5-15
  3. In relation to fasting, 6:16-18
  4. In relation to money, 6:19-24
  5. In relation to anxiety, 6:25-34
  6. In relation to judging, 7:1-5
  7. In relation to prudence, 7:6
  8. In relation to prayer, 7:7-11
  9. In relation to others, 7:12
- D. The Proof of Kingdom Life, 7:13-29

III. The Proof of the King, 8:1-9:38
- A. Exhibit 1: Power, 8:1-34
  1. Power over defilement, 8:1-4
  2. Power over distance, 8:5-13
  3. Power over disease, 8:14-17
  4. Power over disciples, 8:18-22
  5. Power over the deep, 8:23-27
  6. Power over demons, 8:28-34
- B. Exhibit 2: Pardon, 9:1-17
  1. Pardon of a paralytic, 9:1-8
  2. Pardon of a publican, 9:9-13
  3. Problem concerning fasting, 9:14-17

- C. Exhibit 3: Power, 9:18–38
  1. Power over death, 9:18–26
  2. Power over darkness, 9:27–31
  3. Power over dumbness, 9:32–34
  4. Power over disease, 9:35
  5. Pity on the people, 9:36–38

IV. The Program of the King, 10:1–16:12

- A. The Program Announced, 10:1–11:1
- B. The Program Attested, 11:2–12:50
  1. By comforting John's disciples, 11:2–19
  2. By condemning the cities, 11:20–24
  3. By calling all to Himself, 11:25–30
  4. By controversies over the Sabbath, 12:1–13
  5. By condemnation of the Pharisees (the unpardonable sin), 12:14–37
  6. By certain signs, 12:38–45
  7. By changed relationships, 12:46–50
- C. The Program Altered, 13:1–52
  1. The sower, 13:1–23
  2. The wheat and the tares, 13:24–30
  3. The mustard seed, 13:31–32
  4. The leaven, 13:33
  5. The wheat and the tares, 13:34–43
  6. The hidden treasure, 13:44
  7. The pearl of great price, 13:45–46
  8. The dragnet, 13:47–50
  9. The householder, 13:51–52
- D. The Program Attacked, 13:53–16:12
  1. Attack by His own townspeople, 13:53–58
  2. Attack by Herod, followed by miracles (5000 fed and Jesus walks on water), 14:1–36
  3. Attack by the scribes and Pharisees, followed by miracles (Syrophenician woman's daughter healed and 4000 fed), 15:1–39
  4. Attack by the Pharisees and Sadducees, 16:1–12

V. The Pedagogy of the King, 16:13–20:28

- A. Concerning His Church (Peter's Confession of Faith), 16:13–20
- B. Concerning His Death, 16:21–28
- C. Concerning His Glory (the Transfiguration), 17:1–21
- D. Concerning His Betrayal, 17:22–23
- E. Concerning Taxes, 17:24–27
- F. Concerning Humility, 18:1–35
  1. Illustrated in childlike faith, 18:1–6
  2. Illustrated in concern for the lost, 18:7–14
  3. Illustrated in church discipline, 18:15–20
  4. Illustrated in continual forgiveness, 18:21–35
- G. Concerning Human Problems, 19:1–26
  1. Physical problems, 19:1–2
  2. Divorce and remarriage, 19:3–12
  3. Children, 19:13–15
  4. Wealth, 19:16–26
- H. Concerning the Kingdom, 19:27–20:28
  1. Rewards in the kingdom, 19:27–30
  2. Recognition in the kingdom, 20:1–16
  3. Rank in the kingdom, 20:17–28

VI. The Presentation of the King, 20:29–23:39

- A. The Power of the King, 20:29–34
- B. The Presentation of the King, 21:1–11
- C. The Purification by the King, 21:12–17
- D. The Cursing of the Fig Tree, 21:18–22
- E. The Challenge to the King, 21:23–27
- F. The Parables of the King, 21:28–22:14
  1. The rebellion of the nation, 21:28–32
  2. The retribution on the nation, 21:33–46
  3. The rejection of the nation, 22:1–14
- G. The Pronouncements of the King, 22:15–23:39
  1. In answer to the Herodians, 22:15–22
  2. In answer to the Sadducees, 22:23–33
  3. In answer to the Pharisees, 22:34–40
  4. In questioning the Pharisees, 22:41–46
  5. Concerning the Pharisees, 23:1–36
  6. Concerning Jerusalem, 23:37–39

VII. The Predictions of the King, 24:1–25:46

- A. The Destruction of the Temple, 24:1–2
- B. The Disciples' Questions, 24:3
- C. The Signs of the End of the Age, 24:4–28
- D. The Sign of His Coming, 24:29–31
- E. The Illustrations, 24:32–25:46
  1. The fig tree, 24:32–35
  2. The days of Noah, 24:36–39
  3. The two, 24:40–41
  4. The faithful householder, 24:42–44
  5. The wise servant, 24:45–51
  6. The ten virgins, 25:1–13
  7. The talents, 25:14–30
  8. The judgment of Gentiles, 25:31–46

VIII. The Passion of the King, 26:1–27:66

- A. The Preparation, 26:1–16
- B. The Passover, 26:17–30
- C. The Betrayal, 26:31–56
- D. The Hearings, 26:57–27:26
  1. Before the high priest, 26:57–75
  2. Before the Sanhedrin, 27:1–10
  3. Before Pilate, 27:11–26
- E. The Crucifixion, 27:27–66
  1. The preliminaries, 27:27–44
  2. The death, 27:45–56
  3. The burial, 27:57–66

IX. The Power of the King, 28:1–20

- A. The Conquest, 28:1–10
- B. The Conspiracy, 28:11–15
- C. The Commission, 28:16–20

THE GOSPEL ACCORDING TO MATTHEW

I THE PERSON OF THE KING, 1:1–4:25

A His Background, 1:1–17

★ 1 [a]2 Sam. 7:12-16; Ps. 89:3f.; 132:11; Is. 9:6f.; 11:1; Matt. 9:27; Luke 1:32, 69; John 7:42; Acts 13:23; Rom. 1:3; Rev. 22:16 [b]Gen. 22:18; Matt. 1:1-6; *Luke 3:32-34*; Gal. 3:16

1 The book of the genealogy of
Jesus Christ, [a]the son of Da-
vid, [b]the son of Abraham.
2 To Abraham was born
Isaac; and to Isaac, Jacob; and to
Jacob, Judah and his brothers;

3 [a]Ruth 4:18-22; 1 Chr. 2:1-15; Matt. 1:3-6

3 and to Judah were born
Perez and Zerah by Tamar; and to
[a]Perez was born Hezron; and to
Hezron, Ram;
4 and to Ram was born Amminadab; and to Amminadab,
Nahshon; and to Nahshon, Salmon;
5 and to Salmon was born
Boaz by Rahab; and to Boaz was
born Obed by Ruth; and to Obed,
Jesse;

6 [a]2 Sam. 11:27; 12:24

6 and to Jesse was born David the king.
And to David [a]was born Solomon by her *who had been the
wife* of Uriah;

7 [a]1 Chr. 3:10ff.

7 and to Solomon [a]was born
Rehoboam; and to Rehoboam,
Abijah; and to Abijah, Asa;
8 and to Asa was born Je-
hoshaphat; and to Jehoshaphat,
Joram; and to Joram, Uzziah;
9 and to Uzziah was born Jo-
tham; and to Jotham, Ahaz; and to
Ahaz, Hezekiah;
10 and to Hezekiah was born
Manasseh; and to Manasseh,
Amon; and to Amon, Josiah;

★11 [a]2 Kin. 24:14f.; Jer. 27:20; Matt. 1:17

11 and to Josiah were born Jeconiah and his brothers, at the
time of the [a]deportation to Babylon.

12 [a]2 Kin. 24:14f.; Jer. 27:20; Matt. 1:17

12 And after the [a]deportation
to Babylon, to Jeconiah was born
Shealtiel; and to Shealtiel, Zerubbabel;
13 and to Zerubbabel was
born Abiud; and to Abiud, Eliakim; and to Eliakim, Azor;
14 and to Azor was born Zadok; and to Zadok, Achim; and to
Achim, Eliud;
15 and to Eliud was born Eleazar; and to Eleazar, Matthan;
and to Matthan, Jacob;

★16 [a]Matt. 27:17, 22; Luke 2:11; John 4:25

16 and to Jacob was born
Joseph the husband of Mary, by
whom was born Jesus, [a]who is
called Christ.

17 [a]2 Kin. 24:14f.; Jer. 27:20; Matt. 1:11, 12

17 Therefore all the generations from Abraham to David are
fourteen generations; and from
David to the [a]deportation to
Babylon fourteen generations;
and from the [a]deportation to
Babylon to *the time of* Christ
fourteen generations.

B His Birth, 1:18–2:23

1 *The announcement of the birth,* 1:18–25

18 [a]Matt. 12:46; Luke 1:27 [b]Luke 1:35

18 Now the birth of Jesus
Christ was as follows. When His
[a]mother Mary had been be-

1:1 *Jesus Christ.* The name "Jesus" is from the Greek (and Latin) for the Hebrew "Jeshua" (Joshua), which means "the Lord is salvation." "Christ" is from the Greek for the Hebrew *Meshiah* (Messiah), meaning "anointed one." *Son of David* was a highly popular Messianic title of the times. The genealogy is here traced through Joseph, Jesus' legal (though not natural) father, and it establishes His claim and right to the throne of David (1:6). The genealogy in Luke 3:23–38 is evidently that of Mary, though some believe it is also Joseph's, by assuming that Matthan (Matt. 1:15) and Matthat (Luke 3:24) were the same person and Jacob (Matt. 1:16) and Eli (Luke 3:23) were brothers (one being Joseph's father and the other his uncle). See note at Luke 3:23.

1:11 *Jeconiah.* Jehoiachin, king of Judah, who was taken into captivity by Nebuchadnezzar in 597 B.C. Jeremiah contracted "Jeconiah" to "Coniah" (Jer. 22:24, 28; 37:1). A curse was pronounced on Coniah that none of his descendants would prosper sitting on the throne of David. Had our Lord been the natural son of Joseph, He could not have been successful on the throne of David because of this curse. But since He came through Mary's lineage, He was not affected by this curse.

1:16 *by whom.* The word is feminine singular, indicating clearly that Jesus was born of Mary only and not of Mary and Joseph. It is one of the strongest evidences for Jesus' virgin birth.

trothed to Joseph, before they
came together she was [b]found to
be with child by the Holy Spirit.
★19 **19** And Joseph her husband,
being a righteous man, and not
wanting to disgrace her, desired
to put her away secretly.
20 But when he had considered this, behold, an angel of the
Lord appeared to him in a dream,
saying, "Joseph, son of David, do
not be afraid to take Mary as your
wife; for that which has been conceived in her is of the Holy Spirit.
21 [a]Luke 1:31; 2:21 [b]Luke 2:11; John 1:29; Acts 13:23 **21** "And she will bear a Son;
and [a]you shall call His name
Jesus, for it is He who [b]will save
His people from their sins."
22 Now all this took place
that what was spoken by the Lord
through the prophet might be fulfilled, saying,
23 [a]Is. 7:14 **23** "[a]BEHOLD, THE VIRGIN SHALL BE
WITH CHILD, AND SHALL BEAR A SON,
AND THEY SHALL CALL HIS NAME IM-
MANUEL," which translated means,
"GOD WITH US."
24 And Joseph arose from his
sleep, and did as the angel of the
Lord commanded him, and took
her as his wife,
25 [a]Matt. 1:21 **25** and kept her a virgin until
she gave birth to a Son; and [a]he
called His name Jesus.

2 *The adoration of the baby,* 2:1–12

★ 1 [a]Luke 2:4-7 [b]Luke 1:5 **2** Now after Jesus was [a]born in
Bethlehem of Judea in the
days of [b]Herod the king, behold,
magi from the east arrived in Jerusalem, saying,
2 "Where is He who has been 2 [a]Jer. 23:5; 30:9; Zech. 9:9; Matt. 27:11; Luke 19:38; 23:38; John 1:49 [b]Num. 24:17; Rev. 22:16
born [a]King of the Jews? For we
saw [b]His star in the east, and have
come to worship Him."
3 And when Herod the king
heard it, he was troubled, and all
Jerusalem with him.
4 And gathering together all ★ 4
the chief priests and scribes of the
people, he *began* to inquire of
them where the Christ was to be
born.
5 And they said to him, "[a]In 5 [a]John 7:42
Bethlehem of Judea, for so it has
been written by the prophet,

6 '[a]AND YOU, BETHLEHEM, LAND OF JUDAH, ★ 6 [a]Mic. 5:2 [b]John 21:16
ARE BY NO MEANS LEAST AMONG THE LEADERS OF JUDAH;
FOR OUT OF YOU SHALL COME FORTH A RULER,
WHO WILL [b]SHEPHERD MY PEOPLE ISRAEL.' "

7 Then Herod secretly called
the magi, and ascertained from
them the time the star appeared.
8 And he sent them to Bethlehem, and said, "Go and make
careful search for the Child; and
when you have found *Him,* report
to me, that I too may come and
worship Him."
9 And having heard the
king, they went their way; and lo,
the star, which they had seen in
the east, went on before them,
until it came and stood over
where the Child was.

1:19 *her husband.* Although Joseph and Mary were not yet married, so sacred was the period of engagement, or betrothal, that they were by custom considered as if married (cf. Gen. 29:21; Deut. 22:23–30). Consequently, Joseph's only recourse seemed to be to "put her away," which meant to give her a bill of divorcement, a certificate saying, in effect, "This woman is not my wife; I am not her husband" (see Hos. 2:2).

2:1 *Bethlehem.* The town is five miles S. of Jerusalem. *Herod the king.* This was Herod the Great, whose family, though nominally Jewish, were in reality Edomite, and who was king, with Roman help, from 40–4 B.C. He built the temple in Jerusalem which Christ knew. *magi.* These wise men from the east were experts in the study of the stars. Tradition says that there were three and that they were kings.

2:4 *scribes.* Scribes, who belonged mainly to the party of the Pharisees, functioned as members of a highly honored profession. They were professional students and defenders of the law (scriptural and traditional), gathering around them pupils whom they instructed in the law. They were also referred to as lawyers because they were entrusted with the administration of the law as judges in the Sanhedrin (cf. Matt. 22:35).

2:6 *a Ruler.* See Micah 5:2. An earthly king, though a supernatural one, is meant.

10 And when they saw the
star, they rejoiced exceedingly
with great joy.
★11 [a]Matt. 1:18; 12:46 11 And they came into the
house and saw the Child with
[a]Mary His mother; and they fell
down and worshiped Him; and
opening their treasures they presented to Him gifts of gold and
frankincense and myrrh.
12 [a]Matt. 2:13, 19, 22; Luke 2:26; Acts 10:22; Heb. 8:5; 11:7 12 And having been [a]warned
by God in a dream not to return
to Herod, they departed for their
own country by another way.

3 *The advancement of the boy,* 2:13–23

13 [a]Matt. 2:12, 19 **13** Now when they had departed, behold, an angel of the
Lord *[a]appeared to Joseph in a
dream, saying, "Arise and take
the Child and His mother, and
flee to Egypt, and remain there
until I tell you; for Herod is going
to search for the Child to destroy
Him."
14 And he arose and took the
Child and His mother by night,
and departed for Egypt;
★15 [a]Hos. 11:1 [b]Ex. 4:22f. 15 and was there until the
death of Herod, that what was
spoken by the Lord through the
prophet might be fulfilled, saying,
"[a]OUT OF EGYPT DID I CALL [b]MY
SON."
16 Then when Herod saw
that he had been tricked by the
magi, he became very enraged,
and sent and slew all the male
children who were in Bethlehem
and in all its environs, from two
years old and under, according to
the time which he had ascertained
from the magi.
17 Then that which was spo- ★17
ken through Jeremiah the prophet
was fulfilled, saying,

18 "[a]A VOICE WAS HEARD IN RA- 18 [a]Jer. 31:15
MAH,
WEEPING AND GREAT MOURN-
ING,
RACHEL WEEPING FOR HER
CHILDREN;
AND SHE REFUSED TO BE COM-
FORTED,
BECAUSE THEY WERE NO
MORE."

19 But when Herod was dead, 19 [a]Matt. 2:12, 13, 22
behold, an angel of the Lord *[a]ap-
peared in a dream to Joseph in
Egypt, saying,
20 "Arise and take the Child
and His mother, and go into the
land of Israel; for those who
sought the Child's life are dead."
21 And he arose and took the
Child and His mother, and came
into the land of Israel.
22 But when he heard that ★22 [a]Matt. 2:12
Archelaus was reigning over Ju-
dea in place of his father Herod,
he was afraid to go there. And
being [a]warned *by God* in a
dream, he departed for the regions of Galilee,
23 and came and resided in a ★23 [a]Luke 1:26 [b]Is. 11:1 [c]Mark 1:24
city called [a]Nazareth, that what
was spoken through the prophets

2:11 *into the house . . . the Child.* These words need not indicate that the wise men came some time after the birth of Christ. The family would naturally have moved into a house as quickly as possible after Jesus was born, and "child" can mean a newborn (John 16:21). We do not know how many wise men there were. *gold and frankincense and myrrh.* These were gifts worthy of a king. The early church fathers understood the gold to be symbolic of Christ's deity; the frankincense, of His purity; and the myrrh, of His death (since it was used for embalming).

2:15 See Hosea 11:1.

2:17–18 A quotation of Jer. 31:15, which depicts the wailing at the time of Israel's exile. That calamity and Herod's new atrocity are viewed as part of the same broad picture. Since Matthew was writing to those with Jewish background, he used more quotations from the O.T. than the other Gospel writers. There are 93 such quotations in Matthew, 49 in Mark, 80 in Luke, and 33 in John.

2:22 *Archelaus.* On the death of Herod the Great, the Romans divided his kingdom among his sons: Archelaus (Judah and Samaria), Antipas (Galilee and Perea), Philip (NE. Palestine). Archelaus was a bloody king and, worse in the eyes of Rome, ineffective. He was removed by Caesar Augustus in A.D. 6 and banished to Gaul.

2:23 *He shall be called a Nazarene.* Probably a synonym for "contemptible" or "despised" since Nazareth was a most unlikely place for the residence of the Messiah (cf. Isa. 53:3; Ps. 22:6).

might be fulfilled, "[b]He shall be
called a [c]Nazarene."

C His Baptism, 3:1–17

3 Now [a]in those days John the
Baptist *came, preaching in
the [b]wilderness of Judea, saying,
2 "[a]Repent, for [b]the kingdom
of heaven is at hand."
3 For this is the one referred
to by Isaiah the prophet, saying,

"[a]THE VOICE OF ONE CRYING IN
THE WILDERNESS,
'[b]MAKE READY THE WAY OF
THE LORD,
MAKE HIS PATHS STRAIGHT!' "

4 Now John himself had [a]a
garment of camel's hair, and a
leather belt about his waist; and
his food was [b]locusts and wild
honey.
5 Then Jerusalem was going
out to him, and all Judea, and all
[a]the district around the Jordan;

★ 1 [a]Matt. 3:1-12: *Mark 1:3-8; Luke 3:2-17;* John 1:6-8, 19-28 [b]Josh. 15:61 Judg. 1:16
★ 2 [a]Matt. 4:17 [b]Dan. 2:44; Matt. 4:17, 23; 6:10; 10:7; Mark 1:15; Luke 10:9f.; 11:20; 21:31
3 [a]Is. 40:3 [b]John 1:23
4 [a]2 Kin. 1:8; Zech. 13:4 [b]Lev. 11:22
5 [a]Luke 3:3

6 and they were being baptized by him in the Jordan River,
as they confessed their sins.
7 But when he saw many of
the [a]Pharisees and [b]Sadducees
coming for baptism, he said to
them, "You [c]brood of vipers, who
warned you to flee from [d]the
wrath to come?
8 "Therefore bring forth fruit
[a]in keeping with *your* repentance;
9 and do not suppose that
you can say to yourselves, '[a]We
have Abraham for our father'; for
I say to you, that God is able from
these stones to raise up children
to Abraham.
10 "And the axe is already laid
at the root of the trees; [a]every tree
therefore that does not bear good
fruit is cut down and thrown into
the fire.
11 "As for me, [a]I baptize you
in water for repentance, but He
who is coming after me is mightier than I, and I am not *even* fit to

★ 7 [a]Matt. 16:1ff.; 23:13, 15 [b]Matt. 16:1ff.; 22:23; Acts 4:1; 5:17; 23:6ff. [c]Matt. 12:34; 23:33 [d]1 Thess. 1:10
8 [a]Acts 26:20
★ 9 [a]John 8:33, 39
10 [a]Matt. 7:19
★11 [a]John 1:26 [b]John 1:33

3:1 *the wilderness of Judea.* A barren wasteland extending along the W. shore of the Dead Sea.

3:2 *Repent.* Repentance is a change of mind that bears fruit in a changed life (see v. 8). *kingdom of heaven.* This is the rule of heaven over the earth. The Jewish people of Christ's day were looking for this Messianic or Davidic kingdom to be established on the earth, and this is what John proclaimed as being "at hand." The rejection of Christ by the people delayed its establishment until the second coming of Christ (Matt. 25:31). The character of the kingdom today is described in the parables of Matt. 13.

3:7 *Pharisees.* The Pharisees were the most influential of the Jewish sects at the time of Christ. Though holding orthodox doctrines, their zeal for the Mosaic law led them to a degenerate, though strict, outward observance of both the law and their equally authoritative (in their own eyes) interpretations of it. They knew the Scriptures (Matt. 23:2), tithed (Luke 18:12), fasted (Matt. 9:14), prayed (Mark 12:40); but they were also hypocritical (Matt. 23:15), self-righteous (Luke 18:9), and the foremost persecutors of the Lord (Matt. 9:3). *Sadducees.* The Sadducees, whose membership came largely from the priesthood and upper classes, were the anti-supernaturalists of Christ's day. They denied the truth of bodily resurrection, of future punishment and reward, and of the existence of angels (Acts 23:8). Though they upheld the written law of Moses, they were opposed to the oral traditions observed by the Pharisees. They were the party of the high-priestly families of Jerusalem with direct interests in the apparatus of temple worship and generally collaborated with the Roman rulers. They opposed Christ as vigorously as the Pharisees and were condemned by Him as severely, though not so frequently (Matt. 16:1–4, 6).

3:9 *We have Abraham for our father.* The common teaching of that day said that the Jews participated in the merits of Abraham, which made their prayers acceptable, helped in war, expiated sins, appeased the wrath of God, and assured a share in God's eternal kingdom. Consequently the people were startled when John and Jesus preached the necessity of personal repentance.

3:11 *baptize.* Baptism is a form of identification. John's baptism was a sign of an individual's acknowledgment of his need of repentance for the remission of his sins. When Jesus was baptized by John (v. 15) He identified Himself with John's message of righteousness (though, being sinless, He Himself needed no cleansing from sin). The baptism with the Holy Spirit, predicted here, identifies members of the body of Christ with Christ, the risen Head of that body (1 Cor. 12:13). Christian baptism is identification with the Christian message and the Christian group. *and fire.* Probably a reference to the judgments associated with the return of Christ (v. 12; Mal. 3:1–5; 4:1–3).

remove His sandals; [b]He Himself
will baptize you with the Holy
Spirit and fire.

★12 [a]Is. 30:24; Luke 3:17 [b]Matt. 13:30 [c]Mark 9:43, 48

12 "And His [a]winnowing fork
is in His hand, and He will thoroughly
clean His threshing floor;
and He will [b]gather His wheat
into the barn, but He will burn up
the chaff with [c]unquenchable
fire."

13 [a]Matt. 3:13-17: *Mark 1:9-11; Luke 3:21, 22;* John 1:31-34 [b]Matt. 2:22

13 [a]Then Jesus *arrived
[b]from Galilee at the Jordan *coming*
to John, to be baptized by
him.

14 But John tried to prevent
Him, saying, "I have need to be
baptized by You, and do You
come to me?"

15 But Jesus answering said to
him, "Permit *it* at this time; for in
this way it is fitting for us to fulfill
all righteousness." Then he *permitted
Him.

★16 [a]John 1:32

16 And after being baptized,
Jesus went up immediately from
the water; and behold, the heavens
were opened, and [a]he saw the
Spirit of God descending as a
dove, *and* coming upon Him,

17 [a]Is. 42:1; Matt. 12:18; 17:5; Mark 9:7; Luke 9:35

17 and behold, a voice out of
the heavens, saying, "[a]This is My
beloved Son, in whom I am well-pleased."

D His Temptation, 4:1–11

★ 1 [a]Matt. 4:1-11: *Mark 1:12, 13; Luke 4:1-13*
2 [a]Ex. 34:28; 1 Kin. 19:8

4 [a]Then Jesus was led up by
the Spirit into the wilderness
to be tempted by the devil.

2 And after He had [a]fasted
forty days and forty nights, He
then became hungry.

3 [a]1 Thess. 3:5

3 And [a]the tempter came
and said to Him, "If You are the
Son of God, command that these
stones become bread."

★ 4 [a]Deut. 8:3

4 But He answered and said,
"It is written, '[a]MAN SHALL NOT LIVE
ON BREAD ALONE, BUT ON EVERY WORD
THAT PROCEEDS OUT OF THE MOUTH OF
GOD.' "

5 [a]Neh. 11:1, 18; Dan. 9:24; Matt. 27:53

5 Then the devil *took Him
into [a]the holy city; and he stood
Him on the pinnacle of the temple,

★ 6 [a]Ps. 91:11-12

6 and *said to Him, "If You
are the Son of God throw Yourself
down; for it is written,

'[a]HE WILL GIVE HIS ANGELS
CHARGE CONCERNING YOU;
And ON THEIR HANDS THEY
WILL BEAR YOU UP,
LEST YOU STRIKE YOUR FOOT
AGAINST A STONE.' "

★ 7 [a]Deut. 6:16

7 Jesus said to him, "On the
other hand, it is written, '[a]YOU
SHALL NOT TEMPT THE LORD YOUR
GOD.' "

8 Again, the devil *took Him
to a very high mountain, and
*showed Him all the kingdoms of
the world, and their glory;

★ 9

9 and he said to Him, "All
these things will I give You, if
You fall down and worship me."

★10 [a]Deut. 6:13

10 Then Jesus *said to him,
"Begone, Satan! For it is written,
'[a]YOU SHALL WORSHIP THE LORD YOUR
GOD, AND SERVE HIM ONLY.' "

11 [a]Matt. 26:53; Luke 22:43

11 Then the devil *left Him;
and behold, [a]angels came and *began*
to minister to Him.

3:12 *His winnowing fork is in His hand.* A wooden shovel used for tossing grain against the wind after threshing so that the lighter chaff would be blown away, leaving the kernels to settle in a pile.

3:16–17 This is the first clear expression of the concept of the Trinity. The descent of the Spirit upon Christ was for special power at the beginning of His public ministry.

4:1 Satan's intention in the temptation was to make Christ sin so as to thwart God's plan for man's redemption by disqualifying the Savior. God's purpose (note that the Spirit led Jesus to the test) was to prove His Son to be sinless and thus a worthy Savior. It is clear that He was actually tempted; it is equally clear that He was sinless (2 Cor. 5:21). See note on Heb. 4:15.

4:4 See Deut. 8:3.

4:6 Satan, as well as Jesus, quotes the Bible (in this instance, Ps. 91:11–12). But Satan did not quote accurately, for he omitted a phrase which was not suited to his purpose.

4:7 See Deut. 6:16.

4:9 *will I give You.* Satan, as prince of this world, was within his rights to make this offer (John 12:31; see note at 1 John 2:15).

4:10 See Deut. 6:13; 10:20.

12 aMatt. 14:3; Mark 1:14; Luke 3:20; John 3:24 bMark 1:14; Luke 4:14; John 1:43; 2:11 ★13 aMatt. 11:23; Mark 1:21; 2:1; Luke 4:23, 31; John 2:12; 4:46f. ★14 15 aIs. 9:1 16 aIs. 9:2 17 aMark 1:14, 15 bMatt. 3:2 18 aMatt. 4:18-22: *Mark 1:16-20;* Luke 5:2-11; John 1:40-42 bMatt. 15:29; Mark 7:31; Luke 5:1; John 6:1 cMatt. 10:2; 16:18; John 1:40, 42 ★19

E His Inauguration, 4:12-25

12 Now when He heard that
[a]John had been taken into custody, [b]He withdrew into Galilee;
13 and leaving Nazareth, He
came and [a]settled in Capernaum,
which is by the sea, in the region
of Zebulun and Naphtali.
14 *This was* to fulfill what
was spoken through Isaiah the
prophet, saying,

15 "[a]THE LAND OF ZEBULUN AND THE LAND OF NAPHTALI,
BY THE WAY OF THE SEA, BEYOND THE JORDAN, GALILEE OF THE GENTILES—
16 "[a]THE PEOPLE WHO WERE SITTING IN DARKNESS SAW A GREAT LIGHT,
AND TO THOSE WHO WERE SITTING IN THE LAND AND SHADOW OF DEATH,
UPON THEM A LIGHT DAWNED."

17 [a]From that time Jesus began to preach and say, "[b]Repent,
for the kingdom of heaven is at
hand."
18 [a]And walking by [b]the Sea
of Galilee, He saw two brothers,
[c]Simon who was called Peter, and
Andrew his brother, casting a net
into the sea; for they were fishermen.
19 And He *said to them,
"Follow Me, and I will make you
fishers of men."
20 And they immediately left
the nets, and followed Him.
21 And going on from there
He saw two other brothers,
[a]James the *son* of Zebedee, and
John his brother, in the boat with
Zebedee their father, mending
their nets; and He called them.
22 And they immediately left
the boat and their father, and followed Him.
23 And *Jesus* was going about
[a]in all Galilee, [b]teaching in their
synagogues, and [c]proclaiming the
gospel of the kingdom, and [d]heal-
ing every kind of disease and every kind of sickness among the
people.
24 And the news about Him
went out [a]into all Syria; and they
brought to Him all who were ill,
taken with various diseases and
pains, [b]demoniacs, [c]epileptics,
[d]paralytics; and He healed them.
25 And great multitudes [a]fol-
lowed Him from Galilee and [b]De-
capolis and Jerusalem and Judea
and *from* [c]beyond the Jordan.

★21 aMatt. 10:2; 20:20 ★23 aMark 1:39; Luke 4:15, 44 bMatt. 9:35; 13:54; Mark 1:21; 6:2; 10:1; Luke 4:15; 6:6; 13:10; John 6:59; 18:20 cMatt. 3:2; 9:35; 24:14; Mark 1:14; Acts 20:25; 28:31 dMatt. 8:16; 9:35; 14:14; 15:30; 19:2; 21:14; Acts 10:38 24 aMark 7:26; Luke 2:2; Acts 15:23; 18:18; 20:3; 21:3; Gal. 1:21 bMatt. 8:16, 28, 33; 9:32; 12:22; 15:22; Mark 1:32; 5:15, 16, 18; Luke 8:36; John 10:21 cMatt. 17:15 dMatt. 8:6; 9:2, 6; Mark 2:3, 4, 5, 9; ★25 aMark 3:7, 8; Luke 6:17 bMark 5:20; 7:31 cMatt. 4:15

II THE PREACHING OF THE KING, 5:1-7:29

A The Picture of Kingdom Life, 5:1-16

★ 1 aMatt. 5-7; Luke 6:20-49 bMark 3:13;

5 [a]And when He saw the multitudes, He went up on [b]the

4:13 *leaving Nazareth.* According to Luke 4:16-30, He left because of what had happened there.
4:14 See Isa. 9:1-2; 42:6-7.
4:19 *Follow Me.* This was their call to service and illustrates the directness, profundity, and power of Christ's commands ("Go . . . ," 28:19; "love one another," John 13:34).
4:21 *James the son of Zebedee.* This is the apostle James, the brother of John, who was martyred under Herod Agrippa I (Acts 12:2). Other men named James in the N.T. are: James the son of Alphaeus, "the less" (Mark 15:40), also one of The Twelve (Matt. 10:3); James, the half brother of Christ and writer of the epistle of James; James, the father or, less probably, brother of the apostle Judas, to be distinguished from Judas Iscariot (Luke 6:16; Acts 1:13).
4:23 *the gospel of the kingdom.* This is the good news that the presence of the King caused the rule of God on the earth (in fulfillment of many O.T. prophecies) to be "at hand." Prerequisites for entrance into the kingdom included repentance (Matt. 4:17), righteousness (Matt. 5:20), childlike faith (Matt. 18:3), or, in summary, being born again (John 3:3). Because the people rejected these requirements, Christ taught that His earthly reign would not immediately come (Luke 19:11). However, this gospel of the kingdom will be preached again during the tribulation period (Matt. 24:14), just prior to the return of Christ to establish His kingdom on earth (Matt. 25:31, 34).
4:25 *Decapolis.* A district, originally containing ten cities, S. of the Sea of Galilee, mainly to the E. of the Jordan river. These were cities with gentile populations and typical Greco-Roman structures—pagan temples, hippodromes, etc.
5:1 *on the mountain.* Chapters 5-7 contain the widely known and loved Sermon on the Mount. It is one of 5 long discourses by Christ

mountain; and after He sat down,
His disciples came to Him.
2 And [a]opening His mouth
He *began* to teach them, saying,
3 "[a]Blessed are the poor in
spirit, for [b]theirs is the kingdom
of heaven.
4 "Blessed are [a]those who
mourn, for they shall be comforted.
5 "Blessed are [a]the gentle, for
they shall inherit the earth.
6 "Blessed are [a]those who
hunger and thirst for righteousness, for they shall be satisfied.
7 "Blessed are the merciful,
for they shall receive mercy.
8 "Blessed are [a]the pure in
heart, for [b]they shall see God.
9 "Blessed are the peacemak-
ers, for [a]they shall be called sons
of God.
10 "Blessed are those who
have been [a]persecuted for the
sake of righteousness, for [b]theirs
is the kingdom of heaven.
11 "Blessed are you when *men*
[a]revile you, and persecute you,
and say all kinds of evil against
you falsely, on account of Me.
12 "Rejoice, and be glad, for
your reward in heaven is great,
for [a]so they persecuted the
prophets who were before you.
13 "You are the salt of the
earth; but [a]if the salt has become
tasteless, how will it be made
salty *again*? It is good for nothing
any more, except to be thrown
out and trampled under foot by
men.
14 "You are [a]the light of the
world. A city set on a hill cannot
be hidden.

2 [a]Matt. 13:35; Acts 8:35; 10:34; 18:14
★ 3 [a]Matt. 5:3-12; Luke 6:20-23 [b]Matt. 5:10; 19:14; 25:34; Mark 10:14; Luke 6:20; 22:29f.
4 [a]Is. 61:2; John 16:20; Rev. 7:17
5 [a]Ps. 37:11
6 [a]Is. 55:1, 2; John 4:14; 6:48ff.; 7:37
8 [a]Ps. 24:4 [b]Heb. 12:14; 1 John 3:2; Rev. 22:4
9 [a]Matt. 5:45; Luke 6:35; Rom. 8:14
10 [a]1 Pet. 3:14 [b]Matt. 5:3; 19:14; 25:34; Mark 10:14; Luke 6:20; 22:29f.
11 [a]1 Pet. 4:14
12 [a]2 Chr. 36:16; Matt. 23:37; Acts 7:52; 1 Thess. 2:15; Heb. 11:33ff.; James 5:10
13 [a]Mark 9:50; Luke 14:34f.
14 [a]John 8:12

15 "[a]Nor do *men* light a lamp,
and put it under the peck-measure, but on the lampstand; and it
gives light to all who are in the
house.
16 "Let your light shine before
men in such a way that they may
[a]see your good works, and [b]glori-
fy your Father who is in heaven.

15 [a]Mark 4:21; Luke 8:16; 11:33
16 [a]1 Pet. 2:12 [b]Matt. 9:8

B The Precepts for Kingdom Life, 5:17-48

1 *The law of Moses,* 5:17-20

17 "Do not think that I came
to abolish the Law or the Prophets; I did not come to abolish, but
to fulfill.
18 "For truly I say to you, [a]un-
til heaven and earth pass away,
not the smallest letter or stroke
shall pass away from the Law, until all is accomplished.
19 "Whoever then annuls one
of the least of these commandments, and so teaches others,
shall be called least in the kingdom of heaven; but whoever
keeps and teaches *them,* he shall
be called great in the kingdom of
heaven.
20 "For I say to you, that unless your righteousness surpasses
that of the scribes and Pharisees,
you shall not enter the kingdom
of heaven.

★18 [a]Matt. 24:35; Luke 16:17
★20

2 *The law of murder,* 5:21-22

21 "[a]You have heard that the
ancients were told, '[b]YOU SHALL
NOT COMMIT MURDER' and 'Whoever
commits murder shall be liable to
[c]the court.'

21 [a]Matt. 5:27, 33, 38, 43 [b]Ex. 20:13; Deut. 5:17 [c]Deut. 16:18; 2 Chr.

---

found in Matthew, the others being 9:35-10:42; 13:1-52; 17:24-18:35; and 23:1-25:46. The Sermon on the Mount does not present the way of salvation but the way of righteous living for those who are in God's family, contrasting the new Way with the "old one" of the scribes and the Pharisees. For the Jews of Christ's day this message was a detailed explanation of "repent" (3:2; 4:17). It was also an elaboration of the spirit of the law (5:17, 21-22, 27-28). For all of us it is a detailed revelation of the righteousness of God, and its principles are applicable to the children of God today.

5:3-12 The Beatitudes (*blessed* means happy) describe the inner condition of a follower of Christ and promise him blessings in the future.

5:18 *smallest letter or stroke.* The smallest Hebrew letter is *yodh,* which looks like an apostrophe ('). A stroke is a very small extension or protrusion on several Hebrew letters which distinguish these letters from similar ones. The Lord's point is that every letter of every word of the O.T. is vital and will be fulfilled.

5:20 *your righteousness.* We may understand this as "your practice of religion."

★22 [a]Deut. 16:18; 2 Chr. 19:5f. [b]Matt. 10:17; 26:59; Mark 13:9; 14:55; 15:1; Luke 22:66; John 11:47; Acts 4:15; 5:21; 6:12; 22:30; 23:1; 24:20 [c]Matt. 5:29f.; 10:28; 18:9; 23:15, 33; Mark 9:43ff.; Luke 12:5; James 3:6

22 "But I say to you that every one who is angry with his brother shall be guilty before [a]the court; and whoever shall say to his brother, 'Raca,' shall be guilty before [b]the supreme court; and whoever shall say, 'You fool,' shall be guilty *enough to go* into the [c]hell of fire.

3 *The law of reconciliation,* 5:23–26

23 "If therefore you are presenting your offering at the altar, and there remember that your brother has something against you,

24 leave your offering there before the altar, and go your way; first be reconciled to your brother, and then come and present your offering.

25 [a]Luke 12:58

25 "[a]Make friends quickly with your opponent at law while you are with him on the way, in order that your opponent may not deliver you to the judge, and the judge to the officer, and you be thrown into prison.

26 "Truly I say to you, you shall not come out of there, until you have paid up the last cent.

4 *The law of adultery,* 5:27–30

27 [a]Matt. 5:21, 33, 38, 43 [b]Ex. 20:14; Deut. 5:18

27 "[a]You have heard that it was said, '[b]YOU SHALL NOT COMMIT ADULTERY';

28 but I say to you, that every one who looks on a woman to lust for her has committed adultery with her already in his heart. ★28

29 "And [a]if your right eye makes you stumble, tear it out, and throw it from you; for it is better for you that one of the parts of your body perish, than for your whole body to be thrown into [b]hell.

★29 [a]Matt. 17:27; 18:9; Mark 9:47 [b]Matt. 5:22

30 "And [a]if your right hand makes you stumble, cut it off, and throw it from you; for it is better for you that one of the parts of your body perish, than for your whole body to go into [b]hell.

30 [a]Matt. 17:27; 18:8; Mark 9:43 [b]Matt. 5:22

5 *The law of divorce,* 5:31–32

31 "And it was said, '[a]WHOEVER DIVORCES HIS WIFE, LET HIM GIVE HER A CERTIFICATE OF DISMISSAL';

31 [a]Deut. 24:1, 3

32 [a]but I say to you that every one who divorces his wife, except for *the* cause of unchastity, makes her commit adultery; and whoever marries a divorced woman commits adultery.

★32 [a]Matt. 19:9; Mark 10:11f.; Luke 16:18; 1 Cor. 7:11f.

6 *The law of oaths,* 5:33–37

33 "Again, [a]you have heard that the ancients were told, '[b]YOU SHALL NOT MAKE FALSE VOWS, BUT SHALL FULFILL YOUR VOWS TO THE LORD.'

★33 [a]Matt. 5:21, 27, 38, 43; 23:16ff. [b]Lev. 19:12; Num. 30:2; Deut. 23:21

34 "But I say to you, [a]make no oath at all, either by heaven, for it is [b]the throne of God,

34 [a]James 5:12 [b]Is. 66:1; Matt. 23:22

5:22 *Raca.* Probably means "empty-head." *hell of fire.* The word translated "hell" is *Geenna,* or *Gehenna,* a place in the valley of Hinnom where human sacrifices had been offered (cf. Jer. 7:31) and where the continuous burning of rubbish made it an apt illustration of the lake of fire (Mark 9:44; Jas. 3:6; Rev. 20:14).

5:28 The desire itself is sinful, and wrong desire leads to a sinful act.

5:29–30 This is strong language, used to emphasize the comparison; i.e., sin is so dangerous, because it leads to eternal condemnation, that it would be better to lose hands or eyes temporarily than to lose life eternally.

5:32 *except for the cause of unchastity.* See Matt. 19:3-9; Mark 10:2-12; and Luke 16:18 for Jesus' teaching on divorce (cf. 1 Cor. 7:10-11). It is disallowed except for unchastity, which may mean (1) adultery, (2) unfaithfulness during the period of betrothal (see Matt. 1:19), or (3) marriage between near relatives (Lev. 18).

5:33 *make false vows.* Or, "perjure yourself." Oaths taken in the name of the Lord were binding, and perjury was strongly condemned in the law (Ex. 20:7; Lev. 19:12; Deut. 19:16-19). Every oath contained an affirmation or promise and an appeal to God as the omniscient punisher of falsehoods, which made the oath binding. Thus we find phrases like "as the Lord lives" (1 Sam. 14:39). The emphasis on the sanctity of oaths led to the feeling that ordinary phrasing need not be truthful or binding. Jesus, however, taught (Matt. 5:37) that we should say and mean yes or no and never equivocate.

35 [a]Is. 66:1; Acts 7:49 [b]Ps. 48:2

35 or by the earth, for it is the
[a]footstool of His feet, or by Jerusalem, for it is [b]THE CITY OF THE
GREAT KING.
36 "Nor shall you make an
oath by your head, for you cannot
make one hair white or black.

37 [a]Matt. 6:13; 13:19, 38; John 17:15; 2 Thess. 3:3; 1 John 2:13f.; 3:12; 5:18f.

37 "But let your statement be,
'Yes, yes' *or* 'No, no'; and anything beyond these is of [a]evil.

7 The law of nonresistance, 5:38–42

★38 [a]Matt. 5:21, 27, 33, 43 [b]Ex. 21:24; Lev. 24:20; Deut. 19:21

38 "[a]You have heard that it
was said, '[b]AN EYE FOR AN EYE, AND
A TOOTH FOR A TOOTH.'

39 [a]Matt. 5:39-42: *Luke 6:29, 30;* 1 Cor. 6:7

39 "But I say to you, do not resist him who is evil; but [a]whoever
slaps you on your right cheek,
turn to him the other also.
40 "And if any one wants to
sue you, and take your shirt, let
him have your coat also.
41 "And whoever shall force
you to go one mile, go with him
two.

42 [a]Luke 6:34f.

42 "[a]Give to him who asks of
you, and do not turn away from
him who wants to borrow from
you.

8 The law of love, 5:43–48

★43 [a]Matt. 5:21, 27, 33, 38 [b]Lev. 19:18

43 "[a]You have heard that it
was said, '[b]YOU SHALL LOVE YOUR
NEIGHBOR, and hate your enemy.'

★44 [a]Luke 6:27f.; 23:34; Acts 7:60

44 "But I say to you, [a]love your
enemies, and pray for those who
persecute you

45 [a]Matt. 5:9

45 in order that you may be
[a]sons of your Father who is in
heaven; for He causes His sun to
rise on *the* evil and *the* good, and
sends rain on *the* righteous and
the unrighteous.

46 [a]Luke 6:32

46 "For [a]if you love those who
love you, what reward have you?
Do not even the tax-gatherers do
the same?
47 "And if you greet your
brothers only, what do you do
more *than others*? Do not even
the Gentiles do the same?
48 "Therefore [a]you are to be ★48 [a]Lev. 19:2
perfect, as your heavenly Father is
perfect.

C The Practice of Kingdom Life, 6:1–7:12

1 In relation to almsgiving, 6:1–4

6 "Beware of practicing your ★ 1 [a]Matt. 6:5, 16; 23:5
righteousness before men [a]to
be noticed by them; otherwise
you have no reward with your Father who is in heaven.
2 "When therefore you give 2 [a]Matt. 6:5, 16; 23:5 [b]Matt. 6:5, 16; Luke 6:24
alms, do not sound a trumpet be-
fore you, as the hypocrites do in
the synagogues and in the streets,
that they [a]may be honored by
men. [b]Truly I say to you, they
have their reward in full.
3 "But when you give alms,
do not let your left hand know
what your right hand is doing
4 that your alms may be in ★ 4 [a]Matt. 6:6, 18
secret; and [a]your Father who sees
in secret will repay you.

2 In relation to prayer, 6:5–15

5 "And when you pray, you 5 [a]Mark 11:25; Luke 18:11, 13 [b]Matt. 6:1, 16 [c]Matt. 6:2, 16; Luke 6:24
are not to be as the hypocrites; for
they love to [a]stand and pray in
the synagogues and on the street
corners, [b]in order to be seen by
men. [c]Truly I say to you, they
have their reward in full.
6 "But you, when you pray, 6 [a]Is. 26:20 [b]Matt. 6:4, 18
[a]GO INTO YOUR INNER ROOM, AND
WHEN YOU HAVE SHUT YOUR DOOR,
pray to your Father who is in se-

5:38 See Ex. 21:24. The *lex talionis* (law of retaliation) did provide for the ending of feuds, but Christ showed another way to do the same (Matt. 5:39–42).

5:43 See Lev. 19:16–18.

5:44 A new teaching, found nowhere in the O.T.

5:48 *perfect.* Not necessarily without sin, but mature and complete in the likeness of God.

6:1–18 Christ discusses three pharisaic practices of piety: almsgiving, prayer, and fasting.

6:4 *that your alms may be in secret.* Jewish tradition said that there was in the temple a "chamber of secrets" into which the devout used to put their gifts in secret so that the poor could receive support therefrom in secret.

cret, and [b]your Father who sees in secret will repay you.

7 [a]1 Kin. 18:26f.

7 "And when you are praying, do not use meaningless repetition, as the Gentiles do, for they suppose that they will be heard for their [a]many words.

8 [a]Matt. 6:32

8 "Therefore do not be like them; for [a]your Father knows what you need, before you ask Him.

★ 9 [a]Matt. 6:9-13; *Luke 11:2-4*

9 "[a]Pray, then, in this way:

'Our Father who art in heaven,
Hallowed be Thy name.

10 [a]Matt. 3:2

10 '[a]Thy kingdom come.
Thy will be done,
On earth as it is in heaven.

★11 [a]Prov. 30:8

11 '[a]Give us this day our daily bread.

★12

12 'And forgive us our debts, as we also have forgiven our debtors.

13 [a]Matt. 5:37

13 'And do not lead us into temptation, but deliver us from [a]evil. [For Thine is the kingdom, and the power, and the glory, forever. Amen].'

★14 [a]Matt. 18:35; Mark 11:25f.

14 "[a]For if you forgive men for their transgressions, your heavenly Father will also forgive you.

15 "But if you do not forgive men, then your Father will not forgive your transgressions.

3 *In relation to fasting,* 6:16–18

16 [a]Is. 58:5 [b]Matt. 6:2

16 "And [a]whenever you fast, do not put on a gloomy face as the hypocrites *do,* for they neglect their appearance in order to be seen fasting by men. [b]Truly I say to you, they have their reward in full.

17 "But you, when you fast, anoint your head, and wash your face

18 [a]Matt. 6:4, 6

18 so that you may not be seen fasting by men, but by your Father who is in secret; and your [a]Father who sees in secret will repay you.

4 *In relation to money,* 6:19–24

19 "Do not lay up for yourselves treasures upon earth, where moth and rust destroy, and where thieves break in and steal.

20 [a]Matt. 19:21; Luke 12:33; 1 Tim. 6:19

20 "But lay up for yourselves [a]treasures in heaven, where neither moth nor rust destroys, and where thieves do not break in or steal;

21 [a]Luke 12:34

21 for [a]where your treasure is, there will your heart be also.

22 [a]Matt. 6:22, 23; *Luke 11:34, 35*

22 "[a]The lamp of the body is the eye; if therefore your eye is clear, your whole body will be full of light.

23 [a]Matt. 20:15; Mark 7:22

23 "But if [a]your eye is bad, your whole body will be full of darkness. If therefore the light that is in you is darkness, how great is the darkness!

★24 [a]Luke 16:13 [b]Luke 16:9, 11, 13

24 "[a]No one can serve two masters; for either he will hate the one and love the other, or he will hold to one and despise the other. You cannot serve God and [b]mammon.

5 *In relation to anxiety,* 6:25–34

25 [a]Matt. 6:25-33; *Luke 12:22-31* [b]Matt. 6:27, 28, 31, 34; Luke 10:41; 12:11, 22; Phil. 4:6; 1 Pet. 5:7

25 "[a]For this reason I say to you, do not be [b]anxious for your life, *as to* what you shall eat, or what you shall drink; nor for your body, *as to* what you shall put on. Is not life more than food, and the body than clothing?

6:9 *in this way.* The Lord's Prayer is a model for our prayers. It begins with adoration of God (v. 9), acknowledges subjection to His will (v. 10), asks petitions of Him (vv. 11–13a), and ends with an ascription of praise (v. 13b, though this may have been added later).

6:11 *bread.* All necessary food.

6:12 *debts.* These are obligations incurred; i.e., sins of omission and commission. Forgiveness means cancellation of these debts or obligations.

6:14-15 Notice that the only point the Lord emphasizes in the prayer is the necessity for forgiving one another. Forgiveness with the Father depends on forgiveness among the members of the family of God. This is the forgiveness that affects fellowship within the family of God, not the forgiveness that leads to salvation.

6:24 *mammon* = money.

★26 [a]Matt. 10:29ff.

26 "[a]Look at the birds of the air, that they do not sow, neither do they reap, nor gather into barns, and *yet* your heavenly Father feeds them. Are you not worth much more than they?

★27 [a]Matt. 6:25, 28, 31, 34; Luke 10:41; 12:11, 22; Phil. 4:6; 1 Pet. 5:7 [b]Ps. 39:5

27 "And which of you by being [a]anxious can [b]add a *single* cubit to his life's span?

28 [a]Matt. 6:25, 27, 31, 34; Luke 10:41; 12:11, 22; Phil. 4:6; 1 Pet. 5:7

28 "And why are you [a]anxious about clothing? Observe how the lilies of the field grow; they do not toil nor do they spin,

29 [a]1 Kin. 10:4-7

29 yet I say to you that even [a]Solomon in all his glory did not clothe himself like one of these.

30 [a]Matt. 8:26; 14:31; 16:8

30 "But if God so arrays the grass of the field, which is *alive* today and tomorrow is thrown into the furnace, *will He* not much more *do so for* you, [a]O men of little faith?

31 [a]Matt. 6:25, 27, 28, 34; Luke 10:41; 12:11, 22; Phil. 4:6; 1 Pet. 5:7

31 "Do not be [a]anxious then, saying, 'What shall we eat?' or 'What shall we drink?' or 'With what shall we clothe ourselves?'

32 [a]Matt. 6:8

32 "For all these things the Gentiles eagerly seek; for [a]your heavenly Father knows that you need all these things.

33 [a]Matt. 19:28; Mark 10:29f.; Luke 18:29f.; 1 Tim. 4:8

33 "But seek first His kingdom and His righteousness; and [a]all these things shall be added to you.

★34 [a]Matt. 6:25, 27, 28, 31; Luke 10:41; 12:11, 22; Phil. 4:6; 1 Pet. 5:7

34 "Therefore do not be [a]anxious for tomorrow; for tomorrow will care for itself. *Each* day has enough trouble of its own.

6 *In relation to judging,* 7:1–5

★ 1 [a]Matt. 7:1-5: *Luke 6:37f., 41f.* 2 [a]Mark 4:24; Luke 6:38

7 "[a]Do not judge lest you be judged *yourselves.*

2 "For in the way you judge, you will be judged; and [a]by your standard of measure, it shall be measured to you.

3 "And why do you look at the speck in your brother's eye, but do not notice the log that is in your own eye?

4 "Or how can you say to your brother, 'Let me take the speck out of your eye,' and behold, the log is in your own eye?

5 "You hypocrite, first take the log out of your own eye, and then you will see clearly *enough* to take the speck out of your brother's eye.

7 *In relation to prudence,* 7:6

6 "Do not give what is holy to dogs, and do not throw your pearls before swine, lest they trample them under their feet, and turn and tear you to pieces. ★ 6

8 *In relation to prayer,* 7:7–11

7 [a]Matt. 7:7-11: *Luke 11:9-13* [b]Matt. 18:19; 21:22; Mark 11:24; John 14:13; 15:7, 16; 16:23f.; James 1:5f.; 1 John 3:22; 5:14f.

7 "[a]Ask, and [b]it shall be given to you; seek, and you shall find; knock, and it shall be opened to you.

8 "For every one who asks receives, and he who seeks finds, and to him who knocks it shall be opened.

9 "Or what man is there among you, when his son shall ask him for a loaf, will give him a stone?

10 "Or if he shall ask for a fish, he will not give him a snake, will he?

11 "If you then, being evil, know how to give good gifts to your children, how much more shall your Father who is in heaven give what is good to those who ask Him!

6:26 *your heavenly Father feeds them.* God feeds the birds not by miraculous supply of food but through natural processes involving the earth and the birds' use of their faculties. Likewise, the child of God, though sometimes the recipient of a miracle, is usually cared for by normal means.

6:27 *cubit.* About 18 inches.

6:34 *trouble.* Let each day's trouble be enough for that day. This saying is like a proverb.

7:1 *Do not judge.* This does not mean that one is never, in any sense or to any extent, to judge another, for v. 5 indicates that when one's own life is pure he should "cast the mote out" of the brother's eye. It does mean, however, that a follower of Christ is not to be censorious.

7:6 The disciples were expected to make moral distinctions and not allow those who reject the invitation of Christ to treat precious things as cheap.

9 In relation to others, 7:12

★12 [a]Luke 6:31 [b]Matt. 22:40; Rom. 13:8ff.; Gal. 5:14

12 "[a]Therefore whatever you
want others to do for you, do so
for them, for [b]this is the Law and
the Prophets.

D The Proof of Kingdom Life, 7:13–29

★13 [a]Luke 13:24

13 "[a]Enter by the narrow gate;
for the gate is wide, and the way
is broad that leads to destruction,
and many are those who enter by
it.
14 "For the gate is small, and
the way is narrow that leads to
life, and few are those who find it.

15 [a]Matt. 24:11, 24; Mark 13:22; Luke 6:26; Acts 13:6; 2 Pet. 2:1; 1 John 4:1; Rev. 16:13; 19:20; 20:10 [b]Ezek. 22:27; John 10:12; Acts 20:29

16 [a]Matt. 7:20; 12:33; Luke 6:44; James 3:12

15 "Beware of the [a]false
prophets, who come to you in
sheep's clothing, but inwardly are
[b]ravenous wolves.
16 "You will know them [a]by
their fruits. Grapes are not gathered from thorn *bushes,* nor figs
from thistles, are they?
17 "Even so, every good tree
bears good fruit; but the rotten
tree bears bad fruit.
18 "A good tree cannot produce bad fruit, nor can a rotten
tree produce good fruit.

19 [a]Matt. 3:10; Luke 13:7

19 "[a]Every tree that does not
bear good fruit is cut down and
thrown into the fire.

20 [a]Matt. 7:16; 12:33; Luke 6:44; James 3:12

★21 [a]Luke 6:46

20 "So then, you will know
them [a]by their fruits.
21 "[a]Not every one who says
to Me, 'Lord, Lord,' will enter the
kingdom of heaven; but he who
does the will of My Father who is
in heaven.

★22 [a]Matt. 25:11f.; Luke 13:25ff. [b]Matt. 10:15

22 "[a]Many will say to Me on
[b]that day, 'Lord, Lord, did we not
prophesy in Your name, and in
Your name cast out demons, and
in Your name perform many miracles?'

23 [a]Ps. 6:8; Matt. 25:41; Luke 13:27

23 "And then I will declare to
them, 'I never knew you; [a]DEPART
FROM ME, YOU WHO PRACTICE LAW-
LESSNESS.'

24 [a]Matt. 7:24-27: *Luke 6:47-49;* James 1:22-25

24 "Therefore [a]every one who
hears these words of Mine, and
acts upon them, may be compared to a wise man, who built
his house upon the rock.
25 "And the rain descended,
and the floods came, and the
winds blew, and burst against
that house; and *yet* it did not fall,
for it had been founded upon the
rock.
26 "And every one who hears
these words of Mine, and does
not act upon them, will be like a
foolish man, who built his house
upon the sand.
27 "And the rain descended,
and the floods came, and the
winds blew, and burst against
that house; and it fell, and great
was its fall."

28 [a]Matt. 11:1; 13:53; 19:1; 26:1 [b]Matt. 13:54; 22:33; Mark 1:22; 6:2; 11:18; Luke 4:32; John 7:46

★29

28 [a]The result was that when
Jesus had finished these words,
[b]the multitudes were amazed at
His teaching;
29 for He was teaching them
as *one* having authority, and not
as their scribes.

III THE PROOF OF THE KING, 8:1–9:38

A Exhibit 1: Power, 8:1–34

1 Power over defilement, 8:1–4

8 And when He had come
down from the mountain,
great multitudes followed Him.

7:12 The well-known Golden Rule. It was also taught by the great Jewish rabbis, such as Rabbi Hillel.

7:13-29 In these verses notice the two ways (13-14), two trees (15-20), two professions (21-23), and two builders (24-29). The "two ways" was a common teaching method in Judaism and Greco-Roman philosophy.

7:21 Obedience to the will of God comes first.

7:22 *demons.* There is only one devil (Satan) but there are many demons. The demons are those angels who sinned with Satan by following him when he revolted against God. Some are confined (2 Pet. 2:4), but many are active in the world (Matt. 12:43-45). They seek to thwart the purposes of God (Eph. 6:11-12); they promote their own system of doctrine (1 Tim. 4:1); they can inflict diseases (Matt. 9:33) and possess the bodies of men and of animals (Matt. 4:24; Mark 5:13).

7:29 The scribes had to rely on tradition for authority; Christ's authority was His own. It disturbed the Pharisees that He had no "credentials" as an official teacher in their system.

★ 2 [a]Matt. 8:2-4; *Mark 1:40-44; Luke 5:12-14* [b]Matt. 9:18; 15:25; 18:26; 20:20; John 9:38; Acts 10:25

2 And behold, a leper [a]came to Him, and [b]bowed down to Him, saying, "Lord, if You are willing, You can make me clean."

3 And stretching out His hand, He touched him, saying, "I am willing; be cleansed." And immediately his leprosy was cleansed.

★ 4 [a]Matt. 9:30; 12:16; 17:9; Mark 1:44; 3:12; 5:43; 7:36; 8:30; 9:9; Luke 4:41; 8:56; 9:21 [b]Mark 1:44; Luke 5:14; 17:14 [c]Lev. 13:49; 14:2ff.

4 And Jesus *said to him, "[a]See that you tell no one; but [b]go, [c]SHOW YOURSELF TO THE PRIEST, and present the offering that Moses prescribed, for a testimony to them."

2 *Power over distance,* 8:5–13

★ 5 [a]Matt. 8:5-13; *Luke 7:1-10*

5 And [a]when He had entered Capernaum, a centurion came to Him, entreating Him,

6 [a]Matt. 4:24

6 and saying, "Sir, my servant is lying [a]paralyzed at home, suffering great pain."

7 And He *said to him, "I will come and heal him."

8 But the centurion answered and said, "Lord, I am not qualified for You to come under my roof, but just say the word, and my servant will be healed.

★9

9 "For I, too, am a man under authority, with soldiers under me; and I say to this one, 'Go!' and he goes, and to another, 'Come!' and he comes, and to my slave, 'Do this!' and he does *it.*"

10 Now when Jesus heard *this,* He marveled, and said to those who were following, "Truly I say to you, I have not found such great faith with anyone in Israel.

★11 [a]Is. 49:12; 59:19; Mal. 1:11; Luke 13:29

11 "And I say to you, that many [a]shall come from east and west, and recline *at table* with Abraham, and Isaac, and Jacob, in the kingdom of heaven;

★12 [a]Matt. 13:38 [b]Matt. 22:13; 25:30 [c]Matt. 13:42, 50; 22:13; 24:51; 25:30; Luke 13:28

12 but [a]the sons of the kingdom shall be cast out into [b]the outer darkness; in that place [c]there shall be weeping and gnashing of teeth."

13 [a]Matt. 9:22, 29

13 And Jesus said to the centurion, "Go your way; let it be done to you [a]as you have believed." And the servant was healed that *very* hour.

3 *Power over disease,* 8:14–17

★14 [a]Matt. 8:14-16; *Mark 1:29-34; Luke 4:38-41*

14 [a]And when Jesus had come to Peter's home, He saw his mother-in-law lying sick in bed with a fever.

★15

15 And He touched her hand, and the fever left her; and she arose, and began to wait on Him.

16 [a]Matt. 4:24 [b]Matt. 4:23; 8:33

16 And when evening had come, they brought to Him many [a]who were demon-possessed; and He cast out the spirits with a word, and [b]healed all who were ill

★17 [a]Is. 53:4

17 in order that what was spoken through Isaiah the prophet might be fulfilled, saying, "[a]HE HIMSELF TOOK OUR INFIRMITIES, AND CARRIED AWAY OUR DISEASES."

4 *Power over disciples,* 8:18–22

18 [a]Mark 4:35; Luke 8:22

18 Now when Jesus saw a crowd around Him, [a]He gave orders to depart to the other side.

19 [a]Matt. 8:19-22; *Luke 9:57-60*

19 [a]And a certain scribe came and said to Him, "Teacher, I will follow You wherever You go."

★20 [a]Dan. 7:13; Matt. 9:6; 12:8, 32, 40; 13:41; 16:13, 27f.; 17:9; 19:28; 26:64; Mark 8:38; Luke 12:8; 18:8; 21:36; John 1:51; 3:13f.; 6:27; 12:34; Acts 7:56

20 And Jesus *said to him, "The foxes have holes, and the birds of the air *have* nests; but

---

8:2 *a leper.* See note on Luke 5:12.
8:4 *the offering that Moses prescribed.* See Lev. 14:4–32.
8:5 *centurion.* A Roman army officer who commanded 100 men.
8:9 *a man under authority.* If a lesser officer can give orders, certainly Christ, who possesses all authority, can.
8:11 Gentiles will be included in the blessings of the millennial reign of Christ on this earth.
8:12 *sons* = heirs = Jews.
8:14 *his mother-in-law.* Peter was married (see 1 Cor. 9:5).
8:15 *wait on* = serve food.
8:17 See Isa. 53:4.
8:20 *Son of Man.* The title "Son of God" is Jesus' divine name (Matt. 8:29); "Son of David," His Jewish name (Matt. 9:27); but "Son of Man," the name that links Him to the earth and to His mission. It was His favorite designation of Himself (used over 80 times) and was based on Dan. 7:13–14. It emphasizes: (1) His lowliness and humanity (Matt. 8:20); (2) His suffering and death (Luke 19:10); and (3) His future reign as King (Matt. 24:27).

[a]the Son of Man has nowhere to lay His head."

21 And another of the disciples said to Him, "Lord, permit me first to go and bury my father."

22 But Jesus *said to him, "[a]Follow Me; and allow the dead to bury their own dead."

22 [a]Matt. 9:9; Mark 2:14; Luke 9:59; John 1:43; 21:19

5 *Power over the deep,* 8:23–27

23 [a]And when He got into the boat, His disciples followed Him.

23 [a]Matt. 8:23-27: *Mark 4:36-41; Luke 8:22-25*

24 And behold, there arose a great storm in the sea, so that the boat was covered with the waves; but He Himself was asleep.

25 And they came to *Him,* and awoke Him, saying, "Save *us,* Lord; we are perishing!"

26 And He *said to them, "Why are you timid, [a]you men of little faith?" Then He arose, and rebuked the winds and the sea; and it became perfectly calm.

26 [a]Matt. 6:30; 14:31; 16:8

27 And the men marveled, saying, "What kind of a man is this, that even the winds and the sea obey Him?"

6 *Power over demons,* 8:28–34

28 [a]And when He had come to the other side into the country of the Gadarenes, two men who were [b]demon-possessed met Him as they were coming out of the tombs; *they were* so exceedingly violent that no one could pass by that road.

★**28** [a]Matt. 8:28-34: *Mark 5:1-17; Luke 8:26-37* [b]Matt. 4:24

29 And behold, they cried out, saying, "[a]What do we have to do with You, Son of God? Have You come here to torment us before the time?"

29 [a]Judg. 11:12; 2 Sam. 16:10; 19:22; 1 Kin. 17:18; 2 Kin. 3:13; 2 Chr. 35:21; Mark 1:24; 5:7; Luke 4:34; 8:28; John 2:4

30 Now there was at a distance from them a herd of many swine feeding.

31 And the demons *began* to entreat Him, saying, "If You are *going to* cast us out, send us into the herd of swine."

32 And He said to them, "Begone!" And they came out, and went into the swine, and behold, the whole herd rushed down the steep bank into the sea and perished in the waters.

33 And the herdsmen fled, and went away to the city, and reported everything, including the *incident* of the [a]demoniacs.

33 [a]Matt. 4:24

34 And behold, the whole city came out to meet Jesus; and when they saw Him, they entreated *Him* to depart from their region.

B Exhibit 2: Pardon, 9:1–17

1 *Pardon of a paralytic,* 9:1–8

9 And getting into a boat, He crossed over, and came to [a]His own city.

★ **1** [a]Matt. 4:13; Mark 5:21

2 [a]And behold, they were bringing to Him a [b]paralytic, lying on a bed; and Jesus seeing their faith said to the paralytic, "[c]Take courage, *My* son, [d]your sins are forgiven."

★ **2** [a]Matt. 9:2-8: *Mark 2:3-12; Luke 5:18-26* [b]Matt. 4:24; 9:6 [c]Matt. 9:22; 14:27; Mark 6:50; 10:49; John 16:33; Acts 23:11 [d]Mark 2:5, 9; Luke 5:20, 23; 7:48

3 And behold, some of the scribes said to themselves, "This *fellow* blasphemes."

4 And Jesus [a]knowing their thoughts said, "Why are you thinking evil in your hearts?

4 [a]Matt. 12:25; Luke 6:8; 9:47

5 "For which is easier, to say, '[a]Your sins are forgiven,' or to say, 'Rise, and walk'?

★ **5** [a]Mark 2:5, 9; Luke 5:20, 23; 7:48

6 "But in order that you may know that [a]the Son of Man has authority on earth to forgive sins"—then He *said to the [b]paralytic, "Rise, take up your bed, and go home."

6 [a]Matt. 8:20 [b]Matt. 4:24; 9:2

7 And he rose, and went to his home.

8:28 *Gadarenes.* Lived on the E. shore of the Lake of Galilee.

9:1 *His own city.* Capernaum.

9:2 *your sins are forgiven.* This may indicate that the man's sickness was the direct result of sin. Some Jews speculated that such was always the case, but see John 9:2 and note at Phil. 2:30.

9:5 It is obviously easier to *say,* "Your sins are forgiven," since the validity of the statement cannot be tested so easily as "Rise." By making the statement, Christ was asserting a prerogative of God, who alone can forgive sins.

8 [a]Matt. 5:16; 15:31; Mark 2:12; Luke 2:20; 5:25, 26; 7:16; 13:13; 17:15; 23:47; John 15:8; Acts 4:21; 11:18; 21:20; 2 Cor. 9:13; Gal. 1:24

8 But when the multitudes
saw *this,* they were filled with
awe, and [a]glorified God, who had
given such authority to men.

2 *Pardon of a publican,* 9:9–13

9 [a]Matt. 9:9-17: *Mark 2:14-22; Luke 5:27-38* [b]Matt. 10:3; Mark 2:14; 3:18; Luke 6:15; Acts 1:13 [c]Matt. 8:22

9 [a]And as Jesus passed on
from there, He saw a man, called
[b]Matthew, sitting in the tax office;
and He *said to him, "[c]Follow
Me!" And he rose, and followed
Him.

★10

10 And it happened that as
He was reclining *at table* in the
house, behold many tax-gatherers
and sinners came and joined Jesus
and His disciples *at the table.*

11 [a]Matt. 11:19; Mark 2:16; Luke 5:30; 15:2

11 And when the Pharisees
saw *this,* they said to His disciples, "[a]Why does your Teacher
eat with the tax-gatherers and
sinners?"

12 [a]Mark 2:17; Luke 5:31

12 But when He heard this,
He said, "*It is* not [a]those who are
healthy who need a physician,
but those who are ill.

★13 [a]Matt. 12:7 [b]Hos. 6:6 [c]Mark 2:17; Luke 5:32; 1 Tim. 1:15

13 "But go and learn [a]what *this*
means, '[b]I DESIRE COMPASSION, AND
NOT SACRIFICE,' for [c]I did not come
to call *the* righteous, but sinners."

3 *Problem concerning fasting,* 9:14–17

★14 [a]Luke 18:12

14 Then the disciples of John
*came to Him, saying, "Why do
we and [a]the Pharisees fast, but
Your disciples do not fast?"

15 And Jesus said to them,
"The attendants of the bridegroom cannot mourn as long as
the bridegroom is with them, can
they? But the days will come
when the bridegroom is taken
away from them, and then they
will fast.

16 "But no one puts a patch of ★16
unshrunk cloth on an old garment; for the patch pulls away
from the garment, and a worse
tear results.

17 "Nor do *men* put new wine
into old wineskins; otherwise the
wineskins burst, and the wine
pours out, and the wineskins are
ruined; but they put new wine
into fresh wineskins, and both are
preserved."

C **Exhibit 3: Power,** 9:18–38

1 *Power over death,* 9:18–26

18 [a]While He was saying
these things to them, behold,
there came a synagogue official,
and [b]bowed down before Him,
saying, "My daughter has just
died; but come and lay Your hand
on her, and she will live."

18 [a]Matt. 9:18-26: *Mark 5:22-43; Luke 8:41-56* [b]Matt. 8:2

19 And Jesus rose and *began*
to follow him, and *so did* His disciples.

20 And behold, a woman who
had been suffering from a hemorrhage for twelve years, came up
behind Him and touched [a]the
fringe of His cloak;

★20 [a]Num. 15:38; Deut. 22:12; Matt. 14:36; 23:5

21 for she was saying to herself, "If I only [a]touch His garment, I shall get well."

21 [a]Matt. 14:36; Mark 3:10; Luke 6:19

22 But Jesus turning and seeing her said, "Daughter, [a]take
courage; [b]your faith has made
you well." And at once the
woman was made well.

22 [a]Matt. 9:2 [b]Matt. 9:29; 15:28; Mark 5:34; 10:52; Luke 7:50; 8:48; 17:19; 18:42

23 And when Jesus came into
the official's house, and saw [a]the
flute-players, and the crowd in
noisy disorder,

★23 [a]2 Chr. 35:25; Jer. 9:17; 16:6; Ezek. 24:17

24 He *began* to say, "Depart;
for the girl [a]is not dead, but is

24 [a]John 11:13; Acts 20:10

9:10 *tax-gatherers and sinners.* Men who collected taxes for the Romans had a bad reputation for extortion and malpractice. "Sinners" were those whose daily occupations rendered them ceremonially unclean and not, in Pharisaic eyes, to be associated with.

9:13 See Hos. 6:6.

9:14 The Pharisees fasted twice a week—conspicuous piety. John's followers were probably fasting in mourning for him. The required public fasts were only 3 in number: the Day of Atonement; the day before Purim; and the 9th of Ab, commemorating the fall of Jerusalem.

9:16–17 The old and new cannot be combined. See note at Luke 5:37.

9:20 *the fringe of His cloak.* Probably the fringes or tassels at the corners of Christ's mantle. These were religious reminders to the wearer to observe the commandments (Num. 15:37-39).

9:23 *flute-players.* It was customary, even among the very poor, to hire two or more flute-players at times of mourning.

asleep." And they were laughing at Him.

25 But when the crowd had been put out, He entered and took her by the hand; and the girl arose.

26 And [a]this news went out into all that land.

26 [a]Matt. 4:24; 9:31; 14:1; Mark 1:28, 45; Luke 4:14, 37; 5:15; 7:17

2 *Power over darkness,* 9:27-31

27 And as Jesus passed on from there, two blind men followed Him, crying out, and saying, "Have mercy on us, [a]Son of David!"

27 [a]Matt. 1:1; 12:23; 15:22; 20:30, 31; 21:9, 15; 22:42; Mark 10:47, 48; 12:35; Luke 18:38, 39; 20:41f.

28 And after He had come into the house, the blind men came up to Him, and Jesus *said to them, "Do you believe that I am able to do this?" They *said to Him, "Yes, Lord."

29 Then He touched their eyes, saying, "Be it done to you [a]according to your faith."

29 [a]Matt. 8:13; 9:22

30 And their eyes were opened. And Jesus [a]sternly warned them, saying, "See *here,* let no one know *about this!*"

30 [a]Matt. 8:4

31 But they went out, and [a]spread the news about Him in all that land.

31 [a]Matt. 4:24; 9:26; 14:1; Mark 1:28, 45; Luke 4:14, 37; 5:15; 7:17

3 *Power over dumbness,* 9:32-34

32 And as they were going out, behold, [a]a dumb man, [b]demon-possessed, was brought to Him.

32 [a]Matt. 12:22, 24 [b]Matt. 4:24

33 And after the demon was cast out, the dumb man spoke; and the multitudes marveled, saying, "[a]Nothing like this was ever seen in Israel."

33 [a]Mark 2:12

34 But the Pharisees were saying, "He casts out the demons [a]by the ruler of the demons."

34 [a]Matt. 12:24; Mark 3:22; Luke 11:15; John 7:20f

4 *Power over disease,* 9:35

35 And Jesus was going about all the cities and the villages, [a]teaching in their synagogues, and proclaiming the gospel of the kingdom, and [b]healing every kind of disease and every kind of sickness.

35 [a]Matt. 4:23 [b]Matt. 4:23; Mark 1:14

5 *Pity on the people,* 9:36-38

36 And [a]seeing the multitudes, He felt compassion for them, [b]because they were distressed and downcast like sheep without a shepherd.

36 [a]Matt. 14:14; 15:32; Mark 6:34; 8:2 [b]Num. 27:17; Ezek. 34:5; Zech. 10:2; Mark 6:34

37 Then He *said to His disciples, "[a]The harvest is plentiful, but the workers are few.

37 [a]Luke 10:2

38 "[a]Therefore beseech the Lord of the harvest to send out workers into His harvest."

38 [a]Luke 10:2

IV THE PROGRAM OF THE KING, 10:1-16:12

A The Program Announced, 10:1-11:1

10 And [a]having summoned His twelve disciples, He gave them authority over unclean spirits, to cast them out, and to [b]heal every kind of disease and every kind of sickness.

★ 1 [a]Mark 3:13-15; 6:7 [b]Matt. 9:35; Luke 9:1

2 [a]Now the names of the twelve apostles are these: The first, [b]Simon, who is called Peter, and [c]Andrew his brother; and [d]James the *son* of Zebedee, and John his brother;

★ 2 [a]Matt. 10:2-4; *Mark 3:16-19; Luke 6:14-16; Acts 1:13* [b]Matt. 4:18 [c]Matt. 4:18 [d]Matt. 4:21

3 [a]Philip and Bartholomew; [b]Thomas and [c]Matthew the taxgatherer; [d]James the *son* of Alphaeus, and [e]Thaddaeus;

3 [a]John 1:45ff. [b]John 11:16; 14:5; 20:24ff.; 21:2 [c]Matt. 9:9 [d]Mark 15:40 [e]Mark 3:18; Luke 6:16; Acts 1:13

10:1 *disciples.* A disciple is one who is taught by another; he is a learner. In the Gospels the word is frequently used—of disciples of Moses (John 9:28), of John the Baptist (John 3:25), and of Christ. Judas is an example of an unsaved disciple of Christ and there were others who deserted Him as well (John 6:66). The word is used in Acts as a synonym for believer. It does not appear at all in the rest of the N.T.

10:2 *apostles.* The word "apostle" means "one sent forth" as an ambassador who bears a message and who represents the one who sent him. The qualifications included: (1) seeing the Lord and being an eyewitness to His resurrection (Acts 1:22; 1 Cor. 9:1); (2) being invested with miraculous sign-gifts (Acts 5:15-16; Heb. 2:3-4); (3) being chosen by the Lord or the Holy Spirit (Matt. 10:1-2; Acts 1:26).

★ 4 [a]Matt. 26:14; Luke 22:3; John 6:71; 13:2, 26

4 Simon the Cananaean, and [a]Judas Iscariot, the one who betrayed Him.

5 [a]Mark 6:7; Luke 9:2 [b]2 Kin. 17:24ff.; Luke 9:52; 10:33; 17:16; John 4:9, 39f.; 8:48; Acts 8:25

5 [a]These twelve Jesus sent out after instructing them, saying, "Do not go in *the* way of *the* Gentiles, and do not enter *any* city of the [b]Samaritans;

6 [a]Matt. 15:24

6 but rather go to [a]the lost sheep of the house of Israel.

7 [a]Matt. 3:2

7 "And as you go, preach, saying, '[a]The kingdom of heaven is at hand.'

8 "Heal *the* sick, raise *the* dead, cleanse *the* lepers, cast out demons; freely you received, freely give.

9 [a]Matt. 10:9-15: *Mark 6:8-11; Luke 9:3-5; 10:4-12*; Luke 22:35

9 "[a]Do not acquire gold, or silver, or copper for your money belts;

★10 [a]1 Cor. 9:14; 1 Tim. 5:18

10 or a bag for *your* journey, or even two tunics, or sandals, or a staff; for [a]the worker is worthy of his support.

11 "And into whatever city or village you enter, inquire who is worthy in it; and abide there until you go away.

12 [a]1 Sam. 25:6; Ps. 122:7, 8

12 "And as you enter the house, [a]give it your greeting.

13 "And if the house is worthy, let your *greeting of* peace come upon it; but if it is not worthy, let your *greeting of* peace return to you.

14 [a]Acts 13:51

14 "And whoever does not receive you, nor heed your words, as you go out of that house or that city, [a]shake off the dust of your feet.

15 [a]Matt. 11:22, 24 [b]Matt. 11:24; 2 Pet. 2:6; Jude 7 [c]Matt. 7:22; 11:22, 24; 12:36; Acts 17:31; 1 Thess. 5:4; Heb. 10:25; 2 Pet. 2:9; 3:7; 1 John 4:17; Jude 6

15 "Truly I say to you, [a]it will be more tolerable for *the* land of [b]Sodom and Gomorrah in [c]the day of judgment, than for that city.

16 [a]Luke 10:3 [b]Gen. 3:1; Matt. 24:25; Rom. 16:19 [c]Hos. 7:11

16 "[a]Behold, I send you out as sheep in the midst of wolves; therefore be [b]shrewd as serpents, and [c]innocent as doves.

★17 [a]Matt. 5:22 [b]Matt. 23:34; Mark 13:9; Luke 12:11; Acts 5:40; 22:19; 26:11

17 "But beware of men; for they will deliver you up to *the* [a]courts, and scourge you [b]in their synagogues;

18 and you shall even be brought before governors and kings for My sake, as a testimony to them and to the Gentiles.

19 [a]Matt. 10:19-22: *Mark 13:11-13; Luke 21:12-17* [b]Matt. 6:25

19 "[a]But when they deliver you up, [b]do not become anxious about how or what you will speak; for it shall be given you in that hour what you are to speak.

20 [a]Luke 12:12; Acts 4:8; 13:9; 2 Cor. 13:3

20 "For [a]it is not you who speak, but *it is* the Spirit of your Father who speaks in you.

★21 [a]Matt. 10:35, 36 [b]Mic. 7:6

21 "[a]And brother will deliver up brother to death, and a father *his* child; and [b]CHILDREN WILL RISE UP AGAINST PARENTS, and cause them to be put to death.

22 [a]Matt. 24:9; John 15:18ff. [b]Matt. 24:13

22 "And [a]you will be hated by all on account of My name, but [b]it is the one who has endured to the end who will be saved.

23 [a]Matt. 23:34 [b]Matt. 16:27f.

23 "But whenever they [a]persecute you in this city, flee to the next; for truly I say to you, you shall not finish *going through* the cities of Israel, [b]until the Son of Man comes.

24 [a]Luke 6:40; John 13:16; 15:20

24 "[a]A disciple is not above his teacher, nor a slave above his master.

★25 [a]Matt. 9:34 [b]2 Kin. 1:2; Matt. 12:24, 27; Mark 3:22; Luke 11:15, 18, 19

25 "It is enough for the disciple that he become as his teacher, and the slave as his master. [a]If

---

10:4 *Cananaean.* In Luke 6:15 and Acts 1:13 Simon is called "Zelotes" (the Zealot) (the equivalent Greek term for Cananaean, a resident of Cana). He likely belonged, before following the Lord, to the extremist party of Zealots who advocated the overthrow of Rome by force.

10:10 *or a bag for your journey.* They are to travel light; perhaps it was a quick journey. They could count on traditional hospitality at the hands of many devout Jewish householders. Notice the later change of instructions in Luke 22:36.

10:17 *scourge* = to flog with a bastinado (stick or club), a painful punishment.

10:21-23 These verses are a prediction of persecution in the tribulation days and at the second coming of Christ (Matt. 24:9-14). Such unnatural acts against members of one's own family have taken place under totalitarian regimes in the past and in modern times.

10:25 *Beelzebul.* Means "lord of flies," a guardian deity of the Ekronites (2 Kings 1:2), but used by the Jews as an epithet for Satan. The name may have been a mocking Hebrew alteration of Baal-zebul, a local arch-demon of N. Palestine and Syria. For Jesus' enemies to allege that He was possessed by Beelzebul was the worst kind of blasphemy (Mark 3:22).

they have called the head of the house [b]Beelzebul, how much more the members of his household!

26 [a]Matt. 10:26-33; *Luke 12:2-9* [b]Mark 4:22; Luke 8:17; 12:2

26 "Therefore do not [a]fear them, [b]for there is nothing covered that will not be revealed, and hidden that will not be known.

27 [a]Luke 12:3 [b]Matt. 24:17

27 "[a]What I tell you in the darkness, speak in the light; and what you hear *whispered* in *your* ear, proclaim [b]upon the housetops.

★28 [a]Heb. 10:31 [b]Matt. 5:22

28 "And do not fear those who kill the body, but are unable to kill the soul; but rather [a]fear Him who is able to destroy both soul and body in [b]hell.

★29 [a]Luke 12:6

29 "[a]Are not two sparrows sold for a cent? And *yet* not one of them will fall to the ground apart from your Father.

30 [a]1 Sam. 14:45; 2 Sam. 14:11; 1 Kin. 1:52; Luke 21:18; Acts 27:34

30 "But [a]the very hairs of your head are all numbered.

31 [a]Matt. 12:12

31 "Therefore do not fear; [a]you are of more value than many sparrows.

32 [a]Luke 12:8; Rev. 3:5

32 "Every one therefore who shall confess Me before men, I will also confess [a]him before My Father who is in heaven.

33 [a]Mark 8:38; Luke 9:26; 2 Tim. 2:12

33 "But [a]whoever shall deny Me before men, I will also deny him before My Father who is in heaven.

★34 [a]Matt. 10:34, 35; *Luke 12:51-53*

34 "[a]Do not think that I came to bring peace on the earth; I did not come to bring peace, but a sword.

35 [a]Mic. 7:6; Matt. 10:21

35 "For I came to [a]SET A MAN AGAINST HIS FATHER, AND A DAUGHTER AGAINST HER MOTHER, AND A DAUGHTER-IN-LAW AGAINST HER MOTHER-IN-LAW;

36 [a]Mic. 7:6; Matt. 10:21

36 and [a]A MAN'S ENEMIES WILL BE THE MEMBERS OF HIS HOUSEHOLD.

37 [a]Luke 14:26

37 "[a]He who loves father or mother more than Me is not worthy of Me; and he who loves son or daughter more than Me is not worthy of Me.

★38 [a]Matt. 16:24; Mark 8:34; Luke 9:23; 14:27

38 "And [a]he who does not take his cross and follow after Me is not worthy of Me.

39 [a]Matt. 16:25; Mark 8:35; Luke 9:24; 17:33; John 12:25

39 "[a]He who has found his life shall lose it, and he who has lost his life for My sake shall find it.

40 [a]Matt. 18:5; Luke 10:16; John 13:20; Gal. 4:14 [b]Mark 9:37; Luke 9:48; John 12:44

40 "[a]He who receives you receives Me, and [b]he who receives Me receives Him who sent Me.

★41

41 "He who receives a prophet in *the* name of a prophet shall receive a prophet's reward; and he who receives a righteous man in the name of a righteous man shall receive a righteous man's reward.

42 [a]Matt. 25:40; Mark 9:41

42 "And [a]whoever in the name of a disciple gives to one of these little ones even a cup of cold water to drink, truly I say to you he shall not lose his reward."

1 [a]Matt. 7:28 [b]Matt. 9:35

11 [a]And it came about that when Jesus had finished giving instructions to His twelve disciples, He departed from there [b]to teach and preach in their cities.

B The Program Attested, 11:2–12:50

1 *By comforting John's disciples,* 11:2–19

2 [a]Matt. 11:2-19; *Luke 7:18-35* [b]Matt. 14:3; Mark 6:17; Luke 9:7ff.

2 [a]Now when [b]John in prison heard of the works of Christ, he sent *word* by his disciples,

3 [a]Ps. 118:26; Matt. 11:10; John 6:14; 11:27; Heb. 10:37

3 and said to Him, "Are You [a]the Coming One, or shall we look for someone else?"

4 And Jesus answered and said to them, "Go and report to John the things which you hear and see:

10:28 *Him.* i.e., God, not Satan.

10:29 *a cent.* This small copper coin is called, in the Greek of this verse, *assarion.* Its value was 1/16 of a denarius, the basic unit in Roman coinage. One denarius was the day's wage of a rural worker. *apart from your Father.* Without His knowledge.

10:34 Christ's mission involves tension, persecution, death. The gospel divides families (cf. Mic. 7:6). The world will experience true peace only when the King returns again to rule (Isa. 2:4).

10:38 *cross.* This reference to a cross needed no explanation, for the Jews had seen thousands of their countrymen crucified by the Romans. Allegiance even to death is demanded of Christ's followers.

10:41 *in the name of* = because he is.

5 [a]Is. 35:5f.; 61:1

5 [a]*the* BLIND RECEIVE SIGHT and *the* lame walk, *the* lepers are cleansed and *the* deaf hear, and *the* dead are raised up, and *the* POOR HAVE THE GOSPEL PREACHED to them.

★ 6 [a]Matt. 5:29; 13:21, 57; 24:10; 26:31; Mark 6:3; John 6:61; 16:1

6 "And blessed is he who [a]keeps from stumbling over Me."

★ 7 [a]Matt. 3:1

7 And as these were going *away,* Jesus began to say to the multitudes concerning John, "What did you go out into [a]the wilderness to look at? A reed shaken by the wind?

8 "But what did you go out to see? A man dressed in soft *clothing?* Behold, those who wear soft *clothing* are in kings' palaces.

9 [a]Matt. 14:5; 21:26; Luke 1:76; 20:6

9 "But why did you go out? To see [a]a prophet? Yes, I tell you, and one who is more than a prophet.

★10 [a]Mal. 3:1; Mark 1:2

10 "This is the one about whom it was written,

> '[a]BEHOLD, I SEND MY MESSENGER BEFORE YOUR FACE,
> WHO WILL PREPARE YOUR WAY BEFORE YOU.'

★11

11 "Truly, I say to you, among those born of women there has not arisen *anyone* greater than John the Baptist; yet he who is least in the kingdom of heaven is greater than he.

★12 [a]Luke 16:16

12 "And [a]from the days of John the Baptist until now the kingdom of heaven suffers violence, and violent men take it by force.

13 [a]Luke 16:16

13 "For [a]all the prophets and the Law prophesied until John.

★14 [a]Mal. 4:5; Matt. 17:10-13; Mark 9:11-13; Luke 1:17; John 1:21

14 "And if you care to accept *it,* he himself is [a]Elijah, who was to come.

15 [a]Matt. 13:9, 43; Mark 4:9, 23; Luke 8:8; 14:35; Rev. 2:7, 11, 17, 29; 3:6, 13, 22; 13:9

15 "[a]He who has ears to hear, let him hear.

16 "But to what shall I compare this generation? It is like children sitting in the market places, who call out to the other *children,*

17 and say, 'We played the flute for you, and you did not dance; we sang a dirge, and you did not mourn.'

18 [a]Matt. 3:4 [b]Luke 1:15 [c]Matt. 9:34; John 7:20; 8:48f., 52; 10:20

18 "For John came neither [a]eating nor [b]drinking, and they say, '[c]He has a demon!'

★19 [a]Matt. 9:11; Luke 15:2

19 "The Son of Man came eating and drinking, and they say, 'Behold, a gluttonous man and a drunkard, [a]a friend of tax-gatherers and sinners!' Yet wisdom is vindicated by her deeds."

2 *By condemning the cities,* 11:20-24

★21 [a]Matt. 11:21-23: *Luke 10:13-15* [b]Mark 6:45; 8:22; Luke 9:10; John 1:44; 12:21 [c]Matt. 11:22; 15:21; Mark 3:8; 7:24, 31; Luke 4:26; 6:17; Acts 12:20; 27:3 [d]Rev. 11:3

20 Then He began to reproach the cities in which most of His miracles were done, because they did not repent.

21 "[a]Woe to you, Chorazin! Woe to you, [b]Bethsaida! For if the miracles had occurred in [c]Tyre and [c]Sidon which occurred in you, they would have repented long ago in [d]sackcloth and ashes.

22 [a]Matt. 10:15; 11:24 [b]Matt. 10:15

22 "Nevertheless I say to you, [a]it shall be more tolerable for Tyre and Sidon in [b]*the* day of judgment, than for you.

23 [a]Matt. 4:13 [b]Is. 14:13, 15; Ezek. 26:20; 31:14; 32:18, 24 [c]Matt. 16:18; Luke 10:15; 16:23; Acts 2:27, 31; Rev. 1:18; 6:8; 20:13f. [d]Matt. 10:15

23 "And you, [a]Capernaum, will not be exalted to heaven, will you? You shall [b]descend to [c]Hades; for if the miracles had occurred in [d]Sodom which occurred in you, it would have remained to this day.

11:6 *who keeps from stumbling over Me.* I.e., he who can in full faith acknowledge and accept My "mighty work" as evidence of My Messiahship.

11:7-8 These are rhetorical questions expecting negative answers.

11:10 See Isa. 40:3; Mal. 3:1.

11:11 *is greater than he.* The greatness of John the Baptist in the old dispensation before the Cross fades in comparison to the high position every believer has had since Jesus' crucifixion and resurrection, and the descent of the Spirit.

11:12 Since the time John began preaching, the response had been violent, whether by vicious opponents or enthusiastic supporters.

11:14 *he himself is Elijah.* Jesus is saying that if the Jews had received Him, they would also have understood that John fulfilled the O.T. prediction of the coming of Elijah before the day of the Lord (Mal. 4:5; see Matt. 17:12).

11:19 One can always find a reason to carp at prophets rather than repent at their urging.

11:21 *Chorazin* was about 2½ miles N. of Capernaum. *Bethsaida* was at the N. end of the Sea of Galilee. *Tyre and Sidon* were pagan cities in Phoenicia.

24 [a]Matt. 10:15; 11:22 [b]Matt. 10:15

24 "Nevertheless I say to you that [a]it shall be more tolerable for the land of [b]Sodom in [b]*the* day of judgment, than for you."

3 *By calling all to Himself,* 11:25-30

25 [a]Matt. 11:25-27: *Luke 10:21, 22* [b]Acts 3:12 [c]Luke 22:42; 23:34; John 11:41; 12:27, 28 [d]1 Cor. 1:26ff.

25 [a]At that time Jesus [b]answered and said, "I praise Thee, O [c]Father, Lord of heaven and earth, that [d]Thou didst hide these things from *the* wise and intelligent and didst reveal them to babes.

26 [a]Luke 22:42; 23:34; John 11:41; 12:27, 28

26 "Yes, [a]Father, for thus it was well-pleasing in Thy sight.

27 [a]Matt. 28:18; John 3:35; 13:3; 17:2 [b]John 7:29; 10:15; 17:25

27 "[a]All things have been handed over to Me by My Father; and no one knows the Son, except the Father; nor does anyone know the Father, [b]except the Son, and anyone to whom the Son wills to reveal *Him.*

★28 [a]Jer. 31:25; John 7:37

28 "[a]Come to Me, all who are weary and heavy-laden, and I will give you rest.

29 [a]John 13:15; Eph. 4:20; Phil. 2:5; 1 Pet. 2:21; 1 John 2:6 [b]Jer. 6:16

29 "Take My yoke upon you, and [a]learn from Me, for I am gentle and humble in heart; and [b]YOU SHALL FIND REST FOR YOUR SOULS.

30

30 "For My yoke is easy, and My load is light."

4 *By controversies over the Sabbath,* 12:1-13

1 [a]Matt. 12:1-8: *Mark 2:23-28; Luke 6:1-5* [b]Deut. 23:25

12 [a]At that time Jesus went on the Sabbath through the grainfields, and His disciples became hungry and began to [b]pick the heads *of grain* and eat.

★ 2 [a]Matt. 12:10; Luke 13:14; 14:3; John 5:10; 7:23; 9:16

2 But when the Pharisees saw it, they said to Him, "Behold, Your disciples do what [a]is not lawful to do on a Sabbath."

★ 3

3 But He said to them, "Have you not read what David did, when he became hungry, he and his companions;

★ 4 [a]1 Sam. 21:6

4 how he entered the house of God, and [a]they ate the consecrated bread, which was not lawful for him to eat, nor for those with him, but for the priests alone?

5 "Or have you not read in the Law, that on the Sabbath the priests in the temple break the Sabbath, and are innocent?

★ 6 [a]Matt. 12:41, 42

6 "But I say to you, that something [a]greater than the temple is here.

7 [a]Hos. 6:6

7 "But if you had known what this means, '[a]I DESIRE COMPASSION, AND NOT A SACRIFICE,' you would not have condemned the innocent.

8 [a]Matt. 8:20; 12:32, 40

8 "For [a]the Son of Man is Lord of the Sabbath."

9 [a]Matt. 12:9-14: *Mark 3:1-6; Luke 6:6-11*

9 [a]And departing from there, He went into their synagogue.

10 [a]Matt. 12:2; Luke 13:14; 14:3; John 5:10; 7:23; 9:16

10 And behold, *there was* a man with a withered hand. And they questioned Him, saying, "[a]Is it lawful to heal on the Sabbath?"—in order that they might accuse Him.

11 And He said to them, "What man shall there be among you, who shall have one sheep, and if it falls into a pit on the Sabbath, will he not take hold of it, and lift it out?

12 [a]Matt. 10:31

12 "Of [a]how much more value then is a man than a sheep! So then, it is lawful to do good on the Sabbath."

13 Then He *said to the man, "Stretch out your hand!" And he

11:28-30 This great invitation, extended to all, is threefold: (1) to come and receive salvation; (2) to learn in discipleship; and (3) to serve in yoke with the Lord. The yoke involves instruction under discipline. Yet, in contrast to the teaching of the scribes, Jesus' yoke is easy. Through the ages these verses have been among the most beloved in the N.T.

12:2 *not lawful to do on a Sabbath.* It was lawful for persons to pick grain from another's field to satisfy a hunger (Deut. 23:25) but not to do regular work on the Sabbath (Ex. 20:10). The latter was the charge of the Pharisees.

12:3 *what David did.* See 1 Sam. 21:1-6.

12:4 *the consecrated bread.* Better, bread of the Presence. Twelve cakes, made of fine flour, were placed in the Holy Place in the tabernacle each day on the table which stood opposite the candlestick. The old bread was eaten by the priests. It was this bread that David requested of Ahimelech, the priest, for himself and his men.

12:6 *something.* I.e., the kingdom of God.

stretched it out, and it was restored to normal, like the other.

5 By condemnation of the Pharisees (the unpardonable sin), 12:14–37

14 [a]Matt. 26:4; Mark 14:1; Luke 22:2; John 7:30, 44; 8:59; 10:31, 39; 11:53
15 [a]Matt. 4:23

14 But the Pharisees went
out, and [a]counseled together
against Him, *as to* how they
might destroy Him.
15 But Jesus, aware of *this,*
withdrew from there. And many
followed Him, and [a]He healed
them all,

★16 [a]Matt. 8:4

16 and [a]warned them not to
make Him known,
17 in order that what was
spoken through Isaiah the
prophet, might be fulfilled, saying,

★18 [a]Is. 42:1 [b]Matt. 3:17; 17:5 [c]Luke 4:18; John 3:34

18 "[a]BEHOLD, MY SERVANT
WHOM I HAVE CHOSEN;
[b]MY BELOVED IN WHOM MY
SOUL IS WELL-PLEASED;
[c]I WILL PUT MY SPIRIT UPON
HIM,
[a]AND HE SHALL PROCLAIM
JUSTICE TO THE GENTILES.

19 [a]Is. 42:2

19 "[a]HE WILL NOT QUARREL, NOR
CRY OUT;
NOR WILL ANY ONE HEAR HIS
VOICE IN THE STREETS.

20 [a]Is. 42:3

20 "[a]A BATTERED REED HE WILL
NOT BREAK OFF,
AND A SMOLDERING WICK HE
WILL NOT PUT OUT,
UNTIL HE LEADS JUSTICE TO
VICTORY.

21 [a]Is. 42:4; Rom. 15:12

21 "[a]AND IN HIS NAME THE
GENTILES WILL HOPE."

22 [a]Matt. 12:22, 24: *Luke 11:14, 15;* Matt. 9:32, 34 [b]Matt. 4:24

22 [a]Then there was brought
to Him a [b]demon-possessed man
who was blind and dumb, and He
healed him, so that the dumb
man spoke and saw.

23 [a]Matt. 9:27

23 And all the multitudes
were amazed, and *began* to say,
"This *man* cannot be the [a]Son of
David, can he?"

24 [a]Matt. 9:34

24 But when the Pharisees
heard it, they said, "This man
casts out demons only [a]by Beelzebul the ruler of the demons."

25 [a]Matt. 12:25-29; *Mark 3:23-27; Luke 11:17-22* [b]Matt. 9:4

25 [a]And [b]knowing their
thoughts He said to them, "Any
kingdom divided against itself is
laid waste; and any city or house
divided against itself shall not
stand.

26 [a]Matt. 4:10

26 "And if [a]Satan casts out
[a]Satan, he is divided against himself; how then shall his kingdom
stand?

27 [a]Matt. 9:34 [b]Acts 19:13

27 "And if I [a]by Beelzebul cast
out demons, [b]by whom do your
sons cast them out? Consequently
they shall be your judges.
28 "But if I cast out demons by
the Spirit of God, then the kingdom of God has come upon you.
29 "Or how can anyone enter
the strong man's house and carry
off his property, unless he first
binds the strong *man*? And then
he will plunder his house.

30 [a]Mark 9:40; Luke 9:50; 11:23

30 "[a]He who is not with Me is
against Me; and he who does not
gather with Me scatters.

★31 [a]Matt. 12:31, 32; Mark 3:28-30; Luke 12:10

31 "[a]Therefore I say to you,
any sin and blasphemy shall be
forgiven men, but blasphemy
against the Spirit shall not be forgiven.

32 [a]Matt. 13:22, 39; Mark 10:30; Luke 16:8; 18:30; 20:34, 35; Eph. 1:21; 1 Tim. 6:17; 2 Tim. 4:10; Titus 2:12; Heb. 6:5

32 "And whoever shall speak a
word against the Son of Man, it
shall be forgiven him; but whoever shall speak against the Holy
Spirit, it shall not be forgiven
him, either in [a]this age, or in the
age to come.

33 [a]Matt. 7:16

33 "Either make the tree good,
and its fruit good; or make the
tree rotten, and its fruit rotten; for
[a]the tree is known by its fruit.

12:16 *not to make Him known.* Many were drawn to Christ because of His reputation as a healer, which may have been diverting attention from His primary role as Messiah.

12:18–21 See Isa. 42:1–4. Here is one of Matthew's descriptive gems, highlighting Jesus' graciousness and gentleness.

12:31 *blasphemy against the Spirit.* Technically, according to the scribes, blasphemy involved direct and explicit abuse of the divine name. Jesus here teaches that it also may be the reviling of God by attributing the Spirit's work to Satan. The special circumstances involved in this blasphemy cannot be duplicated today.

34 [a]Matt. 3:7; 23:33 [b]1 Sam. 24:13; Matt. 12:34, 35; 15:18; Luke 6:45; Eph. 4:29; James 3:2-12

34 "[a]You brood of vipers, how can you, being evil, speak what is good? [b]For the mouth speaks out of that which fills the heart.

35 "The good man out of *his* good treasure brings forth what is good; and the evil man out of *his* evil treasure brings forth what is evil.

★36 [a]Matt. 10:15

36 "And I say to you, that every careless word that men shall speak, they shall render account for it in [a]the day of judgment.

37 "For by your words you shall be justified, and by your words you shall be condemned."

6 *By certain signs,* 12:38–45

38 [a]Matt. 16:1; Mark 8:11, 12; Luke 11:16; John 2:18; 6:30; 1 Cor. 1:22

38 Then some of the scribes and Pharisees answered Him, saying, "Teacher, [a]we want to see a sign from You."

★39 [a]Matt. 12:39-42: *Luke 11:29-32;* Matt. 16:4

39 But He answered and said to them, "[a]An evil and adulterous generation craves for a sign; and *yet* no sign shall be given to it but the sign of Jonah the prophet;

★40 [a]Jon. 1:17 [b]Matt. 8:20 [c]Matt. 16:21

40 for just as [a]JONAH WAS THREE DAYS AND THREE NIGHTS IN THE BELLY OF THE SEA MONSTER, so shall [b]the Son of Man be [c]three days and three nights in the heart of the earth.

★41 [a]Jon. 1:2 [b]Jon. 3:5 [c]Matt. 12:6, 42

41 "[a]The men of Nineveh shall stand up with this generation at the judgment, and shall condemn it because [b]they repented at the preaching of Jonah; and behold, [c]something greater than Jonah is here.

42 [a]1 Kin. 10:1; 2 Chr. 9:1 [b]Matt. 12:6, 41

42 "[a]*The* Queen of *the* South shall rise up with this generation at the judgment and shall condemn it, because she came from the ends of the earth to hear the wisdom of Solomon; and behold, [b]something greater than Solomon is here.

★43 [a]Matt. 12:43-45: *Luke 11:24-26*

43 "[a]Now when the unclean spirit goes out of a man, it passes through waterless places, seeking rest, and does not find *it.*

44 "Then it says, 'I will return to my house from which I came'; and when it comes, it finds it unoccupied, swept, and put in order.

45 [a]2 Pet. 2:20

45 "Then it goes, and takes along with it seven other spirits more wicked than itself, and they go in and live there; and [a]the last state of that man becomes worse than the first. That is the way it will also be with this evil generation."

7 *By changed relationships,* 12:46–50

46 [a]Matt. 12:46-50: *Mark 3:31-35; Luke 8:19-21* [b]Matt. 1:18; 2:11ff.; 13:55; Luke 1:43; 2:33f., 48, 51; John 2:1, 5, 12; 19:25f.; Acts 1:14 [c]Matt. 13:55; Mark 6:3; John 2:12; 7:3, 5, 10; Acts 1:14; 1 Cor. 9:5; Gal. 1:19

46 [a]While He was still speaking to the multitudes, behold, His [b]mother and His [c]brothers were standing outside, seeking to speak to Him.

47 And someone said to Him, "Behold, Your mother and Your brothers are standing outside seeking to speak to You."

48 But He answered the one who was telling Him and said, "Who is My mother and who are My brothers?"

49 And stretching out His hand toward His disciples, He said, "Behold, My mother and My brothers!

★50

50 "For whoever shall do the will of My Father who is in heaven, he is My brother and sister and mother."

12:36 *careless* = useless.

12:39 *adulterous.* The nation was unfaithful in its vows to the Lord. *the sign of Jonah the prophet.* In Matt. 16:4 and Luke 11:29–32 the sign is the warning of judgment to come (cf. Jonah 1:2; 3:4). Here the sign is related to the death and resurrection of the Son of Man.

12:40 *three days and three nights.* This phrase does not necessarily require that 72 hours elapse between Christ's death and resurrection, for the Jews reckoned part of a day to be as a whole day. Thus this prophecy can be properly fulfilled if the crucifixion occurred on Friday. However, the statement does require an historical Jonah who was actually swallowed by a great fish.

12:41 *something greater.* The Greek word is neuter here and in v. 42 and refers to the kingdom of God.

12:43 *unclean spirit* = a demon. See note at Matt. 7:22.

12:50 This means that the spiritual relation between Christ and believers is closer than the closest of blood ties. Obedience to God takes precedence over responsibilities to family.

C The Program Altered, 13:1–52

1 The sower, 13:1–23

1 [a]Matt. 9:28; 13:36; Mark 3:19 [b]Matt. 13:1-15; *Mark 4:1-12; Luke 8:4-10*
2 [a]Luke 5:3

13 On that day Jesus went out of [a]the house, and was sitting [b]by the sea.

2 And great multitudes gathered about Him, so that [a]He got into a boat and sat down, and the whole multitude was standing on the beach.

★ 3 [a]Matt. 13:10ff.; Mark 4:2ff.

3 And He spoke many things to them in [a]parables, saying, "Behold, the sower went out to sow;

4 and as he sowed, some *seeds* fell beside the road, and the birds came and devoured them.

5 "And others fell upon the rocky places, where they did not have much soil; and immediately they sprang up, because they had no depth of soil.

6 "But when the sun had risen, they were scorched; and because they had no root, they withered away.

7 "And others fell among the thorns, and the thorns came up and choked them out.

8 [a]Gen. 26:12; Matt. 13:23

8 "And others fell on the good soil, and *yielded a crop, some a [a]hundredfold, some sixty, and some thirty.

9 [a]Matt. 11:15

9 "[a]He who has ears, let him hear."

10 And the disciples came and said to Him, "Why do You speak to them in parables?"

11 [a]Matt. 19:11; 20:23; John 6:65; 1 Cor. 2:10; Col. 1:27; 1 John 2:20, 27

11 And He answered and said to them, "[a]To you it has been granted to know the mysteries of the kingdom of heaven, but to them it has not been granted.

12 [a]Matt. 25:29; Mark 4:25; Luke 8:18; 19:26

12 "[a]For whoever has, to him shall *more* be given, and he shall have an abundance; but whoever does not have, even what he has shall be taken away from him.

13 [a]Deut. 29:4; Is. 42:19, 20; Jer. 5:21; Ezek. 12:2

13 "Therefore I speak to them in parables; because while [a]seeing they do not see, and while hearing they do not hear, nor do they understand.

★14 [a]Is. 6:9; Mark 4:12; Luke 8:10; John 12:40; Acts 28:26, 27; Rom. 10:16; 11:8

14 "And in their case the prophecy of Isaiah is being fulfilled, which says,

'[a]YOU WILL KEEP ON HEARING,
BUT WILL NOT UNDERSTAND;
AND YOU WILL KEEP ON SEEING, BUT WILL NOT PERCEIVE;

15 [a]Is. 6:10

15 [a]FOR THE HEART OF THIS PEOPLE HAS BECOME DULL,
AND WITH THEIR EARS THEY SCARCELY HEAR,
AND THEY HAVE CLOSED THEIR EYES
LEST THEY SHOULD SEE WITH THEIR EYES,
AND HEAR WITH THEIR EARS,
AND UNDERSTAND WITH THEIR HEART AND TURN AGAIN,
AND I SHOULD HEAL THEM.'

16 [a]Matt. 13:16, 17; *Luke 10:23, 24*

16 "[a]But blessed are your eyes, because they see; and your ears, because they hear.

17 [a]John 8:56; Heb. 11:13; 1 Pet. 1:10-12

17 "For truly I say to you, that [a]many prophets and righteous men desired to see what you see, and did not see *it;* and to hear what you hear, and did not hear *it.*

18 [a]Matt. 13:18-23; *Mark 4:13-20; Luke 8:11-15*
19 [a]Matt. 4:23 [b]Matt. 5:37

18 "[a]Hear then the parable of the sower.

19 "When any one hears [a]the word of the kingdom, and does not understand it, [b]the evil *one* comes and snatches away what has been sown in his heart. This is the one on whom seed was sown beside the road.

20 "And the one on whom seed was sown on the rocky places, this is the man who hears the word, and immediately receives it with joy;

21 [a]Matt. 11:6

21 yet he has no *firm* root in himself, but is *only* temporary, and when affliction or persecution arises because of the word, immediately he [a]falls away.

13:3 *parables.* A parable is a figure of speech in which a moral or spiritual truth is illustrated by an analogy drawn from everyday experiences. These parables present truths about the kingdom in this present day. These truths are called "mysteries" (v. 11) because they were not revealed in the O.T., and they are revealed by Christ only to those who are properly related to Him (vv. 11–13 and Mark 4:11–12).

13:14 See Isa. 6:9–10.

22 [a]Matt. 12:32; 13:39; Mark 4:19; Rom. 12:2; 1 Cor. 1:20; 2:6, 8; 3:18; 2 Cor. 4:4; Gal. 1:4; Eph. 2:2 [b]Matt. 19:23; 1 Tim. 6:9, 10, 17
23 [a]Matt. 13:8

22 "And the one on whom seed was sown among the thorns, this is the man who hears the word, and the worry of [a]the world, and the [b]deceitfulness of riches choke the word, and it becomes unfruitful.

23 "And the one on whom seed was sown on the good ground, this is the man who hears the word and understands it; who indeed bears fruit, and brings forth, some [a]a hundredfold, some sixty, and some thirty."

2 *The wheat and the tares,* 13:24-30

24 [a]Matt. 13:31, 33, 45, 47; 18:23; 20:1; 22:2; 25:1; Mark 4:30; Luke 13:18, 20 [b]Mark 4:26-29
★25

24 He presented another parable to them, saying, "[a]The kingdom of heaven may be compared to [b]a man who sowed good seed in his field.

25 "But while men were sleeping, his enemy came and sowed tares also among the wheat, and went away.

26 "But when the wheat sprang up and bore grain, then the tares became evident also.

27 "And the slaves of the landowner came and said to him, 'Sir, did you not sow good seed in your field? How then does it have tares?'

28 "And he said to them, 'An enemy has done this!' And the slaves *said to him, 'Do you want us, then, to go and gather them up?'

29 "But he *said, 'No; lest while you are gathering up the tares, you may root up the wheat with them.

30 [a]Matt. 3:12

30 'Allow both to grow together until the harvest; and in the time of the harvest I will say to the reapers, "First gather up the tares and bind them in bundles to burn them up; but [a]gather the wheat into my barn."'"

3 *The mustard seed,* 13:31-32

★31 [a]Matt. 13:31, 32; *Mark 4:30-32; Luke 13:18, 19;* Matt. 13:24 [b]Matt. 17:20; Luke 17:6
32 [a]Ps. 104:12; Ezek. 17:23; 31:6; Dan. 4:12

31 He presented another parable to them, saying, "[a]The kingdom of heaven is like [b]a mustard seed, which a man took and sowed in his field;

32 and this is smaller than all *other* seeds; but when it is full grown, it is larger than the garden plants, and becomes a tree, so that [a]THE BIRDS OF THE AIR come and NEST IN ITS BRANCHES."

4 *The leaven,* 13:33

★33 [a]Matt. 13:33: *Luke 13:21;* Matt. 13:24 [b]Gen. 18:6; Judg. 6:19; 1 Sam. 1:24

33 He spoke another parable to them, "[a]The kingdom of heaven is like leaven, which a woman took, and hid in [b]three pecks of meal, until it was all leavened."

5 *The wheat and the tares,* 13:34-43

34 [a]Mark 4:34; John 10:6; 16:25
★35 [a]Ps. 78:2

34 All these things Jesus spoke to the multitudes in parables, and He was not talking to them [a]without a parable,

35 so that what was spoken through the prophet might be fulfilled, saying,

"[a]I WILL OPEN MY MOUTH IN PARABLES;
I WILL UTTER THINGS HIDDEN SINCE THE FOUNDATION OF THE WORLD."

36 [a]Matt. 13:1 [b]Matt. 15:15
37 [a]Matt. 8:20

36 Then He left the multitudes, and went into [a]the house. And His disciples came to Him, saying, "[b]Explain to us the parable of the tares of the field."

37 And He answered and

13:25 *tares.* Weeds, in this case probably darnel, which in the blade resembles wheat but which can be distinguished from wheat when fully ripe.

13:31 See note on Luke 13:19.

13:33 *leaven.* Since leaven is everywhere else in the Bible regarded as typifying the presence of impurity or evil, some understand it here to indicate the presence of evil within Christendom (Ex. 12:15; Lev. 2:11; Matt. 16:6; 1 Cor. 5:6-9; Gal. 5:9; cf. 1 Tim. 4:1; Jude 12). Others regard the meaning of leaven in this parable in a good sense, as indicating the growth of the kingdom of heaven by means of the penetrating power of the gospel.

13:35 See Ps. 78:2-3.

said, "The one who sows the good
seed is [a]the Son of Man,
38 [a]Matt. 8:12 [b]John 8:44; Acts 13:10; 1 John 3:10 [c]Matt. 5:37
38 and the field is the world;
and *as for* the good seed, these
are [a]the sons of the kingdom; and
the tares are [b]the sons of [c]the evil
one;
39 [a]Matt. 12:32; 13:22, 40, 49; 24:3; 28:20; 1 Cor. 10:11; Heb. 9:26
39 and the enemy who sowed
them is the devil, and the harvest
is [a]the end of the age; and the
reapers are angels.
40 [a]Matt. 12:32; 13:22, 39, 49; 24:3; 28:20; 1 Cor. 10:11; Heb. 9:26
40 "Therefore just as the tares
are gathered up and burned with
fire, so shall it be at [a]the end of
the age.
41 [a]Matt. 8:20 [b]Matt. 24:31 [c]Zeph. 1:3
41 "[a]The Son of Man [b]will
send forth His angels, and they
will gather out of His kingdom all
[c]STUMBLING BLOCKS, AND THOSE WHO
COMMIT LAWLESSNESS,
42 [a]Matt. 13:50 [b]Matt. 8:12
42 and [a]will cast them into
the furnace of fire; in that place
[b]there shall be weeping and
gnashing of teeth.
43 [a]Dan. 12:3 [b]Matt. 11:15
43 "[a]Then THE RIGHTEOUS WILL
SHINE FORTH AS THE SUN in the kingdom of their Father. [b]He who has
ears, let him hear.

6 ***The hidden treasure,*** 13:44

★44 [a]Matt. 13:24 [b]Matt. 13:46
44 "[a]The kingdom of heaven
is like a treasure hidden in the
field, which a man found and hid;
and from joy over it he goes and
[b]sells all that he has, and buys
that field.

7 ***The pearl of great price,*** 13:45-46

45 [a]Matt. 13:24
45 "Again, [a]the kingdom of
heaven is like a merchant seeking
fine pearls,
46 and upon finding one pearl
of great value, he went and sold
all that he had, and bought it.

8 ***The dragnet,*** 13:47-50

47 [a]Matt. 13:44
47 "Again, [a]the kingdom of
heaven is like a dragnet cast into
the sea, and gathering *fish* of every kind;
48 and when it was filled,
they drew it up on the beach; and
they sat down, and gathered the
good *fish* into containers, but the
bad they threw away.
49 [a]Matt. 13:39, 40
49 "So it will be at [a]the end of
the age; the angels shall come
forth, and take out the wicked
from among the righteous,
50 [a]Matt. 13:42 [b]Matt. 8:12
50 and [a]will cast them into
the furnace of fire; [b]there shall be
weeping and gnashing of teeth.

9 ***The householder,*** 13:51-52

51 "Have you understood all
these things?" They *said to Him,
"Yes."
52 And He said to them,
"Therefore every scribe who has
become a disciple of the kingdom
of heaven is like a head of a
household, who brings forth out
of his treasure things new and
old."

D The Program Attacked, 13:53-16:12

1 ***Attack by His own townspeople,*** 13:53-58

53 [a]Matt. 7:28
53 [a]And it came about that
when Jesus had finished these
parables, He departed from there.
54 [a]Matt. 13:54-58: *Mark 6:1-6* [b]Matt. 4:23 [c]Matt. 7:28
54 [a]And coming to His home-
town He [b]*began* teaching them in
their synagogue, so that [c]they became astonished, and said,
"Where *did* this man *get* this wisdom, and *these* miraculous powers?
★55 [a]Matt. 12:46
55 "Is not this the carpenter's

13:44-46 The parables of the treasure and pearl indicate the incomparable value of the kingdom, which will cause a man to do everything possible to possess it. Another possible interpretation equates the man with Christ (as in v. 37) who sacrifices His all to purchase His people.

13:55 *His brothers.* These were the sons of Joseph and Mary born subsequent to the birth of Jesus from Mary alone. To understand them as sons of Joseph by a former marriage or cousins of Jesus is contrary to the usual sense of brothers.

son? Is not [a]His mother called Mary, and His [a]brothers, James and Joseph and Simon and Judas?

56 [a]Mark 6:3

56 "And [a]His sisters, are they not all with us? Where then *did* this man *get* all these things?"

57 [a]Matt. 11:6 [b]Mark 6:4; Luke 4:24; John 4:44

57 And they took [a]offense at Him. But Jesus said to them, "[b]A prophet is not without honor except in his home town, and in his *own* household."

58 And He did not do many miracles there because of their unbelief.

★ 1 [a]Matt. 14:1-12: *Mark 6:14-29;* Matt. 14:1, 2: *Luke 9:7-9* [b]Mark 8:15; Luke 3:1, 19; 8:3; 13:31; 23:7f., 11f., 15; Acts 4:27; 12:1
2 [a]Matt. 16:14; Mark 6:14; Luke 9:7
★ 3 [a]Matt. 14:1-12: *Mark 6:14-29; Matt. 14:1, 2; Luke 9:7-9;* Mark 8:15; Luke 3:1, 19; 8:3; 13:31; 23:7f., 11f., 15; Acts 4:27; 12:1 [b]Matt. 4:12; 11:2 [c]Matt. 14:6; Mark 6:17, 19, 22; Luke 3:19
4 [a]Lev. 18:16; 20:21
5 [a]Matt. 11:9
6 [a]Matt. 14:3; Mark 6:17, 19, 22; Luke 3:19 [b]Matt. 14:1-12: *Mark 6:14-29;* Matt. 14:1, 2: *Luke 9:7-9;* Mark 8:15; Luke 3:1, 19; 8:3; 13:31; 23:7f., 11f., 15; Acts 4:27; 12:1

2 *Attack by Herod, followed by miracles (5000 fed and Jesus walks on water),* 14:1-36

14 [a]At that time [b]Herod the tetrarch heard the news about Jesus,

2 and said to his servants, "[a]This is John the Baptist; he has risen from the dead; and that is why miraculous powers are at work in him."

3 For [a]Herod had seized John, and bound him, and put him [b]in prison on account of [c]Herodias, the wife of his brother Philip.

4 For John had been saying to him, "[a]It is not lawful for you to have her."

5 And although he wanted to put him to death, he feared the multitude, because they regarded him as [a]a prophet.

6 But when Herod's birthday came, the daughter of [a]Herodias danced before *them* and pleased [b]Herod.

7 Thereupon he promised with an oath to give her whatever she asked.

8 And having been prompted by her mother, she *said, "Give me here on a platter the head of John the Baptist."

9 And although he was grieved, the king commanded *it* to be given because of his oaths, and because of his dinner guests.

10 And he sent and had John beheaded in the prison.

11 And his head was brought on a platter and given to the girl; and she brought *it* to her mother.

12 And his disciples came and took away the body and buried it; and they went and reported to Jesus.

13 [a]Now when Jesus heard *it,* He withdrew from there in a boat, to a lonely place by Himself; and when the multitudes heard *of this,* they followed Him on foot from the cities.

13 [a]Matt. 14:13-21: *Mark 6:32-44; Luke 9:10-17; John 6:1-13;* Matt. 15:32-38

14 And when He came out, He [a]saw a great multitude, and felt compassion for them, and [b]healed their sick.

14 [a]Matt. 9:36 [b]Matt. 4:23

15 And when it was evening, the disciples came to Him, saying, "The place is desolate, and the time is already past; so send the multitudes away, that they may go into the villages and buy food for themselves."

★15

16 But Jesus said to them, "They do not need to go away; you give them *something* to eat!"

17 And they *said to Him, "We have here only [a]five loaves and two fish."

17 [a]Matt. 16:9

18 And He said, "Bring them here to Me."

19 And ordering the multitudes to recline on the grass, He took the five loaves and the two fish, and looking up toward heaven, He [a]blessed *the food,* and

19 [a]1 Sam. 9:13; Matt. 15:36; 26:26; Mark 6:41; 8:7; 14:22; Luke 24:30; Acts 27:35; Rom. 14:6

14:1 *Herod the tetrarch.* Herod Antipas, who ruled from 4 B.C.–A.D. 39, son of Herod the Great and brother of Archelaus (see Matt. 2:1, 22).

14:3 *Herodias.* The former wife of Herod's half brother Philip, her uncle. She had been persuaded to leave her husband and marry Herod Antipas, thus committing incest (Lev. 18:16). John condemned him for this, and Antipas knew that John spoke the truth. See Mark 6:20.

14:15 *when it was evening.* The Hebrew day, that is, the interval between dawn and darkness, was divided into three parts: morning, noon, and evening (Ps. 55:17). The Jews distinguished two evenings in the day: the first began about 3 p.m., and the second, at sundown (see Ex. 12:6, lit., "between the evenings.") In this verse the first evening is meant; in v. 23, the second.

breaking the loaves He gave them
to the disciples, and the disciples
gave to the multitudes,
20 [a]Matt. 16:9; Mark 6:43; 8:19; Luke 9:17; John 6:13
20 and they all ate, and were
satisfied. And they picked up
what was left over of the broken
pieces, twelve full [a]baskets.
21 And there were about five
thousand men who ate, aside
from women and children.
22 [a]Matt. 14:22-33; *Mark 6:45-51; John 6:15-21*
22 [a]And immediately He
made the disciples get into the
boat, and go ahead of Him to the
other side, while He sent the multitudes away.
23 [a]Mark 6:46; Luke 6:12; 9:28; John 6:15
23 And after He had sent the
multitudes away, [a]He went up to
the mountain by Himself to pray;
and when it was evening, He was
there alone.
24 But the boat was already
many stadia away from the land,
battered by the waves; for the
wind was contrary.
★25 [a]Matt. 24:43; Mark 13:35
25 And in [a]the fourth watch
of the night He came to them,
walking upon the sea.
26 [a]Luke 24:37
26 And when the disciples
saw Him walking on the sea, they
were frightened, saying, "It is [a]a
ghost!" And they cried out for
fear.
27 [a]Matt. 9:2 [b]Matt. 17:7; 28:5, 10; Mark 6:50; Luke 1:13; 30; 2:10; 5:10; 12:32; John 6:20; Rev. 1:17
27 But immediately Jesus
spoke to them, saying, "[a]Take
courage, it is I; [b]do not be afraid."
28 And Peter answered Him
and said, "Lord, if it is You, command me to come to You on the
water."
29 And He said, "Come!"
And Peter got out of the boat, and
walked on the water and came
toward Jesus.
30 But seeing the wind, he
became afraid, and beginning to
sink, he cried out, saying, "Lord,
save me!"
31 [a]Matt. 6:30; 8:26; 16:8
31 And immediately Jesus
stretched out His hand and took
hold of him, and *said to him,
"[a]O you of little faith, why did
you doubt?"
32 And when they got into
the boat, the wind stopped.
33 And those who were in the 33 [a]Matt. 4:3
boat worshiped Him, saying,
"You are certainly [a]God's Son!"
34 [a]And when they had ★34 [a]Matt. 14:34-36; *Mark 6:53-56;* John 6:24, 25 [b]Mark 6:53; Luke 5:1
crossed over, they came to land at
[b]Gennesaret.
35 And when the men of that
place recognized Him, they sent
into all that surrounding district
and brought to Him all who were
ill;
36 and they *began* to entreat 36 [a]Matt. 9:20 [b]Matt. 9:21; Mark 3:10; 6:56; 8:22; Luke 6:19
Him that they might just touch
[a]the fringe of His cloak; and as
many as [b]touched *it* were cured.

3 *Attack by the scribes and Pharisees, followed by miracles (Syrophoenician woman's daughter healed and 4000 fed),* 15:1-39

15 [a]Then some Pharisees and 1 [a]Matt. 15:1-20; *Mark 7:1-23* [b]Mark 3:22; 7:1; John 1:19; Acts 25:7
scribes *came to Jesus
[b]from Jerusalem, saying,
2 "Why do Your disciples ★ 2 [a]Luke 11:38
transgress the tradition of the elders? For they [a]do not wash their
hands when they eat bread."
3 And He answered and said
to them, "And why do you yourselves transgress the commandment of God for the sake of your
tradition?
4 "For God said, '[a]HONOR 4 [a]Ex. 20:12; Deut. 5:16 [b]Ex. 21:17; Lev. 20:9
YOUR FATHER AND MOTHER,' and,
'[b]HE WHO SPEAKS EVIL OF FATHER OR
MOTHER, LET HIM BE PUT TO DEATH.'
5 "But you say, 'Whoever
shall say to *his* father or mother,
"Anything of mine you might
have been helped by has been
given *to God,"*
6 he is not to honor his father or his mother.' And *thus* you

---

14:25 *fourth watch* = 3-6 a.m.
14:34 *land at Gennesaret.* NW. of the Sea of Galilee.
15:2 Only traditional interpretation and expansion of the law required this. The written law did not (Lev. 22:1-16). Only priests needed to make an ablution before eating to cleanse themselves from anything unclean. Christ accused them of also expanding (and negating) the commandment about honoring parents (vv. 4-6).

invalidated the word of God for
the sake of your tradition.
★7 **7** "You hypocrites, rightly did
Isaiah prophesy of you, saying,

8 [a]Is. 29:13 **8** '[a]THIS PEOPLE HONORS ME
WITH THEIR LIPS,
BUT THEIR HEART IS FAR AWAY
FROM ME.
9 [a]Is. 29:13 [b]Col. 2:22 **9** [a]BUT IN VAIN DO THEY WOR-
SHIP ME,
TEACHING AS THEIR [b]DOC-
TRINES THE PRECEPTS OF
MEN.' "

10 And He called to Himself
the multitude, and said to them,
"Hear, and understand.
11 [a]Matt. 15:18; Acts 10:14, 15; 1 Tim. 4:3 **11** "[a]Not what enters into the
mouth defiles the man, but what
proceeds out of the mouth, this
defiles the man."
12 Then the disciples *came
and *said to Him, "Do You know
that the Pharisees were offended
when they heard this statement?"
13 [a]Is. 60:21; 61:3; John 15:2; 1 Cor. 3:9 **13** But He answered and said,
"[a]Every plant which My heavenly
Father did not plant shall be
rooted up.
14 [a]Matt. 23:16, 24 [b]Luke 6:39 **14** "Let them alone; [a]they are
blind guides of the blind. And [b]if
a blind man guides a blind man,
both will fall into a pit."
★15 [a]Matt. 13:36 **15** And Peter answered and
said to Him, "[a]Explain the parable
to us."
16 And He said, "Are you
also still without understanding?
17 "Do you not understand
that everything that goes into the
mouth passes into the stomach,
and is eliminated?
18 [a]Matt. 12:34; Mark 7:20 **18** "But [a]the things that proceed out of the mouth come from
the heart, and those defile the
man.
19 [a]Gal. 5:19ff. **19** "[a]For out of the heart come
evil thoughts, murders, adulteries,
fornications, thefts, false witness,
slanders.
20 "These are the things which
defile the man; but to eat with
unwashed hands does not defile
the man."
21 [a]And Jesus went away 21 [a]Matt. 15:21-28; *Mark 7:24-30*
from there, and withdrew into the
district of [b]Tyre and [b]Sidon. [b]Matt. 11:21
22 And behold, a Canaanite 22 [a]Matt. 9:27 [b]Matt. 4:24
woman came out from that re-
gion, and *began* to cry out, saying, "Have mercy on me, O Lord,
[a]Son of David; my daughter is
cruelly [b]demon-possessed."
23 But He did not answer her
a word. And His disciples came to
Him and kept asking Him, saying,
"Send her away, for she is shouting out after us."
24 But He answered and said, 24 [a]Matt. 10:6
"I was sent only to [a]the lost sheep
of the house of Israel."
25 But she came and [a]*began* 25 [a]Matt. 8:2
to bow down before Him, saying,
"Lord, help me!"
26 And He answered and ★26
said, "It is not good to take the
children's bread and throw *it* to
the dogs."
27 But she said, "Yes, Lord;
but even the dogs feed on the
crumbs which fall from their master's table."
28 Then Jesus answered and 28 [a]Matt. 9:22
said to her, "O woman, [a]your
faith is great; be it done for you as
you wish." And her daughter was
healed at once.
29 [a]And departing from 29 [a]Matt. 15:29-31; Mark 7:31-37
there, Jesus went along by [b]the
Sea of Galilee, and having gone [b]Matt. 4:18
up to the mountain, He was sit-
ting there.
30 And great multitudes came 30 [a]Matt. 4:23
to Him, bringing with them *those
who were* lame, crippled, blind,
dumb, and many others, and they
laid them down at His feet; and
[a]He healed them,
31 so that the multitude mar- 31 [a]Matt. 9:8
veled as they saw the dumb
speaking, the crippled restored,
and the lame walking, and the
blind seeing; and they [a]glorified
the God of Israel.

15:7 See Isa. 29:13.
15:15 *the parable.* The reference is to v. 11.
15:26 *to the dogs.* Children ("the lost sheep of the house of Israel") must be fed before dogs. This Gentile woman, like the centurion, showed great faith (v. 28) and was rewarded for it.

32 [a]And Jesus summoned to
Himself His disciples, and said,
"[b]I feel compassion for the multitude, because they have remained
with Me now for three days and
have nothing to eat; and I do not
wish to send them away hungry,
lest they faint on the way."
33 And the disciples *said to
Him, "Where would we get so
many loaves in a desert place to
satisfy such a great multitude?"
34 And Jesus *said to them,
"How many loaves do you have?"
And they said, "Seven, and a few
small fish."
35 And He directed the multitude to sit down on the ground;
36 and He took the seven
loaves and the fish; and [a]giving
thanks, He broke *them* and
started giving *them* to the disciples, and the disciples *in turn,* to
the multitudes.
37 And they all ate, and were
satisfied, and they picked up what
was left over of the broken pieces,
seven large [a]baskets full.
38 And those who ate were
four thousand men, besides
women and children.
39 And dismissing the multitudes, He got into [a]the boat, and
came to the region of [b]Magadan.

32 [a]Matt. 15:32-39; *Mark 8:1-10;* Matt. 14:13-21 [b]Matt. 9:36
36 [a]Matt. 14:19
37 [a]Matt. 16:10; Mark 8:8, 20; Acts 9:25
39 [a]Mark 3:9 [b]Mark 8:10

4 *Attack by the Pharisees and Sadducees,* 16:1–12

16 [a]And the [b]Pharisees and
Sadducees came up, and
testing Him [c]asked Him to show
them a sign from heaven.
2 But He answered and said
to them, "[a]When it is evening,
you say, '*It will be* fair weather,
for the sky is red.'
3 "And in the morning,
'*There will be* a storm today, for
the sky is red and threatening.'
Do you know how to discern the
appearance of the sky, but cannot
discern the signs of the times?
4 "[a]An evil and adulterous
generation seeks after a sign; and
a sign will not be given it, except
the sign of Jonah." And He left
them, and went away.
5 And the disciples came to
the other side and had forgotten
to take bread.
6 And Jesus said to them,
"Watch out and [a]beware of the
leaven of the [b]Pharisees and Sadducees."
7 And they began to discuss
among themselves, saying, "*It is*
because we took no bread."
8 But Jesus, aware of this,
said, "[a]You men of little faith,
why do you discuss among yourselves because you have no
bread?
9 "Do you not yet understand
or remember [a]the five loaves of
the five thousand, and how many
[b]baskets you took up?
10 "Or [a]the seven loaves of the
four thousand, and how many
large [b]baskets you took up?
11 "How is it that you do not
understand that I did not speak to
you concerning bread? But [a]be-
ware of the leaven of the [b]Phari-
sees and Sadducees."
12 Then they understood that
He did not say to beware of the
leaven of bread, but of the teaching of the [a]Pharisees and Sadducees.

1 [a]Matt. 16:1-12; *Mark 8:11-21* [b]Matt. 3:7; 16:6, 11, 12 [c]Matt. 12:38
2 [a]Luke 12:54f.
★ 4 [a]Matt. 12:39
6 [a]Matt. 16:11; Mark 8:15; Luke 12:1 [b]Matt. 3:7; 16:1, 11, 12
★ 8 [a]Matt. 6:30; 8:26; 14:31
9 [a]Matt. 14:17-21 [b]Matt. 14:20
10 [a]Matt. 15:34-38 [b]Matt. 15:37
11 [a]Matt. 16:6; Mark 8:15; Luke 12:1 [b]Matt. 3:7; 16:6, 12
12 [a]Matt. 3:7; 16:6, 11

V THE PEDAGOGY OF THE KING, 16:13–20:28

A Concerning His Church (Peter's Confession of Faith), 16:13–20

13 [a]Now when Jesus came
into the district of [b]Caesarea Philippi, He *began* asking His disciples, saying, "Who do people say
that [c]the Son of Man is?"
14 And they said, "Some *say*
[a]John the Baptist; some, [b]Elijah;

★13 [a]Matt. 16:13-16; *Mark 8:27-29; Luke 9:18-20* [b]Mark 8:27 [c]Matt. 8:20; 16:27, 28
★14 [a]Matt. 14:2 [b]Matt. 17:10; Mark 6:15; Luke 9:8; John 1:21

16:4 See note on Matt. 12:39.
16:8 *discuss among yourselves.* Arguing over the fact that they had no bread.
16:13 *district.* This Caesarea was in Herod Philip's tetrarchy, about 25 miles N. of the Sea of Galilee.
16:14 *Elijah . . . Jeremiah.* Some must have seen resemblances between Christ's teachings and those of these two great prophets.

and others, Jeremiah, or one of
the prophets."
15 He *said to them, "But
who do you say that I am?"
16 And Simon Peter answered and said, "Thou art [a]the
Christ, [b]the Son of [c]the living
God."
17 And Jesus answered and
said to him, "Blessed are you, [a]Si-
mon Barjona, because [b]flesh and
blood did not reveal *this* to you,
but My Father who is in heaven.
18 "And I also say to you that
you are [a]Peter, and upon this rock
I will build My church; and the
gates of [b]Hades shall not over-
power it.
19 "I will give you [a]the keys of
the kingdom of heaven; and
[b]whatever you shall bind on earth
shall have been bound in heaven,
and whatever you shall loose on
earth shall have been loosed in
heaven."
20 [a]Then He warned the disciples that they should tell no one
that He was [b]the Christ.

B Concerning His Death, 16:21–28

21 [a]From that time Jesus
Christ began to show His disciples
that He must go to Jerusalem, and
[b]suffer many things from the elders and chief priests and scribes,
and be killed, and be raised up on
the third day.
22 And Peter took Him aside
and began to rebuke Him, saying,
"God forbid *it,* Lord! This shall
never happen to You."
23 But He turned and said to
Peter, "Get behind Me, [a]Satan!
You are a stumbling block to Me;
for you are not setting your mind
on God's interests, but man's."
24 Then Jesus said to His disciples, "If any one wishes to come
after Me, let him deny himself,
and [a]take up his cross, and follow
Me.
25 "For [a]whoever wishes to
save his life shall lose it; but whoever loses his life for My sake
shall find it.
26 "For what will a man be
profited, if he gains the whole
world, and forfeits his soul? Or
what will a man give in exchange
for his soul?
27 "For the [a]Son of Man [b]is
going to come in the glory of His
Father with His angels; and [c]WILL
THEN RECOMPENSE EVERY MAN AC-
CORDING TO HIS DEEDS.
28 "Truly I say to you, there
are some of those who are standing here who shall not taste death

16 [a]Matt. 1:16; 16:20; John 11:27 [b]Matt. 4:3 [c]Ps. 42:2; Matt. 26:63; Acts 14:15; Rom. 9:26; 2 Cor. 3:3; 6:16; 1 Thess. 1:9; 1 Tim. 3:15; 4:10; Heb. 3:12; 9:14; 10:31; 12:22; Rev. 7:2
★17 [a]John 1:42; 21:15-17 [b]1 Cor. 15:50; Gal. 1:16; Eph. 6:12; Heb. 2:14
★18 [a]Matt. 4:18 [b]Matt. 11:23
★19 [a]Is. 22:22; Rev. 1:18; 3:7 [b]Matt. 18:18; John 20:23
20 [a]Matt. 8:4; Mark 8:30; Luke 9:21 [b]Matt. 1:16; 16:16; John 11:27
★21 [a]Matt. 16:21-28: *Mark 8:31-9:1; Luke 9:22-27* [b]Matt. 12:40; 17:9, 12, 22f.; 20:18f.; 27:63; Mark 9:12, 31; Luke 17:25; 18:32; 24:7; John 2:19
★23 [a]Matt. 4:10
★24 [a]Matt. 10:38
★25 [a]Matt. 10:39
27 [a]Matt. 8:20 [b]Matt. 10:23; 24:3, 27, 37, 39; 26:64; Mark 8:38; 13:26; Luke 21:27; John 21:22; Acts 1:11; 1 Cor. 15:23; 1 Thess. 1:10; 4:16; 2 Thess. 1:7, 10; 2:1, 8; James 5:7f.; 2 Pet. 1:16; 3:4, 12; 1 John 2:28; Rev. 1:7 [c]Ps. 62:12; Prov. 24:12; Rom. 2:6; 14:12; 1 Cor. 3:13; 2 Cor. 5:10; Eph. 6:8; Col. 3:25; Rev. 2:23; 20:12; 22:12
★28 [a]Matt. 8:20 [b]Matt. 10:23; 24:3, 27, 37, 39; 26:64; Mark 8:38; 13:26; Luke 21:27; John 21:22; Acts 1:11; 1 Cor. 15:23; 1 Thess. 1:10; 4:16; 2 Thess. 1:7, 10; 2:1, 8; James 5:7f.; 2 Pet. 1:16; 3:4, 12; 1 John 2:28; Rev. 1:7

16:17 *Blessed are you.* Because he had received this insight through divine revelation and not through human influences.

16:18 *you are Peter.* The name Peter (Greek, *Petros*) means rock or rock-man. In the next phrase Christ used *petra* ("upon this rock"), a feminine form for "rock," not a name. Christ used a play on words. He does not say "upon you, Peter" or "upon your successors," but "upon this rock"—upon this divine revelation and profession of faith in Christ. *I will build* shows that the formation of the church was still in the future. It began on the day of Pentecost (Acts 2). The word "church" appears in the Gospels only here and in 18:17.

16:19 *the keys.* The authority to open the doors of Christendom was given to Peter, who used that authority for Jews on the day of Pentecost and for Gentiles in the house of Cornelius (Acts 10). *shall have been bound . . . shall have been loosed.* Heaven, not the apostles, initiates all binding and loosing, while the apostles announce these things. In John 20:22–23 sins are in view; here, things (i.e., practices). An example of the apostles' binding practices on people is found in Acts 15:20.

16:21 This is Matthew's first prediction of the Passion (see also 17:22; 20:18). Notice the number of specific details in this prediction.

16:23 *Satan.* Peter is sharply rebuked for aligning himself with Satan's plan to deter Jesus from fulfilling His mission. The harshness of the rebuke stems from Christ's fierce realism about the principal purpose of His coming to earth, which was to die. *a stumbling block.* Or "rock of offence" (Rom. 9:33), perhaps a further play on the word "rock" in v. 18.

16:24–28 This passage is on discipleship. Verses 13–20 are on Messiahship; 21–23 are on the atonement; 17:1–8 concern eschatology. These four passages together deal with the foundational truths of N.T. theology.

16:24 *cross.* See note on 10:38.

16:25 *whoever wishes to save his life.* By renouncing the Gospel. *shall find it.* Shall find eternal life.

16:28 *see the Son of Man coming in His kingdom.* This was fulfilled when the disciples wit-

until they see the [a]Son of Man
[b]coming in His kingdom."

C Concerning His Glory (the Transfiguration), 17:1-21

★ 1 [a]Matt. **17** [a]And six days later Jesus
17:1-8; *Mark* *took with Him [b]Peter and
9:2-8; Luke James and John his brother, and
9:28-36 [b]Matt. 26:37; *brought them up to a high
Mark 5:37; 13:3 mountain by themselves.
★ 2 **2** And He was transfigured
before them; and His face shone
like the sun, and His garments
became as white as light.
3 And behold, Moses and
Elijah appeared to them, talking
with Him.
★ 4 [a]Acts **4** And Peter [a]answered and
3:12 [b]Mark said to Jesus, "Lord, it is good for
9:5; Luke us to be here; if You wish, [b]I will
9:33 make three tabernacles here, one
for You, and one for Moses, and
one for Elijah."
5 [a]2 Pet. **5** While he was still speak-
1:17f. [b]Matt. ing, behold, a bright cloud over-
3:17 shadowed them; and behold, [a]a
voice out of the cloud, saying,
"[b]This is My beloved Son, with
whom I am well-pleased; hear
Him!"
6 And when the disciples
heard *this,* they fell on their faces
and were much afraid.
7 [a]Matt. **7** And Jesus came to *them*
14:27 and touched them and said,
9 [a]Matt. "Arise, and [a]do not be afraid."
17:9-13: **8** And lifting up their eyes,
Mark 9:9-13 [b]Matt. 8:4 they saw no one, except Jesus
[c]Matt. 8:20; 17:12, 22 Himself alone.
[d]Matt. 16:21 **9** [a]And as they were coming
down from the mountain, Jesus
commanded them, saying, "[b]Tell
the vision to no one until [c]the Son
of Man has [d]risen from the dead."
10 And His disciples asked ★10 [a]Matt.
Him, saying, "Why then do the 11:14; 16:14
scribes say that [a]Elijah must come
first?"
11 And He answered and ★11
said, "Elijah is coming and will restore all things;
12 but I say to you, that Elijah 12 [a]Matt.
already came, and they did not 8:20; 17:9,
recognize him, but did to him 22
whatever they wished. So also
[a]the Son of Man is going to suffer
at their hands."
13 Then the disciples understood that He had spoken to them
about John the Baptist.
14 [a]And when they came to 14 [a]Matt.
the multitude, a man came up to 17:14-19:
Him, falling on his knees before *Mark 9:14-28;* Matt.
Him, and saying, 17:14-18:
15 "Lord, have mercy on my *Luke 9:37-42* 15 [a]Matt.
son, for he is a [a]lunatic, and is 4:24
very ill; for he often falls into the
fire, and often into the water.
16 "And I brought him to Your
disciples, and they could not cure
him."
17 And Jesus answered and
said, "O unbelieving and perverted generation, how long shall
I be with you? How long shall I
put up with you? Bring him here
to Me."
18 And Jesus rebuked him,
and the demon came out of him,
and the boy was cured at once.
19 Then the disciples came to
Jesus privately and said, "Why
could we not cast it out?"

---

nessed the transfiguration (17:1-8), which was, in miniature, a preview of the kingdom, with the Lord appearing in a state of glory (Dan. 7:9-14).

17:1 *six days later.* Luke's "some eight days" includes the beginning and ending days as well as the interval between. *Peter and James and John.* The inner circle of the disciples.

17:2 *transfigured.* Lit., transformed. The transfiguration gave the three disciples a preview of Jesus' future exaltation and the coming kingdom. The Lord was seen in His body of glory; Moses and Elijah illustrated those whom Christ will bring with Him (either through death or translation, 1 Thess. 4:13-18); the disciples represented those who will behold His coming (Rev. 1:7).

17:4 *tabernacles.* Booths or shelters, for temporary residence.

17:10 *scribes.* I.e., the accredited expounders of Hebrew scriptures.

17:11-12 The sequence of thought is as follows: (1) Elijah is coming as the restorer (Mal. 4:5); (2) he came, unrecognized, in the person of John the Baptist, and was killed; (3) the Son of Man faces a like fate. The disciples seem to grasp only the first two points.

★20 aMatt. 21:21f.; Mark 11:23f.; Luke 17:6 bMatt. 13:31; Luke 17:6 cMatt. 17:9; 1 Cor. 13:2 dMark 9:23; John 11:40

20 And He *said to them, "Because of the littleness of your faith; for truly I say to you, [a]if you have faith as [b]a mustard seed, you shall say to [c]this mountain, 'Move from here to there,' and it shall move; and [d]nothing shall be impossible to you.

★21 aMark 9:29

21 [[a]"But this kind does not go out except by prayer and fasting."]

D Concerning His Betrayal, 17:22-23

22 aMatt. 17:22, 23: *Mark 9:30-32; Luke 9:44, 45*

22 [a]And while they were gathering together in Galilee, Jesus said to them, "The Son of Man is going to be delivered into the hands of men;

23 aMatt. 16:21; 17:9

23 and [a]they will kill Him, and He will be raised again on the third day." And they were deeply grieved.

E Concerning Taxes, 17:24-27

★24 aEx. 30:13; 38:26

24 And when they had come to Capernaum, those who collected [a]the two-drachma *tax* came to Peter, and said, "Does your teacher not pay [a]the two-drachma *tax*?"

25 aRom. 13:7 bMatt. 22:17, 19

25 He *said, "Yes." And when he came into the house, Jesus spoke to him first, saying, "What do you think, Simon? From whom do the kings of the earth collect [a]customs or [b]poll-tax, from their sons or from strangers?"

26 And upon his saying, "From strangers," Jesus said to him, "Consequently the sons are exempt.

27 aMatt. 5:29, 30; 18:6, 8, 9; Mark 9:42, 43, 45, 47; Luke 17:2; John 6:61; 1 Cor. 8:13

27 "But, lest we [a]give them offense, go to the sea, and throw in a hook, and take the first fish that comes up; and when you open its mouth, you will find a stater. Take that and give it to them for you and Me."

F Concerning Humility, 18:1-35

1 *Illustrated in childlike faith,* 18:1-6

1 aMatt. 18:1-5: *Mark 9:33-37; Luke 9:46-48*

18 [a]At that time the disciples came to Jesus, saying, "Who then is greatest in the kingdom of heaven?"

2 And He called a child to Himself and stood him in their midst,

★ 3 aMatt. 19:14; Mark 10:15; Luke 18:17; 1 Cor. 14:20; 1 Pet. 2:2

3 and said, "Truly I say to you, unless you are converted and [a]become like children, you shall not enter the kingdom of heaven.

★ 4

4 "Whoever then humbles himself as this child, he is the greatest in the kingdom of heaven.

5 "And whoever receives one such child in My name receives Me;

★ 6 aMark 9:42; Luke 17:2; 1 Cor. 8:12 bMatt. 17:27

6 but [a]whoever [b]causes one of these little ones who believe in Me to stumble, it is better for him that a heavy millstone be hung around his neck, and that he be drowned in the depth of the sea.

17:20 *nothing shall be impossible.* The will of God, of course, governs all things, including this promise.

17:21 Many manuscripts do not contain this verse.

17:24-27 This assessment of a half-stater, or half-shekel (2 drachmas), was collected annually for the support of the temple. Jesus anticipated Peter's confusion by trying to show him that members of the royal family are exempt from the tax. Thus, Jesus, the Son of God, was not personally obligated to pay for the support of God's house. Nevertheless, to avoid offense, He would pay. The miraculously caught fish yielded a stater, or shekel, which was equal to two half-shekels, sufficient for Jesus and Peter.

18:3 *are converted* = turn, an active and voluntary turning from sin.

18:4 *humbles himself.* The sense is, whoever humbles himself until he becomes as this little child—exhibiting trust, openness, and eagerness to learn. These are the childlike qualities that constitute greatness.

18:6-7 *causes . . . to stumble.* I.e., leads into sin. *stumbling blocks* (v. 7) are occasions for stumbling or temptations to sin. *millstone* (v. 6). The milling of grain was done by grinding it between 2 stones, each about 18 inches in diameter and 3 or 4 inches thick. The upper millstone was turned by a donkey walking in a circle.

2 *Illustrated in concern for the lost,* 18:7-14

7 [a]Luke 17:1; 1 Cor. 11:19; 1 Tim. 4:1

7 "Woe to the world because of *its* stumbling blocks! For [a]it is inevitable that stumbling blocks come; but woe to that man through whom the stumbling block comes!

★ 8 [a]Matt. 5:30; 17:27; Mark 9:43 [b]Matt. 17:27

8 "And [a]if your hand or your foot [b]causes you to stumble, cut it off and throw it from you; it is better for you to enter life crippled or lame, than having two hands or two feet, to be cast into the eternal fire.

9 [a]Matt. 5:29; 17:27; Mark 9:47 [b]Matt. 17:27 [c]Matt. 5:22

9 "And [a]if your eye [b]causes you to stumble, pluck it out, and throw it from you. It is better for you to enter life with one eye, than having two eyes, to be cast into the [c]hell of fire.

★10 [a]1 Kin. 10:8; 2 Kin. 25:19; Luke 1:19; Acts 12:15; Rev. 8:2

10 "See that you do not despise one of these little ones, for I say to you, that [a]their angels in heaven continually behold the face of My Father who is in heaven.

11 [a]Luke 19:10

11 ["[a]For the Son of Man has come to save that which was lost.]

12 [a]Matt. 18:12-14; Luke 15:4-7

12 "What do you think? [a]If any man has a hundred sheep, and one of them has gone astray, does he not leave the ninety-nine on the mountains and go and search for the one that is straying?

13 "And if it turns out that he finds it, truly I say to you, he rejoices over it more than over the ninety-nine which have not gone astray.

14 "Thus it is not *the* will of your Father who is in heaven that one of these little ones perish.

3 *Illustrated in church discipline,* 18:15-20

15 [a]Lev. 19:17; Luke 17:3; Gal. 6:1; 2 Thess. 3:15; James 5:19

15 "And [a]if your brother sins, go and reprove him in private; if he listens to you, you have won your brother.

★16 [a]Deut. 19:15; John 8:17; 2 Cor. 13:1; 1 Tim. 5:19; Heb. 10:28

16 "But if he does not listen *to you,* take one or two more with you, so that [a]BY THE MOUTH OF TWO OR THREE WITNESSES EVERY FACT MAY BE CONFIRMED.

★17 [a]1 Cor. 6:1ff. [b]2 Thess. 3:6, 14f.

17 "And if he refuses to listen to them, [a]tell it to the church; and if he refuses to listen even to the church, [b]let him be to you as a Gentile and a tax-gatherer.

★18 [a]Matt. 16:19; John 20:23

18 "Truly I say to you, [a]whatever you shall bind on earth shall have been bound in heaven; and whatever you loose on earth shall have been loosed in heaven.

19 [a]Matt. 7:7

19 "Again I say to you, that if two of you agree on earth about anything that they may ask, [a]it shall be done for them by My Father who is in heaven.

20 "For where two or three have gathered together in My name, there I am in their midst."

4 *Illustrated in continual forgiveness,* 18:21-35

★21 [a]Matt. 18:15 [b]Luke 17:4

21 Then Peter came and said to Him, "Lord, [a]how often shall my brother sin against me and I forgive him? Up to [b]seven times?"

22 [a]Gen. 4:24

22 Jesus *said to him, "I do not say to you, up to seven times, but up to [a]seventy times seven.

23 [a]Matt. 13:24 [b]Matt. 25:19

23 "For this reason [a]the kingdom of heaven may be compared to a certain king who wished to [b]settle accounts with his slaves.

★24

24 "And when he had begun to settle *them,* there was brought to him one who owed him ten thousand talents.

25 [a]Luke 7:42 [b]Ex. 21:2; Lev. 25:39; 2 Kin. 4:1; Neh. 5:5

25 "But since he [a]did not have *the means* to repay, his lord commanded him [b]to be sold, along with his wife and children and all

---

18:8 *cut it off.* See note on Matt. 5:29-30.

18:10 *their angels.* Apparently children have guardian angels (Ps. 91:11; Acts 12:15). *behold the face* = are in the immediate presence.

18:16 *two or three witnesses.* An ancient law (Deut. 19:15) for the purpose of reconciliation.

18:17 *church.* Here and in 16:18 are the only mention of the church in the Gospels. A local congregation is meant here; in 16:18, all the followers of Christ.

18:18 See notes on Matt. 16:19 and John 20:23.

18:21 *Up to seven times?* The rabbis said to forgive 3 times, so Peter thought he was being exceptionally worthy by suggesting 7 times.

18:24 *talents.* A talent was a measure of weight varying in size from about 58-80 lbs. It was used to weigh precious metals.

that he had, and repayment to be
made.
26 aMatt. 8:2 **26** "The slave therefore falling
down, [a]prostrated himself before
him, saying, 'Have patience with
me, and I will repay you everything.'
27 "And the lord of that slave
felt compassion and released him
and forgave him the debt.
★28 **28** "But that slave went out
and found one of his fellow-
slaves who owed him a hundred
denarii; and he seized him and
began to choke *him,* saying, 'Pay
back what you owe.'
29 "So his fellow-slave fell
down and *began* to entreat him,
saying, 'Have patience with me
and I will repay you.'
30 "He was unwilling however,
but went and threw him in prison
until he should pay back what
was owed.
31 "So when his fellow-slaves
saw what had happened, they
were deeply grieved and came
and reported to their lord all that
had happened.
32 "Then summoning him, his
lord *said to him, 'You wicked
slave, I forgave you all that debt
because you entreated me.
33 'Should you not also have
had mercy on your fellow-slave,
even as I had mercy on you?'
34 "And his lord, moved with
anger, handed him over to the
torturers until he should repay all
that was owed him.
35 aMatt. 6:14 **35** "[a]So shall My heavenly Father also do to you, if each of you
does not forgive his brother from
your heart."

G Concerning Human Problems, 19:1–26

1 *Physical problems,* 19:1–2

19 [a]And it came about that ★ 1 aMatt. 7:28 bMatt. 19:1-9; *Mark 10:1-12*
when Jesus had finished
these words, He departed from
Galilee, and [b]came into the region
of Judea beyond the Jordan;
2 and great multitudes fol- 2 aMatt. 4:23
lowed Him, and [a]He healed them
there.

2 *Divorce and remarriage,* 19:3–12

3 And *some* Pharisees came ★ 3 aMatt. 5:31
to Him, testing Him, and saying,
"[a]Is it lawful *for a man* to divorce
his wife for any cause at all?"
4 And He answered and ★ 4 aGen. 1:27; 5:2
said, "Have you not read, [a]that
He who created *them* from the
beginning MADE THEM MALE AND FE-
MALE,
5 and said, '[a]FOR THIS CAUSE A 5 aGen. 2:24; Eph. 5:31 b1 Cor. 6:16
MAN SHALL LEAVE HIS FATHER AND
MOTHER, AND SHALL CLEAVE TO HIS
WIFE; AND [b]THE TWO SHALL BECOME
ONE FLESH'?
6 "Consequently they are no
more two, but one flesh. What
therefore God has joined together, let no man separate."
7 They *said to Him, "[a]Why ★ 7 aDeut. 24:1-4
then did Moses command to GIVE
HER A CERTIFICATE AND DIVORCE HER?"
8 He *said to them, "Be- ★ 8
cause of your hardness of heart,
Moses permitted you to divorce
your wives; but from the beginning it has not been this way.
9 "And I say to you, [a]whoever 9 aMatt. 5:32
divorces his wife, except for im-

18:28 *a hundred denarii.* A 100 days' wages, a trifling sum in comparison.
19:1 *beyond the Jordan* = Perea, not part of Judea but within the tetrarchy of Herod Antipas. Perea was a region east of the Jordan, extending from the Sea of Galilee almost to the Dead Sea.
19:3 *for any cause at all.* The rabbis were divided on what were legitimate grounds for divorce. The followers of Shammai held that a man could not divorce his wife unless he found her guilty of sexual immorality. The followers of Hillel were more lax, allowing divorce for many, including trivial, reasons.
19:4-5 See Gen. 1:27; 2:23-24. Rather than aligning Himself with either rabbinical position, Jesus cites the purpose of God in creation that husband and wife should be one flesh—the oneness of kinship or fellowship with the body as the medium, causing marriage to be the deepest physical and spiritual unity.
19:7 *a certificate.* See note on Matt. 5:32.
19:8 *permitted.* Moses made a concession with regard to God's intention that marriage be lifelong and monogamous (Deut. 24:1-4).

morality, and marries another
commits adultery."
★10 **10** The disciples *said to Him,
"If the relationship of the man
with his wife is like this, it is better not to marry."
11 But He said to them, "[a]Not
all men *can* accept this statement,
but [b]*only* those to whom it has
been given.
12 "For there are eunuchs who
were born that way from their
mother's womb; and there are eunuchs who were made eunuchs
by men; and there are *also* eunuchs who made themselves eunuchs for the sake of the kingdom of heaven. He who is able to
accept *this,* let him accept *it.*"

11 [a]1 Cor. 7:7ff. [b]Matt. 13:11

3 *Children,* 19:13–15

13 [a]Then *some* children were
brought to Him so that He might
lay His hands on them and pray;
and the disciples rebuked them.
14 But Jesus said, "[a]Let the
children alone, and do not hinder
them from coming to Me; for [b]the
kingdom of heaven belongs to
such as these."
15 And after laying His hands
on them, He departed from there.

13 [a]Matt. 19:13-15: *Mark 10:13-16; Luke 18:15-17*
14 [a]Matt. 18:3; Mark 10:15; Luke 18:17; 1 Cor. 14:20; 1 Pet. 2:2 [b]Matt. 5:3

4 *Wealth,* 19:16–26

★16 **16** [a]And behold, one came to
Him and said, "Teacher, what
good thing shall I do that I may
obtain [b]eternal life?"
17 And He said to him, "Why
are you asking Me about what is
good? There is *only* One who is
good; but [a]if you wish to enter
into life, keep the commandments."
18 He *said to Him, "Which
ones?" And Jesus said, "[a]YOU
SHALL NOT COMMIT MURDER; YOU
SHALL NOT COMMIT ADULTERY; YOU
SHALL NOT STEAL; YOU SHALL NOT
BEAR FALSE WITNESS;
19 [a]HONOR YOUR FATHER AND
MOTHER; and [b]YOU SHALL LOVE YOUR
NEIGHBOR AS YOURSELF."
20 The young man *said to
Him, "All these things I have
kept; what am I still lacking?"
★21 **21** Jesus said to him, "If you
wish to be complete, go *and* [a]sell
your possessions and give to *the*
poor, and you shall have [b]treasure
in heaven; and come, follow Me."
22 But when the young man
heard this statement, he went
away grieved; for he was one who
owned much property.
23 And Jesus said to His disciples, "Truly I say to you, [a]it is
hard for a rich man to enter the
kingdom of heaven.
★24 **24** "And again I say to you, [a]it
is easier for a camel to go through
the eye of a needle, than for a rich
man to enter the kingdom of
God."
25 And when the disciples
heard *this,* they were very astonished and said, "Then who can be
saved?"
26 And looking upon *them*
Jesus said to them, "[a]With men
this is impossible, but with God
all things are possible."

16 [a]Matt. 19:16-29: *Mark 10:17-30; Luke 18:18-30;* Luke 10:25-28 [b]Matt. 25:46
17 [a]Lev. 18:5; Neh. 9:29; Ezek. 20:21
18 [a]Ex. 20:13-16; Deut. 5:17-20
19 [a]Ex. 20:12; Deut. 5:16 [b]Lev. 19:18
21 [a]Luke 12:33; 16:9; Acts 2:45; 4:34f. [b]Matt. 6:20
23 [a]Matt. 13:22; Mark 10:23f.; Luke 18:24
24 [a]Mark 10:25; Luke 18:25
26 [a]Gen. 18:14; Job 42:2; Jer. 32:17; Zech. 8:6; Mark 10:27; Luke 1:37; 18:27

19:10 *it is better not to marry.* The disciples seemed to have understood that Christ was teaching a very restricted meaning to "immorality" and that He completely disallowed divorce of married persons (see note on Matt. 5:32). In turn, Christ acknowledges that the saying "it is better not to marry" is valid in some cases, and these are enumerated in v. 12—those congenitally incapable, those made incapable, and those who wish to devote themselves more completely to the service of God (1 Cor. 7:7, 8, 26, 32-35). Celibacy is an acceptable option.

19:16 Jews of the time believed that performing some single act would guarantee salvation.

19:21 *complete.* I.e., genuinely pleasing to God. *go and sell.* The man was being asked to prove his claim to have kept the commandments, especially the one that says "thou shalt love thy neighbor as thyself." His unwillingness to do so belied his claim (v. 20) and showed him as a sinner in need of salvation.

19:24 *needle.* This means a sewing needle. In this proverbial expression, Christ does not say that a rich man could not be saved (v. 26), but only that, for him, it is more difficult, since such a person seldom senses his personal need as readily as a poorer man does.

H Concerning the Kingdom, 19:27–20:28

1 *Rewards in the kingdom,* 19:27–30

★27

27 Then Peter answered and said to Him, "Behold, we have left everything and followed You; what then will there be for us?"

★28 [a]Matt. 25:31 [b]Luke 22:30; Rev. 3:21; 4:4; 11:16; 20:4

28 And Jesus said to them, "Truly I say to you, that you who have followed Me, in the regeneration when [a]the Son of Man will sit on His glorious throne, [b]you also shall sit upon twelve thrones, judging the twelve tribes of Israel.

29 [a]Matt. 6:33; Mark 10:29f.; Luke 18:29f.

29 "And [a]everyone who has left houses or brothers or sisters or father or mother or children or farms for My name's sake, shall receive many times as much, and shall inherit eternal life.

30 [a]Matt. 20:16; Mark 10:31; Luke 13:30

30 "[a]But many *who are* first will be last; and *the* last, first.

2 *Recognition in the kingdom,* 20:1–16

★ 1 [a]Matt. 13:24 [b]Matt. 21:28, 33

20 "For [a]the kingdom of heaven is like a landowner who went out early in the morning to hire laborers for his [b]vineyard.

★ 2

2 "And when he had agreed with the laborers for a denarius for the day, he sent them into his vineyard.

3 "And he went out about the third hour and saw others standing idle in the market place;

4 and to those he said, 'You too go into the vineyard, and whatever is right I will give you.' And *so* they went.

5 "Again he went out about the sixth and the ninth hour, and did the same thing.

6 "And about the eleventh *hour* he went out, and found others standing; and he *said to them, 'Why have you been standing here idle all day long?'

7 "They *said to him, 'Because no one hired us.' He *said to them, 'You too go into the vineyard.'

8 "And when [a]evening had come, the owner of the vineyard *said to his [b]foreman, 'Call the laborers and pay them their wages, beginning with the last *group* to the first.' 8 [a]Lev. 19:13 [b]Luke 8:3

9 "And when those *hired* about the eleventh hour came, each one received a denarius.

10 "And when those *hired* first came, they thought that they would receive more; and they also received each one a denarius.

11 "And when they received it, they grumbled at the landowner,

12 saying, 'These last men have worked *only* one hour, and you have made them equal to us who have borne the burden and the [a]scorching heat of the day.' 12 [a]Jon. 4:8; Luke 12:55; James 1:11

13 "But he answered and said to one of them, '[a]Friend, I am doing you no wrong; did you not agree with me for a denarius? 13 [a]Matt. 22:12; 26:50

14 'Take what is yours and go your way, but I wish to give to this last man the same as to you. ★14

15 'Is it not lawful for me to do what I wish with what is my own? Or is your [a]eye envious because I am generous?' 15 [a]Deut. 15:9; Matt. 6:23; Mark 7:22

16 "Thus [a]the last shall be first, and the first last." 16 [a]Matt. 19:30

3 *Rank in the kingdom,* 20:17–28

17 [a]Matt. 20:17-19: *Mark 10:32-34; Luke 18:31-33*

17 [a]And as Jesus was about to go up to Jerusalem, He took the

---

19:27 Peter must have been thinking, "Well, we disciples certainly don't have any such hindrances of wealth!"

19:28 *in the regeneration* = in the New Age, the millennium, when the earth will be made new. The only other use of the word "regeneration" in the N.T. speaks of people being made new (Titus 3:5). *on His glorious throne.* See Matt. 25:31.

20:1-16 The subject is the reward of willingness to serve, whether one comes early or late. Christ is not teaching economics.

20:2 *a denarius for the day.* A good and normal wage for a rural worker. Additional workers were hired at about 9 a.m., noon, 3 p.m., and 5 p.m.

20:14 *I wish to give.* This is the point of the parable: God's grace and generosity know no bounds, and man's ideas of merit and earned rewards are irrelevant.

twelve *disciples* aside by themselves, and on the way He said to
them,

18 [a]Matt. 16:21

18 "Behold, we are going up to
Jerusalem; and the Son of Man
[a]will be delivered up to the chief
priests and scribes, and they will
condemn Him to death,

19 [a]Matt. 27:2; Acts 2:23; 3:13; 4:27; 21:11 [b]Matt. 16:21

19 and [a]will deliver Him up to
the Gentiles to mock and scourge
and crucify *Him,* and on [b]the
third day He will be raised up."

20 [a]Matt. 20:20-28: *Mark 10:35-45* [b]Matt. 4:21; 10:2 [c]Matt. 8:2

20 [a]Then the mother of [b]the
sons of Zebedee came to Him
with her sons, [c]bowing down, and
making a request of Him.

21 [a]Matt. 19:28

21 And He said to her, "What
do you wish?" She *said to Him,
"Command that in Your kingdom
these two sons of mine [a]may sit,
one on Your right and one on
Your left."

★22 [a]Is. 51:17, 22; Jer. 49:12; Matt. 26:39, 42; Luke 22:42; John 18:11

22 But Jesus answered and
said, "You do not know what you
are asking for. Are you able [a]to
drink the cup that I am about to
drink?" They *said to Him, "We
are able."

23 [a]Acts 12:2; Rev. 1:9 [b]Matt. 13:11 [c]Matt. 25:34

23 He *said to them, "[a]My
cup you shall drink; but to sit on
My right and on *My* left, this is
not Mine to give, [b]but *it is* for
those for whom it has been [c]pre-
pared by My Father."

24 And hearing *this,* the ten
became indignant at the two
brothers.

25 [a]Matt. 20:25-28; Luke 22:25-27

25 [a]But Jesus called them to
Himself, and said, "You know
that the rulers of the Gentiles lord
it over them, and *their* great men
exercise authority over them.

26 [a]Matt. 23:11; Mark 9:35; 10:43

26 "It is not so among you,
[a]but whoever wishes to become
great among you shall be your
servant,

★28 [a]Matt. 8:20 [b]Matt. 26:28; John 13:13ff.; 2 Cor. 8:9; Phil. 2:7; 1 Tim. 2:6; Titus 2:14; Heb. 9:28; Rev. 1:5

27 and whoever wishes to be
first among you shall be your
slave;
28 just as [a]the Son of Man
[b]did not come to be served, but to
serve, and to give His life a ransom for many."

VI THE PRESENTATION OF THE KING, 20:29–23:39

A The Power of the King, 20:29–34

★29 [a]Matt. 20:29-34; *Mark 10:46-52; Luke 18:35-43;* Matt. 9:27-31 ★30 [a]Matt. 20:31 [b]Matt. 9:27

29 [a]And as they were going
out from Jericho, a great multitude followed Him.
30 And behold, two blind
men sitting by the road, hearing
that Jesus was passing by, cried
out, saying, "Lord, [a]have mercy
on us, [b]Son of David!"

31 [a]Matt. 9:27

31 And the multitude sternly
told them to be quiet; but they
cried out all the more, saying,
"Lord, have mercy on us, [a]Son of
David!"
32 And Jesus stopped and
called them, and said, "What do
you wish Me to do for you?"
33 They *said to Him, "Lord,
we want our eyes to be opened."
34 And moved with compassion, Jesus touched their eyes; and
immediately they received their
sight, and followed Him.

B The Presentation of the King, 21:1–11

★ 1 [a]Matt. 21:1-9; *Mark 11:1-10; Luke 19:29-38* [b]Matt. 24:3; 26:30; Mark 11:1; 13:3; 14:26; Luke 19:29, 37; 21:37; 22:39; John 8:1; Acts 1:12

21 [a]And when they had approached Jerusalem and

20:22 *the cup that I am about to drink?* I.e., the cup of suffering. *We are able.* James was the first of the apostles to be martyred (Acts 12:2).

20:28 *ransom for many.* The word "for" undebatably means "in the place of" many. Christ here clearly interprets the meaning of His sacrifice as a substitution for sinners.

20:29–34 The differences in this account (which speaks of 2 blind men and of the miracle being done as Jesus left Jericho) and the accounts in Mark 10:46–52 and Luke 18:35–43 (which mention only 1 blind man and the miracle performed as they entered Jericho) are explained thus: (1) there were actually 2 men involved, but Bartimaeus, being more aggressive, takes the place of prominence; and (2) the men pled with Jesus as He entered Jericho but were not healed until He was leaving. It is also possible that the healing took place after Jesus left old Jericho and was nearing new Jericho.

20:30 *Son of David.* The specific Messianic title (Ps. 72; Isa. 9:7).

21:1 *Bethphage.* A village ½ mile E. of Jerusalem, on the S. side of the Mount of Olives.

had come to Bethphage, to [b]the
Mount of Olives, then Jesus sent
two disciples,
2 saying to them, "Go into
the village opposite you, and immediately you will find a donkey
tied *there* and a colt with her; untie *them,* and bring *them* to Me.
★ 3 **3** "And if anyone says something to you, you shall say, 'The
Lord has need of them,' and immediately he will send them."
4 [a]Matt. 21:4-9; *John 12:12-15* **4** [a]Now this took place that
what was spoken through the
prophet might be fulfilled, saying,

★ 5 [a]Is. 62:11; Zech. 9:9 **5** "[a]SAY TO THE DAUGHTER OF ZION,
'BEHOLD YOUR KING IS COMING TO YOU,
GENTLE, AND MOUNTED UPON A DONKEY,
EVEN UPON A COLT, THE FOAL OF A BEAST OF BURDEN.' "

6 And the disciples went and
did just as Jesus had directed
them,
7 and brought the donkey
and the colt, and laid on them
their garments, on which He sat.
8 [a]2 Kin. 9:13 **8** And most of the multitude
[a]spread their garments in the
road, and others were cutting
branches from the trees, and
spreading them in the road.
★ 9 [a]Ps. 118:26f.; [b]Matt. 9:27; [c]Luke 2:14 **9** And the multitudes going
before Him, and those who fol-
lowed after were crying out, saying,

"[a]HOSANNA to the [b]Son of David;
[a]BLESSED IS HE WHO COMES IN THE NAME OF THE LORD;
HOSANNA [c]in the highest!"

10 And when He had entered
Jerusalem, all the city was stirred,
saying, "Who is this?"
11 And the multitudes were 11 [a]Matt. 21:26; Mark 6:15; Luke 7:16, 39; 13:33; 24:19; John 1:21, 25; 4:19; 6:14; 7:40; 9:17; Acts 3:22f.; 7:37; [b]Matt. 2:23
saying, "This is [a]the prophet
Jesus, from [b]Nazareth in Galilee."

C The Purification by the King, 21:12-17

12 [a]And Jesus entered the ★12 [a]Matt. 21:12-16; *Mark 11:15-18; Luke 19:45-47;* Matt. 21:12, 13; *John 2:13-16* [b]Ex. 30:13 [c]Lev. 1:14; 5:7; 12:8
temple and cast out all those who
were buying and selling in the
temple, and overturned the tables
of the [b]moneychangers and the
seats of those who were selling
[c]doves.
13 And He *said to them, "It ★13 [a]Is. 56:7; Jer. 7:11
is written, '[a]MY HOUSE SHALL BE
CALLED A HOUSE OF PRAYER'; but you
are making it a robbers' den."
14 And *the* blind and *the* ★14 [a]Matt. 4:23
lame came to Him in the temple,
and [a]He healed them.
15 But when the chief priests 15 [a]Matt. 9:27
and the scribes saw the wonderful
things that He had done, and the
children who were crying out in
the temple and saying, "Hosanna
to the [a]Son of David," they became indignant,
16 and said to Him, "Do You ★16 [a]Ps. 8:2
hear what these are saying?" And
Jesus *said to them, "Yes; have
you never read, '[a]OUT OF THE
MOUTH OF INFANTS AND NURSING
BABES THOU HAST PREPARED PRAISE
FOR THYSELF'?"
17 And He left them and 17 [a]Matt. 26:6; Mark 11:1, 11, 12; 14:3; Luke 19:29; 24:50; John 11:1, 18; 12:1
went out of the city to [a]Bethany,
and lodged there.

21:3 *he will send them.* I.e., the owner will.
21:5 See Zech. 9:9.
21:9 *Hosanna* = save now. The acclamation is a quotation based upon Ps. 118:25-27, sung at the Feast of Tabernacles. The crowd wanted salvation from the oppression of Rome, not the spiritual salvation which Christ offered.
21:12 *moneychangers.* Ordinary coinage had to be exchanged for ancient Hebrew or Tyrian shekels, which were of standard weight and without blemish, as an offering to God.
21:13 Jesus here combines parts of 2 O.T. verses, Isa. 56:7 and Jer. 7:11.
21:14 *in the temple.* Doubtless at the gate or in the temple court, for *the blind and the lame* were not permitted into the temple (2 Sam. 5:8).
21:16 Jesus is apparently quoting Ps. 8:2, though *prepared praise* comes from the Septuagint version of the Psalm and may be translated "provided thyself with praise."

D The Cursing of the Fig Tree, 21:18-22

★18 [a]Matt. 21:18-22; *Mark 11:12-14, 20-24*
18 [a]Now in the morning,
when He returned to the city, He
became hungry.
★19
19 And seeing a lone fig tree
by the road, He came to it, and
found nothing on it except leaves
only; and He *said to it, "No
longer shall there ever be *any*
fruit from you." And at once the
fig tree withered.
20 And seeing *this,* the disciples marveled, saying, "How did
the fig tree wither at once?"
21 [a]Matt. 17:20; Mark 11:23; Luke 17:6; James 1:6
21 And Jesus answered and
said to them, "Truly I say to you,
[a]if you have faith, and do not
doubt, you shall not only do what
was done to the fig tree, but even
if you say to this mountain, 'Be
taken up and cast into the sea,' it
shall happen.
22 [a]Matt. 7:7
22 "And [a]everything you ask
in prayer, believing, you shall receive."

E The Challenge to the King, 21:23-27

★23 [a]Matt. 21:23-27; *Mark 11:27-33; Luke 20:1-8*
23 [a]And when He had come
into the temple, the chief priests
and the elders of the people came
to Him as He was teaching, and
said, "By what authority are You
doing these things, and who gave
You this authority?"
24 But Jesus answered and
said to them, "I will ask you one
thing too, which if you tell Me, I
will also tell you by what authority I do these things.
★25
25 "The baptism of John was
from what *source,* from heaven or
from men?" And they *began* reasoning among themselves, saying,
"If we say, 'From heaven,' He will
say to us, 'Then why did you not
believe him?'
26 "But if we say, 'From men,' 26 [a]Matt. 11:9; Mark 6:20
we fear the multitude; for they all
hold John to be [a]a prophet."
27 And they answered Jesus
and said, "We do not know." He
also said to them, "Neither will I
tell you by what authority I do
these things.

F The Parables of the King, 21:28-22:14

1 *The rebellion of the nation,* 21:28-32

28 "But what do you think? A 28 [a]Matt. 20:1; 21:33
man had two sons, and he came
to the first and said, 'Son, go work
today in the [a]vineyard.'
29 "And he answered and said,
'I will, sir'; and he did not go.
30 "And he came to the second
and said the same thing. But he
answered and said, 'I will not'; *yet*
he afterward regretted *it* and
went.
31 "Which of the two did the 31 [a]Luke 7:29, 37-50
will of his father?" They *said,
"The latter." Jesus *said to them,
"Truly I say to you that [a]the tax-
gatherers and harlots will get into
the kingdom of God before you.
32 "For John came to you in 32 [a]Luke 3:12
the way of righteousness and you
did not believe him; but [a]the tax-
gatherers and harlots did believe
him; and you, seeing this, did not
even feel remorse afterward so as
to believe him.

2 *The retribution on the nation,* 21:33-46

33 [a]Matt. 21:33-46; *Mark 12:1-12; Luke 20:9-19* [b]Ps. 80:8; Is. 5:1ff. [c]Matt. 20:1; 21:28 [d]Is. 5:2 [e]Matt. 25:14
33 "Listen to another parable.
[a]There was a landowner who
[b]PLANTED A [c]VINEYARD AND PUT A
WALL AROUND IT AND DUG A [d]WINE
PRESS IN IT, AND [d]BUILT A TOWER, and

21:18 *in the morning.* I.e., on Monday of Holy Week.

21:19 *except leaves only.* Normally the fruit and leaves appear at the same time. The curse on the tree is illustrative of the rejection of Israel, a nation unfruitful despite every advantage.

21:23 This begins Tuesday of Holy Week.

21:23-27 In effect, Jesus refuses to accept their claim of a right to examine Him.

21:25 *from what source.* Christ placed these men on the horns of a dilemma by asking them what test they would apply in the case of John.

rented it out to vine-growers, and
[e]went on a journey.
34 [a]Matt. **34** "And when the harvest
22:3 time approached, he [a]sent his
slaves to the vine-growers to receive his produce.
35 "And the vine-growers took
his slaves and beat one, and killed
another, and stoned a third.
36 [a]Matt. **36** "Again he [a]sent another
22:4 group of slaves larger than the
first; and they did the same thing
to them.
37 "But afterward he sent his
son to them, saying, 'They will respect my son.'
38 "But when the vine-growers
saw the son, they said among
themselves, 'This is the heir;
come, let us kill him, and seize his
inheritance.'
39 "And they took him, and
cast him out of the vineyard, and
killed *him.*
40 "Therefore when the owner
of the vineyard comes, what will
he do to those vine-growers?"
41 [a]Matt. **41** They *said to Him, "He
8:11f.; Acts will bring those wretches to a
13:46; 18:6; wretched end, and [a]will rent out
28:28 the vineyard to other vine-growers, who will pay him the proceeds at the *proper* seasons."
★42 [a]Ps. **42** Jesus *said to them, "Did
118:22; Acts you never read in the Scriptures,
4:11; Rom.
9:33; 1 Pet.
2:7

'[a]THE STONE WHICH THE BUILDERS REJECTED,
THIS BECAME THE CHIEF CORNER *stone;*
THIS CAME ABOUT FROM THE LORD,
AND IT IS MARVELOUS IN OUR EYES'?

★43 **43** "Therefore I say to you, the
kingdom of God will be taken
away from you, and be given to a
nation producing the fruit of it.
44 "And he who falls on this
stone will be broken to pieces;
but on whomever it falls, it will
scatter him like dust."
45 And when the chief priests
and the Pharisees heard His parables, they understood that He
was speaking about them.
46 And when they sought to 46 [a]Matt.
seize Him, they [a]became afraid of 21:26 [b]Matt.
the multitudes, because they held 21:11
Him to be a [b]prophet.

3 The rejection of the nation, 22:1–14

22 And Jesus [a]answered and 1 [a]Acts
spoke to them again in 3:12
parables, saying,
2 "[a]The kingdom of heaven 2 [a]Matt.
may be compared to a king, who 13:24; 22:2-
gave a wedding feast for his son. 14; Luke 14:16-24
3 "And he [a]sent out his slaves 3 [a]Matt.
to call those who had been invited 21:34
to the wedding feast, and they
were unwilling to come.
4 "Again he [a]sent out other 4 [a]Matt.
slaves saying, 'Tell those who 21:36
have been invited, "Behold, I
have prepared my dinner; my
oxen and my fattened livestock
are *all* butchered and everything
is ready; come to the wedding
feast." '
5 "But they paid no attention
and went their way, one to his
own farm, another to his business,
6 and the rest seized his
slaves and mistreated them and
killed them.
7 "But the king was enraged ★ 7
and sent his armies, and destroyed those murderers, and set
their city on fire.
8 "Then he *said to his slaves,
'The wedding is ready, but those
who were invited were not worthy.
9 'Go therefore to [a]the main ★ 9 [a]Ezek.
highways, and as many as you 21:21; Obad.
find *there,* invite to the wedding 14
feast.'
10 "And those slaves went out
into the streets, and gathered together all they found, both evil

---

21:42 See Ps. 118:22–23. The cornerstone figure was popular with N.T. writers (Acts 4:11; Eph. 2:20; 1 Pet. 2:7).

21:43 *taken away from you . . . given to a nation.* I.e., taken from the Jews and given to the Church (1 Pet. 2:9).

22:7 *set their city on fire.* A prediction of the destruction of Jerusalem in A.D. 70.

22:9 *highways.* Better, broad places or plazas.

and good; and the wedding hall
was filled with dinner guests.
11 a2 Kin. 10:22 **11** "But when the king came in
to look over the dinner guests, he
saw there [a]a man not dressed in
wedding clothes,
★12 aMatt. 20:13; 26:50 **12** and he *said to him,
'[a]Friend, how did you come in
here without wedding clothes?'
And he was speechless.
13 aMatt. 8:12 **13** "Then the king said to the
servants, 'Bind him hand and
foot, and cast him into [a]the outer
darkness; in that place [a]there
shall be weeping and gnashing of
teeth.'
★14 aMatt. 24:22; 2 Pet. 1:10; Rev. 17:14 **14** "For many are [a]called, but
few *are* [a]chosen."

G The Pronouncements of the King, 22:15–23:39

1 *In answer to the Herodians,* 22:15–22

15 aMatt. 22:15-22: *Mark 12:13-17; Luke 20:20-26* **15** [a]Then the Pharisees went
and counseled together how they
might trap Him in what He said.
★16 aMark 3:6; 8:15; 12:13 **16** And they *sent their disciples to Him, along with the [a]He-
rodians, saying, "Teacher, we
know that You are truthful and
teach the way of God in truth,
and defer to no one; for You are
★17 aMatt. 17:25 bLuke 2:1; 3:1 not partial to any.
17 "Tell us therefore, what do
You think? Is it lawful to give a
[a]poll-tax to [b]Caesar, or not?"
18 But Jesus perceived their
malice, and said, "Why are you
testing Me, you hypocrites?
19 "Show Me the [a]coin *used* 19 aMatt. 17:25
for the poll-tax." And they
brought Him a denarius.
20 And He *said to them,
"Whose likeness and inscription
is this?"
21 They *said to Him, "Cae- ★21 aMark 12:17; Luke 20:25; Rom. 13:7
sar's." Then He *said to them,
"[a]Then render to Caesar the
things that are Caesar's; and to
God the things that are God's."
22 And hearing *this,* they 22 aMark 12:12
marveled, and [a]leaving Him, they
went away.

2 *In answer to the Sadducees,* 22:23–33

23 [a]On that day *some* [b]Sad- 23 aMatt. 22:23-33: *Mark 12:18-27; Luke 20:27-40* bMatt. 3:7 cActs 23:8
ducees (who say [c]there is no res-
urrection) came to Him and questioned Him,
24 saying, "Teacher, Moses ★24 aDeut. 25:5
said, '[a]IF A MAN DIES, HAVING NO
CHILDREN, HIS BROTHER AS NEXT OF
KIN SHALL MARRY HIS WIFE, AND RAISE
UP AN OFFSPRING TO HIS BROTHER.'
25 "Now there were seven
brothers with us; and the first
married and died, and having no
offspring left his wife to his
brother;

22:12 *without wedding clothes.* This assumes that the guests would have been supplied with robes by the king's servants, since all the guests came in a hurry and most were unsuitably attired.

22:14 An ancient proverb, used 3 times in the apocryphal 4 Ezra. Here it indicates that there is a general call of God to sinners inviting them to receive His salvation, and there is also a specific election that brings some to Him. At the same time, man is held responsible for his rejecting Christ, whether it be because of indifference (Matt. 22:5), rebellion (v. 6), or self-righteousness (v. 12).

22:16 *Herodians.* A Jewish party who favored the Herodian dynasty, the party of "peace at any price" and appeasement of Rome.

22:17 *Is it lawful.* I.e., is it in accordance with the Torah, the sacred law? *to give a poll-tax to Caesar.* The poll-tax was imposed by Rome on every Jew. The burning question in the minds of many Jews of that day was simply this: If God gave the land of Israel to the Hebrews, and if God meant them to live there, and if He received their sacrifices and offerings in acknowledgment of His relationship to them, how could they pay tribute to any other power, king, god, or person? If Christ said that they should pay, they could then charge Him with disloyalty to Judaism; if He said no, they could denounce Him to the Romans.

22:21 Christ recognized the distinction between political and spiritual responsibilities. Caesar should be given taxes and all rightful political obedience; God should be given worship, obedience, service, and the dedication of one's whole life.

22:24 *children.* See Deut. 25:5-6; Gen. 38:8. The object of such a marriage law was to perpetuate the line of the dead brother and to keep his property within the family.

26 so also the second, and the third, down to the seventh.

27 "And last of all, the woman died.

28 "In the resurrection therefore whose wife of the seven shall she be? For they all had her."

29 [a]John 20:9

29 But Jesus answered and said to them, "You are mistaken, [a]not understanding the Scriptures, or the power of God.

★30 [a]Matt. 24:38; Luke 17:27

30 "For in the resurrection they neither [a]marry, nor are given in marriage, but are like angels in heaven.

31 "But regarding the resurrection of the dead, have you not read that which was spoken to you by God, saying,

★32 [a]Ex. 3:6

32 '[a]I AM THE GOD OF ABRAHAM, AND THE GOD OF ISAAC, AND THE GOD OF JACOB'? God is not *the God* of *the* dead but of *the* living."

33 [a]Matt. 7:28

33 And when the multitudes heard *this,* [a]they were astonished at His teaching.

3 *In answer to the Pharisees,* 22:34–40

34 [a]Matt. 22:34-40; *Mark 12:28-31;* Luke 10:25-37 [b]Matt. 3:7

34 [a]But when the Pharisees heard that He had put [b]the Sadducees to silence, they gathered themselves together.

★35 [a]Luke 7:30; 10:25; 11:45, 46, 52; 14:3; Titus 3:13

35 And one of them, [a]a lawyer, asked Him a question, testing Him,

★36

36 "Teacher, which is the great commandment in the Law?"

★37 [a]Deut. 6:5

37 And He said to him, " '[a]YOU SHALL LOVE THE LORD YOUR GOD WITH ALL YOUR HEART, AND WITH ALL YOUR SOUL, AND WITH ALL YOUR MIND.'

38 "This is the great and foremost commandment.

★39 [a]Lev. 19:18; Matt. 19:19; Gal. 5:14

39 "And a second is like it, '[a]YOU SHALL LOVE YOUR NEIGHBOR AS YOURSELF.'

40 [a]Matt. 7:12

40 "[a]On these two commandments depend the whole Law and the Prophets."

4 *In questioning the Pharisees,* 22:41–46

41 [a]Matt. 22:41-46; *Mark 12:35-37; Luke 20:41-44*

41 [a]Now while the Pharisees were gathered together, Jesus asked them a question,

42 [a]Matt. 9:27

42 saying, "What do you think about the Christ, whose son is He?" They *said to Him, "[a]*The son* of David."

★43 [a]2 Sam. 23:2; Rev. 1:10; 4:2

43 He *said to them, "Then how does David [a]in the Spirit call Him 'Lord,' saying,

★44 [a]Ps. 110:1; Matt. 26:64; Mark 16:19; Acts 2:34f.; 1 Cor. 15:25; Heb. 1:13; 10:13

44 '[a]THE LORD SAID TO MY LORD,

"SIT AT MY RIGHT HAND,
UNTIL I PUT THINE ENEMIES
BENEATH THY FEET?" '

45 "If David then calls Him 'Lord', how is He his son?"

46 [a]Mark 12:34; Luke 14:6; 20:40

46 And [a]no one was able to answer Him a word, nor did anyone dare from that day on to ask Him another question.

5 *Concerning the Pharisees,* 23:1–36

1 [a]Matt. 23:1-7; *Mark 12:38, 39; Luke 20:45, 46*

23 [a]Then Jesus spoke to the multitudes and to His disciples,

★2 [a]Deut. 33:3f.; Ezra 7:6, 25; Neh. 8:4

2 saying, "[a]The scribes and the Pharisees have seated themselves in the chair of Moses;

3 therefore all that they tell

22:30 *like angels in heaven.* Christ's argument is: In the resurrection men will not marry and women will not be given in marriage. There is no married state in that life. Thus the whole case cited is irrelevant and immaterial. Resurrected saints will be as angels, neither male nor female.

22:32 See Ex. 3:6. For believers, there is life after death, a truth rooted in the character of God.

22:35 *lawyer* = scribe.

22:36 Other answers to this question are found in Isa. 33:15; Amos 5:4; Mic. 6:8; Hab. 2:4.

22:37 Christ quotes Deut. 6:5, part of the Shema, used by all Jews in their daily prayers.

22:39-40 See Lev. 19:18. Christ was the first to combine these two texts into a summary of the law.

22:43 *in the Spirit.* I.e., inspired by the Holy Spirit.

22:44 *The Lord said to my Lord.* Christ was trying to make the Pharisees see that the Son of David was also the Lord of David (Ps. 110:1); i.e., the Messiah was David's human descendant and divine Lord.

23:2 *seated . . . in the chair of Moses.* I.e., act as teachers of the law.

you, do and observe, but do not
do according to their deeds; for
they say *things,* and do not do
them.
4 "And [a]they tie up heavy
loads, and lay them on men's
shoulders; but they themselves
are unwilling to move them with
so much as a finger.
5 "But they do all their deeds
[a]to be noticed by men; for they
[b]broaden their phylacteries, and
lengthen [c]the tassels *of their garments.*
6 "And they [a]love the place of
honor at banquets, and the chief
seats in the synagogues,
7 and respectful greetings in
the market places, and being
called by men, [a]Rabbi.
8 "But [a]do not be called
[b]Rabbi; for One is your Teacher,
and you are all brothers.
9 "And do not call *anyone* on
earth your father; for [a]One is
your Father, He who is in heaven.
10 "And do not be called leaders; for One is your Leader, *that
is,* Christ.
11 "[a]But the greatest among
you shall be your servant.
12 "And [a]whoever exalts himself shall be humbled; and whoever humbles himself shall be exalted.
13 "[a]But woe to you, scribes
and Pharisees, hypocrites, [b]be-
cause you shut off the kingdom of
heaven from men; for you do not
enter in yourselves, nor do you al-

4 [a]Luke 11:46; Acts 15:10
★ 5 [a]Matt. 6:1, 5, 16 [b]Ex. 13:9; Deut. 6:8; 11:18 [c]Matt. 9:20
6 [a]Luke 11:43; 14:7; 20:46
7 [a]Matt. 23:8; 26:25, 49; Mark 9:5; 10:51; 11:21; John 1:38, 49; 3:2, 26; 4:31; 6:25; 9:2; 11:8; 20:16
8 [a]James 3:1 [b]Matt. 23:7; 26:25, 49; Mark 9:5; 10:51; 11:21; 14:45; John 1:38, 49; 3:2, 26; 4:31; 6:25; 9:2; 11:8; 20:16
9 [a]Matt. 6:9; 7:11
11 [a]Matt. 20:26
12 [a]Luke 14:11; 18:14
★13 [a]Matt. 23:15, (16), 23, 25, 27, 29 [b]Luke 11:52

low those who are entering to go
in.
14 ["Woe to you, scribes and
Pharisees, hypocrites, because
[a]you devour widows' houses,
even while for a pretense you
make long prayers; therefore you
shall receive greater condemnation.]
15 "Woe to you, scribes and
Pharisees, hypocrites, because
you travel about on sea and land
to make one [a]proselyte; and when
he becomes one, you make him
twice as much a son of [b]hell as
yourselves.
16 "Woe to you, [a]blind guides,
who say, '[b]Whoever swears by
the temple, that is nothing; but
whoever swears by the gold of the
temple, he is obligated.'
17 "You fools and blind men;
[a]which is more important, the
gold, or the temple that sanctified
the gold?
18 "And, 'Whoever swears by
the altar, *that* is nothing, but
whoever swears by the offering
upon it, he is obligated.'
19 "You blind men, [a]which is
more important, the offering or
the altar that sanctifies the offering?
20 "Therefore he who swears,
swears *both* by the altar and by
everything on it.
21 "And he who swears by the
temple, swears *both* by the temple and by Him who [a]dwells
within it.

★14 [a]Mark 12:40; Luke 20:47
★15 [a]Acts 2:10; 6:5; 13:43 [b]Matt. 5:22
★16 [a]Matt. 15:14; 23:24; [b]Matt. 5:33-35
17 [a]Ex. 30:29
★18
19 [a]Ex. 29:37
21 [a]1 Kin. 8:13; Ps. 26:8; 132:14

23:5 *phylacteries.* A phylactery was a square leather box which contained four strips of parchment on which were written Deut. 11:13-21, Deut. 6:4-9, Ex. 13:11-16, and Ex. 13:1-10. During prayer one was worn on the forehead between the eyebrows and another on the left arm close to the elbow. They were held in place by leather bands, which the Pharisees made broad to attract more attention to themselves. The custom was based on Ex. 13:9, 16; Deut. 6:8; 11:18, though phylacteries had only begun to be used by the ultrapious in Christ's day. Christ criticizes not the custom itself but the spirit that corrupted it. *lengthen the tassels of their garments.* A hem or fringe on a garment was placed there in accordance with Num. 15:38, but the Pharisees made theirs unnecessarily wide.

23:13–33 This passage is often called "the seven woes," each beginning with the same phrase. (There are 8 if v. 14, omitted in many manuscripts, is included).

23:14 *devour widows' houses.* They used their position as jurists to adjust claims against wealthy widows or to get them to bestow on them their estates.

23:15 *proselyte.* Converts from paganism to Judaism.

23:16 *swears.* Here Christ argues with the Pharisees on their own grounds. *he is obligated.* I.e., his oath is binding. See Matt. 5:33-37.

23:18 *obligated.* I.e., guilty if he fails to carry out his oath.

22 [a]Matt. 5:34
22 "And he who swears by
heaven, [a]swears *both* by the
throne of God and by Him who
sits upon it.
★23 [a]Matt. 23:13; Luke 11:42
23 "[a]Woe to you, scribes and
Pharisees, hypocrites! For you
tithe the mint and dill and cummin,
and have neglected the weightier
provisions of the law: justice and
mercy and faithfulness; but these
are the things you should have
done without neglecting the others.
24 [a]Matt. 23:16
24 "You [a]blind guides, who
strain out a gnat and swallow a
camel!
25 [a]Mark 7:4; Luke 11:39f.
25 "[a]Woe to you, scribes and
Pharisees, hypocrites! For [a]you
clean the outside of the cup and
of the dish, but inside they are
full of robbery and self-indulgence.
26 [a]Mark 7:4; Luke 11:39f.
26 "You blind Pharisee, first
[a]clean the inside of the cup and of
the dish, so that the outside of it
may become clean also.
★27 [a]Luke 11:44; Acts 23:3
27 "[a]Woe to you, scribes and
Pharisees, hypocrites! For you are
like whitewashed tombs which on
the outside appear beautiful, but
inside they are full of dead men's
bones and all uncleanness.
28 "Even so you too outwardly
appear righteous to men, but inwardly
you are full of hypocrisy
and lawlessness.
29 [a]Luke 11:47f.
29 "[a]Woe to you, scribes and
Pharisees, hypocrites! For you
build the tombs of the prophets
and adorn the monuments of the
righteous,
30 and say, 'If we had been
living in the days of our fathers,
we would not have been partners
with them in *shedding* the blood
of the prophets.'
★31 [a]Matt. 23:34, 37; Acts 7:51f.
31 "Consequently you bear
witness against yourselves, that
you [a]are sons of those who murdered
the prophets.
★32
32 "Fill up then the measure *of
the guilt* of your fathers.
33 [a]Matt. 3:7 [b]Matt. 5:22
33 "You serpents, [a]you brood
of vipers, how shall you escape
the sentence of [b]hell?
★34 [a]Matt. 23:34-36; Luke 11:49-51 [b]2 Chr. 36:15, 16 [c]Matt. 10:17 [d]Matt. 10:23
34 "[a]Therefore, behold, [b]I am
sending you prophets and wise
men and scribes; some of them
you will kill and crucify, and
some of them you will [c]scourge in
your synagogues, and [d]persecute
from city to city,
★35 [a]Gen. 4:8ff.; Heb. 11:4 [b]Zech. 1:1 [c]2 Chr. 24:21
35 that upon you may fall *the
guilt of* all the righteous blood
shed on earth, from the blood of
righteous [a]Abel to the blood of
Zechariah, the [b]son of Berechiah,
whom [c]you murdered between
the temple and the altar.
36 [a]Matt. 10:23; 24:34
36 "Truly I say to you, all these
things shall come upon [a]this generation.

6 *Concerning Jerusalem,* 23:37–39

37 [a]Matt. 23:37-39; *Luke 13:34, 35* [b]Matt. 5:12 [c]Ruth 2:12
37 "[a]O Jerusalem, Jerusalem,
who [b]kills the prophets and
stones those who are sent to her!
How often I wanted to gather
your children together, [c]the way a
hen gathers her chicks under her
wings, and you were unwilling.
★38 [a]1 Kin. 9:7f.; Jer. 22:5
38 "Behold, [a]your house is
being left to you desolate!

23:23 *tithe.* The tithing of various herbs was based on Lev. 27:30. Though tithing of grain, fruit, wine, and oil was demanded (see also Num. 18:12; Deut. 14:22–23), the scribes had expanded the items required to be tithed to include even the smallest of herbs. *cummin* = a seed resembling the caraway. *without neglecting the others.* I.e., without neglecting the proper normal tithing.

23:27 *whitewashed tombs.* The outsides of tombs were often whitewashed to make them attractive and easily seen, while inside were death and decay.

23:31 The idea is: "like father, like son."

23:32 *the measure.* I.e., add to the iniquity of your fathers and bring down divine judgment on yourselves.

23:34 The last part of the verse refers to the apostles (see Matt. 10:17, 23).

23:35 *Zechariah, the son of Berechiah.* This murder is recorded in 2 Chron. 24:20–22. Berechiah was likely the father of Zechariah, while the famous Jehoiada was his grandfather. This is not the prophet Zechariah (though his father was also named Berechiah). Since Abel's death is recorded in Genesis, and since 2 Chronicles is the last book in the Hebrew Bible, Christ was saying, in effect, "from the first to the last murder in the Bible." See Luke 11:51.

23:38 *your house* = the temple and the city of Jerusalem.

★39 [a]Ps. 118:26; Matt. 21:9

39 "For I say to you, from now
on you shall not see Me until you
say, '[a]BLESSED IS HE WHO COMES IN
THE NAME OF THE LORD!' "

VII THE PREDICTIONS OF THE KING, 24:1–25:46

A The Destruction of the Temple, 24:1–2

★ 1 [a]Matt. 24:1-51; *Mark 13; Luke 21:5-36* [b]Matt. 21:23

2 [a]Luke 19:44

24 [a]And Jesus [b]came out
from the temple and was
going away when His disciples
came up to point out the temple
buildings to Him.
2 And He answered and said
to them, "Do you not see all these
things? Truly I say to you, [a]not
one stone here shall be left upon
another, which will not be torn
down."

B The Disciples' Questions, 24:3

★ 3 [a]Matt. 21:1 [b]Matt. 16:27f.; 24:27, 37, 39

3 And as He was sitting on
[a]the Mount of Olives, the disciples came to Him privately, saying, "Tell us, when will these
things be, and what *will be* the
sign of [b]Your coming, and of the
end of the age?"

C The Signs of the End of the Age, 24:4–28

4 [a]Jer. 29:8

4 And Jesus answered and
said to them, "[a]See to it that no
one misleads you.
5 "For [a]many will come in My
name, saying, 'I am the Christ,'
and will mislead many.
6 "And you will be hearing of
wars and rumors of wars; see that
you are not frightened, for *those
things* must take place, but *that* is
not yet the end.
7 "For [a]nation will rise
against nation, and kingdom
against kingdom, and in various
places there will be [b]famines and
earthquakes.
8 "But all these things are
merely the beginning of birth
pangs.
9 "[a]Then they will deliver
you up to tribulation, and will kill
you, and [b]you will be hated by all
nations on account of My name.
10 "And at that time many will
[a]fall away and will betray one another and hate one another.
11 "And many [a]false prophets
will arise, and will mislead many.
12 "And because lawlessness is
increased, most people's love will
grow cold.
13 "[a]But the one who endures
to the end, it is he who shall be
saved.
14 "And this [a]gospel of the
kingdom [b]shall be preached in
the whole [c]world for a witness to
all the nations, and then the end
shall come.
15 "Therefore when you see
the [a]ABOMINATION OF DESOLATION
which was spoken of through

5 [a]Matt. 24:11, 24; Acts 5:36f.; 1 John 2:18; 4:3
★ 6
7 [a]2 Chr. 15:6; Is. 19:2 [b]Acts 11:28
★ 9 [a]Matt. 10:17; John 16:2 [b]Matt. 10:22; John 15:18ff.
10 [a]Matt. 11:6
11 [a]Matt. 7:15; 24:24
13 [a]Matt. 10:22
★14 [a]Matt. 4:23 [b]Rom. 10:18; Col. 1:6, 23 [c]Luke 2:1; 4:5; Acts 11:28; 17:6, 31; 19:27; Rom. 10:18; Heb. 1:6; 2:5; Rev. 3:10; 16:14
★15 [a]Dan. 9:27; 11:31; 12:11 [b]Mark 13:14; Luke 21:20; John 11:48; Acts 6:13f.; 21:28 [c]Mark 13:14; Rev. 1:3

23:39 *from now on you shall not see me.* I.e., I will no longer teach publicly. *until you say.* At the second coming of Christ Israel will recognize and welcome their rejected Messiah (Zech. 12:10).

24:1 *the temple buildings.* Herod the Great began the building of this temple in 20 B.C., and it was finished in A.D. 64. The stones, 10–12 feet in length, would have been plainly visible.

24:3 *the Mount of Olives,* just E. of Jerusalem across the Kidron Valley. In this discourse Jesus answered two of the three questions the disciples asked. He does not answer *"when will these things be?"*. He answers *"what will be the sign of Your coming?"* in vv. 29–31 and He speaks of the signs of the end of the age in vv. 4–28. Verses 4–14 list characteristics of the first half of the tribulation period, while vv. 15–28 deal with the second half.

24:6–7 See the same judgments outlined in Rev. 6:1–8.

24:9 *on account of My name.* I.e., because they are His followers.

24:14 *this gospel of the kingdom.* This is the good news that will be preached during the tribulation days concerning the coming of Messiah and the setting up of His kingdom.

24:15 *abomination of desolation.* This is the man of sin (2 Thess. 2:4), the Antichrist, who at this midpoint in the tribulation breaks his covenant which he made at the beginning of the tribulation with the Jewish people (Dan. 9:27), and demands that they and the world worship him. Those who resist will be persecuted and many will be martyred; that is the reason for the urgency of the instructions in vv. 16–22.

Daniel the prophet, standing in
[b]the holy place ([c]let the reader
understand),
16 then let those who are in
Judea flee to the mountains;

17 [a]1 Sam. 9:25; 2 Sam. 11:2; Matt. 10:27; Luke 5:19; 12:3; Acts 10:9

17 let him who is on [a]the
housetop not go down to get the
things out that are in his house;
18 and let him who is in the
field not turn back to get his
cloak.

19 [a]Luke 23:29

19 "But [a]woe to those who are
with child and to those who nurse
babes in those days!
20 "But pray that your flight
may not be in the winter, or on a
Sabbath;

21 [a]Dan. 12:1; Joel 2:2; Matt. 24:29

21 for then there will be a
[a]great tribulation, such as has not
occurred since the beginning of
the world until now, nor ever
shall.

★22 [a]Matt. 22:14; 24:24, 31; Luke 18:7

22 "And unless those days had
been cut short, no life would have
been saved; but for [a]the sake of
the elect those days shall be cut
short.

23 [a]Luke 17:23f.

23 "[a]Then if any one says to
you, 'Behold, here is the Christ,'
or 'There *He is,*' do not believe
him.

24 [a]Matt. 7:15; 24:11 [b]John 4:48; 2 Thess. 2:9 [c]Matt. 22:14 [Gr.]; 24:22, 31; Luke 18:7

★25

24 "For false Christs and [a]false
prophets will arise and will show
great [b]signs and wonders, so as to
mislead, if possible, even [c]the
elect.
25 "Behold, I have told you in
advance.
26 "If therefore they say to
you, 'Behold, He is in the wilderness,' do not go forth, *or,* 'Behold,
He is in the inner rooms,' do not
believe *them.*

27 [a]Luke 17:23f. [b]Matt. 24:3, 37, 39 [c]Matt. 8:20

27 "[a]For just as the lightning
comes from the east, and flashes
even to the west, so shall the
[b]coming of the [c]Son of Man be.

28 [a]Job 39:30; Ezek. 39:17; Hab. 1:8; Luke 17:37

28 "[a]Wherever the corpse is,
there the vultures will gather.

D The Sign of His Coming, 24:29–31

★29 [a]Matt. 24:21 [b]Is. 13:10; 24:23; Ezek. 32:7; Joel 2:10, 31; 3:15; Amos 5:20; 8:9; Zeph. 1:15; Acts 2:20; Rev. 6:12; 8:12 [c]Is. 34:4; Rev. 6:13

29 "But immediately after the
[a]tribulation of those days [b]THE SUN
WILL BE DARKENED, AND THE MOON
WILL NOT GIVE ITS LIGHT, AND [c]THE
STARS WILL FALL from the sky, and
the powers of the heavens will be
shaken,

★30 [a]Matt. 24:3; Rev. 1:7 [b]Dan. 7:13; Matt. 16:27; 24:3, 37, 39

30 and then [a]the sign of the
Son of Man will appear in the
sky, and then all the tribes of the
earth will mourn, and they will
see [b]the SON OF MAN COMING ON
THE CLOUDS OF THE SKY with power
and great glory.

31 [a]Matt. 13:41 [b]Ex. 19:16; Is. 27:13; Zech. 9:14; 1 Cor. 15:52; 1 Thess. 4:16; Heb. 12:19; Rev. 8:2; 11:15 [c]Matt. 24:22 [d]Dan. 7:2; Zech. 2:6; Rev. 7:1 [e]Deut. 4:32

31 "And [a]He will send forth
His angels WITH [b]A GREAT TRUMPET
and THEY WILL GATHER TOGETHER His
[c]elect FROM [d]THE FOUR WINDS, [e]FROM
ONE END OF THE SKY TO THE OTHER.

E The Illustrations, 24:32–25:46

1 *The fig tree,* 24:32–35

32 "Now learn the parable
from the fig tree: when its branch
has already become tender, and
puts forth its leaves, you know
that summer is near;

★33 [a]James 5:9; Rev. 3:20

33 even so you too, when you
see all these things, recognize that
He is near, *right* [a]at the door.

★34 [a]Matt. 10:23; 16:28; 23:36

34 "Truly I say to you, [a]this
generation will not pass away until all these things take place.

24:22 *no life* = no human being. *the elect.* Those redeemed during the tribulation days. The elect of this age (the Church) will have been translated before that time begins.

24:25 *in advance.* This is a warning as well as a prediction.

24:29 *the sun . . . darkened.* These astral phenomena which will accompany the return of the Son of Man are foretold in Isa. 13:9–10 and Joel 2:31, 3:15.

24:30 *the sign.* Some think this is the lightning of v. 27; others, the Shekinah, or glory, of Christ; still others leave it unspecified. At any rate, *the Son of Man* Himself will come visibly (Rev. 1:7). There seems to be no reason for not taking this part of Jesus' teaching as plainly as other parts.

24:33 *all these things.* The signs described in vv. 4–28.

24:34 *this generation.* No one living when Jesus spoke these words lived to see "all these things" come to pass. However, the Greek word can mean "race" or "family," which makes good sense here; i.e., the Jewish race will be preserved, in spite of terrible persecution, until the Lord comes.

35 [a]Matt. 5:18; Mark 13:31; Luke 21:33

35 "[a]Heaven and earth will
pass away, but My words shall
not pass away.

2 *The days of Noah,* 24:36–39

36 [a]Mark 13:32; Acts 1:7

36 "But [a]of that day and hour
no one knows, not even the angels of heaven, nor the Son, but
the Father alone.

37 [a]Matt. 16:27; 24:3, 30, 39 [b]Gen. 6:5; 7:6-23; Luke 17:26f.
38 [a]Matt. 22:30 [b]Gen. 7:7

37 "For the [a]coming of the Son
of Man will be [b]just like the days
of Noah.
38 "For as in those days which
were before the flood they were
eating and drinking, they were
[a]marrying and giving in marriage,
until the day that [b]NOAH ENTERED
THE ARK,

39 [a]Matt. 16:27; 24:3, 30, 37

39 and they did not understand until the flood came and
took them all away, so shall the
[a]coming of the Son of Man be.

3 *The two,* 24:40–41

40 "Then there shall be two
men in the field; one will be
taken, and one will be left.

41 [a]Luke 17:35 [b]Ex. 11:5; Deut. 24:6; Is. 47:2

41 "[a]Two women *will be*
grinding at the [b]mill; one will be
taken, and one will be left.

4 *The faithful householder,* 24:42–44

42 [a]Matt. 24:43, 44; 25:10, 13; Luke 12:39f.; 21:36
43 [a]Matt. 24:42, 44; 25:10, 13; Luke 12:39f.; 21:36 [b]Matt. 14:25; Mark 6:48; 13:35; Luke 12:38
44 [a]Matt. 24:42, 43; 25:10, 13; Luke 12:39f.; 21:36 [b]Matt. 24:27

42 "Therefore [a]be on the alert,
for you do not know which day
your Lord is coming.
43 "But be sure of this, that [a]if
the head of the house had known
[b]at what time of the night the
thief was coming, he would have
been on the alert and would not
have allowed his house to be broken into.
44 "For this reason [a]you be
ready too; for [b]the Son of Man is
coming at an hour when you do
not think *He will.*

5 *The wise servant,* 24:45–51

45 "[a]Who then is the [b]faithful
and [c]sensible slave whom his
master [d]put in charge of his
household to give them their food
at the proper time?
46 "Blessed is that slave whom
his master finds so doing when he
comes.

45 [a]Matt. 24:45-51; *Luke 12:42-46* [b]Matt. 25:21, 23; Luke 16:10 [c]Matt. 7:24; 10:16; 25:2ff. [d]Matt. 25:21, 23

47 "Truly I say to you, that [a]he
will put him in charge of all his
possessions.

47 [a]Matt. 25:21, 23

48 "But if that evil slave says in
his heart, 'My master is not coming for a long time,'
49 and shall begin to beat his
fellow-slaves and eat and drink
with drunkards;
50 the master of that slave
will come on a day when he does
not expect *him* and at an hour
which he does not know,
51 and shall cut him in pieces
and assign him a place with the
hypocrites; [a]weeping shall be
there and the gnashing of teeth.

51 [a]Matt. 8:12

6 *The ten virgins,* 25:1–13

25 "Then [a]the kingdom of
heaven will be comparable
to ten virgins, who took their
[b]lamps, and went out to meet the
bridegroom.
2 "And five of them were
foolish, and five were [a]prudent.
3 "For when the foolish took
their lamps, they took no oil with
them,
4 but the [a]prudent took oil
in flasks along with their lamps.
5 "Now while the bridegroom
was delaying, they all got drowsy
and *began* to sleep.
6 "But at midnight there was

★ 1 [a]Matt. 13:24 [b]John 18:3; Acts 20:8; Rev. 4:5; 8:10 [Gr.]
2 [a]Matt. 7:24; 10:16; 25:2ff.
4 [a]Matt. 7:24; 10:16; 25:2ff.

25:1–13 The story clearly teaches watchfulness (v. 13); i.e., only those who are prepared for His coming will enter the kingdom.

25:1 *to meet the bridegroom.* There were two phases to Jewish weddings. First the bridegroom went to the bride's home to obtain his bride and observe certain religious ceremonies. Then he took his bride to his own home for a resumption of the festivities. Christ will take His bride, the church, to heaven before the tribulation period begins; then He will return with His bride at His second coming to the marriage supper on earth. The virgins represent the professing Jewish remnant on earth at His return.

a shout, 'Behold, the bridegroom!
Come out to meet *him.*'
7 "Then all those virgins
arose, and trimmed their lamps.
8 "And the foolish said to the
prudent, 'Give us some of your
oil, for our lamps are going out.'
9 [a]Matt. 7:24; 10:16; 25:2ff. — 9 "But the [a]prudent answered, saying, 'No, there will not
be enough for us and you *too;* go
instead to the dealers and buy
some for yourselves.'
10 [a]Matt. 24:42ff. [b]Luke 12:35f. [c]Matt. 7:21ff.; Luke 13:25 — 10 "And while they were going
away to make the purchase, the
bridegroom came, and those who
were [a]ready went in with him to
[b]the wedding feast; and [c]the door
was shut.
11 [a]Matt. 7:21ff.; Luke 13:25 — 11 "And later the other virgins
also came, saying, '[a]Lord, lord,
open up for us.'
12 "But he answered and said,
'Truly I say to you, I do not know
you.'
13 [a]Matt. 24:42ff. — 13 "[a]Be on the alert then, for
you do not know the day nor the
hour.

7 *The talents,* 25:14–30

★14 [a]Matt. 25:14-30; Luke 19:12-27 [b]Matt. 21:33 — 14 "[a]For *it is* just like a man
[b]*about* to go on a journey, who
called his own slaves, and entrusted his possessions to them.
★15 [a]Matt. 18:24; Luke 19:13 [b]Matt. 21:33 — 15 "And to one he gave five
[a]talents, to another, two, and to
another, one, each according to
his own ability; and he [b]went on
his journey.
16 [a]Matt. 18:24; Luke 19:13 — 16 "Immediately the one who
had received the five [a]talents
went and traded with them, and
gained five more talents.
17 "In the same manner the
one who had *received* the two *talents* gained two more.
18 "But he who received the
one *talent* went away and dug in
the ground, and hid his master's
money.
19 "Now after a long time the — **19** [a]Matt. 18:23
master of those slaves *came and
*[a]settled accounts with them.
20 "And the one who had re- — **20** [a]Matt. 18:24; Luke 19:13
ceived the five [a]talents came up
and brought five more talents,
saying, 'Master, you entrusted
five talents to me; see, I have
gained five more talents.'
21 "His master said to him, — **★21** [a]Matt. 24:45, 47; 25:23
'Well done, good and [a]faithful
slave; you were faithful with a
few things, I will put you in
charge of many things, enter into
the joy of your master.'
22 "The one also who had *re-* — **22** [a]Matt. 18:24; Luke 19:13
ceived the two [a]talents came up
and said, 'Master, you entrusted
to me two talents; see, I have
gained two more talents.'
23 "His master said to him, — **★23** [a]Matt. 24:45, 47; 25:21
'Well done, good and [a]faithful
slave; you were faithful with a
few things, I will put you in
charge of many things; enter into
the joy of your master.'
24 "And the one also who had — **24** [a]Matt. 18:24; Luke 19:13
received the one [a]talent came up
and said, 'Master, I knew you to
be a hard man, reaping where you
did not sow, and gathering where
you scattered no *seed.*
25 'And I was afraid, and went
away and hid your talent in the
ground; see, you have what is
yours.'
26 "But his master answered — **★26**
and said to him, 'You wicked, lazy
slave, you knew that I reap where
I did not sow, and gather where I
scattered no *seed.*
27 'Then you ought to have put
my money in the bank, and on
my arrival I would have received
my *money* back with interest.
28 'Therefore take away the
talent from him, and give it to the
one who has the ten talents.'
29 "[a]For to everyone who has — **29** [a]Matt. 13:12
shall *more* be given, and he shall
have an abundance; but from the

25:14–30 The contrast here is between those who make use of God's gifts and those who do not.

25:15 *talents.* See note on 18:24. These were silver (the word "money" in v. 18 means silver).

25:21, 23, 26 Two of the men received the same reward, indicating that faithfulness in the use of the different abilities given to each of us is what is required. The third is condemned for his sloth and indifference.

one who does not have, even what he does have shall be taken away.

30 [a]Matt. 8:12

30 "And cast out the worthless slave into [a]the outer darkness; in that place there shall be weeping and gnashing of teeth.

8 The judgment of Gentiles, 25:31–46

31 [a]Matt. 16:27f. [b]Matt. 19:28

31 "But when [a]the Son of Man comes in His glory, and all the angels with Him, then [b]He will sit on His glorious throne.

★32 [a]Ezek. 34:17, 20

32 "And all the nations will be gathered before Him; and He will separate them from one another, [a]as the shepherd separates the sheep from the goats;

★33 [a]1 Kin. 2:19; Ps. 45:9 [b]Eccles. 10:2

33 and He will put the sheep [a]on His right, and the goats [b]on the left.

34 [a]Matt. 5:3; 19:29; Luke 12:32; 1 Cor. 6:9; 15:50; Gal. 5:21; James 2:5 [b]Matt. 13:35; Luke 11:50; John 17:24; Eph. 1:4; Heb. 4:3; 9:26; 1 Pet. 1:20; Rev. 13:8; 17:8

34 "Then the King will say to those on His right, 'Come, you who are blessed of My Father, [a]inherit the kingdom prepared for you [b]from the foundation of the world.

35 [a]Is. 58:7; Ezek. 18:7, 16; James 2:15, 16 [b]Job 31:32; Heb. 13:2

35 'For [a]I was hungry, and you gave Me *something* to eat; I was thirsty, and you gave Me drink; [b]I was a stranger, and you invited Me in;

36 [a]Is. 58:7; Ezek. 18:7, 16; James 2:15, 16 [b]James 1:27 [c]2 Tim. 1:16f.

36 [a]naked, and you clothed Me; I was sick, and you [b]visited Me; [c]I was in prison, and you came to Me.'

★37

37 "Then the righteous will answer Him, saying, 'Lord, when did we see You hungry, and feed You, or thirsty, and give You drink?

38 'And when did we see You a stranger, and invite You in, or naked, and clothe You?

39 'And when did we see You sick, or in prison, and come to You?'

40 [a]Matt. 25:34; Luke 19:38; Rev. 17:14; 19:16 [b]Prov. 19:17; Matt. 10:42; Heb. 6:10

40 "And [a]the King will answer and say to them, 'Truly I say to you, [b]to the extent that you did it to one of these brothers of Mine, *even* the least *of them,* you did it to Me.'

41 [a]Matt. 7:23 [b]Mark 9:48; Luke 16:24; Jude 7 [c]Matt. 4:10; Rev. 12:9

41 "Then He will also say to those on His left, '[a]Depart from Me, accursed ones, into the [b]eternal fire which has been prepared for [c]the devil and his angels;

42 for I was hungry, and you gave Me *nothing* to eat; I was thirsty, and you gave Me nothing to drink;

43 I was a stranger, and you did not invite Me in; naked, and you did not clothe Me; sick, and in prison, and you did not visit Me.'

44 "Then they themselves also will answer, saying, 'Lord, when did we see You hungry, or thirsty, or a stranger, or naked, or sick, or in prison, and did not take care of You?'

45 "Then He will answer them, saying, 'Truly I say to you, to the extent that you did not do it to one of the least of these, you did not do it to Me.'

46 [a]Dan. 12:2; John 5:29; Acts 24:15 [b]Matt. 19:29; John 3:15f., 36; 5:24; 6:27, 40, 47, 54; 17:2f.; Acts 13:46, 48; Rom. 2:7; 5:21; 6:23; Gal. 6:8; 1 John 5:11

46 "And these will go away into [a]eternal punishment, but the righteous into [b]eternal life."

VIII THE PASSION OF THE KING, 26:1–27:66

A The Preparation, 26:1–16

1 [a]Matt. 7:28

★ 2 [a]Matt. 26:2-5: *Mark 14:1-2; Luke 22:1-2* [b]John 11:55; 13:1 [c]Matt. 10:4

26 [a]And it came about that when Jesus had finished all these words, He said to His disciples,

2 "[a]You know that after two days [b]the Passover is coming, and

---

25:32 *all the nations.* Lit., all the Gentiles. This is a judgment of those Gentiles who survive the tribulation and whose heart relation to God is evidenced by their treatment of the Jews (Christ's brethren, v. 40), especially during that time. Surviving Jews will also be judged at this same time (Ezek. 20:33–38).

25:33 *on His right.* The place of honor.

25:37 *when.* They are unconscious of their goodness, in contrast to the ostentation of the Pharisees. In v. 44 we see the opposite, the unconscious neglect of duty.

26:2 *after two days* = two days from now. The events recorded in 26:1–16 occurred on Wednesday. *Passover.* This was the ancient Jewish festival commemorating the deliverance from Egypt. It was followed immediately by the seven days' Feast of Unleavened Bread, and the entire festival was often called "Passover." See note on Acts 2:1.

the Son of Man is *to be* [c]delivered
up for crucifixion."
3 [a]Then the chief priests and
the elders of the people were
gathered together in [b]the court of
the high priest, named [c]Caiaphas;
4 and they [a]plotted together
to seize Jesus by stealth, and kill
Him.
5 But they were saying, "Not
during the festival, [a]lest a riot occur among the people."
6 [a]Now when Jesus was in
[b]Bethany, at the home of Simon
the leper,
7 a woman came to Him
with an alabaster vial of very
costly perfume, and she poured it
upon His head as He reclined *at
table.*
8 But the disciples were indignant when they saw *this,* and
said, "What is the point of this
waste?
9 "For this *perfume* might
have been sold for a high price
and *the money* given to the
poor."
10 But Jesus, aware of this,
said to them, "Why do you
bother the woman? For she has
done a good deed to Me.
11 "For [a]the poor you have
with you always; but you do not
always have Me.
12 "For when she poured this
perfume upon My body, she did
it [a]to prepare Me for burial.
13 "Truly I say to you, [a]wher-
ever this gospel is preached in the
whole world, what this woman

★ 3 [a]John 11:47 [b]Matt. 26:58, 69; 27:27; Mark 14:54, 66; 15:16; Luke 11:21; 22:55; John 18:15 [c]Matt. 26:57; Luke 3:2; John 11:49; 18:13, 14, 24, 28; Acts 4:6
4 [a]Matt. 12:14
5 [a]Matt. 27:24
★ 6 [a]Matt. 26:6-13; *Mark 14:3-9;* Luke 7:37-39; John 12:1-8 [b]Matt. 21:17
★ 7
★11 [a]Deut. 15:11; Mark 14:7; John 12:8
★12 [a]John 19:40
13 [a]Mark 14:9

has done shall also be spoken of
in memory of her."
14 [a]Then one of the twelve,
named [b]Judas Iscariot, went to the
chief priests,
15 and said, "What are you
willing to give me to [a]deliver Him
up to you?" And [b]they weighed
out to him thirty pieces of silver.
16 And from then on he *began* looking for a good opportunity to betray Him.

14 [a]Matt. 26:14-16; *Mark 14:10, 11; Luke 22:3-6* [b]Matt. 10:4; 26:25, 47; 27:3; John 6:71; 12:4; 13:26; Acts 1:16
★15 [a]Matt. 10:4 [b]Ex. 21:32; Zech. 11:12

B The Passover, 26:17-30

17 [a]Now on the first *day* of
[b]the *Feast* of Unleavened Bread
the disciples came to Jesus, saying, "Where do You want us to
prepare for You to eat the Passover?"
18 And He said, "Go into the
city to [a]a certain man, and say to
him, 'The Teacher says, "[b]My
time is at hand; I *am to* keep the
Passover at your house with My
disciples." ' "
19 And the disciples did as
Jesus had directed them; and they
prepared the Passover.
20 [a]Now when evening had
come, He was reclining *at table*
with the twelve disciples.
21 And as they were eating,
He said, "[a]Truly I say to you that
one of you will betray Me."
22 And being deeply grieved,
they each one began to say to
Him, "Surely not I, Lord?"

★17 [a]Matt. 26:17-19; *Mark 14:12-16; Luke 22:7-13* [b]Ex. 12:18-20
★18 [a]Mark 14:13; Luke 22:10 [b]John 7:6, 8
★20 [a]Matt. 26:20-24; *Mark 14:17-21*
21 [a]Luke 22:21-23; John 13:21f.

26:3 *Caiaphas,* high priest A.D. 18-36 and son-in-law and successor of Annas.

26:6 *Simon the leper.* Nothing more of him is known. Perhaps Christ had healed him.

26:7 *very costly perfume.* Mark (14:5) says it was worth 300 denarii or approximately a year's salary for a rural worker.

26:11 *For the poor you have with you always.* This should not be understood callously. Christ says, in effect, that there will be other opportunities to do good to the poor, but not another opportunity to do what had just been done to Him.

26:12 *she did it to prepare Me for burial.* Though the disciples ignored Christ's many predictions of His approaching death, apparently this woman believed them (16:21; 17:22; 20:18). John identifies her as Mary (John 12:3).

26:15 *thirty pieces of silver.* The coin is unidentified. If it was a denarius, this sum represented approximately five weeks' wages. It could have amounted to much more.

26:17 *eat the Passover.* I.e., the Passover lamb (Ex. 12:3-10), meaning the whole sacred meal.

26:18 *My time* (of death) *is at hand.*

26:20 *He was reclining at table.* The order of events that night was: eating the Passover; washing the disciples' feet (John 13:1-20); identifying Judas as the betrayer (Matt. 26:21-25), after which he left (John 13:30); the institution of the Lord's Supper (Matt. 26:26-29); messages in the Upper Room (John 14) and on the way to Gethsemane (John 15-16); Christ's great prayer for His people (John 17); the betrayal and arrest in Gethsemane (Matt. 26:36-56).

23 And He answered and
said, "[a]He who dipped his hand
with Me in the bowl is the one
who will betray Me.
24 "The Son of Man *is to* go,
[a]just as it is written of Him; but
woe to that man through whom
the Son of Man is betrayed! [b]It
would have been good for that
man if he had not been born."
25 And [a]Judas, who was betraying Him, answered and said,
"Surely it is not I, [b]Rabbi?" He
*said to him, "[c]You have said *it*
yourself."
26 [a]And while they were eating, Jesus took *some* bread, and
[b]after a blessing, He broke it and
gave *it* to the disciples, and said,
"Take, eat; this is My body."
27 And He took a cup and
gave thanks, and gave *it* to them,
saying, "Drink from it, all of you;
28 for [a]this is My blood of the
covenant, which is *to be* shed on
behalf of [b]many for forgiveness
of sins.
29 "But I say to you, I will not
drink of this fruit of the vine from
now on until that day when I
drink it new with you in My Father's kingdom."
30 [a]And after singing a
hymn, they went out to [b]the
Mount of Olives.

C The Betrayal, 26:31–56

31 Then Jesus *said to them,
"You will all [a]fall away because of
Me this night, for it is written, '[b]I
WILL STRIKE DOWN THE SHEPHERD, AND
THE SHEEP OF THE FLOCK SHALL BE
[c]SCATTERED.'
32 "But after I have been
raised, [a]I will go before you to
Galilee."
33 But Peter answered and
said to Him, "*Even* though all
may fall away because of You, I
will never fall away."
34 Jesus said to him, "[a]Truly I
say to you that [b]this *very* night,
before a cock crows, you shall
deny Me three times."
35 Peter *said to Him, "[a]Even
if I must die with You, I will not
deny You." All the disciples said
the same thing too.
36 [a]Then Jesus *came with
them to a place called [b]Gethsema-
ne, and *said to His disciples, "Sit
here while I go over there and
pray."
37 And He took with Him
[a]Peter and the two sons of Zebedee, and began to be grieved and
distressed.
38 Then He *said to them,
"[a]My soul is deeply grieved, to
the point of death; remain here
and [b]keep watch with Me."
39 And He went a little beyond *them,* and fell on His face
and prayed, saying, "My Father, if
it is possible, let [a]this cup pass
from Me; [b]yet not as I will, but as
Thou wilt."
40 And He *came to the disciples and *found them sleeping,
and *said to Peter, "So, you *men*
could not [a]keep watch with Me
for one hour?
41 "[a]Keep watching and praying, that you may not enter into

23 [a]John 13:18, 26
24 [a]Matt. 26:31, 54, 56; Mark 9:12; Luke 24:25-27, 46; Acts 17:2f.; 26:22f.; 1 Cor. 15:3; 1 Pet. 1:10f. [b]Matt. 18:7; Mark 14:21
25 [a]Matt. 26:14 [b]Matt. 23:7; 26:49 [c]Matt. 26:64; 27:11; Luke 22:70
26 [a]Matt. 26:26-29: *Mark 14:22-25; Luke 22:17-20; 1 Cor. 11:23-25;* 1 Cor. 10:16 [b]Matt. 14:19
★**28** [a]Heb. 9:20 [b]Matt. 20:28
★**29**
★**30** [a]Matt. 26:30-35: *Mark 14:26-31; Luke 22:31-34* [b]Matt. 21:1
★**31** [a]Matt. 11:6 [b]Zech. 13:7 [c]John 16:32
32 [a]Matt. 28:7, 10, 16; Mark 16:7
34 [a]Matt. 26:75; John 13:38 [b]Mark 14:30
35 [a]John 13:37
★**36** [a]Matt. 26:36-46: *Mark 14:32-42; Luke 22:40-46* [b]Mark 14:32; Luke 22:39; John 18:1
★**37** [a]Matt. 4:21; 17:1; Mark 5:37
★**38** [a]John 12:27 [b]Matt. 26:40, 41
★**39** [a]Matt. 20:22 [b]Matt. 26:42; Mark 14:36; Luke 22:42; John 6:38
40 [a]Matt. 26:38
41 [a]Matt. 26:38 [b]Mark 14:38

26:28 *the covenant.* The new testament, or new covenant, is God's new arrangement with men based on the death of Christ. See Introduction to the New Testament.

26:29 *until that day when I drink it new with you in My Father's kingdom.* The disciples' attention is directed toward their eventual reunion in the future millennial kingdom with its joy and fellowship.

26:30 *hymn.* Probably all or part of Pss. 115–118, the traditional Passover Hallel.

26:31 *You will all fall away.* All the disciples would "fall away" before the night was over (v. 56), not only Peter. See Zech. 13:7.

26:36 *Gethsemane.* The name means "oil press." It was a garden, doubtless containing olive trees, on the side of the Mount of Olives.

26:37 *the two sons of Zebedee.* I.e., James and John.

26:38 *keep watch* = stay awake, be alert. So also in vv. 40, 41.

26:39 *this cup.* The cup was all the suffering involved in the sinless Son of God taking upon Himself the sin of mankind including the necessary, though temporary, separation from God (27:46). He naturally shrank from this, though He willingly submitted to it.

temptation; [b]the spirit is willing, but the flesh is weak."

42 [a]Matt. 20:22 [b]Matt. 26:39; Mark 14:36; Luke 22:42; John 6:38

42 He went away again a second time and prayed, saying, "My Father, if this [a]cannot pass away unless I drink it, [b]Thy will be done."

43 And He came back and found them sleeping, for their eyes were heavy.

44 And He left them again, and went away and prayed a third time, saying the same thing once more.

45 [a]Mark 14:41; John 12:27; 13:1

45 Then He *came to the disciples, and *said to them, "Are you still sleeping and taking your rest? Behold, [a]the hour is at hand and the Son of Man is being betrayed into the hands of sinners.

46 "Arise, let us be going; behold, the one who betrays Me is at hand!"

47 [a]Matt. 26:47-56: *Mark 14:43-50; Luke 22:47-53; John 18:3-11* [b]Matt. 26:14

47 [a]And while He was still speaking, behold, [b]Judas, one of the twelve, came up, accompanied by a great multitude with swords and clubs, from the chief priests and elders of the people.

48 Now he who was betraying Him gave them a sign, saying, "Whomever I shall kiss, He is the one; seize Him."

49 [a]Matt. 23:7; 26:25

49 And immediately he came to Jesus and said, "Hail, [a]Rabbi!" and kissed Him.

★50 [a]Matt. 20:13; 22:12

50 And Jesus said to him, "[a]Friend, *do* what you have come for." Then they came and laid hands on Jesus and seized Him.

★51 [a]Mark 14:47; Luke 22:50; John 18:10 [b]Luke 22:38 [c]Mark 14:47; Luke 22:50; John 18:10

51 And behold, [a]one of those who were with Jesus reached and drew out his [b]sword, and struck the [c]slave of the high priest, and cut off his ear.

52 [a]Gen. 9:6; Rev. 13:10

52 Then Jesus *said to him, "Put your sword back into its place; for [a]all those who take up the sword shall perish by the sword.

★53 [a]Mark 5:9, 15; Luke 8:30 [b]Matt. 4:11

53 "Or do you think that I cannot appeal to My Father, and He will at once put at My disposal more than twelve [a]legions of [b]angels?

54 [a]Matt. 26:24

54 "How then shall [a]the Scriptures be fulfilled, that it must happen this way?"

55 [a]Mark 12:35; 14:49; Luke 4:20; 19:47; 20:1; 21:37; John 7:14, 28; 8:2, 20; 18:20

55 At that time Jesus said to the multitudes, "Have you come out with swords and clubs to arrest Me as though *I were* a robber? [a]Every day I used to sit in the temple teaching and you did not seize Me.

56 [a]Matt. 26:24

56 "But all this has taken place that [a]the Scriptures of the prophets may be fulfilled." Then all the disciples left Him and fled.

D The Hearings, 26:57-27:26

1 Before the high priest, 26:57-75

★57 [a]Matt. 26:57-68: *Mark 14:53-65; John 18:12f., 19-24* [b]Matt. 26:3

57 [a]And those who had seized Jesus led Him away to [b]Caiaphas, the high priest, where the scribes and the elders were gathered together.

58 [a]John 18:15 [b]Matt. 26:3 [c]Matt. 5:25; John 7:32, 45f.; 19:6; Acts 5:22, 26

58 But [a]Peter also followed Him at a distance as far as the [b]courtyard of the high priest, and entered in, and sat down with the [c]officers to see the outcome.

59 [a]Matt. 5:22

59 Now the chief priests and the whole [a]Council kept trying to obtain false testimony against Jesus, in order that they might put Him to death;

★60 [a]Deut. 19:15

60 and they did not find it, even though many false witnesses came forward. But later on [a]two came forward,

61 [a]Matt. 27:40; Mark 14:58; 15:29; John 2:19; Acts 6:14

61 and said, "This man stated, '[a]I am able to destroy the temple

---

26:50 *Friend* = comrade or companion.
26:51 *one of those.* This was Peter (John 18:10).
26:53 *twelve legions.* Christ meant simply a very large, not an exact, number. A Roman legion varied in number from 3000 to 6000.
26:57 The order of Jesus' trials was as follows: (1) the hearing before Annas (John 18:12-14, 19-23); (2) the trial before Caiaphas and the Sanhedrin (Matt. 26:57-68; 27:1); (3) the first appearance before Pilate (Matt. 27:2, 11-14); (4) an appearance before Herod (Luke 23:6-12); (5) a second trial before Pilate (Matt. 27:15-26).
26:60 *false witnesses.* To establish a charge, two witnesses were required under Jewish law, and their testimony had to be in agreement.

of God and to rebuild it in three days.' "

62 And the high priest stood up and said to Him, "Do You make no answer? What is it that these men are testifying against You?"

★63 aMatt. 27:12, 14; John 19:9 bMatt. 26:63-66; Luke 22:67-71 cLev. 5:1 dMatt. 16:16 eMatt. 4:3

63 But [a]Jesus kept silent. [b]And the high priest said to Him, "I [c]adjure You by [d]the living God, that You tell us whether You are the Christ, [e]the Son of God."

64 aMatt. 26:25 bPs. 110:1 cDan. 7:13; Matt. 16:27f.

64 Jesus *said to him, "[a]You have said it *yourself;* nevertheless I tell you, hereafter you shall see [b]THE SON OF MAN SITTING AT THE RIGHT HAND OF POWER, *and* [c]COMING ON THE CLOUDS OF HEAVEN."

★65 aNum. 14:6; Mark 14:63; Acts 14:14

65 Then the high priest [a]tore his robes, saying, "He has blasphemed! What further need do we have of witnesses? Behold, you have now heard the blasphemy;

66 aLev. 24:16; John 19:7

66 what do you think?" They answered and said, "[a]He is deserving of death!"

★67 aMatt. 26:67, 68; Luke 22:63-65; John 18:22 bMatt. 27:30; Mark 10:34

67 [a]Then they [b]spat in His face and beat Him with their fists; and others slapped Him,

★68 aMark 14:65; Luke 22:64

68 and said, "[a]Prophesy to us, You Christ; who is the one who hit You?"

69 aMatt. 26:69-75: *Mark 14:66-72; Luke 22:55-62; John 18:16-18, 25-27* bMatt. 26:3

69 [a]Now Peter was sitting outside in the [b]courtyard, and a certain servant-girl came to him and said, "You too were with Jesus the Galilean."

70 But he denied *it* before them all, saying, "I do not know what you are talking about."

71 And when he had gone out to the gateway, another *servant-girl* saw him and *said to those who were there, "This man was with Jesus of Nazareth."

72 And again he denied *it* with an oath, "I do not know the man."

73 And a little later the bystanders came up and said to Peter, "Surely you too are *one* of them; [a]for the way you talk gives you away." ★73 aMark 14:70; Luke 22:59; John 18:26

74 Then he began to curse and swear, "I do not know the man!" And immediately a cock crowed. ★74

75 And Peter remembered the word which Jesus had said, "[a]Before a cock crows, you will deny Me three times." And he went out and wept bitterly. 75 aMatt. 26:34

2 *Before the Sanhedrin,* 27:1–10

27 [a]Now when morning had come, all the chief priests and the elders of the people took counsel against Jesus to put Him to death; 1 aMark 15:1; Luke 22:66; John 18:28

2 and they bound Him, and led Him away, and [a]delivered Him up to [b]Pilate the governor. ★ 2 aMatt. 20:19 bLuke 3:1; 13:1; 23:12; Acts 3:13; 4:27; 1 Tim. 6:13

3 Then when [a]Judas, who had betrayed Him, saw that He had been condemned, he felt remorse and returned [b]the thirty pieces of silver to the chief priests and elders, ★ 3 aMatt. 26:14 bMatt. 26:15

4 saying, "I have sinned by betraying innocent blood." But they said, "What is that to us? [a]See *to that* yourself!" 4 aMatt. 27:24

5 And he threw the pieces of silver into [a]the sanctuary and departed; and [b]he went away and hanged himself. 5 aMatt. 26:61 marg.; Luke 1:9, 21 bActs 1:18

6 And the chief priests took ★ 6

26:63 *Jesus kept silent.* See Isa. 53:7. *I adjure You* = I command You.

26:65 *the high priest tore his robes.* An action expressive of grief, obligatory on hearing blasphemy.

26:67 *spat.* See Isa. 50:6. *slapped.* See Isa. 52:14.

26:68 *Prophesy to us.* Having blindfolded Him, they suggest He name His taunters (Luke 22:64).

26:73 *the way you talk.* Galilean pronunciation differed from Judean.

26:74 *to curse.* Peter began to call down a curse on himself if he were lying.

27:2 *Pilate.* See note on Mark 15:1. His headquarters were in Caesarea, the city Herod built on the Mediterranean in honor of Caesar Augustus. He had a palace in Jerusalem and was in the city at Passover time, when crowds would be huge and trouble always possible.

27:3-10 Compare Acts 1:16-19.

27:3 *saw that He had been condemned.* Perhaps Judas had only wanted to force Jesus to do something to confound His enemies, not to get Himself condemned.

27:6 *the price of blood.* I.e., "blood money," and thus impure and defiling to the temple.

the pieces of silver and said, "It is
not lawful to put them into the
temple treasury, since it is the
price of blood."
★ 7 — 7 And they counseled together and with the money
bought the Potter's Field as a
burial place for strangers.
8 [a]Acts 1:19 — 8 [a]For this reason that field
has been called the Field of Blood
to this day.
★ 9 [a]Zech. 11:12, 13; cf., Jer. 18:2; 19:2, 11; 32:6-9 — 9 Then that which was spoken through Jeremiah the prophet
was fulfilled, saying, "[a]AND THEY
TOOK THE THIRTY PIECES OF SILVER,
THE PRICE OF THE ONE WHOSE PRICE
HAD BEEN SET BY THE SONS OF ISRAEL;
10 AND THEY GAVE THEM FOR THE
POTTER'S FIELD, AS THE LORD DI-
RECTED ME."

3 *Before Pilate,* 27:11-26

11 [a]Matt. 27:11-14; *Mark 15:2-5; Luke 23:2-3; John 18:29-38* [b]Matt. 2:2 [c]Matt. 26:25 — **11** [a]Now Jesus stood before
the governor, and the governor
questioned Him, saying, "Are
You the [b]King of the Jews?" And
Jesus said to him, "[c]*It is as* you
say."
12 [a]Matt. 26:63; John 19:9 — 12 And while He was being
accused by the chief priests and
elders, [a]He made no answer.
13 Then Pilate *said to Him,
"Do You not hear how many
things they testify against You?"
14 [a]Matt. 27:12; Mark 15:5; Luke 23:9; John 19:9 — 14 And [a]He did not answer
him with regard to even a *single*
charge, so that the governor was
quite amazed.
15 [a]Matt. 27:15-26; *Mark 15:6-15; Luke 23:[17]-25;* John 18:39-19:16 — 15 [a]Now at *the* feast the governor was accustomed to release
for the multitude *any* one prisoner whom they wanted.
16 And they were holding at
that time a notorious prisoner,
called Barabbas.
17 When therefore they were — 17 [a]Matt. 1:16; 27:22
gathered together, Pilate said to
them, "Whom do you want me to
release for you? Barabbas, or
Jesus [a]who is called Christ?"
18 For he knew that because
of envy they had delivered Him
up.
19 And [a]while he was sitting — 19 [a]John 19:13; Acts 12:21 marg.; 18:12, 16f.; 25:6, 10, 17 [b]Matt. 27:24 [c]Gen. 20:6; 31:11; Num. 12:6; Job 33:15; Matt. 1:20; 2:12f., 19, 22
on the judgment seat, his wife
sent to him, saying, "Have nothing to do with that [b]righteous
Man; for last night I suffered
greatly [c]in a dream because of
Him."
20 But the chief priests and — 20 [a]Acts 3:14
the elders persuaded the multi-
tudes to [a]ask for Barabbas, and to
put Jesus to death.
21 But the governor answered
and said to them, "Which of the
two do you want me to release for
you?" And they said, "Barabbas."
22 Pilate *said to them, — 22 [a]Matt. 1:16
"What then shall I do with Jesus
[a]who is called Christ?" They all
*said, "Let Him be crucified!"
23 And he said, "Why, what
evil has He done?" But they kept
shouting all the more, saying,
"Let Him be crucified!"
24 And when Pilate saw that — ★24 [a]Matt. 26:5 [b]Deut. 21:6-8 [c]Matt. 27:19 [d]Matt. 27:4
he was accomplishing nothing,
but rather that [a]a riot was starting, he took water and [b]washed
his hands in front of the multitude, saying, "I am innocent of
[c]this Man's blood; [d]see *to that*
yourselves."
25 And all the people an- — ★25 [a]Josh. 2:19; Acts 5:28
swered and said, "[a]His blood *be*
on us and on our children!"

27:7 *Potter's Field.* A field where potters dug clay for making pottery vessels. It may have been full of holes so as to make it easy to bury people there who had no family tombs.

27:9 *spoken through Jeremiah.* These words are found in Zech. 11:12-13 with allusions to Jer. 18:1-4; 19:1-3. They are ascribed to Jeremiah since, in Jesus' day, the books of the prophets were headed by Jeremiah, not Isaiah as now, and the quotation is identified by the name of the first book of the group, rather than by the name of the specific book within the group. Similarly in Luke 24:44, "Psalms" includes all the books known as the "Writings," because it is the first book of the group.

27:24 *and washed his hands in front of the multitude.* A Jewish custom which when used legitimately (though not so in Pilate's case) was a symbol of absolution of an innocent man from implication in a wrongful death. *this Man's blood.* Pilate found no political or military threat to Rome in Christ, and this was his only concern.

27:25 *all the people.* I.e., all those present, which was only a fractional part of the nation. Some of the leaders opposed the crucifixion (Luke 23:51). See also Luke 23:34; Acts 5:28; 1 Cor. 2:8.

★26 [a]Mark 15:15; Luke 23:16; John 19:1

26 Then he released Barabbas for them; but Jesus he [a]scourged and delivered over to be crucified.

E The Crucifixion, 27:27-66

1 The preliminaries, 27:27-44

★27 [a]Matt. 27:27-31: *Mark 15:16-20* [b]Matt. 26:3; John 18:28, 33; 19:9 [c]Acts 10:1

27 [a]Then the soldiers of the governor took Jesus into [b]the Praetorium and gathered the whole *Roman* [c]cohort around Him.

28 [a]Mark 15:17; John 19:2

28 And they stripped Him, and [a]put a scarlet robe on Him.

29 [a]Mark 15:17; John 19:2 [b]Mark 15:18; John 19:1

29 [a]And after weaving a crown of thorns, they put it on His head, and a reed in His right hand; and they kneeled down before Him and mocked Him, saying, "[b]Hail, King of the Jews!"

30 [a]Matt. 26:67; Mark 10:34; 14:65; 15:19

30 And [a]they spat on Him, and took the reed and *began* to beat Him on the head.

★31 [a]Mark 15:20

31 [a]And after they had mocked Him, they took His robe off and put His garments on Him, and led Him away to crucify *Him.*

★32 [a]Matt. 27:32: *Mark 15:21; Luke 23:26;* John 19:17 [b]Acts 2:10; 6:9; 11:20; 13:1

32 [a]And as they were coming out, they found a certain [b]Cyrenian named Simon; this man they pressed into service to bear His cross.

★33 [a]Matt. 27:34-44: *Mark 15:22-32; Luke 23:33-43; John 19:17-24* [b]Luke 23:33 and marg.; John 19:17

33 [a]And when they had come to a place called [b]Golgotha, which means Place of a Skull,

★34 [a]Ps. 69:21 [b]Mark 15:23

34 [a]THEY GAVE HIM [b]WINE TO DRINK MINGLED WITH GALL; and after tasting *it,* He was unwilling to drink.

★35 [a]Ps. 22:18

35 And when they had crucified Him, [a]THEY DIVIDED UP HIS GARMENTS AMONG THEMSELVES, CASTING LOTS;

36 [a]Matt. 27:54

36 and sitting down, they *began* to [a]keep watch over Him there.

★37 [a]Mark 15:26; Luke 23:38; John 19:19

37 And they put up above His head the charge against Him which read, "[a]THIS IS JESUS THE KING OF THE JEWS."

38 At that time two robbers *were crucified with Him, one on the right and one on the left.

★39 [a]Job 16:4; Ps. 22:7; 109:25; Lam. 2:15; Mark 15:29

39 And those who were passing by were hurling abuse at Him, [a]WAGGING THEIR HEADS,

★40 [a]Matt. 26:61 [b]Matt. 27:42

40 and saying, "[a]You who destroy the temple and rebuild it in three days, save Yourself! [b]If You are the Son of God, come down from the cross."

41 In the same way the chief priests, along with the scribes and elders, were mocking *Him,* and saying,

★42 [a]Mark 15:31; Luke 23:35 [b]Matt. 27:37; Luke 23:37; John 1:49; 12:13

42 "[a]He saved others; He cannot save Himself. [b]He is the King of Israel; let Him now come down

---

27:26 *scourged.* Better, flogged by means of a leather whip that had pieces of bone or metal imbedded in its thongs. It was used by the Romans only on murderers and traitors.

27:27 *Praetorium.* Pilate's residence in Jerusalem. This was probably in the Castle of Antonia, near the temple, though it may have been located near Herod's palace. *cohort.* One-tenth of a legion, about 300-600 men.

27:31 *to crucify Him.* A painful and slow means of execution which the Romans adopted from the Phoenicians. The victim usually died after 2 or 3 days, of thirst, exhaustion, and exposure. The hands were often nailed to the crossbeam, which was then hoisted up and affixed to the upright, to which the feet were then nailed. A peg, astride which the victim sat, supported the main weight of the body. Death was sometimes hastened by breaking the legs, but not in Christ's case (John 19:33).

27:32 *Cyrenian.* From Cyrene, the capital of Cyrenaica in N. Africa. Many Jews lived there. *to bear His cross.* The crossbeam was carried to the place of execution usually by the victim, but Jesus was too weakened by the tortures that had already been inflicted on Him.

27:33 *Golgotha.* Aramaic for "skull," indicating either that the place of crucifixion looked like a skull or that it was a place of execution where skulls accumulated. Its location is uncertain.

27:34 *wine . . . mingled with gall.* A drink given to victims to help deaden their pain. Jesus refused it, preferring to meet His death with all His faculties unimpaired.

27:35 *divided.* The victim's clothes were spoils for his executioners.

27:37 *above His head.* To the soldiers, the charge would be considered insurrection. His cross was in the traditional shape pictured in Christian art, with room over the crossbeam for this sign.

27:39 *wagging their heads.* A Near Eastern gesture of scorn.

27:40 See 26:61.

27:42 See 12:38; 16:1.

from the cross, and we shall believe in Him.
43 [a]Ps. 22:8
43 "[a]HE TRUSTS IN GOD; LET HIM
DELIVER *Him* now, IF HE TAKES PLEA-
SURE IN HIM; for He said, 'I am the
Son of God.' "
44 [a]Luke 23:39-43
44 [a]And the robbers also who
had been crucified with Him were
casting the same insult at Him.

2 *The death,* 27:45-56

★45 [a]Matt. 27:45-56: *Mark 15:33-41; Luke 23:44-49*
45 [a]Now from the sixth hour
darkness fell upon all the land
until the ninth hour.
★46 [a]Ps. 22:1
46 And about the ninth hour
Jesus cried out with a loud voice,
saying, "ELI, ELI, LAMA SABACHTHA-
NI?" that is, "[a]MY GOD, MY GOD,
WHY HAST THOU FORSAKEN ME?"
★47
47 And some of those who
were standing there, when they
heard it, *began* saying, "This man
is calling for Elijah."
★48 [a]Mark 15:36; Luke 23:36; John 19:29
48 And [a]immediately one of
them ran, and taking a sponge, he
filled it with sour wine, and put it
on a reed, and gave Him a drink.
49 But the rest *of them* said,
"Let us see whether Elijah will
come to save Him."
★50 [a]Mark 15:37; Luke 23:46; John 19:30
50 And Jesus [a]cried out again
with a loud voice, and yielded up
His spirit.
★51 [a]Matt. 27:51-56: *Mark 15:38-41;* Luke 23:47-49 [b]Ex. 26:31ff.; Mark 15:38; Luke 23:45; Heb. 9:3 [c]Matt. 27:54
51 [a]And behold, [b]the veil of
the temple was torn in two from
top to bottom, and [c]the earth
shook; and the rocks were split,
★52 [a]Acts 7:60
52 and the tombs were
opened; and many bodies of the
saints who had [a]fallen asleep
were raised;
53 [a]Matt. 4:5
53 and coming out of the
tombs after His resurrection they
entered [a]the holy city and appeared to many.
54 [a]Mark 15:39; Luke 23:47 [b]Matt. 27:36 [c]Matt. 27:51 [d]Matt. 4:3; 27:43
54 [a]Now the centurion, and
those who were with him [b]keep-
ing guard over Jesus, when they
saw [c]the earthquake and the
things that were happening, became very frightened and said,
"Truly this was [d]the Son of God!"
55 [a]Mark 15:40f.; Luke 23:49; John 19:25 [b]Mark 15:41; Luke 8:2, 3
55 [a]And many women were
there looking on from a distance,
who had followed Jesus from
Galilee, [b]ministering to Him,
56 [a]Matt. 28:1; Mark 15:40, 47; 16:9; Luke 8:2; John 19:25; 20:1, 18 [b]Matt. 20:20
56 among whom was [a]Mary
Magdalene, *along with* Mary the
mother of James and Joseph, and
[b]the mother of the sons of Zebedee.

3 *The burial,* 27:57-66

★57 [a]Matt. 27:57-61: *Mark 15:42-47; Luke 23:50-56; John 19:38-42*
57 [a]And when it was evening,
there came a rich man from Arimathea, named Joseph, who himself had also become a disciple of
Jesus.
58 This man came to Pilate
and asked for the body of Jesus.
Then Pilate ordered *it* to be given
over *to him.*
59 And Joseph took the body
and wrapped it in a clean linen
cloth,
★60 [a]Matt. 27:66; 28:2; Mark 16:4
60 and laid it in his own new
tomb, which he had hewn out in
the rock; and he rolled [a]a large
stone against the entrance of the
tomb and went away.
61 [a]Matt. 27:56; 28:1
61 And [a]Mary Magdalene
was there, and the other Mary,
sitting opposite the grave.

27:45 *sixth . . . until the ninth hour.* From noon to 3 p.m.

27:46 *Eli, Eli, lama sabachthani.* Quoting Ps. 22:1 in its Aramaic form, except that *Eloi* (Mark 15:34) has been reconverted to the Hebrew *Eli.* This cry may reflect the desertion Jesus felt as He was bearing the sins of the world (2 Cor. 5:21).

27:47 *Elijah.* Some listeners made a poor guess as to what Christ was saying and mistook "Eli" for "Elijah."

27:48 *put it on a reed.* To raise it to His lips.

27:50 *His spirit.* Christ was not directly killed by anyone nor was He overcome by natural processes; He released His spirit (John 10:18).

27:51 *veil.* I.e., the curtain separating the Holy of Holies from the rest of the temple (Ex. 26:37; 38:18; Heb. 9:3). *from top to bottom.* Showing that God did it, not man. It signified that the new and living way was now open into the presence of God (Heb. 10:20; Eph. 2:11-22). One probable result of this supernatural tearing of the veil is recorded in Acts 6:7b.

27:52-53 *out of the tombs.* These people may have been restored to earthly bodies to die again, or resurrected with glorified bodies.

27:57 *Arimathea.* A town N. of Lydda and E. of Joppa.

27:60 *the tomb.* See Isa. 53:9.

★62 [a]Mark 15:42; Luke 23:54; John 19:14, 31, 42

62 Now on the next day, which is *the one* after [a]the preparation, the chief priests and the Pharisees gathered together with Pilate,

63 [a]Matt. 16:21

63 and said, "Sir, we remember that when He was still alive that deceiver said, '[a]After three days I *am to* rise again.'

64 "Therefore, give orders for the grave to be made secure until the third day, lest the disciples come and steal Him away and say to the people, 'He has risen from the dead,' and the last deception will be worse than the first."

65 [a]Matt. 27:66; 28:11

65 Pilate said to them, "You have a [a]guard; go, make it *as* secure as you know how."

★66 [a]Matt. 27:65; 28:11 [b]Dan. 6:17 [c]Matt. 27:60; 28:2; Mark 16:4

66 And they went and made the grave secure, and along with [a]the guard they set a [b]seal on [c]the stone.

IX THE POWER OF THE KING, 28:1-20

A The Conquest, 28:1-10

★ 1 [a]Matt. 28:1-8; *Mark 16:1-8; Luke 24:1-10;* John 20:1-8 [b]Matt. 27:56, 61

28 [a]Now after the Sabbath, as it began to dawn toward the first *day* of the week, [b]Mary Magdalene and the other Mary came to look at the grave.

2 [a]Luke 24:4; John 20:12 [b]Matt. 27:66; 28:2; Mark 16:4

2 And behold, a severe earthquake had occurred, for [a]an angel of the Lord descended from heaven and came and rolled away [b]the stone and sat upon it.

3 [a]Dan. 7:9; 10:6; Mark 9:3; John 20:12; Acts 1:10

3 And [a]his appearance was like lightning, and his garment as white as snow;

4 and the guards shook for fear of him, and became like dead men.

5 [a]Matt. 14:27; 28:10

5 And the angel answered and said to the women, "[a]Do not be afraid; for I know that you are looking for Jesus who has been crucified.

★ 6 [a]Matt. 12:40; 16:21; 27:63

6 "He is not here, for He has risen, [a]just as He said. Come, see the place where He was lying.

7 [a]Matt. 26:32; 28:10, 16

7 "And go quickly and tell His disciples that He has risen from the dead; and behold, He is going before you [a]into Galilee, there you will see Him; behold, I have told you."

8 And they departed quickly from the tomb with fear and great joy and ran to report it to His disciples.

9 And behold, Jesus met them and greeted them. And they came up and took hold of His feet and worshiped Him.

10 [a]Matt. 14:27; 28:5 [b]John 20:17; Rom. 8:29; Heb. 2:11f., 17 [c]Matt. 26:32; 28:7, 16

10 Then Jesus *said to them, "[a]Do not be afraid; go and take word to [b]My brethren to leave [c]for Galilee, and there they shall see Me."

B The Conspiracy, 28:11-15

11 [a]Matt. 27:65, 66

11 Now while they were on their way, behold, some of [a]the guard came into the city and reported to the chief priests all that had happened.

12 And when they had assembled with the elders and counseled together, they gave a large sum of money to the soldiers,

★13

13 and said, "You are to say, 'His disciples came by night and stole Him away while we were asleep.'

14 [a]Matt. 27:2

14 "And if this should come to [a]the governor's ears, we will win him over and keep you out of trouble."

15 [a]Matt. 9:31; Mark 1:45 [b]Matt. 27:8

15 And they took the money and did as they had been instructed; and this story was

---

27:62 *the next day.* The Sabbath.

27:66 *set a seal on the stone.* This was likely done by connecting the stone to the tomb with a cord and wax so that any tampering could easily be detected.

28:1 *after the Sabbath.* It was now Sunday morning, and the work of preparing Christ's body for permanent burial could be done.

28:6 *He has risen.* This simply stated fact is the basis of our Christian faith. *as He said.* See Matt. 16:21; 17:23; 20:19.

28:13 *while we were asleep.* How would sleeping people know what had happened? Would it be likely that all the soldiers were sleeping at the same time? Why would Roman soldiers risk incriminating themselves even for a large bribe? The story was self-contradictory!

widely [a]spread among the Jews, *and is* [b]to this day.

C The Commission, 28:16-20

★16 [a]Matt. 26:32; 28:7, 10 **16** But the eleven disciples proceeded [a]to Galilee, to the mountain which Jesus had designated.

17 [a]Mark 16:11 **17** And when they saw Him, they worshiped *Him;* but [a]some were doubtful.

18 And Jesus came up and spoke to them, saying, "[a]All authority has been given to Me in heaven and on earth. ★18 [a]Dan. 7:13f.; Matt. 11:27; 26:64; Rom. 14:9; Eph. 1:20-22; Phil. 2:9f.; Col. 2:10

19 "[a]Go therefore and [b]make disciples of [c]all the nations, [d]baptizing them in the name of the Father and the Son and the Holy Spirit, ★19 [a]Mark 16:15f. [b]Matt. 13:52; Acts 14:21 [c]Matt. 25:32 [d]Acts 2:38; 8:16; Rom. 6:3

20 teaching them to observe all that I commanded you; and lo, [a]I am with you always, even to [b]the end of the age." ★20 [a]Matt. 18:20; Acts 18:10 [b]Matt. 13:39

28:16 *designated* = commanded, see 26:32; 28:7.

28:18 *All authority.* The Great Commission which follows is based upon and backed by the authority of the risen and exalted Lord who promises to be ever-present with His people.

28:19 *make disciples of all the nations.* This is the one command in the Commission. It is surrounded by three participles: *go* (lit., going), *baptizing* and *teaching* (v. 20). This is the missionary task of the church. *in the name of the Father and the Son and the Holy Spirit.* Here is evidence for the trinity of God: one God (*the name*) who subsists in three persons (Father, Son and Holy Spirit). Each of the three is distinguished from the others; each possesses all the divine attributes; yet the three are one. This is a mystery which no analogy can illustrate satisfactorily. The sun, sunlight, and the power of the sun may come close to a suitable illustration.

28:20 *end of the age.* The personal and empowering presence of the One vividly portrayed in this Gospel is promised to His followers. In His power the commission can be performed.

INTRODUCTION TO THE GOSPEL ACCORDING TO MARK

AUTHOR: Mark DATE: 50's

Authorship *John Mark was the son of Mary, a woman of wealth and position in Jerusalem (Acts 12:12). Barnabas was his cousin (Col. 4:10). Mark was a close friend (and possibly a convert) of the apostle Peter (1 Pet. 5:13). He had the rare privilege of accompanying Paul and Barnabas on the first missionary journey but failed to stay with them through the entire trip. Because of this, Paul refused to take him on the second journey, so he went with Barnabas to Cyprus (Acts 15:38-40). About a dozen years later he was again with Paul (Col. 4:10; Philem. 24), and just before Paul's execution he was sent for by the apostle (2 Tim. 4:11). His biography proves that one failure in life does not mean the end of usefulness.*

Distinctive Approach of Mark *(1) Mark wrote for Gentile readers in general and Roman readers in particular. For this reason the genealogy of Christ is not included (for it would have meant little to Gentiles), the Sermon on the Mount is not reported, and the condemnations of the Jewish sects receive little attention. As a further indication of his Gentile readership, Mark felt it necessary to interpret Aramaic words (5:41; 7:34; 15:22) and he used Latin words not found in the other Gospels ("executioner," 6:27; "cent," 12:42). (2) There are only about 63 quotations or allusions from the Old Testament in Mark as compared with about 128 in Matthew and between 90 and 100 in Luke. (3) This Gospel emphasizes what Jesus did rather than what He said. It is a book of action (the word "straightway" occurs more than 40 times).*

Mark and Peter *It is generally agreed that Mark received much of the information in his Gospel from Peter. With Peter's apostolic authority behind the Gospel, there was never any challenge to its inclusion in the canon of Scripture.*

Date *If one denies the phenomenon of predictive prophecy, then the book must be dated after* A.D. *70 because of 13:2, but since our Lord could predict the future, this late date is unnecessary. In fact, if Acts must be dated about 61, and if Luke, the companion volume, preceded it, then Mark must be even earlier, since Luke apparently used Mark in writing his Gospel. This points to a date in the 50's for Mark. However, many scholars believe that Mark was not written until after Peter died; i.e., after 67 but before 70.*

Contents *The theme of the book is Christ the Servant. The key verse is 10:45, which divides the Gospel into two major divisions: the service of the Servant (1:1-10:52) and the sacrifice of the Servant (11:1-16:20).*

OUTLINE OF THE GOSPEL OF MARK

I. The Service of the Servant, 1:1-10:52
- A. His Preparation, 1:1-13
  1. By the ministry of John the Baptist, 1:1-8
  2. By His baptism, 1:9-11
  3. By His temptation, 1:12-13
- B. His Preaching, 1:14-20
- C. His Power, 1:21-3:12
  1. Over a demon, 1:21-28
  2. Over disease, 1:29-39
  3. Over leprosy, 1:40-45
  4. Over paralysis, 2:1-12
  5. Over a publican, 2:13-20
  6. Over the old religion, 2:21-22
  7. Over the Sabbath, 2:23-28
  8. Over deformity, 3:1-6
  9. Over demons, 3:7-12
- D. His Personnel, 3:13-35
  1. The call of The Twelve, 3:13-21
  2. The condemnation of rejectors, 3:22-30
  3. The call to be in Jesus' spiritual family, 3:31-35
- E. His Parables, 4:1-34
  1. The sower, 4:1-20
  2. The lamp, 4:21-25
  3. The seed growing gradually, 4:26-29
  4. The mustard seed, 4:30-34
- F. His Prerogatives, 4:35-9:1
  1. Over the storm, 4:35-41
  2. Over demons, 5:1-20
  3. Over sickness and death, 5:21-43
  4. Rejected by His own townspeople, 6:1-6
  5. In commissioning The Twelve, 6:7-13

6. As affecting Herod, who killed John the Baptist, 6:14-29
7. In feeding 5000 men, 6:30-44
8. In walking on water, 6:45-52
9. Over sickness, 6:53-56
10. Over the Pharisees' traditions, 7:1-23
11. Over a Syrophoenician woman, 7:24-30
12. Over a deaf mute, 7:31-37
13. In feeding 4000, 8:1-9
14. In condemning the Pharisees, 8:10-13
15. In His teaching on leaven, 8:14-21
16. Over blindness, 8:22-26
17. Over Peter, 8:27-33
18. Over the lives of His disciples, 8:34-9:1

G. His Previews, 9:2-50
1. Of His glory, 9:2-29
2. Of His death, 9:30-32
3. Of rewards, 9:33-41
4. Of hell, 9:42-50

H. His Preaching in Perea, 10:1-52
1. Concerning divorce, 10:1-12
2. Concerning children, 10:13-16
3. Concerning eternal life, 10:17-31
4. Concerning His own death and resurrection, 10:32-34
5. Concerning ambition, 10:35-45
6. To blind Bartimaeus, 10:46-52

II. The Sacrifice of the Servant, 11:1-15:47

A. Triumphal Entry into Jerusalem on Sunday, 11:1-11

B. Cursing of the Fig Tree and Cleansing of the Temple on Monday, 11:12-19

C. Teaching on Tuesday, 11:20-13:37
1. Concerning faith, 11:20-26
2. Concerning His authority, 11:27-33
3. Concerning the Jewish nation, 12:1-12
4. Concerning taxes, 12:13-17
5. Concerning resurrection, 12:18-27
6. Concerning the greatest commandments, 12:28-34
7. Concerning His deity, 12:35-37
8. Concerning pride, 12:38-40
9. Concerning giving, 12:41-44
10. Concerning the future, 13:1-37

D. Anointing by Mary and Agreement to Betray by Judas, on Wednesday, 14:1-11

E. Supper and Betrayal on Thursday, 14:12-52
1. Preparation for the Last Supper, 14:12-16
2. Partaking of the Last Supper, 14:17-21
3. Institution of the Lord's Supper, 14:22-25
4. Walk to Gethsemane, 14:26-31
5. Prayer in Gethsemane, 14:32-42
6. Betrayal and arrest in Gethsemane, 14:43-52

F. Trials and Crucifixion, on Friday, 14:53-15:47
1. Christ before Caiaphas, 14:53-65
2. Peter's denial of Jesus, 14:66-72
3. Christ before Pilate, 15:1-15
4. Abuse by the soldiers, 15:16-20
5. Crucifixion of Jesus, 15:21-32
6. Death of Jesus, 15:33-41
7. Burial of Jesus, 15:42-47

III. The Success of the Servant, 16:1-20

A. His Resurrection, 16:1-8

B. His Appearances, 16:9-18

C. His Ascension, 16:19-20

Note: This Gospel may also be outlined geographically:

I. Preparation of the Servant, 1:1-13
II. Preaching of the Servant in Galilee, 1:14-9:50
III. Preaching of the Servant in Perea, 10:1-52
IV. Passion of the Servant in Jerusalem, 11:1-16:20

THE GOSPEL ACCORDING TO MARK

I THE SERVICE OF THE SERVANT, 1:1-10:52

A His Preparation, 1:1-13

1 By the ministry of John the Baptist, 1:1-8

★ 1 [a]Matt. 4:3
★ 2 [a]Mark 1:2-8; *Matt. 3:1-11; Luke 3:2-16* [b]Mal. 3:1; Matt. 11:10; Luke 7:27

1 The beginning of the gospel
of Jesus Christ, [a]the Son of
God.
2 [a]As it is written in Isaiah
the prophet,
"[b]BEHOLD, I SEND MY MESSENGER BEFORE YOUR FACE,
WHO WILL PREPARE YOUR WAY;
3 "[a]THE VOICE OF ONE CRYING IN THE WILDERNESS, 3 [a]Is. 40:3; Matt. 3:3; Luke 3:4; John 1:23
'MAKE READY THE WAY OF THE LORD,
MAKE HIS PATHS STRAIGHT.' "
4 John the Baptist appeared ★ 4 [a]Acts 13:24 [b]Luke 1:77

1:1 *The beginning of the gospel.* Here begins the good news—i.e., that Jesus Christ is the Savior.

1:2 *in Isaiah the prophet.* See Isa. 40:3; Mal. 3:1.

1:4 *baptism of repentance for the forgiveness of sins.* The Jews practiced self-immersion as a form of baptism, but John immersed others as a witness to their repentance. Christian baptism is performed in the name of the Trinity as a witness to one's faith in Christ. Some who followed John and who later believed in Christ were rebaptized (Acts 19:5).

in the wilderness [a]preaching a
baptism of repentance for the
[b]forgiveness of sins.
5 And all the country of Judea was going out to him, and all
the people of Jerusalem; and they
were being baptized by him in the
Jordan River, confessing their
sins.
6 And John was clothed with
camel's hair and *wore* a leather
belt around his waist, and his diet
was locusts and wild honey.
★ 7 7 And he was preaching, and
saying, "After me comes One
who is mightier than I, and I am
not *even* fit to stoop down and
untie the thong of His sandals.
★ 8 8 "I baptized you with water;
but He will baptize you with the
Holy Spirit."

2 *By His baptism,* 1:9–11

9 [a]Mark 1:9-11: *Matt. 3:13-17; Luke 3:21, 22* [b]Matt. 2:23; Luke 2:51 9 [a]And it came about in
those days that Jesus [b]came from
Nazareth in Galilee, and was baptized by John in the Jordan.
★10 10 And immediately coming
up out of the water, He saw the
heavens opening, and the Spirit
like a dove descending upon Him;
11 [a]Matt. 3:17; Luke 3:22 11 and a voice came out of
the heavens: "[a]Thou art My be-
loved Son, in Thee I am well-
pleased."

3 *By His temptation,* 1:12–13

★12 [a]Mark 1:12, 13: *Matt. 4:1-11; Luke 4:1-13* 12 [a]And immediately the
Spirit *impelled Him *to go* out
into the wilderness.
13 [a]Matt. 4:10 13 And He was in the wilderness forty days being tempted by
[a]Satan; and He was with the wild
beasts, and the angels were ministering to Him.

B His Preaching, 1:14–20

14 [a]And after John had been ★14 [a]Matt. 4:12 [b]Matt. 4:23
taken into custody, Jesus came
into Galilee, [b]preaching the gospel of God,
15 and saying, "[a]The time is ★15 [a]Gal. 4:4; Eph. 1:10; 1 Tim. 2:6; Titus 1:3 [b]Acts 20:21
fulfilled, and the kingdom of God
is at hand; [b]repent and believe in
the gospel."
16 [a]And as He was going 16 [a]Mark 1:16-20: *Matt. 4:18-22;* Luke 5:2-11; John 1:40-42
along by the Sea of Galilee, He
saw Simon and Andrew, the
brother of Simon, casting a net in
the sea; for they were fishermen.
17 And Jesus said to them,
"Follow Me, and I will make you
become fishers of men."
18 And they immediately left
the nets and followed Him.
19 And going on a little farther, He saw James the *son* of
Zebedee, and John his brother,
who were also in the boat mending the nets.
20 And immediately He
called them; and they left their father Zebedee in the boat with the
hired servants, and went away to
follow Him.

C His Power, 1:21–3:12
1 *Over a demon,* 1:21–28

21 [a]And they *went into Ca- ★21 [a]Mark 1:21-28; Luke 4:31-37 [b]Matt. 4:23; Mark 1:39; 10:1
pernaum; and immediately on the

1:7 *thong of His sandals.* It was usually loosened by a slave as a guest entered a home.
1:8 See note on Matt. 3:11.
1:10 See note on Matt. 3:16–17.
1:12 *the Spirit impelled Him. impelled* reflects Mark's forceful style (the other Gospel writers use "led").
1:14 Between the temptation of Jesus and the imprisonment of John the Baptist occurred the events recorded in John 1:19–4:54. How he came to be imprisoned is told in Mark 6:17–20.
1:15 *the kingdom of God is at hand.* The rule of Messiah on earth, promised in the Old Testament and earnestly longed for by the Jewish people, was near, for the Messiah had now come. However, the people rejected rather than accepted Him, and the fulfillment of the kingdom promises had to be delayed until God's purpose in saving Jews and Gentiles and forming His church was completed. Then Christ will return and set up God's kingdom on this earth (Acts 15:14–16; Rev. 19:15).
1:21 *Capernaum.* Situated on the NW. shore of the Sea of Galilee, this was an important town on the caravan route to Damascus. It was the site of a customs station (2:14), had a Roman garrison (Matt. 8:5-13), and was the home of Peter, Andrew, James, and John.

Sabbath [b]He entered the synagogue and *began* to teach.

★22 [a]Matt. 7:28

22 And [a]they were amazed at
His teaching; for He was teaching
them as *one* having authority, and
not as the scribes.
23 And just then there was in
their synagogue a man with an
unclean spirit; and he cried out,

24 [a]Matt. 8:29 [b]Matt. 2:23; Mark 10:47; 14:67; 16:6; Luke 4:34; 24:19; Acts 24:5 [c]Luke 1:35; 4:34; John 6:69; Acts 3:14

24 saying, "[a]What do we have
to do with You, Jesus of [b]Naza-
reth? Have You come to destroy
us? I know who You are—[c]the
Holy One of God!"
25 And Jesus rebuked him,
saying, "Be quiet, and come out
of him!"
26 And throwing him into
convulsions, the unclean spirit
cried out with a loud voice, and
came out of him.

27 [a]Mark 10:24, 32; 14:33; 16:5, 6

27 And they were all
[a]amazed, so that they debated
among themselves, saying, "What
is this? A new teaching with authority! He commands even the
unclean spirits, and they obey
Him."
28 And immediately the news
about Him went out everywhere
into all the surrounding district of
Galilee.

2 *Over disease,* 1:29–39

29 [a]Mark 1:29-31; *Matt. 8:14, 15; Luke 4:38, 39* [b]Mark 1:21, 23

29 [a]And immediately after
they had come [b]out of the synagogue, they came into the house
of Simon and Andrew, with James
and John.
30 Now Simon's mother-in-
law was lying sick with a fever;
and immediately they *spoke to
Him about her.

★32 [a]Mark 1:32-34; *Matt. 8:16, 17; Luke 4:40, 41* [b]Matt. 8:16; Luke 4:40 [c]Matt. 4:24

31 And He came to her and
raised her up, taking her by the
hand, and the fever left her, and
she began to wait on them.
32 [a]And [b]when evening had
come, [b]after the sun had set, they
began bringing to Him all who
were ill and those who were [c]de-
mon-possessed.
33 And the whole [a]city had
gathered at the door.

33 [a]Mark 1:21

34 And He [a]healed many who
were ill with various diseases, and
cast out many demons; and He
was not permitting the demons to
speak, because they knew who
He was.

34 [a]Matt. 4:23

35 [a]And in the early morning,
while it was still dark, He arose
and went out and departed to a
lonely place, and [b]was praying
there.

35 [a]Mark 1:35-38; *Luke 4:42, 43* [b]Matt. 14:23; Luke 5:16

36 And Simon and his com-
panions hunted for Him;
37 and they found Him, and
*said to Him, "Everyone is look-
ing for You."
38 And He *said to them,
"Let us go somewhere else to the
towns nearby, in order that I may
preach there also; for that is what
I came out for."

★38

39 [a]And He went into their
synagogues throughout all Galilee, preaching and casting out the
demons.

39 [a]Matt. 4:23; Mark 1:23; 3:1

3 *Over leprosy,* 1:40–45

40 [a]And a leper *came to
Him, beseeching Him and [b]falling
on his knees before Him, and saying to Him, "If You are willing,
You can make me clean."

★40 [a]Mark 1:40-44; *Matt. 8:2-4; Luke 5:12-14* [b]Matt. 8:2; Mark 10:17; Luke 5:12

41 And moved with compas-
sion, He stretched out His hand
and touched him, and *said to
him, "I am willing; be cleansed."
42 And immediately the leprosy left him and he was cleansed.
43 And He sternly warned
him and immediately sent him
away,
44 and He *said to him, "[a]See

★44 [a]Matt. 8:4 [b]Matt. 8:4

1:22 *authority.* Jesus' teaching was based on His own personal authority in contrast to that of the scribes, whose manner of teaching was to quote the authoritative statements of scribes who had gone before.

1:32 *after the sun had set.* Burdens could not be carried on the Sabbath (v. 21), but the next day, when they could be, began at sundown.

1:38 *that is what I came out for.* I.e., that is why I left Capernaum.

1:40 *leper.* See note on Luke 5:12. The laws concerning leprosy are found in Lev. 13–14.

1:44 *say nothing to anyone.* Jesus did not want people coming to Him merely to receive physical benefits. The result of the leper's failure to obey is seen in v. 45.

that you say nothing to anyone;
but [b]go, show yourself to the
priest and offer for your cleansing
what Moses commanded, for a
testimony to them."
45 [a]Matt. 28:15; Luke 5:15 [b]Mark 2:2, 13; 3:7; Luke 5:17; John 6:2
45 But he went out and began
to [a]proclaim it freely and to
[a]spread the news about, to such
an extent that Jesus could no
longer publicly enter a city, but
stayed out in unpopulated areas;
and [b]they were coming to Him
from everywhere.

4 *Over paralysis,* 2:1–12

2 And when He had come back
to Capernaum several days
afterward, it was heard that He
was at home.
2 [a]Mark 1:45; 2:13
2 And [a]many were gathered
together, so that there was no
longer room, even near the door;
and He was speaking the word to
them.
3 [a]Mark 2:3-12: *Matt. 9:2-8; Luke 5:18-26* [b]Matt. 4:24
3 [a]And they *came, bringing
to Him a [b]paralytic, carried by
four men.
4 [a]Luke 5:19 [b]Matt. 4:24
4 And being unable to get to
Him on account of the crowd,
they [a]removed the roof above
Him; and when they had dug an
opening, they let down the pallet
on which the [b]paralytic was lying.
★ 5 [a]Matt. 9:2
5 And Jesus seeing their
faith *said to the paralytic, "My
son, [a]your sins are forgiven."
6 But there were some of the
scribes sitting there and reasoning
in their hearts,
7 [a]Is. 43:25
7 "Why does this man speak
that way? He is blaspheming;
[a]who can forgive sins but God
alone?"
★ 8
8 And immediately Jesus,
perceiving in His spirit that they
were reasoning that way within
themselves, *said to them, "Why
are you reasoning about these
things in your hearts?

9 "Which is easier, to say to 9 [a]Matt. 4:24
the [a]paralytic, 'Your sins are forgiven'; or to say, 'Arise, and take
up your pallet and walk'?
10 "But in order that you may ★10
know that the Son of Man has authority on earth to forgive sins,"
He *said to the paralytic,
11 "I say to you, rise, take up
your pallet and go home."
12 And he rose and immedi- 12 [a]Matt. 9:8 [b]Matt. 9:33
ately took up the pallet and went
out in the sight of all; so that they
were all amazed and [a]were glorifying God, saying, "[b]We have
never seen anything like this."

5 *Over a publican,* 2:13–20

13 And He went out again by 13 [a]Mark 1:45
the seashore; and [a]all the multitude were coming to Him, and He
was teaching them.
14 [a]And as He passed by, He 14 [a]Mark 2:14-17: *Matt. 9:9-13; Luke 5:27-32* [b]Matt. 9:9 [c]Matt. 8:22
saw [b]Levi the *son* of Alpheus sit-
ting in the tax office, and He *said
to him, "[c]Follow Me!" And he
rose and followed Him.
15 And it came about that He
was reclining *at table* in his
house, and many tax-gatherers
and sinners were dining with
Jesus and His disciples; for there
were many of them, and they
were following Him.
16 And when [a]the scribes of 16 [a]Luke 5:30; Acts 23:9 [b]Matt. 9:11
the Pharisees saw that He was
eating with the sinners and tax-
gatherers, they *began* saying to
His disciples, "[b]Why is He eating
and drinking with tax-gatherers
and sinners?"
17 And hearing this, Jesus 17 [a]Matt. 9:12, 13; Luke 5:31, 32
*said to them, "[a]*It is* not those
who are healthy who need a physician, but those who are sick; I
did not come to call *the* righteous,
but sinners."
★18 [a]Mark 2:18-22: *Matt. 9:14-17; Luke 5:33-38*
18 [a]And John's disciples and
the Pharisees were fasting; and
they *came and *said to Him,

2:5 See note on Matt. 9:2.
2:8 *in His spirit.* I.e., intuitively.
2:10 *the Son of Man.* A favorite title of Christ, used 14 times in Mark. See note on Matt. 8:20 for its significance.
2:18 Jesus' disciples did not fast because it was incompatible with the joy they had in being with Him. On the Jews' fasting see note on Matt. 9:14. The N.T. church did not fast regularly as a prescribed rite, though it was done on occasion (Acts 13:2–3; 14:23). Whenever practiced, it is never to be done ostentatiously (Matt. 6:16–18).

"Why do John's disciples and the
disciples of the Pharisees fast, but
Your disciples do not fast?"
19 And Jesus said to them,
"While the bridegroom is with
them, the attendants of the bridegroom do not fast, do they? So
long as they have the bridegroom
with them, they cannot fast.
20 [a]Matt. 9:15; Luke 17:22 **20** "But the [a]days will come
when the bridegroom is taken
away from them, and then they
will fast in that day.

6 *Over the old religion,* 2:21–22

21 "No one sews a patch of unshrunk cloth on an old garment;
otherwise the patch pulls away
from it, the new from the old, and
a worse tear results.
★22 **22** "And no one puts new wine
into old wineskins; otherwise the
wine will burst the skins, and the
wine is lost, and the skins *as well;*
but *one puts* new wine into fresh
wineskins."

7 *Over the Sabbath,* 2:23–28

23 [a]Mark 2:23-28; *Matt. 12:1-8; Luke 6:1-5* [b]Deut. 23:25 **23** [a]And it came about that
He was passing through the
grainfields on the Sabbath, and
His disciples began to make their
way along while [b]picking the
heads *of grain.*
24 [a]Matt. 12:2 **24** And the Pharisees were
saying to Him, "See here, [a]why
are they doing what is not lawful
on the Sabbath?"
★25 **25** And He *said to them,
"Have you never read what David
did when he was in need and became hungry, he and his companions:
26 [a]1 Sam. 21:1; 2 Sam. 8:17; 1 Chr. 24:6 **26** how he entered into the
house of God in the time of [a]Abi-
athar *the* high priest, and ate the
consecrated bread, which is not
lawful for *anyone* to eat except
the priests, and he gave *it* also to
those who were with him?"
27 And He was saying to 27 [a]Ex 23:12; Deut. 5:14 [b]Col. 2:16
them, "[a]The Sabbath was made
for man, and [b]not man for the
Sabbath.
28 "Consequently, the Son of
Man is Lord even of the Sabbath."

8 *Over deformity,* 3:1–6

3 [a]And He [b]entered again into 1 [a]Mark 3:1-6; *Matt. 12:9-14; Luke 6:6-11* [b]Mark 1:21, 39
a synagogue; and a man was
there with a withered hand.
2 And [a]they were watching ★ 2 [a]Luke 6:7; 14:1; 20:20 [b]Matt. 12:10; Luke 6:7; 11:54
Him *to see* if He would heal him
on the Sabbath, [b]in order that
they might accuse Him.
3 And He *said to the man
with the withered hand, "Rise
and *come* forward!"
4 And He *said to them, "Is ★ 4
it lawful on the Sabbath to do
good or to do harm, to save a life
or to kill?" But they kept silent.
5 And after [a]looking around 5 [a]Luke 6:10
at them with anger, grieved at
their hardness of heart, He *said
to the man, "Stretch out your
hand." And he stretched it out,
and his hand was restored.
6 And the Pharisees went ★ 6 [a]Matt. 22:16; Mark 12:13
out and immediately *began* tak-
ing counsel with the [a]Herodians
against Him, *as to* how they
might destroy Him.

9 *Over demons,* 3:7–12

7 [a]And Jesus withdrew to 7 [a]Mark 3:7-12; *Matt. 12:15, 16; Luke 6:17-19* [b]Matt. 4:25; Luke 6:17
the sea with His disciples; and [b]a
great multitude from Galilee followed; and *also* from Judea,
8 and from Jerusalem, and ★ 8 [a]Josh. 15:1, 21; Ezek. 35:15; 36:5 [b]Matt. 11:21
from [a]Idumea, and beyond the
Jordan, and the vicinity of [b]Tyre

2:22 *wineskins.* See note on Luke 5:37.

2:25 *what David did.* See 1 Sam. 21:1-6. See note on Matt. 12:2.

3:2 *on the Sabbath.* Rabbinic tradition, not the O.T. law, forbade practicing medicine on the Sabbath unless the person were on the verge of death. Christ's critics were simply determined somehow to stop His activities.

3:4 Christ's argument is: To be able to do good and refuse to do it is evil; not to heal this man would have been evil.

3:6 *Pharisees.* See note on Matt. 3:7. *Herodians.* See note on Matt. 22:16.

3:8 *Idumea.* The former country of Edom, which in the time of Christ included the region around Hebron.

and Sidon, a great multitude
heard of all that He was doing
and came to Him.
9 And He told His disciples
that a boat should stand ready for
Him because of the multitude, in
order that they might not crowd
Him;
10 for He had [a]healed many,
with the result that all those who
had [b]afflictions pressed about
Him in order to [c]touch Him.
11 And whenever the unclean
spirits beheld Him, they would
fall down before Him and cry out,
saying, "You are [a]the Son of
God!"
12 And He [a]earnestly warned
them not to reveal His identity.

10 [a]Matt. 4:23 [b]Mark 5:29, 34; Luke 7:21 [c]Matt. 9:21; 14:36; Mark 6:56; 8:22
11 [a]Matt. 4:3
12 [a]Matt. 8:4

D His Personnel, 3:13–35

1 *The call of The Twelve,* 3:13–21

13 And He *went up to [a]the
mountain and *[b]summoned those
whom He Himself wanted, and
they came to Him.
14 And He appointed twelve,
that they might be with Him, and
that He might send them out to
preach,
15 and to have authority to
cast out the demons.
16 And He appointed the
twelve: [a]Simon (to whom He gave
the name Peter),
17 and James, the *son* of Zebedee, and John the brother of
James (to them He gave the name
Boanerges, which means, "Sons
of Thunder");
18 and Andrew, and Philip,
and Bartholomew, and Matthew,
and Thomas, and James the *son*
of Alphaeus, and Thaddaeus, and
Simon the Cananaean;
19 and Judas Iscariot, who
also betrayed Him.

13 [a]Matt. 5:1; Luke 6:12 [b]Matt. 10:1; Mark 6:7; Luke 9:1-6
★16 [a]Mark 3:16-19: *Matt. 10:2-4; Luke 6:14-16;* Acts 1:13
★17

20 And He *came [a]home, and
the [b]multitude *gathered again,
[c]to such an extent that they could
not even eat a meal.
21 And when [a]His own peo-
ple heard *of this,* they went out to
take custody of Him; for they
were saying, "[b]He has lost His
senses."

20 [a]Mark 2:1; 7:17; 9:28 [b]Mark 1:45; 3:7 [c]Mark 6:31
21 [a]Mark 3:31f. [b]John 10:20; Acts 26:24

2 *The condemnation of rejectors,* 3:22–30

22 And the scribes who came
down [a]from Jerusalem were saying, "He is possessed by [b]Beelze-
bul," and "[c]He casts out the demons by the ruler of the
demons."
23 [a]And He called them to
Himself and began speaking to
them in [b]parables, "How can [c]Sa-
tan cast out Satan?
24 "And if a kingdom is divided against itself, that kingdom
cannot stand.
25 "And if a house is divided
against itself, that house will not
be able to stand.
26 "And if [a]Satan has risen up
against himself and is divided, he
cannot stand, but he is finished!
27 "[a]But no one can enter the
strong man's house and plunder
his property unless he first binds
the strong man, and then he will
plunder his house.
28 "[a]Truly I say to you, all sins
shall be forgiven the sons of men,
and whatever blasphemies they
utter;
29 but whoever blasphemes
against the Holy Spirit never has
forgiveness, but is guilty of an
eternal sin" —
30 because they were saying,
"He has an unclean spirit."

★22 [a]Matt. 15:1 [b]Matt. 10:25; 11:18 [c]Matt. 9:34
23 [a]Mark 3:23-27: *Matt. 12:25-29; Luke 11:17-22* [b]Matt. 13:3ff.; Mark 4:2ff. [c]Matt. 4:10
26 [a]Matt. 4:10
27 [a]Is. 49:24, 25
28 [a]Matt. 12:31, 32; Mark 3:28-30; Luke 12:10
★29

3:16–19 There are 4 lists of the apostles given in the N.T. (Matt. 10:1–4; Luke 6:13–16; Acts 1:13 are the others). Thaddaeus (Matt. 10:3; Mark 3:18) is apparently the same as Judas the son or brother of James (Thaddaeus may represent a corruption of *Yaddai,* a form of Judas).

3:17 *Sons of Thunder.* Probably indicating the fiery zeal and energy of James and John.

3:22 *Beelzebul.* See note on Matt. 10:25.

3:29 *blasphemes against the Holy Spirit.* See note on Matt. 12:31.

3 The call to be in Jesus' spiritual family, 3:31-35

31 [a]Mark 3:31-35; *Matt. 12:46-50; Luke 8:19-21*

31 [a]And His mother and His brothers *arrived, and standing outside they sent *word* to Him, and called Him.

32 And a multitude was sitting around Him, and they *said to Him, "Behold, Your mother and Your brothers are outside looking for You."

33 And answering them, He *said, "Who are My mother and My brothers?"

34 And looking about on those who were sitting around Him, He *said, "Behold, My mother and My brothers!

★35

35 "For whoever does the will of God, he is My brother and sister and mother."

E His Parables, 4:1-34

1 The sower, 4:1-20

1 [a]Mark 4:1-12; *Matt. 13:1-15; Luke 8:4-10* [b]Mark 2:13; 3:7

4 [a]And He began to teach again [b]by the seashore. And such a very great multitude gathered before Him that He got into a boat in the sea and sat down; and all the multitude were by the seashore on the land.

★ 2 [a]Matt. 13:3ff.; Mark 3:23; 4:2ff.

2 And He was teaching them many things in [a]parables, and was saying to them in His teaching,

3 "Listen *to this*! Behold, the sower went out to sow;

4 and it came about that as he was sowing, some *seed* fell beside the road, and the birds came and ate it up.

5 "And other *seed* fell on the rocky *ground* where it did not have much soil; and immediately it sprang up because it had no depth of soil. ★ 5

6 "And after the sun had risen, it was scorched; and because it had no root, it withered away.

7 "And other *seed* fell among the thorns, and the thorns grew up and choked it, and it yielded no crop.

8 "And other *seeds* fell into the good soil and as they grew up and increased, they were yielding a crop and were producing thirty, sixty, and a hundredfold."

9 And He was saying, "[a]He who has ears to hear, let him hear." 9 [a]Matt. 11:15; Mark 4:23

10 And as soon as He was alone, His followers, along with the twelve, *began* asking Him *about* the parables.

11 And He was saying to them, "To you has been given the mystery of the kingdom of God; but [a]those who are outside get everything [b]in parables, ★11 [a]1 Cor. 5:12f.; Col. 4:5; 1 Thess. 4:12; 1 Tim. 3:7 [b]Mark 3:23; 4:2

12 [a]in order that WHILE SEEING, THEY MAY SEE AND NOT PERCEIVE; AND WHILE HEARING, THEY MAY HEAR AND NOT UNDERSTAND LEST THEY RETURN AGAIN AND BE FORGIVEN." 12 [a]Is. 6:9; Matt. 13:14

13 [a]And He *said to them, "Do you not understand this parable? And how will you understand all the parables? 13 [a]Mark 4:13-20; *Matt. 13:18-23; Luke 8:11-15*

14 "The sower sows the word.

15 "And these are the ones who are beside the road where the word is sown; and when they hear, immediately [a]Satan comes and takes away the word which has been sown in them. 15 [a]Matt. 4:10

3:35 Those who belong to God's family are closer to Jesus than His natural family.

4:2 *parables.* A parable is a short discourse that makes a comparison; it is usually designed to inculcate a single truth. Some parables, however, like those of the sower and of the tares, are given detailed interpretations. Also, the Greek word "parable" is used in Luke 4:23 for what we would normally call a proverb. Parables were told by Christ for opposite effects: on the one hand, to make the truth more engaging and clear to those who were willing to hear (Luke 15:3) and, on the other, to make the truth obscure to those who lacked spiritual concern (Mark 4:11-12).

4:5-8 Jesus wanted the people to examine their hearts' responses to His message. Though some of the soils proved barren, nevertheless how great was the harvest.

4:11 *the mystery.* Just as in pagan mystery religions the initiate was instructed in the teaching of the cult, which was not revealed to outsiders, so the purpose of parables was to instruct the disciples without revealing truths to *those who are outside.* Parables test the spiritual responsiveness of those who hear them.

16 "And in a similar way these are the ones on whom seed was sown on the rocky *places,* who, when they hear the word, immediately receive it with joy;

17 and they have no *firm* root in themselves, but are *only* temporary; then, when affliction or persecution arises because of the word, immediately they fall away.

18 "And others are the ones on whom seed was sown among the thorns; these are the ones who have heard the word,

★19 [a]Matt. 13:22

19 and the worries of [a]the world, and the deceitfulness of riches, and the desires for other things enter in and choke the word, and it becomes unfruitful.

20 "And those are the ones on whom seed was sown on the good ground; and they hear the word and accept it, and bear fruit, thirty, sixty, and a hundredfold."

2 *The lamp,* 4:21–25

21 [a]Matt. 5:15; Luke 8:16; 11:33

21 And He was saying to them, "[a]A lamp is not brought to be put under a peck-measure, is it, or under a bed? Is it not *brought* to be put on the lampstand?

22 [a]Matt. 10:26; Luke 8:17; 12:2

22 "[a]For nothing is hidden, except to be revealed; nor has *anything* been secret, but that it should come to light.

23 [a]Matt. 11:15; Mark 4:9

23 "[a]If any man has ears to hear, let him hear."

24 [a]Matt. 7:2; Luke 6:38

24 And He was saying to them, "Take care what you listen to. [a]By your standard of measure it shall be measured to you; and more shall be given you besides.

25 [a]Matt. 13:12

25 "[a]For whoever has, to him shall *more* be given; and whoever does not have, even what he has shall be taken away from him."

3 *The seed growing gradually,* 4:26–29

★26 [a]Matt. 13:24-30; Mark 4:26-29

26 And He was saying, "[a]The kingdom of God is like a man who casts seed upon the ground;

27 and goes to bed at night and gets up by day, and the seed sprouts up and grows — how, he himself does not know.

28 "The earth produces crops by itself; first the blade, then the head, then the mature grain in the head.

29 "But when the crop permits, he immediately puts in the sickle, because the harvest has come."

4 *The mustard seed,* 4:30–34

30 [a]Mark 4:30-32; *Matt. 13:31, 32; Luke 13:18, 19* [b]Matt. 13:24

30 [a]And He said, "How shall we [b]picture the kingdom of God, or by what parable shall we present it?

★31

31 "*It is* like a mustard seed, which, when sown upon the ground, though it is smaller than all the seeds that are upon the ground,

32 yet when it is sown, grows up and becomes larger than all the garden plants and forms large branches; so that the birds of the air can nest under its shade."

33 And with many such parables He was speaking the word to them as they were able to hear it;

34 [a]Matt. 13:34; John 10:6; 16:25

34 and He was not speaking to them [a]without parables; but He was explaining everything privately to His own disciples.

F His Prerogatives, 4:35–9:1

1 *Over the storm,* 4:35–41

35 [a]Mark 4:35-41; *Matt. 8:18, 23-27; Luke 8:22, 25*

35 [a]And on that day, when evening had come, He *said to

4:19 *desires for other things.* I.e., desire for things other than the gospel.

4:26–29 The Word of God, when sown in men's hearts, produces fruit sometimes slowly but always surely (see 1 Pet. 1:23–25).

4:31 *a mustard seed.* Though it has one of the smallest seeds and is an herb, the Palestinian mustard plant grows to a height of 10 or 12 feet. It pictures the phenomenally rapid spread of Christianity from a small beginning.

them, "Let us go over to the other side."

36 [a]Mark 3:9; 4:1; 5:2, 21

36 And leaving the multitude, they *took Him along with them, just as He was, [a]in the boat; and other boats were with Him.

37 And there *arose a fierce gale of wind, and the waves were breaking over the boat so much that the boat was already filling up.

38 And He Himself was in the stern, asleep on the cushion; and they *awoke Him and *said to Him, "Teacher, do You not care that we are perishing?"

39 And being aroused, He rebuked the wind and said to the sea, "Hush, be still." And the wind died down and it became perfectly calm.

40 And He said to them, "Why are you so timid? How is it that you have no faith?"

*41

41 And they became very much afraid and said to one another, "Who then is this, that even the wind and the sea obey Him?"

2 *Over demons,* 5:1-20

1 [a]Mark 5:1-17; *Matt. 8:28-34; Luke 8:26-37*

5 [a]And they came to the other side of the sea, into the country of the Gerasenes.

2 [a]Mark 3:9; 4:1, 36; 5:21 [b]Mark 1:23

2 And when He had come out of [a]the boat, immediately a man from the tombs [b]with an unclean spirit met Him,

3 and he had his dwelling among the tombs. And no one was able to bind him any more, even with a chain;

4 because he had often been bound with shackles and chains, and the chains had been torn apart by him, and the shackles broken in pieces, and no one was strong enough to subdue him.

5 And constantly night and day, among the tombs and in the mountains, he was crying out and gashing himself with stones.

6 And seeing Jesus from a distance, he ran up and bowed down before Him;

★ 7 [a]Matt. 8:29 [b]Matt. 4:3 [c]Luke 8:28; Acts 16:17; Heb. 7:1

7 and crying out with a loud voice, he *said, "[a]What do I have to do with You, Jesus, [b]Son of [c]the Most High God? I implore You by God, do not torment me!"

8 For He had been saying to him, "Come out of the man, you unclean spirit!"

★ 9 [a]Matt. 26:53; Mark 5:15; Luke 8:30

9 And He was asking him, "What is your name?" And he *said to Him, "My name is [a]Legion; for we are many."

10 And he *began* to entreat Him earnestly not to send them out of the country.

11 Now there was a big herd of swine feeding there on the mountain side.

12 And they entreated Him, saying, "Send us into the swine so that we may enter them."

13 And He gave them permission. And coming out, the unclean spirits entered the swine; and the herd rushed down the steep bank into the sea, about two thousand *of them;* and they were drowned in the sea.

14 And those who tended them ran away and reported it in the city and *out* in the country. And *the people* came to see what it was that had happened.

15 [a]Matt. 4:24; Mark 5:16, 18 [b]Luke 8:27 [c]Luke 8:35 [d]Mark 5:9

15 And they *came to Jesus and *observed the man who had been [a]demon-possessed sitting down, [b]clothed and [c]in his right mind, the very man who had had the "[d]legion"; and they became frightened.

4:41 *they became very much afraid.* The disciples were rebuked (v. 40) for being *timid,* literally, "cowardly." In v. 41 the word *afraid* refers to reverential, respectful awe for the Lord. In exclaiming, *Who then is this,* they acknowledged that He was greater than they thought.

5:7 *What do I have to do with You.* Today we would say instead, "What have you to do with me?" *Jesus, Son of the Most High God.* Though this apparently was his first encounter with Jesus, this man knew who He was, such knowledge coming to him from the demons who indwelt him.

5:9 *Legion.* The largest unit of the Roman army, 3000-6000 strong, indicating that many demons possessed the man (see Matt. 12:45 and Luke 8:2).

16 [a]Matt. 4:24; Mark 5:15

16 And those who had seen it described to them how it had happened to the [a]demon-possessed man, and *all* about the swine.

17 And they began to entreat Him to depart from their region.

[a]Mark 18-20; e 8:38, [b]Matt. 4; Mark .15, 16

18 [a]And as He was getting into the boat, the man who had been [b]demon-possessed was entreating Him that he might accompany Him.

19 And He did not let him, but He *said to him, "Go home to your people and report to them what great things the Lord has done for you, and *how* He had mercy on you."

0 [a]Matt. 25; Mark 7:31

20 And he went off and began to proclaim in [a]Decapolis what great things Jesus had done for him; and everyone marveled.

3 Over sickness and death, 5:21–43

21 [a]Matt. 9:1; Luke 8:40 [b]Mark 4:36 [c]Mark 4:1

21 [a]And when Jesus had crossed over again in [b]the boat to the other side, a great multitude gathered about Him; and He stayed [c]by the seashore.

★22 [a]Mark 5:22-43; *Matt 9:18-26; Luke 8:41-56* [b]Matt. 9:18; Mark 5:35, 36, 38; Luke 8:49; 13:14; Acts 13:15; 18:8, 17

22 [a]And one of [b]the synagogue officials named Jairus *came up, and upon seeing Him, *fell at His feet,

23 [a]Mark 6:5; 7:32; 8:23; 16:18; Luke 4:40; 13:13; Acts 6:6; 9:17; 28:8

23 and *entreated Him earnestly, saying, "My little daughter is at the point of death; *please* come and [a]lay Your hands on her, that she may get well and live."

24 And He went off with him; and a great multitude was following Him and pressing in on Him.

25 And a woman who had had a hemorrhage for twelve years,

26 and had endured much at the hands of many physicians, and had spent all that she had and was not helped at all, but rather had grown worse,

27 after hearing about Jesus, came up in the crowd behind *Him,* and touched His cloak.

28 For she thought, "If I just touch His garments, I shall get well."

29 And immediately the flow of her blood was dried up; and she felt in her body that she was healed of her [a]affliction.

29 [a]Mark 3:10; 5:34

30 And immediately Jesus, perceiving in Himself that [a]the power *proceeding* from Him had gone forth, turned around in the crowd and said, "Who touched My garments?"

30 [a]Luke 5:17

31 And His disciples said to Him, "You see the multitude pressing in on You, and You say, 'Who touched Me?' "

32 And He looked around to see the woman who had done this.

33 But the woman fearing and trembling, aware of what had happened to her, came and fell down before Him, and told Him the whole truth.

34 And He said to her, "Daughter, [a]your faith has made you well; [b]go in peace, and be healed of your [c]affliction."

★34 [a]Matt. 9:22 [b]Luke 7:50; 8:48; Acts 16:36; James 2:16 [c]Mark 3:10; 5:29

35 While He was still speaking, they *came from the *house of* the [a]synagogue official, saying, "Your daughter has died; why trouble the Teacher any more?"

35 [a]Mark 5:22

36 But Jesus, overhearing what was being spoken, *said to the [a]synagogue official, "[b]Do not be afraid *any longer,* only believe."

★36 [a]Mark 5:22 [b]Luke 8:50

37 And He allowed no one to follow with Him, except [a]Peter and James and John the brother of James.

37 [a]Matt. 17:1; 26:37

38 And they *came to the

★38 [a]Mark 5:22

5:20 *Decapolis,* the region SE. of the Sea of Galilee, in which were located 10 cities originally, although the number varied from time to time. They were Greek in organization and culture.

5:22 *one of the synagogue officials.* Jairus was an elder in the synagogue at Capernaum which Jesus attended.

5:34 *your faith has made you well.* I.e., your faith has made possible your recovery.

5:36 *only believe.* Lit., just keep on believing! There are no limits, Christ says, to what faith in the power of God can do.

5:38 *loudly weeping and wailing.* These professional mourners were hired by the family.

house of the [a]synagogue official;
and He *beheld a commotion,
and *people* loudly weeping and
wailing.
★39 **39** And entering in, He *said
to them, "Why make a commotion and weep? The child has not
died, but is asleep."
40 And they were laughing at
Him. But putting them all out, He
*took along the child's father and
mother and His own companions,
and *entered the *room* where the
child was.
41 [a]Luke **41** And taking the child by
7:14; Acts the hand, He *said to her, "Tali-
9:40 tha kum!" (which translated
means, "Little girl, [a]I say to you,
arise!")
42 And immediately the girl
got up and *began* to walk; for she
was twelve years old. And immediately they were completely as-
tounded.
43 [a]Matt. 8:4 **43** And He [a]gave them strict
orders that no one should know
about this; and He said that
something should be given her to
eat.

4 *Rejected by His own townspeople,* 6:1-6

★ 1 [a]Mark **6** [a]And He went out from
6:1-6; *Matt. 13:54-58* there, and He *came into
[b]Matt. 13:54, [b]His home town; and His disciples
57; Luke 4:16, 23 *followed Him.
2 [a]Matt. **2** And when the Sabbath
4:23; Mark had come, He began [a]to teach in
10:1 [b]Matt. 7:28 the synagogue; and the [b]many listeners were astonished, saying,
"Where did this man *get* these
things, and what is *this* wisdom
given to Him, and such miracles
★ 3 [a]Matt. as these performed by His hands?
13:55 [b]Matt. **3** "Is not this [a]the carpenter,
12:46 [c]Matt. [b]the son of Mary, and brother of
13:56 [d]Matt. 11:6 James, and Joses, and Judas, and
Simon? Are not [c]His sisters here
with us?" And they took [d]offense
at Him.
4 And Jesus said to them, 4 [a]Matt.
"[a]A prophet is not without honor 13:57 [b]Mark
except in [b]his home town and 6:1
among his *own* relatives and in
his *own* household."
5 And He could do no mir- 5 [a]Mark
acle there except that He [a]laid His 5:23
hands upon a few sick people and
healed them.
6 And He wondered at their 6 [a]Matt.
unbelief. 9:35; Mark
[a]And He was going around the 1:39; 10:1;
villages teaching. Luke 13:22

5 *In commissioning The Twelve,* 6:7-13

7 [a]And [b]He *summoned the 7 [a]Mark
twelve and began to send them 6:7-11; *Matt.*
out [c]in pairs; and He was giving *10:1, 9-14; Luke 9:1, 3-*
them authority over the unclean *5;* Luke 10:4-
spirits; 11 [b]Matt. 10:1, 5; Mark
8 [a]and He instructed them 3:13; Luke
that they should take nothing for 9:1 [c]Luke 10:1
their journey, except a mere staff; 8 [a]Matt. 10:10
no bread, no bag, no money in
their belt;
9 but *to* wear sandals; and
He added, "Do not put on two tunics."
10 And He said to them,
"Wherever you enter a house,
stay there until you leave town.
11 "And any place that does ★11 [a]Matt.
not receive you or listen to you, as 10:14
you go out from there, [a]shake off
the dust from the soles of your
feet for a testimony against
them."
12 [a]And they went out and 12 [a]Matt.
preached that *men* should repent. 11:1; Luke 9:6
13 And they were casting out 13 [a]James
many demons and [a]were anoint- 5:14
ing with oil many sick people and
healing them.

5:39 *is asleep.* The girl had been pronounced dead (Luke 8:53). Christ's reference to death as sleep was intended to suggest that her condition was temporary and that she would come back to life again.

6:1 *His home town.* Lit., His native place; i.e., Nazareth.

6:3 *brother of.* The four half brothers and two or more half sisters were children of Joseph and Mary born after Jesus (Matt. 1:25). James became the leader of the church in Jerusalem and author of the Epistle of James. Jude wrote the letter that bears his name. *they took offense.* Something stood in the way of their believing in Him.

6:11 *shake off the dust.* An action that symbolized a complete break in fellowship and renunciation of all further responsibility. See Acts 13:51; 18:6.

6 *As affecting Herod, who killed John the Baptist,* 6:14–29

★14 [a]Mark 6:14-29: *Matt. 14:1-12;* Mark 6:14-16: *Luke 9:7-9* [b]Matt. 14:2
14 [a]And King Herod heard *of*
it, for His name had become well
known; and *people* were saying,
"[b]John the Baptist has risen from
the dead, and therefore these miraculous powers are at work in
Him."
15 [a]Matt. 16:14; Mark 8:28 [b]Matt. 21:11
15 But others were saying,
"*He is* [a]Elijah." And others were
saying, "*He is* [b]a prophet, like one
of the prophets *of old.*"
16 But when Herod heard *of*
it, he kept saying, "John, whom I
beheaded, has risen!"
★17 [a]Matt. 14:3
17 For Herod himself had
sent and had John arrested and
bound in prison on account of
[a]Herodias, the wife of his brother
Philip, because he had married
her.
★18 [a]Matt. 14:4
18 For John had been saying
to Herod, "[a]It is not lawful for
you to have your brother's wife."
19 [a]Matt. 14:3
19 And [a]Herodias had a
grudge against him and wanted to
kill him; and could not *do so;*
20 [a]Matt. 21:26
20 for [a]Herod was afraid of
John, knowing that he was a
righteous and holy man, and kept
him safe. And when he heard
him, he was very perplexed; but
he used to enjoy listening to him.
21 [a]Esther 1:3; 2:18 [b]Luke 3:1
21 And a strategic day came
when Herod on his birthday
[a]gave a banquet for his lords and
military commanders and the
leading men [b]of Galilee;
22 [a]Matt. 14:3
22 and when the daughter of
[a]Herodias herself came in and
danced, she pleased Herod and
his dinner guests; and the king
said to the girl, "Ask me for whatever you want and I will give it to
you."
23 [a]Esther 5:3, 6; 7:2
23 And he swore to her,
"Whatever you ask of me, I will
give it to you; up to [a]half of my
kingdom."
24 And she went out and said
to her mother, "What shall I ask
for?" And she said, "The head of
John the Baptist."
25 And immediately she came
in haste before the king and
asked, saying, "I want you to give
me right away the head of John
the Baptist on a platter."
26 And although the king was ★26
very sorry, *yet* because of his
oaths and because of his dinner
guests, he was unwilling to refuse
her.
27 And immediately the king
sent an executioner and commanded *him* to bring *back* his
head. And he went and beheaded
him in the prison,
28 and brought his head on a
platter, and gave it to the girl; and
the girl gave it to her mother.
29 And when his disciples
heard *about this,* they came and
took away his body and laid it in
a tomb.

7 *In feeding 5000 men,* 6:30–44

30 [a]And the [b]apostles *gath- 30 [a]Luke 9:10 [b]Matt. 10:2 [Mark 3:14 in Gr.]; Luke 6:13; 9:10; 17:5; 22:14; 24:10; Acts 1:2, 26
ered together with Jesus; and they
reported to Him all that they had
done and taught.
31 And He *said to them, 31 [a]Mark 3:20
"Come away by yourselves to a
lonely place and rest a while."
(For there were many *people*
coming and going, and [a]they did
not even have time to eat.)
32 [a]And they went away in 32 [a]Mark 6:32-44: *Matt. 14:13-21; Luke 9:10-17; John 6:5-13;* Mark 8:2-9 [b]Mark 3:9; 4:36; 6:45
[b]the boat to a lonely place by
themselves.
33 And *the people* saw them
going, and many recognized
them, and they ran there together
on foot from all the cities, and got
there ahead of them.
34 And disembarking, He ★34 [a]Matt. 9:36
[a]saw a great multitude, and He

6:14 *King Herod.* Herod Antipas, tetrarch of Galilee and Perea from 4 B.C.–A.D. 39. Officially he was not a king, but this title for him was popularly used.

6:17 *Philip.* Herod's brother, but not the same Philip mentioned in Luke 3:1. Herodias, who was married to Herod Philip, left him to live with another uncle, Herod Antipas.

6:18 *not lawful.* See Mark 10:11; Lev. 18:16.

6:26 *because of his oaths.* In the ancient Near East an oath was considered to be irrevocable.

6:34 *a shepherd.* See Num. 27:17; 1 Kings 22:17; Ezek. 34:5.

felt compassion for them because [a]they were like sheep without a shepherd; and He began to teach them many things.

35 And when it was already quite late, His disciples came up to Him and *began* saying, "The place is desolate and it is already quite late;

36 send them away so that they may go into the surrounding countryside and villages and buy themselves something to eat."

★37 [a]John 6:7 [b]Matt. 18:28; Luke 7:41

37 But He answered and said to them, "You give them something to eat!" [a]And they *said to Him, "Shall we go and spend two hundred [b]denarii on bread and give them something to eat?"

38 And He *said to them, "How many loaves do you have? Go look!" And when they found out, they *said, "Five and two fish."

39 And He commanded them all to recline by groups on the green grass.

40 And they reclined in companies of hundreds and of fifties.

41 [a]Matt. 14:19

41 And He took the five loaves and the two fish, and looking up toward heaven, He [a]blessed *the food* and broke the loaves and He kept giving *them* to the disciples to set before them; and He divided up the two fish among them all.

42 And they all ate and were satisfied.

43 [a]Matt. 14:20

43 And they picked up twelve full [a]baskets of the broken pieces, and also of the fish.

★44 [a]Matt. 14:21

44 And there were [a]five thousand men who ate the loaves.

★45 [a]Mark 6:45-51: *Matt. 14:22-32; John 6:15-21* [b]Mark 6:32 [c]Matt. 11:21; Mark 8:22

8 *In walking on water,* 6:45–52

45 [a]And immediately He made His disciples get into [b]the boat and go ahead of *Him* to the other side to [c]Bethsaida, while He Himself was sending the multitude away.

46 [a]Acts 18:18, 21; 2 Cor. 2:13 [b]Matt. 14:23

46 And after [a]bidding them farewell, He departed [b]to the mountain to pray.

47 And when it was evening, the boat was in the midst of the sea, and He *was* alone on the land.

★48 [a]Matt. 24:43; Mark 13:35

48 And seeing them straining at the oars, for the wind was against them, at about the [a]fourth watch of the night, He *came to them, walking on the sea; and He intended to pass by them.

49 But when they saw Him walking on the sea, they supposed that it was a ghost, and cried out;

50 [a]Matt. 9:2 [b]Matt. 14:27

50 for they all saw Him and were frightened. But immediately He spoke with them and *said to them, "[a]Take courage; it is I, [b]do not be afraid."

51 [a]Mark 6:32

51 And He got into [a]the boat with them, and the wind stopped; and they were greatly astonished,

★52 [a]Mark 8:17ff. [b]Rom. 11:7

52 for [a]they had not gained any insight from the *incident of* the loaves, but their heart [b]was hardened.

9 *Over sickness,* 6:53–56

★53 [a]Mark 6:53-56: *Matt. 14:34-36; John 6:24, 25*

53 [a]And when they had crossed over they came to land at Gennesaret, and moored to the shore.

54 And when they had come out of the boat, immediately *the people* recognized Him,

55 and ran about that whole country and began to carry about on their pallets those who were sick, to the place they heard He was.

56 [a]Mark 3:10 [b]Matt. 9:20

56 And wherever He entered villages, or cities, or countryside, they were laying the sick in the

---

6:37 *two hundred denarii.* The basic Roman silver coin used in Palestine, the denarius was a rural worker's average daily wage.

6:44 *five thousand men.* The count did not include women and children.

6:45 *Bethsaida.* About 2 miles N. of the Sea of Galilee.

6:48 *the fourth watch.* From 3 to 6 a.m.

6:52 *their heart was hardened.* I.e., they were spiritually insensitive to the truth concerning the deity of Christ which His miracles were continually demonstrating.

6:53 *land at Gennesaret.* On the NE. shore of the Sea of Galilee.

market places, and entreating
Him that they might just [a]touch
[b]the fringe of His cloak; and as
many as touched it were being
cured.

10 *Over the Pharisees' traditions,* 7:1-23

★ 1 aMark 7:1-23; Matt. 15:1-20 bMatt. 15:1 **7** [a]And the Pharisees and some
of the scribes gathered to-
gether around Him when they
had come [b]from Jerusalem,
2 aMatt. 15:2; Mark 7:5; Luke 11:38; Acts 10:14, 28; 11:8; Rom. 14:14; Heb. 10:29; Rev. 21:27 **2** and had seen that some of
His disciples were eating their
bread with [a]impure hands, that is,
unwashed.
★ 3 aMark 7:5, 8, 9, 13; Gal. 1:14 **3** (For the Pharisees and all
the Jews do not eat unless they
carefully wash their hands, *thus*
observing the [a]traditions of the
elders;
4 aMatt. 23:25 **4** and *when they come* from
the market place, they do not eat
unless they cleanse themselves;
and there are many other things
which they have received in order
to observe, such as the washing of
[a]cups and pitchers and copper
pots.)
★ 5 aMark 7:3, 8, 9, 13; Gal. 1:14 bMark 7:2 **5** And the Pharisees and the
scribes *asked Him, "Why do
Your disciples not walk according
to the [a]tradition of the elders, but
eat their bread with [b]impure
hands?"
6 aIs. 29:13 **6** And He said to them,
"Rightly did Isaiah prophesy of
you hypocrites, as it is written,

'[a]THIS PEOPLE HONORS ME
WITH THEIR LIPS,
BUT THEIR HEART IS FAR AWAY
FROM ME.

7 '[a]BUT IN VAIN DO THEY WOR- 7 aIs. 29:13
SHIP ME,
TEACHING AS DOCTRINES THE
PRECEPTS OF MEN.'

8 "Neglecting the command- ★ 8 aMark 7:3, 5, 9, 13; Gal. 1:14
ment of God, you hold to the [a]tra-
dition of men."
9 He was also saying to 9 aMark 7:3, 5, 8, 13; Gal. 1:14
them, "You nicely set aside the
commandment of God in order to
keep your [a]tradition.
10 "For Moses said, '[a]HONOR ★10 aEx. 20:12; Deut. 5:16 bEx. 21:17; Lev. 20:9
YOUR FATHER AND YOUR MOTHER';
and, '[b]HE WHO SPEAKS EVIL OF FA-
THER OR MOTHER, LET HIM BE PUT TO
DEATH';
11 but you say, 'If a man says ★11 aLev. 1:2; Matt. 27:6
to *his* father or *his* mother, any-
thing of mine you might have
been helped by is [a]Corban (that is
to say, given *to God*),'
12 you no longer permit him
to do anything for *his* father or
his mother;
13 *thus* invalidating the word 13 aMark 7:3, 5, 8, 9; Gal. 1:14
of God by your [a]tradition which
you have handed down; and you
do many things such as that."
14 And summoning the multitude again, He *began* saying to
them, "Listen to Me, all of you,
and understand:
15 there is nothing outside
the man which going into him can
defile him; but the things which
proceed out of the man are what
defile the man.
16 ["If any man has ears to ★16
hear, let him hear."]
17 And when leaving the 17 aMark 2:1; 3:19; 9:28 bMatt. 15:15
multitude, He had entered [a]the
house, [b]His disciples questioned
Him about the parable.

7:1 *scribes.* See note on Matt. 2:4.

7:3 *the traditions of the elders.* The unwritten body of commands and teachings of honored rabbis of the past, the authoritative source of scribal teachings.

7:5 *impure hands.* This does not mean dirty hands but hands not washed according to the rules of the elders, and therefore not free of ceremonial defilement.

7:8 Christ is here criticizing the reinterpretation and debasement of the law by the scribes and Pharisees who viewed oral tradition as more authoritative than the written law of the O.T. He then illustrated the point (vv. 9-13).

7:10 *Moses said.* See Ex. 20:12; Deut. 5:16. For *who speaks evil* see Ex. 21:17.

7:11 *Corban.* The transliteration of a Hebrew word meaning a "gift." The word referred to something devoted to God by an inviolable vow. If a son declared that the amount needed to support his parents was Corban, the scribes said that he was exempt from his duty to care for his parents as prescribed in the law. Evidently, too, he was not really obliged to devote that sum to the temple.

7:16 Most manuscripts do not contain this verse.

★18
18 And He *said to them,
"Are you too so uncomprehend-
ing? Do you not see that whatever
goes into the man from outside
cannot defile him;
19 [a]Rom. 14:1-12; Col. 2:16 [b]Luke 11:41; Acts 10:15; 11:9
19 because it does not go into
his heart, but into his stomach,
and is eliminated?" (*Thus He* declared [a]all foods [b]clean.)
20 [a]Matt. 15:18; Mark 7:23
20 And He was saying,
"[a]That which proceeds out of the
man, that is what defiles the man.
21 "For from within, out of the
heart of men, proceed the evil
thoughts and fornications, thefts,
murders, adulteries,
22 [a]Matt. 6:23; 20:15
22 deeds of coveting *and*
wickedness, *as well as* deceit, sensuality, [a]envy, slander, pride *and*
foolishness.
23 "All these evil things proceed from within and defile the
man."

11 Over a Syrophoenician woman, 7:24-30

24 [a]Mark 7:24-30; *Matt. 15:21-28* [b]Matt. 11:21; Mark 7:31
24 [a]And from there He arose
and went away to the region of
[b]Tyre. And when He had entered
a house, He wanted no one to
know *of it;* yet He could not escape notice.
25 But after hearing of Him, a
woman whose little daughter had
an unclean spirit, immediately
came and fell at His feet.
★26
26 Now the woman was a
Gentile, of the Syrophoenician
race. And she kept asking Him to
cast the demon out of her daughter.
★27
27 And He was saying to her,
"Let the children be satisfied first,
for it is not good to take the children's bread and throw it to the
dogs."
28 But she answered and
*said to Him, "Yes, Lord, *but*
even the dogs under the table
feed on the children's crumbs."
29 And He said to her, "Because of this answer go your way;
the demon has gone out of your
daughter."
30 And going back to her ★30
home, she found the child lying
on the bed, the demon having departed.

12 Over a deaf mute, 7:31-37

31 [a]And again He went out 31 [a]Mark 7:31-37; *Matt. 15:29-31* [b]Matt. 11:21; Mark 7:24 [c]Matt. 4:18 [d]Matt. 4:25; Mark 5:20
from the region of [b]Tyre, and
came through Sidon to [c]the Sea of
Galilee, within the region of [d]De-
capolis.
32 And they *brought to Him 32 [a]Mark 5:23
one who was deaf and spoke with
difficulty, and they *entreated
Him to [a]lay His hand upon him.
33 And [a]He took him aside 33 [a]Mark 8:23
from the multitude by himself,
and put His fingers into his ears,
and after [a]spitting, He touched
his tongue *with the saliva;*
34 and looking up to heaven 34 [a]Mark 8:12
with a deep [a]sigh, He *said to
him, "Ephphatha!" that is, "Be
opened!"
35 And his ears were opened,
and the impediment of his tongue
was removed, and he *began*
speaking plainly.
36 And [a]He gave them orders 36 [a]Matt. 8:4 [b]Mark 1:45
not to tell anyone; but the more
He ordered them, the more
widely they [b]continued to proclaim it.
37 And they were utterly astonished, saying, "He has done all
things well; He makes even the
deaf to hear, and the dumb to
speak."

13 In feeding 4000, 8:1-9

8 In those days again, when 1 [a]Mark 8:1-9; *Matt. 15:32-39;* [Mark 6:34-44]
there was a great multitude

7:18 *cannot defile him.* Foods declared to be "unclean" are specified in Lev. 11. Jesus is here not abrogating the law but making the point that sin comes from the heart. Thus the defilement that came to a Jew who ate "unclean" food was caused not by the food itself but by the rebellious heart that acted in disobedience to God.

7:26 *Syrophoenician.* By birth this Gentile woman was a Syrian from the region of Phoenicia.

7:27 *the dogs.* See note on Matt. 15:26.

7:30 This miracle was performed from a distance, without any vocal command from Christ.

and they had nothing to eat, [a]He
summoned His disciples and
*said to them,
2 [a]Matt. 9:36; Mark 6:34 2 "[a]I feel compassion for the
multitude because they have re-
mained with Me now three days,
and have nothing to eat;
3 and if I send them away
fasting to their home, they will
faint on the way; and some of
them have come from a distance."
4 And His disciples an-
swered Him, "Where will anyone
be able to *find enough to* satisfy
these men with bread here in the
wilderness?"
5 And He was asking them,
"How many loaves do you have?"
And they said, "Seven."
6 And He *directed the multitude to sit down on the ground;
and taking the seven loaves, He
gave thanks and broke them, and
began giving them to His disciples
to serve to them, and they served
them to the multitude.
7 [a]Matt. 14:19 7 They also had a few small
fish; and [a]after He had blessed
them, He ordered these to be
served as well.
★ 8 [a]Matt. 15:37; Mark 8:20 8 And they ate and were satisfied; and they picked up seven
large [a]baskets full of what was
left over of the broken pieces.
9 And about four thousand
were *there;* and He sent them
away.

14 In condemning the Pharisees, 8:10–13

★10 [a]Matt. 15:39 10 And immediately He entered the boat with His disciples,
and came to the district of [a]Dal-
★11 [a]Mark 8:11-21: *Matt. 16:1-12* [b]Matt. 12:38 manutha.
11 [a]And the Pharisees came
out and began to argue with Him,
[b]seeking from Him a sign from
heaven, to test Him.
12 And [a]sighing deeply in His 12 [a]Mark 7:34
spirit, He *said, "Why does this
generation seek for a sign? Truly I
say to you, no sign shall be given
to this generation."
13 And leaving them, He
again embarked and went away
to the other side.

15 In His teaching on leaven, 8:14–21

14 And they had forgotten to
take bread; and did not have
more than one loaf in the boat
with them.
15 And He was giving orders ★15 [a]Matt. 16:6; Luke 12:1 [b]Matt. 14:1; 22:16
to them, saying, "[a]Watch out! Be-
ware of the leaven of the Pharisees and the leaven of [b]Herod."
16 And they *began* to discuss
with one another *the fact* that
they had no bread.
17 And Jesus, aware of this, ★17 [a]Mark 6:52
*said to them, "Why do you dis-
cuss *the fact* that you have no
bread? [a]Do you not yet see or understand? Do you have a hardened heart?
18 "[a]HAVING EYES, DO YOU NOT 18 [a]Ezek. 12:2
SEE? AND HAVING EARS, DO YOU NOT
HEAR? And do you not remember,
19 when I broke [a]the five 19 [a]Mark 6:41-44 [b]Matt. 14:20
loaves for the five thousand, how
many [b]baskets full of broken
pieces you picked up?" They
*said to Him, "Twelve."
20 "And when *I broke* [a]the 20 [a]Mark 8:6-9 [b]Mark 8:8
seven for the four thousand, how
many large [b]baskets full of broken pieces did you pick up?" And
they *said to Him, "Seven."
21 And He was saying to 21 [a]Mark 6:52
them, "[a]Do you not yet understand?"

8:8 *seven large baskets.* The word *basket* itself (in the Greek) denotes larger baskets than the word used of the twelve baskets in which the leftovers were collected from the feeding of the 5,000 (6:43). The larger basket was the kind used to let Paul down over the wall of Damascus (Acts 9:25).

8:10 *Dalmanutha.* An unknown location.

8:11 *a sign from heaven.* The Pharisees wanted a startling miracle or celestial portent which would prove that Jesus was the Messiah. They did not believe, however, that He could provide such a sign.

8:15 *the leaven of the Pharisees* was hypocrisy (Luke 12:1) and *the leaven of Herod* was secularism and worldliness.

8:17 *Why do you discuss.* See note on Matt. 16:8.

16 *Over blindness,* 8:22-26

22 [a]Matt. 11:21; Mark 6:45 [b]Mark 3:10

22 And they *came to [a]Bethsaida. And they *brought a blind man to Him, and *entreated Him to [b]touch him.

23 [a]Mark 7:33 [b]Mark 5:23

23 And taking the blind man by the hand, He [a]brought him out of the village; and after [a]spitting on his eyes, and [b]laying His hands upon him, He asked him, "Do you see anything?"

24 And he looked up and said, "I see men, for I am seeing *them* like trees, walking about."

★25

25 Then again He laid His hands upon his eyes; and he looked intently and was restored, and *began* to see everything clearly.

26 [a]Matt. 8:4 [b]Mark 8:23

26 And He sent him to his home, saying, "[a]Do not even enter [b]the village."

17 *Over Peter,* 8:27-33

★27 [a]Mark 8:27-29: *Matt. 16:13-16; Luke 9:18-20* [b]Matt. 16:13

27 [a]And Jesus went out, along with His disciples, to the villages of [b]Caesarea Philippi; and on the way He questioned His disciples, saying to them, "Who do people say that I am?"

28 [a]Mark 6:14

28 [a]And they told Him, saying, "John the Baptist; and others *say* Elijah; but still others, one of the prophets."

29 And He *continued* by questioning them, "But who do you say that I am?" Peter *answered and *said to Him, "Thou art the Christ."

30 [a]Matt. 8:4; 16:20; Luke 9:21

30 And [a]He warned them to tell no one about Him.

★31 [a]Mark 8:31-9:1: *Matt. 16:21-28; Luke 9:22-27* [b]Matt. 16:21

31 [a]And He began to teach them that [b]the Son of Man must suffer many things and be rejected by the elders and the chief priests and the scribes, and be killed, and after three days rise again.

32 [a]John 10:24; 11:14; 16:25, 29; 18:20

32 And He was stating the matter [a]plainly. And Peter took Him aside and began to rebuke Him.

★33 [a]Matt. 4:10

33 But turning around and seeing His disciples, He rebuked Peter, and *said, "Get behind Me, [a]Satan; for you are not setting your mind on God's interests, but man's."

18 *Over the lives of His disciples,* 8:34-9:1

★34 [a]Matt. 10:38

34 And He summoned the multitude with His disciples, and said to them, "If anyone wishes to come after Me, let him deny himself, and [a]take up his cross, and follow Me.

★35 [a]Matt. 10:39

35 "For [a]whoever wishes to save his life shall lose it; and whoever loses his life for My sake and the gospel's shall save it.

36 "For what does it profit a man to gain the whole world, and forfeit his soul?

37 "For what shall a man give in exchange for his soul?

38 [a]Matt. 10:33; Luke 9:26; Heb. 11:16 [b]Matt. 8:20 [c]Matt. 16:27; Mark 13:26; Luke 9:27

38 "For [a]whoever is ashamed of Me and My words in this adulterous and sinful generation, [b]the Son of Man will also be ashamed of him when He [c]comes in the glory of His Father with the holy angels."

★ 1 [a]Matt. 16:27; Mark 13:26; Luke 9:27

9 And He was saying to them, "[a]Truly I say to you, there

8:25 This miracle was performed in stages.

8:27-30 See notes on Matt. 16:13, 14.

8:27 *Caesarea Philippi.* A city about 25 miles N. of the Sea of Galilee, built by Herod Philip in honor of Caesar Augustus.

8:31 *the Son of Man must suffer.* Christ expanded, for the disciples, the concept of Son of Man, who, in Daniel's vision (Dan. 7:13-14) and in the apocryphal book of Enoch, is not described as suffering and dying. The idea was unthinkable, as Peter declared (Mark 8:32). This was Jesus' first prediction of His death (see 9:31; 10:33-34).

8:33 *Get behind Me, Satan.* Peter was used by Satan to try to dissuade Christ from going to the cross.

8:34 *take up his cross.* See notes on Matt. 10:38 and Luke 9:23.

8:35 The verse means: Whoever would save his life (by renouncing the gospel and thus avoiding the risk of martyrdom) will lose it (eternally because he has not believed the gospel); but whoever is willing to lose his life (as a martyr for Christ) will save it (i.e., will prove that he is a follower of Christ and an heir of eternal life).

9:1 *until they see the kingdom of God after it has come with power.* See note on Matt. 16:28.

are some of those who are standing here who shall not taste of
death until they see the kingdom
of God after it has come with
power."

G His Previews, 9:2–50
1 *Of His glory,* 9:2–29

★ 2 [a]Mark 9:2-8: *Matt. 17:1-8; Luke 9:28-36* [b]Mark 5:37
2 [a]And six days later, Jesus
*took with Him [b]Peter and James
and John, and *brought them up
to a high mountain by themselves. And He was transfigured
before them;
3 [a]Matt. 28:3
3 and [a]His garments became
radiant and exceedingly white, as
no launderer on earth can whiten
them.
★ 4
4 And Elijah appeared to
them along with Moses; and they
were conversing with Jesus.
★ 5 [a]Matt. 23:7 [b]Matt. 17:4; Luke 9:33
5 And Peter *answered and
*said to Jesus, "[a]Rabbi, it is good
for us to be here; and [b]let us
make three tabernacles, one for
You, and one for Moses, and one
for Elijah."
6 For he did not know what
to answer; for they became terrified.
7 [a]2 Pet. 1:17f. [b]Matt. 3:17; Mark 1:11
7 Then a cloud formed,
overshadowing them, and [a]a voice
came out of the cloud, "[b]This is
My beloved Son, listen to Him!"
8 And all at once they
looked around and saw no one
with them any more, except Jesus
only.
9 [a]Mark 9:9-13: *Matt. 17:9-13* [b]Matt. 8:4; Mark 5:43; 7:36; 8:30
9 [a]And as they were coming
down from the mountain, He
[b]gave them orders not to relate to
anyone what they had seen, until
the Son of Man should rise from
the dead.
10 And they seized upon that ★10
statement, discussing with one
another what rising from the dead
might mean.
11 And they *began* question- ★11 [a]Matt. 11:14
ing Him, saying, *"Why is it* that
the scribes say that first [a]Elijah
must come?"
12 And He said to them, "Eli- 12 [a]Mark 9:31 [b]Matt. 16:21; 26:24
jah does first come and restore
everything. And *yet* how is it
written of [a]the Son of Man that
[b]He should suffer many things
and be treated with contempt?
13 "But I say to you, that Elijah has indeed come, and they did
to him whatever they wished, just
as it is written of him."
14 [a]And when they came 14 [a]Mark 9:14-28: *Matt. 17:14-19; Luke 9:37-42*
back to the disciples, they saw a
large crowd around them, and
some scribes arguing with them.
15 And immediately, when 15 [a]Mark 14:33; 16:5, 6
the entire crowd saw Him, they
were [a]amazed, and *began* running
up to greet Him.
16 And He asked them,
"What are you discussing with
them?"
17 And one of the crowd answered Him, "Teacher, I brought
You my son, possessed with a
spirit which makes him mute;
18 and whenever it seizes
him, it dashes him *to the ground*
and he foams *at the mouth,* and
grinds his teeth, and stiffens out.

9:2 *six days later.* Luke 9:28 says "some eight days" which includes the beginning and ending days as well as the interval between of six full days. *up to a high mountain.* Either Mt. Tabor, 10 miles SW. of the Sea of Galilee, or Mt. Hermon, 40 miles NE. of the Sea of Galilee. *transfigured* = transformed.

9:4 *Elijah.* Elijah's return was expected (Mal. 4:5–6). *conversing with Jesus.* Luke tells what they were talking about (9:31).

9:5 *and let us make three tabernacles.* Booths of intertwined branches. Peter thought they would be there a while so they might as well get settled down! His suggestion also implied that he viewed Jesus, Moses, and Elijah as being equal. God's answer was to remove Moses and Elijah from view (v. 8) and to declare the uniqueness of His Son (v. 7).

9:10 *rising from the dead.* I.e., Christ's resurrection from the dead, not resurrection in general.

9:11–13 The progression of thought is this: If Elijah is to come before the last day and "restore the hearts" (Mal. 4:5–6), why should the Son of Man have to die? Christ replied that they are correct about Elijah but that their concept of the Son of Man was deficient, since it did not include the truths of His suffering and death (Ps. 22:6; Isa. 53). Then Christ adds (Mark 9:13) that Elijah already had come, and been unrecognized, in John the Baptist. See also the note on Matt. 17:11–12.

And I told Your disciples to cast it out, and they could not *do it.*"

19 And He *answered them and *said, "O unbelieving generation, how long shall I be with you? How long shall I put up with you? Bring him to Me!"

20 And they brought the boy to Him. And when he saw Him, immediately the spirit threw him into a convulsion, and falling to the ground, he *began* rolling about and foaming *at the mouth.*

21 And He asked his father, "How long has this been happening to him?" And he said, "From childhood.

22 "And it has often thrown him both into the fire and into the water to destroy him. But if You can do anything, take pity on us and help us!"

★23 aMatt. 17:20; John 11:40 **23** And Jesus said to him, " 'If You can!' [a]All things are possible to him who believes."

★24 **24** Immediately the boy's father cried out and *began* saying, "I do believe; help my unbelief."

25 aMark 9:15 **25** And when Jesus saw that [a]a crowd was rapidly gathering, He rebuked the unclean spirit, saying to it, "You deaf and dumb spirit, I command you, come out of him and do not enter him again."

26 And after crying out and throwing him into terrible convulsions, it came out; and *the boy* became so much like a corpse that most *of them* said, "He is dead!"

27 But Jesus took him by the hand and raised him; and he got up.

28 aMark 2:1; 7:17 **28** And when He had come [a]into *the* house, His disciples *began* questioning Him privately, "Why is it that we could not cast it out?"

★29 **29** And He said to them, "This kind cannot come out by anything but prayer."

2 *Of His death,* 9:30-32

30 [a]And from there they went out and *began* to go through Galilee, and He was unwilling for anyone to know *about it.* 30 aMark 9:30-32; *Matt. 17:22-23; Luke 9:43-45*

31 For He was teaching His disciples and telling them, "[a]The Son of Man is to be delivered up into the hands of men, and they will kill Him; and when He has been killed, He will rise again three days later." ★31 aMatt. 16:21; Mark 8:31; 9:12

32 But [a]they did not understand *this* statement, and they were afraid to ask Him. ★32 aLuke 2:50; 9:45; 18:34; John 12:16

3 *Of rewards,* 9:33-41

33 [a]And they came to Capernaum; and when He was in [b]the house, He *began* to question them, "What were you discussing on the way?" 33 aMark 9:33-37; *Matt. [17:24] 18:1-5; Luke 9:46-48* bMark 3:19

34 But they kept silent, for on the way [a]they had discussed with one another which *of them was* the greatest. 34 aMark 9:50; Luke 22:24

35 And sitting down, He called the twelve and *said to them, "[a]If any one wants to be first, he shall be last of all, and servant of all." 35 aMatt. 20:26

36 And taking a child, He stood him in the midst of them; and taking him in His arms, He said to them,

37 "[a]Whoever receives one child like this in My name is receiving Me; and whoever receives Me is not receiving Me, but Him who sent Me." 37 aMatt. 10:40

38 [a]John said to Him, "Teacher, we saw someone casting out demons in Your name, and [b]we tried to hinder him because he was not following us." 38 aMark 9:38-40; *Luke 9:49-50* bNum. 11:27-29

39 But Jesus said, "Do not hinder him, for there is no one who shall perform a miracle in

---

9:23 *All things are possible.* See note on Matt. 17:20.

9:24 *help my unbelief.* The man cried for help for his own weak faith.

9:29 *This kind.* I.e., this kind of demon can be conquered only by prayer. Some manuscripts add the words, "and fasting."

9:31 *they will kill Him.* The second prediction of His death (see 8:31; 10:33-34).

9:32 *and they were afraid to ask Him.* Perhaps because of the rebuke to Peter (8:32-33).

My name, and be able soon afterward to speak evil of Me.

40 [a]Matt. 12:30
40 "[a]For he who is not against us is for us.

41 [a]Matt. 10:42
41 "For [a]whoever gives you a cup of water to drink because of your name as *followers* of Christ, truly I say to you, he shall not lose his reward.

4 *Of hell,* 9:42–50

★42 [a]Matt. 18:6; Luke 17:2; 1 Cor. 8:12
42 "And [a]whoever causes one of these little ones who believe to stumble, it would be better for him if, with a heavy millstone hung around his neck, he had been cast into the sea.

43 [a]Matt. 5:30; 17:27; 18:8 [b]Matt. 5:22 [c]Matt. 3:12; 25:41
43 "And [a]if your hand causes you to stumble, cut it off; it is better for you to enter life crippled, than having your two hands, to go into [b]hell, into the [c]unquenchable fire,

★44
44 [where THEIR WORM DOES NOT DIE, AND THE FIRE IS NOT QUENCHED.]

45 [a]Matt. 5:22
45 "And if your foot causes you to stumble, cut it off; it is better for you to enter life lame, than having your two feet, to be cast into [a]hell,

46 [where THEIR WORM DOES NOT DIE, AND THE FIRE IS NOT QUENCHED.]

47 [a]Matt. 5:29; 17:27; 18:9 [b]Matt. 5:22
47 "And [a]if your eye causes you to stumble, cast it out; it is better for you to enter the kingdom of God with one eye, than having two eyes, to be cast into [b]hell,

48 [a]Is. 66:24 [b]Matt. 3:12; 25:41
48 [a]where THEIR WORM DOES NOT DIE, AND [b]THE FIRE IS NOT QUENCHED.

★49
49 "For everyone will be salted with fire.

★50 [a]Matt. 5:13; Luke 14:34f. [b]Col. 4:6 [c]Mark 9:34; Rom. 12:18; 2 Cor. 13:11; 1 Thess. 5:13
50 "Salt is good; but [a]if the salt becomes unsalty, with what will you make it salty *again?* [b]Have salt in yourselves, and [c]be at peace with one another."

H His Preaching in Perea, 10:1–52

1 *Concerning divorce,* 10:1–12

1 [a]Mark 10:1-12; Matt. 19:1-9 [b]Matt. 4:23; 26:55; Mark 1:21; 2:13; 4:2; 6:2, 6, 34; 12:35; 14:49
10 [a]And rising up, He *went from there to the region of Judea, and beyond the Jordan; and crowds *gathered around Him again, and, [b]according to His custom, He once more *began* to teach them.

2 And *some* Pharisees came up to Him, testing Him, and *began* to question Him whether it was lawful for a man to divorce a wife.

3 And He answered and said to them, "What did Moses command you?"

4 [a]Deut. 24:1, 3
4 And they said, "[a]Moses permitted *a man* to write a certificate of divorce and send *her* away."

5 [a]Matt. 19:8
5 But Jesus said to them, "[a]Because of your hardness of heart he wrote you this commandment.

★6 [a]Mark 13:19; 2 Pet. 3:4 [b]Gen. 1:27; 5:2
6 "But [a]from the beginning of creation, *God* [b]MADE THEM MALE AND FEMALE.

7 [a]Gen. 2:24
7 "[a]FOR THIS CAUSE A MAN SHALL LEAVE HIS FATHER AND MOTHER,

8 [a]Gen. 2:24
8 [a]AND THE TWO SHALL BECOME ONE FLESH; consequently they are no longer two, but one flesh.

9 "What therefore God has joined together, let no man separate."

10 And in the house the disciples *began* questioning Him about this again.

★11 [a]Matt. 5:32
11 And He *said to them, "[a]Whoever divorces his wife and marries another woman commits adultery against her;

9:42 *causes . . . to stumble.* I.e., causes to fall into sin. So also in vv. 43, 45, 47.

9:44 Many manuscripts do not contain verses 44 and 46, which are identical to verse 48.

9:49 *salted with fire.* Just as salt preserves, everyone who enters hell will be preserved through an eternity of torment.

9:50 *Have salt in yourselves.* Christ's followers are to be permeated with this preserving power, which influences the world for good.

10:6 *male and female.* See Gen. 2:21–25; it presupposes and enjoins monogamy. The Mosaic law concerning divorce was a concession to the people, not a part of God's original purpose.

10:11–12 See notes on Matt. 5:32 and 19:4–5.

12 a1 Cor. 7:11, 13

12 and [a]if she herself divorces her husband and marries another man, she is committing adultery."

2 Concerning children, 10:13–16

13 aMark 10:13-16; *Matt. 19:13-15; Luke 18:15-17*

13 [a]And they *began* bringing children to Him, so that He might touch them; and the disciples rebuked them.

★14 aMatt. 5:3

14 But when Jesus saw this, He was indignant and said to them, "Permit the children to come to Me; do not hinder them; [a]for the kingdom of God belongs to such as these.

15 aMatt. 18:3; 19:14; Luke 18:17; 1 Cor. 14:20; 1 Pet. 2:2

15 "Truly I say to you, [a]whoever does not receive the kingdom of God like a child shall not enter it *at all.*"

16 aMark 9:36

16 And He [a]took them in His arms and *began* blessing them, laying His hands upon them.

3 Concerning eternal life, 10:17–31

17 aMark 10:17-31; *Matt. 19:16-30; Luke 18:18-30* bMark 1:40 cMatt. 25:34; Luke 10:25; 18:18; Acts 20:32; Eph. 1:18; 1 Pet. 1:4

17 [a]And as He was setting out on a journey, a man ran up to Him and [b]knelt before Him, and *began* asking Him, "Good Teacher, what shall I do to [c]inherit eternal life?"

★18

18 And Jesus said to him, "Why do you call Me good? No one is good except God alone.

19 aEx. 20:12-16; Deut. 5:16-20

19 "You know the commandments, '[a]DO NOT MURDER, DO NOT COMMIT ADULTERY, DO NOT STEAL, DO NOT BEAR FALSE WITNESS, Do not defraud, HONOR YOUR FATHER AND MOTHER.' "

20 aMatt. 19:20

20 And he said to Him, "Teacher, I have kept [a]all these things from my youth up."

★21 aMatt. 6:20

21 And looking at him, Jesus felt a love for him, and said to him, "One thing you lack: go and sell all you possess, and give *it* to the poor, and you shall have [a]treasure in heaven; and come, follow Me."

22 But at these words his face fell, and he went away grieved, for he was one who owned much property.

23 aMatt. 19:23

23 And Jesus, looking around, *said to His disciples, "[a]How hard it will be for those who are wealthy to enter the kingdom of God!"

24 aMark 1:27

24 And the disciples [a]were amazed at His words. But Jesus *answered again and *said to them, "Children, how hard it is to enter the kingdom of God!

★25 aMatt. 19:24

25 "[a]It is easier for a camel to go through the eye of a needle than for a rich man to enter the kingdom of God."

26 And they were even more astonished and said to Him, "Then who can be saved?"

★27 aMatt. 19:26

27 Looking upon them, Jesus *said, "[a]With men it is impossible, but not with God; for all things are possible with God."

28 aMatt. 4:20-22

28 [a]Peter began to say to Him, "Behold, we have left everything and followed You."

29 aMatt. 6:33; 19:29; Luke 18:29f.

29 Jesus said, "Truly I say to you, [a]there is no one who has left house or brothers or sisters or mother or father or children or farms, for My sake and for the gospel's sake,

30 aMatt. 12:32

30 but that he shall receive a hundred times as much now in the present age, houses and brothers and sisters and mothers and children and farms, along with persecutions; and in [a]the world to come, eternal life.

31 aMatt. 19:30

31 "But [a]many *who are* first, will be last; and the last, first."

10:14 *the kingdom of God belongs to such as these.* In order to enter the kingdom we must come to Christ in childlike faith.

10:18 *Why do you call Me good?* "Good" was a designation reserved, in the absolute sense, for God. Jesus was reacting to being addressed thus by someone who had no awareness of His divine nature.

10:21 Christ was trying to show the man that, in reality, his love of money violated the law and made him a sinner.

10:25 *eye of a needle.* See note on Matt. 19:24.

10:27 *all things are possible with God.* Also taught in the O.T. (Gen. 18:14; Job 42:2).

4 *Concerning His own death and resurrection,* 10:32–34

★32 [a]Mark 10:32-34; Matt 20:17-19; Luke 18:31-33 [b]Mark 1:27

32 [a]And they were on the road, going up to Jerusalem, and Jesus was walking on ahead of them; and they [b]were amazed, and those who followed were fearful. And again He took the twelve aside and began to tell them what was going to happen to Him,

★33 [a]Mark 8:31; 9:12

33 *saying,* "Behold, we are going up to Jerusalem, and [a]the Son of Man will be delivered up to the chief priests and the scribes; and they will condemn Him to death, and will deliver Him up to the Gentiles.

34 [a]Matt 16:21; 26:67; 27:30; Mark 9:31; 14:65

34 "And they will mock Him and [a]spit upon Him, and scourge Him, and kill *Him,* and three days later He will rise again."

5 *Concerning ambition,* 10:35–45

35 [a]Mark 10:35-45; Matt 20:20-28

35 [a]And James and John, the two sons of Zebedee, *came up to Him, saying to Him, "Teacher, we want You to do for us whatever we ask of You."

36 And He said to them, "What do you want Me to do for you?"

★37 [a]Matt 19:28

37 And they said to Him, "Grant that we [a]may sit in Your glory, one on Your right, and one on *Your* left."

★38 [a]Matt 20:22 [b]Luke 12:50

38 But Jesus said to them, "You do not know what you are asking for. Are you able [a]to drink the cup that I drink, or [b]to be baptized with the baptism with which I am baptized?"

★39 [a]Acts 12:2; Rev 1:9

39 And they said to Him, "We are able." And Jesus said to them, "The cup that I drink [a]you shall drink; and you shall be baptized with the baptism with which I am baptized.

40 [a]Matt 13:11

40 "But to sit on My right or on *My* left, this is not Mine to give; [a]but *it is for those* for whom it has been prepared."

41 [a]Mark 10:42-45; Luke 22:25-27

41 [a]And hearing this, the ten began to feel indignant toward James and John.

42 And calling them to Himself, Jesus *said to them, "You know that those who are recognized as rulers of the Gentiles lord it over them; and their great men exercise authority over them.

43 [a]Matt 20:26; Mark 9:35

43 "But it is not so among you, [a]but whoever wishes to become great among you shall be your servant;

44 and whoever wishes to be first among you shall be slave of all.

45 [a]Matt 20:28

45 "For even the Son of Man [a]did not come to be served, but to serve, and to give His life a ransom for many."

6 *To blind Bartimaeus,* 10:46–52

★46 [a]Mark 10:46-52; Matt 20:29-34; Luke 18:35-43 [b]Luke 18:35; 19:1

46 [a]And they *came to Jericho. And [b]as He was going out from Jericho with His disciples and a great multitude, a blind beggar *named* Bartimaeus, the son of Timaeus, was sitting by the road.

47 [a]Mark 1:24 [b]Matt 9:27

47 And when he heard that it was Jesus the [a]Nazarene, he began to cry out and say, "Jesus, [b]Son of David, have mercy on me!"

48 [a]Matt 9:27

48 And many were sternly telling him to be quiet, but he *began* crying out all the more, "[a]Son of David, have mercy on me!"

10:32 *going up.* Jerusalem is over 2500 feet above sea level. Their probable route was down the Jordan Valley, below sea level, then up to Jerusalem. *amazed.* At Jesus' determination to go on to Jerusalem.

10:33–34 The third prediction of His death (see 8:31; 9:31).

10:37 *in Your glory.* I.e., in the Messianic kingdom (see Matt. 20:21).

10:38 *the cup . . . the baptism.* Figures of speech for Christ's coming sufferings (see Mark 14:36 and Luke 12:50).

10:39 James did die as a martyr (Acts 12:2) and John suffered exile (Rev. 1:9).

10:46–52 For a comparison of the different accounts of this miracle, see the note on Matt. 20:29–34.

49 [a]Matt. 9:2

49 And Jesus stopped and said, "Call him *here.*" And they *called the blind man, saying to him, "[a]Take courage, arise! He is calling for you."

50 And casting aside his cloak, he jumped up, and came to Jesus.

51 [a]Matt. 23:7; John 20:16

51 And answering him, Jesus said, "What do you want Me to do for you?" And the blind man said to Him, "[a]Rabboni, *I want* to regain my sight!"

★52 [a]Matt. 9:22

52 And Jesus said to him, "Go your way; [a]your faith has made you well." And immediately he received his sight and *began* following Him on the road.

II THE SACRIFICE OF THE SERVANT, 11:1–15:47

A Triumphal Entry into Jerusalem on Sunday, 11:1–11

1 [a]Mark 11:1-10; Matt. 21:1-9; Luke 19:29-38 [b]Matt. 21:17 [c]Matt. 21:1

11 [a]And as they *approached Jerusalem, at Bethphage and [b]Bethany, near [c]the Mount of Olives, He *sent two of His disciples,

★ 2

2 and *said to them, "Go into the village opposite you, and immediately as you enter it, you will find a colt tied *there,* on which no one yet has ever sat; untie it and bring it *here.*

3 "And if anyone says to you, 'Why are you doing this?' you say, 'The Lord has need of it;' and immediately he will send it back here."

4 And they went away and found a colt tied at the door outside in the street; and they *untied it.

5 And some of the bystanders were saying to them, "What are you doing, untying the colt?"

6 And they spoke to them just as Jesus had told *them,* and they gave them permission.

7 [a]Mark 11:7-10; John 12:12-15

7 [a]And they *brought the colt to Jesus and put their garments on it; and He sat upon it.

8 And many spread their garments in the road, and others *spread* leafy branches which they had cut from the fields.

★ 9 [a]Ps. 118:26; Matt. 21:9

9 And those who went before, and those who followed after, were crying out,

"[a]HOSANNA!
BLESSED IS HE WHO COMES IN THE NAME OF THE LORD;

★10 [a]Matt. 21:9

10 Blessed *is* the coming kingdom of our father David;
HOSANNA [a]in the highest!"

11 [a]Matt. 21:12 [b]Matt. 21:17

11 And [a]He entered Jerusalem *and came* into the temple; and after looking all around, [b]He departed for Bethany with the twelve, since it was already late.

B Cursing of the Fig Tree and Cleansing of the Temple on Monday, 11:12–19

12 [a]Mark 11:12-14 [20-24]; Matt. 21:18-22

12 [a]And on the next day, when they had departed from Bethany, He became hungry.

★13

13 And seeing at a distance a fig tree in leaf, He went *to see* if perhaps He would find anything on it; and when He came to it, He found nothing but leaves, for it was not the season for figs.

14 And He answered and said to it, "May no one ever eat fruit from you again!" And His disciples were listening.

★15 [a]Mark 11:15-18; Matt. 21:12-16; Luke 19:45-47; John 2:13-16

15 [a]And they *came to Jerusalem. And He entered the temple and began to cast out those who were buying and selling in the temple, and overturned the

---

10:52 *your faith has made you well.* Cf. 5:34.

11:2 *the village opposite you.* Bethphage, on the S. side of the Mount of Olives.

11:9 *Hosanna* = Save now! This occasion was the fulfillment of Zech. 9:9. In a few days the same crowd who now hailed Him would desert Him.

11:10 *kingdom of our father David.* I.e., the Messianic kingdom.

11:13 *fig tree.* See note on Matt. 21:19.

11:15 *cast out those who were buying and selling.* This is the second time Christ purged the temple (see John 2:13-17, the beginning of His ministry). The animals, guaranteed to be without blemish, were sold for sacrificial purposes,

tables of the moneychangers and
the seats of those who were selling doves;

16 and He would not permit
anyone to carry goods through
the temple.

★17 [a]Is. 56:7 [b]Jer. 7:11 **17** And He *began* to teach
and say to them, "Is it not written,
'[a]MY HOUSE SHALL BE CALLED A
HOUSE OF PRAYER FOR ALL THE NA-
TIONS'? [b]But you have made it a
robbers' den."

18 [a]Matt. 21:46; Mark 12:12; Luke 20:19; John 7:1 [b]Matt. 7:28 **18** And the chief priests and
the scribes heard *this,* and [a]*began*
seeking how to destroy Him; for
they were afraid of Him, for [b]all
the multitude was astonished at
His teaching.

19 [a]Matt. 21:17; Mark 11:11; Luke 21:37 **19** And [a]whenever evening
came, they would go out of the
city.

C Teaching on Tuesday, 11:20–13:37

1 *Concerning faith,* 11:20–26

20 [a]Mark 11:20-24 [Mark 11:12-14]; *Matt. 21:19-22* **20** [a]And as they were passing
by in the morning, they saw the
fig tree withered from the roots
up.

21 [a]Matt. 23:7 **21** And being reminded, Peter
*said to Him, "[a]Rabbi, behold,
the fig tree which You cursed has
withered."

22 [a]Matt. 17:20; 21:21f. **22** And Jesus *answered saying to them, "[a]Have faith in God.

23 "Truly I say to you, whoever says to this mountain, 'Be
taken up and cast into the sea,'
and does not doubt in his heart,
but believes that what he says is
going to happen, it shall be
granted him.

★24 [a]Matt. 7:7f. **24** "Therefore I say to you, [a]all
things for which you pray and
ask, believe that you have received them, and they shall be
granted you.

25 "And whenever you [a]stand ★25 [a]Matt. 6:5 [b]Matt. 6:14
praying, [b]forgive, if you have
anything against anyone; so that
your Father also who is in heaven
may forgive you your transgressions.

26 ["[a]But if you do not for- ★26 [a]Matt. 6:15; 18:35
give, neither will your Father who
is in heaven forgive your transgressions."]

2 *Concerning His authority,* 11:27–33

27 And they *came again to 27 [a]Mark 11:27-33; *Matt. 21:23-27; Luke 20:1-8*
Jerusalem. [a]And as He was walk-
ing in the temple, the chief
priests, and scribes, and elders
*came to Him,

28 and *began* saying to Him, ★28
"By what authority are You doing
these things, or who gave You
this authority to do these things?"

29 And Jesus said to them, "I
will ask you one question, and
you answer Me, and *then* I will
tell you by what authority I do
these things.

30 "Was the baptism of John ★30
from heaven, or from men? Answer Me."

31 And they *began* reasoning
with one another, saying, "If we
say, 'From heaven,' He will say,
'Then why did you not believe
him?'

32 "But shall we say, 'From
men'?" —they were afraid of the
multitude, for all considered John
to have been a prophet indeed.

33 And answering Jesus, they
*said, "We do not know." And
Jesus *said to them, "Neither will
I tell you by what authority I do
these things."

---

and Greek and Roman coinage was changed into the standard half-shekel required for the temple tax. The merchants were guilty of profanation of the temple and of excess profiteering.

11:17 See Isa. 56:7 and Jer. 7:11.

11:24 *all things for which you pray.* This principle is qualified by Christ in other teaching (Matt. 6:10) and in His own life (Mark 14:36).

11:25 *stand praying.* In ancient worship this was the normal position of prayer.

11:26 Many manuscripts do not contain this verse.

11:28 *these things.* I.e., the cleansing of the temple (vv. 15–18).

11:30 *Answer Me.* Christ placed these Jewish leaders on the horns of a dilemma. Whichever answer they gave would have condemned them.

3 *Concerning the Jewish nation,* 12:1-12

★ 1 [a]Mark 3:23; 4:2ff. [b]Mark 12:1-12; *Matt. 21:33-46; Luke 20:9-19* [c]Is. 5:2

12 [a]And He began to speak to them in parables: "[b]A man [c]PLANTED A VINEYARD, AND PUT A WALL AROUND IT, AND DUG A VAT UNDER THE WINE PRESS, AND BUILT A TOWER, and rented it out to vine-growers and went on a journey.

2 "And at the *harvest* time he sent a slave to the vine-growers, in order to receive *some* of the produce of the vineyard from the vine-growers.

3 "And they took him, and beat him, and sent him away empty-handed.

4 "And again he sent them another slave, and they wounded him in the head, and treated him shamefully.

5 "And he sent another, and that one they killed; and *so with* many others, beating some, and killing others.

6 "He had one more *to send,* a beloved son; he sent him last *of all* to them, saying, 'They will respect my son.'

7 "But those vine-growers said to one another, 'This is the heir; come, let us kill him, and the inheritance will be ours!'

8 "And they took him, and killed him, and threw him out of the vineyard.

9 "What will the owner of the vineyard do? He will come and destroy the vine-growers, and will give the vineyard to others.

★10 [a]Ps. 118:22

10 "Have you not even read this scripture:

'[a]THE STONE WHICH THE BUILDERS REJECTED,
THIS BECAME THE CHIEF CORNER *stone;*

11 [a]THIS CAME ABOUT FROM THE LORD,
AND IT IS MARVELOUS IN OUR EYES'?"

11 [a]Ps. 118:23

12 And [a]they were seeking to seize Him; and *yet* they feared the multitude; for they understood that He had spoken the parable against them. And *so* [b]they left Him, and went away.

12 [a]Mark 11:18 [b]Matt. 22:22

4 *Concerning taxes,* 12:13-17

13 [a]And they *sent some of the Pharisees and [b]Herodians to Him, in order to [c]trap Him in a statement.

13 [a]Mark 12:13-17; *Matt. 22:15-22; Luke 20:20-26* [b]Matt. 22:16 [c]Luke 11:54

14 And they *came and *said to Him, "Teacher, we know that You are truthful, and defer to no one; for You are not partial to any, but teach the way of God in truth. Is it lawful to pay a poll-tax to Caesar, or not?

★14

15 "Shall we pay, or shall we not pay?" But He, knowing their hypocrisy, said to them, "Why are you testing Me? Bring Me a denarius to look at."

★15

16 And they brought *one.* And He *said to them, "Whose likeness and inscription is this?" And they said to Him, "Caesar's."

17 And Jesus said to them, "[a]Render to Caesar the things that are Caesar's, and to God the things that are God's." And they were amazed at Him.

17 [a]Matt. 22:21

5 *Concerning resurrection,* 12:18-27

18 [a]And *some* Sadducees (who say that there is no resurrection) *came to Him, and *began* questioning Him, saying,

★18 [a]Mark 12:18-27; *Matt. 22:23-33; Luke 20:27-38*

12:1-12 This parable, addressed to the obdurate religious leaders of Israel, illustrates God's dealings with that people. The man (v. 1) is God. The vineyard (v. 1) is Israel. The servants (vv. 2-5) are the O.T. prophets and John the Baptist. The son whom they killed is Jesus (vv. 6-8). The prediction of the destruction of the vine-growers (v. 9) was fulfilled when Jerusalem was destroyed in A.D. 70.

12:10 *The stone.* See Ps. 118:22-23 and the use of the cornerstone figure in Acts 4:11; 1 Pet. 2:6-7.

12:14 *defer to no one.* I.e., you're no flatterer, you play up to no one. Yet their own opening remark employs flattery. *poll-tax to Caesar.* See note on Matt. 22:17.

12:15 *a denarius.* See note on Mark 6:37.

12:18 *Sadducees.* See note on Matt. 3:7.

★19 [a]Deut. **19** "Teacher, Moses wrote for
25:5 us *a law* that [a]IF A MAN'S BROTHER
DIES, and leaves behind a wife,
AND LEAVES NO CHILD, HIS BROTHER
SHOULD TAKE THE WIFE, AND RAISE UP
OFFSPRING TO HIS BROTHER.
20 "There were seven brothers; and the first one took a wife,
and died, leaving no offspring.
21 "And the second one took
her, and died, leaving behind no
offspring; and the third likewise;
22 and *so* all seven left no offspring. Last of all the woman died
too.
23 "In the resurrection, when
they rise again, which one's wife
will she be? For all seven had her
as wife."
24 Jesus said to them, "Is this
not the reason you are mistaken,
that you do not understand the
Scriptures, or the power of God?
★25 **25** "For when they rise from
the dead, they neither marry, nor
are given in marriage, but are like
angels in heaven.
★26 [a]Luke 20:37; Rom. 11:2 [b]Ex. 3:6 **26** "But regarding the fact that
the dead rise again, have you not
read in the book of Moses, [a]in the
passage about the burning bush,
how God spoke to him, saying, '[b]I
AM THE GOD OF ABRAHAM, AND THE
GOD OF ISAAC, AND THE GOD OF JA-
COB'?
27 [a]Matt. 22:32; Luke 20:38 **27** "[a]He is not *the* God of *the*
dead, but of *the* living; you are
greatly mistaken."

6 *Concerning the greatest commandments,* 12:28–34

28 [a]Mark 12:28-34; *Matt. 22:34-40;* Luke 10:25-28; 20:39f. [b]Matt. 22:34; Luke 20:39 **28** [a]And one of the scribes
came and heard them arguing,
and [b]recognizing that He had answered them well, asked Him,
"What commandment is the foremost of all?"
29 Jesus answered, "The fore- ★29 [a]Deut. 6:4
most is, '[a]HEAR, O ISRAEL; THE
LORD OUR GOD IS ONE LORD;
30 [a]AND YOU SHALL LOVE THE 30 [a]Deut. 6:5
LORD YOUR GOD WITH ALL YOUR
HEART, AND WITH ALL YOUR SOUL, AND
WITH ALL YOUR MIND, AND WITH ALL
YOUR STRENGTH.'
31 "The second is this, '[a]YOU ★31 [a]Lev. 19:18
SHALL LOVE YOUR NEIGHBOR AS YOUR-
SELF.' There is no other command-
ment greater than these."
32 And the scribe said to 32 [a]Deut. 4:35
Him, "Right, Teacher, You have
truly stated that [a]HE IS ONE; AND
THERE IS NO ONE ELSE BESIDES HIM;
33 [a]AND TO LOVE HIM WITH ALL ★33 [a]Deut. 6:5 [b]1 Sam. 15:22; Hos. 6:6; Mic. 6:6-8; Matt. 9:13; 12:7
THE HEART AND WITH ALL THE UNDER-
STANDING AND WITH ALL THE
STRENGTH, AND TO LOVE ONE'S NEIGH-
BOR AS HIMSELF, [b]is much more
than all burnt offerings and sacrifices."
34 And when Jesus saw that 34 [a]Matt. 22:46
he had answered intelligently, He
said to him, "You are not far from
the kingdom of God." [a]And after
that, no one would venture to ask
Him any more questions.

7 *Concerning His deity,* 12:35–37

35 [a]And Jesus answering *be-* ★35 [a]Mark 12:35-37; *Matt. 22:41-46;* Luke *20:41-44* [b]Matt. 26:55; Mark 10:1 [c]Matt. 9:27
gan to say, as He [b]taught in the
temple, "How *is it that* the scribes
say that the Christ is the [c]son of
David?
36 "David himself said in the 36 [a]Ps. 110:1
Holy Spirit,

'[a]THE LORD SAID TO MY LORD,
"SIT AT MY RIGHT HAND,
UNTIL I PUT THINE ENEMIES
BENEATH THY FEET." '

37 "David himself calls Him 37 [a]John 12:9
'Lord'; and *so* in what sense is He
his son?" And [a]the great crowd
enjoyed listening to Him.

12:19 See Deut. 25:5.
12:25 *like angels.* In the resurrection state there will be no conjugal union nor reproduction of children.
12:26 See Ex. 3:6. When God spoke to Moses, He was still associated with the patriarchs, though they had died many years before. Thus there is life after death.
12:29 See Deut. 6:4.
12:31 See Lev. 19:18.
12:33 So taught the prophets (Isa. 1:11–17; Mic. 6:6–8).
12:35 See note on Matt. 22:44.

8 Concerning pride, 12:38–40

★38 [a]Mark 12:38-40; *Matt. 23:1-7; Luke 20:45-47* [b]Matt. 23:6; Luke 11:43

38 [a]And in His teaching He was saying: "Beware of the scribes who like to walk around in long robes, and *like* [b]respectful greetings in the market places,

★39

39 and chief seats in the synagogues, and places of honor at banquets.

★40 [a]Luke 20:47

40 "[a]They *are* the ones who devour widows' houses, and for appearance's sake offer long prayers; these will receive greater condemnation."

9 Concerning giving, 12:41–44

★41 [a]Mark 12:41-44; *Luke 21:1-4* [b]John 8:20 [c]2 Kin. 12:9

41 [a]And He sat down opposite [b]the treasury, and *began* observing how the multitude were [c]putting money into the treasury; and many rich people were putting in large sums.

★42

42 And a poor widow came and put in two small copper coins, which amount to a cent.

43 And calling His disciples to Him, He said to them, "Truly I say to you, this poor widow put in more than all the contributors to the treasury;

44 [a]Luke 8:43; 15:12, 30; 21:4

44 for they all put in out of their surplus, but she, out of her poverty, put in all she owned, all she had [a]to live on."

10 Concerning the future, 13:1–37

★1 [a]Mark 13:1-37; *Matt. 24; Luke 21:5-36*

13 [a]And as He was going out of the temple, one of His disciples *said to Him, "Teacher, behold what wonderful stones and what wonderful buildings!"

2 [a]Luke 19:44

2 And Jesus said to him, "Do you see these great buildings? [a]Not one stone shall be left upon another which will not be torn down."

3 [a]Matt. 21:1 [b]Matt. 17:1

3 And as He was sitting on [a]the Mount of Olives opposite the temple, [b]Peter and James and John and Andrew were questioning Him privately,

★4

4 "Tell us, when will these things be, and what *will be* the sign when all these things are going to be fulfilled?"

5 And Jesus began to say to them, "See to it that no one misleads you.

6 [a]John 8:24

6 "Many will come in My name, saying, '[a]I am *He!*' and will mislead many.

7 "And when you hear of wars and rumors of wars, do not be frightened; *those things* must take place; but *that is* not yet the end.

8 "For nation will arise against nation, and kingdom against kingdom; there will be earthquakes in various places; there will *also* be famines. These things are *merely* the beginning of birth pangs.

★9 [a]Matt. 10:17 [b]Matt. 10:17

9 "But be on your guard; for they will [a]deliver you up to *the* courts, and you will be flogged [b]in *the* synagogues, and you will stand before governors and kings for My sake, as a testimony to them.

10 [a]Matt. 24:14

10 "[a]And the gospel must first be preached to all the nations.

★11 [a]Mark 13:11-13; *Matt. 10:19-22; Luke 21:12-17*

11 "[a]And when they arrest you and deliver you up, do not be anxious beforehand about what

---

12:38 *long robes.* The long flowing robe of a dignitary or wealthy man.

12:39 *chief seats.* Seats in the front row.

12:40 *devour widows' houses.* See note on Matt. 23:14.

12:41 *treasury.* A chest located in the temple area, designed to receive coins dropped in a spout.

12:42 *two small copper coins.* The smallest of copper coins, worth very little.

13:1 See note on Matt. 24:1.

13:4 *when will these things be?* There is a double perspective in Christ's answer: some of the events described were to be fulfilled in the destruction of Jerusalem in A.D. 70 and some are yet to be fulfilled during the tribulation days that precede His second coming.

13:9 *synagogues.* They were used as places of assembly and as courtrooms. Floggings were therefore administered in them (2 Cor. 11:24). These predictions began to be fulfilled in the book of Acts (see Acts 4:5ff.; 5:27ff.; 12:1ff.; 24:1ff.; 25:1ff.).

13:11 *deliver you up.* I.e., denounce you to the authorities.

you are to say, but say whatever
is given you in that hour; for it is
not you who speak, but *it is* the
Holy Spirit.
12 "And brother will deliver
up brother to death, and a father
his child; and children will rise up
against parents and cause them to
be put to death.
★13 [a]John 15:21 13 "And [a]you will be hated by
all on account of My name, but it
is the one who has endured to the
end who will be saved.
★14 [a]Matt. 24:15 [b]Dan. 9:27; 11:31; 12:11 14 "But [a]when you see the [b]A-
BOMINATION OF DESOLATION standing
where it should not be (let the
reader understand), then let those
who are in Judea flee to the
mountains.
15 "And let him who is on the
housetop not go down, or enter
in, to get anything out of his
house;
16 and let him who is in the
field not turn back to get his
cloak.
17 "But woe to those who are
with child and to those who nurse
babes in those days!
18 "But pray that it may not
happen in the winter.
19 [a]Mark 10:6 19 "For those days will be a
time of tribulation such as has not
occurred [a]since the beginning of
the creation which God created,
until now, and never shall.
★20 20 "And unless the Lord had
shortened *those* days, no life
would have been saved; but for
the sake of the elect whom He
chose, He shortened the days.
21 "And then if anyone says to
you, 'Behold, here is the Christ';
or, 'Behold, *He is* there'; do not
believe *him;*
22 [a]Matt. 7:15 [b]Matt. 24:24; John 4:48 22 for false Christs and [a]false
prophets will arise, and will show
[b]signs and [b]wonders, in order, if
possible, to lead the elect astray.
23 "But take heed; behold, I ★23
have told you everything in advance.
24 "But in those days, after 24 [a]Is. 13:10
that tribulation, [a]THE SUN WILL BE
DARKENED, AND THE MOON WILL NOT
GIVE ITS LIGHT,
25 [a]AND THE STARS WILL BE FALL- 25 [a]Is. 34:4
ING from heaven, and the powers
that are in the heavens will be
shaken.
26 "[a]And then they shall see 26 [a]Dan. 7:13 [b]Matt. 16:27; Mark 8:38
the Son of Man [b]coming in clouds
with great power and glory.
27 "And then He will send 27 [a]Deut. 30:4 [b]Zech. 2:6
forth the angels, and [a]WILL GATHER
TOGETHER His elect FROM THE FOUR
WINDS, [b]FROM THE FARTHEST END of
the earth, TO THE FARTHEST END OF
HEAVEN.
28 "Now learn the parable ★28
from the fig tree: when its branch
has already become tender, and
puts forth its leaves, you know
that the summer is near.
29 "Even so you too, when you ★29
see these things happening, recognize that He is near, *right* at the
door.
30 "Truly I say to you, this ★30
generation will not pass away until all these things take place.
31 "Heaven and earth will pass
away, but My words will not pass
away.
32 "[a]But of that day or hour no ★32 [a]Matt. 24:36; Acts 1:7
one knows, not even the angels in
heaven, nor the Son, but the Father *alone.*
33 "Take heed, [a]keep on the ★33 [a]Eph. 6:18; Col. 4:2
alert; for you do not know when
the *appointed* time is.
34 "*It is* like a man, away on a
journey, *who* upon leaving his
house and putting his slaves in
charge, *assigning* to each one his

13:13 *endured.* I.e., remained loyal.
13:14 *abomination of desolation.* See note on Matt. 24:15.
13:20 *the elect.* The elect (saved) remnant of Israel during the tribulation days. At the second coming, these people will be restored to Palestine (v. 27).
13:23 The third warning to be prepared; the others are in v. 5 and v. 9.
13:28 *the parable.* I.e., the principle illustrated by the fig tree.
13:29 *He.* The Son of Man (v. 26).
13:30 *this generation.* See note on Matt. 24:34.
13:32 *nor the Son.* In His humanity, Jesus did not know. See note on Phil. 2:7 on the self-limitation of Christ.
13:33 The fourth and final warning of this chapter.

task, also commanded the doorkeeper to stay on the alert.

35 aMatt. 24:42; Mark 13:37 bMark 14:30 cMatt. 14:25; Mark 6:48

35 "Therefore, [a]be on the alert — for you do not know when the master of the house is coming, whether in the evening, at midnight, at [b]cockcrowing, or [c]in the morning—

36 aRom. 13:11

36 lest he come suddenly and find you [a]asleep.

37 aMatt. 24:42; Mark 13:35

37 "And what I say to you I say to all, '[a]Be on the alert!' "

D Anointing by Mary and Agreement to Betray by Judas, on Wednesday, 14:1–11

★ 1 aMark 14:1, 2: *Matt. 26:2-5; Luke 22:1, 2* bMark 14:12; John 11:55; 13:1 cMatt. 12:14

14 [a]Now *the feast of* [b]the Passover and Unleavened Bread was two days off; and the chief priests and the scribes [c]were seeking how to seize Him by stealth, and kill *Him;*

2 for they were saying, "Not during the festival, lest there be a riot of the people."

★ 3 aMark 14:3-9: *Matt. 26:6-13;* Luke 7:37-39; John 12:1-8 bMatt. 21:17 cMatt. 26:6f.; John 12:3

3 [a]And while He was in [b]Bethany at the home of Simon the leper, and reclining *at table,* there came a woman with an alabaster vial of [c]costly perfume of pure nard; *and* she broke the vial and poured it over His head.

★ 4

4 But some were indignantly *remarking* to one another, "For what purpose has this perfume been wasted?

★ 5

5 "For this perfume might have been sold for over three hundred denarii, and *the money* given to the poor." And they were scolding her.

6 But Jesus said, "Let her alone; why do you bother her? She has done a good deed to Me.

7 "For [a]the poor you always have with you, and whenever you wish, you can do them good; but you do not always have Me.

★ 7 aDeut. 15:11; Matt. 26:11; John 12:8

8 "She has done what she could; [a]she has anointed My body beforehand for the burial.

8 aJohn 19:40

9 "And truly I say to you, [a]wherever the gospel is preached in the whole world, that also which this woman has done shall be spoken of in memory of her."

9 aMatt. 26:13

10 [a]And Judas Iscariot, [b]who was one of the twelve, went off to the chief priests, in order to betray Him to them.

★10 aMark 14:10, 11: *Matt. 26:14-16; Luke 22:3-6* bJohn 6:71

11 And they were glad when they heard *this,* and promised to give him money. And he *began* seeking how to betray Him at an opportune time.

★11

E Supper and Betrayal on Thursday, 14:12–52

1 *Preparation for the Last Supper,* 14:12–16

12 [a]And on the first day of *the feast of* [b]Unleavened Bread, when the Passover *lamb* was being [c]sacrificed, His disciples *said to Him, "Where do You want us to go and prepare for You to eat the Passover?"

12 aMark 14:12-16: *Matt. 26:17-19; Luke 22:7-13* bMatt. 26:17 cDeut. 16:5; Mark 14:1; Luke 22:7; 1 Cor. 5:7

13 And He *sent two of His disciples, and *said to them, "Go into the city, and a man will meet you carrying a pitcher of water; follow him;

★13

14:1 *the feast of the Passover.* One of Israel's three great yearly festivals (the other two were Pentecost and Tabernacles), commemorating their deliverance from Egypt on the night when God "passed over" the homes of the Israelites during the slaughter of the firstborn. It was celebrated on the 14th of Nisan (March–April) and was followed immediately by the Feast of Unleavened Bread, which continued from the 15th to the 21st. See Ex. 12.

14:3 *a woman.* Mary of Bethany (John 12:3). *nard.* A costly aromatic anointing oil extracted from an East Indian plant.

14:4 *wasted.* Judas had instigated the murmuring (John 12:4–6).

14:5 *three hundred denarii.* In purchasing power equivalent to 300 days' wages for a rural worker.

14:7 *the poor.* See note on Matt. 26:11.

14:10–11 Judas' motive in betraying Jesus was, in part, avarice (Matt. 26:15), though it may also have been related to his bitterness at Jesus' failure to be a political Messiah. Basically, however, Judas' act was inspired by Satan (John 12:6; 13:2, 27).

14:11 *opportune time.* I.e., in the absence of the multitude (Luke 22:6).

14:13 *a man . . . carrying a pitcher of water.* Since women usually performed this task, they would easily notice a man carrying water.

14 [a]Luke 2:7; 22:11

14 and wherever he enters, say to the owner of the house, 'The Teacher says, "Where is My [a]guest room in which I may eat the Passover with My disciples?" '

15 "And he himself will show you a large upper room furnished *and* ready; and prepare for us there."

16 And the disciples went out, and came to the city, and found *it* just as He had told them; and they prepared the Passover.

2 *Partaking of the Last Supper,* 14:17–21

17 [a]Mark 14:17-21: *Matt. 26:20-24; Luke 22:14, 21-23;* John 13:18ff.

17 [a]And when it was evening He *came with the twelve.

18 And as they were reclining *at table* and eating, Jesus said, "Truly I say to you that one of you will betray Me—one who is eating with Me."

19 They began to be grieved and to say to Him one by one, "Surely not I?"

20 And He said to them, *"It is* one of the twelve, one who dips with Me in the bowl.

★21

21 "For the Son of Man *is to* go, just as it is written of Him; but woe to that man by whom the Son of Man is betrayed! *It would have been* good for that man if he had not been born."

3 *Institution of the Lord's Supper,* 14:22–25

22 [a]Mark 14:22-25: *Matt. 26:26-29; Luke 22:17-20; 1 Cor. 11:23-25;* Mark 10:16 [b]Matt. 14:19

22 [a]And while they were eating, He took *some* bread, and after a [b]blessing He broke *it;* and gave *it* to them, and said, "Take *it;* this is My body."

23 And He took a cup, and when He had given thanks, He gave *it* to them; and they all drank from it.

★24

24 And He said to them, "This is My blood of the covenant, which is *to be* shed on behalf of many.

★25

25 "Truly I say to you, I shall never again drink of the fruit of the vine until that day when I drink it new in the kingdom of God."

4 *Walk to Gethsemane,* 14:26–31

★26 [a]Matt. 26:30 [b]Matt. 21:1

26 [a]And after singing a hymn, they went out to [b]the Mount of Olives.

27 [a]Mark 14:27-31: *Matt. 26:31-35* [b]Zech. 13:7

27 [a]And Jesus *said to them, "You will all fall away, because it is written, '[b]I WILL STRIKE DOWN THE SHEPHERD, AND THE SHEEP SHALL BE SCATTERED.'

28 "But after I have been raised, I will go before you to Galilee."

29 But Peter said to Him, *"Even* though all may fall away, yet I will not."

30 [a]Matt. 26:34 [b]Mark 14:68, 72; John 13:38

30 And Jesus *said to him, "Truly I say to you, that you yourself [a]this very night, before [b]a cock crows twice, shall three times deny Me."

31 But *Peter* kept saying insistently, *"Even* if I have to die with You, I will not deny You!" And they all were saying the same thing, too.

5 *Prayer in Gethsemane,* 14:32–42

★32 [a]Mark 14:32-42: *Matt. 26:36-46; Luke 22:40-46*

32 [a]And they *came to a place named Gethsemane; and He *said to His disciples, "Sit here until I have prayed."

33 [a]Mark 9:15; 16:5, 6

33 And He *took with Him Peter and James and John, and began to be very [a]distressed and troubled.

34 [a]Matt. 26:38; John 12:27

34 And He *said to them, "[a]My soul is deeply grieved to the point of death; remain here and keep watch."

★35 [a]Matt. 26:45; Mark 14:41

35 And He went a little beyond *them,* and fell to the

14:21 See Ps. 22 and Isa. 53.
14:24 *the covenant.* See Introduction to the New Testament. *shed* = poured out.
14:25 *until that day.* See note on Matt. 26:29.
14:26 *a hymn.* This would have been a portion of Ps. 115–118, traditionally sung at this season.
14:32 *Gethsemane.* See note on Matt. 26:36.
14:35 *if it were possible.* I.e., in accordance with God's will.

ground, and *began* praying that if
it were possible, [a]the hour might
pass Him by.
★36 [a]Rom. 8:15; Gal. 4:6 [b]Matt. 26:39
36 And He was saying, "[a]Ab-
ba! Father! All things are possible
for Thee; remove this cup from
Me; [b]yet not what I will, but what
Thou wilt."
37 And He *came and *found
them sleeping, and *said to Peter,
"Simon, are you asleep? Could
you not keep watch for one hour?
38 [a]Matt. 26:41
38 "[a]Keep watching and praying, that you may not come into
temptation; the spirit is willing,
but the flesh is weak."
39 And again He went away
and prayed, saying the same
words.
40 And again He came and
found them sleeping, for their
eyes were very heavy; and they
did not know what to answer
Him.
★41 [a]Mark 14:35
41 And He *came the third
time, and *said to them, "Are you
still sleeping and taking your rest?
It is enough; [a]the hour has come;
behold, the Son of Man is being
betrayed into the hands of sinners.
42 "Arise, let us be going; behold, the one who betrays Me is
at hand!"

6 *Betrayal and arrest in Gethsemane,* 14:43–52

43 [a]Mark 14:43-50: *Matt. 26:47-56; Luke 22:47-53; John 18:3-11*
43 [a]And immediately while
He was still speaking, Judas, one
of the twelve, *came up, accompanied by a multitude with
swords and clubs, from the chief
priests and the scribes and the elders.
44 Now he who was betray-
ing Him had given them a signal,
saying, "Whomever I shall kiss,
He is the one; seize Him, and lead
Him away under guard."
45 And after coming, he im-
45 [a]Matt. 23:7
mediately went up to Him, saying, "[a]Rabbi!" and kissed Him.
46 And they laid hands on
Him, and seized Him.
47 But a certain one of those
★47
who stood by drew his sword, and
struck the slave of the high priest,
and cut off his ear.
48 And Jesus answered and
said to them, "Have you come out
with swords and clubs to arrest
Me, as though I were a robber?
49 "Every day I was with you
49 [a]Mark 12:35
[a]in the temple teaching, and you
did not seize Me; but *this has
happened* that the Scriptures
might be fulfilled."
50 And they all left Him and
fled.
51 And a certain young man
was following Him, wearing *nothing but* a linen sheet over *his*
naked *body;* and they *seized
him.
52 But he left the linen sheet
behind, and escaped naked.

F Trials and Crucifixion, on Friday, 14:53–15:47

1 *Christ before Caiaphas,* 14:53–65

53 [a]And they led Jesus away
★53 [a]Mark 14:53-65: *Matt. 26:57-68; John 18:12f.; 19-24*
to the high priest; and all the chief
priests and the elders and the
scribes *gathered together.
54 And Peter had followed
54 [a]Mark 14:68 [b]Matt. 26:3 [c]Mark 14:67; John 18:18
Him at a distance, [a]right into [b]the
courtyard of the high priest; and
he was sitting with the officers,
and [c]warming himself at the fire.
55 Now the chief priests and
55 [a]Matt. 5:22
the whole [a]Council kept trying to
obtain testimony against Jesus to

14:36 *this cup.* See note on Matt. 26:39.
14:41 *Sleep on now, and take your rest.* Some understand this as a statement of reproach; others translate it as a question: Are you still sleeping . . .?
14:47 *one of those.* Peter (John 18:10).
14:53 *to the high priest.* The examination before Caiaphas and the Sanhedrin. See note on Matt. 26:57 for the order of Jesus' trials.

put Him to death; and they were
finding none.
★56 **56** For many were giving false
testimony against Him, and *yet*
their testimony was not consistent.
57 And some stood up and
began to give false testimony
against Him, saying,
★58 [a]Matt. 26:61; Mark 15:29 **58** "We heard Him say, '[a]I will
destroy this temple made with
hands, and in three days I will
build another made without
hands.' "
59 And not even in this respect was their testimony consistent.
★60 **60** And the high priest arose
and came forward and questioned
Jesus, saying, "Do You make no
answer to what these men are testifying against You?"
★61 [a]Matt. 26:63 [b]Mark 14:61-63: *Matt. 26:63ff.; Luke 22:67-71* **61** [a]But He kept silent, and
made no answer. [b]Again the high
priest was questioning Him, and
saying to Him, "Are You the
Christ, the Son of the Blessed
One?"
★62 [a]Ps. 110:1; Mark 13:26 [b]Dan. 7:13 **62** And Jesus said, "I am; and
you shall see the [a]SON OF MAN SIT-
TING AT THE RIGHT HAND OF POWER,
and [b]COMING WITH THE CLOUDS OF
HEAVEN."
★63 [a]Num. 14:6; Matt. 26:65; Acts 14:14 **63** And [a]tearing his clothes,
the high priest *said, "What fur-
ther need do we have of witnesses?
★64 **64** "You have heard the blasphemy; how does it seem to
you?" And they all condemned
Him to be deserving of death.
65 And some began to [a]spit at ★65 [a]Matt. 26:67; Mark 10:34 [b]Esther 7:8 [c]Matt. 26:68; Luke 22:64
Him, and [b]to blindfold Him, and
to beat Him with their fists, and
to say to Him, "[c]Prophesy!" And
the officers received Him with
slaps *in the face.*

2 *Peter's denial of Jesus,* 14:66–72

66 [a]And as Peter was below 66 [a]Mark 14:66-72: *Matt. 26:69-75; Luke 22:56-62; John 18:16-18, 25-27* [b]Mark 14:54
in [b]the courtyard, one of the ser-
vant-girls of the high priest
*came,
67 and seeing Peter [a]warming 67 [a]Mark 14:54 [b]Mark 1:24
himself, she looked at him, and
*said, "You, too, were with Jesus
the [b]Nazarene."
68 But he denied *it,* saying, "I ★68 [a]Mark 14:54
neither know nor understand
what you are talking about." And
he [a]went out onto the porch.
69 And the maid saw him,
and began once more to say to the
bystanders, "This is *one* of
them!"
70 But again [a]he was denying ★70 [a]Mark 14:68 [b]Matt. 26:73; Luke 22:59
it. And after a little while the by-
standers were again saying to Peter, "Surely you are *one* of them,
[b]for you are a Galilean too."
71 But he began to curse and
swear, "I do not know this fellow
you are talking about!"
72 And immediately a cock 72 [a]Mark 14:30, 68
crowed a second time. And Peter
remembered how Jesus had made
the remark to him, "Before [a]a
cock crows twice, you will deny
Me three times." And he *began* to
weep.

14:56 Jewish law required two agreeing witnesses to establish a charge (Deut. 19:15).
14:58 This seems to be another version of 13:2.
14:60 The high priest suggested Christ incriminate Himself.
14:61 *kept silent.* Defense seemed irrelevant to Christ.
14:62 *I am.* Christ affirmed that He was the Messiah and assured His judges that He was also the coming Judge of all mankind. *right hand of Power.* The right hand of God.
14:63 *tearing his clothes.* The proper gesture for the high priest to make upon hearing blasphemy.
14:64 *the blasphemy.* The members of the council understood clearly that in Christ's answer (v. 62) He claimed to be equal with God. Since they viewed Him as a mere man, this claim was blasphemy in their minds, and the penalty was death (Lev. 24:16).
14:65 *spit at Him.* See Isa. 50:6. *Prophesy!* Said in mockery. Perhaps they meant: Tell us who is hitting you (as each blow is given).
14:68 *porch.* Better, gateway or forecourt.
14:70 *Galilean.* Galileans spoke a dialect of Aramaic, with noticeable pronunciation differences.

3 *Christ before Pilate,* 15:1-15

★ 1 [a]Matt. 27:1 [b]Matt. 5:22 **15** [a]And early in the morning
the chief priests with the
elders and scribes, and the whole
[b]Council, immediately held a con-
sultation; and binding Jesus, they
led Him away, and delivered Him
up to Pilate.
★ 2 [a]Mark 15:2-5; *Matt. 27:11-14; Luke 23:2, 3; John 18:29-38* **2** [a]And Pilate questioned
Him, "Are You the King of the
Jews?" And answering He *said to
him, "*It is as* you say."
3 And the chief priests *began* to accuse Him harshly.
4 And Pilate was questioning Him again, saying, "Do You
make no answer? See how many
charges they bring against You!"
5 [a]Matt. 27:12 **5** But Jesus [a]made no further
answer; so that Pilate was aston-
ished.
★ 6 [a]Mark 15:6-15; *Matt. 27:15-26; Luke 23:18-25; John 18:39-19:16* **6** [a]Now at *the* feast he used
to release for them *any* one pris-
oner whom they requested.
7 And the man named Barabbas had been imprisoned with
the insurrectionists who had committed murder in the insurrection.
8 And the multitude went
up and began asking him *to do* as
he had been accustomed to do for
them.
9 And Pilate answered them,
saying, "Do you want me to release for you the King of the
Jews?"
10 For he was aware that the
chief priests had delivered Him
up because of envy.
11 [a]Acts 3:14 **11** But the chief priests stirred
up the multitude [a]*to ask* him to
release Barabbas for them instead.
12 And answering again, Pilate was saying to them, "Then
what shall I do to Him whom you
call the King of the Jews?"
13 And they shouted back,
"Crucify Him!"
14 But Pilate was saying to
them, "Why, what evil has He
done?" But they shouted all the
more, "Crucify Him!"
15 And wishing to satisfy the ★15 [a]Matt. 27:26
multitude, Pilate released Barab-
bas for them, and after having
Jesus [a]scourged, he delivered Him
over to be crucified.

4 *Abuse by the soldiers,* 15:16-20

16 [a]And the soldiers took ★16 [a]Mark 15:16-20; *Matt. 27:27-31* [b]Matt. 26:3; 27:27 [c]Acts 10:1
Him away into [b]the palace (that
is, the Praetorium), and they
*called together the whole *Roman*
[c]cohort.
17 And they *dressed Him up
in purple, and after weaving a
crown of thorns, they put it on
Him;
18 and they began to acclaim
Him, "Hail, King of the Jews!"
19 And they kept beating His
head with a reed, and spitting at
Him, and kneeling and bowing
before Him.
20 And after they had
mocked Him, they took the purple off Him, and put His garments
on Him. And they *led Him out
to crucify Him.

15:1 *in the morning.* See note on Luke 22:66. *Pilate.* Pilate was the Roman prefect or governor of Judea (usually referred to as procurator), to which position he was appointed by Tiberius in A.D. 26. He was in charge of the army of occupation, kept the taxes flowing to Rome, had power of life and death over his subjects, appointed the high priests, and decided cases involving capital punishment. He was a capricious, weak governor who let personal and political considerations outweigh his awareness that justice was not being done in Jesus' case. He did not want another report to get to Rome that he had offended Jewish customs or could not control a situation—charges against him made to Tiberius earlier.

15:2 *King of the Jews.* The Jews knew that Pilate would be concerned only with a charge of a political nature, which this was. *It is as you say.* This affirmative answer, according to John 18:34-38, was accompanied by an explanation as to what kind of king Jesus claimed to be.

15:6 *at the feast.* I.e., at Passover.

15:15 *scourged.* See note on Matt. 27:26. *crucified.* See note on Matt. 27:31.

15:16 *Praetorium.* The residence of the governor, perhaps in the fortress of Antonia, where the Roman troops were quartered. *whole . . . cohort.* A company or battalion.

5 *Crucifixion of Jesus,* 15:21–32

★21 [a]Mark 15:21: *Matt. 27:32; Luke 23:26*

21 [a]And they *pressed into service a passerby coming from the country, Simon of Cyrene (the father of Alexander and Rufus), that he might bear His cross.

★22 [a]Mark 15:22-32: *Matt. 27:33-44; Luke 23:33-43; John 19:17-24* [b]Luke 23:33; John 19:17

22 [a]And they *brought Him to the place [b]Golgotha, which is translated, Place of a Skull.

★23 [a]Matt. 27:34

23 And they tried to give Him [a]wine mixed with myrrh; but He did not take it.

★24 [a]Ps. 22:18; John 19:24

24 And they *crucified Him, and *[a]DIVIDED UP HIS GARMENTS AMONG THEMSELVES, CASTING LOTS FOR THEM, *to decide* what each should take.

★25 [a]Mark 15:33; John 19:14

25 And it was the [a]third hour when they crucified Him.

26 [a]Matt. 27:37

26 And the inscription of the charge against Him read, "[a]THE KING OF THE JEWS."

27 And they *crucified two robbers with Him, one on the right and one on the left.

★28

28 [And the Scripture was fulfilled which says, "And He was reckoned with transgessors."]

29 [a]Ps. 22:8; Matt. 27:39 [b]Mark 14:58

29 And those passing by were hurling abuse at Him, [a]WAGGING THEIR HEADS, and saying, "Ha! You who *were going to* [b]destroy the temple and rebuild it in three days,

30 save Yourself, and come down from the cross!"

31 [a]Matt. 27:42; Luke 23:35

31 In the same way the chief priests along with the scribes were also mocking *Him* among themselves and saying, "[a]He saved others; He cannot save Himself.

★32 [a]Matt. 27:42; Mark 15:26 [b]Matt. 27:44; Mark 15:27; Luke 23:39-43

32 "Let *this* Christ, [a]the King of Israel, now come down from the cross, so that we may see and believe!" And [b]those who were crucified with Him were casting the same insult at Him.

6 *Death of Jesus,* 15:33–41

33 [a]Mark 15:33-41: *Matt. 27:45-56; Luke 23:44-49* [b]Matt. 27:45f.; Mark 15:25; Luke 23:44

33 [a]And when the [b]sixth hour had come, darkness fell over the whole land until the [b]ninth hour.

★34 [a]Matt. 27:45f.; Mark 15:25; Luke 23:44 [b]Ps. 22:1; Matt. 27:46

34 And at the [a]ninth hour Jesus cried out with a loud voice, "[b]ELOI, ELOI, LAMA SABACHTHANI?" which is translated, "MY GOD, MY GOD, WHY HAST THOU FORSAKEN ME?"

★35

35 And when some of the bystanders heard it, they *began* saying, "Behold, He is calling for Elijah."

★36

36 And someone ran and filled a sponge with sour wine, put it on a reed, and gave Him a drink, saying, "Let us see whether Elijah will come to take Him down."

37 [a]Matt. 27:50; Luke 23:46; John 19:30

37 [a]And Jesus uttered a loud cry, and breathed His last.

★38 [a]Matt. 27:51; Luke 23:45

38 [a]And the veil of the temple was torn in two from top to bottom.

39 [a]Matt. 27:54; Mark 15:45; Luke 23:47

39 [a]And when the centurion, who was standing right in front of Him, saw the way He breathed His last, he said, "Truly this man was the Son of God!"

★40 [a]Mark 15:40, 41: *Matt. 27:55f.;* Luke 23:49; John 19:25 [b]Luke 19:3 [c]Mark 16:1

40 [a]And there were also *some* women looking on from afar, among whom *were* Mary Magdalene, and Mary the mother of James [b]the Less and Joses, and [c]Salome.

41 [a]Matt. 27:55f.

41 And when He was in Galilee, they used to follow Him and [a]minister to Him; and *there were*

15:21 *coming from the country.* I.e., coming from the country into the city, probably as another pilgrim to Jerusalem at Passover. *Simon of Cyrene.* Cyrene was a port in N. Africa and had a Jewish community.
15:22 *Golgotha.* See note on Matt. 27:33.
15:23 *wine mixed with myrrh.* A sedative.
15:24 *divided up His garments.* The garments of a victim were customarily taken by his executioners. See Ps. 22:18.
15:25 *it was the third hour.* 9 a.m.
15:28 This quotation, from Isa. 53:12, is not contained in many manuscripts.
15:32 *Let this Christ.* I.e., Let the (to them) false Christ.
15:34 *why hast Thou forsaken Me?* See note on Matt. 27:46.
15:35 *Elijah.* See note on Matt. 27:47.
15:36 *sour wine.* See Ps. 69:21.
15:38 *the veil.* See note on Matt. 27:51.
15:40 A list of trustworthy witnesses (the apostles having fled) is given. Compare 16:1.

many other women who had
come up with Him to Jerusalem.

7 *Burial of Jesus,* 15:42-47

42 [a]Mark 15:42-47: *Matt. 27:57-61; Luke 23:50-56; John 19:38-42* [b]Matt. 27:62
★43 [a]Matt. 27:57; Luke 23:51; Acts 13:50; 17:12 [b]Matt. 27:57; Luke 2:25, 38; 23:51; John 19:38 [c]John 19:38
★44
45 [a]Mark 15:39
★46
47 [a]Matt. 27:56; Mark 15:40; 16:1

42 [a]And when evening had
already come, because it was [b]the
preparation day, that is, the day
before the Sabbath,
43 Joseph of Arimathea came,
a [a]prominent member of the
Council, a man who was himself
[b]waiting for the kingdom of God;
and he [c]gathered up courage and
went in before Pilate, and asked
for the body of Jesus.
44 And Pilate wondered if He
was dead by this time, and summoning the centurion, he questioned him as to whether He was
already dead.
45 And ascertaining this from
[a]the centurion, he granted the
body to Joseph.
46 And *Joseph* bought a linen
sheet, took Him down, wrapped
Him in the linen sheet, and laid
Him in a tomb which had been
hewn out in the rock; and he
rolled a stone against the entrance
of the tomb.
47 And [a]Mary Magdalene
and Mary the *mother* of Joses
were looking on *to see* where He
was laid.

III THE SUCCESS OF THE SERVANT, 16:1-20

★ 1 [a]Mark 16:1-8: *Matt. 28:1-8; Luke 24:1-10;* John 20:1-8 [b]Mark 15:47 [c]Luke 23:56; John 19:39f.

A His Resurrection, 16:1-8

16 [a]And when the Sabbath
was over, [b]Mary Magda-
lene, and Mary the *mother* of
James, and Salome, [c]bought
spices, that they might come and
anoint Him.
2 And very early on the first
day of the week, they *came to
the tomb when the sun had risen.
3 And they were saying to ★ 3 [a]Matt. 27:60; Mark 15:46; 16:3, 4
one another, "Who will roll away
[a]the stone for us from the entrance of the tomb?"
4 And looking up, they *saw
that the stone had been rolled
away, although it was extremely
large.
5 And [a]entering the tomb, ★ 5 [a]John 20:11, 12 [b]Mark 9:15
they saw a young man sitting at
the right, wearing a white robe;
and they [b]were amazed.
6 And he *said to them, ★ 6 [a]Mark 9:15 [b]Mark 1:24 [c]Matt. 28:6; Luke 24:6
"[a]Do not be amazed; you are
looking for Jesus the [b]Nazarene,
who has been crucified. [c]He has
risen; He is not here; behold, *here
is* the place where they laid Him.
7 "But go, tell His disciples 7 [a]Matt. 26:32; Mark 14:28
and Peter, '[a]He is going before
you into Galilee; there you will
see Him, just as He said to you.' "
8 And they went out and
fled from the tomb, for trembling
and astonishment had gripped
them; and they said nothing to
anyone, for they were afraid.

B His Appearances, 16:9-18

9 [Now after He had risen ★ 9 [a]Matt. 27:56; John 20:14
early on the first day of the week,
He first appeared to [a]Mary Magdalene, from whom He had cast
out seven demons.

15:43 *Joseph.* See Matt. 27:57; Luke 23:50; and John 19:38.

15:44 *wondered if He was dead by this time.* Pilate wondered because several days of agony on a cross before death came was common. Christ's death after only 6 hours was very unusual. *centurion.* The one who had been in charge of the crucifixion.

15:46 *wrapped Him in the linen.* The linen was wrapped around the body in strips (John 19:40). *tomb.* See Isa. 53:9.

16:1 *when the Sabbath was over.* Work could now be done to prepare the body for permanent burial.

16:3 *the stone.* See note on Luke 24:2.

16:5 *a young man.* Evidently the angel who rolled away the stone (Matt. 28:2).

16:6 *He has risen.* This simply stated fact is the foundation of the Christian faith.

16:9-20 These verses do not appear in two of the most truthworthy manuscripts of the N.T., though they are part of many other manuscripts and versions. If they are not a part of the genuine text of Mark, the abrupt ending at verse 8 is probably because the original closing verses were lost. The doubtful genuineness of verses 9-20 makes it unwise to build a doctrine or base an experience on them (especially vv. 16-18).

10 [a]She went and reported to those who had been with Him, while they were mourning and weeping.

11 And when they heard that He was alive, and had been seen by her, [a]they refused to believe it.

12 And after that, [a]He appeared in a different form [b]to two of them, while they were walking along on their way to the country.

13 And they went away and reported it to the others, but they [a]did not believe them either.

14 And afterward [a]He appeared [b]to the eleven themselves as they were reclining *at table;* and He reproached them for their [c]unbelief and hardness of heart, because they had not believed those who had seen Him after He had risen.

15 And He said to them, "[a]Go into all the world and preach the gospel to all creation.

16 "[a]He who has believed and has been baptized shall be saved; but he who has disbelieved shall be condemned.

17 "And these signs will accompany those who have believed: [a]in My name they will cast out demons, they will [b]speak with new tongues;

18 they will [a]pick up serpents, and if they drink any deadly *poison,* it shall not hurt them; they will [b]lay hands on the sick, and they will recover."

C His Ascension, 16:19–20

19 So then, when the Lord Jesus had [a]spoken to them, He [b]was received up into heaven, and [c]SAT DOWN AT THE RIGHT HAND OF GOD.

20 And they went out and preached everywhere, while the Lord worked with them, and confirmed the word by the signs that followed.]

[*And they promptly reported all these instructions to Peter and his companions. And after that, Jesus Himself sent out through them from east to west the sacred and imperishable proclamation of eternal salvation.*]

10 [a]John 20:18
11 [a]Matt. 28:17; Mark 16:13, 14; Luke 24:11, 41; John 20:25
12 [a]Mark 16:14; John 21:1, 14 [b]Luke 24:13-35
13 [a]Matt. 28:17; Mark 16:11, 14; Luke 24:11, 41; John 20:25
14 [a]Mark 16:12; John 21:1, 14 [b]Luke 24:36; John 20:19, 26; 1 Cor. 15:5 [c]Matt. 28:17; Mark 16:11, 13; Luke 24:11, 41; John 20:25
15 [a]Matt. 28:19
★16 [a]John 3:18, 36; Acts 16:31
17 [a]Mark 9:38; Luke 10:17; Acts 5:16; 8:7; 16:18; 19:12 [b]Acts 2:4; 10:46; 19:6; 1 Cor. 12:10
18 [a]Luke 10:19; Acts 28:3-5
19 [a]Acts 1:3 [b]Luke 9:51; 24:51; John 6:62; 20:17; Acts 1:2; 1 Tim 3:16 [c]Ps. 110:1; Luke 22:69; Acts 7:55f.; Rom. 8:34; Eph. 1:20; Col. 3:1; Heb. 1:3; 8:1; 10:12; 12:2; 1 Pet. 3:22

16:16 *baptized.* This may be a reference to the baptism of the Holy Spirit (1 Cor. 12:13). Water baptism does not save (see notes at Acts 2:38; 1 Pet. 3:21).

INTRODUCTION TO THE GOSPEL ACCORDING TO LUKE

AUTHOR: Luke DATE: 60

Authorship *Luke, the "beloved physician" (Col. 4:14), close friend and companion of Paul, was probably the only Gentile author of any part of the New Testament. We know nothing about his early life or conversion except that he was not an eyewitness of the life of Jesus Christ (Luke 1:2). Though a physician by profession, he was primarily an evangelist, writing this Gospel and the book of Acts and accompanying Paul in missionary work (see the Introduction to Acts). He was with Paul at the time of the apostle's martyrdom (2 Tim. 4:11), but of his later life we have no certain facts.*

Methodology *In his prologue, Luke states that his own work was stimulated by the work of others (1:1), that he consulted eyewitnesses (1:2), and that he sifted and arranged the information (1:3) under the guidance of the Holy Spirit to instruct Theophilus in the historical reliability of the faith (1:4). This is a carefully researched and documented writing.*

Distinctive Approach *Though specifically dedicated to Theophilus, the Gospel is slanted toward all Gentiles. (1) The author displays an unusual interest in medical matters (4:38; 7:15; 8:55; 14:2; 18:15; 22:50). (2) Much attention is given to recounting of the events surrounding the birth of Christ. Only Luke records the annunciation to Zacharias and Mary, the songs of Elizabeth and Mary, the birth and childhood of John the Baptist, the birth of Jesus, the visit of the shepherds, the circumcision, presentation in the Temple, details of Christ's childhood, and the inner thoughts of Mary. (3) Luke shows an uncommon interest in individuals, as seen in his accounts of Zaccheus (19:1-10) and the penitent thief (23:39-43) and in the parables of the prodigal son (15:11-32) and the penitent publican (18:9-14). It is Luke who gives us the story of the good Samaritan (10:29-37) and the one thankful ex-leper (17:11-19). (4) There is in this Gospel a special emphasis on prayer (3:21; 5:16; 6:12; 9:18, 28-29; 10:21; 11:1; 22:39-46; 23:34, 46). (5) The prominent place given to women is another distinctive feature of this Gospel (chapters 1, 2; 7:11-13; 8:1-3; 10:38-42; 21:1-4; 23:27-31, 49). (6) The writer also shows interest in poverty and wealth (1:52-53; 4:16-22; 6:20, 24-25; 12:13-21; 14:12-13; 16:19-31). (7) The book preserves four beautiful hymns: the* Magnificat *of Mary (1:46-55), the* Benedictus *of Zechariah (1:67-79), the* Gloria in Excelsis *of the angels (2:14), and the* Nunc Dimittis *of Simeon (2:29-32). This is a Gospel of the compassionate Son of Man offering salvation to the whole world (19:10).*

Date *Since the conclusion of Acts shows Paul in Rome, and since the Gospel of Luke was written before Acts (Acts 1:1), Luke's Gospel was probably written about* A.D. *60, possibly in Caesarea during Paul's two-year imprisonment there (Acts 24:27).*

Contents *The theme of Luke's Gospel is Christ, the Son of Man, and it narrates many of those events which demonstrated Christ's humanity (see* Distinctive Approach *for a listing of favorite passages).*

OUTLINE OF THE GOSPEL OF LUKE

I. Preface: The Method and Purpose of Writing, 1:1-4

II. The Identification of the Son of Man with Men, 1:5-4:13

A. The Announcement of the Birth of John the Baptist, 1:5-25
B. The Announcement of the Birth of the Son of Man, 1:26-56
C. The Advent of John the Baptist, 1:57-80
D. The Advent of the Son of Man, 2:1-20
E. The Adoration of the Babe, 2:21-38
F. The Advancement of the Boy, 2:39-52
G. The Baptism of the Son of Man, 3:1-22
H. The Genealogy of the Son of Man, 3:23-38
I. The Temptation of the Son of Man, 4:1-13

III. The Ministry of the Son of Man to Men, 4:14-9:50

A. The Announcement of His Ministry, 4:14-30
B. The Authority of His Ministry, 4:31-6:11
1. Over demons, 4:31-37
2. Over disease, 4:38-44
3. Over the disciples, 5:1-11
4. Over defilement (a leper healed), 5:12-16
5. Over defectiveness (a paralytic healed), 5:17-26
6. Over the despised (the call of Matthew and parables), 5:27-39
7. Over days, 6:1-5

8. Over deformity, 6:6-11
C. The Associates of His Ministry, 6:12-49
1. The call of the disciples, 6:12-16
2. The characteristics of disciples (The Great Sermon), 6:17-49
D. The Activities of His Ministry, 7:1-9:50
1. Ministry in sickness, 7:1-10
2. Ministry in death, 7:11-17
3. Ministry in doubt, 7:18-35
4. Ministry to sinners, 7:36-50
5. Ministry financed, 8:1-3
6. Ministry illustrated through parables, 8:4-21
7. Ministry in storms, 8:22-25
8. Ministry over demons, 8:26-39
9. Ministry in death and despair, 8:40-56
10. Ministry through the disciples, 9:1-9
11. Ministry to physical needs, 9:10-17
12. Ministry of prediction, 9:18-50

IV. The Repudiation of the Son of Man by Men, 9:51-19:27

A. Rejection by Samaritans, 9:51-56
B. Rejection by Worldly Men, 9:57-62
C. Commissioning of the Seventy, 10:1-24
D. Rejection by a Lawyer (Parable of the Good Samaritan), 10:25-37
E. Reception at Bethany, 10:38-42
F. Instruction on Prayer, 11:1-13
G. Rejection by the Nation, 11:14-36
H. Rejection by Pharisees and Lawyers, 11:37-54
I. Instruction in the Light of Rejection, 12:1-19:27
1. Concerning hypocrisy, 12:1-12
2. Concerning covetousness, 12:13-34
3. Concerning faithfulness, 12:35-48
4. Concerning division and signs, 12:49-59
5. Concerning repentance, 13:1-9
6. Concerning hypocrisy, 13:10-17
7. Concerning the kingdom, 13:18-35
8. Concerning inflexible people, 14:1-6
9. Concerning inflated people, 14:7-11
10. Concerning invited people, 14:12-14
11. Concerning indifferent people, 14:15-24
12. Concerning indulgent people, 14:25-35
13. Concerning God's love for sinners, 15:1-32
14. Concerning wealth, 16:1-31
15. Concerning forgiveness, 17:1-6
16. Concerning service, 17:7-10
17. Concerning gratitude, 17:11-19
18. Concerning the kingdom, 17:20-37
19. Concerning prayer, 18:1-14
20. Concerning entrance into the kingdom, 18:15-30
21. Concerning His death, 18:31-34
22. Concerning salvation, 18:35-19:10
23. Concerning faithfulness, 19:11-27

V. The Condemnation of the Son of Man for Men, 19:28-23:56

A. Sunday, 19:28-44
B. Monday, 19:45-48
C. Tuesday, 20:1-21:38
1. Authority requested, 20:1-8
2. Authority revealed, 20:9-18
3. Authority resisted, 20:19-40
4. Authority reiterated, 20:41-21:4
5. The apocalyptic discourse, 21:5-38
D. Wednesday, 22:1-6
E. Thursday, 22:7-53
1. The Lord's Supper, 22:7-38
2. The garden of Gethsemane, 22:39-46
3. The arrest, 22:47-53
F. Friday, 22:54-23:55
1. Peter's denial, 22:54-62
2. Christ derided, beaten, 22:63-65
3. Christ before the Sanhedrin, 22:66-71
4. Christ before Pilate, 23:1-5
5. Christ before Herod, 23:6-12
6. Christ again before Pilate, 23:13-25
7. The crucifixion, 23:26-49
8. The burial, 23:50-55
G. Saturday, 23:56

VI. The Vindication of the Son of Man before Men, 24:1-53

A. The Victor over Death, 24:1-12
B. The Fulfiller of the Prophecies (the Emmaus Disciples), 24:13-35
C. The Pattern of Resurrection Life, 24:36-43
D. The Head of the Church, 24:44-48
E. The Giver of the Holy Spirit, 24:49
F. The Ascended Lord, 24:50-53

THE GOSPEL ACCORDING TO LUKE

I PREFACE: THE METHOD AND PURPOSE OF WRITING, 1:1-4

1 [a][Gr., in] Rom. 4:21; 14:5; Col. 2:2; 4:12; 1 Thess. 1:5; 2 Tim. 4:5, 17; Heb. 6:11; 10:22 **2** [a]John 15:27; Acts 1:21f. [b]2 Pet. 1:16; 1 John 1:1 [c]Acts 26:16; 1 Cor. 4:1; Heb. 2:3 [d]Mark 4:14; 16:20; Acts 8:4; 14:25; 16:6; 17:11 ★ **3** [a]1 Tim. 4:6; 2 Tim. 3:10 [in Gr.] [b]Acts 11:4; 18:23 [c]Acts 23:26; 24:3; 26:25 [d]Acts 1:1

1 Inasmuch as many have un-
dertaken to compile an account of the things [a]accomplished
among us,
2 just as those who [a]from
the beginning were [b]eyewitnesses
and [c]servants of [d]the Word have
handed them down to us,
3 it seemed fitting for me as
well, [a]having investigated everything carefully from the beginning, to write *it* out for you [b]in
consecutive order, [c]most excellent
[d]Theophilus;
4 so that you might know
the exact truth about the things
you have been [a]taught.

II THE IDENTIFICATION OF THE SON OF MAN WITH MEN, 1:5-4:13

4 [a]Acts 18:25; Rom. 2:18; 1 Cor. 14:19; Gal. 6:6 [Gr.]

A The Announcement of the Birth of John the Baptist, 1:5-25

★ **5** [a]Matt. 2:1 [b]1 Chr. 24:10

5 [a]In the days of Herod,
king of Judea, there was a certain
priest named Zacharias, of the
[b]division of Abijah; and he had a
wife from the daughters of Aaron,
and her name was Elizabeth.

★ **6** [a]Gen. 7:1; Acts 2:25; 8:21 [b]Phil. 2:15; 3:6; 1 Thess. 3:13 [Gr.]

6 And they were both
[a]righteous in the sight of God,
walking [b]blamelessly in all the
commandments and require-
ments of the Lord.
7 And they had no child, because Elizabeth was barren, and
they were both advanced in years.
8 Now it came about, while
[a]he was performing his priestly
service before God in the *ap-*
pointed order of his division,
9 according to the custom of
the priestly office, he was chosen
by lot [a]to enter the temple of the
Lord and burn incense.
10 And the whole multitude
of the people were in prayer [a]out-
side at the hour of the incense offering.
11 And [a]an angel of the Lord
appeared to him, standing to the
right of the altar of incense.
12 And Zacharias was troubled when he saw *him,* and fear
gripped him.
13 But the angel said to him,
"[a]Do not be afraid, Zacharias, for
your petition has been heard, and
your wife Elizabeth will bear you
a son, and [b]you will give him the
name John.
14 "And you will have joy and
gladness, and many will rejoice at
his birth.
15 "For he will be great in the
sight of the Lord, and he will
[a]drink no wine or liquor; and he
will be filled with the Holy Spirit,
while yet in his mother's womb.
16 "And he will turn back
many of the sons of Israel to the
Lord their God.
17 "And it is he who will [a]go
as a forerunner before Him in the
spirit and power of [b]Elijah, [c]TO

8 [a]1 Chr. 24:19; 2 Chr. 8:14; 31:2 ★ **9** [a]Ex. 30:7f. **10** [a]Lev. 16:17 ★**11** [a]Luke 2:9; Acts 5:19 **13** [a]Matt. 14:27; Luke 1:30 [b]Luke 1:60, 63 **15** [a]Num. 6:3; Judg. 13:4; Matt. 11:18; Luke 7:33 ★**17** [a]Luke 1:76 [b]Matt. 11:14 [c]Mal. 4:6

1:3 *from the beginning* of the Gospel story; i.e., the birth of John the Baptist. The word "beginning" in some instances is translated "from above"; e.g., John 3:31; Jas. 1:17). *most excellent Theophilus.* His name means "dear to God," or "friend of God." He is unknown otherwise, but the form of the address shows that he was a person of high rank.

1:5 *Herod.* Herod the Great. See note on Matt. 2:1. *the division of Abijah.* Work in the temple was divided among "divisions" of priests, each division named for its leader (1 Chron. 24:10). *daughters of Aaron.* Elizabeth, like Zacharias, was of a priestly family.

1:6 *they were both righteous in the sight of God.* In a godless age this couple lived lives that were fully pleasing to God, yet they were without the much-cherished blessing of children.

1:9 *chosen by lot.* The privilege of burning incense was permitted only once in the lifetime of any priest.

1:11 *an angel.* Gabriel (see v. 19).

1:17 *in the spirit and power of Elijah.* The stern prophet who rebuked the idolatrous King Ahab (1 Kings 21:17-24). He preached repentance, as John the Baptist would also do (Luke 3:8). See notes on Matt. 11:14; 17:11-12.

TURN THE HEARTS OF THE FATHERS
BACK TO THE CHILDREN, and the disobedient to the attitude of the
righteous; so as to [a]make ready a
people prepared for the Lord."
18 And Zacharias said to the
angel, "How shall I know this *for*
certain? For I am an old man, and
my wife is advanced in years."
★19 [a]Dan. 8:16; 9:21; Luke 1:26 [b]Matt. 18:10 **19** And the angel answered
and said to him, "I am [a]Gabriel,
who [b]stands in the presence of
God; and I have been sent to
speak to you, and to bring you
this good news.
20 "And behold, you shall be
silent and unable to speak until
the day when these things take
place, because you did not believe
my words, which shall be fulfilled
in their proper time."
★21 **21** And the people were waiting for Zacharias, and were wondering at his delay in the temple.
22 [a]Luke 1:62 **22** But when he came out, he
was unable to speak to them; and
they realized that he had seen a
vision in the temple; and he [a]kept
making signs to them, and remained mute.
★23 **23** And it came about, when
the days of his priestly service
were ended, that he went back
home.
24 And after these days Elizabeth his wife became pregnant;
and she kept herself in seclusion
for five months, saying,
25 [a]Gen. 30:23; Is. 4:1 **25** "This is the way the Lord
has dealt with me in the days
when He looked *with favor* upon
me, to [a]take away my disgrace
among men."

B The Announcement of the Birth of the Son of Man, 1:26–56

26 Now in the sixth month 26 [a]Luke 1:19 [b]Matt. 2:23
the angel [a]Gabriel was sent from
God to a city in Galilee, called
[b]Nazareth,
27 to [a]a virgin engaged to a ★27 [a]Matt. 1:18 [b]Matt. 1:16, 20; Luke 2:4
man whose name was Joseph, [b]of
the descendants of David; and the
virgin's name was Mary.
28 And coming in, he said to ★28
her, "Hail, favored one! The Lord
is with you."
29 But she [a]was greatly trou- 29 [a]Luke 1:12
bled at *this* statement, and kept
pondering what kind of salutation
this might be.
30 And the angel said to her, 30 [a]Matt. 14:27; Luke 1:13
"[a]Do not be afraid, Mary; for you
have found favor with God.
31 "And behold, you will con- ★31 [a]Matt. 1:21, 25; Luke 2:21
ceive in your womb, and bear a
son, and you [a]shall name Him
Jesus.
32 "He will be great, and will ★32 [a]Mark 5:7; Luke 1:35, 76; 6:35; Acts 7:48
be called the Son of [a]the Most
High; and the Lord God will give
Him the throne of His father David;
33 [a]and He will reign over the ★33 [a]Matt. 1:1 [b]Dan. 2:44; 7:14, 18, 27; Matt. 28:18
house of Jacob forever; [b]and His
kingdom will have no end."
34 And Mary said to the an-
gel, "How can this be, since I am a ★35 [a]Matt. 1:18 [b]Luke 1:32 [c]Mark 1:24 [d]Matt. 4:3
virgin?"
35 And the angel answered

1:19 *Gabriel.* The angel's name means "man of God," and his ministry involves making special announcements concerning God's plans (Dan. 8:16; 9:21). He and Michael, the archangel, are the only angels named in the Bible.

1:21 *wondering at his delay.* The people probably wondered if Zacharias had died.

1:23 *he went back home.* After serving in his division for a limited time, Zacharias was free to return to his home in the hill country, probably not far from Jerusalem (cf. 1:39).

1:27 *a virgin engaged.* According to Jewish law, espousal or engagement was as binding as marriage. See note on Matt. 1:19.

1:28 *favored one!* = filled with grace. The term is used in the N.T. elsewhere only in Eph. 1:6, where all believers in Christ also are said to be filled with grace.

1:31 *Jesus.* The name means "the Lord is salvation." See note on Matt. 1:1.

1:32 *His father David.* See 3:31 and note on Matt. 1:1.

1:33 *He will reign.* Jesus is the Davidic Messiah, and though He reigns always, the ultimate fulfillment of this promise in relation to the *house of Jacob* begins in the millennial kingdom. See 2 Sam. 7:16.

1:35 *The Holy Spirit will come upon you.* The incarnation was accomplished by this creative act of the Holy Spirit in the body of Mary. The virgin birth was a special miracle performed by the Third Person of the Trinity, the Holy Spirit, whereby the Second Person of the Trinity, the eternal Son of God, took to Himself a genuine, though sinless, human nature and was born as a man, without surrendering in any aspect His deity.

and said to her, "[a]The Holy Spirit
will come upon you, and the
power of [b]the Most High will
overshadow you; and for that reason [c]the holy offspring shall be
called [d]the Son of God.
36 "And behold, even your
relative Elizabeth has also conceived a son in her old age; and
she who was called barren is now
in her sixth month.
37 [a]Matt. 19:26 **37** "For [a]nothing will be impossible with God."
38 And Mary said, "Behold,
the bondslave of the Lord; be it
done to me according to your
word." And the angel departed
from her.
39 [a]Josh. 20:7; 21:11; Luke 1:65 **39** Now at this time Mary
arose and went with haste to [a]the
hill country, to a city of Judah,
40 and entered the house of
Zacharias and greeted Elizabeth.
41 [a]Luke 1:67 **41** And it came about that
when Elizabeth heard Mary's
greeting, the baby leaped in her
womb; and Elizabeth was [a]filled
with the Holy Spirit.
42 And she cried out with a
loud voice, and said, "Blessed
among women *are* you, and
blessed *is* the fruit of your womb!
43 [a]Luke 2:11 **43** "And how has it *happened*
to me, that the mother of [a]my
Lord should come to me?
44 "For behold, when the
sound of your greeting reached
my ears, the baby leaped in my
womb for joy.
45 [a]Luke 1:20, 48 **45** "And [a]blessed *is* she who
believed that there would be a
fulfillment of what had been spoken to her by the Lord."
★46 [a]Luke 1:46-53; *1 Sam. 2:1-10* [b]Ps. 34:2f. **46** And Mary said:

"[a]My soul [b]exalts the Lord,
47 [a]Ps. 35:9 [b]1 Tim. 1:1; 2:3; Titus 1:3; 2:10; 3:4; Jude 25 **47** "And [a]my spirit has rejoiced in [b]God my Sav-
ior.
48 [a]Luke 1:45 **48** "For He has had regard for
the humble state of His
bondslave;
For behold, from this time
on all generations will
count me [a]blessed.
49 "For the Mighty One has
done great things for
me;
And holy is His name.
50 "[a]AND HIS MERCY IS UPON 50 [a]Ps. 103:17
GENERATION AFTER GENERA-
TION
TOWARDS THOSE WHO FEAR
HIM.
51 "[a]He has done mighty 51 [a]Ps. 98:1; 118:15
deeds with His arm;
He has scattered *those
who were* proud in the
thoughts of their heart.
52 "He has brought down rulers from *their* thrones,
And has exalted those who
were humble.
53 "[a]HE HAS FILLED THE HUNGRY 53 [a]Ps. 107:9
WITH GOOD THINGS;
And sent away the rich
empty-handed.
54 "He has given help to Israel His servant,
In remembrance of His
mercy,
55 [a]As He spoke to our fa- 55 [a]Gen. 17:19; Ps. 132:11; Gal. 3:16
thers,
To Abraham and his off-
spring forever."

56 And Mary stayed with her
about three months, and *then* returned to her home.

C The Advent of John the Baptist, 1:57-80

57 Now the time had come
for Elizabeth to give birth, and
she brought forth a son.
58 And her neighbors and her 58 [a]Gen. 19:19
relatives heard that the Lord had
[a]displayed His great mercy
toward her; and they were rejoic- ★59 [a]Gen. 17:12; Lev. 12:3; Luke 2:21; Phil. 3:5
ing with her.
59 And it came about that on
[a]the eighth day they came to cir-

1:46-56 Often called "the Magnificat," from the first word of the Latin translation. There are 15 discernible quotations from the O.T. in this poem, showing how much the O.T. was known and loved in the home in which Jesus was reared.

1:59 *to circumcise the child.* This ritual act was performed 8 days after birth, and the name was given at this time.

cumcise the child, and they were
going to call him Zacharias, after
his father.

★60 [a]Luke 1:13, 63 — **60** And his mother answered
and said, "No indeed; but [a]he
shall be called John."

61 And they said to her,
"There is no one among your
relatives who is called by that
name."

62 [a]Luke 1:22 — **62** And they [a]made signs to
his father, as to what he wanted
him called.

63 [a]Luke 1:13, 60 — **63** And he asked for a tablet,
and wrote as follows, "[a]His name
is John." And they were all astonished.

64 [a]Luke 1:20 — **64** [a]And at once his mouth
was opened and his tongue
loosed, and he *began* to speak in
praise of God.

65 [a]Luke 1:39 — **65** And fear came on all those
living around them; and all these
matters were being talked about
in all [a]the hill country of Judea.

66 [a]Acts 11:21 — **66** And all who heard them
kept them in mind, saying,
"What then will this child *turn
out to* be?" For [a]the hand of the
Lord was certainly with him.

67 [a]Luke 1:41 [b]Joel 2:28 — **67** And his father Zacharias
[a]was filled with the Holy Spirit,
and [b]prophesied, saying:

68 [a]Luke 1:71; 2:38; Acts 1:6; Heb. 9:12 — **68** "Blessed *be* the Lord God
of Israel,
For He has visited us and
accomplished [a]redemp-
tion for His people,

★69 [a]1 Sam. 2:1, 10; Ps. 18:2; 89:17; 132:17; Ezek. 29:21 [b]Matt. 1:1 — **69** And has raised up a
[a]horn of salvation for us
In the house of David [b]His
servant—

70 [a]Rom. 1:2 [b]Acts 3:21 — **70** [a]As He spoke by the
mouth of His holy
prophets [b]from of old—

71 [a]Luke 1:68 [b]Ps. 106:10 — **71** [a]Salvation [b]FROM OUR EN-
EMIES,
And FROM THE HAND OF ALL
WHO HATE US;

72 [a]Mic. 7:20 [b]Ps. 105:8f.; 106:45 — **72** [a]To show mercy toward
our fathers,
[b]And to remember His
holy covenant,

73 [a]The oath which He
swore to Abraham our
father, — ★73 [a]Gen. 22:16ff.

74 To grant us that we,
being delivered from the
hand of our enemies,
Might serve Him without
fear,

75 In holiness and righteousness before Him all our
days.

76 "And you, child, will be
called the [a]prophet of
[b]the Most High;
For you will go on [c]BEFORE
THE LORD TO [d]PREPARE HIS
WAYS; — 76 [a]Matt. 11:9 [b]Luke 1:32 [c]Mal. 3:1 [d]Luke 1:17

77 To give to His people *the*
knowledge of salvation
By [a]the forgiveness of their
sins, — 77 [a]Jer. 31:34; Mark 1:4

78 Because of the tender
mercy of our God,
With which [a]the Sunrise
from on high shall visit
us, — 78 [a]Mal. 4:2; Eph. 5:14; 2 Pet. 1:19

79 [a]TO SHINE UPON THOSE WHO
SIT IN DARKNESS AND THE
SHADOW OF DEATH,
To guide our feet into the
way of peace." — 79 [a]Is. 9:1, 2; 59:8; Matt. 4:16

80 [a]And the child continued
to grow, and to become strong in
spirit, and he lived in the deserts
until the day of his public appearance to Israel. — 80 [a]Luke 2:40

D The Advent of the Son of Man, 2:1–20

2 Now it came about in those
days that a decree went out
from [a]Caesar Augustus, that a
census be taken of [b]all the inhab-
ited earth. — ★1 [a]Matt. 22:17; Luke 3:1 [b]Matt. 24:14

2 This was the first census
taken while Quirinius was governor of [a]Syria. — ★2 [a]Matt. 4:24

1:60 *John.* The name means "God is gracious."

1:69 *horn of salvation.* Horn is often used as a metaphor for power (cf. 2 Sam. 22:3); thus this phrase means "a powerful Savior."

1:73 *The oath.* The covenant which God made with Abraham, recorded in Gen. 22:16–18.

2:1 *Caesar Augustus* reigned from 27 B.C. to A.D. 14.

2:2 *Quirinius was governor of Syria.* Apparently he was governor of Syria twice: from 4 B.C. to A.D. 1, when this census was taken, and again in A.D. 6.

3 And all were proceeding to register for the census, everyone to his own city.

★ 4 [a]Luke 1:27

4 And Joseph also went up from Galilee, from the city of Nazareth, to Judea, to the city of David, which is called Bethlehem, because [a]he was of the house and family of David,

5 in order to register, along with Mary, who was engaged to him, and was with child.

6 And it came about that while they were there, the days were completed for her to give birth.

★ 7

7 And she gave birth to her first-born son; and she wrapped Him in cloths, and laid Him in a manger, because there was no room for them in the inn.

8 And in the same region there were *some* shepherds staying out in the fields, and keeping watch over their flock by night.

9 [a]Luke 1:11; Acts 5:19 [b]Luke 24:4; Acts 12:7

9 And [a]an angel of the Lord suddenly [b]stood before them, and the glory of the Lord shone around them; and they were terribly frightened.

10 [a]Matt. 14:27

10 And the angel said to them, "[a]Do not be afraid; for behold, I bring you good news of a great joy which shall be for all the people;

★11 [a]Matt. 1:21; John 4:42; Acts 5:31 [b]Matt. 1:16; 16:16, 20; John 11:27 [c]Luke 1:43; Acts 2:36; 10:36

11 for today in the city of David there has been born for you a [a]Savior, who is [b]Christ [c]the Lord.

12 [a]1 Sam. 2:34; 2 Kin. 19:29; 20:8f.; Is. 7:11, 14

12 "And [a]this *will be* a sign for you: you will find a baby wrapped in cloths, and lying in a manger."

13 And suddenly there appeared with the angel a multitude of the heavenly host praising God, and saying,

14 [a]Matt. 21:9; Luke 19:38 [b]Luke 3:22; Eph. 1:9; Phil. 2:13

14 "[a]Glory to God in the highest,
And on earth peace among men [b]with whom He is pleased."

15 And it came about when the angels had gone away from them into heaven, that the shepherds *began* saying to one another, "Let us go straight to Bethlehem then, and see this thing that has happened which the Lord has made known to us."

16 And they came in haste and found their way to Mary and Joseph, and the baby as He lay in the manger.

17 And when they had seen this, they made known the statement which had been told them about this Child.

18 And all who heard it wondered at the things which were told them by the shepherds.

19 [a]Luke 2:51

19 But Mary [a]treasured up all these things, pondering them in her heart.

20 [a]Matt. 9:8

20 And the shepherds went back, [a]glorifying and praising God for all that they had heard and seen, just as had been told them.

E The Adoration of the Babe, 2:21–38

★21 [a]Luke 1:59 [b]Luke 1:31

21 And when [a]eight days were completed before His circumcision, [b]His name was *then* called Jesus, the name given by the angel before He was conceived in the womb.

★22

22 And when the days for their purification according to the

2:4 *to . . . Bethlehem.* To fulfill the prophecy of Mic. 5:2.

2:7 *cloths.* Wrapped around an infant in the Near East in Bible times. *manger.* A feeding trough for animals in a stall or stable. Tradition says that Jesus was born in a cave, in which case the manger may have been cut out of a rock wall.

2:11 Three titles were given to Jesus in the angel's announcement: *Savior, Christ* (Messiah, anointed One), and *Lord* (Yahweh, or God). He was both God and man.

2:21 *before His circumcision.* In accordance with Lev. 12:3.

2:22 *the days for their purification.* According to the Mosaic law the mother of a male child was unclean. On the eighth day the boy was circumcised but she remained unclean for 33 more days, after which she presented a burnt offering and a sin offering for her cleansing (Lev. 12:4–6).

law of Moses were completed,
they brought Him up to Jerusalem to present Him to the Lord
23 [a]Ex 13:2, 12 **23** (as it is written in the Law
of the Lord, "[a]EVERY *first-born*
MALE THAT OPENS THE WOMB SHALL BE
CALLED HOLY TO THE LORD"),
★24 [a]Lev 5:11; 12:8 **24** and to offer a sacrifice according to what was said in the
Law of the Lord, "[a]A PAIR OF TUR-
TLEDOVES, OR TWO YOUNG PIGEONS."
★25 [a]Luke 1:6 [b]Mark 15:43; Luke 2:38; 23:51 **25** And behold, there was a
man in Jerusalem whose name
was Simeon; and this man was
[a]righteous and devout, [b]looking
for the consolation of Israel; and
the Holy Spirit was upon him.
26 [a]Matt 2:12 [b]Ps 89:48; John 8:51; Heb 11:5 **26** And [a]it had been revealed
to him by the Holy Spirit that he
would not [b]see death before he
had seen the Lord's Christ.
27 [a]Luke 2:22 **27** And he came in the Spirit
into the temple; and when the
parents brought in the child Jesus,
[a]to carry out for Him the custom
of the Law,
28 then he took Him into his
arms, and blessed God, and said,

29 [a]Luke 2:26 **29** "Now Lord, Thou dost let
Thy bond-servant de-
part
In peace, [a]according to Thy
word;
30 [a]Is 52:10; Luke 3:6 **30** For my eyes have [a]seen
Thy salvation,
31 Which Thou hast prepared in the presence of
all peoples,
★32 [a]Is 42:6; 49:6; Acts 13:47; 26:23 **32** [a]A LIGHT OF REVELATION TO
THE GENTILES,
And the glory of Thy peo-
ple Israel."

33 [a]Matt 12:46 **33** And His father and [a]moth-
er were amazed at the things
34 [a]Matt 12:46 [b]Matt 21:44; 1 Cor 1:23; 2 Cor 2:16; 1 Pet 2:8 which were being said about Him.
34 And Simeon blessed them,
and said to Mary [a]His mother,
"Behold, this *Child* is appointed
for [b]the fall and rise of many in
Israel, and for a sign to be opposed —
35 and a sword will pierce ★35
even your own soul — to the end
that thoughts from many hearts
may be revealed."
36 And there was a [a]prophet- 36 [a]Luke 2:38; Acts 21:9 [b]Josh 19:24 [c]1 Tim 5:9
ess, Anna the daughter of Phanu-
el, of [b]the tribe of Asher. She was
advanced in years, [c]having lived
with a husband seven years after
her marriage,
37 and then as a widow to the 37 [a]Luke 5:33; Acts 13:3; 14:23; 1 Tim 5:5
age of eighty-four. And she *never*
left the temple, serving night and
day with [a]fastings and prayers.
38 And at that very moment 38 [a]Luke 1:68; 2:25
she came up and *began* giving
thanks to God, and continued to
speak of Him to all those who
were [a]looking for the redemption
of Jerusalem.

F The Advancement of the Boy, 2:39–52

39 And when they had per- 39 [a]Matt 2:23; Luke 1:26; 2:51; 4:16
formed everything according to
the Law of the Lord, they returned to Galilee, to [a]their own
city of Nazareth.
40 [a]And the Child continued 40 [a]Luke 1:80; 2:52
to grow and become strong, in-
creasing in wisdom; and the grace
of God was upon Him.
41 And His parents used to 41 [a]Ex 23:15; Deut 16:1-6
go to Jerusalem every year at [a]the
Feast of the Passover.
42 And when He became ★42
twelve, they went up *there* according to the custom of the
Feast;
43 and as they were return- 43 [a]Ex 12:15
ing, after spending the [a]full number of days, the boy Jesus stayed
behind in Jerusalem. And His
parents were unaware of it,

2:24 *A pair of turtledoves.* This shows the poverty of Christ's family, since they could not afford a lamb for the offering.

2:25 *Simeon.* All we know of Simeon is what Luke tells us here. *the consolation of Israel* is the promised Messiah.

2:32 Christ's salvation was offered to Gentile and Jew alike.

2:35 *a sword.* Refers to the agony which Mary would have to bear.

2:42 *when He became twelve.* At 13 a Jewish boy became a "son of the commandment" and a full member of the religious community. This age was often anticipated by one or two years in the matter of going to the temple.

44 but supposed Him to be in
the caravan, and went a day's
journey; and they *began* looking
for Him among their relatives and
acquaintances.
45 And when they did not
find Him, they returned to Jerusalem, looking for Him.
46 And it came about that after three days they found Him in
the temple, sitting in the midst of
the teachers, both listening to
them, and asking them questions.
47 And all who heard Him
were amazed at His understanding and His answers.
★**48** [a]Matt. 12:46 [b]Luke 2:49; 3:23; 4:22 **48** And when they saw Him,
they were astonished; and [a]His
mother said to Him, "Son, why
have You treated us this way? Behold, [b]Your father and I have
been anxiously looking for You."
49 And He said to them,
"Why is it that you were looking
for Me? Did you not know that I
had to be in My Father's *house?*"
50 [a]Mark 9:32 **50** And [a]they did not understand the statement which He had
made to them.
★**51** [a]Luke 2:39 [b]Matt. 12:46 [c]Luke 2:19 **51** And He went down with
them, and came to [a]Nazareth; and
He continued in subjection to
them; and [b]His mother [c]treasured
all *these* things in her heart.
52 [a]Luke 2:40 **52** And Jesus kept increasing
in wisdom and stature, and in [a]fa-
vor with God and men.

G The Baptism of the Son of Man, 3:1–22

★ **1** [a]Matt. 27:2 [b]Matt. 14:1 **3** Now in the fifteenth year of
the reign of Tiberius Caesar,
when [a]Pontius Pilate was governor of Judea, and [b]Herod was tetrarch of Galilee, and his brother
Philip was tetrarch of the region
of Ituraea and Trachonitis, and
Lysanias was tetrarch of Abilene,
2 in the high priesthood of ★ **2** [a]John 18:13, 24; Acts 4:6 [b]Matt. 26:3 [c]Luke 3:3-10; *Matt. 3:1-10; Mark 1:3-5*
[a]Annas and [b]Caiaphas, [c]the word
of God came to John, the son of
Zacharias, in the wilderness.
3 And he came into all [a]the
district around the Jordan, **3** [a]Matt. 3:5
preaching a baptism of repen-
tance for forgiveness of sins;
4 as it is written in the book **4** [a]Is. 40:3
of the words of Isaiah the
prophet, "[a]THE VOICE OF ONE CRYING
IN THE WILDERNESS,

'MAKE READY THE WAY OF THE
LORD,
MAKE HIS PATHS STRAIGHT.
5 '[a]EVERY RAVINE SHALL BE **5** [a]Is. 40:4
FILLED UP,
AND EVERY MOUNTAIN AND
HILL SHALL BE BROUGHT
LOW;
AND THE CROOKED SHALL BE-
COME STRAIGHT,
AND THE ROUGH ROADS
SMOOTH;
6 [a]AND ALL FLESH SHALL [b]SEE **6** [a]Is. 40:5 [b]Luke 2:30
THE SALVATION OF GOD.' "

7 He therefore *began* saying
to the multitudes who were going
out to be baptized by him, "You
brood of vipers, who warned you
to flee from the wrath to come?
8 "Therefore bring forth ★ **8** [a]Luke 5:21; 13:25, 26; 14:9
fruits in keeping with your repen-
tance, and [a]do not begin to say to
yourselves, 'We have Abraham
for our father,' for I say to you
that God is able from these stones
to raise up children to Abraham.

2:48 *Your father.* As Mary's husband, Joseph was Jesus' legal, though not His natural, father.

2:51 *came to Nazareth.* A veil is drawn over the life of Jesus until the beginning of His public ministry 18 years later.

3:1 *Tiberius Caesar* was the adopted son of Augustus Caesar (2:1) and reigned from A.D. 14–37. *Pilate.* See note on Mark 15:1. *Herod.* Antipas, the son of Herod the Great (Matt. 2:1) ruled over Galilee (*tetrarch* = ruler of one quarter of a given territory). *Philip.* Another son of Herod the Great, he ruled over Ituraea, NE. of Galilee and E. of Mt. Hermon. *Abilene.* A small kingdom on the E. slope of the Lebanon mountains, NE. of Damascus.

3:2 *Annas and Caiaphas.* Caiaphas was the ruling high priest (A.D. 18–36), though Annas, high priest A.D. 6–15, continued to exercise weighty influence (cf. John 18:13; Acts 4:6).

3:8 The meaning is: Do not trust in your religious ancestry, however good it may be; you must personally have a right relation with God.

★9 **9** "And also the axe is already
laid at the root of the trees; every
tree therefore that does not bear
good fruit is cut down and thrown
into the fire."
10 And the multitudes were
questioning him, saying, "Then
what shall we do?"
11 And he would answer and
say to them, "Let the man who
has two tunics share with him
who has none; and let him who
has food do likewise."
★12 **12** And *some* tax-gatherers
also came to be baptized, and
they said to him, "Teacher, what
shall we do?"
13 And he said to them, "Collect
no more than what you have
been ordered to."
★14 **14** And *some* soldiers were
questioning him, saying, "And
what about us, what shall we do?"
And he said to them, "Do not
take money from anyone by
force, or accuse *anyone* falsely,
and be content with your wages."
★15 aJohn 1:19f. **15** Now while the people
were in a state of expectation and
all were wondering in their hearts
about John, [a]as to whether he
might be the Christ,
★16 aLuke 3:16, 17; Matt. 3:11, 12; Mark 1:7, 8 **16** [a]John answered and said to
them all, "As for me, I baptize
you with water; but He who is
mightier than I is coming, and I
am not fit to untie the thong of
His sandals; He Himself will baptize
you in the Holy Spirit and
fire.
17 aIs. 30:24 bMark 9:43, 48 **17** "And His [a]winnowing fork
is in His hand to clean out His
threshing floor, and to gather the
wheat into His barn; but He will
burn up the chaff with [b]unquenchable
fire."
18 So with many other exhortations
also he preached the gospel
to the people.
19 But when [a]Herod the te- ★19 aMatt. 14:3; Mark 6:17 bMatt. 14:1; Luke 3:1
trarch was reproved by him on
account of [a]Herodias, his brother's
wife, and on account of all the
wicked things which [b]Herod had
done,
20 he added this also to them 20 aJohn 3:24
all, that [a]he locked John up in
prison.
21 [a]Now it came about when 21 aLuke 3:21, 22; Matt. 3:13-17; Mark 1:9-11 bMatt. 14:23; Luke 5:16; 9:18, 28f.
all the people were baptized, that
Jesus also was baptized, and while
He was [b]praying, heaven was
opened,
22 and the Holy Spirit de- ★22 aMatt. 3:17
scended upon Him in bodily form
like a dove, and a voice came out
of heaven, "[a]Thou art My beloved
Son, in Thee I am well-pleased."

H The Genealogy of the Son of Man, 3:23–38

23 And [a]when He began His ★23 aMatt. 4:17; Acts 1:1 bMatt. 1:16; Luke 3:23-27
ministry, Jesus Himself was about
thirty years of age, being supposedly
the son of [b]Joseph, the *son* of
Eli,
24 the *son* of Matthat, the *son*
of Levi, the *son* of Melchi, the *son*
of Jannai, the *son* of Joseph,
25 the *son* of Mattathias, the
son of Amos, the *son* of Nahum,
the *son* of Hesli, the *son* of Naggai,
26 the *son* of Maath, the *son*
of Mattathias, the *son* of Semein,
the *son* of Josech, the *son* of Joda,
27 the *son* of Joanan, the *son* 27 aMatt. 1:12

3:9 *the axe is already laid at the root of the trees.* Just as unproductive trees are cut down, so the unfruitful nation of Israel could expect judgment.
3:12 *tax-gatherers.* See notes on Matt. 9:10 and Luke 19:2.
3:14 *soldiers* were often brutal to civilians and practiced extortion.
3:15 *in a state of expectation* of the Messiah's coming.
3:16 *baptize.* See note on Matt. 3:11. *in the Holy Spirit and fire.* The baptism with the Holy Spirit occurred on the day of Pentecost, while the baptism with fire refers to the judgments accompanying the second coming of Christ.
3:19 *Herodias.* See note on Matt. 14:3.
3:22 *like a dove.* The dove was used as a symbol for all kinds of virtues in those days (see Matt. 10:16). All persons of the Trinity were present at Christ's baptism.
3:23 *son of Eli.* Joseph was Jacob's son by birth (Matt. 1:16) and Eli's son by marriage. This is apparently the genealogy of Jesus through His mother, Mary. See note at Matt. 1:1.

of Rhesa, [a]the *son* of Zerubbabel,
the *son* of Shealtiel, the *son* of
Neri,
28 the *son* of Melchi, the *son*
of Addi, the *son* of Cosam, the
son of Elmadam, the *son* of Er,
29 the *son* of Joshua, the *son*
of Eliezer, the *son* of Jorim, the
son of Matthat, the *son* of Levi,
30 the *son* of Simeon, the *son*
of Judah, the *son* of Joseph, the
son of Jonam, the *son* of Eliakim,
31 the *son* of Melea, the *son*
of Menna, the *son* of Mattatha,
the *son* of Nathan, the *son* of David,
32 [a]Luke 3:32-34; *Matt. 1:1-6* **32** [a]the *son* of Jesse, the *son*
of Obed, the *son* of Boaz, the *son*
of Salmon, the *son* of Nahshon,
33 the *son* of Amminadab,
the *son* of Admin, the *son* of
Ram, the *son* of Hezron, the *son*
of Perez, the *son* of Judah,
34 [a]Luke 3:34-36; *Gen. 11:26-30; 1 Chr. 1:24-27* **34** the *son* of Jacob, the *son* of
Isaac, [a]the *son* of Abraham, the
son of Terah, the *son* of Nahor,
35 the *son* of Serug, the *son*
of Reu, the *son* of Peleg, the *son*
of Heber, the *son* of Shelah,
36 [a]Luke 3:36-38; *Gen. 5:3-32; 1 Chr. 1:1-4* **36** the *son* of Cainan, the *son*
of Arphaxad, the *son* of Shem,
[a]the *son* of Noah, the *son* of La-
mech,
37 the *son* of Methuselah, the
son of Enoch, the *son* of Jared, the
son of Mahalaleel, the *son* of Cainan,
38 the *son* of Enosh, the *son*
of Seth, the *son* of Adam, the *son*
of God.

I The Temptation of the Son of Man, 4:1–13

★ 1 [a]Luke 4:1-13; *Matt. 4:1-11; Mark 1:12, 13* [b]Luke 3:3, 21 **4** [a]And Jesus, full of the Holy
Spirit, [b]returned from the
Jordan and was led about by the
Spirit in the wilderness
2 for forty days, while ★ 2
tempted by the devil. And He ate
nothing during those days; and
when they had ended, He became
hungry.
3 And the devil said to Him, ★ 3
"If You are the Son of God, tell
this stone to become bread."
4 And Jesus answered him, ★ 4 [a]Deut. 8:3
"It is written, '[a]MAN SHALL NOT LIVE
ON BREAD ALONE.' "
5 [a]And he led Him up and 5 [a]Matt. 4:8-10 [b]Matt. 24:14
showed Him all the kingdoms of
[b]the world in a moment of time.
6 And the devil said to Him, 6 [a]1 John 5:19
"I will give You all this domain
and its glory; [a]for it has been
handed over to me, and I give it to
whomever I wish.
7 "Therefore if You worship
before me, it shall all be Yours."
8 And Jesus answered and ★ 8 [a]Deut. 6:13
said to him, "It is written, '[a]YOU
SHALL WORSHIP THE LORD YOUR GOD
AND SERVE HIM ONLY.' "
9 [a]And he led Him to Jerusa- ★ 9 [a]Matt. 4:5-7
lem and set Him on the pinnacle
of the temple, and said to Him, "If
You are the Son of God, cast
Yourself down from here;
10 for it is written, ★10 [a]Ps. 91:11

'[a]HE WILL GIVE HIS ANGELS
CHARGE CONCERNING YOU
TO GUARD YOU,'

11 and, 11 [a]Ps. 91:12

'[a]ON THEIR HANDS THEY WILL
BEAR YOU UP,
LEST YOU STRIKE YOUR FOOT
AGAINST A STONE.' "

12 And Jesus answered and ★12 [a]Deut. 6:16
said to him, "It is said, '[a]YOU SHALL

4:1 *the wilderness.* The traditional site of the temptation is NW. of the Dead Sea, near Jericho.
4:2 *tempted by the devil.* See note on Matt. 4:1.
4:3 *If You are the Son of God.* The particular Greek construction used here indicates that the devil did not doubt that Jesus was the Son of God.
4:4 See Deut. 8:3.
4:8 See Deut. 6:13; 10:20.
4:9 *pinnacle of the temple.* One of the battlements or towers that overlooked the courtyard of the temple. If Jesus had cast Himself off and landed unharmed among the crowds below, He surely would have been acclaimed the Messiah.
4:10 See Ps. 91:11–12. Satan omits from the quotation the phrase, "in all your ways," in an attempt to apply the promise to something which was contrary to God's will.
4:12 See Deut. 6:16. The temptations were designed to offer Christ the glory of ruling without the suffering of dying for sin.

NOT FORCE A TEST ON THE LORD YOUR
GOD.' "
13 And when the devil had
finished every temptation, he departed from Him until an opportune time.

III THE MINISTRY OF THE SON OF MAN TO MEN, 4:14–9:50

A The Announcement of His Ministry, 4:14–30

14 [a]Matt. 4:12 [b]Matt. 9:26; Luke 4:37

14 And [a]Jesus returned to
Galilee in the power of the Spirit;
and [b]news about Him spread
through all the surrounding district.

15 [a]Matt. 4:23

15 And He *began* [a]teaching in
their synagogues and was praised
by all.

16 [a]Luke 2:39, 51 [b]Matt. 13:54; Mark 6:1f. [c]Acts 13:14-16

16 And He came to [a]Naza-
reth, where He had been brought
up; and as was His custom, [b]He
entered the synagogue on the
Sabbath, and [c]stood up to read.

★17

17 And the book of the
prophet Isaiah was handed to
Him. And He opened the book,
and found the place where it was
written,

★18 [a]Is. 61:1; Matt. 11:5; 12:18; John 3:34

18 "[a]THE SPIRIT OF THE LORD IS
UPON ME,
BECAUSE HE ANOINTED ME TO
PREACH THE GOSPEL TO THE
POOR.
HE HAS SENT ME TO PROCLAIM
RELEASE TO THE CAPTIVES,
AND RECOVERY OF SIGHT TO
THE BLIND,
TO SET FREE THOSE WHO ARE
DOWNTRODDEN,

19 [a]Lev. 25:10; Is. 61:2

19 [a]TO PROCLAIM THE FAVOR-
ABLE YEAR OF THE LORD."

★20 [a]Luke 4:17 [b]Matt. 26:55

20 And He [a]closed the book,
and gave it back to the attendant,
and [b]sat down; and the eyes of all
in the synagogue were fixed upon
Him.
21 And He began to say to
them, "Today this Scripture has
been fulfilled in your hearing."

22 [a]Matt. 13:55; Mark 6:3; John 6:42

22 And all were speaking well
of Him, and wondering at the gracious words which were falling
from His lips; and they were saying, "[a]Is this not Joseph's son?"

23 [a]Matt. 4:13; Mark 1:21ff.; 2:1ff.; Luke 4:35ff.; John 4:46ff. [b]Mark 6:1; Luke 2:39, 51; 4:16

23 And He said to them, "No
doubt you will quote this proverb
to Me, 'Physician, heal yourself;
whatever we heard was done [a]at
Capernaum, do here in [b]your
home town as well.' "

24 [a]Matt. 13:57; Mark 6:4; John 4:44

24 And He said, "Truly I say
to you, [a]no prophet is welcome in
his home town.

★25 [a]1 Kin. 17:1; 18:1; James 5:17

25 "But I say to you in truth,
there were many widows in Israel
[a]in the days of Elijah, when the
sky was shut up for three years
and six months, when a great
famine came over all the land;

26 [a]1 Kin. 17:9 [b]Matt. 11:21

26 and yet Elijah was sent to
none of them, but [a]only to Zarephath, in the land of [b]Sidon, to a
woman who was a widow.

27 [a]2 Kin. 5:1-14

27 "And there were many lepers in Israel in the time of Elisha
the prophet; and none of them
was cleansed, but [a]only Naaman
the Syrian."
28 And all in the synagogue
were filled with rage as they
heard these things;

29 [a]Num. 15:35; Acts 7:58; Heb. 13:12

29 and they rose up and [a]cast
Him out of the city, and led Him
to the brow of the hill on which
their city had been built, in order
to throw Him down the cliff.

★30 [a]John 10:39

30 But [a]passing through their
midst, He went His way.

4:17 *book.* More correctly, the scroll.

4:18 See Isa. 61:1-2a. Christ stopped reading in the middle of 61:2, since at His first coming He preached only the "favorable year of the Lord" (v. 19). The "day of vengeance of our God" (Isa. 61:2b) was reserved for His second coming. Long-suffering and the cross are associated with His first coming; judgment and a crown, with His second.

4:20 *the attendant* had charge of the scrolls of Scriptures.

4:25-26 The story is in 1 Kings 17:8-24.

4:30 *passing through their midst.* These words do not necessarily imply a miraculous deliverance. Rather, His commanding presence and righteousness had power to thwart the crowd's plan.

B The Authority of His Ministry, 4:31–6:11

1 *Over demons,* 4:31–37

★31 [a]Luke 4:31-37; *Mark 1:21-28* [b]Matt. 4:13; Luke 4:23

31 And [a]He came down to
[b]Capernaum, a city of Galilee.
And He was teaching them on
Sabbath days;

32 [a]Matt. 7:28 [b]Luke 4:36; John 7:46

32 and [a]they were *continually*
amazed at His teaching, for [b]His
message was with authority.

★33

33 And there was a man in
the synagogue possessed by the
spirit of an unclean demon, and
he cried out with a loud voice,

34 [a]Matt. 8:29 [b]Mark 1:24

34 "Ha! [a]What do we have to
do with You, Jesus of [b]Nazareth?
Have You come to destroy us? I
know who You are — [b]the Holy
One of God!"

35 [a]Matt. 8:26; Mark 4:39; Luke 4:39, 41; 8:24

35 And Jesus [a]rebuked him,
saying, "Be quiet and come out of
him!" And when the demon had
thrown him down in *their* midst,
he went out of him without doing
him any harm.

36 [a]Luke 4:32

36 And amazement came
upon them all, and they *began*
discussing with one another, and
saying, "What is this message?
For [a]with authority and power He
commands the unclean spirits,
and they come out."

37 [a]Luke 4:14

37 And [a]the report about Him
was getting out into every locality
in the surrounding district.

2 *Over disease,* 4:38–44

★38 [a]Luke 4:38, 39; *Matt. 8:14, 15; Mark 1:29-31* [b]Matt. 4:24

38 [a]And He arose and *left* the
synagogue, and entered Simon's
home. Now Simon's mother-in-
law was [b]suffering from a high fever; and they made request of
Him on her behalf.

39 [a]Luke 4:35, 41
40 [a]Luke 4:40, 41; *Matt. 8:16, 17; Mark 1:32-34* [b]Mark 1:32 [c]Mark 5:23 [d]Matt. 4:23

39 And standing over her, He
[a]rebuked the fever, and it left her;
and she immediately arose and
began to wait on them.
40 [a]And while [b]the sun was
setting, all who had any sick with
various diseases brought them to
Him; and [c]laying His hands on
every one of them, He was [d]heal-
ing them.

41 [a]Matt. 4:3 [b]Luke 4:35 [c]Matt. 8:4; Mark 1:34

41 And demons also were
coming out of many, crying out
and saying, "You are [a]the Son of
God!" And [b]rebuking them, He
would [c]not allow them to speak,
because they knew Him to be the
Christ.

42 [a]Luke 4:42, 43; *Mark 1:35-38*

42 [a]And when day came, He
departed and went to a lonely
place; and the multitudes were
searching for Him, and came to
Him, and tried to keep Him from
going away from them.

43 [a]Mark 1:38

43 But He said to them, "I
must preach the kingdom of God
to the other cities also, [a]for I was
sent for this purpose."

44 [a]Matt. 4:23

44 And He kept on preaching
in the synagogues [a]of Judea.

3 *Over the disciples,* 5:1–11

★ 1 [a]Matt. 4:18-22; Mark 1:16-20; Luke 5:1-11; John 1:40-42 [b]Num. 34:11; Deut. 3:17; Josh. 12:3; 13:27; Matt. 4:18

5 [a]Now it came about that
while the multitude were
pressing around Him and listening to the word of God, He was
standing by [b]the lake of Gennesaret;

2 and He saw two boats
lying at the edge of the lake; but
the fishermen had gotten out of
them, and were washing their
nets.

3 [a]Matt. 13:2; Mark 4:1

3 And [a]He got into one of
the boats, which was Simon's,
and asked him to put out a little
way from the land. And He sat
down and *began* teaching the
multitudes from the boat.

4 [a]John 21:6

4 And when He had finished
speaking, He said to Simon, "Put
out into the deep water and [a]let
down your nets for a catch."

5 [a]Gr. as in Luke 8:24; 9:33, 49; 17:13

5 And Simon answered and
said, "[a]Master, we worked hard
all night and caught nothing, but
at Your bidding I will let down
the nets."
6 And when they had done
this, they enclosed a great quan-

4:31 *Capernaum.* A city on the shore of the Lake of Galilee, about 25 miles NE. of Nazareth. Jesus carried on an extensive ministry there.

4:33 *demon.* See note on Matt. 7:22.

4:38 *a high fever.* Only Luke, a physician, recorded this fact.

5:1 *the lake of Gennesaret.* The Lake, or Sea, of Galilee.

tity of fish; and their nets *began* to break;

7 and they signaled to their partners in the other boat, for them to come and help them. And they came, and filled both of the boats, so that they began to sink.

★8 8 But when Simon Peter saw *that,* he fell down at Jesus' feet, saying, "Depart from me, for I am a sinful man, O Lord!"

9 For amazement had seized him and all his companions because of the catch of fish which they had taken;

10 [a]Matt. 14:27 [b]2 Tim. 2:26

10 and so also James and John, sons of Zebedee, who were partners with Simon. And Jesus said to Simon, "[a]Do not fear, from now on you will be [b]catching men."

11 [a]Matt. 4:20, 22; 19:29; Mark 1:18, 20; Luke 5:28

11 And when they had brought their boats to land, [a]they left everything and followed Him.

4 *Over defilement (a leper healed),* 5:12-16

★12 [a]Luke 5:12-14: *Matt. 8:2-4; Mark 1:40-44*

12 [a]And it came about that while He was in one of the cities, behold, *there was* a man full of leprosy; and when he saw Jesus, he fell on his face and implored Him, saying, "Lord, if You are willing, You can make me clean."

13 And He stretched out His hand, and touched him, saying, "I am willing; be cleansed." And immediately the leprosy left him.

14 [a]Lev. 13:49; 14:2ff

14 And He ordered him to tell no one, "But go and [a]SHOW YOURSELF TO THE PRIEST, and make an offering for your cleansing, just as Moses commanded, for a testimony to them."

15 [a]Matt. 9:26

15 But [a]the news about Him was spreading even farther, and great multitudes were gathering to hear *Him* and to be healed of their sicknesses.

16 But He Himself would *often* slip away to the wilderness and [a]pray.

★16 [a]Matt. 14:23; Mark 1:35; Luke 6:12

5 *Over defectiveness (a paralytic healed),* 5:17-26

17 And it came about one day that He was teaching; and [a]there were *some* Pharisees and [b]teachers of the law sitting *there,* who had [c]come from every village of Galilee and Judea and *from* Jerusalem; and [d]the power of the Lord was *present* for Him to perform healing.

★17 [a]Matt. 15:1 [b]Luke 2:46 [c]Mark 1:45 [d]Mark 5:30; Luke 6:19; 8:46

18 [a]And behold, *some* men *were* carrying on a bed a man who was paralyzed; and they were trying to bring him in, and to set him down in front of Him.

18 [a]Luke 5:18-26: *Matt. 9:2-8; Mark 2:3-12*

19 And not finding any *way* to bring him in because of the crowd, they went up on [a]the roof and let him down [b]through the tiles with his stretcher, right in the center, in front of Jesus.

19 [a]Matt. 24:17 [b]Mark 2:4

20 And seeing their faith, He said, "Friend, [a]your sins are forgiven you."

★20 [a]Matt. 9:2

21 And the scribes and the Pharisees [a]began to reason, saying, "Who is this *man* who speaks blasphemies? [b]Who can forgive sins, but God alone?"

21 [a]Luke 3:8 [b]Is. 43:25

22 But Jesus, aware of their reasonings, answered and said to them, "Why are you reasoning in your hearts?

23 "Which is easier, to say, 'Your sins have been forgiven you,' or to say, 'Rise and walk'?

5:8 The miracle demonstrated to Peter his own sinfulness and Jesus' deity.

5:12 *leprosy.* See Lev. 13 for 7 forms of this skin disease, generally regarded not to be the leprosy we know today. A leper was ceremonially unclean, had to live outside of the towns, and had to cry "unclean" when other people came near. Leprosy serves as an illustration of sin.

5:16 *pray.* See Introduction, under "Distinctive Approach."

5:17 Only Luke mentions the presence of religious leaders from all parts of the land, listening critically to the claims of Jesus.

5:20 *Friend, your sins are forgiven you.* The Lord began with the man's greater problem, his spiritual need, rather than his physical one. Jesus' statement was considered blasphemy, since it was clearly understood to be a claim of being equal with God. See notes on Matt. 9:2 and 9:5.

24 [a]Matt. 4:24

24 "But in order that you may know that the Son of Man has authority on earth to forgive sins," He said to the [a]paralytic, "I say to you, rise, and take up your stretcher and go home."

25 [a]Matt. 9:8

25 And at once he rose up before them, and took up what he had been lying on, and went home, [a]glorifying God.

26 [a]Matt. 9:8 [b]Luke 1:65; 7:16

26 And they were all seized with astonishment and *began* [a]glorifying God; and they were filled [b]with fear, saying, "We have seen remarkable things today."

6 Over the despised (the call of Matthew and parables), 5:27–39

★27 [a]Luke 5:27-39; *Matt. 9:9-17; Mark 2:14-22* [b]Matt. 9:9

27 [a]And after that He went out, and noticed a tax-gatherer named [b]Levi, sitting in the tax office, and He said to him, "Follow Me."

28 [a]Luke 5:11

28 And he [a]left everything behind, and rose up and *began* to follow Him.

29 [a]Matt. 9:9 [b]Luke 15:1

29 And [a]Levi gave a big reception for Him in his house; and there was a great crowd of [b]tax-gatherers and other *people* who were reclining *at table* with them.

30 [a]Mark 2:16; Acts 23:9

30 And the Pharisees and [a]their scribes *began* grumbling at His disciples, saying, "Why do you eat and drink with the tax-gatherers and sinners?"

31 [a]Matt. 9:12, 13; Mark 2:17

31 And Jesus answered and said to them, "[a]*It is* not those who are well who need a physician, but those who are sick.

32 "I have not come to call righteous men but sinners to repentance."

33 [a]Matt. 9:14; Mark 2:18

33 And they said to Him, "[a]The disciples of John often fast and offer prayers; the *disciples* of the Pharisees also do the same; but Yours eat and drink."

34 And Jesus said to them, "You cannot make the attendants of the bridegroom fast while the bridegroom is with them, can you?

35 [a]Matt. 9:15; Mark 2:20; Luke 17:22

35 "[a]But *the* days will come; and when the bridegroom is taken away from them, then they will fast in those days."

36 And He was also telling them a parable: "No one tears a piece from a new garment and puts it on an old garment; otherwise he will both tear the new, and the piece from the new will not match the old.

★37

37 "And no one puts new wine into old wineskins; otherwise the new wine will burst the skins, and it will be spilled out, and the skins will be ruined.

38 "But new wine must be put into fresh wineskins.

39 "And no one, after drinking old *wine* wishes for new; for he says, 'The old is good *enough.*'"

7 Over days, 6:1–5

1 [a]Luke 5:1-5; *Matt. 12:1-8; Mark 2:23-28* [b]Deut. 23:25

6 [a]Now it came about that on a *certain* Sabbath He was passing through *some* grainfields; and His disciples [b]were picking and eating the heads *of wheat,* rubbing them in their hands.

★ 2 [a]Matt. 12:2

2 But some of the Pharisees said, "Why do you do what [a]is not lawful on the Sabbath?"

★ 3 [a]1 Sam. 21:6

3 And Jesus answering them said, "Have you not even read [a]what David did when he was hungry, he and those who were with him,

4 how he entered the house of God, and took and ate the con-

5:27 *Levi.* Matthew. See Introduction to Matthew and note on Matt. 9:10.

5:37 *wineskins.* Used as containers for liquid. If filled with new wine, old skins lost elasticity and burst when it fermented. The point is that the new teaching of the grace of Christ cannot be contained within the old forms of the law (John 1:17).

6:2 *not lawful on the Sabbath.* Jesus was being charged with working on the Sabbath, though it was lawful to pick grain from another's field to satisfy hunger (Deut. 23:25).

6:3 *what David did.* See 1 Sam. 21:1–6. To the Pharisees' objections Jesus quoted an O.T. example of the spirit of the law taking priority over the letter of the law. See note on Matt. 12:2.

secrated bread which is not lawful
for any to eat except the priests
alone, and gave it to his companions?"
★ 5 **5** And He was saying to
them, "The Son of Man is Lord of
the Sabbath."

8 Over deformity, 6:6–11

6 [a]Luke 5:6-11; *Matt. 12:9-14; Mark 3:1-6* [b]Luke 6:1 [c]Matt. 4:23 **6** [a]And it came about [b]on
another Sabbath, that He entered
[c]the synagogue and was teaching;
and there was a man there whose
right hand was withered.
★ 7 [a]Mark 3:2 **7** And the scribes and the
Pharisees [a]were watching Him
closely, *to see* if He healed on the
Sabbath, in order that they might
find *reason* to accuse Him.
8 [a]Matt. 9:4 **8** But He [a]knew what they
were thinking, and He said to the
man with the withered hand,
"Arise and come forward!" And
he arose and came forward.
9 And Jesus said to them, "I
ask you, is it lawful on the Sabbath to do good, or to do evil, to
save a life, or to destroy it?"
10 [a]Mark 3:5 **10** And after [a]looking around
at them all, He said to him,
"Stretch out your hand!" And he
did *so;* and his hand was *completely* restored.
11 But they themselves were
filled with rage, and discussed together what they might do to
Jesus.

C The Associates of His Ministry, 6:12–49

1 The call of the disciples, 6:12–16

12 [a]Matt. 5:1 [b]Matt. 14:23; Luke 5:16; 9:18, 28 **12** And it was at this time
that He went off to [a]the mountain
to [b]pray, and He spent the whole
night in prayer to God.
13 And when day came, [a]He ★13 [a]Luke 6:13-16; *Matt. 10:2-4; Mark 3:16-19; Acts 1:13* [b]Mark 6:30
called His disciples to Him; and
chose twelve of them, whom He
also named as [b]apostles:
14 Simon, whom He also
named Peter, and Andrew his
brother; James and John; Philip
and Bartholomew;
15 [a]Matthew and Thomas; 15 [a]Matt. 9:9
James *the son* of Alphaeus, and
Simon who was called the Zealot;
16 Judas *the son* of James, and
Judas Iscariot, who became a trai-
tor.

2 The characteristics of disciples (The Great Sermon), 6:17–49

17 And He [a]descended with ★17 [a]Luke 6:12 [b]Matt. 4:25; Mark 3:7, 8 [c]Matt. 11:21
them, and stood on a level place;
and *there was* [b]a great multitude
of His disciples, and a great
throng of people from all Judea
and Jerusalem and the coastal region of [c]Tyre and Sidon,
18 who had come to hear
Him, and to be healed of their
diseases; and those who were
troubled with unclean spirits were
being cured.
19 And all the multitude were 19 [a]Matt. 9:21; 14:36; Mark 3:10 [b]Luke 5:17
trying to [a]touch Him, for [b]power
was coming from Him and healing *them* all.
20 And turning His gaze on 20 [a]Matt. 5:3-12; Luke 6:20-23 [b]Matt. 5:3
His disciples, He *began* to say,
"[a]Blessed *are* you *who are* poor,
for [b]yours is the kingdom of God.
21 "Blessed *are* you who hunger now, for you shall be satisfied.
Blessed *are* you who weep now,
for you shall laugh.
22 "Blessed are you when men 22 [a]John 9:22; 16:2
hate you, and [a]ostracize you, and
heap insults upon you, and spurn

6:5 *Lord of the Sabbath.* Not only had Christ claimed deity (5:20), but now He claimed sovereignty over the Sabbath day and its laws, and asserted His right to interpret its laws without reference to the traditions of the Pharisees.

6:7 *reason to accuse Him.* To heal on the Sabbath would have been a violation, according to the traditions of the Pharisees, of the prohibition against work on that day; but not to heal, as Christ tried to point out, would have been to do evil and to destroy life (v. 9). To heal, and therefore to do a good work, would be no violation of Sabbath laws.

6:13 *apostles.* See note on Matt. 10:2.

6:17–26 This may be Luke's account of the same occasion and teaching recorded in Matt. 5–7 (the Sermon on the Mount) or it may simply be similar teaching given on a different occasion.

your name as evil, for the sake of
the Son of Man.
23 [a]Mal. 4 **23** "Be glad in that day, and
[a]leap *for joy,* for behold, your reward is great in heaven; for in the
same way their fathers used to
treat the prophets.
24 [a]Luke **24** "But woe to [a]you who are
16:25; James rich, for [b]you are receiving your
5:1 [b]Matt. 6:2 comfort in full.
25 "Woe to you who are well-
fed now, for you shall be hungry.
Woe *to you* who laugh now, for
you shall mourn and weep.
26 [a]Matt. **26** "Woe *to you* when all men
7:15 speak well of you, for in the same
way their fathers used to treat the
[a]false prophets.
27 [a]Matt. **27** "But I say to you who hear,
5:44; Luke [a]love your enemies, do good to
6:35 those who hate you,
28 [a]Matt. **28** bless those who curse you,
5:44; Luke [a]pray for those who mistreat you.
6:35
29 [a]Luke **29** "[a]Whoever hits you on the
6:29, 30; cheek, offer him the other also;
Matt. 5:39-42 and whoever takes away your
coat, do not withhold your shirt
from him either.
30 "Give to everyone who asks
of you, and whoever takes away
what is yours, do not demand it
back.
31 [a]Matt. **31** "[a]And just as you want men
7:12 to treat you, treat them in the
same way.
32 [a]Matt. **32** "And [a]if you love those
5:46 who love you, what credit is *that*
to you? For even sinners love
those who love them.
33 "And if you do good to
those who do good to you, what
credit is *that* to you? For even sinners do the same thing.
34 [a]Matt. **34** "[a]And if you lend to those
5:42 from whom you expect to receive,
what credit is *that* to you? Even
sinners lend to sinners, in order to
receive back the same *amount.*
35 [a]Luke **35** "But [a]love your enemies,
6:27 [b]Matt. and do good, and lend, expecting
5:9 [c]Luke nothing in return; and your re-
1:32 ward will be great, and you will
be [b]sons of [c]the Most High; for
He Himself is kind to ungrateful
and evil *men.*
36 "Be merciful, just as your
Father is merciful.
37 "[a]And do not pass judg- 37 [a]Luke
ment and you will not be judged; 6:37-42; *Matt. 7:1-5*
and do not condemn, and you [b]Matt. 6:14;
shall not be condemned; [b]pardon, Luke 23:16; Acts 3:13
and you will be pardoned.
38 "Give, and it will be given ★38 [a]Mark
to you; [a]good measure, pressed 4:24 [b]Ps. 79:12; Is.
down, shaken together, running 65:6, 7; Jer.
over, they will pour [b]into your 32:18
lap. For whatever measure you
deal out *to others,* it will be dealt
to you in return."
39 And He also spoke a par- 39 [a]Matt.
able to them: "[a]A blind man can- 15:14
not guide a blind man, can he?
Will they not both fall into a pit?
40 "[a]A pupil is not above his 40 [a]Matt.
teacher; but everyone, after he 10:24
has been fully trained, will be like
his teacher.
41 "And why do you look at ★41
the speck that is in your brother's
eye, but do not notice the log that
is in your own eye?
42 "Or how can you say to
your brother, 'Brother, let me
take out the speck that is in your
eye,' when you yourself do not
see the log that is in your own
eye? You hypocrite, first take the
log out of your own eye, and then
you will see clearly to take out the
speck that is in your brother's
eye.
43 "[a]For there is no good tree 43 [a]Luke
which produces bad fruit; nor, on 6:43, 44; *Matt. 7:16,*
the other hand, a bad tree which *18, 20*
produces good fruit.
44 "[a]For each tree is known by 44 [a]Matt.
its own fruit. For men do not 7:16
gather figs from thorns, nor do
they pick grapes from a briar
bush.
45 "[a]The good man out of the 45 [a]Matt.
good treasure of his heart brings 12:35 [b]Matt.
forth what is good; and the evil 12:34
man out of the evil *treasure*
brings forth what is evil; [b]for his

6:38 *pressed down, shaken together, running over.* The imagery is of a container of grain filled to the brim and running over the edge. Our liberality should be like that.

6:41 *speck . . . log.* A speck is something tiny like a bit of sawdust, while a log, of course, is large. Perhaps Jesus was drawing on His experience as a carpenter.

mouth speaks from that which fills his heart.

46 aMal. 1:6; Matt. 7:21 **46** "And [a]why do you call Me, 'Lord, Lord,' and do not do what I say?

47 aLuke 6:47-49; *Matt. 7:24-27* **47** "[a]Everyone who comes to Me, and hears My words, and acts upon them, I will show you whom he is like:

48 he is like a man building a house, who dug deep and laid a foundation upon the rock; and when a flood arose, the river burst against that house and could not shake it, because it had been well built.

49 "But the one who has heard, and has not acted *accordingly,* is like a man who built a house upon the ground without any foundation; and the river burst against it and immediately it collapsed, and the ruin of that house was great."

D The Activities of His Ministry, 7:1–9:50

1 Ministry in sickness, 7:1–10

1 aMatt. 7:28 bLuke 7:1-10; *Matt. 8:5-13* **7** [a]When He had completed all His discourse in the hearing of the people, [b]He went to Capernaum.

★ 2 **2** And a certain centurion's slave, who was highly regarded by him, was sick and about to die.

3 aMatt. 8:5 **3** And when he heard about Jesus, [a]he sent some Jewish elders asking Him to come and save the life of his slave.

4 And when they had come to Jesus, they earnestly entreated Him, saying, "He is worthy for You to grant this to him;

★ 5 **5** for he loves our nation, and it was he who built us our synagogue."

6 Now Jesus *started* on His way with them; and when He was already not far from the house, the centurion sent friends, saying to Him, "Lord, do not trouble Yourself further, for I am not fit for You to come under my roof;

7 for this reason I did not even consider myself worthy to come to You, but just say the word, and my servant will be healed.

8 "For indeed, I am a man under authority, with soldiers under me; and I say to this one, 'Go!' and he goes; and to another, 'Come!' and he comes; and to my slave, 'Do this!' and he does it."

9 And when Jesus heard this, He marveled at him, and turned and said to the multitude that was following Him, "I say to you, [a]not even in Israel have I found such great faith." ★ 9 aMatt. 8:10; Luke 7:50

10 And when those who had been sent returned to the house, they found the slave in good health.

2 Ministry in death, 7:11–17

11 And it came about soon afterwards, that He went to a city called Nain; and His disciples were going along with Him, accompanied by a large multitude. ★11

12 Now as He approached the gate of the city, behold, a dead man was being carried out, the only son of his mother, and she was a widow; and a sizeable crowd from the city was with her.

13 And when [a]the Lord saw her, He felt compassion for her, and said to her, "Do not weep." 13 aLuke 7:19; 10:1; 11:1, 39; 12:42; 13:15; 17:5, 6; 18:6; 19:8; 22:61; 24:34; John 4:1; 6:23; 11:2

14 And He came up and touched the coffin; and the bearers came to a halt. And He said, "Young man, I say to you, arise!"

7:2 *centurion.* Here was an atypical Roman officer who loved his servant and the Jewish people.

7:5 *synagogue.* A Jewish house of worship, first established during the Babylonian captivity but also used after the temple was rebuilt by Jews wherever they settled. Services included prescribed readings, prayer, and a sermon (4:20). Any competent teacher might be asked to speak (Acts 13:15). Ruins of a later synagogue can be seen in Capernaum today.

7:9 *such great faith.* This Gentile's faith was a welcome contrast to the unbelief of the Jews.

7:11 *Nain.* About 10 miles SE. of Nazareth.

★15

15 And the dead man sat up, and began to speak. And *Jesus* gave him back to his mother.

16 [a]Luke 5:26 [b]Matt. 9:8 [c]Matt. 21:11; Luke 7:39

16 And [a]fear gripped them all, and they *began* [b]glorifying God, saying, "A great [c]prophet has arisen among us!" and, "God has visited His people!"

17 [a]Matt. 9:26

17 [a]And this report concerning Him went out all over Judea, and in all the surrounding district.

3 *Ministry in doubt,* 7:18–35

18 [a]Luke 7:18-35: *Matt. 11:2-19*

18 [a]And the disciples of John reported to him about all these things.

19 [a]Luke 7:13; 10:1; 11:1, 39; 12:42; 13:15; 17:5, 6; 18:6; 19:8; 22:61; 24:34; John 4:1; 6:23; 11:2

19 And summoning two of his disciples, John sent them to [a]the Lord, saying, "Are You the One who is coming, or do we look for someone else?"

20 And when the men had come to Him, they said, "John the Baptist has sent us to You, saying, 'Are You the One who is coming, or do we look for someone else?' "

21 [a]Matt. 4:23 [b]Mark 3:10

21 At that very time He [a]cured many *people* of diseases and [b]afflictions and evil spirits; and He granted sight to many *who were* blind.

★22 [a]Is. 61:1

22 And He answered and said to them, "Go and report to John what you have seen and heard: *the* [a]BLIND RECEIVE SIGHT, *the* lame walk, *the* lepers are cleansed, and *the* deaf hear, *the* dead are raised up, *the* [a]POOR HAVE THE GOSPEL PREACHED TO THEM.

23 "And blessed is he who keeps from stumbling over Me."

★24

24 And when the messengers of John had left, He began to speak to the multitudes about John, "What did you go out into the wilderness to look at? A reed shaken by the wind?

25 "But what did you go out to see? A man dressed in soft clothing? Behold, those who are splendidly clothed and live in luxury are *found* in royal palaces.

26 "But what did you go out to see? A prophet? Yes, I say to you, and one who is more than a prophet.

27 [a]Mal. 3:1; Matt. 11:10; Mark 1:2

27 "This is the one about whom it is written,

> '[a]BEHOLD, I SEND MY MESSENGER BEFORE YOUR FACE,
> WHO WILL PREPARE YOUR WAY BEFORE YOU.'

★28

28 "I say to you, among those born of women, there is no one greater than John; yet he who is least in the kingdom of God is greater than he."

29 [a]Luke 7:35 [b]Matt. 21:32; Luke 3:12 [c]Acts 18:25; 19:3

29 And when all the people and the tax-gatherers heard *this,* they acknowledged [a]God's justice, [b]having been baptized with [c]the baptism of John.

30 [a]Matt. 22:35

30 But the Pharisees and the [a]lawyers rejected God's purpose for themselves, not having been baptized by John.

31 "To what then shall I compare the men of this generation, and what are they like?

32 "They are like children who sit in the market place and call to one another; and they say, 'We played the flute for you, and you did not dance; we sang a dirge, and you did not weep.'

33 [a]Luke 1:15

33 "For John the Baptist has come [a]eating no bread and drinking no wine; and you say, 'He has a demon!'

34 "The Son of Man has come eating and drinking; and you say, 'Behold, a gluttonous man, and a drunkard, a friend of tax-gatherers and sinners!'

7:15 *And the dead man sat up.* One of three resurrections recorded in the Gospels that Christ effected, the others being those of Jairus' daughter (Mark 5:41) and Lazarus (John 11:44).

7:22 *report to John what you have seen and heard.* These were things the O.T. predicted the Messiah would do, and Jesus had done them; the men, therefore, had their answer.

7:24-25 John the Baptist was not like a reed that bends in whatever direction the wind blows it, but was a man of conviction. Neither was he given to soft living.

7:28 *no one greater than John.* See note on Matt. 11:11.

35 [a]Luke 7:29 35 "Yet wisdom [a]is vindicated
by all her children."

4 *Ministry to sinners,* 7:36–50

★36 36 Now one of the Pharisees
was requesting Him to dine with
him. And He entered the Pharisee's house, and reclined *at table.*
★37 [a]Matt. 26:6-13; Mark 14:3-9; Luke 7:37-39; John 12:1-8 37 [a]And behold, there was a
woman in the city who was a sin-
ner; and when she learned that
He was reclining *at table* in the
Pharisee's house, she brought an
alabaster vial of perfume,
38 and standing behind *Him*
at His feet, weeping, she began to
wet His feet with her tears, and
kept wiping them with the hair of
her head, and kissing His feet,
and anointing them with the perfume.
39 [a]Luke 7:16; John 4:19 39 Now when the Pharisee
who had invited Him saw this, he
said to himself, "If this man were
[a]a prophet He would know who
and what sort of person this
woman is who is touching Him,
that she is a sinner."
40 And Jesus answered and
said to him, "Simon, I have something to say to you." And he replied, "Say it, Teacher."
★41 [a]Matt. 18:28; Mark 6:37 41 "A certain moneylender
had two debtors: one owed five
hundred [a]denarii, and the other
fifty.
42 [a]Matt. 18:25 42 "When they [a]were unable
to repay, he graciously forgave
them both. Which of them therefore will love him more?"
43 Simon answered and said,
"I suppose the one whom he forgave more." And He said to him,
"You have judged correctly."
44 [a]Gen. 18:4; 19:2; 43:24; Judg. 19:21; 1 Tim. 5:10 44 And turning toward the
woman, He said to Simon, "Do
you see this woman? I entered
your house; you [a]gave Me no water for My feet, but she has wet
My feet with her tears, and wiped
them with her hair.
45 "You [a]gave Me no kiss; but 45 [a]2 Sam. 15:5
she, since the time I came in, has
not ceased to kiss My feet.
46 "[a]You did not anoint My 46 [a]2 Sam. 12:20; Ps. 23:5; Eccles. 9:8; Dan. 10:3
head with oil, but she anointed
My feet with perfume.
47 "For this reason I say to
you, her sins, which are many,
have been forgiven, for she loved
much; but he who is forgiven little, loves little."
48 And He said to her, "[a]Your 48 [a]Matt. 9:2
sins have been forgiven."
49 And those who were re-
clining *at table* with Him began to
say to themselves, "Who is this
man who even forgives sins?"
50 And He said to the 50 [a]Matt. 9:22 [b]Mark 5:34; Luke 8:48
woman, "[a]Your faith has saved
you; [b]go in peace."

5 *Ministry financed,* 8:1–3

8 And it came about soon af- 1 [a]Matt. 4:23
terwards, that He *began*
going about from one city and village to another, [a]proclaiming and
preaching the kingdom of God;
and the twelve were with Him,
2 and *also* [a]some women ★ 2 [a]Matt. 27:55f.; Luke 23:49
who had been healed of evil spir-
its and sicknesses: [a]Mary who
was called Magdalene, from
whom seven demons had gone
out,
3 and Joanna the wife of ★ 3 [a]Matt. 14:1 [b]Matt. 20:8
Chuza, [a]Herod's [b]steward, and
Susanna, and many others who
were contributing to their support
out of their private means.

7:36–50 This is not the same as a similar incident which occurred in Bethany of Judea during the last week of Christ's life (Matt. 26:6–31; Mark 14:3–9; John 12:1–8).

7:37 *an alabaster vial of perfume.* A long-necked flask of fine translucent material, used for storing perfume.

7:41 *denarii.* A Roman silver coin (singular, denarius), a day's wage for ordinary workers.

8:2 *Mary who was called Magdalene.* From Magdala, a small town between Capernaum and Tiberius. Other Marys in the N.T. are: (1) the mother of Jesus (1:27); (2) the mother of James and wife of Alphaeus, or Clopas (6:15; John 19:25)—these two Marys were evidently cousins; (3) the sister of Martha and Lazarus (Luke 10:39); (4) the mother of John Mark (Acts 12:12); and (5) a Christian woman in Rome (Rom. 16:6).

8:3 *Herod's steward.* A position of some rank involving the management of Herod's finances. *were contributing to their support.* These women helped finance the ministry of the twelve.

6 *Ministry illustrated through parables,* 8:4–21

4 [a]Luke 8:4-8: *Matt. 13:2-9; Mark 4:1-9*

4 [a]And when a great multitude were coming together, and those from the various cities were journeying to Him, He spoke by way of a parable:

5 "The sower went out to sow his seed; and as he sowed, some fell beside the road; and it was trampled under foot, and the birds of the air devoured it.

★ 6

6 "And other *seed* fell on rocky *soil,* and as soon as it grew up, it withered away, because it had no moisture.

7 "And other *seed* fell among the thorns; and the thorns grew up with it, and choked it out.

8 [a]Matt. 11:15

8 "And other *seed* fell into the good ground, and grew up, and produced a crop a hundred times as great." As He said these things, He would call out, "[a]He who has ears to hear, let him hear."

9 [a]Luke 8:9-15: *Matt. 13:10-23; Mark 4:10-20*

9 [a]And His disciples *began* questioning Him as to what this parable might be.

10 [a]Matt. 13:11 [b]Is. 6:9; Matt. 13:14

10 And He said, "[a]To you it is granted to know the mysteries of the kingdom of God, but to the rest *it is* in parables; in order that [b]SEEING THEY MAY NOT SEE, AND HEARING THEY MAY NOT UNDERSTAND.

11 [a]1 Pet. 1:23

11 "Now the parable is this: [a]the seed is the word of God.

12 "And those beside the road are those who have heard; then the devil comes and takes away the word from their heart, so that they may not believe and be saved.

13 "And those on the rocky *soil are* those who, when they hear, receive the word with joy; and these have no *firm* root; they believe for a while, and in time of temptation fall away.

14 "And the *seed* which fell among the thorns, these are the ones who have heard, and as they go on their way they are choked with worries and riches and pleasures of *this* life, and bring no fruit to maturity.

15 "And the *seed* in the good ground, these are the ones who have heard the word in an honest and good heart, and hold it fast, and bear fruit with perseverance.

16 "Now [a]no one after lighting a lamp covers it over with a container, or puts it under a bed; but he puts it on a lampstand, in order that those who come in may see the light.

★16 [a]Matt. 5:15; Mark 4:21; Luke 11:33

17 "[a]For nothing is hidden that shall not become evident, nor *anything* secret that shall not be known and come to light.

17 [a]Matt. 10:26; Mark 4:22; Luke 12:2

18 "Therefore take care how you listen; [a]for whoever has, to him shall *more* be given; and whoever does not have, even what he thinks he has shall be taken away from him."

18 [a]Matt. 13:12; Luke 19:26

19 [a]And His mother came to Him and *His* brothers *also,* and they were unable to get to Him because of the crowd.

19 [a]Luke 8:19-21: *Matt. 12:46-50; Mark 3:31-35*

20 And it was reported to Him, "Your mother and Your brothers are standing outside, wishing to see You."

21 But He answered and said to them, "My mother and My brothers are these [a]who hear the word of God and do it."

★21 [a]Luke 11:28

7 *Ministry in storms,* 8:22–25

22 [a]Now it came about on one of *those* days, that He and His disciples got into a boat, and He said to them, "Let us go over to the other side of [b]the lake." And they launched out.

22 [a]Luke 8:22-25: *Matt. 8:23-27; Mark 4:36-41* [b]Luke 5:1f.; 8:23

23 But as they were sailing along He fell asleep; and a fierce gale of wind descended upon [a]the

23 [a]Luke 5:1f.; 8:22

8:6 *on rocky soil.* Or on thin soil covering rock. Palestine is a stony land.

8:16 *lamp.* A small clay vessel in which olive oil and a wick were placed. It gave feeble light at best (when placed on a lampstand).

8:21 *My mother and My brothers.* Those who belong to God's spiritual family are closer to Christ than those related to Him by natural birth.

lake, and they *began* to be
swamped and to be in danger.
24 [a]Luke 5:5 [b]Luke 4:39
24 And they came to Him and
woke Him up, saying, "[a]Master,
Master, we are perishing!" And
being aroused, He [b]rebuked the
wind and the surging waves, and
they stopped, and it became calm.
25 And He said to them,
"Where is your faith?" And they
were fearful and amazed, saying
to one another, "Who then is this,
that He commands even the
winds and the water, and they
obey Him?"

8 Ministry over demons, 8:26–39

★26 [a]Luke 8:26-37; *Matt. 8:28-34; Mark 5:1-17*
26 [a]And they sailed to the
country of the Gerasenes, which
is opposite Galilee.
27 And when He had come
out onto the land, He was met by
a certain man from the city who
was possessed with demons; and
who had not put on any clothing
for a long time, and was not living
in a house, but in the tombs.
28 [a]Matt. 8:29 [b]Mark 5:7
28 And seeing Jesus, he cried
out and fell before Him, and said
in a loud voice, "[a]What do I have
to do with You, Jesus, Son of [b]the
Most High God? I beg You, do not
torment me."
29 For He had been commanding the unclean spirit to
come out of the man. For it had
seized him many times; and he
was bound with chains and
shackles and kept under guard;
and *yet* he would burst his fetters
and be driven by the demon into
the desert.
★30 [a]Matt. 26:53
30 And Jesus asked him,
"What is your name?" And he
said, "[a]Legion"; for many demons
had entered him.
★31 [a]Rom. 10:7; Rev. 9:1f., 11; 11:7; 17:8; 20:1, 3
31 And they were entreating
Him not to command them to depart into [a]the abyss.
32 Now there was a herd of
many swine feeding there on the
mountain; and *the demons* entreated Him to permit them to enter the swine. And He gave them
permission.
33 And the demons came out
33 [a]Luke 5:1f.; 8:22
from the man and entered the
swine; and the herd rushed down
the steep bank into [a]the lake, and
were drowned.
34 And when those who
tended them saw what had happened, they ran away and reported it in the city and *out* in the
country.
35 And *the people* went out
35 [a]Luke 10:39
to see what had happened; and
they came to Jesus, and found the
man from whom the demons had
gone out, sitting down [a]at the feet
of Jesus, clothed and in his right
mind; and they became frightened.
36 And those who had seen it
36 [a]Matt. 4:24
reported to them how the man
who was [a]demon-possessed had
been made well.
37 And all the people of the
country of the Gerasenes and the
surrounding district asked Him to
depart from them; for they were
gripped with great fear; and He
got into a boat, and returned.
38 [a]But the man from whom
38 [a]Luke 8:38, 39; *Mark 5:18-20*
the demons had gone out was
begging Him that he might accompany Him; but He sent him
away, saying,
39 "Return to your house and
describe what great things God
has done for you." And he departed, proclaiming throughout
the whole city what great things
Jesus had done for him.

9 Ministry in death and despair, 8:40–56

40 [a]And as Jesus returned,
40 [a]Matt. 9:1; Mark 5:21
the multitude welcomed Him, for
they had all been waiting for
Him.
41 [a]Luke 8:41-56; *Matt. 9:18-26; Mark 5:22-43* [b]Mark 5:22; Luke 8:49
41 [a]And behold, there came a
man named Jairus, and he was an
[b]official of the synagogue; and he

8:26 *Gerasenes.* Lived on the E. shore of the Lake of Galilee.
8:30 *Legion.* See note on Mark 5:9.
8:31 *the abyss.* The place to which all evil spirits will ultimately be consigned (Rev. 9:1; 20:1, 3).

fell at Jesus' feet, and *began* to
entreat Him to come to his house;
42 for he had an only daughter, about twelve years old, and
she was dying. But as He went,
the multitudes were pressing
against Him.
★43 **43** And a woman who had a
hemorrhage for twelve years, and
could not be healed by anyone,
★44 **44** came up behind Him, and
touched the fringe of His cloak;
and immediately her hemorrhage
stopped.
45 [a]Luke 5:5 **45** And Jesus said, "Who is
the one who touched Me?" And
while they were all denying it, Peter said, "[a]Master, the multitudes
are crowding and pressing upon
You."
46 [a]Luke 5:17 **46** But Jesus said, "Someone
did touch Me, for I was aware that
[a]power had gone out of Me."
47 And when the woman saw
that she had not escaped notice,
she came trembling and fell down
before Him, and declared in the
presence of all the people the reason why she had touched Him,
and how she had been immediately healed.
48 [a]Matt. 9:22 [b]Mark 5:34; Luke 7:50 **48** And He said to her,
"Daughter, [a]your faith has made
you well; [b]go in peace."
49 [a]Luke 8:41 **49** While He was still speaking, someone *came from *the
house of* [a]the synagogue official,
saying, "Your daughter has died;
do not trouble the Teacher any
more."
50 [a]Mark 5:36 **50** But when Jesus heard *this,*
He answered him, "[a]Do not be
afraid *any longer;* only believe,
and she shall be made well."
51 And when He had come to
the house, He did not allow anyone to enter with Him, except Peter, John and James, and the girl's
father and mother.
52 Now they were all weeping ★52 [a]Matt. 11:17; Luke 23:27 [b]John 11:13
and [a]lamenting for her; but He
said, "Stop weeping, for she has
not died, but [b]is asleep."
53 And they *began* laughing
at Him, knowing that she had
died.
54 He, however, took her by
the hand and called, saying,
"Child, arise!"
55 And her spirit returned,
and she rose up immediately; and
He gave orders for *something* to
be given her to eat.
56 And her parents were 56 [a]Matt. 8:4
amazed; but He [a]instructed them
to tell no one what had happened.

10 Ministry through the disciples, 9:1–9

9 [a]And He called the twelve to- 1 [a]Matt. 10:5; Mark 6:7
gether, and gave them power
and authority over all the demons, and to heal diseases.
2 And He sent them out to 2 [a]Matt. 10:7
[a]proclaim the kingdom of God,
and to perform healing.
3 And He said to them, ★ 3 [a]Luke 9:3-5: *Matt. 10:9-15; Mark 6:8-11;* Luke 10:4-12; 22:35 [b]Matt. 10:10; Mark 6:8; Luke 22:35f.
"[a]Take nothing for *your* journey,
[b]neither a staff, nor a bag, nor
bread, nor money; and do not
even have two tunics apiece.
4 "And whatever house you
enter, stay there, and take your
leave from there.
5 "And as for those who do ★ 5 [a]Luke 10:11; Acts 13:51
not receive you, when you depart
from that city, [a]shake off the dust
from your feet as a testimony
against them."
6 And departing, they *began* 6 [a]Mark 6:12; Luke 8:1
going about among the villages,
[a]preaching the gospel, and healing everywhere.
7 [a]Now [b]Herod the tetrarch ★ 7 [a]Luke 9:7-9: *Matt. 14:1, 2;* Mark 6:14f. [b]Matt. 14:1; Luke 3:1; 13:31; 23:7 [c]Matt. 14:2
heard of all that was happening;
and he was greatly perplexed, because it was said by some that
[c]John had risen from the dead,

8:43 Luke makes clear that this chronic *hemorrhage* was an incurable condition.
8:44 *the fringe of His cloak.* A tassel which a rabbi wore on his outer garment. The garment was draped over the back so that the tassel of one corner hung between the shoulder blades.
8:52 *she has not died, but is asleep.* The mourners looked on death as irreversible, so Christ called it sleep, since (though the girl was actually dead) she would be awakened to life once again.
9:3 See Luke 22:35–36 for a change of orders. See note on Matt. 10:10.
9:5 *shake off the dust.* See note on Mark 6:11.
9:7 *Herod the tetrarch.* Herod Antipas, tetrarch of Galilee and Perea, 4 B.C.–A.D. 39.

8 aMatt. 16:14 — 8 and by some that [a]Elijah
had appeared, and by others, that
one of the prophets of old had ris-
en again.
9 aLuke 23:8 — 9 And Herod said, "I myself
had John beheaded; but who is
this man about whom I hear such
things?" And [a]he kept trying to
see Him.

11 *Ministry to physical needs,* 9:10–17

★10 aMark 6:30 bMark 6:30 cLuke 9:10-17; *Matt. 14:13-21; Mark 6:32-44; John 6:5-13* dMatt. 11:21 — 10 [a]And when the [b]apostles
returned, they gave an account to
Him of all that they had done.
[c]And taking them with Him, He
withdrew privately to a city called
[d]Bethsaida.
11 But the multitudes were
aware of this and followed Him;
and welcoming them, He *began*
speaking to them about the kingdom of God and curing those who
had need of healing.
12 And the day began to de-
cline, and the twelve came and
said to Him, "Send the multitude
away, that they may go into the
surrounding villages and countryside and find lodging and get
something to eat; for here we are
in a desolate place."
★13 — 13 But He said to them, "You
give them something to eat!" And
they said, "We have no more
than five loaves and two fish, unless perhaps we go and buy food
for all these people."
14 aMark 6:39 — 14 (For there were about five
thousand men). And He said to
His disciples, "Have them recline
to eat [a]in groups of about fifty
each."
15 And they did so, and had
them all recline.
16 And He took the five
loaves and the two fish, and looking up to heaven, He blessed
them, and broke *them,* and kept
giving *them* to the disciples to set
before the multitude.
17 And they all ate and were — 17 aMatt. 14:20
satisfied; and that which was left
over [a]to them of the broken
pieces was picked up, twelve
[a]baskets *full.*

12 *Ministry of prediction,* 9:18–50

18 [a]And it came about that — ★18 aLuke 9:18-20; *Matt. 16:13-16; Mark 8:27-29* bMatt. 14:23; Luke 6:12; 9:28
while He was [b]praying alone, the
disciples were with Him, and He
questioned them, saying, "Who
do the multitudes say that I am?"
19 And they answered and
said, "John the Baptist; but others
say, Elijah; and others, that one of
the prophets of old has risen
again."
20 And He said to them, "But — 20 aJohn 6:68f.
who do you say that I am?" And
Peter answered and said, "[a]The
Christ of God."
21 But He [a]warned them, and — 21 aMatt. 8:4; 16:20; Mark 8:30
instructed *them* not to tell this to
anyone,
22 [a]saying, "[b]The Son of Man — 22 aLuke 9:22-27; *Matt. 16:21-28; Mark 8:31-9:1* bMatt. 16:21; Luke 9:44
must suffer many things, and be
rejected by the elders and chief
priests and scribes, and be killed,
and be raised up on the third
day."
23 And He was saying to — ★23 aMatt. 10:38
them all, "If anyone wishes to
come after Me, let him deny himself, and [a]take up his cross daily,
and follow Me.
24 "For [a]whoever wishes to — 24 aMatt. 10:39
save his life shall lose it, but whoever loses his life for My sake, he
is the one who will save it.
25 "For what is a man profited — 25 aHeb. 10:34
if he gains the whole world, and
[a]loses or forfeits himself?
26 "[a]For whoever is ashamed — 26 aMatt. 10:33; Luke 12:9
of Me and My words, of him will
the Son of Man be ashamed when
He comes in His glory, and *the*

9:10 *Bethsaida.* A small town on the N. shore of the Lake of Galilee.

9:13 *loaves . . . fish.* The loaves were round cakes (like biscuits) and the fish were small smoked or pickled fish, typical food of the poor in Palestine.

9:18–21 See notes on Matt. 16:13–14.

9:23 *cross.* The first mention of a cross in Luke. The cross was well-known as an instrument of death, so it represents here the death or separation from the old life that must mark a disciple (Rom. 8:13). See note on Matt. 10:38.

glory of the Father and of the
holy angels.
27 "But I tell you truly, [a]there
are some of those standing here
who shall not taste death until
they see the kingdom of God."
28 [a]And some eight days after these sayings, it came about
that He took along [b]Peter and
John and James, and [c]went up to
the mountain [d]to pray.
29 And while He was [a]pray-
ing, the appearance of His face
[b]became different, and His clothing *became* white *and* gleaming.
30 And behold, two men
were talking with Him; and they
were Moses and Elijah,
31 who, appearing in glory,
were speaking of His [a]departure
which He was about to accomplish at Jerusalem.
32 Now Peter and his com-
panions [a]had been overcome with
sleep; but when they were fully
awake, they saw His glory and the
two men standing with Him.
33 And it came about, as
these were parting from Him, Peter said to Jesus, "[a]Master, it is
good for us to be here; and [b]let us
make three tabernacles: one for
You, and one for Moses, and one
for Elijah"—[c]not realizing what
he was saying.
34 And while he was saying
this, a cloud formed and *began* to
overshadow them; and they were
afraid as they entered the cloud.
35 And [a]a voice came out of
the cloud, saying, "[b]This is My
Son, *My* Chosen One; listen to
Him!"
36 And when the voice had
spoken, Jesus was found alone.
And [a]they kept silent, and reported to no one in those days
any of the things which they had
seen.
37 [a]And it came about on the
next day, that when they had
come down from the mountain, a
great multitude met Him.
38 And behold, a man from

★27 [a]Matt. 16:28
28 [a]Luke 9:28-36; *Matt. 17:1-8; Mark 9:2-8* [b]Matt. 17:1 [c]Matt. 5:1 [d]Luke 3:21; 5:16; 6:12; 9:18
29 [a]Luke 3:21; 5:16; 6:12; 9:18 [b]Mark 16:12
31 [a]2 Pet. 1:15
32 [a]Matt. 26:43; Mark 14:40
33 [a]Luke 5:5; 9:49 [b]Matt. 17:4; Mark 9:5 [c]Mark 9:6
35 [a]2 Pet. 1:17f. [b]Matt. 3:17; Luke 3:22
36 [a]Matt. 17:9; Mark 9:9f.
37 [a]Luke 9:37-42; *Matt. 17:14-18; Mark 9:14-27*

the multitude shouted out, saying, "Teacher, I beg You to look
at my son, for he is my only *boy,*
39 and behold, a spirit seizes
him, and he suddenly screams,
and it throws him into a convulsion with foaming *at the mouth,*
and as it mauls him, it scarcely
leaves him.
40 "And I begged Your disci- ★40
ples to cast it out, and they could
not."
41 And Jesus answered and
said, "O unbelieving and perverted generation, how long shall
I be with you, and put up with
you? Bring your son here."
42 And while he was still approaching, the demon dashed him
to the ground, and threw him into
a violent convulsion. But Jesus rebuked the unclean spirit, and
healed the boy, and gave him
back to his father.
43 And they were all amazed
at the [a]greatness of God.
[b]**B**ut while everyone was marveling at all that He was doing,
He said to His disciples,
44 "Let these words sink into
your ears; [a]for the Son of Man is
going to be delivered into the
hands of men."
45 But [a]they did not understand this statement, and it was
concealed from them so that they
might not perceive it; and they
were afraid to ask Him about this
statement.
46 [a]And an argument arose
among them as to which of them
might be the greatest.
47 But Jesus, [a]knowing what
they were thinking in their heart,
took a child and stood him by His
side,
48 and said to them, "[a]Who-
ever receives this child in My
name receives Me; and whoever
receives Me receives Him who
sent Me; [b]for he who is least
among you, this is the one who is
great."

43 [a]2 Pet. 1:16 [b]Luke 9:43-45; *Matt. 17:22f.; Mark 9:30-32*
44 [a]Luke 9:22
45 [a]Mark 9:32
46 [a]Luke 9:46-48; *Matt. 18:1-5; Mark 9:33-37*
47 [a]Matt. 9:4
48 [a]Matt. 10:40 [b]Luke 22:26

9:27-36 See notes on Matt. 16:28; 17:1, 2, 4; Mark 9:5.

9:40 *they could not.* The reason was that the disciples failed to pray (Mark 9:29).

49 aLuke 9:49, 50; Mark 9:38-40 bLuke 5:5; 9:33

49 [a]And John answered and
said, "[b]Master, we saw someone
casting out demons in Your name;
and we tried to hinder him because he does not follow along
with us."

★50 aMatt. 12:30; Luke 11:23

50 But Jesus said to him, "Do
not hinder *him;* [a]for he who is not
against you is for you."

IV THE REPUDIATION OF THE SON OF MAN BY MEN, 9:51–19:27

A Rejection by Samaritans, 9:51–56

51 aMark 16:19 bLuke 13:22; 17:11; 18:31; 19:11, 28

51 And it came about, when
the days were approaching for
[a]His ascension, that He resolutely
set His face [b]to go to Jerusalem;

52 aMatt. 10:5; Luke 10:33; 17:16; John 4:4

52 and He sent messengers on
ahead of Him. And they went,
and entered a village of the [a]Sa-
maritans, to make arrangements
for Him.

53 aJohn 4:9

53 And they did not receive
Him, [a]because He was journeying
with His face toward Jerusalem.

★54 aMark 3:17

54 And when His disciples
[a]James and John saw *this,* they
said, "Lord, do You want us to
command fire to come down from
heaven and consume them?"
55 But He turned and rebuked them.
56 And they went on to another village.

B Rejection by Worldly Men, 9:57–62

57 aLuke 9:51 bLuke 9:57-60; Matt. 8:19-22

57 And [a]as they were going
along the road, [b]someone said to
Him, "I will follow You wherever
You go."

★58 aMatt. 8:20

58 And Jesus said to him,
"The foxes have holes, and the
birds of the air *have* nests, but
[a]the Son of Man has nowhere to
lay His head."

★59 aMatt. 8:22

59 And He said to another,
"[a]Follow Me." But he said, "Permit me first to go and bury my
father."

★60 aMatt. 4:23

60 But He said to him, "Allow
the dead to bury their own dead;
but as for you, go and [a]proclaim
everywhere the kingdom of
God."

61 a1 Kin. 19:20

61 And another also said, "I
will follow You, Lord; but [a]first
permit me to say good-bye to
those at home."

★62 aPhil. 3:13

62 But Jesus said to him, "[a]No
one, after putting his hand to the
plow and looking back, is fit for
the kingdom of God."

C Commissioning of the Seventy, 10:1–24

★ 1 aLuke 7:13 bLuke 9:1f., 52 cMark 6:7

10 Now after this [a]the Lord
appointed seventy [b]others,
and sent them [c]two and two
ahead of Him to every city and
place where He Himself was
going to come.

2 aMatt. 9:37, 38; John 4:35

2 And He was saying to
them, "[a]The harvest is plentiful,
but the laborers are few; therefore beseech the Lord of the harvest to send out laborers into His
harvest.

3 aMatt. 10:16

3 "Go your ways; [a]behold, I
send you out as lambs in the
midst of wolves.

★ 4 aMatt. 10:9-14; Mark 6:8-11; Luke 9:3-5; 10:4-12

4 "[a]Carry no purse, no bag,
no shoes; and greet no one on the
way.
5 "And whatever house you

9:50 *he who is not against you is for you.* The test by which others are tried. In 11:23 is a test by which one tries himself.

9:54 *fire . . . from heaven.* See 2 Kings 1:10–12.

9:58 *Son of Man.* For the meaning of this title see note on Matt. 8:20.

9:59 *bury my father.* The father had not died; the speaker meant that he was obligated to care for him until he died.

9:60 *Allow the dead to bury their own dead.* I.e., let those who are spiritually dead bury those who die physically. The claims of the kingdom are paramount.

9:62 *looking back.* This will make the furrow crooked.

10:1 *seventy.* Only Luke records this mission. The fact that 70 people could be sent out shows that Jesus must have had a large following.

10:4 *greet no one on the way.* The urgency of the mission did not allow for the usual elaborate greetings.

enter, first say, 'Peace *be* to this house.'

★ 6

6 "And if a man of peace is there, your peace will rest upon him; but if not, it will return to you.

7 [a]Matt. 10:10; 1 Cor. 9:14; 1 Tim. 5:18

7 "And stay in that house, eating and drinking what they give you; for [a]the laborer is worthy of his wages. Do not keep moving from house to house.

8 [a]1 Cor. 10:27

8 "And whatever city you enter, and they receive you, [a]eat what is set before you;

9 [a]Matt. 3:2; 10:7; Luke 10:11

9 and heal those in it who are sick, and say to them, '[a]The kingdom of God has come near to you.'

10 "But whatever city you enter and they do not receive you, go out into its streets and say,

11 [a]Matt. 10:14; Mark 6:11; Luke 9:5 [b]Matt. 3:2; 10:7; Luke 10:9

11 '[a]Even the dust of your city which clings to our feet, we wipe off *in protest* against you; yet be sure of this, that [b]the kingdom of God has come near.'

★12 [a]Matt. 10:15; 11:24 [b]Matt. 10:15

12 "I say to you, [a]it will be more tolerable in that day for [b]Sodom, than for that city.

13 [a]Luke 10:13-15: *Matt. 11:21-23* [b]Matt. 11:21 [c]Rev. 11:3

13 "[a]Woe to you, [b]Chorazin! Woe to you, [b]Bethsaida! For if the miracles had been performed in [b]Tyre and Sidon which occurred in you, they would have repented long ago, sitting in [c]sackcloth and ashes.

14 [a]Matt. 11:21

14 "But it will be more tolerable for [a]Tyre and Sidon in the judgment, than for you.

15 [a]Matt. 4:13 [b]Matt. 11:23

15 "And you, [a]Capernaum, will not be exalted to heaven, will you? You will be brought down to [b]Hades!

16 [a]Matt. 10:40; John 13:20; Gal. 4:14 [b]John 12:48; 1 Thess. 4:8

16 "[a]The one who listens to you listens to Me, and [b]the one who rejects you rejects Me; and he who rejects Me rejects the One who sent Me."

17 [a]Mark 16:17

17 And the seventy returned with joy, saying, "Lord, even [a]the demons are subject to us in Your name."

★18 [a]Matt. 4:10

18 And He said to them, "I was watching [a]Satan fall from heaven like lightning.

19 [a]Mark 16:18

19 "Behold, I have given you authority to [a]tread upon serpents and scorpions, and over all the power of the enemy, and nothing shall injure you.

20 [a]Ex. 32:32; Ps. 69:28; Is. 4:3; Ezek. 13:9; Dan. 12:1; Phil. 4:3; Heb. 12:23; Rev. 3:5; 13:8; 17:8; 20:12, 15; 21:27

20 "Nevertheless do not rejoice in this, that the spirits are subject to you, but rejoice that [a]your names are recorded in heaven."

21 [a]Luke 10:21, 22: *Matt. 11:25-27*

21 [a]At that very time He rejoiced greatly in the Holy Spirit, and said, "I praise Thee, O Father, Lord of heaven and earth, that Thou didst hide these things from *the* wise and intelligent and didst reveal them to babes. Yes, Father, for thus it was well-pleasing in Thy sight.

22 "All things have been handed over to Me by My Father, and no one knows who the Son is except the Father, and who the Father is except the Son, and anyone to whom the Son wills to reveal *Him.*"

23 [a]Luke 10:23, 24: *Matt. 13:16, 17*

23 [a]And turning to the disciples, He said privately, "Blessed *are* the eyes which see the things you see,

24 for I say to you, that many prophets and kings wished to see the things which you see, and did not see *them,* and to hear the things which you hear, and did not hear *them.*"

D Rejection by a Lawyer (Parable of the Good Samaritan), 10:25–37

★25 [a]Luke 10:25-28: *Matt. 22:34-40; Mark 12:28-31;* Matt. 19:16-19 [b]Matt. 22:35

25 [a]And behold, a certain [b]lawyer stood up and put Him to the test, saying, "Teacher, what shall I do to inherit eternal life?"

26 And He said to him, "What is written in the Law? How does it read to you?"

★27 [a]Lev. 19:18; Deut. 6:5

27 And he answered and said, "[a]YOU SHALL LOVE THE LORD YOUR

10:6 *a man of peace.* A Hebrew idiom meaning "a peaceful man."

10:12 *in that day.* I.e., the day of judgment. The judgment on *Sodom* is recorded in Gen. 19.

10:18 *Satan fall from heaven.* The power of Satan was broken, and the success of the seventy over demons was proof of it (v. 17).

10:25 *a certain lawyer.* I.e., a scribe. See note on Matt. 2:4.

10:27 See Deut. 6:5; Lev. 19:18.

GOD WITH ALL YOUR HEART, AND WITH ALL YOUR SOUL, AND WITH ALL YOUR STRENGTH, AND WITH ALL YOUR MIND; AND YOUR NEIGHBOR AS YOURSELF."

28 [a]Lev. 18:5; Matt. 19:17

28 And He said to him, "You have answered correctly; [a]DO THIS, AND YOU WILL LIVE."

29 [a]Luke 16:15

29 But wishing [a]to justify himself, he said to Jesus, "And who is my neighbor?"

★30 [a]Luke 18:31; 19:28

30 Jesus replied and said, "A certain man was [a]going down from Jerusalem to Jericho; and he fell among robbers, and they stripped him and beat him, and went off leaving him half dead.

31 "And by chance a certain priest was going down on that road, and when he saw him, he passed by on the other side.

32 "And likewise a Levite also, when he came to the place and saw him, passed by on the other side.

★33 [a]Matt. 10:5; Luke 9:52

33 "But a certain [a]Samaritan, who was on a journey, came upon him; and when he saw him, he felt compassion,

34 and came to him, and bandaged up his wounds, pouring oil and wine on *them;* and he put him on his own beast, and brought him to an inn, and took care of him.

35 "And on the next day he took out two denarii and gave them to the innkeeper and said, 'Take care of him; and whatever more you spend, when I return, I will repay you.'

36 "Which of these three do you think proved to be a neighbor to the man who fell into the robbers' *hands?"*

37 And he said, "The one who showed mercy toward him." And Jesus said to him, "Go and do the same."

E Reception at Bethany, 10:38–42

38 Now as they were traveling along, He entered a certain village; and a woman named [a]Martha welcomed Him into her home.

★38 [a]Luke 10:40f.; John 11:1, 5, 19ff., 30, 39; 12:2

39 And she had a sister called [a]Mary, who moreover was listening to the Lord's word, [b]seated at His feet.

39 [a]Luke 10:42; John 11:1f., 19f., 28, 31f., 45; 12:3 [b]Luke 8:35; Acts 22:3

40 But [a]Martha was distracted with all her preparations; and she came up *to Him,* and said, "Lord, do You not care that my sister has left me to do all the serving alone? Then tell her to help me."

40 [a]Luke 10:38, 41; John 11:1, 5, 19ff., 30, 39; 12:2

41 But the Lord answered and said to her, "[a]Martha, Martha, you are [b]worried and bothered about so many things;

41 [a]Luke 10:38, 40; John 11:1, 5, 19ff., 30, 39; 12:2 [b]Matt. 6:25

42 [a]but *only* a few things are necessary, really *only* one, for [b]Mary has chosen the good part, which shall not be taken away from her."

★42 [a]Ps. 27:4; John 6:27 [b]Luke 10:39; John 11:1f., 19f., 28, 31f., 45; 12:3

F Instruction on Prayer, 11:1–13

11 And it came about that while He was praying in a certain place, after He had finished, one of His disciples said to Him, "[a]Lord, teach us to pray just as John also taught his disciples."

★ 1 [a]Luke 7:13

2 And He said to them, "[a]When you pray, say:

★ 2 [a]Luke 11:2-4; *Matt. 6:9-13*

'Father, hallowed be Thy name.
Thy kingdom come.

3 'Give us [a]each day our daily bread.

3 [a]Acts 17:11

4 'And forgive us our sins,
For we ourselves also forgive everyone who [a]is indebted to us.

4 [a]Luke 13:4 marg.

10:30 *was going down from Jerusalem to Jericho.* The steeply descending road winds through rocky places that easily hide robbers.

10:33 *a certain Samaritan.* The Samaritans were descendants of colonists whom the Assyrian kings planted in Palestine after the fall of the Northern Kingdom in 721 B.C. They were despised by the Jews because of their mixed Gentile blood and their different worship, which centered at Mt. Gerizim (John 4:20–22).

10:38 *a certain village.* I.e., Bethany (John 12:1).

10:42 *really only one.* One simple dish for the meal is all that is necessary, rather than the elaborate preparations Martha had made.

11:1 *teach us to pray.* It was customary for famous rabbis to compose special prayers.

11:2–4 See notes on Matt. 6:9, 11, 12.

And lead us not into temptation.' "

5 And He said to them, "Suppose one of you shall have a friend, and shall go to him at midnight, and say to him, 'Friend, lend me three loaves;

6 for a friend of mine has come to me from a journey, and I have nothing to set before him';

7 and from inside he shall answer and say, 'Do not bother me; the door has already been shut and my children and I are in bed; I cannot get up and give you *anything.*'

8 [a]Luke 18:1-6

8 "I tell you, even though he will not get up and give him *anything* because he is his friend, yet [a]because of his persistence he will get up and give him as much as he needs.

9 [a]Luke 11:9-13: *Matt. 7:7-11*

9 "And I say to you, [a]ask, and it shall be given to you; seek, and you shall find; knock, and it shall be opened to you.

10 "For everyone who asks, receives; and he who seeks, finds; and to him who knocks, it shall be opened.

11 "Now suppose one of you fathers is asked by his son for a fish; he will not give him a snake instead of a fish, will he?

12 "Or *if* he is asked for an egg, he will not give him a scorpion, will he?

★13 [a]Luke 18:7f. [b]Matt. 7:11

13 "[a]If you then, being evil, know how to give good gifts to your children, how much more shall *your* heavenly Father give the [b]Holy Spirit to those who ask Him?"

G Rejection by the Nation, 11:14-36

14 [a]Luke 11:14, 15: *Matt. 12:22, 24;* Matt. 9:32-34

14 [a]And He was casting out a demon, *and it was* dumb; and it came about that when the demon had gone out, the dumb man spoke; and the multitudes marveled.

★15 [a]Matt. 9:34 [b]Matt. 10:25

15 But some of them said, "He casts out demons [a]by [b]Beelzebul, the ruler of the demons."

16 [a]Matt. 12:38

16 And others, to test *Him,* [a]were demanding of Him a sign from heaven.

17 [a]Luke 11:17-22: *Matt. 12:25-29; Mark 3:23-27*

17 [a]But He knew their thoughts, and said to them, "Any kingdom divided against itself is laid waste; and a house divided against itself falls.

18 [a]Matt. 4:10 [b]Matt. 10:25

18 "And if [a]Satan also is divided against himself, how shall his kingdom stand? For you say that I cast out demons by [b]Beelzebul.

19 [a]Matt. 10:25

19 "And if I by [a]Beelzebul cast out demons, by whom do your sons cast them out? Consequently they shall be your judges.

20 [a]Ex. 8:19 [b]Matt. 3:2

20 "But if I cast out demons by the [a]finger of God, then [b]the kingdom of God has come upon you.

★21 [a]Matt. 26:3

21 "When a strong *man* fully armed guards his own [a]homestead, his possessions are undisturbed;

22 but when someone stronger than he attacks him and overpowers him, he takes away from him all his armor on which he had relied, and distributes his plunder.

23 [a]Matt. 12:30

23 "[a]He who is not with Me is against Me; and he who does not gather with Me, scatters.

★24 [a]Luke 11:24-26: *Matt. 12:43-45*

24 "[a]When the unclean spirit goes out of a man, it passes through waterless places seeking rest, and not finding any, it says, 'I will return to my house from which I came.'

25 "And when it comes, it finds it swept and put in order.

★26

26 "Then it goes and takes *along* seven other spirits more evil

---

11:13 *give the Holy Spirit.* Since the day of Pentecost, the gift of the Spirit is given to all believers (Acts 10:45; Rom. 8:9).

11:15 *Beelzebul.* See note on Matt. 10:25.

11:21-22 *a strong man* (v. 21) is Satan; the *stronger* (v. 22) is Christ (4:18).

11:24 *my house.* The life of the person the demon indwelt.

11:26 *worse.* See 2 Pet. 2:20-21. Notice also that some demons are more wicked than others.

than itself, and they go in and live
there; and the last state of that
man becomes worse than the
first."
27 [a]Luke 23:29 **27** And it came about while
He said these things, one of the
women in the crowd raised her
voice, and said to Him, "[a]Blessed
is the womb that bore You, and
the breasts at which You nursed."
28 [a]Luke 8:21 **28** But He said, "On the contrary,
blessed are [a]those who hear
the word of God, and observe it."
29 [a]Luke 11:29-32: *Matt. 12:39-42* [b]Matt. 12:38; Luke 11:16 **29** And as the crowds were
increasing, He began to say,
"[a]This generation is a wicked
generation; it [b]seeks for a sign,
and *yet* no sign shall be given to it
but the sign of Jonah.
★30 **30** "For just as Jonah became a
sign to the Ninevites, so shall the
Son of Man be to this generation.
31 "The Queen of the South
shall rise up with the men of this
generation at the judgment and
condemn them, because she came
from the ends of the earth to hear
the wisdom of Solomon; and behold,
something greater than
Solomon is here.
★32 **32** "The men of Nineveh shall
stand up with this generation at
the judgment and condemn it, because
they repented at the
preaching of Jonah; and behold,
something greater than Jonah is
here.
33 [a]Matt. 5:15; Mark 4:21; Luke 8:16 **33** "No [a]one, after lighting a
lamp, puts it away in a cellar, nor
under a peck-measure, but on the
lampstand, in order that those
who enter may see the light.
34 [a]Luke 11:34, 35: *Matt. 6:22, 23* **34** "[a]The lamp of your body is
your eye; when your eye is clear,
your whole body also is full of
light; but when it is bad, your
body also is full of darkness.
35 "Then watch out that the
light in you may not be darkness.
36 "If therefore your whole
body is full of light, with no dark
part in it, it shall be wholly illumined,
as when the lamp illumines
you with its rays."

H Rejection by Pharisees and Lawyers, 11:37-54

37 Now when He had spoken, ★37
a Pharisee *asked Him to
have lunch with him; and He
went in, and reclined *at table.*
38 And when the Pharisee 38 [a]Matt. 15:2; Mark 7:3f.
saw it, he was surprised that He
had not first [a]ceremonially
washed before the meal.
39 But [a]the Lord said to him, 39 [a]Luke 7:13 [b]Matt. 23:25f.
"Now [b]you Pharisees clean the
outside of the cup and of the platter;
but inside of you, you are full
of robbery and wickedness.
40 "[a]You foolish ones, did not 40 [a]Luke 12:20; 1 Cor. 15:36
He who made the outside make
the inside also?
41 "But [a]give that which is 41 [a]Luke 12:33; 16:9 [b]Mark 7:19; Titus 1:15
within as charity, and then all
things are [b]clean for you.
42 "[a]But woe to you Pharisees! ★42 [a]Matt. 23:23 [b]Luke 18:12
For you [b]pay tithe of mint and rue
and every *kind of* garden herb,
and *yet* disregard justice and the
love of God; but these are the
things you should have done
without neglecting the others.
43 "Woe to you Pharisees! For ★43 [a]Matt. 23:6f.; Mark 12:38f.; Luke 14:7; 20:46
you [a]love the front seats in the
synagogues, and the respectful
greetings in the market places.
44 "[a]Woe to you! For you are ★44 [a]Matt. 23:27
like concealed tombs, and the
people who walk over *them* are
unaware *of it.*"
45 And one of the [a]lawyers 45 [a]Matt. 22:35; Luke 11:46, 52
*said to Him in reply, "Teacher,
when You say this, You insult us
too."
46 But He said, "Woe to you 46 [a]Matt. 22:35; Luke 11:45, 52 [b]Matt. 23:4
[a]lawyers as well! For [b]you weigh
men down with burdens hard to
bear, while you yourselves will

11:30 *Jonah became a sign* of judgment. See note on Matt. 12:39.
11:32 *they repented.* See Jonah 3:5-9; 4:11.
11:37 *reclined at table.* Christ often used dinner invitations as opportunities to reach people (Luke 5:29; 7:36; 14:1; 19:5; John 2:1-12; 12:1-2).
11:42 *pay tithe.* See note on Matt. 23:23.
11:43 *the front seats.* Usually reserved for the most important members.
11:44 *concealed tombs.* To step on a grave, even unknowingly, defiled a man (Num. 19:16). Jesus says that the Pharisees cause men to break the law and defile themselves.

not even touch the burdens with
one of your fingers.
47 [a]Matt. 23:29ff.
47 "[a]Woe to you! For you
build the tombs of the prophets,
and *it was* your fathers *who* killed
them.
48 "Consequently, you are witnesses and approve the deeds of
your fathers; because it was they
who killed them, and you build
their tombs.
49 [a]1 Cor. 1:24, 30; Col. 2:3 [b]Matt. 23:34-36; Luke 11:49-51
49 "For this reason also [a]the
wisdom of God said, '[b]I will send
to them prophets and apostles,
and *some* of them they will kill
and *some* they will persecute,
50 [a]Matt. 25:34
50 in order that the blood of
all the prophets, shed [a]since the
foundation of the world, may be
charged against this generation,
★51
51 from the blood of Abel to
the blood of Zechariah, who perished between the altar and the
house *of God;* yes, I tell you, it
shall be charged against this generation.'
52 [a]Matt. 22:35; Luke 11:45, 46 [b]Matt. 23:13
52 "Woe to you [a]lawyers! For
you have taken away the key of
knowledge; [b]you did not enter in
yourselves, and those who were
entering in you hindered."
53 And when He left there,
the scribes and the Pharisees began to be very hostile and to
question Him closely on many
subjects,
54 [a]Mark 3:2; Luke 20:20; Acts 23:21 [b]Mark 12:13
54 [a]plotting against Him, [b]to
catch *Him* in something He might
say.

I Instruction in the Light of Rejection, 12:1–19:27

1 Concerning hypocrisy, 12:1–12

1 [a]Matt. 16:6, 11ff.; Mark 8:15
12 Under these circumstances, after so many
thousands of the multitude had
gathered together that they were
stepping on one another, He began saying to His disciples first *of*
all, "[a]Beware of the leaven of the
Pharisees, which is hypocrisy.
2 [a]Luke 12:2-9: *Matt. 10:26-33;* Matt. 10:26; Mark 4:22; Luke 8:17
2 "[a]But there is nothing cov-
ered up that will not be revealed,
and hidden that will not be
known.
3 [a]Matt. 10:27; 24:17
3 "Accordingly whatever you
have said in the dark shall be
heard in the light, and what you
have whispered in the inner
rooms shall be proclaimed upon
[a]the housetops.
4 [a]John 15:13-15
4 "And I say to you, [a]My
friends, do not be afraid of those
who kill the body, and after that
have no more that they can do.
★ 5 [a]Heb. 10:31 [b]Matt. 5:22
5 "But I will warn you whom
to fear: [a]fear the One who after
He has killed has authority to cast
into [b]hell; yes, I tell you, fear
Him!
★ 6 [a]Matt. 10:29
6 "Are not [a]five sparrows sold
for two cents? And *yet* not one of
them is forgotten before God.
7 [a]Matt. 10:30
7 "[a]Indeed the very hairs of
your head are all numbered. Do
not fear; you are of more value
than many sparrows.
8 [a]Matt. 10:32; Luke 15:10; Rom. 10:9
8 "And I say to you, everyone
who confesses Me before men,
the Son of Man shall confess him
also [a]before the angels of God;
9 [a]Matt. 10:33; Luke 9:26 [b]Matt. 10:32; Luke 15:10; Rom. 10:9
9 but [a]he who denies Me be-
fore men shall be denied [b]before
the angels of God.
★10 [a]Matt. 12:31, 32; Mark 3:28-30
10 "[a]And everyone who will
speak a word against the Son of
Man, it shall be forgiven him; but
he who blasphemes against the
Holy Spirit, it shall not be forgiven him.
11 [a]Matt. 10:17 [b]Matt. 6:25; 10:19; Mark 13:11; Luke 12:22; 21:14
11 "And when they bring you
before [a]the synagogues and the
rulers and the authorities, do not
become [b]anxious about how or
what you should speak in your
defense, or what you should say;
12 [a]Matt. 10:20; Luke 21:15
12 for [a]the Holy Spirit will

11:51 *to the blood of Zechariah.* See note on Matt. 23:35.
12:5 *fear Him.* I.e., God, who alone has the power to cast into hell (Rev. 20:10).
12:6 *five sparrows.* Sparrows were so cheap that, though they sold two for a cent (Matt. 10:29), a fifth one was thrown in for the price of four. Yet the infinite God is concerned for each one.
12:10 *blasphemes against the Holy Spirit.* See note on Matt. 12:31.

teach you in that very hour what
you ought to say."

2 *Concerning covetousness,* 12:13–34

13 And someone in the crowd
said to Him, "Teacher, tell my
brother to divide the *family* inheritance with me."
★14 [a]Mic. 6:8; Rom. 2:1, 3; 9:20 **14** But He said to him, "[a]Man,
who appointed Me a judge or ar-
biter over you?"
15 [a]1 Tim. 6:6-10 **15** And He said to them,
"[a]Beware, and be on your guard
against every form of greed; for
not *even* when one has an abundance does his life consist of his
possessions."
16 And He told them a parable, saying, "The land of a certain rich man was very productive.
17 "And he began reasoning to
himself, saying, 'What shall I do,
since I have no place to store my
crops?'
18 "And he said, 'This is what I
will do: I will tear down my barns
and build larger ones, and there I
will store all my grain and my
goods.
★19 [a]Eccles. 11:9 **19** 'And I will say to my soul,
"Soul, [a]you have many goods laid
up for many years *to come;* take
your ease, eat, drink *and* be merry." '
20 [a]Jer. 17:11; Luke 11:40 [b]Job 27:8 [c]Ps. 39:6 **20** "But God said to him, '[a]You
fool! This *very* night [b]your soul is
required of you; and [c]*now* who
will own what you have prepared?'
21 [a]Luke 12:33 **21** "So is the man who [a]lays up
treasure for himself, and is not
rich toward God."
22 [a]Luke 12:22-31; *Matt. 6:25-33* **22** And He said to His disciples, "[a]For this reason I say to
you, do not be anxious for *your*
life, *as to* what you shall eat; nor
for your body, *as to* what you
shall put on.
23 "For life is more than food,
and the body than clothing.
24 "Consider the [a]ravens, for 24 [a]Job 38:41 [b]Luke 12:18
they neither sow nor reap; and
they have no storeroom nor
[b]barn; and *yet* God feeds them;
how much more valuable you are
than the birds!
25 "And which of you by 25 [a]Ps. 39:5
being anxious can add a *single*
[a]cubit to his life's span?
26 "If then you cannot do even
a very little thing, why are you
anxious about other matters?
27 "Consider the lilies, how ★27 [a]1 Kin. 10:4-7
they grow; they neither toil nor
spin; but I tell you, even [a]Solo-
mon in all his glory did not clothe
himself like one of these.
28 "But if God so *arrays* the 28 [a]Matt. 6:30
grass in the field, which is *alive*
today and tomorrow is thrown
into the furnace, how much more
will He clothe you, [a]O men of little faith!
29 "And do not seek what you 29 [a]Matt. 6:31
shall eat, and what you shall
drink, and do not [a]keep worrying.
30 "For all these things the nations of the world eagerly seek;
but your Father knows that you
need these things.
31 "But seek for His kingdom, 31 [a]Matt. 6:33
and [a]these things shall be added
to you.
32 "[a]Do not be afraid, [b]little 32 [a]Matt. 14:27 [b]John 21:15-17 [c]Eph. 1:5, 9
flock, for [c]your Father has chosen
gladly to give you the kingdom.
33 "[a]Sell your possessions and 33 [a]Matt. 19:21; Luke 11:41; 18:22 [b]Matt. 6:20; Luke 12:21
give to charity; make yourselves
purses which do not wear out, [b]an
unfailing treasure in heaven,
where no thief comes near, nor
moth destroys.
34 "For [a]where your treasure 34 [a]Matt. 6:21
is, there will your heart be also.

3 *Concerning faithfulness,* 12:35–48

35 "[a]Be dressed in [b]readiness, ★35 [a]Matt. 25:1ff.; Luke 12:35, 36 [b]Eph. 6:14; 1 Pet. 1:13
and *keep* your lamps alight.

12:14 *who appointed Me a judge?* Christ refused to assume the position of judge in this secular matter.
12:19–20 Man proposes; God disposes.
12:27 *lilies.* Probably anemones.

12:35 *Be dressed in readiness.* The long, flowing outer robe had to be tucked into a belt before traveling or working. The idea is: "be ready."

★36 36 "And be like men who are
waiting for their master when he
returns from the wedding feast,
so that they may immediately
open *the door* to him when he
comes and knocks.
37 [a]Matt. 24:42 [b]Luke 17:8; John 13:4
37 "Blessed are those slaves
whom the master shall find [a]on
the alert when he comes; truly I
say to you, that [b]he will gird himself *to serve,* and have them recline *at table,* and will come up
and wait on them.
38 [a]Matt. 24:43
38 "Whether he comes in the
[a]second watch, or even in the
[a]third, and finds *them* so, blessed
are those *slaves.*
39 [a]Luke 12:39, 40: *Matt. 24:43, 44* [b]Matt. 6:19
39 "[a]And be sure of this, that
if the head of the house had
known at what hour the thief was
coming, he would not have allowed his house to be [b]broken
into.
40 [a]Mark 13:33; Luke 21:36
40 "[a]You too, be ready; for the
Son of Man is coming at an hour
that you do not expect."
41 [a]Luke 12:47, 48
41 And Peter said, "Lord, are
You addressing this parable to us,
or [a]to everyone *else* as well?"
42 [a]Luke 7:13 [b]Luke 12:42-46: *Matt. 24:45-51* [c]Matt. 24:45; Luke 16:1ff.
42 And [a]the Lord said,
"[b]Who then is the faithful and
sensible [c]steward, whom his master will put in charge of his servants, to give them their rations at
the proper time?
43 [a]Luke 12:42
43 "Blessed is that [a]slave
whom his master finds so doing
when he comes.
44 "Truly I say to you, that he
will put him in charge of all his
possessions.
45 "But if that slave says in his
heart, 'My master will be a long
time in coming,' and begins to
beat the slaves, *both* men and
women, and to eat and drink and
get drunk;
46 the master of that slave
will come on a day when he does
not expect *him,* and at an hour he
does not know, and will cut him
in pieces, and assign him a place
with the unbelievers.
47 "And that slave who knew 47 [a]Deut. 25:2
his master's will and did not get
ready or act in accord with his
will, shall [a]receive many lashes,
48 but the one who did not 48 [a]Lev. 5:17; Num. 15:29f. [b]Matt. 13:12
[a]know *it,* and committed deeds
worthy of a flogging, will receive
but few. [b]And from everyone
who has been given much shall
much be required; and to whom
they entrusted much, of him they
will ask all the more.

4 *Concerning division and signs,* 12:49–59

49 "I have come to cast fire ★49
upon the earth; and how I wish it
were already kindled!
50 "But I have a [a]baptism to ★50 [a]Mark 10:38
undergo, and how distressed I am
until it is accomplished!
51 "[a]Do you suppose that I 51 [a]Luke 12:51-53: *Matt. 10:34-36*
came to grant peace on earth? I
tell you, no, but rather division;
52 for from now on five *members* in one household will be divided, three against two, and two
against three.
53 "They will be divided, [a]fa- 53 [a]Mic. 7:6; Matt. 10:21
ther against son, and son against
father; mother against daughter,
and daughter against mother;
mother-in-law against daughter-
in-law, and daughter-in-law
against mother-in-law."
54 And He was also saying to 54 [a]Matt. 16:2f.
the multitudes, "[a]When you see a
cloud rising in the west, immediately you say, 'A shower is coming,' and so it turns out.
55 "And when *you see* a south 55 [a]Matt. 20:12
wind blowing, you say, 'It will be
a [a]hot day,' and it turns out *that
way.*
56 "You hypocrites! [a]You 56 [a]Matt. 16:3
know how to analyze the appear-
ance of the earth and the sky, but

12:36 *when he returns from the wedding feast.* The groom first had supper with his friends, then went to the house of his bride to claim her, then returned to his own house. Although it might be quite late, he expected his servants to be waiting and ready for him (the second watch was from 9 p.m. to midnight, v. 38). There is no place for slothful ease in the life of a believer while waiting for the return of the Lord.

12:49 *fire.* I.e., judgment.

12:50 *baptism.* I.e., His death.

why do you not analyze this present time?
57 aLuke 21:30 **57** "And [a]why do you not even
on your own initiative judge what
is right?
58 aLuke 12:58, 59; *Matt. 5:25, 26* **58** "For [a]while you are going
with your opponent to appear be-
fore the magistrate, on *your* way
there make an effort to settle with
him, in order that he may not
drag you before the judge, and
the judge turn you over to the
constable, and the constable
throw you into prison.
★59 aMark 12:42 **59** "I say to you, you shall not
get out of there until you have
paid the very last [a]cent."

5 *Concerning repentance,* 13:1–9

★ 1 aMatt. 27 **13** Now on the same occasion
there were some present
who reported to Him about the
Galileans, whose blood [a]Pilate
had mingled with their sacrifices.
2 aJohn 9:2f. **2** And He answered and said
to them, "[a]Do you suppose that
these Galileans were *greater* sinners than all *other* Galileans, because they suffered this *fate?*
3 "I tell you, no, but, unless
you repent, you will all likewise
perish.
4 aIs. 8:6 [Neh. 3:15]; John 9:7, 11 bMatt. 6:12; Luke 11:4 **4** "Or do you suppose that
those eighteen on whom the
tower in [a]Siloam fell and killed
them, were *worse* [b]culprits than
all the men who live in Jerusalem?
5 "I tell you, no, but, unless
you repent, you will all likewise
perish."
★ 6 aMatt. 21:19 **6** And He *began* telling this
parable: "A certain man had [a]a fig
tree which had been planted in
his vineyard; and he came looking
for fruit on it, and did not find
7 aMatt. 3:10; 7:19; Luke 3:9 any.
7 "And he said to the vine-
yard-keeper, 'Behold, for three
years I have come looking for
fruit on this fig tree without finding any. [a]Cut it down! Why does
it even use up the ground?'
8 "And he answered and said ★ 8
to him, 'Let it alone, sir, for this
year too, until I dig around it and
put in fertilizer;
9 and if it bears fruit next
year, *fine;* but if not, cut it
down.' "

6 *Concerning hypocrisy,* 13:10–17

10 And He was [a]teaching in 10 aMatt. 4:23
one of the synagogues on the
Sabbath.
11 And behold, there was a 11 aLuke 13:16
woman who for eighteen years
had had [a]a sickness caused by a
spirit; and she was bent double,
and could not straighten up at all.
12 And when Jesus saw her,
He called her over and said to her,
"Woman, you are freed from
your sickness."
13 And He [a]laid His hands 13 aMark 5:23 bMatt. 9:8
upon her; and immediately she
was made erect again, and *began*
[b]glorifying God.
14 And [a]the synagogue offi- 14 aMark 5:22 bMatt. 12:2; Luke 14:3 cEx. 20:9; Deut. 5:13
cial, indignant because Jesus [b]had
healed on the Sabbath, *began*
saying to the multitude in response, "[c]There are six days in
which work should be done;
therefore come during them and
get healed, and not on the Sabbath day."
15 But [a]the Lord answered 15 aLuke 7:13 bLuke 14:5
him and said, "You hypocrites,
[b]does not each of you on the Sabbath untie his ox or his donkey
from the stall, and lead him away
to water *him?*
16 "And this woman, [a]a ★16 aLuke 19:9 bMatt. 4:10; Luke 13:11
daughter of Abraham as she is,

12:59 *cent.* The smallest of copper coins, worth very little (see 21:2).

13:1 Though there is no other record of this incident, apparently some Galileans were slain by Pilate's soldiers while offering sacrifices at the temple, so that their blood and the blood of the sacrifices were mixed. The point Christ makes is that this did not happen to them because they were worse sinners than other Galileans, but that all need to repent (vv. 2–3).

13:6 *a fig tree.* The fruitless fig tree was symbolic of the Jewish people.

13:8–9 God's judgment is sure, and His patience is great.

13:16 *should she not have been released.* Her healing was obligatory, especially since animals could be watered on the Sabbath (v. 15).

whom [b]Satan has bound for eighteen long years, should she not
have been released from this
bond on the Sabbath day?"
17 [a]Luke 18:43 — 17 And as He said this, all His
opponents were being humiliated;
and [a]the entire multitude was rejoicing over all the glorious things
being done by Him.

7 *Concerning the kingdom,* 13:18–35

18 [a]Luke 13:18, 19: *Matt. 13:31, 32; Mark 4:30-32* [b]Matt. 13:24; Luke 13:20 — 18 Therefore [a]He was saying,
"[b]What is the kingdom of God
like, and to what shall I compare
it?
★19 — 19 "It is like a mustard seed,
which a man took and threw into
his own garden; and it grew and
became a tree; and the birds of
the air nested in its branches."
20 [a]Matt. 13:24; Luke 13:18 — 20 And again He said, "[a]To
what shall I compare the kingdom
of God?
★21 [a]Luke 13:20, 21: *Matt. 13:33* [b]Matt. 13:33 — 21 "[a]It is like leaven, which a
woman took and hid in [b]three
pecks of meal, until it was all
leavened."
22 [a]Luke 9:51 — 22 And He was passing
through from one city and village
to another, teaching, and [a]pro-
ceeding on His way to Jerusalem.
23 And someone said to Him,
"Lord, are there *just* a few who
are being saved?" And He said to
them,
★24 [a]Matt. 7:13 — 24 "[a]Strive to enter by the narrow door; for many, I tell you, will
seek to enter and will not be able.
25 [a]Matt. 25:10 [b]Luke 3:8 [c]Matt. 7:22; 25:11 [d]Matt. 7:23; 25:12; Luke 13:27 — 25 "Once the head of the
house gets up and [a]shuts the
door, and you [b]begin to stand
outside and knock on the door,
saying, '[c]Lord, open up to us!'
then He will answer and say to
you, '[d]I do not know where you
are from.'
26 "Then you will [a]begin to — 26 [a]Luke 3:8
say, 'We ate and drank in Your
presence, and You taught in our
streets';
27 and He will say, 'I tell you, — 27 [a]Luke 13:25 [b]Ps. 6:8; Matt. 25:41
[a]I do not know where you are
from; [b]DEPART FROM ME, ALL YOU
EVILDOERS.'
28 "[a]There will be weeping — 28 [a]Matt. 8:12
and gnashing of teeth there when
you see Abraham and Isaac and
Jacob and all the prophets in the
kingdom of God, but yourselves
being cast out.
29 "And they [a]will come from — 29 [a]Matt. 8:11
east and west, and from north and
south, and will recline *at table* in
the kingdom of God.
30 "And behold, [a]*some* are last — 30 [a]Matt. 19:30
who will be first and *some* are
first who will be last."
31 Just at that time some — 31 [a]Matt. 14:1; Luke 3:1; 9:7; 23:7
Pharisees came up, saying to Him,
"Go away and depart from here,
for [a]Herod wants to kill You."
32 And He said to them, "Go — ★32 [a]Heb. 2:10; 5:9; 7:28
and tell that fox, 'Behold, I cast
out demons and perform cures today and tomorrow, and the third
day I [a]reach My goal.'
33 "Nevertheless [a]I must jour- — 33 [a]John 11:9 [b]Matt. 21:11
ney on today and tomorrow and
the next *day;* for it cannot be that
a [b]prophet should perish outside
of Jerusalem.
34 "[a]O Jerusalem, Jerusalem, — 34 [a]Luke 13:34, 35: *Matt. 23:37-39;* Luke 19:41 [b]Matt. 23:37
the city that kills the prophets
and stones those sent to her! How
often I wanted to gather your
children together, [b]just as a hen
gathers her brood under her
wings, and you would not *have it!*
35 "Behold, your house is left — ★35 [a]Ps. 118:26; Matt. 21:9; Luke 19:38
to you *desolate;* and I say to you,
you shall not see Me until *the
time* comes when you say,
'[a]BLESSED *is* HE WHO COMES IN THE
NAME OF THE LORD!' "

13:19 *mustard seed.* From the smallest of seeds the Palestinian mustard plant grows in one season to a shrub the size of a small tree.

13:21 *leaven.* See note on Matt. 13:33.

13:24 *narrow door.* Christ Himself, apart from Whom there is no other way to heaven (John 14:6).

13:32 *that fox.* Herod Antipas is described as a fox, known for its use of cunning deceit to achieve its aims.

13:35 *your house is left to you desolate.* This was fulfilled when the temple was destroyed in A.D. 70 and the Jews were expelled under Hadrian in A.D. 135. *Blessed is He who comes.* See Ps. 118:26. This will be fulfilled at the second coming of Christ.

8 Concerning inflexible people, 14:1-6

1 aMark 3:2 **14** And it came about when
He went into the house of
one of the leaders of the Pharisees
on *the* Sabbath to eat bread, that
[a]they were watching Him closely.
★ 2 **2** And there, in front of Him
was a certain man suffering from
dropsy.
3 aActs 3:12 bMatt. 22:35 cMatt. 12:2; Luke 13:14 **3** And Jesus [a]answered and
spoke to the [b]lawyers and Pharisees, saying, "[c]Is it lawful to heal
on the Sabbath, or not?"
4 But they kept silent. And
He took hold of him, and healed
him, and sent him away.
5 aLuke 13:15 **5** And He said to them,
"[a]Which one of you shall have a
son or an ox fall into a well, and
will not immediately pull him out
on a Sabbath day?"
6 aMatt. 22:46; Luke 20:40 **6** [a]And they could make no
reply to this.

9 Concerning inflated people, 14:7-11

7 aMatt. 23:6 **7** And He *began* speaking a
parable to the invited guests
when He noticed how [a]they had
been picking out the places of
honor *at the table;* saying to
them,
8 aProv. 25:6, 7 **8** "When you are invited by
someone to a wedding feast, [a]do
not take the place of honor, lest
someone more distinguished than
you may have been invited by
him,
9 aLuke 3:8 **9** and he who invited you
both shall come and say to you,
'Give place to this man', and then
[a]in disgrace you proceed to occupy the last place.
10 aProv. 25:6, 7 **10** "But when you are invited,
go and recline at the last place, so
that when the one who has invited you comes, he may say to
you, 'Friend, [a]move up higher';
then you will have honor in the
sight of all who are at the table
with you.
11 "[a]For everyone who exalts ★11 aMatt. 23:12; Luke 18:14
himself shall be humbled, and he
who humbles himself shall be exalted."

10 Concerning invited people, 14:12-14

12 And He also went on to
say to the one who had invited
Him, "When you give a luncheon
or a dinner, do not invite your
friends or your brothers or your
relatives or rich neighbors, lest
they also invite you in return, and
repayment come to you.
13 "But when you give a reception, invite *the* poor, *the* crippled,
the lame, *the* blind,
14 and you will be blessed, 14 aJohn 5:29; Acts 24:15; Rev. 20:4, 5 [?]
since they do not have *the means*
to repay you; for you will be repaid at [a]the resurrection of the
righteous."

11 Concerning indifferent people, 14:15-24

15 And when one of those ★15 aRev. 19:9
who were reclining *at table* with
Him heard this, he said to Him,
"[a]Blessed is everyone who shall
eat bread in the kingdom of
God!"
16 But He said to him, "[a]A 16 aMatt. 22:2-14; Luke 14:16-24
certain man was giving a big dinner, and he invited many;
17 and at the dinner hour he
sent his slave to say to those who
had been invited, 'Come; for
everything is ready now.'
18 "But they all alike began to
make excuses. The first one said
to him, 'I have bought a piece of
land and I need to go out and look
at it; please consider me excused.'
19 "And another one said, 'I
have bought five yoke of oxen,
and I am going to try them out;
please consider me excused.'

14:2 *dropsy.* A swelling of the body due to retention of excessive liquid.

14:11 Humility is the path to promotion in the kingdom of God.

14:15 *Blessed is everyone.* A seemingly pious remark made for the purpose of dulling the point of Christ's teaching.

20 [a]Deut. 24:5; 1 Cor. 7:33 20 "And another one said, '[a]I
have married a wife, and for that
reason I cannot come.'
21 "And the slave came *back*
and reported this to his master.
Then the head of the household
became angry and said to his
slave, 'Go out at once into the
streets and lanes of the city and
bring in here the poor and crippled and blind and lame.'
22 "And the slave said, 'Master, what you commanded has
been done, and still there is
room.'
23 "And the master said to the
slave, 'Go out into the highways
and along the hedges, and compel
them to come in, that my house
may be filled.
24 'For I tell you, none of those
men who were invited shall taste
of my dinner.' "

12 Concerning indulgent people, 14:25-35

★25 25 Now great multitudes
were going along with Him; and
He turned and said to them,
★26 [a]Matt. 10:37f. 26 "[a]If anyone comes to Me,
and does not hate his own father
and mother and wife and children
and brothers and sisters, yes, and
even his own life, he cannot be
My disciple.
27 [a]Matt. 10:38 27 "Whoever does not [a]carry
his own cross and come after Me
cannot be My disciple.
28 "For which one of you,
when he wants to build a tower,
does not first sit down and calculate the cost, to see if he has
enough to complete it?
29 "Otherwise, when he has
laid a foundation, and is not able
to finish, all who observe it begin
to ridicule him,
30 saying, 'This man began to
build and was not able to finish.'
31 "Or what king, when he
sets out to meet another king in
battle, will not first sit down and
take counsel whether he is strong
enough with ten thousand *men* to
encounter the one coming against
him with twenty thousand?
32 "Or else, while the other is
still far away, he sends a delegation and asks terms of peace.
33 "So therefore, no one of 33 [a]Phil. 3:7; Heb. 11:26
you can be My disciple who [a]does
not give up all his own possessions.
34 "Therefore, salt is good; but 34 [a]Matt. 5:13; Mark 9:50
[a]if even salt has become tasteless,
with what will it be seasoned?
35 "It is useless either for the 35 [a]Matt. 11:15
soil or for the manure pile; it is
thrown out. [a]He who has ears to
hear, let him hear."

13 Concerning God's love for sinners, 15:1-32

15 Now all the [a]tax-gatherers 1 [a]Luke 5:29
and the sinners were com-
ing near Him to listen to Him.
2 And both the Pharisees ★ 2 [a]Matt. 9:11
and the scribes *began* to grumble,
saying, "This man receives sinners and [a]eats with them."
3 And He told them this
parable, saying,
4 "[a]What man among you, if ★ 4 [a]Matt. 18:12-14; Luke 15:4-7
he has a hundred sheep and has
lost one of them, does not leave
the ninety-nine in the open pasture, and go after the one which is
lost, until he finds it?
5 "And when he has found it,
he lays it on his shoulders, rejoicing.
6 "And when he comes home,
he calls together his friends and
his neighbors, saying to them,

14:25-33 The parable that precedes in vv. 16-24 expresses the open, compelling invitation to come to Christ for salvation. The teaching of vv. 25-33 cautions His followers to consider carefully the cost of full commitment to Christ in a life of service.

14:26 *hate.* This saying does not justify malice or ill will toward one's family, but it means that devotion to family must take second place to one's devotion to Christ.

15:2 *This man receives sinners.* Since the Pharisees disdained publicans and sinners, Christ told three parables (15:4-32) to show God's interest in them.

15:4 *lost.* Eight times in this chapter the lostness of man is emphasized (vv. 4 [twice], 6, 8, 9, 17, 24, 32).

'Rejoice with me, for I have found
my sheep which was lost!'
7 "I tell you that in the same
way, there will be *more* joy in
heaven over one sinner who repents, than over ninety-nine
righteous persons who need no
repentance.
★8 8 "Or what woman, if she has
ten silver coins and loses one
coin, does not light a lamp and
sweep the house and search carefully until she finds it?
9 "And when she has found
it, she calls together her friends
and neighbors, saying, 'Rejoice
with me, for I have found the coin
which I had lost!'
10 [a]Matt 10 "In the same way, I tell you,
10:32; Luke there is joy [a]in the presence of the
15:7 angels of God over one sinner
who repents."
11 And He said, "A certain
man had two sons;
12 [a]Deut. 12 and the younger of them
21:17 [b]Mark said to his father, 'Father, give me
12:44; Luke [a]the share of the estate that falls
15:30 to me.' And he divided his
[b]wealth between them.
13 "And not many days later,
the younger son gathered everything together and went on a
journey into a distant country,
and there he squandered his estate with loose living.
14 "Now when he had spent
everything, a severe famine occurred in that country, and he began to be in need.
★15 15 "And he went and attached
himself to one of the citizens of
that country, and he sent him into
his fields to feed swine.
16 "And he was longing to fill
his stomach with the pods that
the swine were eating, and no one
was giving *anything* to him.
17 "But when he came to his
senses, he said, 'How many of my
father's hired men have more
than enough bread, but I am
dying here with hunger!
18 'I will get up and go to my ★18
father, and will say to him, "Father, I have sinned against
heaven, and in your sight;
19 "I am no longer worthy to
be called your son; make me as
one of your hired men." '
20 "And he got up and came to 20 [a]Gen.
his father. But while he was still a 45:14; 46:29;
long way off, his father saw him, Acts 20:37
and felt compassion *for him,* and
ran and [a]embraced him, and
kissed him.
21 "And the son said to him,
'Father, I have sinned against
heaven and in your sight; I am no
longer worthy to be called your
son.'
22 "But the father said to his 22 [a]Zech.
slaves, 'Quickly bring out [a]the 3:4; Rev.
best robe and put it on him, and 6:11 [b]Gen.
[b]put a ring on his hand and san- 41:42
dals on his feet;
23 and bring the fattened calf,
kill it, and let us eat and be merry;
24 for this son of mine was 24 [a]Matt.
[a]dead, and has come to life again; 8:22; Luke
he was lost, and has been found.' 9:60; 15:32;
And they began to be merry. Rom. 11:15;
25 "Now his older son was in Eph. 2:1, 5;
the field, and when he came and 5:14; Col.
approached the house, he heard 2:13; 1 Tim.
music and dancing. 5:6
26 "And he summoned one of
the servants and *began* inquiring
what these things might be.
27 "And he said to him, 'Your
brother has come, and your father
has killed the fattened calf, because he has received him back
safe and sound.'
28 "But he became angry, and ★28
was not willing to go in; and his
father came out and *began* entreating him.
29 "But he answered and said
to his father, 'Look! For so many
years I have been serving you,

15:8 *what woman.* The second parable using a woman suggests that many women followed Christ and heard Him teach.

15:15 *to feed swine.* The lowest possible humiliation for a Jew.

15:18 *I have sinned.* Acknowledging one's personal responsibility for sin is the first step toward reconciliation with God.

15:28 *he became angry.* The elder son's attitude is the same as the Pharisees' (v. 2; 18:11-12). The words reflect self-righteousness.

and I have never neglected a command of yours; and *yet* you have
never given me a kid, that I might
be merry with my friends;
30 [a]Prov. 29:3; Luke 15:12 **30** but when this son of yours
came, who has devoured your
[a]wealth with harlots, you killed
the fattened calf for him.'
31 "And he said to him, *'My*
child, you have always been with
me, and all that is mine is yours.
32 [a]Luke 15:24 **32** 'But we had to be merry and
rejoice, for this brother of yours
was [a]dead and *has begun* to live,
and *was* lost and has been
found.' "

14 Concerning wealth, 16:1–31

1 [a]Luke 15:13 **16** Now He was also saying to
the disciples, "There was a
certain rich man who had a steward, and this *steward* was reported to him as [a]squandering his
possessions.
2 "And he called him and said
to him, 'What is this I hear about
you? Give an account of your
stewardship, for you can no
longer be steward.'
3 "And the steward said to
himself, 'What shall I do, since
my master is taking the stewardship away from me? I am not
strong enough to dig; I am
ashamed to beg.
4 'I know what I shall do, so
that when I am removed from the
stewardship, they will receive me
into their homes.'
5 "And he summoned each
one of his master's debtors, and
he *began* saying to the first, 'How
much do you owe my master?'
6 "And he said, 'A hundred
measures of oil.' And he said to
him, 'Take your bill, and sit down
quickly and write fifty.'
7 "Then he said to another,
'And how much do you owe?'
And he said, 'A hundred measures of wheat.' He *said to him,
'Take your bill, and write eighty.'
8 "And his master praised the ★ 8 [a]Matt. 12:32; Luke 20:34 [b]John 12:36; Eph. 5:8; 1 Thess. 5:5
unrighteous steward because he
had acted shrewdly; for the sons
of [a]this age are more shrewd in
relation to their own kind than
the [b]sons of light.
9 "And I say to you, [a]make ★ 9 [a]Matt. 19:21; Luke 11:41; 12:33 [b]Matt. 6:24; Luke 16:11, 13 [c]Luke 16:4
friends for yourselves by means
of the [b]mammon of unrighteousness; that when it fails, [c]they may
receive you into the eternal dwell-
ings.
10 "[a]He who is faithful in a 10 [a]Matt. 25:21, 23
very little thing is faithful also in
much; and he who is unrighteous
in a very little thing is unrighteous also in much.
11 "If therefore you have not ★11 [a]Luke 16:9
been faithful in the *use of* unrighteous [a]mammon, who will entrust the true *riches* to you?
12 "And if you have not been ★12
faithful in *the use of* that which is
another's, who will give you that
which is your own?
13 "[a]No servant can serve two 13 [a]Matt. 6:24 [b]Luke 16:9
masters; for either he will hate the
one, and love the other, or else he
will hold to one, and despise the
other. You cannot serve God and
[b]mammon."
14 Now the Pharisees, who 14 [a]2 Tim. 3:2 [b]Luke 23:35
were [a]lovers of money, were lis-
tening to all these things, and
they [b]were scoffing at Him.
15 And He said to them, 15 [a]Luke 10:29; 18:9, 14 [b]1 Sam. 16:7; Prov. 21:2; Acts 1:24; Rom. 8:27
"You are those who [a]justify your-
selves in the sight of men, but
[b]God knows your hearts; for that
which is highly esteemed among
men is detestable in the sight of
God.
16 "[a]The Law and the Prophets ★16 [a]Matt. 11:12f. [b]Matt. 4:23
were proclaimed until John; since

16:8 *acted shrewdly.* What is commended is the ingenuity, not the dishonesty, of the steward in using his present opportunities to prepare for the future. Likewise, the believer should use what he has in this life in the service of God in order to assure rewards in heaven (v. 9).

16:9 *mammon* = money and other material possessions.

16:11 *the true riches.* I.e., spiritual responsibilities.

16:12 Unfaithfulness in managing another's goods proves one unworthy to be given much for himself.

16:16 *every one is forcing his way into it.* Men were crowding to enter the kingdom.

then [b]the gospel of the kingdom
of God is preached, and every one
is forcing his way into it.
★17 [a]Matt. 17 "[a]But it is easier for heaven
5:18 and earth to pass away than for
one stroke of a letter of the Law
to fail.
★18 [a]Matt. 18 "[a]Every one who divorces
5:32 his wife and marries another
commits adultery; and he who
marries one who is divorced from
a husband commits adultery.
★19 **19** "Now there was a certain
rich man, and he habitually
dressed in purple and fine linen,
gaily living in splendor every day.
20 [a]Acts 3:2 20 "And a certain poor man
named Lazarus [a]was laid at his
gate, covered with sores,
21 and longing to be fed with
the *crumbs* which were falling
from the rich man's table; besides, even the dogs were coming
and licking his sores.
★22 [a]John 22 "Now it came about that
1:18; 13:23 the poor man died and he was
carried away by the angels to [a]A-
braham's bosom; and the rich
man also died and was buried.
★23 [a]Matt. 23 "And in [a]Hades he lifted up
11:23 his eyes, being in torment, and
*saw Abraham far away, and
Lazarus in his bosom.
24 [a]Luke 24 "And he cried out and said,
3:8; 16:30; '[a]Father Abraham, have mercy on
19:9 [b]Matt. me, and send Lazarus, that he
25:41 may dip the tip of his finger in
water and cool off my tongue; for
I am in agony in [b]this flame.'
25 [a]Luke 25 "But Abraham said, 'Child,
6:24 remember that [a]during your life
you received your good things,
and likewise Lazarus bad things;
but now he is being comforted
here, and you are in agony.
26 'And besides all this, between us and you there is a great
chasm fixed, in order that those
who wish to come over from here
to you may not be able, and *that*
none may cross over from there
to us.'
27 "And he said, 'Then I beg
you, Father, that you send him to
my father's house —
28 for I have five brothers — 28 [a]Acts
that he may [a]warn them, lest they 2:40; 8:25;
also come to this place of tor- 10:42; 18:5;
ment.' 20:21ff.;
29 "But Abraham *said, 'They 23:11; 28:23;
have [a]Moses and the Prophets; let Gal. 5:3;
them hear them.' Eph. 4:17;
30 "But he said, 'No, [a]Father 1 Thess.
Abraham, but if someone goes to 2:11; 4:6
them from the dead, they will re- 29 [a]Luke 4:17; John 5:45-47; Acts 15:21
pent!' 30 [a]Luke 3:8; 16:24; 19:9
31 "But he said to him, 'If they
do not listen to Moses and the
Prophets, neither will they be
persuaded if someone rises from
the dead.'"

15 Concerning forgiveness, 17:1-6

17 And He said to His disci- 1 [a]Matt.
ples, "[a]It is inevitable that 18:7; 1 Cor.
stumbling blocks should come, 11:19; 1 Tim.
but woe to him through whom 4:1
they come!
2 "[a]It would be better for him ★ 2 [a]Matt.
if a millstone were hung around 18:6; Mark
his neck and he were thrown into 9:42; 1 Cor.
the sea, than that he should cause 8:12
one of these little ones to stumble.
3 "Be on your guard! [a]If your 3 [a]Matt.
brother sins, rebuke him; and if 18:15
he repents, forgive him.
4 "And if he sins against you 4 [a]Matt.
[a]seven times a day, and returns to 18:21f.
you seven times, saying, 'I re-
pent,' forgive him."

16:17 *stroke.* See note on Matt. 5:18.
16:18 *divorces.* See notes on Matt. 5:32; 19:10.
16:19 *rich man.* His name is not given. Dives, sometimes said to be his name, is simply Latin for "rich man." Life was one continual party for him.
16:22 *Abraham's bosom.* Figurative speech for paradise, or the presence of God (Luke 23:43; 2 Cor. 12:4).
16:23 *in Hades.* The unseen world in general, but specifically here the abode of the unsaved dead between death and judgment at the great white throne (Rev. 20:11–15). See note on Eph. 4:9. In this saying the Lord taught: (1) conscious existence after death; (2) the reality and torment of hell; (3) no second chance after death; and (4) the impossibility of the dead communicating with the living (v. 26). The two men in this story illustrate two different lives, two different deaths, and two different destinies.
17:2 *a millstone.* See note on Matt. 18:6.

5 [a]Mark 6:30 [b]Luke 7:13
★ 6 [a]Luke 7:13 [b]Matt. 13:31; 17:20; Mark 4:31; Luke 13:19 [c]Luke 19:4

5 And [a]the apostles said to
[b]the Lord, "Increase our faith!"
6 And [a]the Lord said, "If you
had faith like [b]a mustard seed,
you would say to this [c]mulberry
tree, 'Be uprooted and be planted
in the sea'; and it would obey
you.

16 Concerning service, 17:7-10

7 "But which of you, having a
slave plowing or tending sheep,
will say to him when he has come
in from the field, 'Come immediately and sit down to eat'?

8 [a]Luke 12:37

8 "But will he not say to him,
'[a]Prepare something for me to eat,
and *properly* clothe yourself and
serve me until I have eaten and
drunk; and afterward you will eat
and drink'?
9 "He does not thank the
slave because he did the things
which were commanded, does he?
10 "So you too, when you do
all the things which are commanded you, say, 'We are unworthy slaves; we have done *only*
that which we ought to have
done.' "

17 Concerning gratitude, 17:11-19

11 [a]Luke 9:51 [b]Luke 9:52ff.; John 4:3f.
★12 [a]Lev. 13:45f.
13 [a]Luke 5:5
★14 [a]Matt. 8:4; Luke 5:14

11 And it came about while
He was [a]on the way to Jerusalem,
that [b]He was passing between Samaria and Galilee.
12 And as He entered a certain village, there met Him ten
leprous men, who [a]stood at a distance;
13 and they raised their
voices, saying, "Jesus, [a]Master,
have mercy on us!"
14 And when He saw them,
He said to them, "[a]Go and show
yourselves to the priests." And it
came about that as they were
going, they were cleansed.

15 [a]Matt. 9:8
16 [a]Matt. 10:5
18 [a]Matt. 9:8
19 [a]Matt. 9:22; Luke 18:42

15 Now one of them, when he
saw that he had been healed,
turned back, [a]glorifying God with
a loud voice,
16 and he fell on his face at
His feet, giving thanks to Him.
And he was a [a]Samaritan.
17 And Jesus answered and
said, "Were there not ten
cleansed? But the nine — where
are they?
18 "Were none found who
turned back to [a]give glory to God,
except this foreigner?"
19 And He said to him, "Rise,
and go your way; [a]your faith has
made you well."

18 Concerning the kingdom, 17:20-37

20 [a]Luke 19:11; Acts 1:6 [b]Luke 14:1 [Gr.]
★21 [a]Luke 17:23
22 [a]Matt. 9:15; Mark 2:20; Luke 5:35
23 [a]Matt. 24:23; Mark 13:21; Luke 21:8
24 [a]Matt. 24:27

20 Now having been questioned by the Pharisees [a]as to
when the kingdom of God was
coming, He answered them and
said, "The kingdom of God is not
coming with [b]signs to be observed;
21 nor will [a]they say, 'Look,
here *it is!*' or, 'There *it is!*' For behold, the kingdom of God is in
your midst."
22 And He said to the disciples, "[a]The days shall come when
you will long to see one of the
days of the Son of Man, and you
will not see it.
23 "[a]And they will say to you,
'Look there! Look here!' Do not
go away, and do not run after
them.
24 "[a]For just as the lightning,
when it flashes out of one part of
the sky, shines to the other part
of the sky, so will the Son of Man
be in His day.

17:6 *mulberry tree.* A tree whose roots were regarded as being particularly strong, making it virtually impossible to uproot.

17:12 *leprous men.* See note on Luke 5:12.

17:14 *Go and show yourselves to the priests.* The priest had to certify the cleansing of a leper (Lev. 14:1-32). The men exhibited faith by starting on their way to the priest before being cleansed.

17:21 *the kingdom of God is in your midst.* The necessary elements of the kingdom were there present and needed only to be recognized. It cannot mean "within you," for the kingdom certainly was completely unconnected with the Pharisees to whom Jesus was speaking (v. 20).

25 [a]Matt. 16:21; Luke 9:22 **25** "[a]But first He must suffer
many things and be rejected by
this generation.
★26 [a]Luke 17:26, 27; *Matt. 24:37-39* [b]Gen. 7 **26** "[a]And just as it happened
[b]in the days of Noah, so it shall be
also in the days of the Son of
Man:
27 they were eating, they
were drinking, they were marry-
ing, they were being given in
marriage, until the day that Noah
entered the ark, and the flood
came and destroyed them all.
★28 [a]Gen. 19 **28** "It was the same as happened in [a]the days of Lot: they
were eating, they were drinking,
they were buying, they were selling, they were planting, they were
building;
29 but on the day that Lot
went out from Sodom it rained
fire and brimstone from heaven
and destroyed them all.
★30 [a]Matt. 16:27; 1 Cor. 1:7; Col. 3:4; 2 Thess. 1:7; 1 Pet. 1:7; 4:13; 1 John 2:28 **30** "It will be just the same on
the day that the Son of Man [a]is
revealed.
31 "On that day, let not the
one who is [a]on the housetop and
31 [a]Matt. 24:17, 18; Mark 13:15f.; Luke 21:21 whose goods are in the house go
down to take them away; and
likewise let not the one who is in
the field turn back.
32 [a]Gen. 19:26 **32** "[a]Remember Lot's wife.
33 [a]Matt. 10:39 **33** "[a]Whoever seeks to keep
his life shall lose it, and whoever
loses *his life* shall preserve it
alive.
34 "I tell you, on that night
there will be two men in one bed;
one will be taken, and the other
will be left.
35 [a]Matt. 24:41 **35** "[a]There will be two women
grinding at the same place; one
will be taken, and the other will
be left.
36 ["[a]Two men will be in the field; one will be taken and the ★36 [a]Matt. 24:40
field; one will be taken and the
other will be left."]
37 And answering they *said ★37 [a]Matt. 24:28
to Him, "Where, Lord?" And He
said to them, "[a]Where the body
is, there also will the vultures be
gathered."

19 Concerning prayer, 18:1-14

18 Now He was telling them ★ 1 [a]Luke 11:5-10 [b]2 Cor. 4:1
a parable to show that at
all times they [a]ought to pray and
not to [b]lose heart,
2 saying, "There was in a 2 [a]Luke 18:4; 20:13; Heb. 12:9
certain city a judge who did not
fear God, and did not [a]respect
man.
3 "And there was a widow in
that city, and she kept coming to
him, saying, 'Give me legal protection from my opponent.'
4 "And for a while he was un- 4 [a]Luke 18:2; 20:13; Heb. 12:9
willing; but afterward he said to
himself, 'Even though I do not
fear God nor [a]respect man,
5 yet [a]because this widow 5 [a]Luke 11:8 [b]1 Cor. 9:27
bothers me, I will give her legal
protection, lest by continually
coming she [b]wear me out.'"
6 And [a]the Lord said, "Hear 6 [a]Luke 7:13
what the unrighteous judge *said;
7 now shall not God [a]bring 7 [a]Rev. 6:10 [b]Matt. 24:22; Rom. 8:33; Col. 3:12; 2 Tim. 2:10; Titus 1:1 [c]2 Pet. 3:9
about justice for His [b]elect, who
cry to Him day and night, and will
He [c]delay long over them?
8 "I tell you that He will bring ★ 8 [a]Luke 17:26ff
about justice for them speedily.
However, when the Son of Man
comes, [a]will He find faith on the
earth?"
9 And He also told this par- 9 [a]Luke 16:15 [b]Rom. 14:3, 10
able to certain ones who [a]trusted
in themselves that they were

17:26-27 *in the days of Noah.* See Gen. 6. The activities mentioned in v. 27 are not wrong; the people were unprepared for the judgment of the flood because they did not heed God's warnings through Noah.

17:28 *in the days of Lot.* See Gen. 19.

17:30 *It will be just the same.* Until the time of Christ's return, many people will be prosperous, feel secure and be unprepared for His return (as in the days of Noah and Lot).

17:36 Many manuscripts do not contain this verse.

17:37 *body.* I.e., a corpse. *vultures.* A reference to the carnage of Armageddon (Rev. 19:17-19).

18:1 *lose heart.* I.e., be discouraged because answers do not come immediately.

18:8 *speedily.* Not necessarily immediately, but quickly when the answer begins to come. For other uses of the term see Rom. 16:20; Rev. 1:1. *will He find faith on the earth?* This does not augur for improved spiritual conditions in the world before Christ's return.

righteous, and [b]viewed others with contempt:

10 [a]1 Kin. 10:5; 2 Kin. 20:5, 8; Acts 3:1

10 "Two men [a]went up into the temple to pray, one a Pharisee, and the other a tax-gatherer.

11 [a]Matt. 6:5; Mark 11:25; Luke 22:41

11 "The Pharisee [a]stood and was praying thus to himself, 'God, I thank Thee that I am not like other people: swindlers, unjust, adulterers, or even like this tax-gatherer.

★12 [a]Matt. 9:14 [b]Luke 11:42

12 'I [a]fast twice a week; I [b]pay tithes of all that I get.'

★13 [a]Matt. 6:5; Mark 11:25; Luke 22:41 [b]Ezra 9:6 [c]Luke 23:48

13 "But the tax-gatherer, [a]standing some distance away, [b]was even unwilling to lift up his eyes to heaven, but [c]was beating his breast, saying, 'God, be merciful to me, the sinner!'

★14 [a]Matt. 23:12; Luke 14:11

14 "I tell you, this man went down to his house justified rather than the other; [a]for every one who exalts himself shall be humbled, but he who humbles himself shall be exalted."

20 Concerning entrance into the kingdom, 18:15–30

15 [a]Luke 18:15-17: *Matt. 19:13-15; Mark 10:13-16*

15 [a]And they were bringing even their babies to Him, in order that He might touch them, but when the disciples saw it, they *began* rebuking them.

16 But Jesus called for them, saying, "Permit the children to come to Me, and stop hindering them, for the kingdom of God belongs to such as these.

17 [a]Matt. 18:3; 19:14; Mark 10:15; 1 Cor. 14:20; 1 Pet. 2:2

17 "Truly I say to you, [a]whoever does not receive the kingdom of God like a child shall not enter it *at all.*"

18 [a]Luke 18:18-30: *Matt. 19:16-29; Mark 10:17-30;* Luke 10:25-28

18 [a]And a certain ruler questioned Him, saying, "Good Teacher, what shall I do to obtain eternal life?"

19 And Jesus said to him, "Why do you call Me good? No one is good except God alone.

20 [a]Ex. 20:12-16; Deut. 5:16-20

20 "You know the commandments, '[a]Do NOT COMMIT ADULTERY, Do NOT MURDER, Do NOT STEAL, Do NOT BEAR FALSE WITNESS, HONOR YOUR FATHER AND MOTHER.' "

21 And he said, "All these things I have kept from *my* youth."

★22 [a]Matt. 19:21; Luke 12:33 [b]Matt. 6:20

22 And when Jesus heard *this,* He said to him, "One thing you still lack; [a]sell all that you possess, and distribute it to the poor, and you shall have [b]treasure in heaven; and come, follow Me."

23 But when he had heard these things, he became very sad; for he was extremely rich.

24 [a]Matt. 19:23; Mark 10:23f

24 And Jesus looked at him and said, "[a]How hard it is for those who are wealthy to enter the kingdom of God!

★25 [a]Matt. 19:24; Mark 10:25

25 "For [a]it is easier for a camel to go through the eye of a needle, than for a rich man to enter the kingdom of God."

26 And they who heard it said, "Then who can be saved?"

27 [a]Matt. 19:26

27 But He said, "[a]The things impossible with men are possible with God."

28 [a]Luke 5:11

28 And Peter said, "Behold, [a]we have left our own *homes,* and followed You."

29 [a]Matt. 6:33; 19:29; Mark 10:29f

29 And He said to them, "Truly I say to you, [a]there is no one who has left house or wife or brothers or parents or children, for the sake of the kingdom of God,

30 [a]Matt. 12:32

30 who shall not receive many times as much at this time and in [a]the age to come, eternal life."

18:12 *I fast.* See note on Matt. 9:14. *I pay tithes.* See note on Matt. 23:23.

18:13 *God, be merciful.* Lit., God be propitiated or satisfied. Now Christ is the propitiation or satisfaction for our sins (1 John 2:1).

18:14 The Pharisee thought God operated on a merit system, and thus could be put in man's debt through good works. The publican knew God was merciful and was worthy of trust.

18:22 *One thing you still lack.* Apparently the man had kept the laws of v. 20, but Jesus saw his attachment to material things. Rather than admit this, the man turned his back on Christ's help.

18:25 *the eye of a needle.* See note on Matt. 19:24.

21 *Concerning His death,* 18:31-34

31 [a]Luke 18:31-33: Matt. 20:17-19; Mark 10:32-34 [b]Luke 9:51 [c]Ps. 22; Is. 53 **31** [a]And He took the twelve
aside and said to them, "Behold,
[b]we are going up to Jerusalem,
and [c]all things which are written
through the prophets about the
Son of Man will be accomplished.
32 [a]Matt. 16:21 **32** "[a]For He will be delivered
up to the Gentiles, and will be
mocked and mistreated and spit
upon,
33 and after they have
scourged Him, they will kill Him;
and the third day He will rise
again."
34 [a]Mark 9:32; Luke 9:45 **34** And [a]they understood
none of these things, and this say-
ing was hidden from them, and
they did not comprehend the
things that were said.

22 *Concerning salvation,* 18:35-19:10

★35 [a]Luke 18:35-43: Matt. 20:29-34; Mark 10:46-52 [b]Matt. 20:29; Mark 10:46; Luke 19:1 **35** [a]And it came about that
[b]as He was approaching Jericho, a
certain blind man was sitting by
the road, begging.
36 Now hearing a multitude
going by, he *began* to inquire
what this might be.
37 And they told him that
Jesus of Nazareth was passing by.
38 [a]Matt. 9:27; Luke 18:39 **38** And he called out, saying,
"Jesus, [a]Son of David, have mercy
on me!"
39 [a]Luke 18:38 **39** And those who led the
way were sternly telling him to be
quiet; but he kept crying out all
the more, "[a]Son of David, have
mercy on me!"
40 And Jesus stopped and
commanded that he be brought to
Him; and when he had come
near, He questioned him,
41 "What do you want Me to
do for you?" And he said, "Lord, *I*
want to receive my sight!"
42 And Jesus said to him, 42 [a]Matt. 9:22
"Receive your sight; [a]your faith
has made you well."
43 And immediately he re- 43 [a]Matt. 9:8 [b]Luke 9:43; 13:17; 19:37
ceived his sight, and *began* fol-
lowing Him, [a]glorifying God; and
when [b]all the people saw it, they
gave praise to God.
19 And He [a]entered and was 1 [a]Luke 18:35
passing through Jericho.
2 And behold, there was a ★ 2
man called by the name of Zaccheus; and he was a chief tax-
gatherer, and he was rich.
3 And he was trying to see
who Jesus was, and he was unable
because of the crowd, for he was
small in stature.
4 And he ran on ahead and 4 [a]1 Kin. 10:27; 1 Chr. 27:28; 2 Chr. 1:15; 9:27; Ps. 78:47; Is. 9:10; Luke 17:6 [?]
climbed up into a [a]sycamore tree
in order to see Him, for He was
about to pass through that way.
5 And when Jesus came to
the place, He looked up and said
to him, "Zaccheus, hurry and
come down, for today I must stay
at your house."
6 And he hurried and came
down, and received Him gladly.
7 And when they saw it,
they all *began* to grumble, saying,
"He has gone to be the guest of a
man who is a sinner."
8 And Zaccheus stopped and ★ 8 [a]Luke 7:13 [b]Luke 3:14 [c]Ex. 22:1; Lev. 6:5; Num. 5:7; 2 Sam. 12:6
said to [a]the Lord, "Behold, Lord,
half of my possessions I will give
to the poor, and if I have [b]de-
frauded anyone of anything, I will
give back [c]four times as much."
9 And Jesus said to him, 9 [a]Luke 3:8; 13:16; Rom. 4:16; Gal. 3:7
"Today salvation has come to this
house, because he, too, is [a]a son
of Abraham.
10 "For [a]the Son of Man has 10 [a]Matt. 18:11
come to seek and to save that
which was lost."

18:35 *a certain blind man.* Concerning the differences in the accounts in the Gospels see note on Matt. 20:29-34.

19:2 *tax-gatherer.* As a tax collector for the Romans, he therefore had a bad reputation, since the system was open to abuse and extortion was common. The word *chief* implies that Zaccheus was responsible for all the taxes of Jericho and had other collectors under him.

19:8 Zaccheus' declaration of what he intended to do from then on, now that his life had been changed by Christ.

23 *Concerning faithfulness,* 19:11-27

★11 [a]Luke 9:51 [b]Luke 17:20

11 And while they were listening to these things, He went on to tell a parable, because [a]He was near Jerusalem, and they supposed that [b]the kingdom of God was going to appear immediately.

12 [a]Matt. 25:14-30; Luke 19:12-27

12 He said therefore, "[a]A certain nobleman went to a distant country to receive a kingdom for himself, and *then* return.

★13

13 "And he called ten of his slaves, and gave them ten minas, and said to them, 'Do business *with this* until I come *back.*'

14 "But his citizens hated him, and sent a delegation after him, saying, 'We do not want this man to reign over us.'

15 "And it came about that when he returned, after receiving the kingdom, he ordered that these slaves, to whom he had given the money, be called to him in order that he might know what business they had done.

16 "And the first appeared, saying, 'Master, your mina has made ten minas more.'

17 [a]Luke 16:10

17 "And he said to him, 'Well done, good slave, because you have been [a]faithful in a very little thing, be in authority over ten cities.'

18 "And the second came, saying, 'Your mina, master, has made five minas.'

19 "And he said to him also, 'And you are to be over five cities.'

20 "And another came, saying, 'Master, behold your mina, which I kept put away in a handkerchief;

21 for I was afraid of you, because you are an exacting man; you take up what you did not lay down, and reap what you did not sow.'

22 "He *said to him, 'By your own words I will judge you, you worthless slave. Did you know that I am an exacting man, taking up what I did not lay down, and reaping what I did not sow?

23 'Then why did you not put the money in the bank, and having come, I would have collected it with interest?'

24 "And he said to the bystanders, 'Take the mina away from him, and give it to the one who has the ten minas.'

25 "And they said to him, 'Master, he has ten minas *already.*'

26 "[a]I tell you, that to everyone who has shall *more* be given, but from the one who does not have, even what he does have shall be taken away.

26 [a]Matt. 13:12; Luke 8:18

27 "But [a]these enemies of mine, who did not want me to reign over them, bring them here, and [b]slay them in my presence."

27 [a]Luke 19:14 [b]Matt. 22:7; Luke 20:16

V THE CONDEMNATION OF THE SON OF MAN FOR MEN, 19:28-23:56

A Sunday, 19:28-44

28 And after He had said these things, He [a]was going on ahead, [b]ascending to Jerusalem.

28 [a]Mark 10:32 [b]Luke 9:51

29 And it came about that [a]when He approached Bethphage and [b]Bethany, near the mount that is called [c]Olivet, He sent two of the disciples,

★29 [a]Luke 19:29-38: *Matt. 21:1-9; Mark 11:1-10* [b]Matt. 21:17 [c]Luke 21:37; Acts 1:12

30 saying, "Go into the village opposite *you,* in which as you enter you will find a colt tied, on which no one yet has ever sat; untie it, and bring it *here.*

19:11 *they supposed.* The disciples still could not understand why they should not expect the political triumph of the Messianic kingdom immediately (and without the cross).

19:13 *minas.* A mina was a measure of money worth 100 drachmas or denarii. Notice that each servant received the same amount (in contrast to the parable of the talents in which each received according to his ability, Matt. 25:15). The minas represent the equal opportunity of life itself; the talents, the different gifts God gives each individual.

19:29 *Bethphage.* Its site is unknown though it was near *Bethany* which was on the SE. side of the Mount of Olives.

31 "And if anyone asks you, 'Why are you untying it?' thus shall you speak, 'The Lord has need of it.' "

32 And those who were sent went away and found it just as He had told them.

33 And as they were untying the colt, its owners said to them, "Why are you untying the colt?"

34 And they said, "The Lord has need of it."

35 And they brought it to Jesus, [a]and they threw their garments on the colt, and put Jesus *on it.*

35 [a]Luke 19:35-38; *John 12:12-15*

36 And as He was going, they were spreading their garments in the road.

37 And as He was now approaching, near the descent of [a]the Mount of Olives, the whole multitude of the disciples began to [b]praise God joyfully with a loud voice for all the miracles which they had seen,

37 [a]Matt. 21:1; Luke 19:29 [b]Luke 18:43

38 saying,

"[a]BLESSED IS THE [b]King WHO COMES IN THE NAME OF THE LORD;
Peace in heaven and [c]glory in the highest!"

★38 [a]Ps. 118:26 [b]Matt. 2:2; 25:34 [c]Matt. 21:9; Luke 2:14

39 [a]And some of the Pharisees in the multitude said to Him, "Teacher, rebuke Your disciples."

39 [a]Matt. 21:15f.

40 And He answered and said, "I tell you, if these become silent, [a]the stones will cry out!"

40 [a]Hab. 2:11

41 And when He approached, He saw the city and [a]wept over it,

41 [a]Luke 13:34, 35

42 saying, "If you had known in this day, even you, the things which make for peace! But now they have been hidden from your eyes.

43 "For the days shall come upon you when your enemies will [a]throw up a bank before you, and [b]surround you, and hem you in on every side,

★43 [a]Eccles. 9:14; Is. 29:3; 37:33; Jer. 6:6; Ezek. 4:2; 26:8 [b]Luke 21:20

44 and will level you to the ground and your children within you, and [a]they will not leave in you one stone upon another, because you did not recognize [b]the time of your visitation."

44 [a]Matt. 24:2; Mark 13:2; Luke 21:6 [b]1 Pet. 2:12

B Monday, 19:45–48

45 [a]And He entered the temple and began to cast out those who were selling,

★45 [a]Luke 19:45, 46; *Matt. 21:12-16; Mark 11:15-18;* John 2:13-16

46 saying to them, "It is written, '[a]AND MY HOUSE SHALL BE A HOUSE OF PRAYER,' but you have made it a robbers' den."

46 [a]Is. 56:7; Jer. 7:11; Matt. 21:13; Mark 11:17

47 And [a]He was teaching daily in the temple; but the chief priests and the scribes and the leading men among the people [b]were trying to destroy Him,

47 [a]Matt. 26:55 [b]Luke 20:19

48 and they could not find anything that they might do, for all the people were hanging upon His words.

C Tuesday, 20:1–21:38

1 *Authority requested,* 20:1–8

20 [a]And it came about on one of the days while [b]He was teaching the people in the temple and [c]preaching the gospel, that the chief priests and the scribes with the elders [d]confronted *Him,*

★ 1 [a]Luke 20:1-8; *Matt. 21:23-27; Mark 11:27-33* [b]Matt. 26:55 [c]Luke 8:1 [d]Acts 4:1; 6:12

2 and they spoke, saying to Him, "Tell us by what authority You are doing these things, or who is the one who gave You this authority?"

3 And He answered and said to them, "I shall also ask you a question, and you tell Me:

4 "Was the baptism of John from heaven or from men?"

5 And they reasoned among themselves, saying, "If we say, 'From heaven,' He will say, 'Why did you not believe him?'

6 "But if we say, 'From men,' all the people will stone us to death, for they are convinced that John was a [a]prophet."

6 [a]Matt. 11:9; Luke 7:29, 30

19:38 This quotation from Ps. 118:26 was sung as the pilgrims made their way into Jerusalem.
19:43 *your enemies.* The Romans under Titus in A.D. 70.
19:45 *to cast out.* See note on Mark 11:15.
20:1–8 See note on Mark 11:30.

7 And they answered that
they did not know where *it came*
from.
8 And Jesus said to them,
"Neither will I tell you by what
authority I am doing these
things."

2 ***Authority revealed,*** 20:9–18

★ **9** aLuke 20:9-19; *Matt. 21:33-46; Mark 12:1-12*
9 [a]And He began to tell the
people this parable: "A man
planted a vineyard and rented it
out to vine-growers, and went on
a journey for a long time.
10 "And at the *harvest* time he
sent a slave to the vine-growers,
in order that they might give him
some of the produce of the vineyard; but the vine-growers beat
him and sent him away empty-
handed.
11 "And he proceeded to send
another slave; and they beat him
also and treated him shamefully,
and sent him away empty-
handed.
12 "And he proceeded to send
a third; and this one also they
wounded and cast out.
13 aLuke 18:2
13 "And the owner of the vineyard said, 'What shall I do? I will
send my beloved son; perhaps
they will [a]respect him.'
14 "But when the vine-growers
saw him, they reasoned with one
another, saying, 'This is the heir;
let us kill him that the inheritance
may be ours.'
15 "And they cast him out of
the vineyard and killed him.
16 aMatt. 21:41; Mark 12:9; Luke 19:27 bRom. 3:4, 6, 31; 6:2, 15; 7:7, 13; 9:14; 11:1, 11; 1 Cor. 6:15; Gal. 2:17; 3:21; 6:14
What, therefore, will the owner of
the vineyard do to them?
16 "He will come and [a]destroy
these vine-growers and will give
the vineyard to others." And
when they heard it, they said,
"[b]May it never be!"
★**17** aPs. 118:22 bEph. 2:20; 1 Pet. 2:6
17 But He looked at them and
said, "What then is this that is
written,

'[a]THE STONE WHICH THE
BUILDERS REJECTED,
THIS BECAME [b]THE CHIEF COR-
NER *stone*'?

18 "[a]Every one who falls on **18** aMatt. 21:44
that stone will be broken to
pieces; but on whomever it falls,
it will scatter him like dust."

3 ***Authority resisted,*** 20:19–40

19 And the scribes and the **19** aLuke 19:47
chief priests [a]tried to lay hands on
Him that very hour, and they
feared the people; for they understood that He spoke this parable
against them.
20 [a]And they watched Him, **20** aLuke 20:20-26; *Matt. 22:15-22; Mark 12:13-17;* Mark 3:2 bLuke 11:54; 20:26 cMatt. 27:2
and sent spies who pretended to
be righteous, in order [b]that they
might catch Him in some statement, so as to deliver Him up to
the rule and the authority of [c]the
governor.
21 And they questioned Him,
saying, "Teacher, we know that
You speak and teach correctly,
and You are not partial to any,
but teach the way of God in truth.
22 "Is it lawful for us [a]to pay **22** aMatt. 17:25; Luke 23:2
taxes to Caesar, or not?"
23 But He detected their
trickery and said to them,
24 "Show Me a denarius. ★**24**
Whose head and inscription does
it have?" And they said, "Caesar's."
25 And He said to them, ★**25** aMatt. 22:21; Mark 12:17
"Then [a]render to Caesar the
things that are Caesar's, and to
God the things that are God's."
26 And they were unable to **26** aLuke 11:54; 20:26
[a]catch Him in a saying in the
presence of the people; and marveling at His answer, they became
silent.
27 [a]Now there came to Him **27** aLuke 20:27-40; *Matt. 22:23-33; Mark 12:18-27*
some of the Sadducees (who say
that there is no resurrection),

20:9 *a vineyard.* The parable explains God's dealings with Israel (see Isa. 5:1–7 for a similar story). The O.T. prophets are called slaves (vv. 10–12); Jesus Himself is the beloved son (v. 13).

20:17 See Ps. 118:22.

20:24 *a denarius.* A Roman silver coin, bearing Caesar's image. See notes on Matt. 20:2; 22:17, 21.

20:25 A follower of Christ has dual citizenship and responsibility. Of course, God's due takes precedence over Caesar's when there is conflict between them.

★28 aDeut. 25:5 **28** and they questioned Him,
saying, "Teacher, Moses wrote us
that [a]IF A MAN'S BROTHER DIES, having a wife, AND HE IS CHILDLESS, HIS
BROTHER SHOULD TAKE THE WIFE AND
RAISE UP OFFSPRING TO HIS BROTHER.
29 "Now there were seven
brothers; and the first took a wife,
and died childless;
30 and the second
31 and the third took her; and
in the same way the seven also
died, leaving no children.
32 "Finally the woman died
also.
33 "In the resurrection therefore, which one's wife will the
woman be? For the seven had her
as wife."
34 aMatt. 12:32; Luke 16:8 **34** And Jesus said to them,
"The sons of [a]this age marry and
are given in marriage,
35 aMatt. 12:32; Luke 16:8 **35** but those who are considered worthy to attain to [a]that age
and the resurrection from the
dead, neither marry, nor are given
in marriage;
★36 aRom. 8:16f.; 1 John 3:1, 2 **36** for neither can they die
any more, for they are like angels,
and are [a]sons of God, being sons
of the resurrection.
★37 aMark 12:26 bEx. 3:6 **37** "But that the dead are
raised, even Moses showed, in
[a]the *passage about the burning*
bush, where he calls the Lord [b]THE
GOD OF ABRAHAM, AND THE GOD OF
ISAAC, AND THE GOD OF JACOB.
38 aMatt. 22:32; Mark 12:27 bRom. 14:8 **38** "[a]Now He is not the God of
the dead, but of the living; for [b]all
live to Him."
39 And some of the scribes
answered and said, "Teacher, You
have spoken well."
40 aMatt. 22:46; Luke 14:6 **40** For [a]they did not have
courage to question Him any
longer about anything.

4 *Authority reiterated,* 20:41–21:4

41 [a]And He said to them, 41 aLuke 20:41-44; Matt. 22:41-46; Mark 12:35-37 bMatt. 9:27
"How *is it that* they say the Christ
is [b]David's son?
42 "For David himself says in 42 aPs. 110:1
the book of Psalms,

> '[a]THE LORD SAID TO MY LORD,
> "SIT AT MY RIGHT HAND,
>
> **43** [a]UNTIL I MAKE THINE EN- 43 aPs. 110:1
> EMIES A FOOTSTOOL FOR
> THY FEET." '

44 "David therefore calls Him ★44
'Lord,' and how is He his son?"
45 [a]And while all the people 45 aLuke 20:45-47; Matt. 23:1-7; Mark 12:38-40
were listening, He said to the dis-
ciples,
46 "Beware of the scribes, 46 aLuke 11:43; 14:7
[a]who like to walk around in long
robes, and love respectful greetings in the market places, and
chief seats in the synagogues, and
places of honor at banquets,
47 who devour widows'
houses, and for appearance's sake
offer long prayers; these will receive greater condemnation."
21 [a]And He looked up and ★1 aLuke 21:1-4; Mark 12:41-44
saw the rich putting their
gifts into the treasury.
2 And He saw a certain poor ★2 aMark 12:42
widow putting in [a]two small cop-
per coins.
3 And He said, "Truly I say
to you, this poor widow put in
more than all *of them;*
4 for they all out of their 4 aMark 12:44
surplus put into the offering; but
she out of her poverty put in all
that she had [a]to live on."

5 *The apocalyptic discourse,* 21:5–38

5 [a]And while some were 5 aLuke 21:5-36; Matt. 24; Mark 13
talking about the temple, that it

20:28 See Deut. 25:5-10. According to the law, if a man died without an heir, any unmarried brother was obliged to marry the man's widow.
20:36 *like angels.* I.e., in the resurrection state there is no marriage or procreation. See note on Matt. 22:30.
20:37 See Ex. 3:6. God acknowledged a continuing relationship with Abraham, Isaac, and Jacob, though they had died long before.
20:44 *how is He his son?* See note on Matt. 22:44.
21:1 *treasury.* Chests in the court of the temple where gifts were deposited.
21:2 *small copper coins.* See note on Luke 12:59.

was adorned with beautiful
stones and votive gifts, He said,
6 [a]Luke 6 "*As for* these things which
19:44 you are looking at, the days will
come in which [a]there will not be
left one stone upon another
which will not be torn down."
★ 7 7 And they questioned Him,
saying, "Teacher, when therefore
will these things be? And what
will be the sign when these things
are about to take place?"
8 [a]John 8 And He said, "Take heed
8:24 [b]Luke that you be not misled; for many
17:23 will come in My name, saying, '[a]I
am *He,*' and, 'The time is at
hand'; [b]do not go after them.
9 "And when you hear of
wars and disturbances, do not be
terrified; for these things must
take place first, but the end *does*
not *follow* immediately."
10 Then He continued by
saying to them, "Nation will rise
against nation, and kingdom
against kingdom,
11 and there will be great
earthquakes, and in various
places plagues and famines; and
there will be terrors and great
signs from heaven.
12 [a]Luke 12 "But before all these things,
21:12-17; [a]they will lay their hands on you
Matt. 10:19- and will persecute you, delivering
22; Mark you to the synagogues and pris-
13:11-13 ons, bringing you before kings
and governors for My name's
sake.
13 [a]Phil. 13 "[a]It will lead to an opportu-
1:12 nity for your testimony.
14 [a]Luke 14 "[a]So make up your minds
12:11 not to prepare beforehand to defend yourselves;
15 [a]Luke 15 for [a]I will give you utter-
12:12 ance and wisdom which none of
your opponents will be able to resist or refute.
16 "But you will be betrayed
even by parents and brothers and
relatives and friends, and they
will put *some* of you to death,
17 and you will be hated by
all on account of My name.
18 "Yet [a]not a hair of your 18 [a]Matt.
head will perish. 10:30; Luke 12:7
19 "[a]By your perseverance you 19 [a]Matt.
will win your souls. 10:22; 24:13;
20 "But when you see Jerusa- Rom. 2:7;
lem [a]surrounded by armies, then 5:3f.; Heb.
recognize that her desolation is at 10:36; James 1:3; 2 Pet.
hand. 1:6 20 [a]Luke 19:43
21 "Then let those who are in 21 [a]Luke
Judea flee to the mountains, and 17:31
let those who are in the midst of
the city depart, and [a]let not those
who are in the country enter the
city;
22 because these are [a]days of 22 [a]Is. 63:4;
vengeance, in order that all things Dan. 9:24-
which are written may be ful- 27; Hos. 9:7
filled.
23 "Woe to those who are with 23 [a]Dan.
child and to those who nurse 8:19; 1 Cor.
babes in those days; for [a]there 7:26
will be great distress upon the
land, and wrath to this people,
24 and they will fall by [a]the ★24 [a]Gen.
edge of the sword, and will be led 34:26; Ex.
captive into all the nations; and 17:13; Heb.
[b]Jerusalem will be [c]trampled un- 11:34 [b]Is.
derfoot by the Gentiles until [d]the 63:18; Dan.
times of the Gentiles be fulfilled. 8:13; Rev.
25 "And there will be signs in 11:2 [c]Rev. 11:2 [d]Rom. 11:25
sun and moon and stars, and
upon the earth dismay among nations, in perplexity at the roaring
of the sea and the waves,
26 men fainting from fear and
the expectation of the things
which are coming upon the world;
for the powers of the heavens will
be shaken.
27 "And [a]then will they see 27 [a]Matt.
[b]THE SON OF MAN COMING IN A 16:27; 24:30;
CLOUD with power and great glory. 26:64; Mark 13:26 [b]Dan. 7:13
28 "But when these things be- 28 [a]Luke
gin to take place, straighten up 18:7
and lift up your heads, because

21:7 *when . . . will these things be?* There is a double perspective in Christ's answer—the destruction of Jerusalem in A.D. 70 and the tribulation days just prior to His second coming. Verses 8–19 and 25–28 relate particularly to the latter time while vv. 20–24 refer to the former.

21:24 *the times of the Gentiles.* The period of Gentile domination of Jerusalem, which began probably under Nebuchadnezzar (587 B.C.), was certainly in effect in A.D. 70, and which continues into the tribulation days (cf. Rev. 11:2).

[a]your redemption is drawing
near."
29 And He told them a parable: "Behold the fig tree, and all
the trees;

30 [a]Luke 12:57

30 as soon as they put forth
leaves, you see it and [a]know for
yourselves that the summer is
now near.

31 [a]Matt. 3:2

31 "Even so you, too, when
you see these things happening,
recognize that [a]the kingdom of
God is near.

★32

32 "Truly I say to you, this
generation will not pass away until all things take place.

33 [a]Matt. 5:18; Luke 16:17

33 "[a]Heaven and earth will
pass away, but My words will not
pass away.

34 [a]Matt. 24:42-44; Mark 4:19; Luke 12:40, 45; 1 Thess. 5:2ff.

34 "[a]Be on guard, that your
hearts may not be weighted down
with dissipation and drunkenness
and the worries of life, and that
day come on you suddenly like a
trap;
35 for it will come upon all
those who dwell on the face of all
the earth.

36 [a]Mark 13:33; Luke 12:40 [b]Luke 1:19; Rev. 7:9; 8:2; 11:4

36 "But [a]keep on the alert at
all times, praying in order that
you may have strength to escape
all these things that are about to
take place, and to [b]stand before
the Son of Man."

37 [a]Matt. 26:55 [b]Mark 11:19 [c]Matt. 21:1

37 Now during the day He
was [a]teaching in the temple, but
[b]at evening He would go out and
spend the night on [c]the mount
that is called Olivet.

38 [a]John 8:2

38 And all the people would
get up [a]early in the morning *to
come* to Him in the temple to listen to Him.

D Wednesday, 22:1-6

★ 1 [a]Luke 22:1, 2; Matt. 26:2-5; Mark 14:1, 2 [b]John 11:55; 13:1
2 [a]Matt. 12:14

22 [a]Now the Feast of Unleavened Bread, which is called
the [b]Passover, was approaching.
2 And the chief priests and
the scribes [a]were seeking how
they might put Him to death; for
they were afraid of the people.

★ 3 [a]Luke 22:3-6; Matt. 26:14-16; Mark 14:10, 11 [b]Matt. 4:10; John 13:2, 27
4 [a]1 Chr. 9:11; Neh. 11:11; Luke 22:52; Acts 4:1; 5:24, 26

3 [a]And [b]Satan entered into
Judas who was called Iscariot, belonging to the number of the
twelve.
4 And he went away and
discussed with the chief priests
and [a]officers how he might betray
Him to them.
5 And they were delighted,
and agreed to give him money.
6 And he consented, and *began* seeking a good opportunity to
betray Him to them apart from
the multitude.

E Thursday, 22:7-53

1 *The Lord's Supper,* 22:7-38

7 [a]Luke 22:7-13; Matt. 26:17-19; Mark 14:12-16 [b]Mark 14:12
8 [a]Acts 3:1, 11; 4:13, 19; 8:14; Gal. 2:9

7 [a]Then came the day of
Unleavened Bread on which [b]the
Passover *lamb* had to be sacrificed.
8 And He sent [a]Peter and
John, saying, "Go and prepare the
Passover for us, that we may eat
it."
9 And they said to Him,
"Where do You want us to prepare it?"

★10

10 And He said to them, "Behold, when you have entered the
city, a man will meet you carrying
a pitcher of water; follow him into
the house that he enters.
11 "And you shall say to the
owner of the house, 'The Teacher
says to you, "Where is the guest
room in which I may eat the Passover with My disciples?"'
12 "And he will show you a
large, furnished, upper room; prepare it there."
13 And they departed and
found *everything* just as He had
told them; and they prepared the
Passover.

14 [a]Matt. 26:20; Mark 14:17 [b]Mark 6:30

14 [a]And when the hour had
come He reclined *at table,* and
[b]the apostles with Him.

21:32 *this generation.* See note on Matt. 24:34.
22:1 *Passover.* See Ex. 12:1-28 and Lev. 23:5-6 and note on Matt. 26:2.
22:3 *And Satan entered into Judas.* Satan did this twice (see John 13:27).
22:10 *a man . . . carrying a pitcher of water.* He would be easily identifiable, since women usually performed this task.

15 And He said to them, "I have earnestly desired to eat this Passover with you before I suffer;

16 for I say to you, I shall never again eat it [a]until it is fulfilled in the kingdom of God."

17 [a]And having taken a cup, [b]when He had given thanks, He said, "Take this and share it among yourselves;

18 for [a]I say to you, I will not drink of the fruit of the vine from now on until the kingdom of God comes."

19 And having taken *some* bread, [a]when He had given thanks, He broke *it,* and gave *it* to them, saying, "This is My body which is given for you; do this in remembrance of Me."

20 And in the same way *He took* the cup after they had eaten, saying, "This cup which is [a]poured out for you is the [b]new covenant in My blood.

21 "[a]But behold, the hand of the one betraying Me is with Me on the table.

22 "For indeed, the Son of Man is going [a]as it has been determined; but woe to that man through whom He is betrayed!"

23 And they began to discuss among themselves which one of them it might be who was going to do this thing.

24 And there arose also [a]a dispute among them *as to* which one of them was regarded to be greatest.

25 [a]And He said to them, "The kings of the Gentiles lord it over them; and those who have authority over them are called 'Benefactors.'

26 "But not so with you, [a]but let him who is the greatest among you become as [b]the youngest, and the leader as the servant.

27 "For [a]who is greater, the one who reclines *at table,* or the one who serves? Is it not the one who reclines *at table?* But [b]I am among you as the one who serves.

★16 [a]Luke 14:15; 22:18, 30; Rev. 19:9
17 [a]Luke 22:17-20: *Matt. 26:26-29; Mark 14:22-25; 1 Cor. 11:23-25;* 10:16 [b]Matt. 14:19
18 [a]Matt. 26:29; Mark 14:25
★19 [a]Matt. 14:19
★20 [a]Matt. 26:28; Mark 14:24 [b]Ex. 24:8; Jer. 31:31; 1 Cor. 11:25; 2 Cor. 3:6; Heb. 8:8, [13]; 9:15
21 [a]Luke 22:21-23: *Matt. 26:21-24; Mark 14:18-21;* John 13:18, 21, 22, 26
22 [a]Acts 2:23; 4:28; 10:42; 17:31
24 [a]Mark 9:34; Luke 9:46
★25 [a]Luke 22:25-27: *Matt. 20:25-28; Mark 10:42-45*
26 [a]Luke 9:48 [b]1 Pet. 5:5
27 [a]Luke 12:37 [b]Matt. 20:28

28 "And you are those who have stood by Me in My [a]trials;

29 and just as My Father has granted Me a [a]kingdom, I grant you

30 that you may [a]eat and drink at My table in My [b]kingdom, and [c]you will sit on thrones judging the twelve tribes of Israel.

31 "Simon, Simon, behold, [a]Satan has demanded *permission* to [b]sift you like wheat;

32 but I [a]have prayed for you, that your faith may not fail; and you, when once you have turned again, [b]strengthen your brothers."

33 [a]And he said to Him, "Lord, with You I am ready to go both to prison and to death!"

34 And He said, "I tell you, Peter, the cock will not crow today until you have denied three times that you know Me."

35 And He said to them, "[a]When I sent you out without purse and bag and sandals, you did not lack anything, did you?" And they said, "*No,* nothing."

36 And He said to them, "But now, let him who has a purse take it along, likewise also a bag, and let him who has no sword sell his robe and buy one.

37 "For I tell you, that this which is written must be fulfilled in Me, '[a]AND HE WAS CLASSED AMONG CRIMINALS'; for [b]that which refers to Me has *its* fulfillment."

38 And they said, "Lord, look, here are two [a]swords." And He said to them, "It is enough."

2 *The garden of Gethsemane,* 22:39–46

39 [a]And He came out and proceeded [b]as was His custom to

28 [a]Heb. 2:18; 4:15
29 [a]Matt. 5:3; 2 Tim. 2:12
★30 [a]Luke 22:16 [b]Matt. 5:3; 2 Tim. 2:12 [c]Matt. 19:28
31 [a]Job 1:6-12; 2:1-6; Matt. 4:10 [b]Amos 9:9
★32 [a]John 17:9, 15 [b]John 21:15-17
33 [a]Luke 22:33, 34: *Matt. 26:33-35; Mark 14:29-31; John 13:37, 38*
35 [a]Matt. 10:9f.; Mark 6:8; Luke 9:3ff.; 10:4
37 [a]Is. 53:12 [b]John 17:4; 19:30
38 [a]Luke 22:36, 49
39 [a]Matt. 26:30; Mark 14:26; John 18:1 [b]Luke 21:37 [c]Matt. 21:1

22:16 *until it is fulfilled in the kingdom of God.* See note on Matt. 26:29.

22:19 *This is My body.* The bread remains bread but represents His body. It is an illustration, like "I am the door" (John 10:7).

22:20 *the new covenant.* See note on Matt. 26:28.

22:25 *Benefactors.* A favorite title used by the Greek kings of Egypt and Syria.

22:30 See note on Matt. 19:28.

22:32 *I have prayed for you.* An illustration of Heb. 7:25.

[c]the Mount of Olives; and the
disciples also followed Him.
40 aLuke 22:40-46: *Matt. 26:36-46; Mark 14:32-42* bMatt. 6:13; Luke 22:46
40 [a]And when He arrived at
the place, He said to them, "[b]Pray
that you may not enter into temptation."
41 aMatt. 26:39; Mark 14:35; Luke 18:11
41 And He withdrew from
them about a stone's throw, and
He [a]knelt down and *began* to
pray,
★42 aMatt. 20:22 bMatt. 26:39
42 saying, "Father, if Thou art
willing, remove this [a]cup from
Me; [b]yet not My will, but Thine
be done."
★43 aMatt. 4:11
43 Now an [a]angel from
heaven appeared to Him,
strengthening Him.
44 aHeb. 5:7
44 And [a]being in agony He
was praying very fervently; and
His sweat became like drops of
blood, falling down upon the
ground.
45 And when He rose from
prayer, He came to His disciples
and found them sleeping from
sorrow,
46 aLuke 22:40
46 and said to them, "Why
are you sleeping? Rise and [a]pray
that you may not enter into temptation."

3 ***The arrest,*** 22:47-53

47 aLuke 22:47-53: *Matt. 26:47-56; Mark 14:43-50; John 18:3-11*
47 [a]While He was still speak-
ing, behold, a multitude *came,*
and the one called Judas, one of
the twelve, was preceding them;
and he approached Jesus to kiss
Him.
48 But Jesus said to him, "Judas, are you betraying the Son of
Man with a kiss?"
49 aLuke 22:38
49 And when those who were
around Him saw what was going
to happen, they said, "Lord, shall
we strike with the [a]sword?"
★50
50 And a certain one of them
struck the slave of the high priest
and cut off his right ear.
51 But Jesus answered and
said, "Stop! No more of this."
And He touched his ear and
healed him.
52 And Jesus said to the chief 52 aLuke 22:4 bLuke 22:37
priests and [a]officers of the temple
and elders who had come against
Him, "Have you come out with
swords and clubs [b]as against a
robber?
53 "While I was with you daily
in the temple, you did not lay
hands on Me; but this hour and
the power of darkness are yours."

F **Friday,** 22:54-23:55

1 ***Peter's denial,*** 22:54-62

54 [a]And having arrested Him, 54 aMatt. 26:57; Mark 14:53 bMatt. 26:58; Mark 14:54; John 18:15
they led Him *away,* and brought
Him to the house of the high
priest; but [b]Peter was following at
a distance.
55 [a]And after they had kin- 55 aLuke 22:55-62: *Matt. 26:69-75; Mark 14:66-72; John 18:16-18, 25-27* bMatt. 26:3
dled a fire in the middle of [b]the
courtyard and had sat down together, Peter was sitting among
them.
56 And a certain servant-girl,
seeing him as he sat in the fire-
light, and looking intently at him,
said, "This man was with Him
too."
57 But he denied *it,* saying,
"Woman, I do not know Him."
58 And a little later, [a]another 58 aJohn 18:26
saw him and said, "You are *one*
of them too!" But Peter said,
"Man, I am not!"
59 And after about an hour ★59 aMatt. 26:73; Mark 14:70
had passed, another man *began* to
insist, saying, "Certainly this man
also was with Him, [a]for he is a
Galilean too."
60 But Peter said, "Man, I do
not know what you are talking
about." And immediately, while
he was still speaking, a cock
crowed.
61 And [a]the Lord turned and ★61 aLuke 7:13 bLuke 22:34
looked at Peter. And Peter re-
membered the word of the Lord,
how He had told him, "[b]Before a
cock crows today, you will deny
Me three times."
62 And he went outside and
wept bitterly.

22:42 *this cup.* See note on Matt. 26:39.
22:43-44 These verses are not in certain important manuscripts.
22:50 *one of them.* This was Peter (John 18:10).
22:59 *he is a Galilean.* See note on Mark 14:70.
22:61 *Before a cock crows.* A Roman term for the end of the third watch at 3 a.m.

2 *Christ derided, beaten,* 22:63-65

63 [a]Matt. 26:67f.; Mark 14:65; John 18:22f.
64 [a]Matt. 26:68; Mark 14:65
65 [a]Matt. 27:39

63 [a]And the men who were
holding Jesus in custody were
mocking Him, and beating Him,
64 and they blindfolded Him
and were asking Him, saying,
"[a]Prophesy, who is the one who
hit You?"
65 And they were saying
many other things against Him,
[a]blaspheming.

3 *Christ before the Sanhedrin,* 22:66-71

★66 [a]Matt. 27:1f.; Mark 15:1; John 18:28 [b]Acts 22:5 [c]Matt. 5:22
67 [a]Matt. 26:63-66; Mark 14:61-63; Luke 22:67-71; John 18:19-21
69 [a]Matt. 26:64; Mark 14:62; 16:19 [b]Ps. 110:1
70 [a]Matt. 4:3 [b]Matt. 26:64; 27:11; Luke 23:3

66 [a]And when it was day,
[b]the Council of elders of the people assembled, both chief priests
and scribes, and they led Him
away to their [c]council *chamber,*
saying,
67 "[a]If You are the Christ, tell
us." But He said to them, "If I tell
you, you will not believe;
68 and if I ask a question, you
will not answer.
69 "[a]But from now on [b]THE SON
OF MAN WILL BE SEATED AT THE RIGHT
HAND of the power OF GOD."
70 And they all said, "Are
You [a]the Son of God, then?" And
He said to them, "[b]Yes, I am."
71 And they said, "What further need do we have of testimony? For we have heard it ourselves from His own mouth."

4 *Christ before Pilate,* 23:1-5

1 [a]Matt. 27:2; Mark 15:1; John 18:28
★ 2 [a]Luke 23:2, 3: *Matt. 27:11-14; Mark 15:2-5; John 18:29-37* [b]Luke 23:14 [c]Luke 20:22; John 18:33ff.; 19:12; Acts 17:7
3 [a]Luke 22:70
4 [a]Matt. 27:23; Mark 15:14; Luke 23:14, 22; John 18:38; 19:4, 6
5 [a]Matt. 4:12

23 Then the whole body of
them arose and [a]brought
Him before Pilate.
2 [a]And they began to accuse
Him, saying, "We found this man
[b]misleading our nation and [c]for-
bidding to pay taxes to Caesar,
and saying that He Himself is
Christ, a King."
3 And Pilate asked Him,
saying, "Are You the King of the
Jews?" And He answered him and
said, "[a]*It is as* you say."
4 And Pilate said to the chief
priests and the multitudes, "[a]I
find no guilt in this man."
5 But they kept on insisting,
saying, "He stirs up the people,
teaching all over Judea, [a]starting
from Galilee, even as far as this
place."

5 *Christ before Herod,* 23:6-12

★ 7 [a]Matt. 14:1; Mark 6:14; Luke 3:1; 9:7; 13:31
8 [a]Luke 9:9
9 [a]Matt. 27:12, 14; Mark 15:5; John 19:9
★11 [a]Matt. 27:28

6 But when Pilate heard it,
he asked whether the man was a
Galilean.
7 And when he learned that
He belonged to Herod's jurisdiction, he sent Him to [a]Herod, who
himself also was in Jerusalem at
that time.
8 Now Herod was very glad
when he saw Jesus; for [a]he had
wanted to see Him for a long
time, because he had been hearing about Him and was hoping to
see some sign performed by Him.
9 And he questioned Him at
some length; but [a]He answered
him nothing.
10 And the chief priests and
the scribes were standing there,
accusing Him vehemently.
11 And Herod with his soldiers, after treating Him with contempt and mocking Him, [a]dressed
Him in a gorgeous robe and sent
Him back to Pilate.

22:66 *when it was day.* Matthew (26:57-58) and Mark (14:53, 55) mention a preliminary hearing held at night, but the Sanhedrin (70 or 72 elders and teachers of the nation) could not legally convene at night, so this verdict was made official as soon as it was day. Since, however, the Sanhedrin had no power to carry out a capital sentence, the case had to be remanded to Pilate, senior representative of the Roman government in Judea.

23:2 *Christ, a King.* The charge against Jesus made before Pilate was political—that He was a rival "king." Insurrection against Rome was implied. The Jews knew that blasphemy would not be regarded by Rome as sufficient ground for the death penalty.

23:7 *he sent Him to Herod.* Pilate was not required to send Jesus to Herod Antipas but did so hoping to find a way out of his own dilemma and perhaps also as a diplomatic gesture (see v. 12).

23:11 *sent Him back to Pilate.* To Herod the whole matter seemed to be a joke, since he treated the incident as an occasion for amusement and then returned Jesus to Pilate.

12 [a]Acts 4:27 12 Now [a]Herod and Pilate became friends with one another
that very day; for before they had
been at enmity with each other.

6 *Christ again before Pilate,* 23:13–25

13 [a]Luke 23:35; John 7:26, 48; 12:42; Acts 3:17; 4:5, 8; 13:27 13 And Pilate summoned the
chief priests and the [a]rulers and
the people,
14 [a]Luke 23:2 [b]Luke 23:4 14 and said to them, "You
brought this man to me as one
who [a]incites the people to rebellion, and behold, having examined Him before you, I [b]have
found no guilt in this man regarding the charges which you make
against Him.
15 [a]Luke 9:9 15 "No, nor has [a]Herod, for he
sent Him back to us; and behold,
nothing deserving death has been
done by Him.
16 [a]Matt. 27:26; Mark 15:15; Luke 23:22; John 19:1; Acts 16:37 16 "I will therefore [a]punish
Him and release Him."
17 [Now he was obliged to release to them at the feast one
★17 prisoner.]
18 [a]Luke 23:18-25; Matt. 27:15-26; Mark 15:6-15; John 18:39-19:16 18 But they cried out all together, saying, "[a]Away with this
man, and release for us Barabbas!"
19 (He was one who had been
thrown into prison for a certain
insurrection made in the city, and
for murder.)
20 And Pilate, wanting to release Jesus, addressed them again,
21 but they kept on calling
out, saying, "Crucify, crucify
Him!"
★22 [a]Luke 23:16 22 And he said to them the
third time, "Why, what evil has
this man done? I have found in
Him no guilt *demanding* death; I
will therefore [a]punish Him and
release Him."
23 But they were insistent,
with loud voices asking that He
be crucified. And their voices *be-*
gan to prevail.
24 And Pilate pronounced
sentence that their demand
should be granted.
25 And he released the man
they were asking for who had
been thrown into prison for insurrection and murder, but he
turned Jesus over to their will.

7 *The crucifixion,* 23:26–49

26 [a]And when they led Him ★26 [a]Luke 23:26; Matt. 27:32; Mark 15:21; John 19:17 [b]Matt. 27:32
away, they laid hold of one Si-
mon, a [b]Cyrenian, coming in from
the country, and placed on him
the cross to carry behind Jesus.
27 And there were following 27 [a]Luke 8:52
Him a great multitude of the people, and of women who were
[a]mourning and lamenting Him.
28 But Jesus turning to them ★28
said, "Daughters of Jerusalem,
stop weeping for Me, but weep
for yourselves and for your children.
29 "For behold, the days are ★29 [a]Matt. 24:19; Luke 11:27; 21:23
coming when they will say,
'[a]Blessed are the barren, and the
wombs that never bore, and the
breasts that never nursed.'
30 "Then they will begin TO ★30 [a]Is. 2:19, 20; Hos. 10:8; Rev. 6:16
[a]SAY TO THE MOUNTAINS, 'FALL ON
US,' AND TO THE HILLS, 'COVER US.'
31 "For if they do these things ★31
in the green tree, what will happen in the dry?"
32 [a]And two others also, who 32 [a]Matt. 27:38; Mark 15:27; John 19:18
were criminals, were being led
away to be put to death with Him.
33 [a]And when they came to ★33 [a]Luke 23:33-43; Matt. 27:33-44; Mark 15:22-32; John 19:17-24
the place called The Skull, there
they crucified Him and the criminals, one on the right and the other on the left.
34 But Jesus was saying, "[a]Fa- ★34 [a]Matt. 11:25; Luke 22:42 [b]Ps. 22:18; John 19:24
ther forgive them; for they do not
know what they are doing." [b]AND

23:17 Many manuscripts do not contain this verse. See John 18:39.
23:22 *I will therefore punish Him.* Done by scourging (Mark 15:15), i.e., whipping (see note on Matt. 27:26).
23:26 *a Cyrenian.* See note on Matt. 27:32.
23:28 *weep for yourselves and for your children.* The Lord foresaw the destruction of Jerusalem, with its attendant miseries, in A.D. 70.
23:29 See Luke 21:23.
23:30 See Hos. 10:8; Rev. 6:16.
23:31 The meaning is this: If such injustice can be done to an innocent man, as was being done then to Jesus, what would befall the Jews in time of war?
23:33 *The Skull.* See note on Matt. 27:33.
23:34 *dividing up His garments.* See Ps. 22:18 and note on Matt. 27:35.

THEY CAST LOTS, DIVIDING UP HIS
GARMENTS AMONG THEMSELVES.
35 [a]Luke 23:13 [b]Matt. 27:43
35 And the people stood by,
looking on. And even the [a]rulers
were sneering at Him, saying,
"He saved others; [b]let Him save
Himself if this is the Christ of
God, His Chosen One."
36 [a]Matt. 27:48
36 And the soldiers also
mocked Him, coming up to Him,
[a]offering Him sour wine,
37 [a]Matt. 27:43
37 and saying, "[a]If You are
the King of the Jews, save Yourself!"
★38 [a]Matt. 27:37; Mark 15:26; John 19:19
38 Now there was also an inscription above Him, "[a]THIS IS
THE KING OF THE JEWS."
39 [a]Matt. 27:44; Mark 15:32; Luke 23:39-43 [b]Luke 23:35, 37
39 [a]And one of the criminals
who were hanged *there* was hurling abuse at Him, saying, "Are
You not the Christ? [b]Save Yourself and us!"
40 But the other answered,
and rebuking him said, "Do you
not even fear God, since you are
under the same sentence of condemnation?
41 "And we indeed justly, for
we are receiving what we deserve
for our deeds; but this man has
done nothing wrong."
★42
42 And he was saying, "Jesus,
remember me when You come in
Your kingdom!"
★43 [a]Gen. 2:8 [Septuagint]; 2 Cor. 12:4; Rev. 2:7
43 And He said to him,
"Truly I say to you, today you
shall be with Me in [a]Paradise."
★44 [a]Luke 23:44-49: *Matt. 27:45-56; Mark 15:33-41* [b]John 19:14
44 [a]And it was now about
[b]the sixth hour, and darkness fell
over the whole land until the
ninth hour,
★45 [a]Matt. 27:51
45 the sun being obscured;
and [a]the veil of the temple was
torn in two.
46 [a]Matt. 27:50; Mark 15:37; John 19:30 [b]Ps. 31:5
46 And Jesus, [a]crying out
with a loud voice, said, "Father,
[b]INTO THY HANDS I COMMIT MY
SPIRIT." And having said this, He
breathed His last.
47 [a]Matt. 27:54; Mark 15:39 [b]Matt. 9:8
47 [a]Now when the centurion
saw what had happened, he *began* [b]praising God, saying, "Certainly this man was innocent."
48 [a]Luke 8:52; 18:13
48 And all the multitudes
who came together for this spectacle, when they observed what
had happened, *began* to return,
[a]beating their breasts.
49 [a]Matt. 27:55f.; Mark 15:40f.; Luke 8:2; John 19:25
49 [a]And all His acquaintances
and [a]the women who accompanied Him from Galilee, were
standing at a distance, seeing
these things.

8 *The burial,* 23:50–55

★50 [a]Luke 23:50-56: *Matt. 27:57-61; Mark 15:42-47; John 19:38-42* [b]Mark 15:43
50 [a]And behold, a man
named Joseph, who was a [b]member of the Council, a good and
righteous man
★51 [a]Mark 15:43; Luke 2:25
51 (he had not consented to
their plan and action), *a man* from
Arimathea, a city of the Jews, who
was [a]waiting for the kingdom of
God;
52 this man went to Pilate
and asked for the body of Jesus.
★53
53 And he took it down and
wrapped it in a linen cloth, and
laid Him in a tomb cut into the
rock, where no one had ever lain.
★54 [a]Matt. 27:62; Mark 15:42
54 And it was [a]the preparation day, and the Sabbath was
about to begin.
55 [a]Luke 23:49
55 Now [a]the women who had
come with Him out of Galilee followed after, and saw the tomb
and how His body was laid.

G Saturday, 23:56

★56 [a]Mark 16:1; Luke 24:1 [b]Ex. 20:10
56 And they returned and
[a]prepared spices and perfumes.
And on the Sabbath they rested
according to [b]the commandment.

23:38 *an inscription.* See note on Matt. 27:37.

23:42 *when You come in Your kingdom.* Seeing Jesus dying on a cross but believing that He would come into His kingdom shows the amazing faith of the thief.

23:43 *Paradise.* Heaven, the abode of God (Luke 16:22; 2 Cor. 12:4).

23:44 *the sixth hour* = noon.

23:45 *the veil of the temple.* See note on Matt. 27:51.

23:50 *the Council.* I.e., the Sanhedrin.

23:51 *Arimathea.* A town north of Lydda.

23:53 *wrapped it.* The word means "wrap by winding tightly," referring to the linen around the body. See also Isa. 53:9.

23:54 *it was the preparation day.* Friday, the day Jesus died, was the time of the preparation for the Sabbath, which began Friday at sunset.

23:56 *according to the commandment.* I.e., not to work on the Sabbath (Ex. 20:10).

VI THE VINDICATION OF THE SON OF MAN BEFORE MEN, 24:1–53

A The Victor over Death, 24:1–12

1 [a]Luke 24:1-10; *Matt. 28:1-8; Mark 16:1-8;* John 20:1-8
24 [a]But on the first day of the
week, at early dawn, they
came to the tomb, bringing the
spices which they had prepared.
★ 2 **2** And they found the stone
rolled away from the tomb,
3 [a]Luke 7:13; Acts 1:21 **3** but when they entered,
they did not find the body of [a]the
Lord Jesus.
4 [a]John 20:12 [b]Luke 2:9; Acts 12:7 **4** And it happened that
while they were perplexed about
this, behold, [a]two men suddenly
[b]stood near them in dazzling apparel;
5 and as *the women* were
terrified and bowed their faces to
the ground, *the men* said to them,
"Why do you seek the living One
among the dead?
★ 6 [a]Mark 16:6 [b]Matt. 17:22f.; Mark 9:30f.; Luke 9:44; 24:44 **6** "He is not here, but He
[a]has risen. Remember how He
spoke to you [b]while He was still
in Galilee,
7 [a]Matt. 16:21; Luke 24:46 **7** saying that [a]the Son of
Man must be delivered into the
hands of sinful men, and be crucified, and the third day rise again."
8 [a]John 2:22 **8** And [a]they remembered
His words,
9 and returned from the
tomb and reported all these
things to the eleven and to all the
rest.
10 [a]Matt. 27:56 [b]Mark 6:30 **10** Now they were [a]Mary
Magdalene and Joanna and Mary
the *mother* of James; also the other women with them were telling
these things to [b]the apostles.
11 [a]Mark 16:11 **11** And these words appeared
to them as nonsense, and they
[a]would not believe them.
★12 [a]John 20:3-6 [b]John 20:10 **12** [But Peter arose and [a]ran
to the tomb; [a]stooping and look-
ing in, he *saw the linen wrappings only; and he went away [b]to
his home, marveling at that which
had happened.]

B The Fulfiller of the Prophecies (the Emmaus Disciples), 24:13–35

13 And behold, [a]two of them ★13 [a]Mark 16:12
were going that very day to a vil-
lage named Emmaus, which was
about seven miles from Jerusalem.
14 And they were conversing
with each other about all these
things which had taken place.
15 And it came about that
while they were conversing and
discussing, Jesus Himself approached, and *began* traveling
with them.
16 But [a]their eyes were pre- 16 [a]Luke 24:31; John 20:14; 21:4
vented from recognizing Him.
17 And He said to them,
"What are these words that you
are exchanging with one another
as you are walking?" And they
stood still, looking sad.
18 And one of them, named
Cleopas, answered and said to
Him, "Are You the only one visit-
ing Jerusalem and unaware of the
things which have happened here
in these days?"
19 And He said to them, 19 [a]Mark 1:24 [b]Matt. 21:11
"What things?" And they said to
Him, "The things about [a]Jesus the
Nazarene, who was a [b]prophet
mighty in deed and word in the
sight of God and all the people,
20 and how the chief priests 20 [a]Luke 23:13
and our [a]rulers delivered Him up
to the sentence of death, and crucified Him.

24:2 *the stone rolled away.* A circular stone like a solid wheel rolled in front of the entrance to the tomb-cave to keep out intruders.

24:6–7 *Remember.* See 9:31; 18:31–34.

24:12 *the linen wrappings.* The wide bandage-like strips that were wound around the body (23:53). *only.* Or, by themselves. Despite the absence of the body, the clothes retained the same shape and position they had when it was there. If someone had stolen the body but left the clothes, he would have had to unwrap it and the clothes would not have been in this position. See John 20:6–7.

24:13 *two of them.* One is identified as Cleopas (v. 18); the other may have been his wife (v. 32: "our hearts"). Many identify Cleopas as the person mentioned in John 19:25, in which case his wife's name was Mary. *Emmaus.* The location is uncertain, though it was less than 7 miles from Jerusalem.

21 [a]Luke 1:68

21 "But we were hoping that it was He who was going to [a]redeem Israel. Indeed, besides all this, it is the third day since these things happened.

22 [a]Luke 24:1ff

22 "But also some women among us amazed us. [a]When they were at the tomb early in the morning,

23 and did not find His body, they came, saying that they had also seen a vision of angels, who said that He was alive.

24 "And some of those who were with us went to the tomb and found it just exactly as the women also had said; but Him they did not see."

25 [a]Matt. 26:24

25 And He said to them, "O foolish men and slow of heart to believe in all that [a]the prophets have spoken!

26 [a]Luke 24:7, 44ff.; Heb. 2:10; 1 Pet. 1:11

26 "[a]Was it not necessary for the Christ to suffer these things and to enter into His glory?"

★27 [a]Gen. 3:15; 12:3; Num. 21:9 [John 3:14]; Deut. 18:15 [John 1:45]; John 5:46 [b]2 Sam. 7:12-16; Is. 7:14 [Matt. 1:23]; 9:1f. [Matt. 4:15f.]; 42:1 [Matt. 12:18ff.]; 53:4 [Matt. 8:17; Luke 22:37]; Dan. 7:13 [Matt. 24:30]; Mic. 5:2 [Matt. 2:6]; Zech. 9:9 [Matt. 21:5]; Acts 13:27

27 And beginning with [a]Moses and with all the [b]prophets, He explained to them the things concerning Himself in all the Scriptures.

28 [a]Mark 6:48

28 And they approached the village where they were going, and [a]He acted as though He would go farther.

29 And they urged Him, saying, "Stay with us, for it is *getting* toward evening, and the day is now nearly over." And He went in to stay with them.

★30 [a]Matt. 14:19

30 And it came about that when He had reclined *at table* with them, He took the bread and [a]blessed *it,* and breaking *it,* He *began* giving *it* to them.

★31 [a]Luke 24:16

31 And their [a]eyes were opened and they recognized Him; and He vanished from their sight.

32 [a]Luke 24:45

32 And they said to one another, "Were not our hearts burning within us while He was speaking to us on the road, while He [a]was explaining the Scriptures to us?"

33 [a]Mark 16:13 [b]Acts 1:14

33 And they arose that very hour and returned to Jerusalem, and [a]found gathered together the eleven and [b]those who were with them,

★34 [a]Luke 24:6 [b]1 Cor. 15:5

34 saying, "[a]The Lord has really risen, and [b]has appeared to Simon."

35 [a]Luke 24:30f

35 And they *began* to relate their experiences on the road and how [a]He was recognized by them in the breaking of the bread.

C The Pattern of Resurrection Life, 24:36-43

36 [a]Mark 16:14

36 And while they were telling these things, [a]He Himself stood in their midst.

37 [a]Matt. 14:26; Mark 6:49

37 But they were startled and frightened and thought that they were seeing [a]a spirit.

38 And He said to them, "Why are you troubled, and why do doubts arise in your hearts?

★39 [a]John 20:20, 27 [b]John 20:27; 1 John 1:1

39 "[a]See My hands and My feet, that it is I Myself; [b]touch Me and see, for a spirit does not have flesh and bones as you see that I have."

★40

40 [And when He had said this, He showed them His hands and His feet.]

41 [a]Luke 24:11 [b]John 21:5

41 And while they still [a]could not believe *it* for joy and were marveling, He said to them, "[b]Have you anything here to eat?"

42 And they gave Him a piece of a broiled fish;

43 [a]Acts 10:41

43 and He took it and [a]ate *it* in their sight.

24:27 *in all the Scriptures.* E.g., passages like Pss. 16; 22; Isa. 53.

24:30 *He took the bread.* Christ's assuming the position as host, and perhaps something in His gestures, made them recognize Him.

24:31 He vanished from their sight. Lit., He became invisible.

24:34 *appeared to Simon.* There is no other record of this event except the mention in 1 Cor. 15:5.

24:39 The evidences that Jesus' appearance was not as a spirit are: (1) the scars in His hands and feet; (2) His tangibleness in being handled; and (3) His ability to eat (v. 43; Acts 10:41). *touch.* The same word is used in 1 John 1:1.

24:40 Many manuscripts do not contain this verse.

D The Head of the Church, 24:44-48

★44 [a]Luke 9:22, 44f.; 18:31-34; 22:37 [b]Luke 24:27 [c]Ps. 2 [Acts 13:33]; Ps. 16 [Acts 2:27]; Ps. 22 [Matt. 27:34-46]; Ps. 69 [John 19:28ff.]; Ps. 72; 110 [Matt. 22:43f.]; Ps. 118 [Matt. 21:42] 45 [a]Luke 24:32; Acts 16:14; 1 John 5:20 46 [a]Luke 24:26, 44 [b]Luke 24:7 47 [a]Acts 5:31; 10:43; 13:38; 26:18 [b]Matt. 28:19 48 [a]Acts 1:8, 22; 2:32; 3:15; 4:33; 5:32; 10:39, 41; 13:31; 1 Pet. 5:1

44 Now He said to them,
"[a]These are My words which I
spoke to you while I was still with
you, that all things which are
written about Me in the [b]Law of
Moses and [b]the Prophets and [c]the
Psalms must be fulfilled."
45 Then He [a]opened their
minds to understand the Scriptures,
46 and He said to them,
"[a]Thus it is written, that the
Christ should suffer and [b]rise
again from the dead the third day;
47 and that [a]repentance for
forgiveness of sins should be proclaimed in His name to [b]all the
nations, beginning from Jerusalem.
48 "You are [a]witnesses of
these things.

E The Giver of the Holy Spirit, 24:49

49 "And behold, [a]I am sending
forth the promise of My Father
upon you; but [b]you are to stay in
the city until you are clothed with
power from on high."

★49 [a]John 14:26 [b]Acts 1:4

F The Ascended Lord, 24:50-53

50 And He led them out as
far as [a]Bethany, and He lifted up
His hands and blessed them.
51 And it came about that
while He was blessing them, He
parted from them.
52 And they returned to Jerusalem with great joy,
53 and were continually in
the temple, praising God.

★50 [a]Matt. 21:17; Acts 1:12 ★51

24:44 A common Jewish division of the O.T. The *Prophets* included most of the historical books, and the *Psalms* included the "writings."

24:49 *the promise of My Father.* The coming of the Holy Spirit on the day of Pentecost.

24:50 *as far as Bethany.* Or, toward Bethany.

24:51 Luke gives details of the ascension of Christ in his other book; see Acts 1:9.

INTRODUCTION TO THE GOSPEL ACCORDING TO JOHN

AUTHOR: The Apostle John DATE: 85-90

Authorship *The writer of this Gospel is identified in the book only as "the disciple whom Jesus loved" (21:20, 24). He obviously was a Palestinian Jew who was an eyewitness of the events of Christ's life, for he displays knowledge of Jewish customs (7:37-39; 18:28) and of the land of Palestine (1:44, 46; 5:2) and he includes details of an eyewitness (2:6; 13:26; 21:8, 11). Eliminating the other disciples that belonged to the "inner circle" (because James had been martyred before this time, Acts 12:1-5, and because Peter is named in close association with the disciple whom Jesus loved (13:23-24; 20:2-10), one concludes that John was the author. Whether this was the apostle John or a different John (the Elder) is discussed in the Introduction to 1 John.*

John the apostle was the son of Zebedee and Salome and was the older brother of James. He was a Galilean who apparently came from a fairly well-to-do home (Mark 15:40-41). Though often painted centuries later as effeminate, his real character was such that he was known as a "son of thunder" (Mark 3:17). He played a leading role in the work of the early church in Jerusalem (Acts 3:1; 8:14; Gal. 2:9). Later he went to Ephesus and for an unknown reason was exiled to the island of Patmos (Rev. 1:9).

Distinctive Approach *This is the most theological of the four Gospels. It deals with the nature and person of Christ and the meaning of faith in Him. John's presentation of Christ as the divine Son of God is seen in the titles given Him in the book: "the Word was God" (1:1), "the Lamb of God" (1:29), "the Messiah" (1:41), "the Son of God" and "the King of Israel" (1:49), the "Savior of the world" (4:42), "Lord and . . . God" (20:28). His deity is also asserted in the series of "I am . . ." claims (6:35; 8:12; 10:7, 9, 11, 14; 11:25; 14:6; 15:1, 5). In other "I am" statements Christ made implicit and explicit claim to be the I AM-Yahweh of the Old Testament (4:24, 26; 8:24, 28, 58; 13:19). These are the strongest claims to deity that Jesus could have made.*

The structure and style of the Gospel are different from those of the synoptics. It contains no parables, only seven miracles (five of which are not recorded elsewhere), and many personal interviews. The author emphasizes the physical actuality of Jesus' hunger, thirst, weariness, pain, and death as a defense against the Gnostic denial of Jesus' true human nature.

Date *Though the Gospel of John used to be dated by some extreme critics as being written in the middle of the second century, the discovery of the Rylands papyrus fragment (a few verses from John 18 dated about* A.D. *135) forced an earlier date. Several decades would have been required between the original writing of the Gospel and its being copied and circulated as far as the Egyptian hinterland where the fragment was found. The Gospel was apparently being circulated between 89 and 90, though it may have been written from Ephesus earlier (a pre-70 date has been suggested on the basis of 5:2 which may indicate that Jerusalem had not yet been destroyed). Discoveries at Qumran have attested to the genuineness of the Jewish background and thought patterns seen in the book.*

Contents *John's statement of purpose is clearly spelled out in 20:30-31. The Gospel is sometimes called The Book of the Seven Signs, since the author chose seven sign-miracles to reveal the person and mission of Jesus. These are: (1) the turning of water into wine (2:1-11); (2) the cure of the nobleman's son (4:46-54); (3) the cure of the paralytic (5:1-18); (4) the feeding of the multitude (6:6-13); (5) the walking on the water (6:16-21); (6) the giving of sight to the blind (9:1-7); and (7) the raising of Lazarus (11:1-45). Other important themes in the book include the Holy Spirit (14:26; 15:26; 16:7-14), Satan and the world (8:44; 12:31; 17:15), the Word (1:1-14), and the new birth (3:1-12).*

OUTLINE OF THE GOSPEL OF JOHN

I. Incarnation of the Son of God, 1:1-18
II. Presentation of the Son of God, 1:19-4:54
- A. By John the Baptizer, 1:19-34
- B. To John's Disciples, 1:35-51
- C. At a Wedding in Cana, 2:1-11
- D. At the Temple in Jerusalem, 2:12-25
- E. To Nicodemus, 3:1-21
- F. By John the Baptizer, 3:22-36
- G. To the Samaritan Woman, 4:1-42
- H. To an Official of Capernaum, 4:43-54

III. Confrontations with the Son of God, 5:1-12:50
- A. At a Feast in Jerusalem, 5:1-47
  1. The miraculous sign, 5:1-9

2. The reaction, 5:10-18
3. The discourse, 5:19-47

B. At Passover Time in Galilee, 6:1-71
1. The miraculous sign, 6:1-21
2. The discourse, 6:22-40
3. The reactions, 6:41-71

C. At the Feast of Tabernacles in Jerusalem, 7:1-10:21
1. Debate #1—the discourse, 7:1-29
2. The reactions, 7:30-36
3. Debate #2—the discourse, 7:37-39
4. The reactions, 7:40-53
5. Debate #3—the discourses, 8:1-58
6. The reaction, 8:59
7. Debate #4—the miraculous sign, 9:1-12
8. The reactions, 9:13-41
9. Debate #5—the discourse on the Good Shepherd, 10:1-18
10. The reactions, 10:19-21

D. At the Feast of Dedication in Jerusalem, 10:22-42
1. The discourse, 10:22-30
2. The rejection, 10:31-42

E. At Bethany, 11:1-12:11
1. The miraculous sign, 11:1-44
2. The reactions, 11:45-57
3. The anointing by Mary, 12:1-8
4. The reactions, 12:9-11

F. At Jerusalem, 12:12-50
1. The triumphal entry, 12:12-19
2. The teaching, 12:20-50

IV. Instruction by the Son of God, 13:1-16:33
A. Concerning Forgiveness, 13:1-20
B. Concerning His Betrayal, 13:21-30
C. Concerning His Departure, 13:31-38
D. Concerning Heaven, 14:1-14
E. Concerning the Holy Spirit, 14:15-26
F. Concerning Peace, 14:27-31
G. Concerning Fruitfulness, 15:1-17
H. Concerning the World, 15:18-16:6
I. Concerning the Holy Spirit, 16:7-15
J. Concerning His Return, 16:16-33

V. Intercession of the Son of God, 17:1-26

VI. Crucifixion of the Son of God, 18:1-19:42
A. The Arrest, 18:1-11
B. The Trials, 18:12-19:15
1. Before Annas, 18:12-23
2. Before Caiaphas, 18:24-27
3. Before Pilate, 18:28-19:16

C. The Crucifixion, 19:17-37
D. The Burial, 19:38-42

VII. Resurrection of the Son of God, 20:1-21:25
A. The Empty Tomb, 20:1-10
B. The Appearances of the Risen Lord, 20:11-21:25
1. To Mary Magdalene, 20:11-18
2. To the disciples, Thomas absent, 20:19-25
3. To the disciples, Thomas present, 20:26-31
4. To seven disciples, 21:1-14
5. To Peter and the beloved disciple, 21:15-25

THE GOSPEL ACCORDING TO JOHN

I INCARNATION OF THE SON OF GOD, 1:1-18

★ 1 [a]Gen. 1:1; Col. 1:17; 1 John 1:1 [b]John 1:14; Rev. 19:13 [c]John 17:5; 1 John 1:2 [d]Phil. 2:6

1 In the beginning was [b]the
Word, and the Word was
[c]with God, and [d]the Word was
God.
2 He was in the beginning
with God.
3 [a]All things came into
being by Him; and apart from
Him nothing came into being that
has come into being.
4 [a]In Him was life; and the
life was [b]the light of men.
5 And [a]the light shines in
the darkness; and the darkness
did not comprehend it.

★ 3 [a]John 1:10; 1 Cor. 8:6; Col. 1:16; Heb. 1:2

★ 4 [a]John 5:26; 11:25; 14:6 [b]John 8:12; 9:5; 12:46

5 [a]John 3:19

1:1 *In the beginning.* Before time began, Christ was already in existence with God. This is what is meant by the term "the pre-existent Christ." See Gen. 1:1 and 1 John 1:1. *Word* (Greek: *logos*). *Logos* means word, thought, concept, and the expressions thereof. In the O.T. the concept conveyed activity and revelation, and the word or wisdom of God is often personified (Ps. 33:6; Prov. 8). In the Targums (Aramaic paraphrases of the O.T.) it was a designation of God. To the Greek mind it expressed the ideas of reason and creative control. Revelation is the keynote idea in the *logos* concept. Here it is applied to Jesus, who is all that God is and the expression of Him (1:1, 14). In this verse the Word (Christ) is said to be *with God* (i.e., in communion with and yet distinct from God) and to be *God* (i.e., identical in essence with God).

1:3 *came into being by Him.* Christ was active in the work of creation (cf. Col. 1:16).

1:4-5 *life . . . light.* These are two words especially associated with John (8:12; 9:5; 11:25; 14:6). "Light" in John implies revelation which reveals the "life" that is in Christ and which brings into judgment those who refuse it (3:19). "Life" denotes salvation and deliverance, based on Christ's atonement. *the darkness did not comprehend it.* I.e., the darkness did not overcome the light.

6 There came a man, sent
from God, whose name was
[a]John.
7 He came [a]for a witness,
that he might bear witness of the
light, [b]that all might believe
through him.
8 [a]He was not the light, but
came that he might bear witness
of the light.
9 There was [a]the true light
which, coming into the world, enlightens every man.
10 He was in the world, and
[a]the world was made through
Him, and the world did not know
Him.
11 He came to His own, and
those who were His own did not
receive Him.
12 But as many as received
Him, to them He gave the right to
become [a]children of God, *even*
[b]to those who believe in His
name,
13 [a]who were born not of
blood, nor of the will of the flesh,
nor of the will of man, but of
God.
14 And [a]the Word [b]became
flesh, and [c]dwelt among us, and
[d]we beheld His glory, glory as of
the only begotten from the Father, full of [e]grace and [f]truth.
15 John *[a]bore witness of
Him, and cried out, saying, "This
was He of whom I said, '[b]He who
comes after me has a higher rank
than I, [c]for He existed before
me.' "
16 For of His [a]fulness we
have all received, and grace upon
grace.
17 For [a]the law was given
through Moses; [b]grace and [c]truth
were realized through Jesus
Christ.
18 [a]No man has seen God at
any time; [b]the only begotten God,
who is [c]in the bosom of the Father, [d]He has explained *Him.*

II PRESENTATION OF THE SON OF GOD, 1:19–4:54

A By John the Baptizer, 1:19–34

19 And this is [a]the witness of
John, when [b]the Jews sent to him

★ 6 [a]Matt. 3:1
7 [a]John 1:15, 19, 32; 3:26; 5:33 [b]John 1:12; Acts 19:4; Gal. 3:26
8 [a]John 1:20
★ 9 [a]1 John 2:8
★10 [a]1 Cor. 8:6; Col. 1:16; Heb. 1:2
★11
★12 [a]John 11:52; Gal. 3:26 [b]John 1:7; 3:18; 1 John 3:23
★13 [a]John 3:5f.; James 1:18; 1 Pet. 1:23; 1 John 2:29; 3:9
★14 [a]Rev. 19:13 [b]Rom. 1:3; Gal. 4:4; Phil. 2:7f.; 1 Tim. 3:16; 1 John 1:1f.; 4:2; 2 John 7 [c]Rev. 21:3 [d]Luke 9:32; John 2:11; 17:22, 24; 2 Pet. 1:16f.; 1 John 1:1 [e]John 1:17; Rom. 5:21; 6:14 [f]John 8:32; 14:6; 18:37
15 [a]John 1:7 [b]Matt. 3:11; John 1:27, 30 [c]John 1:30
★16 [a]Eph. 1:23; 3:19; 4:13; Col. 1:19; 2:9
★17 [a]John 7:19 [b]John 1:14; Rom. 5:21; 6:14 [c]John 8:32; 14:6; 18:37
★18 [a]Ex. 33:20; John 6:46; Col. 1:15; 1 Tim. 6:16; 1 John 4:12 [b]John 3:16, 18; 1 John 4:9 [c]Luke 16:22; John 13:23 [d]John 3:11
★19 [a]John 1:7 [b]John 2:18, 20; 5:10, 15f., 18; 6:41, 52; 7:1, 11, 13, 15, 35; 8:22, 48, 52, 57; 9:18, 22; 10:24, 31, 33 [c]Matt. 15:1

1:6 *John* (the Baptist). His role, it is made clear in v. 8, was simply as a witness to the Light.

1:9 *enlightens every man.* Not that every man is redeemed automatically, for redemption comes through faith in the Savior (1:12). But this light is available to all men.

1:10 *did not know Him.* The world did not recognize Jesus as the Christ, God's Son, Creator, Savior, etc.

1:11 *He came to His own* (thing or place—i.e., the world which He made). *His own* (people—the Jews) *did not receive Him.*

1:12 *even to those who believe in His name.* An explanation of what it means to "receive" Him.

1:13 The new birth is supernatural and therefore completely distinct from natural birth. It is *not of blood* (lit., bloods), i.e., contains no human element; nor does it lie within the scope of human achievement (it is not *of the will of the flesh* or *man*).

1:14 *the Word became flesh.* Jesus Christ was unique, for He was God from all eternity and yet joined Himself to sinless humanity in the incarnation. The God-man possessed all the attributes of deity (Phil. 2:6) and the attributes common to humanity (apart from sin), and He will exist forever as the God-man in His resurrected body (Acts 1:11; Rev. 5:6). Only the God-man could be an adequate Savior; for He must be human in order to be able to suffer and die, and He must be God to make that death effective as a payment for sin. The use of the word *flesh* contradicts the Gnostic teaching that pure deity could not be united with flesh, which was regarded as entirely evil. *glory.* In the O.T., glory expressed the splendor of divine manifestation and attested the divine presence. Here it means the visible manifestation of God in Christ.

1:16 *grace upon grace.* I.e., grace piled upon grace in the experiences of the Christian life.

1:17 *grace.* Though grace was manifest in the O.T. (Gen. 6:8; Ex. 34:6; Jer. 31:3), it was but a candle compared with the brightness of grace that appeared at the incarnation (Titus 2:11). Grace is the unmerited favor of God and is the basis of our salvation, justification, election, faith, and spiritual gifts (Eph. 1:7; Rom. 3:24; 11:5–6; Eph. 2:8–9; Rom. 12:6).

1:18 *No man has seen God at any time.* I.e., since God is Spirit (John 4:24), no man has ever seen God in His essence, His Spirit-being. Yet He assumed visible form which men saw in O.T. times (Gen. 32:30; Ex. 24:9–10; Judg. 13:22; Isa. 6:1; Dan. 7:9) and in Jesus men could see God (John 14:8–9). Christ gives life (1:12); He reveals (vv. 14, 18); He gives grace and truth (vv. 16–17).

1:19 *the Jews.* I.e., probably the chief priests.

priests and Levites [c]from Jerusalem to ask him, "Who are you?"
20 [a]John 3:28; cf. Luke 3:15f.
20 And he confessed, and did
not deny, and he confessed, "[a]I
am not the Christ."
★21 [a]Matt. 11:14; 16:14 [b]Deut. 18:15, 18; Matt. 21:11; John 1:25
21 And they asked him,
"What then? Are you [a]Elijah?"
And he *said, "I am not." "Are
you [b]the Prophet?" And he answered, "No."
22 They said then to him,
"Who are you, so that we may
give an answer to those who sent
us? What do you say about yourself?"
23 [a]Matt. 3:3; Mark 1:3; Luke 3:4 [b]Is. 40:3
23 He said, "[a]I am a voice of
one crying in the wilderness,
'[b]MAKE STRAIGHT THE WAY OF THE
LORD,' as Isaiah the prophet said."
★24
24 Now they had been sent
from the Pharisees.
★25 [a]Deut. 18:15, 18; Matt. 21:11; John 1:21
25 And they asked him, and
said to him, "Why then are you
baptizing, if you are not the
Christ, nor Elijah, nor [a]the
Prophet?"
26 [a]Matt. 3:11; Mark 1:8; Luke 3:16; Acts 1:5
26 John answered them say-
ing, "[a]I baptize in water, *but*
among you stands One whom
you do not know.
27 [a]Matt. 3:11; John 1:30 [b]Matt. 3:11; Mark 1:7; Luke 3:16
27 "*It is* [a]He who comes after
me, the [b]thong of whose sandal I
am not worthy to untie."
28 [a]John 3:26; 10:40
28 These things took place in
Bethany [a]beyond the Jordan,
where John was baptizing.
★29 [a]Is. 53:7; John 1:36; Acts 8:32; 1 Pet. 1:19; Rev. 5:6, 8, 12f.; 6:1 [b]Matt. 1:21; 1 John 3:5
29 The next day he *saw
Jesus coming to him, and *said,
"Behold, [a]the Lamb of God who
[b]takes away the sin of the world!
30 [a]Matt. 3:11; John 1:27 [b]John 1:15
30 "This is He on behalf of
whom I said, '[a]After me comes a
Man who has a higher rank than
I, [b]for He existed before me.'
31 "And I did not recognize
Him, but in order that He might
be manifested to Israel, I came
baptizing in water."
32 [a]John 1:7 [b]Matt. 3:16; Mark 1:10; Luke 3:22
32 And John [a]bore witness
saying, "[b]I have beheld the Spirit
descending as a dove out of
heaven; and He remained upon
Him.
33 [a]Matt. 3:11; Mark 1:8; Luke 3:16; Acts 1:5
33 "And I did not recognize
Him, but He who sent me to baptize in water said to me, 'He upon
whom you see the Spirit descending and remaining upon Him,
[a]this is the one who baptizes in
the Holy Spirit.'
34 [a]Matt. 4:3; John 1:49
34 "And I have seen, and have
borne witness that this is [a]the Son
of God."

B To John's Disciples, 1:35–51

35 [a]John 1:29
35 Again [a]the next day John
was standing, and two of his disciples;
36 [a]John 1:29
36 and he looked upon Jesus
as He walked, and *said, "Behold,
[a]the Lamb of God!"
37 And the two disciples
heard him speak, and they followed Jesus.
38 [a]Matt. 23:7f.; John 1:49
38 And Jesus turned, and beheld them following, and *said to
them, "What do you seek?" And
they said to Him, "[a]Rabbi (which
translated means Teacher), where
are You staying?"
★39
39 He *said to them, "Come,
and you will see." They came
therefore and saw where He was
staying; and they stayed with Him
that day, for it was about the
tenth hour.
40 [a]Matt. 4:18-22; Mark 1:16-20; Luke 5:2-11; John 1:40-42
40 [a]One of the two who
heard John *speak,* and followed
Him, was Andrew, Simon Peter's
brother.
★41 [a]Dan. 9:25; John 4:25
41 He *found first his own

1:21 *Elijah.* See Mal. 4:5. He was supposed to return to earth before the time of judgment (see note on Matt. 11:14). *the Prophet.* The prophecy referred to (Deut. 18:15) is of Christ, though the Jews did not understand it correctly, since (John 1:25) they distinguished Christ and the Prophet (Acts 3:22–23).

1:24 *Pharisees.* See note on Matt. 3:7.

1:25 They seem to be saying: Since you have no authority, what are you doing baptizing and thus gathering followers?

1:29 *Lamb.* History (the Passover lamb, Ex. 12:3) and prophecy (the Messiah, Isa. 53:7) are linked in this metaphor. *the sin of the world.* No longer just the sins of Israel (Isa. 53:4–12; 1 John 2:2).

1:39 *the tenth hour.* 10 a.m. by Roman time; 4 p.m. by Jewish time.

1:41 *Messiah.* See note on Matt. 1:1.

brother Simon, and *said to him,
"We have found the [a]Messiah"
(which translated means Christ).
42 He brought him to Jesus.
Jesus looked at him, and said,
"You are Simon the son of [a]John;
you shall be called [b]Cephas"
(which translated means [c]Peter).
43 [a]The next day *He* purposed to go forth into [b]Galilee,
and He *found [c]Philip, and Jesus
*said to him, "[d]Follow Me."
44 Now [a]Philip was from
[b]Bethsaida, of the city of Andrew
and Peter.
45 [a]Philip *found [b]Nathanael,
and *said to him, "We have
found Him of whom [c]Moses in
the Law and also [c]the Prophets
wrote, Jesus of [d]Nazareth, [e]the
son of Joseph."
46 And Nathanael *said to
him, "[a]Can any good thing come
out of Nazareth?" [b]Philip *said to
him, "Come and see."
47 Jesus saw Nathanael coming to Him, and *said of him,
"Behold, an [a]Israelite indeed, in
whom is no guile!"
48 Nathanael *said to Him,
"How do You know me?" Jesus
answered and said to him, "Before [a]Philip called you, when you
were under the fig tree, I saw
you."
49 Nathanael answered Him,
"[a]Rabbi, You are [b]the Son of
God; You are the [c]King of Israel."
50 Jesus answered and said to
him, "Because I said to you that I
saw you under the fig tree, do you
believe? You shall see greater
things than these."
51 And He *said to him,
"Truly, truly, I say to you, you
shall see [a]the heavens opened,
and [b]the angels of God ascending
and descending upon [c]the Son of
Man."

42 [a]John 21:15-17 [b]1 Cor. 1:12; 3:22; 9:5; 15:5; Gal. 1:18; 2:9, 11, 14 [c]Matt. 16:18
43 [a]John 1:29, 35 [b]Matt. 4:12; John 1:28; 2:11 [c]Matt. 10:3; John 1:44-48; 6:5, 7; 12:21f.; 14:8f. [d]Matt. 8:22
44 [a]Matt. 10:3; John 1:44-48; 6:5, 7; 12:21f.; 14:8f. [b]Matt. 11:21
45 [a]Matt. 10:3; John 1:44-48; 6:5, 7; 12:21f.; 14:8f. [b]John 1:46-49; 21:2 [c]Luke 24:27 [d]Matt. 2:23 [e]Luke 2:48; 3:23; 4:22; John 6:42
★**46** [a]John 7:41, 52 [b]Matt. 10:3; John 1:44-48; 6:5, 7; 12:21f.; 14:8f.
47 [a]Rom. 9:4
★**48** [a]Matt. 10:3; John 1:44-48; 6:5, 7; 12:21f.; 14:8f.
★**49** [a]John 1:38 [b]John 1:34 [c]Matt. 2:2; 27:42; Mark 15:32; John 12:13
★**50**
★**51** [a]Ezek. 1:1; Matt. 3:16; Luke 3:21; Acts 7:56; 10:11; Rev. 19:11 [b]Gen. 28:12 [c]Matt. 8:20

C At a Wedding in Cana, 2:1-11

2 And on [a]the third day there
was a wedding in [b]Cana of
Galilee; and the [c]mother of Jesus
was there;
2 and Jesus also was invited,
and His [a]disciples, to the wedding.
3 And when the wine gave
out, the mother of Jesus *said to
Him, "They have no wine."
4 And Jesus *said to her,
"[a]Woman, [b]what do I have to do
with you? [c]My hour has not yet
come."
5 His [a]mother *said to the
servants, "Whatever He says to
you, do it."
6 Now there were six stone
waterpots set there [a]for the Jewish custom of purification, containing twenty or thirty gallons
each.
7 Jesus *said to them, "Fill
the waterpots with water." And
they filled them up to the brim.
8 And He *said to them,
"Draw *some* out now, and take it
to the headwaiter." And they
took it *to him.*
9 And when the headwaiter
tasted the water [a]which had become wine, and did not know

1 [a]John 1:29, 35, 43 [b]John 2:11; 4:46; 21:2 [c]Matt. 12:46
2 [a]John 1:40-49; 2:12, 17, 22; 3:22; 4:2, 8, 27ff.; 6:8, 12, 16, 22, 24, 60f., 66; 7:3; 8:31
★ **4** [a]John 19:26 [b]Matt. 8:29 [c]John 7:6, 8, 30; 8:20
5 [a]Matt. 12:46
6 [a]Mark 7:3f.; John 3:25
9 [a]John 4:46

1:46 *Nazareth.* The town had a negative reputation at this period (see 7:52).

1:48 *when you were under the fig tree, I saw you.* Though bodily removed from Philip, the omnipresent Lord was with him under the fig tree.

1:49 *Son of God.* A Messianic title for the One in whom the true destiny of Israel is to be fulfilled; also a claim of deity (5:18). The title *King of Israel* stated the Jewish political Messianic hope.

1:50 *greater things.* I.e., greater proofs of who I am as revealed in the seven great "signs" that comprise chapters 2–12.

1:51 *the heavens opened.* A symbol of the fellowship open to followers of Christ. *Son of Man.* See note on Matt. 8:20. Notice the titles given to Jesus in chapter 1: Word (v. 1), God (v. 1), Creator (v. 3), Light (v. 7), only begotten God (v. 18), Lamb of God (vv. 29, 36), Son of God (vv. 34, 49), Messiah (v. 41), King of Israel (v. 49), and Son of Man (v. 51).

2:4 *Woman, what do I have to do with you?* "Woman" was a term of respectful address (see 19:26). Christ's remark meant: "that concerns you, leave Me alone." The *hour* for manifesting Himself as Messiah had *not yet come* (see 8:20).

where it came from (but the servants who had drawn the water
knew), the headwaiter *called the
bridegroom,

10 [a]Matt. 24:49; Luke 12:45; Acts 2:15; 1 Cor. 11:21; Eph. 5:18; 1 Thess. 5:7; Rev. 17:2, 6

10 and *said to him, "Every
man serves the good wine first,
and when *men* [a]have drunk
freely, *then* that which is poorer;
you have kept the good wine until
now."

★11 [a]John 2:23; 3:2; 4:54; 6:2, 14, 26, 30; 7:31; 9:16; 10:41; 11:47; 12:18, 37; 20:30 [b]John 1:43 [c]John 1:14

11 This beginning of *His*
[a]signs Jesus did in Cana of [b]Gali-
lee, and manifested His [c]glory,
and His disciples believed in Him.

D At the Temple in Jerusalem, 2:12–25

12 [a]Matt. 4:13 [b]Matt. 12:46 [c]John 2:2

12 After this He went down
to [a]Capernaum, He and His
[b]mother, and *His* [b]brothers, and
His [c]disciples; and there they
stayed a few days.

★13 [a]John 5:1 marg.; 6:4; 11:55 [b]Deut. 16:1-6; Luke 2:41; John 2:23

13 And [a]the Passover of the
Jews was at hand, and Jesus [b]went
up to Jerusalem.

★14 [a]John 2:14-16: *Matt. 21:12ff.; Mark 11:15, 17; Luke 19:45f.;* Mal. 3:1ff.

14 [a]And He found in the temple those who were selling oxen
and sheep and doves, and the
moneychangers seated.
15 And He made a scourge of
cords, and drove *them* all out of
the temple, with the sheep and
the oxen; and He poured out the
coins of the moneychangers, and
overturned their tables;

16 [a]Matt. 21:12 [b]Luke 2:49

16 and to those who were
selling [a]the doves He said, "Take
these things away; stop making
[b]My Father's house a house of
merchandise."

★17 [a]John 2:2 [b]Ps. 69:9

17 His [a]disciples remembered
that it was written, "[b]ZEAL FOR
THY HOUSE WILL CONSUME ME."

18 [a]John 1:19 [b]Matt. 12:38

18 [a]The Jews therefore answered and said to Him, "[b]What
sign do You show to us, seeing
that You do these things?"

★19 [a]Matt. 26:61; 27:40; Mark 14:58; 15:29; Acts 6:14

19 Jesus answered and said to
them, "[a]Destroy this temple, and
in three days I will raise it up."

20 [a]John 1:19 [b]Ezra 5:16

20 [a]The Jews therefore said,
"It took [b]forty-six years to build
this temple, and will You raise it
up in three days?"

21 [a]1 Cor. 6:19

21 But He was speaking of
[a]the temple of His body.

22 [a]John 2:2 [b]Luke 24:8; John 2:17; 12:16; 14:26 [c]Ps. 16:10; Luke 24:26f.; John 20:9; Acts 13:33

22 When therefore He was
raised from the dead, His [a]disci-
ples [b]remembered that He said
this; and they believed [c]the Scripture, and the word which Jesus
had spoken.

23 [a]John 2:13 [b]John 2:11

23 Now when He was in Jerusalem at [a]the Passover, during the
feast, many believed in His name,
[b]beholding His signs which He
was doing.
24 But Jesus, on His part, was
not entrusting Himself to them,
for He knew all men,

25 [a]Matt. 9:4; John 1:42, 47; 6:61, 64; 13:11

25 and because He did not
need anyone to bear witness concerning man [a]for He Himself
knew what was in man.

E To Nicodemus, 3:1–21

★ 1 [a]John 7:50; 19:39 [b]Luke 23:13; John 7:26, 48

3 Now there was a man of the
Pharisees, named [a]Nico-
demus, a [b]ruler of the Jews;

2 [a]Matt. 23:7; John 3:26 [b]John 2:11 [c]John 9:33; 10:38; 14:10f.; Acts 2:22; 10:38

2 this man came to Him by
night, and said to Him, "[a]Rabbi,
we know that You have come
from God *as* a teacher; for no one

2:11 *beginning of His signs.* The miracles of Jesus are called signs by John in order to emphasize the significance of the miracles rather than the miracles themselves. They revealed various aspects of the person or work of Christ (here His *glory*), and their purpose was to encourage faith in His followers. For the specific signs in this book see Introduction, under "Contents."

2:13 *Passover.* See note on Mark 14:1.

2:14 The many pilgrims that came to Jerusalem for Passover brought a variety of currency and no animals for sacrifice. The outer courts of the temple became a noisy market for changing money and selling animals.

2:17 See Ps. 69:9. Christ was jealous for the holiness of God's house. The offense of the money-changers was in their defiling it.

2:19 *in three days I will raise it up.* This cryptic expression is explained in v. 21, after a verse which shows how the Jews characteristically misunderstood Jesus.

3:1 *Nicodemus, a ruler of the Jews.* A member of the Sanhedrin (see note on Luke 22:66). He perfectly represents the aristocratic, well-intentioned but unenlightened Judaism of his day. For additional information on Nicodemus see John 7:50–51 and 19:39.

can do these [b]signs that You do unless [c]God is with him."

3 Jesus answered and said to him, "Truly, truly, I say to you, unless one [a]is born again, he cannot see [b]the kingdom of God."

4 Nicodemus *said to Him, "How can a man be born when he is old? He cannot enter a second time into his mother's womb and be born, can he?"

5 Jesus answered, "Truly, truly, I say to you, unless one is born of [a]water and the Spirit, he cannot enter into [b]the kingdom of God.

6 "[a]That which is born of the flesh is flesh; and that which is born of the Spirit is spirit.

7 "Do not marvel that I said to you, 'You must be born again.'

8 "[a]The wind blows where it wishes and you hear the sound of it, but do not know where it comes from and where it is going; so is every one who is born of the Spirit."

9 Nicodemus answered and said to Him, "How can these things be?"

10 Jesus answered and said to him, "Are you [a]the teacher of Israel, and do not understand these things?

11 "Truly, truly, I say to you, [a]we speak that which we know, and [b]bear witness of that which we have seen; and [b]you do not receive our witness.

12 "If I told you earthly things and you do not believe, how shall you believe if I tell you heavenly things?

13 "And [a]no one has ascended into heaven, but [b]He who descended from heaven, *even* [c]the Son of Man.

14 "And as [a]Moses lifted up the serpent in the wilderness, even so must [b]the Son of Man [c]be lifted up;

15 that whoever believes may [a]in Him have eternal life.

16 "For God so [a]loved the world, that He [b]gave His [c]only begotten Son, that whoever [d]believes in Him should not perish, but have eternal life.

17 "For God [a]did not send the Son into the world [b]to judge the world; but that the world should be saved through Him.

18 "[a]He who believes in Him is not judged; he who does not believe has been judged already, because he has not believed in the name of [b]the only begotten Son of God.

19 "And this is the judgment, that [a]the light is come into the world, and men loved the darkness rather than the light; for [b]their deeds were evil.

20 "[a]For everyone who does evil hates the light, and does not come to the light, lest his deeds should be exposed.

★ **3** [a]2 Cor. 5:17; 1 Pet. 1:23 [b]Matt. 19:24; 21:31; Mark 9:47; 10:14f.; John 3:5

★ **5** [a]Ezek. 36:25-27; Eph. 5:26; Titus 3:5 [b]Matt. 19:24; 21:31; Mark 9:47; 10:14f.; John 3:3

6 [a]John 1:13; 1 Cor. 15:50

★ **8** [a]Ps. 135:7; Eccles. 11:5; Ezek. 37:9

10 [a]Luke 2:46; 5:17; Acts 5:34

★**11** [a]John 1:18; 7:16f.; 8:26, 28; 12:49; 14:24 [b]John 3:32

13 [a]Deut. 30:12; Prov. 30:4; Acts 2:34; Rom. 10:6; Eph. 4:9 [b]John 3:31; 6:38, 42 [c]Matt. 8:20

★**14** [a]Num. 21:9 [b]Matt. 8:20 [c]John 8:28; 12:34

15 [a]John 20:31; 1 John 5:11-13

★**16** [a]Rom. 5:8; Eph. 2:4; 2 Thess. 2:16; 1 John 4:10; Rev. 1:5 [b]Rom. 8:32; 1 John 4:9 [c]John 1:18; 3:18; 1 John 4:9 [d]John 3:36; 6:40; 11:25f.

17 [a]John 3:34; 5:36, 38; 6:29, 38, 57; 7:29; 8:42; 10:36; 11:42; 17:3, 8, 18, 21, 23, 25; 20:21 [b]Luke 19:10; John 8:15; 12:47; 1 John 4:14

18 [a]Mark 16:16; John 5:24 [b]John 1:18; 1 John 4:9

19 [a]John 1:4; 8:12; 9:5; 12:46 [b]John 7:7

20 [a]John 3:20, 21; Eph. 5:11, 13

3:3 *born again.* Lit., "from above" (as in 3:31; 19:11), though the word also means "again" (Gal. 4:9). Both ideas (merged in John's Gospel) are combined in the translation "be born anew." The new birth or regeneration (Titus 3:5) is the act of God which gives eternal life to the one who believes in Christ. As a result, he becomes a member of God's family (1 Pet. 1:23) with a new capacity and desire to please his heavenly Father (2 Cor. 5:17).

3:5 *born of water and the Spirit.* Various interpretations have been suggested for the meaning here of "water": (1) It refers to baptism as a requirement for salvation. However, this would contradict many other N.T. passages (Eph. 2:8-9). (2) It stands for the act of repentance which John the Baptist's baptism signified. (3) It refers to natural birth; thus it means "except a man be born the first time by water and the second time by the Spirit . . ." (4) It means the Word of God, as in John 15:3. (5) It is a synonym for the Holy Spirit and may be translated, "by water, even the Spirit." One truth is clear: the new birth is from God through the Spirit.

3:8 *wind.* The Greek word, *pneuma,* means both *wind* and *spirit.*

3:11 *witness.* Or testimony. The witness theme is found throughout John (3:31-36; 5:31-47; 8:12-20).

3:14 *Moses.* The reference is to Num. 21:5-9.

3:16 *eternal life.* A new quality of life, not an everlasting "this-life." Here begins another major theme of John: the dual one of redemption and judgment. It reappears at 5:22; 8:15; 9:39; 12:47. Here the emphasis is on the fact that men judge themselves. The acquitted are those who have believed in Him; the condemned, those who have rejected Him.

★21 a 1 John 1:6

21 "But he who [a]practices the
truth comes to the light, that his
deeds may be manifested as having been wrought in God."

F By John the Baptizer, 3:22–36

22 a John 2:2 b John 4:1, 2

22 After these things Jesus
and His [a]disciples came into the
land of Judea; and there He was
spending time with them, and
[b]baptizing.

★23

23 And John also was baptizing in Aenon near Salim, because
there was much water there; and
they were coming, and were
being baptized.

24 a Matt. 4:12

24 For [a]John had not yet been
thrown into prison.

25 a John 2:6

25 There arose therefore a
discussion on the part of John's
disciples with a Jew about [a]purifi-
cation.

26 a Matt. 23:7; John 3:2 b John 1:28 c John 1:7

26 And they came to John,
and said to him, "[a]Rabbi, He who
was with you [b]beyond the Jordan,
to whom you [c]have borne witness, behold, He is baptizing, and
all are coming to Him."

27 a 1 Cor. 4:7; Heb. 5:4

27 John answered and said,
"[a]A man can receive nothing, unless it has been given him from
heaven.

28 a John 1:20, 23

28 "You yourselves bear me
witness, that I said, '[a]I am not the
Christ', but, 'I have been sent before Him.'

★29 a Matt. 9:15; 25:1 b John 15:11; 16:24; 17:13; Phil. 2:2; 1 John 1:4; 2 John 12

29 "He who has the bride is
[a]the bridegroom; but the friend of
the bridegroom, who stands and
hears him, rejoices greatly because of the bridegroom's voice.
And so this [b]joy of mine has been
made full.

30 "He must increase, but I
must decrease.

★31 a John 3:13; 8:23 b 1 John 4:5

31 "[a]He who comes from
above is above all, he who is of
the earth is from the earth and
speaks [b]of the earth. [a]He who
comes from heaven is above all.

32 a John 3:11

32 "What He has seen and
heard, of that He [a]bears witness;
and [a]no man receives His witness.

33 a John 6:27; Rom. 4:11; 15:28; 1 Cor. 9:2; 2 Cor. 1:22; Eph. 1:13; 4:30; 2 Tim. 2:19; Rev. 7:3-8

33 "He who has received His
witness [a]has set his seal to *this,*
that God is true.

34 a John 3:17 b Matt. 12:18; Luke 4:18; Acts 1:2; 10:38

34 "For He whom God has
[a]sent speaks the words of God;
[b]for He gives the Spirit without
measure.

35 a Matt. 28:18; John 5:20; 17:2

35 "[a]The Father loves the Son,
and has given all things into His
hand.

36 a John 3:16 b Acts 14:2; Heb. 3:18

36 "He who [a]believes in the
Son has eternal life; but he who
[b]does not obey the Son shall not
see life, but the wrath of God
abides on him."

G To the Samaritan Woman, 4:1–42

★ 1 a Luke 7:13 b John 3:22, 26; 1 Cor. 1:17

4 When therefore [a]the Lord
knew that the Pharisees had
heard that Jesus was making and
[b]baptizing more disciples than
John

2 a John 3:22, 26; 1 Cor. 1:17 b John 2:2

2 (although [a]Jesus Himself
was not baptizing, but His [b]disci-
ples were),

3 a John 3:22 b John 2:11f.

3 He left [a]Judea, and departed [b]again into Galilee.

4 a Luke 9:52

4 And He had to pass
through [a]Samaria.

5 a Luke 9:52 b Gen. 33:19; 48:22; Josh. 24:32; John 4:12

5 So He *came to a city of
[a]Samaria, called Sychar, near the
parcel of ground that [b]Jacob gave
to his son Joseph;

★ 6

6 and Jacob's well was there.
Jesus therefore, being wearied
from His journey, was sitting thus
by the well. It was about the sixth
hour.

3:21 *truth.* I.e., what is true or right.

3:23 *Aenon . . . Salim.* Though not positively identified, they are thought to be in Samaria.

3:29 *the friend of the bridegroom.* As the bridegroom, Christ must occupy the prominent place, though John the Baptist's place as the friend was unique, and he vicariously participated in the joy of the bridegroom.

3:31 This verse picks up where 3:13 left off. *He who comes* is the Son of Man.

4:1-3 The meaning is this: When the Lord knew that the Pharisees had heard that He was making and baptizing more disciples than John (though actually Jesus' disciples did the baptizing, not Jesus Himself), He determined to leave the area and go into Galilee to avoid trouble with the Pharisees.

4:6 *the sixth hour.* 6 p.m. by Roman time and 12 noon by Jewish. The latter, at the sun's zenith, seems indicated.

★ 7
7 There *came a woman of Samaria to draw water. Jesus *said to her, "Give Me a drink."

8 [a]John 2:2 [b]John 4:5, 39
8 For His [a]disciples had gone away into [b]the city to buy food.

9 [a]Luke 9:52 [b]Ezra 4:3-6, 11ff.; Matt. 10:5; John 8:48
9 The [a]Samaritan woman therefore *said to Him, "How is it that You, being a Jew, ask me for a drink since I am a Samaritan woman?" (For [b]Jews have no dealings with Samaritans.)

★10 [a]John 7:37f.; Rev. 21:6; 22:17
10 Jesus answered and said to her, "If you knew the gift of God, and who it is who says to you, 'Give Me a drink,' you would have asked Him, and He would have given you [a]living water."

11 [a]John 7:37f.; Rev. 21:6; 22:17
11 She *said to Him, "Sir, You have nothing to draw with and the well is deep; where then do You get that [a]living water?

12 [a]John 4:6
12 "You are not greater than our father Jacob, are You, who [a]gave us the well, and drank of it himself, and his sons, and his cattle?"

13 Jesus answered and said to her, "Everyone who drinks of this water shall thirst again;

14 [a]John 6:35; 7:38 [b]Matt. 25:46; John 6:27
14 but whoever drinks of the water that I shall give him [a]shall never thirst; but the water that I shall give him shall become in him a well of water springing up to [b]eternal life."

15 [a]John 6:34
15 The woman *said to Him, "Sir, [a]give me this water, so I will not be thirsty, nor come all the way here to draw."

16 He *said to her, "Go, call your husband, and come here."

17 The woman answered and said, "I have no husband." Jesus *said to her, "You have well said, 'I have no husband';

18 for you have had five husbands; and the one whom you now have is not your husband; this you have said truly."

19 The woman *said to Him, "Sir, I perceive that You are [a]a prophet.
19 [a]Matt. 21:11; Luke 7:39

20 "[a]Our fathers worshiped in [b]this mountain; and you *people* say that [c]in Jerusalem is the place where men ought to worship."
★20 [a]Gen. 33:20 [John 4:12] [b]Deut. 11:29; Josh. 8:33 [c]Luke 9:53

21 Jesus *said to her, "Woman, believe Me, [a]an hour is coming when [b]neither in this mountain, nor in Jerusalem, shall you worship the Father.
21 [a]John 4:23; 5:25, 28; 16:2, 32 [b]Mal. 1:11; 1 Tim. 2:8

22 "[a]You worship that which you do not know; we worship that which we know; for [b]salvation is from the Jews.
★22 [a]2 Kin. 17:28-41 [b]Is. 2:3; Rom. 3:1f.; 9:4f.

23 "But [a]an hour is coming, and now is, when the true worshipers shall worship the Father [b]in spirit and truth; for such people the Father seeks to be His worshipers.
23 [a]John 4:21; 5:25, 28; 16:2, 32 [b]Phil. 3:3

24 "God is spirit; and those who worship Him must worship [a]in spirit and truth."
★24 [a]Phil.

25 The woman *said to Him, "I know that [a]Messiah is coming ([b]He who is called Christ); when that One comes, He will declare all things to us."
★25 [a]John 1:41 [b]Matt. 1:16

26 Jesus *said to her, "[a]I who speak to you am *He.*"
26 [a]John 8:24; 9:35-37

27 And at this point His [a]disciples [b]came, and they marveled that He had been speaking with a woman; yet no one said, "What do You seek?" or, "Why do You speak with her?"
27 [a]John 4:8 [b]John 2:2

28 So the woman left her waterpot, and went into the city, and *said to the men,

---

4:7 *a woman of Samaria.* On the Samaritans, see note on Luke 10:33.

4:10 *living water.* New life through the Spirit (see Jer. 2:13; Zech. 14:8; John 7:37–39). Salvation is a gift from Jesus Christ, the Son of God and Messiah. Notice that Christ asked the woman to receive Him and His gift without any prerequisite change in her life. After she believed, and because she believed, her way of living would be changed.

4:20 *in this mountain.* On Mt. Gerizim the Samaritans had built a temple to rival the one in Jerusalem, from which they had long been separated politically and religiously.

4:22 *salvation is from the Jews.* The Savior was a Jew and the Jews were the first messengers of the good news.

4:24 *must worship in spirit and truth.* The English word "worship" was originally spelled "worthship" and means to acknowledge the worth of the object worshiped. We should acknowledge God's worth *in spirit* (in contrast to material ways) and *in truth* (in contrast to falsehood).

4:25 The Samaritans also believed in a coming Messiah.

29 [a]John 4:17f. [b]Matt. 12:23; John 7:26, 31

29 "Come, see a man [a]who told me all the things that I *have* done; [b]this is not the Christ, is it?"

30 They went out of the city, and were coming to Him.

31 [a]Matt. 23:7

31 In the meanwhile the disciples were requesting Him, saying, "[a]Rabbi, eat."

32 But He said to them, "I have food to eat that you do not know about."

33 [a]John 2:2

33 The [a]disciples therefore were saying to one another, "No one brought Him *anything* to eat, did he?"

34 [a]John 5:30; 6:38 [b]John 5:36; 17:4; 19:28, 30

34 Jesus *said to them, "My food is to [a]do the will of Him who sent Me, and to [b]accomplish His work.

★35 [a]Luke 10:2

35 "Do you not say, 'There are yet four months, and *then* comes the harvest'? Behold, I say to you, lift up your eyes, and look on the fields, that they are white [a]for harvest.

36 [a]1 Cor. 9:17f. [b]Rom. 1:13 [c]John 4:14

36 "Already he who reaps is receiving [a]wages, and is gathering [b]fruit for [c]life eternal; that he who sows and he who reaps may rejoice together.

37 [a]Job 31:8; Mic. 6:15

37 "For in this *case* the saying is true, '[a]One sows, and another reaps.'

38 "I sent you to reap that for which you have not labored; others have labored, and you have entered into their labor."

39 [a]John 4:5, 30 [b]John 4:29

39 And from [a]that city many of the Samaritans believed in Him because of the word of the woman who testified, "[b]He told me all the things that I *have* done."

40 So when the Samaritans came to Him, they were asking Him to stay with them; and He stayed there two days.

41 And many more believed because of His word;

42 [a]Luke 2:11; Acts 5:31; 13:23; 1 Tim. 4:10; 1 John 4:14

42 and they were saying to the woman, "It is no longer because of what you said that we believe, for we have heard for ourselves and know that this One is indeed [a]the Savior of the world."

H To an Official of Capernaum, 4:43–54

43 [a]John 4:40

43 And after [a]the two days He went forth from there into Galilee.

44 [a]Matt. 13:57

44 For Jesus Himself testified that [a]a prophet has no honor in his own country.

45 [a]John 2:23

45 So when He came to Galilee, the Galileans received Him, [a]having seen all the things that He did in Jerusalem at the feast; for they themselves also went to the feast.

46 [a]John 2:1 [b]John 2:9 [c]Luke 4:23; John 2:12

46 He came therefore again to [a]Cana of Galilee [b]where He had made the water wine. And there was a certain royal official, whose son was sick at [c]Capernaum.

47 [a]John 4:3, 54

47 When he heard that Jesus had come [a]out of Judea into Galilee, he went to Him, and was requesting *Him* to come down and heal his son; for he was at the point of death.

48 [a]Dan. 4:2f.; 6:27; Matt. 24:24; Mark 13:22; Acts 2:19, 22, 43; 4:30; 5:12; 6:8; 7:36; 14:3; 15:12; Rom. 15:19; 1 Cor. 1:22; 2 Cor. 12:12; 2 Thess. 2:9; Heb. 2:4

48 Jesus therefore said to him, "Unless you *people* see [a]signs and [a]wonders, you *simply* will not believe."

49 The royal official *said to Him, "Sir, come down before my child dies."

50 Jesus *said to him, "Go your way; your son lives." The man believed the word that Jesus spoke to him, and he started off.

51 And as he was now going down, *his* slaves met him, saying that his son was living.

52 So he inquired of them the hour when he began to get better. They said therefore to him, "Yesterday at the seventh hour the fever left him."

53 [a]Acts 11:14

53 So the father knew that *it was* at that hour in which Jesus

---

4:35 *they are white for harvest.* The mission fields, Christ says, are ripe and waiting for harvesters.

said to him, "Your son lives"; and he himself believed, and [a]his whole household.

54 [a]John 2:11 [b]John 4:45f.

54 This is again a [a]second sign that Jesus performed, when He had [b]come out of Judea into Galilee.

III CONFRONTATIONS WITH THE SON OF GOD, 5:1-12:50

A At a Feast in Jerusalem, 5:1-47

1 *The miraculous sign,* 5:1-9

5 After these things there was a feast of the Jews; and Jesus went up to Jerusalem.

★ 2 [a]Neh. 3:1, 32; 12:39 [b]John 19:13, 17, 20; 20:16; Acts 21:40; Rev. 9:11; 16:16
★ 3

2 Now there is in Jerusalem by [a]the sheep *gate* a pool, which is called [b]in Hebrew Bethesda, having five porticoes.

3 In these lay a multitude of those who were sick, blind, lame, and withered, [waiting for the moving of the waters;

4 for an angel of the Lord went down at certain seasons into the pool, and stirred up the water; whoever then first, after the stirring up of the water, stepped in was made well from whatever disease with which he was afflicted.]

5 And a certain man was there, who had been thirty-eight years in his sickness.

6 When Jesus saw him lying there, and knew that he had already been a long time *in that condition,* He *said to him, "Do you wish to get well?"

7 [a]John 5:4

7 The sick man answered Him, "Sir, I have no man to put me into the pool when [a]the water is stirred up, but while I am coming, another steps down before me."

★ 8 [a]Matt. 9:6; Mark 2:11; Luke 5:24
9 [a]John 9:14

8 Jesus *said to him, "[a]Arise, take up your pallet, and walk."

9 And immediately the man became well, and took up his pallet and *began* to walk.

[a]Now it was the Sabbath on that day.

2 *The reaction,* 5:10-18

★10 [a]John 1:19; 5:15, 16, 18 [b]Neh. 13:19; Jer. 17:21f.; Matt. 12:2; John 7:23; 9:16

10 Therefore [a]the Jews were saying to him who was cured, "It is the Sabbath, and [b]it is not permissible for you to carry your pallet."

11 But he answered them, "He who made me well was the one who said to me, 'Take up your pallet and walk.'"

12 They asked him, "Who is the man who said to you, 'Take up *your* pallet, and walk'?"

13 But he who was healed did not know who it was; for Jesus had slipped away while there was a crowd in *that* place.

14 [a]Mark 2:5; John 8:11 [b]Ezra 9:14

14 Afterward Jesus *found him in the temple, and said to him, "Behold, you have become well; do not [a]sin any more, [b]so that nothing worse may befall you."

★15 [a]John 1:19; 5:16, 18

15 The man went away, and told [a]the Jews that it was Jesus who had made him well.

16 [a]John 1:19; 5:10, 15, 18

16 And for this reason [a]the Jews were persecuting Jesus, because He was doing these things on the Sabbath.

★17

17 But He answered them, "My Father is working until now, and I Myself am working."

18 [a]John 1:19; 5:15, 16 [b]John 5:16; 7:1 [c]John 10:33; 19:7

18 For this cause therefore [a]the Jews [b]were seeking all the more to kill Him, because He not only was breaking the Sabbath,

---

5:2 *the sheep gate.* See Neh. 3:1; 12:39. *five porticoes.* I.e., colonnades or cloisters to shelter the sick.

5:3 *waiting for the moving of the waters.* This phrase and all of v. 4 are not found in some manuscripts.

5:8 *pallet.* The bed of the very poor.

5:10 *it is not permissible for you to carry your pallet.* Carrying furniture on the Sabbath was a kind of work which the rabbis taught that the fourth commandment prohibited.

5:15 *the Jews.* I.e., the Jewish authorities; here as in vv. 10, 16, 18.

5:17-47 In this important Christological passage, Jesus asserts His authority, which He bases on His special relation to the Father. The Jews were perfectly aware that Jesus was claiming full deity—equality with God (v. 18).

but also was calling God His own
Father, [c]making Himself equal
with God.

3 *The discourse,* 5:19-47

19 [a]John 5:30; 8:28; 12:49; 14:10

19 Jesus therefore answered
and was saying to them, "Truly,
truly, I say to you, [a]the Son can
do nothing of Himself, unless *it is*
something He sees the Father
doing; for whatever *the Father*
does, these things the Son also
does in like manner.

20 [a]John 3:35 [b]John 14:12

20 "[a]For the Father loves the
Son, and shows Him all things
that He Himself is doing; and
[b]greater works than these will He
show Him, that you may marvel.

★21 [a]Rom. 4:17; 8:11 [b]John 11:25

21 "For just as the Father raises
the dead and [a]gives them life,
even so [b]the Son also gives life to
whom He wishes.

22 [a]John 5:27; 9:39; Acts 10:42; 17:31

22 "For not even the Father
judges any one, but [a]He has given
all judgment to the Son,

23 [a]Luke 10:16; 1 John 2:23

23 in order that all may honor
the Son, even as they honor the
Father. [a]He who does not honor
the Son does not honor the Father
who sent Him.

24 [a]John 3:18; 12:44; 20:31; 1 John 5:13 [b]John 3:18 [c]1 John 3:14

24 "Truly, truly, I say to you,
he who hears My word, and [a]be-
lieves Him who sent Me, has eternal life, and [b]does not come into
judgment, but has [c]passed out of
death into life.

25 [a]John 4:21, 23; 5:28 [b]Luke 15:24 [c]John 6:60; 8:43, 47; 9:27

25 "Truly, truly, I say to you,
[a]an hour is coming and now is,
when [b]the dead shall hear the
voice of the Son of God; and
those who [c]hear shall live.

26 [a]John 1:4; 6:57

26 "For just as the Father has
life in Himself, even so He [a]gave
to the Son also to have life in
Himself;

27 [a]John 9:39; Acts 10:42; 17:31

27 and He gave Him authority to [a]execute judgment, because
He is *the* Son of Man.

28 [a]John 4:21 [b]John 11:24; 1 Cor. 15:52

28 "Do not marvel at this; for
[a]an hour is coming, in which [b]all
who are in the tombs shall hear
His voice,

29 [a]Dan. 12:2; Matt. 25:46; Acts 24:15

29 and shall come forth;
[a]those who did the good *deeds,* to
a resurrection of life, those who
committed the evil *deeds* to a resurrection of judgment.

30 [a]John 5:19 [b]John 8:16 [c]John 4:34; 6:38

30 "[a]I can do nothing on My
own initiative. As I hear, I judge;
and [b]My judgment is just, because I do not seek My own will,
but [c]the will of Him who sent Me.

★31 [a]John 8:14

31 "[a]If I *alone* bear witness of
Myself, My testimony is not true.

32 [a]John 5:37

32 "There is [a]another who
bears witness of Me; and I know
that the testimony which He
bears of Me is true.

33 [a]John 1:7

33 "You have sent to John, and
he [a]has borne witness to the
truth.

34 [a]John 5:32; 1 John 5:9

34 "But [a]the witness which I
receive is not from man; but I say
these things, that you may be
saved.

35 [a]2 Sam. 21:17; 2 Pet. 1:19 [b]Mark 1:5

35 "He was [a]the lamp that was
burning and was shining and you
[b]were willing to rejoice for a
while in his light.

36 [a]Matt. 11:4; John 2:23; 10:25, 38; 14:11; 15:24 [b]John 4:34 [c]John 3:17

36 "But the witness which I
have is greater than *that of* John;
for [a]the works which the Father
has given Me [b]to accomplish, the
very works that I do, bear witness
of Me, that the Father [c]has sent
Me.

37 [a]Luke 24:27; John 8:18

37 "And the Father who sent
Me, [a]He has borne witness of Me.
You have neither heard His voice
at any time, nor seen His form.

38 [a]1 John 2:14 [b]John 3:17

38 "And you do not have [a]His
word abiding in you, for you do
not believe Him whom He [b]sent.

★39 [a]John 7:52; Rom. 2:17ff. [b]Luke 24:25, 27; Acts 13:27

39 "[a]You search the Scriptures,
because you think that in them
you have eternal life; and it is
[b]these that bear witness of Me;

5:21-27 Christ's authority is seen in the spheres of resurrection (vv. 21, 25, 26) and judgment (vv. 22-23, 27). God will make Christ the judge in order that the Son may be honored. Those who believe will escape judgment (v. 24).

5:31 Here Christ acquiesces to the arguments of His opponents that His witness alone (without other witnesses) is not true. But He goes on to remind them that *another,* His Father, witnesses to the validity of His claims (vv. 32, 37). Other witnesses cited are John the Baptist (v. 33), His miracles (v. 36), the Scriptures (v. 39), and Moses (v. 46). In 8:14 He claims that His witness is indeed true.

5:39 *search the Scriptures.* This may be either a command or a statement of fact, probably the latter.

40 and you are unwilling to come to Me, that you may have life.

41 [a]John 5:44; 7:18

41 "[a]I do not receive glory from men;

42 but I know you, that you do not have the love of God in yourselves.

★43 [a]Matt. 24:5

43 "I have come in My Father's name, and you do not receive Me; [a]if another shall come in his own name, you will receive him.

44 [a]John 5:41 [b]Rom. 2:29 [c]John 17:3; 1 Tim. 1:17

44 "How can you believe, when you [a]receive glory from one another, and you do not seek [b]the glory that is from [c]the *one and* only God?

45 [a]John 9:28; Rom. 2:17ff.

45 "Do not think that I will accuse you before the Father; the one who accuses you is [a]Moses, in whom you have set your hope.

46 [a]Luke 24:27

46 "For if you believed Moses, you would believe Me; for [a]he wrote of Me.

47 [a]Luke 16:29, 31

47 "But [a]if you do not believe his writings, how will you believe My words?"

B At Passover Time in Galilee, 6:1-71

1 *The miraculous sign,* 6:1-21

★ 1 [a]John 6:1-13: *Matt. 14:13-21; Mark 6:32-44; Luke 9:10-17* [b]Matt. 4:18; Luke 5:1 [c]John 6:23; 21:1
2 [a]John 2:11

6 After these things [a]Jesus went away to the other side of [b]the Sea of Galilee (or [c]Tiberias).

2 And a great multitude was following Him, because they were seeing the [a]signs which He was performing on those who were sick.

3 [a]Matt. 5:1; John 6:15

3 And Jesus went up on [a]the mountain, and there He sat with His disciples.

4 [a]John 2:13

4 Now [a]the Passover, the feast of the Jews, was at hand.

5 Jesus therefore lifting up His eyes, and seeing that a great multitude was coming to Him, *said to [a]Philip, "Where are we to buy bread, that these may eat?"

5 [a]John 1:43

6 And this He was saying to [a]test him; for He Himself knew what He was intending to do.

6 [a]Compare 2 Cor. 13:5 and Rev. 2:2 in Gr.

7 [a]Philip answered Him, "[b]Two hundred denarii worth of bread is not sufficient for them, for every one to receive a little."

★ 7 [a]John 1:43 [b]Mark 6:37

8 One of His [a]disciples, [b]Andrew, Simon Peter's brother, *said to Him,

8 [a]John 2:2 [b]John 1:40

9 "There is a lad here, who has five barley loaves, and two [a]fish; but what are these for so many people?"

★ 9 [a]John 6:11; 21:9, 10, 13

10 Jesus said, "Have the people sit down." Now there was [a]much grass in the place. So the men sat down, in number about [b]five thousand.

10 [a]Mark 6:39; John 6:4 [b]Matt. 14:21

11 Jesus therefore took the loaves; and [a]having given thanks, He distributed to those who were seated; likewise also of the [b]fish as much as they wanted.

11 [a]Matt. 15:36; John 6:23 [b]John 6:9; 21:9, 10, 13

12 And when they were filled, He *said to His [a]disciples, "Gather up the leftover fragments that nothing may be lost."

12 [a]John 2:2

13 And so they gathered them up, and filled twelve [a]baskets with fragments from the five barley loaves, which were left over by those who had eaten.

13 [a]Matt. 14:20

14 When therefore the people saw the sign which He had performed, they said, "This is of a truth the [a]Prophet who is to come into the world."

★14 [a]Matt. 11:3; 21:11; John 1:21

15 Jesus therefore perceiving that they were intending to come and take Him by force, [a]to make

★15 [a]John 18:36f. [b]John 6:15-21: *Matt. 14:22-33; Mark 6:45-51* [c]John 6:3

5:43 *in My Father's name.* I.e., as His representative. Though you won't follow Me, Christ says, you will, ironically, follow false Messiahs—which the Jews did periodically until finally crushed by Rome in A.D. 135.

6:1 *Sea of Galilee.* An earlier name for this lake was Gennesaret; later it was called *Galilee,* and finally *Tiberias,* after the city built on its shore by Herod Antipas in honor of the Roman emperor Tiberius.

6:7 *Two hundred denarii.* For the denarius, see note on Matt. 20:2.

6:9 *barley loaves.* The cheap food of the common people.

6:14 *the Prophet.* See Deut. 18:15 and John 1:21.

6:15 *to make Him king.* Jesus had to escape from the enthusiasm of the crowd, which would have forced Him to lead them in revolt against the Roman government. Jesus refused to become a political revolutionist.

Him king, [b]withdrew again to
[c]the mountain by Himself alone.
16 [a]John 2:2 **16** Now when evening came,
His [a]disciples went down to the
sea,
17 [a]Mark 6:45; John 6:24, 59 **17** and after getting into a
boat, they *started to* cross the sea
[a]to Capernaum. And it had already become dark, and Jesus had
not yet come to them.
18 And the sea *began* to be
stirred up because a strong wind
was blowing.
19 When therefore they had
rowed about three or four miles,
they *beheld Jesus walking on the
sea and drawing near to the boat;
and they were frightened.
20 [a]Matt. 14:27 **20** But He *said to them, "It is
I; [a]do not be afraid."
21 They were willing therefore to receive Him into the boat;
and immediately the boat was at
the land to which they were
going.

2 *The discourse,* 6:22-40

22 [a]John 6:2 [b]John 6:15ff. **22** The next day [a]the multitude that stood on the other side
of the sea saw that there was no
other small boat there, except
one, and that Jesus [b]had not entered with His disciples into the
boat, but *that* His disciples had
gone away alone.
23 [a]John 6:1 [b]Luke 7:13 [c]John 6:11 **23** There came other small
boats from [a]Tiberias near to the
place where they ate the bread after the [b]Lord [c]had given thanks.
24 [a]Matt. 14:34; Mark 6:53; John 6:17, 59 **24** When the multitude therefore saw that Jesus was not there,
nor His disciples, they themselves
got into the small boats, and
[a]came to Capernaum, seeking
Jesus.
25 [a]Matt. 23:7 **25** And when they found Him
on the other side of the sea, they
said to Him, "[a]Rabbi, when did
You get here?"
26 [a]John 6:24 [b]John 6:2, 14, 30 **26** Jesus answered them and
said, "Truly, truly, I say to you,
you [a]seek Me, not because you
saw [b]signs, but because you ate of
the loaves, and were filled.
27 "Do not [a]work for the food 27 [a]Is. 55:2 [b]John 3:15f.; 4:14; 6:40, 47, 54; 10:28; 17:2f. [c]Matt. 8:20; John 6:53, 62 [d]John 3:33
which perishes, but for the food
which endures to [b]eternal life,
which [c]the Son of Man shall give
to you, for on Him the Father,
even God, [d]has set His seal."
28 They said therefore to
Him, "What shall we do, that we
may work the works of God?"
29 Jesus answered and said to ★29 [a]1 Thess. 1:3; James 2:22; 1 John 3:23; Rev. 2:26 [b]John 3:17
them, "This is [a]the work of God,
that you believe in Him whom He
[b]has sent."
30 They said therefore to
Him, "[a]What then do You do for 30 [a]Matt. 12:38 [b]John 6:2, 14, 26
a [b]sign, that we may see, and be-
lieve You? What work do You
perform?
31 "[a]Our fathers ate the man- ★31 [a]Ex. 16:21; Num. 11:8; John 6:49, 58 [b]Ex. 16:4, 15; Neh. 9:15; Ps. 78:24; 105:40
na in the wilderness; as it is writ-
ten, '[b]HE GAVE THEM BREAD OUT OF
HEAVEN TO EAT.' "
32 Jesus therefore said to
them, "Truly, truly, I say to you,
it is not Moses who has given you
the bread out of heaven, but it is
My Father who gives you the true
bread out of heaven.
33 "For the bread of God is 33 [a]John 6:41, 50
that which [a]comes down out of
heaven, and gives life to the
world."
34 They said therefore to 34 [a]John 4:15
Him, "Lord, evermore [a]give us
this bread."
35 Jesus said to them, "[a]I am 35 [a]John 6:48, 51 [b]John 4:14
the bread of life; he who comes to
Me shall not hunger, and he who
believes in Me [b]shall never thirst.
36 "But [a]I said to you, that you 36 [a]John 6:26
have seen Me, and yet do not be-
lieve.
37 "[a]All that the Father gives 37 [a]John 6:39; 17:2, 24
Me shall come to Me; and the one 38 [a]John 3:13 [b]Matt. 26:39 [c]John 4:34; 5:30 [d]John 6:29
who comes to Me I will certainly
not cast out.
38 "For [a]I have come down ★39 [a]John 6:37; 17:2, 24 [b]John 17:12; 18:9 [c]Matt. 10:15; John 6:40, 44, 54; 11:24
from heaven, [b]not to do My own
will, but [c]the will of Him who
[d]sent Me.
39 "And this is the will of Him

6:29 The only "work" that a man can do that is acceptable to God is to believe in Christ (cf. 1 John 3:23).

6:31 *manna.* See Ex. 16:15; Num. 11:8; Neh. 9:15.

6:39 It is the Father's will to preserve those who come to Christ.

who sent Me, that of [a]all that He
has given Me I [b]lose nothing, but
[c]raise it up on the last day.
40 "For this is the will of My
Father, that every one who [a]be-
holds the Son, and [b]believes in
Him, may have eternal life; and I
Myself will [c]raise him up on the
last day."

40 [a]John 12:45; 14:17, 19 [b]John 3:16 [c]Matt. 10:15; John 6:39, 44, 54; 11:24

3 *The reactions,* 6:41–71

41 [a]The Jews therefore were
grumbling about Him, because
He said, "I am the bread that
[b]came down out of heaven."
42 And they were saying, "[a]Is
not this Jesus, the son of Joseph,
whose father and mother [b]we
know? How does He now say, '[c]I
have come down out of heaven'?"
43 Jesus answered and said to
them, "Do not grumble among
yourselves.
44 "No one can come to Me,
unless the Father who sent Me
[a]draws him; and I will [b]raise him
up on the last day.
45 "It is written [a]in the prophets, '[b]AND THEY SHALL ALL BE
[c]TAUGHT OF GOD.' Every one who
has heard and learned from the
Father, comes to Me.
46 "[a]Not that any man has
seen the Father, except the One
who is from God; He has seen the
Father.
47 "Truly, truly, I say to you,
he who believes [a]has eternal life.
48 "[a]I am the bread of life.
49 "[a]Your fathers ate the manna in the wilderness, and they
died.
50 "This is the bread which
[a]comes down out of heaven, so
that one may eat of it and [b]not
die.
51 "[a]I am the living bread that
[b]came down out of heaven; if any
one eats of this bread, [c]he shall
live forever; and the bread also
which I shall give [d]for the life of
the world is [e]My flesh."
52 [a]The Jews therefore [b]*began* to argue with one another,
saying, "How can this man give
us *His* flesh to eat?"
53 Jesus therefore said to
them, "Truly, truly, I say to you,
unless you eat the flesh of [a]the
Son of Man and drink His blood,
you have no life in yourselves.
54 "He who eats My flesh and
drinks My blood has eternal life;
and I will [a]raise him up on the last
day.
55 "For My flesh is true food,
and My blood is true drink.
56 "He who eats My flesh and
drinks My blood [a]abides in Me,
and I in him.
57 "As the [a]living Father [b]sent
Me, and I live because of the Father, so he who eats Me, he also
shall live because of Me.
58 "This is the bread which
[a]came down out of heaven; not as
[b]the fathers ate, and died, he who
eats this bread [c]shall live forever."
59 These things He said [a]in
the synagogue, as He taught [b]in
Capernaum.
60 Many therefore of His
[a]disciples, when they heard *this*
said, "[b]This is a difficult statement; who can listen to it?"
61 But Jesus, [a]conscious that
His disciples grumbled at this,
said to them, "Does this [b]cause
you to stumble?
62 "*What* then if you should
behold [a]the Son of Man [b]ascend-
ing where He was before?
63 "[a]It is the Spirit who gives
life; the flesh profits nothing; [b]the
words that I have spoken to you
are spirit and are life.
64 "But there are [a]some of you
who do not believe." For Jesus
[b]knew from the beginning who
they were who did not believe,

41 [a]John 1:19; 6:52 [b]John 6:33, 51, 58
42 [a]Luke 4:22 [b]John 7:27f. [c]John 6:38, 62
44 [a]Jer. 31:3; Hos. 11:4; John 6:65; 12:32 [b]John 6:39
★45 [a]Acts 7:42; 13:40; Heb. 8:11 [b]Is. 54:13; Jer. 31:34 [c]Phil. 3:15; 1 Thess. 4:9; 1 John 2:27
★46 [a]John 1:18
47 [a]John 3:36; 5:24; 6:51, 58; 11:26
48 [a]John 6:35, 51
49 [a]John 6:31, 58
50 [a]John 6:33 [b]John 3:36; 5:24; 6:47, 51, 58; 11:26
★51 [a]John 6:35, 48 [b]John 6:41, 58 [c]John 3:36; 5:24; 6:47, 58; 11:26 [d]John 1:29; 3:14f.; Heb. 10:10; 1 John 4:10 [e]John 6:53-56
52 [a]John 1:19; 6:41 [b]John 9:16; 10:19
★53 [a]Matt. 8:20; John 6:27, 62
★54 [a]John 6:39
56 [a]John 15:4f.; 17:23; 1 John 2:24; 3:24; 4:15f.
57 [a]Matt. 16:16; John 5:26 [b]John 3:17; 6:29, 38
58 [a]John 6:33, 41, 51 [b]John 6:31, 49 [c]John 3:36; 5:24; 6:47, 51; 11:26
59 [a]Matt. 4:23 [b]John 6:24
★60 [a]John 2:2; 6:66; 7:3 [b]John 6:52
61 [a]John 6:64 [b]Matt. 11:6
62 [a]Matt. 8:20; John 6:27, 53 [b]Mark 16:19; John 3:13
★63 [a]2 Cor. 3:6 [b]John 6:68
64 [a]John 6:60, 66 [b]John 2:25 [c]Matt. 10:4; John 6:71; 13:11

6:45 See Isa. 54:13.
6:46 On seeing God, see note on 1:18.
6:51 *the bread . . . which I shall give.* A reference to His sacrificial death on the cross.
6:53–56 Just as one eats and drinks in order to have physical life, so it is necessary to appropriate Christ in order to have eternal life.
6:54 *has eternal life.* I.e., already has it, and so can count on being raised.
6:60 *listen to it.* I.e., accept it.
6:63 *profits nothing.* I.e., is of no account.

and [c]who it was that would betray Him.
65 And He was saying, "For
this reason I have [a]said to you,
that no one can come to Me, unless [b]it has been granted him
from the Father."
66 As a result of this many of
His [a]disciples [b]withdrew, and
were not walking with Him any
more.
67 Jesus said therefore to [a]the
twelve, "You do not want to go
away also, do you?"
68 [a]Simon Peter answered
Him, "Lord, to whom shall we go?
You have [b]words of eternal life.
69 "And we have believed and
have come to know that You are
[a]the Holy One of God."
70 Jesus answered them,
"[a]Did I Myself not choose you,
[b]the twelve, and *yet* one of you is
[c]a devil?"
71 Now He meant Judas [a]*the*
son of Simon Iscariot, for he, [b]one
of [c]the twelve, was going to betray Him.

65 aJohn 6:37, 44 bMatt 13:11; John 3:27
66 aJohn 2:2; 7:3 bJohn 6:60, 64
67 aMatt 10:2; John 2:2; 6:70f.; 20:24
68 aMatt 16:16 bJohn 6:63; 12:49f.; 17:8
69 aMark 1:24
70 aJohn 15:16, 19 bMatt 10:2; John 2:2; 6:71; 20:24 cJohn 8:44; 13:2, 27; 17:12
71 aJohn 12:4; 13:2, 26 bMark 14:10 cMatt 10:2; John 2:2; 6:70f.; 20:24

C At the Feast of Booths in Jerusalem, 7:1–10:21

1 *Debate #1—the discourse,* 7:1–29

7 And after these things Jesus
[a]was walking in Galilee; for
He was unwilling to walk in Judea, because [b]the Jews [c]were
seeking to kill Him.
2 Now the feast of the Jews,
[a]the Feast of Booths, was at hand.
3 His [a]brothers therefore
said to Him, "Depart from here,
and go into Judea, that Your [b]dis-
ciples also may behold Your
works which You are doing.
4 "For no one does anything
in secret, when he himself seeks
to be *known* publicly. If You do
these things, show Yourself to the
world."
5 For not even His [a]brothers
were believing in Him.
6 Jesus therefore *said to
them, "[a]My time is not yet at
hand; but your time is always opportune.
7 "[a]The world cannot hate
you; but it hates Me, because I
testify of it, that [b]its deeds are
evil.
8 "Go up to the feast yourselves; I do not go up to this feast
because [a]My time has not yet fully come."
9 And having said these
things to them, He stayed in Galilee.
10 But when His [a]brothers
had gone up to the feast, then He
Himself also went up, not publicly, but as it were, in secret.
11 [a]The Jews therefore [b]were
seeking Him at the feast, and
were saying, "Where is He?"
12 And there was much
grumbling among the multitudes
concerning Him; [a]some were saying, "He is a good man"; others
were saying, "No, on the contrary, He leads the multitude
astray."
13 Yet no one was speaking
openly of Him for [a]fear of the
Jews.
14 But when it was now the
midst of the feast Jesus went up
into the temple, and *began to*
[a]teach.
15 [a]The Jews therefore were
marveling, saying, "How has this
man [b]become learned, having
never been educated?"
16 Jesus therefore answered
them, and said, "[a]My teaching is
not Mine, but His who sent Me.
17 "[a]If any man is willing to do

1 aJohn 4:3; 6:1; 11:54 bJohn 1:19; 7:11, 13, 15, 35 cJohn 5:18; 7:19; 8:37, 40; 11:53
★ 2 aLev 23:34; Deut 16:16; Zech 14:16-19
3 aMatt 12:46; Mark 3:21; John 7:5, 10 bJohn 6:60
5 aMatt 12:46; Mark 3:21; John 7:3, 10
★ 6 aMatt 26:18; John 2:4; 7:8, 30
★ 7 aJohn 15:18f bJohn 3:19f
8 aJohn 7:6
10 aMatt 12:46; Mark 3:21; John 7:3, 5
11 aJohn 7:13, 15, 35 bJohn 11:56
12 aJohn 7:40-43
★13 aJohn 9:22; 12:42; 19:38; 20:19
14 aMatt 26:55; John 7:28
★15 aJohn 1:19; 7:11, 13, 35 bActs 26:24 [Gr.]
16 aJohn 3:11
★17 aPs 25:9, 14; Prov 3:32; Dan 12:10; John 3:21; 8:43f

7:2 *Feast of Booths.* This was one of the three pilgrimage festivals of the Jewish year, occurring in the autumn after harvest. The Jews dwelt in booths made of the boughs of trees for the seven days of the festival.

7:6 *your time is always opportune.* I.e., it doesn't make any difference when you go.

7:7 The world rejected Jesus because His words and acts were a witness against its evil deeds.

7:13 *the Jews.* Since *the multitude* (v. 12) were all Jews, here the Jewish authorities must be meant.

7:15 *having never been educated.* Jesus was not trained in the rabbinical schools (Acts 4:13).

7:17 The thought is: Anyone who does God's will will be able to judge the authority of My teaching.

His will, he shall know of the teaching, whether it is of God, or *whether* I speak from Myself.

18 [a]John 5:41; 8:50, 54; 12:43

18 "He who speaks from himself [a]seeks his own glory; but He who is seeking the glory of the one who sent Him, He is true, and there is no unrighteousness in Him.

19 [a]John 1:17 [b]Mark 11:18; John 7:1

19 "[a]Did not Moses give you the law, and *yet* none of you carries out the law? Why do you [b]seek to kill Me?"

★20 [a]Matt. 11:18; John 8:48f., 52; 10:20

20 The multitude answered, "[a]You have a demon! Who seeks to kill You?"

★21 [a]John 5:2-9, 16; 7:23

21 Jesus answered and said to them, "I did [a]one deed, and you all marvel.

22 [a]Lev. 12:3 [b]Gen. 17:10ff.; 21:4; Acts 7:8

22 "On this account [a]Moses has given you circumcision (not because it is from Moses, but from [b]the fathers); and on *the* Sabbath you circumcise a man.

★23 [a]Matt. 12:2; John 5:10

23 "[a]If a man receives circumcision on *the* Sabbath that the Law of Moses may not be broken, are you angry with Me because I made an entire man well on *the* Sabbath?

24 [a]Lev. 19:15; Is. 11:3; Zech. 7:9; John 8:15

24 "Do not [a]judge according to appearance, but judge with righteous judgment."

25 Therefore some of the people of Jerusalem were saying, "Is this not the man whom they are seeking to kill?

26 [a]Luke 23:13; John 3:1

26 "And look, He is speaking publicly, and they are saying nothing to Him. [a]The rulers do not really know that this is the Christ, do they?

★27 [a]John 6:42; 7:41f.; 9:29

27 "However [a]we know where this man is from; but whenever the Christ may come, no one knows where He is from."

★28 [a]John 7:14 [b]John 6:42; 7:14f.; 9:29 [c]John 8:42

28 Jesus therefore cried out in the temple, [a]teaching and saying, "[b]You both know Me, and know where I am from; and [c]I have not come of Myself, but He who sent Me is true, whom you do not know.

29 [a]Matt. 11:27; John 8:55; 17:25 [b]John 6:46 [c]John 3:17

29 "[a]I know Him; because [b]I am from Him, and [c]He sent Me."

2 *The reactions,* 7:30-36

30 [a]Matt. 21:46; John 7:32, 44; 10:39 [b]John 7:6; 8:20

30 They [a]were seeking therefore to seize Him; and no man laid his hand on Him, because His [b]hour had not yet come.

31 [a]John 2:23; 8:30; 10:42; 11:45; 12:11, 42 [b]John 7:26 [c]John 2:11

31 But [a]many of the multitude believed in Him; and they were saying, "[b]When the Christ shall come, He will not perform more [c]signs than those which this man has, will He?"

32 [a]Matt. 26:58; John 7:45f. [b]Matt. 12:14

32 The Pharisees heard the multitude muttering these things about Him; and the chief priests and the Pharisees sent [a]officers to [b]seize Him.

33 [a]John 12:35; 13:33; 14:19; 16:16-19 [b]John 14:12, 28; 16:5, 10, 17, 28; 20:17

33 Jesus therefore said, "[a]For a little while longer I am with you, then [b]I go to Him who sent Me.

★34 [a]John 7:36; 8:21; 13:33

34 "[a]You shall seek Me, and shall not find Me; and where I am, you cannot come."

35 [a]John 7:1 [b]John 8:22 [c]Ps. 147:2; Is. 11:12; 56:8; Zeph. 3:10; James 1:1; 1 Pet. 1:1 [d]John 12:20; Acts 14:1; 17:4; 18:4; Rom. 1:16

35 [a]The Jews therefore said to one another, "[b]Where does this man intend to go that we shall not find Him? He is not intending to go to [c]the Dispersion among [d]the Greeks, and teach the Greeks, is He?

36 [a]John 7:34; 8:21; 13:33

36 "What is this statement that He said, '[a]You will seek Me, and will not find Me; and where I am, you cannot come'?"

3 *Debate #2—the discourse,* 7:37-39

★37 [a]Lev. 23:36; Num. 29:35; Neh. 8:18 [b]John 4:10, 14; 6:35

37 Now on [a]the last day, the great *day* of the feast, Jesus stood

---

7:20 *a demon.* See Mark 3:22. The question of the last half of this verse seems strange in light of 5:18.

7:21 The *one deed* which, at this time, most turned the authorities against Him was the healing of the man on the Sabbath day (5:1-9).

7:23 If circumcision be allowed on the Sabbath (Lev. 12:3), should not also a deed of mercy like the healing of a whole man?

7:27 A popular idea associated with the coming of Messiah was that He would be a man of mystery, coming out of nowhere. Jesus was known to have come from Nazareth and so did not fulfill the requirement.

7:28 Christ says, in effect, If you knew God, you would recognize Me.

7:34 The Jewish authorities would die in their sins (8:24) and so could not come to be with Him in heaven.

7:37-39 Though it is not mentioned in the O.T.,

and cried out, saying, "[b]If any
man is thirsty, let him come to
Me and drink.
38 "He who believes in Me, [a]as
the Scripture said, 'From his innermost being shall flow rivers of
[b]living water.' "
39 But this He spoke [a]of the
Spirit, whom those who believed
in Him were to receive; for [b]the
Spirit was not yet *given,* because
Jesus was not yet [c]glorified.

★38 [a]Is. 44:3; 55:1; 58:11 [b]John 4:10
★39 [a]Joel 2:28; John 1:33 [b]John 20:22; Acts 1:4f.; 2:4, 33; 19:2 [c]John 12:16, 23; 13:31f.; 16:14; 17:1

4 *The reactions,* 7:40-53

40 *Some* of the multitude
therefore, when they heard these
words, were saying, "This certainly is [a]the Prophet."
41 Others were saying, "This
is the Christ." Still others were
saying, "[a]Surely the Christ is not
going to come from Galilee, is He?
42 "Has not the Scripture said
that the Christ comes from [a]the
offspring of David, and from
Bethlehem, the village where David was?"
43 So [a]there arose a division
in the multitude because of Him.
44 And [a]some of them
wanted to seize Him, but no one
laid hands on Him.
45 The [a]officers therefore
came to the chief priests and
Pharisees, and they said to them,
"Why did you not bring Him?"
46 The [a]officers answered,
"[b]Never did a man speak the way
this man speaks."
47 The Pharisees therefore
answered them, "[a]You have not
also been led astray, have you?
48 "[a]No one of [b]the rulers or
Pharisees has believed in Him,
has he?
49 "But this multitude which
does not know the Law is accursed."
50 [a]Nicodemus *said to them
(he who came to Him before,
being one of them),
51 "[a]Our Law does not judge a
man, unless it first hears from
him and knows what he is doing,
does it?"
52 They answered and said to
him, "[a]You are not also from
Galilee, are you? Search, and see
that no prophet arises out of Galilee."
53 [And everyone went to his
home.

40 [a]Matt. 21:11; John 1:21
41 [a]John 1:46; 7:52
★42 [a]Ps. 89:4; Mic. 5:2; Matt. 1:1; 2:5f.; Luke 2:4ff.
★43 [a]John 9:16; 10:19
44 [a]John 7:30
45 [a]John 7:32
46 [a]John 7:32 [b]Matt. 7:28
47 [a]John 7:12
48 [a]John 12:42 [b]Luke 23:13; John 7:26
★49
50 [a]John 3:1; 19:39
51 [a]Ex. 23:1; Deut. 17:6; 19:15; Prov. 18:13; Acts 23:3
52 [a]John 1:46; 7:41
★53

5 *Debate #3—the discourses,* 8:1-58

8 But Jesus went to [a]the Mount
of Olives.
2 And early in the morning
He came again into the temple,
and all the people were coming to
Him; and [a]He sat down and *began* to teach them.
3 And the scribes and the
Pharisees *brought a woman
caught in adultery, and having set
her in the midst,
4 they *said to Him,
"Teacher, this woman has been
caught in adultery, in the very act.
5 "Now in the Law [a]Moses
commanded us to stone such
women; what then do You say?"
6 And they were saying this,
[a]testing Him, [b]in order that they
might have grounds for accusing

1 [a]Matt. 21:1
2 [a]Matt. 26:55; John 8:20
★ 5 [a]Lev. 20:10; Deut. 22:22f.
6 [a]Matt. 16:1; 19:3; 22:18, 35; Mark 8:11; 10:2; 12:15; Luke 10:25; 11:16 [b]Mark 3:2

---

the Jews had a ceremony of carrying water from the Pool of Siloam and pouring it into a silver basin by the altar of burnt offering each day for the first seven days of the Feast of Tabernacles. On the eighth day this was not done, making Christ's offer of the water of eternal life from Himself even more startling.

7:38 *innermost being.* The O.T. reference is probably to Isa. 55:1.

7:39 *was not yet given.* Though the Spirit had been active in the world from the beginning (Gen. 1:2), the epoch of the Spirit, in which He would indwell God's people, empowering and energizing them, would not begin until the day of Pentecost (see 14:26; 15:26; 16:7).

7:42 *offspring of David.* See 2 Sam. 7:12. *Bethlehem.* See Mic. 5:2.

7:43 *So there arose a division.* John records three occasions of division regarding Christ: here concerning His person; in 9:16 concerning His power; and in 10:19 concerning His passion.

7:49 *this multitude.* I.e., the crowd, the *am ha-arez,* the people of the land, whom the Pharisees despised because they no longer observed the minutiae of the Jewish law.

7:53-8:11 This story, though probably authentic, is omitted in many manuscripts and may not have been originally a part of this Gospel.

8:5 See Lev. 20:10; Deut. 22:22-24.

Him. But Jesus stooped down, and
with His finger wrote on the
ground.
7 But when they persisted in
asking Him, [a]He straightened up,
and said to them, "[b]He who is
without sin among you, let him
be the [c]first to throw a stone at
her."
8 And again He stooped
down, and wrote on the ground.
9 And when they heard it,
they *began* to go out one by one,
beginning with the older ones,
and He was left alone, and the
woman, *where she had been,* in
the midst.
10 And [a]straightening up,
Jesus said to her, "Woman, where
are they? Did no one condemn
you?"
11 And she said, "No one,
Lord." And Jesus said, "[a]Neither
do I condemn you; go your way;
from now on [b]sin no more."]
12 Again therefore Jesus
spoke to them, saying, "[a]I am the
light of the world; [b]he who follows Me shall not walk in the
darkness, but shall have the light
of life."
13 The Pharisees therefore
said to Him, "[a]You are bearing
witness of Yourself; Your witness
is not true."
14 Jesus answered and said to
them, "[a]Even if I bear witness of
Myself, My witness is true; for I
know [b]where I came from, and
where I am going; but [c]you do not
know where I come from, or
where I am going.
15 "[a]You people judge according to the flesh; [b]I am not judging
any one.
16 "But even [a]if I do judge, My
judgment is true; for I am not
alone *in it,* but I and He who sent
Me.
17 "Even in [a]your law it has

7 [a]John 8:10 [b]Matt. 7:1; Rom. 2:1 [c]Deut. 17:7
10 [a]John 8:7
11 [a]John 3:17 [b]John 5:14
★12 [a]John 1:4; 12:35 [b]Matt. 5:14
13 [a]John 5:31
★14 [a]John 18:37; Rev. 1:5; 3:14 [b]John 8:42; 13:3; 16:28 [c]John 7:28; 9:29
15 [a]1 Sam. 16:7; John 7:24 [b]John 3:17
16 [a]John 5:30
17 [a]Deut. 17:6; 19:15 [b]Matt. 18:16

been written, that the testimony
of [b]two men is true.
18 "I am He who bears witness
of Myself, and [a]the Father who
sent Me bears witness of Me."
19 And so they were saying to
Him, "Where is Your Father?"
Jesus answered, "You know neither Me, nor My Father; [a]if you
knew Me, you would know My
Father also."
20 These words He spoke in
[a]the treasury, as [b]He taught in the
temple; and no one seized Him,
because [c]His hour had not yet
come.
21 He said therefore again to
them, "I go away, and [a]you shall
seek Me, and [b]shall die in your
sin; where I am going, you cannot
come."
22 Therefore [a]the Jews were
saying, "Surely He will not kill
Himself, will He, since He says,
'[b]Where I am going, you cannot
come'?"
23 And He was saying to
them, "[a]You are from below, I am
from above; [b]you are of this
world; [c]I am not of this world.
24 "I said therefore to you, that
you [a]shall die in your sins; for unless you believe that [b]I am *He,*
[a]you shall die in your sins."
25 And so they were saying to
Him, "Who are You?" Jesus said
to them, "What have I been saying to you *from* the beginning?
26 "I have many things to
speak and to judge concerning
you, but [a]He who sent Me is true;
and [b]the things which I heard
from Him, these I speak to the
world."
27 They did not realize that
He had been speaking to them
about the Father.
28 Jesus therefore said,
"When you [a]lift up the Son of
Man, then you will know that [b]I
am *He,* and [c]I do nothing on My

18 [a]John 5:37; 1 John 5:9
19 [a]John 7:28; 8:55; 14:7, 9; 16:3
20 [a]Mark 12:41, 43; Luke 21:1 [b]John 7:14; 8:2 [c]John 7:30
21 [a]John 7:34 [b]John 8:24
22 [a]John 1:19; 8:48, 52, 57 [b]John 7:35
23 [a]John 3:31 [b]1 John 4:5 [c]John 17:14, 16
★24 [a]John 8:21 [b]Mark 13:6; Luke 21:8 [Matt. 24:5]; John 4:26; 8:28; 13:19
26 [a]John 3:33; 7:28 [b]John 8:40; 12:49; 15:15
28 [a]John 3:14; 12:32 [b]Mark 13:6; Luke 21:8 [Matt. 24:5]; John 4:26; 8:24; 13:19 [c]John 3:11; 5:19

8:12 *I am the light of the world.* Our Lord here draws an analogy between the sun as the physical light of the world and Himself as the spiritual light of the world (see 9:4–5; 11:9–10). This theme also permeates chapter 9.

8:14 *Even if.* Even, Christ says, if I am testifying about Myself, My testimony is to be believed and trusted. Furthermore, My testimony is attested to by the Father (v. 18).

8:24 This remark doubtlessly infuriated the Jewish authorities, since it ranked them with sinners.

own initiative, but I speak these
things as the Father taught Me.
29 "And He who sent Me is
with Me; [a]He has not left Me
alone, for [b]I always do the things
that are pleasing to Him."
30 As He spoke these things,
[a]many came to believe in Him.
31 Jesus therefore was saying
to those Jews who had believed
Him, "[a]If you abide in My word,
then you are truly [b]disciples of
Mine;
32 and [a]you shall know the
truth, and [b]the truth shall make
you free."
33 They answered Him, "[a]We
are Abraham's offspring, and
have never yet been enslaved to
anyone; how is it that You say,
'You shall become free'?"
34 Jesus answered them,
"Truly, truly, I say to you, [a]every
one who commits sin is the slave
of sin.
35 "And [a]the slave does not remain in the house forever; [b]the
son does remain forever.
36 "If therefore the Son [a]shall
make you free, you shall be free
indeed.
37 "I know that you are [a]Abra-
ham's offspring; yet [b]you seek to
kill Me, because My word has no
place in you.
38 "I speak the things which I
have seen with *My* Father; therefore you also do the things which
you heard from [a]*your* father."
39 They answered and said to
Him, "Abraham is [a]our father."
Jesus *said to them, "[b]If you are
Abraham's children, do the deeds
of Abraham.
40 "But as it is, [a]you are seeking to kill Me, a man who has
[b]told you the truth, which I heard

29 [a]John 8:16; 16:32 [b]John 4:34
30 [a]John 7:31
31 [a]John 15:7; 2 John 9 [b]John 2:2
★**32** [a]John 1:14, 17 [b]John 8:36; Rom. 8:2; 2 Cor. 3:17; Gal. 5:1, 13; James 2:12; 1 Pet. 2:16
33 [a]Matt. 3:9; John 8:37, 39
34 [a]Rom. 6:16; 2 Pet. 2:19
35 [a]Gen. 21:10; Gal. 4:30 [b]Luke 15:31
36 [a]John 8:32
37 [a]Matt. 3:9; John 8:39 [b]John 7:1; 8:40
38 [a]John 8:41, 44
★**39** [a]Matt. 3:9; John 8:37 [b]Rom. 9:7; Gal. 3:7
40 [a]John 7:1; 8:37 [b]John 8:26

from God; this Abraham did not
do.
41 "You are doing the deeds of
[a]your father." They said to Him,
"We were not born of fornication;
[b]we have one Father, *even* God."
42 Jesus said to them, "If God
were your Father, [a]you would
love Me; [b]for I proceeded forth
and have come from God, for I
have [c]not even come on My own
initiative, but [d]He sent Me.
43 "Why do you not understand [a]what I am saying? *It is* because you cannot [b]hear My word.
44 "[a]You are of [b]*your* father
the devil, and [c]you want to do the
desires of your father. [d]He was a
murderer from the beginning,
and does not stand in the truth,
because [e]there is no truth in him.
Whenever he speaks a lie, he
[f]speaks from his own *nature;* for
he is a liar, and the father of lies.
45 "But because [a]I speak the
truth, you do not believe Me.
46 "Which one of you convicts
Me of sin? If [a]I speak truth, why
do you not believe Me?
47 "[a]He who is of God hears
the words of God; for this reason
you do not hear *them,* because
you are not of God."
48 [a]The Jews answered and
said to Him, "Do we not say
rightly that You are a [b]Samaritan
and [c]have a demon?"
49 Jesus answered, "I do not
[a]have a demon; but I honor My
Father, and you dishonor Me.
50 "But [a]I do not seek My glory; there is One who seeks and
judges.
51 "Truly, truly, I say to you, if
anyone [a]keeps My word he shall
never [b]see death."

41 [a]John 8:38, 44 [b]Deut. 32:6; Is. 63:16; 64:8
42 [a]1 John 5:1 [b]John 13:3; 16:28, 30; 17:8 [c]John 7:28 [d]John 3:17
★**43** [a]John 8:33, 39, 41 [b]John 5:25
★**44** [a]1 John 3:8 [b]John 8:38, 41 [c]John 7:17 [d]Gen. 3:4; 1 John 3:8, 15 [e]1 John 2:4 [f]Matt. 12:34
45 [a]John 18:37
46 [a]John 18:37
47 [a]1 John 4:6
48 [a]John 1:19 [b]Matt. 10:5; John 4:9 [c]John 7:20
49 [a]John 7:20
50 [a]John 5:41; 8:54
★**51** [a]John 8:55; 14:23; 15:20; 17:6 [b]Matt. 16:28; Luke 2:26; John 8:52; Heb. 2:9; 11:5

8:32 *the truth.* I.e., of the divine revelation, not some current Gnostic truth about the cosmos, the soul, its relation to the body, etc.

8:39 *If you are Abraham's children.* The Jews were the natural descendants of Abraham (vv. 33, 37) but, because of their unbelief, not all were spiritual descendants. The father of all unbelievers is the devil (v. 44; see also Eph. 2:2–3; 1 John 3:8–10).

8:43 *cannot hear.* I.e., do not wish to, cannot bear to, accept His teaching. It is not a matter of intellectual capacity but of inner response.

8:44 The true reason for their failure to receive Christ was their relationship to the devil. Notice a similar harsh condemnation in Matt. 23:15.

8:51 *he shall never see death.* The believer shall not see spiritual death (separation from God), because through faith he possesses spiritual life (5:24). It may also have the meaning that he shall not see death forever; that is, though the believer dies physically, this death is only temporary, being eventually overcome by the resurrection of the body.

52 [a]John 1:19 [b]John 7:20 [c]John 8:55; 14:23; 15:20; 17:6 [d]John 8:51

52 [a]The Jews said to Him,
"Now we know that You [b]have a
demon. Abraham died, and the
prophets *also;* and You say, 'If
anyone [c]keeps My word, he shall
never [d]taste of death.'

53 [a]John 4:12

53 "Surely You [a]are not
greater than our father Abraham,
who died? The prophets died too;
whom do You make Yourself out
to be?"

54 [a]John 8:50 [b]John 7:39

54 Jesus answered, "[a]If I glorify Myself, My glory is nothing;
[b]it is My Father who glorifies Me,
of whom you say, 'He is our God';

55 [a]John 8:19; 15:21 [b]John 7:29 [c]John 8:44 [d]John 8:51; 15:10

55 and [a]you have not come to
know Him, [b]but I know Him; and
if I say that I do not know Him, I
shall be [c]a liar like you, [b]but I do
know Him, and [d]keep His word.

56 [a]John 8:37, 39 [b]Matt. 13:17; Heb. 11:13

56 "[a]Your father Abraham [b]re-
joiced to see My day; and he saw
it, and was glad."

57 [a]John 1:19

57 [a]The Jews therefore said to
Him, "You are not yet fifty years
old, and have You seen Abraham?"

★58 [a]John 1:1; 17:5, 24

58 Jesus said to them, "Truly,
truly, I say to you, before Abraham was born, [a]I AM."

6 *The reaction,* 8:59

59 [a]Matt. 12:14; John 10:31; 11:8 [b]John 12:36

59 Therefore they [a]picked up
stones to throw at Him; but Jesus
[b]hid Himself, and went out of the
temple.

7 *Debate #4—the miraculous sign,* 9:1-12

★ 2 [a]Matt. 23:7 [b]Luke 13:2; John 9:34; Acts 28:4 [c]Ex. 20:5
3 [a]John 11:4

9 And as He passed by, He saw
a man blind from birth.
2 And His disciples asked
Him, saying, "[a]Rabbi, who
sinned, [b]this man or his [c]parents,
that he should be born blind?"
3 Jesus answered, "*It was*
neither *that* this man sinned, nor
his parents; but *it was* in order
[a]that the works of God might be
displayed in him.

4 [a]John 7:33; 11:9; 12:35; Gal. 6:10

4 "We must work the works
of Him who sent Me, [a]as long as
it is day; night is coming, when no
man can work.

5 [a]John 1:4; 8:12; 12:46
6 [a]Mark 7:33; 8:23

5 "While I am in the world, I
am [a]the light of the world."
6 When He had said this, He
[a]spat on the ground, and made
clay of the spittle, and applied the
clay to his eyes,

★ 7 [a]Luke 13:4; John 9:11 [b]John 11:37

7 and said to him, "Go, wash
in [a]the pool of Siloam" (which is
translated, Sent). And so he went
away and washed, and [b]came
back seeing.

8 [a]Acts 3:2, 10

8 The neighbors therefore,
and those who previously saw
him as a beggar, were saying, "Is
not this the one who used to [a]sit
and beg?"
9 Others were saying, "This
is he," *still* others were saying,
"No, but he is like him." He kept
saying, "I am the one."
10 Therefore they were saying to him, "How then were your
eyes opened?"

11 [a]John 9:7

11 He answered, "The man
who is called Jesus made clay, and
anointed my eyes, and said to me,
'Go to [a]Siloam, and wash'; so I
went away and washed, and I received sight."
12 And they said to him,
"Where is He?" He *said, "I do
not know."

8 *The reactions,* 9:13-41

13 They *brought to the
Pharisees him who was formerly
blind.

14 [a]John 5:9

14 [a]Now it was a Sabbath on
the day when Jesus made the clay,
and opened his eyes.

8:58 *before Abraham was born, I AM.* The "I AM" denotes absolute eternal existence, not simply existence prior to Abraham. It is a claim to be Yahweh of the O.T. That the Jews understood the significance of this claim is clear from their reaction (v. 59) to the supposed blasphemy.

9:2 Sickness and suffering were commonly held to be the consequences of one's sin. The religious problem became troublesome, however, when the victim was *born* with a handicap such as blindness. Jesus first corrected this false idea and then focused on the purpose of this particular suffering, which provided an occasion for revealing God's glory.

9:7 *pool of Siloam.* This lay at the southern extremity of the Tyropoeon Valley, at the southern end of Hezekiah's tunnel.

15 [a]John 9:10 **15** [a]Again, therefore, the Pharisees also were asking him how he received his sight. And he said to them, "He applied clay to my eyes, and I washed, and I see."

★16 [a]Matt. 12:2 [b]John 2:11 [c]John 6:52; 7:43; 10:19 **16** Therefore some of the Pharisees were saying, "[a]This man is not from God, because He does not keep the Sabbath." But others were saying, "How can a man who is a sinner perform such [b]signs?" And [c]there was a division among them.

17 [a]John 9:15 [b]Matt. 21:11 **17** They *said therefore to the blind man [a]again, "What do you say about Him, since He opened your eyes?" And he said, "He is a [b]prophet."

18 [a]John 1:19; 9:22 **18** [a]The Jews therefore did not believe *it* of him, that he had been blind, and had received sight, until they called the parents of the very one who had received his sight,

19 and questioned them, saying, "Is this your son, who you say was born blind? Then how does he now see?"

20 His parents answered them and said, "We know that this is our son, and that he was born blind;

21 but how he now sees, we do not know; or who opened his eyes, we do not know. Ask him; he is of age, he shall speak for himself."

★22 [a]John 7:13 [b]John 7:45-52 [c]Luke 6:22; John 12:42; 16:2 **22** His parents said this because they [a]were afraid of the Jews; for the Jews [b]had already agreed, that if any one should confess Him to be Christ, [c]he should be put out of the synagogue.

23 [a]John 9:21 **23** For this reason his parents said, "[a]He is of age; ask him."

24 [a]Josh. 7:19; Ezra 10:11; Rev. 11:13 [b]John 9:16 **24** So a second time they called the man who had been blind, and said to him, "[a]Give glory to God; we know that [b]this man is a sinner."

25 He therefore answered, "Whether He is a sinner, I do not know; one thing I do know, that, whereas I was blind, now I see."

26 They said therefore to him, "What did He do to you? How did He open your eyes?"

27 He answered them, "[a]I told you already, and you did not [b]listen; why do you want to hear *it* again? You do not want to become His disciples too, do you?" 27 [a]John 9:15 [b]John 5:25

28 And they reviled him, and said, "You are His disciple; but [a]we are disciples of Moses. 28 [a]John 5:45; Rom. 2:17

29 "We know that God has spoken to Moses; but as for this man, [a]we do not know where He is from." ★29 [a]John 8:14

30 The man answered and said to them, "Well, here is an amazing thing, that you do not know where He is from, and *yet* He opened my eyes.

31 "We know that [a]God does not hear sinners; but if any one is God-fearing, and does His will, He hears him. 31 [a]Job 27:8f.; 35:13; Ps. 34:15f.; 66:18; 145:19; Prov. 15:29; 28:9; Is. 1:15; James 5:16ff.

32 "Since the beginning of time it has never been heard that any one opened the eyes of a person born blind.

33 "[a]If this man were not from God, He could do nothing." 33 [a]John 3:2; 9:16

34 They answered and said to him, "[a]You were born entirely in sins, and are you teaching us?" And they [b]put him out. ★34 [a]John 9:2 [b]John 9:22, 35; 3 John 10

35 Jesus heard that they had [a]put him out; and finding him, He said, "Do you believe in the [b]Son of Man?" 35 [a]John 9:22, 34; 3 John 10 [b]Matt. 4:3

36 He answered and said, "And [a]who is He, Lord, that I may believe in Him?" 36 [a]Rom. 10:14

37 Jesus said to him, "You have both seen Him, and [a]He is the one who is talking with you." 37 [a]John 4:26

38 And he said, "Lord, I believe." And he [a]worshiped Him. 38 [a]Matt. 8:2

9:16 *He does not keep the Sabbath.* The Pharisees considered the making of clay (v. 14) a work that violated the Sabbath (see 5:10).

9:22 *be put out of the synagogue.* I.e., excommunicated from worship and fellowship.

9:29 A typical statement of Pharisaic orthodoxy. But the man refused to be coerced away from the plain fact that he had been cured (vv. 25, 30).

9:34 Their hostility now bordered on fanaticism.

39 And Jesus said, "[a]For judgment I came into this world, that
[b]those who do not see may see;
and that [c]those who see may become blind."
40 Those of the Pharisees
who were with Him heard these
things, and said to Him, "[a]We are
not blind too, are we?"
41 Jesus said to them, "[a]If you
were blind, you would have no
sin; but since you say, '[b]We see';
your sin remains.

9 Debate #5—the discourse on the Good Shepherd, 10:1–18

10 "Truly, truly, I say to you,
he who does not enter by
the door into the fold of the
sheep, but climbs up some other
way, he is [a]a thief and a robber.
2 "But he who enters by the
door is [a]a shepherd of the sheep.
3 "To him the doorkeeper
opens, and the sheep hear [a]his
voice, and he calls his own sheep
by name, and [b]leads them out.
4 "When he puts forth all his
own, he goes before them, and
the sheep follow him because
they know [a]his voice.
5 "And a stranger they simply
will not follow, but will flee from
him, because they do not know
[a]the voice of strangers."
6 This [a]figure of speech
Jesus spoke to them, but they did
not understand what those things
were which He had been saying
to them.
7 Jesus therefore said to
them again, "Truly, truly, I say to
you, I am [a]the door of the sheep.
8 "All who came before Me
are [a]thieves and robbers; but the
sheep did not hear them.
9 "[a]I am the door; if anyone
enters through Me, he shall be
saved, and shall go in and out,
and find pasture.
10 "The thief comes only to
steal, and kill, and destroy; I came
that they [a]might have life, and
might have *it* abundantly.
11 "[a]I am the good shepherd;
the good shepherd [b]lays down His
life for the sheep.
12 "He who is a hireling, and
not a [a]shepherd, who is not the
owner of the sheep, beholds the
wolf coming, and leaves the
sheep, and flees, and the wolf
snatches them, and scatters *them.*
13 *"He flees* because he is a
hireling, and is not concerned
about the sheep.
14 "[a]I am the good shepherd;
and [b]I know My own, and My
own know Me,
15 even as [a]the Father knows
Me and I know the Father; and [b]I
lay down My life for the sheep.
16 "And I have [a]other sheep,
which are not of this fold; I must
bring them also, and they shall
hear My voice; and they shall become [b]one flock *with* [c]one shepherd.
17 "For this reason the Father
loves Me, because I [a]lay down My
life that I may take it again.
18 "[a]No one has taken it away
from Me, but I [b]lay it down on
My own initiative. I have authority to lay it down, and I have authority to take it up again. [c]This
commandment I received from
My Father."

10 The reactions, 10:19–21

19 [a]There arose a division
again among the Jews because of
these words.
20 And many of them were

★39 [a]John 3:19; 5:22, 27 [b]Luke 4:18 [c]Matt. 13:13; 15:14
40 [a]Rom. 2:19
★41 [a]John 15:22, 24 [b]Prov. 26:12
1 [a]John 10:8
2 [a]John 10:11f.
3 [a]John 10:4f., 16, 27 [b]John 10:9
4 [a]John 10:5, 16, 27
5 [a]John 10:4f., 16, 27
6 [a]John 16:25, 29; 2 Pet. 2:22
7 [a]John 10:1f., 9
★8 [a]Jer. 23:1f.; Ezek. 34:2ff.; John 10:1
9 [a]John 10:1f., 9
10 [a]John 5:40
★11 [a]Is. 40:11; Ezek. 34:11-16, 23; John 10:14; Heb. 13:20; 1 Pet. 5:4; Rev. 7:17 [b]John 10:15, 17, 18; 15:13; 1 John 3:16
12 [a]John 10:2
14 [a]John 10:11 [b]John 10:27
15 [a]Matt. 11:27 [b]John 10:11, 17, 18
★16 [a]Is. 56:8 [b]John 11:52; 17:20f.; Eph. 2:13-18; 1 Pet. 2:25 [c]Ezek. 34:23; 37:24
17 [a]John 10:11, 15, 18
18 [a]Matt. 26:53; John 2:19; 5:26 [b]John 10:11, 15, 17 [c]John 14:31; 15:10; Phil. 2:8; Heb. 5:8
19 [a]John 7:43; 9:16
20 [a]John 7:20 [b]Mark 3:21

9:39 *For judgment I came into this world.* Jesus' coming was not for the purpose of judgment (3:17), but it inevitably resulted in judgment, because some decided against Him. Compare Mark 4:12 and Isa. 6:9.

9:41 The Pharisees' insistence that they could see made their sin willful.

10:8 *thieves and robbers.* I.e., false Messiahs, false teachers, of whom Palestine knew many in the first century A.D.

10:11 *I am the good shepherd.* As Good Shepherd, Christ gave His life for His sheep and became the door to God's fold (v. 7); as the Great Shepherd (Heb. 13:20–21), He rose from the dead to care for His sheep; as Chief Shepherd (1 Pet. 5:4) He will come again for His sheep.

10:16 *I have other sheep.* These are the Gentiles who would believe and, with converted Jews, form one spiritual body (Eph. 2:16).

saying, "He [a]has a demon, and [b]is
insane; why do you listen to
Him?"

21 [a]Matt. 4:24 [b]Ex. 4:11; John 9:32f.

21 Others were saying,
"These are not the sayings of one
[a]demon-possessed. [b]A demon
cannot open the eyes of the blind,
can he?"

D At the Feast of Dedication in Jerusalem, 10:22-42

1 *The discourse,* 10:22-30

★22

22 At that time the Feast of
the Dedication took place at Jerusalem;

23 [a]Acts 3:11; 5:12

23 it was winter, and Jesus
was walking in the temple in the
portico of [a]Solomon.

24 [a]John 1:19; 10:31, 33 [b]Luke 22:67; John 16:25

24 [a]The Jews therefore gathered around Him, and were saying to Him, "How long will You
keep us in suspense? If You are
the Christ, tell us [b]plainly."

25 [a]John 8:56, 58 [b]John 5:36; 10:38

25 Jesus answered them, "[a]I
told you, and you do not believe;
[b]the works that I do in My Father's name, these bear witness of
Me.

26 [a]John 8:47

26 "But you do not believe, because [a]you are not of My sheep.

27 [a]John 10:4, 16 [b]John 10:14

27 "My sheep [a]hear My voice,
and [b]I know them, and they follow Me;

28 [a]John 17:2f.; 1 John 2:25; 5:11 [b]John 6:37, 39

28 and I give [a]eternal life to
them, and they shall never perish;
and [b]no one shall snatch them out
of My hand.
29 "My Father, who has given
them to Me, is greater than all;
and no one is able to snatch *them*
out of the Father's hand.
30 "[a]I and the Father are one." ★30 [a]John 17:21ff.

2 *The rejection,* 10:31-42

31 The Jews [a]took up stones 31 [a]John 8:59
again to stone Him.
32 Jesus answered them, "I
showed you many good works
from the Father; for which of
them are you stoning Me?"
33 The Jews answered Him, ★33 [a]Lev. 24:16 [b]John 5:18
"For a good work we do not stone
You, but for [a]blasphemy; and because You, being a man, [b]make
Yourself out *to be* God."
34 Jesus answered them, "Has ★34 [a]John 8:17 [b]John 12:34; 15:25; Rom. 3:19; 1 Cor. 14:21 [c]Ps. 82:6
it not been written in [a]your [b]Law,
'I said, [c]YOU ARE GODS'?
35 "If he called them gods, to
whom the word of God came (and ★35
the Scripture cannot be broken),
36 do you say of Him, whom 36 [a]Jer. 1:5; John 6:69 [b]John 3:17 [c]John 5:17f.; 10:30
the Father [a]sanctified and [b]sent
into the world, 'You are blaspheming,' because I said, '[c]I am
the Son of God'?
37 "[a]If I do not do the works of 37 [a]John 10:25; 15:24
My Father, do not believe Me;
38 but if I do them, though ★38 [a]John 10:25; 14:11 [b]John 14:10f., 20; 17:21, 23
you do not believe Me, believe
[a]the works, that you may know
and understand that [b]the Father is
in Me, and I in the Father."
39 Therefore [a]they were ★39 [a]John 7:30 [b]Luke 4:30; John 8:59
seeking again to seize Him; and
[b]He eluded their grasp.
40 And He went away [a]again 40 [a]John 1:28
beyond the Jordan to the place
where John was first baptizing;
and He was staying there.
41 And many came to Him; 41 [a]John 2:11 [b]John 1:27, 30, 34; 3:27-30
and they were saying, "While

10:22 *the Feast of the Dedication.* This was instituted in 165 B.C. by Judas Maccabeus in commemoration of the cleansing and reopening of the temple after its desecration by the Syrian ruler Antiochus Epiphanes in 168 B.C. (Dan. 11:31; 1 Macc. 4:52-59). It is also called the Feast of Lights or Hanukkah. The date falls near the winter solstice, Dec. 22.

10:30 *one.* The Father and Son are in perfect unity in their natures and actions, but the neuter form of "one" rules out the meaning that they are one person.

10:33 *blasphemy.* See note on Mark 14:64.

10:34 *written in your Law.* I.e., in Ps. 82:6. The term "law" was sometimes applied to the entire O.T. Christ's point is that if the O.T. uses the word "God" (Elohim) of men who were representative of God, then the Jews should not oppose Him for calling Himself the Son of God.

10:35 *the Scripture cannot be broken.* I.e., deprived of its binding authority. Jesus here employs rather technical exegesis of the O.T.

10:38 *believe the works.* Even if the leaders could not test Jesus' verbal claims, they could see His works, and these miracles should have led them to acknowledge the truth of His claims.

10:39 *He eluded their grasp.* Apparently He moved without walking, another supernatural phenomenon.

John performed no [a]sign, yet [b]ev-
erything John said about this man
was true."
42 [a]John 7:31
42 And [a]many believed in
Him there.

E At Bethany, 11:1–12:11

1 *The miraculous sign,* 11:1–44

1 [a]Matt. 21:17; John 11:18 [b]Luke 10:38; John 11:5, 19ff.
11 Now a certain man was
sick, Lazarus of [a]Bethany,
the village of Mary and her sister
[b]Martha.
★ 2 [a]Luke 7:38; John 12:3 [b]Luke 7:13; John 11:3, 21, 32; 13:13f.
2 And it was the Mary who
[a]anointed [b]the Lord with ointment, and wiped His feet with her
hair, whose brother Lazarus was
sick.
3 [a]Luke 7:13; John 11:2, 21, 32; 13:13f. [b]John 11:5, 11, 36
3 The sisters therefore sent
to Him, saying, "[a]Lord, behold,
[b]he whom You love is sick."
★ 4 [a]John 9:3; 10:38; 11:40
4 But when Jesus heard it,
He said, "This sickness is not
unto death, but for [a]the glory of
God, that the Son of God may be
glorified by it."
5 [a]John 11:1
5 Now Jesus loved [a]Martha,
and her sister, and Lazarus.
6 When therefore He heard
that he was sick, He stayed then
two days *longer* in the place
where He was.
7 [a]John 10:40
7 Then after this He *said to
the disciples, "[a]Let us go to Judea
again."
★ 8 [a]Matt. 23:7 [b]John 8:59; 10:31
8 The disciples *said to Him,
"[a]Rabbi, the Jews were just now
seeking [b]to stone You; and are
You going there again?"
9 [a]Luke 13:33; John 9:4; 12:35
9 Jesus answered, "[a]Are
there not twelve hours in the day?
If anyone walks in the day, he
does not stumble, because he sees
the light of this world.
10 "But if anyone walks in the
night, he stumbles, because the
light is not in him."

11 This He said, and after that
He *said to them, "Our [a]friend
Lazarus [b]has fallen asleep; but I
go, that I may awaken him out of
sleep."
★11 [a]John 11:3 [b]Matt. 27:52; Mark 5:39; John 11:13; Acts 7:60
12 The disciples therefore
said to Him, "Lord, if he has
fallen asleep, he will recover."
13 Now [a]Jesus had spoken of
his death; but they thought that
He was speaking of literal sleep.
13 [a]Matt. 9:24; Luke 8:52
14 Then Jesus therefore said
to them plainly, "Lazarus is dead,
15 and I am glad for your
sakes that I was not there, so that
you may believe; but let us go to
him."
16 [a]Thomas therefore, who is
called [b]Didymus, said to *his* fellow disciples, "Let us also go, that
we may die with Him."
★16 [a]Matt. 10:3; Mark 3:18; Luke 6:15; John 14:5; 20:26-28; Acts 1:13 [b]John 20:24; 21:2
17 So when Jesus came, He
found that he had already been in
the tomb [a]four days.
17 [a]John 11:39
18 Now [a]Bethany was near
Jerusalem, about two miles off;
18 [a]John 11:1
19 and many of [a]the Jews had
come to [b]Martha and Mary, [c]to
console them concerning *their*
brother.
19 [a]John 1:19; 11:8 [b]John 11:1 [c]1 Sam. 31:13; 1 Chr. 10:12; Job 2:11; John 11:31
20 [a]Martha therefore, when
she heard that Jesus was coming,
went to meet Him; but [a]Mary still
sat in the house.
20 [a]Luke 10:38-42
21 Martha therefore said to
Jesus, "[a]Lord, [b]if You had been
here, my brother would not have
died.
21 [a]John 11:2 [b]John 11:32, 37
22 "Even now I know that
[a]whatever You ask of God, God
will give You."
22 [a]John 9:31; 11:41f.
23 Jesus *said to her, "Your
brother shall rise again."
24 Martha *said to Him, "[a]I
know that he will rise again in the
resurrection on the last day."
24 [a]Dan. 12:2; John 5:28f.; Acts 24:15
25 Jesus said to her, "[a]I am
the resurrection and the life; he
★25 [a]John 1:4; 5:26; 6:39f.; Rev. 1:18

11:2 *Mary.* See John 12:3; Matt. 26:7; Mark 14:3.

11:4 *for the glory of God.* The resurrection of Lazarus would demonstrate the glory of God even more than restoration from a sick bed.

11:8–10 Jesus states that He could safely go back to Judea, where an attempt had been made to stone Him (11:8), as long as He was walking in the light of His Father's will.

11:11 *fallen asleep.* Though the disciples understood this to mean natural sleep (v. 12), Jesus used it as a metaphor to denote death (Mark 5:39; cf. Acts 7:60; 1 Thess. 4:13).

11:16 *Didymus* = twin. Possibly Thomas was a twin of Matthew, with whose name his own is coupled in Matt. 10:3, Mark 3:18, and Luke 6:15.

11:25–26 *he who believes in Me,* even if he

who believes in Me shall live even
if he dies,
26 and everyone who lives
and believes in Me [a]shall never
die. Do you believe this?"
27 She *said to Him, "Yes,
Lord; I have believed that You are
[a]the Christ, the Son of God, *even*
[b]He who comes into the world."
28 And when she had said
this, she [a]went away, and called
Mary her sister, saying secretly,
"[b]The Teacher is here, and is calling for you."
29 And when she heard it,
she *arose quickly, and was coming to Him.
30 Now Jesus had not yet
come into the village, but [a]was
still in the place where Martha
met Him.
31 [a]The Jews then who were
with her in the house, and [b]con-
soling her, when they saw that
Mary rose up quickly and went
out, followed her, supposing that
she was going to the tomb to
weep there.
32 Therefore, when Mary
came where Jesus was, she saw
Him, and fell at His feet, saying to
Him, "[a]Lord, [b]if You had been
here, my brother would not have
died."
33 When Jesus therefore saw
her weeping, and [a]the Jews who
came with her, *also* weeping, He
[b]was deeply moved in spirit, and
[c]was troubled,
34 and said, "Where have you
laid him?" They *said to Him,
"Lord, come and see."
35 Jesus [a]wept.
36 And so [a]the Jews were saying, "Behold how He [b]loved him!"
37 But some of them said,
"Could not this man, who
[a]opened the eyes of him who was
blind, have kept this man also
from dying?"
38 Jesus therefore again being
deeply moved within, *came to
the tomb. Now it was a [a]cave, and
a stone was lying against it.
39 Jesus *said, "Remove the
stone." Martha, the sister of the
deceased, *said to Him, "Lord, by
this time there will be a stench;
for he *has been dead* [a]four days."
40 Jesus *said to her, "[a]Did I
not say to you, if you believe, you
will see the glory of God?"
41 And so they removed the
[a]stone. And Jesus [b]raised His
eyes, and said, "[c]Father, I thank
Thee that Thou heardest Me.
42 "And I knew that Thou
hearest Me always; but [a]because
of the people standing around I
said it, that they may believe that
[b]Thou didst send Me."
43 And when He had said
these things, He cried out with a
loud voice, "Lazarus, come forth."
44 He who had died came
forth, [a]bound hand and foot with
wrappings; and [b]his face was
wrapped around with a cloth.
Jesus *said to them, "Unbind
him, and let him go."

2 *The reactions,* 11:45–57

45 [a]Many therefore of the
Jews, [b]who had come to Mary and
[c]beheld what He had done, believed in Him.
46 But some of them went
away to the [a]Pharisees, and told
them the things which Jesus had
done.
47 Therefore [a]the chief
priests and the Pharisees [b]con-
vened a [c]council, and were saying, "What are we doing? For this
man is performing many [d]signs.
48 "If we let Him *go on* like
this, all men will believe in Him,
and the Romans will come and
take away both our [a]place and
our nation."
49 But a certain one of them,
[a]Caiaphas, [b]who was high priest

26 [a]John 6:47, 50, 51; 8:51
27 [a]Matt. 16:16; Luke 2:11 [b]John 6:14
28 [a]John 11:30 [b]Matt. 26:18; Mark 14:14; Luke 22:11; John 13:13
30 [a]John 11:20
31 [a]John 11:19, 33 [b]John 11:19
32 [a]John 11:2 [b]John 11:21
★**33** [a]John 11:19 [b]John 11:38 [c]John 12:27; 13:21
35 [a]Luke 19:41; John 11:33
36 [a]John 11:19 [b]John 11:3
37 [a]John 9:7
38 [a]Matt. 27:60; Mark 15:46; Luke 24:2; John 20:1
39 [a]John 11:17
40 [a]John 11:4, 23ff.
41 [a]Matt. 27:60; Mark 15:46; Luke 24:2; John 20:1 [b]John 17:1; Acts 7:55 [c]Matt. 11:25
42 [a]John 12:30; 17:21 [b]John 3:17
★**43**
44 [a]John 19:40 [b]John 20:7
45 [a]John 7:31 [b]John 11:19; 12:17f. [c]John 2:23
46 [a]John 7:32, 45; 11:57
47 [a]John 7:32, 45; 11:57 [b]Matt. 26:3 [c]Matt. 5:22 [d]John 2:11
★**48** [a]Matt. 24:15
49 [a]Matt. 26:3 [b]John 11:51; 18:13

---

dies physically shall live spiritually and eternally. *everyone who lives* physically *and believes in Me shall never die* spiritually and eternally.

11:33 *deeply moved.* Because of the sorrow that sickness and death brought.

11:43 *Lazarus, come forth.* Only Jesus can call the dead to life (5:25); others could move the stone (11:39) and grave clothes (v. 44).

11:48 *our place.* I.e., the holy place, the temple.

that year, said to them, "You
know nothing at all,

★50 [a]John 18:14

50 nor do you take into account that [a]it is expedient for you
that one man should die for the
people, and that the whole nation
should not perish."

51 [a]John 18:13 [b]Ex. 28:30; Num. 27:21; 1 Sam. 23:9; 30:7; Ezra 2:63

51 Now this he did not say on
his own initiative; but [a]being high
priest that year, he [b]prophesied
that Jesus was going to die for the
nation;

52 [a]John 10:16

52 and not for the nation
only, but that He might also
[a]gather together into one the children of God who are scattered
abroad.

53 [a]Matt. 26:4

53 So from that day on they
[a]planned together to kill Him.

54 [a]John 7:1 [b]2 Chr. 13:19 marg.

54 Jesus therefore [a]no longer
continued to walk publicly among
the Jews, but went away from
there to the country near the wilderness, into a city called [b]Ephra-
im; and there He stayed with the
disciples.

55 [a]Matt. 26:1f.; Mark 14:1; Luke 22:1; John 2:13; 12:1; 13:1 [b]Num. 9:10; 2 Chr. 30:17f.; John 18:28

55 Now [a]the Passover of the
Jews was at hand, and many went
up to Jerusalem out of the country before the Passover, [b]to purify
themselves.

★56 [a]John 7:11

56 Therefore they [a]were
seeking for Jesus, and were saying
to one another, as they stood in
the temple, "What do you think;
that He will not come to the feast
at all?"

57 [a]John 11:47

57 Now [a]the chief priests and
the Pharisees had given orders
that if any one knew where He
was, he should report it, that they
might seize Him.

3 *The anointing by Mary,* 12:1–8

1 [a]John 12:1-8: *Matt. 26:6-13; Mark 14:3-9; Luke 7:37-39* [b]John 11:55; 12:20 [c]Matt. 21:17; John 11:43f.

12 [a]Jesus, therefore, six days
before [b]the Passover, came
to [c]Bethany where Lazarus was,
whom Jesus had raised from the
dead.

2 [a]Luke 10:38

2 So they made Him a sup-
per there; and [a]Martha was serving; but Lazarus was one of those
reclining *at the table* with Him.

3 [a]John 11:2 [b]Mark 14:3

3 [a]Mary therefore took a
pound of very costly, [b]genuine
spikenard ointment, and anointed
the feet of Jesus, and wiped His
feet with her hair; and the house
was filled with the fragrance of
the ointment.

4 [a]John 6:71

4 But [a]Judas Iscariot, one of
His disciples, who was intending
to betray Him, *said,

★5

5 "Why was this ointment
not sold for three hundred denarii, and given to poor *people?*"

★6 [a]John 13:29 [b]Luke 8:3

6 Now he said this, not because he was concerned about the
poor, but because he was a thief,
and as he [a]had the money box, he
used to pilfer [b]what was put into
it.

7 [a]John 19:40

7 Jesus therefore said, "Let
her alone, in order that she may
keep it for [a]the day of My burial.

8 [a]Deut. 15:11; Matt. 26:11; Mark 14:7

8 "[a]For the poor you always
have with you; but you do not always have Me."

4 *The reactions,* 12:9–11

9 [a]Mark 12:37; John 12:12 marg. [b]John 11:43f.; 12:1, 17f.

9 The [a]great multitude
therefore of the Jews learned that
He was there; and they came, not
for Jesus' sake only, but that they
might also see Lazarus, [b]whom
He raised from the dead.

10 But the chief priests took
counsel that they might put Lazarus to death also;

11 [a]John 11:45f.; 12:18 [b]John 7:31; 11:42

11 because [a]on account of
him [b]many of the Jews were
going away, and were believing in
Jesus.

F At Jerusalem, 12:12–50

1 *The triumphal entry,* 12:12–19

12 [a]John 12:12-15: *Matt. 21:4-9; Mark 11:7-10; Luke 19:35-38* [b]John 12:1

12 On the next day [a]the great
multitude who had come to [b]the

11:50 Caiaphas could hardly realize the full meaning of his own words (18:14). He was simply expressing the thought of a political collaborator with Rome; and yet those words express the central doctrine of the Christian faith, the substitutionary atonement of Christ.

11:56 *stood in the temple,* after undergoing the purification rites (v. 55).

12:5 *three hundred denarii,* approximately what a rural worker would earn in one year.

12:6 *had the money box.* Judas was evidently the treasurer of the group.

feast, when they heard that Jesus was coming to Jerusalem,

13 took the branches of the palm trees, and went out to meet Him, and *began* to cry out, "[a]Hosanna! Blessed *is* He who comes in the name of the Lord, even the [b]King of Israel."

14 And Jesus, finding a young donkey, sat on it; as it is written,

15 "[a]Fear not, daughter of Zion; behold, your King comes sitting on a donkey's colt."

16 [a]These things His disciples did not understand at the first; but when Jesus [b]was glorified, then they remembered that these things were written of Him, and that they had done these things to Him.

17 And so [a]the multitude who were with Him when He called Lazarus out of the tomb, and raised him from the dead, were bearing Him witness.

18 [a]For this cause also the multitude went and met Him, [b]because they heard that He had performed this sign.

19 The Pharisees therefore said to one another, "You see that you are not doing any good; look, the world has gone after Him."

13 [a]Ps. 118:25f. [b]John 1:49
15 [a]Zech. 9:9
★16 [a]Mark 9:32; John 2:22; 14:26 [b]John 7:39; 12:23
17 [a]John 11:42
18 [a]Luke 19:37; John 12:12 [b]John 12:11

2 *The teaching,* 12:20–50

20 Now there were certain [a]Greeks among those who were going up to worship at [b]the feast;

21 these therefore came to [a]Philip, who was from [b]Bethsaida of Galilee, and *began to* ask him, saying, "Sir, we wish to see Jesus."

22 Philip *came and *told [a]Andrew; Andrew and Philip *came, and they *told Jesus.

23 And Jesus *answered them, saying, "[a]The hour has come for the Son of Man to [b]be glorified.

24 "Truly, truly, I say to you, [a]unless a grain of wheat falls into the earth and dies, it remains by itself alone; but if it dies, it bears much fruit.

25 "[a]He who loves his life loses it; and he who [b]hates his life in this world shall keep it to life eternal.

26 "If any one serves Me, let him follow Me; and [a]where I am, there shall My servant also be; if any one serves Me, the Father will [b]honor him.

27 "[a]Now My soul has become troubled; and what shall I say, '[b]Father, save Me from [c]this hour'? But for this purpose I came to this hour.

28 "[a]Father, glorify Thy name." There came therefore a [b]voice out of heaven: "I have both glorified it, and will glorify it again."

29 The multitude therefore, who stood by and heard it, were saying that it had thundered; others were saying, "[a]An angel has spoken to Him."

30 Jesus answered and said, "[a]This voice has not come for My sake, but for your sakes.

31 "[a]Now judgment is upon this world; now [b]the ruler of this world shall be cast out.

32 "And I, if I [a]be lifted up from the earth, will [b]draw all men to Myself."

33 But He was saying this [a]to indicate the kind of death by which He was to die.

34 The multitude therefore answered Him, "We have heard out of [a]the Law that [b]the Christ is to remain forever; and how can

20 [a]John 7:35 [b]John 12:1
21 [a]John 1:44 [b]Matt. 11:21
22 [a]John 1:44
★23 [a]Matt. 26:45; Mark 14:35, 41; John 13:1, 32; 17:1 [b]John 7:39; 12:16
24 [a]Rom. 14:9; 1 Cor. 15:36
25 [a]Matt. 10:39 [b]Luke 14:26
26 [a]John 14:3; 17:24; 2 Cor. 5:8; Phil. 1:23; 1 Thess. 4:17 [b]1 Sam. 2:30; Ps. 91:15; Luke 12:37
27 [a]Matt. 26:38; Mark 14:34; John 11:33 [b]Matt. 11:25 [c]John 12:23
28 [a]Matt. 11:25 [b]Matt. 3:17; 17:5; Mark 1:11; 9:7; Luke 3:22; 9:35
29 [a]Acts 23:9
30 [a]John 11:42
★31 [a]John 3:19; 9:39; 16:11 [b]John 14:30; 16:11; 2 Cor. 4:4; Eph. 2:2; 6:12; 1 John 4:4; 5:19
★32 [a]John 3:14; 8:28; 12:34 [b]John 6:44
33 [a]John 18:32; 21:19
★34 [a]John 10:34 [b]Ps. 110:4; Is. 9:7; Ezek. 37:25; Dan. 7:14 [c]Matt. 8:20 [d]John 3:14; 8:28; 12:32

12:16 *that these things were written of Him.* I.e., in the Hebrew Scriptures, which Christ's followers searched carefully after His death.

12:23 *The hour has come.* The time had come for which He had been working throughout His ministry; namely, the time of His death and resurrection. This is the beginning of the climax of His ministry.

12:31 *judgment is upon this world.* The cross is the condemnation of, the judgment upon, those who reject it; it is also the basis for the ultimate victory over Satan.

12:32 *lifted up* on the cross. *will draw all men.* His saving grace will be available to Greeks (like those present, v. 20) as well as to Jews.

12:34 They could not conceive of the heavenly Son of Man being lifted up to die.

You say, 'The [c]Son of Man must be [d]lifted up'? Who is this [c]Son of Man?"

35 [a]John 7:33; 9:4; 1 John 2:10 [b]John 12:46 [c]Gal. 6:10; Eph. 5:8 [d]1 John 1:6; 2:11

35 Jesus therefore said to them, "[a]For a little while longer [b]the light is among you. [c]Walk while you have the light, that darkness may not overtake you; he who [d]walks in the darkness does not know where he goes.

36 [a]John 12:46 [b]Luke 16:8; John 8:12 [c]John 8:59

36 "While you have the light, [a]believe in the light, in order that you may become [b]sons of light."

These things Jesus spoke, and He departed and [c]hid Himself from them.

★37

37 But though He had performed so many signs before them, *yet* they were not believing in Him;

★38 [a]Is. 53:1; Rom. 10:16

38 that the word of Isaiah the prophet might be fulfilled, which he spoke, "[a]LORD, WHO HAS BELIEVED OUR REPORT? AND TO WHOM HAS THE ARM OF THE LORD BEEN REVEALED?"

39 For this cause they could not believe, for Isaiah said again,

40 [a]Is. 6:10; Matt. 13:14f. [b]Mark 6:52

40 "[a]HE HAS BLINDED THEIR EYES, AND HE [b]HARDENED THEIR HEART; LEST THEY SEE WITH THEIR EYES, AND PERCEIVE WITH THEIR HEART, AND BE CONVERTED, AND I HEAL THEM."

41 [a]Is. 6:1ff. [b]Luke 24:27

41 These things Isaiah said, because [a]he saw His glory, and [b]he spoke of Him.

42 [a]John 7:48; 12:11 [b]Luke 23:13 [c]John 7:13 [d]John 9:22

42 Nevertheless [a]many even of [b]the rulers believed in Him, but [c]because of the Pharisees they were not confessing *Him,* lest they should be [d]put out of the synagogue;

43 [a]John 5:41, 44

43 [a]for they loved the approval of men rather than the approval of God.

44 [a]Matt. 10:40; John 5:24

44 And Jesus cried out and said, "[a]He who believes in Me does not believe in Me, but in Him who sent Me.

45 [a]John 14:9

45 "And [a]he who beholds Me beholds the One who sent Me.

46 [a]John 1:4; 3:19; 8:12; 9:5; 12:35f.

46 "[a]I have come *as* light into the world, that everyone who believes in Me may not remain in darkness.

★47 [a]John 3:17; 8:15f.

47 "And if any one hears My sayings, and does not keep them, I do not judge him; for [a]I did not come to judge the world, but to save the world.

48 [a]Luke 10:16 [b]Deut. 18:18f.; John 5:45ff.; 8:47 [c]Matt. 10:15

48 "[a]He who rejects Me, and does not receive My sayings, has one who judges him; [b]the word I spoke is what will judge him at [c]the last day.

49 [a]John 3:11 [b]John 14:31; 17:8

49 "[a]For I did not speak on My own initiative, but the Father Himself who sent Me [b]has given Me commandment, what to say, and what to speak.

50 [a]John 6:68 [b]John 8:28

50 "And I know that [a]His commandment is eternal life; therefore the things I speak, I speak [b]just as the Father has told Me."

IV INSTRUCTION BY THE SON OF GOD, 13:1–16:33

A Concerning Forgiveness, 13:1–20

★ 1 [a]John 2:13; 11:55 [b]John 12:23 [c]John 13:3; 16:28

13 Now before the Feast of [a]the Passover, Jesus knowing that [b]His hour had come that He should depart out of this world [c]to the Father, having loved His own who were in the world, He loved them to the end.

2 [a]John 6:70; 13:27 [b]John 6:71

2 And during supper, [a]the devil having already put into the heart of [b]Judas Iscariot, *the son* of Simon, to betray Him,

★ 3 [a]John 3:35 [b]John 8:42

3 *Jesus,* [a]knowing that the Father had given all things into His hands, and that [b]He had come forth from God, and was going back to God,

4 [a]Luke 12:37

4 *rose from supper, and *laid aside His garments; and taking a towel, [a]girded Himself about.

5 [a]Luke 7:44

5 Then He *poured water into the basin, and began to

12:37–50 These verses summarize the public ministry of Jesus Christ, and explain the rejections which are equated with the rejection of God.

12:38–41 See Isa. 6:10; 53:1.

12:47 See note on 9:39.

13:1 *to the end.* Lit., to the fullest extent.

13:3–11 This dramatic scene of the foot-washing is an acted parable, a lesson in humility, and a vivid portrayal of Christ's self-humiliation.

[a]wash the disciples' feet, and to
wipe them with the towel with
which He was girded.
6 And so He *came to Simon
Peter. He *said to Him, "Lord, do
You wash my feet?"
7 Jesus answered and said to
him, "What I do you do not realize now; but you shall understand
[a]hereafter."
8 Peter *said to Him, "Never
shall You wash my feet!" Jesus
answered him, "If I do not wash
you, [a]you have no part with Me."
9 Simon Peter *said to Him,
"Lord, not my feet only, but also
my hands and my head."
10 Jesus *said to him, "He
who has bathed needs only to
wash his feet, but is completely
clean; and [a]you are clean, but not
all *of you.*"
11 For [a]He knew the one who
was betraying Him; for this reason He said, "Not all of you are
clean."
12 And so when He had
washed their feet, and [a]taken His
garments, and reclined *at table*
again, He said to them, "Do you
know what I have done to you?
13 "You call Me [a]Teacher and
[b]Lord; and you are right; for *so* I
am.
14 "If I then, [a]the Lord and the
Teacher, washed your feet, you
also ought to wash one another's
feet.
15 "For I gave you [a]an example
that you also should do as I did to
you.
16 "Truly, truly, I say to you,
[a]a slave is not greater than his
master; neither [b]one who is sent

7 [a]John 13:12ff.
8 [a]Deut. 12:12; 2 Sam. 20:1; 1 Kin. 12:16
★10 [a]John 15:3
11 [a]John 6:64; 13:2
12 [a]John 13:4
13 [a]John 11:28 [b]John 11:2; 1 Cor. 12:3; Phil. 2:11
★14 [a]John 11:2; 1 Cor. 12:3; Phil. 2:11
15 [a]1 Pet. 5:3
16 [a]Matt. 10:24 [b]2 Cor. 8:23; Phil. 2:25

greater than the one who sent
him.
17 "If you know these things,
you are [a]blessed if you do them.
18 "[a]I do not speak of all of
you. I know the ones I have [b]cho-
sen; but *it is* [c]that the Scripture
may be fulfilled, '[d]HE WHO EATS
MY BREAD HAS LIFTED UP HIS HEEL
AGAINST ME.'
19 "From now on [a]I am telling
you before *it* comes to pass, so
that when it does occur, you may
believe that [b]I am *He.*
20 "Truly, truly, I say to you,
[a]he who receives whomever I
send receives Me; and he who receives Me receives Him who sent
Me."

17 [a]Matt. 7:24ff.; Luke 11:28; James 1:25
★18 [a]John 13:10f. [b]John 6:70; 15:16, 19 [c]John 15:25; 17:12; 18:32; 19:24, 36; [d]Ps. 41:9; Matt. 26:21ff.; Mark 14:18f.; Luke 22:21ff.; John 13:18, 21, 22, 26
★19 [a]John 14:29; 16:4 [b]John 8:24
★20 [a]Matt. 10:40; Luke 10:16; Gal. 4:14

B Concerning His Betrayal 13:21–30

21 When Jesus had said this,
He [a]became troubled in spirit,
and testified, and said, "Truly,
truly, I say to you, that [b]one of
you will betray Me."
22 The disciples *began* looking at one another, [a]at a loss *to
know* of which one He was
speaking.
23 There was reclining on [a]Je-
sus' breast one of His disciples,
[b]whom Jesus loved.
24 Simon Peter therefore
*gestured to him, and *said to
him, "Tell *us* who it is of whom
He is speaking."
25 He, [a]leaning back thus on
Jesus' breast, *said to Him, "Lord,
who is it?"
26 Jesus therefore *answered,
"That is the one for whom I shall

21 [a]John 11:33 [b]Matt. 26:21f.; Mark 14:18ff.; Luke 22:21ff.; John 13:18, 21, 22, 26
22 [a]Matt. 26:21ff.; Mark 14:18ff.; Luke 22:21ff.; John 13:18, 21, 22, 26
★23 [a]John 1:18 [b]John 19:26; 20:2; 21:7, 20
25 [a]John 21:20
★26 [a]John 6:71

13:10 *He who has bathed needs only to wash his feet.* Just as in the natural life a man who has bathed needs only to wash the dust off his sandaled feet when he returns home, so in the spiritual life a man who has been cleansed from sin need not think that all is lost when he sins in his walk through life. He need only confess these sins to be entirely clean again (1 John 1:9).

13:14 *you also ought to wash one another's feet.* Since the illustration has to do with forgiveness, this phrase means that believers ought to forgive one another (Matt. 5:23–24; Eph. 4:32).

13:18 *Scripture.* Ps. 41:9 is referred to.

13:19 *I am He.* I.e., the one to whom Ps. 41:9 refers.

13:20 Those who are sent are the apostles, as in v. 16.

13:23 *one of His disciples, whom Jesus loved.* I.e., John.

13:26 *the morsel.* At Eastern meals it was customary for the host to offer one of the guests a morsel of bread as a gesture of special friendship. By this Jesus was showing His love for the betrayer.

dip the morsel and give it to him."
So when He had dipped the morsel, He *took and *gave it to Judas, [a]*the son* of Simon Iscariot.
27 And after the morsel, [a]Sa-
tan then [b]entered into him. Jesus
therefore *said to him, "What
you do, do quickly."
28 Now no one of those reclining *at table* knew for what
purpose He had said this to him.
29 For some were supposing,
because Judas [a]had the money
box, that Jesus was saying to him,
"Buy the things we have need of
[b]for the feast"; or else, that he
should [c]give something to the
poor.
30 And so after receiving the
morsel he went out immediately;
and [a]it was night.

27 [a]Matt. 4:10 [b]Luke 22:3; John 13:2
29 [a]John 12:6 [b]John 13:1 [c]John 12:5
★30 [a]Luke 22:53

C Concerning His Departure, 13:31–38

31 When therefore he had
gone out, Jesus *said, "Now is
[a]the Son of Man [b]glorified, and
[c]God is glorified in Him;
32 if God is glorified in Him,
[a]God will also glorify Him in
Himself, and will glorify Him immediately.
33 "[a]Little children, I am with
you [b]a little while longer. [c]You
shall seek Me; and as I said to the
Jews, 'Where I am going, you cannot come,' now I say to you also.
34 "A [a]new commandment I
give to you, [b]that you love one
another, [c]even as I have loved
you, that you also love one another.
35 "[a]By this all men will know
that you are My disciples, if you
have love for one another."
36 Simon Peter *said to Him,
"Lord, where are You going?"
Jesus answered, "[a]Where I go,
you cannot follow Me now; but
[b]you shall follow later."
37 Peter *said to Him, "Lord,
why can I not follow You right
now? [a]I will lay down my life for
You."
38 Jesus *answered, "Will
you lay down your life for Me?
Truly, truly, I say to you, [a]a cock
shall not crow, until you deny Me
three times.

★31 [a]Matt. 8:20 [b]John 7:39 [c]John 14:13; 17:4; 1 Pet. 4:11
32 [a]John 17:1
33 [a]1 John 2:1 [b]John 7:33 [c]John 7:34
34 [a]John 15:12, 17; 1 John 2:7f.; 3:11, 23; 2 John 5 [b]Lev. 19:18; Matt. 5:44; Gal. 5:14; 1 Thess. 4:9; Heb. 13:1; 1 Pet. 1:22; 1 John 4:7 [c]Eph. 5:2; 1 John 4:10f.
★35 [a]1 John 3:14; 4:20
36 [a]John 13:33; 14:2; 16:5 [b]John 21:18f.; 2 Pet. 1:14
37 [a]John 13:37, 38; *Matt. 26:33-35; Mark 14:29-31; Luke 22:33-34*
38 [a]Mark 14:30; John 18:27

D Concerning Heaven, 14:1–14

14 "[a]Let not your heart be
troubled; believe in God,
believe also in Me.
2 "In My Father's house are
many dwelling places; if it were
not so, I would have told you; for
[a]I go to prepare a place for you.
3 "And if I go and prepare a
place for you, [a]I will come again,
and receive you to Myself; that
[b]where I am, *there* you may be
also.
4 "And you know the way
where I am going."
5 [a]Thomas *said to Him,
"Lord, we do not know where
You are going; how do we know
the way?"
6 Jesus *said to him, "I am
[a]the way, and [b]the truth, and [c]the
life; no one comes to the Father,
but through Me.
7 "[a]If you had known Me,
you would have known My Father also; from now on you

★ 1 [a]John 14:27; 16:22, 24
★ 2 [a]John 13:33, 36
★ 3 [a]John 14:18, 28 [b]John 12:26
5 [a]John 11:16
6 [a]John 10:9; Rom. 5:2; Eph. 2:18; Heb. 10:20 [b]John 1:14 [c]John 1:4; 11:25; 1 John 5:20
7 [a]John 8:19 [b]1 John 2:13 [c]John 6:46

13:30 *and it was night.* The "hour" for which Christ, the light of the world, had been waiting, when the powers of darkness would engulf Him, begins in darkness.

13:31–32 In His death Christ and the Father will be glorified (v. 31). In the resurrection and exaltation the Father will glorify Christ and validate all His claims (v. 32).

13:35 I.e., their mutual love would be the strongest possible argument for the Christian faith.

14:1 In view of His departure from them, Christ gave the disciples (in this chapter) specific encouragements. These include the provision in the Father's house (v. 2), the promise to return (v. 3), the prospect of doing greater works (v. 12), the promise of answered prayer (v. 14), the coming of the Holy Spirit (v. 16), and the legacy of peace (v. 27).

14:2 *dwelling places.* The same word is used elsewhere in the N.T. only in v. 23, where it is translated "abode."

14:3 *I will come again.* See 1 Thess. 4:13–18. This is not the coming of the Spirit nor the believer's death, but Christ's personal return.

[b]know Him, and have [c]seen
Him."
8 [a]Philip *said to Him,
"Lord, show us the Father, and it
is enough for us."
9 Jesus *said to him, "Have I
been so long with you, and *yet*
you have not come to know Me,
Philip? [a]He who has seen Me has
seen the Father; how do you say,
'Show us the Father'?
10 "Do you not believe that [a]I
am in the Father, and the Father is
in Me? [b]The words that I say to
you I do not speak on My own
initiative, but the Father abiding
in Me does His works.
11 "Believe Me that [a]I am in
the Father, and the Father in Me;
otherwise [b]believe on account of
the works themselves.
12 "Truly, truly, I say to you,
he who believes in Me, the works
that I do shall he do also; and
[a]greater *works* than these shall he
do; because [b]I go to the Father.
13 "And [a]whatever you ask in
My name, that will I do, that [b]the
Father may be glorified in the
Son.
14 "If you ask Me anything [a]in
My name, I will do *it*.

8 [a]John 1:43
★ **9** [a]John 1:14; 12:45; Col. 1:15; Heb. 1:3
10 [a]John 10:38; 14:11, 20 [b]John 5:19; 14:24
11 [a]John 10:38; 14:10, 20 [b]John 5:36
★**12** [a]John 4:37f.; 5:20 [b]John 7:33; 14:28
★**13** [a]Matt. 7:7 [b]John 13:31
14 [a]John 15:16; 16:23f.
15 [a]John 14:21, 23; 15:10; 1 John 5:3; 2 John 6
★**16** [a]John 7:39; 14:26; 15:26; 16:7; Rom. 8:26; 1 John 2:1 marg.

E Concerning the Holy Spirit, 14:15–26

15 "[a]If you love Me, you will
keep My commandments.
16 "And I will ask the Father,
and He will give you another
[a]Helper, that He may be with you
forever;
17 *that is* [a]the Spirit of truth,
[b]whom the world cannot receive,
because it does not behold Him or
know Him, *but* you know Him
because He abides with you, and
will be in you.
18 "I will not leave you as orphans; [a]I will come to you.
19 "[a]After a little while [b]the
world will behold Me no more;
but you *will* behold Me; [c]because
I live, you shall live also.
20 "[a]In that day you shall
know that [b]I am in My Father,
and you in Me, and I in you.
21 "[a]He who has My commandments and keeps them, he it
is who loves Me; and [b]he who
loves Me shall be loved by My Father, and I will love him, and will
[c]disclose Myself to him."
22 [a]Judas (not Iscariot) *said
to Him, "Lord, what then has
happened [b]that You are going to
disclose Yourself to us, and not to
the world?"
23 Jesus answered and said to
him, "[a]If anyone loves Me, he will
[b]keep My word; and [c]My Father
will love him, and We [d]will come
to him, and make Our abode with
him.
24 "He who does not love Me
[a]does not keep My words; and
[b]the word which you hear is not
Mine, but the Father's who sent
Me.

★**17** [a]John 15:26; 16:13; 1 John 4:6; 5:7 [b]1 Cor. 2:14
18 [a]John 14:3, 28
19 [a]John 7:33 [b]John 16:16, 22 [c]John 6:57
20 [a]John 16:23, 26 [b]John 10:38; 14:11
★**21** [a]John 14:15, 23; 15:10; 1 John 5:3; 2 John 6 [b]John 14:23; 16:27 [c]Ex. 33:18f.; Prov. 8:17
22 [a]Matt. 10:3; Luke 6:16; Acts 1:13 [b]Acts 10:40, 41
23 [a]John 14:15, 21; 15:10; 1 John 5:3; 2 John 6 [b]John 8:51; 1 John 2:5 [c]John 14:21 [d]2 Cor. 6:16 for O.T.; Eph. 3:17; 1 John 2:24; Rev. 3:20; 21:3
24 [a]John 14:23 [b]John 7:16; 14:10

14:9 *He who has seen Me has seen the Father.* See note on 1:18.

14:12 *greater works than these shall he do.* Greater in extent (through the worldwide preaching of the gospel) and effect (the spiritual redemption and placing in the body of Christ multitudes of people since the day of Pentecost). These will be done through prayer in His name (v. 13).

14:13 *in My name.* This is not a formula to be tacked on to the end of prayers, but means praying for the same things which Christ would desire to see accomplished. It is like using a power of attorney which a very dear loved one has given you.

14:16 *another Helper.* The Holy Spirit is called the Helper (Greek: *paraclete,* as also in 14:26; 15:26; 16:7). In the root of this word are the ideas of advising, exhorting, comforting, strengthening, interceding, and encouraging. The only other occurrence of the word outside this discourse in the N.T. is in 1 John 2:1 applied to Christ and translated "Advocate." Here and in the other passages in John cited above, Christ teaches that the Holy Spirit (1) will indwell Christians (vv. 16–17); (2) will help the disciples recall the events of His life (14:26); (3) will convince the world of sin, righteousness and judgment (16:7–11); (4) will teach believers the truth (15:26; 16:13–15).

14:17 *He abides with you, and will be in you.* The Holy Spirit was active in O.T. times, but His dwelling in the lives of believers after Pentecost is different in that (1) it is permanent and (2) it is true of every individual believer.

14:21 The Christian faith works through love, and the measure of one's love is the extent to which one keeps Christ's commandments.

25 "These things I have spoken to you, while abiding with you.

26 [a]John 14:16 [b]Luke 24:49; John 1:33; 15:26; 16:7; Acts 2:33 [c]John 16:13f.; 1 John 2:20, 27 [d]John 2:22

26 "But the [a]Helper, the Holy Spirit, [b]whom the Father will send in My name, [c]He will teach you all things, and [d]bring to your remembrance all that I said to you.

F Concerning Peace, 14:27-31

27 [a]John 16:33; 20:19; Phil. 4:7; Col. 3:15 [b]John 14:1

27 "[a]Peace I leave with you; My peace I give to you; not as the world gives, do I give to you. [b]Let not your heart be troubled, nor let it be fearful.

28 [a]John 14:2-4 [b]John 14:3, 18 [c]John 14:12 [d]John 10:29; Phil. 2:6

28 "[a]You heard that I said to you, 'I go away, and [b]I will come to you.' If you loved Me, you would have rejoiced, because [c]I go to the Father; for [d]the Father is greater than I.

29 [a]John 13:19

29 "And now [a]I have told you before it comes to pass, that when it comes to pass, you may believe.

★30 [a]John 12:31 [b]Heb. 4:15

30 "I will not speak much more with you, for [a]the ruler of the world is coming, and [b]he has nothing in Me;

31 [a]John 10:18; 12:49 [b]John 13:1; 18:1

31 but that the world may know that I love the Father, and as [a]the Father gave Me commandment, even so I do. Arise, [b]let us go from here.

G Concerning Fruitfulness, 15:1-17

★ 1 [a]Ps. 80:8ff.; Is. 5:1ff.; Ezek. 19:10ff.; Matt. 21:33ff. [b]Matt. 15:13; Rom. 11:17; 1 Cor. 3:9

15 "[a]I am the true vine, and My Father is the [b]vinedresser.

★ 2

2 "Every branch in Me that does not bear fruit, He takes away; and every *branch* that bears fruit, He prunes it, that it may bear more fruit.

3 [a]John 13:10; 17:17; Eph. 5:26

3 "[a]You are already clean because of the word which I have spoken to you.

★ 4 [a]John 6:56; 15:4-7; 1 John 2:6

4 "[a]Abide in Me, and I in you. As the branch cannot bear fruit of itself, unless it abides in the vine, so neither *can* you, unless you abide in Me.

5 [a]John 15:16

5 "I am the vine, you are the branches; he who abides in Me, and I in him, he [a]bears much fruit; for apart from Me you can do nothing.

★ 6 [a]John 15:2

6 "If anyone does not abide in Me, he is [a]thrown away as a branch, and dries up; and they gather them, and cast them into the fire, and they are burned.

7 [a]Matt. 7:7; John 15:16

7 "If you abide in Me, and My words abide in you, [a]ask whatever you wish, and it shall be done for you.

★ 8 [a]Matt. 5:16 [b]John 8:31

8 "[a]By this is My Father glorified, that you bear much fruit, and *so* [b]prove to be My disciples.

9 [a]John 3:35; 17:23, 24, 26

9 "Just as [a]the Father has loved Me, I have also loved you; abide in My love.

10 [a]John 14:15 [b]John 8:29

10 "[a]If you keep My commandments, you will abide in My love; just as [b]I have kept My Father's commandments, and abide in His love.

11 [a]John 17:13 [b]John 3:29

11 "[a]These things I have spoken to you, that My joy may be in

---

14:30 *and he has nothing in Me.* Satan (*the ruler of the world*) possesses nothing in the person of Christ and has no power over Him whatsoever. This is another evidence of Christ's sinlessness.

15:1 Chapters 15 and 16 contain the second Farewell Discourse. In 15 are the themes of fruit-bearing and the hatred of the world for Christ's disciples. The theme of persecution is continued in chapter 16 along with teaching concerning the ministry of the Holy Spirit.

15:2 *takes away.* The word may mean this literally (as "Remove" in 11:39) and would therefore be a reference to the physical death of fruitless Christians (1 Cor. 11:30); or it may mean lift up (as "picked up" in 8:59) which would indicate that the vinedresser encourages and makes it easier for the fruitless believer, hoping he will respond and begin to bear fruit. *prunes.* This is done through the Word of God, which cleans the life (same root word as *clean* in v. 3).

15:4 *Abide in Me.* John explains what this means when he uses the same word in 1 John 3:24. Abiding depends on keeping Christ's commandments (15:10).

15:6 *they are burned.* This refers to the works of the believer. The Christian who does not abide in Christ cannot do what pleases God; therefore, his works will be burned at the judgment seat of Christ, though he himself will be saved (1 Cor. 3:11-15).

15:8 *By this.* I.e., by answered prayer. Note the progression: the step from fruit to more fruit

you, and *that* your [b]joy may be made full.

12 [a]John 13:34; 15:17

12 "This is [a]My commandment, that you love one another, just as I have loved you.

★13 [a]Rom. 5:7f. [b]John 10:11

13 "[a]Greater love has no one than this, that one [b]lay down his life for his friends.

14 [a]Luke 12:4 [b]Matt. 12:50

14 "You are My [a]friends, if [b]you do what I command you.

15 [a]John 8:26; 16:12

15 "No longer do I call you slaves; for the slave does not know what his master is doing; but I have called you friends, for [a]all things that I have heard from My Father I have made known to you.

16 [a]John 6:70; 13:18; 15:19 [b]John 15:5 [c]John 14:13; 15:7; 16:23

16 "[a]You did not choose Me, but I chose you, and appointed you, that you should go and [b]bear fruit, and *that* your fruit should remain, that [c]whatever you ask of the Father in My name, He may give to you.

17 [a]John 15:12

17 "This [a]I command you, that you love one another.

H Concerning the World, 15:18–16:6

18 [a]John 7:7; 1 John 3:13

18 "[a]If the world hates you, you know that it has hated Me before *it hated* you.

19 [a]Matt. 10:22; 24:9 [b]John 15:16 [c]John 17:14

19 "[a]If you were of the world, the world would love its own; but because you are not of the world, but [b]I chose you out of the world, [c]therefore the world hates you.

20 [a]John 13:16 [b]1 Cor. 4:12; 2 Cor. 4:9; 2 Tim. 3:12 [c]John 8:51

20 "Remember the word that I said to you, '[a]A slave is not greater than his master.' If they persecuted Me, [b]they will also persecute you; if they [c]kept My word, they will keep yours also.

★21 [a]Matt. 10:22; 24:9; Mark 13:13; Luke 21:12, 17; Acts 4:17; 5:41; 9:14; 26:9; 1 Pet. 4:14; Rev. 2:3 [b]John 8:19, 55; 16:3; 17:25; Acts 3:17; 1 John 3:1

21 "But all these things they will do to you [a]for My name's sake, [b]because they do not know the One who sent Me.

22 [a]John 9:41; 15:24

22 "[a]If I had not come and spoken to them, they would not have sin, but now they have no excuse for their sin.

23 "He who hates Me hates My Father also.

24 [a]John 9:41; 15:21 [b]John 5:36; 10:37

24 "[a]If I had not done among them [b]the works which no one else did, they would not have sin; but now they have both seen and hated Me and My Father as well.

★25 [a]John 10:34 [b]Ps. 35:19; 69:4

25 "But *they have done this* in order that the word may be fulfilled that is written in their [a]Law, '[b]They hated Me without a cause.'

★26 [a]John 14:16 [b]John 14:26 [c]John 14:17 [d]1 John 5:7

26 "When the [a]Helper comes, [b]whom I will send to you from the Father, *that is* [c]the Spirit of truth, who proceeds from the Father, [d]He will bear witness of Me,

27 [a]Luke 24:48; John 19:35; 21:24; 1 John 1:2; 4:14 [b]Luke 1:2

27 and [a]you *will* bear witness also, because you have been with Me [b]from the beginning.

★ 1 [a]John 15:18-27 [b]Matt. 11:6

16 "[a]These things I have spoken to you, that you may be kept from [b]stumbling.

★ 2 [a]John 9:22 [b]John 4:21; 16:25 [c]Is. 66:5; Acts 26:9-11; Rev. 6:9

2 "They will [a]make you outcasts from the synagogue; but [b]an hour is coming for everyone [c]who kills you to think that he is offering service to God.

3 [a]John 8:19, 55; 15:21; 17:25; Acts 3:17; 1 John 3:1

3 "And these things they will do, [a]because they have not known the Father, or Me.

4 [a]John 13:19 [b]Luke 1:2

4 "But these things I have spoken to you, [a]that when their hour comes, you may remember that I told you of them. And these things I did not say to you [b]at the

---

involves pruning (cleansing) through the Word of God (v. 2), and the step from more fruit to much fruit involves a life of answered prayer.

15:13 The highest expression of love is a self-sacrifice which spares not life itself (see 1 John 3:16).

15:21 *for My name's sake.* Better, on My account, i.e., because you are My followers.

15:25 The reference is to Ps. 35:19; 69:4. In this section Christ states: (1) the world hates Me (v. 18); (2) My followers are aliens in the world (v. 19); (3) the world will persecute you because you are My followers (v. 20); (4) the persecutors do not know God (v. 21); (5) My words (v. 22) and My works (v. 24) rebuke them. These arguments are found in many early Christian writings, as instruction to the faithful and as warning to pagans and Jews.

15:26 *Helper.* See note on 14:16. *who proceeds from the Father.* The mission of the Spirit is from the Father; the Spirit's witness, therefore, is also that of the Father Himself.

16:1 *stumbling.* Or, falling away.

16:2 *everyone who kills you* (will) *think that he is offering service to God.* The history of religious persecution clearly portrays the fulfillment of this prophecy (e.g., Acts 7:57–60).

beginning, because I was with
you.
5 [a]John 7:33; 16:10, 17, 28 [b]John 13:36; 14:5
5 "But now [a]I am going to
Him who sent Me; and none of
you asks Me, '[b]Where are You
going?'
6 [a]John 14:1; 16:22
6 "But because I have said
these things to you, [a]sorrow has
filled your heart.

I Concerning the Holy Spirit, 16:7–15

7 [a]John 14:16 [b]John 14:26
7 "But I tell you the truth, it is
to your advantage that I go away;
for if I do not go away, the [a]Help-
er shall not come to you; but if I
go, [b]I will send Him to you.
★ 8
8 "And He, when He comes,
will convict the world concerning
sin, and righteousness, and judgment;
★ 9 [a]John 15:22, 24
9 concerning sin, [a]because
they do not believe in Me;
10 [a]Acts 3:14; 7:52; 17:31; 1 Pet. 3:18 [b]John 16:5
10 and concerning [a]righteous-
ness, because [b]I go to the Father,
and you no longer behold Me;
★11 [a]John 12:31
11 [a]and concerning judgment,
because the ruler of this world
has been judged.
★12
12 "I have many more things
to say to you, but you cannot bear
them now.
★13 [a]John 14:17 [b]John 14:26
13 "But when He, [a]the Spirit of
truth, comes, He will [b]guide you
into all the truth; for He will not
speak on His own initiative, but
whatever He hears, He will speak;
and He will disclose to you what
is to come.
14 "He shall [a]glorify Me; for ★14 [a]John 7:39
He shall take of Mine, and shall
disclose *it* to you.
15 "[a]All things that the Father ★15 [a]John 17:10
has are Mine; therefore I said,
that He takes of Mine, and will
disclose *it* to you.

J Concerning His Return, 16:16–33

16 "[a]A little while, and [b]you 16 [a]John 7:33 [b]John 14:18-24; 16:16-24 [c]John 16:22
will no longer behold Me; and
again a little while, and [c]you will
see Me."
17 *Some* of His disciples 17 [a]John 16:16 [b]John 16:5
therefore said to one another,
"What is this thing He is telling
us, '[a]A little while, and you *will*
not behold Me; and again a little
while, and you will see Me'; and,
'because [b]I go to the Father'?"
18 And so they were saying,
"What is this that He says, 'A little while'? We do not know what
He is talking about."
19 [a]Jesus knew that they 19 [a]Mark 9:32; John 6:61
wished to question Him, and He
said to them, "Are you deliberat-
ing together about this, that I
said, 'A little while, and you *will*
not behold Me, and again a little
while, and you *will* see Me'?
20 "Truly, truly, I say to you, 20 [a]Mark 16:10; Luke 23:27 [b]John 20:20
that [a]you will weep and lament,
but the world will rejoice; you

16:8–11 The Spirit, through apostles, evangelists, and preachers, will *convict* the world. To convict means to set forth the truth of the Gospel in such a clear light that men are able to accept or reject it intelligently; i.e., to convince men of the truthfulness of the Gospel. The Spirit will help break down the indifference of the typical pagan who has no conviction of sin, who holds a low regard for righteousness, and who pays no heed to warnings of the coming judgment.

16:9 *because they do not believe in Me.* The greatest, and basic, sin is unbelief. Jesus' return to the Father will vindicate His righteous life and the truthfulness of all He said (v. 10).

16:11 *the ruler of this world has been judged.* At the cross, Christ triumphed over Satan, serving notice on unbelievers of their judgment to come.

16:12 *many more things . . . but you cannot bear them now.* These things would become clear after the resurrection.

16:13 *He will disclose to you what is to come.* These things include the meaning of Christ's death and resurrection (which the disciples did not fully understand) as well as things yet in the future concerning the return of Christ. See Paul's statement in 1 Cor. 2:10.

16:14 *take of Mine.* I.e., My teachings and whatever relates to Me.

16:15 The teaching ministry of the Holy Spirit has guided the church since the Spirit's coming. Doctrine, therefore, does not have to be traced back to the earthly ministry of Jesus to be authoritative, because *He* (the Spirit) *takes of Mine* (Christ's), *and will disclose it to you* (the apostles). These truths were then recorded in the New Testament.

will be sorrowful, but [b]your sorrow will be turned to joy.
21 "[a]Whenever a woman is in
travail she has sorrow, because
her hour has come; but when she
gives birth to the child, she remembers the anguish no more,
for joy that a child has been born
into the world.
22 "Therefore [a]you, too, now
have sorrow; but [b]I will see you
again, and your heart will rejoice,
and no one takes your joy away
from you.
23 "And [a]in that day [b]you will
ask Me no question. Truly, truly,
I say to you, [c]if you shall ask the
Father for anything, He will give
it to you in My name.
24 "[a]Until now you have asked
for nothing in My name; ask, and
you will receive, that your [b]joy
may be made full.
25 "These things I have spoken to you in [a]figurative language; [b]an hour is coming, when I
will speak no more to you in figurative language, but will tell you
plainly of the Father.
26 "[a]In that day [b]you will ask
in My name; and I do not say to
you that I will request the Father
on your behalf;
27 for [a]the Father Himself
loves you, because you have
loved Me, and [b]have believed that
[c]I came forth from the Father.
28 "[a]I came forth from the Father, and have come into the
world; I am leaving the world
again, and [b]going to the Father."
29 His disciples *said, "Lo,
now You are speaking plainly,

21 [a]Is. 13:8; 21:3; 26:17; 66:7; Hos. 13:13; Mic. 4:9; 1 Thess. 5:3
22 [a]John 16:6 [b]John 16:16
★23 [a]John 14:20; 16:26 [b]John 16:19, 30 [c]John 15:16
24 [a]John 14:14 [b]John 3:29; 15:11
★25 [a]Matt. 13:34; John 10:6; 16:29 [b]John 16:2
★26 [a]John 14:20; 16:23 [b]John 16:19, 30
27 [a]John 14:21, 23 [b]John 2:11; 16:30 [c]John 8:42; 16:30
28 [a]John 8:42; 16:30 [b]John 13:1, 3; 16:5, 10, 17
29 [a]Matt. 13:34; John 10:6; 16:25

and are not using [a]a figure of
speech.
30 "Now we know that You
know all things, and have no need
for anyone to question You; by
this we [a]believe that You [b]came
from God."
31 Jesus answered them, "Do
you now believe?
32 "Behold, [a]an hour is coming, and has *already* come, for
[b]you to be scattered, each to [c]his
own *home*, and to leave Me
alone; and *yet* [d]I am not alone,
because the Father is with Me.
33 "These things I have spoken
to you, that [a]in Me you may have
peace. [b]In the world you have
tribulation, but [c]take courage; [d]I
have overcome the world."

30 [a]John 2:11; 16:27 [b]John 8:42; 16:28
32 [a]John 4:23; 16:2, 25 [b]Zech. 13:7; Matt. 26:31 [c]John 19:27 [d]John 8:29
★33 [a]John 14:27 [b]John 15:18ff. [c]Matt. 9:2 [d]Rom. 8:37; 2 Cor. 2:14; 4:7ff.; 6:4ff.; Rev. 3:21; 12:11

V INTERCESSION OF THE SON OF GOD, 17:1–26

17 These things Jesus spoke;
and [a]lifting up His eyes to
heaven, He said, "Father, the
hour has come; [b]glorify Thy Son,
that the Son may glorify Thee,
2 even as [a]Thou gavest Him
authority over all mankind, that
[b]to all whom Thou hast given
Him, [c]He may give eternal life.
3 "And this is eternal life,
that they may know Thee, [a]the
only true God, and Jesus Christ
whom [b]Thou hast sent.
4 "[a]I glorified Thee on the
earth, [b]having accomplished the
work which Thou hast given Me
to do.
5 "And now, [a]glorify Thou
Me together with Thyself, Father,

★ 1 [a]John 11:41 [b]John 7:39; 13:31f.
2 [a]John 3:35 [b]John 6:37, 39; 17:6, 9, 24 [c]John 10:28
★ 3 [a]John 5:44 [b]John 3:17; 17:8, 21, 23, 25
4 [a]John 13:31 [b]Luke 22:37; John 4:34
★ 5 [a]John 17:1 [b]John 1:1; 8:58; 17:24; Phil. 2:6

16:23 *in that day.* I.e., after His ascension.
16:25 *in figurative language* (see v. 29).
16:26 *ask in My name.* To address the Father through the Son has been the normal Christian practice ever since. See also note on 14:13.
16:33 *In the world you have tribulation.* There are three aspects of this: (1) general trials which come simply because we live in a sinful world (Rom. 8:35-36); (2) afflictions which God allows to come into our lives (2 Cor. 12:7); and (3) chastisement which comes more directly from God (Heb. 12:6). *I have overcome the world.* See Rom. 8:37; 1 John 5:4.
17:1 In this great so-called "high-priestly" prayer the Lord prays for: (1) His own glorification (vv. 1, 5); (2) believers' protection (v. 11); (3) believers' sanctification (v. 17); (4) the unity of believers (vv. 21–23); (5) the ultimate glorification of believers (v. 24). It is essentially an intercession for those who will form the church (vv. 6–26).
17:3 This is Christ's definition of salvation, especially if we add what is clearly understood: *sent* to be the Savior of the world (3:16; 4:42; 6:33; 1 John 4:14; 5:20).
17:5 *with Thyself.* I.e., in thy presence, "at the right hand of God."

with the glory which I had [b]with Thee before the world was.

6 "[a]I manifested Thy name to the men whom [b]Thou gavest Me out of the world; [c]Thine they were, and Thou gavest them to Me, and they have [d]kept Thy word.

7 "Now they have come to know that everything Thou hast given Me is from Thee;

8 for [a]the words which [a]Thou gavest Me [b]I have given to them; and they received *them,* and truly understood that [c]I came forth from Thee, and they believed that [d]Thou didst send Me.

9 "[a]I ask on their behalf; [b]I do not ask on behalf of the world, but of those whom [c]Thou hast given Me; for [d]they are Thine;

10 and [a]all things that are Mine are Thine, and Thine are Mine; and I have been glorified in them.

11 "And I am no more in the world; and *yet* [a]they themselves are in the world, and [b]I come to Thee. [c]Holy Father, keep them in Thy name, *the name* [d]which Thou hast given Me, that [e]they may be one, even as We *are.*

12 "While I was with them, I was keeping them in Thy name [a]which Thou hast given Me; and I guarded them, and [b]not one of them perished but [c]the son of perdition, that the [d]Scripture might be fulfilled.

13 "But now [a]I come to Thee; and [b]these things I speak in the world, that they may have My [c]joy made full in themselves.

14 "I have given them Thy word; and [a]the world has hated them, because [b]they are not of the world, even as I am not of the world.

15 "I do not ask Thee to take them out of the world, but to keep them from [a]the evil *one.*

16 "[a]They are not of the world, even as I am not of the world.

17 "[a]Sanctify them in the truth; Thy word is truth.

18 "As [a]Thou didst send Me into the world, [b]I also have sent them into the world.

19 "And for their sakes I [a]sanctify Myself, that they themselves also may be [b]sanctified [c]in truth.

20 "I do not ask in behalf of these alone, but for those also who believe in Me through their word;

21 that they may all be one; [a]even as Thou, Father, *art* in Me, and I in Thee, that they also may be in Us; [b]that the world may believe that [c]Thou didst send Me.

22 "And the [a]glory which Thou hast given Me I have given to them; that they may be one, just as We are one;

23 [a]I in them, and Thou in Me, that they may be perfected in unity, that the world may know that [b]Thou didst send Me, and didst [c]love them, even as Thou didst love Me.

24 "Father, I desire that [a]they also, whom Thou hast given Me, [b]be with Me where I am, in order that they may behold My [c]glory, which Thou hast given Me; for Thou didst love Me before [d]the foundation of the world.

25 "O [a]righteous Father, although [b]the world has not known Thee, yet I have known Thee; and

★ 6 [a]John 17:26 [b]John 6:37, 39; 17:2, 9, 24 [c]John 17:9 [d]John 8:51
★ 8 [a]John 6:68; 12:49 [b]John 15:15; 17:14, 26 [c]John 8:42; 16:27, 30 [d]John 3:17; 17:18, 21, 23, 25
9 [a]Luke 22:32; John 14:16 [b]Luke 23:34; John 17:20f. [c]John 6:37, 39; 17:2, 6, 24 [d]John 17:6
10 [a]John 16:15
11 [a]John 13:1 [b]John 7:33; 17:13 [c]John 17:25 [d]John 17:6; Phil. 2:9; Rev. 19:12 [e]John 17:21f.; Rom. 12:5; Gal. 3:28
★12 [a]John 17:6; Phil. 2:9; Rev. 19:12 [b]John 6:39; 18:9 [c]John 6:70 [d]Ps. 41:9
13 [a]John 7:33; 17:11 [b]John 15:11 [c]John 3:29
14 [a]John 15:19 [b]John 8:23; 17:16
★15 [a]Matt. 5:37
16 [a]John 17:14
★17 [a]John 15:3
★18 [a]John 3:17; 17:3, 8, 21, 23, 25 [b]Matt. 10:5; John 4:38; 20:21
19 [a]John 15:13 [b]John 15:3 [c]2 Cor. 7:14; Col. 1:6; 1 John 3:18
★21 [a]John 10:38; 17:11, 23 [b]John 17:8 [c]John 3:17; 17:3, 8, 18, 23, 25
22 [a]John 1:14; 17:24
23 [a]John 10:38; 17:11, 21 [b]John 3:17; 17:3, 8, 18, 21, 25 [c]John 16:27
24 [a]John 17:2 [b]John 12:26 [c]John 1:14; 17:22 [d]Matt. 25:34; John 17:5
25 [a]John 17:11; 1 John 1:9 [b]John 7:29; 15:21 [c]John 3:17; 17:3, 8, 18, 21, 23

17:6 *manifested Thy name.* I.e., revealed your true nature. This divine revelation is the basis on which the church is established.

17:8 *the words.* I.e., the divine message.

17:12 *the son of perdition.* Judas. See Ps. 41:9.

17:15 *from the evil one.* The word can be neuter *(from evil)* or masculine (*from the evil one,* Satan). It should be noted that Christ does not teach withdrawal from the world but that Christians should be in the world but not of it (vv. 14-16).

17:17 *Sanctify* means to set apart for God and His holy purposes, so also v. 19.

17:18 A great text for the mission of the church.

17:21 *that they may all be one.* All believers belong to the one body of Christ (1 Cor. 12:13) and to the same household of God (Eph. 2:19). This spiritual unity should be visibly expressed in the exercise of spiritual gifts (Eph. 4:3-16), prayer, and exhortation (2 Cor. 1:11; Heb. 10:25).

these have known that [c]Thou
didst send Me;

26 [a]John 17:6 [b]John 15:9

26 and [a]I have made Thy
name known to them, and will
make it known; that [b]the love
wherewith Thou didst love Me
may be in them, and I in them."

VI CRUCIFIXION OF THE SON OF GOD, 18:1–19:42

A The Arrest, 18:1–11

★ 1 [a]Matt. 26:30, 36; Mark 14:26, 32; Luke 22:39 [b]2 Sam. 15:23; 1 Kin. 2:37; 15:13; 2 Kin. 23:4, 6, 12; 2 Chr. 15:16; 29:16; 30:14; Jer. 31:40 [c]Matt. 26:36; Mark 14:32; John 18:26
2 [a]Luke 21:37; 22:39
★ 3 [a]John 18:3-11: *Matt. 26:47-56; Mark 14:43-50; Luke 22:47-53* [b]John 18:12; Acts 10:1 [c]John 7:32; 18:12, 18 [d]Matt. 25:1 and marg.
4 [a]John 6:64; 13:1, 11 [b]John 18:7

18 When Jesus had spoken
these words, [a]He went
forth with His disciples over [b]the
ravine of the Kidron, where there
was [c]a garden, into which He
Himself entered, and His disciples.
2 Now Judas also, who was
betraying Him, knew the place;
for Jesus had [a]often met there
with His disciples.
3 [a]Judas then, having received [b]the *Roman* cohort, and
[c]officers from the chief priests
and the Pharisees, *came there
with lanterns and [d]torches and
weapons.
4 Jesus therefore, [a]knowing
all the things that were coming
upon Him, went forth, and *said
to them, "[b]Whom do you seek?"
5 They answered Him,
"Jesus the Nazarene." He *said to
them, "I am *He.*" And Judas also
who was betraying Him, was
standing with them.
6 When therefore He said to
them, "I am *He*", they drew back,
and fell to the ground.

7 [a]John 18:4

7 Again therefore He asked
them, "[a]Whom do you seek?"
And they said, "Jesus the Nazarene."
8 Jesus answered, "I told you
that I am *He;* if therefore you
seek Me, let these go their way,"

9 [a]John 17:12

9 that the word might be
fulfilled which He spoke, "[a]Of
those whom Thou hast given Me I
lost not one."

★10 [a]Matt. 26:51; Mark 14:47

10 Simon Peter therefore
[a]having a sword, drew it, and
struck the high priest's slave, and
cut off his right ear; and the
slave's name was Malchus.

11 [a]Matt. 20:22

11 Jesus therefore said to Peter, "Put the sword into the
sheath; [a]the cup which the Father
has given Me, shall I not drink
it?"

B The Trials, 18:12–19:15

1 Before Annas, 18:12–23

★12 [a]John 18:12f.: *Matt. 26:57ff.* [b]John 18:3

12 [a]So [b]the *Roman* cohort
and the commander, and the [b]of-
ficers of the Jews, arrested Jesus
and bound Him,

★13 [a]Luke 3:2; John 18:24 [b]Matt. 26:3; John 11:49, 51

13 and led Him to [a]Annas
first; for he was father-in-law of
[b]Caiaphas, who was high priest
that year.

14 [a]John 11:50

14 Now Caiaphas was the one
who had advised the Jews that [a]it
was expedient for one man to die
on behalf of the people.

★15 [a]Matt. 26:58; Mark 14:54; Luke 22:54 [b]Matt. 26:3; John 18:24, 28

15 And [a]Simon Peter was following Jesus, and *so was* another
disciple. Now that disciple was
known to the high priest, and entered with Jesus into [b]the court of
the high priest,

16 [a]John 18:16-18: *Matt. 26:69f.; Mark 14:66-68; Luke 22:55-57*

16 [a]but Peter was standing at
the door outside. So the other disciple, who was known to the high
priest, went out and spoke to the
doorkeeper, and brought in Peter.

17 [a]Acts 12:13 [b]John 18:25

17 [a]The slave-girl therefore
who kept the door *said to Peter,
"[b]You are not also *one* of this
man's disciples, are you?" He
*said, "I am not."

18 [a]John 18:3 [b]Mark 14:54, 67 [c]John 21:9

18 Now the slaves and the
[a]officers were standing *there,*
[b]having made [c]a charcoal fire, for
it was cold and they were warm-

18:1 *ravine of the Kidron.* A ravine E. of Jerusalem, between the city and the Mount of Olives.

18:3 *Roman cohort.* A group of 300-600 Roman soldiers.

18:10 *cut off his right ear.* For the sequel see Luke 22:51.

18:12 *officers of the Jews.* Better, servants of the Jewish authorities (high priests).

18:13 A small inner circle of high priests, headed by Annas and Caiaphas, ruled Jerusalem regardless of who was officially *the* high priest. See note on Luke 3:2.

18:15 *another disciple.* John.

ing themselves; and Peter also
was with them, standing and
warming himself.
19 [a]The high priest therefore
questioned Jesus about His disciples, and about His teaching.
20 Jesus answered him, "I
[a]have spoken openly to the world;
I always [b]taught in synagogues,
and [c]in the temple, where all the
Jews come together; and I spoke
nothing in secret.
21 "Why do you question Me?
Question those who have heard
what I spoke to them; behold,
these know what I said."
22 And when He had said
this, one of the [a]officers standing
by [b]gave Jesus a blow, saying, "Is
that the way You answer the high
priest?"
23 [a]Jesus answered him, "If I
have spoken wrongly, bear witness of the wrong; but if rightly,
why do you strike Me?"

19 [a]John 18:19-24: *Matt. 26:59-68; Mark 14:55-65; Luke 22:63-71*
20 [a]John 7:26; 8:26 [b]Matt. 4:23; John 6:59 [c]Matt. 26:55
22 [a]John 18:3 [b]John 19:3
23 [a]Matt. 5:39; Acts 23:2-5

2 *Before Caiaphas,* 18:24-27

24 [a]Annas therefore sent Him
bound to [a]Caiaphas the high
priest.
25 [a]Now [b]Simon Peter was
standing and warming himself.
They said therefore to him, "[c]You
are not also *one* of His disciples,
are you?" He denied *it,* and said,
"I am not."
26 One of the slaves of the
high priest, being a relative of the
one [a]whose ear Peter cut off,
*said, "Did I not see you in [b]the
garden with Him?"
27 Peter therefore denied *it*
again; and immediately [a]a cock
crowed.

★24 [a]John 18:13
25 [a]John 18:25-27: *Matt. 26:71-75; Mark 14:69-72; Luke 22:58-62* [b]John 18:18 [c]John 18:17
26 [a]John 18:10 [b]John 18:1
27 [a]John 13:38

3 *Before Pilate,* 18:28-19:16

28 [a]They *led Jesus therefore
from [b]Caiaphas into [c]the Praetorium; and it was early; and they
themselves did not enter into [c]the
Praetorium in order that [d]they
might not be defiled, but might
eat the Passover.
29 [a]Pilate therefore went out
to them, and *said, "What accusation do you bring against this
Man?"
30 They answered and said to
him, "If this Man were not an
evildoer, we would not have delivered Him up to you."
31 Pilate therefore said to
them, "Take Him yourselves, and
judge Him according to your
law." The Jews said to him, "We
are not permitted to put any one
to death,"
32 that [a]the word of Jesus
might be fulfilled, which He
spoke, signifying by what kind of
death He was about to die.
33 Pilate therefore [a]entered
again into the Praetorium, and
summoned Jesus, and said to
Him, "[b]You are the King of the
Jews?"
34 Jesus answered, "Are you
saying this on your own initiative,
or did others tell you about Me?"
35 Pilate answered, "I am not
a Jew, am I? Your own nation and
the chief priests delivered You up
to me; what have You done?"
36 Jesus answered, "[a]My
kingdom is not of this world. If

★28 [a]Matt. 27:2; Mark 15:1; Luke 23:1 [b]John 18:13 [c]Matt. 27:27; John 18:33; 19:9 [d]John 11:55; Acts 11:3
29 [a]John 18:29-38: *Matt. 27:11-14; Mark 15:2-5; Luke 23:2, 3*
★31
32 [a]Matt. 20:19; 26:2; Mark 10:33f.; Luke 18:32f.; John 3:14; 8:28; 12:32f.
33 [a]John 18:28, 29; 19:9 [b]Luke 23:3; John 19:12
★34
★36 [a]Matt. 26:53; Luke 17:21; John 6:15

18:24 No examination before *Caiaphas* is reported by John. See note on Matt. 26:57. Under Roman law, as in free societies today, a prisoner was assumed to be innocent until proved guilty.

18:28 *they themselves did not enter into the Praetorium.* The Roman headquarters, the barracks (also in v. 33). As a dwelling place of Gentiles it was unclean. Thus the Jewish authorities would not enter, lest they be defiled for the Passover. They were willing, however, to see the murder of Jesus committed without fearing defilement! See note on Matt. 27:27.

18:31 *We are not permitted.* The Sanhedrin could condemn a man to death, but the Roman government had to approve and execute the sentence. See note on Luke 22:66.

18:34 Jesus asked whether Pilate's question arose from his own Roman viewpoint *(Are you saying this on your own initiative)* or from a Jewish viewpoint *(or did others tell you about Me?).*

18:36 Because Pilate's answer indicated that he was concerned only about a rival political kingdom to Rome (v. 35), our Lord replied as He did in this verse, indicating that His was not such a kingdom. Pilate was then satisfied that Jesus was not a political threat and there-

My kingdom were of this world,
then My servants would be fighting, that I might not be delivered
up to the Jews; but as it is, My
kingdom is not of this realm."

37 [a]Matt. 27:11; Mark 15:2; Luke 22:70; 23:3 [b]John 1:14; 3:32; 8:14 [c]John 8:47; 1 John 4:6

37 Pilate therefore said to
Him, "So You are a king?" Jesus
answered, "[a]You say *correctly*
that I am a king. For this I have
been born, and for this I have
come into the world, [b]to bear witness to the truth. [c]Every one who
is of the truth hears My voice."

★38 [a]John 18:33; 19:4 [b]Luke 23:4; John 19:4

38 Pilate *said to Him, "What
is truth?"
And when he had said this, he
[a]went out again to the Jews, and
*said to them, "[b]I find no guilt in
Him.

39 [a]John 18:39-19:16: *Matt. 27:15-18, 20-23; Mark 15:6-15; Luke 23:18-25*

39 "[a]But you have a custom,
that I should release someone for
you at the Passover; do you wish
then that I release for you the
King of the Jews?"

40 [a]Acts 3:14

40 Therefore they cried out
again, saying, "[a]Not this Man, but
Barabbas." Now Barabbas was a
robber.

★ 1 [a]Matt. 27:26

19 Then Pilate therefore took
Jesus, and [a]scourged Him.

2 [a]Matt. 27:27-30: *Mark 15:16-19*

2 [a]And the soldiers wove a
crown of thorns and put it on His
head, and arrayed Him in a purple robe;

3 [a]Matt. 27:29; Mark 15:18 [b]John 18:22

3 and they *began* to come up
to Him, and say, "[a]Hail, King of
the Jews!" and to [b]give Him blows
in the face.

★ 4 [a]John 18:33, 38 [b]Luke 23:4; John 18:38; 19:6

4 And Pilate [a]came out
again, and *said to them, "Behold, I am bringing Him out to
you, that you may know that [b]I
find no guilt in Him."

★ 5 [a]John 19:2

5 Jesus therefore came out,
[a]wearing the crown of thorns and
the purple robe. And *Pilate* *said
to them, "Behold, the Man!"

6 [a]Matt. 26:58; John 18:3 [b]Luke 23:4; John 18:38; 19:4

6 When therefore the chief
priests and the [a]officers saw Him,
they cried out, saying, "Crucify,
crucify!" Pilate *said to them,
"Take Him yourselves, and crucify Him, for [b]I find no guilt in
Him."

★ 7 [a]Lev. 24:16; Matt. 26:63-66 [b]John 5:18; 10:33

7 The Jews answered him,
"[a]We have a law, and by that law
He ought to die because He
[b]made Himself out *to be* the Son
of God."

★ 8

8 When Pilate therefore
heard this statement, he was the
more afraid;

★ 9 [a]John 18:33 [b]Matt. 26:63; 27:12, 14; John 18:34-37

9 and he [a]entered into the
Praetorium again, and *said to
Jesus, "Where are You from?"
But [b]Jesus gave him no answer.

10 Pilate therefore *said to
Him, "You do not speak to me?
Do You not know that I have authority to release You, and I have
authority to crucify You?"

★11 [a]Rom. 13:1 [b]John 18:13f., 28ff.; Acts 3:13

11 Jesus answered, "[a]You
would have no authority over Me,
unless it had been given you from
above; for this reason [b]he who
delivered Me up to you has *the*
greater sin."

★12 [a]Luke 23:2; John 18:33ff.

12 As a result of this Pilate
made efforts to release Him, but
the Jews cried out, saying, "[a]If
you release this Man, you are no
friend of Caesar; every one who
makes himself out *to be* a king
opposes Caesar."

---

fore wished to release Him. *kingdom.* Better, kingship; i.e., My authority is not of human origin.

18:38 *What is truth?* Pilate was not being philosophical but was simply expressing frustration and irritation at Jesus' avoidance of a direct answer to what seemed to him to be a simple question. He did not really understand the charges (18:31, 35, 38; 19:4, 12).

19:1 *scourged.* See note on Matt. 27:26.

19:4 Perhaps Pilate now sought a compromise.

19:5 *Behold, the Man!* Pilate's remark was sarcastic: "Look at your so-called king now!"

19:7 *by that law He ought to die.* A reference to Jesus' alleged blasphemy because He claimed to be God.

19:8 *afraid.* Perhaps of several things: of possible violence; of loss of favor in Rome for his inability to control the turbulent Jews (v. 15); of some sense of Jesus' true nature (this may be indicated by the question in v. 9).

19:9 *no answer.* See Isa. 53:7.

19:11 *he who delivered Me.* Evidently a reference to Caiaphas (18:28).

19:12 The Jewish authorities reverted to the political charge against Jesus, suggesting a potent threat to a provincial governor who served at the whim of the emperor (Tiberius). The Jews had already protested to Rome Pilate's actions in other matters where he was insensitive to their customs (see note on Mark 15:1).

13 When Pilate therefore
heard these words, he brought
Jesus out, and [a]sat down on the
judgment seat at a place called
The Pavement, but [b]in Hebrew,
Gabbatha.
14 Now it was [a]the day of
preparation for the Passover; it
was about the [b]sixth hour. And
he *said to the Jews, "Behold,
[c]your King!"
15 They therefore cried out,
"[a]Away with *Him,* away with
Him, crucify Him!" Pilate *said to
them, "Shall I crucify your King?"
The chief priests answered, "We
have no king but Caesar."
16 And so he then [a]delivered
Him up to them to be crucified.

★13 [a]Matt. 27:19 [b]John 5:2; 19:17, 20
★14-15
★14 [a]Matt. 27:62; John 19:31, 42 [b]Matt. 27:45; Mark 15:25 [c]John 19:19, 21
15 [a]Luke 23:18
★16 [a]Matt. 27:26; Mark 15:15; Luke 23:25

C The Crucifixion, 19:17-37

17 [a]They took Jesus therefore, and He went out, [b]bearing
His own cross, to the place called
[c]the Place of a Skull, which is
called [d]in Hebrew, Golgotha.
18 There they crucified Him,
and with Him [a]two other men,
one on either side, and Jesus in
between.
19 And Pilate wrote an inscription also, and put it on the
cross. And it was written, "[a]JE-
SUS THE NAZARENE, [b]THE
KING OF THE JEWS."
20 Therefore this inscription
many of the Jews read, for the
place where Jesus was crucified
was near the city; and it was written [a]in Hebrew, Latin, *and* in
Greek.
21 And so the chief priests of
the Jews were saying to Pilate,
"Do not write, '[a]The King of the
Jews'; but that He said, 'I am
[a]King of the Jews.'"
22 Pilate answered, "[a]What I
have written I have written."
23 [a]The soldiers therefore,
when they had crucified Jesus,
took His outer garments and
made [b]four parts, a part to every
soldier and *also* the tunic; now
the tunic was seamless, woven in
one piece.
24 They said therefore to one
another, "[a]Let us not tear it, but
cast lots for it, *to decide* whose it
shall be"; [b]that the Scripture
might be fulfilled, "THEY [c]DIVIDED
MY OUTER GARMENTS AMONG THEM,
AND FOR MY CLOTHING THEY CAST
LOTS."
25 Therefore the soldiers did
these things. [a]But there were
standing by the cross of Jesus
[b]His mother, and His mother's
sister, Mary the *wife* of [c]Clopas,
and [d]Mary Magdalene.
26 When Jesus therefore saw
His mother, and [a]the disciple
whom He loved standing nearby,
He *said to His mother, "[b]Wom-
an, behold, your son!"
27 Then He *said to the disciple, "Behold, your mother!" And
from that hour the disciple took
her into [a]his own *household.*
28 After this, Jesus, [a]knowing
that all things had already been
accomplished, [b]in order that the
Scripture might be fulfilled, *said,
"[c]I am thirsty."
29 A jar full of sour wine was
standing there; so [a]they put a
sponge full of the sour wine upon
a branch of hyssop, and brought
it up to His mouth.
30 When Jesus therefore had
received the sour wine, He said,

★17 [a]John 19:17-24: *Matt. 27:33-44; Mark 15:22-32; Luke 23:33-43* [b]Matt. 27:32; Mark 15:21; Luke 14:27; 23:26 [c]Luke 23:33 and marg. [d]John 19:13
18 [a]Luke 23:32
19 [a]Matt. 27:37; Mark 15:26; Luke 23:38 [b]John 19:14, 21
20 [a]John 19:13
21 [a]John 19:14, 19
22 [a]Gen. 43:14; Esth. 4:16
23 [a]Matt. 27:35; Mark 15:24; Luke 23:34 [b]Acts 12:4
★24 [a]Ex. 28:32; Matt. 27:35; Mark 15:24; Luke 23:34 [b]John 19:28, 36f. [c]Ps. 22:18
★25 [a]Matt. 27:55f.; Mark 15:40f.; Luke 23:49 [b]Matt. 12:46 [c]Luke 24:18 [d]Luke 8:2; John 20:1, 18
26 [a]John 13:23 [b]John 2:4
27 [a]Luke 18:28; John 1:11; 16:32; Acts 21:6 [Gr.]
28 [a]John 13:1; 17:4 [b]John 19:24, 36f. [c]Ps. 69:21
★29 [a]John 19:29, 30: *Matt. 27:48, 50; Mark 15:36f.; Luke 23:36*
30 [a]John 17:4 [b]Matt. 27:50; Mark 15:37; Luke 23:46

19:13 *Pavement.* Almost certainly the large paved area that was part of the Castle of Antonia at the NW. corner of the temple area beneath Ecce Homo Arch.

19:14-15 Pilate's sarcasm was directed to the chief priests (whom he hates and mistrusts) and to their clique. He draws from them the response, *"We have no king but Caesar,"* a blasphemous denial of the kingship of God over their nation.

19:14 *preparation for the Passover.* Friday of Passover week. In v. 31 *preparation* refers to Friday as the day of preparation for the Sabbath (see note on Luke 23:54).

19:16 *to be crucified.* See note on Matt. 27:31.

19:17 *Golgotha.* See note on Matt. 27:33.

19:24 See note on Matt. 27:35.

19:25 *Mary.* On the Marys of the N.T. see note on Luke 8:2.

19:29 *sour wine . . . hyssop.* The vinegar was a sour, cheap wine. Hyssop was likely the caper plant, which has stems 2-3 feet long.

"[a]It is finished!" And He bowed His head, and [b]gave up His spirit.

31 The Jews therefore, because it was [a]the day of preparation, so that [b]the bodies should not remain on the cross on the Sabbath (for that Sabbath was a [c]high *day),* asked Pilate that their legs might be broken, and *that* they might be taken away.

★31 [a]John 19:14, 42 [b]Deut. 21:23; Josh. 8:29; 10:26f. [c]Ex. 12:16

32 The soldiers therefore came, and broke the legs of the first man, and of the other man who was [a]crucified with Him;

32 [a]John 19:18

33 but coming to Jesus, when they saw that He was already dead, they did not break His legs;

34 but one of the soldiers pierced His side with a spear, and immediately there came out [a]blood and water.

34 [a]1 John 5:6, 8

35 And he who has seen has [a]borne witness, and his witness is true; and he knows that he is telling the truth, so that you also may believe.

35 [a]John 15:27; 21:24

36 For these things came to pass, [a]that the Scripture might be fulfilled, "[b]Not a bone of Him shall be broken."

★36 [a]John 19:24, 28 [b]Ex. 12:46; Num. 9:12; Ps. 34:20

37 And again another Scripture says, "[a]They shall look on Him whom they pierced."

★37 [a]Zech. 12:10

D The Burial, 19:38–42

★38 [a]John 19:38-42; *Matt. 27:57-61; Mark 15:42-47; Luke 23:50-56* [b]Mark 15:43 [c]John 7:13

38 [a]And after these things Joseph of Arimathea, being a disciple of Jesus, but a [b]secret *one,* for [c]fear of the Jews, asked Pilate that he might take away the body of Jesus; and Pilate granted permission. He came therefore, and took away His body.

39 And [a]Nicodemus came also, who had first come to Him by night; [b]bringing a mixture of [c]myrrh and aloes, about a [d]hundred pounds *weight.*

★39 [a]John 3:1 [b]Mark 16:1 [c]Ps. 45:8; Prov. 7:17; Song of Sol. 4:14; Matt. 2:11 [d]John 12:3

40 And so they took the body of Jesus, and [a]bound it in [b]linen wrappings with the spices, as is the burial custom of the Jews.

★40 [a]Matt. 26:12; Mark 14:8; John 11:44 [b]Luke 24:12; John 20:5, 7

41 Now in the place where He was crucified there was a garden; and in the garden a [a]new tomb, [b]in which no one had yet been laid.

★41 [a]Matt. 27:60 [b]Luke 23:53

42 Therefore on account of the Jewish day of [a]preparation, because the tomb was [b]nearby, they laid Jesus there.

42 [a]John 19:14, 31 [b]John 19:20, 41

VII RESURRECTION OF THE SON OF GOD, 20:1–21:25

A The Empty Tomb, 20:1–10

20 [a]Now on the first *day* of the week [b]Mary Magdalene *came early to the tomb, while it *was still dark, and *saw [c]the stone *already* taken away from the tomb.

★1 [a]John 20:1-8: *Matt. 28:1-8; Mark 16:1-8; Luke 24:1-10* [b]John 19:25; 20:18 [c]Matt. 27:60, 66; 28:2; Mark 15:46; 16:3f.; Luke 24:2; John 11:38

2 And so she *ran and *came to Simon Peter, and to the other [a]disciple whom Jesus loved, and *said to them, "[b]They have taken away the Lord out of the tomb, and we do not know where they have laid Him."

2 [a]John 13:23 [b]John 20:13

19:31 *for that Sabbath was a high day.* I.e., the first day of the Feast of Unleavened Bread fell that year on a Sabbath, making it a "high" festival (Ex. 12:16; Lev. 23:7). They were anxious that the body not remain on the cross (see Deut. 21:22–23). *their legs might be broken.* This was done to hasten death, since the victim could no longer raise himself up on the nail through his feet in order to allow himself to breathe.

19:36 See Ex. 12:46; Num. 9:12; Ps. 34:20.

19:37 See Zech. 12:10.

19:38 *Arimathea.* A town 20 miles NW. of Jerusalem.

19:39 *Nicodemus* apparently became a secret follower of Christ.

19:40 *linen wrappings.* I.e., long strips of linen.

19:41 See Isa. 53:9.

20:1 The order of Christ's appearances after His resurrection seems to be as follows: (1) To Mary Magdalene and the other women (Matt. 28:8–10; John 20:11–18; Mark 16:9–10); (2) to Peter, probably in the afternoon (Luke 24:34; 1 Cor. 15:5); (3) to the disciples on the Emmaus road toward evening (Luke 24:13–32; Mark 16:12); (4) to the disciples, except Thomas, in the upper room (Luke 24:36–43; John 20:19–25); (5) to the disciples, including Thomas, on the next Sunday night (Mark 16:14; John 20:26–29); (6) to seven disciples beside the Sea of Galilee (John 21:1–24); (7) to the apostles and more than 500 brethren and James, the Lord's half brother (1 Cor. 15:6–7); (8) to those who witnessed the ascension (Matt. 28:18–20; Mark 16:19; Luke 24:44–53; Acts 1:3–12).

3 [a]Luke 24:12; John 20:3-10

3 [a]Peter therefore went forth, and the other disciple, and they were going to the tomb.

4 And the two were running together; and the other disciple ran ahead faster than Peter, and came to the tomb first;

5 [a]John 20:11 [b]John 19:40

5 and [a]stooping and looking in, he *saw the [b]linen wrappings lying *there;* but he did not go in.

★ 6

6 Simon Peter therefore also *came, following him, and entered the tomb; and he *beheld the linen wrappings lying *there,*

7 [a]John 11:44 [b]John 19:40

7 and [a]the face-cloth, which had been on His head, not lying with the [b]linen wrappings, but rolled up in a place by itself.

8 [a]John 20:4

8 Then entered in therefore the other disciple also, who [a]had first come to the tomb, and he saw, and believed.

9 [a]Matt. 22:29; John 2:22 [b]Luke 24:26ff., 46

9 For as yet [a]they did not understand the Scripture, [b]that He must rise again from the dead.

10 [a]Luke 24:12

10 So the disciples went away again [a]to their own homes.

B The Appearances of the Risen Lord, 20:11–21:25

1 *To Mary Magdalene,* 20:11–18

11 [a]Mark 16:5 [b]John 20:5

11 [a]But Mary was standing outside the tomb weeping; and so, as she wept, she [b]stooped and looked into the tomb;

12 [a]Matt. 28:2f.; Mark 16:5; Luke 24:4

12 and she *beheld [a]two angels in white sitting, one at the head, and one at the feet, where the body of Jesus had been lying.

13 [a]John 20:15 [b]John 20:2

13 And they *said to her, "[a]Woman, why are you weeping?" She *said to them, "Because [b]they have taken away my Lord, and I do not know where they have laid Him."

14 [a]Matt. 28:9; Mark 16:9 [b]John 21:4

14 When she had said this, she turned around, and *[a]beheld Jesus standing *there,* and [b]did not know that it was Jesus.

15 [a]John 20:13

15 Jesus *said to her, "[a]Woman, why are you weeping? Whom are you seeking?" Supposing Him to be the gardener, she *said to Him, "Sir, if you have carried Him away, tell me where you have laid Him, and I will take Him away."

16 [a]John 5:2 [b]Matt. 23:7; Mark 10:51

16 Jesus *said to her, "Mary!" She *turned and *said to Him [a]in Hebrew, "[b]Rabboni!" (which means, Teacher).

★17 [a]Matt. 28:10 [b]Mark 12:26; 16:19; John 7:33

17 Jesus *said to her, "Stop clinging to Me; for I have not yet ascended to the Father; but go to [a]My brethren, and say to them, 'I [b]ascend to My Father and your Father, and My God and your God.' "

18 [a]John 20:1 [b]Mark 16:10; Luke 24:10, 23

18 [a]Mary Magdalene *came, [b]announcing to the disciples, "I have seen the Lord," and *that* He had said these things to her.

2 *To the disciples, Thomas absent,* 20:19–25

★19 [a]John 7:13 [b]Luke 24:36; John 14:27; 20:21, 26

19 When therefore it was evening, on that day, the first *day* of the week, and when the doors were shut where the disciples were, for [a]fear of the Jews, Jesus came and stood in their midst, and *said to them, "[b]Peace *be* with you."

20 [a]Luke 24:39, 40; John 19:34 [b]John 16:20, 22

20 And when He had said this, [a]He showed them both His hands and His side. The disciples therefore [b]rejoiced when they saw the Lord.

★21 [a]Luke 24:36; John 14:27; 20:19, 26 [b]John 17:18

21 Jesus therefore said to them again, "[a]Peace *be* with you; [b]as the Father has sent Me, I also send you."

★22

22 And when He had said this, He breathed on them, and

20:6 *beheld the linen wrappings lying.* If the body had been stolen, the thieves would not have taken time to unwrap it; but even if they had, the wrappings would have been strewn around the tomb, not lying in perfect order as they were. See note on Luke 24:12.

20:17 *Stop clinging to Me.* I.e., in order to restrain Him. Inappropriate because of His new relationship as resurrected Lord.

20:19 *the Jews.* I.e., the Jewish authorities.

20:21 Another great verse on the mission of the church (see also 17:18).

20:22 *Receive the Holy Spirit.* This was a filling with the Spirit for power until the regularized relationship of the Spirit began at Pentecost.

*said to them, "Receive the Holy
Spirit.
★23 [a]Matt. 16:19; 18:18 **23** "[a]If you forgive the sins of
any, *their sins* have been forgiven
them; if you retain the *sins* of
any, they have been retained."
24 [a]John 11:16 [b]John 6:67 **24** But [a]Thomas, one of [b]the
twelve, called [a]Didymus, was not
with them when Jesus came.
25 [a]John 20:20 [b]Mark 16:11 **25** The other disciples therefore were saying to him, "We
have seen the Lord!" But he said
to them, "Unless I shall see in
[a]His hands the imprint of the
nails, and put my finger into the
place of the nails, and put my
hand into His side, [b]I will not believe."

3 *To the disciples, Thomas present,* 20:26–31

26 [a]Luke 24:36; John 14:27; 20:19, 21 **26** And after eight days again
His disciples were inside, and
Thomas with them. Jesus *came,
the doors having been shut, and
stood in their midst, and said,
"[a]Peace *be* with you."
27 [a]Luke 24:40; John 20:25 **27** Then He *said to Thomas,
"[a]Reach here your finger, and see
My hands; and reach here your
hand, and put it into My side; and
be not unbelieving, but believing."
★28 **28** Thomas answered and said
to Him, "My Lord and my God!"
29 [a]1 Pet. 1:8 **29** Jesus *said to him, "Because you have seen Me, have
you believed? [a]Blessed *are* they
who did not see, and *yet* believed."
30 [a]John 21:25 [b]John 2:11 **30** [a]Many other [b]signs therefore Jesus also performed in the
31 [a]John 19:35 [b]Matt. 4:3 [c]John 3:15 presence of the disciples, which
are not written in this book;
31 but these have been written [a]that you may believe that
Jesus is the Christ, [b]the Son of
God; and that [c]believing you may
have life in His name.

4 *To seven disciples,* 21:1–14

21 After these things Jesus 1 [a]Mark 16:12; John 21:14 [b]John 20:19, 26 [c]John 6:1
[a]manifested Himself
[b]again to the disciples at the [c]Sea
of Tiberias; and He manifested
Himself in this way.
2 There were together Si- 2 [a]John 11:16 [b]John 1:45ff. [c]John 2:1 [d]Matt. 4:21; Mark 1:19; Luke 5:10
mon Peter, and [a]Thomas called
Didymus, and [b]Nathanael of
[c]Cana in Galilee, and [d]the *sons* of
Zebedee, and two others of His
disciples.
3 Simon Peter *said to them, ★ 3 [a]Luke 5:5
"I am going fishing." They *said
to him, "We will also come with
you." They went out, and got into
the boat; and [a]that night they
caught nothing.
4 But when the day was now 4 [a]Luke 24:16; John 20:14
breaking, Jesus stood on the
beach; yet the disciples did not
[a]know that it was Jesus.
5 Jesus therefore *said to ★ 5 [a]Luke 24:41
them, "Children, [a]you do not
have any fish, do you?" They answered Him, "No."
6 And He said to them, 6 [a]Luke 5:4ff.
"[a]Cast the net on the right-hand
side of the boat, and you will find
a catch." They cast therefore, and
then they were not able to haul it
in because of the great number of
fish.
7 [a]That disciple therefore ★ 7 [a]John 13:23; 21:20
whom Jesus loved *said to Peter,
"It is the Lord." And so when Simon Peter heard that it was the
Lord, he put his outer garment on
(for he was stripped *for work),*
and threw himself into the sea.

20:23 *have been forgiven . . . have been retained.* Since only God can forgive sins (Mark 2:7), the disciples and the church are here given the authority to declare what God does when a man either accepts or rejects His Son. See note on Matt. 16:19.

20:28 *My Lord and my God.* Thomas, the doubter, finally recognized the full deity of Jesus Christ. This marks the climax of John's Gospel. The Lord had claimed deity throughout His ministry. Note: (1) the names of deity which He uses (Matt. 22:42–45; John 8:58); (2) the attributes of deity which He claimed (holiness, John 8:46; omnipotence and omnipresence, Matt. 28:20; omniscience, John 11:11–14); (3) the things He claimed to be able to do which only God can do (forgive sins, Mark 2:5–7; raise the dead, John 5:28–30; 11:43; judge all men, John 5:22, 27).

21:3 *boat.* A Galilean fishing boat was about 15 feet long.

21:5 *Children* = boys or lads.

21:7 *stripped for work.* I.e., not completely dressed. Peter swam ashore, while others followed in the boat, dragging the net behind them as they rowed ashore.

8 But the other disciples
came in the little boat, for they
were not far from the land, but
about one hundred yards away,
dragging the net *full* of fish.
9 [a]John 18:18 [b]John 6:9, 11; 21:10, 13 9 And so when they got out
upon the land, they *saw a char-
coal [a]fire *already* laid, and [b]fish
placed on it, and bread.
10 [a]John 6:9, 11; 21:10, 13 10 Jesus *said to them, "Bring
some of the [a]fish which you have
now caught."
11 Simon Peter went up, and
drew the net to land, full of large
fish, a hundred and fifty-three;
and although there were so many,
the net was not torn.
12 [a]John 21:15 12 Jesus *said to them,
"Come *and* have [a]breakfast."
None of the disciples ventured to
question Him, "Who are You?"
knowing that it was the Lord.
13 [a]John 21:9 [b]John 6:9, 11; 21:9, 10 13 Jesus *came and *took
[a]the bread, and *gave them, and
the [b]fish likewise.
★14 [a]John 20:19, 26 14 This is now the [a]third time
that Jesus was manifested to the
disciples, after He was raised from
the dead.

5 *To Peter and the beloved disciple,* 21:15-25

★15 [a]John 21:12 [b]Matt. 26:33; Mark 14:29; John 13:37 [c]Luke 12:32 15 So when they had [a]fin-
ished breakfast, Jesus *said to Si-
mon Peter, "Simon, *son* of John,
do you [b]love Me more than
these?" He *said to Him, "Yes,
Lord; You know that I love You."
He *said to him, "Tend [c]My
lambs."
16 [a]Matt. 2:6; Acts 20:28; 1 Pet. 5:2; Rev. 7:17 16 He *said to him again a
second time, "Simon, *son* of John,
do you love Me?" He *said to
Him, "Yes, Lord; You know that I
love You." He *said to him,
"[a]Shepherd My sheep."
17 [a]John 13:38 [b]John 16:30 [c]John 21:16 17 He *said to him the third
time, "Simon, *son* of John, do you
love Me?" Peter was grieved because He said to him [a]the third
time, "Do you love Me?" And he
said to Him, "Lord, [b]You know all
things; You know that I love
You." Jesus *said to him, "[c]Tend
My sheep.
18 "Truly, truly, I say to you, ★18
when you were younger, you
used to gird yourself, and walk
wherever you wished; but when
you grow old, you will stretch out
your hands, and someone else
will gird you, and bring you
where you do not wish to *go.*"
19 Now this He said, [a]signify- 19 [a]John 12:33; 18:32 [b]2 Pet. 1:14 [c]Matt. 8:22; 16:24; John 21:22
ing by [b]what kind of death he
would glorify God. And when He
had spoken this, He *said to him,
"[c]Follow Me!"
20 Peter, turning around, 20 [a]John 21:7 [b]John 13:25
*saw the [a]disciple whom Jesus
loved following *them;* the one
who also had [b]leaned back on His
breast at the supper, and said,
"Lord, who is the one who betrays You?"
21 Peter therefore seeing him
*said to Jesus, "Lord, and what
about this man?"
22 Jesus *said to him, "If I ★22 [a]Matt. 16:27f.; 1 Cor. 4:5; 11:26; James 5:7; Rev. 2:25 [b]Matt. 8:22; 16:24; John 21:19
want him to remain [a]until I come,
what *is that* to you? You [b]follow
Me!"
23 This saying therefore went 23 [a]Acts 1:15 [b]Matt. 16:27f.; 1 Cor. 4:5; 11:26; James 5:7; Rev. 2:25
out among [a]the brethren that that
disciple would not die; yet Jesus
did not say to him that he would
not die, but *only,* "If I want him
to remain [b]until I come, what *is
that* to you?"
24 This is the disciple who 24 [a]John 15:27
[a]bears witness of these things,
and wrote these things; and we
know that his witness is true.
25 And there are also [a]many ★25 [a]John 20:30
other things which Jesus did,
which if they *were written in detail, I suppose that even the world
itself *would not contain the
books which *were written.

21:14 *the third time.* See 20:19 and 20:26 for the other two occasions.

21:15-17 Peter's three denials are here offset by three protestations of his love for Christ. John probably used the two different words for love in these verses synonymously (compare 3:35, *agapao,* with 5:20, *phileo*). *more than these* (v. 15) means "more than the other disciples" (see Matt. 26:33; Mark 14:29).

21:18-19 A prophecy of the martyrdom of Peter.

21:22 The Lord rebuked Peter for being distracted over John's future. Peter's only responsibility was to *follow* Christ.

21:25 The Gospels were not intended to be complete accounts of the life of Christ.

INTRODUCTION TO THE ACTS OF THE APOSTLES

AUTHOR: Luke DATE: 61

Authorship *That the author of Acts was a companion of Paul is clear from the passages in the book in which "we" and "us" are used (16:10-17; 20:5-21:18; 27:1-28:16). These sections themselves eliminate known companions of Paul other than Luke, and Colossians 4:14 and Philemon 24 point affirmatively to Luke, who was a physician. The frequent use of medical terms also substantiates this conclusion (1:3; 3:7ff.; 9:18, 33; 13:11; 28:1-10). Luke answered the Macedonian call with Paul, was in charge of the work at Philippi for about six years, and later was with Paul in Rome during the time of Paul's house arrest. It was probably during this last period that the book was written. If it were written later it would be very difficult to explain the absence of mention of such momentous events as the burning of Rome, the martyrdom of Paul, or the destruction of Jerusalem.*

Importance of the Book *(1) Acts gives us the record of the spread of Christianity from the coming of the Spirit on the day of Pentecost to Paul's arrival in Rome to preach the gospel in the world's capital. In this regard, then, it is the record of the continuation of those things which Jesus began while on earth and which He continued as the risen Head of the Church and the One who sent the Holy Spirit (1:2; 2:33). The book is sometimes called The Acts of the Holy Spirit.*

(2) The thirty years covered by the book were important years of transition. The gospel was preached first only to Jews, and the early church was composed largely of Jewish believers. As more and more Gentiles were included, the Church became distinct from Judaism.

(3) Doctrines which are later developed in the epistles appear in seed form in Acts (the Spirit, 1:8; the kingdom, 3:21; 15:16; elders, 11:30; Gentile salvation, 15:14). However, the book emphasizes the practice of doctrine more than the statement of doctrine.

(4) Acts furnishes principles for missionary work. (5) The book reveals patterns for church life. (6) Archaeological discoveries confirm in a remarkable way the historical accuracy of Luke's writing.

Contents *In the first twelve chapters of the book the important figures are Peter, Stephen, Philip, Barnabas, and James. From chapter 13 to the end, the dominant person is Paul. The book may also be divided according to the geographical divisions mentioned in the Great Commission (1:8).*

OUTLINE OF THE ACTS

I. Christianity in Jerusalem, 1:1-8:3

- A. The Risen Lord, 1:1-26
  1. The Lord confirming, 1:1-5
  2. The Lord commissioning, 1:6-11
  3. The Lord choosing, 1:12-26
- B. Pentecost: Birthday of the Church, 2:1-47
  1. The power of Pentecost, 2:1-13
  2. The preaching of Pentecost, 2:14-36
  3. The results of Pentecost, 2:37-47
- C. The Healing of a Lame Man, 3:1-26
  1. The miracle, 3:1-11
  2. The message, 3:12-26
- D. The Beginning of Persecution, 4:1-37
  1. The persecution, 4:1-22
  2. The prayer, 4:23-31
  3. The provision, 4:32-37
- E. Purging and Persecution, 5:1-42
  1. Purging from within, 5:1-11
  2. Purging from without, 5:12-42
- F. Choosing Colaborers, 6:1-7
- G. Stephen, the First Martyr, 6:8-8:3
  1. The stirring of the people, 6:8-15
  2. The sermon of Stephen, 7:1-53
  3. The stoning of Stephen, 7:54-8:3

II. Christianity in Palestine and Syria, 8:4-12:25

- A. The Christians Scattered, 8:4-40
  1. The preaching in Samaria, 8:4-25
  2. The preaching on the Gaza road, 8:26-40
- B. The Conversion of Paul, 9:1-31
  1. The account of Paul's conversion, 9:1-19
  2. The aftermath of Paul's conversion, 9:20-31
- C. The Conversion of Gentiles, 9:32-11:30
  1. The preparation of Peter, 9:32-10:22
  2. The preaching of Peter, 10:23-48
  3. The plea of Peter, 11:1-18
  4. The church at Antioch, 11:19-30
- D. The Christians Persecuted by Herod, 12:1-25
  1. The death of James, 12:1-2
  2. The deliverance of Peter, 12:3-19
  3. The death of Herod, 12:20-23
  4. The dissemination of the Word, 12:24-25

III. Christianity to the Uttermost Part of the World, 13:1–28:31

A. The First Missionary Journey, 13:1–14:28
   1. Events in Antioch, 13:1–3
   2. Events in Cyprus, 13:4–12
   3. Events in Galatian cities, 13:13–14:20
   4. Events on the return to Antioch, 14:21–28

B. The Council at Jerusalem, 15:1–35
   1. The dissension, 15:1–5
   2. The discussion, 15:6–18
   3. The decision, 15:19–29
   4. The letter delivered to Antioch, 15:30–35

C. The Second Missionary Journey, 15:36–18:22
   1. The personnel chosen, 15:36–40
   2. The churches revisited, 15:41–16:5
   3. The call to Europe, 16:6–10
   4. The work at Philippi, 16:11–40
   5. The work at Thessalonica, Berea, and Athens, 17:1–34
   6. The ministry at Corinth, 18:1–17
   7. The journey completed, 18:18–22

D. The Third Missionary Journey, 18:23–21:26
   1. Ephesus: The power of the Word, 18:23–19:41
   2. Greece, 20:1–5
   3. Asia Minor: Troas and the elders of Ephesus, 20:6–38
   4. From Miletus to Caesarea, 21:1–14
   5. Paul with the Jerusalem church, 21:15–26

E. The Journey to Rome, 21:27–28:31
   1. Paul's arrest and defense, 21:27–22:29
   2. Paul brought before the Sanhedrin, 22:30–23:10
   3. Paul escorted to Caesarea, 23:11–35
   4. Paul's defense before Felix, 24:1–27
   5. Paul's defense before Festus, 25:1–27
   6. Paul's defense before Agrippa, 26:1–32
   7. Paul's voyage and shipwreck, 27:1–44
   8. Paul in Malta and on to Rome, 28:1–16
   9. Paul in Rome, 28:17–31

THE ACTS OF THE APOSTLES

I CHRISTIANITY IN JERUSALEM, 1:1–8:3

A The Risen Lord, 1:1–26

1 The Lord confirming, 1:1–5

1 The first account I composed,
[a]Theophilus, about all that
Jesus [b]began to do and teach,
2 until the day when He
[a]was taken up, after He [b]had by
the Holy Spirit given orders to
[c]the apostles whom He had [d]chosen.
3 To these [a]He also presented Himself alive, after His
suffering, by many convincing
proofs, appearing to them over *a*
period of forty days, and speaking
of [b]the things concerning the
kingdom of God.
4 And gathering them together, He commanded them [a]not
to leave Jerusalem, but to wait for
[b]what the Father had promised,
"Which," *He said,* "you heard of
from Me;
5 for [a]John baptized with
water, but you shall be baptized
with the Holy Spirit [b]not many
days from now."

★ 1 [a]Luke 1:3 [b]Luke 3:23
2 [a]Mark 16:19; Acts 1:9, 11, 22 [b]Matt. 28:19f.; Mark 16:15; John 20:21f.; Acts 10:42 [c]Mark 6:30 [d]John 13:18; Acts 10:41
★ 3 [a]Matt. 28:17; Mark 16:12, 14; Luke 24:34, 36; John 20:19, 26; 21:1, 14; 1 Cor. 15:5-7 [b]Acts 8:12; 19:8; 28:23, 31
4 [a]Luke 24:49 [b]John 14:16, 26; 15:26; Acts 2:33
★ 5 [a]Matt. 3:11; Acts 11:16 [b]Acts 2:1-4

2 The Lord commissioning, 1:6–11

6 And so when they had
come together, they were asking
Him, saying, "Lord, [a]is it at this
time You are restoring the kingdom to Israel?"
7 He said to them, "It is not
for you to know times or epochs
which [a]the Father has fixed by
His own authority;
8 but you shall receive
power [a]when the Holy Spirit has

★ 6 [a]Matt. 17:11; Mark 9:12; Luke 17:20; 19:11
★ 7 [a]Matt. 24:36; Mark 13:32
8 [a]Acts 2:1-4 [b]Luke 24:48; John 15:27 [c]Acts 8:1, 5, 14 [d]Matt. 28:19; Mark 16:15; Rom. 10:18; Col. 1:23

1:1 *The first account.* I.e., the Gospel of Luke. *Theophilus* means "dear to God" or "friend of God." He was probably a Roman official, since the title "most excellent" (Luke 1:3) indicates an official position in Acts 23:26; 24:3; 26:25.

1:3 *forty days.* The only reference to the length of Christ's ministry on earth between His resurrection and His ascension.

1:5 *baptized with the Holy Spirit.* This promise was first fulfilled on the day of Pentecost (see 11:15–16) and affects every believer by joining him to the body of Christ (1 Cor. 12:13). See notes on Matt. 3:11.

1:6 *the kingdom to Israel.* The Messianic, Davidic, millennial kingdom on earth. The time of its coming is unrevealed (Matt. 24:36, 42).

1:7 There is no rebuke in Christ's answer, for God is not through with Israel and the kingdom will eventually come (Rom. 11:26). In the meantime, the gospel must be preached throughout the whole world (Acts 1:8).

come upon you; and you shall be
[b]My witnesses both in Jerusalem,
and in all Judea and [c]Samaria,
and even to [d]the remotest part of
the earth."
9 And after He had said
these things, [a]He was lifted up
while they were looking on, and a
cloud received Him out of their
sight.
10 And as they were gazing
intently into the sky while He was
departing, behold, [a]two men in
white clothing stood beside them;
11 and they also said, "[a]Men
of Galilee, why do you stand
looking into the sky? This Jesus,
who [b]has been taken up from you
into heaven, will [c]come in just the
same way as you have watched
Him go into heaven."

3 *The Lord choosing,* 1:12–26

12 Then they [a]returned to Jerusalem from the [b]mount called
Olivet, which is near Jerusalem, a
Sabbath day's journey away.
13 And when they had en-
tered, they went up to [a]the upper
room, where they were staying;
[b]that is, Peter and John and James
and Andrew, Philip and Thomas,
Bartholomew and Matthew,
James *the son* of Alphaeus, and
Simon the Zealot, and [c]Judas *the
son* of James.
14 These all with one mind
[a]were continually devoting themselves to prayer, along with [b]*the*
women, and Mary the [c]mother of
Jesus, and with His [c]brothers.
15 And at this time Peter
stood up in the midst of [a]the
brethren (a gathering of about
one hundred and twenty persons
was there together), and said,
16 "Brethren, [a]the Scripture
had to be fulfilled, which the

9 [a]Acts 1:2
10 [a]Luke 24:4; John 20:12
★11 [a]Acts 2:7; 13:31 [b]Mark 16:19; Acts 1:9, 22 [c]Matt. 16:27f.; Acts 3:21
★12 [a]Luke 24:50, 52 [b]Matt. 21:1
★13 [a]Mark 14:15; Luke 22:12; Acts 9:37, 39; 20:8 [b]Acts 1:13: *Matt. 1:2-4; Mark 3:16-19; Luke 6:14-16* [c]John 14:22
14 [a]Acts 2:42; 6:4; Rom. 12:12; Eph. 6:18; Col. 4:2 [b]Luke 8:2f. [c]Matt. 12:46
★15 [a]John 21:23; Acts 6:3; 9:30; 10:23; 11:1, 12, 26, 29; 12:17; 14:2; 15:1, 3, 22, 23, 32f., 40; 16:2, 40; 17:6, 10; 14; 18:18, 27;21:7, 17; 22:5; 28:14f.; Rom. 1:13
★16 [a]John 13:18; 17:12; Acts 1:20 [b]Matt. 26:47; Mark 14:43; Luke 22:47; John 18:3

Holy Spirit foretold by the mouth
of David concerning Judas, [b]who
became a guide to those who arrested Jesus.
17 "For he was [a]counted
among us, and received his portion in [b]this ministry."
18 (Now this man [a]acquired a
field with [b]the price of his wickedness; and falling headlong, he
burst open in the middle and all
his bowels gushed out.
19 And it became known to
all who were living in Jerusalem;
so that in [a]their own language
that field was called Hakeldama,
that is, Field of Blood).
20 "For it is written in the
book of Psalms,

'[a]LET HIS HOMESTEAD BE MADE
DESOLATE,
AND LET NO MAN DWELL IN
IT';

and,

'[b]HIS OFFICE LET ANOTHER MAN
TAKE.'

21 "It is therefore necessary
that of the men who have accompanied us all the time that [a]the
Lord Jesus went in and out among
us—
22 [a]beginning with the baptism of John, until the day that He
[b]was taken up from us—one of
these should become a [c]witness
with us of His resurrection."
23 And they put forward two
men, Joseph called Barsabbas
(who was also called Justus), and
[a]Matthias.
24 And they [a]prayed, and
said, "Thou, Lord, [b]who knowest
the hearts of all men, show which
one of these two Thou hast chosen

17 [a]John 6:70f. [b]Acts 1:25; 20:24; 21:19
★18 [a]Matt. 27:3-10 [b]Matt. 26:14f.
19 [a]Matt. 27:8; Acts 21:40
★20 [a]Ps. 69:25 [b]Ps. 109:8
21 [a]Luke 24:3
22 [a]Mark 1:1-4 [b]Acts 1:2 [c]Acts 1:8; 2:32
23 [a]Acts 1:26
24 [a]Acts 6:6; 13:3; 14:23 [b]1 Sam. 16:7; Jer. 17:10; Acts 15:8; Rom. 8:27

1:11 *in just the same way.* The second coming of Christ, like the ascension, will be personal and visible (Rev. 1:8; 19:11–16).

1:12 *a Sabbath day's journey.* About 2000 cubits, or a little more than half a mile—the distance the rabbis allowed Jews to journey on the Sabbath. This limitation was apparently arrived at on the basis of Ex. 16:29 interpreted by Num. 35:5.

1:13 *Simon the Zealot.* See note on Matt. 10:4.

1:15 *Peter* had made a full recovery of confidence and authority from the night of his denial and was now fulfilling Matt. 16:19.

1:16 See Ps. 41:9.

1:18 *burst open in the middle.* Probably due to Judas' ineptness in trying to hang himself (Matt. 27:5).

1:20 See Ps. 69:25; 109:8.

25 to occupy [a]this ministry
and [b]apostleship from which Judas turned aside to go to his own
place."
26 And they [a]drew lots for
them, and the lot fell to [b]Matthi-
as; and he was numbered with
[c]the eleven apostles.

25 [a]Acts 1:17 [b]Rom. 1:5; 1 Cor. 9:2; Gal. 2:8
★26 [a]Lev. 16:8; Josh. 14:2; 1 Sam. 14:41f.; Neh. 10:34; 11:1; Prov. 16:33 [b]Acts 1:23 [c]Acts 2:14

B Pentecost: Birthday of the Church, 2:1–47

1 *The power of Pentecost,* 2:1–13

2 And when [a]the day of Pentecost had come, they were all
together in one place.
2 And suddenly there came
from heaven a noise like a violent, rushing wind, and it filled
[a]the whole house where they
were sitting.
3 And there appeared to
them tongues as of fire distributing themselves, and they rested
on each one of them.
4 And they were all [a]filled
with the Holy Spirit and began to
[b]speak with other tongues, as the
Spirit was giving them utterance.
5 Now there were Jews living in Jerusalem, [a]devout men,
from every nation under heaven.
6 And when [a]this sound occurred, the multitude came together, and were bewildered, because they were each one hearing
them speak in his own language.
7 And [a]they were amazed
and marveled, saying, "Why, are
not all these who are speaking
[b]Galileans?
8 "And how is it that we each
hear *them* in our own language to
which we were born?
9 "Parthians and Medes and
Elamites, and residents of Mesopotamia, Judea and [a]Cappadocia,
[b]Pontus and [c]Asia,
10 [a]Phrygia and [b]Pamphylia,
Egypt and the districts of Libya
around [c]Cyrene, and [d]visitors
from Rome, both Jews and [e]pros-
elytes,
11 Cretans and Arabs—we
hear them in our *own* tongues
speaking of the mighty deeds of
God."
12 And [a]they continued in
amazement and great perplexity,
saying to one another, "What
does this mean?"
13 But others were mocking
and saying, "[a]They are full of
sweet wine."

★ 1 [a]Lev. 23:15f.; Acts 20:16; 1 Cor. 16:8
★ 2 [a]Acts 4:31
★ 3
★ 4 [a]Matt. 10:20; Acts 1:5, 8; 4:8, 31; 6:3, 5; 7:55; 8:17; 9:17; 11:15; 13:9, 52 [b]Mark 16:17; 1 Cor. 12:10f.; 14:21
5 [a]Luke 2:25; Acts 8:2
6 [a]Acts 2:2
7 [a]Acts 2:12 [b]Matt. 26:73; Acts 1:11
★ 9–11
9 [a]1 Pet. 1:1 [b]Acts 18:2; 1 Pet. 1:1 [c]Acts 6:9; 16:6; 19:10; 20:4; 21:27; 24:18; 27:2; Rom. 16:5; 1 Cor. 16:19; 2 Cor. 1:8; 2 Tim. 1:15; Rev. 1:4
10 [a]Acts 16:6; 18:23 [b]Acts 13:13; 14:24; 15:38; 27:5 [c]Matt. 27:32 [d]Acts 17:21 [e]Matt. 23:15
12 [a]Acts 2:7
13 [a]1 Cor. 14:23

2 *The preaching of Pentecost,* 2:14–36

14 But Peter, taking his stand
with [a]the eleven, raised his voice
and declared to them: "Men of Judea, and all you who live in Jerusalem, let this be known to you,
and give heed to my words.
15 "For these men are not
drunk, as you suppose, [a]for it is
only the third hour of the day;
16 but this is what was spoken of through the prophet Joel:

★14 [a]Acts 1:26
★15 [a]1 Thess. 5:7
★16–21

1:26 *drew lots.* Two names were written on stones and placed in an urn. The one that fell out first was taken to be the Lord's choice (cf. Prov. 16:33; Jon. 1:7). The occasion was unique, for the Lord was not there in person to appoint and the Spirit had not been given in the special way of Pentecost.

2:1 *the day of Pentecost.* The fourth of the annual feasts of the Jews (after Passover, Unleavened Bread, and Firstfruits), it came 50 days after Firstfruits (a type of the resurrection of Christ, 1 Cor. 15:23). Pentecost was the Greek name for the Jewish Feast of Weeks, so called because it fell seven (a week of) weeks after Firstfruits. It celebrated the wheat harvest (Ex. 23:16). This day of Pentecost in Acts 2 marked the beginning of the Church (Matt. 16:18).

2:2 *a noise.* It was like a wind but was not wind.

2:3 Possibly at this point the group left the house and went to the temple.

2:4 *with other tongues.* Actual languages unknown to the speakers but understood by the hearers (v. 8).

2:9–11 These countries form a circuit around the Mediterranean Sea.

2:14 Here begins Peter's great sermon, with an explanation of the phenomena they were witnessing (vv. 14–21). He then proclaimed the gospel (vv. 22–35) and applied the message (v. 36).

2:15 *the third hour* = 9 a.m. Jews engaged in the exercises of the synagogue on feast days abstained from eating and drinking until 10 a.m. or noon; therefore, this could not be drunkenness.

2:16–21 The fulfillment of this prophecy will be in the last days, immediately preceding the re-

17 [a]Joel 2:28-32

17 '[a]And it shall be in the last
days,' God says,
'That I will pour forth of
My Spirit upon all mankind;
And your sons and your
daughters shall prophesy,
And your young men shall
see visions,
And your old men shall
dream dreams;
18 Even upon My bondslaves,
both men and women,
I will in those days pour
forth of My Spirit
And they shall prophesy.
19 'And I will grant wonders
in the sky above,
And signs on the earth beneath,
Blood, and fire, and vapor
of smoke.
20 'The sun shall be turned
into darkness,
And the moon into blood,
Before the great and glorious day of the Lord
shall come.

21 [a]Rom. 10:13

21 'And it shall be, that [a]every
one who calls on the
name of the Lord shall
be saved.'

★22-36

22 [a]Acts 3:6; 4:10; 10:38 [b]John 3:2 [c]John 4:48; Acts 2:19, 43

23 [a]Luke 22:22; Acts 3:18; 4:28; 1 Pet. 1:20 [b]Luke 24:20; Acts 3:13

22 "Men of Israel, listen to
these words: [a]Jesus the Nazarene,
[b]a man attested to you by God
with miracles and [c]wonders and
signs which God performed
through Him in your midst, just
as you yourselves know—
23 this *Man,* delivered up by
the [a]predetermined plan and
foreknowledge of God, [b]you
nailed to a cross by the hands of
godless men and put *Him* to
death.

24 [a]Acts 2:32; 3:15, 26; 4:10; 5:30; 10:40; 13:30, 33, 34, 37; 17:31; Rom. 4:24; 6:4; 8:11; 10:9; 1 Cor. 6:14; 15:15; 2 Cor. 4:14; Gal. 1:1; Eph. 1:20; Col. 2:12; 1 Thess. 1:10; Heb. 13:20; 1 Pet. 1:21 [b]John 20:9

25 [a]Ps. 16:8-11

24 "And [a]God raised Him up
again, putting an end to the agony
of death, since it [b]was impossible
for Him to be held in its power.
25 "For David says of Him,

'[a]I was always beholding
the Lord in my presence;
For He is at my right hand,
that I may not be shaken.
26 'Therefore my heart was
glad and my tongue exulted;
Moreover my flesh also
will abide in hope;

★27 [a]Matt. 11:23; Acts 2:31 [b]Acts 13:35

27 Because Thou wilt not
abandon my soul to
[a]Hades,
[b]Nor allow Thy Holy One
to undergo decay.
28 'Thou hast made known to
me the ways of life;
Thou wilt make me full of
gladness with Thy presence.'

29 [a]Acts 7:8f.; Heb. 7:4 [b]Acts 13:36 [c]1 Kin. 2:10 [d]Neh. 3:16

30 [a]Matt. 22:43 [b]2 Sam. 7:12f.; Ps. 89:3f.; 132:11

31 [a]Matt. 11:23; Acts 2:27

32 [a]Acts 2:24; 3:15, 26; 4:10; 5:30; 10:40; 13:30, 33, 34, 37; 17:31; Rom. 4:24; 6:4; 8:11; 10:9; 1 Cor. 6:14; 15:15; 2 Cor. 4:14; Gal. 1:1; Eph. 1:20; Col. 2:12; 1 Thess. 1:10; Heb. 13:20; 1 Pet. 1:21 [b]Acts 1:8

★33 [a]Mark 16:19; Acts 5:31 [b]Acts 1:4 [c]John 7:39; Gal. 3:14 [d]Acts 2:17; 10:45

29 "Brethren, I may confidently say to you regarding the
[a]patriarch David that he both
[b]died and [c]was buried, and [d]his
tomb is with us to this day.
30 "And so, because he was [a]a
prophet, and knew that [b]God had
sworn to him with an oath to seat
one of his descendants upon his
throne,
31 he looked ahead and spoke
of the resurrection of the Christ,
that He was neither abandoned to
[a]Hades, nor did His flesh suffer
decay.
32 "This Jesus [a]God raised up
again, to which we are all [b]witnesses.
33 "Therefore having been ex-

---

turn of Christ, when all the particulars (e.g., v. 20 and Rev. 6:12) of the prophecy will come to pass. Peter reminded his hearers that, knowing Joel's prophecy, they should have recognized what they were seeing as a work of the Spirit, not a result of drunkenness.

2:22-36 Peter reviewed the life and death of Jesus of Nazareth (vv. 22-24) and then recited the prophecy of the resurrection, (vv. 25-31), quoting Ps. 16:8-11. Since David was speaking of the Messiah (v. 31), Peter continued, and since Jesus was raised from the dead (v. 32), Jesus must be the Messiah (v. 36).

2:27 *Hades.* The unseen world, sometimes specifically a place of torment (see note on Luke 16:23) and sometimes merely the grave, as here. The meaning is that Christ's body and spirit would not be allowed to remain separated (v. 31).

2:33 Returning to the original point, Peter declared that it is the exalted Jesus who sent the Holy Spirit.

alted [a]to the right hand of God,
and [b]having received from the Father [c]the promise of the Holy
Spirit, He has [d]poured forth this
which you both see and hear.
34 "For it was not David who
ascended into heaven, but he
himself says:

'[a]THE LORD SAID TO MY LORD,
"SIT AT MY RIGHT HAND,
35 UNTIL I MAKE THINE ENEMIES
A FOOTSTOOL FOR THY
FEET." '

36 "Therefore let all the
[a]house of Israel know for certain
that God has made Him both
[b]Lord and Christ—this Jesus
[c]whom you crucified."

3 *The results of Pentecost,* 2:37–47

37 Now when they heard
this, they were pierced to the
heart, and said to Peter and the
rest of the apostles, "Brethren,
[a]what shall we do?"
38 And Peter *said* to them,
"[a]Repent, and let each of you be
[b]baptized in the name of Jesus
Christ for the forgiveness of your
sins; and you shall receive the gift
of the Holy Spirit.
39 "For [a]the promise is for you
and your children, and for all who
are [b]far off, as many as the Lord
our God shall call to Himself."
40 And with many other
words he solemnly [a]testified and
kept on exhorting them, saying,
"Be saved from this [b]perverse
generation!"

34 [a]Ps. 110:1; Matt. 22:44f.
36 [a]Ezek. 36:22, 32, 37; 45:6 [b]Luke 2:11 [c]Acts 2:23
37 [a]Luke 3:10, 12, 14
★38 [a]Mark 1:15; Luke 24:47; Acts 3:19; 5:31; 20:21 [b]Mark 16:16; Acts 8:12, 16; 22:16
39 [a]Is. 44:3; 54:13; 57:19; Joel 2:32; Rom. 9:4; Eph. 2:12 [b]Eph. 2:13, 17
40 [a]Luke 16:28 [b]Deut. 32:5; Matt. 17:17; Phil. 2:15

41 So then, those who had received his word were baptized;
and there were added that day
about three thousand [a]souls.
42 And they were [a]continual-
ly devoting themselves to the
apostles' teaching and to fellowship, to [b]the breaking of bread
and [a]to prayer.
43 And everyone kept feeling
a sense of awe; and many [a]won-
ders and signs were taking place
through the apostles.
44 And all those who had believed were together, and [a]had all
things in common;
45 and they [a]*began* selling
their property and possessions,
and were sharing them with all, as
anyone might have need.
46 [a]And day by day continuing with one mind in the temple,
and [b]breaking bread from house
to house, they were taking their
meals together with gladness and
sincerity of heart,
47 praising God, and [a]having
favor with all the people. And the
Lord [b]was adding to their number
day by day [c]those who were
being saved.

C The Healing of a Lame Man, 3:1–26

1 *The miracle,* 3:1–11

3 Now [a]Peter and John were
going up to the temple at the
ninth *hour,* [b]the hour of prayer.
2 And [a]a certain man who
had been lame from his mother's

41 [a]Acts 3:23; 7:14; 27:37; Rom. 13:1; 1 Pet. 3:20; Rev. 16:3
★42 [a]Acts 1:14 [b]Luke 24:30; Acts 2:46; 20:7; 1 Cor. 10:16
43 [a]Acts 2:22
★44 [a]Acts 4:32, 37; 5:2
45 [a]Matt. 19:21; Acts 4:34
46 [a]Acts 5:42 [b]Luke 24:30; Acts 2:42; 20:7; 1 Cor. 10:16
47 [a]Acts 5:13 [b]Acts 2:41; 4:4; 5:14; 6:1, 7; 9:31, 35, 42; 11:21, 24; 14:1, 21; 16:5; 17:12 [c]1 Cor. 1:18
★ 1 [a]Luke 22:8; Acts 3:3, 4, 11 [b]Ps. 55:17; Matt. 27:45; Acts 10:30
★ 2 [a]Acts 14:8 [b]Luke 16:20 [c]John 9:8; Acts 3:10

2:38 *Repent.* To change one's mind; specifically, here, about Jesus of Nazareth, and to acknowledge Him as Lord (= God) and Christ (= Messiah). Such repentance brings salvation. There is also a repentance needed in the Christian life in relation to specific sins (2 Cor. 7:9; Rev. 2:5). *be baptized . . . for the forgiveness of your sins.* On baptism see note on Matt. 3:11. Water baptism is the outward sign of repentance and forgiveness of sins. Forgiveness is through faith in Christ, not through the act of baptism (*for* may here mean "because of," as in Matt. 12:41). *the gift of the Holy Spirit.* The Spirit is a gift to all who believe, not a reward to some.

2:42 *breaking of bread.* I.e., celebrating the Lord's Supper.

2:44 *had all things in common.* This community of goods seems to have been limited to the early years of the Jerusalem church only. It may have been necessitated by the many pilgrims who lingered in Jerusalem to learn more of their new Christian faith.

3:1 *the ninth hour.* =3 p.m., the hour of prayer associated with the evening sacrifice.

3:2 *the gate . . . Beautiful.* Probably the Nicanor Gate, the eastern gate of the temple buildings, leading from the Court of the Gentiles into the Women's Court.

womb was being carried along, whom they [b]used to set down every day at the gate of the temple which is called Beautiful, [c]in order to beg alms of those who were entering the temple.

3 [a]Luke 22:8; Acts 3:1, 4, 11

3 And when he saw [a]Peter and John about to go into the temple, he *began* asking to receive alms.

4 [a]Acts 10:4

4 And Peter, along with John, [a]fixed his gaze upon him and said, "Look at us!"

5 And he *began* to give them his attention, expecting to receive something from them.

★ 6 [a]Acts 2:22; 3:16; 4:10

6 But Peter said, "I do not possess silver and gold, but what I do have I give to you: [a]In the name of Jesus Christ the Nazarene—walk!"

7 And seizing him by the right hand, he raised him up; and immediately his feet and his ankles were strengthened.

8 [a]Acts 14:10

8 [a]And with a leap, he stood upright and *began* to walk; and he entered the temple with them, walking and leaping and praising God.

9 [a]Acts 4:16, 21

9 And [a]all the people saw him walking and praising God;

10 [a]John 9:8; Acts 3:2

10 and they were taking note of him as being the one who used to [a]sit at the Beautiful Gate of the temple to *beg* alms, and they were filled with wonder and amazement at what had happened to him.

★11 [a]Luke 22:8; Acts 3:3, 4 [b]John 10:23; Acts 5:12

11 And while he was clinging to [a]Peter and John, all the people ran together to them at the so-called [b]portico of Solomon, full of amazement.

2 *The message,* 3:12–26

12 [a]Matt. 11:25; 17:4; 22:1; Luke 14:3; Acts 5:8; 10:46

12 But when Peter saw *this,* he [a]replied to the people, "Men of Israel, why do you marvel at this, or why do you gaze at us, as if by our own power or piety we had made him walk?

★13 [a]Matt. 22:32 [b]Ex. 3:13, 15; Acts 5:30; 7:32; 22:14 [c]Acts 3:26; 4:27, 30 [d]Matt. 20:19; John 19:11; Acts 2:23 [e]Matt. 27:2 [f]Luke 23:4

13 "[a]The God of Abraham, Isaac, and Jacob, [b]the God of our fathers, has glorified His [c]servant Jesus, *the one* whom [d]you delivered up, and disowned in the presence of [e]Pilate, when he had [f]decided to release Him.

14 [a]Mark 1:24; Acts 4:27; 7:52; 2 Cor. 5:21 [b]Matt. 27:20; Mark 15:11; Luke 23:18-25

14 "But you disowned [a]the Holy and Righteous One, and [b]asked for a murderer to be granted to you,

★15 [a]Acts 5:31; Heb. 2:10; 12:2 [b]Acts 2:24 [c]Luke 24:48

15 but put to death the [a]Prince of life, *the one* whom [b]God raised from the dead, *a fact* to which we are [c]witnesses.

★16 [a]Acts 3:6

16 "And on the basis of faith [a]in His name, *it is* the name of Jesus which has strengthened this man whom you see and know; and the faith which *comes* through Him has given him this perfect health in the presence of you all.

17 [a]Luke 23:34; John 15:21; Acts 13:27; 26:9; Eph. 4:18 [b]Luke 23:13

17 "And now, brethren, I know that you acted [a]in ignorance, just as your [b]rulers did also.

18 [a]Acts 2:23 [b]Luke 24:27; Acts 17:3; 26:23

18 "But the things which [a]God announced beforehand by the mouth of all the prophets, [b]that His Christ should suffer, He has thus fulfilled.

★19 [a]Acts 2:38; 26:20 [b]2 Thess. 1:7; Heb. 4:1ff.

19 "[a]Repent therefore and return, that your sins may be wiped away, in order that [b]times of refreshing may come from the presence of the Lord;

20 and that He may send Jesus, the Christ appointed for you,

21 [a]Acts 1:11 [b]Matt. 17:11; Rom. 8:21 [c]Luke 1:70

21 [a]whom heaven must receive until *the* period of [b]restoration of all things about which [c]God spoke by the mouth of His holy prophets from ancient time.

3:6 *In the name of Jesus Christ.* His power and authority are invoked.

3:11 *the . . . portico of Solomon.* A colonnade running the length of the E. side of the outer court of the temple.

3:13 *His servant.* I.e., the "servant" of Isa. 42:1–9; 49:1–13; 52:13–53:12.

3:15 *Prince of life.* Lit., Author of life; i.e., originator.

3:16 *on the basis of faith.* I.e., through the apostles' faith or possibly the lame man's faith.

3:19 *return.* I.e., turn from sin to God by reversing their verdict about Jesus and confessing Him as the Messiah. *times of refreshing* and *restoration of all things* (v. 21) refer to the millennial kingdom.

★22 [a]Deut. 18:15; Acts 7:37

22 "Moses said, '[a]THE LORD
GOD SHALL RAISE UP FOR YOU A
PROPHET LIKE ME FROM YOUR BRETH-
REN; TO HIM YOU SHALL GIVE HEED IN
EVERYTHING HE SAYS TO YOU.

★23 [a]Deut. 18:19 [b]Acts 2:41

23 '[a]AND IT SHALL BE THAT EVERY
[b]SOUL THAT DOES NOT HEED THAT
PROPHET SHALL BE UTTERLY DESTROYED
FROM AMONG THE PEOPLE.'

24 [a]Luke 24:27; Acts 17:3; 26:23

24 "And likewise, [a]all the
prophets who have spoken, from
Samuel and *his* successors on-
ward, also announced these days.

25 [a]Acts 2:39 [b]Rom. 9:4f. [c]Gen. 22:18

25 "It is you who are [a]the sons
of the prophets, and of the [b]cove-
nant which God made with your
fathers, saying to Abraham, '[c]AND
IN YOUR SEED ALL THE FAMILIES OF THE
EARTH SHALL BE BLESSED.'

★26 [a]Matt. 15:24; John 4:22; Acts 13:46; Rom. 1:16; 2:9f. [b]Acts 2:24

26 "For you [a]first, God [b]raised
up His Servant, and sent Him to
bless you by turning every one *of*
you from your wicked ways."

D The Beginning of Persecution, 4:1–37

1 *The persecution,* 4:1–22

★ 1 [a]Luke 22:4 [b]Matt. 3:7 [c]Luke 20:1; Acts 6:12

4 And as they were speaking to
the people, the priests and
[a]the captain of the temple *guard,*
and [b]the Sadducees, [c]came upon
them,

2 [a]Acts 3:15; 17:18

2 being greatly disturbed because they were teaching the people and proclaiming [a]in Jesus the
resurrection from the dead.

3 [a]Acts 5:18

3 And they laid hands on
them, and [a]put them in jail until
the next day, for it was already
evening.

4 [a]Acts 2:41

4 But many of those who
had heard the message believed;
and [a]the number of the men
came to be about five thousand.

5 [a]Luke 23:13; Acts 4:8

5 And it came about on the
next day, that their [a]rulers and elders and scribes were gathered together in Jerusalem;

★ 6 [a]Luke 3:2 [b]Matt. 26:3

6 and [a]Annas the high priest
was there, and [b]Caiaphas and
John and Alexander, and all who
were of high-priestly descent.

7 And when they had placed
them in the center, they *began to*
inquire, "By what power, or in
what name, have you done this?"

★ 8-12
8 [a]Acts 2:4; 13:9 [b]Luke 23:13; Acts 4:5

8 Then Peter, [a]filled with the
Holy Spirit, said to them, "[b]Rulers
and elders of the people,

9 [a]Acts 3:7f.

9 if we are on trial today for
[a]a benefit done to a sick man, as
to how this man has been made
well,

10 [a]Acts 2:22; 3:6 [b]Acts 2:24

10 let it be known to all of
you, and to all the people of Israel, that [a]by the name of Jesus
Christ the Nazarene, whom you
crucified, whom [b]God raised from
the dead—by this *name* this man
stands here before you in good
health.

11 [a]Matt. 21:42 [b]Ps. 118:22 [c]Mark 9:12

11 "[a]He is the [b]STONE WHICH
WAS [c]REJECTED by you, THE BUILDERS,
but WHICH BECAME THE VERY CORNER
stone.

12 [a]Matt. 1:21; Acts 10:43; 1 Tim. 2:5

12 "And there is salvation in
[a]no one else; for there is no other
name under heaven that has been
given among men, by which we
must be saved."

★13 [a]Acts 4:31 [b]Luke 22:8; Acts 4:19 [c]John 7:15

13 Now as they observed the
[a]confidence of [b]Peter and John,
and understood that they were
uneducated and untrained men,

3:22 The Jews expected a *prophet* and the Messiah—two distinct persons (John 1:20–21; 7:40–41). The Christian view united them in the one person of Jesus Christ (cf. Deut. 18:15).

3:23 See Lev. 23:29; Deut. 18:19.

3:26 *His Servant* (see note on 3:13).

4:1 *the captain of the temple guard.* An official second only to the high priest. He was responsible for order in the temple. The *Sadducees* hated the idea of resurrection which the apostles were preaching (v. 2).

4:6 *Annas . . . and Caiaphas.* See note on Luke 3:2. We know nothing about *John and Alexander.*

4:8-12 In his answer, Peter actually puts his hearers on trial. He calls attention to the fact that the miracle was a good deed, not a crime (v. 9) and that it was performed by the power of Jesus whom they had crucified (v. 10). Jesus' rejection was predicted in the O.T. (v. 11; Ps. 118:22) and salvation is only through Him (v. 12).

4:13 *uneducated and untrained men.* This means that Peter and John were not formally trained in the rabbinic schools; they were not professional scholars or ordained teachers (see also John 7:15).

they were marveling, and [c]*began*
to recognize them as having been
with Jesus.
14 And seeing the man who
had been healed standing with
them, they had nothing to say in
reply.
★15-17 **15** But when they had or-
15 [a]Matt. 5:22 dered them to go aside out of the
[a]Council, they *began* to confer
with one another,
16 [a]John 11:47 [b]Acts 3:7-10 **16** saying, "[a]What shall we do
with these men? For the fact that
a [b]noteworthy miracle has taken
place through them is apparent to
all who live in Jerusalem, and we
cannot deny it.
17 [a]John 15:21 **17** "But in order that it may
not spread any further among the
people, let us warn them to speak
no more to any man [a]in this
name."
18 [a]Acts 5:28f. **18** And when they had summoned them, they [a]commanded
them not to speak or teach at all
in the name of Jesus.
19 [a]Acts 4:13 [b]Acts 5:28f. **19** But [a]Peter and John answered and said to them,
"[b]Whether it is right in the sight
of God to give heed to you rather
than to God, you be the judge;
20 [a]1 Cor. 9:16 **20** for [a]we cannot stop speaking what we have seen and
heard."
21 [a]Acts 5:26 [b]Matt. 9:8 **21** And when they had
threatened them further, they let
them go (finding no basis on
which they might punish them)
[a]on account of the people, because they were all [b]glorifying
God for what had happened;
22 for the man was more than
forty years old on whom this miracle of healing had been performed.

2 *The prayer,* 4:23-31

23 And when they had been
released, they went to their own
companions, and reported all that
the chief priests and the elders
had said to them.
24 And when they heard *this,* ★24-30
they lifted their voices to God 24 [a]Ex. 20:11; Ps. 146:6
with one accord and said, "O
Lord, it is Thou who [a]DIDST MAKE
THE HEAVEN AND THE EARTH AND THE
SEA, AND ALL THAT IS IN THEM,
25 who [a]by the Holy Spirit, 25 [a]Acts 1:16 [b]Ps. 2:1
through the mouth of our father
David Thy servant, didst say,

> '[b]WHY DID THE GENTILES
> RAGE,
> AND THE PEOPLES DEVISE FU-
> TILE THINGS?

26 '[a]THE KINGS OF THE EARTH 26 [a]Ps. 2:2 [b]Dan. 9:24f.; Luke 4:18; Acts 10:38; Heb. 1:9
> TOOK THEIR STAND,
> AND THE RULERS WERE GATH-
> ERED TOGETHER
> AGAINST THE LORD, AND
> AGAINST HIS [b]CHRIST.'

27 "For truly in this city there ★27 [a]Acts 3:13; 4:30 [b]Matt. 14:1 [c]Matt. 27:2; Luke 23:12 [d]Matt. 20:19
were gathered together against
Thy holy [a]servant Jesus, whom
Thou didst anoint, both [b]Herod
and [c]Pontius Pilate, along with
[d]the Gentiles and the peoples of
Israel,
28 to do whatever Thy hand 28 [a]Acts 2:23
and [a]Thy purpose predestined to
occur.
29 "And now, Lord, take note 29 [a]Phil. 1:14 [b]Acts 4:13, 31; 14:3
of their threats, and grant that
Thy bond-servants may [a]speak
Thy word with all [b]confidence,
30 while Thou dost extend 30 [a]John 4:48 [b]Acts 3:13; 4:27
Thy hand to heal, and [a]signs and
wonders take place through the
name of Thy holy [b]servant Jesus." ★31 [a]Acts 2:1 [b]Acts 2:4 [c]Phil. 1:14 [d]Acts 4:13; 14:3
31 And when they had
prayed, the [a]place where they had

4:15-17 Though the Sanhedrin forbade further preaching, they did not try to disprove the resurrection of Jesus, which would have been the simplest way to discredit the apostles.

4:24-30 A prayer of thanksgiving for the sovereign power of God, not a prayer for deliverance from further opposition. The only petition in the prayer is for boldness (v. 29-31).

4:27 Responsibility for the death of Christ is laid upon both Jews and Gentiles.

4:31 *the Holy Spirit.* There are a number of references to the activity of the Holy Spirit in Acts: (1) He baptizes believers into the body of Christ, thus forming the Church (1:5; 11:15-16). (2) His presence in the believer is evidence of the new birth (2:38; 5:32; 10:44; 15:8). (3) He fills believers for witnessing (4:8), for leadership (6:3), for strength (7:55), and for special discernment (13:9). (4) He leads (13:4; 16:7).

gathered together was shaken, and they were all [b]filled with the Holy Spirit, and *began* to [c]speak the word of God with [d]boldness.

3 *The provision,* 4:32–37

★32 [a]Acts 2:44

32 And the congregation of those who believed were of one heart and soul; and not one *of them* claimed that anything belonging to him was his own; but [a]all things were common property to them.

33 [a]Acts 1:8 [b]Luke 24:48

33 And [a]with great power the apostles were giving [b]witness to the resurrection of the Lord Jesus, and abundant grace was upon them all.

34 [a]Matt. 19:21; Acts 2:45

34 For there was not a needy person among them, for all who were owners of land or houses [a]would sell them and bring the proceeds of the sales,

35 [a]Acts 4:37; 5:2 [b]Acts 2:45; 6:1

35 and [a]lay them at the apostles' feet; and they would be [b]distributed to each, as any had need.

36 [a]Acts 11:19f.; 13:4; 15:39; 21:3, 16; 27:4 [b]Acts 9:27; 11:22, 30; 12:25; 13:15; 1 Cor. 9:6; Gal. 2:1, 9, 13; Col. 4:10 [c]Acts 2:40; 11:23; 13:15; 1 Cor. 14:3; 1 Thess. 2:3

36 And Joseph, a Levite of [a]Cyprian birth, who was also called [b]Barnabas by the apostles (which translated means, Son of [c]Encouragement),

37 [a]Acts 4:35; 5:2

37 and who owned a tract of land, sold it and brought the money and [a]laid it at the apostles' feet.

E Purging and Persecution, 5:1–42

1 *Purging from within,* 5:1–11

5 But a certain man named Ananias, with his wife Sapphira, sold a piece of property,

2 [a]Acts 5:3 [b]Acts 4:35, 37

2 and [a]kept back *some* of the price for himself, with his wife's full knowledge, and bringing a portion of it, he [b]laid it at the apostles' feet.

★ 3 [a]Matt. 4:10; Luke 22:3; John 13:2, 27 [b]Acts 5:4, 9 [c]Acts 5:2

3 But Peter said, "Ananias, why has [a]Satan filled your heart to lie [b]to the Holy Spirit, and to [c]keep back *some* of the price of the land?

4 [a]Acts 5:3, 9

4 "While it remained *unsold,* did it not remain your own? And after it was sold, was it not under your control? Why is it that you have conceived this deed in your heart? You have not lied to men, but [a]to God."

5 [a]Ezek. 11:13; Acts 5:10 [b]Acts 2:43; 5:11

5 And as he heard these words, Ananias [a]fell down and breathed his last; and [b]great fear came upon all who heard of it.

6 [a]John 19:40

6 And the young men arose and [a]covered him up, and after carrying him out, they buried him.

7 Now there elapsed an interval of about three hours, and his wife came in, not knowing what had happened.

8 [a]Acts 3:12 [b]Acts 5:2

8 And Peter [a]responded to her, "Tell me whether you sold the land [b]for such and such a price?" And she said, "Yes, that was the price."

★ 9 [a]Acts 15:10 [b]Acts 5:3, 4

9 Then Peter *said* to her, "Why is it that you have agreed together to [a]put [b]the Spirit of the Lord to the test? Behold, the feet of those who have buried your husband are at the door, and they shall carry you out *as well.*"

10 [a]Ezek. 11:13; Acts 5:5

10 And she [a]fell immediately at his feet, and breathed her last; and the young men came in and found her dead, and they carried her out and buried her beside her husband.

11 [a]Acts 2:43; 5:5

11 And [a]great fear came upon the whole church, and upon all who heard of these things.

4:32 *all things were common property to them.* This display of Christian charity did not abolish the right of personal property. Such community of goods was not compulsory but voluntary, as a way of eliminating need among them.

5:3 *to lie.* The sin of Ananias and Sapphira was not in not selling all their property, or in keeping part of the proceeds of the sale, but in lying about how much they had received. Lying to the Spirit is lying to God, because the Holy Spirit is God (v. 4).

5:9 *to put . . . to the test.* I.e., to see how far they could go in presuming on God's goodness.

2 *Purging from without,* 5:12–42

★12 [a]John 4:48 [b]John 10:23; Acts 3:11

12 And at the hands of the apostles many [a]signs and wonders were taking place among the people; and they were all with one accord in [b]Solomon's portico.

13 [a]Acts 2:47; 4:21

13 But none of the rest dared to associate with them; however, [a]the people held them in high esteem.

14 [a]2 Cor. 6:15 [b]Acts 2:47; 11:24

14 And all the more [a]believers in the Lord, multitudes of men and women, were constantly [b]added to *their number;*

15 [a]Acts 19:12

15 to such an extent that they even carried the sick out into the streets, and laid them on cots and pallets, so that when Peter came by, [a]at least his shadow might fall on any one of them.

16 And also the people from the cities in the vicinity of Jerusalem were coming together, bringing people who were sick or afflicted with unclean spirits; and they were all being healed.

★17 [a]Acts 15:5 [b]Matt. 3:7; Acts 4:1

17 But the high priest rose up, along with all his associates (that is [a]the sect of [b]the Sadducees), and they were filled with jealousy;

18 [a]Acts 4:3

18 and they laid hands on the apostles, and [a]put them in a public jail.

19 [a]Matt. 1:20, 24; 2:13, 19; 28:2; Luke 1:11; 2:9; Acts 8:26; 10:3; 12:7, 23; 27:23

19 But [a]an angel of the Lord during the night opened the gates of the prison, and taking them out he said,

20 [a]John 6:63, 68

20 "Go your way, stand and speak to the people in the temple [a]the whole message of this Life."

★21 [a]John 8:2 [b]Acts 4:6 [c]Matt. 5:22; Acts 5:27, 34, 41

21 And upon hearing *this,* they entered into the temple [a]about daybreak, and *began* to teach. Now when [b]the high priest and his associates had come, they called [c]the Council together, even all the Senate of the sons of Israel, and sent *orders* to the prison house for them to be brought.

22 [a]Matt. 26:58; Acts 5:26

22 But [a]the officers who came did not find them in the prison; and they returned, and reported back,

23 saying, "We found the prison house locked quite securely and the guards standing at the doors; but when we had opened up, we found no one inside."

24 [a]Acts 4:1; 5:26

24 Now when [a]the captain of the temple *guard* and the chief priests heard these words, they were greatly perplexed about them as to what would come of this.

25 But someone came and reported to them, "Behold, the men whom you put in prison are standing in the temple and teaching the people!"

26 [a]Acts 5:24 [b]Acts 5:22 [c]Acts 4:21; 5:13

26 Then [a]the captain went along with [b]the officers and *proceeded* to bring them *back* without violence; (for [c]they were afraid of the people, lest they should be stoned).

27 [a]Matt. 5:22; Acts 5:21, 34, 41

27 And when they had brought them, they stood them before [a]the Council. And the high priest questioned them,

28 [a]Acts 4:18 [b]Matt. 23:35; 27:25; Acts 2:23, 36; 3:14f.; 7:52

28 saying, "We gave you [a]strict orders not to continue teaching in this name, and behold, you have filled Jerusalem with your teaching, and [b]intend to bring this man's blood upon us."

29 [a]Acts 4:19

29 But Peter and the apostles answered and said, "[a]We must obey God rather than men.

30 [a]Acts 3:13 [b]Acts 2:24 [c]Acts 10:39; 13:29; Gal. 3:13; 1 Pet. 2:24

30 "[a]The God of our fathers [b]raised up Jesus, whom you had [c]put to death by hanging Him on a cross.

★31 [a]Acts 2:33 [b]Acts 3:15 [c]Luke 2:11 [d]Luke 24:47; Acts 2:38

31 "[a]He is the one whom God exalted to His right hand as a [b]Prince and a [c]Savior, to grant [d]repentance to Israel, and forgiveness of sins.

5:12 *Solomon's portico.* See note on 3:11.

5:17 Again the *Sadducees,* who did not believe in resurrection (23:8), were particularly riled at the disciples' preaching the resurrection of Christ (4:33).

5:21 *Council . . . Senate.* These are the same body, the Jewish Sanhedrin.

5:31 *Prince* = Author (Heb. 12:2), or Leader (cf. Acts 3:15).

32 [a]Luke 24:48 [b]John 15:26; Acts 15:28; Rom. 8:16; Heb. 2:4

32 "And we are [a]witnesses of these things; and [b]*so is* the Holy Spirit, whom God has given to those who obey Him."

33 [a]Acts 2:37; 7:54

33 But when they heard this, they were [a]cut to the quick and were intending to slay them.

★34 [a]Acts 22:3 [b]Luke 2:46; 5:17 [c]Acts 5:21

34 But a certain Pharisee named [a]Gamaliel, a [b]teacher of the Law, respected by all the people, stood up in [c]the Council and gave orders to put the men outside for a short time.

35 And he said to them, "Men of Israel, take care what you propose to do with these men.

★36 [a]Acts 8:9; Gal. 2:6; 6:3

36 "For some time ago Theudas rose up, [a]claiming to be somebody; and a group of about four hundred men joined up with him. And he was slain; and all who followed him were dispersed and came to nothing.

★37 [a]Luke 2:2

37 "After this man Judas of Galilee rose up in the days of [a]the census, and drew away *some* people after him, he too perished, and all those who followed him were scattered.

38 [a]Mark 11:30

38 "And so in the present case, I say to you, stay away from these men and let them alone, for if this plan or action should [a]be of men, it will be overthrown;

39 [a]Prov. 21:30; Acts 11:17

39 but if it is of God, you will not be able to overthrow them; or else you may even be found [a]fighting against God."

40 [a]Matt. 10:17

40 And they took his advice; and after calling the apostles in, they [a]flogged them and ordered them to speak no more in the name of Jesus, and *then* released them.

41 [a]Acts 5:21 [b]1 Pet. 4:14, 16 [c]John 15:21

41 So they went on their way from the presence of the [a]Council, [b]rejoicing that they had been considered worthy to suffer shame [c]for *His* name.

42 [a]Acts 2:46 [b]Acts 8:35; 11:20; 17:18; Gal. 1:16

42 [a]And every day, in the temple and from house to house, they kept right on teaching and [b]preaching Jesus *as* the Christ.

F Choosing Colaborers, 6:1–7

★ 1 [a]Acts 11:26 [b]Acts 2:47; 6:7 [c]Acts 9:29; 11:20 marg. [d]2 Cor. 11:22; Phil. 3:5 [e]Acts 9:39, 41; 1 Tim. 5:3 [f]Acts 4:35; 11:29

6 Now at this time while the [a]disciples were increasing [b]*in number,* a complaint arose on the part of the [c]Hellenistic *Jews* against the *native* [d]Hebrews, because their [e]widows were being overlooked in [f]the daily serving *of food.*

★ 2

2 And the twelve summoned the congregation of the disciples and said, "It is not desirable for us to neglect the word of God in order to serve tables.

3 [a]John 21:23; Acts 1:15 [b]Acts 2:4

3 "But select from among you, [a]brethren, seven men of good reputation, [b]full of the Spirit and of wisdom, whom we may put in charge of this task.

4 [a]Acts 1:14

4 "But we will [a]devote ourselves to prayer, and to the ministry of the word."

★ 5 [a]Acts 6:8ff.; 11:19; 22:20 [b]Acts 6:3; 11:24 [c]Acts 8:5ff.; 21:8 [d]Matt. 23:15 [e]Acts 11:19

5 And the statement found approval with the whole congregation; and they chose [a]Stephen, a man [b]full of faith and of the Holy Spirit, and [c]Philip, Prochorus, Nicanor, Timon, Parmenas and Nicolas, a [d]proselyte from [e]Antioch.

5:34 *Gamaliel.* A respected rabbi who followed the liberal interpretations of Hillel, another rabbi who lived shortly before the time of Christ. His popularity demanded that the Sanhedrin listen to him. Paul was a student of Gamaliel (22:3).

5:36 *Theudas.* This is the only historical reference to him.

5:37 *Judas . . . rose up.* This revolt (in A.D. 6) is described by the historian Josephus. The followers of this Judas became the "Zealots."

6:1 *Hellenistic Jews . . . Hebrews.* The former were Greek-speaking Jewish Christians and the latter, Aramaic-speaking Jewish Christians.

6:2 *serve tables.* I.e., tables of food for the widows or of money (as in John 2:15). The Greek word for "serve" is the one from which we derive "deacon," but these men were "deacons" only in the sense of being servants. They were not yet deacons in the later sense of officers in the church (see note on 1 Tim. 3:8).

6:5 All seven had Greek, not Jewish, names; two, Stephen and Philip, quickly achieved prominence for their vigorous evangelism.

★ 6 aActs 1:24 bNum. 8:10; 27:18; Deut. 34:9; Mark 5:23; Acts 8:17ff.; 9:17; 13:3; 19:6; 1 Tim. 4:14; 2 Tim. 1:6; Heb. 6:2
7 aActs 12:24; 19:20 bActs 6:1 cActs 13:8; 14:22; Gal. 1:23; 6:10; Jude 3, 20

6 And these they brought before the apostles; and after [a]praying, they [b]laid their hands on them.

7 And [a]the word of God kept on spreading; and [b]the number of the disciples continued to increase greatly in Jerusalem, and a great many of the priests were becoming obedient to [c]the faith.

G Stephen, the First Martyr, 6:8–8:3

1 *The stirring of the people,* 6:8–15

8 aJohn 4:48

8 And Stephen, full of grace and power, was performing great [a]wonders and signs among the people.

★ 9 aMatt. 27:32; Acts 2:10 bActs 18:24 cActs 15:23, 41; 21:39; 22:3; 23:34; 27:5; Gal. 1:21 dActs 16:6; 19:10; 21:27; 24:18

9 But some men from what was called the Synagogue of the Freedmen, *including* both [a]Cyrenians and [b]Alexandrians, and some from [c]Cilicia and [d]Asia, rose up and argued with Stephen.

10 And *yet* they were unable to cope with the wisdom and the Spirit with which he was speaking.

11 Then they secretly induced men to say, "We have heard him speak blasphemous words against Moses and *against* God."

★12 aLuke 20:1; Acts 4:1 bMatt. 5:22

12 And they stirred up the people, the elders and the scribes, and they [a]came upon him and dragged him away, and brought him before [b]the Council.

13 aMatt. 26:59-61; Acts 7:58 bMatt. 24:15; Acts 21:28; 25:8

13 And they put forward [a]false witnesses who said, "This man incessantly speaks against this [b]holy place, and the Law;

14 for we have heard him say that [a]this Nazarene, Jesus, will destroy this place and alter [b]the customs which Moses handed down to us."

14 aMatt. 26:61 bActs 15:1; 21:21; 26:3; 28:17

15 And fixing their gaze on him, all who were sitting in the [a]Council saw his face like the face of an angel.

15 aMatt. 5:22

2 *The sermon of Stephen,* 7:1–53

7 And the high priest said, "Are these things so?" ★1

2 And he said, "Hear me, [a]brethren and fathers! [b]The God of glory [c]appeared to our father Abraham when he was in Mesopotamia, before he lived in Haran,

★ 2-53
★ 2 aActs 22:1 bPs. 29:3; 1 Cor. 2:8 cGen. 11:31; 15:7

3 AND SAID TO HIM, '[a]DEPART FROM YOUR COUNTRY AND YOUR RELATIVES, AND COME INTO THE LAND THAT I WILL SHOW YOU.'

3 aGen. 12:1

4 "[a]Then he departed from the land of the Chaldeans, and settled in Haran. And [b]from there, after his father died, God removed him into this country in which you are now living.

4 aGen. 11:31; 15:7 bGen. 12:5

5 "And He gave him no inheritance in it, not even a foot of ground; and *yet,* even when he had no child, [a]He promised that HE WOULD GIVE IT TO HIM AS A POSSESSION, AND TO HIS OFFSPRING AFTER HIM.

5 aGen. 12:7; 17:8

6 "But [a]God spoke to this effect, that HIS OFFSPRING WOULD BE ALIENS IN A FOREIGN LAND, AND THAT THEY WOULD BE ENSLAVED AND MISTREATED FOR FOUR HUNDRED YEARS.

6 aGen. 15:13f.

7 " '[a]AND WHATEVER NATION TO WHICH THEY SHALL BE IN BONDAGE I

7 aEx. 3:12

6:6 *laid their hands on them.* The laying on of hands was a formal sign of appointment to this service. The rite indicates a link or association between the parties involved. Sometimes it was related to healing (Mark 5:23) or to the impartation of the Spirit (Acts 8:17; 9:17; 19:6) or, as here, was a sign of ordination for special service (13:3; 1 Tim. 4:14).

6:9 *Freedmen.* These were Jewish freedmen, or descendants of freedmen, from the various places mentioned in the verse. They had their own synagogue in Jerusalem.

6:12 *the Council.* The Sanhedrin. See note on Luke 22:66.

7:1 *the high priest.* Caiaphas.

7:2-53 Stephen's sermon is the longest recorded in Acts. The text is: "you are doing just as your fathers did" (v. 51). Stephen recited the privileges of the nation Israel and their rejection of God's messengers; then he laid blame for the slaying of Jesus squarely on his hearers (v. 52).

7:2 God's call to *Abraham* came first when he was in *Mesopotamia* (Gen. 15:7; Neh. 9:7). Later he went to Haran (Gen. 11:31-32) and later to Palestine.

MYSELF WILL JUDGE,' said God, 'AND [a]AFTER THAT THEY WILL COME OUT AND SERVE ME IN THIS PLACE.'

★ 8 [a]Gen. 17:10ff. [b]Gen. 21:2-4 [c]Gen. 25:26 [d]Gen. 29:31ff.; 30:5ff.; 35:23ff. [e]Acts 2:29

8 "And He [a]gave him the covenant of circumcision; and so [b]*Abraham* became the father of Isaac, and circumcised him on the eighth day; and [c]Isaac *became the father of* Jacob, and [d]Jacob *of* the twelve [e]patriarchs.

★ 9 [a]Gen. 37:11, 28; 39:2, 21f.; 45:4

9 "And the patriarchs [a]BECAME JEALOUS OF JOSEPH AND SOLD HIM INTO EGYPT. And *yet* God WAS WITH HIM,

10 [a]Gen. 39:21; 41:40-46; Ps. 105:21

10 and rescued him from all his afflictions, and [a]GRANTED HIM FAVOR and wisdom IN THE SIGHT OF PHARAOH, KING OF EGYPT; AND HE MADE HIM GOVERNOR OVER EGYPT AND ALL HIS HOUSEHOLD.

11 [a]Gen. 41:54f.; 42:5

11 "Now [a]A FAMINE CAME OVER ALL EGYPT AND CANAAN, and great affliction *with it;* and our fathers could find no food.

12 [a]Gen. 42:2

12 "But [a]WHEN JACOB HEARD THAT THERE WAS GRAIN IN EGYPT, he sent our fathers *there* the first time.

13 [a]Gen. 45:1-4

13 "And on the second *visit* [a]Joseph made himself known to his brothers, and Joseph's family was disclosed to Pharaoh.

★14 [a]Gen. 45:9f. [b]Gen. 46:26f.; Ex. 1:5; Deut. 10:22 [c]Acts 2:41

14 "And [a]Joseph sent *word* and invited Jacob his father and all his relatives to come to him, [b]seventy-five [c]persons *in all.*

★15-16
15 [a]Gen. 46:5; 49:33; Ex. 1:6

15 "And [a]Jacob WENT DOWN TO EGYPT AND *there* PASSED AWAY, he and our fathers.

16 [a]Gen. 23:16; 33:19; 50:13; Josh. 24:32

16 "And *from there* they were removed to [a]Shechem, and laid in the tomb which Abraham had purchased for a sum of money from the sons of Hamor in Shechem.

17 [a]Ex. 1:7f.

17 "But as the time of the promise was approaching which God had assured to Abraham, [a]the people increased and multiplied in Egypt,

18 [a]Ex. 1:8

18 until [a]THERE AROSE ANOTHER KING OVER EGYPT WHO KNEW NOTHING ABOUT JOSEPH.

19 [a]Ex. 1:10f., 16ff.

19 "It was he who took [a]shrewd advantage of our race, and mistreated our fathers so that they would expose their infants and they would not survive.

★20 [a]Ex. 2:2

20 "And it was at this time that [a]Moses was born; and he was lovely in the sight of God; and he was nurtured three months in his father's home.

21 [a]Ex. 2:5f., 10

21 "And after he had been exposed, [a]Pharaoh's daughter took him away, and nurtured him as her own son.

22 [a]1 Kin. 4:30; Is. 19:11

22 "And Moses was educated in all [a]the learning of the Egyptians, and he was a man of power in words and deeds.

23 [a]Ex. 2:11f.

23 "But when he was approaching the age of forty, [a]it entered his mind to visit his brethren, the sons of Israel.

24 "And when he saw one *of them* being treated unjustly, he defended him and took vengeance for the oppressed by striking down the Egyptian.

25 "And he supposed that his brethren understood that God was granting them deliverance through him; but they did not understand.

26 [a]Ex. 2:13f.

26 "[a]And on the following day he appeared to them as they were fighting together, and he tried to reconcile them in peace, saying, 'Men, you are brethren, why do you injure one another?'

27 [a]Ex. 2:14; Acts 7:35

27 "[a]BUT THE ONE WHO WAS INJURING HIS NEIGHBOR pushed him away, saying, 'WHO MADE YOU A RULER AND JUDGE OVER US?

28 [a]Ex. 2:14

28 '[a]YOU DO NOT MEAN TO KILL ME

7:8 *circumcision.* See Gen. 17:9–14.

7:9 *Joseph.* See Gen. 37:11.

7:14 *seventy-five persons.* This number follows the Septuagint (Greek translation of the O.T.), which arrived at 75 by including the son and grandson of Manasseh and two sons and a grandson of Ephraim. See Gen. 46:27, which reflects a different way of numbering Jacob's family, totaling 70.

7:15–16 Jacob was buried at Hebron in the Cave of Machpelah, which Abraham bought from Ephron the Hittite (Gen. 23:16). Joseph was buried at Shechem in a piece of ground Jacob bought from the sons of Hamor (Josh. 24:32). The two transactions are simply telescoped in these verses because of the pressure of Stephen's circumstances and need for brevity.

7:20 *Moses.* See Ex. 2 and Heb. 11:24–26.

AS YOU KILLED THE EGYPTIAN YESTER-
DAY, DO YOU?'
29 [a]Ex. 2:15, 22 **29** "AND AT THIS REMARK [a]MOSES
FLED, AND BECAME AN ALIEN IN THE
LAND OF MIDIAN, where he became
the father of two sons.
30 [a]Ex. 3:1f. **30** "And after forty years had
passed, [a]AN ANGEL APPEARED TO HIM
IN THE WILDERNESS OF MOUNT Sinai,
IN THE FLAME OF A BURNING THORN
BUSH.
31 "And when Moses saw it,
he *began* to marvel at the sight;
and as he approached to look
more closely, there came the voice
of the Lord:
32 [a]Ex. 3:6 **32** '[a]I AM THE GOD OF YOUR FA-
THERS, THE GOD OF ABRAHAM AND
ISAAC AND JACOB.' And Moses
shook *with fear* and would not
venture to look.
33 [a]Ex. 3:5 **33** "BUT THE LORD SAID TO HIM,
'[a]TAKE OFF THE SANDALS FROM YOUR
FEET, FOR THE PLACE ON WHICH YOU
ARE STANDING IS HOLY GROUND.
34 [a]Ex. 3:7 [b]Ex. 3:10 **34** '[a]I HAVE CERTAINLY SEEN THE
OPPRESSION OF MY PEOPLE IN EGYPT,
AND HAVE HEARD THEIR GROANS, AND I
HAVE COME DOWN TO DELIVER THEM;
[b]COME NOW, AND I WILL SEND YOU TO
EGYPT.'
35 [a]Acts 7:27 **35** "This Moses whom they
[a]disowned, saying, 'WHO MADE
YOU A RULER AND A JUDGE?' is the
one whom God sent *to be* both a
36 [a]Ex. 12:41; 33:1; Heb. 8:9 [b]Ex. 7:3; John 4:48 [c]Ex. 16:35; Num. 14:33; Ps. 95:8-10; Acts 7:42; 13:18; Heb. 3:8f. ruler and a deliverer with the help
of the angel who appeared to him
in the thorn bush.
36 "[a]This man led them out,
performing [b]wonders and signs in
the land of Egypt and in the Red
Sea and in the [c]wilderness for
forty years.
37 [a]Deut. 18:15; Acts 3:22 **37** "This is the Moses who said
to the sons of Israel, 'GOD SHALL
RAISE UP FOR YOU [a]A PROPHET LIKE ME
FROM YOUR BRETHREN.'
38 "This is the one who was in ★38 [a]Ex. 19:17 [b]Acts 7:53 [c]Deut. 32:47; Heb. 4:12 [d]Rom. 3:2; Heb. 5:12; 1 Pet. 4:11
[a]the congregation in the wilder-
ness together with [b]the angel who
was speaking to him on Mount
Sinai, and *who was* with our fathers; and he received [c]living [d]or-
acles to pass on to you.
39 "And our fathers were un- 39 [a]Num. 14:3f.
willing to be obedient to him, but
[a]repudiated him and in their
hearts turned back to Egypt,
40 SAYING TO AARON, '[a]MAKE 40 [a]Ex. 32:1, 23
FOR US GODS WHO WILL GO BEFORE US;
FOR THIS MOSES WHO LED US OUT OF
THE LAND OF EGYPT—WE DO NOT
KNOW WHAT HAPPENED TO HIM.'
41 "And at that time [a]they 41 [a]Ex. 32:4, 6 [b]Rev. 9:20
made a calf and brought a sacri-
fice to the idol, and were rejoicing
in [b]the works of their hands.
42 "But God [a]turned away and 42 [a]Josh. 24:20; Is. 63:10; Jer. 19:13; Ezek. 20:39 [b]Amos 5:25 [c]Acts 7:36
delivered them up to serve the
host of heaven; as it is written in
the book of the prophets, '[b]IT WAS
NOT TO ME THAT YOU OFFERED VIC-
TIMS AND SACRIFICES [c]FORTY YEARS IN
THE WILDERNESS, WAS IT, O HOUSE OF
ISRAEL?
43 '[a]YOU ALSO TOOK ALONG THE ★43 [a]Amos 5:26, 27
TABERNACLE OF MOLOCH AND THE
STAR OF THE GOD ROMPHA, THE IM-
AGES WHICH YOU MADE TO WORSHIP
THEM. I ALSO WILL REMOVE YOU BE-
YOND BABYLON.'
44 "Our fathers had [a]the tab- ★44 [a]Ex. 25:8, 9; 38:21
ernacle of testimony in the wil-
derness, just as He who spoke to
Moses directed *him* to make it according to the pattern which he
had seen.
45 "And having received it in 45 [a]Deut. 32:49; Josh. 3:14ff.; 18:1; 23:9; 24:18; Ps. 44:2f.
their turn, our fathers [a]brought it
in with Joshua upon dispossessing
the nations whom God drove out

7:38 *the congregation in the wilderness.* Lit., the assembly in the wilderness; i.e., the gathering of the people to receive the law. The word translated "church" (or congregation, assembly, gathering) is used in the N.T. of four kinds of groups: (1) the children of Israel gathered as a nation; (2) in Acts 19:32, 39, 41, a group of townspeople assembled in a town meeting; (3) in a technical sense, all believers who are gathered together in the one body of Christ, the Church universal (Col. 1:18); and (4) most frequently, in reference to a local group of professing Christians; e.g., the church at Antioch (Acts 13:1).

7:43 *Moloch . . . Rompha.* Moloch was a title for various Canaanite deities to whom human sacrifices were offered. Rompha, (better, Rephan) was the name of a god connected with the planet Saturn.

7:44 *tabernacle of testimony.* I.e., the tabernacle was a testimony to the presence of God in their midst.

before our fathers, until the time
of David.
46 "And [a]*David* found favor in
God's sight, and asked that he
might find a dwelling place for
the God of Jacob.
47 "But it was [a]Solomon who
built a house for Him.
48 "However, [a]the Most High
does not dwell in *houses* made by
human hands; as the prophet
says:

49 '[a]HEAVEN IS MY THRONE,
AND EARTH IS THE FOOTSTOOL
OF MY FEET;
WHAT KIND OF HOUSE WILL
YOU BUILD FOR ME?' says
the Lord;
'OR WHAT PLACE IS THERE FOR
MY REPOSE?
50 '[a]WAS IT NOT MY HAND
WHICH MADE ALL THESE
THINGS?'

51 "You men who are [a]stiff-
necked and uncircumcised in
heart and ears are always resisting
the Holy Spirit; you are doing just
as your fathers did.
52 "[a]Which one of the prophets did your fathers not persecute? And they killed those who
had previously announced the
coming of [b]the Righteous One,
whose betrayers and murderers
[c]you have now become;
53 you who received the law
as [a]ordained by angels, and *yet*
did not keep it."

3 *The stoning of Stephen,* 7:54–8:3

54 Now when they heard
this, they were [a]cut to the quick,
and they *began* gnashing their
teeth at him.
55 But being [a]full of the Holy
Spirit, he [b]gazed intently into
heaven and saw the glory of God,
and Jesus standing [c]at the right
hand of God;
56 and he said, "Behold, I see
the [a]heavens opened up and [b]the
Son of Man standing at the right
hand of God."
57 But they cried out with a
loud voice, and covered their ears,
and they rushed upon him with
one impulse.
58 And when they had
[a]driven him out of the city, they
began stoning *him*, and [b]the witnesses [c]laid aside their robes at
the feet of [d]a young man named
Saul.
59 And they went on stoning
Stephen as he [a]called upon *the*
Lord and said, "Lord Jesus, receive
my spirit!"
60 And [a]falling on his knees,
he cried out with a loud voice,
"Lord, [b]do not hold this sin
against them!" And having said
this, he [c]fell asleep.
8 And [a]Saul was in hearty
agreement with putting him
to death.
1 And on that day a great persecution arose against [b]the church
in Jerusalem; and they were all
[c]scattered throughout the regions
of Judea and [d]Samaria, except the
apostles.
2 And *some* devout men
buried Stephen, and made loud
lamentation over him.
3 But [a]Saul *began* ravaging
the church, entering house after
house; and [b]dragging off men and
women, he would put them in
prison.

46 [a]2 Sam. 7:8ff.; Ps. 132:1-5; Acts 13:22
47 [a]1 Kin. 8:20
48 [a]Luke 1:32
49 [a]Is. 66:1; Matt. 5:34f.
50 [a]Is. 66:2
★51-53
51 [a]Ex. 32:9; 33:3, 5; Lev. 26:41; Num. 27:14; Is. 63:10; Jer. 6:10; 9:26
52 [a]2 Chr. 36:15f.; Matt. 5:12; 23:31, 37 [b]Acts 3:14; 22:14; 1 John 2:1 [c]Acts 3:14; 5:28
53 [a]Deut. 33:2 [Septuagint]; Acts 7:38; Gal. 3:19; Heb. 2:2
54 [a]Acts 5:33
★55 [a]Acts 2:4 [b]John 11:41 [c]Mark 16:19
56 [a]John 1:51 [b]Matt. 8:20
★58 [a]Lev. 24:14, 16; Luke 4:29 [b]Deut. 13:9f.; 17:7; Acts 6:13 [c]Acts 22:20 [d]Acts 8:1; 22:20; 26:10
59 [a]Acts 9:14, 21; 22:16; Rom. 10:12, 13f.; 1 Cor. 1:2; 2 Tim. 2:22
★60 [a]Luke 22:41 [b]Matt. 5:44; Luke 23:34 [c]Dan. 12:2; Matt. 27:52; John 11:11f.; Acts 13:36; 1 Cor. 15:6, 18, 20; 1 Thess. 4:13ff.; 2 Pet. 3:4
1 [a]Acts 7:58; 22:20; 26:10 [b]Acts 9:31 [c]Acts 8:4; 11:19 [d]Acts 1:8; 8:5, 14; 9:31
3 [a]Acts 9:1, 13, 21; 22:4, 19; 26:10f.; 1 Cor. 15:9; Gal. 1:13; Phil. 3:6; 1 Tim. 1:13 [b]James 2:6

7:51–53 Stephen's indictment of unbelieving Jews, amply illustrated in the previously cited history of Israel.

7:55 *Jesus standing at the right hand of God.* Jesus' priestly work of offering a sacrifice for sin was finished on the cross; He is therefore sometimes pictured as seated at the right hand of God (Heb. 1:3). But His priestly work of sustaining His people continues (as here with Stephen); therefore, He is portrayed as standing to minister (cf. Rev. 2:1).

7:58 The mention of *witnesses* suggests that they went through the motions of a legal execution (Lev. 24:14), though probably without securing the official approval of Pilate.

7:60 *he fell asleep.* This expression is used of the physical death of believers (John 11:11; 1 Thess. 4:13, 15).

II CHRISTIANITY IN PALESTINE AND SYRIA, 8:4–12:25

A The Christians Scattered, 8:4–40

1 *The preaching in Samaria,* 8:4–25

★ 4 [a]Acts 8:1 [b]Acts 8:12; 15:35 **4** Therefore, those [a]who had
been scattered went about
[b]preaching the word.
★ 5 [a]Acts 6:5; 8:26, 30 **5** And [a]Philip went down to
the city of Samaria and *began*
proclaiming Christ to them.
6 And the multitudes with
one accord were giving attention
to what was said by Philip, as
they heard and saw the signs
which he was performing.
7 [a]Mark 16:17 [b]Matt. 4:24 **7** For *in the case of* many
who had [a]unclean spirits, they
were coming out *of them* shouting with a loud voice; and many
who had been [b]paralyzed and
lame were healed.
8 [a]John 4:40-42; Acts 8:39 **8** And there was [a]much rejoicing in that city.
★ 9 [a]Acts 8:11; 13:6 [b]Acts 5:36 **9** Now there was a certain
man named Simon, who formerly
was practicing [a]magic in the city,
and astonishing the people of Samaria, [b]claiming to be someone
great;
10 [a]Acts 14:11; 28:6 **10** and they all, from smallest
to greatest, were giving attention
to him, saying, "[a]This man is
what is called the Great Power of
God."
11 [a]Acts 8:9; 13:6 **11** And they were giving him
attention because he had for a
long time astonished them with
his [a]magic arts.

12 But when they believed 12 [a]Acts 1:3; 8:4 [b]Acts 2:38
Philip [a]preaching the good news
about the kingdom of God and
the name of Jesus Christ, they
were being [b]baptized, men and
women alike.
13 And even Simon himself ★13 [a]Acts 8:6 [b]Acts 19:11
believed; and after being bap-
tized, he continued on with
Philip; and as he observed [a]signs
and [b]great miracles taking place,
he was constantly amazed.
14 Now when [a]the apostles in 14 [a]Acts 8:1 [b]Luke 22:8
Jerusalem heard that Samaria had
received the word of God, they ★14-17
sent them [b]Peter and John,
15 who came down and 15 [a]Acts 2:38; 19:2
prayed for them, [a]that they might
receive the Holy Spirit.
16 For He had not yet fallen 16 [a]Matt. 28:19
upon any of them; they had sim-
ply been [a]baptized in the name of
the Lord Jesus.
17 Then they [a]*began* laying 17 [a]Mark 5:23; Acts 6:6 [b]Acts 2:4
their hands on them, and they
were [b]receiving the Holy Spirit.
18 Now when Simon saw that ★18-24
the Spirit was bestowed through
the laying on of the apostles'
hands, he offered them money,
19 saying, "Give this authority to me as well, so that everyone
on whom I lay my hands may receive the Holy Spirit."
20 But Peter said to him, 20 [a]2 Kin. 5:16; Is. 55:1; Dan. 5:17; Matt. 10:8; Acts 2:38
"May your silver perish with you,
because you thought you could
[a]obtain the gift of God with money!
21 "You have [a]no part or por- 21 [a]Deut. 10:9; 12:12; Eph. 5:5 [b]Ps. 78:37
tion in this matter, for your heart
is not [b]right before God.
22 "Therefore repent of this
wickedness of yours, and pray the

8:4 *went about.* See 11:19 for details.
8:5 *Philip.* See 6:5. *the city of Samaria* was then called Sebaste. Some texts read "a city of Samaria," which would mean some smaller city in Samaria. On the Samaritans see the note on Luke 10:33.
8:9 *magic.* Simon was a practitioner of magic, quackery, and various kinds of sorcery. He may also have made Messianic claims.
8:13 *Simon himself believed.* Peter's denunciation (vv. 20–23) indicates that Simon's faith was not unto salvation (Jas. 2:14–20).
8:14–17 Though the Samaritans had been baptized in water (v. 12), the gift of the Holy Spirit was delayed until Peter and John came and laid their hands on them. Normally the Spirit is given at the moment of faith (10:44; 19:2; Eph. 1:13). In this instance, however, it was imperative that the Samaritans be identified with the apostles and the Jerusalem church so that there would be no rival Samaritan Christian church.
8:18–24 Simon thought he could buy the gift of God (v. 20). When Peter urged him to repent, Simon replied, in effect, "Pray for me that I may escape punishment" (v. 24). He was still thinking in terms of magical powers rather than repentance of heart.

Lord that if possible, the intention
of your heart may be forgiven
you.
23 [a]Is. 58:6 **23** "For I see that you are in
the gall of bitterness and in [a]the
bondage of iniquity."
24 But Simon answered and
said, "Pray to the Lord for me
yourselves, so that nothing of
what you have said may come
upon me."
25 [a]Luke 16:28 [b]Acts 13:12 [c]Acts 8:40 [d]Matt. 10:5 **25** And so, when they had
solemnly [a]testified and spoken
[b]the word of the Lord, they
started back to Jerusalem, and
were [c]preaching the gospel to
many villages of the [d]Samaritans.

2 *The preaching on the Gaza road,* 8:26–40

★26 [a]Acts 5:19; 8:29 [b]Acts 8:5 [c]Gen. 10:19 **26** But [a]an angel of the Lord
spoke to [b]Philip saying, "Arise
and go south to the road that de-
scends from Jerusalem to [c]Gaza."
(This is a desert *road.*)
★27 [a]Ps. 68:31; 87:4; Is. 56:3ff. [b]1 Kin. 8:41f.; John 12:20 **27** And he arose and went;
and behold, [a]there was an Ethi-
opian eunuch, a court official of
Candace, queen of the Ethiopians,
who was in charge of all her treasure; and he [b]had come to Jerusalem to worship.
28 And he was returning and
sitting in his chariot, and was
reading the prophet Isaiah.
29 [a]Acts 8:39; 10:19; 11:12; 13:2; 16:6, 7; 20:23; 21:11; 28:25; Heb. 3:7 **29** And [a]the Spirit said to
Philip, "Go up and join this
chariot."
30 And when Philip had run
up, he heard him reading Isaiah
the prophet, and said, "Do you
understand what you are reading?"
31 And he said, "Well, how
could I, unless someone guides
me?" And he invited Philip to
come up and sit with him.
32 Now the passage of Scrip- 32 [a]Is. 53:7
ture which he was reading was
this:

"[a]HE WAS LED AS A SHEEP TO
SLAUGHTER;
AND AS A LAMB BEFORE ITS
SHEARER IS SILENT,
SO HE DOES NOT OPEN HIS
MOUTH.
33 "[a]IN HUMILIATION HIS JUDG- 33 [a]Is. 53:8f.
MENT WAS TAKEN AWAY;
WHO SHALL RELATE HIS GEN-
ERATION?
FOR HIS LIFE IS REMOVED
FROM THE EARTH."

34 And the eunuch answered
Philip and said, "Please *tell me,* of
whom does the prophet say this?
Of himself, or of someone else?"
35 And Philip [a]opened his ★35 [a]Matt. 5:2 [b]Luke 24:27; Acts 17:2; 18:28; 28:23 [c]Acts 5:42
mouth, and [b]beginning from this
Scripture he [c]preached Jesus to
him.
36 And as they went along 36 [a]Acts 10:47
the road they came to some wa-
ter; and the eunuch *said, "Look!
Water! [a]What prevents me from
being baptized?"
37 [And Philip said, "If you ★37
believe with all your heart, you
may." And he answered and said,
"I believe that Jesus Christ is the
Son of God."]
38 And he ordered the chariot 39 [a]1 Kin. 18:12; 2 Kin. 2:16; Ezek. 3:12, 14; 8:3; 11:1, 24; 43:5; 2 Cor. 12:2
to stop; and they both went down
into the water, Philip as well as
the eunuch; and he baptized him.
39 And when they came up ★40 [a]Josh. 11:22; 1 Sam. 5:1 [b]Acts 8:25 [c]Acts 9:30; 10:1, 24; 11:11; 12:19; 18:22; 21:8, 16; 23:23, 33; 25:1, 4, 6, 13
out of the water, [a]the Spirit of the
Lord snatched Philip away; and
the eunuch saw him no more, but
went on his way rejoicing.
40 But Philip found himself at
[a]Azotus; and as he passed
through he [b]kept preaching the

8:26 *a desert road.* Possibly the road to Desert Gaza, the old city which had been destroyed in 93 B.C. and which was inland from the Gaza of N.T. times.

8:27 *Ethiopian.* Not from present-day Abyssinia but ancient Nubia, south of Aswan. The story shows how far the gospel was spreading. *Candace.* The hereditary title of Ethiopian queens.

8:35 *preached Jesus to him.* Before the coming of Jesus, the Jews understood Isa. 53 as referring to the Messiah. This interpretation was abandoned as Christians applied the prophecy to Jesus of Nazareth, and Isa. 53 was then considered by the Jews to be referring either to Isaiah himself or to the people of Israel, who would be a light to the nations, etc.

8:37 Most manuscripts do not contain this verse.

8:40 *Azotus* = O.T. Ashdod, 20 miles N. of Gaza.

gospel to all the cities, until he
came to [c]Caesarea.

B The Conversion of Paul, 9:1–31

1 The account of Paul's conversion, 9:1–19

9 [a]Now Saul, still [b]breathing
threats and murder against
the disciples of the Lord, went to
the high priest,
2 and asked for [a]letters from
him to [b]the synagogues at [c]Da-
mascus, so that if he found any
belonging to [d]the Way, both men
and women, he might bring them
bound to Jerusalem.
3 And it came about that as
he journeyed, he was approaching
Damascus, and [a]suddenly a light
from heaven flashed around him;
4 and [a]he fell to the ground,
and heard a voice saying to him,
"Saul, Saul, why are you persecuting Me?"
5 And he said, "Who art
Thou, Lord?" And He *said,* "I am
Jesus whom you are persecuting,
6 but rise, and enter the city,
and [a]it shall be told you what you
must do."
7 And the men who traveled
with him [a]stood speechless,
[b]hearing the voice, but seeing no
one.
8 And Saul got up from the
ground, and [a]though his eyes
were open, he could see nothing;
and leading him by the hand,
they brought him into [b]Damas-
cus.

★ 1-19
1 [a]Acts 9:1-22; 22:3-16; 26:9-18 [b]Acts 8:3; 9:13-21
★ 2 [a]Acts 9:14, 21; 22:5; 26:10 [b]Matt. 10:17 [c]Gen. 14:15; 2 Cor. 11:32; Gal. 1:17 [d]John 14:6; Acts 18:25f.; 19:9, 23; 22:4; 24:14, 22
3 [a]1 Cor. 15:8
4 [a]Acts 22:7; 26:14
★5
6 [a]Acts 9:16
7 [a]Acts 26:14 [b]Acts 22:9 [John 12:29f.]
8 [a]Acts 9:18; 22:11 [b]Gen. 14:15; 2 Cor. 11:32; Gal. 1:17

9 And he was three days
without sight, and neither ate nor
drank.
10 Now there was a certain
disciple at [a]Damascus, named
[b]Ananias; and the Lord said to
him in [c]a vision, "Ananias." And
he said, "Behold, *here am* I,
Lord."
11 And the Lord *said* to him,
"Arise and go to the street called
Straight, and inquire at the house
of Judas for a man from [a]Tarsus
named Saul, for behold, he is
praying,
12 and he has seen in a vision
a man named Ananias come in
and [a]lay his hands on him, so that
he might regain his sight."
13 But Ananias answered,
"Lord, I have heard from many
about this man, [a]how much harm
he did to [b]Thy saints at Jerusalem;
14 and here he [a]has authority
from the chief priests to bind all
who [b]call upon Thy name."
15 But the Lord said to him,
"Go, for [a]he is a chosen instrument of Mine, to bear My name
before [b]the Gentiles and [c]kings
and the sons of Israel;
16 for [a]I will show him how
much he must suffer for My
name's sake."
17 And Ananias departed and
entered the house, and after [a]lay-
ing his hands on him said,
"[b]Brother Saul, the Lord Jesus,
who appeared to you on the road
by which you were coming, has
sent me so that you may regain

★10 [a]Gen. 14:15; 2 Cor. 11:32; Gal. 1:17 [b]Acts 22:12 [c]Acts 10:3, 17, 19; 11:5; 12:9; 16:9f.; 18:9
11 [a]Acts 9:30; 11:25; 21:39; 22:3
12 [a]Mark 5:23; Acts 6:6; 9:17
13 [a]Acts 8:3 [b]Acts 9:32, 41; 26:10; Rom 1:7; 15:25f., 31; 16:2, 15; 1 Cor. 1:2
14 [a]Acts 9:2, 21 [b]Acts 7:59
15 [a]Acts 13:2; Rom. 1:1; 9:23; Gal. 1:15; Eph. 3:7 [b]Acts 22:21; 26:17; Rom. 1:5; 11:13; 15:16; Gal. 1:16; 2:7ff.; Eph. 3:2, 8; 1 Tim. 2:7; 2 Tim. 4:17 [c]Acts 25:22f.; 26:1, 32; 2 Tim. 4:16
16 [a]Acts 20:23; 21:11 [4 and 13]; 1 Thess. 3:3; 2 Cor. 6:4f.; 11:23-27
★17 [a]Mark 5:23; Acts 6:6; 9:12 [b]Acts 22:13 [c]Acts 2:4

9:1–19 Luke here records Paul's conversion (22:4 ff. and 26:12ff. also give accounts of it, to the crowd in Jerusalem and to Herod Agrippa II). In his own writings, Paul refers to it only a few times. He related it to the supernatural purposes of God (Gal. 1:15); he spoke of its suddenness (1 Cor. 15:8; Phil. 3:12); he called it an act of new creation by God (2 Cor. 4:6); he acknowledged the merciful character of it (1 Tim. 1:13); and he claimed that during it he saw the Lord (1 Cor. 9:1). He was, therefore, just as qualified as the other apostles, for his conversion experience was just as objective a reality as their meetings with the risen Christ before the ascension.

9:2 *belonging to the Way.* I.e., Christians.

9:5 *I am Jesus.* In this moment Paul identified the Lord Yahweh (or Jehovah) of the O.T., whom he had attempted so zealously to serve, with Jesus of Nazareth, whom he had so ferociously persecuted through His saints. The phrase, *"it is hard for thee to kick against the pricks"* (AV), is not found in most manuscripts.

9:10 *Ananias.* According to 22:12 Ananias was an unimpeachable witness to the reality of Paul's conversion.

9:17 Through Ananias' *laying his hands on him,* Paul is identified with the people he had been persecuting.

your sight, and be [c]filled with the
Holy Spirit."
18 And immediately there fell
from his eyes something like
scales, and he regained his sight,
and he arose and was baptized;
19 and he took food and was
strengthened.
Now [a]for several days he was
with [b]the disciples who were at
Damascus,

19 [a]Acts 26:20 [b]Acts 9:26, 38; 11:26

2 *The aftermath of Paul's conversion,* 9:20-31

20 and immediately he *began*
to proclaim Jesus [a]in the synagogues, saying, "He is [b]the Son of
God."
21 And all those hearing him
continued to be amazed, and were
saying, "Is this not he who in Jerusalem [a]destroyed those who
[b]called on this name, and *who*
had come here for the purpose of
bringing them bound before the
chief priests?"
22 But Saul kept increasing in
strength and confounding the
Jews who lived at Damascus by
proving that this *Jesus* is the
Christ.
23 And when [a]many days
had elapsed, [b]the Jews plotted together to do away with him,
24 but [a]their plot became
known to Saul. And [b]they were
also watching the gates day and
night so that they might put him
to death;
25 but his disciples took him
by night, and let him down
through *an opening in* the wall,
lowering him in a large basket.
26 And [a]when he had come
to Jerusalem, he was trying to associate with the disciples; and
they were all afraid of him, not
believing that he was a disciple.
27 But [a]Barnabas took hold of
him and brought him to the apostles and described to them how he
had [b]seen the Lord on the road,
and that He had talked to him,
and how [c]at Damascus he had
[d]spoken out boldly in the name of
Jesus.
28 And he was with them
moving about freely in Jerusalem,
[a]speaking out boldly in the name
of the Lord.
29 And he was talking and arguing with the [a]Hellenistic *Jews;*
but they were attempting to put
him to death.
30 But when [a]the brethren
learned *of it,* they brought him
down to [b]Caesarea and [c]sent him
away to [d]Tarsus.
31 So [a]the church throughout
all Judea and Galilee and Samaria
enjoyed peace, being built up;
and, going on in the fear of the
Lord and in the comfort of the
Holy Spirit, it continued to increase.

20 [a]Acts 13:5, 14; 14:1; 16:13; 17:2, 10; 18:4, 19; 19:8; 28:17 [b]Matt. 4:3; Acts 9:22; 13:33
21 [a]Acts 8:3; 9:13; Gal. 1:13, 23 [b]Acts 9:14
★23 [a]Gal. 1:17, 18 [b]1 Thess. 2:16
24 [a]Acts 20:3, 19; 23:12, 30; 25:3 [b]2 Cor. 11:32f.
26 [a]Acts 22:17-20; 26:20
27 [a]Acts 4:36 [b]Acts 9:3-6 [c]Acts 9:20, 22 [d]Acts 4:13, 29; 9:29
28 [a]Acts 4:13, 29; 9:29
★29 [a]Acts 6:1
30 [a]Acts 1:15 [b]Acts 8:40 [c]Gal. 1:21 [d]Acts 9:11
31 [a]Acts 5:11; 8:1; 16:5

C The Conversion of Gentiles, 9:32-11:30

1 *The preparation of Peter,* 9:32-10:22

32 Now it came about that as
Peter was traveling through all
those parts, he came down also to
[a]the saints who lived at [b]Lydda.
33 And there he found a certain man named Aeneas, who had
been bedridden eight years, for
he was paralyzed.
34 And Peter said to him,
"Aeneas, Jesus Christ heals you;
arise, and make your bed." And
immediately he arose.
35 And all who lived at [a]Lyd-
da and [b]Sharon saw him, and
they [c]turned to the Lord.
36 Now in [a]Joppa there was a
certain disciple named Tabitha
(which translated *in Greek* is

★32 [a]Acts 9:13 [b]1 Chr. 8:12; Ezra 2:33; Neh. 7:37; 11:35
★35 [a]1 Chr. 8:12; Ezra 2:33; Neh. 7:37; 11:35 [b]1 Chr. 5:16; 27:29; Is. 33:9; 35:2; 65:10 [c]Acts 2:47; 9:42; 11:21
★36 [a]Josh. 19:46; 2 Chr. 2:16; Ezra 3:7; Jon. 1:3; Acts 9:38, 42f.; 10:5, 8, 23, 32; 11:5, 13

9:23 *when many days had elapsed.* During this time Paul went to Arabia (see note on Gal. 1:17), so that three years elapsed between his conversion and his going to Jerusalem (Acts 9:26).
9:29 *Hellenistic Jews* = Greek-speaking Jews.
9:32 *Lydda* = Lod, 11 miles SE of Joppa.
9:35 *Sharon.* The plain extending southward for 50 miles along the Mediterranean Sea from modern Haifa, which stands on Mt. Carmel.
9:36 *Tabitha* means "gazelle" (*Dorcas* is Greek for the same).

called Dorcas); this woman was
abounding with deeds of kindness and charity, which she continually did.
37 And it came about at that
time that she fell sick and died;
and when they had washed her
body, they laid it in an [a]upper
room.
38 And since Lydda was near
[a]Joppa, [b]the disciples, having
heard that Peter was there, sent
two men to him, entreating him,
"Do not delay to come to us."
39 And Peter arose and went
with them. And when he had
come, they brought him into the
[a]upper room; and all the [b]widows
stood beside him weeping, and
showing all the tunics and garments that Dorcas used to make
while she was with them.
40 But Peter [a]sent them all
out and [b]knelt down and prayed,
and turning to the body, he said,
"[c]Tabitha, arise." And she
opened her eyes, and when she
saw Peter, she sat up.
41 And he gave her his hand
and raised her up; and calling [a]the
saints and [b]widows, he presented
her alive.
42 And it became known all
over [a]Joppa, and [b]many believed
in the Lord.
43 And it came about that he
stayed many days in [a]Joppa with
[b]a certain tanner, Simon.

10

Now *there was* a certain
man at [a]Caesarea named
Cornelius, a centurion of what
was [b]called the Italian cohort,
2 a devout man, and [a]one
who feared God with all his
household, and [b]gave many alms
to the *Jewish* people, and prayed
to God continually.
3 About [a]the ninth hour of
the day he clearly saw [b]in a vision
[c]an angel of God who had *just*
come in to him, and said to him,
"Cornelius!"
4 And [a]fixing his gaze upon
him and being much alarmed, he
said, "What is it, Lord?" And he
said to him, "Your prayers and
alms [b]have ascended [c]as a memo-
rial before God.
5 "And now dispatch *some*
men to [a]Joppa, and send for a
man *named* Simon, who is also
called Peter;
6 he is staying with a certain
tanner *named* [a]Simon, whose
house is by the sea."
7 And when the angel who
was speaking to him had departed, he summoned two of his
servants and a devout soldier of
those who were in constant at-
tendance upon him,
8 and after he had explained
everything to them, he sent them
to [a]Joppa.
9 And on the next day, as
they were on their way, and approaching the city, [a]Peter went up
on [b]the housetop about [c]the sixth
hour to pray.
10 And he became hungry,
and was desiring to eat; but while
they were making preparations,
he [a]fell into a trance;
11 and he *beheld [a]the sky
opened up, and a certain object
like a great sheet coming down,
lowered by four corners to the
ground,
12 and there were in it all
kinds of four-footed animals and
crawling creatures of the earth
and birds of the air.
13 And a voice came to him,
"Arise, Peter, kill and eat!"
14 But Peter said, "By no
means, [a]Lord, for [b]I have never
eaten anything unholy and unclean."
15 And again a voice *came* to
him a second time, "[a]What God

37 [a]Acts 1:13; 9:39
38 [a]Josh. 19:46; 2 Chr. 2:16; Ezra 3:7; Jon. 1:3; Acts 9:36, 42f.; 10:5, 8, 23, 32; 11:5, 13 [b]Acts 11:26
39 [a]Acts 1:13; 9:37 [b]Acts 6:1
40 [a]Matt. 9:25 [b]Luke 22:41; Acts 7:60 [c]Mark 5:41
41 [a]Acts 9:13 [b]Acts 6:1
42 [a]Josh. 19:46; 2 Chr. 2:16; Jon. 1:3; Acts 9:38, 42f.; 10:5, 8, 23, 32; 11:5, 13 [b]Acts 9:35
43 [a]Josh. 19:46; 2 Chr. 2:16; Ezra 3:7; Jon. 1:3; Acts 9:38, 42f.; 10:5, 8, 23, 32; 11:13, 15 [b]Acts 10:6
★ 1 [a]Acts 8:40; 10:24 [b]Matt. 27:27; Mark 15:16; John 18:3, 12; Acts 21:31; 27:1
★ 2 [a]Acts 10:22, 35; 13:16, 26 [b]Luke 7:4f.
3 [a]Acts 3:1 [b]Acts 9:10; 10:17, 19 [c]Acts 5:19
4 [a]Acts 3:4 [b]Rev. 8:4 [c]Matt. 26:13; Phil. 4:18; Heb. 6:10
5 [a]Acts 9:36
6 [a]Acts 9:43
8 [a]Acts 9:36
9 [a]Acts 10:9-32; 11:5-14 [b]Jer. 19:13; 32:29; Zeph. 1:5; Matt. 24:17 [c]Ps. 55:17; Acts 10:3
10 [a]Acts 11:5; 22:17
11 [a]John 1:51
★14 [a]Matt. 8:2ff.; John 4:11ff.; Acts 9:5; 22:8 [b]Lev. 11:20-25; Deut. 14:4-20; Ezek. 4:14; Dan. 1:8; Acts 10:28
15 [a]Matt. 15:11; Mark 7:19; Rom. 14:14; 1 Cor. 10:25ff.; 1 Tim. 4:4f.; Titus 1:15

10:1 *a centurion* was a noncommissioned officer who was in command of 100 men. Cornelius was a commander in the *Italian* cohort (see note on John 18:3).

10:2 Cornelius was a semi-proselyte to Judaism, accepting Jewish beliefs and practices but stopping short of circumcision.

10:14 *unholy and unclean.* The Mosaic law prohibited the eating of certain unclean animals (Lev. 11). God was teaching Peter a lesson about people (see v. 28).

has cleansed, no *longer* consider unholy."

16 And this happened three times; and immediately the object was taken up into the sky.

17 [a]Acts 10:3 [b]Acts 10:8

17 Now while Peter was greatly perplexed in mind as to what [a]the vision which he had seen might be, behold, [b]the men who had been sent by Cornelius, having asked directions for Simon's house, appeared at the gate;

18 and calling out, they were asking whether Simon, who was also called Peter, was staying there.

19 [a]Acts 10:3 [b]Acts 8:29

19 And while Peter was reflecting on [a]the vision, [b]the Spirit said to him, "Behold, three men are looking for you.

20 [a]Acts 15:7-9

20 "But arise, go downstairs, and [a]accompany them without misgivings; for I have sent them Myself."

21 And Peter went down to the men and said, "Behold, I am the one you are looking for; what is the reason for which you have come?"

22 [a]Acts 10:2 [b]Matt. 2:12 [c]Mark 8:38; Luke 9:26; Rev. 14:10 [d]Acts 11:14

22 And they said, "Cornelius, a centurion, a righteous and [a]God-fearing man well spoken of by the entire nation of the Jews, [b]was *divinely* directed by a [c]holy angel to send for you *to come* to his house and hear [d]a message from you."

2 *The preaching of Peter,* 10:23–48

★23 [a]Acts 10:45; 11:12 [b]Acts 1:15 [c]Acts 9:36

23 And so he invited them in and gave them lodging.

And on the next day he arose and went away with them, and [a]some of [b]the brethren from [c]Joppa accompanied him.

24 [a]Acts 8:40; 10:1

24 And on the following day he entered [a]Caesarea. Now Cornelius was waiting for them, and had called together his relatives and close friends.

25 And when it came about that Peter entered, Cornelius met him, and fell at his feet and [a]worshiped *him.*

25 [a]Matt. 8:2

26 But Peter raised him up, saying, "[a]Stand up; I too am *just* a man."

26 [a]Acts 14:15; Rev. 19:10; 22:8f.

27 And as he talked with him, he entered, and found [a]many people assembled.

27 [a]Acts 10:24

28 And he said to them, "You yourselves know how [a]unlawful it is for a man who is a Jew to associate with a foreigner or to visit him; and *yet* [b]God has shown me that I should not call any man unholy or unclean.

★28 [a]John 4:9; 18:28; Acts 11:3 [b]Acts 10:14f., 35; 15:9

29 "That is why I came without even raising any objection when I was sent for. And so I ask for what reason you have sent for me."

30 And Cornelius said, "[a]Four days ago to this hour, I was praying in my house during [b]the ninth hour; and behold, [c]a man stood before me in shining garments,

30 [a]Acts 10:9, 22f. [b]Acts 3:1; 10:3 [c]Acts 10:3-6, 30-32

31 and he *said, 'Cornelius, your prayer has been heard and your alms have been remembered before God.

32 'Send therefore to [a]Joppa and invite Simon, who is also called Peter, to come to you; he is staying at the house of Simon *the* tanner by the sea.'

32 [a]John 4:9; 18:28; Acts 11:3

33 "And so I sent to you immediately, and you have been kind enough to come. Now then, we are all here present before God to hear all that you have been commanded by the Lord."

34 And [a]opening his mouth, Peter said:

★34 [a]Matt. 5:2 [b]Deut. 10:17; 2 Chr. 19:7; Rom. 2:11; Gal. 2:6; Eph. 6:9; Col. 3:25; 1 Pet. 1:17

"I most certainly understand *now* that [b]God is not one to show partiality,

35 but [a]in every nation the

35 [a]Acts 10:28 [b]Acts 10:2

10:23 *some of the brethren.* There were six of them (11:12).

10:28 The case of Cornelius was the first of its kind and crucial to the spread of Christianity. It answered the question, "Can the new faith (still so closely associated with Judaism) admit into fellowship an uncircumcised Gentile?" The issue, however, would not be completely resolved for some time.

10:34 *God is not one to show partiality.* This fact was taught in the O.T. (Deut. 10:17; 2 Chron. 19:7).

man who [b]fears Him and does what is right, is welcome to Him.

36 "The word which He sent to the sons of Israel, [a]preaching [b]peace through Jesus Christ (He is [c]Lord of all)—

36 [a]Acts 13:32 [b]Luke 1:79; 2:14; Rom. 5:1; Eph. 2:17 [c]Matt. 28:18; Acts 2:36; Rom. 10:12

37 you yourselves know the thing which took place throughout all Judea, starting from Galilee, after the baptism which John proclaimed.

38 *"You know of* [a]Jesus of Nazareth, how God [b]anointed Him with the Holy Spirit and with power, [c]and *how* He went about doing good, and healing all who were oppressed by the devil; for [d]God was with Him.

38 [a]Acts 2:22 [b]Acts 4:26 [c]Matt. 4:23 [d]John 3:2

39 "And we are [a]witnesses of all the things He did both in the land of the Jews and in Jerusalem. And they also [b]put Him to death by hanging Him on a cross.

39 [a]Luke 24:48; Acts 10:41 [b]Acts 5:30

40 "[a]God raised Him up on the third day, and granted that He should become visible,

40 [a]Acts 2:24

41 [a]not to all the people, but to [b]witnesses who were chosen beforehand by God, *that is,* to us, [c]who ate and drank with Him after He arose from the dead.

41 [a]John 14:19, 22; 15:27 [b]Luke 24:48; Acts 10:39 [c]Luke 24:43; Acts 1:4 marg.

42 "And He [a]ordered us to preach to the people, and solemnly to [b]testify that this is the One who has been [c]appointed by God as [d]Judge of the living and the dead.

42 [a]Acts 1:2 [b]Luke 16:28 [c]Luke 22:22 [d]John 5:22, 27; Acts 17:31; 2 Tim. 4:1; 1 Pet. 4:5

43 "Of Him [a]all the prophets bear witness that through [b]His name every one who believes in Him receives forgiveness of sins."

43 [a]Acts 3:18 [b]Luke 24:47; Acts 2:38; 4:12

44 While Peter was still speaking these words, [a]the Holy Spirit fell upon all those who were listening to the message.

★44 [a]Acts 11:15; 15:8

45 And [a]all the circumcised believers who had come with Peter were amazed, because the gift of the Holy Spirit had been [b]poured out upon the Gentiles also.

45 [a]Acts 10:23 [b]Acts 2:33, 38

46 For they were hearing them [a]speaking with tongues and exalting God. Then Peter [b]answered,

46 [a]Mark 16:17; Acts 2:4; 19:6 [b]Acts 3:12

47 "[a]Surely no one can refuse the water for these to be baptized who [b]have received the Holy Spirit just as we *did,* can he?"

47 [a]Acts 8:36 [b]Acts 2:4; 10:44f.; 11:17; 15:8

48 And he [a]ordered them to be baptized [b]in the name of Jesus Christ. Then they asked him to stay on for a few days.

48 [a]1 Cor. 1:14-17 [b]Acts 2:38; 8:16; 19:5

3 The plea of Peter, 11:1-18

11 Now the apostles and [a]the brethren who were throughout Judea heard that the Gentiles also had received the word of God.

1 [a]Acts 1:15

2 And when Peter came up to Jerusalem, [a]those who were circumcised took issue with him,

★ 2 [a]Acts 10:45

3 saying, "[a]You went to uncircumcised men and ate with them."

3 [a]Matt. 9:11; Acts 10:28; Gal. 2:12

4 But Peter began *speaking* and *proceeded* to explain to them [a]in orderly sequence, saying,

4 [a]Luke 1:3

5 "[a]I was in the city of Joppa praying; and in a trance I saw [b]a vision, a certain object coming down like a great sheet lowered by four corners from the sky; and it came right down to me,

5 [a]Acts 10:9-32; 11:5-14 [b]Acts 9:10

6 and when I had fixed my gaze upon it and was observing it I saw the four-footed animals of the earth and the wild beasts and the crawling creatures and the birds of the air.

7 "And I also heard a voice saying to me, 'Arise, Peter; kill and eat.'

8 "But I said, 'By no means, Lord, for nothing unholy or un-

10:44 *the Holy Spirit fell upon all.* In the case of these Gentile converts, the gift of the Spirit came before they were baptized in water (v. 48). The authentication of the gift was the speaking in tongues (v. 46), entirely apart from the laying on of hands. All this demonstrated, especially to the Jewish brethren who accompanied Peter, that God had received these Gentiles into the Church on an equal basis with Jewish believers because they had believed in Christ (v. 43).

11:2 *those who were circumcised.* Jewish Christians, the so-called "circumcision party," who were unhappy at the report that Gentiles were being saved without ritual induction into Judaism. After Peter's review of what happened, they were satisfied that this was God's doing (v. 18).

clean has ever entered my mouth.'

9 [a]Acts 10:15

9 "But a voice from heaven answered a second time, '[a]What God has cleansed, no longer consider unholy.'

10 "And this happened three times, and everything was drawn back up into the sky.

11 [a]Acts 8:40

11 "And behold, at that moment three men appeared before the house in which we were *staying,* having been sent to me from [a]Caesarea.

12 [a]Acts 8:29 [b]Acts 15:9; Rom. 3:22 [c]Acts 10:23

12 "And [a]the Spirit told me to go with them [b]without misgivings. And [c]these six brethren also went with me, and we entered the man's house.

13 "And he reported to us how he had seen the angel standing in his house, and saying, 'Send to Joppa, and have Simon, who is also called Peter, brought here;

14 [a]Acts 10:22 [b]John 4:53; Acts 10:2; 16:15, 31-34; 18:8; 1 Cor. 1:16

14 and he shall speak [a]words to you by which you will be saved, you and [b]all your household.'

★15 [a]Acts 10:44 [b]Acts 2:4

15 "And as I began to speak, [a]the Holy Spirit fell upon them, just [b]as *He did* upon us at the beginning.

16 [a]Acts 1:5

16 "And I remembered the word of the Lord, how He used to say, '[a]John baptized with water, but you shall be baptized with the Holy Spirit.'

17 [a]Acts 10:45, 47 [b]Acts 5:39

17 "If [a]God therefore gave to them the same gift as *He gave* to us also after believing in the Lord Jesus Christ, [b]who was I that I could stand in God's way?"

18 [a]Matt. 9:8 [b]2 Cor. 7:10

18 And when they heard this, they quieted down, and [a]glorified God, saying, "Well then, God has granted to the Gentiles also the [b]repentance *that leads* to life."

4 The church at Antioch, 11:19–30

★19 [a]Acts 8:1, 4 [b]Acts 15:3; 21:2 [c]Acts 4:36 [d]Acts 6:5; 11:20, 22, 27; 13:1; 14:26; 15:22f., 30, 35; 18:22; Gal. 2:11

19 [a]So then those who were scattered because of the persecution that arose in connection with Stephen made their way to [b]Phoenicia and [c]Cyprus and [d]Antioch, speaking the word to no one except to Jews alone.

20 [a]Acts 4:36 [b]Matt. 27:32; Acts 2:10; 6:9; 13:1 [c]Acts 6:5; 11:19, 22, 27; 13:1; 14:26; 15:22f., 30, 35; 18:22; Gal. 2:11 [d]John 7:35 [e]Acts 5:42

20 But there were some of them, men of [a]Cyprus and [b]Cyrene, who came to [c]Antioch and *began* speaking to the [d]Greeks also, [e]preaching the Lord Jesus.

21 [a]Luke 1:66 [b]Acts 2:47

21 And [a]the hand of the Lord was with them, and [b]a large number who believed turned to the Lord.

★22 [a]Acts 4:36 [b]Acts 6:5; 11:19, 20, 27; 13:1; 14:26; 15:22f., 30, 35; 18:22; Gal. 2:11

22 And the news about them reached the ears of the church at Jerusalem, and they sent [a]Barnabas off to [b]Antioch.

23 [a]Acts 13:43; 14:26; 15:40; 20:24, 32

23 Then when he had come and witnessed [a]the grace of God, he rejoiced and *began* to encourage them all with resolute heart to remain *true* to the Lord;

24 [a]Acts 2:4 [b]Acts 2:47; 5:14; 11:21

24 for he was a good man, and [a]full of the Holy Spirit and of faith. And [b]considerable numbers were brought to the Lord.

★25 [a]Acts 9:11

25 And he left for [a]Tarsus to look for Saul;

11:15 *at the beginning.* I.e., on the day of Pentecost. Since God had done for the Gentiles in Cornelius' house the same as He had done for the Jews at Pentecost, to refuse to accept these Gentile converts would be to resist the work of God (v. 17).

11:19 *Antioch* on the Orontes River about 300 miles from Jerusalem was the capital of the Roman province of Syria. It was the third largest city in the empire, with a population of about 500,000. It was one of the cosmopolitan centers of the world of that day and a center of commerce, Seleucia (16 miles away) being its seaport (13:4). Replacing Jerusalem as the number one Christian city, it was the center of the early missionary activity of the Church (6:5; 13:1; 14:26; 15:35; 18:22).

11:22 *Barnabas.* Described by Luke as one who consoles or encourages (4:36). *a good man* who was *full of the Holy Spirit* (11:24), he played an important role in the early life of the church on four occasions: (1) he convinced the apostles of the genuineness of Paul's conversion (Acts 9:27); (2) he represented the apostles at Antioch and recognized that the movement there was the work of God (11:22-24); (3) he and Paul were sent by the Spirit on the first missionary journey (13:2); and (4) he defended the work among Gentiles at the Jerusalem council (15:12, 22, 25).

11:25 *to look for Saul.* Paul had been in Tarsus, his home city, and in Syria and Cilicia (Gal. 1:21) about 9 years since going there from Jerusalem (Acts 9:30).

26 and when he had found
him, he brought him to [a]Antioch.
And it came about that for an entire year they met with the
church, and taught considerable
numbers; and [b]the disciples were
first called [c]Christians in [a]Anti-
och.
27 Now at this time [a]some
prophets [b]came down from Jerusalem to [c]Antioch.
28 And one of them named
[a]Agabus stood up and *began* to
indicate by the Spirit that there
would certainly be a great famine
[b]all over the world. And this took
place in the *reign* of [c]Claudius.
29 And in the proportion that
any of [a]the disciples had means,
each of them determined to send
a contribution for the relief of
[b]the brethren living in Judea.
30 [a]And this they did, sending it in charge of [b]Barnabas and
Saul to the [c]elders.

★26 [a]Acts 6:5; 11:20, 22, 27; 13:1; 14:26; 15:22f., 30, 35; 18:22; Gal. 2:11 [b]John 2:2; Acts 1:15; 6:1f.; 9:19, 25, 26, 38; 11:29; 13:52; 14:20, 22, 28 [c]Acts 26:28; 1 Pet. 4:16
27 [a]Luke 11:49; Acts 2:17; 13:1; 1 Cor. 12:10, 28f. [b]Acts 18:22 [c]Acts 6:5; 11:20, 22, 26; 13:1; 14:26; 15:22f., 30, 35; 18:22; Gal. 2:11
★28 [a]Acts 21:10 [b]Matt. 24:14 [c]Acts 18:2
29 [a]John 2:2; Acts 1:15; 6:1f.; 9:19, 25, 26, 38; 11:26; 13:52; 14:20, 22, 28 [b]Acts 11:1
★30 [a]Acts 12:25 [b]Acts 4:36 [c]Acts 14:23; 15:2, 4, 6, 22f.; 16:4; 20:17; 21:18; 1 Tim. 5:17, 19; Titus 1:5; James 5:14; 1 Pet. 5:1; 2 John 1; 3 John 1

D The Christians Persecuted by Herod, 12:1–25

1 *The death of James,* 12:1–2

12 Now about that time Herod the king laid hands on
some who belonged to the
church, in order to mistreat them.
2 And he [a]had James the
brother of John [b]put to death with
a sword.

★ 1
★ 2 [a]Matt. 4:21; 20:23 [b]Mark 10:39

2 *The deliverance of Peter,* 12:3–19

3 And when he saw that it
[a]pleased the Jews, he proceeded
to arrest Peter also. Now it was
during [b]the days of *the Feast of*
Unleavened Bread.
4 And when he had seized
him, he put him in prison, delivering him to four [a]squads of soldiers to guard him, intending after [b]the Passover to bring him out
before the people.
5 So Peter was kept in the
prison, but prayer for him was
being made fervently by the
church to God.
6 And on the very night
when Herod was about to bring
him forward, Peter was sleeping
between two soldiers, [a]bound
with two chains; and guards in
front of the door were watching
over the prison.
7 And behold, [a]an angel of
the Lord suddenly [b]appeared, and
a light shone in the cell; and he
struck Peter's side and roused
him, saying, "Get up quickly."
And [c]his chains fell off his hands.
8 And the angel said to him,
"Gird yourself and put on your
sandals." And he did so. And he
*said to him, "Wrap your cloak
around you and follow me."
9 And he went out and continued to follow, and he did not
know that what was being done
by the angel was real, but thought
he was seeing [a]a vision.
10 And when they had passed
the first and second guard, they
came to the iron gate that leads
into the city, which [a]opened for
them by itself; and they went out
and went along one street; and
immediately the angel departed
from him.
11 And when Peter [a]came to
himself, he said, "Now I know for
sure that [b]the Lord has sent forth
His angel and rescued me from
the hand of Herod and from all
that the Jewish people were expecting."

3 [a]Acts 24:27; 25:9 [b]Ex. 12:15; 23:15; Acts 20:6
★ 4 [a]John 19:23 [b]Mark 14:1; Acts 12:3
★ 6 [a]Acts 21:33
7 [a]Acts 5:19 [b]Luke 2:9; 24:4 [c]Acts 16:26
9 [a]Acts 9:10
10 [a]Acts 5:19; 16:26
★11 [a]Luke 15:17 [b]Dan. 3:28; 6:22

11:26 *Christians.* The word appears only here, in 26:28, and in 1 Pet. 4:16. It means partisans or followers of Christ, "Christ's men."
11:28 *great famine.* Josephus reports that a famine occurred in about A.D. 46.
11:30 *elders.* See note on 1 Tim. 3:1.
12:1 *Herod.* Herod Agrippa I, grandson of the Herod the Great who ruled at the birth of Jesus. Agrippa, at least on the surface, was a zealous practicer of Jewish rites and a religious patriot.
12:2 *James.* The first of the Twelve to be martyred.
12:4 *Passover.* See note on Mark 14:1.
12:6 *Peter was sleeping.* He had Christ's promise that he would live to an old age (John 21:18).
12:11 *rescued me.* God's ways are inscrutable—Peter was delivered, but James was killed (v. 2).

★12 [a]Acts 12:25; 13:5, 13; 15:37, 39; Col. 4:10; 2 Tim. 4:11; Philem. 24; 1 Pet. 5:13 [b]Acts 12:5

12 And when he realized *this,*
he went to the house of Mary, the
mother of [a]John who was also
called Mark, where many were
gathered together and [b]were
praying.

13 [a]John 18:16f.

13 And when he knocked at
the door of the gate, [a]a servant-
girl named Rhoda came to answer.

14 [a]Luke 24:41

14 And when she recognized
Peter's voice, [a]because of her joy
she did not open the gate, but ran
in and announced that Peter was
standing in front of the gate.

★15 [a]Matt. 18:10

15 And they said to her, "You
are out of your mind!" But she
kept insisting that it was so. And
they kept saying, "It is [a]his angel."

16 But Peter continued
knocking; and when they had
opened *the door,* they saw him
and were amazed.

17 [a]Acts 13:16; 19:33; 21:40 [b]Mark 6:3; Acts 15:13; 21:18; 1 Cor. 15:7; Gal. 1:19; 2:9, 12 [c]Acts 1:15

17 But [a]motioning to them
with his hand to be silent, he described to them how the Lord had
led him out of the prison. And he
said, "Report these things to
[b]James and [c]the brethren." And
he departed and went to another
place.

18 Now when day came,
there was no small disturbance
among the soldiers *as to* what
could have become of Peter.

19 [a]Acts 16:27; 27:42 [b]Acts 8:40

19 And when Herod had
searched for him and had not
found him, he examined the
guards and ordered that they [a]be
led away *to execution.* And he
went down from Judea to [b]Caesa-
rea and was spending time there.

3 The death of Herod, 12:20–23

20 Now he was very angry
with the people of [a]Tyre and Sidon; and with one accord they
came to him, and having won
over Blastus the king's chamber-
lain, they were asking for peace,
because [b]their country was fed by
the king's country.

★20 [a]Matt. 11:21 [b]1 Kin. 5:11; Ezra 3:7; Ezek. 27:17

21 And on an appointed day
Herod, having put on his royal
apparel, took his seat on the ros-
trum and *began* delivering an address to them.

22 And the people kept crying out, "The voice of a god and
not of a man!"

23 And immediately [a]an angel of the Lord struck him because he did not give God the glory, and he was eaten by worms
and died.

★23 [a]2 Sam. 24:16; 2 Kin. 19:35; Acts 5:19

4 The dissemination of the Word, 12:24–25

24 But [a]the word of the Lord
continued to grow and to be multiplied.

24 [a]Acts 6:7; 19:20

25 And [a]Barnabas and [a]Saul
returned from Jerusalem [b]when
they had fulfilled their mission,
taking along with *them* [c]John,
who was also called Mark.

25 [a]Acts 4:36; 13:1ff. [b]Acts 11:30 [c]Acts 12:12

III CHRISTIANITY TO THE UTTERMOST PART OF THE WORLD, 13:1–28:31

A The First Missionary Journey, 13:1–14:28

1 Events in Antioch, 13:1–3

13 Now there were at [a]Anti-
och, in the [b]church that

★ 1 [a]Acts 11:19 [b]Acts 11:26 [c]Acts 11:27; 15:32; 19:6; 21:9; 1 Cor. 11:4f.; 13:2, 8f.; 14:29, 32, 37 [d]Rom. 12:6f.; 1 Cor. 12:28f.; Eph. 4:11; James 3:1 [e]Acts 4:36; [f]Matt. 27:32; Acts 11:20 [g]Matt. 14:1

12:12 *the house of Mary.* Traditionally it was here that the Last Supper was held and here now was the nerve center of the church in Jerusalem.

12:15 *his angel.* For other guardian angels in Scripture, see Gen. 48:16; Dan. 10:20–21; 12:1; Matt. 18:10; Heb. 1:14.

12:20 *Tyre and Sidon* had to import grain; the fields of Galilee produced large supplies (1 Kings 5:9).

12:23 Josephus states that Herod was struck down while delivering his oration and, after five days of suffering, died (A.D. 44).

13:1 Here begins what has been called "The Acts of Paul," because Paul becomes the dominant figure. *Simeon who was called Niger.* Niger was his Latin name and probably indicates that he was an African. *who had been brought up with.* Lit., foster brother, a designation given to boys of the same age as royal children with whom they were brought up. *Herod the tetrarch.* Herod Antipas, who ruled Galilee during the public ministry of Christ.

was *there,* [c]prophets and [d]teach-
ers: [e]Barnabas, and Simeon who
was called Niger, and Lucius of
[f]Cyrene, and Manaen who had
been brought up with [g]Herod the
tetrarch, and [e]Saul.

2 [a]Acts 8:29; 13:4 [b]Acts 4:36; 13:1ff. [c]Acts 9:15

2 And while they were ministering to the Lord and fasting,
[a]the Holy Spirit said, "Set apart
for Me [b]Barnabas and Saul for
[c]the work to which I have called
them."

★ 3 [a]Acts 1:24 [b]Acts 6:6 [c]Acts 13:4; 14:26

3 Then, when they had
fasted and [a]prayed and [b]laid their
hands on them, [c]they sent them
away.

2 *Events in Cyprus,* 13:4–12

4 [a]Acts 13:2f. [b]Acts 4:36

4 So, being [a]sent out by the
Holy Spirit, they went down to
Seleucia and from there they
sailed to [b]Cyprus.

★ 5 [a]Acts 9:20; 13:14 [b]Acts 12:12

5 And when they reached
Salamis, they *began* to proclaim
the word of God in [a]the synagogues of the Jews; and they also
had [b]John as their helper.

6 [a]Acts 8:9 [b]Matt. 7:15

6 And when they had gone
through the whole island as far as
Paphos, they found a certain [a]ma-
gician, a Jewish [b]false prophet
whose name was Bar-Jesus,

★ 7 [a]Acts 13:8, 12; 18:12; 19:38

7 who was with the [a]procon-
sul, Sergius Paulus, a man of in-
telligence. This man summoned
Barnabas and Saul and sought to
hear the word of God.

★ 8 [a]Acts 8:9 [b]Acts 13:7, 12; 18:12; 19:38 [c]Acts 6:7

8 But Elymas the [a]magician
(for thus his name is translated)
was opposing them, seeking to
turn the [b]proconsul away from
[c]the faith.

★ 9 [a]Acts 2:4; 4:8 10 [a]Matt. 13:38; John 8:44 [b]Hos. 14:9; 2 Pet. 2:15

9 But Saul, who was also
known as Paul, [a]filled with the
Holy Spirit, fixed his gaze upon
him,
10 and said, "You who are
full of all deceit and fraud, you
[a]son of the devil, you enemy of all
righteousness, will you not cease
to make crooked [b]the straight
ways of the Lord?

11 [a]Ex. 9:3; 1 Sam. 5:6f.; Job 19:21; Ps. 32:4; Heb. 10:31

11 "And now, behold, [a]the
hand of the Lord is upon you, and
you will be blind and not see the
sun for a time." And immediately
a mist and a darkness fell upon
him, and he went about seeking
those who would lead him by the
hand.

12 [a]Acts 13:7, 8; 18:12; 19:38 [b]Acts 8:25; 13:49; 15:35f.; 19:10, 20

12 Then the [a]proconsul believed when he saw what had
happened, being amazed at [b]the
teaching of the Lord.

3 *Events in Galatian cities,* 13:13–14:20

13 [a]Acts 13:6 [b]Acts 14:25 [c]Acts 2:10; 14:24; 15:38; 27:5 [d]Acts 12:12

13 Now Paul and his com-
panions put out to sea from [a]Pa-
phos and came to [b]Perga in [c]Pam-
phylia; and [d]John left them and
returned to Jerusalem.

★14 [a]Acts 14:24 [b]Acts 14:19, 21; 2 Tim. 3:11 [c]Acts 13:42, 44; 16:13; 17:2; 18:4 [d]Acts 9:20; 13:5

14 But going on from Perga,
they arrived at [a]Pisidian [b]Anti-
och, and on [c]the Sabbath day
they went into [d]the synagogue
and sat down.

15 [a]Acts 15:21; 2 Cor. 3:14f. [b]Acts 13:27 [c]Mark 5:22

15 And after [a]the reading of
the Law and [b]the Prophets [c]the
synagogue officials sent to them,
saying, "Brethren, if you have any
word of exhortation for the people, say it."

16 [a]Acts 12:17 [b]Acts 10:2; 13:26

16 And Paul stood up, and
[a]motioning with his hand, he
said,
"Men of Israel, and [b]you who
fear God, listen:

17 [a]Ex. 6:1, 6; 13:14, 16; Deut. 7:6-8; Acts 7:17ff.

17 "The God of this people Israel [a]chose our fathers, and made
the people great during their stay
in the land of Egypt, and with an
uplifted arm He led them out
from it.

13:3 *laid their hands on them.* See note on 6:6.
13:5 *John as their helper.* This was John Mark, son of Mary (12:12) and cousin to Barnabas (Col. 4:10). See 13:13; 15:38–40; 2 Tim. 4:11.
13:7 *who was with the proconsul.* Cyprus was a Roman senatorial province.
13:8 *Elymas* was the name given to Bar-Jesus by Greek-speaking acquaintances.
13:9 *Saul, who was also known as Paul.* Saul was his Jewish name and Paul his Roman or Gentile name. Both were given him at the time of his birth, but he now begins to use his Gentile name in this Gentile environment.
13:14 *Pisidian Antioch.* Actually it was in Phrygia, but near the border of Pisidia. This Antioch was so called to distinguish it from the larger Antioch in Syria.

18 [a]Acts 7:36 [b]Deut. 1:31

18 "And for [a]a period of about forty years [b]He put up with them in the wilderness.

★19 [a]Acts 7:45 [b]Deut. 7:1 [c]Josh. 19:51; Ps. 78:55 [d]Judg. 11:26; 1 Kin. 6:1

19 "And [a]when He had destroyed [b]seven nations in the land of Canaan, He [c]distributed their land as an inheritance—*all of which took* [d]about four hundred and fifty years.

20 [a]Judg. 2:16 [b]Acts 3:24

20 "And after these things He [a]gave *them* judges until [b]Samuel the prophet.

21 [a]1 Sam. 8:5 [b]1 Sam. 9:1f.; 10:1

21 "And then they [a]asked for a king, and God gave them [b]Saul the son of Kish, a man of the tribe of Benjamin, for forty years.

22 [a]1 Sam. 15:23, 26, 28; 16:1, 13 [b]1 Sam. 13:14; Ps. 89:20; Acts 7:46

22 "And after He had [a]removed him, He raised up David to be their king, concerning whom He also testified and said, 'I have found [b]David the son of Jesse, a man after My heart, who will do all My will.'

23 [a]Matt. 1:1 [b]Acts 13:32f. [c]Luke 2:11; John 4:42

23 "[a]From the offspring of this man, [b]according to promise, God has brought to Israel [c]a Savior, Jesus,

24 [a]Mark 1:1-4; Acts 1:22; 19:4

24 after [a]John had proclaimed before His coming a baptism of repentance to all the people of Israel.

25 [a]Acts 20:24 [b]Matt. 3:11; Mark 1:7; Luke 3:16; John 1:20, 27

25 "And while John [a]was completing his course, [b]he kept saying, 'What do you suppose that I am? I am not *He.* But behold, one is coming after me the sandals of whose feet I am not worthy to untie.'

26 [a]John 6:68; Acts 4:12; 5:20; 13:46; 28:28

26 "Brethren, sons of Abraham's family, and those among you who fear God, to us the word of [a]this salvation is sent out.

27 [a]Luke 23:13 [b]Acts 3:17 [c]Luke 24:27 [d]Acts 13:15

27 "For those who live in Jerusalem, and their [a]rulers, [b]recognizing neither Him nor the utterances of [c]the prophets which are [d]read every Sabbath, fulfilled *these* by condemning *Him.*

28 [a]Acts 3:14

28 "And though they found no ground for *putting Him to* death, they [a]asked Pilate that He be executed.

29 [a]Acts 26:22 [b]Luke 23:53 [c]Acts 5:30

29 "And when they had [a]carried out all that was written concerning Him, [b]they took Him down from [c]the cross and laid Him in a tomb.

30 [a]Acts 2:24; 13:33, 34, 37

30 "But God [a]raised Him from the dead;

31 [a]Acts 1:11 [b]Luke 24:48

31 and for many days He appeared to those who came up with Him [a]from Galilee to Jerusalem, the very ones who are now [b]His witnesses to the people.

32 [a]Acts 5:42; 14:15 [b]Acts 13:23; 26:6; Rom. 1:2; 4:13; 9:4

32 "And we [a]preach to you the good news of [b]the promise made to the fathers,

33 [a]Acts 2:24; 13:30, 34, 37 [b]Ps. 2:7

33 that God has fulfilled this *promise* to our children in that He [a]raised up Jesus, as it is also written in the second Psalm, '[b]THOU ART MY SON; TODAY I HAVE BEGOTTEN THEE.'

34 [a]Acts 2:24; 13:30, 33, 37 [b]Is. 55:3

34 "*And as for the fact* that He [a]raised Him up from the dead, no more to return to decay, He has spoken in this way: '[b]I WILL GIVE YOU THE HOLY *and* SURE *blessings* OF DAVID.'

35 [a]Ps. 16:10; Acts 2:27

35 "Therefore He also says in another *Psalm,* '[a]THOU WILT NOT ALLOW THY HOLY ONE TO UNDERGO DECAY.'

36 [a]Acts 2:29 [b]Acts 13:22; 20:27 [c]1 Kin. 2:10; Acts 8:1

36 "For [a]David, after he had served [b]the purpose of God in his own generation, [c]fell asleep, and was laid among his fathers, and underwent decay;

37 [a]Acts 2:24; 13:30, 33, 34

37 but He whom God [a]raised did not undergo decay.

38 [a]Luke 24:47; Acts 2:38

38 "Therefore let it be known to you, brethren, that [a]through Him forgiveness of sins is proclaimed to you,

39 [a]Acts 10:43; Rom. 3:28; 10:4

39 and through Him [a]everyone who believes is freed from all things, from which you could not be freed through the Law of Moses.

40 [a]Luke 24:44; John 6:45; Acts 7:42

40 "Take heed therefore, so that the thing spoken of [a]in the Prophets may not come upon *you:*

41 [a]Hab. 1:5

41 '[a]BEHOLD, YOU SCOFFERS, AND MARVEL, AND PERISH;
FOR I AM ACCOMPLISHING A WORK IN YOUR DAYS,
A WORK WHICH YOU WILL NEVER BELIEVE, THOUGH SOMEONE SHOULD DESCRIBE IT TO YOU.' "

13:19 The *four hundred and fifty years* extends from the Patriarchs to the Judges.

42 [a]Acts 13:14

42 And as Paul and Barnabas were going out, the people kept begging that these things might be spoken to them the next [a]Sabbath.

43 [a]Acts 13:50; 16:14; 17:4, 17; 18:7 [b]Matt. 23:15 [c]Acts 11:23

43 Now when *the meeting of* the synagogue had broken up, many of the Jews and of the [a]God-fearing [b]proselytes followed Paul and Barnabas, who, speaking to them, were urging them to continue in [c]the grace of God.

44 [a]Acts 13:14

44 And the next [a]Sabbath nearly the whole city assembled to hear the word of God.

45 [a]Acts 13:50; 14:2, 4, 5, 19; 1 Thess. 2:16

45 But when [a]the Jews saw the crowds, they were filled with jealousy, and *began* contradicting the things spoken by Paul, and were blaspheming.

46 [a]Acts 3:26; 9:20; 13:5, 14 [b]Acts 18:6; 19:9, 15; 22:21; 26:20; 28:28

46 And Paul and Barnabas spoke out boldly and said, "It was necessary that the word of God should be spoken to you [a]first; since you repudiate it, and judge yourselves unworthy of eternal life, behold, [b]we are turning to the Gentiles.

47 [a]Is. 49:6 [b]Luke 2:32

47 "For thus the Lord has commanded us,

> '[a]I HAVE PLACED YOU AS A
> [b]LIGHT FOR THE GENTILES,
> THAT YOU SHOULD BRING
> SALVATION TO THE END OF
> THE EARTH.' "

★48 [a]Acts 13:12 [b]Rom. 8:28ff.; Eph. 1:4f., 11

48 And when the Gentiles heard this, they *began* rejoicing and glorifying [a]the word of the Lord; and as many as [b]had been appointed to eternal life believed.

49 [a]Acts 13:12

49 And [a]the word of the Lord was being spread through the whole region.

50 [a]Acts 13:45; 14:2, 4, 5, 19; 1 Thess. 2:16 [b]Acts 13:43; 16:14; 17:4, 17; 18:7 [c]Mark 15:43

50 But [a]the Jews aroused the [b]devout women [c]of prominence and the leading men of the city, and instigated a persecution against Paul and Barnabas, and drove them out of their district.

★51 [a]Matt. 10:14; Acts 18:6 [b]Acts 14:1, 19, 21; 16:2; 2 Tim. 3:11

51 But [a]they shook off the dust of their feet *in protest* against them and went to [b]Iconium.

52 [a]Acts 2:4

52 And the disciples were continually [a]filled with joy and with the Holy Spirit.

1 [a]Acts 13:51; 14:19, 21; 16:2; 2 Tim. 3:11 [b]Acts 13:5 [c]Acts 2:47 [d]John 7:35; Acts 18:4

14 And it came about that in [a]Iconium [b]they entered the synagogue of the Jews together, and spoke in such a manner [c]that a great multitude believed, both of Jews and of [d]Greeks.

2 [a]Acts 13:45, 50; 14:4, 5, 19; 1 Thess. 2:16 [b]John 3:36 [c]Acts 1:15

2 But [a]the Jews who [b]disbelieved stirred up the minds of the Gentiles, and embittered them against [c]the brethren.

3 [a]Acts 4:29f.; 20:32; Heb. 2:4 [b]John 4:48

3 Therefore they spent a long time *there* [a]speaking boldly *with reliance* upon the Lord, who was bearing witness to the word of His grace, granting that [b]signs and wonders be done by their hands.

4 [a]Acts 17:4f.; 19:9; 28:24 [b]Acts 13:45, 50; 14:2, 5, 19; 1 Thess. 2:16 [c]Acts 14:14

4 [a]But the multitude of the city was divided; and some sided with [b]the Jews, and some with [c]the apostles.

5 [a]Acts 13:45, 50; 14:2, 4, 19; 1 Thess. 2:16 [b]Acts 14:19

5 And when an attempt was made by both the Gentiles and [a]the Jews with their rulers, to mistreat and to [b]stone them,

★ 6 [a]Acts 14:11 [b]Acts 14:8, 21; 16:1f.; 2 Tim. 3:11 [c]Acts 14:20; 16:1; 20:4

6 they became aware of it and fled to the cities of [a]Lycaonia, [b]Lystra and [c]Derbe, and the surrounding region;

7 [a]Acts 14:15, 21; 16:10

7 and there they continued to [a]preach the gospel.

8 [a]Acts 14:6, 21; 16:1f.; 2 Tim. 3:11 [b]Acts 3:2

8 And at [a]Lystra there was sitting [b]a certain man, without strength in his feet, lame from his mother's womb, who had never walked.

9 [a]Acts 3:4; 10:4 [b]Matt. 9:28

9 This man was listening to Paul as he spoke, who, [a]when he had fixed his gaze upon him, and had seen that he had [b]faith to be made well,

---

13:48 *they began rejoicing.* The Gentiles' reception and the Jews' rejection (v. 50) of the gospel is, from here on, a recurring theme in Acts.

13:51 *they shook off the dust.* A good Jew took pains not to carry back into Palestine any dust from non-Jewish countries. To "shake off the dust" was a vivid gesture of complete break of fellowship and renunciation of responsibility for the person or community gestured at. See Christ's command at Luke 9:5; 10:11; and note on Mark 6:11.

14:6 *Lystra.* About 20 miles from Iconium.

10 said with a loud voice, "Stand upright on your feet." [a]And he leaped up and *began* to walk.

11 And when the multitudes saw what Paul had done, they raised their voice, saying in the [a]Lycaonian language, "[b]The gods have become like men and have come down to us."

12 And they *began* calling Barnabas, Zeus, and Paul, Hermes, because he was the chief speaker.

13 And the priest of Zeus, whose *temple* was just outside the city, brought oxen and garlands to the gates, and [a]wanted to offer sacrifice with the crowds.

14 But when [a]the apostles, Barnabas and Paul, heard of it, they [b]tore their robes and rushed out into the crowd, crying out

15 and saying, "Men, why are you doing these things? We are also [a]men of the same nature as you, and [b]preach the gospel to you in order that you should turn from these [c]vain things to a [d]living God, [e]WHO MADE THE HEAVEN AND THE EARTH AND THE SEA, AND ALL THAT IS IN THEM.

16 "And in the generations gone by He [a]permitted all the nations to [b]go their own ways;

17 and yet [a]He did not leave Himself without witness, in that He did good and [b]gave you rains from heaven and fruitful seasons, satisfying your hearts with food and gladness."

18 And *even* saying these things, they with difficulty restrained the crowds from offering sacrifice to them.

19 But [a]Jews came from [b]Antioch and [c]Iconium, and having won over the multitudes, they [d]stoned Paul and dragged him out of the city, supposing him to be dead.

20 But while [a]the disciples stood around him, he arose and entered the city. And the next day he went away with Barnabas to [b]Derbe.

4 *Events on the return to Antioch,* 14:21-28

21 And after they had [a]preached the gospel to that city and had [b]made many disciples, they returned to [c]Lystra and to [d]Iconium and to [e]Antioch,

22 strengthening the souls of [a]the disciples, encouraging them to continue in [b]the faith, and *saying,* "[c]Through many tribulations we must enter the kingdom of God."

23 And when [a]they had appointed [b]elders for them in every church, having [c]prayed with fasting, they [d]commended them to the Lord in whom they had believed.

24 And they passed through [a]Pisidia and came into [b]Pamphylia.

25 And when they had spoken the word in [a]Perga, they went down to Attalia;

26 and from there they sailed to [a]Antioch, from [b]which they had been [c]commended to the grace of God for the work that they had accomplished.

27 And when they had arrived and gathered the church together, they *began* to [a]report all things that God had done with them and how He had opened a [b]door of faith to the Gentiles.

28 And they spent a long time with [a]the disciples.

10 [a]Acts 3:8
11 [a]Acts 14:6 [b]Acts 8:10; 28:6
★**12**
13 [a]Dan. 2:46
14 [a]Acts 14:4 [b]Num. 14:6; Matt. 26:65; Mark 14:63
15 [a]Acts 10:26; James 5:17 [b]Acts 13:32; 14:7, 21 [c]Deut. 32:21; 1 Sam. 12:21; Jer. 8:19; 14:22; 1 Cor. 8:4 [d]Matt. 16:16 [e]Ex. 20:11; Ps. 146:6; Acts 4:24; 17:24; Rev. 14:7
16 [a]Acts 17:30 [b]Ps. 81:12; Mic. 4:5
17 [a]Acts 17:26f.; Rom. 1:19f. [b]Deut. 11:14; Job 5:10; Ps. 65:10f.; Ezek. 34:26f.; Joel 2:23
★**19** [a]Acts 13:45, 50; 14:2, 4, 5; 1 Thess. 2:16 [b]Acts 13:14; 14:21, 26 [c]Acts 13:51; 14:1, 21 [d]Acts 14:5; 2 Cor. 11:25; 2 Tim. 3:11
20 [a]Acts 11:26; 14:22, 28 [b]Acts 14:6
21 [a]Acts 14:7 [b]Acts 2:47 [c]Acts 14:6 [d]Acts 13:51; 14:1, 19 [e]Acts 13:14; 14:19, 26
22 [a]Acts 11:26; 14:28 [b]Acts 6:7 [c]Mark 10:30; John 15:18, 20; 16:33; Acts 9:16; 1 Thess. 3:3; 2 Tim. 3:12; 1 Pet. 2:21; Rev. 1:9
★**23** [a]2 Cor. 8:19; Titus 1:5 [b]Acts 11:30 [c]Acts 1:24; 13:3 [d]Acts 20:32
24 [a]Acts 13:14 [b]Acts 13:13
25 [a]Acts 13:13
26 [a]Acts 11:19 [b]Acts 13:3 [c]Acts 11:23; 15:40
27 [a]Acts 15:3, 4, 12; 21:19 [b]1 Cor. 16:9; 2 Cor. 2:12; Col. 4:3; Rev. 3:8
28 [a]Acts 11:26; 14:22

14:12 *Zeus.* The chief god of the Greek Pantheon. *Hermes.* The patron god of orators. In two Greek legends connected with Lystra (and familiar to Paul's listeners) Zeus and Hermes had come down and had "become like men" (v. 11).

14:19 *they stoned Paul.* After suffering the crushing blows of the stones, the victim was dragged outside the city and left to the dogs and beasts. It was a miracle that Paul could get up and leave the next day. Some think the vision mentioned in 2 Cor. 12:1-5 occurred at this time, and it is also possible that he received the marks spoken of in Gal. 6:17 during this stoning.

14:23 *appointed elders.* See note on 1 Tim. 3:1.

B The Council at Jerusalem, 15:1-35

1 *The dissension,* 15:1-5

15 And [a]some men came
down from Judea and *be-
gan* teaching [b]the brethren, "Unless you are [c]circumcised according to [d]the custom of Moses, you
cannot be saved."
2 And when Paul and Barnabas had great dissension and [a]de-
bate with them, [b]*the brethren* determined that Paul and Barnabas
and certain others of them,
should go up to Jerusalem to the
[c]apostles and elders concerning
this issue.
3 Therefore, being [a]sent on
their way by the church, they
were passing through both [b]Phoe-
nicia and Samaria, [c]describing in
detail the conversion of the Gentiles, and were bringing great joy
to all [d]the brethren.
4 And when they arrived at
Jerusalem, they were received by
the church and [a]the apostles and
the elders, and they [b]reported all
that God had done with them.
5 But certain ones of [a]the
sect of the [b]Pharisees who had
believed, stood up, saying, "It is
necessary to [c]circumcise them,
and to direct them to observe the
Law of Moses."

★ 1 [a]Acts 15:24 [b]Acts 1:15; 15:3, 22, 32 [c]Acts 15:5; 1 Cor. 7:18; Gal. 2:11, 14; 5:2f. [d]Acts 6:14
2 [a]Acts 15:7 [b]Gal. 2:2 [c]Acts 11:30; 15:4, 6, 22, 23; 16:4
3 [a]Acts 20:38; 21:5; Rom. 15:24; 1 Cor. 16:6, 11; 2 Cor. 1:16; Titus 3:13; 3 John 6 [b]Acts 11:19 [c]Acts 14:27; 15:4, 12 [d]Acts 1:15; 15:22, 32
4 [a]Acts 11:30; 15:6, 22, 23; 16:4 [b]Acts 14:27; 15:12
5 [a]Acts 5:17; 24:5, 14; 26:5; 28:22 [b]Matt. 3:7; Acts 26:5 [c]1 Cor. 7:18; Gal. 2:11, 14; 5:2f.

2 *The discussion,* 15:6-18

6 And [a]the apostles and the
elders came together to look into
this matter.
7 And after there had been
much [a]debate, Peter stood up and
said to them, "Brethren, you
know that in the early days [b]God
made a choice among you, that by
my mouth the Gentiles should
hear the word of [c]the gospel and
believe.
8 "And God, [a]who knows the
heart, bore witness to them, [b]giv-
ing them the Holy Spirit, just as
He also did to us;
9 and [a]He made no distinction between us and them,
[b]cleansing their hearts by faith.
10 "Now therefore why do you
[a]put God to the test by placing
upon the neck of the disciples a
yoke which [b]neither our fathers
nor we have been able to bear?
11 "But we believe that we are
saved through [a]the grace of the
Lord Jesus, in the same way as
they also are."
12 And all the multitude kept
silent, and they were listening to
Barnabas and Paul as they were
[a]relating what [b]signs and wonders
God had done through them
among the Gentiles.
13 And after they had
stopped speaking, [a]James answered, saying, "Brethren, listen
to me.
14 "[a]Simeon has related how
God first concerned Himself
about taking from among the
Gentiles a people for His name.

6 [a]Acts 11:30; 15:4, 22, 23; 16:4
★ 7 [a]Acts 15:2 [b]Acts 10:19f. [c]Acts 20:24
8 [a]Acts 1:24 [b]Acts 10:47
9 [a]Acts 10:28, 34; 11:12 [b]Acts 10:43
★10 [a]Acts 5:9 [b]Matt. 23:4; Gal. 5:1
★11 [a]Rom. 3:24; 5:15; 2 Cor. 13:14; Eph. 2:5-8
12 [a]Acts 14:27; 15:3, 4 [b]John 4:48
★13 [a]Acts 12:17
14 [a]Acts 15:7; 2 Pet. 1:1

15:1 *Unless you are circumcised . . . you cannot be saved.* The problems raised by the presence of Gentiles in the Church now came to a head. Peter had learned that no man should be called unclean—not even Gentiles (10:34), and the Jerusalem church had accepted the first Gentile converts on an equal basis with Jewish converts and without the necessity of being circumcised. However, the ultra-Judaistic party went on the offensive and insisted that Gentile converts be circumcised. A parallel question was also being raised: Should there be unrestricted social contact between Jewish and Gentile Christians? The Judaistic party separated themselves from those who did not follow the dietary laws and would not partake of the common meals. Chapter 15 is concerned with these two questions: circumcision and foods (socializing). Had the division over these questions prevailed, the unity of the Church would have been shattered from the start.

15:7 *by my mouth the Gentiles.* A reference to Peter's ministry in the house of Cornelius (10:44).

15:10 *a yoke.* I.e., that of the law, which in its complexities had become a burden, almost literally impossible to keep.

15:11 Peter means that both Jew and Gentile will be saved through grace without the yoke of the law.

15:13 *James.* See notes on Matt. 4:21 and the Introduction to James.

★15-17 15 [a]Acts 13:40

15 "And with this the words of [a]the Prophets agree, just as it is written,

16 [a]Amos 9:11 [b]Jer. 12:15

16 '[a]AFTER THESE THINGS [b]I WILL RETURN,
AND I WILL REBUILD THE TABERNACLE OF DAVID WHICH HAS FALLEN,
AND I WILL REBUILD ITS RUINS,
AND I WILL RESTORE IT,

17 [a]Amos 9:12 [b]Deut. 28:10; Is. 63:19; Jer. 14:9; Dan. 9:19; James 2:7

17 [a]IN ORDER THAT THE REST OF MANKIND MAY SEEK THE LORD,
AND ALL THE GENTILES [b]WHO ARE CALLED BY MY NAME,

18 [a]Amos 9:12 [b]Is. 45:21

18 [a]SAYS THE LORD, WHO [b]MAKES THESE THINGS KNOWN FROM OF OLD.'

3 *The decision,* 15:19-29

★19 [a]Acts 15:28; 21:25 ★20 [a]Dan. 1:8; Acts 15:29; 1 Cor. 8:7, 13; 10:7f., 14-28; Rev. 2:14, 20 [b]Gen. 9:4; Lev. 3:17; 7:26; 17:10, 14; 19:26; Deut. 12:16, 23; 15:23; 1 Sam. 14:33 21 [a]Acts 13:15; 2 Cor. 3:14f. 22 [a]Acts 15:2 [b]Acts 11:20 [c]Acts 15:27, 32, 40; 16:19, 25, 29; 17:4, 10, 14f.; 18:5; 2 Cor. 1:19; 1 Thess. 1:1; 2 Thess. 1:1; 1 Pet. 5:12 [d]Acts 15:1

19 "Therefore it is [a]my judgment that we do not trouble those who are turning to God from among the Gentiles,

20 but that we write to them that they abstain from [a]things contaminated by idols and from fornication and from [b]what is strangled and from blood.

21 "For [a]Moses from ancient generations has in every city those who preach him, since he is read in the synagogues every Sabbath."

22 Then it seemed good to [a]the apostles and the elders, with the whole church, to choose men from among them to send to [b]Antioch with Paul and Barnabas—Judas called Barsabbas, and [c]Silas, leading men among [d]the brethren,

23 and they sent this letter by them,

23 [a]Acts 15:2 [b]Acts 15:1 [c]Acts 11:20 [d]Matt. 4:24; Acts 15:41; Gal. 1:21 [e]Acts 6:9 [f]Acts 23:26; James 1:1; 2 John 10f.

"[a]The apostles and the brethren who are elders, to [b]the brethren in [c]Antioch and [d]Syria and [e]Cilicia who are from the Gentiles, [f]greetings.

24 "Since we have heard that [a]some of our number to whom we gave no instruction have [b]disturbed you with *their* words, unsettling your souls,

24 [a]Acts 15:1 [b]Gal. 1:7; 5:10

25 [a]it seemed good to us, having become of one mind, to select men to send to you with our beloved Barnabas and Paul,

25 [a]Acts 15:28

26 men who have [a]risked their lives for the name of our Lord Jesus Christ.

★26 [a]Acts 9:23ff.; 14:19

27 "Therefore we have sent [a]Judas and [b]Silas, who themselves will also report the same things by word *of mouth.*

27 [a]Acts 15:22, 32 [b]Acts 15:22

28 "For [a]it seemed good to [b]the Holy Spirit and to [c]us to lay upon you no greater burden than these essentials:

28 [a]Acts 15:25 [b]Acts 5:32; 15:8 [c]Acts 15:19, 25

29 that you abstain from [a]things sacrificed to idols and from [a]blood

★29 [a]Acts 15:20

15:15-17 The quotation is from the Septuagint (Greek) version of Amos 9:11-12. James specifies that the prophecy of Amos will be fulfilled "after these things," i.e., after the present worldwide witness. Then, after the return of Christ, the tabernacle of David (in the millennial kingdom) will be established, and Jew and Gentile will know the Lord. James assured the council that God's program for Israel had not been abandoned by the coming of Gentiles into the Church.

15:19 *we do not trouble those.* The clear verdict of James, as president of the council, was that Gentile converts need not be circumcised.

15:20 In order to promote peace between Jewish and Gentile believers, the Gentiles were asked to abstain from any practice abhorrent to Jewish Christians. The Jewish Christians would then socialize with them (cf. 1 Cor. 8:13). *fornication.* It does not seem likely that the word means illicit sexual relations in this instance (though it does elsewhere), for this would be wrong for any Christian, Gentile or Jew. It evidently has the special meaning here of marriages contracted between too-near relatives, as forbidden in Lev. 18.

15:26 *risked their lives.* For some of the risks incurred see 13:50; 14:5, 19.

15:29 *do well.* I.e., act rightly.

and from [a]things
strangled and from
[a]fornication; if you
keep yourselves free
from such things, you
will do well. Fare-
well."

4 *The letter delivered to Antioch,* 15:30-35

30 [a]Acts **30** So, when they were sent
15:22f. away, [a]they went down to Antioch; and having gathered the congregation together, they delivered
the letter.
31 And when they had read
it, they rejoiced because of its encouragement.
32 [a]Acts **32** And [a]Judas and [b]Silas, also
15:22, 27 being [c]prophets themselves, en-
[b]Acts 15:22 [c]Acts 13:1 couraged and strengthened [d]the
[d]Acts 15:1 brethren with a lengthy message.
33 [a]Mark **33** And after they had spent
5:34; Acts time *there,* they were sent away
16:36; 1 Cor. 16:11; Heb. from the brethren [a]in peace to
11:31 [b]Acts 15:22 those who had [b]sent them out.
★34 **34** [But it seemed good to Si-
las to remain there.]
35 [a]Acts **35** But [a]Paul and Barnabas
12:25 [b]Acts stayed in Antioch, teaching and
8:4 [c]Acts [b]preaching, with many others
13:12 also, [c]the word of the Lord.

C The Second Missionary Journey, 15:36-18:22

1 *The personnel chosen,* 15:36-40

36 [a]Acts **36** And after some days Paul
13:4, 13, 14, said to Barnabas, "Let us return
51; 14:6, 24f. and visit the brethren in [a]every
[b]Acts 13:12 city in which we proclaimed [b]the
word of the Lord, *and see* how
they are."
37 And Barnabas was desir- 37 [a]Acts
ous of taking [a]John, called Mark, 12:12
along with them also.
38 But Paul kept insisting that 38 [a]Acts
they should not take him along 13:13
who had [a]deserted them in Pamphylia and had not gone with
them to the work.
39 And there arose such a ★39 [a]Acts
sharp disagreement that they 12:12; 15:37;
separated from one another, and Col. 4:10
Barnabas took [a]Mark with him [b]Acts 4:36
and sailed away to [b]Cyprus.
40 But Paul chose [a]Silas and 40 [a]Acts
departed, being [b]committed by 15:22 [b]Acts
the brethren to the grace of the 11:23; 14:26
Lord.

2 *The churches revisited,* 15:41-16:5

41 And he was traveling 41 [a]Matt. 4:24; Acts
through [a]Syria and [b]Cilicia, 15:23 [b]Acts
strengthening the churches. 6:9 ★ 1 [a]Acts
16 And he came also to 14:6 [b]Acts
[a]Derbe and to [a]Lystra. 17:14f.; 18:5; 19:22; 20:4;
And behold, a certain disciple was Rom. 16:21; 1 Cor. 4:17;
there, named [b]Timothy, the son 16:10; 2 Cor.
of a [c]Jewish woman who was a 1:1, 19; Phil. 1:1; 2:19;
believer, but his father was a Col. 1:1;
Greek, 1 Thess. 1:1; 3:2, 6;
2 and he was well spoken of 2 Thess. 1:1;
by [a]the brethren who were in 1 Tim. 1:2, 18; 6:20;
[b]Lystra and [c]Iconium. 2 Tim. 1:2;
3 Paul wanted this man to go Philem. 1; Heb. 13:23
with him; and he [a]took him and [c]2 Tim. 1:5;
circumcised him because of the 3:15 2 [a]Acts
Jews who were in those parts, for 16:40 [b]Acts
they all knew that his father was 14:6 [c]Acts 13:51
a Greek. ★ 3 [a]Gal. 2:3
4 Now while they were pass- ★ 4 [a]Acts
ing through the cities, they were 15:28f. [b]Acts
delivering [a]the decrees, which 15:2 [c]Acts 11:30

15:34 Some manuscripts do not contain this verse.

15:39 *they separated from one another.* Here is an example of separation because of personality or practicality, not doctrine, and it seemed to be the only solution to the problem. God brought good out of it in that two missionary teams were sent out, and Barnabas' continued interest in John Mark rescued him from possible uselessness. (For separation on doctrinal grounds see Gal. 1:8; 2 Thess. 3:14; 2 Tim. 2:18; 1 John 2:18; 2 John 10.)

16:1 *Timothy.* See Introduction to 1 Timothy.

16:3 *circumcised him.* The Jerusalem council had declared that circumcision was not necessary for salvation or for acceptance into the Christian Church (15:19), but because of Timothy's part-Jewish background it seemed expedient in his case, in order to enlarge his local usefulness in witnessing. In the case of Gentile Titus, Paul insisted that he *not* be circumcised (Gal. 2:3).

16:4 *the decrees.* The decisions arrived at in Jerusalem, 15:23-29.

had been decided upon by [b]the
apostles and [c]elders who were in
Jerusalem, for them to observe.
5 So [a]the churches were
being strengthened in the faith,
and were [b]increasing in number
daily.

3 *The call to Europe,* 16:6–10

6 And they passed through
the [a]Phrygian and [b]Galatian region, having been forbidden by
the Holy Spirit to speak the word
in [c]Asia;
7 and when they had come
to [a]Mysia, they were trying to go
into [b]Bithynia, and the [c]Spirit of
Jesus did not permit them;
8 and passing by [a]Mysia,
they came down to [b]Troas.
9 And [a]a vision appeared to
Paul in the night: a certain man of
[b]Macedonia was standing and appealing to him, and saying,
"Come over to Macedonia and
help us."
10 And when he had seen
[a]the vision, immediately [b]we
sought to go into Macedonia, concluding that God had called us to
[c]preach the gospel to them.

4 *The work at Philippi,* 16:11–40

11 Therefore putting out to
sea from [a]Troas, we ran [b]a
straight course to Samothrace,
and on the day following to Neapolis;
12 and from there to [a]Philip-
pi, which is a leading city of the
district of [b]Macedonia, [c]a *Roman*
colony; and we were staying in
this city for some days.

5 aActs 9:31 bActs 2:47
★ **6** aActs 2:10; 18:23 bActs 18:23; 1 Cor. 16:1; Gal. 1:2; 3:1; 2 Tim. 4:10; 1 Pet. 1:1 cActs 2:9
7 aActs 16:8 b1 Pet. 1:1 cLuke 24:49; Acts 8:29; Rom. 8:9; Gal. 4:6; Phil. 1:19; 1 Pet. 1:11
8 aActs 16:7 bActs 16:11; 20:5f.; 2 Cor. 2:12; 2 Tim. 4:13
9 aActs 9:10 bActs 16:10, 12; 18:5; 19:21f., 29; 20:1, 3; 27:2; Rom. 15:26
★**10** aActs 9:10 b[we] Acts 16:10-17; 20:5-15; 21:1-18; 27:1-28:16 cActs 14:7
11 aActs 16:8; 20:5f.; 2 Cor. 2:12; 2 Tim. 4:13 bActs 21:1
★**12** aActs 20:6; Phil. 1:1; 1 Thess. 2:2 bActs 16:9, 10; 18:5; 19:21f., 29; 20:1, 3; 27:2; Rom. 15:26 cActs 16:21

13 And on [a]the Sabbath day
we went outside the gate to a riverside, where we were supposing
that there would be a place of
prayer; and we sat down and began speaking to the women who
had assembled.
14 And a certain woman
named Lydia, from the city of
[a]Thyatira, a seller of purple fabrics, [b]a worshiper of God, was listening; and the Lord [c]opened her
heart to respond to the things
spoken by Paul.
15 And when she and [a]her
household had been baptized, she
urged us, saying, "If you have
judged me to be faithful to the
Lord, come into my house and
stay." And she prevailed upon us.
16 And it happened that as
we were going to [a]the place of
prayer, a certain slave-girl having
[b]a spirit of divination met us, who
was bringing her masters much
profit by fortunetelling.
17 Following after Paul and
us, she kept crying out, saying,
"These men are bond-servants of
[a]the Most High God, who are
proclaiming to you the way of salvation."
18 And she continued doing
this for many days. But Paul was
greatly annoyed, and turned and
said to the spirit, "I command you
[a]in the name of Jesus Christ to
come out of her!" And it came out
at that very moment.
19 But when her masters saw
that their hope of [a]profit was
gone, they seized [b]Paul and Silas
and [c]dragged them into the market place before the authorities,

★**13** aActs 13:14
★**14** aRev. 1:11; 2:18, 24 bActs 13:43; 18:7 cLuke 24:45
15 aActs 11:14
★**16** aActs 16:13 bLev. 19:31; 20:6, 27; Deut. 18:11; 1 Sam. 28:3, 7; 2 Kin. 21:6; 1 Chr. 10:13; Is. 8:19
17 aMark 5:7
18 aMark 16:17
19 aActs 16:16; 19:25f. bActs 15:22, 40; 16:25, 29 cActs 8:3; 17:6f.; 21:30; James 2:6

16:6 Paul traveled in a northwesterly direction around Asia, to Troas and on to Greece. On the *Galatian region,* see the Introduction to Galatians.

16:10 *we.* Luke joined Paul and his group at Troas and went with them to Philippi, where he remained when the others left (v. 40). Six or seven years later he rejoined Paul (20:5) and remained with him until the end of the narrative.

16:12 *Philippi.* See the Introduction to Philippians. *a Roman colony* was like a piece of Rome transplanted abroad, so that those who held citizenship in a colony enjoyed the same rights they would have had if they had lived in Italy. Other colonies mentioned in Acts are Antioch in Pisidia, Lystra, Troas, Ptolemais, and Corinth.

16:13 *outside the gate to a riverside.* Apparently there was no synagogue in Philippi; it required at least ten men to organize one.

16:14 *seller of purple fabrics.* Thyatira in Asia Minor was famous for its purple dye.

16:16 *a spirit of divination.* The girl was demon-possessed and was being exploited by her masters (v. 19).

★20 **20** and when they had
brought them to the chief magistrates, they said, "These men are
throwing our city into confusion,
being Jews,
21 [a]Esther 3:8 [b]Acts 16:12 **21** and [a]are proclaiming customs which it is not lawful for us
to accept or to observe, being
[b]Romans."
22 [a]2 Cor. 11:25; 1 Thess. 2:2 **22** And the crowd rose up together against them, and the chief
magistrates tore their robes off
them, and proceeded to order
them to be [a]beaten with rods.
23 [a]Acts 16:27, 36 **23** And when they had inflicted many blows upon them,
they threw them into prison,
commanding [a]the jailer to guard
them securely;
24 [a]Job 13:27; 33:11; Jer. 20:2f.; 29:26 **24** and he, having received
such a command, threw them into
the inner prison, and fastened
their feet in [a]the stocks.
25 [a]Acts 16:19 [b]Eph. 5:19 **25** But about midnight [a]Paul
and Silas were praying and [b]sing-
ing hymns of praise to God, and
the prisoners were listening to
them;
26 [a]Acts 4:31 [b]Acts 12:10 [c]Acts 12:7 **26** and suddenly [a]there came
a great earthquake, so that the
foundations of the prison house
were shaken; and immediately
[b]all the doors were opened, and
everyone's [c]chains were unfas-
tened.
27 [a]Acts 16:23, 36 [b]Acts 12:19 **27** And when [a]the jailer had
been roused out of sleep and had
seen the prison doors opened, he
drew his sword and was about [b]to
kill himself, supposing that the
prisoners had escaped.
28 But Paul cried out with a
loud voice, saying, "Do yourself
no harm, for we are all here!"
29 [a]Acts 16:19 **29** And he called for lights
and rushed in and, trembling with
fear, he fell down before [a]Paul
and Silas,

30 and after he brought them 30 [a]Acts 2:37; 22:10
out, he said, "Sirs, [a]what must I
do to be saved?"
31 And they said, "[a]Believe in ★31 [a]Mark 16:16 [b]Acts 11:14; 16:15
the Lord Jesus, and you shall be
saved, you and [b]your household."
32 And they spoke the word
of the Lord to him together with
all who were in his house.
33 And he took them [a]that 33 [a]Acts 16:25
very hour of the night and
washed their wounds, and immediately he was baptized, he and all
his *household.*
34 And he brought them into 34 [a]Acts 11:14; 16:15
his house and set food before
them, and rejoiced greatly, having
believed in God with [a]his whole
household.
35 Now when day came, the
chief magistrates sent their policemen, saying, "Release those
men."
36 And [a]the jailer reported 36 [a]Acts 16:27 [b]Acts 15:33
these words to Paul, *saying,* "The
chief magistrates have sent to release you. Now therefore come
out and go [b]in peace."
37 But Paul said to them, ★37 [a]Acts 22:25-29
"They have beaten us in public
without trial, [a]men who are Romans, and have thrown us into
prison; and now are they sending
us away secretly? No indeed! But
let them come themselves and
bring us out."
38 And the policemen re- 38 [a]Acts 22:29
ported these words to the chief
magistrates. And [a]they were
afraid when they heard that they
were Romans,
39 and they came and ap- 39 [a]Matt. 8:34
pealed to them, and when they
had brought them out, they kept
begging them [a]to leave the city.
40 And they went out of the 40 [a]Acts 16:14 [b]Acts 1:15; 16:2
prison and entered *the house of*
[a]Lydia, and when they saw [b]the

16:20 *throwing our city into confusion, being Jews.* Judaism was not a prohibited religion (the cult of the emperor being the official religion), but propagating it was regarded as a menace. Paul and Silas were regarded as Jews, since, at this time, the Romans considered Christianity to be a Jewish sect. See also note on 18:14-16.

16:31 *and your household.* These words must be connected with "believe" as well as "be saved." Each member of the household must believe in order to be saved.

16:37 *Romans.* Paul was born a Roman citizen (22:28), which gave him certain rights, including a public hearing. Scourging of any Roman citizen was prohibited by law; the rights of Paul and Silas, therefore, had already been violated.

brethren, they encouraged them
and departed.

5 *The work at Thessalonica, Berea, and Athens,* 17:1–34

★ 1 [a]Acts 17:11, 13; 20:4; 27:2; Phil. 4:16; 1 Thess. 1:1; 2 Thess. 1:1; 2 Tim. 4:10

17 Now when they had traveled through Amphipolis
and Apollonia, they came to
[a]Thessalonica, where there was a
synagogue of the Jews.

2 [a]Acts 9:20; 17:10, 17 [b]Acts 13:14 [c]Acts 8:35

2 And [a]according to Paul's
custom, he went to them, and for
three [b]Sabbaths reasoned with
them from [c]the Scriptures,

3 [a]Acts 3:18 [b]John 20:9 [c]Acts 9:22; 18:5, 28

3 explaining and giving evidence that the Christ [a]had to suffer and [b]rise again from the dead,
and *saying,* "[c]This Jesus whom I
am proclaiming to you is the
Christ."

4 [a]Acts 14:4 [b]Acts 15:22, 40; 17:10, 14f. [c]Acts 13:43; 17:17 [d]John 7:35 [e]Acts 13:50

4 [a]And some of them were
persuaded and joined [b]Paul and
Silas, along with a great multitude
of the [c]God-fearing [d]Greeks and
a number of the [e]leading women.

5 [a]Acts 17:13; 1 Thess. 2:16 [b]Acts 17:6, 7, 9; Rom. 16:21

5 But [a]the Jews, becoming
jealous and taking along some
wicked men from the market
place, formed a mob and set the
city in an uproar; and coming
upon the house of [b]Jason, they
were seeking to bring them out to
the people.

6 [a]Acts 16:19f. [b]Matt. 24:14; Acts 17:31

6 And when they did not
find them, they *began* [a]dragging
Jason and some brethren before
the city authorities, shouting,
"These men who have upset [b]the
world have come here also;

7 [a]Luke 10:38; James 2:25 [b]Luke 23:2

7 and Jason [a]has welcomed
them, and they all act [b]contrary to
the decrees of Caesar, saying that
there is another king, Jesus."
8 And they stirred up the
crowd and the city authorities
who heard these things.

★ 9 [a]Acts 17:5

9 And when they had re-
ceived a pledge from [a]Jason and
the others, they released them.

10 [a]Acts 1:15; 17:6, 14f. [b]Acts 17:4 [c]Acts 17:13; 20:4 [d]Acts 17:2

10 And [a]the brethren immediately sent [b]Paul and Silas away
by night to [c]Berea; and when they
arrived, they went into [d]the synagogue of the Jews.

11 [a]Acts 17:1

11 Now these were more
noble-minded than those in
[a]Thessalonica, for they received
the word with great eagerness, examining the Scriptures daily, *to
see* whether these things were so.

12 [a]Acts 2:47 [b]Mark 15:43 [c]Acts 13:50

12 [a]Many of them therefore
believed, along with a number of
[b]prominent Greek [c]women and
men.

13 [a]Acts 17:1 [b]Acts 17:10; 20:4

13 But when the Jews of
[a]Thessalonica found out that the
word of God had been proclaimed
by Paul in [b]Berea also, they came
there likewise, agitating and stirring up the crowds.

14 [a]Acts 1:15; 17:6, 10 [b]Acts 15:22; 17:4, 10 [c]Acts 16:1

14 And then immediately
[a]the brethren sent Paul out to go
as far as the sea; and [b]Silas and
[c]Timothy remained there.

15 [a]Acts 15:3 [b]Acts 17:16, 21f.; 18:1; 1 Thess. 3:1 [c]Acts 17:14 [d]Acts 18:5

15 Now [a]those who con-
ducted Paul brought him as far as
[b]Athens; and receiving a command for [c]Silas and Timothy to
[d]come to him as soon as possible,
they departed.

16 [a]Acts 17:15, 21f.; 18:1; 1 Thess. 3:1

16 Now while Paul was wait-
ing for them at [a]Athens, his spirit
was being provoked within him
as he was beholding the city full
of idols.

17 [a]Acts 9:20; 17:2 [b]Acts 17:4

17 So he was reasoning [a]in
the synagogue with the Jews and
[b]the God-fearing *Gentiles,* and in
the market place every day with
those who happened to be present.

★18 [a]1 Cor. 1:20; 4:10 [b]Acts 4:2; 17:31f.

18 And also some of the Epicurean and Stoic philosophers
were conversing with him. And
some were saying, "What would
[a]this idle babbler wish to say?"

17:1 *Thessalonica.* See the Introduction to 1 Thessalonians.

17:9 *received a pledge from Jason.* I.e., made Jason put up a bond, forfeitable if there was further trouble.

17:18 *Epicurean . . . philosophers.* Followers of Epicurus (341–270 B.C.), who believed that happiness was the chief end of life. The *Stoic* philosophers, who regarded Zeno (340–265 B.C.) as their founder and whose name came from *Stoa Poikile* (Painted Porch) where he taught in Athens, emphasized the rational over the emotional. They were pantheistic. Their ethics were characterized by moral earnestness and a high sense of duty, advocating conduct "according to nature."

Others, "He seems to be a pro-
claimer of strange deities,"—because he was preaching [b]Jesus
and the resurrection.

★19 [a]Acts 23:19 [b]Acts 17:22 [c]Mark 1:27

19 And they [a]took him and
brought him to the [b]Areopagus,
saying, "May we know what [c]this
new teaching is which you are
proclaiming?
20 "For you are bringing some
strange things to our ears; we
want to know therefore what
these things mean."

21 [a]Acts 2:10

21 (Now all the Athenians
and the strangers [a]visiting there
used to spend their time in nothing other than telling or hearing
something new.)

22 [a]Acts 17:15 [b]Acts 25:19

22 And Paul stood in the
midst of the Areopagus and said,
"Men of [a]Athens, I observe that
you are very [b]religious in all respects.

23 [a]2 Thess. 2:4 [b]John 4:22

23 "For while I was passing
through and examining the [a]ob-
jects of your worship, I also found
an altar with this inscription, 'TO
AN UNKNOWN GOD.' What
therefore [b]you worship in ignorance, this I proclaim to you.

★24 [a]Is. 42:5; Acts 14:15 [b]Deut. 10:14; Ps. 115:16; Matt. 11:25 [c]Acts 7:48

24 "[a]The God who made the
world and all things in it, since He
is [b]Lord of heaven and earth, does
not [c]dwell in temples made with
hands;

25 [a]Job 22:2; Ps. 50:10-12

25 neither is He served by human hands, [a]as though He
needed anything, since He Himself gives to all life and breath and
all things;

26 [a]Mal. 2:10 [b]Deut. 32:8; Job 12:23

26 and [a]He made from one,
every nation of mankind to live
on all the face of the earth, having
[b]determined *their* appointed
times, and the boundaries of their
habitation,

27 [a]Deut. 4:7; Jer. 23:23f.; Acts 14:17

27 that they should seek God,
if perhaps they might grope for
Him and find Him, [a]though He is
not far from each one of us;
28 for [a]in Him we live and
move and exist, as even some of
your own poets have said, 'For we
also are His offspring.'

28 [a]Job 12:10; Dan. 5:23

29 "Being then the offspring of
God, we [a]ought not to think that
the Divine Nature is like gold or
silver or stone, an image formed
by the art and thought of man.

★29 [a]Is. 40:18ff.; Rom. 1:23

30 "Therefore having [a]over-
looked [b]the times of ignorance,
God is [c]now declaring to men that
all everywhere should repent,

30 [a]Acts 14:16; Rom. 3:25 [b]Acts 17:23 [c]Luke 24:47; Acts 26:20; Titus 2:11f.

31 because He has fixed [a]a
day in which [b]He will judge [c]the
world in righteousness through a
Man whom He has [d]appointed,
having furnished proof to all men
by [e]raising Him from the dead."

31 [a]Matt. 10:15 [b]Ps. 9:8; 96:13; 98:9; John 5:22, 27; Acts 10:42 [c]Matt. 24:14; Acts 17:6 [d]Luke 22:22 [e]Acts 2:24

32 Now when they heard of
[a]the resurrection of the dead,
some *began* to sneer, but others
said, "We shall hear you again
concerning this."
33 So Paul went out of their
midst.

32 [a]Acts 17:18, 31

34 But some men joined him
and believed, among whom also
was Dionysius the [a]Areopagite
and a woman named Damaris and
others with them.

★34 [a]Acts 17:19, 22

6 The ministry at Corinth, 18:1–17

★ 1 [a]Acts 17:15 [b]Acts 18:8; 19:1; 1 Cor. 1:2; 2 Cor. 1:1, 23; 6:11; 2 Tim. 4:20

18 After these things he left
[a]Athens and went to [b]Cor-
inth.
2 And he found a certain
Jew named [a]Aquila, a native of
[b]Pontus, having recently come
from [c]Italy with his wife [a]Pris-
cilla, because [d]Claudius had com-

★ 2 [a]Acts 18:18, 26; Rom. 16:3; 1 Cor. 16:19; 2 Tim. 4:19 [b]Acts 2:9 [c]Acts 27:1, 6; Heb. 13:24 [d]Acts 11:28

17:19 *Areopagus.* The venerable council that had charge of religious and educational matters in Athens. It met on the Hill of Ares W. of the Acropolis, the hill also being known as the Areopagus.

17:24. Notice this echo of Stephen's words which Paul had heard years before (7:48–50).

17:29 *Being then the offspring of God.* Because God is the Creator of all.

17:34 *Dionysius the Areopagite.* Membership in the Areopagus was a high distinction. There is no record of a church in Athens. Paul calls certain Corinthians the first converts on mainland Greece (1 Cor. 16:15).

18:1 *Corinth.* See the Introduction to 1 Corinthians.

18:2 *Aquila . . . his wife Priscilla.* See Rom. 16:3; 1 Cor. 16:19; 2 Tim. 4:19, where Priscilla is called Prisca. *because Claudius had commanded all the Jews to leave Rome.* This imperial edict was issued in A.D. 49 or 50.

manded all the Jews to leave
Rome. He came to them,
3 and because he was of the
same trade, he stayed with them
and [a]they were working; for by
trade they were tent-makers.
4 And he was reasoning [a]in
the synagogue every [b]Sabbath
and trying to persuade [c]Jews and
Greeks.
5 But when [a]Silas and Timothy [b]came down from [c]Macedo-
nia, Paul *began* devoting himself
completely to the word, solemnly
[d]testifying to the Jews that [e]Jesus
was the Christ.
6 And when they resisted
and blasphemed, he [a]shook out
his garments and said to them,
"[b]Your blood *be* upon your own
heads! I am clean. From now on I
shall go [c]to the Gentiles."
7 And he departed from
there and went to the house of a
certain man named Titius Justus,
[a]a worshiper of God, whose house
was next to the synagogue.
8 And [a]Crispus, [b]the leader
of the synagogue, believed in the
Lord [c]with all his household, and
many of the [d]Corinthians when
they heard were believing and
being baptized.
9 And the Lord said to Paul
in the night by [a]a vision, "Do not
be afraid *any longer*, but go on
speaking and do not be silent;
10 for I am with you, and no
man will attack you in order to
harm you, for I have many people
in this city."
11 And he settled *there* a year
and six months, teaching the
word of God among them.

★ **3** [a]Acts 20:34; 1 Cor. 4:12; 9:15; 2 Cor. 11:7; 12:13; 1 Thess. 2:9; 4:11; 2 Thess. 3:8
4 [a]Acts 9:20; 18:19 [b]Acts 13:14 [c]Acts 14:1
5 [a]Acts 15:22; 16:1; 17:14 [b]Acts 17:15 [c]Acts 16:9 [d]Luke 16:28; Acts 20:21 [e]Acts 17:3; 18:28
6 [a]Neh. 5:13; Acts 13:51 [b]2 Sam. 1:16; 1 Kin. 2:33; Ezek. 18:13; 33:4, 6, 8; Matt. 27:25; Acts 20:26 [c]Acts 13:46
7 [a]Acts 13:43; 16:14
8 [a]1 Cor. 1:14 [b]Mark 5:22 [c]Acts 11:14 [d]Acts 18:1; 19:1; 1 Cor. 1:2; 2 Cor. 1:1, 23; 6:11; 2 Tim. 4:20
9 [a]Acts 9:10

12 But while Gallio was [a]pro-
consul of [b]Achaia, [c]the Jews with
one accord rose up against Paul
and brought him before [d]the
judgment seat,
13 saying, "This man per-
suades men to worship God contrary to [a]the law."
14 But when Paul was about
to [a]open his mouth, Gallio said to
the Jews, "If it were a matter of
wrong or of vicious crime, O Jews,
it would be reasonable for me to
put up with you;
15 but if there are [a]questions
about words and names and your
own law, look after it yourselves;
I am unwilling to be a judge of
these matters."
16 And he drove them away
from [a]the judgment seat.
17 And they all took hold of
[a]Sosthenes, [b]the leader of the
synagogue, and *began* beating
him in front of [c]the judgment
seat. And Gallio was not concerned about any of these things.

7 *The journey completed,* 18:18–22

18 And Paul, having remained many days longer, [a]took
leave of [b]the brethren and put out
to sea for [c]Syria, and with him
were [d]Priscilla and [d]Aquila. In
[e]Cenchrea he [f]had his hair cut,
for he was keeping a vow.
19 And they came to [a]Ephe-
sus, and he left them there. Now
he himself entered [b]the synagogue and reasoned with the
Jews.

★**12** [a]Acts 13:7 [b]Acts 18:27; 19:21; Rom. 15:26; 1 Cor. 16:15; 2 Cor. 1:1; 9:2; 11:10; 1 Thess. 1:7f. [c]1 Thess. 2:16 [d]Matt. 27:19
13 [a]John 19:7; Acts 18:15
★**14–16**
14 [a]Matt. 5:2
15 [a]Acts 23:29; 25:19
16 [a]Matt. 27:19
★**17** [a]1 Cor. 1:1 [b]Acts 18:8 [c]Matt. 27:19
★**18** [a]Mark 6:46 [b]Acts 1:15; 18:27 [c]Matt. 4:24 [d]Acts 18:2, 26 [e]Rom. 16:1 [f]Num. 6:2, 5, 9, 18; Acts 21:24
19 [a]Acts 18:21, 24; 19:1, 17, 26 [28, 34f.]; 20:16f.; [21:29]; 1 Cor. 15:32; 16:8; Eph. 1:1; 1 Tim. 1:3; 2 Tim. 1:18; 4:12; Rev. 1:11; 2:1 [b]Acts 18:4

18:3 *tent-makers.* Jewish fathers were urged to teach their sons a trade, and Paul learned tent-making, an important industry in Tarsus.

18:12 *proconsul.* Gallio was proconsul of Achaia in 51. He was characterized by contemporaries as an amiable, witty, and lovable person.

18:14–16 Judaism was a "licensed religion" under Roman law. Christianity could take advantage of this protection as long as it sheltered itself under the tent of Judaism. The Jews must have complained that these Christians were not a division or sect of Judaism, and Gallio refuses to see it their way. He says, in effect, "Settle your own religious squabbles yourselves." This ruling was probably important for the spread of the gospel. See also note on 16:20.

18:17 *Sosthenes* became the victim of the Greeks' anti-Jewish feelings. Obviously he was the head of the anti-Pauline faction in the synagogue and a Jew. If this is the same Sosthenes mentioned in 1 Cor. 1:1, perhaps the beating helped him to become a Christian!

18:18 *he had his hair cut.* The sign of the conclusion of a Nazarite vow (Num. 6:18; Acts 21:24). Just why he took the vow is not known. *Cenchrea.* The eastern port of Corinth.

20 And when they asked him to stay for a longer time, he did not consent,

21 but [a]taking leave of them and saying, "I will return to you again [b]if God wills," he set sail from [c]Ephesus.

22 And when he had landed at [a]Caesarea, he went up and greeted the church, and went down to [b]Antioch.

21 [a]Mark 6:46 [b]Rom. 1:10; 15:32; 1 Cor. 4:19; 16:7; Heb. 6:3; James 4:15; 1 Pet. 3:17 [c]Acts 18:19, 24; 19:1, 17, 26 [28, 34f.]; 20:16f.; [21:29]; 1 Cor. 15:32; 16:8; Eph. 1:1; 1 Tim. 1:3; 2 Tim. 1:18; 4:12; Rev. 1:11; 2:1
22 [a]Acts 8:40 [b]Acts 11:19

D The Third Missionary Journey, 18:23–21:26

1 *Ephesus: The power of the Word,* 18:23–19:41

23 And having spent some time *there,* he departed and passed successively through the [a]Galatian region and Phrygia, strengthening all the disciples.

24 Now a certain Jew named [a]Apollos, an [b]Alexandrian by birth, an eloquent man, came to [c]Ephesus; and he was mighty in the Scriptures.

25 This man had been instructed in [a]the way of the Lord; and being fervent in spirit, he was speaking and teaching accurately the things concerning Jesus, being acquainted only with [b]the baptism of John;

26 and he began to speak out boldly in the synagogue. But when [a]Priscilla and Aquila heard him, they took him aside and explained to him [b]the way of God more accurately.

27 And when he wanted to go across to [a]Achaia, [b]the brethren encouraged him and wrote to [c]the disciples to welcome him; and when he had arrived, he helped greatly those who had believed through grace;

23 [a]Acts 16:6
★24 [a]Acts 19:1; 1 Cor. 1:12; 3:5, 6, 22; 4:6; 16:12; Titus 3:13 [b]Acts 6:9 [c]Acts 18:19
25 [a]Acts 9:2; 18:26 [b]Luke 7:29; Acts 19:3
26 [a]Acts 18:2, 18 [b]Acts 18:25
27 [a]Acts 18:12; 19:1 [b]Acts 18:18 [c]Acts 11:26

28 for he powerfully refuted the Jews in public, demonstrating [a]by the Scriptures that [b]Jesus was the Christ.

19 And it came about that while [a]Apollos was at [b]Corinth, Paul having passed through the [c]upper country came to [d]Ephesus, and found some disciples,

2 and he said to them, "[a]Did you receive the Holy Spirit when you believed?" And they *said* to him, "No, [b]we have not even heard whether there is a Holy Spirit."

3 And he said, "Into what then were you baptized?" And they said, "[a]Into John's baptism."

4 And Paul said, "[a]John baptized with the baptism of repentance, telling the people [b]to believe in Him who was coming after him, that is, in Jesus."

5 And when they heard this, they were [a]baptized in the name of the Lord Jesus.

6 And when Paul had [a]laid his hands upon them, the Holy Spirit came on them, and they *began* [b]speaking with tongues and [c]prophesying.

7 And there were in all about twelve men.

8 And he entered [a]the synagogue and continued speaking out boldly for three months, reasoning and persuading *them* [b]about the kingdom of God.

9 But when [a]some were becoming hardened and disobedient, speaking evil of [b]the Way before the multitude, he withdrew from them and took away [c]the disciples, reasoning daily in the school of Tyrannus.

10 And this took place for [a]two years, so that all who lived

28 [a]Acts 8:35 [b]Acts 18:5
★ 1 [a]Acts 18:24; 1 Cor. 1:12; 3:5, 6, 22; 4:6; 16:12; Titus 3:13 [b]Acts 18:1 [c]Acts 18:23 [d]Acts 18:21, 24; 19:1, 17, 26 [28, 34f.]; 20:16f.; [21:29]; 1 Cor. 15:32; 16:8; Eph. 1:1; 1 Tim. 1:3; 2 Tim. 1:18; 4:12; Rev. 1:11; 2:1
★ 2 [a]Acts 8:15f.; 11:16f. [b]John 7:39
3 [a]Luke 7:29; Acts 18:25
4 [a]Acts 13:24 [b]John 1:7
★ 5 [a]Acts 8:12, 16; 10:48
6 [a]Acts 6:6; 8:17 [b]Mark 16:17; Acts 2:4; 10:46 [c]Acts 13:1
★ 8 [a]Acts 9:20; 18:26 [b]Acts 1:3
★ 9 [a]Acts 14:4 [b]Acts 9:2; 19:23 [c]Acts 11:26; 19:30
10 [a]Acts 19:8; 20:31 [b]Acts 16:6; 19:22, 26, 27 [c]Acts 13:12; 19:20

18:24 *Apollos.* See note on 1 Cor. 1:12.

19:1 *Ephesus.* See the Introduction to Ephesians and note on Rev. 2:1.

19:2 *Did you receive the Holy Spirit when you believed?* The gift of the Spirit is given at the time of believing (10:44).

19:5 *they were baptized in the name of the Lord Jesus.* Though these men had been baptized by John the Baptist, baptism in the name of Christ was in order as a testimony to their new faith in Christ.

19:8 *synagogue.* Again Paul, on arriving at a city, used the synagogue as his center of witness.

19:9 *school.* I.e., lecture hall owned by Tyrannus, probably used by him to teach students of rhetoric, and made available by him to traveling philosophers or teachers.

in [b]Asia heard [c]the word of the
Lord, both Jews and Greeks.
11 And God was performing
[a]extraordinary miracles by the
hands of Paul,
12 [a]so that handkerchiefs or
aprons were even carried from his
body to the sick, and the diseases
left them and [b]the evil spirits
went out.
13 But also some of the Jewish [a]exorcists, who went from
place to place, attempted to name
over those who had the evil spirits
the name of the Lord Jesus, saying, "I adjure you by Jesus whom
Paul preaches."
14 And seven sons of one
Sceva, a Jewish chief priest, were
doing this.
15 And the evil spirit answered and said to them, "I recognize Jesus, and I know about Paul,
but who are you?"
16 And the man, in whom
was the evil spirit, leaped on them
and subdued both of them and
overpowered them, so that they
fled out of that house naked and
wounded.
17 And this became known to
all, both Jews and Greeks, who
lived in [a]Ephesus; and fear fell
upon them all and the name of
the Lord Jesus was being magni-
fied.
18 Many also of those who
had believed kept coming, confessing and disclosing their practices.
19 And many of those who
practiced magic brought their
books together and *began* burning them in the sight of all; and

★**11** [a]Acts 8:13
12 [a]Acts 5:15 [b]Mark 16:17
★**13** [a]Matt. 12:27; Luke 11:19
17 [a]Acts 18:19
★**19** [a]Luke 15:8

they counted up the price of them
and found it fifty thousand
[a]pieces of silver.
20 So [a]the word of the Lord
[b]was growing mightily and prevailing.
21 Now after these things
were finished, Paul purposed in
the spirit to [a]go to Jerusalem [b]af-
ter he had passed through [c]Mace-
donia and [d]Achaia, saying, "After
I have been there, [e]I must also see
Rome."
22 And having sent into
[a]Macedonia two of [b]those who
ministered to him, [c]Timothy and
[d]Erastus, he himself stayed in
[e]Asia for a while.
23 And about that time there
arose no small disturbance concerning [a]the Way.
24 For a certain man named
Demetrius, a silversmith, who
made silver shrines of Artemis,
[a]was bringing no little business to
the craftsmen;
25 these he gathered together
with the workmen of similar
trades, and said, "Men, you know
that our prosperity depends upon
this business.
26 "And you see and hear that
not only in [a]Ephesus, but in almost all of [b]Asia, this Paul has
persuaded and turned away a
considerable number of people,
saying that [c]gods made with
hands are no gods *at all.*
27 "And not only is there danger that this trade of ours fall into
disrepute, but also that the temple of the great goddess Artemis
be regarded as worthless and that
she whom all of [a]Asia and [b]the

20 [a]Acts 19:10 [b]Acts 6:7; 12:24
21 [a]Acts 20:16, 22; 21:15; Rom. 15:25; 2 Cor. 1:16 [b]Acts 20:1; 1 Cor. 16:5 [c]Acts 16:9; 19:22, 29; Rom. 15:26; 1 Thess. 1:7f. [d]Acts 18:12 [e]Acts 23:11; Rom. 15:24, 28
22 [a]Acts 16:9; 19:21, 29 [b]Acts 13:5; 19:29; 20:34; 2 Cor. 8:19 [c]Acts 16:1 [d]Rom. 16:23; 2 Tim. 4:20 [e]Acts 19:10
23 [a]Acts 19:9
★**24** [a]Acts 16:16, 19f.
26 [a]Acts 18:19 [b]Acts 19:10 [c]Deut. 4:28; Ps. 115:4; Is. 44:10-20; Jer. 10:3ff.; Acts 17:29; 1 Cor. 8:4; 10:19; Rev. 9:20
★**27** [a]Acts 19:10 [b]Matt. 24:14

19:11 *extraordinary miracles.* On other occasions Paul did not have this power (2 Cor. 12:8; Phil. 2:27; 1 Tim. 5:23; 2 Tim. 4:20).

19:13 *exorcists.* Magicians who could cast out demons. The lesson of this story (vv. 13–17) is that to use the name of Jesus effectively in exorcism one must be totally devoted to Him. Contrary to theories of magic of the time, the name by itself could do nothing; this misuse, in fact, backfired (v. 16).

19:19 *magic.* Magical spells written on scrolls. *pieces of silver.* If the silver drachma is meant, the value would have been more than $10,000.

19:24 *silver shrines.* Small shrines in a niche, representing Artemis (Latin, Diana), for worshipers to dedicate in the temple. No silver ones have been found, only some in terra-cotta. *bringing no little business.* Big profits are clearly implied.

19:27 The gospel was endangering the business of these idol-makers. In order to stir up opposition against the Christians, the craftsmen appealed to the civic pride of the Ephesians. The temple of Artemis was one of the Seven Wonders of the ancient world—a magnificent structure with 127 columns 60 feet high standing on an area 425 feet long and 220 feet wide.

world worship should even be de-
throned from her magnificence."
28 [a]Acts 18:19 **28** And when they heard *this*
and were filled with rage, they *be-*
gan crying out, saying, "Great is
Artemis of the [a]Ephesians!"
29 [a]Acts 20:4 [b]Acts 20:4; 27:2; Col. 4:10; Philem. 24 [c]Acts 13:5; 19:22; 20:34; 2 Cor. 8:19 [d]Acts 16:9; 19:22 **29** And the city was filled
with the confusion, and they
rushed with one accord into the
theater, dragging along [a]Gaius
and [b]Aristarchus, Paul's traveling
[c]companions from [d]Macedonia.
30 [a]Acts 19:9 **30** And when Paul wanted to
go into the assembly, [a]the disciples would not let him.
31 And also some of the
Asiarchs who were friends of his
sent to him and repeatedly urged
him not to venture into the theater.
★32 [a]Acts 21:34 **32** [a]So then, some were
shouting one thing and some an-
other, for the assembly was in
confusion, and the majority did
not know for what cause they had
come together.
33 [a]Acts 12:17 **33** And some of the crowd
concluded *it was* Alexander, since
the Jews had put him forward;
and having [a]motioned with his
hand, Alexander was intending to
make a defense to the assembly.
34 But when they recognized
that he was a Jew, a *single* outcry
arose from them all as they
shouted for about two hours,
"Great is Artemis of the Ephesians!"
35 [a]Acts 18:19 **35** And after quieting the
multitude, the town clerk *said,
"Men of [a]Ephesus, what man is
there after all who does not know
that the city of the Ephesians is
guardian of the temple of the
great Artemis, and of the *image*
which fell down from heaven?
36 "Since then these are unde-
niable facts, you ought to keep
calm and to do nothing rash.
37 [a]Rom. 2:22 **37** "For you have brought
these men *here* who are neither
[a]robbers of temples nor blas-
phemers of our goddess.
38 "So then, if Demetrius and 38 [a]Acts 13:7
the craftsmen who are with him
have a complaint against any
man, the courts are in session and
[a]proconsuls are *available;* let
them bring charges against one
another.
39 "But if you want anything ★39
beyond this, it shall be settled in
the lawful assembly.
40 "For indeed we are in danger of being accused of a riot in
connection with today's affair,
since there is no *real* cause *for it;*
and in this connection we shall be
unable to account for this disor-
derly gathering."
41 And after saying this he ★41
dismissed the assembly.

2 ***Greece,*** 20:1–5

20 And after the uproar had ★ 1-4 1 [a]Acts 11:26 [b]Acts 19:21 [c]Acts 16:9; 20:3
ceased, Paul sent for [a]the
disciples and when he had exhorted them and taken his leave
of them, he departed [b]to go to
[c]Macedonia.
2 And when he had gone
through those districts and had
given them much exhortation, he
came to Greece.
3 And *there* he spent three 3 [a]Acts 9:24; 20:19 [b]Matt. 4:24 [c]Acts 16:9; 20:1
months, and when [a]a plot was
formed against him by the Jews as
he was about to set sail for [b]Syria,
he determined to return through
[c]Macedonia.
4 And he was accompanied 4 [a]Acts 17:10 [b]Acts 19:29 [c]Acts 17:1 [d]Acts 19:29 [e]Acts 14:6 [f]Acts 16:1 [g]Eph. 6:21; Col. 4:7; 2 Tim. 4:12; Titus 3:12 [h]Acts 21:29; 2 Tim. 4:20 [i]Acts 16:6; 20:16, 18
by Sopater of [a]Berea, *the son* of
Pyrrhus; and by [b]Aristarchus and
Secundus of the [c]Thessalonians;
and [d]Gaius of [e]Derbe, and [f]Timo-
thy; and [g]Tychicus and [h]Trophi-
mus of [i]Asia.
5 But these had gone on 5 [a]Acts 16:10; 20:5-15 [b]Acts 16:8
ahead and were waiting for [a]us at
[b]Troas.

19:32, 39, 41 *assembly.* The people of Ephesus had the right to meet in a legislative assembly, though this particular gathering was an unlawful one. See note on 7:38.

20:1–4 Luke's brevity here, a mere mention of the missionary team and a journey through Macedonia revisiting established communities, suggests that Acts could have been a much longer book.

3 *Asia Minor: Troas and the elders of Ephesus,* 20:6–38

6 And [a]we sailed from [b]Phil-
ippi after [c]the days of Unleavened
Bread, and came to them at
[d]Troas within five days; and there
we stayed seven days.
7 And on [a]the first day of
the week, when [b]we were gathered together to [c]break bread,
Paul *began* talking to them, intending to depart the next day,
and he prolonged his message until midnight.
8 And there were many
[a]lamps in the [b]upper room where
we were gathered together.
9 And there was a certain
young man named Eutychus sitting on the window sill, sinking
into a deep sleep; and as Paul
kept on talking, he was overcome
by sleep and fell down from the
third floor, and was picked up
dead.
10 But Paul went down and
[a]fell upon him and after embracing him, he [b]said, "Do not be
troubled, for his life is in him."
11 And when he had gone
back up, and had [a]broken the
bread and eaten, he talked with
them a long while, until daybreak, and so departed.
12 And they took away the
boy alive, and were greatly comforted.
13 But [a]we, going ahead to
the ship, set sail for Assos, intending from there to take Paul
on board; for thus he had arranged it, intending himself to go
by land.
14 And when he met us at
Assos, we took him on board and
came to Mitylene.
15 And sailing from there, we
arrived the following day opposite
Chios; and the next day we
crossed over to Samos; and the
day following we came to [a]Mile-
tus.
16 For Paul had decided to
sail past [a]Ephesus in order that he
might not have to spend time in
[b]Asia; for he was hurrying [c]to be
in Jerusalem, if possible, [d]on the
day of Pentecost.
17 And from Miletus he sent
to [a]Ephesus and called to him
[b]the elders of the church.
18 And when they had come
to him, he said to them,
"You yourselves know, [a]from
the first day that I set foot in Asia,
how I was with you the whole
time,
19 serving the Lord with all
humility and with tears and with
trials which came upon me
through [a]the plots of the Jews;
20 how I [a]did not shrink from
declaring to you anything that
was profitable, and teaching you
publicly and from house to house,
21 solemnly [a]testifying to
both Jews and Greeks of [b]repent-
ance toward God and [c]faith in our
Lord Jesus Christ.
22 "And now, behold, bound
in spirit, [a]I am on my way to Jerusalem, not knowing what will
happen to me there,
23 except that [a]the Holy
Spirit solemnly [b]testifies to me in
every city, saying that [c]bonds and
afflictions await me.
24 "But [a]I do not consider my
life of any account as dear to myself, in order that I may [b]finish
my course, and [c]the ministry
which I received from the Lord
Jesus, to [d]testify solemnly of the
gospel of [e]the grace of God.
25 "And now, behold, I know
that you all, among whom I went
about [a]preaching the kingdom,
will see my face no more.
26 "Therefore I testify to you

6 [a]Acts 16:10; 20:5-15 [b]Acts 16:12 [c]Acts 12:3 [d]Acts 16:8
★ 7 [a]1 Cor. 16:2; Rev. 1:10 [b]Acts 16:10; 20:5-15 [c]Acts 2:42; 20:11
8 [a]Matt. 25:1 [b]Acts 1:13
10 [a]1 Kin. 17:21; 2 Kin. 4:34 [b]Matt. 9:23f.; Mark 5:39
11 [a]Acts 2:42; 20:7
13 [a]Acts 16:10; 20:5-15
15 [a]Acts 20:17; 2 Tim. 4:20
★16 [a]Acts 18:19 [b]Acts 16:6; 20:4, 18 [c]Acts 19:21; 20:6, 22; 1 Cor. 16:8 [d]Acts 2:1
★17 [a]Acts 18:19 [b]Acts 11:30
18 [a]Acts 18:19; 19:1, 10; 20:4, 16
19 [a]Acts 20:3
20 [a]Acts 20:27
21 [a]Luke 16:28; Acts 18:5; 20:23, 24 [b]Acts 2:38; 11:18; 26:20 [c]Acts 24:24; 26:18; Eph. 1:15; Col. 2:5; Philem. 5
22 [a]Acts 17:16; 20:16
23 [a]Acts 8:29 [b]Luke 16:28; Acts 18:5; 20:21, 24 [c]Acts 9:16; 21:33
★24 [a]Acts 21:13 [b]Acts 13:25 [c]Acts 1:17 [d]Luke 16:28; Acts 18:5; 20:21 [e]Acts 11:23; 20:32
25 [a]Matt. 4:23; Acts 28:31
26 [a]Acts 18:6

20:7 *on the first day of the week.* This became the regular day of worship for Christians in remembrance of Christ's resurrection on Sunday.

20:16 If Paul had stopped at Ephesus, friends would surely have delayed him. He *decided* to take a boat that would not stop at Ephesus.

20:17 *elders.* These leaders of the group were recognized by all, since the church knew whom to send when Paul *called to him the elders.* See note on 1 Tim. 3:1.

20:24 Compare Paul's words in 2 Tim. 4:7.

this day, that [a]I am innocent of
the blood of all men.
27 "For I [a]did not shrink from
declaring to you the whole [b]pur-
pose of God.
28 "Be on guard for yourselves
and for all [a]the flock, among
which the Holy Spirit has made
you overseers, to shepherd [b]the
church of God which [c]He purchased with His own blood.
29 "I know that after my departure [a]savage wolves will come
in among you, not sparing [b]the
flock;
30 and from among your own
selves men will arise, speaking
perverse things, to draw away
[a]the disciples after them.
31 "Therefore be on the alert,
remembering that night and day
for a period of [a]three years I did
not cease to admonish each one
[b]with tears.
32 "And now I [a]commend you
to God and to [b]the word of His
grace, which is able to [c]build *you*
up and to give *you* [d]the inheritance among all those who are
sanctified.
33 "[a]I have coveted no one's
silver or gold or clothes.
34 "You yourselves know that
[a]these hands ministered to my
own needs and to the [b]men who
were with me.
35 "In every thing I showed
you that by working hard in this
manner you must help the weak
and remember the words of the
Lord Jesus, that He Himself said,
'It is more blessed to give than to
receive.' "
36 And when he had said
these things, he [a]knelt down and
prayed with them all.
37 And they *began* to weep
aloud and [a]embraced Paul, and
repeatedly kissed him,
38 grieving especially over
[a]the word which he had spoken,

27 [a]Acts 20:20 [b]Acts 13:36
★28-30
★28 [a]Luke 12:32; John 21:15-17; Acts 20:29; 1 Pet. 5:2f. [b]Matt. 16:18; Rom. 16:16; 1 Cor. 10:32 [c]Eph. 1:7, 14; Titus 2:14; 1 Pet. 1:19; 2:9; Rev. 5:9
29 [a]Ezek. 22:27; Matt. 7:15 [b]Luke 12:32; John 21:15-17; Acts 20:28; 1 Pet. 5:2f.
30 [a]Acts 11:26
31 [a]Acts 19:1, 8, 10; 24:17 [b]Acts 20:19
32 [a]Acts 14:23 [b]Acts 14:3; 20:24 [c]Acts 9:31 [d]Acts 26:18; Eph. 1:14; 5:5; Col. 1:12; 3:24; Heb. 9:15; 1 Pet. 1:4
33 [a]1 Cor. 9:4-18; 2 Cor. 11:7-12; 12:14-18; 1 Thess. 2:5f.
34 [a]Acts 18:3 [b]Acts 19:22
★35
36 [a]Acts 9:40; 21:5; Luke 22:41
37 [a]Luke 15:20
38 [a]Acts 20:25 [b]Acts 15:3

that they should see his face no
more. And they were [b]accompa-
nying him to the ship.

4 *From Miletus to Caesarea,* 21:1–14

21 And when it came about
that [a]we had parted from
them and had set sail, we ran [b]a
straight course to Cos and the
next day to Rhodes and from
there to Patara;
2 and having found a ship
crossing over to [a]Phoenicia, we
went aboard and set sail.
3 And when we had come in
sight of [a]Cyprus, leaving it on the
left, we kept sailing to [b]Syria and
landed at [c]Tyre; for [d]there the
ship was to unload its cargo.
4 And after looking up [a]the
disciples, we stayed there seven
days; and they kept telling Paul
[b]through the Spirit not to set foot
in Jerusalem.
5 And when it came about
that our days there were ended,
we departed and started on our
journey, while they all, with
wives and children, [a]escorted us
until *we were* out of the city. And
after [b]kneeling down on the
beach and praying, we said farewell to one another.
6 Then we went on board
the ship, and they returned
[a]home again.
7 And when we had finished
the voyage from [a]Tyre, we arrived
at Ptolemais; and after greeting
[b]the brethren, we stayed with
them for a day.
8 And on the next day we
departed and came to [a]Caesarea;
and entering the house of [b]Philip
the [c]evangelist, who was [b]one of
the seven, we stayed with him.
9 Now this man had four
virgin daughters who were
[a]prophetesses.

★1 [a][we] Acts 16:10; 21:1-18 [b]Acts 16:11
2 [a]Acts 11:19; 21:3
3 [a]Acts 4:36; 21:16 [b]Matt. 4:24 [c]Acts 12:20; 21:7 [d]Acts 21:2
4 [a]Acts 11:26; 21:16 [b]Acts 20:23; 21:11
5 [a]Acts 15:3 [b]Luke 22:41; Acts 9:40; 20:36
6 [a]John 19:27
7 [a]Acts 12:20; 21:3 [b]Acts 1:15; 21:17
★8 [a]Acts 8:40; 21:16 [b]Acts 6:5 [c]Eph. 4:11; 2 Tim. 4:5
9 [a]Luke 2:36; Acts 13:1; 1 Cor. 11:5

20:28–30 For what happened at Ephesus later, see 1 Tim. 1:3-7.
20:28 *with His own blood.* Lit., with the blood of His own (Son).
20:35 *remember the words of the Lord Jesus.* This saying is not recorded in the Gospels.
21:1 Luke obviously enjoyed describing a sea voyage. His masterpiece comes later (ch. 27).
21:8 *Philip the evangelist.* He was previously mentioned in 6:5 and 8:5.

★10 [a]Acts 11:28
10 And as we were staying
there for some days, a certain
prophet named [a]Agabus came
down from Judea.

11 [a]1 Kin. 22:11; Is. 20:2; Jer. 13:1-11; 19:1, 11; John 18 [b]Acts 8:29 [c]Acts 9:16; 21:33 [d]Matt. 20:19
11 And coming to us, he
[a]took Paul's belt and bound his
own feet and hands, and said,
"This [b]is what the Holy Spirit
says: 'In this way the Jews at Jerusalem will [c]bind the man who
owns this belt and [d]deliver him
into the hands of the Gentiles.' "

12 [a]Acts 21:15
12 And when we had heard
this, we as well as the local residents *began* begging him [a]not to
go up to Jerusalem.

13 [a]Acts 20:24 [b]Acts 5:41; 9:16
13 Then Paul answered,
"What are you doing, weeping
and breaking my heart? For [a]I am
ready not only to be bound, but
even to die at Jerusalem for [b]the
name of the Lord Jesus."

14 [a]Luke 22:42
14 And since he would not be
persuaded, we fell silent, remarking, "[a]The will of the Lord be
done!"

5 Paul with the Jerusalem church, 21:15–26

15 [a]Acts 21:12
15 And after these days we
got ready and [a]started on our way
up to Jerusalem.

16 [a]Acts 21:4 [b]Acts 8:40 [c]Acts 4:36; 21:3 [d]Acts 15:7
16 And *some* of [a]the disciples
from [b]Caesarea also came with us,
taking us to Mnason of [c]Cyprus, a
[d]disciple of long standing with
whom we were to lodge.

17 [a]Acts 1:15; 21:7
17 And when we had come to
Jerusalem, [a]the brethren received
us gladly.

18 [a]Acts 12:17 [b]Acts 11:30
18 And now the following
day Paul went in with us to
[a]James, and all [b]the elders were
present.

19 [a]Acts 14:27 [b]Acts 1:17
19 And after he had greeted
them, he [a]*began* to relate one by
one the things which God had
done among the Gentiles through
his [b]ministry.

★20 [a]Matt. 9:8 [b]Acts 15:1; 22:3; Rom. 10:2; Gal. 1:14
20 And when they heard it
they *began* [a]glorifying God; and
they said to him, "You see,
brother, how many thousands
there are among the Jews of those
who have believed, and they are
all [b]zealous for the Law;

21 [a]Acts 21:28 [b]Acts 15:19ff.; 1 Cor. 7:18f. [c]Acts 6:14
21 and they have been told
about you, that you are [a]teaching
all the Jews who are among the
Gentiles to forsake Moses, telling
them [b]not to circumcise their children nor to walk according to [c]the
customs.

22 "What, then, is *to be done?*
They will certainly hear that you
have come.

23 [a]Acts 18:18
23 "Therefore do this that we
tell you. We have four men who
[a]are under a vow;

★24 [a]John 11:55; Acts 21:26; 24:18 [b]Acts 18:18
24 take them and [a]purify
yourself along with them, and pay
their expenses in order that they
may [b]shave their heads; and all
will know that there is nothing to
the things which they have been
told about you, but that you
yourself also walk orderly, keeping the Law.

★25 [a]Acts 15:19f., 29
25 "But concerning the Gentiles who have believed, we wrote,
[a]having decided that they should
abstain from meat sacrificed to
idols and from blood and from
what is strangled and from fornication."

26 [a]John 11:55; Acts 21:24; 24:18 [b]Num. 6:13; Acts 24:18
26 Then Paul took the men,
and the next day, [a]purifying himself along with them, [b]went into
the temple, giving notice of the
completion of the days of purification, until the sacrifice was offered for each one of them.

E The Journey to Rome, 21:27–28:31

1 Paul's arrest and defense, 21:27–22:29

27 [a]Num. 6:9, 13-20 [b]Acts 20:19; 24:18 [c]Acts 16:6
27 And when [a]the seven days
were almost over, [b]the Jews from

21:10 *Agabus.* Presumably the same one who prophesied (11:28).

21:20 The old division reappears (see note on 15:1).

21:24 *pay their expenses.* Paul was being asked to pay the expenses involved in the offerings required at the completion of the Nazarite vow these four men had taken (cf. Num. 6:13-21). He was being urged to take actions that would indicate that he was, after all, a "middle-of-the-road" Jewish-Christian.

21:25 See note on 15:19.

[c]Asia, upon seeing him in the
temple, *began* to stir up all the
multitude and laid hands on him,
28 crying out, "Men of Israel,
come to our aid! [a]This is the man
who preaches to all men everywhere against our people, and the
Law, and this place; and besides
he has even brought Greeks into
the temple and has [b]defiled this
[a]holy place."
29 For they had previously
seen [a]Trophimus the [b]Ephesian in
the city with him, and they supposed that Paul had brought him
into the temple.
30 And all the city was
aroused, and the people rushed
together; and taking hold of Paul,
they [a]dragged him out of the temple; and immediately the doors
were shut.
31 And while they were seeking to kill him, a report came up
to the commander of the [a]*Roman*
cohort that all Jerusalem was in
confusion.
32 And at once he [a]took
along *some* soldiers and centurions, and ran down to them; and
when they saw the commander
and the soldiers, they stopped
beating Paul.
33 Then the commander
came up and took hold of him,
and ordered him to be [a]bound
with [b]two chains; and he *began*
asking who he was and what he
had done.
34 But among the crowd
[a]some were shouting one thing
and some another, and when he
could not find out the facts on account of the uproar, he ordered
him to be brought into [b]the barracks.
35 And when he got to [a]the
stairs, it so happened that he was
carried by the soldiers because of
the violence of the mob;
36 for the multitude of the
people kept following behind,
crying out, "[a]Away with him!"
37 And as Paul was about to
be brought into [a]the barracks, he
said to the commander, "May I
say something to you?" And he
*said, "Do you know Greek?
38 "Then you are not [a]the
Egyptian who some time ago
stirred up a revolt and led the
four thousand men of the Assas-
sins out [b]into the wilderness?"
39 But Paul said, "[a]I am a Jew
of Tarsus in [b]Cilicia, a citizen of
no insignificant city; and I beg
you, allow me to speak to the
people."
40 And when he had given
him permission, Paul, standing on
[a]the stairs, [b]motioned to the people with his hand; and when there
was a great hush, he spoke to
them in the [c]Hebrew dialect, saying,

22 "[a]Brethren and fathers,
hear my defense which I
now *offer* to you."
2 And when they heard that
he was addressing them in the
[a]Hebrew dialect, they became
even more quiet; and he *said,
3 "[a]I am [b]a Jew, born in [c]Tar-
sus of [d]Cilicia, but brought up in
this city, [e]educated under [f]Gama-
liel, [g]strictly according to the law
of our fathers, being zealous for
God, just as [h]you all are today.
4 "And [a]I persecuted this
[b]Way to the death, binding and
putting both men and women
into prisons,
5 as also [a]the high priest and
all [b]the Council of the elders can
testify. From them I also [c]received
letters to [d]the brethren, and
started off for [e]Damascus in order
to bring even those who were
there to Jerusalem as prisoners to
be punished.
6 "[a]And it came about that as
I was on my way, approaching

★28 [a]Acts 6:13 [b]Matt. 24:15; Acts 6:13f.; 24:6
29 [a]Acts 20:4 [b]Acts 18:19
30 [a]2 Kin. 11:15; Acts 16:19; 26:21
31 [a]Acts 10:1
32 [a]Acts 23:27
33 [a]Acts 20:23; 21:11; 22:29; 26:29; 28:20; Eph. 6:20; 2 Tim. 1:16; 2:9 [b]Acts 12:6
34 [a]Acts 19:32 [b]Acts 21:37; 22:24; 23:10, 16, 32
35 [a]Acts 21:40
36 [a]Luke 23:18; John 19:15; Acts 22:22
37 [a]Acts 21:34; 22:24; 23:10, 16, 32
★38 [a]Acts 5:36 [b]Matt. 24:26
39 [a]Acts 9:11; 22:3 [b]Acts 6:9
40 [a]Acts 21:35 [b]Acts 12:17 [c]John 5:2; Acts 1:19; 22:2; 26:14
1 [a]Acts 7:2
2 [a]Acts 21:40
3 [a]Acts 9:1-22; 22:3-16; 26:9-18 [b]Acts 21:39 [c]Acts 9:11 [d]Acts 6:9 [e]Deut. 33:3; 2 Kin. 4:38; Luke 10:39 [f]Acts 5:34 [g]Acts 23:6; 26:5; Phil. 3:6 [h]Acts 21:20
4 [a]Acts 8:3; 22:19f. [b]Acts 9:2
5 [a]Acts 9:1 [b]Luke 22:66 [Gr.]; Acts 5:21 [Gr.]; 1 Tim. 4:14 [Gr.] [c]Acts 9:2 [d]Acts 2:29; 3:17; 13:26; 23:1; 28:17, 21; Rom. 9:3 [e]Acts 9:2
6 [a]Acts 22:6-11: *Acts 9:3-8; 26:12-18*

21:28 *brought Greeks into the temple.* Verse 29 explains that the crowd assumed (though it was untrue) that Paul had taken Trophimus, a Gentile, into the inner courts of the temple, which were reserved for Jews only. This was an offense punishable by death.

21:38 *the Egyptian.* The historian Josephus records such an event in A.D. 54. The leader disappeared. The tribune jumps to the conclusion that Paul is he.

Damascus about noontime, a very
bright light suddenly flashed from
heaven all around me,
7 and I fell to the ground
and heard a voice saying to me,
'Saul, Saul, why are you persecuting Me?'
8 "And I answered, 'Who art
Thou, Lord?' And He said to me,
'I am [a]Jesus the Nazarene, whom
you are persecuting.'
9 "And those who were with
me [a]beheld the light, to be sure,
but [b]did not understand the voice
of the One who was speaking to
me.
10 "And I said, '[a]What shall I
do, Lord?' And the Lord said to
me, 'Arise and go on into Damascus; and there you will be told of
all that has been appointed for
you to do.'
11 "But since I [a]could not see
because of the brightness of that
light, I was led by the hand by
those who were with me, and
came into Damascus.
12 "And a certain [a]Ananias, a
man who was devout by the standard of the Law, *and* [b]well spoken
of by all the Jews who lived there,
13 came to me, and standing
near said to me, '[a]Brother Saul,
receive your sight!' And [b]at that
very time I looked up at him.
14 "And he said, '[a]The God of
our fathers has [b]appointed you to
know His will, and to [c]see the
[d]Righteous One, and to hear an
utterance from His mouth.
15 'For you will be [a]a witness
for Him to all men of [b]what you
have seen and heard.
16 'And now why do you delay? [a]Arise, and be baptized, and
[b]wash away your sins, [c]calling on
His name.'
17 "And it came about when I
[a]returned to Jerusalem and was
praying in the temple, that I [b]fell
into a trance,

8 [a]Acts 26:9
9 [a]Acts 26:13 [b]Acts 9:7
10 [a]Acts 16:30
11 [a]Acts 9:8
12 [a]Acts 9:10 [b]Acts 6:3; 10:22
13 [a]Acts 9:17 [b]Acts 9:18
14 [a]Acts 3:13 [b]Acts 9:15; 26:16 [c]Acts 9:17; 26:16; 1 Cor. 9:1; 15:8 [d]Acts 7:52
15 [a]Acts 23:11; 26:16 [b]Acts 22:14
★16 [a]Acts 9:18 [b]Acts 2:38; 1 Cor. 6:11; Eph. 5:26; Heb. 10:22 [c]Acts 7:59
17 [a]Acts 9:26; 26:20 [b]Acts 10:10

18 and I saw Him saying to
me, '[a]Make haste, and get out of
Jerusalem quickly, because they
will not accept your testimony
about Me.'
19 "And I said, 'Lord, they
themselves understand that in
one synagogue after another [a]I
used to imprison and [b]beat those
who believed in Thee.
20 'And [a]when the blood of
Thy witness Stephen was being
shed, I also was standing by ap-
proving, and watching out for the
cloaks of those who were slaying
him.'
21 "And He said to me, 'Go!
For I will send you far away [a]to
the Gentiles.' "
22 And they listened to him
up to this statement, and *then*
they raised their voices and said,
"[a]Away with such a fellow from
the earth, for [b]he should not be
allowed to live!"
23 And as they were crying
out and [a]throwing off their cloaks
and [b]tossing dust into the air,
24 the commander ordered
him to be brought into [a]the barracks, stating that he should be
[b]examined by scourging so that
he might find out the reason why
they were shouting against him
that way.
25 And when they stretched
him out with thongs, Paul said to
the centurion who was standing
by, "Is it lawful for you to scourge
[a]a man who is a Roman and un-
condemned?"
26 And when the centurion
heard *this,* he went to the commander and told him, saying,
"What are you about to do? For
this man is a Roman."
27 And the commander came
and said to him, "Tell me, are you
a Roman?" And he said, "Yes."
28 And the commander an-

18 [a]Acts 9:29
19 [a]Acts 8:3; 22:4 [b]Matt. 10:17; Acts 26:11
20 [a]Acts 7:58f.; 8:1; 26:10
★21-23
21 [a]Acts 9:15
22 [a]Acts 21:36; 1 Thess. 2:16 [b]Acts 25:24
23 [a]Acts 7:58 [b]2 Sam. 16:13
24 [a]Acts 21:34 [b]Acts 22:29
25 [a]Acts 16:37
★28

22:16 Lit., "Having arisen, be baptized; and wash away your sins, having called on the name of the Lord." Baptism does not wash away sins.

22:21–23 The reference to the Gentiles, joined with Paul's claiming a divine commission, set off the mob again.

22:28 *with a large sum.* In the reign of Claudius, contemporaneous with these events, Roman citizenship could be purchased for what would be a princely sum for a soldier. Somehow Paul's parents had earned Roman citizenship before Paul's birth. See note on 16:37.

swered, "I acquired this citizenship with a large sum of money." And Paul said, "But I was actually born *a citizen.*"

29 [a]Acts 22:24 [b]Acts 16:38 [c]Acts 22:24f.

29 Therefore those who were about to [a]examine him immediately let go of him; and the commander also [b]was afraid when he found out that he was a Roman, and because he had [c]put him in chains.

2 *Paul brought before the Sanhedrin,* 22:30–23:10

★**30** [a]Acts 23:28 [b]Acts 21:33 [c]Matt. 5:22

30 But on the next day, [a]wishing to know for certain why he had been accused by the Jews, he [b]released him and ordered the chief priests and all [c]the Council to assemble, and brought Paul down and set him before them.

1 [a]Acts 22:30; 23:6, 15, 20, 28 [b]Acts 22:5 [c]Acts 24:16; 2 Cor. 1:12; 2 Tim. 1:3

23 And Paul, looking intently at [a]the Council, said, "[b]Brethren, [c]I have lived my life with a perfectly good conscience before God up to this day."

★ **2** [a]Acts 24:1 [b]John 18:22

2 And the high priest [a]Ananias commanded those standing beside him [b]to strike him on the mouth.

3 [a]Matt. 23:27 [b]Lev. 19:15; Deut. 25:2; John 7:51

3 Then Paul said to him, "God is going to strike you, [a]you whitewashed wall! And do you [b]sit to try me according to the Law, and in violation of the Law order me to be struck?"

4 But the bystanders said, "Do you revile God's high priest?"

★ **5** [a]Ex. 22:28

5 And Paul said, "I was not aware, brethren, that he was high priest; for it is written, '[a]YOU SHALL NOT SPEAK EVIL OF A RULER OF YOUR PEOPLE.' "

★ **6** [a]Matt. 3:7; 22:23 [b]Acts 22:30; 23:1, 15, 20, 28 [c]Acts 22:5 [d]Acts 26:5; Phil. 3:5 [e]Acts 24:15, 21; 26:8

6 But perceiving that one part were [a]Sadducees and the other Pharisees, Paul *began* crying out in [b]the Council, "[c]Brethren, [d]I am a Pharisee, a son of Pharisees; I am on trial for [e]the hope and resurrection of the dead!"

7 And as he said this, there arose a dissension between the Pharisees and Sadducees; and the assembly was divided.

8 [a]Matt. 22:23; Acts 3:7

8 For [a]the Sadducees say that there is no resurrection, nor an angel, nor a spirit; but the Pharisees acknowledge them all.

9 [a]Mark 2:16; Luke 5:30 [b]Acts 23:29 [c]John 12:29; Acts 22:6ff.

9 And there arose a great uproar; and some of [a]the scribes of the Pharisaic party stood up and *began* to argue heatedly, saying, "[b]We find nothing wrong with this man; [c]suppose a spirit or an angel has spoken to him?"

10 [a]Acts 21:34; 23:16, 32

10 And as a great dissension was developing, the commander was afraid Paul would be torn to pieces by them and ordered the troops to go down and take him away from them by force, and bring him into [a]the barracks.

3 *Paul escorted to Caesarea,* 23:11–35

★**11** [a]Acts 18:9 [b]Matt. 9:2 [c]Acts 19:21 [d]Luke 16:28; Acts 28:23

11 But on [a]the night *immediately* following, the Lord stood at his side and said, "[b]Take courage; for [c]as you have [d]solemnly witnessed to My cause at Jerusalem, so you must witness at Rome also."

12 [a]Acts 9:23; 23:30; 1 Thess. 2:16 [b]Acts 23:14, 21

12 And when it was day, [a]the Jews formed a conspiracy and [b]bound themselves under an oath, saying that they would nei-

---

22:30 *the Council* = the Sanhedrin. See note on Luke 22:66. Somehow the Sanhedrin had interposed itself so that Paul's case did not get directly and immediately referred to the Roman governor in Caesarea.

23:2 *commanded . . . to strike him.* Ananias (high priest about A.D. 48–58) was reportedly insolent and overbearing. He was probably angered at Paul's bold claims and ordered him struck.

23:5 *I was not aware, brethren, that he was high priest.* Some think Paul's weak eyes caused him to fail to recognize the high priest; however, the remark may have been sarcasm—"I didn't think the high priest would ever speak like that!"

23:6 In effect Paul said, "I, a Pharisee by inheritance and training, can hardly be regarded as a subversive teacher!" He then proceeded to split the Sanhedrin into its two factions.

23:11 Christ appeared to Paul four times: at his conversion (9:5), in Corinth (18:9–10), on his first visit to Jerusalem (22:17–18), and here during his last visit to Jerusalem.

ther eat nor drink until they had
killed Paul.
13 And there were more than
forty who formed this plot.
14 [a]Acts 23:12, 21
14 And they came to the chief
priests and the elders, and said,
"We have [a]bound ourselves under a solemn oath to taste nothing
until we have killed Paul.
15 [a]Acts 22:30; 23:1, 6, 20, 28
15 "Now, therefore, you and
[a]the Council notify the commander to bring him down to
you, as though you were going to
determine his case by a more
thorough investigation; and we
for our part are ready to slay him
before he comes near *the place.*"
★16 [a]Acts 21:34; 23:10, 32
16 But the son of Paul's sister
heard of their ambush, and he
came and entered [a]the barracks
and told Paul.
17 And Paul called one of the
centurions to him and said, "Lead
this young man to the commander, for he has something to
report to him."
18 [a]Eph. 3:1
18 So he took him and led
him to the commander and *said,
"Paul [a]the prisoner called me to
him and asked me to lead this
young man to you since he has
something to tell you."
19 And the commander took
him by the hand and stepping
aside, *began* to inquire of him privately, "What is it that you have
to report to me?"
20 [a]Acts 23:14f. [b]Acts 22:30; 23:1, 6, 15, 28
20 And he said, "[a]The Jews
have agreed to ask you to bring
Paul down tomorrow to [b]the
Council, as though they were
going to inquire somewhat more
thoroughly about him.
21 [a]Luke 11:54 [b]Acts 23:12, 14
21 "So do not listen to them,
for more than forty of them are
[a]lying in wait for him who have
[b]bound themselves under a curse
not to eat or drink until they slay
him; and now they are ready and
waiting for the promise from
you."
22 Therefore the commander
let the young man go, instructing
him, "Tell no one that you have
notified me of these things."
23 And he called to him two
of the centurions, and said, "Get
two hundred soldiers ready by
the third hour of the night to proceed to [a]Caesarea, with seventy
horsemen and two hundred
spearmen."
23 [a]Acts 8:40; 23:33
24 *They were* also to provide
mounts to put Paul on and bring
him safely to [a]Felix the governor.
★24 [a]Acts 23:26, 33; 24:1, 3, 10; 25:14
25 And he wrote a letter having this form:

26 "Claudius Lysias, to
the [a]most excellent
governor Felix,
[b]greetings.
26 [a]Luke 1:3; Acts 24:3; 26:25 [b]Acts 15:23

27 "When this man was
arrested by the Jews
and [a]was about to be
slain by them, I came
upon them with the
troops and rescued
him, [b]having learned
that he was a Roman.
27 [a]Acts 21:32f. [b]Acts 22:25-29

28 "And [a]wanting to ascertain the charge for
which they were ac-
cusing him, I [b]brought
him down to their
[c]Council;
28 [a]Acts 22:30 [b]Acts 23:10 [c]Acts 23:1

29 and I found him to be
accused over [a]ques-
tions about their Law,
but under [b]no accusa-
tion deserving death
or imprisonment.
29 [a]Acts 18:15; 25:19 [b]Acts 23:9; 25:25; 26:31; 28:18

30 "And when I was [a]in-
formed that there
would be [b]a plot
against the man, I sent
him to you at once,
also instructing [c]his
accusers to bring
charges against him
before you."
30 [a]Acts 23:20f. [b]Acts 9:24; 23:12 [c]Acts 23:35; 24:19; 25:16

31 So the soldiers, in accordance with their orders, took Paul
and brought him by night to
Antipatris.
32 [a]Acts 23:23 [b]Acts 23:10
32 But the next day, leaving

23:16 *son of Paul's sister.* Only here is any mention made of Paul's immediate relatives.
23:24 *Felix the governor.* Roman procurator of Judea (A.D. 52 to probably 58) with headquarters in Caesarea.

[a]the horsemen to go on with him,
they returned to [b]the barracks.
33 [a]Acts 8:40; 23:23 [b]Acts 23:24, 26; 24:1, 3, 10; 25:14 **33** And when these had come
to [a]Caesarea and delivered the
letter to [b]the governor, they also
presented Paul to him.
★34 [a]Acts 25:1 [b]Acts 6:9; 21:39 **34** And when he had read it,
he asked from what [a]province he
was; and when he learned that
[b]he was from Cilicia,
35 [a]Acts 23:30; 24:19; 25:16 [b]Acts 24:27 **35** he said, "I will give you a
hearing after your [a]accusers ar-
rive also," giving orders for him
to be [b]kept in Herod's Praetorium.

4 *Paul's defense before Felix,* 24:1–27

★ 1 [a]Acts 24:11 [b]Acts 23:2 [c]Acts 23:24 **24** And after [a]five days the
high priest [b]Ananias came
down with some elders, with a
certain attorney *named* Tertullus;
and they brought charges to [c]the
governor against Paul.
2 And after *Paul* had been
summoned, Tertullus began to
accuse him, saying *to the governor,*
"Since we have through you attained much peace, and since by
your providence reforms are
being carried out for this nation,
3 [a]Acts 23:26; 26:25 **3** we acknowledge *this* in every way and everywhere, [a]most
excellent Felix, with all thankfulness.
4 "But, that I may not weary
you any further, I beg you to
grant us, by your kindness, a
brief hearing.
★ 5 [a]Acts 15:5; 24:14 **5** "For we have found this
man a real pest and a fellow who
stirs up dissension among all the
Jews throughout the world, and a
ringleader of the [a]sect of the
Nazarenes.
6 "And he even tried to [a]des- ★ 6–8 6 [a]Acts 21:28
ecrate the temple; and then we ar-
rested him. [And we wanted to
judge him according to our own
Law.
7 "But Lysias the commander came along, and with
much violence took him out of
our hands,
8 ordering his accusers to ★8
come before you.] And by examining him yourself concerning all
these matters, you will be able to
ascertain the things of which we
accuse him."
9 And [a]the Jews also joined 9 [a]1 Thess. 2:16
in the attack, asserting that these
things were so.
10 And when [a]the governor 10 [a]Acts 23:24
had nodded for him to speak,
Paul responded:
"Knowing that for many years
you have been a judge to this nation, I cheerfully make my defense,
11 since you can take note of 11 [a]Acts 21:18, 27; 24:1
the fact that no more than [a]twelve
days ago I went up to Jerusalem to
worship.
12 "And [a]neither in the tem- 12 [a]Acts 25:8 [b]Acts 24:18
ple, nor in the synagogues, nor in
the city *itself* did they find me
carrying on a discussion with anyone or [b]causing a riot.
13 "[a]Nor can they prove to you 13 [a]Acts 25:7
the charges of which they now ac-
cuse me.
14 "But this I admit to you, 14 [a]Acts 9:2; 24:22 [b]Acts 15:5; 24:5 [c]Acts 3:13 [d]Acts 25:8; 26:4ff., 22f.; 28:23
that according to [a]the Way which
they call a [b]sect I do serve [c]the
God of our fathers, [d]believing
everything that is in accordance

23:34 *from what province he was.* Roman law required that this question be asked at the opening of a hearing, for Paul had the right to be tried in his home province or in the province where the alleged crime was committed. Tarsus was in Cilicia. Felix was a deputy of the legate of Syria and Cilicia, and so claimed the right to conduct the hearing, whichever choice Paul made. Such a detail is strong proof that Luke was with Paul at the hearing.

24:1 *Ananias* headed the group that presented the complaint against Paul. *Tertullus* (Roman name) was probably a lawyer hired by the Jews in Caesarea to present their case.

24:5 Tertullus broadened the charge, and made it more serious in Roman eyes by, for the first time, accusing Paul of being an insurrectionist *(stirs up dissension).*

24:6–8 Most manuscripts do not contain a concluding sentence in verse 6, verse 7, or an opening phrase in verse 8.

24:8 Tertullus now argued that Lysias had exceeded his authority in removing Paul from trial by Jewish authorities on the charge of profaning the temple.

with the Law, and that is written
in the Prophets;

15 [a]Dan. 12:2; John 5:28f.; 11:24; Acts 23:6

15 having a hope in God,
which [a]these men cherish themselves, that there shall certainly
be a resurrection of both the
righteous and the wicked.

16 [a]Acts 23:1

16 "In view of this, [a]I also do
my best to maintain always a
blameless conscience *both* before
God and before men.

17 [a]Acts 20:31 [b]Acts 11:29f.; Rom. 15:25-28; 1 Cor. 16:1-4; 2 Cor. 8:1-4; 9:1, 2, 12; Gal. 2:10

17 "Now [a]after several years I
[b]came to bring alms to my nation
and to present offerings;

18 [a]Acts 21:26 [b]Acts 24:12 [c]Acts 21:27

18 in which they found me
occupied in the temple, having
been [a]purified, without *any*
[b]crowd or uproar. But *there were*
certain [c]Jews from Asia—

★19 [a]Acts 23:30

19 who ought to have been
present before you, and to [a]make
accusation, if they should have
anything against me.

20 [a]Matt. 5:22

20 "Or else let these men
themselves tell what misdeed
they found when I stood before
[a]the Council,

21 [a]Acts 23:6; 24:15

21 other than for this one
statement which [a]I shouted out
while standing among them, 'For
the resurrection of the dead I am
on trial before you today.' "

★22 [a]Acts 24:14

22 But Felix, having a more
exact knowledge about [a]the Way,
put them off, saying, "When Lysias the commander comes down, I
will decide your case."

★23 [a]Acts 23:35 [b]Acts 28:16 [c]Acts 23:16; 27:3

23 And he gave orders to the
centurion for him to be [a]kept in
custody and *yet* [b]have *some* freedom, and not to prevent any of
[c]his friends from ministering to
him.

24 [a]Acts 20:21

24 But some days later, Felix
arrived with Drusilla, his wife
who was a Jewess, and sent for
Paul, and heard him *speak* about
[a]faith in Christ Jesus.

★25 [a]Titus 2:12 [b]Gal. 5:23; Titus 1:8; 2 Pet. 1:6 [c]Acts 10:42

25 And as he was discussing
[a]righteousness, [b]self-control and
[c]the judgment to come, Felix became frightened and said, "Go
away for the present, and when I
find time, I will summon you."

26 [a]Acts 24:17

26 At the same time too, he
was hoping that [a]money would be
given him by Paul; therefore he
also used to send for him quite
often and converse with him.

★27 [a]Acts 25:1, 4, 9, 12; 26:24f., 32 [b]Acts 12:3; 25:9 [c]Acts 23:35; 25:14

27 But after two years had
passed, Felix was succeeded by
Porcius [a]Festus; and [b]wishing to
do the Jews a favor, Felix left Paul
[c]imprisoned.

5 *Paul's defense before Festus,* 25:1-27

★ 1 [a]Acts 23:34 [b]Acts 8:40; 25:4, 6, 13

25 Festus therefore, having
arrived in [a]the province,
three days later went up to Jerusalem from [b]Caesarea.

2 [a]Acts 24:1; 25:15

2 And the chief priests and
the leading men of the Jews
[a]brought charges against Paul;
and they were urging him,

3 [a]Acts 9:24

3 requesting a concession
against Paul, that he might have
him brought to Jerusalem, (*at the
same time,* [a]setting an ambush to
kill him on the way).

4 [a]Acts 25:16 [b]Acts 24:23 [c]Acts 8:40; 25:1, 6, 13

4 Festus then [a]answered that
Paul [b]was being kept in custody
at [c]Caesarea and that he himself
was about to leave shortly.
5 "Therefore," he *said, "let
the influential men among you go
there with me, and if there is anything wrong about the man, let
them prosecute him."

6 [a]Acts 8:40; 25:1, 4, 13 [b]Matt. 27:19; Acts 25:10, 17

6 And after he had spent not
more than eight or ten days

24:19 *who.* I.e., the Jews from Asia. They were not there as witnesses, Paul points out.

24:22 *put them off.* Because Lysias wasn't there to be heard from.

24:23 *have some freedom.* Paul was under a relatively loose military confinement.

24:25 *Felix became frightened.* Felix had stolen Drusilla from her first husband. He also was corrupt as a governor (v. 26), and Paul may have challenged him concerning his low morality.

24:27 *Porcius Festus* was Felix's successor. The change came about A.D. 58. A Roman magistrate could decide when a case would be called; often the delays were long, as here.

25:1 *to Jerusalem.* Since there was much unrest, Festus thought it prudent to make an early visit to the religious capital, Jerusalem. The Jews saw in this an opportunity to ask that Paul be returned there. If the request were granted they would try to kill him on the way (v. 3).

among them, he went down to
[a]Caesarea; and on the next day he
took his seat on [b]the tribunal and
ordered Paul to be brought.
7 [a]Acts 24:5f. [b]Acts 24:13
7 And after he had arrived,
the Jews who had come down
from Jerusalem stood around him,
bringing [a]many and serious
charges against him [b]which they
could not prove;
8 [a]Acts 6:13; 24:12; 28:17
8 while Paul said in his own
defense, "[a]I have committed no
offense either against the Law of
the Jews or against the temple or
against Caesar."
9 [a]Acts 12:3; 24:27 [b]Acts 25:20
9 But Festus, [a]wishing to do
the Jews a favor, answered Paul
and said, "[b]Are you willing to go
up to Jerusalem and stand trial
before me on these charges?"
10 [a]Matt. 27:19; Acts 25:10, 17
10 But Paul said, "I am standing before Caesar's [a]tribunal,
where I ought to be tried. I have
done no wrong to *the* Jews, as you
also very well know.
★11 [a]Acts 25:21, 25; 26:32; 28:19
11 "If then I am a wrongdoer,
and have committed anything
worthy of death, I do not refuse to
die; but if none of those things is
true of which these men accuse
me, no one can hand me over to
them. I [a]appeal to Caesar."
12 Then when Festus had
conferred with his council, he answered, "You have appealed to
Caesar, to Caesar you shall go."
★13 [a]Acts 8:40; 25:1, 4, 6
13 Now when several days
had elapsed, King Agrippa and
Bernice arrived at [a]Caesarea, and
paid their respects to Festus.
14 [a]Acts 24:27
14 And while they were
spending many days there, Festus
laid Paul's case before the king,
saying, "There is a certain man
[a]left a prisoner by Felix;
15 [a]Acts 24:1; 25:2
15 and when I was at Jerusalem, the chief priests and the elders of the Jews [a]brought charges
against him, asking for a sentence
of condemnation upon him.
16 [a]Acts 25:4f. [b]Acts 23:30
16 "And I [a]answered them that
it is not the custom of the Romans
to hand over any man before [b]the
accused meets his accusers face to
face, and has an opportunity to
make his defense against the
charges.
17 [a]Matt. 27:19; Acts 25:6, 10
17 "And so after they had assembled here, I made no delay,
but on the next day took my seat
on [a]the tribunal, and ordered the
man to be brought.
18 "And when the accusers
stood up, they *began* bringing
charges against him not of such
crimes as I was expecting;
19 [a]Acts 18:15; 23:29 [b]Acts 17:22
19 but they *simply* had some
[a]points of disagreement with him
about their own [b]religion and
about a certain dead man, Jesus,
whom Paul asserted to be alive.
20 [a]Acts 25:9
20 "And [a]being at a loss how
to investigate such matters, I
asked whether he was willing to
go to Jerusalem and there stand
trial on these matters.
21 [a]Acts 25:11f.
21 "But when Paul [a]appealed
to be held in custody for the Emperor's decision, I ordered him to
be kept in custody until I send
him to Caesar."
22 [a]Acts 9:15
22 And [a]Agrippa *said* to Festus, "I also would like to hear the
man myself." "Tomorrow," he
*said, "you shall hear him."
23 [a]Acts 25:13; 26:30
23 And so, on the next day
when [a]Agrippa had come together with [a]Bernice, amid great
pomp, and had entered the audi-
torium accompanied by the commanders and the prominent men
of the city, at the command of
Festus, Paul was brought in.
24 [a]Acts 25:2, 7 [b]Acts 22:22
24 And Festus *said, "King
Agrippa, and all you gentlemen
here present with us, you behold

25:11 *I appeal to Caesar.* Festus' suggestion that Paul appear in Jerusalem for trial (v. 9) provoked this appeal to Caesar. Paul realized that the trial would not be impartial if conducted by Festus, especially if the case were transferred to Jerusalem, and that he would be in great danger if he was returned to the jurisdiction of the Sanhedrin. The right of appeal was one of the most ancient and cherished rights of a Roman citizen. Nero was emperor at this time (A.D. 54–68).

25:13 *Agrippa.* Herod Agrippa II, son of Herod Agrippa I (12:1) and great-grandson of Herod the Great (Matt. 2:1), both of whose territories he ultimately ruled under Rome's jurisdiction. *Bernice* was his sister, with whom he was living incestuously. Paul was not required to defend himself before them, since he had already appealed to Caesar, but he took this opportunity to witness to the Jewish king.

this man about whom [a]all the
people of the Jews appealed to
me, both at Jerusalem and here,
loudly declaring that [b]he ought
not to live any longer.

25 [a]Acts 23:29 [b]Acts 25:11f.

25 "But I found that he had
committed [a]nothing worthy of
death; and since he himself [b]ap-
pealed to the Emperor, I decided
to send him.
26 "Yet I have nothing definite
about him to write to my lord.
Therefore I have brought him before you *all* and especially before
you, King Agrippa, so that after
the investigation has taken place,
I may have something to write.
27 "For it seems absurd to me
in sending a prisoner, not to indicate also the charges against
him."

6 *Paul's defense before Agrippa,* 26:1-32

1 [a]Acts 9:15

26 And [a]Agrippa said to Paul,
"You are permitted to
speak for yourself." Then Paul
stretched out his hand and *proceeded* to make his defense:
2 "In regard to all the things
of which I am accused by the
Jews, I consider myself fortunate,
King Agrippa, that I am about to
make my defense before you today;

3 [a]Acts 6:14; 25:19; 26:7

3 especially because you are
an expert in all [a]customs and
questions among *the* Jews; therefore I beg you to listen to me pa-
tiently.

4 [a]Gal. 1:13f.; Phil. 3:5

4 "So then, all Jews know
[a]my manner of life from my
youth up, which from the beginning was spent among my *own*
nation and at Jerusalem;

5 [a]Acts 23:6 [b]Acts 22:3 [c]Acts 15:5

5 since they have known
about me for a long time previously, if they are willing to testify,
that I lived *as* a [a]Pharisee [b]accord-
ing to the strictest [c]sect of our religion.

★ 6 [a]Acts 24:15; 28:20 [b]Acts 13:32

6 "And now I am standing
trial [a]for the hope of [b]the promise
made by God to our fathers;

7 [a]James 1:1 [b]Acts 24:15; 28:20 [c]Acts 26:2

7 *the promise* [a]to which our
twelve tribes hope to attain, as
they earnestly serve *God* night
and day. And for this [b]hope, O
King, I am being [c]accused by
Jews.

★ 8 [a]Acts 23:6

8 "Why is it considered incredible among you *people* [a]if
God does raise the dead?

9 [a]John 16:2; 1 Tim. 1:13 [b]John

9 "So then, [a]I thought to myself that I had to do many things
hostile to [b]the name of Jesus of
Nazareth.

10 [a]Acts 8:3; 9:13 [b]Acts 9:1f. [c]Acts 22:20

10 "And this is just what I [a]did
in Jerusalem; not only did I lock
up many of the saints in prisons,
having [b]received authority from
the chief priests, but also when
they were being put to death I
[c]cast my vote against them.

★11 [a]Matt. 10:17; Acts 22:19 [b]Acts 9:1 [c]Acts 22:5

11 "And [a]as I punished them
often in all the synagogues, I tried
to force them to blaspheme; and
being [b]furiously enraged at them,
I kept pursuing them [c]even to
foreign cities.

12 [a]Acts 26:12-18: *9:3-8; 22:6-11*

12 "While thus engaged [a]as I
was journeying to Damascus with
the authority and commission of
the chief priests,
13 at midday, O King, I saw
on the way a light from heaven,
brighter than the sun, shining all
around me and those who were
journeying with me.

14 [a]Acts 9:7 [b]Acts 21:40

14 "And when we had [a]all
fallen to the ground, I heard a
voice saying to me in the [b]He-
brew dialect, 'Saul, Saul, why are
you persecuting Me? It is hard for
you to kick against the goads.'
15 "And I said, 'Who art Thou,
Lord?' And the Lord said, 'I am
Jesus whom you are persecuting.

16 [a]Ezek. 2:1; Dan. 10:11 [b]Acts 22:14 [c]Luke 1:2 [d]Acts 22:15

16 'But arise, and [a]stand on
your feet; for this purpose I have
appeared to you, to [b]appoint you
a [c]minister and [d]a witness not
only to the things which you have
seen, but also to the things in
which I will appear to you;

26:6 *the promise.* I.e., of the Messiah (Gen. 22:18; 49:10).

26:8 That Paul preached the resurrection of Jesus Christ was the heart of the complaint of the Jewish authorities.

26:11 *force them to blaspheme.* I.e., to blaspheme against Christ, which would not have been blasphemy to the Jews.

17 [a]delivering you [b]from the *Jewish* people and from the Gentiles, to whom I am sending you,

17 [a]Jer. 1:8, 19 [b]1 Chr. 16:35; Acts 9:15

18 to [a]open their eyes so that they may turn from [b]darkness to light and from the dominion of [c]Satan to God, in order that they may receive [d]forgiveness of sins and an [e]inheritance among those who have been sanctified by [f]faith in Me.'

18 [a]Is. 35:5; 42:7, 16; Eph. 5:8; Col. 1:13; 1 Pet. 2:9 [b]John 1:5; Eph. 5:8; Col. 1:12f.; 1 Thess. 5:5; 1 Pet. 2:9 [c]Matt. 4:10 [d]Luke 24:47; Acts 2:38 [e]Acts 20:32 [f]Acts 20:21

19 "Consequently, King Agrippa, I did not prove disobedient to the heavenly vision,

20 but *kept* declaring both [a]to those of Damascus first, and *also* [b]at Jerusalem and *then* throughout all the region of Judea, and *even* [c]to the Gentiles, that they should [d]repent and turn to God, performing deeds [e]appropriate to repentance.

20 [a]Acts 9:19ff. [b]Acts 9:26-29; 22:17-20 [c]Acts 9:15; 13:46 [d]Acts 3:19 [e]Matt. 3:8; Luke 3:8

21 "For this reason *some* Jews [a]seized me in the temple and tried [b]to put me to death.

21 [a]Acts 21:27, 30 [b]Acts 21:31

22 "And so, having obtained help from God, I stand to this day [a]testifying both to small and great, stating nothing but what [b]the Prophets and Moses said was going to take place;

22 [a]Luke 16:28 [b]Acts 10:43; 24:14

23 [a]that the Christ was to suffer, *and* that [b]by reason of *His* resurrection from the dead He should be the first to proclaim [c]light both to the *Jewish* people and to the Gentiles."

23 [a]Matt. 26:24; Acts 3:18 [b]1 Cor. 15:20, 23; Col. 1:18; Rev. 1:5 [c]Luke 2:32; 2 Cor. 4:4

24 And while *Paul* was saying this in his defense, Festus *said in a loud voice, "Paul, you are out of your mind! *Your* great [a]learning is driving you mad."

★24 [a]John 7:15; 2 Tim. 3:15

25 But Paul *said, "I am not out of my mind, [a]most excellent Festus, but I utter words of sober truth.

25 [a]Acts 23:26; 24:3

26 "For the king [a]knows about these matters, and I speak to him also with confidence, since I am persuaded that none of these things escape his notice; for this has not been done in a corner.

26 [a]Acts 26:3

27 "King Agrippa, do you believe the Prophets? I know that you do."

28 And Agrippa *replied* to Paul, "In a short time you will persuade me to become a [a]Christian."

★28 [a]Acts 11:26

29 And Paul *said,* "I would to God, that whether in a short or long time, not only you, but also all who hear me this day, might become such as I am, except for these [a]chains."

29 [a]Acts 21:33

30 And [a]the king arose and the governor and Bernice, and those who were sitting with them,

30 [a]Acts 25:23

31 and when they had drawn aside, they *began* talking to one another, saying, "[a]This man is not doing anything worthy of death or imprisonment."

31 [a]Acts 23:29

32 And Agrippa said to Festus, "This man might have been [a]set free if he had not [b]appealed to Caesar."

32 [a]Acts 28:18 [b]Acts 25:11

7 *Paul's voyage and shipwreck,* 27:1–44

27 And when it was decided that [a]we [b]should sail for [c]Italy, they proceeded to deliver Paul and some other prisoners to a centurion of the Augustan [d]cohort named Julius.

★ 1 [a][we] Acts 16:10; 27:1-28 [b]Acts 25:12, 25 [c]Acts 18:2; 27:6 [d]Acts 10:1

2 And embarking in an Adramyttian ship, which was about to sail to the regions along the coast of [a]Asia, we put out to sea, accompanied by [b]Aristarchus, a [c]Macedonian of [d]Thessalonica.

★ 2 [a]Acts 2:9 [b]Acts 19:29 [c]Acts 16:9 [d]Acts 17:1

3 And the next day we put in at [a]Sidon; and Julius [b]treated Paul with consideration and [c]allowed him to go to his friends and receive care.

3 [a]Matt. 11:21 [b]Acts 27:43 [c]Acts 24:23

26:24 *Paul, you are out of your mind!* Festus, a Roman, simply could not comprehend Paul's line of thought and language. Agrippa, a Jew, had no such semantic problems.

26:28 *In a short time.* Lit., In a little . . . This enigmatic statement may mean: "In such a short time are you trying to make a Christian of me?" or "With so few words you are persuading me to be a Christian."

27:1 *centurion.* A commander of 100 Roman soldiers.

27:2 *Adramyttian.* From Adramyttium, a port on the west coast of Asia Minor (modern Turkey), just south of Troas.

★ 4 [a]Acts 4:36 [b]Acts 27:7
4 And from there we put out
to sea and sailed under the shelter
of [a]Cyprus because [b]the winds
were contrary.
5 [a]Acts 6:9 [b]Acts 13:13
5 And when we had sailed
through the sea along the coast of
[a]Cilicia and [b]Pamphylia, we
landed at Myra in Lycia.
6 [a]Acts 28:11 [b]Acts 18:2; 27:1
6 And there the centurion
found an [a]Alexandrian ship sailing for [b]Italy, and he put us
aboard it.
7 [a]Acts 27:4 [b]Acts 2:11; 27:12f., 21; Titus 1:5, 12
7 And when we had sailed
slowly for a good many days, and
with difficulty had arrived off Cnidus, [a]since the wind did not permit us *to go* farther, we sailed under the shelter of [b]Crete, off
Salmone;
8 [a]Acts 27:13 [Gr.]
8 and with difficulty [a]sailing
past it we came to a certain place
called Fair Havens, near which
was the city of Lasea.
★ 9 [a]Lev. 16:29-31; 23:27-29; Num. 29:7
9 And when considerable
time had passed and the voyage
was now dangerous, since even
[a]the fast was already over, Paul
began to admonish them,
10 [a]Acts 27:21
10 and said to them, "Men, I
perceive that the voyage will certainly be *attended* with [a]damage
and great loss, not only of the cargo and the ship, but also of our
lives."
11 [a]Rev. 18:17
11 But the centurion was
more persuaded by the [a]pilot and
the captain of the ship, than by
what was being said by Paul.
12 [a]Acts 2:11; 27:13, 21; Titus 1:5, 12
12 And because the harbor
was not suitable for wintering,
the majority reached a decision to
put out to sea from there, if somehow they could reach Phoenix, a
harbor of [a]Crete, facing northeast
and southeast, and spend the
winter *there.*
13 And when a moderate
south wind came up, supposing
that they had gained their purpose, they weighed anchor and
began [a]sailing along [b]Crete, close
inshore.
13 [a]Acts 27:8 [Gr.] [b]Acts 2:11; 27:12f., 21; Titus 1:5, 12
14 But before very long there
[a]rushed down from the land a
violent wind, called Euraquilo;
★14 [a]Mark 4:37
15 and when the ship was
caught *in it,* and could not face
the wind, we gave way *to it,* and
let ourselves be driven along.
16 And running under the
shelter of a small island called
Clauda, we were scarcely able to
get the *ship's* boat under control.
★16
17 And after they had hoisted
it up, they used supporting cables
in undergirding the ship; and
fearing that they might [a]run
aground on *the shallows* of Syrtis,
they let down the sea anchor, and
so let themselves be driven along.
★17 [a]Acts 27:26, 29
18 The next day as we were
being violently storm-tossed, they
began to [a]jettison the cargo;
18 [a]Jon. 1:5; Acts 27:38
19 and on the third day they
threw the ship's tackle overboard
with their own hands.
20 And since neither sun nor
stars appeared for many days, and
no small storm was assailing *us,*
from then on all hope of our
being saved was gradually abandoned.
21 And when they had gone a
long time without food, then Paul
stood up in their midst and said,
"[a]Men, you ought to have followed my advice and not to have
set sail from [b]Crete, and incurred
this [a]damage and loss.
21 [a]Acts 27:10 [b]Acts 27:7

27:4 *under the shelter of Cyprus.* The prevailing early autumn winds came from the northwest, making headwinds difficult for a coastal vessel to handle in open ocean. So the ship sailed around the east end of Cyprus, the lee side, and headed north for the coast of Cilicia, where it would then head west, close to shore for many miles.

27:9 *the fast was already over.* Only one fast was prescribed by the law and that was on the Day of Atonement (Lev. 16:29-34). If this was the year 59, the fast was on Oct. 5. This means Paul left Caesarea in August or September and did not arrive in Rome until the following March.

27:14 *Euraquilo.* A hybrid word, half Greek, half Latin, meaning east-north and standing for a treacherous east-northeast wind.

27:16 *to get the ship's boat under control.* I.e., the dinghy, probably being towed and starting to fill up.

27:17 *supporting cables in undergirding the ship.* Some sort of rope truss to stiffen the timbers seems indicated.

22 [a]Acts 27:25, 36 22 "And *yet* now I urge you to
[a]keep up your courage, for there
shall be no loss of life among you,
but *only* of the ship.
23 [a]Acts 5:19 [b]Rom. 1:9 [c]Acts 18:9; 23:11; 2 Tim. 4:17 23 "For this very night [a]an angel of the God to whom I belong
and [b]whom I serve [c]stood before
me,
24 [a]Acts 23:11 [b]Acts 27:31, 42, 44 24 saying, 'Do not be afraid,
Paul; [a]you must stand before
Caesar; and behold, God has
granted you [b]all those who are
sailing with you.'
25 [a]Acts 27:22, 36 25 "Therefore, [a]keep up your
courage, men, for I believe God,
that it will turn out exactly as I
have been told.
26 [a]Acts 27:17, 29 [b]Acts 28:1 26 "But we must [a]run aground
on a certain [b]island."
★27 **27** But when the fourteenth
night had come, as we were being
driven about in the Adriatic Sea,
about midnight the sailors *began*
to surmise that they were approaching some land.
★28 28 And they took soundings,
and found *it to be* twenty fathoms; and a little farther on they
took another sounding and found
it to be fifteen fathoms.
29 [a]Acts 27:17, 26 29 And fearing that we might
[a]run aground somewhere on the
rocks, they cast four anchors from
the stern and wished for daybreak.
30 [a]Acts 27:16 30 And as the sailors were
trying to escape from the ship,
and had let down [a]the *ship's* boat
into the sea, on the pretense of
intending to lay out anchors from
the bow,
★31-36 31 Paul said to the centurion
and to the soldiers, "Unless these
men remain in the ship, you
yourselves cannot be saved."
32 [a]John 2:15 [Gr.] 32 Then the soldiers cut away
the [a]ropes of the *ship's* boat, and
let it fall away.
33 And until the day was
about to dawn, Paul was encouraging them all to take some food,
saying, "Today is the fourteenth
day that you have been constantly watching and going without eating, having taken nothing.
34 "Therefore I encourage you 34 [a]Matt. 10:30
to take some food, for this is for
your preservation; for [a]not a hair
from the head of any of you shall
perish."
35 And having said this, he 35 [a]Matt. 14:19
took bread and [a]gave thanks to
God in the presence of all; and he
broke it and began to eat.
36 And all [a]of them were en- 36 [a]Acts 27:22, 25
couraged, and they themselves
also took food.
37 And all of us in the ship 37 [a]Acts 2:41
were two hundred and seventy-
six [a]persons.
38 And when they had eaten ★38 [a]Jon. 1:5; Acts 27:18
enough, they *began* to lighten the
ship by [a]throwing out the wheat
into the sea.
39 And when day came, [a]they 39 [a]Acts 28:1
could not recognize the land; but
they did observe a certain bay
with a beach, and they resolved to
drive the ship onto it if they
could.
40 And casting off [a]the an- 40 [a]Acts 27:29
chors, they left them in the sea
while at the same time they were
loosening the ropes of the rud-
ders, and hoisting the foresail to
the wind, they were heading for
the beach.
41 But striking a reef where ★41
two seas met, they ran the vessel
aground; and the prow stuck fast
and remained immovable, but the
stern *began* to be broken up by
the force *of the waves.*
42 And the soldiers' plan was 42 [a]Acts 12:19
to [a]kill the prisoners, that none *of*
them should swim away and escape;
43 but the centurion, [a]want- 43 [a]Acts 27:3
ing to bring Paul safely through,
kept them from their intention,

27:27 *the Adriatic Sea.* In this period the Adriatic Sea was a name applied to the Mediterranean E. of Sicily, and not merely to the present Adriatic Sea.

27:28 *fathoms.* A fathom is about 6 feet.

27:31–36 Paul the prisoner has risen to a place of commanding leadership.

27:38 The purpose of lightening the ship was to raise her in the water and let her run as far up the beach as possible before grounding.

27:41 *a reef where two seas met.* They did not reach the shore but ran aground on a shoal.

and commanded that those who
could swim should jump overboard first and get to land,
44 [a]Acts 27:22, 31 — 44 and the rest *should follow,*
some on planks, and others on
various things from the ship. And
thus it happened that [a]they all
were brought safely to land.

8 ***Paul in Malta and on to Rome,*** 28:1-16

1 [a][we] Acts 16:10; 27:1 [b]Acts 27:39 [c]Acts 27:26 — **28** And when [a]they had been
brought safely through,
[b]then we found out that [c]the island was called Malta.
★ 2 [a]Acts 28:4; Rom. 1:14; 1 Cor. 14:11; Col. 3:11 [b]Rom. 14:1 — 2 And [a]the natives showed
us extraordinary kindness; for be-
cause of the rain that had set in
and because of the cold, they kindled a fire and [b]received us all.
3 But when Paul had gath-
ered a bundle of sticks and laid
them on the fire, a viper came out
because of the heat, and fastened
on his hand.
4 [a]Acts 28:2 [b]Luke 13:2, 4 — 4 And when [a]the natives
saw the creature hanging from his
hand, they *began* saying to one
another, "[b]Undoubtedly this man
is a murderer, and though he has
been saved from the sea, justice
has not allowed him to live."
5 [a]Mark 16:18 — 5 However [a]he shook the
creature off into the fire and suffered no harm.
6 [a]Acts 14:11 — 6 But they were expecting
that he was about to swell up or
suddenly fall down dead. But after they had waited a long time
and had seen nothing unusual
happen to him, they changed
their minds and [a]*began* to say
that he was a god.
7 Now in the neighborhood
of that place were lands belonging
to the leading man of the island,
named Publius, who welcomed us
8 [a]Acts 9:40; James 5:14f. [b]Mark 5:23 — and entertained us courteously
three days.
8 And it came about that the
father of Publius was lying *in bed*
afflicted with *recurrent* fever and
dysentery; and Paul went in *to see*
him and after he had [a]prayed, he
[b]laid his hands on him and healed
him.
9 And after this had hap-
pened, the rest of the people on
the island who had diseases were
coming to him and getting cured.
10 And they also honored us
with many marks of respect; and
when we were setting sail, they
supplied *us* with all we needed.
11 And at the end of three — ★11 [a]Acts 27:6
months we set sail on [a]an Alexandrian ship which had wintered at
the island, and which had the
Twin Brothers for its figurehead.
12 And after we put in at
Syracuse, we stayed there for
three days.
13 And from there we sailed — ★13
around and arrived at Rhegium,
and a day later a south wind
sprang up, and on the second day
we came to Puteoli.
14 There we found *some* — 14 [a]Acts 1:15
[a]brethren, and were invited to
stay with them for seven days;
and thus we came to Rome.
15 And the [a]brethren, when — 15 [a]Acts 1:15
they heard about us, came from
there as far as the Market of Ap-
pius and Three Inns to meet us;
and when Paul saw them, he
thanked God and took courage.
16 And when we entered — 16 [a]Acts 24:23
Rome, Paul was [a]allowed to stay
by himself, with the soldier who
was guarding him.

9 ***Paul in Rome,*** 28:17-31

17 And it happened that after — ★17 [a]Acts 13:50; 25:2 [b]Acts 22:5 [c]Acts 25:8 [d]Acts 6:14
three days he called together
those who were [a]the leading men
of the Jews, and when they had
come together, he *began* saying to
them, "[b]Brethren, [c]though I had
done nothing against our people,

28:2 *natives.* The primary meaning of the Greek word is "people who speak a foreign tongue," i.e., non-Greeks.

28:11 *at the end of three months.* I.e., in the middle of February.

28:13 *Rhegium.* A town on the "toe" of Italy, modern Reggio di Calabria. *Puteoli.* A port on the bay of Naples. Ostia, Rome's harbor, wasn't a deep enough harbor at this time to receive Alexandrian grain ships.

28:17 Paul wanted to prevent any derogatory report from his Jewish enemies in Jerusalem.

or [d]the customs of our fathers, yet
I was delivered prisoner from Jerusalem into the hands of the Romans.
18 "And when they had exam- 18 [a]Acts 26:32 [b]Acts 23:29
ined me, they [a]were willing to re-
lease me because there was [b]no
ground for putting me to death.
19 "But when the Jews ob- 19 [a]Acts 25:11
jected, I was forced to [a]appeal to
Caesar; not that I had any accusation against my nation.
20 "For this reason therefore, I ★20 [a]Acts 21:33 [b]Acts 26:6f.
requested to see you and to speak
with you, for I am wearing [a]this
chain for [b]the sake of the hope of
Israel."
21 And they said to him, "We 21 [a]Acts 22:5
have neither received letters from
Judea concerning you, nor have
any of [a]the brethren come here
and reported or spoken anything
bad about you.
22 "But we desire to hear from 22 [a]Acts 24:14 [b]1 Pet. 2:12; 3:16; 4:14, 16
you what your views are; for con-
cerning this [a]sect, it is known to
us that [b]it is spoken against
everywhere."
23 And when they had set a ★23 [a]Philem. 22 [b]Luke 16:28; Acts 1:3; 23:11 [c]Acts 8:35
day for him, they came to him at
[a]his lodging in large numbers;
and he was explaining to them by
solemnly [b]testifying about the
kingdom of God, and trying to
persuade them concerning Jesus,
[c]from both the Law of Moses and
from the Prophets, from morning
until evening.
24 And [a]some were being 24 [a]Acts 14:4
persuaded by the things spoken,
but others would not believe.

25 And when they did not ★25-27
agree with one another, they *be-*
gan leaving after Paul had spoken
one parting word, "The Holy
Spirit rightly spoke through Isaiah the prophet to your fathers,
26 saying, 26 [a]Is. 6:9 [b]Matt. 13:14f.; Acts 28:26, 27

'[a]GO TO THIS PEOPLE AND SAY,
"[b]YOU WILL KEEP ON HEARING,
BUT WILL NOT UNDERSTAND;
AND YOU WILL KEEP ON SEE-
ING, BUT WILL NOT PER-
CEIVE;
27 [a]FOR THE HEART OF THIS PEO- 27 [a]Is. 6:10
PLE HAS BECOME DULL,
AND WITH THEIR EARS THEY
SCARCELY HEAR,
AND THEY HAVE CLOSED THEIR
EYES;
LEST THEY SHOULD SEE WITH
THEIR EYES,
AND HEAR WITH THEIR EARS,
AND UNDERSTAND WITH THEIR
HEART AND TURN AGAIN,
AND I SHOULD HEAL THEM." '

28 "Let it be known to you 28 [a]Ps. 98:3; Luke 2:30; Acts 13:26 [b]Acts 9:15; 13:46
therefore, that [a]this salvation of
God has been sent [b]to the Gentiles; they will also listen."
29 [And when he had spoken ★29
these words, the Jews departed,
having a great dispute among
themselves.]
30 And he stayed two full ★30
years in his own rented quarters,
and was welcoming all who came
to him,
31 [a]preaching the kingdom of 31 [a]Matt. 4:23; Acts 20:25; 28:23 [b]2 Tim. 2:9
God, and teaching concerning the
Lord Jesus Christ [b]with all openness, unhindered.

28:20 *the hope of Israel.* The Messianic hope, incarnate in Jesus Christ and climaxed in His resurrection.

28:23 *trying to persuade* the Jews meant proving to them from Scripture and His resurrection that Jesus was the Messiah (see 13:30-39).

28:25-27 Paul's citation of this passage (Isa. 6:9-10) has been regarded as a parting shot at their obtuseness. He followed with a declaration that henceforth salvation will be preached to the Gentiles, the Jews having refused it.

28:29 Many manuscripts do not contain this verse.

28:30 *two full years in his own rented quarters.* During this time of confinement Paul wrote Ephesians, Philippians, Colossians, and Philemon. See the Introduction to Ephesians. Knowing that they could not get a verdict of guilty, his accusers probably never showed up and therefore lost the case by default. Paul would then have been released and become free to engage in the ministry reflected in the Pastoral Epistles before being rearrested and finally martyred. See the Introduction to Titus.

INTRODUCTION TO THE LETTER OF PAUL TO THE ROMANS

AUTHOR: Paul DATE: 58

The Church at Rome *Though both Paul and Peter were apparently martyred in Rome, it is unlikely that either was the founder of the church in that city. Possibly some who were converted on the day of Pentecost (Acts 2:10) carried the gospel back to the imperial city; or it may be that converts of Paul or of other apostles founded the church there. The membership was predominantly Gentile (1:13; 11:13; 15:5-6).*

Occasion of the Letter *Paul was anxious to minister in this church which was already widely known (1:8), so he wrote the letter to prepare the way for his visit (15:14-17). It was written from Corinth, where Paul was completing the collection for the poor in Palestine. From there he went to Jerusalem to deliver the money, intending to continue on to Rome and Spain (15:24). These plans were, of course, changed by his arrest in Jerusalem, though Paul did eventually get to Rome as a prisoner. Phoebe, who belonged to the church at Cenchrea near Corinth (16:1), probably carried the letter to Rome.*

The Question about Chapter 16 *The mention by name of 26 people in a church Paul had never visited (and particularly Priscilla and Aquila, who were most recently associated with Ephesus, Acts 18:18-19) has caused some scholars to consider chapter 16 as part of an epistle sent to Ephesus. It would be natural, however, for Paul to mention to a church to which he was a stranger his acquaintance with mutual friends. Paul's only other long series of greetings is in Colossians—a letter also sent to a church he had not visited.*

Contents *More formal than Paul's other letters, Romans sets forth the doctrine of justification by faith (and its ramifications) in a systematic way. The theme of the epistle is the righteousness of God (1:16-17). A number of basic Christian doctrines are discussed: natural revelation (1:19-20), universality of sin (3:9-20), justification (3:24), propitiation (3:25), faith (chap. 4), original sin (5:12), union with Christ (chap. 6), the election and rejection of Israel (chaps. 9-11), spiritual gifts (12:3-8), and respect for government (13:1-7).*

OUTLINE OF ROMANS

I. Salutation and Statement of Theme, 1:1-17
- A. Greeting, 1:1-7
- B. Paul's Interest, 1:8-15
- C. Theme, 1:16-17

II. Righteousness Needed; Condemnation, Sin, 1:18-3:20
- A. The Condemnation of the Gentile, 1:18-32
  - 1. The cause of the condemnation: willful ignorance, 1:18-23
  - 2. The consequences of the condemnation: divine abandonment, 1:24-32
- B. The Condemnation of the Moralist, 2:1-16
- C. The Condemnation of the Jew, 2:17-3:8
  - 1. He did not keep the law of God, 2:17-29
  - 2. He did not believe the promises of God, 3:1-8
- D. The Condemnation of All Men, 3:9-20

III. Righteousness Imputed; Justification, Salvation, 3:21-5:21
- A. The Description of Righteousness, 3:21-31
- B. The Illustration of Righteousness, 4:1-25
  - 1. Abraham's faith was apart from works, 4:1-8
  - 2. Abraham's faith was apart from circumcision, 4:9-12
  - 3. Abraham's faith was apart from the law, 4:13-15
  - 4. Abraham's faith was in God, 4:16-25
- C. The Benefits of Righteousness, 5:1-11
- D. The Applicability of Righteousness, 5:12-21

IV. Righteousness Imparted; Sanctification, Separation, 6:1-8:39
- A. The Principles of Sanctification; The Question of License, 6:1-23
  - 1. Shall we continue in sin? 6:1-14
  - 2. Shall we continue to sin? 6:15-23
- B. The Practice of Sanctification; The Question of Law, 7:1-25
  - 1. Is the believer under law? 7:1-6
  - 2. Is the law evil? 7:7-12
  - 3. Is the law a cause of death? 7:13-14
  - 4. How can I resolve the struggle within myself? 7:15-25
- C. The Power of Sanctification; The Question of Living, 8:1-39
  - 1. Emancipated living, 8:1-11

2. Exalted living, 8:12-17
3. Expectant living, 8:18-30
4. Exultant living, 8:31-39

V. Righteousness Vindicated; Dispensation, Sovereignty, 9:1-11:36

A. Israel's Past; Election, 9:1-29
   1. Paul's sorrow, 9:1-5
   2. God's sovereignty, 9:6-29

B. Israel's Present; Rejection, 9:30-10:21

C. Israel's Future; Salvation, 11:1-36
   1. The extent of Israel's rejection (partial), 11:1-10
   2. The purpose of Israel's rejection, 11:11-24
   3. The duration of Israel's rejection (temporary), 11:25-32
   4. Discourse on God's wisdom, 11:33-36

VI. Righteousness Practiced; Application, Service, 12:1-15:13

A. In Relation to Ourselves, 12:1-2

B. In Relation to the Church, 12:3-8

C. In Relation to Society, 12:9-21

D. In Relation to Government, 13:1-14

E. In Relation to Other Believers, 14:1-15:13
   1. Do not judge one another, 14:1-12
   2. Do not hinder one another, 14:13-23
   3. Do imitate Christ, 15:1-13

VII. Personal Messages and Benediction, 15:14-16:27

A. Paul's Plans, 15:14-33

B. Paul's Personal Greetings, 16:1-16

C. Paul's Concluding Admonition and Benediction, 16:17-27

THE LETTER OF PAUL TO THE ROMANS

I SALUTATION AND STATEMENT OF THEME, 1:1-17

A Greeting, 1:1-7

1 Paul, a bond-servant of
Christ Jesus, [a]called *as* an
apostle, [b]set apart for [c]the gospel
of God,
2 which He [a]promised beforehand through His [b]prophets
in the holy Scriptures,
3 concerning His Son, who
was born [a]of a descendant of David [b]according to the flesh,
4 who was declared [a]the Son
of God with power by the resurrection from the dead, according
to the Spirit of holiness, Jesus
Christ our Lord,
5 through whom we have received grace and [a]apostleship to
bring about *the* [b]obedience of
faith among [c]all the Gentiles, for
His name's sake,
6 among whom you also are
the [a]called of Jesus Christ;
7 to all who are [a]beloved of
God in Rome, called *as* [b]saints:
[c]Grace to you and peace from
God our Father and the Lord Jesus
Christ.

★ 1 [a]1 Cor. 1:1; 9:1; 2 Cor. 1:1 [b]Acts 9:15; 13:2; Gal. 1:15 [c]Mark 1:14; Rom. 15:16; 2 Cor. 2:12; 11:7; 1 Thess. 2:2, 8, 9; 1 Pet. 4:17
2 [a]Titus 1:2 [b]Luke 1:70; Rom. 3:21; 16:26
★ 3 [a]Matt. 1:1 [b]John 1:14; Rom. 4:1; 9:3, 5; 1 Cor. 10:18
★ 4 [a]Matt. 4:3
5 [a]Acts 1:25; Gal. 1:16 [b]Acts 6:7; Rom. 16:26 [c]Acts 9:15

B Paul's Interest, 1:8-15

8 First, [a]I thank my God
through Jesus Christ for you all,
because [b]your faith is being proclaimed throughout the whole
world.
9 For [a]God, whom I [b]serve in
my spirit in the *preaching of the*
gospel of His Son, is my witness
as to how unceasingly [c]I make
mention of you,

★ 6 [a]Jude 1; Rev. 17:14
★ 7 [a]Rom. 5:5ff.; 8:39; 1 Thess. 1:4 [b]Acts 9:13; Rom. 8:28ff.; 1 Cor. 1:2, 24 [c]Num. 6:25f.; 1 Cor. 1:3; 2 Cor. 1:2; Gal. 1:3;
8 [a]1 Cor. 1:4; Eph. 1:15f.; Phil. 1:3f.; Col. 1:3f.; 1 Thess. 1:2; 2:13; 2 Thess. 1:3; 2:13; 2 Tim. 1:3; Philem. 4 [b]Acts 28:22; Rom. 16:19
9 [a]Rom. 9:1; 2 Cor. 1:23; 11:31; Phil. 1:8; 1 Thess. 2:5, 10 [b]Acts 24:14; 2 Tim. 1:3 [c]Eph. 1:16; Phil. 1:3f

---

1:1 *bond-servant.* Lit., slave, from a word that means "to bind." The believer who voluntarily takes the position of slave to Christ has no rights or will of his own. He does always and only the will of his Master. For His part, the Lord binds Himself to care for His servant (cf. Deut. 15:12-18). *the gospel* is the good news that the death of Jesus Christ provided the full payment for the penalty of sin, and that anyone who trusts that living Christ is forgiven and has eternal life.

1:3 *born of a descendant of David according to the flesh.* Jesus was descended from David. See notes on Matt. 1:1, 1:11; John 1:14.

1:4 *declared.* Better, designated; i.e., Jesus was designated or proved to be the Son of God by His own *resurrection from the dead.* Some understand *according to the Spirit of holiness* to refer to the Holy Spirit, while others consider it a reference to Christ's own holy being. Thus the verse may be understood this way: the resurrection of Jesus is the mighty proof of His deity, and this is declared by the Holy Spirit.

1:6 *the called.* I.e., those who have been summoned by God to salvation (8:30).

1:7 *saints.* The word means "holy ones" or "set-apart ones." The N.T. designates all believers as "saints" because they are by position holy and set apart to God (Phil. 4:21; Col. 1:2).

★10 [a]Acts 18:21; Rom. 15:32
★11 [a]Acts 19:21; Rom. 15:23
13 [a]Rom. 11:25; 1 Cor. 10:1; 12:1; 2 Cor. 1:8; 1 Thess. 4:13 [b]Acts 1:15; Rom. 7:1; 1 Cor. 1:10; 14:20, 26; Gal. 3:15 [c]Acts 19:21; Rom. 15:22f. [d]John 4:36; 15:16; Phil. 1:22; Col. 1:6
★14 [a]1 Cor. 9:16 [b]Acts 28:2
15 [a]Rom. 12:18 [b]Rom. 15:20

10 always in my prayers making request, if perhaps now at last
by [a]the will of God I may succeed
in coming to you.
11 For [a]I long to see you in
order that I may impart some
spiritual gift to you, that you may
be established;
12 that is, that I may be encouraged together with you *while*
among you, each of us by the other's faith, both yours and mine.
13 And [a]I do not want you to
be unaware, [b]brethren, that often
I [c]have planned to come to you
(and have been prevented thus
far) in order that I might obtain
some [d]fruit among you also, even
as among the rest of the Gentiles.
14 [a]I am under obligation
both to Greeks and to [b]barbari-
ans, both to the wise and to the
foolish.
15 Thus, [a]for my part, I am
eager to [b]preach the gospel to you
also who are in Rome.

C Theme, 1:16–17

★16 [a]2 Tim. 1:8, 12, 16 [b]1 Cor. 1:18, 24 [c]Acts 3:26; Rom. 2:9 [d]John 7:35
★17 [a]Rom. 3:21; 9:30; Phil. 3:9 [b]Hab. 2:4; Gal. 3:11; Heb. 10:38

16 For I am not [a]ashamed of
the gospel, for [b]it is the power of
God for salvation to every one
who believes, to the [c]Jew first and
also to [d]the Greek.
17 For in it [a]*the* righteousness
of God is revealed from faith to
faith; as it is written, "[b]BUT THE
RIGHTEOUS *man* SHALL LIVE BY
FAITH."

II RIGHTEOUSNESS NEEDED; CONDEMNATION, SIN, 1:18–3:20

A The Condemnation of the Gentile, 1:18–32

1 The cause of the condemnation: willful ignorance, 1:18–23

★18 [a]Rom. 5:9; Eph. 5:6; Col. 3:6 [b]2 Thess. 2:6f. [Gr.]
19 [a]Acts 14:17; 17:24ff.
★20 [a]Mark 10:6 [b]Job 12:7-9; Ps. 19:1-6; Jer. 5:21f.
21 [a]2 Kin. 17:15; Jer. 2:5; Eph. 4:17f.

18 For [a]the wrath of God is
revealed from heaven against all
ungodliness and unrighteousness
of men, who [b]suppress the truth
in unrighteousness,
19 because [a]that which is
known about God is evident
within them; for God made it evident to them.
20 For [a]since the creation of
the world His invisible attributes,
His eternal power and divine nature, have been clearly seen,
[b]being understood through what
has been made, so that they are
without excuse.
21 For even though they
knew God, they did not honor
Him as God, or give thanks; but
they became [a]futile in their
speculations, and their foolish
heart was darkened.

1:10 *making request.* Arrest, trial, two years' languishing in prison (Acts 24:27), and shipwreck intervened before Paul's prayer was answered.

1:11 *impart.* I.e., exercise his gifts for their benefit (as explained in v. 12).

1:14 *Greeks.* Those who spoke Greek and who had adopted Hellenistic culture, in contrast to *barbarians* who had not. However, in v. 16 *Greek* means "Gentile." *wise* = educated.

1:16 *salvation* has three facets: past salvation from the penalties of sin (Luke 7:50); present salvation from the power of sin in the daily life (Rom. 5:10); and future salvation from the actual presence of sin (in heaven) (1 Cor. 3:15; 5:5). This salvation comes *to every one who believes.* We receive and experience it through faith, which is both assent to the truths of the gospel and genuine confidence in the Savior Himself.

1:17 *the righteousness of God.* I.e., the restoration of right relations between man and God which proceeds from God's gift through His Son (see note on 3:21). *from faith to faith.* I.e., faith from start to finish. *The righteous man shall live by faith.* Quoting Hab. 2:4, Paul is emphasizing that one can be righteous in God's sight only through faith; i.e., he who is just through faith shall live now and forever by faith. See notes on Gal. 3:11 and Heb. 10:38. In vv. 16–17 is the essence of Paul's theology: Believe in the Lord Jesus, and you will be saved.

1:18 From here to 3:20 is God's indictment of the world, showing why man needs the righteousness of God. *suppress.* Man is condemned because truth was given to him (vv. 19–20) and because he by his actions rejected it (vv. 21–32).

1:20 *they are without excuse.* The things that are made (creation) reveal to all men the *power and divine nature* of the true God, so that the rejection of this truth makes a man without excuse before God.

22 [a]Jer. 10:14; 1 Cor. 1:20
23 [a]Ps. 106:20; Jer. 2:11; Acts 17:29

22 [a]Professing to be wise,
they became fools,
23 and [a]exchanged the glory
of the incorruptible God for an
image in the form of corruptible
man and of birds and four-footed
animals and crawling creatures.

2 *The consequences of the condemnation: divine abandonment,* 1:24–32

★24 [a]Rom. 1:26, 28; Eph. 4:19 [b]Eph. 2:3
25 [a]Is. 44:20; Jer. 10:14; 13:25; 16:19 [b]Rom. 9:5; 2 Cor. 11:31
26 [a]Rom. 1:24 [b]1 Thess. 4:5
27 [a]Lev. 18:22; 20:13; 1 Cor. 6:9
28 [a]Rom. 1:24
29 [a]2 Cor. 12:20
30 [a]Ps. 5:5 [b]2 Tim. 3:2
31 [a]2 Tim. 3:3

24 Therefore [a]God gave them
over in the lusts of their hearts to
impurity, that their bodies might
be [b]dishonored among them.
25 For they exchanged the
truth of God for a [a]lie, and worshiped and served the creature
rather than the Creator, [b]who is
blessed forever. Amen.
26 For this reason [a]God gave
them over to [b]degrading passions;
for their women exchanged the
natural function for that which is
unnatural,
27 and in the same way also
the men abandoned the natural
function of the woman and
burned in their desire towards
one another, [a]men with men
committing indecent acts and receiving in their own persons the
due penalty of their error.
28 And just as they did not
see fit to acknowledge God any
longer, [a]God gave them over to a
depraved mind, to do those things
which are not proper,
29 being filled with all unrighteousness, wickedness, greed,
malice; full of envy, murder,
strife, deceit, malice; *they are*
[a]gossips,
30 slanderers, [a]haters of God,
insolent, arrogant, boastful, in-
ventors of evil, [b]disobedient to
parents,
31 without understanding,
untrustworthy, [a]unloving, unmer-
ciful;
32 and, although they know
the ordinance of God, that those
who practice such things are worthy of [a]death, they not only do
the same, but also [b]give hearty
approval to those who practice
them.

★32 [a]Rom. 6:21 [b]Luke 11:48; Acts 8:1; 22:20

B The Condemnation of the Moralist, 2:1–16

2 Therefore you are [a]without
excuse, [b]every man *of you*
who passes judgment, for in that
[c]you judge another, you condemn
yourself; for you who judge practice the same things.
2 And we know that the
judgment of God rightly falls
upon those who practice such
things.
3 And do you suppose this,
[a]O man, when you pass judgment
upon those who practice such
things and do the same *yourself,*
that you will escape the judgment
of God?
4 Or do you think lightly of
[a]the riches of His [b]kindness and
[c]forbearance and [d]patience, not
knowing that [e]the kindness of
God leads you to repentance?
5 But because of your stub-
bornness and unrepentant heart
[a]you are storing up wrath for
yourself [b]in the day of wrath and
revelation of the righteous judgment of God,
6 [a]who WILL RENDER TO EVERY
MAN ACCORDING TO HIS DEEDS:
7 to those who by [a]persever-
ance in doing good seek for [b]glory
and honor and [c]immortality,
[d]eternal life;

★ 1 [a]Rom. 1:20 [b]Luke 12:14; Rom. 2:3; 9:20 [c]2 Sam. 12:5-7; Matt. 7:1; Rom. 14:22
3 [a]Luke 12:14; Rom. 2:1; 9:20
4 [a]Rom. 9:23; 11:33; 2 Cor. 8:2; Eph. 1:7, 18; 2:7; Phil. 4:19; Col. 1:27; 2:2; Titus 3:6 [b]Rom. 11:22 [c]Rom. 3:25 [d]Ex. 34:6; Rom. 9:22; 1 Tim. 1:16; 1 Pet. 3:20; 2 Pet. 3:15 [e]2 Pet. 3:9
★ 5 [a]Deut. 32:34f.; Prov. 1:18 [b]Ps. 110:5; 2 Cor. 5:10; 2 Thess. 1:5; Jude 6
6 [a]Ps. 62:12; Matt. 16:27
★ 7 [a]Luke 8:15; Heb. 10:36 [b]Rom. 2:10; Heb. 2:7; 1 Pet. 1:7 [c]1 Cor. 15:42, 50, 53f.; Eph. 6:24; 2 Tim. 1:10 [d]Matt. 25:46

1:24 *God gave them over.* Note the repetition of this phrase in vv. 26 and 28. Paul is attacking the frank idolatry of most of the Gentile world, in which animals were considered gods (v. 23), sexual perversion was prevalent (vv. 26–27), and sin in general was rampant (vv. 29–32).

1:32 *give hearty approval to those who practice them.* Not only did the people themselves sin but they encouraged and vicariously enjoyed the sins of others.

2:1 Paul now shows, first subtly (vv. 1–16), then openly, that the Jews are defenseless.

2:5 *wrath* results when grace is rejected.

2:7 *eternal life.* Good works do not save (Eph. 2:8–9) but are evidence of a changed life. Much of Romans is devoted to this extremely important thesis.

8 but to those who are [a]selfishly ambitious and [b]do not obey the truth, but obey unrighteousness, wrath and indignation.

9 *There will be* [a]tribulation and distress for every soul of man who does evil, of the Jew [b]first and also of the Greek,

10 but [a]glory and honor and peace to every man who does good, to the Jew [b]first and also to the Greek.

11 For [a]there is no partiality with God.

12 For all who have sinned [a]without the Law will also perish without the Law; and all who have sinned under the Law will be judged by the Law;

13 for [a]not the hearers of the Law are just before God, but the doers of the Law will be justified.

14 For when Gentiles who do not have the Law do [a]instinctively the things of the Law, these, not having the Law, are a law to themselves,

15 in that they show [a]the work of the Law written in their hearts, their conscience bearing witness, and their thoughts alternately accusing or else defending them,

16 on the day when, [a]according to my gospel, [b]God will judge the secrets of men through Christ Jesus.

8 [a]2 Cor. 12:20; Gal. 5:20; Phil. 1:17; 2:3; James 3:14, 16 [b]2 Thess. 2:12
★ 9-10
9 [a]Rom. 8:35 [b]Acts 3:26; Rom. 1:16; 1 Pet. 4:17
10 [a]Rom. 2:7; Heb. 2:7; 1 Pet. 1:7 [b]Rom. 2:9
11 [a]Acts 10:34
★12 [a]Acts 2:23; 1 Cor. 9:21
13 [a]Matt. 7:21, 24ff.; John 13:17; James 1:22f., 25
★14 [a]Acts 10:35; Rom. 1:19; 2:15
15 [a]Rom. 2:14, 27
16 [a]Rom. 16:25; 1 Cor. 15:1; Gal. 1:11; 1 Tim. 1:11; 2 Tim. 2:8 [b]Acts 10:42; 17:31; Rom. 3:6; 14:10

C The Condemnation of the Jew, 2:17–3:8

1 *He did not keep the law of God,* 2:17–29

17 But if you bear the name "Jew," and [a]rely upon the Law, and boast in God,

★17 [a]Mic. 3:11; John 5:45; Rom. 2:23; 9:4

18 and know *His* will, and [a]approve the things that are essential, being instructed out of the Law,

19 and are confident that you yourself are a guide to the blind, a light to those who are in darkness,

20 a corrector of the foolish, a teacher of the immature, having in the Law [a]the embodiment of knowledge and of the truth,

21 you, therefore, [a]who teach another, do you not teach yourself? You who preach that one should not steal, do you steal?

22 You who say that one should not commit adultery, do you commit adultery? You who abhor idols, do you [a]rob temples?

23 You who [a]boast in the Law, through your breaking the Law, do you dishonor God?

24 For "[a]THE NAME OF GOD IS BLASPHEMED AMONG THE GENTILES [b]BECAUSE OF YOU," just as it is written.

25 For indeed circumcision is of value, if you [a]practice the Law; but if you are a transgressor of the Law, [b]your circumcision has become uncircumcision.

26 [a]If therefore [b]the uncircumcised man [c]keeps the requirements of the Law, will not his uncircumcision be regarded as circumcision?

27 And will not [a]he who is physically uncircumcised, if he keeps the Law, will he not [b]judge you who though having the letter *of the Law* and circumcision are a transgressor of the Law?

28 For [a]he is not a Jew who is one outwardly; neither is circum-

18 [a]Phil. 1:10
20 [a]Rom. 3:31; 2 Tim. 1:13
21 [a]Matt. 23:3ff.
22 [a]Acts 19:37
23 [a]Mic. 3:11; John 5:45; Rom. 2:17; 9:4
24 [a]Is. 52:5 [b]Ezek. 36:20ff.; 2 Pet. 2:2
★25 [a]Rom. 2:13f., 27 [b]Jer. 4:4; 9:25f.
26 [a]1 Cor. 7:19 [b]Rom. 3:30; Eph. 2:11 [c]Rom. 2:25, 27; 8:4
27 [a]Rom. 3:30; Eph. 2:11 [b]Matt. 12:41
28 [a]John 8:39; Rom. 2:17; 9:6; Gal. 6:15

2:9–10 *the Jew first.* The Jews' priority of privilege was also one of responsibility, and the principles of God's judgment are the same for all (v. 11).

2:12 *without the Law.* I.e., Gentiles, to whom the Mosaic law had not been given (9:4).

2:14 *instinctively.* The interaction of conscience and innate morality may result in a good life. To such persons God sends the gospel (Acts 4:12; Rom. 10:4).

2:17 *you bear the name "Jew."* The failure of the Jew makes him culpable because of privileges he had in the law and the promises of God. He could and should have become a *guide* and *light* to those in darkness (v. 19).

2:25 *your circumcision has become uncircumcision.* I.e., a Jewish lawbreaker stands before God in the same place as a pagan. Paul emphasizes that the Jewish law was impossible to keep perfectly.

cision that which is outward in
the flesh.
29 But [a]he is a Jew who is one
inwardly; and circumcision is that
which is of the heart, by the
[b]Spirit, not by the letter; [c]and his
praise is not from men, but from
God.

★29 [a]Phil. 3:3; Col. 2:11 [b]Rom. 2:27; 7:6; 2 Cor. 3:6 [c]John 5:44; 12:43; 1 Cor. 4:5; 2 Cor. 10:18

2 *He did not believe the promises of God,* 3:1-8

★1

3 Then what advantage has the
Jew? Or what is the benefit of
circumcision?
2 Great in every respect.
First of all, that [a]they were entrusted with the [b]oracles of God.
3 What then? If [a]some did
not believe, their unbelief will not
nullify the faithfulness of God,
will it?
4 [a]May it never be! Rather,
let God be found true, though every man *be found* [b]a liar, as it is
written,

"[c]That Thou mightest be
justified in Thy words,
And mightest prevail when
Thou art judged."

5 But if our unrighteousness
[a]demonstrates the righteousness
of God, [b]what shall we say? The
God who inflicts wrath is not unrighteous, is He? ([c]I am speaking
in human terms.)
6 [a]May it never be! For otherwise how will [b]God judge the
world?
7 But if through my lie [a]the
truth of God abounded to His glory, [b]why am I also still being
judged as a sinner?
8 And why not *say* (as we
are slanderously reported and as
some affirm that we say), "[a]Let us
do evil that good may come"?
Their condemnation is just.

★ 2 [a]Deut. 4:8; Ps. 147:19; Rom. 9:4 [b]Acts 7:38
3 [a]Rom. 10:16; Heb. 4:2
★ 4 [a]Luke 20:16; Rom. 3:6, 31 [b]Ps. 116:11; Rom. 3:7 [c]Ps. 51:4
★ 5 [a]Rom. 5:8; 2 Cor. 6:4; 7:11 [Gr.]; Gal. 2:18 [Gr.] [b]Rom. 4:1; 7:7; 8:31; 9:14, 30 [c]Rom. 6:19; 1 Cor. 9:8; 15:32; Gal. 3:15
6 [a]Luke 20:16; Rom. 3:4, 31 [b]Rom. 2:16
7 [a]Rom. 3:4 [b]Rom. 9:19
8 [a]Rom. 6:1

D **The Condemnation of All Men,** 3:9-20

9 What then? [a]Are we better
than they? Not at all; for we have
already charged that both [b]Jews
and [c]Greeks are [d]all under sin;
10 as it is written,

"[a]There is none righteous,
not even one;
11 There is none who understands,
There is none who seeks for
God;
12 All have turned aside, together they have become
useless;
There is none who does
good,
There is not even one."
13 "[a]Their throat is an open
grave,
With their tongues they
keep deceiving,"
"The poison of asps is under
their lips;"
14 "[a]Whose mouth is full of
cursing and bitterness;"
15 "[a]Their feet are swift to
shed blood,
16 Destruction and misery
are in their paths,
17 And the path of peace
have they not known."

★ 9 [a]Rom. 3:1 [b]Rom. 2:1-29 [c]Rom. 1:18-32 [d]Rom. 3:19, 23; 11:32; Gal. 3:22
★10-18
10 [a]Ps. 14:1-3; 53:1-4
13 [a]Ps. 5:9; 140:3
14 [a]Ps. 10:7
15 [a]Is. 59:7f.

2:29 *circumcision is that which is of the heart.* Circumcision is used in three senses in this passage: (1) it stands for the Jews (note that *uncircumcised* in v. 27 means Gentiles; see also Gen. 17:10); (2) it indicates the physical rite commanded in the law (v. 25a and Lev. 12:3); (3) it represents a life that is separated from the flesh and unto God (v. 27 and Deut. 10:16). See note on Acts 16:3.

3:1 *advantage.* A Jew had the advantage of special revelation of God's law. Yet this could not save him, for he was not able to keep it. The law increased his responsibility, but demonstrated his inability to live up to God's standards.

3:2 *the oracles of God.* The promises of God to the Jews, found in the Scriptures.

3:4 *though every man be found a liar.* Men should believe that they all have broken their word rather than that God has broken His. See Ps. 51:4.

3:5 Does God use man's sin to glorify Himself? No, otherwise He would have to abandon all judgment.

3:9 *Are we better than they?* Possibly this should be translated, "Are we Jews disadvantaged?" i.e., in a worse position than Gentiles.

3:10-18 In these verses Paul quotes and paraphrases a number of O.T. passages, Ps. 5:9; 10:7; 14:1-3; 36:1; 140:3; Isa. 59:7-8. His indictment of the Jews has the authority of Scripture behind it.

18 [a]Ps. 36:1

18 "[a]THERE IS NO FEAR OF GOD
BEFORE THEIR EYES."

19 [a]John 10:34 [b]Rom. 2:12 [c]Rom. 3:9

19 Now we know that what-
ever the [a]Law says, it speaks to
[b]those who are under the Law,
that every mouth may be closed,
and [c]all the world may become
accountable to God;

★20 [a]Ps. 143:2; Acts 13:39; Gal. 2:16 [b]Rom. 4:15; 5:13, 20; 7:7

20 because [a]by the works of
the Law no flesh will be justified
in His sight; for [b]through the Law
comes the knowledge of sin.

III RIGHTEOUSNESS IMPUTED; JUSTIFICATION, SALVATION, 3:21–5:21

A The Description of Righteousness, 3:21–31

★21 [a]Rom. 1:17; 9:30 [b]Acts 10:43
22 [a]Rom. 1:17; 9:30 [b]Rom. 4:5 [c]Acts 3:16; Gal. 2:16 [d]Rom. 4:11, 16; 10:4 [e]Rom. 10:12; Gal. 3:28
★23 [a]Rom. 3:9
★24 [a]Rom. 4:4f., 16; Eph. 2:8 [b]1 Cor. 1:30; Eph. 1:7; Col. 1:14
★25 [a]1 John 2:2; 4:10 [b]1 Cor. 5:7; Rev. 1:5 [c]Rom. 2:4 [d]Acts 14:16; 17:30

21 But now apart from the
Law [a]*the* righteousness of God
has been manifested, being [b]wit-
nessed by the Law and the Prophets,
22 even *the* [a]righteousness of
God through [b]faith [c]in Jesus
Christ for [d]all those who believe;
for [e]there is no distinction;
23 for all [a]have sinned and
fall short of the glory of God,
24 being justified as a gift [a]by
His grace through [b]the redemption which is in Christ Jesus;
25 whom God displayed publicly as [a]a propitiation [b]in His
blood through faith. *This was* to
demonstrate His righteousness,
because in the [c]forbearance of
God He [d]passed over the sins previously committed;
26 for the demonstration, *I* ★26
say, of His righteousness at the
present time, that He might be
just and the justifier of the one
who has faith in Jesus.
27 Where then is [a]boasting? It
is excluded. By [b]what kind of law?
Of works? No, but by a law of
faith.
28 For [a]we maintain that a
man is justified by faith apart
from works of the Law.
29 Or [a]is God *the God* of Jews
only? Is He not *the God* of Gentiles also? Yes, of Gentiles also,
30 since indeed [a]God [b]who
will justify the circumcised by
faith and the uncircumcised
through faith [c]is one.
31 Do we then nullify the
Law through faith? [a]May it never
be! On the contrary, we [b]establish
the Law.

27 [a]Rom. 2:17, 23; 4:2; 1 Cor. 1:29ff. [b]Rom. 9:31
28 [a]Acts 13:39; Rom. 3:20, 21; Eph. 2:9; James 2:20, 24, 26
29 [a]Acts 10:34f.; Rom. 9:24; 10:12; 15:9; Gal. 3:28
30 [a]Rom. 10:12 [b]Rom. 3:22; 4:11f., 16; Gal. 3:8 [c]Deut. 6:4
★31 [a]Luke 20:16; Rom. 3:4 [b]Matt. 5:17; Rom. 4:3; 8:4

B The Illustration of Righteousness, 4:1–25

1 *Abraham's faith was apart from works,* 4:1–8

★ 1ff
1 [a]Rom. 1:3

4 What then shall we say that
Abraham, our forefather [a]ac-
cording to the flesh, has found?

3:20 The function of the law, Paul says, is to give knowledge of or about sin, not to save from sin (Acts 13:39; 1 Tim. 1:9–10).

3:21 *righteousness.* Used in various ways in the Bible, righteousness refers: (1) to God's character (John 17:25); (2) to the gift which is given to everyone who receives Christ (here and 5:17); and (3) to standards of right living (6:18; 2 Tim. 2:22).

3:23 *all have sinned.* Sin is defined in 1 John 3:4 as lawlessness, and here as lack of conformity to the *glory of God.* These are complementary ideas, since the law of God is an expression of His character.

3:24 *justified.* To justify was a legal term meaning to secure a favorable verdict, to acquit, to vindicate, to declare righteous (Deut. 25:1). It is an act of God (Rom. 8:33), who takes the initiative and provides the means *through the redemption which is in Christ Jesus.* The sinner who believes in Christ receives God's gift of righteousness (5:17), which then enables God to pronounce him righteous. On *redemption* see note on Eph. 1:7.

3:25 *propitiation.* Here this may mean the "place of propitiation"; i.e., the mercy seat (as in Heb. 9:5). Christ is pictured as the mercy seat where God's holy demands were satisfied (cf. Lev. 16:14). See note on Heb. 2:17. *sins previously committed.* The death of Christ also paid fully for sins committed before He died.

3:26 *that He might be just and the justifier of the one who has faith in Jesus.* Because of the death of Christ, God can remain just when declaring righteous the one who believes in Jesus and who is thus forgiven of his sins.

3:31 *we establish the Law.* The role of the law in making men conscious of sin (v. 20) is confirmed by everyone who acknowledges sin and turns to Christ in faith.

4:1ff. Paul's point in this chapter is that the faith-righteousness principle is not new, and he uses Abraham as proof.

2 [a]1 Cor. 1:31

2 For if Abraham was justified by works, he has something to boast about; but [a]not before God.

★ 3 [a]Gen. 15:6; Rom. 4:9, 22; Gal. 3:6; James 2:23

3 For what does the Scripture say? "[a]AND ABRAHAM BELIEVED GOD, AND IT WAS RECKONED TO HIM AS RIGHTEOUSNESS."

★ 4 [a]Rom. 11:6

4 Now to the one who [a]works, his wage is not reckoned as a favor but as what is due.

5 [a]John 6:29; Rom. 3:22

5 But to the one who does not work, but [a]believes in Him who justifies the ungodly, his faith is reckoned as righteousness,

6 just as David also speaks of the blessing upon the man to whom God reckons righteousness apart from works:

★ 7 [a]Ps. 32:1

7 "[a]BLESSED ARE THOSE WHOSE LAWLESS DEEDS HAVE BEEN FORGIVEN,
AND WHOSE SINS HAVE BEEN COVERED.

8 [a]Ps. 32:2 [b]2 Cor. 5:19

8 "[a]BLESSED IS THE MAN WHOSE SIN THE LORD WILL NOT [b]TAKE INTO ACCOUNT."

2 *Abraham's faith was apart from circumcision,* 4:9–12

★ 9-25
9 [a]Rom. 3:30 [b]Rom. 4:3 [c]Gen. 15:6

9 Is this blessing then upon [a]the circumcised, or upon the uncircumcised also? For [b]we say, "[c]FAITH WAS RECKONED TO ABRAHAM AS RIGHTEOUSNESS."

★10

10 How then was it reckoned? While he was circumcised, or uncircumcised? Not while circumcised, but while uncircumcised;

11 [a]Gen. 17:10f. [b]John 3:33 [c]Luke 19:9; Rom. 4:16f. [d]Rom. 3:22; 4:16

11 and he [a]received the sign of circumcision, [b]a seal of the righteousness of the faith which he had while uncircumcised, that he might be [c]the father of [d]all who believe without being circumcised, that righteousness might be reckoned to them,

12 and the father of circumcision to those who not only are of the circumcision, but who also follow in the steps of the faith of our father Abraham which he had while uncircumcised.

3 *Abraham's faith was apart from the law,* 4:13–15

13 For [a]the promise to Abraham or to his descendants [b]that he would be heir of the world was not through the Law, but through the righteousness of faith.

13 [a]Rom. 9:8; Gal. 3:16 [b]Gen. 17:4-6; 22:17f.

14 For [a]if those who are of the Law are heirs, faith is made void and the promise is nullified;

14 [a]Gal. 3:18

15 for [a]the Law brings about wrath, but [b]where there is no law, neither is there violation.

15 [a]Rom. 7:7, 10-25; 1 Cor. 15:56; Gal. 3:10 [b]Rom. 3:20

4 *Abraham's faith was in God,* 4:16–25

16 For this reason *it is* by faith, that *it might be* in accordance with [a]grace, in order that the promise may be certain to [b]all the descendants, not only to those who are of the Law, but also to those who are of the faith of Abraham, who is [c]the father of us all,

16 [a]Rom. 3:24 [b]Rom. 4:11; 9:8; 15:8 [c]Luke 19:9; Rom. 4:11

17 (as it is written, "[a]A FATHER OF MANY NATIONS HAVE I MADE YOU") in the sight of Him whom he believed, *even* God, [b]who gives life to the dead and [c]calls into being [d]that which does not exist.

★17 [a]Gen. 17:5 [b]John 5:21 [c]Is. 48:13; 51:2 [d]1 Cor. 1:28

18 In hope against hope he believed, in order that he might become [a]a father of many nations, according to that which had been spoken, "[b]SO SHALL YOUR DESCENDANTS BE."

★18 [a]Rom. 4:17 [b]Gen. 15:5

19 And without becoming weak in faith he contemplated his

★19 [a]Heb. 11:12 [b]Gen. 17:17 [c]Gen. 18:11

4:3 *Abraham* was justified by faith, not by works (Gen. 15:6).
4:4 Wages have nothing to do with grace (unmerited favor) but with what is due.
4:7 See Ps. 32:1–2.
4:9–25 The points Paul makes from the illustrations are these: (1) justification did not come to Abraham by faith plus circumcision (vv. 9–12); (2) justification was not by faith plus keeping the law (vv. 13–17); (3) justification was by faith alone (vv. 18–25).
4:10 Abraham's acceptance by God on the basis of faith preceded his circumcision (Gen. 15 is before Gen. 17).
4:17 See Gen. 17:5.
4:18 See Gen. 15:5.
4:19 Abraham fully faced the difficulty, yet he believed God.

own body, now [a]as good as dead
since [b]he was about a hundred
years old, and [c]the deadness of
Sarah's womb;
20 yet, with respect to the
promise of God, he did not waver
in unbelief, but grew strong in
faith, [a]giving glory to God,
21 and [a]being fully assured
that [b]what He had promised, He
was able also to perform.
22 Therefore also [a]IT WAS
RECKONED TO HIM AS RIGHTEOUSNESS.
23 Now [a]not for his sake only
was it written, that "IT WAS RECK-
ONED TO HIM,"
24 but for our sake also, to
whom it will be reckoned, as
those [a]who believe in Him who
[b]raised Jesus our Lord from the
dead,
25 *He* who was [a]delivered up
because of our transgressions,
and was [b]raised because of our
justification.

20 [a]Matt. 9:8
21 [a]Rom. 14:5 [b]Gen. 18:14; Heb. 11:19
22 [a]Rom. 4:3
23 [a]Rom. 15:4; 1 Cor. 9:9f.; 10:11; 2 Tim. 3:16f.
★24 [a]Rom. 10:9; 1 Pet. 1:21 [b]Acts 2:24
★25 [a]Rom. 5:6, 8; 8:32; Gal. 2:20; Eph. 5:2 [b]Rom. 5:18; 1 Cor. 15:17; 2 Cor. 5:15

C The Benefits of Righteousness, 5:1-11

5 [a]Therefore having been justified by faith, [b]we have peace
with God through our Lord Jesus
Christ,
2 through whom also we
have [a]obtained our introduction
by faith into this grace [b]in which
we stand; and we exult in hope of
the glory of God.
3 [a]And not only this, but we
also [b]exult in our tribulations,
knowing that tribulation brings
about [c]perseverance;
4 and [a]perseverance, [b]prov-
en character; and proven character, hope;
5 and hope [a]does not disap-
point, because the love of God
has been [b]poured out within our
hearts through the Holy Spirit
who was given to us.
6 For while we were still
[a]helpless, [b]at the right time
[c]Christ died for the ungodly.
7 For one will hardly die for
a righteous man; though perhaps
for the good man someone would
dare even to die.
8 But God [a]demonstrates
[b]His own love toward us, in that
while we were yet sinners, [c]Christ
died for us.
9 Much more then, having
now been justified [a]by His blood,
we shall be saved [b]from the wrath
of God through Him.
10 For if while we were [a]en-
emies, we were reconciled to God
through the death of His Son,
much more, having been reconciled, we shall be saved [b]by His
life.
11 [a]And not only this, but we
also exult in God through our
Lord Jesus Christ, through whom
we have now received [b]the reconciliation.

★ 1-11
1 [a]Rom. 3:28 [b]Rom. 5:11
★ 2 [a]Eph. 2:18; 3:12; Heb. 10:19f.; 1 Pet. 3:18 [b]1 Cor. 15:1
3 [a]Rom. 5:11; 8:23; 9:10; 2 Cor. 8:19 [b]Matt. 5:12; James 1:2f. [c]Luke 21:19
4 [a]Luke 21:19 [b]Phil. 2:22; James 1:12
5 [a]Ps. 119:116; Rom. 9:33; Heb. 6:18f. [b]Acts 2:33; 10:45; Gal. 4:6; Titus 3:6
★ 6-8
6 [a]Rom. 5:8, 10 [b]Gal. 4:4 [c]Rom. 4:25; 5:8; 8:32; Gal. 2:20; Eph. 5:2
8 [a]Rom. 3:5 [b]John 3:16; 15:13; Rom. 8:39 [c]Rom. 4:25; 5:6; 8:32; Gal. 2:20; Eph. 5:2
★ 9 [a]Rom. 3:25 [b]Rom. 1:18; 1 Thess. 1:10
★10 [a]Rom. 11:28; 2 Cor. 5:18f.; Eph. 2:3; Col. 1:21f. [b]Rom. 8:34; Heb. 7:25; 1 John 2:1
★11 [a]Rom. 5:3; 8:23; 9:10; 2 Cor. 8:19 [b]Rom. 5:10; 11:15; 2 Cor. 5:18f.

D The Applicability of Righteousness, 5:12-21

12 Therefore, just as through
[a]one man sin entered into the
world, and [b]death through sin,
and [c]so death spread to all men,
because all sinned—

★12-21
★12 [a]Gen. 2:17; 3:6, 19; Rom. 5:15, 16, 17 [b]Rom. 6:23; 1 Cor. 15:56; James 1:15 [c]Rom. 5:14, 19, 21; 1 Cor. 15:22

4:24 Saving faith is faith in the Giver of miraculous life, demonstrated in the resurrection of Jesus.

4:25 *because of our justification.* Christ's resurrection was because of our justification; i.e., as a proof of God's acceptance of His Son's sacrifice.

5:1-11 For Paul, justification is not sterile doctrine, but a source of blessing in one's life. *we have* (v. 1). Some manuscripts read "let us have."

5:2 *exult in hope of the glory of God.* Better, we boast in the hope of the glory which God will manifest.

5:6-8 The extent of God's love is shown in the fact that Christ died for men in whom there was nothing that evoked that love.

5:9 *Much more.* Note the repetition of this emphasis in vv. 10, 15, 17, 20. Paul is teaching the vicarious, sacrificial significance of Christ's death.

5:10 *we shall be saved by His life.* Christ's present resurrection ministry in heaven keeps us saved (Heb. 7:25).

5:11 *the reconciliation.* See note on 2 Cor. 5:18.

5:12-21 In the closely worded argument of this section Paul contrasts death in Adam with life in Christ. Just as Adam's sin brought certain

★13 [a]Rom. 4:15

13 for until the Law sin was in
the world; but [a]sin is not imputed
when there is no law.

14 [a]Hos. 6:7 [b]1 Cor. 15:45

14 Nevertheless death reigned
from Adam until Moses, even
over those who had not sinned [a]in
the likeness of Adam's offense,
who is a [b]type of Him who was to
come.

15 [a]Rom. 5:12, 18 [b]Rom. 5:18, 19 [c]Acts 15:11

15 But the free gift is not like
the transgression. For if by the
transgression of [a]the one [b]the
many died, much more did the
grace of God and the gift by [c]the
grace of the one Man, Jesus
Christ, abound to [b]the many.

16 [a]1 Cor. 11:32 [Gr.]

16 And the gift is not like *that*
which came through the one who
sinned; for on the one hand [a]the
judgment *arose* from one *trans-*
gression resulting in condemnation, but on the other hand the
free gift *arose* from many transgressions resulting in justification.

17 [a]Gen. 2:17; 3:6, 19; Rom. 5:12, 15, 16; 1 Cor. 15:21f. [b]2 Tim. 2:12; Rev. 22:5

17 For if by the transgression
of the one, death reigned
[a]through the one, much more
those who receive the abundance
of grace and of the gift of righteousness will [b]reign in life
through the One, Jesus Christ.

★18 [a]Rom. 5:12, 15 [b]Rom. 3:25 [c]Rom. 4:25

18 So then as through [a]one
transgression there resulted condemnation to all men, even so
through one [b]act of righteousness
there resulted [c]justification of life
to all men.

19 For as through the one
man's disobedience [a]the many
[b]were made sinners, even so
through [c]the obedience of the
One [a]the many will be made
righteous.

19 [a]Rom. 5:15, 18 [b]Rom. 5:12; 11:32 [c]Phil. 2:8

20 And [a]the Law came in that
the transgression might increase;
but where sin increased, [b]grace
abounded all the more,

20 [a]Rom. 3:20; 7:7f.; Gal. 3:19 [b]Rom. 6:1; 1 Tim. 1:14

21 that, as [a]sin reigned in
death, even so [b]grace might reign
through righteousness to eternal
life through Jesus Christ our Lord.

21 [a]Rom. 5:12, 14 [b]John 1:17; Rom. 6:23

IV RIGHTEOUSNESS IMPARTED; SANCTIFICATION, SEPARATION, 6:1–8:39

A The Principles of Sanctification; The Question of License, 6:1–23

1 Shall we continue in sin? 6:1–14

★ 1 [a]Rom. 3:5 [b]Rom. 3:8; 6:15 ★ 2 [a]Luke 20:16; Rom. 6:15 [b]Rom. 6:11; 7:4, 6; Gal. 2:19; Col. 2:20; 3:3; 1 Pet. 2:24 ★ 3 [a]Matt. 28:19 [b]Acts 2:38; 8:16; 19:5; Gal. 3:27

6 [a]What shall we say then? Are
we to [b]continue in sin that
grace might increase?

2 [a]May it never be! How
shall we who [b]died to sin still live
in it?

3 Or do you not know that
all of us who have been [a]baptized

---

results, so did the death of Christ. Yet this does not mean automatic salvation, for men must receive the *grace* God offers (v. 17).

5:12 *as through one man sin entered into the world.* After Adam sinned, he and his descendants could only beget sinners, so that all men are under the sentence of death, the penalty of sin. *all sinned.* True because of the solidarity of the race just explained (see Heb. 7:9–10).

5:13 *sin is not imputed.* I.e., sin is not charged as a specific violation of a particular command *when there is no law.* However, this does not mean that sin was not sin during the period from Adam to Moses, as proved by the fact of death during that period (v. 14). Sin could never be anything but evil.

5:18 Notice here, and often in this passage, the contrasts between Adam and Christ—between their deeds and the results of those deeds. The contrasts would lose meaning if Adam had not been an historical person.

6:1 If grace abounds in the presence of sin (5:20), then *Are we to continue in sin that grace might increase?*

6:2 *May it never be!* Grace cannot be exploited for evil ends! Because of our union with Christ we *died to sin* and are *alive to God* (v. 11). The new moral life is based on: (1) our union with Christ (6:1–14); (2) our being slaves to righteousness (6:15–23); and (3) the new marriage union we have with Christ (7:1–6). *died to sin.* Death is separation, not extinction: (1) Physical death is the separation of body from spirit (Jas. 2:26). (2) Spiritual death is the separation of a person from God (Eph. 2:1). (3) The second death is eternal separation from God (Rev. 20:14). (4) Death to sin is separation from the ruling power of sin in one's own life (Rom. 6:14).

6:3 *baptized into Christ Jesus.* Baptism with the Holy Spirit joins the believer to Christ, separating him from the old life and associating him with the new. He is no longer "in Adam" but is "in Christ." Water baptism is a reminder of this truth.

into [b]Christ Jesus have been baptized into His death?
4 Therefore we have been
[a]buried with Him through baptism into death, in order that as
Christ was [b]raised from the dead
through the [c]glory of the Father,
so we too might walk in [d]newness
of life.
5 For [a]if we have become
united with *Him* in the likeness of
His death, certainly we shall be
also *in the likeness* of His resurrection,
6 knowing this, that our [a]old
self was [b]crucified with *Him,* that
our [c]body of sin might be done
away with, that we should no
longer be slaves to sin;
7 for [a]he who has died is
freed from sin.
8 Now [a]if we have died with
Christ, we believe that we shall
also live with Him,
9 knowing that Christ, having been [a]raised from the dead, is
never to die again; [b]death no
longer is master over Him.
10 For the death that He died,
He died to sin, once for all; but
the life that He lives, He lives to
God.
11 Even so consider your-
selves to be [a]dead to sin, but alive
to God in Christ Jesus.
12 Therefore do not let sin
[a]reign in your mortal body that
you should obey its lusts,
13 and do not go on [a]present-
ing the members of your body to
sin *as* instruments of unrighteousness; but [b]present yourselves
to God as those alive from the
dead, and your members *as* instruments of righteousness to
God.

4 [a]Col. 2:12 [b]Acts 2:24; Rom. 6:9 [c]John 11:40; 2 Cor. 13:4 [d]Rom. 7:6; 2 Cor. 5:17; Gal. 6:15; Eph. 4:23f.; Col. 3:10
5 [a]2 Cor. 4:10; Phil. 3:10f.; Col. 2:12; 3:1
★ 6 [a]Eph. 4:22; Col. 3:9 [b]Gal. 2:20; 5:24; 6:14 [c]Rom. 7:24
7 [a]1 Pet. 4:1
8 [a]Rom. 6:4; 2 Cor. 4:10; 2 Tim. 2:11
9 [a]Acts 2:24; Rom. 6:4 [b]Rev. 1:18
★11 [a]Rom. 6:2; 7:4, 6; Gal. 2:19; Col. 2:20; 3:3; 1 Pet. 2:24
★12 [a]Rom. 6:14
★13 [a]Rom. 6:16, 19; 7:5; Col. 3:5 [b]Rom. 12:1; 2 Cor. 5:14f.; 1 Pet. 2:24

14 For [a]sin shall not [b]be master over you, for [c]you are not under law, but [d]under grace.

2 *Shall we continue to sin?* 6:15–23

15 What then? [a]Shall we sin
because we are not under law but
under grace? [b]May it never be!
16 Do you not [a]know that
when you present yourselves to
someone *as* [b]slaves for obedience,
you are slaves of the one whom
you obey, either of [c]sin resulting
in death, or of obedience resulting
in righteousness?
17 But [a]thanks be to God that
though you were slaves of sin,
you became obedient from the
heart to that [b]form of teaching to
which you were committed,
18 and having been [a]freed
from sin, you became slaves of
righteousness.
19 [a]I am speaking in human
terms because of the weakness of
your flesh. For just [b]as you presented your members *as* slaves to
impurity and to lawlessness, resulting in *further* lawlessness, so
now present your members *as*
slaves to righteousness, resulting
in sanctification.
20 For [a]when you were slaves
of sin, you were free in regard to
righteousness.
21 Therefore what [a]benefit
were you then deriving from the
things of which you are now
ashamed? For the outcome of
those things is [b]death.
22 But now having been
[a]freed from sin and [b]enslaved to
God, you derive your [c]benefit, re-

14 [a]Rom. 8:2, 12 [b]Rom. 6:12 [c]Rom. 5:18; 7:4, 6; Gal. 4:21 [d]Rom. 5:17, 21
★15-23
15 [a]Rom. 6:1 [b]Luke 20:16; Rom. 6:2
16 [a]Rom. 11:2; 1 Cor. 3:16; 5:6; 6:2, 3, 9, 15, 16, 19; 9:13, 24 [b]John 8:34; 2 Pet. 2:19 [c]Rom. 6:21, 23
★17 [a]Rom. 1:8; 2 Cor. 2:14 [b]2 Tim. 1:13
18 [a]John 8:32; Rom. 6:22; 8:2
★19 [a]Rom. 3:5 [b]Rom. 6:13
20 [a]Matt. 6:24; Rom. 6:16
★21 [a]Jer. 12:13; Ezek. 16:63; Rom. 7:5 [b]Rom. 1:32; 5:12; 6:16, 23; 8:6, 13; Gal. 6:8
22 [a]John 8:32; Rom. 6:18; 8:2 [b]1 Cor. 7:22; 1 Pet. 2:16 [c]Rom. 7:4 [d]1 Pet. 1:9

6:6 *old self.* I.e., all that a person is before salvation which is made "old" by reason of the presence of the new life in Christ. *done away.* I.e., made ineffective or impotent (as in 2 Thess. 2:8).

6:11 *consider.* This means "calculate," i.e., by adding up the facts presented in vv. 1–10 and then acting accordingly.

6:12 We must either dethrone sin or obey its evil desires.

6:13 *do not go on presenting the members of your body . . . but present yourselves to God.* The tenses may imply "stop presenting your members . . . but present yourselves once for all unto God."

6:15–23 This passage is the ethical application of 5:12–21. When we were in Adam sin was master, demanding shameful living and repaying with death. In Christ we can be slaves of righteousness.

6:17 *that form of teaching.* I.e., Christian truth.

6:19 Paul uses the illustration of slaves and masters because of the dullness of understanding of those to whom he wrote.

6:21 *then.* I.e., when you were slaves to sin what benefit did you have?

sulting in sanctification, and [d]the outcome, eternal life.

★23 [a]Rom. 1:32; 5:12; 6:16, 21; 8:6, 13; Gal. 6:8 [b]Matt. 25:46; Rom. 5:21; 8:39

23 For the wages of [a]sin is death, but the free gift of God is [b]eternal life in Christ Jesus our Lord.

B The Practice of Sanctification; The Question of Law, 7:1-25

1 *Is the believer under law?* 7:1-6

★ 1-6 ★ 1 [a]Rom. 1:13

7 Or do you not know, [a]brethren (for I am speaking to those who know the law), that the law has jurisdiction over a person as long as he lives?

2 [a]1 Cor. 7:39

2 For [a]the married woman is bound by law to her husband while he is living; but if her husband dies, she is released from the law concerning the husband.

3 So then if, while her husband is living, she is joined to another man, she shall be called an adulteress; but if her husband dies, she is free from the law, so that she is not an adulteress, though she is joined to another man.

★ 4 [a]Rom. 6:2; 7:6 [b]Rom. 8:2; Gal. 2:19; 5:18 [c]Col. 1:22

4 Therefore, my brethren, you also were [a]made to die [b]to the Law [c]through the body of Christ, that you might be joined to another, to Him who was raised from the dead, that we might bear fruit for God.

★ 5 [a]Rom. 8:8f.; 2 Cor. 10:3 [b]Rom. 7:7f. [c]Rom. 6:13, 21, 23

5 For while we were [a]in the flesh, the sinful passions, which were [b]*aroused* by the Law, were at work [c]in the members of our body to bear fruit for death.

6 [a]Rom. 7:2 [b]Rom. 6:2 [c]Rom. 6:4 [d]Rom. 2:29

6 But now we have been [a]released from the Law, having [b]died to that by which we were bound, so that we serve in [c]newness of [d]the Spirit and not in oldness of the letter.

2 *Is the law evil?* 7:7-12

7 [a]What shall we say then? Is the Law sin? [b]May it never be! On the contrary, [c]I would not have come to know sin except through the Law; for I would not have known about coveting if the Law had not said, "[d]YOU SHALL NOT COVET."

7 [a]Rom. 3:5 [b]Luke 20:16 [c]Rom. 3:20; 4:15; 5:20 [d]Ex. 20:17; Deut. 5:21

8 But sin, [a]taking opportunity [b]through the commandment, produced in me coveting of every kind; for [c]apart from the Law sin *is* dead.

8 [a]Rom. 7:11 [b]Rom. 3:20; 7:11 [c]1 Cor. 15:56

9 And I was once alive apart from the Law; but when the commandment came, sin became alive, and I died;

★ 9

10 and this commandment, which was [a]to result in life, proved to result in death for me;

10 [a]Lev. 18:5; Luke 10:28; Rom. 10:5; Gal. 3:12

11 for sin, [a]taking opportunity [b]through the commandment, [c]deceived me, and through it killed me.

11 [a]Rom. 7:8 [b]Rom. 3:20; 7:8 [c]Gen. 3:13

12 [a]So then, the Law is holy, and the commandment is holy and righteous and good.

★12 [a]Rom. 7:16; 1 Tim. 1:8

3 *Is the law a cause of death?* 7:13-14

13 Therefore did that which is good become *a cause of* death for me? [a]May it never be! Rather it was sin, in order that it might be shown to be sin by effecting my death through that which is good,

13 [a]Luke 20:16

6:23 *the free gift of God.* Sanctification of life does not earn eternal life; it is still God's gracious gift.

7:1-6 Paul here introduces a new metaphor, that of a fruitful marriage. The Christian, because of his death with Christ, is free from his marriage to the law and is brought into a new marriage with Christ. The new union demands good living as its progeny.

7:1 *know the law.* Legal principles, not the Mosaic law here.

7:4 The believer who has died with Christ is released from bondage to the law and hence from bondage to sin, and is free to experience the abundant life of Christ.

7:5 *while we were in the flesh.* I.e., before we were saved.

7:9 When Paul came to understand the true meaning of the Law, he realized that he was a sinner and worthy of death.

7:12 The law is fundamentally good, but the result of the law is to bring into the open the power of sin. It is sin, not the law which exposes it, that deceives and kills (v. 11).

that through the commandment
sin might become utterly sinful.
14 For we know that the Law
is [a]spiritual; but I am [a]of flesh,
[b]sold [c]into bondage to sin.

14 [a]1 Cor. 3:1 [b]1 Kin. 21:20, 25; 2 Kin. 17:17; Rom. 6:6; Gal. 4:3 [c]Rom. 3:9

4 *How can I resolve the struggle within myself?* 7:15-25

15 For that which I am doing,
[a]I do not understand; for I am not
practicing [b]what I *would* like to
do, but I am doing the very thing
I hate.
16 But if I do the very thing I
do not wish *to do,* I agree with
[a]the Law, *confessing* that it is
good.
17 So now, [a]no longer am I
the one doing it, but sin which indwells me.
18 For I know that nothing
good dwells in me, that is, in my
[a]flesh; for the wishing is present
in me, but the doing of the good
is not.
19 For [a]the good that I wish, I
do not do; but I practice the very
evil that I do not wish.
20 But if I am doing the very
thing I do not wish, [a]I am no
longer the one doing it, but sin
which dwells in me.
21 I find then [a]the principle
that evil is present in me, the one
who wishes to do good.
22 For I joyfully concur with
the law of God in [a]the inner man,
23 but I see [a]a different law in
the members of my body, waging
war against the [b]law of my mind,
and making me a prisoner of [c]the
law of sin which is in my members.
24 Wretched man that I am!
Who will set me free from [a]the
body of this [b]death?
25 [a]Thanks be to God
through Jesus Christ our Lord! So
then, on the one hand I myself
with my mind am serving the law
of God, but on the other, with my
flesh [b]the law of sin.

★15-25
15 [a]John 15:15 [b]Rom. 7:19; Gal. 5:17
16 [a]Rom. 7:12; 1 Tim. 1:8
★17 [a]Rom. 7:20
★18 [a]John 3:6; Rom. 7:25; 8:3
19 [a]Rom. 7:15
20 [a]Rom. 7:17
21 [a]Rom. 7:23, 25; 8:2
22 [a]2 Cor. 4:16; Eph. 3:16; 1 Pet. 3:4
23 [a]Rom. 6:19; Gal. 5:17; James 4:1; 1 Pet. 2:11 [b]Rom. 7:25 [c]Rom. 7:21, 25; 8:2
★24 [a]Rom. 6:6; Col. 2:11 [b]Rom. 8:2
25 [a]1 Cor. 15:57 [b]Rom. 7:21, 23; 8:2

C The Power of Sanctification; The Question of Living, 8:1-39

1 *Emancipated living,* 8:1-11

8 There is therefore now no
[a]condemnation for those who
are [b]in [c]Christ Jesus.
2 For [a]the law of the Spirit of
life in [b]Christ Jesus [c]has set you
free from the law of sin and of
death.
3 For [a]what the Law could
not do, [b]weak as it was through
the flesh, God *did:* sending His
own Son in [c]the likeness of sinful
flesh and *as an offering* for sin, He
condemned sin in the flesh,
4 in order that the [a]require-
ment of the Law might be fulfilled
in us, who [b]do not walk according
to the flesh, but according to the
Spirit.
5 For those who are according to the flesh set their minds on
[a]the things of the flesh, but those
who are according to the Spirit,
[b]the things of the Spirit.

1 [a]Rom. 5:16; 8:34 [b]Rom. 8:9f. [c]Rom. 8:2, 11, 39; 16:3
★ 2 [a]1 Cor. 15:45 [b]Rom. 8:1, 11, 39; 16:3 [c]John 8:32, 36; Rom. 6:14, 18; 7:4
★ 3 [a]Acts 13:39; Heb. 10:1ff. [b]Rom. 7:18f; Heb. 7:18 [c]Phil. 2:7; Heb. 2:14, 17; 4:15
★ 4-8
4 [a]Luke 1:6; Rom. 2:26 [b]Gal. 5:16, 25
5 [a]Gal. 5:19-21 [b]Gal. 5:22-25

7:15-25 The intensely personal character of these verses seems to indicate that this was Paul's own experience as a believer. This is his diagnosis of what happens when one tries to be sanctified by keeping the law.

7:17 *sin which indwells me.* Though Paul has written of acts of sin (1:21-32), here he speaks of sin as a disposition deep in a man's life which produces those acts.

7:18 *flesh.* Paul uses flesh in several ways. (1) It denotes the personality of man controlled by sin and directed to selfish pursuits rather than the service of God (here; v. 25; 8:5-7; Gal. 5:17). (2) It sometimes refers simply to physical descent (1:3; 9:3). (3) It also stands for the physical existence of a person, i.e., being in the body (Eph. 2:15; Philem. 16). There is no blame attached to the last two meanings of the word.

7:24 The *body* dominated by sin endures a "living" *death.*

8:2 *the law of the Spirit of life.* The working of the Holy Spirit in the life of a believer is regular (like a *law*) but not mechanical (for it is *life*).

8:3 *in the likeness of sinful flesh.* The word "likeness" is crucial, for it indicates that Jesus was a true man but not a sinful man. *flesh* = body.

8:4-8 The contrast here is between a life dominated by the flesh (= sinful nature within) and one controlled by the Holy Spirit.

6 [a]Gal. 6:8 [b]Rom. 6:21; 8:13
7 [a]James 4:4
8 [a]Rom. 7:5
★ 9 [a]Rom. 7:5 [b]John 14:23; Rom. 8:11; 1 Cor. 3:16; 6:19; 2 Cor. 6:16; 2 Tim. 1:14 [c]John 14:17; Gal. 4:6; Phil. 1:19; 1 John 4:13
10 [a]John 17:23; Gal. 2:20; Eph. 3:17; Col. 1:27
11 [a]Acts 2:24; Rom. 6:4 [b]John 5:21 [c]Rom. 8:1, 2, 39; 16:3

6 [a]For the mind set on the
flesh is [b]death, but the mind set
on the Spirit is life and peace,
7 because the mind set on
the flesh is [a]hostile toward God;
for it does not subject itself to the
law of God, for it is not even able
to do so;
8 and those who are [a]in the
flesh cannot please God.
9 However you are not [a]in
the flesh but in the Spirit, if indeed the Spirit of God [b]dwells in
you. But [c]if anyone does not have
the Spirit of Christ, he does not
belong to Him.
10 And [a]if Christ is in you,
though the body is dead because
of sin, yet the spirit is alive because of righteousness.
11 But if the Spirit of Him
who [a]raised Jesus from the dead
dwells in you, [b]He who raised
[c]Christ Jesus from the dead will
also give life to your mortal bodies through His Spirit who indwells you.

2 *Exalted living,* 8:12–17

★13 [a]Rom. 8:6 [b]Col. 3:5
14 [a]Gal. 5:18 [b]Hos. 1:10; [Rom. 9:26]; Matt. 5:9; John 1:12; Rom. 8:16, 19; 9:8; 2 Cor. 6:18; Gal. 3:26; 1 John 3:1; Rev. 21:7
★15 [a]2 Tim. 1:7; Heb. 2:15 [b]Rom. 8:23; Gal. 4:5f. [c]Mark 14:36; Gal. 4:6

12 So then, brethren, we are
under obligation, not to the flesh,
to live according to the flesh—
13 for [a]if you are living according to the flesh, you must die;
but if by the Spirit you are [b]put-
ting to death the deeds of the
body, you will live.
14 For all who are [a]being led
by the Spirit of God, these are
[b]sons of God.
15 For you [a]have not received
a spirit of slavery leading to fear
again, but you [b]have received a
spirit of adoption as sons by
which we cry out, "[c]Abba! Father!"
16 The Spirit Himself [a]bears
witness with our spirit that we are
[b]children of God,
17 and if children, [a]heirs also,
heirs of God and fellow-heirs
with Christ, [b]if indeed we suffer
with *Him* in order that we may
also be glorified with *Him.*

16 [a]Acts 5:32 [b]Hos. 1:10; [Rom. 9:26]; Matt. 5:9; John 1:12; Rom. 8:14, 19; 9:8
17 [a]Acts 20:32; Gal. 3:29; 4:7; Eph. 3:6; Titus 3:7; Heb. 1:14; Rev. 21:7 [b]2 Cor. 1:5, 7; Phil. 3:10; Col. 1:24

3 *Expectant living,* 8:18–30

★18-25
18 [a]2 Cor. 4:17; 1 Pet. 4:13 [b]Col. 3:4; Titus 2:13
19 [a]Phil. 1:20 [b]Rom. 8:18; 1 Cor. 1:7f.; Col. 3:4; 1 Pet. 1:7, 13 [c]Hos. 1:10; Matt. 5:9; John 1:12; 2 Cor. 6:18; Gal. 3:26
★20 [a]Gen. 3:17-19 [b]Ps. 39:5f.; Eccl. 1:2 [c]Gen. 3:17; 5:29
21 [a]Acts 3:21; 2 Pet. 3:13; Rev. 21:1
22 [a]Jer. 12:4, 11
★23 [a]Rom. 5:3 [b]Rom. 8:16; 2 Cor. 1:22 [c]2 Cor. 5:2, 4 [d]Rom. 8:15, 19, 25; [e]Rom. 7:24
★24 [a]Rom. 8:20; 1 Thess. 5:8; Titus 3:7 [b]Rom. 4:18; 2 Cor. 5:7

18 For I consider that the sufferings of this present time [a]are
not worthy to be compared with
the [b]glory that is to be revealed to
us.
19 For the [a]anxious longing of
the creation waits eagerly for [b]the
revealing of the [c]sons of God.
20 For the creation [a]was subjected to [b]futility, not of its own
will, but [c]because of Him who
subjected it, in hope
21 that [a]the creation itself
also will be set free from its slavery to corruption into the freedom of the glory of the children
of God.
22 For we know that the
whole creation [a]groans and suffers the pains of childbirth together until now.
23 [a]And not only this, but
also we ourselves, having [b]the
first fruits of the Spirit, even we
ourselves [c]groan within ourselves,
[d]waiting eagerly for *our* adoption
as sons, [e]the redemption of our
body.
24 For [a]in hope we have been
saved, but [b]hope that is seen is

8:9 *if indeed* = since. There is no doubt in the statement; those who belong to Christ have the Holy Spirit.

8:13 *putting to death.* I.e., separating from the deeds of the body (see Col. 3:5).

8:15 *adoption.* The act of God which places the believer in His family as an adult son (v. 23; 9:4; Gal. 4:5; Eph. 1:5). At the same time he is born into the family of God as a child who needs to grow and develop. His position is one of full privilege; his practice involves growth in grace. *Abba.* Aramaic for father.

8:18–25 A statement of the Christian hope as it affects the individual (v. 18) and the entire creation (vv. 19-25). Compare 2 Cor. 4:17.

8:20 *was subjected to futility.* After Adam sinned, God was obliged to subject the creation to futility so that man in his sinful state might retain some measure of dominion over creation. Nature was involved for evil in man's fall; she will be emancipated when man receives the adoption as sons (v. 23).

8:23 The culmination of our position as adopted sons is the resurrection state.

8:24 *in hope.* I.e., in the just-expressed hope (vv. 21-23) of the future redemption of the body.

not hope; for why does one also
hope for what he sees?
25 But [a]if we hope for what
we do not see, with perseverance
we wait eagerly for it.
26 And in the same way the
Spirit also helps our weakness; for
[a]we do not know how to pray as
we should, but [b]the Spirit Himself
intercedes for *us* with groanings
too deep for words;
27 and [a]He who searches the
hearts knows what [b]the mind of
the Spirit is, because He [c]inter-
cedes for the saints according to
the will of God.
28 And we know that God
causes [a]all things to work together for good to those who love
God, to those who are [b]called according to *His* purpose.
29 For whom He [a]foreknew,
He also [b]predestined *to become*
[c]conformed to the image of His
Son, that He might be the [d]first-
born among many brethren;
30 and whom He [a]predes-
tined, these He also [b]called; and
whom He called, these He also
[c]justified; and whom He justified,
these He also [d]glorified.

25 [a]1 Thess. 1:3
★26 [a]Matt. 20:22; 2 Cor. 12:8 [b]John 14:16; Rom. 8:15f.
27 [a]Ps. 139:1f.; Luke 16:15; Acts 1:24; Rev. 2:23 [b]Rom. 8:6 [c]Rom. 8:34
★28 [a]Rom. 8:32 [b]Rom. 8:30; 9:24; 11:29; 1 Cor. 1:9; Gal. 1:6
★29 [a]Rom. 11:2; 1 Cor. 8:3; 2 Tim. 1:9 [b]Rom. 9:23; 1 Cor. 2:7; [c]1 Cor. 15:49; Phil. 3:21; Col. 3:10; 1 John 3:2 [d]Col. 1:18
★30 [a]Rom. 9:23; 11:29; 1 Cor. 2:7; Eph. 1:5, 11 [b]Rom. 8:28; 9:24; 1 Cor. 1:9; Gal. 1:6 [c]1 Cor. 6:11 [d]John 17:22; Rom. 8:21

4 *Exultant living,* 8:31–39

31 [a]What then shall we say to
these things? [b]If God *is* for us,
who *is* against us?
32 He who [a]did not spare His
own Son, but [b]delivered Him up
for us all, how will He not also
with Him freely give us all things?
33 Who will bring a charge
against [a]God's elect? [b]God is the
one who justifies;
34 who is the one who [a]con-
demns? Christ Jesus is He who
[b]died, yes, rather who was
[c]raised, who is [d]at the right hand
of God, who also [e]intercedes for
us.
35 Who shall separate us
from [a]the love of Christ? Shall
[b]tribulation, or distress, or [c]perse-
cution, or [c]famine, or [c]nakedness,
or [c]peril, or sword?
36 Just as it is written,

"[a]For Thy sake we are being
put to death all day
long;
We were considered as
sheep to be slaughtered."

37 But in all these things we
overwhelmingly [a]conquer
through [b]Him who loved us.
38 For I am convinced that
neither [a]death, nor life, nor [b]an-
gels, nor principalities, nor
[c]things present, nor things to
come, nor powers,
39 nor height, nor depth, nor
any other created thing, shall be
able to separate us from [a]the love
of God, which is [b]in Christ Jesus
our Lord.

31 [a]Rom. 3:5; 4:1 [b]Ps. 118:6; Matt. 1:23
32 [a]John 3:16; Rom. 5:8 [b]Rom. 4:25
★33-34
33 [a]Luke 18:7 [b]Is. 50:8f.
34 [a]Rom. 8:1 [b]Rom. 5:6f. [c]Acts 2:24 [d]Mark 16:19 [e]Rom. 8:27; Heb. 7:25; 9:24; 1 John 2:1
35 [a]Rom. 8:37f. [b]Rom. 2:9; 2 Cor. 4:8 [c]1 Cor. 4:11; 2 Cor. 11:26f.
★36 [a]Ps. 44:22; Acts 20:24; 1 Cor. 4:9; 15:30f.; 2 Cor. 1:9; 4:10f.; 6:9; 11:23
37 [a]John 16:33; 1 Cor. 15:57 [b]Gal. 2:20; Eph. 5:2; Rev. 1:5
38 [a]1 Cor. 3:22 [b]1 Cor. 15:24; Eph. 1:21; 1 Pet. 3:22 [c]1 Cor. 3:22
★39 [a]Rom. 5:8 [b]Rom. 8:1

V RIGHTEOUSNESS VINDICATED; DISPENSATION, SOVEREIGNTY, 9:1–11:36

A Israel's Past; Election, 9:1–29

1 *Paul's sorrow,* 9:1–5

9 [a]I am telling the truth in
Christ, I am not lying, my

★ 1 [a]Rom. 1:9; 2 Cor. 11:10; Gal. 1:20; 1 Tim. 2:7

8:26 The Holy Spirit helps our *weakness* (our inability to pray intelligently about situations) by praying with unutterable *groanings* (= sighs). Such intercession is in accord with God's will (v. 27).

8:28 A promise only for *those who love God.*

8:29 *predestined.* See note on Eph. 1:5. The destiny of the elect is to be conformed to Christ.

8:30 *called.* See note on 1:6. *justified.* See note on 3:24. *glorified.* The tense of this word shows that our future glorification is so certain that it can be said to be accomplished. Those who were foreknown will all be glorified without loss of a single one.

8:33–34 The Father has declared us righteous; therefore, He will not condemn us. Christ died, rose, and lives for us; therefore neither will He condemn us.

8:36 Difficulties are not necessarily obstacles for God's children, but His appointed way.

8:39 *nor any other created thing.* Nothing in the universe is outside God's control; therefore, nothing can separate us from His eternal love.

9:1 Here begins Paul's discussion of perplexing questions about the Jewish people. Why were they refusing the gospel? How does this new scheme of righteousness apart from the law relate to the privileged position of the Jews? Have the promises contained in their covenants failed?

conscience bearing me witness in
the Holy Spirit,
2 that I have great sorrow
and unceasing grief in my heart.
3 For [a]I could wish that I
myself were [b]accursed, *separated*
from Christ for the sake of my
brethren, my kinsmen [c]according
to the flesh,
4 who are [a]Israelites, to
whom belongs [b]the adoption as
sons and [c]the glory and [d]the covenants and [e]the giving of the Law
and [f]the *temple* service and [g]the
promises,
5 whose are [a]the fathers, and
[b]from whom is the Christ according to the flesh, [c]who is over all,
[d]God [e]blessed forever. Amen.

2 *God's sovereignty,* 9:6–29

6 But *it is* not as though [a]the
word of God has failed. [b]For they
are not all Israel who are *de-*
scended from Israel;
7 neither are they all children [a]because they are Abraham's descendants, but:
"[b]THROUGH ISAAC YOUR DESCENDANTS
WILL BE NAMED."
8 That is, it is not the children of the flesh who are [a]chil-
dren of God, but the [b]children of
the promise are regarded as descendants.
9 For this is a word of promise: "[a]AT THIS TIME I WILL COME, AND
SARAH SHALL HAVE A SON."
10 [a]And not only this, but
there was [b]Rebekah also, when
she had conceived *twins* by one
man, our father Isaac;

3 [a]Ex. 32:32 [b]1 Cor. 12:3; 16:22; Gal. 1:8f. [c]Rom. 1:3; 11:14; Eph. 6:5
★ 4-5
4 [a]Rom. 9:6 [b]Ex. 4:22; Rom. 8:15 [c]Ex. 40:34; 1 Kin. 8:11; Ezek. 1:28; Heb. 9:5 [d]Gen. 17:2; Deut. 29:14; Luke 1:72; Acts 3:25; Eph. 2:12 [e]Deut. 4:13f.; Ps. 147:19 [f]Deut. 7:6; 14:1f.; Heb. 9:1, 6 [g]Acts 2:39; 13:32; Eph. 2:12
★ 5 [a]Acts 3:13; Rom. 11:28 [b]Matt. 1:1-16; Rom. 1:3 [c]Col. 1:16-19 [d]John 1:1; Col. 2:9 [e]Rom. 1:25
6 [a]Num. 23:19 [b]John 1:47; Rom. 2:28f.; Gal. 6:16
7 [a]John 8:33, 39; Gal. 4:23 [b]Gen. 21:12; Heb. 11:18
8 [a]Rom. 8:14 [b]Rom. 4:13, 16; Gal. 3:29; 4:28; Heb. 11:11
★ 9 [a]Gen. 18:10
10 [a]Rom. 5:3 [b]Gen. 25:21

11 for though *the twins* were
not yet born, and had not done
anything good or bad, in order
that [a]God's purpose according to
His choice might stand, not because of works, but because of
Him who calls,
12 it was said to her, "[a]THE
OLDER WILL SERVE THE YOUNGER."
13 Just as it is written, "[a]JACOB
I LOVED, BUT ESAU I HATED."
14 [a]What shall we say then?
[b]There is no injustice with God, is
there? [c]May it never be!
15 For He says to Moses, "[a]I
WILL HAVE MERCY ON WHOM I HAVE
MERCY, AND I WILL HAVE COMPASSION
ON WHOM I HAVE COMPASSION."
16 So then it *does* not *depend*
on the man who wills or the man
who [a]runs, but on [b]God who has
mercy.
17 For the Scripture says to
Pharaoh, "[a]FOR THIS VERY PURPOSE I
RAISED YOU UP, TO DEMONSTRATE MY
POWER IN YOU, AND THAT MY NAME
MIGHT BE PROCLAIMED THROUGHOUT
THE WHOLE EARTH."
18 So then He has mercy on
whom He desires, and He [a]hard-
ens whom He desires.
19 [a]You will say to me then,
"[b]Why does He still find fault?
For [c]who resists His will?"
20 On the contrary, who are
you, [a]O man, who [b]answers back
to God? [c]The thing molded will
not say to the molder, "Why did
you make me like this," will it?
21 Or does not the potter
have a right over the clay, to
make from the same lump one

11 [a]Rom. 4:17; 8:28
★12 [a]Gen. 25:23
★13 [a]Mal. 1:2f.
14 [a]Rom. 3:5 [b]2 Chr. 19:7; Rom. 2:11 [c]Luke 20:16
★15 [a]Ex. 33:19
16 [a]Gal. 2:2 [b]Eph. 2:8
17 [a]Ex. 9:16
18 [a]Ex. 4:21; 7:3; 9:12; 10:20, 27; 11:10; 14:4, 17; Deut. 2:30; Josh. 11:20; John 12:40; Rom. 11:7, 25
★19 [a]Rom. 11:19; 1 Cor. 15:35; James 2:18 [b]Rom. 3:7 [c]2 Chr. 20:6; Job 9:12; Dan. 4:35
20 [a]Rom. 2:1 [b]Job 33:13 [c]Is. 29:16; 45:9; 64:8; Jer. 18:6; Rom. 9:22f.; 2 Tim. 2:20

9:4-5 The privileges of the Jewish people included adoption as a nation (Ex. 4:22), glory (Ex. 16:10), covenants (Eph. 2:12), the Mosaic Law, service in the tabernacle and temple, thousands of promises, the patriarchs, and Christ.

9:5 *who is over all . . . Amen.* Some regard these words as comprising a grammatically separate sentence, a doxology. Although early manuscripts were not punctuated, the punctuation in the present text seems correct. Paul's anguish over the Jew's rejection of Christ drives him to avow his own recognition of Him as God. A doxology does not fit the train of thought here.

9:9 See Gen. 18:10.

9:12 See Gen. 25:23.

9:13 See Mal. 1:2-3.

9:15 See Ex. 33:19. If God were not free to show His mercy, no one would be blessed, for no one deserves His grace, and it cannot be earned.

9:19 An opponent might say that Paul's conclusion in v. 18 leads to fatalism. Paul, however, does not give an analytical answer but rebukes the questioner for such a preposterous conclusion. If a potter can do what he wishes with his vessels, certainly God can with His.

vessel for honorable use, and another for common use?

22 [a]Rom. 2:4 [b]Prov. 16:4; 1 Pet. 2:8

22 What if God, although
willing to demonstrate His wrath
and to make His power known,
endured with much [a]patience vessels of wrath [b]prepared for destruction?

23 [a]Rom. 2:4; Eph. 3:16 [b]Acts 9:15 [c]Rom. 8:29f.

23 And *He did so* in order
that He might make known [a]the
riches of His glory upon [b]vessels
of mercy, which He [c]prepared beforehand for glory,

24 [a]Rom. 8:28 [b]Rom. 3:29

24 *even* us, whom He also
[a]called, [b]not from among Jews
only, but also from among Gentiles.

★25 [a]Hos. 2:23; 1 Pet. 2:10

25 As He says also in Hosea,

"[a]I WILL CALL THOSE WHO WERE
NOT MY PEOPLE, 'MY PEO-
PLE,'
AND HER WHO WAS NOT BE-
LOVED, 'BELOVED.'"

26 [a]Hos. 1:10 [b]Matt. 16:16

26 "[a]AND IT SHALL BE THAT IN
THE PLACE WHERE IT WAS
SAID TO THEM, 'YOU ARE
NOT MY PEOPLE,'
THERE THEY SHALL BE CALLED
SONS OF [b]THE LIVING GOD."

★27 [a]Is. 10:22 [b]Gen. 22:17; Hos. 1:10 [c]Rom. 11:5

27 And Isaiah cries out con-
cerning Israel, "[a]THOUGH THE NUM-
BER OF THE SONS OF ISRAEL BE [b]AS THE
SAND OF THE SEA, IT IS [c]THE REMNANT
THAT WILL BE SAVED;

28 [a]Is. 10:23

28 [a]FOR THE LORD WILL EXECUTE
HIS WORD UPON THE EARTH, THOR-
OUGHLY AND QUICKLY."

★29 [a]Is. 1:9 [b]James 5:4 [c]Deut. 29:23; Is. 13:19; Jer. 49:18; 50:40; Amos 4:11

29 And just as Isaiah foretold,

"[a]EXCEPT [b]THE LORD OF SABA-
OTH HAD LEFT TO US A POS-
TERITY,
[c]WE WOULD HAVE BECOME AS
SODOM, AND WOULD HAVE
RESEMBLED GOMORRAH."

B Israel's Present; Rejection, 9:30–10:21

30 [a]Rom. 9:14 [b]Rom. 1:17; 3:21f.; 10:6; Gal. 2:16; 3:24; Phil. 3:9; Heb. 11:7

30 [a]What shall we say then?
That Gentiles, who did not pursue righteousness, attained righteousness, even [b]the righteousness
which is by faith;

31 [a]Is. 51:1; Rom. 9:30; 10:2f., 20; 11:7 [b]Gal. 5:4

31 but Israel, [a]pursuing a law
of righteousness, did not [b]arrive
at *that* law.

32 [a]Is. 8:14; 1 Pet. 2:6, 8

32 Why? Because *they did* not
pursue it by faith, but as though
it were by works. They stumbled
over [a]THE STUMBLING STONE,

★33 [a]Is. 28:16 [b]Rom. 10:11 [c]Rom. 5:5

33 just as it is written,

"[a]BEHOLD, I LAY IN ZION A
STONE OF STUMBLING AND A
ROCK OF OFFENSE,
[b]AND HE WHO BELIEVES IN
HIM [c]WILL NOT BE DISAP-
POINTED."

★ 1-21

10 Brethren, my heart's desire and my prayer to God
for them is for *their* salvation.

2 [a]Acts 21:20

2 For I bear them witness
that they have [a]a zeal for God,
but not in accordance with
knowledge.

3 [a]Rom. 1:17 [b]Is. 51:1; Rom. 8:30; 10:2f., 20; 11:7

3 For not knowing about
[a]God's righteousness, and [b]seek-
ing to establish their own, they
did not subject themselves to the
righteousness of God.

★ 4 [a]Rom. 7:1-4; Gal. 3:24; 4:5 [b]Rom. 3:22

4 For [a]Christ is the end of
the law for righteousness to [b]ev-
eryone who believes.

5 [a]Lev. 18:5; Neh. 9:29; Ezek. 20:11, 13, 21; Rom. 7:10

5 For Moses writes that the
man who practices the righteousness which is based on law [a]shall
live by that righteousness.

★ 6-8 6 [a]Rom. 9:30 [b]Deut. 30:12f.

6 But [a]the righteousness
based on faith speaks thus, "[b]DO
NOT SAY IN YOUR HEART, 'WHO WILL

9:25 See Hos. 1:9-10.
9:27 See Isa. 10:22-23.
9:29 See Isa. 1:9.
9:33 See Isa. 28:16. The stumbling-stone was Christ (1 Pet. 2:8).
10:1-21 Paul expresses his deep longing for the salvation of Israel (v. 1), who tried to substitute law-righteousness for faith-righteousness (vv. 2-4), though the latter was universally available (vv. 5-13). God gave the Jews every opportunity to receive the gospel but they had not responded in faith (vv. 14-21).
10:4 Christ is the termination of the law. It could not provide righteousness based on merit, but Christ provides righteousness based on God's grace in response to faith (3:20; Acts 13:39).
10:6-8 Quoting Deut. 30:12-14, which emphasizes the initiative of divine grace and humble reception of God's word, Paul applies this truth to the gospel, which is *near*, ready for a man to take on his lips and into his heart (Rom. 10:9).

ASCEND INTO HEAVEN?' (that is, to bring Christ down),

7 [a]Luke 8:31 [b]Heb. 13:20

7 or 'WHO WILL DESCEND INTO THE [a]ABYSS?' (that is, to [b]bring Christ up from the dead)."

8 [a]Deut. 30:14

8 But what does it say? "[a]THE WORD IS NEAR YOU, IN YOUR MOUTH AND IN YOUR HEART"—that is, the word of faith which we are preaching,

★ 9 [a]Matt. 10:32; Luke 12:8; Rom. 14:9; 1 Cor. 12:3; Phil. 2:11 [b]Acts 16:31; Rom. 4:24 [c]Acts 2:24

9 that [a]if you confess with your mouth Jesus *as* Lord, and [b]believe in your heart that [c]God raised Him from the dead, you shall be saved;

10 for with the heart man believes, resulting in righteousness, and with the mouth he confesses, resulting in salvation.

★11 [a]Is. 28:16; Rom. 9:33

11 For the Scripture says, "[a]WHOEVER BELIEVES IN HIM WILL NOT BE DISAPPOINTED."

12 [a]Rom. 3:22, 29 [b]Acts 10:36 [c]Rom. 3:29

12 For [a]there is no distinction between Jew and Greek; for the same *Lord* is [b]Lord of [c]all, abounding in riches for all who call upon Him;

★13 [a]Joel 2:32; Acts 2:21

13 for "[a]WHOEVER WILL CALL UPON THE NAME OF THE LORD WILL BE SAVED."

★14-15 14 [a]Eph. 2:17; 4:21 [b]Acts 8:31; Titus 1:3

14 How then shall they call upon Him in whom they have not believed? And how shall they believe in Him [a]whom they have not heard? And how shall they hear without [b]a preacher?

15 [a]Is. 52:7 [b]Rom. 1:15; 15:20

15 And how shall they preach unless they are sent? Just as it is written, "[a]HOW BEAUTIFUL ARE THE FEET OF THOSE WHO [b]BRING GLAD TIDINGS OF GOOD THINGS!"

★16 [a]Rom. 3:3 [b]Is. 53:1; John 12:38

16 However, they [a]did not all heed the glad tidings; for Isaiah says, "[b]LORD, WHO HAS BELIEVED OUR REPORT?"

★17 [a]Gal. 3:2, 5 [b]Col. 3:16

17 So faith *comes* from [a]hearing, and hearing by [b]the word of Christ.

★18 [a]Ps. 19:4; Rom. 1:8; Col. 1:6, 23; 1 Thess. 1:8

18 But I say, surely they have never heard, have they? Indeed they have:

"[a]THEIR VOICE HAS GONE OUT
INTO ALL THE EARTH,
AND THEIR WORDS TO THE
ENDS OF THE WORLD."

★19 [a]Deut. 32:21 [b]Rom. 11:11, 14

19 But I say, surely Israel did not know, did they? At the first Moses says,

"[a]I WILL [b]MAKE YOU JEALOUS
BY THAT WHICH IS NOT A
NATION,
BY A NATION WITHOUT UNDERSTANDING WILL I ANGER
YOU."

★20 [a]Is. 65:1; Rom. 9:30

20 And Isaiah is very bold and says,

"[a]I WAS FOUND BY THOSE WHO
SOUGHT ME NOT,
I BECAME MANIFEST TO THOSE
WHO DID NOT ASK FOR
ME."

21 [a]Is. 65:2

21 But as for Israel He says, "[a]ALL THE DAY LONG I HAVE STRETCHED OUT MY HANDS TO A DISOBEDIENT AND OBSTINATE PEOPLE."

C Israel's Future; Salvation, 11:1–36

1 *The extent of Israel's rejection (partial),* 11:1–10

★ 1-36 1 [a]1 Sam. 12:22; Jer. 31:37; 33:24-26 [b]Luke 20:16 [c]2 Cor. 11:22; Phil. 3:5

11 I say then, God has not [a]rejected His people, has He? [b]May it never be! For [c]I too

---

10:9 *Jesus as Lord.* Lord, or Yahweh, is the O.T. name for God; thus he who confesses that Jesus is Lord affirms His deity.
10:11 See Isa. 28:16; 49:23.
10:13 See Joel 2:32.
10:14-15 Though God's election of His people is of His own free choice and not based on human merit (9:11, 23), the elect are not saved without believing the message which is preached by those who are sent (Isa. 52:7).
10:16 See Isa. 53:1.
10:17 *by the word of Christ.* The spoken word rather than the written Word (Bible). Our oral testimony (our preaching of Christ) is, of course, based on the Bible.
10:18 See Ps. 19:4.
10:19 See Deut. 32:21.
10:20 See Isa. 65:1-2.
11:1-36 In this chapter Paul assures us that God has not forgotten His people, the Jews, and His promises to them. After the full number of Gentiles have been incorporated into the Church, all Jews will turn to the Lord, not a mere handful as now. Paul does not assert that the O.T. promises to Israel have been transferred to the largely Gentile Church.

am an Israelite, a descendant of
Abraham, of the tribe of Benjamin.
2 God [a]has not rejected His
people whom He [b]foreknew. [c]Or
do you not know what the Scripture says in *the passage about* Elijah, how he pleads with God
against Israel?

2 [a]Ps. 94:14 [b]Rom. 8:29 [c]Rom. 6:16

3 "Lord, [a]THEY HAVE KILLED THY
PROPHETS, THEY HAVE TORN DOWN
THINE ALTARS, AND I ALONE AM LEFT,
AND THEY ARE SEEKING MY LIFE."

★ 3 [a]1 Kin. 19:10

4 But what is the divine re-
sponse to him? "[a]I HAVE KEPT for
Myself SEVEN THOUSAND MEN WHO
HAVE NOT BOWED THE KNEE TO BAAL."

4 [a]1 Kin. 19:18

5 In the same way then,
there has also come to be at the
present time [a]a remnant according to *God's* gracious choice.

5 [a]2 Kin. 19:4; Rom. 9:27

6 But [a]if it is by grace, it is
no longer on the basis of works,
otherwise grace is no longer
grace.

6 [a]Rom. 4:4

7 What then? That which
[a]Israel is seeking for, it has not
obtained, but those who were
chosen obtained it, and the rest
were [b]hardened;

★ 7 [a]Rom. 9:31 [b]Mark 6:52; Rom. 9:18; 11:25; 2 Cor. 3:14

8 just as it is written,

"[a]GOD GAVE THEM A SPIRIT OF
STUPOR,
EYES TO SEE NOT AND EARS TO
HEAR NOT,
DOWN TO THIS VERY DAY."

8 [a]Deut. 29:4; Is. 29:10; Matt. 13:13f.

9 And David says,

"[a]LET THEIR TABLE BECOME A
SNARE AND A TRAP,
AND A STUMBLING BLOCK AND
A RETRIBUTION TO THEM.

★ 9 [a]Ps. 69:22f.

10 "[a]LET THEIR EYES BE DARK-
ENED TO SEE NOT,
AND BEND THEIR BACKS FOR-
EVER."

10 [a]Ps. 69:23

2 The purpose of Israel's rejection, 11:11-24

11 [a]I say then, they did not
stumble so as to fall, did they?
[b]May it never be! But by their
transgression [c]salvation *has come*
to the Gentiles, to [d]make them
jealous.

11 [a]Rom. 11:1 [b]Luke 20:16 [c]Acts 28:28 [d]Rom. 11:14

12 Now if their transgression
be riches for the world and their
failure be riches for the Gentiles,
how much more will their [a]fulfill-
ment be!

12 [a]Rom. 11:25

13 But I am speaking to you
who are Gentiles. Inasmuch then
as [a]I am an apostle of Gentiles, I
magnify my ministry,

13 [a]Acts 9:15

14 if somehow I might [a]move
to jealousy [b]my fellow-country-
men and [c]save some of them.

14 [a]Rom. 11:11 [b]Gen. 29:14; 2 Sam. 19:12f.; Rom. 9:3 [c]1 Cor. 1:21; 7:16; 9:22; 1 Tim. 1:15; 2:4; 2 Tim. 1:9; Titus 3:5

15 For if their rejection be the
[a]reconciliation of the world, what
will *their* acceptance be but [b]life
from the dead?

★15 [a]Rom. 5:11 [b]Luke 15:24, 32

16 And if the [a]first piece *of*
dough be holy, the lump is also;
and if the root be holy, the
branches are too.

16 [a]Num. 15:18ff.; Neh. 10:37; Ezek. 44:30

17 But if some of the
[a]branches were broken off, and
[b]you, being a wild olive, were
grafted in among them and became partaker with them of the
rich root of the olive tree,

★17-24
17 [a]Jer. 11:16; John 15:2 [b]Eph. 2:11ff.

18 do not be arrogant toward
the branches; but if you are arrogant, *remember that* [a]it is not you
who supports the root, but the
root *supports* you.

18 [a]John 4:22

19 [a]You will say then,
"Branches were broken off so that
I might be grafted in."

19 [a]Rom. 9:19

20 Quite right, they were broken off for their unbelief, and you

20 [a]Rom. 5:2; 1 Cor. 10:12; 2 Cor. 1:24 [b]Rom. 12:16; 1 Tim. 6:17; 1 Pet. 1:17

11:3 See 1 Kings 19:10-18.

11:7 *those who were chosen.* I.e., the elect minority of Jews who are being saved today.

11:9 See Ps. 69:22-23.

11:15 When Israel rejected Jesus Christ, the nation lost her favored position before God, and the gospel was then preached also to Gentiles. Hopefully the Jews would become jealous and be saved (v. 11). But the casting off is only temporary. When the Lord returns, the Jewish people will be regathered, judged, restored to favor, and redeemed (v. 26).

11:17-24 The olive tree is the place of privilege which was first occupied by the natural branches (the Jews). The wild branches are Gentiles who, because of the unbelief of Israel, now occupy the place of privilege. The root of the tree is the Abrahamic covenant which promised blessing to both Jew and Gentile through Christ.

[a]stand *only* by your faith. [b]Do not
be conceited, but fear;
21 for if God did not spare the
natural branches, neither will He
spare you.

22 [a]Rom. 2:4 [b]1 Cor. 15:2; Heb. 3:6, 14 [c]John 15:2

22 Behold then the kindness
and severity of God; to those who
fell, severity, but to you, God's
[a]kindness, [b]if you continue in His
kindness; otherwise you also [c]will
be cut off.

23 [a]2 Cor. 3:16

23 And they also, [a]if they do
not continue in their unbelief,
will be grafted in; for God is able
to graft them in again.
24 For if you were cut off
from what is by nature a wild olive tree, and were grafted contrary to nature into a cultivated
olive tree, how much more shall
these who are the natural
branches be grafted into their
own olive tree?

3 *The duration of Israel's rejection (temporary),* 11:25-32

★25 [a]Rom. 1:13 [b]Matt. 13:11; Rom. 16:25; 1 Cor. 2:7-10; Eph. 3:3-5, 9 [c]Rom. 12:16 [d]Rom. 11:7 [e]Luke 21:24; John 10:16; Rom. 11:12
★26 [a]Is. 59:20, 21

25 For [a]I do not want you,
brethren, to be uninformed of
this [b]mystery, lest you be [c]wise in
your own estimation, that a partial [d]hardening has happened to
Israel until the [e]fulness of the
Gentiles has come in;
26 and thus all Israel will be
saved; just as it is written,

"[a]The Deliverer will come
from Zion,
He will remove ungodliness
from Jacob."

27 [a]Is. 27:9; Heb. 8:10, 12

27 "[a]And this is My covenant
with them,
When I take away their
sins."

28 [a]Rom. 5:10 [b]Deut. 7:8; 10:15; Rom. 9:5

28 From the standpoint of the
gospel they are [a]enemies for your
sake, but from the standpoint of
God's choice they are beloved for
[b]the sake of the fathers;
29 for the gifts and the [a]call-
ing of God [b]are irrevocable.
30 For just as you once were
disobedient to God but now have
been shown mercy because of
their disobedience,
31 so these also now have
been disobedient, in order that
because of the mercy shown to
you they also may now be shown
mercy.

29 [a]Rom. 8:28; 1 Cor. 1:26; Eph. 1:18; 4:1, 4; Phil. 3:14; 2 Thess. 1:11; 2 Tim. 1:9; Heb. 3:1; 2 Pet. 1:10 [b]Heb. 7:21

32 For [a]God has shut up all in
disobedience that He might show
mercy to all.

★32 [a]Rom. 3:9; Gal. 3:22f.

4 *Discourse on God's wisdom,* 11:33-36

33 Oh, the depth of [a]the
riches both of the [b]wisdom and
knowledge of God! [c]How un-
searchable are His judgments and
unfathomable His ways!
34 For [a]who has known the
mind of the Lord, or who became
His counselor?
35 Or [a]who has first given to
Him that it might be paid back to
him again?
36 For [a]from Him and
through Him and to Him are all
things. [b]To Him *be* the glory forever. Amen.

33 [a]Rom. 2:4; Eph. 3:8 [b]Eph. 3:10; Col. 2:3 [c]Job 5:9; 11:7; 15:8
34 [a]Is. 40:13f.; 1 Cor. 2:16
35 [a]Job 35:7; 41:11
★36 [a]1 Cor. 8:6; 11:12; Col. 1:16; Heb. 2:10 [b]Rom. 16:27; Eph. 3:21; Phil. 4:20; 1 Tim. 1:17; 2 Tim. 4:18; 1 Pet. 4:11; 5:11; 2 Pet. 3:18; Jude 25; Rev. 1:6; 5:13; 7:12

VI RIGHTEOUSNESS PRACTICED; APPLICATION, SERVICE, 12:1-15:13

A In Relation to Ourselves, 12:1-2

12 [a]I urge you therefore,
brethren, by the mercies
of God, to [b]present your bodies a
living and holy sacrifice, acceptable to God, *which is* your spiritual service of worship.
2 And do not [a]be conformed

★ 1 [a]1 Cor. 1:10; 2 Cor. 10:2; Eph. 4:1; 1 Pet. 2:11 [b]Rom. 6:13, 16, 19
★ 2 [a]1 Pet. 1:14 [b]Matt. 13:22 [c]Eph. 4:23; Titus 3:5 [d]Eph. 5:10, 17

11:25 *the fulness of the Gentiles.* I.e., the full number of Gentiles who will be saved (Acts 15:14). After this, God will turn again to the Jews and will save "all Israel" at the Lord's return (v. 26).
11:26 See Isa. 59:20-21.
11:32 *all . . . all.* I.e., Jews and Gentiles alike.
11:36 God is the source *(from Him),* sustainer *(through Him),* and goal *(to Him)* of all things.
12:1 *by the mercies of God,* which have been described in the preceding chapters.
12:2 *do not be conformed.* I.e., do not live according to the style or manner of this present age, but live as if the new age had already arrived. The only other occurrence of this Greek word in the N.T. is in 1 Pet. 1:14.

to [b]this world, but be transformed by the [c]renewing of your mind, that you may [d]prove what the will of God is, that which is good and acceptable and perfect.

B In Relation to the Church, 12:3–8

3 For through [a]the grace given to me I say to every man among you [b]not to think more highly of himself than he ought to think; but to think so as to have sound judgment, as God has allotted to [c]each a measure of faith.

4 For [a]just as we have many members in one body and all the members do not have the same function,

5 so we, [a]who are many, are [b]one body in Christ, and individually members one of another.

6 And since we have gifts that [a]differ according to the grace given to us, *let each exercise them accordingly:* if [b]prophecy, according to the proportion of his faith;

7 if [a]service, in his serving; or he who [b]teaches, in his teaching;

8 or he who [a]exhorts, in his exhortation; he who gives, with [b]liberality; [c]he who leads, with diligence; he who shows mercy, with [d]cheerfulness.

★ **3** [a]Rom. 1:5; 15:15; 1 Cor. 3:10; 15:10; Gal. 2:9; Eph. 3:7f. [b]Rom. 11:20; 12:16 [c]1 Cor. 7:17; 2 Cor. 10:13; Eph. 4:7; 1 Pet. 4:11
★ **4** [a]1 Cor. 12:12-14; Eph. 4:4, 16
5 [a]1 Cor. 10:17, 33 [b]1 Cor. 12:20, 27; Eph. 4:12, 25
★ **6** [a]Rom. 12:3; 1 Cor. 7:7; 12:4; 1 Pet. 4:10f. [b]Acts 13:1; 1 Cor. 12:10
7 [a]Acts 6:1; 1 Cor. 12:5, 28 [b]Acts 13:1; 1 Cor. 12:28; 14:26
8 [a]Acts 4:36; 11:23; 13:15 [b]2 Cor. 8:2; 9:11, 13 [c]1 Cor. 12:28; 1 Tim. 5:17 [d]2 Cor. 9:7

C In Relation to Society, 12:9–21

9 Let [a]love be without hypocrisy. [b]Abhor what is evil; cling to what is good.

10 Be [a]devoted to one another in brotherly love; give preference to one another [b]in honor;

11 not lagging behind in diligence, [a]fervent in spirit, [b]serving the Lord;

12 [a]rejoicing in hope, [b]persevering in tribulation, [c]devoted to prayer,

13 [a]contributing to the needs of the saints, [b]practicing hospitality.

14 [a]Bless those who persecute you; bless and curse not.

15 [a]Rejoice with those who rejoice, and weep with those who weep.

16 [a]Be of the same mind toward one another; do not be haughty in mind, [b]but associate with the lowly. [c]Do not be wise in your own estimation.

17 [a]Never pay back evil for evil to anyone. [b]Respect what is right in the sight of all men.

18 If possible, [a]so far as it depends on you, [b]be at peace with all men.

19 [a]Never take your own revenge, beloved, but leave room for the wrath *of God,* for it is written, "[b]VENGEANCE IS MINE, I WILL REPAY, SAYS THE LORD."

20 "[a]BUT IF YOUR ENEMY IS HUNGRY, FEED HIM, AND IF HE IS THIRSTY, GIVE HIM A DRINK; FOR [b]IN SO DOING YOU WILL HEAP BURNING COALS UPON HIS HEAD."

21 Do not be overcome by evil, but overcome evil with good.

9 [a]2 Cor. 6:6; 1 Tim. 1:5 [b]1 Thess. 5:21f.
10 [a]John 13:34; 1 Thess. 4:9; Heb. 13:1; 2 Pet. 1:7 [b]Rom. 13:7; Phil. 2:3; 1 Pet. 2:17
★**11** [a]Acts 18:25 [b]Acts 20:19
12 [a]Rom. 5:2 [b]Heb. 10:32, 36 [c]Acts 1:14
13 [a]Rom. 15:25; 1 Cor. 16:15; 2 Cor. 9:1; Heb. 6:10 [b]Matt. 25:35; 1 Tim. 3:2
14 [a]Matt. 5:44; Luke 6:28; 1 Cor. 4:12
15 [a]Job 30:25; Heb. 13:3
16 [a]Rom. 15:5; 2 Cor. 13:11; Phil. 2:2; 4:2; 1 Pet. 3:8 [b]Rom. 11:20; 12:3 [c]Prov. 3:7; Rom. 11:25
17 [a]Prov. 20:22; 24:29; Rom. 12:19 [b]2 Cor. 8:21
18 [a]Rom. 1:15 [b]Mark 9:50; Rom. 14:19
★**19** [a]Prov. 20:22; 24:29; Rom. 12:17 [b]Deut. 32:35; Ps. 94:1; 1 Thess. 4:6; Heb. 10:30
20 [a]Prov. 25:21f.; Matt. 5:44; Luke 6:27 [b]2 Kin. 6:22

D In Relation to Government, 13:1–14

13 Let every [a]person be in [b]subjection to the governing authorities. For [c]there is no authority except from God, and those which exist are established by God.

★ **1** [a]Acts 2:41 [b]Titus 3:1; 1 Pet. 2:13f. [c]Dan. 2:21; 4:17; John 19:11

12:3 In introducing the subject of the use of spiritual gifts, Paul warns against high-mindedness and exhorts sober-mindedness, based on the *measure of faith* to work for God which has been given each one.

12:4 *one body.* For this concept see the note on 1 Cor. 12:12–31.

12:6 *gifts.* On spiritual gifts see note on 1 Cor. 1:7. *according to the proportion of his faith;* i.e., the revelations that come through the prophet must be in agreement with the body of truth already revealed.

12:11 *not lagging behind in diligence* = Do not let your zeal slacken. *fervent in* = boiling with.

12:19 See Deut. 32:35.

13:1 *be in subjection.* From the same Greek verb used by Paul in Tit. 3:1 and by Peter in 1

2 Therefore he who resists
authority has opposed the ordinance of God; and they who have
opposed will receive condemnation upon themselves.
3 For [a]rulers are not a cause
of fear for good behavior, but for
evil. Do you want to have no fear
of authority? Do what is good,
and you will have praise from the
same;
4 for it is a minister of God
to you for good. But if you do
what is evil, be afraid; for it does
not bear the sword for nothing;
for it is a minister of God, an [a]a-
venger who brings wrath upon
the one who practices evil.
5 Wherefore it is necessary
to be in subjection, not only because of wrath, but also [a]for conscience' sake.
6 For because of this you
also pay taxes, for *rulers* are servants of God, devoting themselves to this very thing.
7 [a]Render to all what is due
them: [b]tax to whom tax *is due;*
[c]custom to whom custom; fear to
whom fear; honor to whom hon-
or.
8 Owe nothing to anyone
except to love one another; for
[a]he who loves his neighbor has
fulfilled *the* law.
9 For this, "[a]YOU SHALL NOT
COMMIT ADULTERY, YOU SHALL NOT
MURDER, YOU SHALL NOT STEAL, YOU
SHALL NOT COVET," and if there is
any other commandment, it is
summed up in this saying, "[b]YOU
SHALL LOVE YOUR NEIGHBOR AS YOUR-
SELF."
10 Love does no wrong to a
neighbor; [a]love therefore is the
fulfillment of *the* law.
11 And this *do,* knowing the
time, that it is [a]already the hour
for you to [b]awaken from sleep;
for now salvation is nearer to us
than when we believed.
12 [a]The night is almost gone,
and [b]the day is at hand. Let us
therefore lay aside [c]the deeds of
darkness and put on [d]the armor
of light.
13 Let us [a]behave properly as
in the day, [b]not in carousing and
drunkenness, not in sexual pro-
miscuity and sensuality, not in
strife and jealousy.
14 But [a]put on the Lord Jesus
Christ, and make no provision for
the flesh [b]in regard to *its* lusts.

3 [a]1 Pet. 2:14
★ 4 [a]1 Thess. 4:6
5 [a]Eccl. 8; 1 Pet. 2:13, 19
7 [a]Matt. 22:21 [b]Luke 20:22; 23:2 [c]Matt. 17:25
★ 8 [a]Matt. 7:12; 22:39f.; John 13:34; Rom. 13:10; Gal. 5:14; James 2:8
★ 9 [a]Ex. 20:13ff.; Deut. 5:17ff. [b]Lev. 19:18; Matt. 19:19
10 [a]Matt. 7:12; 22:39f.; John 13:34; Rom. 13:8; Gal. 5:14; James 2:8
★11 [a]1 Cor. 7:29f.; 10:11; James 5:8; 1 Pet. 4:7 [b]Mark 13:37; 1 Cor. 15:34
12 [a]1 Cor. 7:29f.; 10:11; James 5:8; 1 Pet. 4:7; 2 Pet. 3:9, 11; 1 John 2:18; Rev. 1:3; 22:10 [b]Heb. 10:25; 1 John 2:8; Rev. 1:3; 22:10 [c]Eph. 5:11 [d]2 Cor. 6:7; 10:4
13 [a]1 Thess. 4:12 [b]Luke 21:34; Gal. 5:21
★14 [a]Job 29:14; Gal. 3:27; Eph. 4:24 [b]Gal. 5:16; 1 Pet. 2:11

E In Relation to Other Believers, 14:1–15:13

1 *Do not judge one another,* 14:1–12

14 Now [a]accept the one who
is [b]weak in faith, *but* not
for *the purpose of* passing judgment on his opinions.
2 [a]One man has faith that he
may eat all things, but he who is
[b]weak eats vegetables *only.*
3 Let not him who eats [a]re-
gard with contempt him who does

★ 1-12
★ 1 [a]Acts 28:2; Rom. 11:15; 14:3; 15:7 [b]Rom. 14:2; 15:1
2 [a]Rom. 14:14 [b]Rom. 14:1; 15:1
3 [a]Luke 18:9; Rom. 14:10 [b]Rom. 14:10, 13 [c]Acts 28:2; Rom. 11:15

Pet. 2:13, where essentially the same view of the individual's proper attitude to the state is set forth. *there is no authority except from God.* This does not say that only certain forms of government are ordained of God. God established and upholds the principle of government even though some governments do not fulfill His desires.

13:4 *it does not bear the sword for nothing.* God has given the state the power of life and death over its subjects in order to maintain order. Therefore, one should hold government in healthy respect.

13:8 Love is a debt one can never fully discharge.

13:9 See Ex. 20:13–17; Lev. 19:18.

13:11 *from sleep.* I.e., out of insensitivity to sin. *salvation.*The future culmination of our salvation at the return of the Lord is nearer every day.

13:14 An illustration of obedience to this command is in Acts 19:19.

14:1-12 Paul here discusses the proper attitude Christians should have toward each other in debatable areas of conduct (things which are not clearly stated to be wrong). He says that we are not to judge one another, in such matters, because God has received both the weaker and stronger believer (vv. 1–3), because we can differ in good conscience (vv. 4–6), and because we shall all be judged by the Lord (vv. 7–12).

14:1 *weak in faith.* I.e., one who does not yet have full knowledge of how to live as a Christian. In this case it is one who eats only *vegetables,* v. 2, and not meat.

not eat, and let not him who does
not eat [b]judge him who eats, for
God has [c]accepted him.

4 [a]Rom. 9:20; James 4:12

4 [a]Who are you to judge the
servant of another? To his own
master he stands or falls; and
stand he will, for the Lord is able
to make him stand.

5 [a]Gal. 4:10 [b]Luke 1:1; Rom. 4:21; 14:23

5 [a]One man regards one day
above another, another regards
every day *alike.* Let each man be
[b]fully convinced in his own mind.

6 [a]Matt. 14:19; 1 Cor. 10:30; 1 Tim. 4:3f.

6 He who observes the day,
observes it for the Lord, and he
who eats, does so for the Lord, for
he [a]gives thanks to God; and he
who eats not, for the Lord he does
not eat, and gives thanks to God.

7 [a]Rom. 8:38; 2 Cor. 5:15; Gal. 2:20; Phil. 1:20f.

7 For not one of us [a]lives for
himself, and not one dies for himself;

8 [a]Luke 20:38; Phil. 1:20; 1 Thess. 5:10; Rev. 14:13

8 for if we live, we live for
the Lord, or if we die, we die for
the Lord; therefore [a]whether we
live or die, we are the Lord's.

9 [a]Rev. 1:18; 2:8 [b]Matt. 28:18; John 12:24; Phil. 2:11; 1 Thess. 5:10

9 For to this end [a]Christ died
and lived *again,* that He might be
[b]Lord both of the dead and of the
living.

★10 [a]Luke 18:9; Rom. 14:3 [b]Rom. 2:16; 2 Cor. 5:10

10 But you, why do you judge
your brother? Or you again, why
do you [a]regard your brother with
contempt? For [b]we shall all stand
before the judgment seat of God.

11 [a]Is. 45:23 [b]Phil. 2:10f.

11 For it is written,

"[a]AS I LIVE, SAYS THE LORD,
[b]EVERY KNEE SHALL BOW TO
ME,
AND EVERY TONGUE SHALL
GIVE PRAISE TO GOD."

12 [a]Matt. 12:36; 16:27; 1 Pet. 4:5

12 So then [a]each one of us
shall give account of himself to
God.

2 *Do not hinder one another,* 14:13–23

★13 [a]Matt. 7:1; Rom. 14:3 [b]1 Cor. 8:13

13 Therefore let us not [a]judge
one another any more, but rather
determine this — [b]not to put an
obstacle or a stumbling block in a
brother's way.

★14 [a]Acts 10:15; Rom. 14:2, 20 [b]1 Cor. 8:7

14 I know and am convinced
in the Lord Jesus that [a]nothing is
unclean in itself; but to him who
[b]thinks anything to be unclean, to
him it is unclean.

15 [a]Eph. 5:2 [b]Rom. 14:20; 1 Cor. 8:11

15 For if because of food your
brother is hurt, you are no longer
[a]walking according to love. [b]Do
not destroy with your food him
for whom Christ died.

16 [a]1 Cor. 10:30; Titus 2:5

16 Therefore [a]do not let what
is for you a good thing be spoken
of as evil;

17 [a]1 Cor. 8:8 [b]Rom. 15:13; Gal. 5:22

17 for the kingdom of God [a]is
not eating and drinking, but
righteousness and [b]peace and [b]joy
in the Holy Spirit.

18 [a]Rom. 16:18 [b]2 Cor. 8:21; Phil. 4:8; 1 Pet. 2:12

18 For he who in this *way*
[a]serves Christ is [b]acceptable to
God and approved by men.

19 [a]Ps. 34:14; Rom. 12:18; 1 Cor. 7:15; 2 Tim. 2:22; Heb. 12:14 [b]Rom. 15:2; 1 Cor. 10:23; 14:3f., 26; 2 Cor. 12:19; Eph. 4:12, 29

19 So then let us [a]pursue the
things which make for peace and
the [b]building up of one another.

20 [a]Rom. 14:15 [b]Acts 10:15; Rom. 14:2, 14 [c]1 Cor. 8:9-12

20 [a]Do not tear down the
work of God for the sake of food.
[b]All things indeed are clean, but
[c]they are evil for the man who
eats and gives offense.

21 [a]1 Cor. 8:13

21 [a]It is good not to eat meat
or to drink wine, or *to do anything* by which your brother
stumbles.

★22 [a]1 John 3:21

22 The faith which you have,
have as your own conviction before God. Happy is he who [a]does
not condemn himself in what he
approves.

23 [a]Rom. 14:5

23 But [a]he who doubts is condemned if he eats, because *his
eating is* not from faith; and
whatever is not from faith is sin.

3 *Do imitate Christ,* 15:1–13

1 [a]Rom. 14:1; Gal. 6:2; 1 Thess. 5:14

15 Now we who are strong
ought to bear the weak-

14:10 *the judgment seat of God.* See 1 Cor. 3:10–15; 2 Cor. 5:10.

14:13 *stumbling block.* I.e., temptation to sin.

14:14 *unclean.* This refers to foods not permitted by the law (Lev. 11). Though these restrictions no longer applied (Rom. 14:20), some immature believers still applied them to their own lives. The mature brother is exhorted to abstain from those foods and also from wine, so as not to be a hindrance to his less mature brothers (v. 21). Abstention, though one may personally think it unnecessary, is better than placing temptation in a brother's way.

14:22 *faith.* I.e., a conviction or standard in regard to these matters. Every believer should have standards, but should see that they are used to help others, never to hinder them (15:2).

nesses of [a]those without strength
and not *just* please ourselves.

2 [a]1 Cor. 9:22; 10:24, 33; 2 Cor. 13:9 [b]Rom. 14:19; 1 Cor. 10:23; 14:3f., 26; 2 Cor. 12:19; Eph. 4:12, 29

2 Let each of us [a]please his
neighbor for his good, to his [b]edi-
fication.

★ 3 [a]2 Cor. 8:9 [b]Ps. 69:9

3 For even [a]Christ did not
please Himself; but as it is written, "[b]THE REPROACHES OF THOSE
WHO REPROACHED THEE FELL UPON
ME."

4 [a]Rom. 4:23f.; 2 Tim. 3:16

4 For [a]whatever was written
in earlier times was written for
our instruction, that through perseverance and the encouragement
of the Scriptures we might have
hope.

5 [a]2 Cor. 1:3 [b]Rom. 12:16

5 Now may the [a]God who
gives perseverance and encouragement grant you [b]to be of the
same mind with one another according to Christ Jesus;

6 [a]Rev. 1:6

6 that with one accord you
may with one voice glorify [a]the
God and Father of our Lord Jesus
Christ.

7 [a]Rom. 14:1

7 Wherefore, [a]accept one
another, just as Christ also accepted us to the glory of God.

★ 8 [a]Matt. 15:24; Acts 3:26 [b]Rom. 4:16; 2 Cor. 1:20

8 For I say that Christ has
become a servant to [a]the circumcision on behalf of the truth of
God to confirm [b]the promises *giv-
en* to the fathers,

★ 9-12
9 [a]Rom. 3:29; 11:30 [b]Matt. 9:8 [c]2 Sam. 22:50; Ps. 18:49

9 and for [a]the Gentiles to
[b]glorify God for His mercy; as it is
written,

> "[c]THEREFORE I WILL GIVE PRAISE TO THEE AMONG THE GENTILES,
> AND I WILL SING TO THY NAME."

10 [a]Deut. 32:43

10 And again he says,

> "[a]REJOICE, O GENTILES, WITH HIS PEOPLE."

11 [a]Ps. 117:1

11 And again,

> "[a]PRAISE THE LORD ALL YOU GENTILES,
> AND LET ALL THE PEOPLES PRAISE HIM."

12 And again Isaiah says,

12 [a]Is. 11:10 [b]Rev. 5:5; 22:16 [c]Matt. 12:21

> "[a]THERE SHALL COME [b]THE ROOT OF JESSE,
> AND HE WHO ARISES TO RULE OVER THE GENTILES,
> [c]IN HIM SHALL THE GENTILES HOPE."

13 Now may the God of hope
fill you with all [a]joy and peace in
believing, that you may abound
in hope [b]by the power of the Holy
Spirit.

13 [a]Rom. 14:17 [b]Rom. 15:19; 1 Cor. 2:4; 1 Thess. 1:5

VII PERSONAL MESSAGES AND BENEDICTION, 15:14–16:27

A Paul's Plans, 15:14–33

14 And concerning you, my
brethren, I myself also am convinced that you yourselves are
full of [a]goodness, filled with [b]all
knowledge, and able also to admonish one another.

14 [a]Eph. 5:9; 2 Thess. 1:11 [b]1 Cor. 1:5; 8:1, 7, 10; 12:8; 13:2

15 But I have written very
boldly to you on some points, so
as to remind you again, because
of [a]the grace that was given me
from God,

15 [a]Rom. 12:3

16 to be [a]a minister of Christ
Jesus to the Gentiles, ministering
as a priest the [b]gospel of God,
that *my* [c]offering of the Gentiles
might become acceptable, sanctified by the Holy Spirit.

★16 [a]Acts 9:15; Rom. 11:13 [b]Rom. 1:1; 15:19, 20 [c]Rom. 12:1; Eph. 5:2; Phil. 2:17

17 Therefore in Christ Jesus I
have found [a]reason for boasting
in [b]things pertaining to God.

17 [a]Phil. 3:3 [b]Heb. 2:17; 5:1

18 For I will not presume to
speak of anything except what
[a]Christ has accomplished through
me, resulting in the obedience of
the Gentiles by word and deed,

18 [a]Acts 15:12; 21:19; Rom. 1:5; 2 Cor. 3:5

19 in the power of [a]signs and
[a]wonders, [b]in the power of the
Spirit; so that [c]from Jerusalem
and round about as [d]far as Illyricum I have fully preached the
gospel of Christ.

★19 [a]John 4:48 [b]Rom. 15:13; 1 Cor. 2:4; 1 Thess. 1:5 [c]Acts 22:17-21 [d]Acts 20:1f.

15:3 By pointing to the example of Christ and quoting from Psalm 69:9, Paul answers the question, Why should I restrict myself?

15:8 *a servant to the circumcision.* Jesus ministered to his fellow-Jews.

15:9-12 All the quotations in these verses (see marg. refs.) are from the Greek version of the O.T.

15:16 *to the Gentiles.* See Gal. 2:9.

15:19 *Illyricum.* The eastern shore of the Adriatic (present-day Yugoslavia).

★20 [a]Rom. 1:15; 10:15; 15:16 [b]1 Cor. 3:10; 2 Cor. 10:15f.

20 And thus I aspired to [a]preach the gospel, not where Christ was *already* named, [b]that I might not build upon another man's foundation;

21 [a]Is. 52:15

21 but as it is written,

"[a]THEY WHO HAD NO NEWS OF HIM SHALL SEE,
AND THEY WHO HAVE NOT HEARD SHALL UNDERSTAND."

22 [a]Rom. 1:13; 1 Thess. 2:18

22 For this reason [a]I have often been hindered from coming to you;

★23 [a]Acts 19:21; Rom. 1:10f.; 15:29, 32

23 but now, with no further place for me in these regions, and since I [a]have had for many years a longing to come to you

24 [a]Rom. 15:28 [b]Acts 15:3 [c]Rom. 1:12

24 whenever I [a]go to Spain — for I hope to see you in passing, and to be [b]helped on my way there by you, when I have first [c]enjoyed your company for a while —

★25 [a]Acts 19:21 [b]Acts 24:17

25 but now, [a]I am going to Jerusalem [b]serving the saints.

26 [a]Acts 16:9; 1 Cor. 16:5; 2 Cor. 1:16; 2:13; 7:5; 8:1; 9:2, 4; 11:9; Phil. 4:15; 1 Thess. 1:7f.; 4:10; 1 Tim. 1:3 [b]Acts 18:12; 19:21

26 For [a]Macedonia and [b]Achaia have been pleased to make a contribution for the poor among the saints in Jerusalem.

27 [a]1 Cor. 9:11

27 Yes, they were pleased *to do so,* and they are indebted to them. For [a]if the Gentiles have shared in their spiritual things, they are indebted to minister to them also in material things.

★28 [a]John 3:33 [b]Rom. 15:24

28 Therefore, when I have finished this, and [a]have put my seal on this fruit of theirs, I will [b]go on by way of you to Spain.

29 [a]Acts 19:21; Rom. 1:10f.; 15:23, 32

29 And I know that when [a]I come to you, I will come in the fulness of the blessing of Christ.

30 [a]Gal. 5:22; Col. 1:8 [b]2 Cor. 1:11; Col. 4:12

30 Now I urge you, brethren, by our Lord Jesus Christ and by [a]the love of the Spirit, to [b]strive together with me in your prayers to God for me,

31 [a]2 Cor. 1:10; 2 Thess. 3:2; 2 Tim. 3:11; 4:17 [b]Rom. 15:25f.; 2 Cor. 8:4; 9:1 [c]Acts 9:13, 15

31 that I may be [a]delivered from those who are disobedient in Judea, and *that* my [b]service for Jerusalem may prove acceptable to the [c]saints;

32 [a]Rom. 15:23 [b]Acts 18:21; Rom. 1:10

32 so that [a]I may come to you in joy by [b]the will of God and find *refreshing* rest in your company.

33 [a]Rom. 16:20; 2 Cor. 13:11; Phil. 4:9; 1 Thess. 5:23

33 Now [a]the God of peace be with you all. Amen.

B Paul's Personal Greetings, 16:1–16

★ 1 [a]2 Cor. 3:1 [b]Acts 18:18

16 I [a]commend to you our sister Phoebe, who is a servant of the church which is at [b]Cenchrea;

2 [a]Phil. 2:29 [b]Acts 9:13, 15

2 that you [a]receive her in the Lord in a manner worthy of the [b]saints, and that you help her in whatever matter she may have need of you; for she herself has also been a helper of many, and of myself as well.

★ 3 [a]Acts 18:2 [b]Rom. 8:1ff.; 16:7, 9, 10; 2 Cor. 5:17; 12:2; Gal. 1:22 [c]Rom. 8:1

3 Greet [a]Prisca and [a]Aquila, my fellow-workers [b]in [c]Christ Jesus,

4 who for my life risked their own necks, to whom not only do I give thanks, but also all the churches of the Gentiles;

★ 5 [a]1 Cor. 16:19; Col. 4:15; Philem. 2 [b]1 Cor. 16:15 [c]Acts 16:6

5 also *greet* [a]the church that is in their house. Greet Epaenetus, my beloved, who is the [b]first convert to Christ from [c]Asia.

6 Greet Mary, who has worked hard for you.

15:20 *not where Christ was already named.* I.e., where Christ was unknown.

15:23 *no further place.* I.e., no more opportunity to preach Christ where He was unknown. Therefore, Paul proposed to go to Spain, stopping off in Rome on his way (v. 24).

15:25 *serving.* I.e., taking the money that had been collected in Greece (see 2 Cor. 8–9).

15:28 *this fruit.* I.e., the money he was collecting.

16:1 *Phoebe. . . a servant of the church.* The word here translated "servant" is often translated "deacon," which leads some to believe that Phoebe was a deaconess. However, the word is more likely used here in an unofficial sense of helper. *Cenchrea.* The eastern port of Corinth.

16:3 *Prisca and Aquila.* See Acts 18:2, 26; 1 Cor. 16:19; 2 Tim 4:19. Just how they risked their lives for Paul (Rom. 16:4), he does not say.

16:5 *the church that is in their house.* Early congregations met in homes (1 Cor. 16:19; Col. 4:15; Philem. 2). The several house churches in one city would constitute the church in that city (1 Cor. 1:2).

7 Greet Andronicus and Ju-
nias, my [a]kinsmen, and my [b]fel-
low prisoners, who are outstanding among the apostles, who also
were [c]in Christ before me.
8 Greet Ampliatus, my be-
loved in the Lord.
9 Greet Urbanus, our fellow-
worker [a]in Christ, and Stachys
my beloved.
10 Greet Apelles, the ap-
proved [a]in Christ. Greet [b]those
who are of the *household* of Aris-
tobulus.
11 Greet Herodion, my [a]kins-
man. [b]Greet those of the *household* of Narcissus, who are in the
Lord.
12 Greet Tryphaena and Try-
phosa, workers in the Lord. Greet
Persis the beloved, who has
worked hard in the Lord.
13 Greet [a]Rufus, a choice
man in the Lord, also his mother
and mine.
14 Greet Asyncritus, Phlegon,
Hermes, Patrobas, Hermas and
the brethren with them.
15 Greet Philologus and Julia,
Nereus and his sister, and Olym-
pas, and all [a]the saints who are
with them.
16 [a]Greet one another with a
holy kiss. All the churches of
Christ greet you.

★ 7 aRom. 9:3; 16:11, 21 bCol. 4:10; Philem. 23 cRom. 8:1ff.; 16:3, 9, 10; 2 Cor. 5:17; 12:2; Gal. 1:22
9 aRom. 8:1ff.; 16:3, 7, 10; 2 Cor. 5:17; 12:2; Gal. 1:22
10 aRom. 8:1ff.; 16:3, 7, 9; 2 Cor. 5:17; 12:2; Gal. 1:22 b1 Cor. 1:11
11 aRom. 9:3; 16:7, 21 b1 Cor. 1:11
13 aMark 15:21
15 aRom. 16:2, 14
16 a1 Cor. 16:20; 2 Cor. 13:12; 1 Thess. 5:26; 1 Pet. 5:14

C Paul's Concluding Admonition and Benediction, 16:17–27

17 Now I urge you, brethren,
keep your eye on those who cause
dissensions and hindrances [a]con-
trary to the teaching which you
learned, and [b]turn away from
them.
18 For such men are [a]slaves
not of our Lord Christ but of
[b]their own appetites; and by their
[c]smooth and flattering speech
they deceive the hearts of the un-
suspecting.
19 For the report of your obedience [a]has reached to all; therefore I am rejoicing over you, but
[b]I want you to be wise in what is
good, and innocent in what is evil.
20 And [a]the God of peace will
soon crush [b]Satan under your
feet.
[c]The grace of our Lord Jesus be
with you.
21 [a]Timothy my fellow-
worker greets you; and *so do* [b]Lu-
cius and [c]Jason and [d]Sosipater,
my [e]kinsmen.
22 I, Tertius, who [a]write this
letter, greet you in the Lord.
23 [a]Gaius, host to me and to
the whole church, greets you. [b]E-
rastus, the city treasurer greets
you, and Quartus, the brother.
24 [The grace of our Lord
Jesus Christ be with you all.
Amen.]
25 [a]Now to Him who is able
to establish you [b]according to my
gospel and the preaching of Jesus
Christ, according to the revelation
of [c]the mystery which has been
kept secret for [d]long ages past,
26 but now is manifested, and
by [a]the Scriptures of the prophets, according to the commandment of the eternal God, has been
made known to all the nations,
leading to [b]obedience of faith;
27 to the only wise God,
through Jesus Christ, [a]be the glory forever. Amen.

17 a1 Tim. 1:3; 6:3 bMatt. 7:15; Gal. 1:8f.; 2 Thess. 3:6, 14; Titus 3:10; 2 John 10
18 aRom. 14:18 bPhil. 3:19 cCol. 2:4; 2 Pet. 2:3
★19 aRom. 1:8 bJer. 4:22; Matt. 10:16; 1 Cor. 14:20
20 aRom. 15:33 bMatt. 4:10 c1 Cor. 16:23; 2 Cor. 13:14; Gal. 6:18; Phil. 4:23; 1 Thess. 5:28; 2 Thess. 3:18; Rev. 22:21
★21 aActs 16:1 bActs 13:1 [?] cActs 17:5 [?] dActs 20:4 [?] eRom. 9:3; 16:7, 11
★22 a1 Cor. 16:21; Gal. 6:11; Col. 4:18; 2 Thess. 3:17; Philem. 19
★23 aActs 20:4 [?]; 1 Cor. 1:14 bActs 19:22
★24
★25 aEph. 3:20; Jude 24 bRom. 2:16 cMatt. 13:35; Rom. 11:25; 1 Cor. 2:1, 7; 4:1; Eph. 1:9; 3:3, 9; 6:19; Col. 1:26f.; 2:2; 4:3; 1 Tim. 3:16 d2 Tim. 1:9; Titus 1:2
26 aRom. 1:2 bRom. 1:5
27 aRom. 11:36

16:7 *outstanding among the apostles.* Better, well-known to the apostles.

16:19 *innocent in what is evil.* I.e., guileless. The believer should not mix with evil; rather, he should be knowledgeable about good things.

16:21 *my kinsmen.* Not relatives, but fellow countrymen (also v. 7).

16:22 *Tertius.* Paul's stenographer.

16:23 *Gaius.* Presumably the Gaius of 1 Cor. 1:14, whom Paul had baptized. *Erastus'* name has been found on a pavement which he donated to Corinth.

16:24 Many manuscripts do not contain this verse.

16:25 *the mystery.* A definition of a scriptural mystery: something unknown in times past but revealed in the N.T. See note on Eph. 3:3.

INTRODUCTION TO THE FIRST LETTER OF PAUL TO THE CORINTHIANS

AUTHOR: Paul DATE: 56

The City of Corinth *Located on the narrow isthmus between the Aegean and Adriatic Seas, Corinth was a port city and wealthy commercial center. Ships wanting to avoid the dangerous trip around the southern tip of Greece were dragged across that isthmus. The city boasted an outdoor theater that accommodated 20,000 people; athletic games second only to the Olympics; a Greek, Roman, and Oriental population; and the great temple of Aphrodite with its 1,000 prostitutes. The immoral condition of Corinth is vividly seen in the fact that the Greek term* Korinthiazomai *(literally, to act the Corinthian) came to mean "to practice fornication." There were taverns on the south side of the marketplace, and many drinking vessels have been dug up from those liquor lockers. Corinth was noted for everything sinful.*

The Church in Corinth *The gospel was first preached in Corinth by Paul on his second missionary journey (A.D. 50). While living and working with Aquila and Priscilla, he preached in the synagogue until opposition forced him to move next door, to the house of Titius Justus. The Jews accused him before the Roman governor Gallio but the charge was dismissed, and Paul remained 18 months in the city (Acts 18:1-17; 1 Cor. 2:3). After leaving, Paul wrote the church a letter which has been lost (5:9), but disturbing news about the believers and questions they asked Paul in a letter they sent to him (7:1) prompted the writing of 1 Corinthians. Problems there included divisions in the church (1:11), immorality (chap. 5; 6:9-20), and the questions concerning marriage, food, worship, and the resurrection. Aberrant beliefs and practices of an astonishing variety characterized this church.*

Place of Writing *This letter was written from Ephesus (16:8).*

Contents *The letter is largely practical in emphasis, dealing with spiritual and moral problems and questions. It is a casebook of pastoral theology. Important emphases include: the judgment seat of Christ (3:11-15), the temple of the Holy Spirit (6:19-20), the glory of God (10:31), the Lord's Supper (11:23-34), love (chap. 13), the exercise of gifts (chaps. 12-14), and resurrection (chap. 15).*

OUTLINE OF 1 CORINTHIANS

I. Introduction, 1:1-9
- A. The Salutation, 1:1-3
- B. The Expression of Thanks, 1:4-9

II. Divisions in the Church, 1:10-4:21
- A. The Fact of Divisions, 1:10-17
- B. The Causes of Divisions, 1:18-2:16
  1. The misunderstanding of God's message of the cross, 1:18-2:5
  2. The misunderstanding of the Spirit's ministry of revealing, 2:6-16
- C. The Consequences of Divisions, 3:1-4:5
  1. Spiritual growth is stunted, 3:1-9
  2. Rewards will be lost, 3:10-4:5
- D. The Example of Paul, 4:6-21

III. Moral Disorders in the Church, 5:1-6:20
- A. The Case of Incest, 5:1-13
  1. The problem stated, 5:1-2
  2. The punishment prescribed, 5:3-13
- B. The Problem of Litigation in Heathen Courts, 6:1-8
- C. The Warning against Moral Laxity, 6:9-20

IV. Discussion Concerning Marriage, 7:1-40
- A. Marriage and Celibacy, 7:1-9
- B. Marriage and Divorce, 7:10-24
- C. Marriage and Christian Service, 7:25-38
- D. Marriage and Remarriage, 7:39-40

V. Discussion Concerning Food Offered to Idols, 8:1-11:1
- A. Enquiry: May a Christian Eat Food Consecrated to a Pagan God? 8:1-13
- B. Example of Paul, 9:1-27
  1. Paul's rights, 9:1-14
  2. Paul's restrictions, 9:15-27
- C. Exhortations, 10:1-11:1
  1. Avoid self-indulgence, 10:1-13
  2. Do not participate in idol feasts, 10:14-22
  3. Glorify God by seeking the welfare of your brother, 10:23-11:1

VI. Discussion Concerning Public Worship, 11:2-14:40
- A. The Veiling of Women, 11:2-16
- B. The Lord's Supper, 11:17-34
- C. The Use of Spiritual Gifts, 12:1-14:40
  1. The varieties of gifts, 12:1-11
  2. The purpose of gifts: unity in diversity, 12:12-31

3. The supremacy of love over gifts, 13:1-13
4. The superiority of prophecy over tongues, 14:1-25
5. The regulations for the use of gifts, 14:26-40

VII. The Doctrine of the Resurrection, 15:1-58
A. The Importance of the Resurrection, 15:1-11
B. The Consequences of Denying the Resurrection, 15:12-19
C. The Christian Hope, 15:20-34
D. The Resurrection Body, 15:35-50
E. The Christian's Victory through Christ, 15:51-58

VIII. Practical and Personal Matters, 16:1-24
A. The Collection for the Saints in Jerusalem, 16:1-4
B. The Planned Visit of Paul, 16:5-9
C. Exhortations, Greetings, and Benediction, 16:10-24

THE FIRST LETTER OF PAUL TO THE CORINTHIANS

I INTRODUCTION, 1:1-9

A The Salutation, 1:1-3

1 Paul, [a]called *as* an apostle of
Jesus Christ by [b]the will of
God, and [c]Sosthenes our [d]broth-
er,
2 to [a]the church of God
which is at [b]Corinth, to those who
have been sanctified in Christ
Jesus, saints [c]by calling, with all
who in every place [d]call upon the
name of our Lord Jesus Christ,
their *Lord* and ours:
3 [a]Grace to you and peace
from God our Father and the Lord
Jesus Christ.

★ 1 [a]Rom. 1:1 [b]Rom. 1:10; 15:32; 2 Cor. 1:1; 8:5; Eph. 1:1; Col. 1:1; 2 Tim. 1:1 [c]Acts 18:17 [d]Acts 1:15
★ 2 [a]1 Cor. 10:32 [b]Acts 18:1 [c]Rom. 1:7; 8:28 [d]Acts 7:59
3 [a]Rom. 1:7

B The Expression of Thanks, 1:4-9

4 [a]I thank my God always
concerning you, for the grace of
God which was given you in
Christ Jesus,
5 that in everything you
were [a]enriched in Him, in all
[b]speech and [b]all knowledge,
6 even as [a]the testimony
concerning Christ was confirmed
in you,
7 so that you are not lacking
in any gift, [a]awaiting eagerly the
revelation of our Lord Jesus
Christ,
8 [a]who shall also confirm
you to the end, blameless in [b]the
day of our Lord Jesus Christ.
9 [a]God is faithful, through
whom you were [b]called into [c]fel-
lowship with His Son, Jesus Christ
our Lord.

4 [a]Rom. 1:8
5 [a]2 Cor. 9:11 [b]Rom. 15:14; 2 Cor. 8:7
6 [a]2 Thess. 1:10; 1 Tim. 2:6; 2 Tim. 1:8; Rev. 1:2
★ 7 [a]Luke 17:30; Rom. 8:19, 23; Phil. 3:20; 2 Pet. 3:12
★ 8 [a]Rom. 8:19; Phil. 1:6; Col. 2:7; 1 Thess. 3:13; 5:23 [b]Luke 17:24, 30; 1 Cor. 5:5; 2 Cor. 1:14; Phil. 1:6, 10; 2:16; 1 Thess. 5:2; 2 Thess. 2:2
9 [a]Deut. 7:9; Is. 49:7; 1 Cor. 10:13; 2 Cor. 1:18; 1 Thess. 5:24; 2 Thess. 3:3 [b]Rom. 8:28 [c]1 John 1:3

II DIVISIONS IN THE CHURCH, 1:10-4:21

A The Fact of Divisions, 1:10-17

10 Now [a]I exhort you, [b]breth-
ren, by the name of our Lord
Jesus Christ, that you all agree,
and there be no [c]divisions among

★10 [a]Rom. 12:1 [b]Rom. 1:13 [c]1 Cor. 11:18 [d]Rom. 12:16; Phil. 1:27

1:1 *Sosthenes.* Possibly the ruler of the synagogue mentioned in Acts 18:17.

1:2 *sanctified.* I.e., set apart for God's possession and use. See note on 6:11. This was true of the Corinthians because of their position in Christ (1 Cor. 12:13), in spite of their blatant imperfections.

1:7 *gift.* I.e., spiritual gift (cf. 12:4-11). Spiritual gifts are abilities which God gives believers in order that they may serve Him. Every Christian has at least one gift (1 Pet. 4:10). At Corinth all the various gifts were found within the group. Spiritual gifts are discussed in Rom. 12:3-8; 1 Cor. 12:1-14:40 and Eph. 4:7-16.

1:8 *confirm* = guarantee. The Corinthians had God's guarantee that they would be in Christ's presence when He returns and that they would then be *blameless.* This assurance is based on the wonderful fact that *God is faithful* (v. 9).

1:10 *divisions.* Or, "schisms," "parties." This letter was written to a church divided over personalities (v. 12). Though severely condemned, these factions were allowed to exist in order that "approved" believers could be recognized (11:19). *made complete.* Paul appeals for adjustments to be made in these personality divisions so that there might be unity in the church. Other issues that divided the church included libertinism (6:13), the relation of men and women in the church (11:2-16), food laws (8:10; 10:25), speaking in tongues (chap. 14), and resurrection of the dead (chap. 15).

you, but you be made complete in [d]the same mind and in the same judgment.

11 For I have been informed concerning you, my brethren, by [a]Chloe's *people,* that there are quarrels among you.

12 Now I mean this, that [a]each one of you is saying, "I am of Paul," and "I of [b]Apollos," and "I of [c]Cephas," and "I of Christ."

13 Has Christ been divided? Paul was not crucified for you, was he? Or were you [a]baptized in the name of Paul?

14 I thank God that I [a]baptized none of you except [a]Crispus and [b]Gaius,

15 that no man should say you were baptized in my name.

16 Now I did baptize also the [a]household of Stephanas; beyond that, I do not know whether I baptized any other.

17 [a]For Christ did not send me to baptize, but to preach the gospel, [b]not in cleverness of speech, that the cross of Christ should not be made void.

★11 [a]Rom. 16:10f.
★12 [a]Matt. 23:8-10; 1 Cor. 3:4 [b]Acts 18:24; 1 Cor. 3:22 [c]John 1:42; 1 Cor. 3:22; 9:5; 15:5
★13 [a]Matt. 28:19; Acts 2:38
14 [a]Acts 18:8 [b]Rom. 16:23
16 [a]1 Cor. 16:15, 17
★17 [a]John 4:2; Acts 10:48 [b]1 Cor. 2:1, 4, 13; 2 Cor. 10:10; 11:6

B The Causes of Divisions, 1:18–2:16

1 *The misunderstanding of God's message of the cross,* 1:18–2:5

18 For the word of the cross is to [a]those who are perishing [b]foolishness, but to us who are being saved it is [c]the power of God.

19 For it is written,

"[a]I WILL DESTROY THE WISDOM OF THE WISE,
AND THE CLEVERNESS OF THE CLEVER I WILL SET ASIDE."

20 [a]Where is the wise man? Where is the scribe? Where is the debater of [b]this age? Has not God [c]made foolish the wisdom of [d]the world?

21 For since in the wisdom of God [a]the world through its wisdom did not *come to* know God, [b]God was well-pleased through the [c]foolishness of the message preached to [d]save those who believe.

22 For indeed [a]Jews ask for signs, and Greeks search for wisdom;

23 but we preach [a]Christ crucified, [b]to Jews a stumbling block, and to Gentiles [c]foolishness,

24 but to those who are [a]the called, both Jews and Greeks, Christ [b]the power of God and [c]the wisdom of God.

25 Because the [a]foolishness of God is wiser than men, and [b]the weakness of God is stronger than men.

26 For consider your [a]calling, brethren, that there were [b]not many wise according to the flesh, not many mighty, not many noble;

27 but [a]God has chosen the foolish things of [b]the world to shame the wise, and God has chosen the weak things of [b]the world to shame the things which are strong,

★18 [a]Acts 2:47; 2 Cor. 2:15; 4:3; 2 Thess. 2:10 [b]1 Cor. 1:21, 23, 25; 2:14; 4:10 [c]Rom. 1:16; 1 Cor. 1:24
19 [a]Is. 29:14
20 [a]Job 12:17; Is. 19:11f.; 33:18 [b]Matt. 13:22; 1 Cor. 2:6, 8; 3:18, 19 [c]Rom. 1:20ff. [d]John 12:31; 1 Cor. 1:27f.; 6:2; 11:32; James 4:4
21 [a]John 12:31; 1 Cor. 1:27f.; 6:2; 11:32; James 4:4 [b]Luke 12:32; Gal. 1:15; Col. 1:19 [c]1 Cor. 1:18, 23, 25; 2:14; 4:10 [d]Rom. 11:14; 1 Tim. 4:16; 2 Tim. 2:10; 3:15; 4:18; Heb. 7:25; James 5:20
22 [a]Matt. 12:38
23 [a]1 Cor. 2:2; Gal. 3:1; 5:11 [b]Luke 2:34; 1 Pet. 2:8 [c]1 Cor. 1:18, 21, 25; 2:14; 4:10
24 [a]Rom. 8:28 [b]Rom. 1:16; 1 Cor. 1:18 [c]Luke 11:49; 1 Cor. 1:30
25 [a]1 Cor. 1:18, 21, 23; 2:14; 4:10 [b]2 Cor. 13:4
★26 [a]Rom. 11:29 [b]Matt. 11:25; 1 Cor. 1:20; 2:8
27 [a]James 2:5 [b]1 Cor. 1:20

1:11 *quarrels.* Or strife, which, according to Gal. 5:20, is a work of the flesh, or old nature.

1:12 The party of *Apollos* apparently preferred a polished style in preaching (Acts 18:24). The party of *Cephas* (Peter) appealed to the traditionalists, who wanted a leader who had walked with Christ. The party of *Christ* included those who disdained attachment to any group and flaunted their liberty in Christ (6:12).

1:13 The impossibility of these things being true demonstrates the fallacies of these factions.

1:17 *For Christ did not send me to baptize, but to preach the gospel.* Though Paul did baptize some (vv. 14, 16), it is clear from this statement that he did not consider baptism necessary for salvation.

1:18–25 In these verses Paul shows that worldly wisdom, which the Corinthians prized so highly, is the very antithesis of the wisdom of God.

1:26–31 Not only is the message of the cross foolishness to the perishing (v. 18), but God uses those who would commonly be considered foolish, weak, and of no consequence to convey that message. An illustration of this truth was their own church group, which did not include many *wise, mighty,* or *noble* (v. 26). God's purpose is to exclude all boasting in self (v. 29).

28 [a]1 Cor. 1:20 [b]Rom. 4:17 [c]Job 34:19; 1 Cor. 2:6; 2 Thess. 2:8; Heb. 2:14
29 [a]Eph. 2:9
30 [a]Rom. 8:1; 1 Cor. 4:15 [b]1 Cor. 1:24 [c]Jer. 23:5f.; 33:16; 2 Cor. 5:21; Phil. 3:9 [d]1 Cor. 1:2; 6:11; 1 Thess. 5:23 [e]Rom. 3:24; Eph. 1:7, 14; Col. 1:4
31 [a]Jer. 9:23f.; 2 Cor. 10:17
1 [a]1 Cor. 1:17; 2:4, 13 [b]1 Cor. 2:7
2 [a]1 Cor. 1:23; Gal. 6:14
★ 3 [a]Acts 18:1, 6, 12 [b]1 Cor. 4:10; 2 Cor. 11:30; 12:5, 9f.; 13:9 [c]Is. 19:16; 2 Cor. 7:15; Eph. 6:5
4 [a]1 Cor. 1:17; 2:1, 13 [b]Rom. 15:19; 1 Cor. 4:20
★ 5 [a]2 Cor. 4:7; 6:7; 12:9

28 and the base things of [a]the
world and the despised, God has
chosen, [b]the things that are not,
that He might [c]nullify the things
that are,
29 that [a]no man should boast
before God.
30 But by His doing you are
in [a]Christ Jesus, who became to
us [b]wisdom from God, and [c]right-
eousness and [d]sanctification, and
[e]redemption,
31 that, just as it is written,
"[a]LET HIM WHO BOASTS, BOAST IN THE
LORD."

2 And when I came to you,
brethren, I [a]did not come
with superiority of speech or of
wisdom, proclaiming to you [b]the
testimony of God.
2 For I determined to know
nothing among you except [a]Jesus
Christ, and Him crucified.
3 And I [a]was with you in
[b]weakness and in [c]fear and in
much trembling.
4 And my message and my
preaching were [a]not in persuasive
words of wisdom, but in demonstration of [b]the Spirit and of
power,
5 that your faith should not
rest on the wisdom of men, but
on [a]the power of God.

6 [a]Eph. 4:13; Phil. 3:15 marg.; Heb. 5:14; 6:1 [b]Matt. 13:22; 1 Cor. 1:20 [c]1 Cor. 1:28
7 [a]Rom. 11:25; 16:25f.; 1 Cor. 2:1 [b]Rom. 8:29f. [c]Heb. 1:2; 11:3

2 *The misunderstanding of the Spirit's ministry of revealing,* 2:6–16

6 Yet we do speak wisdom
among those who are [a]mature; a
wisdom, however, not of [b]this
age, nor of the rulers of [b]this age,
who are [c]passing away;
7 but we speak God's wis-
dom in a [a]mystery, the hidden
wisdom, which God [b]predestined
before the [c]ages to our glory;
8 *the wisdom* [a]which none
of the rulers of [b]this age has understood; for if they had understood it, they would not have crucified [c]the Lord of glory;
9 but just as it is written,

"[a]THINGS WHICH EYE HAS NOT
SEEN AND EAR HAS NOT
HEARD,
AND *which* HAVE NOT EN-
TERED THE HEART OF MAN,
ALL THAT GOD HAS PREPARED
FOR THOSE WHO LOVE
HIM."

10 [a]For to us God revealed
them [b]through the Spirit; for the
Spirit searches all things, even the
[c]depths of God.
11 For who among men
knows the *thoughts* of a man except the [a]spirit of the man, which
is in him? Even so the *thoughts* of
God no one knows except the
Spirit of God.
12 Now we [a]have received,
not the spirit of [b]the world, but
the Spirit who is from God, that
we might know the things freely
given to us by God,
13 which things we also
speak, [a]not in words taught by
human wisdom, but in those
taught by the Spirit, combining
spiritual *thoughts* with spiritual
words.
14 But a [a]natural man [b]does
not accept the things of the Spirit
of God; for they are [c]foolishness
to him, and he cannot understand
them, because they are spiritually
appraised.

★ 8 [a]1 Cor. 1:26; 2:6 [b]Matt. 13:22; 1 Cor. 1:20 [c]Acts 7:2; James 2:1
★ 9 [a]Is. 64:4; 65:17
10 [a]Matt. 11:25; 13:11; 16:17; Gal. 1:12; Eph. 3:3, 5 [b]John 14:26 [c]Rom. 11:33ff.
11 [a]Prov. 20:27
12 [a]Rom. 8:15 [b]1 Cor. 1:27
★13 [a]1 Cor. 1:17; 2:1, 4
★14 [a]1 Cor. 15:44, 46; James 3:15; Jude 19 marg. [b]John 14:17 [c]1 Cor. 1:18

2:3 Paul arrived in Corinth after a discouraging experience in Athens and was anxious about the believers he had just left in Thessalonica (Acts 17). The overwhelming wickedness of Corinth undoubtedly added to his anxiety.

2:5 *wisdom of men.* Paul did not want their faith to be placed in clever arguments but in *the power of God.*

2:8 *the rulers of this age.* I.e., those who crucified Christ.

2:9 A free quotation of Isa. 64:4. These things, long hidden, are now revealed by the Spirit (1 Cor. 2:10).

2:13 *combining spiritual thoughts with spiritual words.* This difficult phrase may perhaps mean, "interpreting spiritual truths to spiritual minds."

2:14 *a natural man.* I.e., an unsaved man. See Jude 19, where the same word is used (translated "worldly-minded") and explained as indicating a person who does not have the Spirit (see also Rom. 8:9).

15 But he who is [a]spiritual appraises all things, yet he himself is
appraised by no man.
16 For [a]WHO HAS KNOWN THE
MIND OF THE LORD, THAT HE SHOULD
INSTRUCT HIM? But [b]we have the
mind of Christ.

★15 [a]1 Cor. 3:1; 14:37; Gal. 6:1
16 [a]Is. 40:13; Rom. 11:34 [b]John 15:15

C The Consequences of Divisions, 3:1–4:5

1 *Spiritual growth is stunted,* 3:1–9

3 And I, brethren, could not
speak to you as to [a]spiritual
men, but as to [b]men of flesh, as to
[c]babes in Christ.
2 I gave you [a]milk to drink,
not solid food; for you [b]were not
yet able *to receive it.* Indeed, even
now you are not yet able,
3 for you are still fleshly. For
since there is [a]jealousy and strife
among you, are you not fleshly,
and are you not walking [b]like
mere men?
4 For when [a]one says, "I am
of Paul," and another, "I am of
Apollos," are you not *mere* [b]men?
5 What then is Apollos? And
what is Paul? [a]Servants through
whom you believed, even [b]as the
Lord gave *opportunity* to each
one.
6 [a]I planted, [b]Apollos watered, but [c]God was causing the
growth.
7 So then neither the one
who plants nor the one who waters is anything, but God who
causes the growth.
8 Now he who plants and he
who waters are one; but each will
[a]receive his own reward according
to his own labor.
9 For we are God's [a]fellow-
workers; you are God's [b]field,
God's [c]building.

★ 1 [a]1 Cor. 2:15; 14:37; Gal. 6:1 [b]Rom. 7:14; 1 Cor. 2:14 [c]1 Cor. 2:6; Eph. 4:14; Heb. 5:13
2 [a]Heb. 5:12f.; 1 Pet. 2:2 [b]John 16:12
★ 3 [a]Rom. 13:13; 1 Cor. 1:10f.; 11:18 [b]1 Cor. 3:4
4 [a]1 Cor. 1:12 [b]1 Cor. 3:3
5 [a]Rom. 15:16; 2 Cor. 3:3, 6; 4:1; 5:18; 6:4; Eph. 3:7; Col. 1:25; 1 Tim. 1:12 [b]Rom. 12:6; 1 Cor. 3:10
6 [a]Acts 18:4-11, 18; 1 Cor. 4:15; 9:1; 15:1; 2 Cor. 10:14f. [b]Acts 18:27; 1 Cor. 1:12 [c]1 Cor. 15:10
★ 8 [a]1 Cor. 3:14; 4:5; 9:17; Gal. 6:4
9 [a]Mark 16:20; 2 Cor. 6:1 [b]Is. 61:3; Matt. 15:13 [c]1 Cor. 3:16; Eph. 2:20-22; Col. 2:7; 1 Pet. 2:5

2 *Rewards will be lost,* 3:10–4:5

10 According to [a]the grace of
God which was given to me, as a
wise master builder [b]I laid a foundation, and [c]another is building
upon it. But let each man be careful how he builds upon it.
11 For no man can lay a
[a]foundation other than the one
which is laid, which is Jesus
Christ.
12 Now if any man builds
upon the foundation with gold,
silver, precious stones, wood, hay,
straw,
13 [a]each man's work will become evident; for [b]the day will
show it, because it is *to be* revealed with fire; and the fire itself
will test the quality of each man's
work.
14 If any man's work which
he has built upon it remains, he
shall [a]receive a reward.
15 If any man's work is
burned up, he shall suffer loss;

★10 [a]Rom. 12:3; 1 Cor. 15:10 [b]Rom. 15:20; 1 Cor. 3:11f. [c]1 Thess. 3:2
11 [a]Is. 28:16; Eph. 2:20; 1 Pet. 2:4ff.
★12
13 [a]1 Cor. 4:5 [b]Matt. 10:15; 1 Cor. 1:8; 4:3 marg.; 2 Thess. 1:7-10; 2 Tim. 1:12, 18; 4:8
★14 [a]1 Cor. 3:8; 4:5; 9:17; Gal. 6:4
★15 [a]Job 23:10; Ps. 66:10, 12; Jude 23

2:15 *he who is spiritual.* The mature Christian, who is led and taught by the Spirit, *appraises all things,* i.e., he can scrutinize, sift, and thereby understand all things; but unbelievers and even carnally-minded Christians cannot appraise (understand) him.

3:1 *men of flesh.* The Greek word *sarkinos* means "fleshly" or "of the flesh," with the idea of weakness; in v. 3 *fleshly* has the overtone of willfulness. Fleshly Christians (brethren) are *babes in Christ* (i.e., undeveloped) who cannot understand the deeper truths of the Word of God (v. 2) and who are characterized by strife (v. 3).

3:3 *still.* Their condition was inexcusable, for they had been saved long enough to have grown up. *walking like mere men.* Carnal Christians are scarcely distinguishable from natural or unsaved men.

3:8 *are one.* I.e., in harmony, not competition.

3:10-15 This passage refers to the judgment seat of Christ (cf. 2 Cor. 5:10). The works discussed here have nothing to do with earning or losing salvation. The rewards (or loss of them) pertain only to Christians.

3:12 *gold.* Those works which are valuable and enduring. *wood.* Those which are ultimately worthless.

3:14 *reward.* Salvation is a free gift, but rewards, for those who are saved, are earned. The *quality* of our service (v. 13) is the criterion. Rewards are often spoken of as crowns (cf. 9:25; 1 Thess. 2:19; 2 Tim. 4:8; Jas. 1:12; 1 Pet. 5:4; Rev. 2:10; 3:11; 4:4, 10).

3:15 *suffer loss.* I.e., of reward not salvation, as is made clear in the latter part of the verse.

but he himself shall be saved, yet [a]so as through fire.

16 [a]Do you not know that [b]you are a temple of God, and *that* the Spirit of God dwells in you?

17 If any man destroys the temple of God, God will destroy him, for the temple of God is holy, and that is what you are.

18 [a]Let no man deceive himself. [b]If any man among you thinks that he is wise in [c]this age, let him become foolish that he may become wise.

19 For [a]the wisdom of this world is foolishness before God. For it is written, "*He is* [b]THE ONE WHO CATCHES THE WISE IN THEIR CRAFTINESS";

20 and again, "[a]THE LORD KNOWS THE REASONINGS of the wise, THAT THEY ARE USELESS."

21 So then [a]let no one boast in men. For [b]all things belong to you,

22 [a]whether Paul or Apollos or Cephas or the world or [b]life or death or things present or things to come; all things belong to you,

23 and [a]you belong to Christ; and [b]Christ belongs to God.

4 Let a man regard us in this manner, as [a]servants of Christ, and [b]stewards of [c]the mysteries of God.

2 In this case, moreover, it is required of stewards that one be found trustworthy.

3 But to me it is a very small thing that I should be examined by you, or by *any* human court; in fact, I do not even examine myself.

4 I [a]am conscious of nothing against myself, yet I am not by this [b]acquitted; but the one who examines me is the Lord.

5 Therefore [a]do not go on passing judgment before the time, *but wait* [b]until the Lord comes who will both [c]bring to light the things hidden in the darkness and disclose the motives of *men's* hearts; and then each man's [d]praise will come to him from God.

★16 [a]Rom. 6:16 [b]Rom. 8:9; 1 Cor. 6:19; 2 Cor. 6:16; Eph. 2:21f.
★18 [a]Is. 5:21 [b]1 Cor. 8:2; Gal. 6:3 [c]1 Cor. 1:20
19 [a]1 Cor. 1:20 [b]Job 5:13
20 [a]Ps. 94:11
21 [a]1 Cor. 4:6 [b]Rom. 8:32
22 [a]1 Cor. 1:12; 3:5, 6 [b]Rom. 8:38
23 [a]1 Cor. 15:23; 2 Cor. 10:7; Gal. 3:29 [b]1 Cor. 11:3; 15:28
★ 1 [a]Luke 1:2 [b]1 Cor. 9:17; Titus 1:7; 1 Pet. 4:10 [c]Rom. 11:25; 16:25
★ 2
★ 4 [a]Acts 23:1; 2 Cor. 1:12 [b]Ps. 143:2; Rom. 2:13
5 [a]Matt. 7:1; Rom. 2:1 [b]John 21:22; Rom. 2:16 [c]1 Cor. 3:13 [d]Rom. 2:29; 1 Cor. 3:8; 2 Cor. 10:18

D The Example of Paul, 4:6–21

6 Now these things, brethren, I have figuratively applied to myself and Apollos for your sakes, that in us you might learn not to exceed [a]what is written, in order that no one of you might [b]become arrogant [c]in behalf of one against the other.

7 For who regards you as superior? And [a]what do you have that you did not receive? But if you did receive it, why do you boast as if you had not received it?

8 You are [a]already filled, you have already become rich, you have become kings without us; and *I* would indeed that you had become kings so that we also might reign with you.

9 For, I think, God has exhibited us apostles last of all, as men [a]condemned to death; because we [b]have become a spectacle to the world, both to angels and to men.

★ 6 [a]1 Cor. 1:19, 31; 3:19f. [b]1 Cor. 4:18f.; 8:1; 13:4 [c]1 Cor. 1:12; 3:4
7 [a]John 3:27; Rom. 12:3, 6; 1 Pet. 4:10
★ 8 [a]Rev. 3:17f.
9 [a]Rom. 8:36; 1 Cor. 15:31; 2 Cor. 11:23 [b]Heb. 10:33

3:16 *a temple of God.* Here the local church is viewed as a temple of God inhabited by the Spirit; in 6:19 the individual is a temple of God.

3:18 *let him become foolish* by accepting God's wisdom, which the world regards as folly.

4:1 *servants.* The word denotes subordination (originally an under-rower in a trireme, a ship with 3 banks of oars) and is different from the "servants" used in 3:5. *mysteries.* See note on Eph. 3:3.

4:2 *trustworthy.* Reliability was the one necessary virtue for stewards, who were managers or administrators of large estates.

4:4 *against myself.* Paul is saying, I have a clear conscience, but my final judgment rests with God.

4:6 *I have figuratively applied.* I.e., though Paul had been speaking of himself and Apollos (3:5–4:5), others, whom he did not name, were the real culprits. *that in us you might learn not to exceed what is written.* I.e., that you might learn by us to live faithfully according to the Scriptures.

4:8–13 With biting irony, Paul contrasts the imagined exaltation of the Corinthians with the degradation and distress which were the apostles' daily lot.

10 We are [a]fools for Christ's
sake, but [b]you are prudent in
Christ; [c]we are weak, but you are
strong; you are distinguished, but
we are without honor.
11 To this present hour we
are both [a]hungry and thirsty, and
are poorly clothed, and are
roughly treated, and are home-
less;
12 and we toil, [a]working with
our own hands; when we are [b]re-
viled, we bless; when we are [c]per-
secuted, we endure;
13 when we are slandered, we
try to conciliate; we have [a]become
as the scum of the world, the
dregs of all things, *even* until
now.
14 I do not write these things
to [a]shame you, but to admonish
you as my beloved [b]children.
15 For if you were to have
countless [a]tutors in Christ, yet
you would not *have* many fathers;
for in [b]Christ Jesus I [c]became
your father through the [d]gospel.
16 I exhort you therefore, be
[a]imitators of me.
17 For this reason I [a]have sent
to you [b]Timothy, who is my [c]be-
loved and faithful child in the
Lord, and he will remind you of
my ways which are in Christ,
[d]just as I teach everywhere in every church.
18 Now some have become
[a]arrogant, as though I were not
[b]coming to you.
19 But I [a]will come to you
soon, [b]if the Lord wills, and I shall
find out, not the words of those
who are [c]arrogant, but their
power.
20 For the kingdom of God
does [a]not consist in words, but in
power.
21 What do you desire? [a]Shall
I come to you with a rod or with
love and a spirit of gentleness?

10 [a]Acts 17:18; 26:24; 1 Cor. 1:18 [b]1 Cor. 1:19f.; 3:18; 2 Cor. 11:19 [c]1 Cor. 2:3; 2 Cor. 13:9
11 [a]Rom. 8:35; 2 Cor. 11:23-27
12 [a]Acts 18:3 [b]1 Pet. 3:9 [c]John 15:20; Rom. 8:35
13 [a]Lam. 3:45
14 [a]1 Cor. 6:5; 15:34 [b]2 Cor. 6:13; 12:14; 1 Thess. 2:11; 1 John 2:1; 3 John 4
★15 [a]Gal. 3:24f. [b]1 Cor. 1:30; [c]Num. 11:12; 1 Cor. 3:8; Gal. 4:19; Philem. 10 [d]1 Cor. 9:12, 14, 18, 23; 15:1
16 [a]1 Cor. 11:1; Phil. 3:17; 4:9; 1 Thess. 1:6; 2 Thess. 3:9
17 [a]1 Cor. 16:10 [b]Acts 16:1 [c]1 Cor. 4:14; 1 Tim. 1:2, 18; 2 Tim. 1:2 [d]1 Cor. 7:17; 11:34; 14:33; 16:1; Titus 1:5
18 [a]1 Cor. 4:6 [b]1 Cor. 4:21
19 [a]Acts 19:21; 20:2; 1 Cor. 11:34; 16:5f.; 16:8; 2 Cor. 1:15f. [b]Acts 18:21 [c]1 Cor. 4:6
20 [a]1 Cor. 2:4
21 [a]2 Cor. 1:23; 2:1, 3; 12:20; 13:2, 10

III MORAL DISORDERS IN THE CHURCH, 5:1–6:20

A The Case of Incest, 5:1–13

1 The problem stated, 5:1-2

5 It is actually reported that
there is immorality among
you, and immorality of such a
kind as does not exist even among
the Gentiles, that someone has
[a]his father's wife.
2 And you [a]have become arrogant, and have not [b]mourned
instead, in order that the one who
had done this deed might be [c]re-
moved from your midst.

2 The punishment prescribed, 5:3-13

3 For I, on my part, though
[a]absent in body but present in
spirit, have already judged him
who has so committed this, as
though I were present.
4 [a]In the name of our Lord
Jesus, when you are assembled,
and I with you in spirit, [b]with the
power of our Lord Jesus,
5 *I have decided* to [a]deliver
such a one to [b]Satan for the destruction of his flesh, that his
spirit may be saved in [c]the day of
the Lord Jesus.
6 [a]Your boasting is not good.
[b]Do you not know that [c]a little
leaven leavens the whole lump *of
dough?*
7 Clean out the old leaven,
that you may be a new lump, just

★ 1 [a]Lev. 18:8; Deut. 22:30; 27:20
★ 2 [a]1 Cor. 4:6 [b]2 Cor. 7:7-10 [c]1 Cor. 5:13
3 [a]Col. 2:5; 1 Thess. 2:17
4 [a]2 Thess. 3:6 [b]John 20:23; 2 Cor. 2:6, 10; 13:3, 10; 1 Tim. 5:20
★ 5 [a]Prov. 23:14; Luke 22:31; 1 Tim. 1:20 [b]Matt. 4:10 [c]1 Cor. 1:8
6 [a]1 Cor. 5:2; James 4:16 [b]Rom. 6:16 [c]Hos. 7:4; Matt. 16:6, 12; Gal. 5:9
★ 7 [a]Mark 14:12; 1 Pet. 1:19

4:15 *tutors.* The same word is used in Gal. 3:24 (see the note there). The Corinthians had many tutors but only one spiritual father, Paul.

5:1 *immorality.* I.e., incest, forbidden by the law (Lev. 18:8; Deut. 22:22). *has.* Suggesting some sort of permanent relationship. *his father's wife.* Not the offender's mother, but a stepmother, possibly divorced from his father.

5:2 *removed* refers to church discipline and excommunication.

5:5 *to deliver such a one to Satan for the destruction of his flesh.* This evidently means that the church was to discipline this sinning brother by committing him to Satan's domain, the world (1 John 5:19) and to Satan's chastisement, the destruction or ruin of his body (*flesh* means "body" here) through sickness or even death. *destruction* does not mean annihilation, but ruin. Persistent sin often leads to physical punishment (1 Cor. 11:30; 1 John 5:16–17).

5:7 *leaven.* A symbol of impurity (see note on

as you are *in fact* unleavened. For
Christ our [a]Passover also has
been sacrificed.

★ 8 [a]Ex. 12:19; 13:7; Deut. 16:3

8 Let us therefore celebrate
the feast, [a]not with old leaven,
nor with the leaven of malice and
wickedness, but with the unleavened bread of sincerity and truth.

★ 9 [a]2 Cor. 6:14; Eph. 5:11; 2 Thess. 3:6

9 I wrote you in my letter
[a]not to associate with immoral
people;

10 [a]1 Cor. 10:27

10 I *did* not at all *mean* with
the immoral people of this world,
or with the covetous and swindlers, or with [a]idolaters; for then
you would have to go out of the
world.

11 [a]Acts 1:15; 2 Thess. 3:6 [b]1 Cor. 10:7, 14, 20f.

11 But actually, I wrote to you
not to associate with any so-called
[a]brother if he should be an immoral person, or covetous, or [b]an
idolater, or a reviler, or a drunkard, or a swindler—not even to
eat with such a one.

★12 [a]Mark 4:11 [b]1 Cor. 5:3-5; 6:1-4

12 For what have I to do with
judging [a]outsiders? [b]Do you not
judge those who are within *the
church?*

13 [a]Deut. 13:5; 17:7, 12; 21:21; 22:21; 1 Cor. 5:2

13 But those who are outside,
God judges. [a]Remove the wicked
man from among yourselves.

B The Problem of Litigation in Heathen Courts, 6:1-8

1 [a]Matt. 18:17

6 Does any one of you, when
he has a case against his
neighbor, dare to go to law before
the unrighteous, and [a]not before
the saints?

★ 2 [a]Rom. 6:16 [b]Dan. 7:18, 22, 27; Matt. 19:28 [c]1 Cor. 1:20

2 Or [a]do you not know that
[b]the saints will judge [c]the world?
And if the world is judged by
you, are you not competent *to
constitute* the smallest law courts?

3 [a]Rom. 6:16

3 [a]Do you not know that we
shall judge angels? How much
more, matters of this life?

★ 4

4 If then you have law courts
dealing with matters of this life,
do you appoint them as judges
who are of no account in the
church?

5 [a]1 Cor. 4:14; 15:34 [b]Acts 1:15; 9:13; 1 Cor. 6:1

5 [a]I say *this* to your shame.
Is it so, *that* there is not among
you one wise man who will be
able to decide between his
[b]brethren,

6 [a]2 Cor. 6:14f.; 1 Tim. 5:8

6 but brother goes to law
with brother, and that before [a]un-
believers?

★ 7 [a]Matt. 5:39f.

7 Actually, then, it is already
a defeat for you, that you have
lawsuits with one another. [a]Why
not rather be wronged? Why not
rather be defrauded?

8 [a]1 Thess. 4:6

8 On the contrary, you yourselves wrong and defraud, and
that *your* [a]brethren.

C The Warning against Moral Laxity, 6:9-20

★ 9 [a]Rom. 6:16 [b]Acts 20:32; 1 Cor. 15:50; Gal. 5:21; Eph. 5:5 [c]Luke 21:8; 1 Cor. 15:33; Gal. 6:7; James 1:16; 1 John 3:7 [d]Rom. 13:13; 1 Cor. 5:11; Gal. 5:19-21; Eph. 5:5; 1 Tim. 1:10; Rev. 21:8; 22:15

9 Or [a]do you not know that
the unrighteous shall not [b]inherit

Matt. 13:33). By position they were *unleavened;* Paul urges that their practice correspond. *Passover.* See Ex. 12:1-28. Christ was already sacrificed, and, just as Passover was followed by the Feast of Unleavened Bread, so should the Corinthians, who were already cleansed, now walk in holiness.

5:8 *the feast.* I.e., of Unleavened Bread (cf. Ex. 12:15-20; 13:1-10).

5:9 *to associate.* I.e., have familiar fellowship. It is impossible not to have some contact with the evil people of the world in the daily pursuits of life (v. 10). But, Paul says, it is improper to have fellowship with a Christian who is under discipline (v. 11).

5:12-13 The church should leave the judgment of unbelievers to God and concentrate on setting its own house in order.

6:2 *the saints will judge the world.* Because of our union with Christ, we will be associated with Him in this judgment (during the millennium, see Matt. 19:28). We will also *judge angels* (v. 3). See 2 Pet. 2:4, 9; Jude 6.

6:4 *appoint them . . .* Better, are you appointing them . . .?

6:7 *a defeat.* Going to court against a brother brings defeat before the case is even heard. It is better to be wronged and take a loss.

6:9 *effeminate, nor homosexuals.* Both expressions refer to homosexuals, the first to those who allow themselves to be used unnaturally, and the second to active homosexuals. Paul's warning is given against the background of incest, homosexuality, pederasty, and other unnatural sexual vices which were prevalent among the Greeks and Romans. Paul did not want Christianity confused with sects that permitted such things.

the kingdom of God? [c]Do not be
deceived; [d]neither fornicators, nor
idolaters, nor adulterers, nor effeminate, nor homosexuals,
10 nor thieves, nor *the* covetous, nor drunkards, nor revilers,
nor swindlers, shall [a]inherit the
kingdom of God.
11 And [a]such were some of
you; but you were [b]washed, but
you were [c]sanctified, but you
were [d]justified in the name of the
Lord Jesus Christ, and in the
Spirit of our God.
12 [a]All things are lawful for
me, but not all things are profitable. All things are lawful for me,
but I will not be mastered by anything.
13 [a]Food is for the stomach,
and the stomach is for food; but
God will [b]do away with both of
them. Yet the body is not for immorality, but [c]for the Lord; and
[d]the Lord is for the body.
14 Now God has not only
[a]raised the Lord, but [b]will also
raise us up through His power.
15 [a]Do you not know that
[b]your bodies are members of
Christ? Shall I then take away the
members of Christ and make
them members of a harlot? [c]May
it never be!
16 Or [a]do you not know that
the one who joins himself to a
harlot is one body *with her?* For
He says, "[b]THE TWO WILL BECOME
ONE FLESH."
17 But the one who joins
himself to the Lord is [a]one spirit
with Him.
18 [a]Flee immorality. Every
other sin that a man commits is
outside the body, but the immoral
man sins against his own body.
19 Or [a]do you not know that
[b]your body is a temple of the
Holy Spirit who is in you, whom
you have from God, and that [c]you
are not your own?
20 For [a]you have been bought
with a price: therefore glorify God
in [b]your body.

10 [a]Acts 20:32; 1 Cor. 15:50; Gal. 5:21; Eph. 5:5
★11 [a]1 Cor. 12:2; Eph. 2:2f.; Col. 3:5-7; Titus 3:3-7 [b]Acts 22:16; Eph. 5:26 [c]1 Cor. 1:2, 30 [d]Rom. 8:30
★12 [a]1 Cor. 10:23
★13 [a]Matt. 15:17 [b]Col. 2:22 [c]1 Cor. 6:15, 19 [d]Gal. 5:24; Eph. 5:23
14 [a]Acts 2:24 [b]John 6:39f.; 1 Cor. 15:23
15 [a]1 Cor. 6:3 [b]Rom. 12:5, 27; 1 Cor. 6:13; Eph. 5:30 [c]Luke 20:16
16 [a]1 Cor. 6:3 [b]Gen. 2:24; Matt. 19:5; Mark 10:8; Eph. 5:31
17 [a]John 17:21-23; Rom. 8:9-11; 1 Cor. 6:15; Gal. 2:20
★18 [a]1 Cor. 6:9; 2 Cor. 12:21; Eph. 5:3; Col. 3:5; Heb. 13:4
★19 [a]1 Cor. 6:3 [b]John 2:21 [c]Rom. 14:7f.
20 [a]Acts 20:28; 1 Cor. 7:23; 1 Pet. 1:18f.; 2 Pet. 2:1; Rev. 5:9 [b]Rom. 12:1; Phil. 1:20

IV DISCUSSION CONCERNING MARRIAGE, 7:1-40

A Marriage and Celibacy, 7:1-9

7 Now concerning the things
about which you wrote, it is
[a]good for a man not to touch a
woman.
2 But because of immorali-
ties, let each man have his own
wife, and let each woman have
her own husband.
3 Let the husband fulfill his
duty to his wife, and likewise also
the wife to her husband.

★ 1 [a]1 Cor. 7:8, 26
★2

6:11 *washed.* I.e., regenerated (Tit. 3:5). *sanctified.* I.e., set apart for God's use. There are three aspects to sanctification: (1) positional sanctification, possessed by every believer from the moment of his conversion (his perfect standing in holiness, Acts 20:32; 1 Cor. 1:2); (2) progressive sanctification, the daily growth in grace, becoming in practice more and more set apart for God's use (John 17:17; Eph. 5:26); and (3) ultimate sanctification, attained only when we are fully and completely set apart to God in heaven (1 Thess. 5:23). *justified.* See note on Rom. 3:24.

6:12 *are lawful.* Apparently some of the Corinthians were trying to use their Christian freedom to justify their sins. Paul here insists that Christian liberty is limited by two considerations: Is the practice expedient (helpful) and will it enslave?

6:13 Some were saying that just as *food* and the belly necessarily go together, so the body and sexual indulgence go together. Not so, says Paul. Rather, the body should always glorify the Lord.

6:18 *Flee immorality.* I.e., make it your habit to flee immorality. Joseph's reaction to the advances of Potiphar's wife (Gen. 39:12) literally illustrates this principle.

6:19 *your body is a temple.* A sharp contrast to the temple of Aphrodite in Corinth where the priestesses were prostitutes.

7:1 *you wrote.* In this chapter Paul is not writing a treatise on marriage but answering questions which had been sent to him. We have only one side of the correspondence. It is clear that Paul favored celibacy (vv. 1, 7, 8, 9, 27, 38), though he approved marriage (vv. 2, 27, 28). For more complete N.T. teaching concerning marriage, see John 2:1-11; Eph. 5:21-33; 1 Tim. 5:14; Heb. 13:4; 1 Pet. 3:1-7. *it is good . . .* Probably a position taken by some at Corinth. Paul grants its validity but states that marriage is better for those who might be overcome by the practices of the evil society in which they live (v. 2).

7:2-5 In the mutuality of marriage, each partner has rights of his or her own and debts to the other.

4 The wife does not have authority over her own body, but
the husband *does;* and likewise
also the husband does not have
authority over his own body, but
the wife *does.*
5 [a]Ex. 19:15; 1 Sam. 21:5 [b]Matt. 4:10
5 [a]Stop depriving one an-
other, except by agreement for a
time that you may devote yourselves to prayer, and come together again lest [b]Satan tempt
you because of your lack of self-
control.
6 [a]2 Cor. 8:8
6 But this I say by way of
concession, [a]not of command.
★ 7 [a]1 Cor. 7:8; 9:5 [b]Matt. 19:11f.; Rom. 12:6; 1 Cor. 12:4, 11
7 Yet I wish that all men
were [a]even as I myself am. However, [b]each man has his own gift
from God, one in this manner,
and another in that.
★ 8 [a]1 Cor. 7:1, 26 [b]1 Cor. 7:7; 9:5
8 But I say to the unmarried
and to widows that it is [a]good for
them if they remain [b]even as I.
★ 9 [a]1 Tim. 5:14
9 But if they do not have
self-control, [a]let them marry; for
it is better to marry than to burn.

B Marriage and Divorce, 7:10–24

★10 [a]Mal. 2:16; Matt. 5:32; 19:3-9; Mark 10:2-12; Luke 16:18; 1 Cor. 7:6
10 But to the married I give
instructions, [a]not I, but the Lord,
that the wife should not leave her
husband
11 (but if she does leave, let
her remain unmarried, or else be
reconciled to her husband), and
that the husband should not send
his wife away.
★12 [a]1 Cor. 7:6; 2 Cor. 11:17
12 But to the rest [a]I say, not
the Lord, that if any brother has a
wife who is an unbeliever, and
she consents to live with him, let
him not send her away.
13 And a woman who has an
unbelieving husband, and he consents to live with her, let her not
send her husband away.
★14 [a]Ezra 9:2; Mal. 2:15
14 For the unbelieving husband is sanctified through his
wife, and the unbelieving wife is
sanctified through her believing
husband; for otherwise your children are unclean, but now they
are [a]holy.
★15 [a]Rom. 14:19
15 Yet if the unbelieving one
leaves, let him leave; the brother
or the sister is not under bondage
in such *cases,* but God has called
us [a]to peace.
16 [a]Rom. 11:14; 1 Pet. 3:1
16 For how do you know, O
wife, whether you will [a]save your
husband? Or how do you know,
O husband, whether you will save
your wife?
★17 [a]Rom. 12:3 [b]1 Cor. 4:17 [c]1 Cor. 11:16; 14:33; 2 Cor. 8:18; 11:28; Gal. 1:22; 1 Thess. 2:14; 2 Thess. 1:4
17 Only, [a]as the Lord has as-
signed to each one, as God has
called each, in this manner let
him walk. And [b]thus I direct in
[c]all the churches.
18 [a]Acts 15:1ff.
18 Was any man called *already* circumcised? Let him not
become uncircumcised. Has anyone been called in uncircumcision? [a]Let him not be circumcised.

7:7 *one in this manner* (i.e., celibate), *and another in that* (i.e., married).

7:8 *even as I.* Paul was obviously unmarried when he wrote these words. He might have been a widower. It is difficult, however, to substantiate that he had been married on the basis that he was a member of the Sanhedrin (Acts 26:10). It is uncertain that he was a member and also uncertain that members had to be married in the period before A.D. 70.

7:9 *burn.* I.e., with passion.

7:10–11 According to both Paul's and Christ's teachings (Mark 10:1–12), believers should not divorce. If separation does occur, the believer must either remain unmarried permanently or be reconciled permanently.

7:12–13 These verses deal with marriages in which one partner becomes a believer after the marriage. *I say, not the Lord.* I.e., Christ did not give any teaching concerning spiritually mixed marriages, but Paul does, and his teaching is authoritative.

7:14 *sanctified.* The presence of a believer in the home sets the home apart and gives it a Christian influence it would not otherwise have. A believing partner, therefore, should stay with the unbeliever. However, this does not mean that children born into such a home are automatically Christians. They are *holy* in the sense of being set apart by the presence of one believing parent.

7:15 *leaves.* If the unbelieving partner chooses to separate, the believer must accept it, though everything should be done to prevent the separation. Nothing is said about a second marriage for the believer.

7:17–24 The principle of remaining in one's marital relationship is part of a more general principle: in everything the Christian is to remain in his calling, unless it is immoral (v. 24).

19 [a]Rom. 2:27, 29; Gal. 3:28; 5:6; 6:15; Col. 3:11 [b]Rom. 2:25

20 [a]1 Cor. 7:24

19 [a]Circumcision is nothing, and uncircumcision is nothing, but *what matters is* [b]the keeping of the commandments of God.

20 [a]Let each man remain in that condition in which he was called.

21 Were you called while a slave? Do not worry about it; but if you are able also to become free, rather do that.

22 [a]John 8:32, 36; Philem. 16 [b]Eph. 6:6; Col. 3:24; 1 Pet. 2:16

22 For he who was called in the Lord while a slave, is [a]the Lord's freedman; likewise he who was called while free, is [b]Christ's slave.

23 [a]1 Cor. 6:20

23 [a]You were bought with a price; do not become slaves of men.

24 [a]1 Cor. 7:20

24 Brethren, [a]let each man remain with God in that *condition* in which he was called.

C Marriage and Christian Service, 7:25–38

★25 [a]1 Cor. 7:6 [b]2 Cor. 4:1; 1 Tim. 1:13, 16

25 Now concerning virgins I have [a]no command of the Lord, but I give an opinion as one who [b]by the mercy of the Lord is trustworthy.

★26 [a]Luke 21:23; 2 Thess. 2:2 [b]1 Cor. 7:1, 8

26 I think then that this is good in view of the present [a]distress, that [b]it is good for a man to remain as he is.

27 Are you bound to a wife? Do not seek to be released. Are you released from a wife? Do not seek a wife.

28 But if you should marry, you have not sinned; and if a virgin should marry, she has not sinned. Yet such will have trouble in this life, and I am trying to spare you.

29 [a]Rom. 13:11f.; 1 Cor. 7:31

29 But this I say, brethren, [a]the time has been shortened, so that from now on both those who have wives should be as though they had none;

30 and those who weep, as though they did not weep; and those who rejoice, as though they did not rejoice; and those who buy, as though they did not possess;

31 [a]1 Cor. 9:18 [b]1 Cor. 7:29; 1 John 2:17

31 and those who use the world, as though they did not [a]make full use of it; for [b]the form of this world is passing away.

32 [a]1 Tim. 5:5

32 But I want you to be free from concern. One who is [a]unmarried is concerned about the things of the Lord, how he may please the Lord;

33 but one who is married is concerned about the things of the world, how he may please his wife,

34 and *his interests* are divided. And the woman who is unmarried, and the virgin, is concerned about the things of the Lord, that she may be holy both in body and spirit; but one who is married is concerned about the things of the world, how she may please her husband.

35 And this I say for your own benefit; not to put a restraint upon you, but to promote what is seemly, and *to secure* undistracted devotion to the Lord.

★36

36 But if any man thinks that he is acting unbecomingly toward his virgin *daughter,* if she should be of full age, and if it must be so, let him do what he wishes, he does not sin; let her marry.

37 But he who stands firm in his heart, being under no constraint, but has authority over his own will, and has decided this in his own heart, to keep his own virgin *daughter,* he will do well.

38 So then both he who gives his own virgin *daughter* in marriage does well, and he who does not give her in marriage will do better.

7:25–35 Celibacy is presented as desirable, though not necessary.

7:26 *the present distress.* Probably a particularly difficult circumstance through which the Corinthian Christians were passing.

7:36 *if she should be of full age.* I.e., if a virgin daughter is getting beyond marriageable age, then her father may arrange a marriage *if it must be so.*

D Marriage and Remarriage, 7:39–40

★39 [a]Rom. 7:2 [b]2 Cor. 6:14

39 [a]A wife is bound as long
as her husband lives; but if her
husband is dead, she is free to be
married to whom she wishes, only
[b]in the Lord.

40 [a]1 Cor. 7:6, 25

40 But [a]in my opinion she is
happier if she remains as she is;
and I think that I also have the
Spirit of God.

V DISCUSSION CONCERNING FOOD OFFERED TO IDOLS, 8:1–11:1

A Enquiry: May a Christian Eat Food Consecrated to a Pagan God? 8:1–13

★ 1 [a]Acts 15:20; 1 Cor. 8:4, 7, 10 [b]Rom. 15:14; 1 Cor. 8:7, 10; 10:15 [c]1 Cor. 4:6 [d]Rom. 14:19

8 Now concerning [a]things sacrificed to idols, we know that
we all have [b]knowledge. Knowledge [c]makes arrogant, but love
[d]edifies.

2 [a]1 Cor. 3:18 [b]1 Cor. 13:8, 9, 12; 1 Tim. 6:4

2 [a]If any one supposes that
he knows anything, he has not
yet [b]known as he ought to know;

3 [a]Ps. 1:6; Jer. 1:5; Amos 3:2; Rom. 8:29; 11:2; Gal. 4:9

3 but if any one loves God,
he [a]is known by Him.

★ 4 [a]Acts 15:20; 1 Cor. 8:1, 7, 10 [b]Acts 14:15; 1 Cor. 10:19; Gal. 4:8 [c]Deut. 4:35, 39; 6:4; 1 Cor. 8:6

4 Therefore concerning the
eating of [a]things sacrificed to
idols, we know that there is [b]no
such thing as an idol in the world,
and that [c]there is no God but one.

5 [a]2 Thess. 2:4

5 For even if [a]there are so-
called gods whether in heaven or
on earth, as indeed there are
many gods and many lords,

6 [a]Deut. 4:35, 39; 6:4; 1 Cor. 8:4 [b]Mal. 2:10; Eph. 4:6 [c]Rom. 11:36 [d]John 13:13; 1 Cor. 1:2; Eph. 4:5; 1 Tim. 2:5 [e]John 1:3; Col. 1:16

6 yet for us [a]there is *but* one
God, [b]the Father, [c]from whom are
all things, and we *exist* for Him;
and [d]one Lord, Jesus Christ,
[e]through whom are all things, and
we *exist* through Him.

7 [a]1 Cor. 8:4ff. [b]Rom. 14:14, 22f.

7 However not all men
[a]have this knowledge; but [b]some,
being accustomed to the idol until
now, eat food as if it were sacrificed to an idol; and their conscience being weak is defiled.

8 [a]Rom. 14:17

8 But [a]food will not com-
mend us to God; we are neither
the worse if we do not eat, nor the
better if we do eat.

9 [a]Rom. 14:13, 21; 1 Cor. 10:28; Gal. 5:13 [b]Rom. 14:1; 1 Cor. 8:10f.

9 But [a]take care lest this liberty of yours somehow become a
stumbling block to the [b]weak.

★10 [a]1 Cor. 8:4ff. [b]Acts 15:20; 1 Cor. 8:1, 4, 7

10 For if someone sees you,
who have [a]knowledge, dining in
an idol's temple, will not his conscience, if he is weak, be
strengthened to eat [b]things sacrificed to idols?

★11 [a]1 Cor. 8:4ff. [b]Rom. 14:15, 20

11 For through [a]your knowledge he who is weak [b]is ruined,
the brother for whose sake Christ
died.

12 [a]Matt. 18:6; Rom. 14:20 [b]Matt. 25:45

12 [a]And thus, by sinning
against the brethren and wound-
ing their conscience when it is
weak, you sin [b]against Christ.

★13 [a]Rom. 14:21; 1 Cor. 10:32; 2 Cor. 6:3; 11:29

13 Therefore, [a]if food causes
my brother to stumble, I will never eat meat again, that I might not
cause my brother to stumble.

B Example of Paul, 9:1–27

1 *Paul's rights,* 9:1–14

★ 1 [a]1 Cor. 9:19; 10:29 [b]Acts 14:14; Rom. 1:1; 2 Cor. 12:12; 1 Thess. 2:6; 1 Tim. 2:7; 2 Tim. 1:11 [c]Acts 9:3, 17; 18:9; 22:14, 18; 23:11; 1 Cor. 15:8 [d]1 Cor. 3:6; 4:15

9 Am I not [a]free? Am I not an
[b]apostle? Have I not [c]seen
Jesus our Lord? Are you not [d]my
work in the Lord?

2 [a]John 3:33; 2 Cor. 3:2f. [b]Acts 1:25

2 If to others I am not an
apostle, at least I am to you; for
you are the [a]seal of my [b]apostle-
ship in the Lord.

3 My defense to those who
examine me is this:

7:39 *only in the Lord.* I.e., only to another Christian.

8:1 *things sacrificed to idols.* The remainders of animals which had been sacrificed to heathen idols. If the offering was private, the remainders were claimed by the offerer; if public, they were sold in the market. The question discussed here concerned what a Christian should do about buying such meat or eating it when served to him at a banquet.

8:4 *there is no such thing as an idol in the world.* Yet Paul recognizes (v. 5) that *there are so-called gods.*

8:10 *in an idol's temple.* Probably refers to some official function or festival.

8:11 *ruined,* not eternally, but in his spiritual life.

8:13 Here is the great principle that regulates conduct in morally indifferent matters. It is the principle of love voluntarily regulating liberty (Gal. 5:13).

9:1 This chapter gives an illustration from Paul's own life of the principle of 8:13. He did not take advantage of the rightful privileges he had as an apostle.

4 [a]Do we not have a right to eat and drink?

4 a1 Cor. 9:14; 1 Thess. 2:6, 9; 2 Thess. 3:8f.

5 [a]Do we not have a right to take along a believing wife, even as the rest of the apostles, and the [b]brothers of the Lord, and [c]Cephas?

★ 5 a1 Cor. 7:7f. bMatt. 12:46 cMatt. 8:14; John 1:42

6 Or do only [a]Barnabas and I not have a right to refrain from working?

★ 6 aActs 4:36

7 Who at any time serves [a]as a soldier at his own expense? Who [b]plants a vineyard, and does not eat the fruit of it? Or who tends a flock and does not use the milk of the flock?

7 a2 Cor. 10:4; 1 Tim. 1:18; 2 Tim. 2:3f. bDeut. 20:6; Prov. 27:18; 1 Cor. 3:6, 8

8 I am not speaking these things [a]according to human judgment, am I? Or does not the Law also say these things?

8 aRom. 3:5

9 For it is written in the Law of Moses, "[a]YOU SHALL NOT MUZZLE THE OX WHILE HE IS THRESHING." God is not concerned about [b]oxen, is He?

★ 9 aDeut. 25:4; 1 Tim. 5:18 bDeut. 22:1-4; Prov. 12:10

10 Or is He speaking altogether for our sake? Yes, [a]for our sake it was written, because [b]the plowman ought to plow in hope, and the thresher *to thresh* in hope of sharing *the crops.*

10 aRom. 4:23f. b2 Tim. 2:6

11 [a]If we sowed spiritual things in you, is it too much if we should reap material things from you?

★11 aRom. 15:27; 1 Cor. 9:14

12 If others share the right over you, do we not more? Nevertheless, we [a]did not use this right, but we endure all things, [b]that we may cause no hindrance to the [c]gospel of Christ.

12 aActs 18:3; 20:33; 1 Cor. 9:15, 18 b2 Cor. 6:3; 11:12 c1 Cor. 4:15; 9:14, 16, 18, 23; 2 Cor. 2:12

13 [a]Do you not know that those who [b]perform sacred services eat the *food* of the temple, *and* those who attend regularly to the altar have their share with the altar?

★13 aRom. 6:16 bLev. 6:16, 26; 7:6, 31ff.; Num. 5:9f.; 18:8-20, 31; Deut. 18:1

14 So also [a]the Lord directed those who proclaim the [b]gospel to [c]get their living from the gospel.

14 aMatt. 10:10; Luke 10:7; 1 Tim. 5:18 b1 Cor. 4:15; 9:12, 16, 18, 23; 2 Cor. 2:12 cLuke 10:8; 1 Cor. 9:4

2 *Paul's restrictions,* 9:15–27

15 But I have [a]used none of these things. And I am not writing these things that it may be done so in my case; for it would be better for me to die than have any man make [b]my boast an empty one.

15 aActs 18:3; 20:33; 1 Cor. 9:12, 18 b2 Cor. 11:10

16 For if I preach the gospel, I have nothing to boast of, for [a]I am under compulsion; for woe is me if I do not preach [b]the gospel.

16 aActs 9:15; Rom. 1:14 b1 Cor. 4:15; 9:12, 14, 18, 23; 2 Cor. 2:12

17 For if I do this voluntarily, I have a [a]reward; but if against my will, I have a [b]stewardship entrusted to me.

★17 aJohn 4:36 [Gr.]; 1 Cor. 3:8; 9:18 b1 Cor. 4:1; Gal. 2:7; Eph. 3:2; Phil. 1:16; Col. 1:25

18 What then is my [a]reward? That, when I preach the gospel, I may offer the gospel [b]without charge, so as [c]not to make full use of my right in the gospel.

18 aJohn 4:36 [Gr.]; 1 Cor. 3:8; 9:17 bActs 18:3; 2 Cor. 11:7; 12:13 c1 Cor. 7:31; 9:12

19 For though I am [a]free from all *men,* I have made myself [b]a slave to all, that I might [c]win the more.

19 a1 Cor. 9:1 b2 Cor. 4:5; Gal. 5:13 cMatt. 18:15; 1 Pet. 3:1

20 And [a]to the Jews I became as a Jew, that I might win Jews; to those who are under the Law, as under the Law, though [b]not being myself under the Law, that I might win those who are under the Law;

★20 aActs 16:3; 21:23-26; Rom. 11:14 bGal. 2:19

21 to those who are [a]without law, [b]as without law, though not being without the law of God but [c]under the law of Christ, that I might win those who are without law.

21 aRom. 2:12, 14 bGal. 2:3; 3:2 c1 Cor. 7:22; Gal. 6:2

9:5 *to take along a believing wife.* I.e., to be married. Peter was married (Matt. 8:14), as were *the rest of the apostles* and Christ's brothers.

9:6 *to refrain from working.* I.e., Is it only Barnabas and I who must work for a living? Paul had the right to be supported by those to whom he ministered, but he did not insist on this right (1 Thess. 2:9).

9:9 *the Law* (Deut. 25:4) vindicates Paul's claim.

9:11 *material things.* I.e., your material support.

9:13 The priests were supported by the people (Num. 18:8–24).

9:17 Willingly or unwillingly, Paul could not escape his responsibility to preach the gospel, because *a stewardship* (responsibility) had been committed to him and he was under orders to preach even though he was never paid (cf. Luke 17:10).

9:20 *as under the Law.* I.e., I became as one under the Law. Though Paul had broken with the law of Moses, he adds (v. 21) that he was not lawless, *but under the law of Christ.*

22 [a]Rom. 14:1; 15:1; 2 Cor. 11:29 [b]1 Cor. 10:33 [c]Rom. 11:14

22 To the [a]weak I became
weak, that I might win the weak; I
have become [b]all things to all
men, [c]that I may by all means
save some.
23 And I do all things for the
sake of the gospel, that I may become a fellow-partaker of it.

★24 [a]1 Cor. 9:13 [b]Phil. 3:14; Col. 2:18 [c]Gal. 2:2; 2 Tim. 4:7; Heb. 12:1

24 [a]Do you not know that
those who run in a race all run,
but *only* one receives [b]the prize?
[c]Run in such a way that you may
win.

★25 [a]Eph. 6:12; 1 Tim. 6:12; 2 Tim. 2:5; 4:7 [b]2 Tim. 4:8; James 1:12; 1 Pet. 5:4; Rev. 2:10; 3:11

25 And everyone who [a]com-
petes in the games exercises self-
control in all things. They then *do*
it to receive a perishable [b]wreath,
but we an imperishable.

★26 [a]Gal. 2:2; 2 Tim. 4:7; Heb. 12:1 [b]1 Cor. 14:9

26 Therefore I [a]run in such a
way, as not without aim; I box in
such a way, as not [b]beating the
air;

★27 [a]Rom. 8:13

27 but I buffet [a]my body and
make it my slave, lest possibly,
after I have preached to others, I
myself should be disqualified.

C Exhortations, 10:1–11:1

1 Avoid self-indulgence, 10:1–13

★ 1 [a]Rom. 1:13 [b]Ex. 13:21; Ps. 105:39 [c]Ex. 14:22, 29; Ps. 66:6
★ 2 [a]Rom. 6:3; 1 Cor. 1:13; Gal. 3:27

10 For [a]I do not want you to
be unaware, brethren, that
our fathers were all [b]under the
cloud, and all [c]passed through the
sea;
2 and all were [a]baptized into
Moses in the cloud and in the sea;
3 and all [a]ate the same spiritual food;
4 and all [a]drank the same
spiritual drink, for they were
drinking from a spiritual rock
which followed them; and the
rock was Christ.
5 Nevertheless, with most of
them God was not well-pleased;
for [a]they were laid low in the wilderness.

★ 3 [a]Ex. 16:4, 35; Deut. 8:3; Neh. 9:15, 20; Ps. 78:24f.; John 6:31
★ 4 [a]Ex. 17:6; Num. 20:11; Ps. 78:15
5 [a]Num. 14:29ff., 37; 26:65; Heb. 3:17; Jude 5

6 Now these things happened as [a]examples for us, that
we should not crave evil things, as
[b]they also craved.

★ 6 [a]1 Cor. 10:11 [b]Num. 11:4, 34; Ps. 106:14

7 And do not be [a]idolaters,
as some of them were; as it is
written, "[b]THE PEOPLE SAT DOWN TO
EAT AND DRINK, AND STOOD UP TO
[c]PLAY."

★ 7 [a]Ex. 32:4; 1 Cor. 5:11; 10:14 [b]Ex. 32:6 [c]Ex. 32:19

8 Nor let us act immorally,
as [a]some of them did, and [b]twen-
ty-three thousand fell in one day.

★ 8 [a]Num. 25:1ff. [b]Num. 25:9

9 Nor let us try the Lord, as
[a]some of them did, and were destroyed by the serpents.

★ 9 [a]Num. 21:5f.

10 Nor grumble, [a]as some of
them did, and [b]were destroyed by
the [c]destroyer.

★10 [a]Num. 16:41; 17:5, 10 [b]Num. 16:49 [c]Ex. 12:23; 2 Sam. 24:16; 1 Chr. 21:15; Heb. 11:28

11 Now these things happened to them as an [a]example,
and [b]they were written for our instruction, upon whom [c]the ends
of the ages have come.

11 [a]1 Cor. 10:6 [b]Rom. 4:23 [c]Rom. 13:11

12 Therefore let him who
[a]thinks he stands take heed lest
he fall.

12 [a]Rom. 11:20; 2 Pet. 3:17

9:24 *race.* Paul draws on his readers' knowledge of the Isthmian games, which were held every two years near Corinth.

9:25 *exercises self-control.* To be a winner one must train diligently. *a perishable wreath.* In the Isthmian games it was a wreath of pine.

9:26 *as not beating the air.* This does not refer to shadowboxing but to wild misses during an actual boxing match.

9:27 *I buffet my body.* Paul changes the metaphor: his opponent is now his own body. By self-discipline he gives it knockout blows. *disqualified.* A reference to the possible loss of reward (see note on 3:14; cf. 2 John 8).

10:1 *our fathers.* The nation Israel is now used as an illustration of some who were disqualified (9:27). *under the cloud* that guided them (Ex. 13:21–22; 14:19). *through the sea.* See Ex. 14:15–22.

10:2 *baptized into Moses.* I.e., united to Moses as their leader.

10:3 *spiritual food.* I.e., the manna (Ex. 16:1–36; Ps. 78:25).

10:4 *from a spiritual rock* which provided water (Ex. 17:1–9; Num. 20:1–13). Since the rock is mentioned twice, and is in different settings, a rabbinic legend held that a material rock actually followed the Israelites. Paul, however, says that it was Christ who was with Israel all the way.

10:6 *craved.* I.e., desired, when they preferred the food of Egypt to God's manna (Num. 11:4).

10:7 *idolaters.* See Ex. 32:1–14 for the making of the golden calf.

10:8 *twenty-three thousand* was the number killed *in one day.* Num. 25:9 indicates that there were additional deaths afterwards.

10:9 *try the Lord . . . destroyed by the serpents.* See Num. 21:6.

10:10 *grumble,* as some did after the judgment on the rebels who were led by Korah (Num. 16:41–50).

★13 [a]1 Cor. 1:9 [b]2 Pet. 2:9

13 No temptation has over-
taken you but such as is common
to man; and [a]God is faithful, who
will not allow you to be [b]tempted
beyond what you are able, but
with the temptation will provide
the way of escape also, that you
may be able to endure it.

2 *Do not participate in idol feasts,* 10:14–22

★14 [a]Heb. 6:9 [b]1 Cor. 10:7, 19f.; 1 John 5:21
16 [a]Matt. 26:27f.; 1 Cor. 11:25 [b]Matt. 26:26; Acts 2:42; 1 Cor. 11:32f.
17 [a]Rom. 12:5; 1 Cor. 12:12f., 27; Eph. 4:4, 16; Col. 3:15
18 [a]Rom. 1:3 [b]Lev. 7:6, 14f.; Deut. 12:17f.
19 [a]1 Cor. 8:4
20 [a]Deut. 32:17; Ps. 106:37; Gal. 4:8; Rev. 9:20
21 [a]2 Cor. 6:16 [b]Is. 65:11
22 [a]Deut. 32:21 [b]Eccl. 6:10; Is. 45:9

14 Therefore, my [a]beloved,
flee from [b]idolatry.
15 I speak as to wise men;
you judge what I say.
16 Is not the [a]cup of blessing
which we bless a sharing in the
blood of Christ? Is not the [b]bread
which we break a sharing in the
body of Christ?
17 Since there is one bread,
we [a]who are many are one body;
for we all partake of the one
bread.
18 Look at the nation [a]Israel;
are not those who [b]eat the sacrifices sharers in the altar?
19 What do I mean then?
That a thing sacrificed to idols is
anything, or [a]that an idol is anything?
20 No, but *I say* that the
things which the Gentiles sacrifice, they [a]sacrifice to demons,
and not to God; and I do not want
you to become sharers in demons.
21 [a]You cannot drink the cup
of the Lord and the cup of demons; you cannot partake of the
table of the Lord and [b]the table of
demons.
22 Or do we [a]provoke the
Lord to jealousy? We are not
[b]stronger than He, are we?

3 *Glorify God by seeking the welfare of your brother,* 10:23–11:1

23 [a]1 Cor. 6:12 [b]Rom. 14:19
★24 [a]Rom. 15:2; 1 Cor. 10:33; 13:5; 2 Cor. 12:14; Phil. 2:21
★25 [a]Acts 10:15; 1 Cor. 8:7
26 [a]Ps. 24:1; 50:12; 1 Tim. 4:4
27 [a]1 Cor. 5:10 [b]Luke 10:8
28 [a]1 Cor. 8:7, 10-12
29 [a]Rom. 14:16; 1 Cor. 9:19
30 [a]1 Cor. 9:1 [b]Rom. 14:6
★31 [a]Col. 3:17; 1 Pet. 4:11
32 [a]Acts 24:16; 1 Cor. 8:13 [b]Acts 20:28; 1 Cor. 1:2; 7:17; 11:22; 15:9; 2 Cor. 1:1; Gal. 1:13; Phil. 3:6; 1 Tim. 3:5, 15

23 [a]All things are lawful, but
not all things are profitable. All
things are lawful, but not all
things [b]edify.
24 Let no one [a]seek his own
good, but that of his neighbor.
25 [a]Eat anything that is sold
in the meat market, without asking questions for conscience'
sake;
26 [a]FOR THE EARTH IS THE
LORD'S, AND ALL IT CONTAINS.
27 If [a]one of the unbelievers
invites you, and you wish to go,
[b]eat anything that is set before
you, without asking questions for
conscience' sake.
28 But [a]if anyone should say
to you, "This is meat sacrificed to
idols," do not eat *it,* for the sake
of the one who informed *you,* and
for conscience' sake;
29 I mean not your own conscience, but the other *man's;* for
[a]why is my freedom judged by
another's conscience?
30 If I partake with thankfulness, [a]why am I slandered concerning that for which I [b]give
thanks?
31 Whether, then, you eat or
drink or [a]whatever you do, do all
to the glory of God.
32 [a]Give no offense either to
Jews or to Greeks or to [b]the
church of God;

10:13 *the way of escape.* Lit., the way out. Not necessarily relief, but power to be able to bear the testing.

10:14–22 Paul's point is that partaking in a religious feast means fellowshipping with the one worshiped at that feast. This is true of the Lord's Supper (vv. 16–17), it was true of Israel in O.T. times (v. 18), and it is true of a pagan feast (vv. 19–22). Therefore, believers must not fellowship at pagan feasts since they may thereby open themselves up to demonic attacks (v. 20).

10:24 *good* = welfare.

10:25 *the meat market.* The subject now changes from meat sacrificed to idols and served at pagan feasts to meat sacrificed to idols that is bought in the market and served at private dinner parties (v. 27). Again, liberty should be voluntarily restricted.

10:31 *do all to the glory of God.* This is the all-inclusive principle concluding the discussion that began in 8:1. It is: Test all conduct by whether or not it manifests the characteristics of God. Other principles for guiding the believer's conduct in this book are: (1) is it beneficial (6:12)? (2) is it enslaving (6:12)? (3) will it hinder the spiritual growth of a brother (8:13)? (4) does it edify (build up, 10:23)?

33 just as I also [a]please all
men in all things, [b]not seeking
my own profit, but the *profit* of
the many, [c]that they may be
saved.

11 [a]Be imitators of me, just as
I also am of Christ.

33 [a]Rom 15:2; 1 Cor. 9:22; Gal. 1:10 [b]Rom. 15:2; 2 Cor. 12:14; Phil. 2:21 [c]Rom. 11:14
★ 1 [a]1 Cor. 4:16

VI DISCUSSION CONCERNING PUBLIC WORSHIP, 11:2–14:40

A The Veiling of Women, 11:2–16

2 Now [a]I praise you because
you [b]remember me in everything,
and [c]hold firmly to the traditions,
just as I delivered them to you.
3 But I want you to understand that Christ is the [a]head of
every man, and [b]the man is the
head of a woman, and God is the
[c]head of Christ.
4 Every man who has *some-*
thing on his head while praying
or [a]prophesying, disgraces his
head.
5 But every [a]woman who
has her head uncovered while
praying or prophesying, disgraces
her head; for she is one and the
same with her whose head is
[b]shaved.
6 For if a woman does not
cover her head, let her also have
her hair cut off; but if it is disgraceful for a woman to have her
hair cut off or her head shaved, let
her cover her head.
7 For a man ought not to
have his head covered, since he is
the [a]image and glory of God; but
the woman is the glory of man.
8 For [a]man does not originate from woman, but woman
from man;
9 for indeed man was not
created for the woman's sake, but
[a]woman for the man's sake.
10 Therefore the woman
ought to have *a symbol of* authority on her head, because of the
angels.
11 However, in the Lord, neither is woman independent of
man, nor is man independent of
woman.
12 For as the woman origi-
nates from the man, so also the
man has his birth through the
woman; and [a]all things originate
[b]from God.
13 [a]Judge for yourselves: is it
proper for a woman to pray to
God *with head* uncovered?
14 Does not even nature itself
teach you that if a man has long
hair, it is a dishonor to him,
15 but if a woman has long
hair, it is a glory to her? For her
hair is given to her for a covering.
16 But if one is inclined to be
contentious, [a]we have no other
practice, nor have [b]the churches
of God.

★ 2 [a]1 Cor. 11:17, 22 [b]1 Cor. 4:17; 15:2; 1 Thess. 1:6; 3:6 [c]2 Thess. 2:15; 3:6
★ 3 [a]Eph. 1:22; 4:15; 5:23; Col. 1:18; 2:19 [b]Gen. 3:16; Eph. 5:23 [c]1 Cor. 3:23
4 [a]Acts 13:1; 1 Thess. 5:20
★ 5 [a]Luke 2:36; Acts 21:9; 1 Cor. 14:34 [b]Deut. 21:12
7 [a]Gen. 1:26; 5:1; 9:6; James 3:9
8 [a]Gen. 2:21-23; 1 Tim. 2:13
9 [a]Gen. 2:18
★10
12 [a]2 Cor. 5:18 [b]Rom. 11:36
13 [a]Luke 12:57
★15
★16 [a]1 Cor. 4:5; 9:1-3, 6 [b]1 Cor. 7:17

B The Lord's Supper, 11:17–34

17 But in giving this instruction, [a]I do not praise you, because

17 [a]1 Cor. 11:2, 22

11:1 This verse belongs in thought with chapter 10. The Corinthians are urged to imitate the self-sacrificing example of Paul and Christ.

11:2 *traditions.* I.e., oral teaching.

11:3 *the man is the head of a woman.* This teaching is based on Gen. 3:16, and Paul makes it the basis for the wearing of a covering.

11:5 *who has her head uncovered.* Women should be veiled or covered in the meeting of the church, and men should not. Paul's reasons were based on theology (headship, v. 3), the order in creation (vv. 7-9), and the presence of angels in the meeting (v. 10). None of these reasons was based on contemporary social custom. *praying or prophesying.* In the light of what he says in 14:34-35, it is doubtful that Paul approved of those activities by the women at Corinth. He simply acknowledges that these were unauthorized practices.

11:10 *a symbol.* I.e., the covering is the sign of man's authority over the woman. *because of the angels.* The insubordination of an uncovered woman (signifying her refusal to recognize the authority of her husband) would offend the angels who observe the conduct of believers in their church gatherings (1 Pet. 1:12).

11:15 *her hair is given to her for a covering.* This is not the same word as that used in vv. 5-6. The point here is that as the hair represents the proper covering in the natural realm, so the veil is the proper covering in the religious.

11:16 *no other practice.* I.e., no custom of women worshiping without some form of a covering.

you come together not for the
better but for the worse.
18 For, in the first place, when
you come together as a church, I
hear that [a]divisions exist among
you; and in part, I believe it.
19 For there [a]must also be
factions among you, [b]in order
that those who are approved may
have become evident among you.
20 Therefore when you meet
together, it is not to eat the Lord's
Supper,
21 for in your eating each one
takes his own supper first; and
one is hungry and [a]another is
drunk.
22 What! Do you not have
houses in which to eat and drink?
Or do you despise the [a]church of
God, and [b]shame those who have
nothing? What shall I say to you?
Shall [c]I praise you? In this I will
not praise you.
23 For [a]I received from the
Lord that which I also delivered to
you, that [b]the Lord Jesus in the
night in which He was betrayed
took bread;
24 and when He had given
thanks, He broke it, and said,
"This is My body, which is for
you; do this in remembrance of
Me."
25 In the same way *He took*
[a]the cup also, after supper, saying, "This cup is the [b]new covenant in My blood; do this, as often as you drink *it,* in
remembrance of Me."
26 For as often as you eat this
bread and drink the cup, you proclaim the Lord's death [a]until He
comes.
27 Therefore whoever eats
the bread or drinks the cup of the
Lord in an unworthy manner,
shall be [a]guilty of the body and
the blood of the Lord.
28 But let a man [a]examine
himself, and so let him eat of the
bread and drink of the cup.
29 For he who eats and
drinks, eats and drinks judgment
to himself, if he does not judge
the body rightly.
30 For this reason many
among you are weak and sick,
and a number [a]sleep.
31 But if we judged ourselves
rightly, we should not be judged.
32 But when we are judged,
we are [a]disciplined by the Lord in
order that we may not be condemned along with [b]the world.
33 So then, my brethren,
when you come together to eat,
wait for one another.
34 If anyone is [a]hungry, let
him eat [b]at home, so that you
may not come together for judgment. And the remaining matters
I shall [c]arrange [d]when I come.

18 [a]1 Cor. 1:10; 3:3
19 [a]Matt. 18:7; Luke 17:1; 1 Tim. 4:1; 2 Pet. 2:1 [b]Deut. 13:3; 1 John 2:19
★**20**
21 [a]Jude 12
22 [a]1 Cor. 10:32 [b]James 2:6 [c]1 Cor. 11:2, 17
23 [a]1 Cor. 15:3; Gal. 1:12; Col. 3:24 [b]1 Cor. 11:23-25: *Matt. 26:26-28; Mark 14:22-24; Luke 22:17-20;* 1 Cor. 10:16
★**24**
★**25** [a]1 Cor. 10:16 [b]Luke 22:20; 2 Cor. 3:6
★**26** [a]John 21:22; 1 Cor. 4:5
★**27** [a]Heb. 10:29
28 [a]Matt. 26:22; 2 Cor. 13:5; Gal. 6:4
30 [a]Acts 7:60
32 [a]2 Sam. 7:14; Ps. 94:12; Heb. 12:7-10; Rev. 3:19 [b]1 Cor. 1:20
34 [a]1 Cor. 11:21 [b]1 Cor. 11:22 [c]1 Cor. 4:17; 7:17; 16:1 [d]1 Cor. 4:19

C The Use of Spiritual Gifts, 12:1–14:40

1 The varieties of gifts, 12:1-11

12 Now concerning [a]spiritual
gifts, brethren, [b]I do not
want you to be unaware.
2 [a]You know that when you
were pagans, *you were* [b]led astray

★ **1** [a]1 Cor. 12:4; 14:1 [b]Rom. 1:13
2 [a]1 Cor. 6:11; Eph. 2:11f.; 1 Pet. 4:3 [b]1 Thess. 1:9 [c]Ps. 115:5; Is. 46:7; Jer. 10:5; Hab. 2:18f.

11:20 *when you meet together.* The early Christians held a love feast in connection with the Lord's Supper, during which they gathered for a fellowship meal, sent and received communications from other churches, and collected money for widows and orphans. Apparently some of the wealthier members were not sharing their food but greedily consumed it before the poor showed up (v. 21). If the purposes of the love feast were not being realized, it was better to eat at home (v. 22).

11:24 *This is My body.* The bread represents Christ's body and the *cup* (v. 25) His blood. See note on Luke 22:19.

11:25 *the new covenant.* See note on Matt. 26:28.

11:26 *you proclaim the Lord's death until He comes.* The Lord's Supper is an acted sermon (proclaim), looking back on Christ's life and death and looking forward to His second coming.

11:27 *in an unworthy manner.* I.e., with unconfessed sin. This may result in judgment, even sickness or physical death (v. 30). Therefore, each one is to examine himself before partaking (vv. 28, 31).

12:1 In chapters 12–14 Paul deals with the subject of *spiritual gifts,* against the background of divisions and moral laxity in a church that lacked no gift (1:7, see note). Chapter 12 deals with the unity and diversity of the gifts, chap. 13 with the power of love, and chap. 14 with the specific gifts of prophecy and tongues.

3 [a]Matt. 22:43; 1 John 4:2f.; Rev. 1:10 [b]Rom. 9:3 [c]John 13:13; Rom. 10:9
4 [a]Rom. 12:6f.; 1 Cor. 12:11; Eph. 4:4ff., 11; Heb. 2:4
6 [a]1 Cor. 15:28; Eph. 1:23; 4:6
7 [a]1 Cor. 12:12-30; 14:26; Eph. 4:12
★ **8** [a]1 Cor. 2:6; 2 Cor. 1:12 [b]Rom. 15:14; 1 Cor. 2:11, 16; 2 Cor. 2:14; 4:6; 8:7; 11:6
9 [a]1 Cor. 13:2; 2 Cor. 4:13 [b]1 Cor. 12:28, 30
10 [a]1 Cor. 12:28f.; Gal. 3:5 [b]1 Cor. 11:4; 13:2, 8 [c]1 Cor. 14:29; 1 John 4:1 [d]Mark 16:17; 1 Cor. 12:28, 30; 13:1; 14:2ff. [e]1 Cor. 12:30; 14:26
11 [a]1 Cor. 12:4 and ref.

to the [c]dumb idols, however you
were led.
3 Therefore I make known
to you, that no one speaking [a]by
the Spirit of God says, "Jesus is
[b]accursed"; and no one can say,
"Jesus is [c]Lord," except [a]by the
Holy Spirit.
4 Now there are [a]varieties of
gifts, but the same Spirit.
5 And there are varieties of
ministries, and the same Lord.
6 And there are varieties of
effects, but the same [a]God who
works all things in all *persons.*
7 But to each one is given
the manifestation of the Spirit
[a]for the common good.
8 For to one is given the
word of [a]wisdom through the
Spirit, and to another the word of
[b]knowledge according to the
same Spirit;
9 to another [a]faith by the
same Spirit, and to another [b]gifts
of healing by the one Spirit,
10 and to another the effecting of [a]miracles, and to another
[b]prophecy, and to another the
[c]distinguishing of spirits, to another *various* [d]kinds of tongues,
and to another the [e]interpretation
of tongues.
11 But one and the same
Spirit works all these things, [a]dis-
tributing to each one individually
just as He wills.

2 *The purpose of gifts: unity in diversity,* 12:12–31

★**12** [a]Rom. 12:4; 1 Cor. 10:17 [b]1 Cor. 12:27

12 For even [a]as the body is
one and *yet* has many members,
and all the members of the body,
though they are many, are one
body, [b]so also is Christ.
13 For [a]by one Spirit we were
all baptized into one body,
whether [b]Jews or Greeks, whether
slaves or free, and we were all
made to [c]drink of one Spirit.
14 For [a]the body is not one
member, but many.
15 If the foot should say, "Because I am not a hand, I am not *a*
part of the body," it is not for this
reason any the less *a part* of the
body.
16 And if the ear should say,
"Because I am not an eye, I am
not *a part* of the body," it is not
for this reason any the less *a part*
of the body.
17 If the whole body were an
eye, where would the hearing be?
If the whole were hearing, where
would the sense of smell be?
18 But now God has [a]placed
the members, each one of them,
in the body, [b]just as He desired.
19 And if they were all one
member, where would the body
be?
20 But now [a]there are many
members, but one body.
21 And the eye cannot say to
the hand, "I have no need of
you"; or again the head to the
feet, "I have no need of you."
22 On the contrary, it is much
truer that the members of the
body which seem to be weaker
are necessary;
23 and those *members* of the
body, which we deem less honorable, on these we bestow more

★**13** [a]Eph. 2:18 [b]Rom. 3:22; Gal. 3:28; Eph. 2:13-18; Col. 3:11 [c]John 7:37-39
14 [a]1 Cor. 12:20
18 [a]1 Cor. 12:28 [b]Rom. 12:6; 1 Cor. 12:11
20 [a]1 Cor. 12:12, 14
★**23**

12:8–10 *the word of wisdom* (v. 8). I.e., the communication of spiritual wisdom. *the word of knowledge* (v. 8). I.e., the communication of practical truth. *faith* (v. 9). I.e., unusual reliance on God. *gifts of healing* (v. 9). Included restoration of life (Acts 9:40; 20:12). *prophecy* (v. 10). The ability to proclaim new revelation from God. *tongues* and *interpretation of tongues* (v. 10). Ability to speak and interpret languages unknown to the speaker or the interpreter. These gifts were necessary before the Word of God was written.

12:12–31 Here Paul describes the relationship of gifted believers to each other, using the analogy of the human body. The Spirit has formed a spiritual organic unity of the many dissimilar members of the body of Christ (vv. 12–13). The constitutions both of the human body and of the body of Christ demand that all members (even those which seem unimportant) function in harmony (vv. 14–20). Finally, the need for mutual dependence, respect, and care for each other is emphasized (vv. 21–31).

12:13 *we were all baptized.* The Spirit joins all believers to the body of Christ. The tense of the verb indicates a past action, and it is something all believers (even carnal ones) have experienced.

12:23 *we bestow more abundant honor.* I.e., by way of clothing.

abundant honor, and our un-
seemly *members come to* have
more abundant seemliness,
24 whereas our seemly *members* have no need *of it.* But God
has *so* composed the body, giving
more abundant honor to that
member which lacked,
25 that there should be no division in the body, but *that* the
members should have the same
care for one another.
26 And if one member suffers, all the members suffer with
it; if *one* member is honored, all
the members rejoice with it.
27 Now you are [a]Christ's
body, and [b]individually members
of it.
28 And God has [a]appointed
in [b]the church, first [c]apostles, second [d]prophets, third [e]teachers,
then [f]miracles, then [g]gifts of healings, helps, [h]administrations, *various* [i]kinds of tongues.
29 All are not apostles, are
they? All are not prophets, are
they? All are not teachers, are
they? All are not *workers of* miracles, are they?
30 All do not have gifts of
healings, do they? All do not
speak with tongues, do they? All
do not [a]interpret, do they?
31 But [a]earnestly desire the
greater gifts.
And I show you a still more excellent way.

3 *The supremacy of love over gifts,* 13:1–13

13 If I speak with the
[a]tongues of men and of
[b]angels, but do not have love, I
have become a noisy gong or a
[c]clanging cymbal.
2 And if I have *the gift of*
[a]prophecy, and know all [b]mys-
teries and all [c]knowledge; and if I
have [d]all faith, so as to [e]remove
mountains, but do not have love, I
am nothing.
3 And if I [a]give all my possessions to feed *the poor,* and if I
[b]deliver my body to be burned,
but do not have love, it profits me
nothing.
4 Love [a]is patient, love is
kind, *and* [b]is not jealous; love
does not brag *and* is not [c]arro-
gant,
5 does not act unbecomingly; it [a]does not seek its own, is
not provoked, [b]does not take into
account a wrong *suffered,*
6 [a]does not rejoice in unrighteousness, but [b]rejoices with
the truth;
7 [a]bears all things, believes
all things, hopes all things, endures all things.
8 Love never fails; but if
there are gifts of [a]prophecy, they
will be done away; if *there are*
[b]tongues, they will cease; if *there
is* knowledge, it will be done
away.
9 For we [a]know in part, and
we prophesy in part;
10 but when the perfect
comes, the partial will be done
away.
11 When I was a child, I used
to speak as a child, think as a
child, reason as a child; when I

27 [a]1 Cor. 1:2; 12:12; Eph. 1:23; 4:12; Col. 1:18, 24; 2:19 [b]Rom. 12:5; Eph. 5:30
★28 [a]1 Cor. 12:18 [b]1 Cor. 10:32 [c]Eph. 4:11 [d]Acts 13:1; Eph. 2:20; 3:5 [e]Acts 13:1 [f]1 Cor. 12:10, 29 [g]1 Cor. 12:9, 30 [h]Rom. 12:8 [i]1 Cor. 12:10
★29
30 [a]1 Cor. 12:10
★31 [a]1 Cor. 14:1, 39
★ 1 [a]1 Cor. 12:10 [b]2 Cor. 12:4; Rev. 14:2 [c]Ps. 150:5 [Septuagint]
2 [a]Matt. 7:22; Acts 13:1; 1 Cor. 11:4; 13:8; 14:1, 39 [b]1 Cor. 14:2; 15:51 [c]Rom. 15:14 [d]1 Cor. 12:9 [e]Matt. 17:20; 21:21
3 [a]Matt. 6:2 [b]Dan. 3:28
4 [a]Prov. 10:12; 17:9; 1 Thess. 5:14; 1 Pet. 4:8 [b]Acts 7:9 [c]1 Cor. 4:6
★ 5 [a]1 Cor. 10:24; Phil. 2:21 [b]2 Cor. 5:19
6 [a]2 Thess. 2:12 [b]2 John 4; 3 John 3f.
7 [a]1 Cor. 9:12
8 [a]1 Cor. 13:2 [b]1 Cor. 13:1
9 [a]1 Cor. 8:2; 13:12
★10
★11

12:28 *first . . .* The gifts are ranked in order of honor.

12:29–30 The answer expected to all of these questions is "No."

12:31 *the greater gifts* (as ranked in v. 28).

13:1 *love.* The Greek word is *agape.* The Greek word for love of an adorable object, especially for love between man and woman, is *eros.* Another Greek word, *phileo,* refers to the love of friendship. *Agape* characterizes God (1 John 4:8) and what He manifested in the gift of His Son (John 3:16). It is more than mutual affection; it expresses unselfish esteem of the object loved. Christ's love for us is undeserved and without thought of return. The love which His followers show, Paul now says, should be the same. *a noisy gong* and *a clanging cymbal.* Associated with pagan worship.

13:5 *unbecomingly* (see 7:36; 11:5–6, 21). *does not seek its own.* See 6:7.

13:10 *the perfect.* A reference to Christ's second coming.

13:11 There are stages of growth within the present imperfect time before Christ's return. After the church began, there was a period of immaturity, during which spectacular gifts were needed for growth and authentication (Heb. 2:3–4). With the completion of the N.T. and the growing maturity of the church, the need for such gifts disappeared.

became a man, I did away with
childish things.
12 For now we [a]see in a mirror dimly, but then [b]face to face;
now I know in part, but then I
shall know fully just as I also
[c]have been fully known.
13 But now abide faith, hope,
love, these three; but the greatest
of these is [a]love.

12 [a]2 Cor. 5:7; Phil. 3:12; James 1:23 [b]Gen. 32:30; Num. 12:8; 1 John 3:2 [c]1 Cor. 8:3
★13 [a]Gal. 5:6

4 *The superiority of prophecy over tongues,* 14:1-25

14 [a]Pursue love, yet [b]desire
earnestly [c]spiritual *gifts,*
but especially that you may
[d]prophesy.
2 For one who [a]speaks in a
tongue does not speak to men,
but to God; for no one understands, but in *his* spirit he speaks
[b]mysteries.
3 But one who prophesies
speaks to men for [a]edification and
[b]exhortation and consolation.
4 One who [a]speaks in a
tongue [b]edifies himself; but one
who [c]prophesies [b]edifies the
church.
5 Now I wish that you all
[a]spoke in tongues, but [b]*even*
more that you would prophesy;
and greater is one who prophesies
than one who [a]speaks in tongues,
unless he interprets, so that the
church may receive [c]edifying.
6 But now, brethren, if I
come to you speaking in tongues,
what shall I profit you, unless I
speak to you either by way of
[a]revelation or of [b]knowledge or of
[c]prophecy or of [d]teaching?
7 Yet *even* lifeless things, either flute or harp, in producing a
sound, if they do not produce a
distinction in the tones, how will
it be known what is played on the
flute or on the harp?

★ 1 [a]1 Cor. 16:14 [b]1 Cor. 12:31; 14:39 [c]1 Cor. 12:1 [d]1 Cor. 13:2
★ 2 [a]Mark 16:17; 1 Cor. 12:10, 28, 30; 13:1; 14:18ff. [b]1 Cor. 13:2
3 [a]Rom. 14:19; 1 Cor. 14:5, 12, 17, 26 [b]Acts 4:36
4 [a]Mark 16:17; 1 Cor. 12:10, 28, 30; 13:1; 14:18ff., 26f. [b]Rom. 14:19; 1 Cor. 14:5, 12, 17, 26 [c]1 Cor. 13:2
5 [a]Mark 16:17; 1 Cor. 12:10, 28, 30; 13:1; 14:18ff., 26f. [b]Num. 11:29 [c]Rom. 14:19; 1 Cor. 14:4, 12, 17, 26
★ 6 [a]1 Cor. 14:26; Eph. 1:17 [b]1 Cor. 12:8 [c]1 Cor. 13:2 [d]Acts 2:42; Rom. 6:17; 1 Cor. 14:26

8 For if [a]the bugle produces
an indistinct sound, who will prepare himself for battle?
9 So also you, unless you utter by the tongue speech that is
clear, how will it be known what
is spoken? For you will be [a]speak-
ing into the air.
10 There are, perhaps, a great
many kinds of languages in the
world, and no *kind* is without
meaning.
11 If then I do not know the
meaning of the language, I shall
be to the one who speaks a [a]bar-
barian, and the one who speaks
will be a barbarian to me.
12 So also you, since you are
zealous of spiritual *gifts,* seek to
abound for the [a]edification of the
church.
13 Therefore let one who
speaks in a tongue pray that he
may interpret.
14 For if I pray in a tongue,
my spirit prays, but my mind is
unfruitful.
15 [a]What is *the outcome*
then? I shall pray with the spirit
and I shall pray with the mind
also; I shall [b]sing with the spirit
and I shall sing with the mind
also.
16 Otherwise if you bless in
the spirit *only,* how will the one
who fills the place of the ungifted
say [a]the "Amen" at your [b]giving
of thanks, since he does not know
what you are saying?
17 For you are giving thanks
well enough, but the other man is
not [a]edified.
18 I thank God, I speak in
tongues more than you all;
19 however, in the church I
desire to speak five words with
my mind, that I may instruct others also, rather than ten thousand
words in a tongue.

8 [a]Num. 10:9; Jer. 4:19; Ezek. 33:3-6; Joel 2:1
9 [a]1 Cor. 9:26
11 [a]Acts 28:2
12 [a]Rom. 14:19; 1 Cor. 14:4, 5, 17, 26
15 [a]Acts 21:22; 1 Cor. 14:26 [b]Eph. 5:19; Col. 3:16
★16 [a]Deut. 27:15-26; 1 Chr. 16:36; Neh. 5:13; 8:6; Ps. 106:48; Jer. 11:5; 28:6; Rev. 5:14; 7:12 [b]Matt. 15:36
17 [a]Rom. 14:19; 1 Cor. 14:4, 5, 12, 26

13:13 *abide.* Since these three virtues remain after all the gifts have ceased, they should be cultivated. Love is the *greatest,* since it expressed God and Calvary.

14:1 *especially that you may prophesy.* Prophecy is preferred over tongues because it is clear (v. 2) and it edifies the church (v. 4).

14:2 *a tongue.* Though many understand these tongues to be ecstatic speech, it may well be that they were languages, as in Acts 2:4, 6, 8, 11.

14:6-15 *tongues* are useless without interpretation.

14:16 *the place of the ungifted.* I.e., the untaught believer, or perhaps the outsider.

★20 [a]Rom. 1:13 [b]Eph. 4:14; Heb. 5:12f. [c]Ps. 131:2; Matt. 18:3; Rom. 16:19; 1 Pet. 2:2
★21 [a]John 10:34; 1 Cor. 14:34 [b]Is. 28:11f.

20 [a]Brethren, [b]do not be children in your thinking; yet in evil
[c]be babes, but in your thinking
be mature.
21 In [a]the Law it is written,
"[b]BY MEN OF STRANGE TONGUES AND
BY THE LIPS OF STRANGERS I WILL
SPEAK TO THIS PEOPLE, AND EVEN SO
THEY WILL NOT LISTEN TO ME," says
the Lord.

22 [a]1 Cor. 14:1

22 So then tongues are for a
sign, not to those who believe,
but to unbelievers; but [a]prophecy
is for a sign, not to unbelievers,
but to those who believe.

23 [a]Acts 2:13

23 If therefore the whole
church should assemble together
and all speak in tongues, and ungifted men or unbelievers enter,
will they not say that [a]you are
mad?

24 [a]1 Cor. 14:1 [b]John 16:8

24 But if all [a]prophesy, and
an unbeliever or an ungifted man
enters, he is [b]convicted by all, he
is called to account by all;

25 [a]John 4:19 [b]Luke 17:16 [c]Is. 45:14; Dan. 2:47; Zech. 8:23; Acts 4:13

25 [a]the secrets of his heart are
disclosed; and so he will [b]fall on
his face and worship God, [c]de-
claring that God is certainly
among you.

5 *The regulations for the use of gifts,* 14:26–40

★26 [a]1 Cor. 14:15 [b]Rom. 1:13 [c]1 Cor. 12:8-10 [d]Eph. 5:19 [e]1 Cor. 14:6 [f]1 Cor. 14:2 [g]1 Cor. 12:10; 14:5, 13, 27f. [h]Rom. 14:19
★27 [a]1 Cor. 14:2 [b]1 Cor. 12:10; 14:5, 13, 26ff.

26 [a]What is *the outcome*
then, [b]brethren? When you assemble, [c]each one has a [d]psalm,
has a [e]teaching, has a [e]revelation,
has a [f]tongue, has an [g]interpreta-
tion. Let [h]all things be done for
edification.
27 If any one speaks in a
[a]tongue, *it should be* by two or at
the most three, and *each* in turn,
and let one [b]interpret;
28 but if there is no interpreter, let him keep silent in the
church; and let him speak to himself and to God.
29 And let two or three
[a]prophets speak, and let the others [b]pass judgment.

★29 [a]1 Cor. 13:2; 14:32, 37 [b]1 Cor. 12:10

30 But if a revelation is made
to another who is seated, let the
first keep silent.
31 For you can all prophesy
one by one, so that all may learn
and all may be exhorted;
32 and the spirits of prophets
are subject to prophets;

★32

33 for God is not *a God* of
[a]confusion but of peace, as in [b]all
the churches of the [c]saints.
34 Let the women [a]keep silent in the churches; for they are
not permitted to speak, but [b]let
them subject themselves, just as
[c]the Law also says.

33 [a]1 Cor. 14:40 [b]1 Cor. 4:17; 7:17 [c]Acts 9:13
★34 [a]1 Cor. 11:5, 13 [b]1 Tim. 2:11f.; 1 Pet. 3:1 [c]1 Cor. 14:21

35 And if they desire to learn
anything, let them ask their own
husbands at home; for it is improper for a woman to speak in
church.
36 Was it from you that the
word of God *first* went forth? Or
has it come to you only?

★36

37 [a]If any one thinks he is a
prophet or [b]spiritual, let him recognize that the things which I
write to you [c]are the Lord's commandment.

37 [a]2 Cor. 10:7 [b]1 Cor. 2:15 [c]1 Cor. 7:40; 1 John 4:6

38 But if any one does not
recognize *this,* he is not recognized.

★38

14:20–25 Prophecy is not only more profitable for those within the church, but also for outsiders.

14:21 See Isa. 28:11–12. Tongues were given as a sign to provoke the Jews to consider the truth of the Christian message.

14:26 Free participation in the service is indicated by this verse, but not to the point of disorder.

14:27 *in turn.* Only *two* or *three* should speak in tongues in a service; never at the same time, but in turn; and not at all if no interpreter is present (v. 28).

14:29 *Two* or *three* prophets can be heard profitably during a meeting.

14:32 I.e., the spiritual activities of the prophets are under the full control of the prophets. No true prophet can claim a hearing on the ground that he is under a power over which he has no control.

14:34 *Let the women keep silent in the churches.* Whatever this restriction means, it must include tongues and prophecy (see vv. 27, 29, where the same Greek verb for *speak* is used). See also 1 Tim. 2:12.

14:36 I.e., Is Corinth the sole repository of the truth?

14:38 *he is not recognized.* One who does not respect and accept Paul's words should not have his own words respected or accepted. A variant translation is, "he is ignored" (i.e., by God).

39 Therefore, my brethren,
[a]desire earnestly to [b]prophesy,
and do not forbid to speak in
tongues.
40 But [a]let all things be done
properly and in an orderly manner.

39 a1 Cor. 12:31 b1 Cor. 13:2; 14:1
40 a1 Cor. 14:33

VII THE DOCTRINE OF THE RESURRECTION, 15:1–58

A The Importance of the Resurrection, 15:1–11

15 Now [a]I make known to
you, brethren, the [b]gospel
which I preached to you, which
also you received, [c]in which also
you stand,
2 by which also you are
saved, [a]if you hold fast the word
which I preached to you, [b]unless
you believed in vain.
3 For [a]I delivered to you as
of first importance what I also received, that Christ died [b]for our
sins [c]according to the Scriptures,
4 and that He was buried,
and that He was [a]raised on the
third day [b]according to the Scriptures,
5 and that [a]He appeared to
[b]Cephas, then [c]to the twelve.
6 After that He appeared to
more than five hundred brethren
at one time, most of whom remain until now, but some [a]have
fallen asleep;
7 then He appeared to
[a]James, then to [b]all the apostles;
8 and last of all, as it were to
one untimely born, [a]He appeared
to me also.
9 For I am [a]the least of the
apostles, who am not fit to be
called an apostle, because I [b]per-
secuted the church of God.
10 But by [a]the grace of God I
am what I am, and His grace
toward me did not prove vain; but
I [b]labored even more than all of
them, yet [c]not I, but the grace of
God with me.
11 Whether then *it was* I or
they, so we preach and so you believed.

1 aRom. 2:16; Gal. 1:11 bRom. 2:16; 1 Cor. 3:6; 4:15 cRom. 5:2; 11:20; 2 Cor. 1:24
★ 2 aRom. 11:22 bGal. 3:4
3 a1 Cor. 11:23 bJohn 1:29; Gal. 1:4; Heb. 5:1, 3; 1 Pet. 2:24 cIs. 53:5-12; Matt. 26:24; Luke 24:25-27; Acts 8:32f.; 17:2f.; 26:22
★ 4 aMatt. 16:21; John 2:21f.; Acts 2:24 bPs. 16:8ff.; Acts 2:31; 26:22f.
5 aLuke 24:34 b1 Cor. 1:12 cMark 16:14
★ 6 aActs 7:60; 1 Cor. 15:18, 20
★ 7 aActs 12:17 bLuke 24:33, 36f.; Acts 1:3f.
★ 8 aActs 9:3-8; 22:6-11; 26:12-18; 1 Cor. 9:1
9 a2 Cor. 12:11; Eph. 3:8; 1 Tim. 1:15 bActs 8:3
10 aRom. 12:3 b2 Cor. 11:23; Col. 1:29; 1 Tim. 4:10 c1 Cor. 3:6; 2 Cor. 3:5; Phil. 2:13

B The Consequences of Denying the Resurrection, 15:12–19

12 Now if Christ is preached,
that He has been raised from the
dead, how do some among you
say that there [a]is no resurrection
of the dead?
13 But if there is no resurrection of the dead, not even Christ
has been raised;
14 and [a]if Christ has not been
raised, then our preaching is vain,
your faith also is vain.
15 Moreover we are even
found *to be* false witnesses of

★12 aActs 17:32; 23:8; 2 Tim. 2:18
★13
14 a1 Thess. 4:14
15 aActs 2:24

15:2 *unless you believed in vain.* That would be the case if the resurrection of Christ were not true.

15:4 *and that He was buried.* Certain proof that Christ actually died. *and that He was raised.* The perfect tense indicates that He is still alive.

15:6 *five hundred brethren.* The citation of these and other witnesses to Christ's resurrection is of great apologetic value, especially in view of the fact that the resurrection was still being attested to by living witnesses 25 years after the event.

15:7 *He appeared to James.* Our Lord's half brother, the author of the letter of James (see John 7:5; Acts 1:14). This appearance is nowhere else recorded in the N.T.

15:8 *one untimely born.* Paul may be referring to his own conversion as premature when viewed in relation to Israel's future conversion (Rom. 11:26); or, more likely, he is regarding himself as a miscarried infant when compared to the other apostles; that is, one thrust suddenly into apostleship without the nurture of Christ's friendship and direct teaching.

15:12 *no resurrection of the dead.* Nothing in the Greek background of the Gentile converts at Corinth led them to believe in the resurrection of the dead. In general, they believed in the immortality of the soul, but not the resurrection of the body. To them, the body was the source of man's weakness and sin; death, therefore, was the welcome means by which the soul was liberated from the body. Resurrection, in their thinking, would only enslave the soul again.

15:13–19 If the bodily resurrection of Christ is untrue, then preaching the Gospel is a lie (v. 15), Christian faith is without meaningful content (v. 17), and Christians are hopeless concerning their prospects for the future (vv. 18–19).

God, because we witnessed
against God that He [a]raised
Christ, whom He did not raise, if
in fact the dead are not raised.
16 For if the dead are not
raised, not even Christ has been
raised;
17 and if Christ has not been
raised, your faith is worthless;
[a]you are still in your sins.
18 Then those also who [a]have
fallen asleep in Christ have perished.
19 If we have only hoped in
Christ in this life, we are [a]of all
men most to be pitied.

17 [a]Rom. 4:25
18 [a]1 Cor. 15:6; 1 Thess. 4:16; Rev. 14:13
19 [a]1 Cor. 4:9; 2 Tim. 3:12

C The Christian Hope, 15:20-34

20 But now Christ [a]has been
raised from the dead, the [b]first
fruits of those who [c]are asleep.
21 For since [a]by a man *came*
death, by a man also *came* the
resurrection of the dead.
22 For [a]as in Adam all die, so
also in Christ all shall be made
alive.
23 But each in his own order:
Christ [a]the first fruits, after that
[b]those who are Christ's at [c]His
coming,
24 then *comes* the end, when
He delivers up [a]the kingdom to
the [b]God and Father, when He
has abolished [c]all rule and all authority and power.
25 For He must reign [a]until
He has put all His enemies under
His feet.

★20 [a]Acts 2:24; 1 Pet. 1:3 [b]Acts 26:23; 1 Cor. 15:23; Rev. 1:5 [c]1 Cor. 15:6; 1 Thess. 4:16; Rev. 14:13
21 [a]Rom. 5:12
★22 [a]Rom. 5:14-18
★23 [a]Acts 26:23; 1 Cor. 15:20; Rev. 1:5 [b]1 Cor. 6:14; 15:52; 1 Thess. 4:16 [c]1 Thess. 2:19
24 [a]Dan. 2:44; 7:14, 27; 2 Pet. 1:11 [b]Eph. 5:20 [c]Rom. 8:38
25 [a]Ps. 110:1; Matt. 22:44

26 The last enemy that will be
[a]abolished is death.
27 For [a]HE HAS PUT ALL THINGS
IN SUBJECTION UNDER HIS FEET. But
when He says, "[b]All things are
put in subjection," it is evident
that He is excepted who put all
things in subjection to Him.
28 And when [a]all things are
subjected to Him, then the Son
Himself also will be subjected to
the One who subjected all things
to Him, that [b]God may be all in
all.
29 Otherwise, what will those
do who are baptized for the dead?
If the dead are not raised at all,
why then are they baptized for
them?
30 Why are we also [a]in danger every hour?
31 I protest, brethren, by the
boasting in you, which I have in
Christ Jesus our Lord, [a]I die daily.
32 If from human motives I
[a]fought with wild beasts at [b]Eph-
esus, what does it profit me? If the
dead are not raised, [c]LET US EAT
AND DRINK, FOR TOMORROW WE DIE.
33 [a]Do not be deceived: "Bad
company corrupts good morals."
34 [a]Become sober-minded as
you ought, and stop sinning; for
some have [b]no knowledge of
God. [c]I speak *this* to your shame.

26 [a]2 Tim. 1:10; Rev. 20:14; 21:4
27 [a]Ps. 8:6 [b]Matt. 11:27; 28:18; Eph. 1:22; Heb. 2:8
28 [a]Phil. 3:21 [b]1 Cor. 3:23; 12:6
★29
30 [a]2 Cor. 11:26
★31 [a]Rom. 8:36
32 [a]2 Cor. 1:8 [b]Acts 18:19; 1 Cor. 16:8f. [c]Is. 22:13; 56:12; Luke 12:19
★33 [a]1 Cor. 6:9
34 [a]Rom. 13:11 [b]Matt. 22:29; Acts 26:8 [c]1 Cor. 6:5

D The Resurrection Body, 15:35-50

35 But [a]some one will say,
"How are [b]the dead raised? And

★35 [a]Rom. 9:19 [b]Ezek. 37:3

15:20 *the first fruits.* Christ's resurrection is an earnest or prototype of resurrections to come (see Lev. 23:9-14).

15:22 *in Christ all shall be made alive.* This refers only to the resurrection of believers (those *in Christ*).

15:23-24 The order of resurrections is as follows: first, Christ's; then that of believers at His coming (1 Thess. 4:13-18); and finally, the resurrection at the end of the millennial kingdom.

15:29 *baptized for the dead.* Various interpretations have been given for this difficult expression. (1) It sanctions being baptized vicariously for another in order to assure him a place in heaven—a view which is heretical. (2) It refers to those who were baptized because of the testimony of those who had died. (3) Most likely it means being baptized in the place of those who had died; i.e., new converts taking the place of older ones who had died. Paul's point is: unless one believes in the resurrection of the dead (rather than the Greek idea of "immortality") what's the point of such a practice?

15:31 *I die daily.* Paul was exposed to so many physical dangers and to such violent attacks on himself and on his teachings that "daily" cannot be an exaggeration.

15:33 *Do not be deceived.* The same Greek phrase occurs in 6:9; Gal. 6:7; Jas. 1:16. The verse is a Greek proverb, first appearing in a play by Menander.

15:35-50 Here Paul deals with two common er-

with what kind of body do they
come?"

36 [a]Luke 11:40 [b]John 12:24

36 [a]You fool! That which you
[b]sow does not come to life unless
it dies;
37 and that which you sow,
you do not sow the body which is
to be, but a bare grain, perhaps of
wheat or of something else.

38 [a]Gen. 1:11

38 But God gives it a body
just as He wished, and [a]to each of
the seeds a body of its own.
39 All flesh is not the same
flesh, but there is *one flesh* of
men, and another flesh of beasts,
and another flesh of birds, and
another of fish.
40 There are also heavenly
bodies and earthly bodies, but the
glory of the heavenly is one, and
the *glory* of the earthly is another.
41 There is one glory of the
sun, and another glory of the
moon, and another glory of the
stars; for star differs from star in
glory.

★42 [a]Dan. 12:3; Matt. 13:43 [b]Rom. 8:21; 1 Cor. 15:50; Gal. 6:8 [c]Rom. 2:7

42 [a]So also is the resurrection
of the dead. It is sown [b]a perishable *body*, it is raised [c]an imperishable *body;*

43 [a]Phil. 3:21; Col. 3:4

43 it is sown in dishonor, it is
raised in [a]glory; it is sown in
weakness, it is raised in power;

44 [a]1 Cor. 2:14 [b]1 Cor. 15:50

44 it is sown a [a]natural body,
it is raised a [b]spiritual body. If
there is a natural body, there is
also a spiritual *body.*

45 [a]Gen. 2:7 [b]Rom. 5:14 [c]John 5:21; 6:57f.; Rom. 8:2

45 So also it is written, "The
first [a]MAN, Adam, BECAME A LIVING
SOUL." The [b]last Adam *became* a
[c]life-giving spirit.
46 However, the spiritual is
not first, but the natural; then the
spiritual.

47 [a]John 3:31 [b]Gen. 2:7; 3:19

47 The first man is [a]from the
earth, [b]earthy; the second man is
from heaven.

48 [a]Phil. 3:20f.

48 As is the earthy, so also are
those who are earthy; and as is
the heavenly, [a]so also are those
who are heavenly.

★49 [a]Gen. 5:3 [b]Rom. 8:29

49 And just as we have
[a]borne the image of the earthy,
we [b]shall also bear the image of
the heavenly.

50 [a]Matt. 16:17; John 3:5f. [b]1 Cor. 6:9 [c]Rom. 2:7

50 Now I say this, brethren,
that [a]flesh and blood cannot [b]in-
herit the kingdom of God; nor
does the perishable inherit [c]the
imperishable.

E The Christian's Victory through Christ, 15:51-58

★51 [a]1 Cor. 13:2 [b]2 Cor. 5:2, 4

51 Behold, I tell you a [a]mys-
tery; we shall not all sleep, but we
shall all be [b]changed,

52 [a]Matt. 24:31 [b]John 5:28 [c]1 Thess. 4:15, 17

52 in a moment, in the twin-
kling of an eye, at the last trumpet; for [a]the trumpet will sound,
and [b]the dead will be raised imperishable, and [c]we shall be
changed.

★53 [a]Rom. 2:7 [b]2 Cor. 5:4

53 For this perishable must
put on [a]the imperishable, and this
[b]mortal must put on immortality.

54 [a]Is. 25:8

54 But when this perishable
will have put on the imperishable,
and this mortal will have put on
immortality, then will come about
the saying that is written,
"[a]DEATH IS SWALLOWED UP IN VIC-
TORY.

55 [a]Hos. 13:14

55 "[a]O DEATH, WHERE IS YOUR
VICTORY? O DEATH, WHERE IS YOUR
STING?"

★56 [a]Rom. 5:12 [b]Rom. 3:20; 4:15; 7:8

56 The sting of [a]death is sin,
and [b]the power of sin is the law;

---

rors in regard to the nature of the resurrection body: (1) that it is the same body that was laid in the grave, simply reconstituted; and (2) that the new body is unrelated to the original one. Paul here explains that it is the body God has chosen (v. 38), related to the former (v. 36) yet different (vv. 39-41).

15:42 *raised an imperishable body.* With no possibility of decay.

15:49 *the image of the heavenly.* I.e., the resurrection body will be like Christ's.

15:51-58 Here Paul answers the question, What happens to those who do not die?

15:51 *we shall not all sleep.* I.e., not all die (1 Thess. 4:15). Some will be alive when the Lord returns, but all will *be changed.*

15:53 *perishable.* I.e., those who have died. *mortal.* I.e., those who are living.

15:56 *The sting of death is sin* because it is by sin that death gains authority over man, *and the power of sin is the law,* because the law stirs up sin (Rom. 5:12; 7:8-11).

57 [a]Rom. 7:25; 2 Cor. 2:14 [b]Rom. 8:37; Heb. 2:14f.; 1 John 5:4; Rev. 21:4
★58 [a]2 Pet. 3:14 [b]1 Cor. 16:10

57 but [a]thanks be to God, who gives us the [b]victory through our Lord Jesus Christ.

58 [a]Therefore, my beloved brethren, be steadfast, immovable, always abounding in [b]the work of the Lord, knowing that your toil is not *in* vain in the Lord.

VIII PRACTICAL AND PERSONAL MATTERS, 16:1–24

A The Collection for the Saints in Jerusalem, 16:1–4

★ 1 [a]Acts 24:17 [b]Acts 9:13 [c]1 Cor. 4:17 [d]Acts 16:6
★ 2 [a]Acts 20:7 [b]2 Cor. 9:4f.
★ 3 [a]2 Cor. 3:1; 8:18f.

16 Now concerning [a]the collection for [b]the saints, as [c]I directed the churches of [d]Galatia, so do you also.

2 On [a]the first day of every week let each one of you put aside and save, as he may prosper, that [b]no collections be made when I come.

3 And when I arrive, [a]whomever you may approve, I shall send them with letters to carry your gift to Jerusalem;

4 and if it is fitting for me to go also, they will go with me.

B The Planned Visit of Paul, 16:5–9

5 [a]1 Cor. 4:19 [b]Rom. 15:26 [c]Acts 19:21
6 [a]Acts 15:3; 1 Cor. 16:11
7 [a]2 Cor. 1:15f. [b]Acts 18:21
8 [a]Acts 18:19 [b]Acts 2:1
★ 9 [a]Acts 14:27 [b]Acts 19:9

5 But I [a]shall come to you after I go through [b]Macedonia, for I [c]am going through Macedonia;

6 and perhaps I shall stay with you, or even spend the winter, that you may [a]send me on my way wherever I may go.

7 For I do not wish to see you now [a]*just* in passing; for I hope to remain with you for some time, [b]if the Lord permits.

8 But I shall remain in [a]Ephesus until [b]Pentecost;

9 for a [a]wide door for effective *service* has opened to me, and [b]there are many adversaries.

C Exhortations, Greetings, and Benediction, 16:10–24

10 [a]Acts 16:1; 1 Cor. 4:17; 2 Cor. 1:1 [b]1 Cor. 15:58
11 [a]1 Tim. 4:12; Titus 2:15 [b]Acts 15:3; 1 Cor. 16:6 [c]Acts 15:33
★12 [a]Acts 18:24 [1 Cor. 1:12; 3:5f.]
13 [a]Matt. 24:42 [b]1 Cor. 15:1; Gal. 5:1; Phil. 1:27; 4:1; 1 Thess. 3:8; 2 Thess. 2:15 [c]1 Sam. 4:9; 2 Sam. 10:12; Is. 46:8 [d]Ps. 31:24; Eph. 3:16; 6:10; Col. 1:11
14 [a]1 Cor. 14:1
★15 [a]1 Cor. 1:16 [b]Rom. 16:5 [c]Acts 18:12 [d]Rom. 15:31 [e]1 Cor. 16:1
16 [a]1 Thess. 5:12; Heb. 13:17
★17 [a]2 Cor. 7:6f. [b]2 Cor. 11:9; Phil. 2:30
18 [a]2 Cor. 7:13; Philem. 7, 20 [b]Phil. 2:29; 1 Thess. 5:12
19 [a]Acts 16:6 [b]Acts 18:2 [c]Rom. 16:5

10 Now if [a]Timothy comes, see that he is with you without cause to be afraid; for he is doing [b]the Lord's work, as I also am.

11 [a]Let no one therefore despise him. But [b]send him on his way [c]in peace, so that he may come to me; for I expect him with the brethren.

12 But concerning [a]Apollos our brother, I encouraged him greatly to come to you with the brethren; and it was not at all *his* desire to come now, but he will come when he has opportunity.

13 [a]Be on the alert, [b]stand firm in the faith, [c]act like men, [d]be strong.

14 Let all that you do be done [a]in love.

15 Now I urge you, brethren (you know the [a]household of Stephanas, that they were the [b]first fruits of [c]Achaia, and that they have devoted themselves for [d]ministry to [e]the saints),

16 that [a]you also be in subjection to such men and to everyone who helps in the work and labors.

17 And I rejoice over the [a]coming of Stephanas and Fortunatus and Achaicus; because they have supplied [b]what was lacking on your part.

18 For they [a]have refreshed my spirit and yours. Therefore [b]acknowledge such men.

19 The churches of [a]Asia greet you. [b]Aquila and Prisca greet you heartily in the Lord,

---

15:58 A firm belief in the resurrection and a solid hope for the future gives incentive for service in the present.

16:1 *the saints.* I.e., those in Jerusalem.

16:2 The Christian's giving is to be done (1) regularly on Sunday; (2) into a private fund ("put aside") at home from which fund he makes distributions; and (3) in proportion to God's prospering.

16:3 Paul would let others handle the money.

16:9 *door.* I.e., of opportunity.

16:12 *his desire.* I.e., Apollos'.

16:15 *first fruits.* I.e., first converts.

16:17 *Stephanas and Fortunatus and Achaicus* probably brought Paul the letter from the Corinthians mentioned in 7:1.

with [c]the church that is in their
house.
20 All the brethren greet you.
[a]Greet one another with a holy
kiss.
21 The greeting is in [a]my
own hand—Paul.
22 If any one does not love
the Lord, let him be [a]accursed.
[b]Maranatha.
23 [a]The grace of the Lord
Jesus be with you.
24 My love be with you all in
Christ Jesus. Amen.

★20 [a]Rom. 16:16
21 [a]Rom. 16:22; Gal. 6:11; Col. 4:18; 2 Thess. 3:17; Philem. 19
★22 [a]Rom. 9:3 [b]Phil. 4:5; Rev. 22:20
23 [a]Rom. 16:20

16:20 *a holy kiss.* See note on 1 Pet. 5:14.
16:22 *accursed* (cf. 12:3; Rom. 9:3; Gal. 1:8–9). *Maranatha* = our Lord, come! See also Rev. 22:20.

INTRODUCTION TO THE SECOND LETTER OF PAUL TO THE CORINTHIANS

AUTHOR: Paul DATE: 57

Occasion *After writing 1 Corinthians, Paul found it necessary to make a hurried, painful visit to Corinth, since the problems that occasioned the first letter had not been resolved (2 Cor. 2:1; 12:14; 13:1-2). Following this visit, he wrote the church a severe and sorrowful letter, to which he refers in 2:4 but which has been lost to us. Titus delivered that letter. Paul, unable to wait to meet Titus on his return to Troas, hurried on to Macedonia where Titus related the good news that the church finally had repented of their rebelliousness against Paul. From Macedonia Paul wrote 2 Corinthians and followed it up with his final recorded visit to the church (Acts 20:1-4).*

A popular theory claims that chapters 10-13 are part of that lost "sorrowful letter." Although some features of those chapters correspond to what must have been the contents of the lost letter, the principal subject of that letter (the offender of 2 Corinthians 2-5) is nowhere mentioned in these chapters. Further, there is no evidence for so partitioning 2 Corinthians.

Purpose *The purpose of this letter was threefold: (1) to express joy at the favorable response of the church to Paul's ministry (1-7); (2) to remind the believers of their commitment to the offering for the Christians in Judea (8-9); and (3) to defend Paul's apostolic authority (10-13).*

Contents *The letter contains many personal and autobiographical glimpses into Paul's life (4:8-18; 11:22-33). The longest discussion of giving in the New Testament is in chapters 8 and 9. Important verses include 5:10, 20-21; 6:14; 8:9; 10:5; 11:14; 12:9; and 13:14.*

OUTLINE OF 2 CORINTHIANS

I. Introduction, 1:1-11
- A. Salutation, 1:1-2
- B. Paul's Gratitude for God's Goodness, 1:3-11

II. The Apostle's Conciliation with Respect to the Problem at Corinth, 1:12-2:13
- A. The Change in Paul's Plans, 1:12-2:4
- B. The Change in the Offender's Punishment, 2:5-11
- C. The Meeting with Titus, 2:12-13

III. The Apostolic Ministry, 2:14-6:10
- A. The Confidence of the Ministry: Victory, 2:14-17
- B. The Commendation of the Ministry: Changed Lives, 3:1-3
- C. The Covenant for the Ministry: The New Covenant, 3:4-18
- D. The Character of the Ministry: Supernatural, 4:1-7
- E. The Circumstances of the Ministry, 4:8-18
- F. The Compulsions of the Ministry, 5:1-21
  1. The assurance of resurrection, 5:1-9
  2. The judgment seat of Christ, 5:10-13
  3. The love of Christ, 5:14-21
- G. The Conduct of the Ministry, 6:1-10

IV. The Apostle's Exhortations to the Corinthians, 6:11-7:16
- A. Be Open toward Him, 6:11-13
- B. Be Separated from Evil, 6:14-7:1
- C. Be Assured of His Joy over Their Repentance, 7:2-16

V. The Apostle's Collection for the Judean Saints, 8:1-9:15
- A. Principles for Giving, 8:1-6
- B. Purposes for Giving, 8:7-15
- C. Policies in Giving, 8:16-9:5
- D. Promises in Giving, 9:6-15

VI. The Apostle's Vindication of Himself, 10:1-12:18
- A. The Authority of His Apostleship, 10:1-18
- B. The Marks of His Apostleship, 11:1-12:18
  1. Paul's conduct, 11:1-15
  2. Paul's sufferings, 11:16-33
  3. Paul's vision, 12:1-10
  4. Paul's unselfishness, 12:11-18

VII. Concluding Remarks, 12:19-13:14
- A. Appeal for Repentance, 12:19-21
- B. Statement of Plans, 13:1-10
- C. Greetings and Benediction, 13:11-14

THE SECOND LETTER OF PAUL TO THE CORINTHIANS

I INTRODUCTION, 1:1-11

A Salutation, 1:1-2

★ 1 [a]Rom. 1:1; Gal. 1:1; Eph. 1:1; Col. 1:1; 2 Tim. 1:1; Titus 1:1 [b]Gal. 3:26 [c]1 Cor. 1:1 [d]Acts 16:1; 1 Cor. 16:10; 2 Cor. 1:19 [e]1 Cor. 10:32 [f]Acts 18:1 [g]Acts 18:12

1 Paul, [a]an apostle of [b]Christ
Jesus [c]by the will of God, and
[d]Timothy *our* brother, to [e]the
church of God which is at [f]Corinth with all the saints who are
throughout [g]Achaia:

★ 2 [a]Rom. 1:7

2 [a]Grace to you and peace
from God our Father and the Lord
Jesus Christ.

B Paul's Gratitude for God's Goodness, 1:3-11

3 [a]Eph. 1:3; 1 Pet. 1:3 [b]Rom. 15:5

3 [a]Blessed *be* the God and
Father of our Lord Jesus Christ,
the Father of mercies and [b]God of
all comfort;

4 [a]Is. 51:12; 66:13; 2 Cor. 7:6, 7, 13

4 who [a]comforts us in all our
affliction so that we may be able
to comfort those who are in any
affliction with the comfort with
which we ourselves are comforted
by God.

★ 5 [a]2 Cor. 4:10; Phil. 3:10; Col. 1:24

5 For just [a]as the sufferings
of Christ are ours in abundance,
so also our comfort is abundant
through Christ.

6 [a]2 Cor. 4:15; 12:15; Eph. 3:1, 13; 2 Tim. 2:10

6 But if we are afflicted, it is
[a]for your comfort and salvation;
or if we are comforted, it is for
your comfort, which is effective in
the patient enduring of the same
sufferings which we also suffer;

7 [a]Rom. 8:17

7 and our hope for you is
firmly grounded, knowing that
[a]as you are sharers of our sufferings, so also you are *sharers* of
our comfort.

★ 8 [a]Rom. 1:13 [b]Acts 19:23; 1 Cor. 15:32 [c]Acts 16:6

8 For [a]we do not want you to
be unaware, brethren, of our [b]affliction which came *to us* in [c]Asia,
that we were burdened excessively, beyond our strength, so
that we despaired even of life;
9 indeed, we had the sentence of death within ourselves in
order that we should not trust in
ourselves, but in God who raises
the dead;

10 [a]Rom. 15:31 [b]1 Tim. 4:10

10 who [a]delivered us from so
great a *peril of* death, and will deliver *us,* He [b]on whom we have
set our hope. And He will yet deliver us,

★11 [a]Rom. 15:30; Phil. 1:19; Philem. 22 [b]2 Cor. 4:15; 9:11f.

11 you also joining in [a]helping us through your prayers, that
thanks may be given by [b]many
persons on our behalf for the favor bestowed upon us through
the prayers of many.

II THE APOSTLE'S CONCILIATION WITH RESPECT TO THE PROBLEM AT CORINTH, 1:12-2:13

A The Change in Paul's Plans, 1:12-2:4

12 [a]Acts 23:1; 1 Thess. 2:10; Heb. 13:18 [b]2 Cor. 2:17 [c]1 Cor. 1:17

12 For our proud confidence
is this, the testimony of [a]our con-

1:1 *Achaia.* The Roman province comprising all of southern Greece below Macedonia, including Athens and Corinth, the capital.

1:2 *God our Father.* Paul teaches a number of truths about God the Father in this epistle: (1) He is the living God (3:3; 6:16); (2) He is the God of grace, mercy, and comfort (1:2-3); (3) He is faithful (1:18); (4) His power is available to His people (4:7; 6:7; 13:4); and (5) He is the Father of Christ (1:3) and of His people (6:18). Concerning *the Lord Jesus Christ* Paul says: (1) He is the Son of God (1:19); (2) He is the image of God (4:4); and (3) He is sinless (5:21). But Paul seems to be most interested in explaining what Christ does: (1) He gives victory (2:14); (2) He judges (5:10); (3) He reconciles (5:19; 8:9); (4) He appoints and motivates His ambassadors (5:20); and (5) He makes men new creatures (5:17).

1:5 *the sufferings of Christ are ours in abundance.* Paul's own sufferings are identified as Christ's sufferings (see 4:10; Phil. 3:10; Col. 1:24). What Paul suffered was intended to encourage others (2 Cor. 1:6).

1:8 *our affliction which came to us in Asia.* Since Paul offers no details, it seems probable the Corinthians knew what the trouble was. It may have been one of the dangers described in 11:23-26, the mob violence of Acts 19:23-41, or some serious illness *(we despaired even of life).*

1:11 *your prayers.* The good report of the church brought by Titus encouraged Paul to exhort the Corinthians to prayer. Paul's great confidence in intercessory prayer is seen also in Rom. 15:30-31; Phil. 1:9; Col. 4:12.

science, that in holiness and [b]god-
ly sincerity, [c]not in fleshly wisdom but in the grace of God, we
have conducted ourselves in the
world, and especially toward you.
13 [a]1 Cor. 1:8 **13** For we write nothing else
to you than what you read and
understand, and I hope you will
understand [a]until the end;
14 [a]1 Cor. 1:8 **14** just as you also partially
did understand us, that we are
your reason to be proud as you
also are ours, in [a]the day of our
Lord Jesus.
15 [a]1 Cor. 4:19 [b]Rom. 1:11; 15:29 **15** And in this confidence I
intended at first to [a]come to you,
that you might twice receive a
[b]blessing;
★16 [a]Acts 19:21; 1 Cor. 16:5-7 [b]Rom. 15:26 [c]Acts 15:3; 1 Cor. 16:6, 11 [d]Acts 19:21 **16** that is, to [a]pass your way
into [b]Macedonia, and again from
Macedonia to come to you, and
by you to be [c]helped on my journey [d]to Judea.
★17 [a]2 Cor. 10:2f.; 11:18 **17** Therefore, I was not vacil-
lating when I intended to do this,
was I? Or that which I purpose, do
I purpose [a]according to the flesh,
that with me there should be yes,
yes and no, no *at the same time?*
18 [a]1 Cor. 1:9 [b]2 Cor. 2:17 **18** But as [a]God is faithful,
[b]our word to you is not yes and
no.
19 [a]Matt. 4:3; 16:16; 26:63 [b]Acts 15:22; 1 Thess. 1:1; 2 Thess. 1:1; 1 Pet. 5:12 [c]2 Cor. 1:1 [d]Heb. 13:8 **19** For [a]the Son of God, Christ
Jesus, who was preached among
you by us—by me and [b]Silvanus
and [c]Timothy—was not yes and
no, but is yes [d]in Him.
★20 [a]Rom. 15:8 [b]Heb. 13:8 [c]1 Cor. 14:16; Rev. 3:14 **20** For [a]as many as may be
the promises of God, [b]in Him
they are yes; wherefore also by
Him is [c]our Amen to the glory of
God through us.

21 Now He who [a]establishes 21 [a]1 Cor. 1:8 [b]1 John 2:20, 27
us with you in Christ and [b]anoint-
ed us is God,
22 who also [a]sealed us and ★22 [a]John 3:33 [b]Rom. 8:16; 2 Cor. 5:5; Eph. 1:14
[b]gave *us* the Spirit in our hearts as
a pledge.
23 But [a]I call God as witness 23 [a]Rom. 1:9; Gal. 1:20 [b]1 Cor. 4:21; 2 Cor. 2:1, 3 [c]2 Cor. 1:1
to my soul, that [b]to spare you I
came no more to [c]Corinth.
24 Not that we [a]lord it over ★24 [a]2 Cor. 4:5; 11:20; 1 Pet. 5:3 [b]Rom 11:20; 1 Cor. 15:1
your faith, but are workers with
you for your joy; for in your faith
you are [b]standing firm.
2 But I determined this for my 1 [a]1 Cor. 4:21; 2 Cor. 12:21
own sake, that I [a]would not
come to you in sorrow again.
2 For if I [a]cause you sorrow, ★ 2 [a]2 Cor. 7:8
who then makes me glad but the
one whom I made sorrowful?
3 And this is the very thing I 3 [a]2 Cor. 2:9; 7:8, 12 [b]1 Cor. 4:21; 2 Cor. 12:21 [c]Gal. 5:10; 2 Thess. 3:4; Philem. 21
[a]wrote you, lest, [b]when I came, I
should have sorrow from those
who ought to make me rejoice;
having [c]confidence in you all, that
my joy would be *the joy* of you
all.
4 For out of much affliction ★ 4 [a]2 Cor. 2:9; 7:8, 12
and anguish of heart I [a]wrote to
you with many tears; not that you
should be made sorrowful, but
that you might know the love
which I have especially for you.

B The Change in the Offender's Punishment, 2:5–11

5 But [a]if any has caused sor- 5 [a]1 Cor. 5:1f.
row, he has caused sorrow not to

1:16 Paul intended to visit them twice, going to and returning from Macedonia, but he changed his plans. This change was dubbed vacillation and unspirituality (*according to the flesh,* v. 17) by his opponents, charges he denies.

1:17 The verse may be paraphrased like this: Did my change of plans indicate that I couldn't make up my mind? Am I like a worldly man who says "Yes" and "No" at the same time? In 1 Cor. 16:5 Paul had promised to go to Corinth. In the second (lost) letter (between 1 and 2 Cor.) he may have said something different, which seemed to make him say yes and no at the same time. His present itinerary was Ephesus to Troas to Macedonia to Corinth.

1:20 *in Him they are yes.* I.e., the promises of God find their certain fulfillment, their Yes, in Christ. *by Him is our Amen.* I.e., we give our concurrence through saying Amen.

1:22 The seal indicates security, and the *pledge* is a guarantee that God will fulfill His promises. See notes on Eph. 1:13 and 1:14.

1:24 *Not that we lord it over your faith.* Apostolic authority did not give Paul any such right (see 1 Pet. 5:1–3). They stand *in . . . faith,* i.e., their own faith, not by Paul's control.

2:2 The meaning is this: If I hurt you, who will be left to make me glad but sad people? That wouldn't be any comfort!

2:4 *I wrote to you.* See the Introduction to 2 Corinthians for a discussion of this "sorrowful letter."

me, but in some degree—in order not to say too much—to all of you.

6 Sufficient for such a one is [a]this punishment which was *inflicted by* the majority,

7 so that on the contrary you should rather [a]forgive and comfort *him,* lest somehow such a one be overwhelmed by excessive sorrow.

8 Wherefore I urge you to reaffirm *your* love for him.

9 For to this end also [a]I wrote that I might [b]put you to the test, whether you are [c]obedient in all things.

10 But whom you forgive anything, I *forgive* also; for indeed what I have forgiven, if I have forgiven anything, *I did it* for your sakes [a]in the presence of Christ,

11 in order that no advantage be taken of us by [a]Satan; for [b]we are not ignorant of his schemes.

★ **6** [a]1 Cor. 5:4f.; 2 Cor. 7:11
7 [a]Gal. 6:1; Eph. 4:32
★ **9** [a]2 Cor. 2:3f. [b]2 Cor. 8:2; Phil. 2:22 [c]2 Cor. 7:15; 10:6
10 [a]1 Cor. 5:4; 2 Cor. 4:6
★**11** [a]Matt. 4:10 [b]Luke 22:31; 2 Cor. 4:4; 1 Pet. 5:8

C The Meeting with Titus, 2:12–13

12 Now when I came to [a]Troas for the [b]gospel of Christ and when a [c]door was opened for me in the Lord,

13 I [a]had no rest for my spirit, not finding [b]Titus my brother; but [c]taking my leave of them, I went on to [d]Macedonia.

12 [a]Acts 16:8 [b]Rom. 1:1; 2 Cor. 4:3, 4; 8:18; 9:13; 10:14; 11:4, 7; 1 Thess. 3:2 [c]Acts 14:27
★**13** [a]2 Cor. 7:5 [b]2 Cor. 7:6, 13f.; 8:6, 16, 23; 12:18; Gal. 2:1, 3; 2 Tim. 4:10; Titus 1:4 [c]Mark 6:46 [d]Rom. 15:26

III THE APOSTOLIC MINISTRY, 2:14–6:10

A The Confidence of the Ministry: Victory, 2:14–17

14 [a]But thanks be to God, who always [b]leads us in His triumph in Christ, and manifests through us the [c]sweet aroma of the [d]knowledge of Him in every place.

15 For we are a [a]fragrance of Christ to God among [b]those who are being saved and among those who are perishing;

16 [a]to the one an aroma from death to death, to the other an aroma from life to life. And who is [b]adequate for these things?

17 For we are not like many, [a]peddling the word of God, but [b]as from sincerity, but as from God, we speak in Christ [c]in the sight of God.

★**14** [a]Rom. 1:8; 6:17; 1 Cor. 15:57; 2 Cor. 8:16; 9:15 [b]Col. 2:15 [Gr.] [c]Song of Sol. 1:3; Ezek. 20:41; Eph. 5:2; Phil. 4:18 [d]1 Cor. 12:8
★**15** [a]Song of Sol. 1:3; Ezek. 20:41; Eph. 5:2; Phil. 4:18 [b]1 Cor. 1:18
16 [a]Luke 2:34; John 9:39; 1 Pet. 2:7f. [b]2 Cor. 3:5f.
17 [a]2 Cor. 4:2; Gal. 1:6-9 [b]1 Cor. 5:8; 2 Cor. 1:12; 1 Thess. 2:4; 1 Pet. 4:11 [c]2 Cor. 12:19

B The Commendation of the Ministry: Changed Lives, 3:1–3

3 Are we beginning to [a]commend ourselves again? Or do we need, as some, [b]letters of commendation to you or from you?

2 [a]You are our letter, written in our hearts, known and read by all men;

3 being manifested that you are a letter of Christ, [a]cared for by us, written not with ink, but with

★ **1** [a]2 Cor. 5:12; 10:12, 18; 12:11 [b]Acts 18:27; Rom. 16:1; 1 Cor. 16:3
2 [a]1 Cor. 9:2
3 [a]2 Cor. 3:6 [b]Matt. 16:16 [c]Ex. 24:12; 31:18; 32:15f.; 2 Cor. 3:7 [d]Prov. 3:3; 7:3; Jer. 17:1 [e]Jer. 31:33; Ezek. 11:19

2:6 *by the majority.* The rebel had been punished sufficiently and had repented. Apparently some wanted a severer penalty (vv. 6–8).

2:9 *whether you are obedient.* Though they had accepted Paul's authority in the case of the rebel, they had yet to prove that they accepted it *in all things* (cf. 10:6).

2:11 *that no advantage be taken of us by Satan.* The forgiven brother needed to be restored to fellowship, lest Satan put him under the pressure of continued self-accusation and introspection. Also, as long as the matter was not settled, Satan kept Paul and the church estranged.

2:13 *I had no rest.* Because of wondering how his severe letter had been received.

2:14 *who always leads us in His triumph in Christ.* The picture is of a Roman conqueror leading his captives in triumph. Paul gladly considered himself one of Christ's captives being led in triumph, to the glory of Christ.

2:15–16 The same gospel brings life to the believer and death to the rejector.

3:1–3 The work of the Spirit in the lives of the Corinthians was sufficient recommendation of Paul's ministry.

the Spirit of [b]the living God, not
on [c]tablets of stone, but on [d]tab-
lets of [e]human hearts.

C The Covenant for the Ministry: The New Covenant, 3:4–18

4 [a]Eph. 3:12
4 And such [a]confidence we
have through Christ toward God.
★ 5 [a]1 Cor. 15:10
5 Not that we are adequate
in ourselves to consider anything
as *coming* from ourselves, but
[a]our adequacy is from God,
★ 6 [a]1 Cor. 3:5 [b]Luke 22:20 [c]Rom. 2:29 [d]John 6:63; Rom. 7:6
6 who also made us ade-
quate *as* [a]servants of a [b]new covenant, not of [c]the letter, but of
the Spirit; for the letter kills, but
[d]the Spirit gives life.
★ 7 [a]Rom. 4:15; 5:20; 7:5f.; 2 Cor. 3:9; Gal. 3:10, 21f. [b]Ex. 24:12; 31:18; 32:15f.; 2 Cor. 3:3 [c]Ex. 34:29-35; 2 Cor. 3:13
7 But if the [a]ministry of
death, [b]in letters engraved on
stones, came with glory, [c]so that
the sons of Israel could not look
intently at the face of Moses because of the glory of his face, fading *as* it was,
★8
8 how shall the ministry of
the Spirit fail to be even more
with glory?
9 [a]Deut. 27:26; 2 Cor. 3:7; Heb. 12:18-21 [b]Rom. 1:17; 3:21f.
9 For if [a]the ministry of con-
demnation has glory, much more
does the [b]ministry of righteousness abound in glory.
10 For indeed what had glory,
in this case has no glory on account of the glory that surpasses
it.
11 For if that which fades ★11
away *was* with glory, much more
that which remains *is* in glory.
12 [a]Having therefore such a 12 [a]2 Cor. 7:4 [b]Acts 4:13, 29; 2 Cor. 7:4; Eph. 6:19; 1 Thess. 2:2
hope, [b]we use great boldness in
our speech,
13 and *are* not as Moses, ★13 [a]2 Cor. 3:7
[a]*who* used to put a veil over his
face that the sons of Israel might
not look intently at the end of
what was fading away.
14 But their minds were 14 [a]Rom. 11:7; 2 Cor. 4:4 [b]Acts 13:15 [c]2 Cor. 3:6
[a]hardened; for until this very day
at the [b]reading of [c]the old covenant the same veil remains un-
lifted, because it is removed in
Christ.
15 But to this day whenever ★15
Moses is read, a veil lies over their
heart;
16 [a]BUT WHENEVER A MAN TURNS 16 [a]Ex. 34:34; Rom. 11:23
TO THE LORD, THE VEIL IS TAKEN
AWAY.
17 Now the Lord is the Spirit; ★17 [a]Is. 61:1f.; Gal. 4:6 [b]John 8:32; Gal. 5:1, 13
and where [a]the Spirit of the Lord
is, [b]*there* is liberty.
18 But we all, with unveiled
face [a]beholding as in a mirror the ★18 [a]1 Cor. 13:12 [b]2 Cor. 4:4, 6; John 17:22, 24 [c]Rom. 8:29 [d]2 Cor. 3:17
[b]glory of the Lord, are being
[c]transformed into the same image
from glory to glory, just as from
[d]the Lord, the Spirit.

3:5 *our adequacy is from God.* This answers the question raised in 2:16.

3:6 *a new covenant.* The message of the grace of Christ (Matt. 26:28). *the letter kills, but the Spirit gives life.* The *letter* stands for the whole Mosaic law. It kills because, of itself, it could not give life (Acts 13:39). The work of the law was to make men conscious of sin (Gal. 3:21–25; 1 Tim. 1:9). The Spirit, by contrast, gives life to believers.

3:7 *the ministry of death.* Refers to the law and particularly to the Ten Commandments, which were *engraved on stones* (Deut. 9:10). Since the law showed man his sinfulness and gave him no power to break out of it, it ministered death. Note that the law *fades away* (2 Cor. 3:11). Moses stood before God with unveiled face (see Ex. 34:29–35).

3:8 *even more with glory.* I.e., more glorious than the old order.

3:11 There is no question that the law was glorious for its time and purpose, but its temporariness and limited purpose caused that glory to fade in the blazing light of the grace of Christ, which has as its eternal purpose the bringing of many sons into glory (John 1:17; Heb. 2:10).

3:13 Paul means here that Moses veiled his face that the Israelites might not see the fading away of the transitory glory reflected in his countenance.

3:15 *a veil lies over their heart.* I.e., as long as they consider the law as permanent and do not turn to Christ, who takes away the veil (v. 14).

3:17 *Now the Lord is the Spirit.* A strong statement that Christ and the Holy Spirit are one in essence, though Paul also recognized the distinctions between them (13:14).

3:18 *with unveiled face beholding.* Paul builds on the experience of Moses in Ex. 34:29–35. We Christians, he says, behold constantly Christ's divine glory; and this beholding changes or transforms us *from glory to glory;* i.e., from one degree of glory to another.

D The Character of the Ministry: Supernatural, 4:1–7

4 Therefore, since we have this [a]ministry, as we [b]received mercy, we [c]do not lose heart,

2 but we have renounced the [a]things hidden because of shame, not walking in craftiness or [b]adulterating the word of God, but by the manifestation of truth [c]commending ourselves to every man's conscience in the sight of God.

3 And even if our [a]gospel is [b]veiled, it is veiled to [c]those who are perishing,

4 in whose case [a]the god of [b]this world has [c]blinded the minds of the unbelieving, that they might not see the [d]light of the gospel of the [e]glory of Christ, who is the [f]image of God.

5 For we [a]do not preach ourselves but Christ Jesus as Lord, and ourselves as your bond-servants for Jesus' sake.

6 For God, who said, "[a]Light shall shine out of darkness," is the One who has [b]shone in our hearts to give the [c]light of the knowledge of the glory of God in the face of Christ.

7 But we have this treasure in [a]earthen vessels, that the surpassing greatness of [b]the power may be of God and not from ourselves;

★ **1** [a]1 Cor. 3:5 [b]1 Cor. 7:25 [c]Luke 18:1; 2 Cor. 4:16; Gal. 6:9; Eph. 3:13; 2 Thess. 3:13
2 [a]Rom. 6:21; 1 Cor. 4:5 [b]2 Cor. 2:17 [c]2 Cor. 5:11f.
3 [a]2 Cor. 2:12 [b]1 Cor. 2:6ff.; 2 Cor. 3:14 [c]1 Cor. 1:18; 2 Cor. 2:15
★ **4** [a]John 12:31 [b]Matt. 13:22 [c]2 Cor. 3:14 [d]Acts 26:18; 2 Cor. 4:6 [e]2 Cor. 3:18; 4:6 [f]John 1:18; Phil. 2:6; Col. 1:15; Heb. 1:3
5 [a]1 Cor. 4:15f.; 1 Thess. 2:6f.
6 [a]Gen. 1:3 [b]2 Pet. 1:19 [c]Acts 26:18; 2 Cor. 4:4
★ **7** [a]Job 4:19; 10:9; 33:6; Lam. 4:2; 2 Cor. 5:1; 2 Tim. 2:20 [b]Judg. 7:2; 1 Cor. 2:5

E The Circumstances of the Ministry, 4:8–18

8 *we are* [a]afflicted in every way, but not [b]crushed; [c]perplexed, but not despairing;

9 [a]persecuted, but not [b]forsaken; [c]struck down, but not destroyed;

10 [a]always carrying about in the body the dying of Jesus, that [b]the life of Jesus also may be manifested in our body.

11 For we who live are constantly being delivered over to death for Jesus' sake, that the life of Jesus also may be manifested in our mortal flesh.

12 So death works in us, but life in you.

13 But having the same [a]spirit of faith, according to what is written, "[b]I BELIEVED, THEREFORE I SPOKE," we also believe, therefore also we speak;

14 knowing that He who [a]raised the Lord Jesus [b]will raise us also with Jesus and will [c]present us with you.

15 For all things *are* [a]for your sakes, that the grace which is [b]spreading to more and more people may cause the giving of thanks to abound to the glory of God.

16 Therefore we [a]do not lose heart, but though our outer man is decaying, yet our [b]inner man is [c]being renewed day by day.

17 For momentary, [a]light affliction is producing for us an eternal weight of glory far beyond all comparison,

18 while we [a]look not at the things which are seen, but at the things which are not seen; for the things which are seen are temporal, but the things which are not seen are eternal.

8 [a]2 Cor. 1:8; 7:5 [b]2 Cor. 6:12 [c]Gal. 4:20
9 [a]John 15:20; Rom. 8:35f. [b]Ps. 129:2; Heb. 13:5 [c]Ps. 37:24; Prov. 24:16; Mic. 7:8
★**10** [a]Rom. 6:5; 8:36; Gal. 6:17 [b]Rom. 6:8
★**12**
13 [a]1 Cor. 12:9 [b]Ps. 116:10
14 [a]Acts 2:24 [b]1 Thess. 4:14 [c]Luke 21:36; Eph. 5:27; Col. 1:22; Jude 24
15 [a]Rom. 8:28; 2 Cor. 1:6 [b]1 Cor. 9:19; 2 Cor. 1:11
16 [a]2 Cor. 4:1 [b]Rom. 7:22 [c]Is. 40:29, 31; Col. 3:10
17 [a]Rom. 8:18
18 [a]Rom. 8:24; 2 Cor. 5:7; Heb. 11:1, 13

4:1 *we do not lose heart.* (Cf. Luke 18:1; 2 Cor. 4:16; Gal. 6:9; Eph. 3:13; 2 Thess. 3:13.) Paul credits his effectiveness to the *mercy* of God.

4:4 *the god of this world.* I.e., Satan.

4:7 *this treasure.* I.e., the glorious gospel of Jesus Christ. *in earthen vessels.* I.e., in our frail human bodies. *the surpassing greatness of the power.* Paul makes clear that this power belongs to God, not to any leader within the church (see 1 Cor. 1:12).

4:10–11 Paul here compares his own constant persecution and suffering with that of Jesus, in Whose dying and resurrection life the apostle will consequently share (Gal. 2:20; Col. 1:24).

4:12 Paul's physical sufferings *(death works in us)* are the means by which spiritual *life* comes to the Corinthians.

4:13–18 Though he is oppressed, Paul's outlook is one of hope (v. 14). Therefore, he does not lose heart (v. 16), though his *outer man is decaying,* for this *affliction* is *light* and temporary.

F The Compulsions of the Ministry, 5:1-21

1 *The assurance of resurrection,* 5:1-9

★ 1 [a]Job 4:19; 1 Cor. 15:47; 2 Cor. 4:7 [b]2 Pet. 1:13f. [c]Mark 14:58; Acts 7:48; Heb. 9:11, 24

5 For we know that if the [a]earthly [b]tent which is our house is torn down, we have a building from God, a house [c]not made with hands, eternal in the heavens.

★ 2 [a]Rom. 8:23; 2 Cor. 5:4 [b]1 Cor. 15:53f.; 2 Cor. 5:4

2 For indeed in this *house* we [a]groan, longing to be [b]clothed with our dwelling from heaven;

★3

3 inasmuch as we, having put it on, shall not be found naked.

★ 4 [a]2 Cor. 5:2 [b]1 Cor. 15:53f.; 2 Cor. 5:2 [c]1 Cor. 15:54

4 For indeed while we are in this tent, we [a]groan, being burdened, because we do not want to be unclothed, but to be [b]clothed, in order that what is [c]mortal may be swallowed up by life.

5 [a]Rom. 8:23; 2 Cor. 1:22

5 Now He who prepared us for this very purpose is God, who [a]gave to us the Spirit as a pledge.

6 [a]Heb. 11:13f.

6 Therefore, being always of good courage, and knowing that [a]while we are at home in the body we are absent from the Lord—

7 [a]1 Cor. 13:12; 2 Cor. 4:18

7 for [a]we walk by faith, not by sight—

8 [a]Phil. 1:23 [b]John 12:26; Phil. 1:23

8 we are of good courage, I say, and [a]prefer rather to be absent from the body and [b]to be at home with the Lord.

★ 9 [a]Rom. 14:18; Col. 1:10; 1 Thess. 4:1

9 Therefore also we have as our ambition, whether at home or absent, to be [a]pleasing to Him.

2 *The judgment seat of Christ,* 5:10-13

★10 [a]Matt. 16:27; Acts 10:42; Rom. 2:16; 14:10, 12; Eph. 6:8

10 For we must all appear before [a]the judgment seat of Christ, that each one may be recompensed for his deeds in the body, according to what he has done, whether good or bad.

★11 [a]Heb. 10:31; 12:29; Jude 23 [b]2 Cor. 4:2

11 Therefore knowing the [a]fear of the Lord, we persuade men, but we are made manifest to God; and I hope that we are [b]made manifest also in your consciences.

12 [a]2 Cor. 3:1 [b]2 Cor. 1:14; Phil. 1:26

12 We are not [a]again commending ourselves to you but *are* giving you an [b]occasion to be proud of us, that you may have *an answer* for those who take pride in appearance, and not in heart.

★13 [a]Mark 3:21; 2 Cor. 11:1, 16ff.; 12:11

13 For if we are [a]beside ourselves, it is for God; if we are of sound mind, it is for you.

3 *The love of Christ,* 5:14-21

★14 [a]Acts 18:5 [b]Rom. 5:15; 6:6f.; Gal. 2:20; Col. 3:3

14 For the love of Christ [a]controls us, having concluded this, that [b]one died for all, therefore all died;

★15 [a]Rom. 14:7-9

15 and He died for all, that they who live should no longer [a]live for themselves, but for Him who died and rose again on their behalf.

5:1 *the earthly tent . . . a house not made with hands.* The present earthly body is contrasted with the resurrection body.

5:2 *in this* earthly body *we groan* because of the burdens of life (cf. Rom. 8:23). *our dwelling from heaven.* Lit., dwelling place which is from heaven.

5:3 *shall not be found naked.* We shall not be bodiless after resurrection.

5:4 While in this body we are burdened; so we do not long to be disembodied but to have the resurrection body God will give us (v. 5).

5:9 *we have as our ambition.* The Greek word is found elsewhere only in Rom. 15:20 and 1 Thess. 4:11.

5:10 *the judgment seat of Christ.* The *bema* (judgment seat) was well-known to the Corinthians (see Acts 18:12). Believers will be judged in a review of their works for the purpose of rewards (see note on 1 Cor. 3:14). *bad* = worthless.

5:11 *fear.* Or awe of the Lord (Christ) in view of His judging us.

5:13 *beside ourselves.* Lit., "we went mad," probably referring to some specific occasion when Paul's critics charged him with madness. (For a similar charge against Jesus, see Mark 3:21; see also Acts 26:24.)

5:14 *For the love of Christ controls us.* Christ's love for us (and possibly it may also mean our love for Christ) controls us; i.e., keeps us within bounds. *therefore all died.* Believers are regarded by God as having died in Christ so that they may be able to live to please Him (Rom. 6:8).

5:15 Christ's death was, in part, for the purpose of bringing His followers into the experience of unselfish living for others.

16 Therefore from now on we recognize no man [a]according to the flesh; even though we have known Christ according to the flesh, yet now we know *Him thus* no longer.

17 Therefore if any man is [a]in Christ, *he is* [b]a new creature; [c]the old things passed away; behold, new things have come.

18 Now [a]all *these* things are from God, [b]who reconciled us to Himself through Christ, and gave us the [c]ministry of reconciliation,

19 namely, that [a]God was in Christ reconciling the world to Himself, [b]not counting their trespasses against them, and He has committed to us the word of reconciliation.

20 Therefore, we are [a]ambassadors for Christ, [b]as though God were entreating through us; we beg you on behalf of Christ, be [c]reconciled to God.

21 He made Him who [a]knew no sin *to be* [b]sin on our behalf, that we might become the [c]righteousness of God in Him.

★**16** [a]John 8:15; 2 Cor. 11:18; Phil. 3:4
★**17** [a]Rom. 16:7 [b]John 3:3; Rom. 6:4; Gal. 6:15 [c]Is. 43:18f.; 65:17; Eph. 4:24; Rev. 21:4f.
★**18** [a]1 Cor. 11:12 [b]Rom. 5:10; Col. 1:20 [c]1 Cor. 3:5
★**19** [a]Col. 2:9 [b]Rom. 4:8; 1 Cor. 13:5
20 [a]Mal. 2:7; Eph. 6:20 [b]2 Cor. 6:1 [c]Rom. 5:10; Col. 1:20
★**21** [a]Acts 3:14; Heb. 4:15; 7:26; 1 Pet. 2:22; 1 John 3:5 [b]Rom. 3:25; 4:25; 8:3; Gal. 3:13 [c]Rom. 1:17; 3:21f.; 1 Cor. 1:30

G The Conduct of the Ministry, 6:1–10

6 And [a]working together *with Him,* [b]we also urge you not to receive [c]the grace of God in vain—

2 for He says,

"[a]At the acceptable time I listened to you,
And on the day of salvation I helped you";

behold, now is "the acceptable time," behold, now is "the day of salvation"—

3 [a]giving no cause for offense in anything, in order that the ministry be not discredited,

4 but in everything [a]commending ourselves as [b]servants of God, [c]in much endurance, in afflictions, in hardships, in distresses,

5 in [a]beatings, in [a]imprisonments, in [b]tumults, in labors, in sleeplessness, in [c]hunger,

6 in purity, in [a]knowledge, in [b]patience, in kindness, in the [c]Holy Spirit, in [d]genuine love,

7 in [a]the word of truth, in [b]the power of God; by [c]the weapons of righteousness for the right hand and the left,

8 by glory and [a]dishonor, by [b]evil report and good report; *regarded* as [c]deceivers and yet [d]true;

9 as unknown yet well-known, as [a]dying yet behold, [b]we live; as punished yet not put to death,

10 as [a]sorrowful yet always [a]rejoicing, as [b]poor yet making many rich, as [c]having nothing yet possessing [d]all things.

1 [a]1 Cor. 3:9 [b]2 Cor. 5:20 [c]Acts 11:23
★ **2** [a]Is. 49:8
★ **3** [a]1 Cor. 8:9, 13; 9:12
4 [a]Rom. 3:5 [b]1 Cor. 3:5; 2 Tim. 2:24f. [c]Acts 9:16; 2 Cor. 4:8-11; 6:4ff.; 11:23-27; 12:10
★ **5** [a]Acts 16:23 [b]Acts 19:23ff. [c]1 Cor. 4:11
★ **6** [a]1 Cor. 12:8; 2 Cor. 11:6 [b]2 Cor. 1:23; 2:10; 13:10 [c]1 Cor. 2:4; 1 Thess. 1:5 [d]Rom. 12:9
7 [a]2 Cor. 2:17; 4:2 [b]1 Cor. 2:5 [c]Rom. 13:12; 2 Cor. 10:4; Eph. 6:11ff.
★ **8** [a]1 Cor. 4:10 [b]Rom. 3:8; 1 Cor. 4:13; 2 Cor. 12:16 [c]Matt. 27:63 [d]2 Cor. 1:18; 4:2; 1 Thess. 2:3f.
★ **9** [a]Rom. 8:36 [b]2 Cor. 1:8, 10; 4:11
10 [a]John 16:22; 2 Cor. 7:4; Phil. 2:17; 4:4; Col. 1:24; 1 Thess. 1:6 [b]1 Cor. 1:5; 2 Cor. 8:9 [c]Acts 3:6 [d]Rom. 8:32; 1 Cor. 3:21

5:16 Before his conversion, Paul regarded Christ as merely another man.

5:17 *a new creature.* Lit., a new creation. Old things are passed away (aorist tense indicating the decisive change salvation brings); *behold, new things have come.* (Perfect tense indicating abiding results of the new life in Christ.) The grace of God not only justifies but also makes "a new creation" which results in a changed style of life (v. 15).

5:18 *reconciliation* involves a changed relationship because our trespasses are not counted against us (v. 19). We are now to announce to others this message of God's grace.

5:19 *namely.* Paul here restates v. 18.

5:21 Here is the heart of the gospel: the sinless Savior has taken our sins that we might have God's righteousness.

6:2 The quotation is from Isa. 49:8, Greek version (Septuagint). Paul's emphasis is on the *now.*

6:3-10 The theme of the apostolic ministry, first introduced in 2:14, is here recapitulated.

6:5 See 11:23–24.

6:6 God-given qualities of character are proof of Paul's integrity.

6:8 *as deceivers.* Paul was hardly a deceiver, but apparently was called one by his enemies (cf. Matt. 27:63). Paul says he fights his way through the slanders and faithfully carries on for Christ.

6:9 *as unknown.* His opponents said Paul was an insignificant teacher, a "nobody."

IV THE APOSTLE'S EXHORTATIONS TO THE CORINTHIANS, 6:11-7:16

A Be Open toward Him, 6:11-13

★11 [a]Ezek. 33:22; Eph. 6:19 [b]Is. 60:5; 2 Cor. 7:3
12 [a]2 Cor. 7:2
13 [a]Gal. 4:12 [b]1 Cor. 4:14

11 [a]Our mouth has spoken
freely to you, O Corinthians, our
[b]heart is opened wide.
12 You are not restrained by
us, but [a]you are restrained in
your own affections.
13 Now in a like [a]exchange—
I speak as to [b]children—open
wide *to us* also.

B Be Separated from Evil, 6:14-7:1

★14 [a]Deut. 22:10; 1 Cor. 5:9f. [b]1 Cor. 6:6 [c]Eph. 5:7, 11; 1 John 1:6
★15 [a]1 Cor. 10:21 [b]Acts 5:14; 1 Pet. 1:21 [c]1 Cor. 6:6
16 [a]1 Cor. 10:21 [b]1 Cor. 3:16 [c]Matt. 16:16 [d]Ex. 29:45; Lev. 26:12; Jer. 31:1; Ezek. 37:27 [e]Ex. 25:8; John 14:23 [f]Rev. 2:1
★17 [a]Is. 52:11 [b]Rev. 18:4
18 [a]Is. 43:6; Hos. 1:10 [b]Rom. 8:14

14 [a]Do not be bound together
with [b]unbelievers; for what [c]part-
nership have righteousness and
lawlessness, or what fellowship
has light with darkness?
15 Or what [a]harmony has
Christ with Belial, or what has a
[b]believer in common with an [c]un-
believer?
16 Or [a]what agreement has
the temple of God with idols? For
we are [b]the temple of [c]the living
God; just as God said,

"[d]I WILL [e]DWELL IN THEM AND
[f]WALK AMONG THEM;
AND I WILL BE THEIR GOD,
AND THEY SHALL BE MY
PEOPLE.
17 "[a]Therefore, [b]COME OUT
FROM THEIR MIDST AND BE
SEPARATE," says the Lord.
"AND DO NOT TOUCH WHAT IS
UNCLEAN;
AND I WILL WELCOME YOU.
18 "[a]AND I WILL BE A FATHER TO
YOU,
AND YOU SHALL BE [b]SONS and
daughters TO ME,"
SAYS THE LORD ALMIGHTY.

1 [a]Heb. 6:9 [b]1 Pet. 1:15f.

7 Therefore, having these
promises, [a]beloved, [b]let us
cleanse ourselves from all defilement of flesh and spirit, perfect-
ing holiness in the fear of God.

C Be Assured of His Joy over Their Repentance, 7:2-16

2 [a]2 Cor. 6:12f.; 12:15
3 [a]2 Cor. 6:11f. [b]Phil. 1:7
4 [a]2 Cor. 3:12 [b]2 Cor. 7:14; 8:24; 9:2f.; 10:8; Phil. 1:26; 2 Thess. 1:4 [c]2 Cor. 1:4 [d]2 Cor. 6:10
★ 5 [a]Rom. 15:26; 2 Cor. 2:13 [b]2 Cor. 4:8 [c]Deut. 32:25
★ 6 [a]2 Cor. 1:3f. [b]2 Cor. 7:13 [c]2 Cor. 2:13; 7:13f.
8 [a]2 Cor. 2:2

2 [a]Make room for us *in your
hearts;* we wronged no one, we
corrupted no one, we took advantage of no one.
3 I do not speak to condemn
you; for I have said [a]before that
you are [b]in our hearts to die together and to live together.
4 Great is my [a]confidence in
you, great is my [b]boasting on
your behalf; I am filled with
[c]comfort. I am overflowing with
[d]joy in all our affliction.
5 For even when we came
into [a]Macedonia our flesh had no
rest, but we were [b]afflicted on every side: [c]conflicts without, fears
within.
6 But [a]God, who comforts
the depressed, [b]comforted us by
the coming of [c]Titus;
7 and not only by his coming, but also by the comfort with
which he was comforted in you,
as he reported to us your longing,
your mourning, your zeal for me;
so that I rejoiced even more.
8 For though I [a]caused you
sorrow by my letter, I do not regret it; though I did regret it—*for*
I see that that letter caused you
sorrow, though only for a while—

6:11 I.e., our speech is frank and our heart is ready to take you in.
6:14 *Do not be bound together with unbelievers.* This injunction applies to marriage, business, and to ecclesiastical and intimate personal relationships.
6:15 *Belial* = Satan.
6:17 *separate.* Personal separation involves not being unequally yoked (v. 14); not loving the world (1 John 2:15-17), though using it (1 Cor. 7:31); not having fellowship with sinning brethren (1 Cor. 5:11); and, on the positive side, exhibiting Christlikeness. See note on Acts 15:39.
7:5-13a resumes the discussion of Paul's journey to Macedonia introduced in 2:13. He describes his relief because of the good news Titus brought (vv. 5-7) and his reflections on the severe letter he had written and its consequences.
7:6 *the coming of Titus.* I.e., from Corinth, with the news that the church had accepted the severe letter.

9 I now rejoice, not that you were made sorrowful, but that you were made sorrowful to *the point of* repentance; for you were made sorrowful according to *the will of* God, in order that you might not suffer loss in anything through us.

10 [a]Acts 11:18

10 For the sorrow that is according to *the will of* God produces a [a]repentance without regret, *leading* to salvation; but the sorrow of the world produces death.

★**11** [a]2 Cor. 7:7 [b]2 Cor. 2:6 [c]Rom. 3:5

11 For behold what earnestness this very thing, this godly sorrow, has produced in you: what vindication of yourselves, what indignation, what fear, what [a]longing, what zeal, what [b]avenging of wrong! In everything you [c]demonstrated yourselves to be innocent in the matter.

★**12** [a]2 Cor. 2:3, 9; 7:8 [b]1 Cor. 5:1f.

12 So although [a]I wrote to you *it was* not for the sake of [b]the offender, nor for the sake of the one offended, but that your earnestness on our behalf might be made known to you in the sight of God.

13 [a]2 Cor. 7:6 [b]2 Cor. 2:13; 7:6, 14 [c]1 Cor. 16:18

13 For this reason we have been [a]comforted.

And besides our comfort, we rejoiced even much more for the joy of [b]Titus, because his [c]spirit has been refreshed by you all.

14 [a]2 Cor. 7:4; 8:24; 9:2f.; 10:8; Phil. 1:26; 2 Thess. 1:4 [b]2 Cor. 2:13; 7:6, 13

14 For if in anything I have [a]boasted to him about you, I was not put to shame; but as we spoke all things to you in truth, so also our boasting before [b]Titus proved to be *the* truth.

15 [a]2 Cor. 2:9 [b]1 Cor. 2:3; Phil. 2:12

15 And his affection abounds all the more toward you, as he remembers the [a]obedience of you all, how you received him with [b]fear and trembling.

16 I rejoice that in everything [a]I have confidence in you.

16 [a]2 Cor. 2:3

V THE APOSTLE'S SOLICITATION (OR COLLECTION) FOR THE JUDEAN SAINTS, 8:1–9:15

A Principles for Giving, 8:1–6

8 Now, brethren, we *wish to* make known to you the grace of God which has been [a]given in the churches of [b]Macedonia,

★ **1** [a]2 Cor. 8:5 [b]Acts 16:9

2 that in a great ordeal of affliction their abundance of joy and their deep poverty overflowed in the [a]wealth of their liberality.

2 [a]Rom. 2:4

3 For I testify that [a]according to their ability, and beyond their ability *they gave* of their own accord,

3 [a]1 Cor. 16:2; 2 Cor. 8:11

4 begging us with much entreaty for the [a]favor of participation in the [b]support of the saints,

4 [a]Acts 24:17; Rom. 15:25f. [b]Rom. 15:31; 2 Cor. 8:19f.; 9:1, 12f.

5 and *this,* not as we had expected, but they first [a]gave themselves to the Lord and to us by [b]the will of God.

5 [a]2 Cor. 8:1 [b]1 Cor. 1:1

6 Consequently we [a]urged [b]Titus that as he had previously [c]made a beginning, so he would also complete in you [d]this gracious work as well.

6 [a]2 Cor. 8:17; 12:18 [b]2 Cor. 2:13; 8:16, 23 [c]2 Cor. 8:10 [d]Acts 24:17; Rom. 15:25f.

B Purposes for Giving, 8:7–15

7 But just as you [a]abound [b]in everything, in faith and utterance and knowledge and in all earnestness and in the love we inspired in you, *see* that you [a]abound in this gracious work also.

★ **7** [a]2 Cor. 9:8 [b]Rom. 15:14; 1 Cor. 1:5; 12:8

8 I [a]am not speaking *this* as a command, but as proving through the earnestness of others the sincerity of your love also.

8 [a]1 Cor. 7:6

7:11 *vindication of yourselves.* I.e., with regard to Paul's accusations by their change of behavior. Their sorrow had worked the right kind of repentance.

7:12 *the offender.* See 2:6. *the one offended.* I.e., Paul.

8:1–6 Truths about N.T. giving presented here are: (1) it is a grace (vv. 1, 6); (2) it can be exercised even during poverty (v. 2); (3) it is a form of fellowship (v. 4); and (4) it should be preceded by the dedication of self (v. 5). Apparently the church at Corinth had never, up to this time at least, supported Paul financially (see 11:8–9; 12:13; 1 Cor. 9:11–12).

8:7–15 Some purposes in giving are: (1) to abound in all aspects of Christian experience (v. 7); (2) to prove the reality of one's love (v. 8); (3) to imitate Christ (v. 9); and (4) to help meet the needs of others (v. 14).

9 For you know [a]the grace of
our Lord Jesus Christ, that
[b]though He was rich, yet for your
sake He became poor, that you
through His poverty might become rich.
10 And I [a]give *my* opinion in
this matter, for this is to your advantage, who were the first to begin [b]a year ago not only to do
this, but also to desire *to do it.*
11 But now finish doing it
also; that just as *there was* the
[a]readiness to desire it, so *there*
may be also the completion of it
by your ability.
12 For if the readiness is present, it is acceptable [a]according to
what *a man* has, not according to
what he does not have.
13 For *this* is not for the ease
of others *and* for your affliction,
but by way of equality—
14 at this present time your
abundance *being a supply* for
[a]their want, that their abundance
also may become *a supply* for
[a]your want, that there may be
equality;
15 as it is written, "[a]HE WHO
gathered MUCH DID NOT HAVE TOO
MUCH, AND HE WHO *gathered* LITTLE
HAD NO LACK."

9 [a]2 Cor. 13:14 [b]Matt. 20:28; 2 Cor. 6:10; Phil. 2:6f.
10 [a]1 Cor. 7:25, 40 [b]1 Cor. 16:2f.; 2 Cor. 9:2
11 [a]2 Cor. 8:12, 19; 9:2
12 [a]Mark 12:43f.; Luke 21:3; 2 Cor. 9:7
14 [a]Acts 4:34; 2 Cor. 9:12
15 [a]Ex. 16:18

C Policies in Giving, 8:16–9:5

16 But [a]thanks be to God,
who [b]puts the same earnestness
on your behalf in the heart of [c]Ti-
tus.
17 For he not only accepted
our [a]appeal, but being himself
very earnest, he has gone to you
of his own accord.
18 And we have sent along
with him [a]the brother whose
fame in *the things of* the [b]gospel
has spread through [c]all the
churches;
19 [a]and not only *this,* but he
has also been [b]appointed by the
churches to travel with us in [c]this
gracious work, which is being administered by us for the glory of
the Lord Himself, and *to show*
our [d]readiness,
20 taking precaution that no
one should discredit us in our administration of this generous gift;
21 for we [a]have regard for
what is honorable, not only in
[b]the sight of the Lord, but also in
the sight of men.
22 And we have sent with
them our brother, whom we have
often tested and found diligent in
many things, but now even more
diligent, because of *his* great confidence in you.
23 As for [a]Titus, *he is* my
[b]partner and fellow-worker
among you; as for our [c]brethren,
they are [d]messengers of the
churches, [e]a glory to Christ.
24 Therefore openly before
the churches show them the proof
of your love and of our [a]reason
for boasting about you.

16 [a]2 Cor. 2:14 [b]Rev. 17:17 [c]2 Cor. 2:13; 8:6, 23
17 [a]2 Cor. 8:6; 12:18
★18 [a]1 Cor. 16:3; 2 Cor. 12:18 [b]2 Cor. 2:12 [c]1 Cor. 4:17; 7:17
19 [a]Rom. 5:3 [b]Acts 14:23; 1 Cor. 16:3f. [c]2 Cor. 8:4, 6 [d]2 Cor. 8:11, 12; 9:2
21 [a]Rom. 12:17 [b]Rom. 14:18
23 [a]2 Cor. 8:6 [b]Philem. 17 [c]2 Cor. 8:18, 22 [d]John 13:16; Phil. 2:25 [e]1 Cor. 11:7
24 [a]2 Cor. 7:4

9 For [a]it is superfluous for me
to write to you about this
[b]ministry to the saints;
2 for I know your readiness,
of which I [a]boast about you to the
[b]Macedonians, *namely,* that [c]A-
chaia has been prepared since
[d]last year, and your zeal has
stirred up most of them.
3 But I have sent the brethren, that our [a]boasting about you
may not be made empty in this
case, that, [b]as I was saying, you
may be prepared;
4 lest if any [a]Macedonians
come with me and find you unprepared, we (not to speak of you)
should be put to shame by this
confidence.
5 So I thought it necessary to
urge the [a]brethren that they

1 [a]1 Thess. 4:9 [b]2 Cor. 8:4
★ 2 [a]2 Cor. 7:4 [b]Rom. 15:26 [c]Acts 18:12 [d]2 Cor. 8:10
3 [a]2 Cor. 7:4 [b]1 Cor. 16:2
4 [a]Rom. 15:26
5 [a]2 Cor. 9:3 [b]Gen. 33:11; Judg. 1:15; 2 Cor. 9:6 [c]Phil. 4:17 [d]2 Cor. 12:17f.

8:18 *the brother.* I.e., fellow Christian. Although we do not know who he was (perhaps Luke or Trophimus), this man was obviously well-known for preaching the gospel. Titus, this unnamed brother and a third brother (also unnamed, v. 22), acted as trustees of the money to insure complete propriety in the handling of it (v. 21).

9:2 *readiness* = eagerness (8:10). The Corinthians' *zeal* had been an example and incentive to others to give also. If they did not now fulfill their promise, it would be a disgrace to them and to Paul (v. 4).

would go on ahead to you and arrange beforehand your previously
promised [b]bountiful gift, that the
same might be ready as a [c]bounti-
ful gift, and not [d]affected by covetousness.

D Promises in Giving, 9:6–15

6 Now this *I say,* [a]he who
sows sparingly shall also reap
sparingly; and he who sows bountifully shall also reap bountifully.
7 Let each one *do* just as he
has purposed in his heart; not
[a]grudgingly or under compulsion;
for [b]God loves a cheerful giver.
8 And [a]God is able to make
all grace abound to you, that always having all sufficiency in
everything, you may have an
abundance for every good deed;
9 as it is written,

"[a]HE SCATTERED ABROAD, HE GAVE TO THE POOR,
HIS RIGHTEOUSNESS ABIDES FOREVER."

10 Now He who supplies
[a]seed to the sower and bread for
food, will supply and multiply
your seed for sowing and [b]in-
crease the harvest of your righteousness;
11 you will be [a]enriched in
everything for all liberality, which
through us is producing [b]thanks-
giving to God.
12 For the ministry of this
service is not only fully supplying
[a]the needs of the saints, but is
also overflowing [b]through many
thanksgivings to God.
13 Because of the proof given
by this [a]ministry they will [b]glori-
fy God for *your* obedience to your
[c]confession of the [d]gospel of
Christ, and for the liberality of
your contribution to them and to
all,
14 while they also, by prayer
on your behalf, yearn for you because of the surpassing grace of
God in you.
15 [a]Thanks be to God for His
indescribable [b]gift!

★ 6 [a]Prov. 11:24f.; 22:9; Gal. 6:7, 9
7 [a]Deut. 15:10; 1 Chr. 29:17; Rom. 12:8; 2 Cor. 8:12 [b]Ex. 25:2; Prov. 22:8 [Septuagint]; 2 Cor. 8:12
★ 8 [a]Eph. 3:20
★ 9 [a]Ps. 112:9
★10 [a]Is. 55:10 [b]Hos. 10:12
11 [a]1 Cor. 1:5 [b]2 Cor. 1:11
★12 [a]2 Cor. 8:14 [b]2 Cor. 1:11
13 [a]Rom. 15:31; 2 Cor. 8:4 [b]Matt. 9:8 [c]1 Tim. 6:12f.; Heb. 3:1; 4:14; 10:23 [d]2 Cor. 2:12
15 [a]2 Cor. 2:14 [b]Rom. 5:15f.

VI THE APOSTLE'S VINDICATION OF HIMSELF, 10:1–12:18

A The Authority of His Apostleship, 10:1–18

10 Now [a]I, Paul, myself [b]urge
you by the [c]meekness and
gentleness of Christ—I who [d]am
meek when face to face with you,
but bold toward you when absent!
2 I ask that [a]when I am present I may not be bold with the
confidence with which I propose
to be courageous against [b]some,
who regard us as if we walked
[c]according to the flesh.
3 For though we walk in the
flesh, we do not war [a]according to
the flesh,
4 for the [a]weapons of our
warfare are not of the flesh, but
[b]divinely powerful [c]for the destruction of fortresses.
5 *We are* destroying speculations and every [a]lofty thing
raised up against the knowledge
of God, and *we are* taking every
thought captive to the [b]obedience
of Christ,
6 and we are ready to punish
all disobedience, whenever [a]your
obedience is complete.

★ 1 [a]Gal. 5:2; Eph. 3:1; Col. 1:23 [b]Rom. 12:1 [c]Matt. 11:29; 1 Cor. 4:21; Phil. 4:5 [d]1 Cor. 2:3f.; 2 Cor. 10:10
2 [a]1 Cor. 4:21; 2 Cor. 13:2, 10 [b]1 Cor. 4:18f. [c]Rom. 8:4; 2 Cor. 1:17
★ 3 [a]Rom. 8:4; 2 Cor. 1:17
4 [a]1 Cor. 9:7; 2 Cor. 6:7; 1 Tim. 1:18 [b]Acts 7:20 [c]Jer. 1:10; 2 Cor. 10:8; 13:10
5 [a]Is. 2:11f. [b]2 Cor. 9:13
6 [a]2 Cor. 2:9

9:6 See Prov. 11:24; 19:17; Luke 6:38.

9:8 God will supply the generous giver with enough to meet his own needs and enough to give for *every good deed.*

9:9 The same thought as in v. 8.

9:10 The generous giver will be given increasing means to give *(multiply your seed for sowing)* and increasing fruit. See Hos. 10:12.

9:12–14 The gift of money will (1) supply need (v. 12); (2) be a cause for thanksgiving (v. 12); (3) prove their obedience (v. 13); (4) draw the Jerusalem Christians to them (v. 14, *yearn for you*).

10:1 In spite of Paul's general satisfaction with the Corinthian church, there were still some there who challenged his apostolic authority and followed certain leaders whom Paul calls "false apostles" (11:13). These leaders were apparently Jewish Christians (11:22) who claimed higher authority than Paul's (10:7) and who lorded over the church (11:20).

10:3 *in the flesh.* I.e., in a human body (with its limitations). *according to the flesh.* I.e., after the impulses of the sinful nature.

7 [a]You are looking at things
as they are outwardly. [b]If any one
is confident in himself that he is
Christ's, let him consider this
again within himself, that just as
he is Christ's, [c]so also are we.
8 For even if [a]I should boast
somewhat further about our [b]au-
thority, which the Lord gave for
building you up and not for destroying you, I shall not be put to
shame,
9 for I do not wish to seem
as if I would terrify you by my
letters.
10 For they say, "His letters
are weighty and strong, but his
personal presence is [a]unimpres-
sive, and [b]his speech contemptible."
11 Let such a person consider
this, that what we are in word by
letters when absent, such persons
we are also in deed when present.
12 For we are not bold to class
or compare ourselves with some
of those who [a]commend themselves; but when they measure
themselves by themselves, and
compare themselves with themselves, they are without understanding.
13 But we will not boast [a]be-
yond *our* measure, but [b]within
the measure of the sphere which
God apportioned to us as a measure, to reach even as far as you.
14 For we are not overextend-
ing ourselves, as if we did not
reach to you, for [a]we were the
first to come even as far as you in
the [b]gospel of Christ;
15 not boasting [a]beyond *our*
measure, *that is,* in [b]other men's
labors, but with the hope that as
[c]your faith grows, we shall be,
within our sphere, [d]enlarged even
more by you,
16 so as to [a]preach the gospel
even to [b]the regions beyond you,
and not to boast [c]in what has
been accomplished in the sphere
of another.
17 But [a]HE WHO BOASTS, LET HIM
BOAST IN THE LORD.
18 For not he who [a]com-
mends himself is approved, but
[b]whom the Lord commends.

★ 7 [a]John 7:24; 2 Cor. 5:12 [b]1 Cor. 1:12; 14:37 [c]1 Cor. 9:1; 2 Cor. 11:23; Gal. 1:12
8 [a]2 Cor. 7:4 [b]2 Cor. 13:10
★10 [a]1 Cor. 2:3; 2 Cor. 12:7; Gal. 4:13f. [b]1 Cor. 1:17; 2 Cor. 11:6
12 [a]2 Cor. 3:1; 10:18
★13 [a]2 Cor. 10:15 [b]Rom. 12:3; 2 Cor. 10:15f.
14 [a]1 Cor. 3:6 [b]2 Cor. 2:12
★15 [a]2 Cor. 10:13 [b]Rom. 15:20 [c]2 Thess. 1:3 [d]Acts 5:13
16 [a]2 Cor. 11:7 [b]Acts 19:21 [c]Rom. 15:20
17 [a]Jer. 9:24; 1 Cor. 1:31
18 [a]2 Cor. 10:12 [b]Rom. 2:29; 1 Cor. 4:5

B The Marks of His Apostleship, 11:1–12:18

1 *Paul's conduct,* 11:1–15

11 I wish that you would
[a]bear with me in a little
[b]foolishness; but indeed you are
bearing with me.
2 For I am jealous for you
with a godly jealousy; for I [a]be-
trothed you to one husband, that
to Christ I might [b]present you *as* a
pure virgin.
3 But I am afraid, lest as the
[a]serpent deceived Eve by his
craftiness, your minds should be
led astray from the simplicity and
purity *of devotion* to Christ.
4 For if one comes and
preaches [a]another Jesus whom we
have not preached, or you receive
a [b]different spirit which you have
not received, or a [c]different gospel
which you have not accepted, you
[d]bear *this* [e]beautifully.
5 For I consider myself [a]not
in the least inferior to the most
eminent apostles.
6 But even if I am [a]unskilled
in speech, yet I am not *so* in
[b]knowledge; in fact, in every way

★ 1 [a]Matt. 17:17; 2 Cor. 11:4, 16, 19f. [b]2 Cor. 5:13; 11:17, 21
2 [a]Hos. 2:19f.; Eph. 5:26f. [b]2 Cor. 4:14
★ 3 [a]Gen. 3:4, 13; John 8:44; 1 Thess. 3:5; 1 Tim. 2:14; Rev. 12:9, 15
★ 4 [a]1 Cor. 3:11 [b]Rom. 8:15 [c]Gal. 1:6 [d]2 Cor. 11:1 [e]Mark 7:9
5 [a]2 Cor. 12:11; Gal. 2:6
★ 6 [a]1 Cor. 1:17 [b]1 Cor. 12:8; Eph. 3:4 [c]2 Cor. 4:2

10:7–9 You look, Paul says, only at what lies before your eyes. I belong to Christ as much as they do (v. 7). As a matter of fact, I could claim higher authority (v. 8), but that might frighten you (v. 9)!

10:10 *contemptible* = of no account.

10:13 *beyond our measure.* I.e., beyond his limits or assigned region, the territory God had assigned to Paul. In that territory, which included Corinth, he would boast, but not in areas in which others had labored.

10:15–16 As their *faith grows* and his presence is no longer necessary, Paul could turn to other fields.

11:1 *a little foolishness.* I.e., the boasting of vv. 21–33. But Paul knows he must do it to make the false apostles appear in their true colors.

11:3 Some texts read, "from the simplicity and purity which is in Christ."

11:4 Paul here and in v. 5 is speaking sarcastically. Of course he did not want them to submit to false teachers, nor did he regard these smooth talkers as "apostles" in any sense.

11:6 *unskilled in speech.* I.e., not an orator.

we have [c]made *this* evident to
you in all things.
7 Or [a]did I commit a sin in
humbling myself that you might
be exalted, because I preached the
[b]gospel of God to you [c]without
charge?
8 I robbed other churches,
[a]taking wages *from them* to serve
you;
9 and when I was present
with you and was in need, I was
[a]not a burden to anyone; for
when [b]the brethren came from
[c]Macedonia, they fully supplied
my need, and in everything I kept
myself from [a]being a burden to
you, and will continue to do so.
10 [a]As the truth of Christ is in
me, [b]this boasting of mine will
not be stopped in the regions of
[c]Achaia.
11 Why? [a]Because I do not
love you? [b]God knows *I do!*
12 But what I am doing, I will
continue to do, [a]that I may cut off
opportunity from those who desire an opportunity to be regarded
just as we are in the matter about
which they are boasting.
13 For such men are [a]false
apostles, [b]deceitful workers, dis-
guising themselves as apostles of
Christ.
14 And no wonder, for even
[a]Satan disguises himself as an
[b]angel of light.
15 Therefore it is not surprising if his servants also disguise
themselves as servants of righteousness; [a]whose end shall be according to their deeds.

7 [a]2 Cor. 12:13 [b]Rom. 1:1; 2 Cor. 2:12 [c]Acts 18:3; 1 Cor. 9:18
★ **8** [a]1 Cor. 4:12; 9:6; Phil. 4:15, 18
9 [a]2 Cor. 12:13f., 16 [b]Acts 18:5 [c]Rom. 15:26
10 [a]Rom. 1:9; 9:1; 2 Cor. 1:23; Gal. 2:20 [b]1 Cor. 9:15 [c]Acts 18:12
11 [a]2 Cor. 12:15 [b]Rom. 1:9; 2 Cor. 2:17; 11:31; 12:2f.
★**12** [a]1 Cor. 9:12
13 [a]Acts 20:30; Gal. 1:7; 2:4; Phil. 1:15; Titus 1:10f.; 2 Pet. 2:1; Rev. 2:2 [b]Phil. 3:2
★**14** [a]Matt. 4:10; Eph. 6:12; Col. 1:13 [b]Col. 1:12
15 [a]Rom. 2:6; 3:8

2 *Paul's sufferings,* 11:16–33

16 [a]Again I say, let no one
think me foolish; but if *you do,*
receive me even as foolish, that I
also may boast a little.
17 That which I am speaking,
I am not speaking [a]as the Lord
would, but as [b]in foolishness, in
this confidence of boasting.
18 Since [a]many boast [b]ac-
cording to the flesh, I will boast
also.
19 For you, [a]being *so* wise,
bear with the foolish gladly.
20 For you bear with anyone
if he [a]enslaves you, if he [b]devours
you, if he [c]takes advantage of
you, if he [d]exalts himself, if he
[e]hits you in the face.
21 To *my* [a]shame I *must* say
that we have been [b]weak *by comparison.* But in whatever respect
anyone *else* [c]is bold (I [d]speak in
foolishness), I am just as bold myself.
22 Are they [a]Hebrews? [b]So
am I. Are they [c]Israelites? [c]So am
I. Are they [d]descendants of Abraham? [e]So am I.
23 Are they [a]servants of
Christ? (I speak as if insane) I
more so; in [b]far more labors, in
[c]far more imprisonments, [d]beaten
times without number, often in
[e]danger of death.
24 Five times I received from
the Jews [a]thirty-nine *lashes.*
25 Three times I was [a]beaten
with rods, once I was [b]stoned,
three times I was shipwrecked, a
night and a day I have spent in
the deep.

16 [a]2 Cor. 11:1
★**17** [a]1 Cor. 7:12, 25 [b]2 Cor. 11:21
18 [a]Phil. 3:3f. [b]2 Cor. 5:16
19 [a]1 Cor. 4:10
★**20** [a]2 Cor. 1:24; Gal. 2:4; 4:3, 9; 5:1 [b]Mark 12:40 [c]Luke 5:5; 2 Cor. 11:3; 12:16 [d]2 Cor. 10:5 [e]1 Cor. 4:11
21 [a]2 Cor. 6:8 [b]2 Cor. 10:10 [c]2 Cor. 10:2 [d]2 Cor. 11:17
22 [a]Acts 6:1 [b]Phil. 3:5 [c]Rom. 9:4 [d]Gal. 3:16 [e]Rom. 11:1
23 [a]1 Cor. 3:5; 2 Cor. 3:6; 10:7 [b]1 Cor. 15:10 [c]2 Cor 6:5 [d]Acts 16:23; 2 Cor. 6:5 [e]Rom. 8:36
★**24** [a]Deut. 25:3
★**25** [a]Acts 16:22 [b]Acts 14:19

11:8 *robbed.* In the sense of having accepted gifts from other churches who could ill afford to give them, in order not to be a financial burden to the Corinthians.

11:12 By not accepting support, Paul cut off his opponents' *opportunity,* or opening, for attacking him.

11:14–15 Satan's masterful deception is to appear in the guise of an angel of light. These teachers, Satan's servants, appeared as preachers of righteousness.

11:17 *as the Lord would.* Paul means that his forced boasting finds no example in the life of Christ. He had to indulge in it, he says, against his natural instincts, so that he could call some significant facts to their attention.

11:20 *devours.* I.e., by exacting money (cf. Mark 12:40).

11:24 *thirty-nine lashes.* This refers to beatings administered in the synagogue. The law prescribed forty lashes (Deut. 25:1–3), but only 39 were given in order to be certain of not exceeding the limit.

11:25 *beaten with rods.* A Roman punishment, administered to Paul at Philippi (Acts 16:23). *stoned.* At Lystra (Acts 14:11–19). *shipwrecked.* On the island of Malta (Acts 27:41–28:1).

26 *I have been* on frequent
journeys, in dangers from rivers,
dangers from robbers, dangers
from *my* [a]countrymen, dangers
from the [b]Gentiles, dangers in the
[c]city, dangers in the wilderness,
dangers on the sea, dangers
among [d]false brethren;
27 *I have been* in [a]labor and
hardship, through many sleepless
nights, in [b]hunger and thirst, often [c]without food, in cold and
[d]exposure.
28 Apart from *such* external
things, there is the daily pressure
upon me *of* concern for [a]all the
churches.
29 Who is [a]weak without my
being weak? Who is led into sin
without my intense concern?
30 If I have to boast, I will
boast of what pertains to my
[a]weakness.
31 The God and Father of the
Lord Jesus, [a]He who is blessed
forever, [b]knows that I am not
lying.
32 In [a]Damascus the ethnarch
under Aretas the king was
[b]guarding the city of the Dama-
scenes in order to seize me,
33 and I was let down in a
basket [a]through a window in the
wall, and *so* escaped his hands.

26 [a]Acts 9:23; 13:45, 50; 14:5; 17:5, 13; 18:12; 20:3, 19; 21:27; 23:10, 12; 25:3; 1 Thess. 2:15 [b]Acts 14:5, 19; 19:23ff.; 27:42 [c]Acts 21:31 [d]Gal. 2:4
27 [a]1 Thess. 2:9; 2 Thess. 3:8 [b]1 Cor. 4:11; Phil. 4:12 [c]2 Cor. 6:5 [d]1 Cor. 4:11
28 [a]1 Cor. 7:17
29 [a]1 Cor. 8:9, 13; 9:22
30 [a]1 Cor. 2:3
31 [a]Rom. 1:25 [b]2 Cor. 11:11
★**32** [a]Acts 9:2 [b]Acts 9:24
33 [a]Acts 9:25

3 *Paul's vision,* 12:1–10

12 [a]Boasting is necessary,
though it is not profitable;
but I will go on to visions and
[b]revelations of the Lord.
2 I know a man [a]in Christ
who fourteen years ago—whether
in the body I do not know, or out
of the body I do not know, [b]God
knows—such a man was [c]caught
up to the [d]third heaven.
3 And I know how such a
man—whether in the body or
apart from the body I do not
know, [a]God knows—
4 was [a]caught up into [b]Para-
dise, and heard inexpressible
words, which a man is not permitted to speak.
5 [a]On behalf of such a man
will I boast; but on my own behalf I will not boast, except in regard to *my* [b]weaknesses.
6 For if I do wish to boast I
shall not be [a]foolish, [b]for I shall
be speaking the truth; but I refrain *from this,* so that no one
may credit me with more than he
sees *in* me or hears from me.
7 And because of the surpassing greatness of the
[a]revelations, for this reason, to
keep me from exalting myself,
there was given me a [b]thorn in
the flesh, a [c]messenger of Satan
to buffet me—to keep me from
exalting myself!
8 Concerning this I entreated
the Lord [a]three times that it might
depart from me.
9 And He has said to me,
"My grace is sufficient for you,
for [a]power is perfected in weakness." Most gladly, therefore, I
will rather [b]boast about my weaknesses, that the power of Christ
may dwell in me.
10 Therefore [a]I am well content with weaknesses, with insults, with [b]distresses, with [c]per-
secutions, with [b]difficulties, [d]for
Christ's sake; for [e]when I am
weak, then I am strong.

1 [a]2 Cor. 11:16, 18, 30; 12:5, 9 [b]1 Cor. 14:6; 2 Cor. 12:7; Gal. 1:12; 2:2; Eph. 3:3
★ **2** [a]Rom. 16:7 [b]2 Cor. 11:11 [c]Ezek. 8:3; Acts 8:39; 2 Cor. 12:4; 1 Thess. 4:17; Rev. 12:5 [d]Deut. 10:14; Ps. 148:4; Eph. 4:10; Heb. 4:14
3 [a]2 Cor. 11:11
4 [a]Ezek. 8:3; Acts 8:39; 2 Cor. 12:2; 1 Thess. 4:17; Rev. 12:5 [b]Luke 23:43
5 [a]2 Cor. 12:1 [b]1 Cor. 2:3; 2 Cor. 12:9f.
★ **6** [a]2 Cor. 5:13; 11:16f.; 12:11 [b]2 Cor. 7:14
★ **7** [a]2 Cor. 12:1 [b]Num. 33:55; Ezek. 28:24; Hos. 2:6 [c]Job 2:6; Matt. 4:10; 1 Cor. 5:5
8 [a]Matt. 26:44
★ **9** [a]1 Cor. 2:5; Eph. 3:16; Phil. 4:13 [b]1 Cor. 2:3; 2 Cor. 12:5
10 [a]Rom. 5:3; 8:35 [b]2 Cor. 6:4 [c]2 Thess. 1:4; 2 Tim. 3:11 [d]2 Cor. 5:15, 20 [e]2 Cor. 13:4

4 *Paul's unselfishness,* 12:11–18

11 I have become [a]foolish;
you yourselves compelled me.
Actually I should have been com-

11 [a]2 Cor. 5:13; 11:16f.; 12:6 [b]1 Cor. 15:10; 2 Cor. 11:5 [c]1 Cor. 3:7; 13:2; 15:9

11:32 The record of the events in *Damascus* is found in Acts 9:24–25.

12:2–4 Paul here speaks of a personal and actual experience when he was caught up into heaven and given revelations he could not speak about. Some think this occurred when he was stoned (Acts 14:19).

12:6 Paul wanted to be judged only on the evidence before their eyes.

12:7 *a thorn in the flesh.* This seems to have been some recurrent physical affliction. Migraine headaches, eye trouble (ophthalmia ?), malaria, and epilepsy have all been seriously suggested (but see note on Gal. 4:12–15). Paul views it as the work of Satan, permitted by God for a good purpose (keeping him humble). It could not be relieved through prayer (2 Cor. 12:8).

12:9 *the power of Christ* in him was more important than freedom from pain.

mended by you, for [b]in no respect
was I inferior to the most eminent
apostles, even though [c]I am a nobody.
12 The [a]signs of a true apostle
were performed among you with
all perseverance, by signs and
wonders and miracles.
13 For in what respect were
you treated as inferior to the rest
of the churches, except that [a]I
myself did not become a burden
to you? Forgive me [b]this wrong!
14 Here [a]for this third time I
am ready to come to you, and I
[b]will not be a burden to you; for
I [c]do not seek what is yours, but
[d]you; for [e]children are not responsible to save up for *their* parents, but [f]parents for *their* children.
15 And I will [a]most gladly
spend and be expended for your
souls. If [b]I love you the more, am
I to be loved the less?
16 But be that as it may, I [a]did
not burden you myself; nevertheless, crafty fellow that I am, I
[b]took you in by deceit.
17 [a]Certainly I have not taken
advantage of you through any of
those whom I have sent to you,
have I?
18 I [a]urged [b]Titus *to go,* and
sent [c]the brother with him. Titus
did not take any advantage of
you, did he? Did we not conduct
ourselves in the same [d]spirit *and
walk* [e]in the same steps?

12 [a]John 4:48; Rom. 15:19; 1 Cor. 9:1
★13 [a]1 Cor. 9:12, 18; 2 Cor. 11:9; 12:14 [b]2 Cor. 11:7
14 [a]2 Cor. 1:15; 13:1, 2 [b]1 Cor. 9:12, 18; 2 Cor. 11:9; 12:13 [c]1 Cor. 10:24, 33 [d]1 Cor. 9:19 [e]1 Cor. 4:14f.; Gal. 4:19 [f]Prov. 19:14; Ezek. 34:2
★15 [a]Rom. 9:3; 2 Cor. 1:6; Phil. 2:17; Col. 1:24; 1 Thess. 2:8; 2 Tim. 2:10 [b]2 Cor. 11:11
★16 [a]2 Cor. 11:9 [b]2 Cor. 11:20
17 [a]2 Cor. 9:5
18 [a]2 Cor. 8:6 [b]2 Cor. 2:13 [c]2 Cor. 8:18 [d]1 Cor. 4:21 [e]Rom. 4:12

VII CONCLUDING REMARKS, 12:19–13:14

A Appeal for Repentance, 12:19–21

19 All this time you have
been thinking that we are defending ourselves to you. *Actually,* [a]it
is in the sight of God that we have
been speaking in Christ; and [b]all
for your upbuilding, [c]beloved.
20 For I am afraid that perhaps [a]when I come I may find you
to be not what I wish and may be
found by you to be not what you
wish; that perhaps *there may be*
[b]strife, jealousy, [c]angry tempers,
[d]disputes, [e]slanders, [f]gossip, [g]ar-
rogance, [h]disturbances;
21 I am afraid that when I
come again my God may humiliate me before you, and I may
mourn over many of those who
have [a]sinned in the past and not
repented of the [b]impurity, immorality and sensuality which they
have practiced.

19 [a]Rom. 9:1; 2 Cor. 2:17 [b]Rom. 14:19; 2 Cor. 10:8; 1 Thess. 5:11 [c]Heb. 6:9
20 [a]1 Cor. 4:21; 2 Cor. 2:1-4 [b]1 Cor. 1:11; 3:3 [c]Gal. 5:20 [d]Rom. 2:8; 1 Cor. 11:19 [e]Rom. 1:30; James 4:11; 1 Pet. 2:1 [f]Rom. 1:29 [g]1 Cor. 4:6, 18; 5:2 [h]1 Cor. 14:33
★21 [a]2 Cor. 13:2 [b]1 Cor. 6:9, 18; Gal. 5:19; Col. 3:5

B Statement of Plans, 13:1–10

13 [a]This is the third time I am
coming to you. [b]EVERY FACT
IS TO BE CONFIRMED BY THE TESTIMONY
OF TWO OR THREE WITNESSES.
2 I have previously said
when present the second time,
and though now absent I say in
advance to those who have
[a]sinned in the past and to all the
rest as well, that [b]if I come again,
I will not [c]spare *anyone,*
3 since you are [a]seeking for
proof of the [b]Christ who speaks
in me, and who is not weak
toward you, but [c]mighty in you.
4 For indeed He was [a]cruci-
fied because of weakness, yet He
lives [b]because of the power of
God. For we also are [c]weak in
Him, yet [d]we shall live with Him
because of the power of God *directed* toward you.

★ 1 [a]2 Cor. 12:14 [b]Deut. 19:15; Matt. 18:16
2 [a]2 Cor. 12:21 [b]1 Cor. 4:21; 2 Cor. 13:10 [c]2 Cor. 1:23; 10:11
3 [a]2 Cor. 10:1, 10 [b]Matt. 10:20; 1 Cor. 5:4; 7:40 [c]2 Cor. 9:8; 10:4
4 [a]Phil. 2:7f.; 1 Pet. 3:18 [b]Rom. 1:4; 6:4; 1 Cor. 6:14 [c]1 Cor. 2:3; 2 Cor. 13:9 [d]Rom. 6:8

12:13 Do you think I made you *inferior to the rest of the churches* because I didn't sponge off you?

12:15 *for your souls.* I.e., for your spiritual good.

12:16 After *nevertheless* add, "they say." To be sure, they said, he didn't take any money while he was here, but what about that collection for the saints? Who knows in whose pockets that will go?

12:21 *God may humiliate me before you.* I.e., if when Paul comes he finds them still acting like pagans (v. 20).

13:1 *This is the third time I am coming to you.* Acts 18:1 records the first visit; the second was likely the "painful visit" (2 Cor. 2:1); and the third is the one he is about to undertake. *by the testimony of two or three witnesses.* Paul warned that, if necessary, trials were going to be held when he came, in which Jewish rules of evidence-giving would be applied (Deut. 19:15).

★ 5 [a]John 6:6 [b]1 Cor. 11:28 [c]1 Cor. 9:27

5 [a]Test yourselves *to see* if
you are in the faith; [b]examine
yourselves! Or do you not recognize this about yourselves, that
Jesus Christ is in you—unless indeed you [c]fail the test?
6 But I trust that you will realize that we ourselves do not fail
the test.
7 Now we pray to God that
you do no wrong; not that we
ourselves may appear approved,
but that you may do what is right,
even though we should appear
unapproved.
8 For we can do nothing
against the truth, but *only* for the
truth.
9 For we rejoice when we
ourselves are [a]weak but you are
strong; this we also pray for, that
you be [b]made complete.
10 For this reason I am writing these things while absent, in
order that when present [a]I may
not use [b]severity, in accordance
with the [c]authority which the
Lord gave me, for building up and
not for tearing down.

★ 9 [a]2 Cor. 12:10; 13:4 [b]1 Cor. 1:10; 2 Cor. 13:11; Eph. 4:12; 1 Thess. 3:10
10 [a]2 Cor. 2:3 [b]Titus 1:13 [c]1 Cor. 5:4; 2 Cor. 10:8

C Greetings and Benediction, 13:11–14

11 [a]Finally, brethren, rejoice,
[b]be made complete, be comforted, [c]be like-minded, [d]live in
peace; and [e]the God of love and
peace shall be with you.
12 [a]Greet one another with a
holy kiss.
13 [a]All the saints greet you.
14 [a]The grace of the Lord
Jesus Christ, and the [b]love of God,
and the [c]fellowship of the Holy
Spirit, be with you all.

11 [a]1 Thess. 4:1; 2 Thess. 3:1 [b]1 Cor. 1:10; 2 Cor. 13:9; Eph. 4:12; 1 Thess. 3:10 [c]Rom. 12:16 [d]Mark 9:50 [e]Rom. 15:33; Eph. 6:23
★12 [a]Rom. 16:16
13 [a]Phil. 4:22
★14 [a]Rom. 16:20; 2 Cor. 8:9 [b]Rom. 5:5; Jude 21 [c]Phil. 2:1

13:5 *yourselves* is emphatic; i.e., it is yourselves, not I, whom you should examine. *fail the test.* I.e., they failed to pass the test and were not members of the household of faith (also cf. v. 6).

13:9 *that you be made complete.* I.e., be fully restored to spiritual health (also v. 11).

13:12 *a holy kiss.* See note on 1 Pet. 5:14.

13:14 An early and clear witness to belief in the Trinity.

INTRODUCTION TO THE LETTER OF PAUL TO THE GALATIANS

AUTHOR: Paul DATE: 49 or 55

Galatia *At the time of the writing of this letter the term "Galatia" was used both in a geographical and a political sense. The former referred to north central Asia Minor, north of the cities of Pisidian Antioch, Iconium, Lystra, and Derbe; the latter referred to the Roman province (organized in 25 B.C.) which included southern districts and those cities just mentioned. If the letter was written to Christians in North Galatia, the churches were founded on the second missionary journey and the epistle was written on the third missionary journey, either early from Ephesus (about 53) or later (about 55) from Macedonia. In favor of this is the fact that Luke seems to use "Galatia" only to describe North Galatia (Acts 16:6; 18:23).*

If the letter was written to Christians in South Galatia, the churches were founded on the first missionary journey, the letter was written after the end of the journey (probably from Antioch, about 49, making it the earliest of Paul's epistles), and the Jerusalem council (Acts 15) convened shortly afterward. In favor of this dating is the fact that Paul does not mention the decision of the Jerusalem council which bore directly on his Galatian argument concerning the Judaizers, indicating that the council had not yet taken place.

The Problem *How can men (sinful by nature) come to God (holy by nature)? Paul's answer is: There is only one way—accept the salvation God's grace makes available through Christ's death and resurrection. Forget about merit-salvation through obedience to the law of Moses. Man is too weak by nature to accomplish self-salvation or self-sanctification. Certain Jewish Christians (the Judaizers) were teaching that such works are necessary, that Paul's gospel was not correct, and that he was not a genuine apostle. Paul's answer was to proclaim the doctrine of justification by faith plus nothing, and of sanctification by the Holy Spirit, not the Mosaic law. This answer was given in the full apostolic authority received from Christ. All theologies that teach salvation by faith plus human effort are forcefully negated by this great letter.*

Contents *The theme, justification by faith, is defended, explained, and applied. Other significant subjects include Paul's three years in Arabia (1:17), his correcting Peter (2:11), the law as a tutor (3:24), and the fruit of the Spirit (5:22-23).*

OUTLINE OF GALATIANS

I. Introduction: The Rightness of Paul's Gospel Asserted, 1:1-10

II. Justification by Faith Defended: Paul's Authority, 1:11-2:21

- A. His Authority Acquired through Revelation, 1:11-24
- B. His Authority Approved by the Church in Jerusalem, 2:1-10
- C. His Authority Acknowledged in the Rebuke of Peter, 2:11-21

III. Justification by Faith Explained: Paul's Gospel, 3:1-4:31

- A. The Argument from Experience, 3:1-5
- B. The Argument from Abraham, 3:6-9
- C. The Argument from the Law, 3:10-4:11
- D. The Argument from Personal Testimony, 4:12-20
- E. The Argument from an Allegory, 4:21-31

IV. Justification by Faith Applied: Paul's Ethics, 5:1-6:10

- A. In Relation to Christian Liberty, 5:1-12
- B. In Relation to License and Love, 5:13-15
- C. In Relation to the Flesh and the Spirit, 5:16-26
- D. In Relation to a Sinning Brother, 6:1-5
- E. In Relation to Giving, 6:6-10

V. Conclusion: The Substance of Paul's Instruction, 6:11-18

THE LETTER OF PAUL TO THE GALATIANS

I INTRODUCTION: THE RIGHTNESS OF PAUL'S GOSPEL ASSERTED, 1:1–10

1 Paul, [a]an apostle ([b]not *sent*
from men, nor through the
agency of man, but [c]through
Jesus Christ, and God the Father,
who [d]raised Him from the dead),
2 and all [a]the brethren who
are with me, to [b]the churches of
Galatia:
3 [a]Grace to you and peace
from God our Father, and the
Lord Jesus Christ,
4 who [a]gave Himself for our
sins, that He might deliver us out
of [b]this present evil age, according
to the will of [c]our God and Father,
5 [a]to whom *be* the glory forevermore. Amen.
6 I am amazed that you are
[a]so quickly deserting [b]Him who
called you by the grace of Christ,
for a [c]different gospel;
7 which is *really* not another;
only there are some who
are [a]disturbing you, and want to
distort the gospel of Christ.
8 But even though we, or
[a]an angel from heaven, should
preach to you a gospel contrary to
that which we have preached to
you, let him be [b]accursed.
9 As we [a]have said before,
so I say again now, [b]if any man is
preaching to you a gospel contrary to that which you received,
let him be [c]accursed.
10 For am I now [a]seeking the
favor of men, or of God? Or am I
striving to please men? If I were
still trying to please men, I would
not be a [b]bond-servant of Christ.

★ 1 [a]2 Cor. 1:1 [b]Gal. 1:11f. [c]Acts 9:15; 20:24; Gal. 1:15f. [d]Acts 2:24
2 [a]Phil. 4:21 [b]Acts 16:6; 1 Cor. 16:1
★ 3 [a]Rom. 1:7
4 [a]Matt. 20:28; Rom. 4:25; 1 Cor. 15:3; Gal. 2:20 [b]Matt. 13:22; Rom. 12:2; 2 Cor. 4:4 [c]Phil. 4:20; 1 Thess. 1:3; 3:11, 13
5 [a]Rom. 11:36
★ 6 [a]Acts 16:6; 18:23; Gal. 4:13 [b]Rom. 8:28; Gal. 1:15; 5:8 [c]2 Cor. 11:4; Gal. 1:7, 11; 2:2, 7; 5:14; 1 Tim. 1:3
★ 7 [a]Acts 15:24; Gal. 5:10
★ 8 [a]2 Cor. 11:14 [b]Rom. 9:3
9 [a]Acts 18:23 [b]Rom. 16:17 [c]Rom. 9:3
★10 [a]1 Cor. 10:33; 1 Thess. 2:4 [b]Rom. 1:1; Phil. 1:1

II JUSTIFICATION BY FAITH DEFENDED: PAUL'S AUTHORITY, 1:11–2:21

A His Authority Acquired through Revelation, 1:11–24

11 For [a]I would have you
know, brethren, that the gospel
which was preached by me is [b]not
according to man.
12 For [a]I neither received it
from man, nor was I taught it, but
I received it through a [b]revelation
of Jesus Christ.
13 For you have heard of [a]my
former manner of life in Judaism,
how I [b]used to persecute [c]the
church of God beyond measure,
and [d]tried to destroy it;
14 and I [a]was advancing in Judaism
beyond many of my contemporaries
among my countrymen,
being more extremely
zealous for my [b]ancestral traditions.
15 But when He who had set

★11 [a]Rom. 2:16; 1 Cor. 15:1 [b]1 Cor. 3:4; 9:8
12 [a]1 Cor. 11:23; Gal. 1:1 [b]1 Cor. 2:10; 2 Cor. 12:1; Gal. 1:16; 2:2
13 [a]Acts 26:4f. [b]Acts 8:3 [c]1 Cor. 10:32 [d]Acts 9:21
14 [a]Acts 22:3 [b]Jer. 9:14; Matt. 15:2; Mark 7:3; Col. 2:8
★15 [a]Gal. 1:6 [b]Is. 49:1, 5; Jer. 1:5; Acts 9:15; Rom. 1:1

1:1 Paul's apostleship was *not . . . from men.* I.e., it did not originate from any man, but God. *nor through the agency of man.* I.e., it was not mediated through any man, but came directly from *Jesus Christ.*

1:3–5 In this greeting Paul neatly summarizes his whole preaching message.

1:6 *deserting Him who called you.* I.e., God the Father. They were deserting grace to retreat into law, and they bore the responsibility for their defection.

1:7 *the gospel of Christ.* The good news of God's grace in Christ, who gave Himself for our sins (v. 4). Those who taught any other way threatened the true gospel.

1:8 *accursed.* Lit., anathema, or devoted to destruction. Ecclesiastically, it was accompanied by excommunication.

1:10 *seeking the favor of men.* I.e., by toning down his message. Paul was being accused of preaching a cheap form of admission to God's kingdom. He counters by saying that he is a *bond-servant of Christ* (lit., slave). How can this cross-centered way be viewed as seeking *to please men?*

1:11–17 In these verses Paul defends his authority as an apostle. On the one hand, he shows that his teaching was not derived from any human agency; on the other, that it was acknowledged by the other apostles as truly from God.

1:15 Paul was set apart from birth for his work (as was Jeremiah, 1:5).

me apart, *even* from my mother's
womb, and [a]called me through
His grace, was [b]pleased

★16 [a]Acts 9:15; Gal. 2:9 [b]Acts 9:20 [c]Matt. 16:17

16 to reveal His Son in me,
that I might [a]preach Him among
the Gentiles, [b]I did not immediately consult with [c]flesh and
blood,

★17 [a]Acts 9:19-22 [b]Acts 9:2

17 [a]nor did I go up to Jerusalem to those who were apostles
before me; but I went away to
Arabia, and returned once more
to [b]Damascus.

★18 [a]Acts 9:22f. [b]Acts 9:26f. [c]John 1:42; Gal. 2:9, 11, 14

18 Then [a]three years later I
went up [b]to Jerusalem to become
acquainted with [c]Cephas, and
stayed with him fifteen days.

19 [a]Matt. 12:46; Acts 12:17

19 But I did not see any other
of the apostles except [a]James, the
Lord's brother.

20 [a]Rom. 9:1; 2 Cor. 1:23; 11:31

20 (Now in what I am writing
to you, I assure you [a]before God
that I am not lying.)

21 [a]Acts 9:30 [b]Acts 15:23, 41 [c]Acts 6:9

21 Then [a]I went into the regions of [b]Syria and [c]Cilicia.

22 [a]1 Cor. 7:17; 1 Thess. 2:14 [b]Rom. 16:7

22 And I was *still* unknown
by sight to [a]the churches of Judea
which were [b]in Christ;

23 [a]Acts 6:7; Gal. 6:10 [b]Acts 9:21

23 but only, they kept hearing, "He who once persecuted us
is now preaching [a]the faith which
he once [b]*tried to* destroy."

24 [a]Matt. 9:8

24 And they [a]were glorifying
God because of me.

B His Authority Approved by the Church in Jerusalem, 2:1–10

★ 1 [a]Acts 15:2 [b]Acts 4:36; Gal. 2:9, 13 [c]2 Cor. 2:13; Gal. 2:3

2 Then after an interval of
fourteen years I [a]went up
again to Jerusalem with [b]Barna-
bas, taking [c]Titus along also.

2 [a]Acts 15:2; Gal. 1:12 [b]Gal. 1:6 [c]Rom. 9:16; 1 Cor. 9:24ff.; Gal. 5:7; Phil. 2:16; 2 Tim. 4:7; Heb. 12:1

2 And it was because of a
[a]revelation that I went up; and I
submitted to them the [b]gospel
which I preach among the Gentiles, but I did so in private to
those who were of reputation, for
fear that I might be [c]running, or
had run, in vain.

★ 3 [a]2 Cor. 2:13; Gal. 2:1 [b]Acts 16:3; 1 Cor. 9:21

3 But not even [a]Titus who
was with me, though he was a
Greek, was [b]compelled to be circumcised.

4 [a]Acts 15:1, 24; 2 Cor. 11:13, 26; Gal. 1:7 [b]2 Pet. 2:1; Jude 4 [c]Gal. 5:1, 13; James 1:25 [d]Rom. 8:15; 2 Cor. 11:20

4 But *it was* because of the
[a]false brethren who [b]had sneaked
in to spy out our [c]liberty which
we have in Christ Jesus, in order
to [d]bring us into bondage.

★ 5 [a]Gal. 1:6; 2:14; Col. 1:5

5 But we did not yield in
subjection to them for even an
hour, so that [a]the truth of the
gospel might remain with you.

6 [a]2 Cor. 11:5; 12:11; Gal. 2:9; 6:3 [b]Acts 10:34

6 But from those who were
of high [a]reputation (what they
were makes no difference to me;
[b]God shows no partiality)—well,
those who were of reputation
contributed nothing to me.

★ 7 [a]1 Cor. 9:17; 1 Thess. 2:4; 1 Tim. 1:11 [b]Acts 9:15; Gal. 1:16 [c]Gal. 1:18; 2:9, 11, 14

7 But on the contrary, seeing

1:16 *with flesh and blood.* I.e., with other people.

1:17 *Arabia.* This may mean anywhere in the kingdom of the Nabataeans, from near Damascus down to the Sinaitic peninsula. Paul's point is not to pinpoint the location but to emphasize that it was a place, in contrast to Jerusalem, where there was no apostle to instruct him. In Arabia he was alone with God, thinking through the implications of his encounter with the risen Christ on the Damascus road. Though not mentioned in Acts, this period in Paul's life would probably fit between Acts 9:21 and 9:22.

1:18–2:21 Paul's account of his relations with the Jerusalem apostles. Though independent of men, Paul makes it clear that he is within the stream of apostolic tradition represented by James, Peter, and John.

1:18 *become acquainted.* The purpose of Paul's visit to Cephas (Peter) was to become acquainted with him rather than to confer with him. He also saw James, the Lord's half brother (v. 19), but did not visit the Judean churches (v. 22).

2:1–10 Paul's account of the events recorded in Acts 11 (if the letter was written to the churches in South Galatia) or Acts 15 (if written to North Galatia).

2:3 *Titus.* A test case: if he were compelled to be circumcised, then other Gentile believers could be too; if not, then freedom from the law was confirmed.

2:5 *the truth of the gospel.* I.e., grace is everything, and for everyone; to compromise these truths was unthinkable.

2:7 *the gospel to the uncircumcised.* I.e., the gospel to the Gentiles. Paul was especially responsible for spreading the gospel to Gentiles (Rom. 1:5) and Peter *to the circumcised,* the Jews.

that I had been [a]entrusted with
the [b]gospel to the uncircumcised,
just as [c]Peter with *the gospel* to
the circumcised
8 (for He who effectually
worked for Peter in *his* [a]apostle-
ship to the circumcised effectually
worked for me also to the Gentiles),
9 and recognizing [a]the grace
that had been given to me, [b]James
and [c]Cephas and John, who were
[d]reputed to be [e]pillars, gave to me
and [f]Barnabas the [g]right hand of
fellowship, that we might [h]go to
the Gentiles, and they to the circumcised.
10 *They* only *asked* us to remember the poor—[a]the very
thing I also was eager to do.

8 [a]Acts 1:25 **9** [a]Rom. 12:3 [b]Acts 12:17; Gal. 2:12 [c]Luke 22:8; Gal. 1:18; 2:7, 11, 14 [d]2 Cor. 11:5; 12:11; Gal. 2:2, 6; 6:3 [e]1 Tim. 3:15; Rev. 3:12 [f]Acts 4:36; Gal. 2:1, 13 [g]2 Kin. 10:15; Ezra 10:19 [h]Gal. 1:16 **★10** [a]Acts 24:17

C His Authority Acknowledged in the Rebuke of Peter, 2:11–21

11 But when [a]Cephas came to
[b]Antioch, I opposed him to his
face, because he stood condemned.
12 For prior to the coming of
certain men from [a]James, he used
to [b]eat with the Gentiles; but
when they came, he *began* to
withdraw and hold himself aloof,
[c]fearing the party of the circumcision.
13 And the rest of the Jews
joined him in hypocrisy, with the
result that even [a]Barnabas was
carried away by their hypocrisy.
14 But when I saw that they
[a]were not straightforward about
[b]the truth of the gospel, I said to
[c]Cephas in the presence of all, "If
you, being a Jew, [d]live like the
Gentiles and not like the Jews,
how *is it that* you compel the
Gentiles to live like Jews?
15 "We *are* [a]Jews by nature,
and not [b]sinners from among the
Gentiles;
16 nevertheless knowing that
[a]a man is not justified by the
works of the Law but through
faith in Christ Jesus, even we have
believed in Christ Jesus, that we
may be justified by [b]faith in
Christ, and not by the works of
the Law; since [c]by the works of
the Law shall no flesh be justified.
17 "But if, while seeking to be
justified in Christ, we ourselves
have also been found [a]sinners, is
Christ then a minister of sin?
[b]May it never be!
18 "For if I rebuild what I have
once destroyed, I [a]prove myself to
be a transgressor.
19 "For through the Law I
[a]died to the Law, that I might live
to God.
20 "I have been [a]crucified with
Christ; and it is no longer I who
live, but [b]Christ lives in me; and
the *life* which I now live in the
flesh I live by faith in [c]the Son of
God, who [d]loved me, and [e]deliv-
ered Himself up for me.
21 "I do not nullify the grace of
God; for [a]if righteousness *comes*
through the Law, then Christ died
needlessly."

★11 [a]Gal. 1:18; 2:6, 9, 14 [b]Acts 11:19; 15:1 **12** [a]Acts 12:17; Gal. 2:9 [b]Acts 11:3 [c]Acts 11:2 **13** [a]Acts 4:36; Gal. 2:1, 9 **14** [a]Heb. 12:13 [b]Gal. 1:6; 2:5; Col. 1:5 [c]Gal. 1:18; 2:7, 9, 11 [d]Acts 10:28; Gal. 2:12

15 [a]Phil. 3:4f. [b]1 Sam. 15:18; Luke 24:7; 1 Cor. 6:1 **★16** [a]Acts 13:39; Gal. 3:11 [b]Rom. 9:30 [c]Ps. 143:2; Rom. 3:20 **17** [a]Gal. 2:15 [b]Luke 20:16; Gal. 3:21 **18** [a]Rom. 3:5 [Gr.] **★19** [a]Rom. 6:2; 7:4; 1 Cor. 9:20 **★20** [a]Rom. 6:6; Gal. 5:24; 6:14 [b]Rom. 8:10 [c]Matt. 4:3 [d]Rom. 8:37 [e]Gal. 1:4 **★21** [a]Gal. 3:21

2:10 *the poor.* The saints in Jerusalem were notoriously poor (Rom. 15:26; see also 1 Cor. 16:1–4).

2:11–13 *Cephas* (Peter) was not preaching heresy but neither was he consistently practicing the gospel of grace. He withdrew from eating with uncircumcised Gentile believers when pressured to do so by some of the Hebrew Christians.

2:16 *justified.* I.e., to be declared righteous in God's sight and to be vindicated of any charge of sin in connection with failure to keep God's law.

2:19 *died to the Law,* because Christ paid the penalty for sin that the Law demanded. Paul could cease giving further thought to legal obedience as a means of winning God's acceptance.

2:20 *I have been crucified with Christ.* Crucifixion with Christ means death to or separation from the reigning power of the old sinful life and freedom to experience the power of the resurrection life of Christ by faith (see Rom. 6:6). *it is no longer I who live, but Christ . . .* Christ had taken up His abode in Paul, yet He did so without submerging Paul's own personality.

2:21 *nullify* = set aside. It was the Galatians, not Paul, who nullified the grace of God by wanting to retain law. If God wanted obedience through law, why would He send His Son to suffer and die on a cross?

III JUSTIFICATION BY FAITH EXPLAINED: PAUL'S GOSPEL, 3:1–4:31

A The Argument from Experience, 3:1–5

1 [a]Gal. 1:2 3 You foolish [a]Galatians, who
[b]1 Cor. 1:23; has bewitched you, before
Gal. 5:11 whose eyes Jesus Christ [b]was
publicly portrayed *as* crucified?
2 [a]Rom. 2 This is the only thing I
10:17 want to find out from you: did
you receive the Spirit by the
works of the Law, or by [a]hearing
with faith?
★ 3 3 Are you so foolish? Having
begun by the Spirit, are you now
being perfected by the flesh?
4 [a]1 Cor. 4 Did you suffer so many
15:2 things in vain—[a]if indeed it was
in vain?
5 [a]2 Cor. 5 Does He then, who [a]pro-
9:10; Phil. vides you with the Spirit and
1:19 [b]1 Cor. 12:10 [c]Rom. [b]works miracles among you, do it
10:17 by the works of the Law, or by
[c]hearing with faith?

B The Argument from Abraham, 3:6–9

★ 6 [a]Rom. 6 Even so [a]Abraham [b]BE-
4:3 [b]Gen. LIEVED GOD, AND IT WAS RECKONED
15:6 TO HIM AS RIGHTEOUSNESS.
★ 7 [a]Gal. 7 Therefore, be sure that [a]it
3:9 [b]Luke 19:9; Gal. is those who are of faith that are
6:16 [b]sons of Abraham.
8 [a]Gen. 8 And the Scripture, foresee-
12:3 ing that God would justify the
Gentiles by faith, preached the
gospel beforehand to Abraham,
saying, "[a]ALL THE NATIONS SHALL BE
BLESSED IN YOU."
9 So then [a]those who are of 9 [a]Gal. 3:7
faith are blessed with Abraham,
the believer.

C The Argument from the Law, 3:10–4:11

10 For as many as are of the ★10 [a]Deut.
works of the Law are under a 27:26
curse; for it is written, "[a]CURSED IS
EVERY ONE WHO DOES NOT ABIDE BY
ALL THINGS WRITTEN IN THE BOOK OF
THE LAW, TO PERFORM THEM."
11 Now that [a]no one is justi- ★11 [a]Gal.
fied by the Law before God is evi- 2:16 [b]Hab. 2:4; Rom.
dent; for, "[b]THE RIGHTEOUS MAN 1:17; Heb.
SHALL LIVE BY FAITH." 10:38
12 However, the Law is not of 12 [a]Lev.
faith; on the contrary, "[a]HE WHO 18:5; Rom.
PRACTICES THEM SHALL LIVE BY THEM." 10:5
13 Christ [a]redeemed us from ★13 [a]Gal.
the curse of the Law, having be- 4:5 [b]Deut.
come a curse for us—for it is writ- 21:23 [c]Acts
ten, "[b]CURSED IS EVERY ONE WHO 5:30
HANGS ON [c]A TREE"—
14 in order that [a]in Christ 14 [a]Rom.
Jesus the blessing of Abraham 4:9, 16; Gal. 3:28 [b]Gal.
might come to the Gentiles, so 3:2 [c]Acts
that we [b]might receive [c]the prom- 2:33; Eph. 1:13
ise of the Spirit through faith.
15 [a]Brethren, [b]I speak in 15 [a]Acts 1:15; Rom.
terms of human relations: [c]even 1:13; Gal.
though it is *only* a man's cov- 6:18 [b]Rom. 3:5 [c]Heb.
enant, yet when it has been rati- 6:16
fied, no one sets it aside or adds ★16 [a]Luke 1:55; Rom.
conditions to it. 4:13, 16; 9:4
16 Now the promises were [b]Acts 3:25

3:3 Paul brought the gospel to them and the *Spirit* worked in them. Yet now they were reverting to flesh-works in the hope that a combination of faith (Spirit) and works (flesh) would work more easily or better.

3:6 Paul now appealed to Scripture (Gen. 15:6) to show that the patriarch Abraham depended on faith for *righteousness.*

3:7 *sons of Abraham.* Abraham's physical descendants through Isaac and Jacob are the Jewish people, but his spiritual descendants are those who believe in God for salvation, men of faith, as contrasted with men of works or men of circumcision.

3:10 Having shattered the Jews' confidence in their physical relation to Abraham, Paul now shows that the law brings a curse. Paul quotes Deut. 27:26 (from the Greek O.T.) and argues that man cannot possibly keep all the laws, hence his bondage (cf. Jas. 2:10).

3:11 *The righteous man shall live by faith.* Paul's use of this quotation from Hab. 2:4 is to stress that one can become justified in God's sight only by faith; i.e., he who is righteous by faith (rather than works) shall live. See note on Heb. 10:38.

3:13 The law brings a curse. The believer is delivered from that curse through Christ, who became *a curse for us.* The crucifixion brought Him under the curse of the law, as explained in the last half of the verse (quoted from Deut. 21:23).

3:16 *seed.* Since Paul's argument here is based on the singular form of the word in the O.T. (Gen. 22:17, 18), he must have believed in the accuracy of the very words of Scripture.

spoken [a]to Abraham and to his
seed. He does not say, "AND TO
SEEDS," as *referring* to many, but
rather to one, "[b]AND TO YOUR
SEED," that is, Christ.
17 What I am saying is this:
the Law, which came [a]four hundred and thirty years later, does
not invalidate a covenant previously ratified by God, so as to
nullify the promise.
18 For [a]if the inheritance is
based on law, it is no longer based
on a promise; but [b]God has
granted it to Abraham by means
of a promise.
19 [a]Why the Law then? It was
added because of transgressions,
having been [b]ordained through
angels [c]by the agency of a mediator, until [d]the seed should come
to whom the promise had been
made.
20 Now [a]a mediator is not for
one *party only;* whereas God is
only one.
21 Is the Law then contrary to
the promises of God? [a]May it
never be! For [b]if a law had been
given which was able to impart
life, then righteousness would indeed have been based on law.
22 But the Scripture has [a]shut
up all [b]men under sin, that the
promise by faith in Jesus Christ
might be given to those who believe.
23 But before faith came, we
were kept in custody under the
law, [a]being shut up to the faith
which was later to be revealed.
24 Therefore the Law has become our [a]tutor *to lead us* to

★17 [a]Gen. 15:13f.; Ex. 12:40; Acts 7:6
18 [a]Rom. 4:14 [b]Heb. 6:14
★19 [a]Rom. 5:20 [b]Acts 7:53 [c]Ex. 20:19; Deut. 5:5 [d]Gal. 3:16
20 [a]1 Tim. 2:5; Heb. 8:6; 9:15; 12:24
21 [a]Luke 20:16; Gal. 2:17 [b]Gal. 2:21
22 [a]Rom. 11:32 [b]1 Cor. 1:27
23 [a]Rom. 11:32
★24 [a]1 Cor. 4:15 [b]Gal. 2:16

Christ, that [b]we may be justified
by faith.
25 But now that faith has
come, we are no longer under a
[a]tutor.
26 For you are all [a]sons of
God through faith in [b]Christ
Jesus.
27 For all of you who were
[a]baptized into Christ have
[b]clothed yourselves with Christ.
28 [a]There is neither Jew nor
Greek, there is neither slave nor
free man, there is neither male
nor female; for [b]you are all one in
[c]Christ Jesus.
29 And if [a]you belong to
Christ, then you are Abraham's
offspring, heirs according to
[b]promise.
4 Now I say, as long as the heir
is a child, he does not differ at
all from a slave although he is
owner of everything,
2 but he is under guardians
and managers until the date set
by the father.
3 So also we, while we were
children, were held [a]in bondage
under the [b]elemental things of
the world.
4 But when [a]the fulness of
the time came, God sent forth His
Son, [b]born of a woman, born [c]un-
der the Law,
5 in order that He might redeem those who were under the
Law, that we might receive the
adoption as [a]sons.
6 And because you are sons,
[a]God has sent forth the Spirit of
His Son into our hearts, crying,
"[b]Abba! Father!"

25 [a]1 Cor. 4:15
26 [a]Rom. 8:14; Gal. 4:5 [b]Rom. 8:1; Gal. 3:28; 4:14; 5:6, 24; Eph. 1:1; Phil. 1:1; Col. 1:4; 1 Tim. 1:12; 2 Tim. 1:1; Titus 1:4
★27 [a]Matt. 28:19; Rom. 6:3; 1 Cor. 10:2 [b]Rom. 13:14
28 [a]Rom. 3:22; 1 Cor. 12:13; Col. 3:11 [b]John 17:11; Eph. 2:15 [c]Rom. 8:1; Gal. 3:26; 4:14; 5:6, 24; Eph. 1:1; Phil. 1:1; Col. 1:4; 1 Tim. 1:12; 2 Tim. 1:1; Titus 1:4
29 [a]1 Cor. 3:23 [b]Rom. 9:8; Gal. 3:18; 4:28
★ 3 [a]Gal. 2:4; 4:8f., 24f. [b]Gal. 4:9; Col. 2:8, 20; Heb. 5:12
★ 4 [a]Mark 1:15 [b]John 1:14; Rom. 1:3; 8:3; Phil. 2:7 [c]Luke 2:21f., 27
★ 5 [a]Rom. 8:14; Gal. 3:26
★ 6 [a]Acts 16:7; Rom. 5:5; 8:9, 16; 2 Cor. 3:17 [b]Mark 14:36; Rom. 8:15

3:17 The Mosaic law did not set aside the promises made to Abraham. And, during those hundreds of years before the law, God had also justified men only by faith.

3:19-20 The law was mediated through angels and Moses, whereas the covenant with Abraham was given directly by God (Gen. 15:18). The presence of a *mediator* assumes two parties, and the need of a mediator shows the inferiority of the law.

3:24 *tutor.* The Greek word here means not a "teacher" but an attendant, a custodian, usually a slave whose job it was to insure the safe arrival of the child at school. Christ is the true teacher.

3:27 *baptized into Christ.* Not water baptism but Spirit baptism, which brings believers into a living union with Christ (cf. 1 Cor. 12:13). *have clothed yourselves with Christ.* A responsible act of appropriating all that Jesus Christ is.

4:3 *the elemental things of the world.* I.e., the bondage of a legalistic practice of Judaism (also v. 9).

4:4 *born under the Law.* Christ was reared in conformity to the Mosaic law.

4:5 *the adoption as sons.* See note on Rom. 8:15.

4:6 The Holy *Spirit* in the heart of the believer shows his acceptance with God as a son and heir (v. 7). *Abba* is the Aramaic word for father.

7 Therefore you are no
longer a slave, but a son; and [a]if a
son, then an heir through God.
8 However at that time,
[a]when you did not know God,
you were [b]slaves to [c]those which
by nature are no gods.
9 But now that you have
come to know God, or rather to
be [a]known by God, [b]how is it that
you turn back again to the weak
and worthless [c]elemental things,
to which you desire to be enslaved all over again?
10 You [a]observe days and
months and seasons and years.
11 I fear for you, that perhaps
I have labored over you in vain.

7 [a]Rom. 8:17
★ 8 [a]1 Cor. 1:21; Eph. 2:12; 1 Thess. 4:5; 2 Thess. 1:8 [b]Gal. 4:3 [c]2 Chr. 13:9; Is. 37:19; Jer. 2:11; 1 Cor. 8:4f.; 10:20
9 [a]1 Cor. 8:3 [b]Col. 2:20 [c]Gal. 4:3
10 [a]Rom. 14:5; Col. 2:16

D The Argument from Personal Testimony, 4:12–20

12 I beg of you, [a]brethren,
[b]become as *I am,* for I also *have*
become as you *are.* You have
done me no wrong;
13 but you know that it was
because of a bodily illness that I
preached the gospel to you the
first time;
14 and that which was a trial
to you in my bodily condition you
did not despise or loathe, but
[a]you received me as an angel of
God, as [b]Christ Jesus *Himself.*
15 Where then is that sense
of blessing you had? For I bear
you witness, that if possible, you
would have plucked out your
eyes and given them to me.
16 Have I therefore become
your enemy [a]by telling you the
truth?
17 They eagerly seek you, not
commendably, but they wish to
shut you out, in order that you
may seek them.
18 But it is good always to be
eagerly sought in a commendable
manner, and [a]not only when I am
present with you.
19 [a]My children, with whom
[b]I am again in labor until [c]Christ
is formed in you —
20 but I could wish to be present with you now and to change
my tone, for [a]I am perplexed
about you.

★12 [a]Gal. 6:18 [b]2 Cor. 6:11, 13
14 [a]Matt. 10:40; 1 Thess. 2:13 [b]Gal. 3:26
16 [a]Amos 5:10
★17
★18 [a]Gal. 4:13f.
19 [a]1 John 2:1 [b]1 Cor. 4:15 [c]Eph. 4:13
20 [a]2 Cor. 4:8

E The Argument from an Allegory, 4:21–31

21 Tell me, you who want to
be under law, do you not [a]listen
to the law?
22 For it is written that Abraham had two sons, one by the
bondwoman and one by the free
woman.
23 But [a]the son by the bondwoman was born according to the
flesh, and [b]the son by the free
woman through the promise.
24 [a]This is allegorically
speaking: for these *women* are
two covenants, one *proceeding*
from [b]Mount Sinai bearing children who are to be [c]slaves; she is
Hagar.
25 Now this Hagar is Mount
Sinai in Arabia, and corresponds
to the present Jerusalem, for she
is in slavery with her children.
26 But [a]the Jerusalem above
is free; she is our mother.
27 For it is written,

"[a]REJOICE, BARREN WOMAN
WHO DOES NOT BEAR;

21 [a]Luke 16:29
23 [a]Rom. 9:7; Gal. 4:29 [b]Gen. 17:16ff.; 18:10ff.; 21:1; Gal. 4:28; Heb. 11:11
★24 [a]1 Cor. 10:11 [b]Deut. 33:2 [c]Gal. 4:3
26 [a]Heb. 12:22; Rev. 3:12; 21:2, 10
27 [a]Is. 54:1

4:8–11 Paul tells the Galatians they are not acting like heirs of God!

4:12–15 Paul is saying that he has had a good relationship with the Galatians: you have in the past been ready to "pluck out your eyes for me" (a common expression of the time for giving up everything for another), not an indication of eye trouble. Though he was ill on his former visit, they had not scorned him but had treated him as Christ had treated them. Now he wanted them to hold firm to the truth he had taught them.

4:17 The Judaizers were apparently using flattery and threats on the Galatians.

4:18 *not only when I am present with you.* I.e., Paul was not averse to having others minister to them, as long as it was done sincerely in the truth.

4:24 The allegory Paul offers here—of Ishmael and Isaac (Gen. 16:15; 21:3, 9)—expresses truth in addition to the simple facts of the case, in this instance that the Judaizers (related to Hagar, Sinai, and the law) did not have the authority or blessing of God.

> BREAK FORTH AND SHOUT, YOU WHO ARE NOT IN LABOR;
> FOR MORE ARE THE CHILDREN OF THE DESOLATE
> THAN OF THE ONE WHO HAS A HUSBAND."

28 [a]Gal. 4:23 [b]Rom. 9:7ff.; Gal. 3:29

28 And you brethren, [a]like Isaac, are [b]children of promise.

29 [a]Gal. 4:23 [b]Gen. 21:9 [c]Gal. 5:11

29 But as at that time [a]he who was born according to the flesh [b]persecuted him *who was born* according to the Spirit, [c]so it is now also.

30 [a]Gen. 21:10, 12 [b]John 8:35

30 But what does the Scripture say?

> "[a]CAST OUT THE BONDWOMAN AND HER SON,
> FOR [b]THE SON OF THE BONDWOMAN SHALL NOT BE AN HEIR WITH THE SON OF THE FREE WOMAN."

31 So then, brethren, we are not children of a bondwoman, but of the free woman.

IV JUSTIFICATION BY FAITH APPLIED: PAUL'S ETHICS, 5:1–6:10

A In Relation to Christian Liberty, 5:1–12

1 [a]John 8:32, 36; Rom. 8:15; 2 Cor. 3:17; Gal. 2:4; 5:13 [b]1 Cor. 16:13 [c]Acts 15:10; Gal. 2:4

5 [a]It was for freedom that Christ set us free; therefore [b]keep standing firm and do not be subject again to a [c]yoke of slavery.

★ 2 [a]2 Cor. 10:1 [b]Acts 15:1; Gal. 5:3, 6, 11

2 Behold I, [a]Paul, say to you that if you receive [b]circumcision, Christ will be of no benefit to you.

3 [a]Luke 16:28 [b]Acts 15:1; Gal. 5:2, 6, 11 [c]Rom. 2:25

3 And I [a]testify again to every man who receives [b]circumcision, that he is under obligation to [c]keep the whole Law.

★ 4 [a]Heb. 12:15; 2 Pet. 3:17

4 You have been severed from Christ, you who are seeking to be justified by law; you have [a]fallen from grace.

5 [a]Rom. 8:23; 1 Cor. 1:7

5 For we through the Spirit, by faith, are [a]waiting for the hope of righteousness.

6 [a]Gal. 3:26 [b]1 Cor. 7:19; Gal. 6:15 [c]Col. 1:4f.; 1 Thess. 1:3; James 2:18, 20, 22

6 For in [a]Christ Jesus [b]neither circumcision nor uncircumcision means anything, but [c]faith working through love.

7 [a]Gal. 2:2

7 You were [a]running well; who hindered you from obeying the truth?

8 [a]Rom. 8:28; Gal. 1:6

8 This persuasion *did* not *come* from [a]Him who calls you.

9 [a]1 Cor. 5:6

9 [a]A little leaven leavens the whole lump *of dough*.

10 [a]2 Cor. 2:3 [b]Gal. 5:7; Phil. 3:15 [c]Gal. 1:7; 5:12

10 [a]I have confidence in you in the Lord, that you [b]will adopt no other view; but the one who is [c]disturbing you shall bear his judgment, whoever he is.

★11 [a]Gal. 4:29; 6:12 [b]Rom. 9:33; 1 Cor. 1:23

11 But I, brethren, if I still preach circumcision, why am I still [a]persecuted? Then [b]the stumbling block of the cross has been abolished.

12 [a]Gal. 2:4; 5:10 [b]Deut. 23:1

12 Would that [a]those who are troubling you would even [b]mutilate themselves.

B In Relation to License and Love, 5:13–15

13 [a]Gal. 5:1 [b]1 Cor. 8:9; 1 Pet. 2:16 [c]1 Cor. 9:19; Eph. 5:21

13 For you were called to [a]freedom, brethren; [b]only *do* not *turn* your freedom into an opportunity for the flesh, but through love [c]serve one another.

★14 [a]Matt. 7:12; 22:40; Rom. 13:8, 10; Gal. 6:2 [b]Lev. 19:18; Matt. 19:19; John 13:34

14 For [a]the whole Law is fulfilled in one word, in the *statement*, "[b]YOU SHALL LOVE YOUR NEIGHBOR AS YOURSELF."

15 [a]Gal. 5:20; Phil. 3:2

15 But if you [a]bite and devour one another, take care lest you be consumed by one another.

C In Relation to the Flesh and the Spirit, 5:16–26

★16 [a]Rom. 8:4; 13:14; Gal. 5:24f. [b]Rom. 13:14; Eph. 2:3

16 But I say, [a]walk by the Spirit, and you will not carry out [b]the desire of the flesh.

5:2 Law (circumcision) and grace (Christ) simply do not mix, Paul says.

5:4 *fallen from grace.* To use the impossible ground of justification by law is to leave, abandon, fall from the way of grace as the only basis for justification.

5:11 *the stumbling block of the cross.* That a man can be saved only by faith is an offense to his pride.

5:14 Compare Rom. 13:8–10.

5:16 *by the Spirit,* which will give victory over the flesh and its works.

17 For [a]the flesh sets its desire
against the Spirit, and the Spirit
against the flesh; for these are in
opposition to one another, [b]so
that you may not do the things
that you please.
18 But if you are [a]led by the
Spirit, [b]you are not under the
Law.
19 Now the deeds of the flesh
are evident, which are: [a]immorali-
ty, impurity, sensuality,
20 idolatry, [a]sorcery, enmi-
ties, [b]strife, jealousy, outbursts of
anger, [c]disputes, dissensions,
[d]factions,
21 envyings, [a]drunkenness,
carousings, and things like these,
of which I forewarn you just as I
have forewarned you that those
who practice such things shall not
[b]inherit the kingdom of God.
22 But [a]the fruit of the Spirit
is [b]love, joy, peace, patience,
kindness, goodness, faithfulness,
23 gentleness, [a]self-control;
against such things [b]there is no
law.
24 Now those who belong to
[a]Christ Jesus have [b]crucified the
flesh with its passions and [c]de-
sires.
25 If we live by the Spirit, let
us also walk [a]by the Spirit.
26 Let us not become [a]boast-
ful, challenging one another, en-
vying one another.

17 [a]Rom. 7:18, 23; 8:5ff. [b]Rom. 7:15ff.
18 [a]Rom. 8:14 [b]Rom. 6:14; 7:4; 1 Tim. 1:9
★19 [a]1 Cor. 6:9, 18; 2 Cor. 12:21
★20 [a]Rev. 21:8 [b]2 Cor. 12:20 [c]Rom. 2:8; James 3:14ff. [d]1 Cor. 11:19
21 [a]Rom. 13:13 [b]1 Cor. 6:9
★22 [a]Matt. 7:16ff.; Rom. 6:21; Eph. 5:9 [b]Rom. 5:1-5; 1 Cor. 13:4; Col. 3:12-15
23 [a]Acts 24:25 [b]Gal. 5:18
★24 [a]Gal. 3:26 [b]Rom. 6:6; Gal. 2:20; 6:14 [c]Gal. 5:16f.
25 [a]Gal. 5:16
26 [a]Phil. 2:3
★ **1** [a]Gal. 6:18; 1 Thess. 4:1 [b]1 Cor. 2:15 [c]2 Cor. 2:7; 2 Thess. 3:15; Heb. 12:13; James 5:19f. [d]1 Cor. 4:21

D In Relation to a Sinning Brother, 6:1–5

6 [a]Brethren, even if a man is
caught in any trespass, you
who are [b]spiritual, [c]restore such a
one [d]in a spirit of gentleness; *each
one* looking to yourself, lest you
too be tempted.
2 [a]Bear one another's burdens, and thus fulfill [b]the law of
Christ.
3 For [a]if anyone thinks he is
something when he is nothing, he
deceives himself.
4 But let each one [a]examine
his own work, and then he will
have *reason for* [b]boasting in regard to himself alone, and not in
regard to another.
5 For [a]each one shall bear
his own load.

★ **2** [a]Rom. 15:1 [b]Rom. 8:2; 1 Cor. 9:21; James 1:25; 2:12; 2 Pet. 3:2
3 [a]Acts 5:36; 1 Cor. 3:18; 2 Cor. 12:11
4 [a]1 Cor. 11:28 [b]Phil. 1:26
5 [a]Prov. 9:12; Rom. 14:12; 1 Cor. 3:8

E In Relation to Giving, 6:6–10

6 And [a]let the one who is
taught [b]the word share all good
things with him who teaches.
7 [a]Do not be deceived, [b]God
is not mocked; for [c]whatever a
man sows, this he will also reap.
8 [a]For the one who sows to
his own flesh shall from the flesh
reap [b]corruption, but [c]the one
who sows to the Spirit shall from
the Spirit reap eternal life.
9 And [a]let us not lose heart
in doing good, for in due time we
shall reap if we [b]do not grow
weary.
10 So then, [a]while we have
opportunity, let us do good to all
men, and especially to those who
are of the [b]household of [c]the
faith.

★ **6** [a]1 Cor. 9:11, 14 [b]2 Tim. 4:2
7 [a]1 Cor. 6:9 [b]Job 13:9 [c]2 Cor. 9:6
8 [a]Job 4:8; Hos. 8:7; Rom. 6:21 [b]1 Cor. 15:42 [c]Rom. 8:11; James 3:18
9 [a]1 Cor. 15:58; 2 Cor. 4:1 [b]Matt. 10:22; Heb. 12:3, 5; James 5:7f.
★10 [a]Prov. 3:27; John 12:35 [b]Eph. 2:19; Heb. 3:6; 1 Pet. 2:5; 4:17 [c]Acts 6:7; Gal. 1:23

5:19 *evident* = plain, or open, with overtones of being unashamed and blatant.
5:20 *sorcery.* The use of drugs and magical potions (see also Rev. 9:21; 18:23; 21:8; 22:15).
5:22 *faithfulness* in word and deed.
5:24 *crucified.* See note on 2:20.
6:1 *caught* = apprehended, taken by surprise, caught red-handed.
6:2 *burdens.* I.e., the excess burdens which we need to share with one another, in contrast to the *load* (different Greek word) in v. 5 which means the normal amount each must carry for himself. *the law of Christ.* I.e., the commands of Christ, especially the new commandment to love one another (John 13:34). Living under grace is not license; it is a life of love and service (Gal. 5:6, 13).
6:6 *all good things.* I.e., material things.
6:10 *the household of the faith* = believers. Concern for this group is a special obligation of the children of God.

V CONCLUSION: THE SUBSTANCE OF PAUL'S INSTRUCTION, 6:11–18

11 See with what large letters
I am writing to you [a]with my own
hand.
12 Those who desire [a]to make
a good showing in the flesh try to
[b]compel you to be circumcised,
simply that they [c]may not be persecuted for the cross of Christ.
13 For those who are circumcised do not even [a]keep the Law
themselves, but they desire to
have you circumcised, that they
may [b]boast in your flesh.

★**11** [a]1 Cor. 16:21
12 [a]Matt. 23:27f. [b]Acts 15:1 [c]Gal. 5:11
13 [a]Rom. 2:25 [b]Phil. 3:3

14 But [a]may it never be that I
should boast, [b]except in the cross
of our Lord Jesus Christ, [c]through
which the world has been crucified to me, and [d]I to the world.
15 For [a]neither is circumcision anything, nor uncircumcision, but a [b]new creation.
16 And those who will walk
by this rule, peace and mercy *be*
upon them, and upon the [a]Israel
of God.
17 From now on let no one
cause trouble for me, for I bear on
my body the [a]brand-marks of
Jesus.
18 [a]The grace of our Lord
Jesus Christ be [b]with your spirit,
[c]brethren. Amen.

14 [a]Luke 20:16 [in the Gr.]; Gal. 2:17; 3:21 [b]1 Cor. 2:2 [c]Gal. 2:20 [d]Rom. 6:2, 6; Gal. 2:19f.; 5:24
15 [a]Rom. 2:26, 28; 1 Cor. 7:19 [b]2 Cor. 5:17; Eph. 2:10, 15; 4:24
★**16** [a]Rom. 9:6; Gal. 3:7, 29; Phil. 3:3
★**17** [a]Is. 44:5; Ezek. 9:4; 2 Cor. 4:10; 11:23; Rev. 13:16
18 [a]Rom. 16:20 [b]2 Tim. 4:22 [c]Acts 1:15; Rom. 1:13

6:11 *with what large letters.* Paul took the pen from his scribe to write this closing section in large letters for emphasis (though some think this indicates that his illness was in his eyes, 4:15).

6:16 *the Israel of God.* I.e., Christian Jews, those who are both the physical and spiritual seed of Abraham.

6:17 *brand-marks.* I.e., scars suffered in persecution, which spoke more eloquently than the mark of circumcision, which the Judaizers sought to impose.

INTRODUCTION TO THE LETTER OF PAUL TO THE EPHESIANS

AUTHOR: Paul DATE: 61

The Prison Epistles *Ephesians, Philippians, Colossians, and Philemon are sometimes referred to as the Prison Epistles, since they were all written during Paul's Roman imprisonment (Eph. 3:1; Phil. 1:7; Col. 4:10; Philem. 9). Whether he was imprisoned once or twice in Rome is debated, though two imprisonments seem to fit the facts better. During the first, Paul was kept in or near the barracks of the Praetorian Guard or in rental quarters at his own expense for two years (Acts 28:30), during which these epistles were written. He anticipated being released (Philem. 22) and following his release he made several trips, wrote 1 Timothy and Titus, was rearrested, wrote 2 Timothy, and was martyred (see the Introduction to Titus). These, then, are the first Roman imprisonment letters, while 2 Timothy is the second Roman imprisonment letter.*

An Encyclical *Several things indicate that Ephesians was a circular letter, a doctrinal treatise in the form of a letter, to the churches in Asia Minor. Some good Greek manuscripts omit the words "at Ephesus" in 1:1. There is an absence of controversy in this epistle, and it does not deal with problems of particular churches. Since Paul had worked at Ephesus for about three years, and since he normally mentioned many friends in the churches to whom he wrote, the absence of personal names in this letter strongly supports the idea of its encyclical character. It was likely sent first to Ephesus by Tychicus (Eph. 6:21-22; Col. 4:7-8) and is probably the same letter that is called "my letter . . . from Laodicea" in Colossians 4:16.*

The City of Ephesus *Christianity probably came first to Ephesus with Aquila and Priscilla when Paul made a brief stop there on his second missionary journey (Acts 18:18-19). On his third journey he stayed in the city for about three years and the gospel spread throughout all of Asia Minor (Acts 19:10). The city was a commercial, political, and religious center, the great temple of Artemis (Diana) being there. As a major trading center, it ranked with Alexandria and Antioch. After Paul, Timothy had charge of the church in Ephesus for a time (1 Tim. 1:3) and later the apostle John made the city his headquarters.*

Contents *The great theme of this letter is God's eternal purpose to establish and complete His body, the church of Christ. In developing this theme, Paul discusses predestination (1:3-14), Christ's headship over the body (1:22-23; 4:15-16), the church as the building and temple of God (2:21-22), the mystery of Christ (3:1-21), spiritual gifts (4:7-16), and the Church as the bride of Christ.*

OUTLINE OF EPHESIANS

I. Greetings, 1:1-2
II. The Position of Believers, 1:3-3:21
- A. Chosen and Sealed, 1:3-23
- B. Saved by Grace, 2:1-10
- C. United in One Body, 2:11-22
- D. Equal in the Body (the Mystery), 3:1-21

III. The Practice of Believers, 4:1-6:9
- A. In Relation to Other Believers, 4:1-6
- B. In Relation to Spiritual Gifts, 4:7-16
- C. In Relation to the Former Life, 4:17-32
- D. In Relation to Evil, 5:1-17
- E. In Relation to the Holy Spirit, 5:18-21
- F. In Relation to Home Life, 5:22-6:4
- G. In Relation to Slaves and Masters, 6:5-9

IV. The Protection for Believers, 6:10-20
- A. Against Whom? 6:10-12
- B. With What? 6:13-20

V. Concluding Words, 6:21-24

THE LETTER OF PAUL TO THE EPHESIANS

I GREETINGS, 1:1-2

1 Paul, [a]an apostle of [b]Christ
Jesus [c]by the will of God, to
the [d]saints who are at [e]Ephesus,
and [f]*who are* faithful in [b]Christ
Jesus:
2 [a]Grace to you and peace
from God our Father and the Lord
Jesus Christ.

1 [a]2 Cor. 1:1 [b]Rom. 8:1; Gal. 3:26; Eph. 2:6, 7, 10, 13, 20; 3:1, 6, 11, 21; Col. 1:4; 2:6; 4:12 [c]1 Cor. 1:1 [d]Acts 9:13; Phil. 1:1; Col. 1:1 [e]Acts 18:19 [f]Col. 1:2
2 [a]Rom. 1:7

II THE POSITION OF BELIEVERS, 1:3-3:21

A Chosen and Sealed, 1:3-23

3 [a]Blessed *be* the God and
Father of our Lord Jesus Christ,
who has blessed us with every
spiritual blessing in [b]the heavenly
places in Christ,
4 just as [a]He chose us in
Him before [b]the foundation of
the world, that we should be
[c]holy and blameless before Him.
[d]In love
5 He [a]predestined us to [b]adoption as sons through Jesus
Christ to Himself, [c]according to
the kind intention of His will,
6 [a]to the praise of the glory
of His grace, which He freely bestowed on us in [b]the Beloved.

★ 3 [a]2 Cor. 1:3 [b]Eph. 1:20; 2:6; 3:10; 6:12; Phil. 3:20
4 [a]Eph. 2:10; 2 Thess. 2:13f. [b]Matt. 25:34 [c]Eph. 5:27; Col. 1:22; 2 Tim. 1:9 [d]Eph. 4:2, 15, 16; 5:2
★ 5 [a]Acts 13:48; Rom. 8:29f.; Eph. 1:11 [b]Rom. 8:14ff.; Gal. 4:5 [c]Luke 12:32; 1 Cor. 1:21; Gal. 1:15; Phil. 2:13; Col. 1:19
★ 6 [a]Eph. 1:12, 14 [b]Matt. 3:17

7 [a]In Him we have [b]redemption [c]through His blood, the [d]forgiveness of our trespasses, according to [e]the riches of His grace,
8 which He lavished upon
us. In all wisdom and insight
9 He [a]made known to us the
mystery of His will, [b]according to
His kind intention which He
[c]purposed in Him
10 with a view to an administration suitable to [a]the fulness of
the times, *that is,* [b]the summing
up of all things in Christ, things in
the heavens and things upon the
earth. In Him
11 also we [a]have obtained an
inheritance, having been [b]predestined [c]according to His purpose
who works all things [d]after the
counsel of His will,
12 to the end that we who
were the first to hope in Christ
should be [a]to the praise of His
glory.
13 In Him, you also, after listening to [a]the message of truth,
the gospel of your salvation—
having also believed, you were
[b]sealed in Him with [c]the Holy
Spirit of promise,
14 who is [a]given as a pledge
of [b]our inheritance, with a view to

★ 7 [a]Col. 1:14 [b]Rom. 3:24; 1 Cor. 1:30; Eph. 1:14 [c]Acts 20:28; Rom. 3:25 [d]Acts 2:38 [e]Rom. 2:4; Eph. 1:18; 2:7; 3:8, 16
★ 9 [a]Rom. 11:25; 16:25; Eph. 3:3 [b]Luke 12:32; 1 Cor. 1:21; Gal. 1:15; Phil. 2:13; Col. 1:19 [c]Rom. 8:28; Eph. 1:11
★10 [a]Mark 1:15 [b]Eph. 3:15; Phil. 2:9f
★11 [a]Deut. 4:20; 9:26 29; 32:9; Eph. 1:14, 18; Titus 2:14 [b]Eph. 1:5 [c]Rom. 8:28f.; Eph. 3:11 [d]Rom. 9:11; Heb. 6:17
12 [a]Eph. 1:6, 14
★13 [a]Acts 13:26; Eph. 4:21; Col. 1:5 [b]John 3:33; Eph. 4:30 [c]Acts 1:4f.; 2:33
★14 [a]2 Cor. 1:22 [b]Acts 20:32 [c]Eph. 1:7 [d]Eph. 1:11 [e]Eph. 1:6, 12

1:3 *in the heavenly places.* Lit., in the heavenlies, i.e., in the realm of heavenly possessions and experiences into which the Christian is brought because of his association with the risen Christ. The term also occurs in 1:20; 2:6; 3:10; 6:12; cf. John 3:12.

1:5 *predestined.* God has determined beforehand that those who believe in Christ will be adopted into His family and conformed to His Son (cf. Rom. 8:29). It involves a choice on His part (Eph. 1:4); it is done in love (v. 4); it is based on the good pleasure of His perfect will (vv. 5, 9, 11); its purpose is to glorify God (v. 14); but it does not relieve man of his responsibility to believe the gospel in order to bring to pass personally God's predestination (v. 13). *adoption as sons.* See note on Rom. 8:15.

1:6 *in the Beloved.* I.e., in Christ.

1:7 *redemption.* Three ideas are involved in the doctrine of redemption: (1) paying the ransom with the blood of Christ (1 Cor. 6:20; Rev. 5:9); (2) removal from the curse of the law (Gal. 3:13; 4:5); and (3) release from the bondage of sin into the freedom of grace (1 Pet. 1:18). Redemption is always *through His blood;* i.e., through the death of Christ (Col. 1:14).

1:9 *mystery.* See note on 3:3.

1:10 *an administration suitable to the fulness of the times.* I.e., the plan, the arrangement, of the millennial kingdom. *The summing up of all things in Christ.* I.e., that God might head up everything in Christ and bring everything into harmony (Col. 1:16).

1:11 *we have obtained an inheritance.* May be translated "we were made His inheritance." Both ideas are true: we are Christ's inheritance as He is ours.

1:13 *having also believed.* The time of sealing coincides with the time of believing. *sealed . . . with the Holy Spirit.* A seal indicates possession and security. The presence of the Holy Spirit, the seal, is the believer's guarantee of the security of his salvation.

1:14 *pledge* = deposit, down payment. The presence of the Spirit is God's pledge that our salvation will be consummated.

the [c]redemption of [d]*God's own*
possession, [e]to the praise of His
glory.
15 For this reason I too, [a]hav-
ing heard of the faith in the Lord
Jesus which *exists* among you,
and your love for [b]all the saints,
16 [a]do not cease giving
thanks for you, [b]while making
mention *of you* in my prayers;
17 that the [a]God of our Lord
Jesus Christ, [b]the Father of glory,
may give to you a spirit of [c]wis-
dom and of [d]revelation in the
knowledge of Him.
18 *I pray that* [a]the eyes of
your heart may be enlightened, so
that you may know what is the
[b]hope of His [c]calling, what are
[d]the riches of the glory of [e]His inheritance in [f]the saints,
19 and what is the surpassing
greatness of His power toward us
who believe. [a]*These are* in accordance with the working of the
[b]strength of His might
20 which He brought about in
Christ, when He [a]raised Him
from the dead, and [b]seated Him
at His right hand in [c]the heavenly
places,
21 far above [a]all rule and authority and power and dominion,
and every [b]name that is named,
not only in [c]this age, but also in
the one to come.
22 And He [a]put all things in
subjection under His feet, and
gave Him as [b]head over all things
to the church,
23 which is His [a]body, the
[b]fulness of Him who [c]fills [d]all in
all.

15 [a]Rom. 1:8; Col. 1:4; Philem. 5 [b]Eph. 1:1; 3:18
16 [a]Rom. 1:8f.; Col. 1:9 [b]Rom. 1:9
17 [a]John 20:17; Rom. 15:6 [b]Acts 7:2; 1 Cor. 2:8 [c]Col. 1:9 [d]1 Cor. 14:6
★**18** [a]Acts 26:18; 2 Cor. 4:6; Heb. 6:4 [b]Eph. 4:4 [c]Rom. 11:29 [d]Eph. 1:7 [e]Eph. 1:11 [f]Acts 9:13; Col. 1:12
19 [a]Eph. 3:7; Phil. 3:21; Col. 1:29 [b]Eph. 6:10
★**20** [a]Acts 2:24 [b]Mark 16:19 [c]Eph. 1:3
★**21** [a]Matt. 28:18; Rom. 8:38; Eph. 3:10; Col. 1:16 [b]John 17:11; Phil. 2:9; Heb. 1:4; Rev. 19:12 [c]Matt. 12:32; Eph. 2:2
★**22** [a]1 Cor. 15:27 [Ps. 8:6] [b]1 Cor. 11:3; Eph. 4:15; 5:23; Col. 1:18; 2:19
23 [a]1 Cor. 12:27; Eph. 4:12; 5:30; Col. 1:18, 24; 2:19 [b]John 1:16; Eph. 3:19 [c]Eph. 4:10 [d]Col. 3:11

B Saved by Grace, 2:1–10

2 And you were [a]dead in your
trespasses and sins,
2 in which you [a]formerly
walked according to the course of
[b]this world, according to [c]the
prince of the power of the air, of
the spirit that is now working in
[d]the sons of disobedience.
3 Among them we too all
[a]formerly lived in [b]the lusts of
our flesh, indulging the desires of
the flesh and of the mind, and
were [c]by nature [d]children of
wrath, [e]even as the rest.
4 But God, being [a]rich in
mercy, because of [b]His great love
with which He loved us,
5 even when we were [a]dead
in our transgressions, made us
alive together with Christ ([b]by
grace you have been saved),
6 and [a]raised us up with
Him, and [b]seated us with Him in
[c]the heavenly *places,* in [d]Christ
Jesus,
7 in order that in the ages to
come He might show the surpassing [a]riches of His grace in [b]kind-
ness toward us in Christ Jesus.
8 For [a]by grace you have

★ **1** [a]Luke 15:24, 32; Eph. 2:5; Col. 2:13
★ **2** [a]Rom. 13:13; 1 Cor. 6:11; Eph. 2:3, 11, 13; 5:8; Col. 3:7; 1 Pet. 4:3 [b]Eph. 1:21 [c]John 12:31; Eph. 6:12 [d]Eph. 5:6
★ **3** [a]Eph. 2:2 [b]Gal. 5:16f. [c]Rom. 2:14; Gal. 2:15 [d]Rom. 5:10; Col. 1:21; 2 Pet. 2:14 [e]Rom. 5:12, 19; 1 Thess. 4:13; 5:6
4 [a]Eph. 1:7 [b]John 3:16
★ **5** [a]Eph. 2:1 [b]Acts 15:11; Eph. 2:8
6 [a]Col. 2:12 [b]Eph. 1:20 [c]Eph. 1:3 [d]Eph. 1:1; 2:10, 13
★ **7** [a]Rom. 2:4; Eph. 1:7 [b]Titus 3:4
★ **8** [a]Acts 15:11; Eph. 2:5 [b]1 Pet. 1:5 [c]John 4:10; Heb. 6:4

1:18 *of your heart.* "Heart" in scripture is considered the very center and core of life.

1:20 *at His right hand.* See Ps. 110:1. The right hand is a figure for the place of honor and sovereign power.

1:21 *rule and authority and power and dominion.* These words, in rabbinic thought of the time, described different orders of angels (see Rom. 8:38; Eph. 3:10; 6:12; Col. 1:16; 2:10, 15; Titus 3:1).

1:22–23 *the church, which is His body.* The universal church to which every true believer belongs, regardless of local church affiliation. It is a spiritual organism entered by means of the baptism of the Spirit (1 Cor. 12:13). Christ is the risen Head of the church and its members are subject to Him (Eph. 5:24). Local churches should be miniatures of the body of Christ, though it is possible to have unbelieving members in local churches who are not, therefore, members of the body of Christ.

2:1 *dead.* I.e., separated from God because of sins. This is spiritual death. If a man continues in this state, by continuing to reject Christ, spiritual death becomes the second death, eternal separation from God (Rev. 20:14).

2:2 *prince . . . spirit.* Both words refer to Satan. *sons of disobedience.* A Hebraism for "disobedient people."

2:3 Man's basic *nature* has been affected by sin. *children of wrath.* A Hebraism, difficult to translate, but meaning "deserving of wrath."

2:5 *grace.* See note on John 1:17.

2:7 Believers will be an eternal display of the grace of God.

2:8 Salvation is *by grace . . . through faith.* Faith involves knowledge of the gospel (Rom. 10:14), acknowledgment of the truth of its message, and personal reception of the Savior (John 1:12). Works cannot save (Eph. 2:9), but good works always accompany salvation (v. 10; Jas. 2:17).

been saved [b]through faith; and that not of yourselves, *it is* [c]the gift of God;

9 [a]not as a result of works, that [b]no one should boast.

10 For we are His workmanship, [a]created in [b]Christ Jesus for [c]good works, which God [d]prepared beforehand, that we should [e]walk in them.

C United in One Body, 2:11–22

11 Therefore remember, that [a]formerly [b]you, the Gentiles in the flesh, who are called "[c]Uncircumcision" by the so-called "[c]Circumcision," *which is* performed in the flesh by human hands—

12 *remember* that you were at that time separate from Christ, [a]excluded from the commonwealth of Israel, and strangers to [b]the covenants of promise, having [c]no hope and [d]without God in the world.

13 But now in [a]Christ Jesus you who [b]formerly were [c]far off have [c]been brought near [d]by the blood of Christ.

14 For He Himself is [a]our peace, [b]who made both *groups into* one, and broke down the barrier of the dividing wall,

15 by [a]abolishing in His flesh the enmity, *which is* [b]the Law of commandments *contained* in ordinances, that in Himself He might [c]make the two into [d]one new man, *thus* establishing [e]peace,

16 and might [a]reconcile them both in [b]one body to God through the cross, by it having [c]put to death the enmity.

17 AND [a]HE CAME AND PREACHED [b]PEACE TO YOU WHO WERE [c]FAR AWAY, AND PEACE TO THOSE WHO WERE [c]NEAR;

18 for through Him we both have [a]our access in [b]one Spirit to [c]the Father.

19 So then you are no longer [a]strangers and aliens, but you are [b]fellow-citizens with the saints, and are of [c]God's household,

20 having been [a]built upon [b]the foundation of [c]the apostles and prophets, [d]Christ Jesus Himself being the [e]corner *stone,*

21 [a]in whom the whole building, being fitted together is growing into [b]a holy temple in the Lord;

22 in whom you also are being [a]built together into a [b]dwelling of God in the Spirit.

D Equal in the Body (the Mystery), 3:1–21

3 For this reason I, Paul, [a]the prisoner of [b]Christ Jesus [c]for the sake of you [d]Gentiles—

2 if indeed you have heard of the [a]stewardship of God's grace which was given to me for you;

3 [a]that [b]by revelation there was [c]made known to me [d]the mystery, [e]as I wrote before in brief.

9 [a]Rom. 3:28; 2 Tim. 1:9; Titus 3:5 [b]1 Cor. 1:29
10 [a]Eph. 2:15; 4:24; Col. 3:10 [b]Eph. 1:1; 2:6, 13 [c]Titus 2:14 [d]Eph. 1:4 [e]Eph. 4:1
★11 [a]Rom. 13:13; 1 Cor. 6:11; Eph. 2:2, 3, 13; 5:8; Col. 3:7; 1 Pet. 4:3 [b]1 Cor. 12:2; Eph. 5:8 [c]Rom. 2:28f.; Col. 2:11, 13
12 [a]Rom. 9:4; Col. 1:21 [b]Gal. 3:17; Heb. 8:6 [c]1 Thess. 4:13 [d]Gal. 4:8; Eph. 4:18
★13 [a]Eph. 1:1; 2:6, 10 [b]Rom. 13:13; 1 Cor. 6:11; Eph. 2:2, 3, 11; 5:8; Col. 3:7; 1 Pet. 4:3 [c]Is. 57:19; Acts 2:39; Eph. 2:17 [d]Rom. 3:25
★14 [a]Is. 9:6; Gal. 3:28; Eph. 2:15; Col. 3:11, 15 [b]1 Cor. 12:13
★15 [a]Eph. 2:16; Col. 1:21f. [b]Col. 2:14, 20 [c]Eph. 2:10; 4:24; Col. 3:10 [d]Gal. 3:28; Col. 3:10f. [e]Is. 9:6; Gal. 3:28
16 [a]2 Cor. 5:18 [b]1 Cor. 10:17; Eph. 4:4 [c]Eph. 2:15
17 [a]Is. 57:19; Rom. 10:14; Eph. 4:21 [b]Acts 10:36; Eph. 2:14 [c]Is. 57:19
18 [a]Rom. 5:2; Eph. 3:12 [b]1 Cor. 12:13; Eph. 4:4 [c]Col. 1:12
19 [a]Eph. 2:12; Heb. 11:13; 1 Pet. 2:11 [b]Phil. 3:20; Heb. 12:22f. [c]Gal. 6:10
★20 [a]1 Cor. 3:9 [b]Matt. 16:18 [c]1 Cor. 12:28; Eph. 3:5 [d]1 Cor. 3:11 [e]Luke 20:17
21 [a]Eph. 4:15f.; Col. 2:19 [b]1 Cor. 3:16f.
22 [a]1 Cor. 3:9, 16; 2 Cor. 6:16 [b]Eph. 3:17
1 [a]Acts 23:18; Eph. 4:1 [b]Gal. 5:24 [c]2 Cor. 1:6; Eph. 3:13 [d]Eph. 3:8
★ 2 [a]Eph. 1:10; 3:9
★ 3 [a]Acts 22:17, 21; 26:16ff. [b]Gal. 1:12 [c]Eph. 1:9; 3:4, 9 [d]Rom. 11:25; 16:25 [e]Eph. 1:9f.

2:11–22 Paul now expands the concept of the body of Christ put forward in 1:23.

2:13 *near* (to God).

2:14 *the barrier of the dividing wall.* An allusion to the wall which separated the Court of the Gentiles from the Court of the Jews in the temple. An inscription warned Gentiles of the death penalty for going beyond it.

2:15 *in His flesh.* For an explanation of Paul's understanding of this "shorthand" phrase, see Gal. 4:4 and Heb. 2:14. *the Law.* The whole Jewish legal system. *the two.* I.e., Jew and Gentile.

2:20–21 In the figure of the church as a temple, Christ is the *corner stone,* the *apostles and* N.T. *prophets* are the *foundation,* and each Christian is a stone in the building (1 Pet. 2:4–8). In 1 Cor. 3:11 Paul speaks of Christ as the sole foundation.

3:2 *stewardship.* Paul was entrusted with the message of the grace of God as the apostle to the Gentiles (v. 1; Gal. 2:7).

3:3 *the mystery.* A mystery was not something mysterious (in the modern sense) but something unknown until revealed to the initiated (cf. Rom. 16:25). The mystery spoken of here is not that Gentiles would be blessed (for that was predicted in the O.T.), but that Jews and Gentiles would be equal heirs in the one body of Christ (Eph. 3:6). This was unknown in O.T. prophecy but was revealed by the N.T. apostles and prophets (v. 5). Other mysteries revealed in the N.T. are found in Matt. 13:11; Rom. 11:25; 1 Cor. 15:51–52; Eph. 5:32; 6:19; Col. 1:27; 2:2; 4:3; 2 Thess. 2:7; 1 Tim. 3:16; Rev. 1:20; 17:5, 7.

4 And by referring to this,
when you read you can understand [a]my insight into the [b]mys-
tery of Christ,
5 which in other generations
was not made known to the sons
of men, as it has now been revealed to His holy [a]apostles and
prophets in the Spirit;
6 *to be specific,* that the
Gentiles are [a]fellow-heirs and
[b]fellow-members of the body,
and [c]fellow-partakers of the
promise in [d]Christ Jesus through
the gospel,
7 [a]of which I was made a
[b]minister, according to the gift of
[c]God's grace which was given to
me [d]according to the working of
His power.
8 To me, [a]the very least of
all saints, this grace was given, to
[b]preach to the Gentiles the unfathomable [c]riches of Christ,
9 and to bring to light what
is the administration of the [a]mys-
tery which for ages has been [b]hid-
den in God, [c]who created all
things;
10 in order that the manifold
[a]wisdom of God might now be
[b]made known through the church
to the [c]rulers and the authorities
in [d]the heavenly *places.*
11 *This was* in [a]accordance
with the eternal purpose which
He carried out in [b]Christ Jesus our
Lord,
12 in whom we have [a]bold-
ness and [b]confident [c]access
through faith in Him.
13 Therefore I ask you not [a]to
lose heart at my tribulations [b]on
your behalf, for they are your glory.
14 For this reason, I [a]bow my
knees before the Father,
15 from whom every family
in heaven and on earth derives its
name,
16 that He would grant you,
according to [a]the riches of His
glory, to be [b]strengthened with
power through His Spirit in [c]the
inner man;
17 so that [a]Christ may dwell
in your hearts through faith; *and*
that you, being [b]rooted and
[c]grounded in love,
18 may be able to compre-
hend with [a]all the saints what is
[b]the breadth and length and
height and depth,
19 and to know [a]the love of
Christ which [b]surpasses knowledge, that you may be [c]filled up
to all the [d]fulness of God.
20 [a]Now to Him who is [b]able
to do exceeding abundantly beyond all that we ask or think, [c]ac-
cording to the power that works
within us,
21 [a]to Him *be* the glory in the
church and in Christ Jesus to all
generations forever and ever.
Amen.

4 [a]2 Cor. 11:6 [b]Rom. 11:25; 16:25; Eph. 3:3, 9; 6:19; Col. 1:26f.; 4:3
5 [a]1 Cor. 12:28; Eph. 2:20
6 [a]Gal. 3:29 [b]Eph. 2:16 [c]Eph. 5:7 [d]Gal. 5:24
★ 7 [a]Col. 1:23, 25 [b]1 Cor. 3:5 [c]Acts 9:15; Rom. 12:3; Eph. 3:2 [d]Eph. 1:19; 3:20
8 [a]1 Cor. 15:9 [b]Acts 9:15; Eph. 3:1f. [c]Rom. 2:4; Eph. 1:7; 3:16
9 [a]Rom. 11:25; 16:25; Eph. 3:3, 4; 6:19; Col. 1:26f.; 4:3 [b]Col. 3:3 [c]Rev. 4:11
10 [a]Rom. 11:33; 1 Cor. 2:7 [b]Eph. 1:23; 1 Pet. 1:12 [c]Eph. 1:21; 6:12; Col. 2:10, 15 [d]Eph. 1:3
11 [a]Eph. 1:11 [b]Gal. 5:24; Eph. 3:1
12 [a]Heb. 4:16; 10:19 35; 1 John 2:28; 3:21 [b]2 Cor. 3:4 [c]Eph. 2:18
13 [a]2 Cor. 4:1 [b]Eph. 3:1
★14 [a]Phil. 2:10
16 [a]Eph. 1:18; 3:8 [b]1 Cor. 16:13; Phil. 4:13; Col. 1:11 [c]Rom. 7:22
★17 [a]John 14:23; Rom. 8:9f.; 2 Cor. 13:5; Eph. 2:22 [b]1 Cor. 3:6; Col. 2:7 [c]Col. 1:23
18 [a]Eph. 1:15 [b]Job 11:8f.
19 [a]Rom. 8:35, 39 [b]Phil. 4:7 [c]Col. 2:10 [d]Eph. 1:23
★20 [a]Rom. 16:25 [b]2 Cor. 9:8 [c]Eph. 3:7
21 [a]Rom. 11:36

III THE PRACTICE OF BELIEVERS, 4:1–6:9

A In Relation to Other Believers, 4:1–6

4 I, therefore, [a]the prisoner of
the Lord, [b]entreat you to
[c]walk in a manner worthy of the
[d]calling with which you have
been [e]called,
2 with all [a]humility and gentleness, with patience, showing
forbearance to one another [b]in
love,
3 being diligent to preserve
the unity of the Spirit in the
[a]bond of peace.

★ 1 [a]Eph. 3:1 [b]Rom. 12:1 [c]Eph. 2:10; Col. 1:10; 2:6; 1 Thess. 2:12 [d]Rom. 11:29 [e]Rom. 8:28f.
2 [a]Col. 3:12f. [b]Eph. 1:4
3 [a]Col. 3:14f.

3:7–10 Paul here gives his concept of his own mission. Note that this was God's doing (v. 7); that he was to make available to all mankind Israel's hope for a Messiah (v. 8); that he was to be a theologian-teacher as well as a missionary (v. 9); that his ministry would even bring angelic beings to see the wisdom of God in His plan for the church (v. 10). On *rulers and . . . authorities* see note on 1:21.

3:14 *For this reason.* Here Paul resumes the thought begun in 3:1.

3:17 *dwell* = be completely at home.

3:20 *the power that works within us.* I.e., the Holy Spirit.

4:1 Here begins Paul's exhortation for his readers to promote the unity of the church through godly living (vv. 1–6) and, through a diversity of gifts, contribute to the common welfare (vv. 7–16).

4 [a]1 Cor. 12:4ff.; Eph. 2:16, 18 [b]Eph. 1:18
★ 5 [a]1 Cor. 8:6
★ 6 [a]Rom. 11:36; Col. 1:16

4 *There is* [a]one body and one Spirit, just as also you were called in one [b]hope of your calling;

5 [a]one Lord, one faith, one baptism,

6 one God and Father of all [a]who is over all and through all and in all.

B In Relation to Spiritual Gifts, 4:7–16

★ 7 [a]1 Cor. 12:7, 11 [b]Eph. 3:2 [c]Rom. 12:3
★ 8 [a]Ps. 68:18 [b]Judg. 5:12; Col. 2:15
★ 9 [a]John 3:13 [b]Ps. 63:9; Is. 44:23
10 [a]Eph. 1:20f.; Heb. 4:14; 7:26; 9:24 [b]Eph. 1:23
★11 [a]Eph. 4:8 [b]Acts 13:1; 1 Cor. 12:28 [c]Acts 21:8 [d]Acts 13:1
12 [a]2 Cor. 13:9 [b]1 Cor. 12:27; Eph. 1:23

7 But [a]to each one of us [b]grace was given [c]according to the measure of Christ's gift.

8 Therefore it says,

> "[a]WHEN HE ASCENDED ON HIGH,
> HE [b]LED CAPTIVE A HOST OF CAPTIVES,
> AND HE GAVE GIFTS TO MEN."

9 (Now this *expression,* "He [a]ascended," what does it mean except that He also had descended into [b]the lower parts of the earth?

10 He who descended is Himself also He who ascended [a]far above all the heavens, that He might [b]fill all things.)

11 And He [a]gave [b]some *as* apostles, and some *as* prophets, and some *as* [c]evangelists, and some *as* pastors and [d]teachers,

12 [a]for the equipping of the saints for the work of service, to the building up of [b]the body of Christ;

13 [a]Eph. 4:3, 5 [b]John 6:69; Eph. 1:17; Phil. 3:10 [c]1 Cor. 14:20; Col. 1:28; Heb. 5:14 [d]John 1:16; Gal. 4:19; Eph. 1:23
14 [a]1 Cor. 14:20 [b]James 1:6; Jude 12 [c]1 Cor. 3:19; 2 Cor. 4:2; 11:3 [d]Eph. 6:11
15 [a]Eph. 1:4 [b]Eph. 2:21 [c]Eph. 1:22
16 [a]Rom. 12:4f.; 1 Cor. 10:17; Col. 2:19 [b]Eph. 1:4

13 until we all attain to [a]the unity of the faith, and of the [b]knowledge of the Son of God, to a [c]mature man, to the measure of the stature which belongs to the [d]fulness of Christ.

14 As a result, we are [a]no longer to be children, [b]tossed here and there by waves, and carried about by every wind of doctrine, by the trickery of men, by [c]craftiness in [d]deceitful scheming;

15 but speaking the truth [a]in love, we are to [b]grow up in all *aspects* into Him, who is the [c]head, *even* Christ,

16 from whom [a]the whole body, being fitted and held together by that which every joint supplies, according to the proper working of each individual part, causes the growth of the body for the building up of itself [b]in love.

C In Relation to the Former Life, 4:17–32

★17 [a]Col. 2:4 [b]Luke 16:28 [c]Eph. 2:2; 4:22 [d]Rom. 1:21; Col. 2:18; 1 Pet. 1:18; 2 Pet. 2:18
18 [a]Rom. 1:21 [b]Eph. 2:1, 12 [c]Acts 3:17; 17:30; 1 Cor. 2:8; Heb. 5:2; 9:7; 1 Pet. 1:14 [d]Mark 3:5; Rom. 11:7, 25; 2 Cor. 3:14

17 [a]This I say therefore, and [b]affirm together with the Lord, [c]that you walk no longer just as the Gentiles also walk, in the [d]futility of their mind,

18 being [a]darkened in their understanding, excluded from [b]the life of God, because of the [c]ignorance that is in them, be-

---

4:5 *one baptism.* I.e., the baptism of the Spirit, which brings us into the unity of the body of Christ.

4:6 God is *Father* in four relationships: (1) here, of all men by virtue of being their Creator; (2) of the Lord Jesus Christ (Matt. 3:17); (3) of Israel (Ex. 4:22); and (4) of believers in the Lord Jesus Christ (Gal. 3:26).

4:7 In 1 Cor. 12:7-11 Paul attributes the giving of spiritual gifts to the Spirit; here to the ascended Christ.

4:8 *He led captive a host of captives.* Paul uses an illustration from Ps. 68:18, in which the triumphant warrior is elevated when he returns with hosts of prisoners, receiving gifts from the conquered people, and distributing gifts to his followers. Christ conquered Satan and all that had conquered us.

4:9–10 These verses are a parenthetical aside, to comment on *He ascended* (v. 8) and to prove that only Christ fits the description.

4:9 *lower parts of the earth.* May mean that Christ descended into Hades between His death and resurrection; or "of the earth" may be an appositional phrase, meaning that He descended (at His incarnation) into the lower parts (of the universe), namely, the earth.

4:11 *apostles.* See note on Matt. 10:2. *prophets.* Strictly speaking, those who were given direct revelation by God to communicate to men. *evangelists.* I.e., preachers of the gospel. *pastors and teachers.* The two ministries are linked together here, though separated elsewhere (Rom. 12:7; 1 Pet. 5:2).

4:17 Here begins a long passage (ending at 6:9) in which Paul draws the logical conclusions, in terms of life and morals, that follow from membership in Christ's body.

cause of the [d]hardness of their heart;

19 and they, having [a]become callous, [b]have given themselves over to [c]sensuality, for the practice of every kind of impurity with greediness.

20 But you did not [a]learn Christ in this way,

21 if indeed you [a]have heard Him and have [b]been taught in Him, just as truth is in Jesus,

22 that, in reference to your former manner of life, you [a]lay aside the [b]old self, which is being corrupted in accordance with the [c]lusts of deceit,

23 and that you be [a]renewed in the spirit of your mind,

24 and [a]put on the [b]new self, which [c]in *the likeness of* God has been created in righteousness and holiness of the truth.

25 Therefore, [a]laying aside falsehood, [b]SPEAK TRUTH, EACH ONE *of you*, WITH HIS NEIGHBOR, for we are [c]members of one another.

26 [a]BE ANGRY, AND *yet* DO NOT SIN; do not let [b]the sun go down on your anger,

27 and do not [a]give the devil an opportunity.

28 Let him who steals steal no longer; but rather [a]let him labor, [b]performing with his own hands what is good, [c]in order that he may have *something* to share with him who has need.

29 Let no [a]unwholesome word proceed from your mouth, but only such *a word* as is good for [b]edification according to the need *of the moment,* that it may give grace to those who hear.

30 And [a]do not grieve the Holy Spirit of God, by whom you were [b]sealed for the day of redemption.

31 [a]Let all bitterness and wrath and anger and clamor and slander be [b]put away from you, along with all [c]malice.

32 And [a]be kind to one another, tender-hearted, forgiving each other, [b]just as God in Christ also has forgiven you.

19 [a]1 Tim. 4:2 [b]Rom. 1:24 [c]Col. 3:5
20 [a]Matt. 11:29
21 [a]Rom. 10:14; Eph. 1:13; 2:17; Col. 1:5 [b]Col. 2:7
★22 [a]Eph. 4:25, 31; Col. 3:8; Heb. 12:1 [Gr.]; James 1:21; 1 Pet. 2:1 [b]Rom. 6:6 [c]2 Cor. 11:3; Heb. 3:13
23 [a]Rom. 12:2
24 [a]Rom. 13:14 [b]Rom. 6:4; 7:6; 12:2; 2 Cor. 5:17; Col. 3:10 [c]Eph. 2:10
25 [a]Eph. 4:22, 31; Col. 3:8; Heb. 12:1 [Gr.]; James 1:21; 1 Pet. 2:1 [b]Zech. 8:16; Eph. 4:15; Col. 3:9 [c]Rom. 12:5
★26 [a]Ps. 4:4 [b]Deut. 24:15
27 [a]Rom. 12:19; James 4:7
28 [a]Acts 20:35; 1 Cor. 4:12; Gal. 6:10 [b]1 Thess. 4:11; 2 Thess. 3:8, 11f.; Titus 3:8, 14 [c]Luke 3:11; 1 Thess. 4:12
29 [a]Matt. 12:34; Eph. 5:4; Col. 3:8 [b]Eccl. 10:12; Rom. 14:19; Col. 4:6
★30 [a]Is. 63:10; 1 Thess. 5:19 [b]John 3:33; Eph. 1:13
31 [a]Rom. 3:14; Col. 3:8, 19 [b]Eph. 4:22 [c]1 Pet. 2:1
32 [a]1 Cor. 13:4; Col. 3:12f.; 1 Pet. 3:8 [b]Matt. 6:14f.; 2 Cor. 2:10

D In Relation to Evil, 5:1–17

5 [a]Therefore be imitators of God, as beloved children;

2 and [a]walk in love, just as Christ also [b]loved you, and [c]gave Himself up for us, an [d]offering and a sacrifice to God as a [e]fragrant aroma.

3 But do not let [a]immorality or any impurity or greed even be named among you, as is proper among saints;

4 and *there must be no* [a]filthiness and silly talk, or coarse jesting, which [b]are not fitting, but rather [c]giving of thanks.

5 For this you know with certainty, that [a]no immoral or impure person or covetous man, who is an idolater, has an inheritance in the kingdom [b]of Christ and God.

6 [a]Let no one deceive you with empty words, for because of these things [b]the wrath of God comes upon [c]the sons of disobedience.

7 Therefore do not be [a]partakers with them;

8 for [a]you were formerly [b]darkness, but now you are light in the Lord; walk as [c]children of light

9 (for [a]the fruit of the light *consists* in all [b]goodness and righteousness and truth),

10 [a]trying to learn what is pleasing to the Lord.

1 [a]Matt. 5:48; Luke 6:36; Eph. 4:32
★ 2 [a]Rom. 14:15; Col. 3:14 [b]John 13:34; Rom. 8:37 [c]John 6:51; Rom. 4:25; Gal. 2:20; Eph. 5:25 [d]Heb. 7:27; 9:14; 10:10, 12 [e]Ex. 29:18, 25; 2 Cor. 2:14
3 [a]Col. 3:5
★ 4 [a]Matt. 12:34; Eph. 4:29; Col. 3:8 [b]Rom. 1:28 [c]Eph. 5:20
5 [a]1 Cor. 6:9; Col. 3:5 [b]Col. 1:13
6 [a]Col. 2:8 [b]Rom. 1:18; Col. 3:6 [c]Eph. 2:2; Col. 3:6
7 [a]Eph. 3:6
8 [a]Eph. 2:2 [b]Acts 26:18; Col. 1:12f. [c]Luke 16:8; John 12:36; Rom. 13:12
9 [a]Gal. 5:22 [b]Rom. 15:14
10 [a]Rom. 12:2

4:22–24 *the old self . . . the new self.* The *old* is what we were before we were saved, and the *new* is the new life we have in Christ. See 2 Cor. 5:17; Gal. 2:20.

4:26 There is an anger which is not sinful, but even this must not be allowed to stay and fester and give the devil an opportunity.

4:30 *the Holy Spirit* is grieved or pained by sin, especially the sins of the tongue (vv. 29, 31). *sealed.* See note on 1:13.

5:2 *a fragrant aroma.* The soothing aroma offerings of Lev. 1–3 prefigured the voluntary character of Christ's sacrifice.

5:4 *silly talk, or coarse jesting.* I.e., unclean speech, often veiled in innuendo or double meaning.

11 [a]1 Cor. 5:9; 2 Cor. 6:14 [b]Rom. 13:12 [c]Acts 26:18; Col. 1:12f. [d]1 Tim. 5:20

11 And [a]do not participate in
the unfruitful [b]deeds of [c]dark-
ness, but instead even [d]expose
them;
12 for it is disgraceful even to
speak of the things which are
done by them in secret.

13 [a]John 3:20f.

13 But all things become visible [a]when they are exposed by
the light, for everything that becomes visible is light.

14 [a]Is. 26:19; 51:17; 52:1; 60:1 [b]Rom. 13:11 [c]Eph. 2:1 [d]Luke 1:78f.

14 For this reason [a]it says,

"[b]AWAKE, SLEEPER,
AND ARISE FROM [c]THE DEAD,
AND CHRIST [d]WILL SHINE ON
YOU."

15 [a]Eph. 5:2 [b]Col. 4:5

15 Therefore be careful how
you [a]walk, not [b]as unwise men,
but as wise,

16 [a]Col. 4:5 [b]Gal. 1:4; Eph. 6:13
17 [a]Rom. 12:2; Col. 1:9; 1 Thess. 4:3

16 [a]making the most of your
time, because [b]the days are evil.
17 So then do not be foolish,
but [a]understand what the will of
the Lord is.

E In Relation to the Holy Spirit, 5:18–21

★18 [a]Prov. 20:1; 23:31f.; Rom. 13:13; 1 Cor. 5:11; 1 Thess. 5:7 [b]Titus 1:6; 1 Pet. 4:4 [c]Luke 1:15
★19 [a]Col. 3:16; James 5:13 [b]1 Cor. 14:26 [c]Acts 16:25 [d]Rev. 5:9 [e]1 Cor. 14:15
20 [a]Rom. 1:8; Eph. 5:4; Col. 3:17 [b]1 Cor. 15:24

18 And [a]do not get drunk
with wine, for that is [b]dissipation,
but be [c]filled with the Spirit,
19 [a]speaking to one another
in [b]psalms and [c]hymns and spiritual [d]songs, [e]singing and making
melody with your heart to the
Lord;
20 [a]always giving thanks for
all things in the name of our Lord
Jesus Christ to [b]God, even the Father;

★21 [a]Gal. 5:13; Phil. 2:3; 1 Pet. 5:5 [b]2 Cor. 5:11

21 [a]and be subject to one another in the [b]fear of Christ.

F In Relation to Home Life, 5:22–6:4

★22 [a]Eph. 5:22-6:9; *Col. 3:18-4:1* [b]1 Cor. 14:34f.; Titus 2:5; 1 Pet. 3:1 [c]Eph. 6:5
23 [a]1 Cor. 11:3 [b]Eph. 1:22 [c]1 Cor. 6:13

22 [a]Wives, [b]*be subject* to
your own husbands, [c]as to the
Lord.
23 For [a]the husband is the
head of the wife, as Christ also is
the [b]head of the church, He Himself [c]*being* the Savior of the body.
24 But as the church is sub-
ject to Christ, so also the wives
ought to be to their husbands in
everything.

★25 [a]Eph. 5:28, 33; 1 Pet. 3:7 [b]Eph. 5:2
26 [a]Heb. 10:10, 14, 29; 13:12; Titus 2:14 [b]2 Pet. 1:9 [c]Acts 22:16; 1 Cor. 6:11; Titus 3:5 [d]John 15:3; 17:17; Rom. 10:8f.; Eph. 6:17
27 [a]2 Cor. 4:14; 11:2; Col. 1:22 [b]Eph. 1:4
28 [a]Eph. 5:25, 33; 1 Pet. 3:7

25 [a]Husbands, love your
wives, just as Christ also loved the
church and [b]gave Himself up for
her;
26 [a]that He might sanctify
her, having [b]cleansed her by the
[c]washing of water with [d]the
word,
27 that He might [a]present to
Himself the church in all her glory, having no spot or wrinkle or
any such thing; but that she
should be [b]holy and blameless.
28 So husbands ought also to
[a]love their own wives as their
own bodies. He who loves his
own wife loves himself;
29 for no one ever hated his
own flesh, but nourishes and
cherishes it, just as Christ also
does the church,

30 [a]1 Cor. 6:15; 12:27 [b]Eph. 1:23
★31 [a]Gen. 2:24; Matt. 19:5; Mark 10:7f.

30 because we are [a]members
of His [b]body.
31 [a]FOR THIS CAUSE A MAN SHALL
LEAVE HIS FATHER AND MOTHER, AND

5:18 *be filled with the Spirit.* Paul has taught in this epistle that all believers are sealed with the Spirit when they believe (1:13–14; 4:30), but not all are filled, since this depends on yieldedness to God's will (5:17). "Filling" describes an experience that can be repeated (Acts 2:4; 4:31), and here, as in Acts, it is connected with joy, courage, spirituality, and Christian character.

5:19 *to one another.* Making music in one's heart is mentioned at the end of this verse.

5:21 *be subject.* The key thought for understanding Paul's view of proper personal relationships in a Christian household; the subjection is to be mutual and based on reverence for God.

5:22 *Wives* are to submit to the leadership of their husbands in the home (vv. 22, 24); they are to respect their husbands (v. 33); they are to love their husbands (Tit. 2:4), and live with them until death (Rom. 7:2–3).

5:25 *Husbands* are to love their wives, lead them (v. 23), nurture them in the things of Christ (v. 29), and live with them faithfully for life (Matt. 19:3–9).

5:31 See Gen. 2:24.

SHALL CLEAVE TO HIS WIFE; AND THE
TWO SHALL BECOME ONE FLESH.
★32 **32** This mystery is great; but I
am speaking with reference to
Christ and the church.
33 Nevertheless let each individual among you also [a]love his
own wife even as himself; and *let*
the wife *see to it* that she [b]respect
her husband.

33 [a]Eph. 5:25, 28; 1 Pet. 3:7 [b]1 Pet. 3:2, 5f.

6 [a]Children, obey your parents
in the Lord, for this is right.
2 [a]HONOR YOUR FATHER AND
MOTHER (which is the first commandment with a promise),
3 [a]THAT IT MAY BE WELL WITH
YOU, AND THAT YOU MAY LIVE LONG
ON THE EARTH.
4 And, [a]fathers, do not provoke your children to anger; but
[b]bring them up in the discipline
and instruction of the Lord.

★ **1** [a]Prov. 6:20; 23:22; Col. 3:20
★ **2** [a]Ex. 20:12; Deut. 5:16
3 [a]Ex. 20:12; Deut. 5:16
★ **4** [a]Col. 3:21 [b]Gen. 18:19; Deut. 6:7; 11:19; Ps. 78:4; Prov. 22:6; 2 Tim. 3:15

G In Relation to Slaves and Masters, 6:5–9

5 [a]Slaves, be obedient to
those who are your masters according to the flesh, with [b]fear
and trembling, in the sincerity of
your heart, [c]as to Christ;
6 [a]not by way of eyeservice,
as [b]men-pleasers, but as [c]slaves
of Christ, doing the will of God
from the heart.
7 With good will render service, [a]as to the Lord, and not to
men,
8 [a]knowing that [b]whatever
good thing each one does, this he
will receive back from the Lord,
[c]whether slave or free.
9 And, masters, do the same
things to them, and [a]give up
threatening, knowing that [b]both
their Master and yours is in
heaven, and there is [c]no partiality
with Him.

5 [a]Col. 3:22; 1 Tim. 6:1; Titus 2:9 [b]1 Cor. 2:3 [c]Eph. 5:22
6 [a]Col. 3:22 [b]Gal. 1:10 [c]1 Cor. 7:22
7 [a]Col. 3:23
8 [a]Col. 3:24 [b]Matt. 16:27; 2 Cor. 5:10; Col. 3:24f. [c]1 Cor. 12:13; Col. 3:11
9 [a]Lev. 25:43 [b]Job 31:13ff.; John 13:13 [c]Acts 10:34; Col. 3:25

IV THE PROTECTION FOR BELIEVERS, 6:10–20

A Against Whom? 6:10–12

10 Finally, [a]be strong in the
Lord, and in [b]the strength of His
might.
11 [a]Put on the full armor of
God, that you may be able to
stand firm against the [b]schemes
of the devil.
12 For our [a]struggle is not
against [b]flesh and blood, but
[c]against the rulers, against the
powers, against the [d]world forces
of this [e]darkness, against the
[f]spiritual *forces* of wickedness in
[g]the heavenly *places.*

10 [a]1 Cor. 16:13; 2 Tim. 2:1 [b]Eph. 1:19
★**11** [a]Rom. 13:12; Eph. 6:13 [b]Eph. 4:14
★**12** [a]1 Cor. 9:25 [b]Matt. 16:17 [c]Eph. 1:21; 2:2; 3:10 [d]John 12:31 [e]Acts 26:18; Col. 1:13 [f]Eph. 3:10 [g]Eph. 1:3

B With What? 6:13–20

13 Therefore, take up [a]the
full armor of God, that you may
be able to [b]resist in [c]the evil day,
and having done everything, to
stand firm.
14 Stand firm therefore, [a]HAV-
ING GIRDED YOUR LOINS WITH TRUTH,
and HAVING [b]PUT ON THE [c]BREAST-
PLATE OF RIGHTEOUSNESS,
15 and having [a]shod YOUR FEET
WITH THE PREPARATION OF THE GOSPEL
OF PEACE;
16 in addition to all, taking up
the [a]shield of faith with which
you will be able to extinguish all
the [b]flaming missiles of [c]the evil
one.
17 And take the [a]HELMET OF
SALVATION, and the [b]sword of the
Spirit, which is [c]the word of God.
18 With all [a]prayer and petition [b]pray at all times [c]in the
Spirit, and with this in view, [d]be

13 [a]Eph. 6:11 [b]James 4:7 [c]Eph. 5:16
14 [a]Is. 11:5; Luke 12:35; 1 Pet. 1:13 [b]Rom. 13:12; Eph. 6:13 [c]Is. 59:17; 1 Thess. 5:8
15 [a]Is. 52:7; Rom. 10:15
16 [a]1 Thess. 5:8 [b]Ps. 7:13; 120:4 [c]Matt. 5:37
★**17** [a]Is. 59:17 [b]Is. 49:2; Hos. 6:5; Heb. 4:12 [c]Eph. 5:26; Heb. 6:5
18 [a]Phil. 4:6 [b]Luke 18:1; Col. 1:3; 4:2; 1 Thess. 5:17 [c]Rom. 8:26f. [d]Mark 13:33 [e]Acts 1:14 [Gr.] [f]1 Tim. 2:1

5:32 The relationship between believing husbands and wives illustrates that which exists between Christ (the bridegroom) and the church (His bride). See also Matt. 25:1–13; Rev. 19:7–8; 21:2.

6:1 *in the Lord.* I.e., obedience to parents is part of a child's obligation to Christ. See the example of Christ in Luke 2:51 and Heb. 5:8.

6:2 When a child marries, his relationship to his parents changes (5:31), but not his responsibility to provide for them (1 Tim. 5:4).

6:4 *do not provoke.* I.e., do not nag or arbitrarily assert authority.

6:11 *schemes* = craftiness.

6:12 The believer's enemies are the demonic hosts of Satan, always assembled for mortal combat.

6:17 *take.* Lit., receive, a different word from that in v. 16. Salvation is a gift. *sword.* The only offensive weapon mentioned.

★19 [a]Col. 4:3; 1 Thess. 5:25 [b]2 Cor. 6:11 [c]2 Cor. 3:12 [d]Eph. 3:3
20 [a]2 Cor. 5:20; Philem. 9 marg. [b]Acts 21:33; 28:20; Eph. 3:1; Phil. 1:7; Col. 4:3 [c]2 Cor. 3:12 [d]Col. 4:4

on the alert with all [e]perseverance
and [f]petition for all the saints,
19 and [a]*pray* on my behalf,
that utterance may be given to me
[b]in the opening of my mouth, to
make known with [c]boldness [d]the
mystery of the gospel,
20 for which I am an [a]ambas-
sador [b]in chains; that in *proclaim-*
ing it I may speak [c]boldly, [d]as I
ought to speak.

V CONCLUDING WORDS, 6:21-24

21 [a]Eph. 6:21, 22 [b]Acts 20:4 [c]Col. 4:7

21 [a]But that you also may
know about my circumstances,
how I am doing, [b]Tychicus, [c]the
beloved brother and faithful minister in the Lord, will make everything known to you.
22 And [a]I have sent him to
you for this very purpose, so that
you may know about us, and that
he may [b]comfort your hearts.
23 [a]Peace be to the brethren,
and [b]love with faith, from God
the Father and the Lord Jesus
Christ.
24 Grace be with all those
who love our Lord Jesus Christ
with *a love* incorruptible.

22 [a]Col. 4:8 [b]Col. 2:2; 4:8
23 [a]Rom. 15:33; Gal. 6:16; 2 Thess. 3:16; 1 Pet. 5:14 [b]Gal. 5:6; 1 Thess. 5:8

6:19 Even in prison Paul was not thinking of his own welfare but of his testimony for Christ.

INTRODUCTION TO THE LETTER OF PAUL TO THE PHILIPPIANS

AUTHOR: Paul DATE: 61

The Church at Philippi *Founded by Paul on his second missionary journey, this was the first church to be established by him in Europe (Acts 16). Philippi was a small city, founded by King Philip of Macedonia, father of Alexander the Great. Its greatest fame came from the battle fought nearby, in 42 B.C., between the forces of Brutus and Cassius and those of Antony and Octavian (later Caesar Augustus). It became a Roman "colony," a military outpost city with special privileges.*

Paul's relationship with the church at Philippi was always close and cordial. Having helped him financially at least two times before this letter was written (4:16), and having heard of his confinement in Rome, the church sent Epaphroditus with another gift. Philippians is a thank-you letter for that gift, and it is the most personal letter Paul wrote to a church. Epaphroditus had become almost fatally ill while with Paul (2:27) and on his recovery Paul sent him back with this letter. Though somewhat obscured by Paul's gentleness in this letter, some of the problems in the church are seen beneath the surface. These included: rivalries and personal ambition (2:3-4; 4:2), the teaching of the Judaizers (3:1-3), perfectionism (3:12-14), and the influence of antinomian libertines (3:18-19).

Place of Writing *Paul was imprisoned when this letter was written, but there is disagreement as to where. Some think he was in Caesarea, others Ephesus; yet he must undoubtedly have been in Rome. In 1:13 (see note there) he mentions the* praetorium, *a Roman body of troops assigned to the emperor in Rome (see also 4:22). It is also clear that, in the trial facing Paul, his life was at stake, indicating that the trial was before Caesar in Rome (1:20). Although Paul was confined in Caesarea for two years, no final decision of his case was even in prospect there (Acts 24). Ephesus has been suggested as the place of writing on the basis of 1 Corinthians 15:32, but there is no clear reference in that verse to an imprisonment.*

Contents *One of the most important doctrinal passages in the New Testament is Philippians 2:5-8, in which Paul presents the doctrine of the* kenosis*—the self-humiliating, or self-emptying, of Christ. Important verses on prayer are 4:6-7. Other favorite verses include 1:21, 23b; 3:10, 20; 4:8, 13. A significant autobiographical sketch appears in 3:4-14.*

OUTLINE OF PHILIPPIANS

I. Greetings and Expressions of Gratitude, 1:1-11

II. Paul's Personal Circumstances: The Preaching of Christ, 1:12-30

III. The Pattern of the Christian Life: The Humility of Christ, 2:1-30
- A. The Exhortation to Humility, 2:1-4
- B. The Epitome of Humility, 2:5-11
- C. The Exercise of Humility, 2:12-18
- D. The Examples of Timothy and Epaphroditus, 2:19-30

IV. The Prize of the Christian Life: The Knowledge of Christ, 3:1-21
- A. The Warning against Judaizers, 3:1-3
- B. The Example of Paul, 3:4-14
- C. The Exhortation to Others, 3:15-21

V. The Peace of the Christian Life: The Presence of Christ, 4:1-23
- A. Peace with Others, 4:1-4
- B. Peace with Self, 4:5-9
- C. Peace with Circumstances, 4:10-23

THE LETTER OF PAUL TO THE PHILIPPIANS

I GREETINGS AND EXPRESSIONS OF GRATITUDE, 1:1-11

★ 1 [a]2 Cor. 1:1; Col. 1:1; 1 Thess. 1:1 [b]Acts 16:1 [c]Rom. 1:1; Gal. 1:10 [d]Gal. 3:26; Phil. 1:8; 2:5, [e]2 Cor. 1:1; Col. 1:2 [f]Acts 9:13 [g]Acts 16:12 [h]Acts 20:28; 1 Tim. 3:1f. [i]1 Tim. 3:8ff.
2 [a]Rom. 1:7
3 [a]Rom. 1:8
4 [a]Rom. 1:9
★ 5 [a]Acts 2:42; Phil. 4:15 [b]Phil. 1:7, 12, 16, 27; 2:22; 4:3, 15 [c]Acts 16:12-40
★ 6 [a]1 Cor. 1:8; Phil. 1:10; 2:16
★ 7 [a]2 Pet. 1:13 [b]2 Cor. 7:3 [c]Acts 21:33; Eph. 6:20 [d]Phil. 1:16 [e]Phil. 1:5
8 [a]Rom. 1:9 [b]Gal. 3:26; Phil. 1:1; 2:5; 3:3, 8, 12, 14; 4:7, 19, 21
9 [a]1 Thess. 3:12 [b]Col. 1:9

1 [a]Paul and [b]Timothy, [c]bond-servants of [d]Christ Jesus, to [e]all the [f]saints in Christ Jesus who are in [g]Philippi, including the [h]overseers and [i]deacons:

2 [a]Grace to you and peace from God our Father and the Lord Jesus Christ.

3 [a]I thank my God in all my remembrance of you,

4 always offering prayer with joy in [a]my every prayer for you all,

5 in view of your [a]participation in the [b]gospel [c]from the first day until now.

6 *For I am* confident of this very thing, that He who began a good work in you will perfect it until [a]the day of Christ Jesus.

7 For [a]it is only right for me to feel this way about you all, because I [b]have you in my heart, since both in my [c]imprisonment and in the [d]defense and confirmation of the [e]gospel, you all are partakers of grace with me.

8 For [a]God is my witness, how I long for you all with the affection of [b]Christ Jesus.

9 And this I pray, that [a]your love may abound still more and more in [b]real knowledge and all discernment,

10 so that you may [a]approve the things that are excellent, in order to be sincere and blameless until [b]the day of Christ;

11 having been filled with the [a]fruit of righteousness which *comes* through Jesus Christ, to the glory and praise of God.

★10 [a]Rom. 2:18 [b]1 Cor. 1:8; Phil. 1:6; 2:16
11 [a]James 3:18

II PAUL'S PERSONAL CIRCUMSTANCES: THE PREACHING OF CHRIST, 1:12-30

12 Now I want you to know, brethren, that my circumstances [a]have turned out for the greater progress of the [b]gospel,

13 so that my [a]imprisonment in *the cause of* Christ has become well known throughout the whole praetorian guard and to [b]everyone else,

14 and that most of the brethren, trusting in the Lord because of my [a]imprisonment, have [b]far more courage to speak the word of God without fear.

15 [a]Some, to be sure, are preaching Christ even from envy

★12-30
12 [a]Luke 21:13 [b]Phil. 1:5, 7, 16, 27; 2:22; 4:3, 15
★13 [a]Phil. 1:7; 2 Tim. 2:9 [b]Acts 28:30
14 [a]Phil. 1:7; 2 Tim. 2:9 [b]Acts 4:31; 2 Cor. 3:12; 7:4; Phil. 1:20
15 [a]2 Cor. 11:13

1:1 *Timothy* had helped Paul found this church. *saints.* See note on Rom. 1:7. *overseers.* Or bishops. See note on 1 Tim. 3:1. *deacons.* See note on 1 Tim. 3:8. Both bishops and deacons were recognizable groups within the church at this time.

1:5 Paul is here complimenting them on their having cooperated with him from the beginning (see Acts 16:40; Phil. 4:15-16).

1:6 *He* (God) *who began.* God will continue His good work of grace in them until the consummation at *the day of Christ Jesus* (the day when Christ returns).

1:7 *right.* The Greek words underlying *imprisonment, defense,* and *confirmation* were courtroom terms. Paul is saying that the Philippian believers shared with him in his courageous witness in the court of law. Whether Paul had already appeared at trial or whether he was still anticipating it is unclear.

1:10 *approve the things that are excellent.* I.e., to differentiate between highest matters and side issues.

1:12-30 This passage tells us about all we know of this imprisonment. Paul knew he was facing a great ordeal, but took great pains not to alarm his friends. His all-consuming concern was for the advancement of the gospel. People were beginning to talk about his bonds and his Christ, the church in Rome was becoming more confident, and he intended to follow his course. He existed only to help forward the cause of Christ (v. 21).

1:13 *praetorian guard.* This group of imperial guards, distinct from the army or Roman police, was about 9000 strong in Rome. They had heard the gospel through their various members who had been assigned the duty of guarding Paul. Guard and prisoner were chained together, making a captive audience for the gospel (see Eph. 6:20).

and strife, but some also from
good will;
16 the latter *do it* out of love,
knowing that I am [a]appointed for
the defense of the [b]gospel;
17 the former proclaim Christ
[a]out of selfish ambition, rather
than from pure motives, thinking
to cause me distress in my [b]im-
prisonment.
18 What then? Only that in
every way, whether in pretense or
in truth, Christ is proclaimed; and
in this I rejoice, yes, and I will rejoice.
19 For I know that this shall
turn out for my deliverance
[a]through your prayers and the
provision of [b]the Spirit of Jesus
Christ,
20 according to my [a]earnest
expectation and [b]hope, that I shall
not be put to shame in anything,
but *that* with [c]all boldness, Christ
shall even now, as always, be [d]ex-
alted in my body, [e]whether by
life or by death.
21 For to me, [a]to live is Christ,
and to die is gain.
22 But if *I am* to live *on* in the
flesh, this *will mean* [a]fruitful labor for me; and I do not know
which to choose.
23 But I am hard-pressed
from both *directions,* having the
[a]desire to depart and [b]be with
Christ, for *that* is very much better;
24 yet to remain on in the
flesh is more necessary for your
sake.
25 And [a]convinced of this, I
know that I shall remain and continue with you all for your progress and joy in the faith,

16 [a]1 Cor. 9:17 [b]Phil. 1:5, 7, 12, 27; 2:22; 4:3, 15
17 [a]Rom. 2:8; Phil. 2:3 [b]Phil. 1:7; 2 Tim. 2:9
★**18**
★**19** [a]2 Cor. 1:11 [b]Acts 16:7
20 [a]Rom. 8:19 [b]Rom. 5:5; 1 Pet. 4:16 [c]Acts 4:31; 2 Cor. 3:12; 7:4; Phil. 1:14 [d]1 Cor. 6:20 [e]Rom. 14:8
★**21** [a]Gal. 2:20
22 [a]Rom. 1:13
23 [a]2 Cor. 5:8; 2 Tim. 4:6 [b]John 12:26
★**25** [a]Phil. 2:24

26 so that your [a]proud confidence in me may abound in
Christ Jesus through my coming
to you again.
27 Only conduct yourselves
in a manner [a]worthy of the [b]gos-
pel of Christ; so that whether I
come and see you or remain absent, I may hear of you that you
are [c]standing firm in [d]one spirit,
with one mind [e]striving together
for the faith of the gospel;
28 in no way alarmed by *your*
opponents—which is a [a]sign of
destruction for them, but of salvation for you, and that *too,* from
God.
29 For to you [a]it has been
granted for Christ's sake, not only
to believe in Him, but also to
[b]suffer for His sake,
30 experiencing the same
[a]conflict which [b]you saw in me,
and now hear *to be* in me.

III THE PATTERN OF THE CHRISTIAN LIFE: THE HUMILITY OF CHRIST, 2:1–30

A The Exhortation to Humility, 2:1–4

2 If therefore there is any encouragement in Christ, if
there is any consolation of love, if
there is any [a]fellowship of the
Spirit, if any [b]affection and compassion,
2 [a]make my joy complete by
[b]being of the same mind, main-
taining the same love, united in
spirit, intent on one purpose.
3 Do nothing from [a]selfish-
ness or [b]empty conceit, but with

26 [a]2 Cor. 5:12; 7:4; Phil. 2:16
27 [a]Eph. 4:1 [b]Phil. 1:5 [c]1 Cor. 16:13; Phil. 4:1 [d]Acts 4:32 [e]Jude 3
28 [a]2 Thess. 1:5
29 [a]Matt. 5:12 [b]Acts 14:22
★**30** [a]Col. 1:29; 2:1; 1 Thess. 2:2; 1 Tim. 6:12; 2 Tim. 4:7; Heb. 10:32; 12:1 [Gr.] [b]Acts 16:19-40; Phil. 1:13
★ **1** [a]2 Cor. 13:14 [Gr.] [b]Col. 3:12
★ **2** [a]John 3:29 [b]Rom. 12:16; Phil. 4:2
3 [a]Rom. 2:8; Phil. 1:17 [b]Gal. 5:26 [c]Rom. 12:10; Eph. 5:21

1:18 Regardless of the motive (cf. v. 15), if Christ is preached, Paul rejoiced.
1:19 *my deliverance.* Paul's trial had probably begun. He was confident that either release or death would advance the cause of Christ (v. 20).
1:21 *to me, to live is Christ.* I.e., his life found all its meaning in Christ. *to die is gain.* Because then there will be union with Christ, without the limitations of this life.
1:25 Here Paul seems certain that he will be acquitted, but the only reason one can see for his momentary confidence is that he believed that he was still needed on earth in the Lord's service.
1:30 The Philippians were in the same basic *conflict* he was in.
2:1 If men will count on Christ, they can do the things described in the following verses.
2:2 *make my joy complete.* I.e., they would cap off his pleasure if they would work together harmoniously and clear up their petty quarrels. Paul particularly had in mind the division caused by two women, Euodia and Syntyche (4:2).

humility of mind let [c]each of you
regard one another as more important than himself;
4 [a]do not *merely* look out for
your own personal interests, but
also for the interests of others.

★ 4 [a]Rom. 15:1f.

B The Epitome of Humility, 2:5–11

5 [a]Have this attitude in
yourselves which was also in
[b]Christ Jesus,
6 who, although He [a]existed
in the [b]form of God, [c]did not regard equality with God a thing to
be grasped,
7 but [a]emptied Himself, taking the form of a [b]bond-servant,
and [c]being made in the likeness
of men.
8 And being found in ap-
pearance as a man, [a]He humbled
Himself by becoming [b]obedient
to the point of death, even [c]death
on a cross.
9 [a]Therefore also God
[b]highly exalted Him, and bestowed on Him [c]the name which
is above every name,
10 that at the name of Jesus
[a]every knee should bow, of
[b]those who are in heaven, and on
earth, and under the earth,

★ 5-11 5 [a]Matt. 11:29; Rom. 15:3 [b]Phil. 1:1
★ 6 [a]John 1:1 [b]2 Cor. 4:4 [c]John 5:18; 10:33; 14:28
★ 7 [a]2 Cor. 8:9 [b]Matt. 20:28 [c]John 1:14; Rom. 8:3; Gal. 4:4; Heb. 2:17
8 [a]2 Cor. 8:9 [b]Matt. 26:39; John 10:18; Rom. 5:19; Heb. 5:8 [c]Heb. 12:2
★ 9 [a]Heb. 1:9 [b]Matt. 28:18; Acts 2:33; Heb. 2:9 [c]Eph. 1:21
10 [a]Rom. 14:11 [b]Eph. 1:10

11 and that every tongue
should confess that Jesus Christ is
[a]Lord, to the glory of God the Father.

11 [a]John 13:13; Rom. 10:9; 14:9

C The Exercise of Humility, 2:12–18

12 So then, my beloved, [a]just
as you have always obeyed, not as
in my presence only, but now
much more in my absence, work
out your [b]salvation with [c]fear and
trembling;
13 for it is [a]God who is at
work in you, both to will and to
work [b]for *His* good pleasure.
14 Do all things without
[a]grumbling or disputing;
15 that you may prove yourselves to be [a]blameless and innocent, [b]children of God above reproach in the midst of a [c]crooked
and perverse generation, among
whom you [d]appear as [e]lights in
the world,
16 holding fast the word of
life, so that in [a]the day of Christ I
may have cause to glory because I
did not [b]run in vain nor [c]toil in
vain.
17 But even if I am being
[a]poured out as a drink offering
upon [b]the sacrifice and service of

★12-18 12 [a]Phil. 1:5, 6; 4:15 [b]Heb. 5:9 [c]2 Cor. 7:15
13 [a]Rom. 12:3; 1 Cor. 12:6; 15:10; Heb. 13:21 [b]Eph. 1:5
14 [a]1 Cor. 10:10; 1 Pet. 4:9
15 [a]Luke 1:6; Phil. 3:6 [b]Matt. 5:45; Eph. 5:1 [c]Acts 2:40 [d]Matt. 24:27 [e]Gen. 1:16
16 [a]Phil. 1:6 [b]Gal. 2:2 [c]Is. 49:4; Gal. 4:11; 1 Thess. 3:5
17 [a]2 Cor. 12:15; 2 Tim. 4:6 [b]Num. 28:6, 7; Rom. 15:16

2:4 The church was apparently evidencing petty jealousies among members over honors and rewards. Paul commends humility and the right disposition that Christ Himself demonstrated and wants to give to His followers (v. 5).

2:5-11 This passage on the humility of Christ is the high mark of the epistle. Unlike the informal, conversational style of the rest of the letter, vv. 5-11 are highly polished. It is also noteworthy in that they convey in a few verses Paul's conception of the uniqueness of the person and work of Christ. Paul's point is that the disposition, the temper, of church members ought always to be that of Christ.

2:6 *the form of God.* Christ is the same nature and essence as God. *to be grasped.* The verse may be paraphrased: Who, though of the same nature as God, did not think this something to be exploited to His own advantage.

2:7 *emptied Himself.* The *kenosis* (emptying) of Christ during His incarnation does not mean that He surrendered any attributes of deity, but that He took on the limitations of humanity. This involved a veiling of His preincarnate glory (John 17:5) and the voluntary waiving of some of His divine prerogatives during the time He was on earth (Matt. 24:36).

2:9 Through self-denial and obedience Christ won sovereignty over all peoples and things (v. 10).

2:12-18 Paul now turns to the obligations that the example of Christ lays on the Philippian Christians. They must learn to stand on their own feet, with a sense of human frailty, but knowing that God was behind them (v. 13). They should so live in corrupt human society that they would reflect the light that comes from a heavenly source (vv. 14-15), constantly proclaiming the gospel of the new life (v. 16a). Thus at Christ's coming Paul would have reason to rejoice in them (v. 16b). In vv. 17-18 Paul employed the language of the Jewish offerings and compares his death to a drink-offering which accompanied the Philippians' presentation of themselves as a burnt-offering (cf. Num. 15:10; 28:7).

your faith, I rejoice and share my
joy with you all.
18 And you too, *I urge you,*
rejoice in the same way and share
your joy with me.

D The Examples of Timothy and Epaphroditus, 2:19–30

★19-30 19 [a]Phil. 2:23 [b]Phil. 1:1
19 But I hope in the Lord
Jesus to [a]send [b]Timothy to you
shortly, so that I also may be encouraged when I learn of your
condition.
20 [a]1 Cor. 16:10; 2 Tim. 3:10
20 For I have no one *else* [a]of
kindred spirit who will genuinely
be concerned for your welfare.
21 [a]1 Cor. 10:24; 13:5; Phil. 2:4
21 For they all [a]seek after
their own interests, not those of
Christ Jesus.
22 [a]Rom. 5:4 [Gr.] [b]1 Cor. 16:10; 2 Tim. 3:10 [c]1 Cor. 4:17
22 But you know [a]of his
proven worth that [b]he served
with me in the furtherance of the
gospel [c]like a child *serving* his father.
23 [a]Phil. 2:19
23 [a]Therefore I hope to send
him immediately, as soon as I see
how things *go* with me;
24 [a]Phil. 1:25
24 and [a]I trust in the Lord
that I myself also shall be coming
shortly.
25 [a]Phil. 4:18 [b]Rom. 16:3, 9, 21; Phil. 4:3; Philem. 1, 24 [c]Philem. 2 [d]John 13:16; 2 Cor. 8:23 [e]Phil. 4:18
25 But I thought it necessary
to send to you [a]Epaphroditus, my
brother and [b]fellow-worker and
[c]fellow-soldier, who is also your
[d]messenger and [e]minister to my
need;
26 because he was longing for
you all and was distressed because you had heard that he was
sick.
27 For indeed he was sick to
the point of death, but God had
mercy on him, and not on him
only but also on me, lest I should
have sorrow upon sorrow.
28 Therefore I have sent him
all the more eagerly in order that
when you see him again you may
rejoice and I may be less concerned *about you.*
29 Therefore [a]receive him in 29 [a]Rom. 16:2 [b]1 Cor. 16:18
the Lord with all joy, and [b]hold
men like him in high regard;
30 because he came close to ★30 [a]Acts 20:24 [b]1 Cor. 16:17; Phil. 4:10
death [a]for the work of Christ,
risking his life to [b]complete what
was deficient in your service to
me.

IV THE PRIZE OF THE CHRISTIAN LIFE: THE KNOWLEDGE OF CHRIST, 3:1–21

A The Warning against Judaizers, 3:1–3

3 Finally, my brethren, [a]rejoice ★ 1 [a]Phil. 2:18; 4:4
in the Lord. To write the
same things *again* is no trouble to
me, and it is a safeguard for you.
2 Beware of the [a]dogs, be- ★ 2 [a]Ps. 22:16, 20; Gal. 5:15; Rev. 22:15 [b]2 Cor. 11:13
ware of the [b]evil workers, beware
of the false circumcision;
3 for [a]we are the *true* cir- 3 [a]Rom. 2:29; 9:6; Gal. 6:15 [b]Gal. 5:25 [c]Rom. 15:17; Gal. 6:14 [d]Rom. 8:39; Phil. 1:1; 3:12
cumcision, who [b]worship in the
Spirit of God and [c]glory in
[d]Christ Jesus and put no confidence in the flesh,

B The Example of Paul, 3:4–14

4 although [a]I myself might ★ 4-14 4 [a]2 Cor. 5:16; 11:18
have confidence even in the flesh.

2:19–30 The letter now returns to personal matters. Paul was going to send Timothy later and send Epaphroditus then; and he wanted them to be accepted as his representative with his authority. No one else with him then, except Timothy, had the interest of Christ at heart (v. 21). Epaphroditus was a leader in the Philippian church whom Paul sent home with this letter (v. 25).

2:30 *close to death.* Epaphroditus was dangerously ill from overwork.

3:1 *the same things.* I.e., the content of vv. 2–3, a basic lesson which Paul as their teacher had undoubtedly gone over with them many times while with them: Do not let Christianity be debased into some form of the Jewish ritualistic religion, obviously a danger then in Philippi.

3:2 Paul here becomes polemical. He labels the Judaizers (who taught that circumcision was necessary for salvation) *dogs* (a term they used to describe Gentiles), *evil workers,* and *false circumcision,* (which meant mutilators). All three epithets are directed at the same people.

3:4–14 Paul reflected on the whole course of his life, which gave him the right to criticize false Judaism.

If anyone else has a mind to put
confidence in the flesh, I far more:
5 [a]circumcised the eighth
day, of the [b]nation of Israel, of the
[c]tribe of Benjamin, a [b]Hebrew of
Hebrews; as to the Law, [d]a Pharisee;
6 as to zeal, [a]a persecutor of
the church; as to the [b]righteous-
ness which is in the Law, found
[c]blameless.
7 But [a]whatever things were
gain to me, those things I have
counted as loss for the sake of
Christ.
8 More than that, I count all
things to be loss in view of the
surpassing value of [a]knowing
[b]Christ Jesus my Lord, for whom I
have suffered the loss of all
things, and count them but rubbish in order that I may gain
Christ,
9 and may be found in Him,
not having [a]a righteousness of my
own derived from *the* Law, but
that which is through faith in
Christ, [b]the righteousness which
comes from God on the basis of
faith,
10 that I may [a]know Him,
and [b]the power of His resurrection and [c]the fellowship of His
sufferings, being [d]conformed to
His death;
11 in order that I may [a]attain
to the resurrection from the dead.
12 Not that I have already
[a]obtained *it,* or have already [b]be-
come perfect, but I press on in order that I may [c]lay hold of that
for which also I [d]was laid hold of
by [e]Christ Jesus.
13 Brethren, I do not regard
myself as having laid hold of *it*
yet; but one thing *I do:* [a]forgetting
what *lies* behind and reaching
forward to what *lies* ahead,
14 I [a]press on toward the goal
for the prize of the [b]upward call
of God in [c]Christ Jesus.

5 [a]Luke 1:59 [b]Rom. 11:1; 2 Cor. 11:22 [c]Rom. 11:1 [d]Acts 22:3; 23:6; 26:5
6 [a]Acts 8:3 [b]Phil. 3:9 [c]Phil. 2:15
7 [a]Luke 14:33
8 [a]Jer. 9:23f.; John 17:3; Eph. 4:13; Phil. 3:10; 2 Pet. 1:3 [b]Rom. 8:39; Phil. 1:1; 3:12
★ **9** [a]Rom. 10:5; Phil. 3:6 [b]Rom. 9:30; 1 Cor. 1:30
★**10** [a]Jer. 9:23f.; John 17:3; Eph. 4:13; Phil. 3:8; 2 Pet. 1:13 [b]Rom. 6:5 [c]Rom. 8:17 [d]Rom. 6:5; 8:36; Gal. 6:17
11 [a]Acts 26:7; 1 Cor. 15:23; Rev. 20:5f.
★**12** [a]1 Cor. 9:24f.; 1 Tim. 6:12, 19 [b]1 Cor. 13:10 [c]1 Tim. 6:12, 19 [d]Acts 9:5f. [e]Rom. 8:39; Phil. 1:1; 3:3, 8
13 [a]Luke 9:62
14 [a]1 Cor. 9:24; Heb. 6:1 [b]Rom. 8:28; 11:29; 2 Tim. 1:9 [c]Phil. 3:3

C The Exhortation to Others, 3:15–21

15 Let us therefore, as many
as are [a]perfect, have this attitude;
and if in anything you have a
[b]different attitude, [c]God will reveal that also to you;
16 however, let us keep [a]liv-
ing by that same *standard* to
which we have attained.
17 Brethren, [a]join in following my example, and observe
those who walk according to the
[b]pattern you have in us.
18 For [a]many walk, of whom
I often told you, and now tell you
even [b]weeping, *that they are* enemies of [c]the cross of Christ,
19 whose end is destruction,
whose god is *their* [a]appetite, and
whose [b]glory is in their shame,
who [c]set their minds on earthly
things.
20 For [a]our citizenship is in
heaven, from which also we eagerly [b]wait for a Savior, the Lord
Jesus Christ;
21 who will [a]transform the
body of our humble state into
[b]conformity with the [c]body of His
glory, [d]by the exertion of the
power that He has even to [e]sub-
ject all things to Himself.

★**15** [a]Matt. 5:48; 1 Cor. 2:6 [b]Gal. 5:10 [c]John 6:45; Eph. 1:17; 1 Thess. 4:9
16 [a]Gal. 6:16
17 [a]1 Cor. 4:16; Phil. 4:9 [b]1 Pet. 5:3
★**18** [a]2 Cor. 11:13 [b]Acts 20:31 [c]Gal. 6:14
19 [a]Rom. 16:18; Titus 1:12 [b]Rom. 6:21; Jude 13 [c]Rom. 8:5f.; Col. 3:2
★**20** [a]Eph. 2:19; Phil. 1:27; Col. 3:1; Heb. 12:22 [b]1 Cor. 1:7
★**21** [a]1 Cor. 15:43-53 [b]Rom. 8:29; Col. 3:4 [c]1 Cor. 15:43, 49 [d]Eph. 1:19 [e]1 Cor. 15:28

3:9 Here Paul contrasts works-righteousness, which is based on the law, with faith-righteousness, which is from God through faith in Christ. Rom. 3:21-5:21 is a commentary on this truth.

3:10 *being conformed to His death* means becoming like Him in His death—passing through death into a new life, dying and rising with Christ (cf. Rom. 6).

3:12 Paul makes it clear that he had not "arrived" but was still very much in the race of life.

3:15 *perfect* = mature. In the latter half of the verse Paul says, in effect, "If you don't agree, God will give you light on the subject."

3:18 *enemies of the cross of Christ.* Evil living (by the libertines) is in view. Their principal concern was their *appetite* (v. 19); i.e., all sensual indulgences.

3:20 *citizenship.* This figure would have been particularly appreciated by the Philippians in view of their city's status as a Roman colony, whose inhabitants were Roman citizens.

3:21 *body of our humble state.* Our present state of mortality is a lowly one.

V THE PEACE OF THE CHRISTIAN LIFE: THE PRESENCE OF CHRIST, 4:1–23

A Peace with Others, 4:1–4

★ 1 [a]Phil. 1:8 [b]1 Cor. 16:13; Phil. 1:27

4 Therefore, my beloved brethren whom I [a]long *to see,* my joy and crown, so [b]stand firm in the Lord, my beloved.

2 [a]Phil. 2:2

2 I urge Euodia and I urge Syntyche to [a]live in harmony in the Lord.

★ 3 [a]Phil. 2:25 [b]Luke 10:20

3 Indeed, true comrade, I ask you also to help these women who have shared my struggle in *the cause of* the gospel, together with Clement also, and the rest of my [a]fellow-workers, whose [b]names are in the book of life.

4 [a]Phil. 3:1

4 [a]Rejoice in the Lord always; again I will say, rejoice!

B Peace with Self, 4:5–9

5 [a]1 Cor. 16:22 marg.; Heb. 10:37; James 5:8f.

5 Let your forbearing *spirit* be known to all men. [a]The Lord is near.

6 [a]Matt. 6:25 [b]Eph. 6:18; 1 Tim. 2:1; 5:5

6 [a]Be anxious for nothing, but in everything by [b]prayer and supplication with thanksgiving let your requests be made known to God.

7 [a]Is. 26:3; John 14:27; Phil. 4:9; Col. 3:15 [b]Phil. 3:19 [c]1 Pet. 1:5 [d]2 Cor. 10:5 [e]Phil. 1:1; 4:19, 21

7 And [a]the peace of God, which [b]surpasses all comprehension, shall [c]guard your hearts and your [d]minds in [e]Christ Jesus.

★ 8 [a]Rom. 14:18; 1 Pet. 2:12

8 Finally, brethren, [a]whatever is true, whatever is honorable, whatever is right, whatever is pure, whatever is lovely, whatever is of good repute, if there is any excellence and if anything worthy of praise, let your mind dwell on these things.

9 [a]Phil. 3:17 [b]Rom. 15:33

9 The things you have learned and received and heard and seen [a]in me, practice these things; and [b]the God of peace shall be with you.

C Peace with Circumstances, 4:10–23

10 [a]2 Cor. 11:9; Phil. 2:30

10 But I rejoiced in the Lord greatly, that now at last [a]you have revived your concern for me; indeed, you were concerned *before,* but you lacked opportunity.

★11 [a]2 Cor. 9:8; 1 Tim. 6:6, 8; Heb. 13:5

11 Not that I speak from want; for I have learned to be [a]content in whatever circumstances I am.

12 [a]1 Cor. 4:11 [b]2 Cor. 11:9

12 I know how to get along with humble means, and I also know how to live in prosperity; in any and every circumstance I have learned the secret of being filled and going [a]hungry, both of having abundance and [b]suffering need.

13 [a]2 Cor. 12:9; Eph. 3:16; Col. 1:11

13 I can do all things through Him who [a]strengthens me.

★14 [a]Heb. 10:33; Rev. 1:9, [in Gr.]

14 Nevertheless, you have done well to [a]share *with me* in my affliction.

15 [a]Phil. 1:5 [b]Rom. 15:26 [c]2 Cor. 11:9

15 And you yourselves also know, Philippians, that at the [a]first preaching of the gospel, after I departed from [b]Macedonia, no church [c]shared with me in the matter of giving and receiving but you alone;

16 [a]Acts 17:1; 1 Thess. 2:9

16 for even in [a]Thessalonica you sent *a gift* more than once for my needs.

17 [a]1 Cor. 9:11f.; 2 Cor. 9:5

17 [a]Not that I seek the gift itself, but I seek for the profit which increases to your account.

18 [a]Phil. 2:25 [b]2 Cor. 2:14; Eph. 5:2

18 But I have received everything in full, and have an abundance; I am amply supplied, having received from [a]Epaphroditus what you have sent, [b]a fragrant aroma, an acceptable sacrifice, well-pleasing to God.

★19 [a]2 Cor. 9:8 [b]Rom. 2:4

19 And [a]my God shall supply all your needs according to His [b]riches in glory in Christ Jesus.

4:1 Here begins Paul's closing section, consisting first of practical advice followed by personal messages.

4:3 The identity of the *true comrade* is not revealed.

4:8 *honorable* = worthy of respect. *lovely* = winsome.

4:11 *content.* Lit., self-sufficient, independent of external circumstances. The secret of such contentment is found in v. 13.

4:14 *to share with me.* Paul refers to the sending of monetary gifts (vv. 10, 16).

4:19 The church that gives to missionaries will have its own needs supplied.

20 [a]Gal. 1:4 [b]Rom. 11:36
21 [a]Gal. 1:2

20 Now to [a]our God and Father [b]*be* the glory forever and ever. Amen.
21 Greet every saint in Christ Jesus. [a]The brethren who are with me greet you.
22 [a]All the [b]saints greet you, especially those of Caesar's household.
23 [a]The grace of the Lord Jesus Christ [b]be with your spirit.

★22 [a]2 Cor. 13:13 [b]Acts 9:13
23 [a]Rom. 16:20 [b]2 Tim. 4:22

4:22 *Caesar's household.* Probably employees in the emperor's palace. There is no evidence of the conversion of a member of the imperial family until a generation later.

INTRODUCTION TO
THE LETTER OF PAUL TO THE COLOSSIANS

AUTHOR: Paul DATE: 61

The Church at Colossae *About 100 miles east of Ephesus, and near Laodicea and Hierapolis (4:13), Colossae was an ancient but declining commercial center. The gospel may have been taken there during Paul's ministry at Ephesus (Acts 19:10), though it was Epaphras who played the major role in the evangelism and growth of the Colossians. Paul was personally unacquainted with the believers there (2:1), but Epaphras either visited Paul in prison or was imprisoned with him (Philem. 23) and reported on conditions in this church.*

Place of Writing *Like Ephesians, Philippians, and Philemon, Colossians was written during Paul's first imprisonment in Rome (see the Introduction to Titus and the Introduction to Philippians for other suggestions as to the place of writing). The many personal references common to Colossians and Philemon and the many similarities of ideas in Colossians and Ephesians link these letters. Tychicus was apparently the bearer of the letter (Eph. 6:21; Col. 4:7).*

The Colossian Heresy *From Paul's counteremphases in the epistle, we can discern some of the features of the false teaching at Colossae. It was a syncretistic, fusing Jewish legalism, Greek philosophic speculation, and Oriental mysticism. Specifics included dietary and Sabbath observances and circumcision rites (2:11, 16), the worship of angels (2:18), and the practice of asceticism, which stemmed from the belief that the body was inherently evil (2:21-23). In combating this heresy, Paul emphasizes the cosmic significance of Christ as Lord of creation and Head of the Church. Any teaching, practice, or intermediary that detracts from the uniqueness and centrality of Christ, is against the faith.*

Contents *The theme is the supremacy and all-sufficiency of Christ. Important subjects include Christ's person and work (1:15-23), heresy (2:8-23), and believers' union with Christ (3:1-4).*

OUTLINE OF COLOSSIANS

I. Introduction, 1:1-14
- A. Greetings, 1:1-2
- B. Gratitude for the Colossians' Faith, 1:3-8
- C. Prayer for the Colossians' Growth, 1:9-14

II. The Exalted Christ, 1:15-29
- A. Christ's Character, 1:15-23
- B. Christ's Commission to Paul, 1:24-29

III. The Exalted Christianity, 2:1-23
- A. Exalted Over Philosophy, 2:1-10
- B. Exalted Over Legalism, 2:11-17
- C. Exalted Over Mystical Teaching, 2:18-19
- D. Exalted Over Asceticism, 2:20-23

IV. The Exalted Calling, 3:1-4:6
- A. The Certainties of Our Calling, 3:1-4
- B. The Characteristics of Our Calling, 3:5-4:6
  1. In everyday life, 3:5-17
  2. In the home, 3:18-21
  3. In servant-master relationships, 3:22-4:1
  4. In prayer, 4:2-4
  5. In witness and speech, 4:5-6

V. Concluding Personal Remarks, 4:7-18

THE LETTER OF PAUL TO THE COLOSSIANS

I INTRODUCTION, 1:1-14

A Greetings, 1:1-2

1 [a]Phil. 1:1 [b]2 Cor. 1:1 [c]1 Cor. 1:1 [d]2 Cor. 1:1; 1 Thess. 3:2; Philem. 1; Heb. 13:23
2 [a]Acts 9:13; Eph. 1:1; Phil. 1:1 [b]Rom. 1:7; Col. 4:18

1 [a]Paul, [b]an apostle of Jesus
Christ [c]by the will of God,
and [d]Timothy our brother,
2 to the [a]saints and faithful
brethren in Christ *who are* at Colossae: [b]Grace to you and peace
from God our Father.

B Gratitude for the Colossians' Faith, 1:3-8

3 [a]Rom. 1:8 [b]Rom. 15:6; 2 Cor. 1:3
★ 4-5
4 [a]Eph. 1:15 [b]Gal. 5:6 [c]Eph. 6:18
5 [a]Acts 23:6; Rom. 5:2; Col. 1:23; 1 Thess. 5:8; Titus 1:2 [b]2 Tim. 4:8; 1 Pet. 1:4 [c]Eph. 1:13; Col. 1:6, 23
6 [a]Rom. 10:18; Col. 1:23; 1 Tim. 3:16 [b]Rom. 1:13 [c]Eph. 4:21; Col. 1:5
★ 7 [a]Col. 4:12; Philem. 23 [b]Col. 4:7
8 [a]Rom. 15:30

3 [a]We give thanks to God,
[b]the Father of our Lord Jesus
Christ, praying always for you,
4 [a]since we heard of your
faith in Christ Jesus and the [b]love
which you have for [c]all the saints;
5 because of the [a]hope [b]laid
up for you in heaven, of which
you previously [c]heard in the word
of truth, the gospel,
6 which has come to you,
just as [a]in all the world also it is
constantly bearing [b]fruit and increasing, even as *it has been
doing* in you also since the day
you [c]heard *of it* and understood
the grace of God in truth;
7 just as you learned *it* from
[a]Epaphras, our [b]beloved fellow
bond-servant, who is a faithful
servant of Christ on our behalf,
8 and he also informed us of
your [a]love in the Spirit.

C Prayer for the Colossians' Growth, 1:9-14

9 [a]Col. 1:4 [b]Eph. 1:16 [c]Eph. 5:17; Phil. 1:9 [d]Eph. 1:17
★10 [a]Eph. 4:1; Col. 2:6 [b]2 Cor. 5:9; Eph. 5:10 [c]Rom. 1:13
★11 [a]1 Cor. 16:13; Eph. 3:16 [b]Eph. 4:2
12 [a]Eph. 2:18 [b]Acts 20:32 [c]Acts 26:18; Eph. 6:12
★13 [a]Acts 26:18; Eph. 6:12 [b]Matt. 3:17; Eph. 1:6
★14 [a]Rom. 3:24; Eph. 1:7

9 For this reason also, [a]since
the day we heard *of it,* [b]we have
not ceased to pray for you and to
ask that you may be filled with
the [c]knowledge of His will in all
spiritual [d]wisdom and understanding,
10 so that you may [a]walk in a
manner worthy of the Lord, [b]to
please *Him* in all respects, [c]bear-
ing fruit in every good work and
increasing in the knowledge of
God;
11 [a]strengthened with all
power, according to His glorious
might, for the attaining of all
steadfastness and patience; [b]joy-
ously
12 giving thanks to [a]the Father, who has qualified us to
share in [b]the inheritance of the
saints in [c]light.
13 For He delivered us from
the [a]domain of darkness, and
transferred us to the kingdom of
[b]His beloved Son,
14 [a]in whom we have re-
demption, the forgiveness of sins.

II THE EXALTED CHRIST, 1:15-29

A Christ's Character, 1:15-23

★15 [a]2 Cor. 4:4 [b]John 1:18; 1 Tim. 1:17; Heb. 11:27 [c]Rom. 8:29; Col. 1:17f.
★16 [a]Eph. 1:10 [b]Eph. 1:20f.; Col. 2:15 [c]John 1:3; Rom. 11:36; 1 Cor. 8:6
17 [a]John 1:1; 8:58

15 And He is the [a]image of
the [b]invisible God, the [c]first-born
of all creation.
16 For [a]by Him all things
were created, [a]*both* in the heavens and on earth, visible and invisible, whether [b]thrones or do-
minions or rulers or authorities—
[c]all things have been created by
Him and for Him.
17 And He [a]is before all

1:4-5 Notice the Colossian believers' triad of Christian graces: *faith, love,* and *hope* (cf. 1 Cor. 13:13).

1:7 *Epaphras* (see 4:12; Philem. 23). Apparently the man who evangelized the cities of the Lycus Valley and founded the churches of Colossae, Hierapolis, and Laodicea. It was his report, brought to Paul in Rome, about the condition of these churches that prompted the writing of this letter. The Epaphroditus of Phil. 2:25 and 4:18 is evidently a different individual.

1:10 *walk in a manner worthy of the Lord* = live a life worthy of the Lord.

1:11 *joyously.* This is what distinguishes the Christian's *steadfastness and patience* from the Stoic's.

1:13 *the kingdom of His beloved Son.* Lit., the kingdom of the Son of His love. Christians are already within the sphere of the new age.

1:14 *redemption.* See note on Eph. 1:7.

1:15 *the first-born of all creation.* I.e., the Son has all the rights belonging to the first-born, because of His preeminent position over all creation (v. 16).

1:16 *rulers or authorities.* See note on Eph. 1:21.

things, and in Him all things hold together.

18 He is also [a]head of [b]the body, the church; and He is [c]the beginning, [d]the first-born from the dead; so that He Himself might come to have first place in everything.

★18 [a]Eph. 1:22 [b]Eph. 1:23; Col. 1:24; 2:19 [c]Rev. 3:14 [d]Acts 26:23

19 For it was [a]the *Father's* good pleasure for all [b]the fulness to dwell in Him,

★19 [a]Eph. 1:5 [b]John 1:16

20 and through Him to [a]reconcile all things to Himself, having made [b]peace through [c]the blood of His cross; through Him, *I say,* [d]whether things on earth or things in heaven.

★20 [a]2 Cor. 5:18; Eph. 2:16 [b]Rom. 5:1; Eph. 2:14 [c]Eph. 2:13 [d]Col. 1:16

21 And although you were [a]formerly alienated and hostile in mind, *engaged* in evil deeds,

21 [a]Rom. 5:10; Eph. 2:3, 12

22 yet He has now [a]reconciled you in His fleshly [b]body through death, in order to [c]present you before Him [d]holy and blameless and beyond reproach—

22 [a]2 Cor. 5:18; Eph. 2:16 [b]Rom. 7:4 [c]Eph. 5:27; Col. 1:28 [d]Eph. 1:4

23 if indeed you continue in the faith firmly [a]established and steadfast, and not moved away from the [b]hope of the gospel that you have heard, which was proclaimed [c]in all creation under heaven, [d]and of which I, Paul, was made a [e]minister.

23 [a]Eph. 3:17; Col. 2:7 [b]Col. 1:5 [c]Mark 16:15; Acts 2:5; Col. 1:6 [d]Eph. 3:7; Col. 1:25 [e]1 Cor. 3:5

B Christ's Commission to Paul, 1:24–29

24 [a]Now I rejoice in my sufferings for your sake, and in my flesh [b]I do my share on behalf of [c]His body (which is the church) in filling up that which is lacking in Christ's afflictions.

★24 [a]Rom. 8:17; 2 Cor. 1:5; 12:15; Phil. 2:17 [b]2 Tim. 1:8; 2:10 [c]Col. 1:18

25 [a]Of *this church* I was made a minister according to the [b]stewardship from God bestowed on me for your benefit, that I might fully carry out the *preaching of* the word of God,

★25 [a]Col. 1:23 [b]Eph. 3:2

26 *that is,* [a]the mystery which has been hidden from the *past* ages and generations; but has now been manifested to His saints,

★26 [a]Rom. 16:25f.; Eph. 3:3f.; Col. 2:2; 4:3

27 to whom [a]God willed to make known what is [b]the riches of the glory of this mystery among the Gentiles, which is [c]Christ in you, the [d]hope of glory.

27 [a]Matt. 13:11 [b]Eph. 1:7, 18; 3:16 [c]Rom. 8:10 [d]1 Tim. 1:1

28 And we proclaim Him, [a]admonishing every man and teaching every man with all [b]wisdom, that we may [c]present every man [d]complete in Christ.

28 [a]Acts 20:31; Col. 3:16 [b]1 Cor. 2:6f.; Col. 2:3 [c]Col. 1:22 [d]Matt. 5:48; Eph. 4:13

29 And for this purpose also I [a]labor, [b]striving [c]according to His power, which mightily works within me.

29 [a]1 Cor. 15:10 [b]Col. 2:1; 4:12 [c]Eph. 1:19; Col. 2:12

III THE EXALTED CHRISTIANITY, 2:1–23

A Exalted Over Philosophy, 2:1–10

2 For I want you to know how great a [a]struggle I have on your behalf, and for those who are at [b]Laodicea, and for all those who have not personally seen my face,

1 [a]Col. 1:29; 4:12 [b]Col. 4:13, 15f.; Rev. 1:11

2 that their [a]hearts may be encouraged, having been [b]knit together in love, and *attaining* to all [c]the wealth that comes from the [d]full assurance of understanding, *resulting* in a [e]true knowledge of [f]God's mystery, *that is,* Christ *Himself,*

2 [a]1 Cor. 14:31; Eph. 6:22; Col. 4:8 [b]Col. 2:19 [c]Eph. 1:7, 18; 3:16 [d]Luke 1:1 [Gr.] [e]Matt. 13:11 [f]Rom. 16:25f.; Eph. 3:3f.; Col. 1:26; 4:3

3 in whom are hidden all [a]the treasures of wisdom and knowledge.

3 [a]Is. 11:2; Rom. 11:33

4 [a]I say this in order that no one may delude you with [b]persuasive argument.

4 [a]Eph. 4:17 [b]Rom. 16:18

1:18 *the church.* See note on Eph. 1:22–23. *the first-born from the dead.* I.e., the first one to rise from the dead with a resurrection body (Rev. 1:5).

1:19 *all the fulness.* The full essence (powers and attributes) of deity dwells in Christ (see 2:9).

1:20 *to reconcile all things to Himself.* Christ is the remedy for alienation from God, and eventually all things will be changed and brought into a unity in Him, even though this will involve judgment (1 Cor. 15:24–28).

1:24 Because of the union of believers with Christ, Paul's *sufferings* for the sake of the church can be called Christ's *afflictions* as well.

1:25 *the stewardship,* assignment, office (1 Cor. 4:1).

1:26 *the mystery.* The secret known only by divine revelation of the indwelling of Christ (see note on Eph. 3:3).

5 For even though I am [a]absent in body, nevertheless I am with you in spirit, rejoicing to see your [b]good discipline and the [c]stability of your faith in Christ.

6 As you therefore have received [a]Christ Jesus the Lord, *so* [b]walk in Him,

7 having been firmly [a]rooted *and now* being [b]built up in Him and [c]established in your faith, just as you [d]were instructed, *and* overflowing with gratitude.

8 [a]See to it that no one takes you captive through [b]philosophy and empty deception, according to the tradition of men, according to the [c]elementary principles of the world, rather than according to Christ.

9 For in Him all the [a]fulness of Deity dwells in bodily form,

10 and in Him you have been [a]made complete, and [b]He is the head over all [c]rule and authority;

5 [a]1 Cor. 5:3 [b]1 Cor. 14:40 [c]1 Pet. 5:9
★ 6 [a]Gal. 3:26 [b]Col. 1:10
7 [a]Eph. 3:17 [b]1 Cor. 3:9; Eph. 2:20 [c]1 Cor. 1:8 [d]Eph. 4:21
★ 8 [a]1 Cor. 8:9; 10:12; Gal. 5:15; Heb. 3:12 [b]Eph. 5:6; Col. 2:23; 1 Tim. 6:20 [c]Gal. 4:3; Col. 2:20
★ 9 [a]2 Cor. 5:19; Col. 1:19
10 [a]Eph. 3:19 [b]Eph. 1:21f. [c]1 Cor. 15:24; Eph. 3:10; Col. 2:15

B Exalted Over Legalism, 2:11–17

11 and in Him [a]you were also circumcised with a circumcision made without hands, in the removal of [b]the body of the flesh by the circumcision of Christ;

12 having been [a]buried with Him in baptism, in which you were also [b]raised up with Him through faith in the working of God, who [c]raised Him from the dead.

13 And when you were [a]dead in your transgressions and the uncircumcision of your flesh, He [b]made you alive together with Him, having forgiven us all our transgressions,

14 having cancelled out [a]the certificate of debt consisting of decrees against us *and* which was hostile to us; and [b]He has taken it out of the way, having nailed it to the cross.

15 When He had [a]disarmed the [b]rulers and authorities, He [c]made a public display of them, having [d]triumphed over them through Him.

16 Therefore let no one [a]act as your judge in regard to [b]food or [b]drink or in respect to a [c]festival or a [d]new moon or a [e]Sabbath day—

17 things which are [a]a *mere* shadow of what is to come; but the substance belongs to Christ.

★11–12
11 [a]Rom. 2:29; Eph. 2:11 [b]Rom. 6:6; 7:24; Gal. 5:24; Col. 3:5
12 [a]Rom. 6:4f. [b]Rom. 6:5; Eph. 2:6; Col. 2:13; 3:1 [c]Acts 2:24
13 [a]Eph. 2:1 [b]Eph. 2:1, 5; Col. 2:12
★14 [a]Eph. 2:15; Col. 2:20 [b]1 Pet. 2:24
★15 [a]Eph. 4:8 [b]1 Cor. 15:24; Eph. 3:10; Col. 2:10 [c]Is. 53:12; Matt. 12:29; Luke 10:18; John 12:31; Eph. 4:8 [d]2 Cor. 2:14 [Gr.]
★16 [a]Rom. 14:3 [b]Mark 7:19; Rom. 14:17; Heb. 9:10 [c]Lev. 23:2; Rom. 14:5 [d]1 Chr. 23:31; 2 Chr. 31:3; Neh. 10:33 [e]Mark 2:27f.; Gal. 4:10f.
17 [a]Heb. 8:5; 10:1

C Exalted Over Mystical Teaching, 2:18–19

18 Let no one keep [a]defrauding you of your prize by [b]delighting in self-abasement and the

★18 [a]1 Cor. 9:24; Phil. 3:14 [b]Col. 2:23 [c]1 Cor. 4:6 [d]Rom. 8:7

2:6 *As . . . so.* Just as Christ is received by faith, the believer is also to walk (live) by faith, acknowledging the Lordship of Christ over his life (2 Cor. 5:7).

2:8 *empty deception.* Paul's belittlement of the Colossian "philosophy." *according to the elementary principles* after the elemental spirits of the universe; i.e., the cosmic spirits of Hellenistic syncretism. Apparently their philosophy involved regulating their religious life by observing the movements of the stars, which they associated with the powers of the angels who were worshiped by some (v. 18). In this passage Paul uses the vocabulary of the heretics, giving the words their proper meaning. He confutes them with their own terms (e.g., *complete,* 1:28; *mystery,* 2:2; *wisdom and knowledge,* 2:3; *elementary principles of the world,* 2:8; *head,* 2:10).

2:9 In Jesus Christ, deity (the divine attributes and nature) dwelt in His earthly body—a strong statement of the deity and humanity of the God-man.

2:11–12 *removal of the body of the flesh* (the old nature, which is corrupt in its unregenerate state of rebellion against God) is illustrated in the rite of circumcision and the ordinance of baptism, but is accomplished by a spiritual circumcision and Spirit baptism.

2:14 *certificate of debt* = an acknowledgment of debt in the handwriting of the debtor. The Mosaic law (which Paul's phrase symbolizes) put us in debt to God with sin; this debt He has canceled by nailing it to the cross of Christ. Christ has made full payment.

2:15 *disarmed.* Lit., stripped (as was done to enemies).

2:16 False teachers were evidently insisting on abstinence from certain foods and observance of certain days. These, Paul says, are shadows which have been dispersed by the coming of Christ (v. 17).

2:18 Some were also teaching a false humility and the worship of angels as proper, claiming

worship of the angels, taking his
stand on *visions* he has seen, [c]in-
flated without cause by his [d]flesh-
ly mind,
19 and not holding fast to
[a]the head, from whom [b]the entire
body, being supplied and held together by the joints and liga-
ments, grows with a growth
which is from God.

19 [a]Eph. 1:22 [b]Eph. 1:23; 4:16

D Exalted Over Asceticism, 2:20–23

20 [a]If you have died with
Christ to the [b]elementary principles of the world, [c]why, as if you
were living in the world, do you
submit yourself to [d]decrees, such
as,
21 "Do not handle, do not
taste, do not touch!"
22 (which all *refer* [a]*to* things
destined to perish with the
using)—in accordance with the
[b]commandments and teachings of
men?
23 These are matters which
have, to be sure, the appearance
of wisdom in [a]self-made religion
and self-abasement and [b]severe
treatment of the body, *but are* of
no value against [c]fleshly indulgence.

★20-23 20 [a]Rom. 6:2 [b]Col. 2:8 [c]Gal. 4:9 [d]Col. 2:14, 16
22 [a]1 Cor. 6:13 [b]Is. 29:13; Matt. 15:9; Titus 1:14
23 [a]Col. 2:18 [b]1 Tim. 4:3 [c]Rom. 13:14; 1 Tim. 4:8

IV THE EXALTED CALLING, 3:1–4:6

A The Certainties of Our Calling, 3:1–4

3 If then you have been [a]raised
up with Christ, keep seeking
the things above, where Christ is,
[b]seated at the right hand of God.
2 [a]Set your mind on the
things above, not on the things
that are on earth.
3 For you have [a]died and
your life is hidden with Christ in
God.
4 When Christ, [a]who is our
life, is revealed, [b]then you also
will be revealed with Him in glory.

★ 1 [a]Col. 2:12 [b]Mark 16:19
2 [a]Matt. 16:23; Phil. 3:19, 20
3 [a]Rom. 6:2; 2 Cor. 5:14; Col. 2:20
4 [a]John 11:25; Gal. 2:20 [b]1 Cor. 1:7; Phil. 3:21; 1 Pet. 1:13; 1 John 2:28; 3:2

B The Characteristics of Our Calling, 3:5–4:6

1 *In everyday life,* 3:5–17

5 [a]Therefore consider [b]the
members of your earthly body as
dead to [c]immorality, impurity,
passion, evil desire, and greed,
which amounts to idolatry.
6 For it is on account of
these things that [a]the wrath of
God will come,
7 and [a]in them you also once
walked, when you were living in
them.
8 But now you also, [a]put
them all aside: [b]anger, wrath,
malice, slander, *and* [c]abusive
speech from your mouth.
9 [a]Do not lie to one another,
since you [b]laid aside the old self
with its *evil* practices,
10 and have [a]put on the new
self who is being [b]renewed to a
true knowledge [c]according to the
image of the One who [d]created
him,
11 —*a renewal* in which
[a]there is no *distinction between*

5 [a]Rom. 8:13 [b]Col. 2:11 [c]Mark 7:21f.; 1 Cor. 6:9f., 18; 2 Cor. 12:21; Gal. 5:19; Eph. 4:19; 5:3, 5
6 [a]Rom. 1:18; Eph. 5:6
7 [a]Eph. 2:2
8 [a]Eph. 4:22 [b]Eph. 4:31 [c]Eph. 4:29
★ 9 [a]Eph. 4:25 [b]Eph. 4:22
★10 [a]Eph. 4:24 [b]Rom. 12:2; 2 Cor. 4:16; Eph. 4:23 [c]Rom. 8:29 [d]Eph. 2:10
★11 [a]Rom. 10:12; 1 Cor. 12:13; Gal. 3:28 [b]1 Cor. 7:19; Gal. 5:6 [c]Acts 28:2 [d]Eph. 6:8 [e]Eph. 1:23

---

special mystic insights by way of visions *(taking his stand on visions he has seen).* The basic problem was their egoistic or *fleshly mind.*

2:20–23 Christ had freed them from the taboos of asceticism, which can only give a pretense of wisdom, promote a self-made religion, and deal severely with the body. Yet it cannot succeed in combating the desires of the flesh.

3:1 Here begins the ethical section of the letter. Paul's appeal is simple: Become in experience what you already are by God's grace. The Christian is risen with Christ; let him exhibit that new life.

3:9 *the old self.* I.e., the old nature, the predisposition to leave God out of one's life and actions, which characterized the unregenerate state.

3:10 *the new self.* I.e., the new nature, or disposition, received when one is saved, with which one may serve God and righteousness (Rom. 6:18). Continual renewing is necessary, however, in order that the new life may have full dominion over moral conduct.

3:11 *barbarian.* At this time the word was applied to those who did not speak Greek or had not adopted Greek culture. *Scythian* represents the lowest type of uncouth barbarian nomads of southern Russia. In Christ, distinctions of race, class, and culture are transcended.

Greek and Jew, [b]circumcised and uncircumcised, [c]barbarian, Scythian, [d]slave and freeman, but [e]Christ is all, and in all.

12 And so, as those who have been [a]chosen of God, holy and beloved, [b]put on a [c]heart of compassion, kindness, [d]humility, gentleness and [e]patience;

12 [a]Luke 18:7 [b]Eph. 4:24 [c]Luke 1:78; Gal. 5:22f.; Phil. 2:1 [d]Eph. 4:2; Phil. 2:3 [e]1 Cor. 13:4; 2 Cor. 6:6

13 [a]bearing with one another, and [b]forgiving each other, whoever has a complaint against any one; [b]just as the Lord forgave you, so also should you.

13 [a]Eph. 4:2 [b]Rom. 15:7; Eph. 4:32

14 And beyond all these things *put on* love, which is [a]the perfect bond of [b]unity.

14 [a]Eph. 4:3 [b]John 17:23; Heb. 6:1

15 And let [a]the peace of Christ rule in your hearts, to which indeed you were called in [b]one body; and be thankful.

15 [a]John 14:27 [b]Eph. 2:16

16 Let [a]the word of Christ richly dwell within you, with all wisdom [b]teaching and admonishing one another [c]with psalms *and* hymns *and* spiritual songs, [d]singing with thankfulness in your hearts to God.

★16 [a]Rom. 10:17; Eph. 5:26; 1 Thess. 1:8 [b]Eph. 5:19; Col. 1:28 [c]Eph. 5:19 [d]1 Cor. 14:15

17 And [a]whatever you do in word or deed, *do* all in the name of the Lord Jesus, [b]giving thanks through Him to God the Father.

17 [a]1 Cor. 10:31 [b]Eph. 5:20; Col. 3:15

2 *In the home,* 3:18–21

18 [a]Wives, [b]be subject to your husbands, as is fitting in the Lord.

18 [a]Col. 3:18-4:1: *Eph. 5:22-6:9* [b]Eph. 5:22

19 [a]Husbands, love your wives, and do not be embittered against them.

★19 [a]Eph. 5:25

20 [a]Children, be obedient to your parents in all things, for this is well-pleasing to the Lord.

20 [a]Eph. 6:1

21 [a]Fathers, do not exasperate your children, that they may not lose heart.

21 [a]Eph. 6:4

3 *In servant-master relationships,* 3:22–4:1

22 [a]Slaves, in all things obey those who are your masters on earth, [b]not with external service, as those who *merely* please men, but with sincerity of heart, fearing the Lord.

22 [a]Eph. 6:5 [b]Eph. 6:6

23 Whatever you do, do your work heartily, [a]as for the Lord rather than for men;

23 [a]Eph. 6:7

24 [a]knowing that from the Lord you will receive the reward of [b]the inheritance. It is the Lord Christ whom you [c]serve.

24 [a]Eph. 6:8 [b]Acts 20:32; 1 Pet. 1:4 [c]1 Cor. 7:22

25 For [a]he who does wrong will receive the consequences of the wrong which he has done, and [b]that without partiality.

★25 [a]Eph. 6:8 [b]Acts 10:34; Eph. 6:9

4 Masters, grant to your slaves justice and fairness, knowing that you too have a Master in heaven.

4 *In prayer,* 4:2–4

2 [a]Devote yourselves to prayer, keeping alert in it with *an attitude of* thanksgiving;

2 [a]Acts 1:14; Eph. 6:18

3 praying at the same time [a]for us as well, that God may open up to us a [b]door for [c]the word, so that we may speak forth [d]the mystery of Christ, for which I have also [e]been imprisoned;

★ 3 [a]Eph. 6:19 [b]Acts 14:27 [c]2 Tim. 4:2 [d]Eph. 3:3, 4; 6:19 [e]Eph. 6:20

4 in order that I may make it clear [a]in the way I ought to speak.

4 [a]Eph. 6:20

5 *In witness and speech,* 4:5–6

5 [a]Conduct yourselves with wisdom toward [b]outsiders, [c]making the most of the opportunity.

★ 5 [a]Eph. 5:15 [b]Mark 4:11 [c]Eph. 5:16

6 [a]Let your speech always be with grace, seasoned, *as it were,* with [b]salt, so that you may know

★ 6 [a]Eph. 4:29 [b]Mark 9:50 [c]1 Pet. 3:15

3:16 The *psalms and hymns and spiritual songs* must be those which teach and admonish.

3:19 *Husbands.* See note on Eph. 5:25.

3:25 *without partiality.* God will show no favoritism, either for the unfaithful slave or for the unjust master (4:1).

4:3 *a door for the word.* I.e., an opportunity to *speak . . . the mystery.*

4:5 *outsiders.* I.e., those who are not Christians, but pagans. The division between them was sharp; the church was the community and all others were shut-out unbelievers.

4:6 *seasoned . . . with salt.* Salt is a preservative that retards spoilage. Our speech should be tempered so as never to be insipid, corrupt, or obscene. *each person.* I.e., those that are without.

how you should [c]respond to each person.

V CONCLUDING PERSONAL REMARKS, 4:7-18

★ 7 [a]Col. 4:7-9: *Eph. 6:21, 22* [b]Acts 20:4 [c]Eph. 6:21; Col. 1:7

7 [a]As to all my affairs, [b]Tychicus, *our* [c]beloved brother and faithful servant and fellow-bondslave in the Lord, will bring you information.

8 [a]Eph. 6:22 [b]Col. 2:2

8 [a]For I have sent him to you for this very purpose, that you may know *about* our circumstances and that he may [b]encourage your hearts;

★ 9 [a]Philem. 10 [b]Col. 1:7 [c]Col. 4:12

9 and with him [a]Onesimus, *our* faithful and [b]beloved brother, [c]who is one of your *number.* They will inform you about the whole situation here.

★10 [a]Acts 19:29 [b]Rom. 16:7 [c]Acts 4:36; 12:12; 15:37, 39 [d]2 Tim. 4:11

10 [a]Aristarchus, my [b]fellow prisoner, sends you his greetings; and *also* [c]Barnabas' cousin Mark (about whom you received instructions: [d]if he comes to you, welcome him);

★11 [a]Rom. 16:3 [b]Acts 11:2

11 and *also* Jesus who is called Justus; these are the only [a]fellow-workers for the kingdom of God [b]who are from the circumcision; and they have proved to be an encouragement to me.

12 [a]Epaphras, [b]who is one of your number, a bondslave of Jesus Christ, sends you his greetings, always [c]laboring earnestly for you in his prayers, that you may stand [d]perfect and [e]fully assured in all the will of God.

12 [a]Col. 1:7 [b]Col. 4:9 [c]Rom. 15:30 [d]Col. 1:28 [e]Luke 1:1 and marg.

13 For I bear him witness that he has a deep concern for you and for those who are in [a]Laodicea and Hierapolis.

13 [a]Col. 2:1; 4:15f.

14 [a]Luke, the beloved physician, sends you his greetings, and *also* [b]Demas.

★14 [a]2 Tim. 4:11; Philem. 24 [b]2 Tim. 4:10; Philem. 24

15 Greet the brethren who are in [a]Laodicea and also Nympha and [b]the church that is in her house.

★15 [a]Col. 2:1; 4:13, 16 [b]Rom. 16:5

16 And [a]when this letter is read among you, have it also read in the church of the Laodiceans; and you, for your part [a]read my letter *that is coming* from [b]Laodicea.

★16 [a]1 Thess. 5:27; 2 Thess. 3:14 [b]Col. 2:1; 4:13, 15

17 And say to [a]Archippus, "Take heed to the [b]ministry which you have received in the Lord, that you may fulfill it."

★17 [a]Philem. 2 [b]2 Tim. 4:5

18 I, Paul, [a]write this greeting with my own hand. [b]Remember my [c]imprisonment. [d]Grace be with you.

18 [a]1 Cor. 16:21 [b]Heb. 13:3 [c]Phil. 1:7; Col. 4:3 [d]1 Tim. 6:21; 2 Tim. 4:22; Titus 3:15; Heb. 13:25

4:7 *Tychicus.* One of the bearers of this letter (Acts 20:4).

4:9 *Onesimus.* See the Introduction to Philemon.

4:10 *Aristarchus.* See Acts 19:29; 20:4; 27:2. *Mark,* the author of the second Gospel. He had been restored to Paul's favor after his lapse on the first missionary journey (Acts 15:36-39).

4:11 *Jesus who is called Justus.* Nothing else is known of him.

4:14 *Luke.* The author of the third Gospel. *Demas.* A helper who later defected (2 Tim. 4:10).

4:15 *the church that is in her house.* See note on Rom. 16:5.

4:16 *my letter . . . from Laodicea.* Some think this is the circular letter Ephesians.

4:17 *Archippus.* See Philem. 2.

INTRODUCTION TO THE FIRST LETTER OF PAUL TO THE THESSALONIANS

AUTHOR: Paul DATE: 51

The Work at Thessalonica *Paul, Silas, and Timothy first went to the Macedonian port city of Thessalonica on the second missionary journey (Acts 17:1–14). This was the second place the gospel was preached in Europe, Philippi being the first. Because the preaching of the gospel depleted the ranks of the synagogue, the Jews charged Paul's host, Jason, with harboring traitors to Caesar. The rulers of the city took Jason as security (like a peace bond) and let the missionaries leave the city. When they arrived in Athens, Paul sent Timothy back to Thessalonica (1 Thess. 3:1–2, 5) to encourage the believers and then to report back on the condition of the church there. Timothy rejoined Paul in Corinth (3:6), where the two Thessalonian letters were written.*

Some feel that Paul was in Thessalonica less than a month (only three Sabbaths are mentioned in Acts 17:2). He must, however, have had an extended ministry outside the synagogue and the Jewish community, since the church was largely Gentile (see under 1 Thess. 1:9). In any case, he was concerned about his departing under pressure and about having to leave the church without experienced leadership. Timothy's report gave Paul cause only for praise for the healthy state of the church. This is a letter from a relieved and grateful pastor to his growing flock.

Purpose *In addition (1) to expressing his thankfulness, Paul (2) defended himself against a campaign to slander his ministry which asserted that it was done only for profit (2:9–10); (3) encouraged the new converts to stand not only against persecution but also against the pressure to revert to their former pagan standards (3:2–3; 4:1–12); (4) answered the question about what happens to Christians who die before the return of the Lord (4:13–18); and finally (5) discussed some problems in their church life which needed to be dealt with (5:12–13, 19–20).*

Contents *The key passages in this letter are eschatological; that is, related to events of the last days, such as the rapture of the Church (4:13–18) and the day of the Lord (5:1–11).*

OUTLINE OF 1 THESSALONIANS

I. Personal and Historical, 1:1–3:13
- A. Paul's Greeting, 1:1
- B. Paul's Commendation of the Thessalonians, 1:2–10
- C. Paul's Conduct among the Thessalonians, 2:1–12
  - 1. His uprightness, 2:1–4
  - 2. His industry, 2:5–9
  - 3. His blameless behavior, 2:10–12
- D. Paul's Concern for the Thessalonians, 2:13–3:13
  - 1. For their sufferings, 2:13–20
  - 2. For their testings (Timothy's visit), 3:1–8
  - 3. For their continued growth, 3:9–13

II. Practical and Hortatory, 4:1–5:28
- A. Teaching Concerning Development, 4:1–12
  - 1. In sexual relations, 4:1–8
  - 2. In brotherly love, 4:9–10
  - 3. In orderly living, 4:11–12
- B. Teaching Concerning the Dead, 4:13–18
- C. Teaching Concerning the Day of the Lord, 5:1–11
- D. Teaching Concerning Various Duties, 5:12–28

THE FIRST LETTER OF PAUL TO THE THESSALONIANS

I PERSONAL AND HISTORICAL, 1:1–3:13

A Paul's Greeting, 1:1

1 [a]Paul and [b]Silvanus and
[c]Timothy to the [d]church of
the Thessalonians in God the Father and the Lord Jesus Christ:
[e]Grace to you and peace.

B Paul's Commendation of the Thessalonians, 1:2–10

2 [a]We give thanks to God
always for all of you, [b]making
mention *of you* in our prayers;
3 constantly bearing in mind
your [a]work of faith and labor of
[b]love and [c]steadfastness of hope
in our Lord Jesus Christ in the
presence of [d]our God and Father,
4 knowing, [a]brethren beloved by God, [b]*His* choice of you;
5 for our [a]gospel did not
come to you in word only, but
also [b]in power and in the Holy
Spirit and with [c]full conviction;
just as you know [d]what kind of
men we proved to be among you
for your sake.
6 You also became [a]imitators of us and of the Lord, [b]having
received [c]the word in much tribulation with the [d]joy of the Holy
Spirit,
7 so that you became an example to all the believers in
[a]Macedonia and in [b]Achaia.
8 For [a]the word of the Lord
has [b]sounded forth from you, not
only in [c]Macedonia and [d]Achaia,
but also [e]in every place your faith
toward God has gone forth, so
that we have no need to say anything.
9 For they themselves report
about us what kind of a [a]reception we had with you, and how
you [b]turned to God [c]from idols to
serve [d]a living and true God,
10 and to [a]wait for His Son
from heaven, whom He [b]raised
from the dead, *that is* Jesus, who
[c]delivers us from [d]the wrath to
come.

★ 1 [a]2 Thess. 1:1 [b]2 Cor. 1:19 [c]Acts 16:1 [2 Thess. 1:1] [d]Acts 17:1; 2 Thess. 1:1 [e]Rom. 1:7
2 [a]Rom. 1:8; Eph. 5:20; 1 Thess. 2:13; 2 Thess. 1:3 [b]Rom. 1:9
3 [a]John 6:29; Gal. 5:6; 2 Thess. 1:11 [b]1 Cor. 13:13; 1 Thess. 3:6; 2 Thess. 1:3f. [c]Rom. 8:25; 15:4 [d]Gal. 1:4
★ 4 [a]Rom. 1:7; 2 Thess. 2:13 [b]Rom. 9:11; 2 Pet. 1:10
★ 5 [a]1 Cor. 9:14; 2 Cor. 2:12; 1 Thess. 2:2, 4, 8f.; 3:2; 2 Thess. 2:14 [b]Rom. 15:19; 1 Cor. 2:4; 2 Cor. 6:6 [c]Luke 1:1 [Gr.]; Col. 2:2 [d]1 Thess. 2:10
★ 6 [a]1 Cor. 4:16; 11:1f. [b]Acts 17:5-10 [c]2 Tim. 4:2 [d]Acts 13:52; 2 Cor. 6:10; Gal. 5:22
★ 7 [a]Rom. 15:26 [b]Acts 18:12
8 [a]Col. 3:16; 2 Thess. 3:1 [b]Rom. 10:18 [c]Rom. 15:26 [d]Acts 18:12 [e]Rom. 1:8; 16:19; 2 Cor. 2:14
★ 9 [a]1 Thess. 2:1 [b]Acts 14:15 [c]1 Cor. 12:2 [d]Matt. 16:16
★10 [a]Matt. 16:27f.; 1 Cor. 1:7 [b]Acts 2:24 [c]Rom. 5:9 [d]Matt. 3:7; 1 Thess. 2:16; 5:9

C Paul's Conduct among the Thessalonians, 2:1–12

1 *His uprightness,* 2:1–4

2 For you yourselves know,
brethren, that our [a]coming to
you [b]was not in vain,
2 but after we had already
suffered and been [a]mistreated in
[b]Philippi, as you know, we had
the boldness in our God [c]to speak
to you the [d]gospel of God amid
much [e]opposition.

★ 1 [a]1 Thess. 1:9 [b]2 Thess. 1:10
★ 2 [a]Acts 14:5; Phil. 1:30 [b]Acts 16:22-24 [c]Acts 17:1-9 [d]Rom. 1:1 [e]Phil. 1:30

1:1 *Silvanus* = Silas, who replaced Barnabas on the second missionary journey (Acts 15:22–18:5).

1:4 *His choice.* In relation to believers, God's choosing is sovereign (Rom. 9:11), it is pretemporal (Eph. 1:4), it is for salvation (2 Thess. 2:13), and it is proved by the fruits which accompany salvation (1 Thess. 1:5; Col. 3:12).

1:5 *what kind of men.* Paul elaborates on this in 2:3–12.

1:6 *imitators* (see 1 Cor. 4:16; 11:1). The Thessalonian Christians imitated the Lord and the apostles in that they responded to the gospel in spite of affliction.

1:7 *an example* = pattern or model. *Macedonia* was the northern province of Greece; *Achaia,* the southern.

1:9 *they themselves.* I.e., people everywhere gave testimony to the conversion of the Thessalonians. *turned to God from idols.* This church was comprised largely of converts from pagan religions and not from Judaism (see also 2:14-16). The last part of this verse and v. 10 summarize the message Paul, Silvanus, and Timothy preached. *to serve,* as bond-slaves. *a living* (in contrast to lifeless idols) *and true God* (not false gods).

1:10 *to wait.* The Christian's hope of the return of Christ is rooted in the fact that He was *raised from the dead. who delivers* = the Deliverer. *the wrath to come.* I.e., the judgments to come (5:9; Rev. 6:16).

2:1 This verse builds on 1:5. *not in vain* = not without results. Paul returns to this subject in v. 13, after reviewing his ministry (vv. 1–12).

2:2 *in Philippi.* The account is in Acts 16:12–40.

3 For our [a]exhortation does
not *come* from [b]error or [c]impur-
ity or by way of [d]deceit;
4 [a]but just as we have been
approved by God to be [b]entrusted
with the gospel, so we speak, [c]not
as pleasing men but God, who
[d]examines our hearts.

★ 3 [a]Acts 13:15 [b]2 Thess. 2:11 [c]1 Thess. 4:7 [d]2 Cor. 4:2
4 [a]2 Cor. 2:17 [b]Gal. 2:7 [c]Gal. 1:10 [d]Rom. 8:27

2 *His industry,* 2:5–9

5 For we never came with
flattering speech, as you know,
nor with [a]a pretext for greed—
[b]God is witness —
6 nor did we [a]seek glory
from men, either from you or
from others, even though as
[b]apostles of Christ we might have
asserted our authority.
7 But we proved to be
[a]gentle among you, [b]as a nursing
mother tenderly cares for her own
children.
8 Having thus a fond affection for you, we were well-
pleased to [a]impart to you not only
the [b]gospel of God but also our
own lives, because you had become very dear to us.
9 For you recall, brethren,
our [a]labor and hardship, *how*
[b]working night and day so as not
to be a [c]burden to any of you, we
proclaimed to you the [d]gospel of
God.

★ 5 [a]Acts 20:33; 2 Pet. 2:3 [b]Rom. 1:9; 1 Thess. 2:10
★ 6 [a]John 5:41, 44; 2 Cor. 4:5 [b]1 Cor. 9:1f.
7 [a]2 Tim. 2:24 [b]Gal. 4:19; 1 Thess. 2:11
★ 8 [a]2 Cor. 12:15; 1 John 3:16 [b]Rom. 1:1
9 [a]Phil. 4:16; 2 Thess. 3:8 [b]Acts 18:3 [c]1 Cor. 9:4f.; 2 Cor. 11:9 [d]Rom. 1:1

3 *His blameless behavior,* 2:10–12

10 You are witnesses, and *so*
is [a]God, [b]how devoutly and up-
rightly and blamelessly we behaved toward you believers;
11 just as you know how we
were [a]exhorting and encouraging
and [b]imploring each one of you as
[c]a father *would* his own children,
12 so that you may [a]walk in a
manner worthy of the God who
[b]calls you into His own kingdom
and [c]glory.

10 [a]1 Thess. 2:5 [b]2 Cor. 1:12; 1 Thess. 1:5
11 [a]1 Thess. 5:14 [b]Luke 16:28; 1 Thess. 4:6 [c]1 Cor. 4:14; 1 Thess. 2:7
★12 [a]Eph. 4:1 [b]Rom. 8:28; 1 Thess. 5:24; 2 Thess. 2:14 [c]2 Cor. 4:6; 1 Pet. 5:10

D Paul's Concern for the Thessalonians, 2:13–3:13

1 *For their sufferings,* 2:13–20

13 And for this reason we
also constantly [a]thank God that
when you received from us the
[b]word of God's message, you accepted *it* [c]not *as* the word of men,
but *for* what it really is, the word
of God, [d]which also performs its
work in you who believe.
14 For you, brethren, became
[a]imitators of [b]the churches of
God in Christ Jesus that are [c]in
Judea, for [d]you also endured the
same sufferings at the hands of
your own countrymen, [e]even as
they *did* from the Jews,
15 [a]who both killed the Lord
Jesus and [b]the prophets, and
drove us out. They are not pleasing to God, but hostile to all men,
16 [a]hindering us from speaking to the Gentiles [b]that they
might be saved; with the result
that they always [c]fill up the measure of their sins. But [d]wrath has
come upon them to the utmost.
17 But we, brethren, having
been bereft of you for a short
while—[a]in person, not in spirit—

13 [a]Rom. 1:8; 1 Thess. 1:2 [b]Rom. 10:17; Heb. 4:2 [c]Matt. 10:20; Gal. 4:14 [d]Heb. 4:12
★14 [a]1 Thess. 1:6 [b]1 Cor. 7:17; 10:32 [c]Gal. 1:22 [d]Acts 17:5; 1 Thess. 3:4; 2 Thess. 1:4f. [e]Heb. 10:33f.
15 [a]Luke 24:20; Acts 2:23 [b]Matt. 5:12; Acts 7:52
★16 [a]Acts 9:23; 13:45, 50; 14:2, 5, 19; 17:5, 13; 18:12; 21:21f., 27; 25:2, 7 [b]1 Cor. 10:33 [c]Gen. 15:16; Dan. 8:23; Matt. 23:32 [d]1 Thess. 1:10
★17–18
17 [a]1 Cor. 5:3 [b]1 Thess. 3:10

2:3 Paul attacks what must have been charges against him: of *error* (i.e., that the gospel he preached was based on error), of *impurity* (that Christianity encouraged sexual immorality), and of *deceit* (that his methods were underhanded).

2:5 *flattering speech* = cajolery, i.e., an attempt to persuade by use of insincere speech.

2:6 *asserted our authority.* Better, made demands (on you), i.e., for support. Paul makes clear his right as an apostle to financial support, but says he behaved as selflessly as a nursing mother (v. 7).

2:8 *fond affection.* An unusual word indicating the yearning love of a mother for her children. Paul's pastoral heart is laid bare in these verses.

2:12 *walk* = live.

2:14 *imitators.* Paul compared the problems of the Christians at Thessalonica among their fellow Greeks with those of the Christians in Judea, persecuted by Jews.

2:16 *fill up the measure of their sins.* God sometimes allows His people to be persecuted in order to show the evil nature of men and the rightness of His judgment when it falls (cf. Gen. 15:16). These persecutors were heaping sin upon sin.

2:17–18 Paul had several times planned to return to Thessalonica. *Satan thwarted us.*

were all the more eager with great
desire [b]to see your face.
18 For [a]we wanted to come to
you—I, Paul, [b]more than once—
and *yet* [c]Satan [d]thwarted us.
19 For who is our hope or [a]joy
or crown of exultation? Is it not
even you, in the presence of our
Lord Jesus at His [b]coming?
20 For you are [a]our glory and
joy.

18 [a]Rom. 15:22 [b]Phil. 4:16 [c]Matt. 4:10 [d]Rom. 1:13; 15:22 **19** [a]Phil. 4:1 [b]Matt. 16:27; Mark 8:38; John 21:22; 1 Thess. 3:13; 4:15; 5:23 **20** [a]2 Cor. 1:14

2 *For their testings (Timothy's visit),* 3:1–8

3 Therefore [a]when we could
endure *it* no longer, we
thought it best to be left behind
at [b]Athens alone;
2 and we sent [a]Timothy, our
brother and God's fellow-worker
in the gospel of Christ, to
strengthen and encourage you as
to your faith,
3 so that no man may be disturbed by these afflictions; for
you yourselves know that [a]we
have been destined for this.
4 For indeed when we were
with you, we *kept* telling you in
advance that we were going to
suffer affliction; [a]and so it came to
pass, as you know.
5 For this reason, [a]when I
could endure *it* no longer, I also
[b]sent to find out about your faith,
for fear that [c]the tempter might
have tempted you, and [d]our labor
should be in vain.
6 But now that [a]Timothy has
come to us from you, and has
brought us good news of [b]your
faith and love, and that you always [c]think kindly of us, longing
to see us just as we also long to
see you,
7 for this reason, brethren,
in all our distress and affliction we
were comforted about you
through your faith;
8 for now we *really* live, if
you [a]stand firm in the Lord.

1 [a]Phil. 2:19; 1 Thess. 3:5 [b]Acts 17:15f. **2** [a]2 Cor. 1:1; Col. 1:1 ★ **3** [a]Acts 9:16; 14:22 ★ **4** [a]1 Thess. 2:14 ★ **5** [a]Phil. 2:19; 1 Thess. 3:1 [b]1 Thess. 3:2 [c]Matt. 4:3 [d]2 Cor. 6:1; Phil. 2:16 **6** [a]Acts 18:5 [b]1 Thess. 1:3 [c]1 Cor. 11:2 ★ **8** [a]1 Cor. 6:13

3 *For their continued growth,* 3:9–13

9 For [a]what thanks can we
render to God for you in return
for all the joy with which we rejoice before our God on your account,
10 as we [a]night and day keep
praying most earnestly that we
may [b]see your face, and may
[c]complete what is lacking in your
faith?
11 [a]Now may [b]our God and
Father [c]Himself and Jesus our
Lord [d]direct our way to you;
12 and may the Lord cause
you to increase and [a]abound in
love for one another, and for all
men, just as we also *do* for you;
13 so that He may [a]establish
your hearts [b]unblamable in holiness before [c]our God and Father
at the [d]coming of our Lord Jesus
[e]with all His saints.

9 [a]1 Thess. 1:2 ★**10** [a]2 Tim. 1:3 [b]1 Thess. 2:17 [c]2 Cor. 13:9 ★**11-13** **11** [a]2 Thess. 2:16 [b]Gal. 1:4; 1 Thess. 3:13 [c]1 Thess. 4:16; 5:23; 2 Thess. 2:16; 3:16; Rev. 21:3 [d]2 Thess. 3:5 **12** [a]Phil. 1:9; 1 Thess. 4:1, 10; 2 Thess. 1:3 ★**13** [a]1 Cor. 1:8; 1 Thess. 3:2 [b]Luke 1:6 [c]Gal. 1:4; 1 Thess. 3:11 [d]1 Thess. 2:19 [e]Matt. 25:31; Mark 8:38; 1 Thess. 4:17; 2 Thess. 1:7

II PRACTICAL AND HORTATORY, 4:1–5:28

A Teaching Concerning Development, 4:1–12

1 *In sexual relations,* 4:1–8

4 [a]Finally then, [b]brethren, we
request and exhort you in the
Lord Jesus, that, as you received
from us *instruction* as to how you
ought to [c]walk and [d]please God

1 [a]2 Cor. 13:11; 2 Thess. 3:1 [b]Gal. 6:1; 1 Thess. 5:12; 2 Thess. 1:3; 2:1; 3:1, 13 [c]Eph. 4:1 [d]2 Cor. 5:9 [e]Phil. 1:9; 1 Thess. 3:12; 4:10

Likely refers to the security taken of Jason (Acts 17:9), which probably included a guarantee that Paul would not return to the city.

3:3 *disturbed.* I.e., that they be not seduced away from the faith by the heathen who were urging them to reject their faith.

3:4 *suffer affliction.* To endure the normal afflictions that come to a believer in this life. Paul had told them these would come (v. 3).

3:5 *the tempter.* Again (as in 2:18) Paul traces events to Satan's working.

3:8 The good news of their spiritual well-being was a breath of life to Paul.

3:10 *complete.* I.e., to make complete as one might repair fishing nets (Matt. 4:21) or restore saints (cf. Gal. 6:1; Eph. 4:12).

3:11-13 The thanksgiving portion of the letter ends in a three-verse prayer.

3:13 *saints.* Lit., holy ones. Probably refers here to angels who will accompany the return of Christ (Mark 8:38), or possibly also holy men (cf. 1 Thess. 4:14).

(just as you actually do walk), that
you may [e]excel still more.
2 For you know what com-
mandments we gave you by *the
authority of* the Lord Jesus.
3 For this is the will of God,
your sanctification; *that is,* that
you [a]abstain from sexual immorality;
4 that [a]each of you know
how to possess his own [b]vessel in
sanctification and [c]honor,
5 not in [a]lustful passion, like
the Gentiles who [b]do not know
God;
6 *and* that no man transgress
and [a]defraud his brother [b]in the
matter because [c]the Lord is *the*
avenger in all these things, just as
we also [d]told you before and solemnly warned *you.*
7 For [a]God has not called us
for [b]the purpose of impurity, but
in sanctification.
8 Consequently, he who rejects *this* is not rejecting man but
the God who [a]gives His Holy
Spirit to you.

★ **3** [a]1 Cor. 6:18
★ **4** [a]1 Cor. 7:2, 9 [b]2 Cor. 4:7; 1 Pet. 3:7 [c]Rom. 1:24
5 [a]Rom. 1:26 [b]Gal. 4:8
★ **6** [a]1 Cor. 6:8 [b]2 Cor. 7:11 [c]Rom. 12:19; 13:4; Heb. 13:4 [d]Luke 16:28; 1 Thess. 2:11; Heb. 2:6
7 [a]1 Pet. 1:15 [b]1 Thess. 2:3
★ **8** [a]Rom. 5:5; 2 Cor. 1:22; Gal. 4:6; 1 John 3:24

2 *In brotherly love,* 4:9-10

9 Now as to the [a]love of the
brethren, you [b]have no need for
anyone to write to you, for you
yourselves are [c]taught by God to
love one another;

9 [a]John 13:34; Rom. 12:10 [b]2 Cor. 9:1; 1 Thess. 5:1 [c]Jer. 31:33f.; John 6:45; 1 John 2:27

10 for indeed [a]you do practice
it toward all the brethren who are
in all Macedonia. But we urge
you, brethren, to [b]excel still more,

★**10** [a]1 Thess. 1:7 [b]1 Thess. 3:12

3 *In orderly living,* 4:11-12

11 and to make it your ambi-
tion [a]to lead a quiet life and [b]at-
tend to your own business and
[c]work with your hands, just as we
commanded you;
12 so that you may [a]behave
properly toward [b]outsiders and
[c]not be in any need.

★**11** [a]2 Thess. 3:12 [b]1 Pet. 4:15 [c]Acts 18:3; Eph. 4:28
★**12** [a]Rom. 13:13; Col. 4:5 [b]Mark 4:11 [c]Eph. 4:28

B Teaching Concerning the Dead, 4:13-18

13 But [a]we do not want you
to be uninformed, brethren,
about those who [b]are asleep, that
you may not grieve, as do [c]the
rest who have [d]no hope.
14 For if we believe that Jesus
died and rose again, [a]even so God
will bring with Him [b]those who
have fallen asleep in Jesus.
15 For this we say to you [a]by
the word of the Lord, that [b]we
who are alive, and remain until
[c]the coming of the Lord, shall not
precede [d]those who have fallen
asleep.
16 For the Lord [a]Himself [b]will
descend from heaven with a

★**13-18**
13 [a]Rom. 1:13 [b]Acts 7:60 [c]Eph. 2:3; 1 Thess. 5:6 [d]Eph. 2:12
★**14** [a]Rom. 14:9; 2 Cor. 4:14 [b]1 Cor. 15:18
15 [a]1 Kin. 13:17f.; 20:35; 2 Cor. 12:1; Gal. 1:12 [b]1 Cor. 15:52; 1 Thess. 5:10 [c]1 Thess. 2:19 [d]1 Cor. 15:18; 1 Thess. 4:13
★**16-17**
16 [a]1 Thess. 3:11 [b]1 Thess. 1:10; 2 Thess. 1:7 [c]Joel 2:11 [d]Jude 9 [e]Matt. 24:31 [f]1 Cor. 15:23; 2 Thess. 2:1; Rev. 14:13

4:3 *will of God.* I.e., His desire or purpose. *sanctification* (holiness) is viewed in three aspects in the N.T.: (1) a position of being set apart to God, which every believer has at the moment of his salvation (1 Cor. 6:11); (2) a progressive holiness of life that ought to be true of every believer (1 Thess. 4:3); and (3) our condition in heaven, in which we shall be "unblamable in holiness" (3:13). *immorality.* The Greek word means all kinds of illicit or unnatural sexual indulgence. Greek cities like Thessalonica were wide open to all kinds of sexual looseness, even in connection with religious rites.

4:4 *possess his own vessel.* This means either mastery over one's body, keeping it pure (1 Cor. 9:24-27), or refers to an honorable marriage (*vessel* = wife, as 1 Pet. 3:7).

4:6 *transgress.* In this context (vv. 3-8), the reference is to sexual conduct.

4:8 *rejects.* Treats lightly these commands for sexual purity.

4:10 *excel still more.* I.e., practice brotherly love more and more with your fellow Macedonian Christians.

4:11 *make it your ambition.* Or, aspire. The Greek word is used only here, in Rom. 15:20, and in 2 Cor. 5:9. The problems mentioned in 2 Thess. 3:11-12 gave rise to these exhortations.

4:12 *outsiders.* I.e., non-Christians.

4:13-18 The question is this: Does the death of a believer before the Lord comes cause him to lose all hope of sharing in the glorious reign of Christ? Paul's answer is the reassuring affirmation that the dead will be raised and will share in the kingdom.

4:13 *are asleep.* The body (not the soul) of the believer who dies is said to sleep during the time between death and resurrection.

4:14 *if we believe.* Better, since we do believe. The certainty of the Christian's resurrection is based on the fact of Christ's resurrection.

4:16-17 *the trumpet of God.* See 1 Cor. 15:52. *the dead in Christ shall rise first,* when the Lord comes for His people (v. 17). Then living

[c]shout, with the voice of [d]*the*
archangel, and with the [e]trumpet
of God; and [f]the dead in Christ
shall rise first.
17 Then [a]we who are alive
and remain shall be [b]caught up
together with them [c]in the clouds
to meet the Lord in the air, and
thus we shall always [d]be with the
Lord.
18 Therefore comfort one another with these words.

17 [a]1 Cor. 15:52; 1 Thess. 5:10 [b]2 Cor. 12:2 [c]Dan. 7:13; Acts 1:9; Rev. 11:12 [d]John 12:26
★18

C Teaching Concerning the Day of the Lord, 5:1-11

5 Now as to the [a]times and the
epochs, brethren, you [b]have
no need of anything to be written
to you.
2 For you yourselves know
full well that [a]the day of the Lord
will come [b]just like a thief in the
night.
3 While they are saying,
"[a]Peace and safety!" then [b]de-
struction will come upon them
suddenly like [c]birth pangs upon a
woman with child; and they shall
not escape.
4 But you, brethren, are not
in [a]darkness, that the day should
overtake you [b]like a thief;
5 for you are all [a]sons of
light and sons of day. We are not
of night nor of [b]darkness;
6 so then let us not [a]sleep as
[b]others do, but let us be alert and
[c]sober.
7 For those who sleep do
their sleeping at night, and those
who get drunk get [a]drunk at
night.
8 But since [a]we are of *the*
day, let us [b]be sober, having put
on the [c]breastplate of [d]faith and
love, and as a [e]helmet, the [f]hope
of salvation.
9 For God has not destined
us for [a]wrath, but for [b]obtaining
salvation through our Lord Jesus
Christ,
10 [a]who died for us, that
whether we are awake or asleep,
we may live together with Him.
11 Therefore encourage one
another, and [a]build up one another, just as you also are doing.

1 [a]Acts 1:7 [b]1 Thess. 4:9
★ 2 [a]1 Cor. 1:8 [b]Luke 21:34; 1 Thess. 5:4; 2 Pet. 3:10; Rev. 3:3; 16:15
3 [a]Jer. 6:14; 8:11; Ezek. 13:10 [b]2 Thess. 1:9 [c]John 16:21
★ 4 [a]Acts 26:18; 1 John 2:8 [b]Luke 21:34; 1 Thess. 5:2; 2 Pet. 3:10; Rev. 3:3; 16:15
5 [a]Luke 16:8 [b]Acts 26:18; 1 John 2:8
★ 6 [a]Rom. 13:11; 1 Thess. 5:10 [b]Eph. 2:3; 1 Thess. 4:13 [c]1 Pet. 1:13
7 [a]Acts 2:15; 2 Pet. 2:13
8 [a]1 Thess. 5:5 [b]1 Pet. 1:13 [c]Eph. 6:14 [d]Eph. 6:23 [e]Eph. 6:17 [f]Rom. 8:24
★ 9 [a]1 Thess. 1:10 [b]2 Thess. 2:13f.
10 [a]Rom. 14:9
11 [a]Eph. 4:29

D Teaching Concerning Various Duties, 5:12-28

12 But we request of you,
brethren, that you [a]appreciate
those [b]who diligently labor
among you, and [c]have charge
over you in the Lord and give you
instruction,
13 and that you esteem them
very highly in love because of
their work. [a]Live in peace with
one another.
14 And we urge you, brethren, admonish [a]the unruly, encourage [b]the fainthearted, help
[c]the weak, be [d]patient with all
men.
15 See that [a]no one repays
another with evil for evil, but always [b]seek after that which is
good for one another and for all
men.
16 [a]Rejoice always;

12 [a]Ps. 144:3; 1 Cor. 16:18; 1 Tim. 5:17 [b]Rom. 16:6, 12; 1 Cor. 15:10; 16:16 [c]Heb. 13:17
13 [a]Mark 9:50
14 [a]2 Thess. 3:6, 7, 11 [b]Is. 35:4 [Septuagint] [c]Rom. 14:1f.; 1 Cor. 8:7ff. [Rom. 15:1] [d]1 Cor. 13:4
15 [a]Matt. 5:44; Rom. 12:17; 1 Pet. 3:9 [b]Rom. 12:9; Gal. 6:10; 1 Thess. 5:21
★16-22
16 [a]Phil. 4:4

---

lievers will be *caught up.* From the Latin for "caught up" comes the term "rapture." The rapture or catching up of believers described here involves both those who have died and those who are living when the Lord comes. His coming here is *in the air,* not to the earth, and will occur just prior to the beginning of the tribulation period (see Rev. 3:10). That period will end with His coming to the earth (see Matt. 24:29-30; Rev. 19:11-16).

4:18 The *comfort* of the Christian's hope in resurrection is in sharp contrast to the hopelessness of the heathen in the face of death.

5:2 *the day of the Lord.* An extended period of time, beginning with the tribulation and including the events of the second coming of Christ and the millennial kingdom on earth. It will begin *(come)* unexpectedly *(like a thief in the night).*

5:4 *darkness.* A figure of the unbeliever's moral state and separation from God.

5:6 *sleep.* Not physical but moral (as in Mark 13:36; Eph. 5:14).

5:9 *wrath.* I.e., the anguish and tribulation associated with the beginning of the day of the Lord (v. 3), from which the believer is to be delivered (1:10).

5:16-22 Verses 16-18 are closely related; vv. 19-22 form another paragraph.

★17 [a]Eph. 6:18
18 [a]Eph. 5:20
★19 [a]Eph. 4:30
20 [a]Acts 13:1; 1 Cor. 14:31
21 [a]1 Cor. 14:29 [b]Rom. 12:9; Gal. 6:10
★23-24
23 [a]Rom. 15:33 [b]1 Thess. 3:11 [c]Luke 1:46f.; Heb. 4:12 [d]James 1:4 [e]1 Thess. 2:19

17 [a]pray without ceasing;
18 in everything [a]give thanks;
for this is God's will for you in
Christ Jesus.
19 [a]Do not quench the Spirit;
20 do not despise [a]prophetic
utterances.
21 But [a]examine everything
carefully; [b]hold fast to that which
is good;
22 abstain from every form of
evil.
23 Now [a]may the God of
peace [b]Himself sanctify you entirely; and may your [c]spirit and
soul and body be preserved complete, [d]without blame at [e]the
coming of our Lord Jesus Christ.
24 [a]Faithful is He who [b]calls
you, and He also will bring it to
pass.
25 Brethren, [a]pray for us.
26 [a]Greet all the brethren
with a holy kiss.
27 I adjure you by the Lord to
[a]have this letter read to all the
[b]brethren.
28 [a]The grace of our Lord
Jesus Christ be with you.

24 [a]1 Cor. 1:9; 2 Thess. 3:3 [b]1 Thess. 2:12
25 [a]Eph. 6:19; 2 Thess. 3:1; Heb. 13:18
★26 [a]Rom. 16:16
27 [a]Col. 4:16 [b]Acts 1:15
28 [a]Rom. 16:20; 2 Thess. 3:18

5:17 *without ceasing.* Paul prayed thus for the Thessalonians (1:3; 2:13).

5:19 *quench. the Spirit* is often likened to fire (Matt. 3:11; Luke 3:16; Acts 2:3). The Spirit is quenched whenever His ministry is stifled in an individual or in the church.

5:23-24 A two-verse prayer that closes the section of instruction and exhortation begun at 4:1. *spirit and soul and body* should not be understood as defining the parts of man, but as representing the whole man.

5:26 *holy kiss.* For the kiss as a symbol of welcome in Jewish life see Luke 7:45; 22:48. As a symbol of Christian fellowship see note on 1 Pet. 5:14. Paul uses the phrase in Rom. 16:16; 1 Cor. 16:20; and 2 Cor. 13:12.

INTRODUCTION TO
THE SECOND LETTER OF PAUL TO THE THESSALONIANS

AUTHOR: Paul DATE: 51

Purpose *This letter was sent by Paul to the church at Thessalonica, not long after 1 Thessalonians, to meet a new situation. Word had reached Paul that somehow there had been misunderstanding, if not misrepresentation (2:2), of his teaching concerning the coming of the day of the Lord (1 Thess. 5:1-11). Some thought that its judgments had already begun; yet they understood Paul to have taught that they would be exempt from those judgments. The practical ramification of this doctrinal confusion was that some, thinking the end of the world was at hand, had stopped working and were creating an embarrassing situation (3:6, 11). Paul corrects the teaching and reprimands the idlers.*

Contents *The major section on the man of sin (2:1-12) should be compared with other passages which tell of this Antichrist (Dan. 9:27; Matt. 24:15; Rev. 11:7, 13:1-10).*

OUTLINE OF 2 THESSALONIANS

I. Salutation, 1:1-2
II. Thanksgiving and Encouragement in Persecution, 1:3-12
III. Correction Concerning the Day of the Lord, 2:1-17
A. Its Relation to the Present, 2:1-2
B. Its Relation to the Apostasy, 2:3a
C. Its Relation to the Man of Lawlessness, 2:3b-5
D. Its Relation to the Restrainer, 2:6-9
E. Its Relation to Unbelievers, 2:10-12
F. Its Relation to Believers, 2:13-17
IV. Exhortations to Prayer and Discipline, 3:1-15
A. Paul's Confidence, 3:1-5
B. Paul's Commands, 3:6-15
V. Concluding Benediction and Greeting, 3:16-18.

THE SECOND LETTER OF PAUL TO THE THESSALONIANS

I SALUTATION, 1:1-2

1 [a]Paul and [b]Silvanus and
[c]Timothy to the [d]church of
the Thessalonians in God our Father and the Lord Jesus Christ:
2 [a]Grace to you and peace
from God the Father and the Lord
Jesus Christ.

1 [a]1 Thess. 1:1 [b]2 Cor. 1:19 [c]Acts 16:1 [1 Thess. 1:1] [d]Acts 17:1; 1 Thess. 1:1
2 [a]Rom. 1:7

II THANKSGIVING AND ENCOURAGEMENT IN PERSECUTION, 1:3-12

3 We ought always [a]to give
thanks to God for you, [b]brethren,
as is *only* fitting, because your
faith is greatly enlarged, and the
[c]love of each one of you toward
one another grows *ever* greater;
4 therefore, we ourselves
[a]speak proudly of you among
[b]the churches of God for your
perseverance and faith [b]in the
midst of all your persecutions and
afflictions which you endure.
5 *This is* a [a]plain indication
of God's righteous judgment so
that you may be [b]considered worthy of the kingdom of God, for
which indeed you are suffering.
6 For after all [a]it is *only* just
for God to repay with affliction
those who afflict you,

★ 3-4
3 [a]Rom. 1:8; Eph. 5:20 [b]1 Thess. 4:1 [c]1 Thess. 3:12
4 [a]2 Cor. 7:4; 1 Thess. 2:19 [b]1 Cor. 7:17; 1 Thess. 2:14
5 [a]Phil. 1:28 [b]Luke 20:35; 2 Thess. 1:11
6 [a]Ex. 23:22; Col. 3:25; Heb. 6:10

1:3-4 *your faith is greatly enlarged.* Paul's earlier fears about their faith (1 Thess. 3:5, 10) have disappeared in the light of their exceptional growth. *love* (see 1 Thess. 3:12).

7 and *to give* relief to you
who are afflicted and to us as well
[a]when the Lord Jesus shall be revealed [b]from heaven [c]with His
mighty angels [d]in flaming fire,
8 dealing out retribution to
those who [a]do not know God and
to those who [b]do not obey the
gospel of our Lord Jesus.
9 And these will pay the
penalty of [a]eternal destruction,
[b]away from the presence of the
Lord and from the glory of His
power,
10 when He comes to be [a]glo-
rified in His saints on that [b]day,
and to be marveled at among all
who have believed—for our [c]tes-
timony to you was believed.
11 To this end also we [a]pray
for you always that our God may
[b]count you worthy of your [c]call-
ing, and fulfill every desire for
[d]goodness and the [e]work of faith
with power;
12 in order that the [a]name of
our Lord Jesus may be glorified in
you, and you in Him, according to
the grace of our God and the Lord
Jesus Christ.

★ **7** [a]Luke 17:30 [b]1 Thess. 4:16 [c]Jude 14 [d]Ex. 3:2; 19:18; Is. 66:15; Ezek. 1:13f.; Dan. 7:9; Matt. 25:41; 1 Cor. 3:13; Heb. 10:27; 12:29; 2 Pet. 3:7; Jude 7; Rev. 14:10

8 [a]Gal. 4:8 [b]Rom 2:8

★ **9** [a]Phil. 3:19; 1 Thess. 5:3 [b]Is. 2:10, 19, 21; 2 Thess. 2:8

★**10** [a]Is. 49:3; John 17:10; 1 Thess. 2:12 [b]Is. 2:11ff.; 1 Cor. 3:13 [c]1 Cor. 1:6; 1 Thess. 2:1

11 [a]Col. 1:9 [b]2 Thess. 1:5 [c]Rom. 11:29 [d]Rom. 15:14 [e]1 Thess. 1:3

12 [a]Is. 24:15; 66:5; Mal. 1:11; Phil. 2:9ff.

III CORRECTION CONCERNING THE DAY OF THE LORD, 2:1–17

A Its Relation to the Present, 2:1–2

2 Now we request you, [a]breth-
ren, with regard to the [b]com-
ing of our Lord Jesus Christ, and
our [c]gathering together to Him,
2 that you may not be
quickly shaken from your compo-
sure or be disturbed either by a
[a]spirit or a [b]message or a [c]letter as
if from us, to the effect that [d]the
day of the Lord [e]has come.

★ **1** [a]2 Thess. 1:3 [b]1 Thess. 2:19 [c]Mark 13:27; 1 Thess. 4:15-17

★ **2** [a]1 Cor. 14:32; 1 John 4:1 [b]1 Thess. 5:2; 2 Thess. 2:15 [c]2 Thess. 3:17 [d]1 Cor. 1:8 [e]1 Cor. 7:26

B Its Relation to the Apostasy, 2:3a

3 [a]Let no one in any way deceive you, for *it will not come* unless the [b]apostasy comes first,

C Its Relation to the Man of Lawlessness, 2:3b–5

and the [c]man of lawlessness is revealed, the [d]son of destruction,
4 who opposes and exalts
himself above [a]every so-called

★ **3** [a]Eph. 5:6 [b]1 Tim. 4:1 [c]Dan. 7:25; 8:25; 11:36; 2 Thess. 2:8; Rev. 13:5ff. [d]John 17:12

★ **4** [a]1 Cor. 8:5 [b]Is. 14:14; Ezek. 28:2

1:7 *relief . . . to us.* I.e., to Paul, Silvanus, and Timothy who knew what it was to be under persecution and pressure for their faith (1 Thess. 1:6; 2:14–18). *Relief* is promised at the return of Christ, who will then judge those who afflict His people (v. 6).

1:9 *eternal destruction.* Not annihilation, but ruin by reason of separation from the presence of the Lord. In 1 Thess. 5:3 the destruction is said to be sudden; here, eternal.

1:10 *on that day.* I.e., the day when the Lord Jesus shall be revealed (v. 7) at His return.

2:1 *with regard to the coming of our Lord Jesus.* I.e., concerning, or in the interest of the truth concerning, the Lord's coming. Paul denies the teaching, ascribed to him, that the day of the Lord had already begun. *our gathering together.* A reference to the rapture of the church (1 Thess. 4:13–18).

2:2 *shaken* = excited, violently disturbed. The Thessalonians were being greatly disturbed by false teaching concerning future events, and Paul seeks to bring them back to true doctrine (2:1–12) and proper living (3:6–16). The false teaching was *by a spirit* (some prophetic utterance), by *a message* (some spoken teaching), and by *a letter as if from us* (some written communication purporting to be from Paul). The source of these teachings is not given. *day of the Lord* (see note on 1 Thess. 5:2).

2:3 *the apostasy.* An aggressive and climactic revolt against God which will prepare the way for the appearance of the man of sin (see 1 Tim. 4:1–5; 2 Tim. 3:1–5). *man of lawlessness.* While it is true that the forces of lawlessness were at work in Paul's time and are at work today (note v. 7, *the mystery of lawlessness is already at work),* the man of lawlessness (also called *that lawless one,* v. 8) is an individual of the future who will come to power during the tribulation days. John also recognized the presence of many antichrists in his time (1 John 2:18) as well as the coming of one great Antichrist in the future (Rev. 11:7; 13:1–10).

2:4 *takes his seat in the temple of God.* At the midpoint of the tribulation period the Antichrist will desecrate the rebuilt Jewish temple in Jerusalem by placing himself there to be worshiped (see note on Matt. 24:15). This will be the climax of man's great sin of self-deification, in open defiance of God.

god or object of worship, so that
he takes his seat in the temple of
God, [b]displaying himself as being
God.
5 Do you not remember that
[a]while I was still with you, I was
telling you these things?

5 [a]1 Thess. 3:4

D Its Relation to the Restrainer, 2:6–9

6 And you know [a]what restrains him now, so that in his
time he may be revealed.
7 For [a]the mystery of lawlessness is already at work; only
[b]he who now restrains *will do so*
until he is taken out of the way.
8 And then that lawless one
[a]will be revealed whom the Lord
will slay [b]with the breath of His
mouth and bring to an end by the
[c]appearance of His coming;
9 *that is,* the one whose
coming is in accord with the activity of [a]Satan, with all power
and [b]signs and false wonders,

6 [a]2 Thess. 2:7
★ 7 [a]Rev. 17:5, 7 [b]2 Thess. 2:6
★ 8 [a]Dan. 7:25; 8:25; 11:36; 2 Thess. 2:3; Rev. 13:5ff. [b]Is. 11:4; Rev. 2:16; 19:15 [c]1 Tim. 6:14; 2 Tim. 1:10; 4:1, 8; Titus 2:13
9 [a]Matt. 4:10 [b]Matt. 24:24; John 4:48

E Its Relation to Unbelievers, 2:10–12

10 and with all the deception
of wickedness for [a]those who perish, because they did not receive
the love of [b]the truth so as to be
saved.
11 And for this reason [a]God
will send upon them a [b]deluding
influence so that they might believe what is false,
12 in order that they all may
be judged who [a]did not believe
the truth, but [b]took pleasure in
wickedness.

10 [a]1 Cor. 1:18 [b]2 Thess. 2:12, 13
★11–12
11 [a]1 Kin. 22:22; Rom. 1:28 [b]1 Thess. 2:3; 2 Tim. 4:4
12 [a]Rom. 2:8 [b]Rom. 1:32; 1 Cor. 13:6

F Its Relation to Believers, 2:13–17

13 [a]But we should always
give thanks to God for you,
[b]brethren beloved by the Lord,
because [c]God has chosen you
from the beginning [d]for salvation
[e]through sanctification by the
Spirit and faith in the truth.
14 And it was for this He
[a]called you through [b]our gospel,
that you may gain the glory of
our Lord Jesus Christ.
15 So then, brethren, [a]stand
firm and [b]hold to the traditions
which you were taught, whether
[c]by word *of mouth* or [c]by letter
from us.
16 [a]Now may our Lord Jesus
Christ [b]Himself and God our Father, who has [c]loved us and given
us eternal comfort and [d]good
hope by grace,
17 [a]comfort and [b]strengthen
your hearts in every good work
and word.

★13 [a]2 Thess. 1:3 [b]1 Thess. 1:4 [c]Eph. 1:4ff. [d]1 Cor. 1:21; 1 Thess. 2:12; 5:9; 1 Pet. 1:5 [e]1 Thess. 4:7; 1 Pet. 1:2
14 [a]1 Thess. 2:12 [b]1 Thess. 1:5
★15 [a]1 Cor. 16:13 [b]1 Cor. 11:2; 2 Thess. 3:6 [c]2 Thess. 2:2
★16–17
16 [a]1 Thess. 3:11 [b]1 Thess. 3:11 [c]John 3:16 [d]Titus 3:7; 1 Pet. 1:3
17 [a]1 Thess. 3:2, 13 [b]2 Thess. 3:3

2:7 *he who now restrains will do so until.* Antichrist is now being held back by a restrainer. Some understand this to be God indwelling His church by the Holy Spirit, while others see human government as the restraint. According to the former view, the removal will be at the rapture of the church (1 Thess. 4:13–18); according to the latter, at the overthrow of human government by Antichrist.

2:8 *then that lawless one will be revealed.* Paul's argument is: The day of the Lord will not begin until the Antichrist is revealed (v. 3); the Antichrist cannot begin to act until the restrainer is removed (v. 7); since the restrainer has not yet been removed, the Thessalonians could be certain that the day of the Lord had not yet begun, regardless of what the false teachers were saying.

2:11–12 The *deluding influence* comes from God; it is both a punishment and a moral result of their rejection of the truth (vv. 10, 12). These verses reflect the O.T. concept that God is sovereign even in the activities of the powers of evil (cf. Ex. 4:21; Josh. 11:20; 1 Kings 22:19–23; 1 Chron. 21:1; cf. 2 Sam. 24:1). The result will be that men will believe *what is false,* as Satan works through Antichrist.

2:13 *through sanctification by the Spirit and faith in the truth.* God's activity (the Holy Spirit's work of regeneration) and man's responsibility (faith) are equally necessary in salvation.

2:15 *the traditions.* I.e., all the teachings Paul had shared with the Thessalonians.

2:16–17 Paul's prayer for steadfastness on the part of the Thessalonians closes this crucial section. Notice the closing prayers of this letter: for their lives to be such as could be commended by the Lord (1:11–12), for their love and steadfastness (3:5), and for their peace (3:16).

IV EXHORTATIONS TO PRAYER AND DISCIPLINE, 3:1-15

A Paul's Confidence, 3:1-5

3 [a]Finally, brethren, [b]pray for
us that [c]the word of the Lord
may spread rapidly and be glorified, just as *it did* also with you;
2 and that we may be [a]deliv-
ered from perverse and evil men;
for not all have faith.
3 But [a]the Lord is faithful,
and He will strengthen and pro-
tect you from [b]the evil *one.*
4 And we have [a]confidence
in the Lord concerning you, that
you [b]are doing and will continue
to do what we command.
5 And may the Lord [a]direct
your hearts into the love of God
and into the steadfastness of
Christ.

1 [a]1 Thess. 4:1 [b]1 Thess. 5:25 [c]1 Thess. 1:8
★ 2 [a]Rom. 15:31
★ 3 [a]1 Cor. 1:9; 1 Thess. 5:24 [b]Matt. 5:37
4 [a]2 Cor. 2:3 [b]1 Thess. 4:10
★ 5 [a]1 Thess. 3:11

B Paul's Commands, 3:6-15

6 Now we command you,
brethren, [a]in the name of our
Lord Jesus Christ, that you [b]keep
aloof from every brother who
leads an [c]unruly life and not according to [d]the tradition which
you received from us.
7 For you yourselves know
how you ought to [a]follow our example, because we did not act in
an undisciplined manner among
you,
8 nor did we [a]eat anyone's
bread without paying for it, but
with [b]labor and hardship we *kept*
[c]working night and day so that
we might not be a burden to any
of you;
9 not because we do not
have [a]the right *to this,* but in order to offer ourselves [b]as a model
for you, that you might follow our
example.
10 For even [a]when we were
with you, we used to give you this
order: [b]if anyone will not work,
neither let him eat.
11 For we hear that some
among you are [a]leading an undisciplined life, doing no work at all,
but acting like [b]busybodies.
12 Now such persons we
command and [a]exhort in the Lord
Jesus Christ to [b]work in quiet
fashion and eat their own bread.
13 But as for you, [a]brethren,
[b]do not grow weary of doing
good.
14 And if anyone does not
obey our instruction [a]in this letter, take special note of that man
[b]and do not associate with him, so
that he may be [c]put to shame.
15 And *yet* [a]do not regard
him as an enemy, but [b]admonish
him as a [c]brother.

★ 6 [a]1 Cor. 5:4 [b]Rom. 16:17; 1 Cor. 5:11; 2 Thess. 3:14 [c]1 Thess. 5:14; 2 Thess. 3:7, 11 [d]1 Cor. 11:2; 2 Thess. 2:15
7 [a]1 Thess. 1:6; 2 Thess. 3:9
8 [a]1 Cor. 9:4 [b]1 Thess. 2:9 [c]Acts 18:3; Eph. 4:28
9 [a]1 Cor. 9:4ff. [b]2 Thess. 3:7
10 [a]1 Thess. 3:4 [b]1 Thess. 4:11
11 [a]2 Thess. 3:6 [b]1 Tim. 5:13; 1 Pet. 4:15
12 [a]1 Thess. 4:1 [b]1 Thess. 4:11
13 [a]1 Thess. 4:1 [b]2 Cor. 4:1; Gal. 6:9
★14 [a]Col. 4:16 [b]2 Thess. 3:6 [c]1 Cor. 4:14
★15 [a]Gal. 6:1 [b]1 Thess. 5:14 [c]2 Thess. 3:6, 13

V CONCLUDING BENEDICTION AND GREETING, 3:16-18

16 Now [a]may the Lord of
peace [b]Himself continually grant
you peace in every circumstance.
[c]The Lord be with you all!
17 I, Paul, write this greeting
[a]with my own hand, and this is a
distinguishing mark in every letter; this is the way I write.
18 [a]The grace of our Lord
Jesus Christ be with you all.

16 [a]Rom. 15:33 [b]1 Thess. 3:11 [c]Ruth 2:4
17 [a]1 Cor. 16:21
18 [a]Rom. 16:20; 1 Thess. 5:28

3:2 *perverse and evil men.* Those "who did not believe the truth" (2:10-12), Jews and Gentiles, whom Paul encountered in virtually every city he visited. His experiences at Thessalonica are recorded in Acts 17:5-10 and those at Corinth (where he wrote this letter) in Acts 18:6-17.

3:3 *But.* I.e., in contrast to this wickedness of men.

3:5 *steadfastness of Christ.* This may refer to our expectation of Christ's coming or it may mean that the endurance or steadfastness of Christ during His life on earth should be our example.

3:6 *who leads an unruly life.* Paul had instructed them on this point earlier (1 Thess. 4:1; 5:14).

3:14 *do not associate with him.* Idlers were to be ostracized from the company of believers in order to shame them into changing their ways. This was not formal excommunication but group disapproval and social ostracism, a serious thing for a believer in a heathen society at that time.

3:15 *admonish him.* The aim of the discipline was reformation and restoration of the offender.

INTRODUCTION TO THE FIRST LETTER OF PAUL TO TIMOTHY

AUTHOR: Paul DATE: 63

The Pastoral Epistles *The two letters to Timothy and the one to Titus are called the "Pastoral Epistles" because they contain principles for the pastoral care of churches and qualifications for ministers.*

Authorship *Some have questioned whether Paul himself wrote these letters, on the grounds that: (1) Paul's travels described in the Pastorals do not fit anywhere into the historical account of the book of Acts; (2) the church organization described in them is that of the second century; (3) the vocabulary and style are significantly different from that of the other Pauline letters. Those who hold to the Pauline authorship reply that: (1) there is no compelling reason to believe that Acts contains the complete history of the life of Paul. Since his death is not recorded in Acts, he was apparently released from his first imprisonment in Rome, traveled over the empire for several years (perhaps even to Spain), was rearrested, imprisoned a second time in Rome, and martyred under Nero. (2) Nothing in the church organization reflected in the Pastorals requires a later date (see Acts 14:23; Phil. 1:1). (3) The question of authorship cannot be decided solely on the basis of vocabulary, without considering how subject matter affects a writer's choice of words. Vocabulary used to describe church organization, for instance, would be expected to be different from that used to teach the doctrine of the Holy Spirit. There is no argument against Pauline authorship that does not have a reasonable answer. And, of course, the letters themselves claim to have been written by Paul.*

Background *Timothy, the son of a Greek Gentile father and a devout Jewish mother named Eunice, was intimately associated with Paul from the time of the second missionary journey, on (2 Tim. 1:5; Acts 16:1-3). When Paul wrote 1 Timothy, probably from Macedonia (1:3), he was on his way to Nicopolis (Tit. 3:12), but Timothy had been left in charge of the work in Ephesus and Asia Minor. Though Paul desired to visit Timothy (3:14; 4:13), this letter, in the meantime, would guide Timothy in the conduct of his pastoral responsibilities.*

Contents *In relation to Timothy personally, the theme is "fighting the good fight" (1:18). In relation to the church corporately, the theme is "behaving in the house of God" (3:15). Important subjects discussed in the epistle include the law (1:7-11), prayer (2:1-8), appearance and activity of women (2:9-15), qualifications for bishops or elders and for deacons (3:1-13), the last days (4:1-3), care of widows (5:3-16), and use of money (6:6-19).*

OUTLINE OF 1 TIMOTHY

I. Opening Greetings, 1:1-2
II. Instruction Concerning Doctrine, 1:3-20
A. Paul's Warning against False Doctrines, 1:3-11
B. Paul's Testimony Concerning the Grace of God, 1:12-17
C. Paul's Charge to Timothy, 1:18-20
III. Instruction Concerning Worship, 2:1-15
A. Prayer in the Church, 2:1-8
B. Women in the Church, 2:9-15
IV. Instruction Concerning Leaders, 3:1-16
A. Bishops, 3:1-7
B. Deacons, 3:8-16
V. Instruction Concerning Dangers, 4:1-16
A. Description of the Dangers, 4:1-5
B. Defenses against the Dangers, 4:6-16
VI. Instruction Concerning Various Duties, 5:1-6:21
A. Toward those Older and Younger, 5:1-2
B. Toward Widows, 5:3-16
C. Toward Elders, 5:17-25
D. Toward Masters and Slaves, 6:1-2
E. Toward False Teachers, 6:3-5
F. Toward Money and Godliness, 6:6-19
G. Toward One's Trust, 6:20-21

THE FIRST LETTER OF PAUL TO TIMOTHY

I OPENING GREETINGS, 1:1-2

1 Paul, [a]an apostle of [b]Christ Jesus [c]according to the commandment of [d]God our Savior, and of [b]Christ Jesus, *who is* our [e]hope;

2 to [a]Timothy, [b]*my* true child in *the* faith: [c]Grace, mercy *and* peace from God the Father and [d]Christ Jesus our Lord.

★ **1** [a]2 Cor. 1:1; 2 Tim. 1:1 [b]1 Tim. 1:12 [c]Titus 1:3 [d]Luke 1:47; Titus 1:3 [e]Col. 1:27
2 [a]Acts 16:1; 2 Tim. 1:2 [b]2 Tim. 1:2; Titus 1:4 [c]Rom. 1:7 [d]1 Tim. 1:12

II INSTRUCTION CONCERNING DOCTRINE, 1:3-20

A Paul's Warning against False Doctrines, 1:3-11

3 As I urged you upon my departure for [a]Macedonia, remain on at [b]Ephesus, in order that you may instruct certain men not to [c]teach strange doctrines,

4 nor to pay attention to [a]myths and endless [b]genealogies, which give rise to mere [c]speculation rather than [d]*furthering* the administration of God which is by faith.

5 But the goal of our [a]instruction is love [b]from a pure heart and a [c]good conscience and a sincere [d]faith.

6 For some men, straying from these things, have turned aside to [a]fruitless discussion,

7 [a]wanting to be [b]teachers of the Law, even though they do not understand either what they are saying or the matters about which they make confident assertions.

8 But we know that [a]the Law is good, if one uses it lawfully,

9 realizing the fact that [a]law is not made for a righteous man, but for those who are lawless and [b]rebellious, for the [c]ungodly and sinners, for the unholy and [d]profane, for those who kill their fathers or mothers, for murderers

10 and [a]immoral men and [b]homosexuals and [c]kidnappers and [d]liars and [e]perjurers, and whatever else is contrary to [f]sound teaching,

11 according to [a]the glorious gospel of [b]the blessed God, with which I have been [c]entrusted.

★ **3** [a]Rom. 15:26 [b]Acts 18:19 [c]Rom. 16:17; 2 Cor. 11:4; Gal. 1:6f.; 1 Tim. 6:3
★ **4** [a]1 Tim. 4:7; 2 Tim. 4:4; Titus 1:14; 2 Pet. 1:16 [b]Titus 3:9 [c]1 Tim. 6:4; 2 Tim. 2:23; Titus 3:9 [d]Eph. 3:2
5 [a]1 Tim. 1:18 [b]2 Tim. 2:22 [c]1 Tim. 1:19; 3:9; 2 Tim. 1:3; 1 Pet. 3:16, 21 [d]2 Tim. 1:5
6 [a]Titus 1:10
7 [a]James 3:1 [b]Luke 2:46
★ **8** [a]Rom. 7:12, 16
9 [a]Gal. 5:23 [b]Titus 1:6, 10 [c]1 Pet. 4:18; Jude 15 [d]1 Tim. 4:7
★**10** [a]1 Cor. 6:9 [b]Lev. 18:22 [c]Ex. 21:16; Rev. 18:13 [d]Rev. 21:8, 27; 22:15 [e]Matt. 5:33; 23:16 [f]1 Tim. 4:6; 6:3; 2 Tim. 1:13; 4:3; Titus 1:9, 13
11 [a]2 Cor. 4:4 [b]1 Tim. 6:15 [c]Gal. 2:7

B Paul's Testimony Concerning the Grace of God, 1:12-17

12 I thank [a]Christ Jesus our Lord, who has [b]strengthened me, because He considered me faithful, [c]putting me into service;

13 even though I was formerly a blasphemer and a [a]persecutor and a violent aggressor. And yet I was [b]shown mercy, because [c]I acted ignorantly in unbelief;

14 and the [a]grace of our Lord was more than abundant, with the [b]faith and love which are *found* in Christ Jesus.

15 [a]It is a trustworthy statement, deserving full acceptance, that [b]Christ Jesus came into the world to [c]save sinners, among whom [d]I am foremost *of all.*

12 [a]Gal. 3:26; 1 Tim. 1:1, 2, 15; 2:5; 6:13; Titus 1:4 [b]Acts 9:22; Phil. 4:13; 2 Tim. 4:17 [c]Acts 9:15
13 [a]Acts 8:3; Phil. 3:6 [b]1 Cor. 7:25; 1 Tim. 1:16 [c]Acts 26:9
14 [a]Rom. 5:20; 1 Cor. 1:13-16; 3:10; 2 Cor. 4:15 [b]1 Thess. 1:3; 1 Tim. 2:15; 4:12; 6:11; 2 Tim. 1:13; 2:22; Titus 2:2
★**15** [a]1 Tim. 3:1; 4:9; 2 Tim. 2:11; Titus 3:8 [b]Mark 2:17; Luke 15:2ff.; 19:10 [c]Rom. 11:14 [d]1 Cor. 15:9

1:1 *apostle.* Paul's title of authority, indicating his status above elders and deacons. An apostle had the right to expect obedience from the churches. *God our Savior.* 1 Timothy (here; 2:3; 4:10) and Titus (1:3; 2:10; 3:4) especially among N.T. books continue the O.T. title "Savior" applied to God, so frequent in the Psalms (106:21) and in Isaiah (45:21). The title also came to be ascribed to Christ (Phil. 3:20; Tit. 1:4).

1:3 *my departure for Macedonia.* This journey evidently occurred after the close of Acts (see the Introduction to Titus). *strange doctrines.* I.e., doctrines different from what Paul taught.

1:4 *myths and endless genealogies.* Mythical legends added to O.T. history which may have led to Gnostic teachings concerning emanations extending from God to the creation (see discussion of Gnosticism in the Introduction to 1 John).

1:8 *the Law is good.* When used lawfully, it restrains evil people.

1:10 *sound teaching.* Lit., healthy or wholesome doctrine in contrast to false, which is diseased. See also 6:3; 2 Tim. 1:13; 4:3; Tit. 1:9, 13; 2:1, 2.

1:15 *It is a trustworthy statement.* This formula, which introduces an axiomatic truth, appears only in the pastoral letters (here; 3:1; 4:9; 2 Tim. 2:11; Tit. 3:8). *I am foremost.* Paul considered himself the foremost of sinners even at the end of his illustrious life.

16 And yet for this reason I [a]found mercy, in order that in me as the foremost, Jesus Christ might [b]demonstrate His perfect patience, as an example for those who would believe in Him for eternal life.

17 Now to the [a]King eternal, [b]immortal, [c]invisible, the [d]only God, [e]*be* honor and glory forever and ever. Amen.

16 [a]1 Cor. 7:25; 1 Tim. 1:13 [b]Eph. 2:7
17 [a]Rev. 15:3 [Gr.] [b]1 Tim. 6:16 [c]Col. 1:15 [d]John 5:44; 1 Tim. 6:15; Jude 25 [e]Rom. 2:7, 10; 11:36; Heb. 2:7

C Paul's Charge to Timothy, 1:18–20

18 This [a]command I entrust to you, Timothy, [b]my son, in accordance with the [c]prophecies previously made concerning you, that by them you may [d]fight the good fight,

19 keeping [a]faith and a good conscience, which some have rejected and suffered shipwreck in regard to [b]their faith.

20 Among these are [a]Hymenaeus and [b]Alexander, whom I have [c]delivered over to Satan, so that they may be [d]taught not to blaspheme.

18 [a]1 Tim. 1:5 [b]1 Tim. 1:2 [c]1 Tim. 4:14 [d]2 Cor. 10:4; 1 Tim. 6:12; 2 Tim. 2:3f.; 4:7
19 [a]1 Tim. 1:5 [b]1 Tim. 6:12, 21; 2 Tim. 2:18
★20 [a]2 Tim. 2:17 [b]2 Tim. 4:14 [c]1 Cor. 5:5 [d]1 Cor. 11:32; Heb. 12:5ff.

III INSTRUCTION CONCERNING WORSHIP, 2:1–15

A Prayer in the Church, 2:1–8

2 First of all, then, I urge that [a]entreaties *and* prayers, petitions *and* thanksgivings, be made on behalf of all men,

2 [a]for kings and all who are in authority, in order that we may lead a tranquil and quiet life in all godliness and dignity.

3 This is good and acceptable in the sight of [a]God our Savior,

4 [a]who desires all men to be [b]saved and to [c]come to the knowledge of the truth.

5 For there is [a]one God, *and* [b]one mediator also between God and men, *the* [c]man Christ Jesus,

6 who [a]gave Himself as a ransom for all, the [b]testimony *borne* at [c]the proper time.

7 [a]And for this I was appointed a preacher and [b]an apostle ([c]I am telling the truth, I am not lying) as a teacher of [d]the Gentiles in faith and truth.

8 Therefore [a]I want the men [b]in every place to pray, [c]lifting up [d]holy hands, without wrath and dissension.

1 [a]Eph. 6:18
2 [a]Ezra 6:10; Rom. 13:1
3 [a]Luke 1:47; 1 Tim. 1:1; 4:10
★ 4 [a]Ezek. 18:23, 32; John 3:17; 1 Tim. 4:10; Titus 2:11; 2 Pet. 3:9 [b]Rom. 11:14 [c]2 Tim. 2:25; 3:7; Titus 1:1; Heb. 10:26
★ 5 [a]Rom. 3:30; 10:12; 1 Cor. 8:4 [b]1 Cor. 8:6; Gal. 3:20 [c]Matt. 1:1; Rom. 1:3
6 [a]Matt. 20:28; Gal. 1:4 [b]1 Cor. 1:6 [c]Mark 1:15; Gal. 4:4; 1 Tim. 6:15; Titus 1:3
7 [a]Eph. 3:8; 1 Tim. 1:11; 2 Tim. 1:11 [b]1 Cor. 9:1 [c]Rom. 9:1 [d]Acts 9:15
★ 8 [a]Phil. 1:12; 1 Tim. 5:14; Titus 3:8, [in Gr.] [b]John 4:21; 1 Cor. 1:2; 2 Cor. 2:14; 1 Thess. 1:8 [c]Ps. 63:4; Luke 24:50 [d]Ps. 24:4; James 4:8

B Women in the Church, 2:9–15

9 Likewise, *I want* [a]women to adorn themselves with proper clothing, modestly and discreetly, not with braided hair and gold or pearls or costly garments;

10 but rather by means of good works, as befits women making a claim to godliness.

11 [a]Let a woman quietly receive instruction with entire submissiveness.

12 [a]But I do not allow a

★ 9 [a]1 Pet. 3:3
11 [a]1 Cor. 14:34; Titus 2:5
★12 [a]1 Cor. 14:34; Titus 2:5

1:20 *Hymenaeus and Alexander.* How they made shipwreck of their faith (v. 19) is not stated, though the false teaching of Hymenaeus is described in 2 Tim. 2:17-18. *I have delivered over to Satan.* A remedial discipline (as in 1 Cor. 5:5), which excluded such persons from the help and fellowship of the church—a kind of last-resort punishment.

2:4 *who desires.* An expression of God's wish, not His decree.

2:5 *one mediator.* All other mediators are ruled out in bringing God and man together; Jesus mediates through His death on the cross (Heb. 9:15; 12:24).

2:8 *men.* I.e., males who are to lead in public prayer. *lifting up holy hands.* A common posture for prayer, and representative of the purity of life which is necessary for proper fellowship in prayer. *without wrath and dissension.* When these attitudes are present, prayer is impossible.

2:9 *proper clothing.* Respectable and honorable apparel reflects a godly woman's inner life. Elaborate interweaving of the hair with gold and pearls was discouraged; and orderliness, not ostentation, was the standard. *good works* (v. 10) will be their ornament.

2:12 *I do not allow a woman to teach.* Women are not to assume the office of teacher in the church (see 1 Cor. 14:34). Women may teach as long as they do not usurp the place of leadership and authority of men in the church. The injunction is based on the relationship of man and woman in the original creation (Gen. 2:18; 3:6).

woman to teach or exercise authority over a man, but to remain
quiet.
13 [a]For it was Adam who was
first created, *and* then Eve.
14 And *it was* not Adam *who*
was deceived, but [a]the woman
being quite deceived, fell into
transgression.
15 But women shall be preserved through the bearing of
children if *they* continue in [a]faith
and love and sanctity with self-re-
straint.

13 [a]Gen. 2:7, 22; 3:16; 1 Cor. 11:8ff. **14** [a]Gen. 3:6, 13; 2 Cor. 11:3 ★**15** [a]1 Tim. 1:14

IV INSTRUCTION CONCERNING LEADERS, 3:1–16

A Bishops, 3:1–7

3 [a]It is a trustworthy statement;
if any man aspires to the [b]of-
fice of overseer, it is a fine work
he desires *to do.*
2 [a]An overseer, then, must
be above reproach, [b]the husband
of one wife, [c]temperate, prudent,
respectable, [d]hospitable, [e]able to
teach,
3 [a]not addicted to wine or
pugnacious, but gentle, uncontentious, [b]free from the love of money.
4 *He must be* one who
[a]manages his own household
well, keeping his children under
control with all dignity
5 (but if a man does not
know how to manage his own
household, how will he take care
of [a]the church of God?);
6 *and* not a new convert, lest
he become [a]conceited and fall
into the [b]condemnation incurred
by the devil.
7 And he must [a]have a good
reputation with [b]those outside *the
church,* so that he may not fall
into reproach and [c]the snare of
the devil.

★ **1** [a]1 Tim. 1:15 [b]Acts 20:28; Phil. 1:1 ★ **2** [a]1 Tim. 3:2-4; Titus 1:6-8 [b]Luke 2:36f.; 1 Tim. 5:9; Titus 1:6 [c]1 Tim. 3:8 [d]Rom. 12:13 [e]2 Tim. 2:24 **3** [a]Titus 1:7 [b]1 Tim. 3:8; 6:10; Titus 1:7; Heb. 13:5 ★ **4-5** **4** [a]1 Tim. 3:12 **5** [a]1 Cor. 10:32; 1 Tim. 3:15 ★ **6** [a]1 Tim. 6:4; 2 Tim. 3:4 [b]1 Tim. 3:7 **7** [a]2 Cor. 8:21 [b]Mark 4:11 [c]1 Tim. 6:9; 2 Tim. 2:26

B Deacons, 3:8–16

8 [a]Deacons likewise *must be*
men of dignity, not double-
tongued, [b]or addicted to much
wine [c]or fond of sordid gain,
9 [a]*but* holding to the mystery of the faith with a clear conscience.
10 And [a]let these also first be
tested; then let them serve as deacons if they are beyond reproach.
11 Women *must* likewise *be*
dignified, [a]not malicious gossips,
but [b]temperate, faithful in all
things.
12 Let [a]deacons be [b]husbands
of *only* one wife, *and* [c]good man-

★ **8** [a]Phil. 1:1; 1 Tim. 3:12 [b]1 Tim. 5:23; Titus 2:3 [c]1 Tim. 3:3; Titus 1:7; 1 Pet. 5:2 ★ **9** [a]1 Tim. 1:5, 19 **10** [a]1 Tim. 5:22 ★**11** [a]2 Tim. 3:3; Titus 2:3 [b]1 Tim. 3:2 **12** [a]Phil. 1:1; 1 Tim. 3:8 [b]1 Tim. 3:2 [c]1 Tim. 3:4

2:15 *preserved through.* This may mean: (1) brought safely through childbirth; (2) saved through the birth of a Child, Jesus the Savior; or (3) that a woman's greatest achievement is found in her devotion to her divinely ordained role: to help her husband, to bear children, and to follow a faithful, chaste way of life.

3:1 *overseer.* Or bishop. Also referred to as an elder in the N.T. (see Tit. 1:5, 7, where the terms are used interchangeably). The elder, the principal official in a local church, was called by the Holy Spirit (Acts 20:28), recognized by other elders (1 Tim. 4:14), and qualified according to the standards listed in this passage. His duties included ruling (5:17), pastoring or shepherding the flock (Acts 20:28; 1 Pet. 5:2), guarding the truth (Tit. 1:9), and general oversight of the work, including finances (Acts 11:30).

3:2 *the husband of one wife* = married only once (see note on Tit. 1:6).

3:4–5 The elder's home provides him with a training-ground for the exercise of his leadership duties in the church.

3:6 *not a new convert.* Lest rapid advancement into a place of leadership cause him to become proud.

3:8 *Deacons.* The word means "minister" or "servant." Deacons were originally the helpers of the elders. Thus their qualifications were practically the same as those for the elders. The office had its beginnings in Jerusalem (Acts 6:1–6). However, the word deacon is used in an unofficial sense throughout the N.T. of anyone who serves (cf. Eph. 6:21), as well as in an official sense, designating those who occupy the office of deacon (cf. Phil. 1:1).

3:9 *the mystery of the faith.* I.e., the body of revealed doctrine. Truth must be united to a life lived with *a clear conscience.*

3:11 *Women.* Most likely a reference to the wives of the deacons, rather than to a separate office of deaconess, since the qualifications for deacons are continued in v. 12. If he had a different group in mind, it would seem more natural for Paul to have finished the qualifications for deacons before introducing the office of deaconess.

agers of *their* children and their
own households.

13 [a]Matt. 25:21

13 For those who have served
well as deacons [a]obtain for themselves a high standing and great
confidence in the faith that is in
Christ Jesus.

14 I am writing these things
to you, hoping to come to you before long;

★15 [a]1 Cor. 3:16; 2 Cor. 6:16; Eph. 2:21f.; 1 Pet. 2:5; 4:17 [b]1 Tim. 3:5 [c]Matt. 16:16; 1 Tim. 4:10 [d]Gal. 2:9; 2 Tim. 2:19

15 but in case I am delayed, *I
write* so that you may know how
one ought to conduct himself in
[a]the household of God, which is
the [b]church of [c]the living God,
the [d]pillar and support of the
truth.

★16 [a]Rom. 16:25 [b]John 1:14; 1 Pet. 1:20; 1 John 3:5, 8 [c]Rom. 3:4 [d]Luke 2:13; 24:4; 1 Pet. 1:12 [e]Rom. 16:26; 2 Cor. 1:19; Col. 1:23 [f]2 Thess. 1:10 [g]Mark 16:19; Acts 1:9

16 And by common confession great is [a]the mystery of godliness:

He who was [b]revealed in
the flesh,
Was [c]vindicated in the
Spirit,
[d]Beheld by angels,
[e]Proclaimed among the
nations,
[f]Believed on in the world,
[g]Taken up in glory.

V INSTRUCTION CONCERNING DANGERS, 4:1-16

A Description of the Dangers, 4:1-5

★ 1-5
1 [a]John 16:13; Acts 20:23; 21:11; [b]2 Thess. 2:3ff.; 2 Tim. 3:1; 2 Pet. 3:3; Jude 18 [c]1 John 4:6 [d]James 3:15
2 [a]Eph. 4:19
3 [a]Heb. 13:4 [b]Col. 2:16, 23 [c]Gen. 1:29; 9:3 [d]Rom. 14:6; 1 Cor. 10:30f.; 1 Tim. 4:4,

4 But [a]the Spirit explicitly says
that [b]in later times some will
fall away from the faith, paying
attention to [c]deceitful spirits and
[d]doctrines of demons,

2 by means of the hypocrisy
of liars [a]seared in their own conscience as with a branding iron,

3 *men* who [a]forbid marriage
and advocate [b]abstaining from
foods, which [c]God has created to
be [d]gratefully shared in by those
who believe and know the truth.

4 For [a]everything created by
God is good, and nothing is to be
rejected, if it is [b]received with
gratitude;

4 [a]1 Cor. 10:26 [b]Rom. 14:6; 1 Cor. 10:30f.; 1 Tim. 4:3

5 for it is sanctified by
means of [a]the word of God and
prayer.

5 [a]Gen. 1:25, 31; Heb. 11:3

B Defenses against the Dangers, 4:6-16

6 In pointing out these
things to [a]the brethren, you will
be a good [b]servant of Christ Jesus,
constantly nourished on the
words of the faith and of the
[c]sound doctrine which you [d]have
been following.

6 [a]Acts 1:15 [b]2 Cor. 11:23 [c]1 Tim. 1:10 [d]Luke 1:3 [Gr.]; Phil. 2:20, 22; 2 Tim. 3:10

7 But have nothing to do
with [a]worldly [b]fables fit only for
old women. On the other hand,
discipline yourself for the purpose
of [c]godliness;

★ 7 [a]1 Tim. 1:9 [b]1 Tim. 1:4 [c]1 Tim. 4:8; 6:3, 5f.; 2 Tim. 3:5

8 for [a]bodily discipline is
only of little profit, but [b]godliness
is profitable for all things, since it
[c]holds promise for the [d]present
life and *also* for the *life* to come.

★ 8 [a]Col. 2:23 [b]1 Tim. 4:7; 6:3, 5f.; 2 Tim. 3:5 [c]Ps. 37:9, 11; Prov. 19:23; 22:4; Matt. 6:33 [d]Matt. 6:33; 12:32; Mark 10:30

9 [a]It is a trustworthy statement deserving full acceptance.

9 [a]1 Tim. 1:15

10 For it is for this we labor
and strive, because we have fixed
[a]our hope on [b]the living God,
who is [c]the Savior of all men, especially of believers.

10 [a]2 Cor. 1:10; 1 Tim. 6:17 [b]1 Tim. 3:15 [c]John 4:42; 1 Tim. 2:4

11 [a]Prescribe and teach these
things.

11 [a]1 Tim. 5:7; 6:2

12 [a]Let no one look down on
your youthfulness, but *rather* in
speech, conduct, [b]love, faith *and*
purity, show yourself [c]an example of those who believe.

12 [a]1 Cor. 16:11; Titus 2:15 [b]1 Tim. 1:14 [c]Titus 2:7; 1 Pet. 5:3

3:15 *the truth.* I.e., the Christian faith.

3:16 This seems to be a summary of the truth contained in what was likely a part of an early Christian hymn. *He who was revealed in the flesh* refers to the incarnation of Christ (cf. 2 Tim. 1:10; Tit. 2:11). *vindicated in the Spirit.* The vindication of Christ by the Spirit in His resurrection. *Taken up in glory.* Christ's ascension into heaven.

4:1-5 Paul returns to his attack on heresy. False teaching is inspired by *demons* and promulgated by means of *the hypocrisy of liars.* The Christian should live affirmatively, neither renouncing the world for a life of self-denial nor plunging into indulgence (vv. 3-5).

4:7 *fables . . . for old women.* See note on 1:4.

4:8 *little.* The benefits of bodily training are limited and transient when contrasted with the extensive and permanent benefits of godliness.

★13 [a]1 Tim. 3:14 [b]2 Tim. 3:15ff.

13 [a]Until I come, give attention to the *public* [b]reading *of Scripture,* to exhortation and teaching.

★14 [a]1 Tim. 1:18 [b]Acts 6:6; 1 Tim. 5:22; 2 Tim. 1:6 [c]Acts 11:30 [Gr.]

14 Do not neglect the spiritual gift within you, which was bestowed upon you through [a]prophetic utterance with [b]the laying on of hands by the [c]presbytery.

15 Take pains with these things; be *absorbed* in them, so that your progress may be evident to all.

16 [a]Acts 20:28 [b]1 Cor. 1:21

16 [a]Pay close attention to yourself and to your teaching; persevere in these things; for as you do this you will [b]insure salvation both for yourself and for those who hear you.

VI INSTRUCTION CONCERNING VARIOUS DUTIES, 5:1–6:21

A Toward those Older and Younger, 5:1–2

1 [a]Lev. 19:32 [b]Titus 2:2 [c]Titus 2:6

5 [a]Do not sharply rebuke an [b]older man, *but rather* appeal to him as a father, *to* [c]the younger men as brothers,

2 the older women as mothers, *and* the younger women as sisters, in all purity.

B Toward Widows, 5:3–16

★ 3-16 3 [a]Acts 6:1; 9:39, 41; 1 Tim. 5:5, 16 4 [a]Eph. 6:2 [b]1 Tim. 2:3

3 Honor widows who are [a]widows indeed;

4 but if any widow has children or grandchildren, [a]let them first learn to practice piety in regard to their own family, and to make some return to their parents; for this is [b]acceptable in the sight of God.

5 [a]Acts 6:1; 9:39, 41; 1 Tim. 5:3, 16 [b]1 Cor. 7:34; 1 Pet. 3:5 [c]Luke 2:37; 1 Tim. 2:1; 2 Tim. 1:3

5 Now she who is a [a]widow, indeed, and who has been left alone [b]has fixed her hope on God, and continues in [c]entreaties and prayers night and day.

6 [a]James 5:5 [b]Luke 15:24; 2 Tim. 3:6; Rev. 3:1

6 But she who [a]gives herself to wanton pleasure is [b]dead even while she lives.

★ 7 [a]1 Tim. 4:11

7 [a]Prescribe these things as well, so that they may be above reproach.

8 [a]2 Tim. 2:12; Titus 1:16; 2 Pet. 2:1; Jude 4

8 But if any one does not provide for his own, and especially for those of his household, he has [a]denied the faith, and is worse than an unbeliever.

9 [a]1 Tim. 5:16 [b]1 Tim. 3:2

9 Let a widow be [a]put on the list only if she is not less than sixty years old, *having been* [b]the wife of one man,

10 [a]Acts 9:36; 1 Tim. 6:18; Titus 2:7; 3:8; 1 Pet. 2:12 [b]1 Tim. 3:2 [c]Luke 7:44; John 13:14 [d]1 Tim. 5:16

10 having a reputation for [a]good works; *and* if she has brought up children, if she has [b]shown hospitality to strangers, if she [c]has washed the saints' feet, if she has [d]assisted those in distress, *and* if she has devoted herself to every good work.

11 [a]Rev. 18:7

11 But refuse *to put* younger widows *on the list,* for when they feel [a]sensual desires in disregard of Christ, they want to get married,

12 *thus* incurring condemnation, because they have set aside their previous pledge.

13 [a]3 John 10 [Gr.] [b]2 Thess. 3:11 [c]Titus 1:11

13 And at the same time they also learn *to be* idle, as they go around from house to house; and not merely idle, but also [a]gossips and [b]busybodies, talking about [c]things not proper *to mention.*

14 [a]1 Tim. 2:8 [b]1 Cor. 7:9; 1 Tim. 4:3 [c]Titus 2:5 [d]1 Tim. 6:1

14 Therefore, [a]I want younger *widows* to get [b]married, bear children, [c]keep house, *and* [d]give the enemy no occasion for reproach;

4:13 *reading.* The public reading of the Scriptures, to be accompanied by *exhortation* (preaching) and *teaching.*

4:14 *the presbytery.* The body of elders.

5:3-16 Widows, who ordinarily would have no financial means of support, were to be cared for by their families, if possible (v. 4). If support were not available from that source, the church should care for them (in such cases the women were called *widows indeed,* v. 3). Younger widows were encouraged to remarry (v. 14), but those over 60 and destitute could be placed on the official relief roll of the church (v. 9). These "enrolled widows" constituted a kind of "order of widows," who were expected to devote themselves to prayer and good works (vv. 5, 10).

5:7 The meaning is: See that these regulations are followed so that both widows and their families will be above criticism in their conduct.

15 [a]1 Tim. 1:20 [b]Matt. 4:10
★16 [a]1 Tim. 5:4 [b]1 Tim. 5:10 [c]1 Tim. 5:3

15 for some [a]have already
turned aside to follow [b]Satan.
16 If any woman who is a believer [a]has *dependent* widows, let
her [b]assist them, and let not the
church be burdened, so that it
may assist those who are [c]widows
indeed.

C Toward Elders, 5:17–25

★17 [a]Acts 11:30; 1 Tim. 4:14 [Gr.]; 5:19 [b]Rom. 12:8 [c]1 Thess. 5:12
18 [a]Deut. 25:4; 1 Cor. 9:9 [b]Lev. 19:13; Deut. 24:15; Matt. 10:10; Luke 10:7; 1 Cor. 9:14
19 [a]Acts 11:30; 1 Tim. 4:14 [Gr.]; 5:17 [b]Matt. 18:16
★20 [a]Gal. 2:14; Eph. 5:11; 2 Tim. 4:2 [b]2 Cor. 7:11
21 [a]Luke 9:26; 1 Tim. 6:13; 2 Tim. 2:14; 4:1
★22 [a]1 Tim. 3:10; 4:14 [b]Eph. 5:11; 1 Tim. 3:2-7
★23 [a]1 Tim. 3:8
24 [a]Rev. 14:13

17 Let [a]the elders who [b]rule
well be considered worthy of
double honor, especially those
who [c]work hard at preaching and
teaching.
18 For the Scripture says,
"[a]YOU SHALL NOT MUZZLE THE OX
WHILE HE IS THRESHING," and "[b]The
laborer is worthy of his wages."
19 Do not receive an accusation against an [a]elder except on
the basis of [b]two or three witnesses.
20 Those who continue in sin,
[a]rebuke in the presence of all, [b]so
that the rest also may be fearful
of sinning.
21 [a]I solemnly charge you in
the presence of God and of Christ
Jesus and of *His* chosen angels, to
maintain these *principles* without
bias, doing nothing in a *spirit of*
partiality.
22 [a]Do not lay hands upon
any one *too* hastily and thus share
[b]*responsibility for* the sins of others; keep yourself free from sin.
23 No longer drink water *exclusively,* but [a]use a little wine for
the sake of your stomach and
your frequent ailments.
24 The sins of some men are
quite evident, going before them
to judgment; for others, their *sins*
[a]follow after.
25 Likewise also, deeds that
are good are quite evident, and
[a]those which are otherwise cannot be concealed.

25 [a]Prov. 10:9

D Toward Masters and Slaves, 6:1–2

★ 1-2
1 [a]Eph. 6:5; Titus 2:9; 1 Pet. 2:18 [b]Titus 2:5
2 [a]Acts 1:15; Gal. 3:28; Philem. 16 [b]1 Tim. 4:11

6 [a]Let all who are under the
yoke as slaves regard their
own masters as worthy of all hon-
or so [b]that the name of God and
our doctrine may not be spoken
against.
2 And let those who have
believers as their masters not be
disrespectful to them because
they are [a]brethren, but let them
serve them all the more, because
those who partake of the benefit
are believers and beloved. [b]Teach
and preach these *principles.*

E Toward False Teachers, 6:3–5

3 [a]1 Tim. 1:3 [b]1 Tim. 1:10 [c]Titus 1:1
★ 4-5
4 [a]1 Tim. 3:6 [b]1 Tim. 1:4 [c]Acts 18:15; 2 Tim. 2:14

3 If any one [a]advocates a
different doctrine, and does not
agree with [b]sound words, those of
our Lord Jesus Christ, and with
the doctrine [c]conforming to godliness,
4 he is [a]conceited *and* understands nothing; but he has a
morbid interest in [b]controversial
questions and [c]disputes about
words, out of which arise envy,
strife, abusive language, evil sus-
picions,

5:16 Relatives should assume the support of widows in their family (cf. vv. 4, 8).

5:17 *double honor.* Respect and remuneration (v. 18). The church was beginning to face the problem of financial support of its workers.

5:20 *Those who continue in sin.* I.e., elders who sin.

5:22 *lay hands . . . too hastily.* Often understood as forbidding hasty ordination, it may well refer to over-hasty receiving of a penitent backslider back into full fellowship.

5:23 *use a little wine.* The words imply that Timothy was a total abstainer and that the advice is given in relation to a medical problem.

6:1-2 The problems of the master-slave relationship are discussed in 1 Cor. 7:21; Eph. 6:5-9; Col. 3:22-4:1; Tit. 2:9-10; and Philem. 10-17. The N.T. writers do not question the institution of slavery, but try to mitigate it through improved attitudes of both masters and slaves. In the church, they met on equal terms as members of the fellowship, though there may have been instances when slaves were elders and thus, in the church, were over masters whom they served all week.

6:4-5 Again heretical teachers are excoriated. Perhaps they charged fees (v. 5).

5 and constant friction between [a]men of depraved mind
and deprived of the truth, who
[b]suppose that godliness is a
means of gain.

5 [a]2 Tim. 3:8; Titus 1:15 [b]Titus 1:11; 2 Pet. 2:3

F Toward Money and Godliness, 6:6-19

6 [a]But godliness *actually* is a
means of [b]great gain, when accompanied by [c]contentment.
7 For [a]we have brought
nothing into the world, so we cannot take anything out of it either.
8 And if we [a]have food and
covering, with these we shall be
content.
9 [a]But those who want to get
rich fall into temptation and [b]a
snare and many foolish and
harmful desires which plunge
men into ruin and destruction.
10 For [a]the love of money is a
[b]root of all sorts of evil, and some
by longing for it have [c]wandered
away from the faith, and pierced
themselves with many a pang.
11 But [a]flee from these
things, you [b]man of God; and
pursue righteousness, godliness,
[c]faith, [d]love, perseverance *and*
gentleness.
12 [a]Fight the good fight of
[b]faith; [c]take hold of the eternal
life [d]to which you were called,
and you made the good [e]confes-
sion in the presence of [f]many witnesses.
13 [a]I charge you in the presence of God, who gives life to all
things, and of [b]Christ Jesus, who
testified the [c]good confession
[d]before Pontius Pilate,

★ 6 [a]Luke 12:15-21; 1 Tim. 6:6-10 [b]1 Tim. 4:8 [c]Phil. 4:11; Heb. 13:5
7 [a]Job 1:21; Eccl. 5:15
8 [a]Prov. 30:8
9 [a]Prov. 15:27; 23:4; 28:20; Luke 12:21; 1 Tim. 6:17 [b]1 Tim. 3:7
10 [a]Col. 3:5; 1 Tim. 3:3; 6:9 [b]Rom. 11:16ff. [c]James 5:19
11 [a]2 Tim. 2:22 [b]2 Tim. 3:17 [c]1 Tim. 1:14 [d]2 Tim. 3:10
★12 [a]1 Cor. 9:25f.; Phil. 1:30; 1 Tim. 1:18 [b]1 Tim. 1:19 [c]Phil. 3:12; 1 Tim. 6:19 [d]Col. 3:15 [e]2 Cor. 9:13; 1 Tim. 6:13 [f]1 Tim. 4:14; 2 Tim. 2:2
13 [a]1 Tim. 5:21 [b]Gal. 3:26; 1 Tim. 1:12, 15; 2:5 [c]2 Cor. 9:13; 1 Tim. 6:12 [d]Matt. 27:2; John 18:37

14 that you keep the commandment without stain or reproach, until the [a]appearing of
our Lord Jesus Christ,
15 which He will bring about
at [a]the proper time—He who is
[b]the blessed and [c]only Sovereign,
[d]the King of kings and [e]Lord of
lords;
16 [a]who alone possesses immortality and [b]dwells in unap-
proachable light; [c]whom no man
has seen or can see. [d]To Him *be*
honor and eternal dominion!
Amen.
17 Instruct those who are rich
in [a]this present world [b]not to be
conceited or to [c]fix their hope on
the uncertainty of riches, but on
God, [d]who richly supplies us with
all things to enjoy.
18 *Instruct them* to do good,
to be rich in [a]good works, [b]to be
generous and ready to share,
19 [a]storing up for themselves
the treasure of a good foundation
for the future, so that they may
[b]take hold of that which is life indeed.

14 [a]2 Thess. 2:8
★15 [a]1 Tim. 2:6 [b]1 Tim. 1:11 [c]1 Tim. 1:17 [d]Deut. 10:17; Rev. 17:14; 19:16 [e]Ps. 136:3
16 [a]1 Tim. 1:17 [b]Ps. 104:2; James 1:17; 1 John 1:5 [c]John 1:18 [d]1 Tim. 1:17
17 [a]Matt. 12:32; 2 Tim. 4:10; Titus 2:12 [b]Ps. 62:10; Luke 12:20; Rom. 11:20; 1 Tim. 6:9 [c]1 Tim. 4:10 [d]Acts 14:17
18 [a]1 Tim. 5:10 [b]Rom. 12:8; Eph. 4:28
19 [a]Matt. 6:20 [b]1 Tim. 6:12

G Toward One's Trust, 6:20-21

20 O [a]Timothy, guard [b]what
has been entrusted to you, avoiding [c]worldly *and* empty chatter
and the opposing arguments of
what is falsely called "knowledge"—
21 which some have professed and thus [a]gone astray from
[b]the faith.
[c]Grace be with you.

20 [a]1 Tim. 1:2 [b]2 Tim. 1:12, 14 [c]1 Tim. 1:9; 2 Tim. 2:16
21 [a]2 Tim. 2:18 [b]1 Tim. 1:19 [c]Col. 4:18

6:6 In contrast to the material gain of the heretics (v. 5), the Christian finds his gain of a nonfinancial sort, *godliness* and *contentment,* or self-sufficiency, which results from an inner satisfaction with the situation that God has ordained for him.

6:12 *made the good confession.* Timothy's public confession of Christ at his baptism.

6:15 This (His appearing, v. 14) will be manifest at the proper time by *the blessed and only Sovereign.* In other words, the return of Christ (v. 14) will occur at the time ordered and appointed by God.

INTRODUCTION TO THE SECOND LETTER OF PAUL TO TIMOTHY

AUTHOR: Paul DATE: 66

Authorship *See Introduction to 1 Timothy.*

Background *See* Probable Order of Events *under the Introduction to Titus. Paul, imprisoned in Rome as the result of persecution under Nero, realized, when he wrote this letter, that his death was near (1:8, 16; 4:6–8). Alone and cold in his dungeon (4:10–12), the veteran missionary wrote his young son in the faith this intensely personal letter. Soon afterward, according to tradition, he was beheaded on the Ostian Way, west of Rome.*

Contents *The theme may be taken from 2:3, "a good soldier of Christ Jesus." Important subjects mentioned include the apostasy of the last days (3:1–9, cf. 1 Tim. 4:1–3), the inspiration of the Scriptures (3:16), and the crown of righteousness (4:8).*

OUTLINE OF 2 TIMOTHY

I. The Salutation, 1:1–2
II. The Expression of Thanks for Timothy, 1:3–7
III. The Call of a Soldier of Christ, 1:8–18
- A. A Call to Courage, 1:8–12
- B. A Call to Faithfulness, 1:13–18

IV. The Character of a Soldier of Christ, 2:1–26
- A. He Is Strong, 2:1–2
- B. He Is Single-minded, 2:3–4
- C. He Is Strict, 2:5–10
- D. He Is Secure, 2:11–13
- E. He Is Sound of Faith, 2:14–19
- F. He Is Sanctified, 2:20–23
- G. He Is a Servant, 2:24–26

V. The Caution for a Soldier of Christ, 3:1–17
- A. The Peril of Apostasy, 3:1–9
- B. The Protection from Apostasy, 3:10–17

VI. The Charge to a Soldier of Christ, 4:1–5
VII. The Comfort of a Soldier of Christ, 4:6–18
- A. A Good Finish to Life, 4:6–7
- B. A Good Future after Life, 4:8
- C. Good Friends in Life, 4:9–18

VIII. Concluding Greetings, 4:19–22

THE SECOND LETTER OF PAUL TO TIMOTHY

I THE SALUTATION, 1:1–2

★ 1 [a]2 Cor. 1:1 [b]Gal. 3:26; 1 Tim. 1:12; 2 Tim. 1:2, 9, 13 [c]1 Cor. 1:1 [d]1 Tim. 6:19
2 [a]Acts 16:1; 1 Tim. 1:2 [b]1 Tim. 1:2; 2 Tim. 2:1; Titus 1:4 [c]1 Tim. 1:2

1 Paul, [a]an apostle of [b]Christ
Jesus [c]by the will of God, according to the promise of [d]life in
Christ Jesus,
2 to [a]Timothy, my beloved
[b]son: [c]Grace, mercy *and* peace
from God the Father and Christ
Jesus our Lord.

II THE EXPRESSION OF THANKS FOR TIMOTHY, 1:3–7

3 [a]I thank God, whom I
[b]serve with a [c]clear conscience
the way my forefathers did, [d]as I
constantly remember you in my
prayers night and day,
4 [a]longing to see you, [b]even
as I recall your tears, so that I may
be filled with joy.

3 [a]Rom. 1:8 [b]Acts 24:14 [c]Acts 23:1; 24:16; 1 Tim. 1:5 [d]Rom. 1:9
★ 4 [a]2 Tim. 4:9, 21 [b]Acts 20:37

1:1 *life in Christ Jesus.* I.e., in union with Christ Jesus.
1:4 *your tears.* Possibly those shed at some parting, such as in Acts 20:37; or perhaps a reference to tears Paul knows Timothy has shed in the course of his service for Christ.

★ 5 [a]1 Tim. 1:5 [b]Acts 16:1; 2 Tim. 3:15

5 For I am mindful of the
[a]sincere faith within you, which
first dwelt in your grandmother
Lois, and [b]your mother Eunice,
and I am sure that *it is* in you as
well.

6 [a]1 Tim. 4:14

6 And for this reason I remind you to kindle afresh [a]the
gift of God which is in you
through [a]the laying on of my
hands.

★ 7 [a]John 14:27; Rom. 8:15

7 For God has not given us a
[a]spirit of timidity, but of power
and love and discipline.

III THE CALL OF A SOLDIER OF CHRIST, 1:8-18

A A Call to Courage, 1:8-12

★ 8 [a]Mark 8:38; Rom. 1:16; 2 Tim. 1:12, 16 [b]1 Cor. 1:6 [c]Eph. 3:1; 2 Tim. 1:16 [d]2 Tim. 2:3, 9; 4:5 [e]2 Tim. 1:10; 2:8

8 Therefore [a]do not be
ashamed of the [b]testimony of our
Lord, or of me [c]His prisoner; but
join with *me* in [d]suffering for the
[e]gospel according to the power of
God,

9 [a]Rom. 11:14 [b]Rom. 8:28f. [c]Rom. 11:29 [d]Eph. 2:9 [e]2 Tim. 1:1 [f]Rom. 16:25; Eph. 1:4; Titus 1:2

9 who has [a]saved us, and
[b]called us with a holy [c]calling,
[d]not according to our works, but
according to His own [b]purpose
and grace which was granted us
in [e]Christ Jesus from [f]all eternity,

★10 [a]Rom. 16:26 [b]2 Thess. 2:8; 2 Tim. 4:1, 8; Titus 2:11 [c]2 Tim. 1:1 [d]1 Cor. 15:26; Heb. 2:14f.

10 but [a]now has been revealed by the [b]appearing of our
Savior [c]Christ Jesus, who [d]abol-
ished death, and brought life and
immortality to light through the
gospel,

11 [a]1 Tim. 2:7

11 [a]for which I was appointed
a preacher and an apostle and a
teacher.

★12 [a]2 Tim. 1:8, 16 [b]Titus 3:8 [c]1 Tim. 6:20; 2 Tim. 1:14 [d]1 Cor. 1:8; 3:13; 2 Tim. 1:18; 4:8

12 For this reason I also suffer
these things, but [a]I am not
ashamed; for I know [b]whom I
have believed and I am convinced
that He is able to [c]guard what I
have entrusted to Him until [d]that
day.

B A Call to Faithfulness, 1:13-18

13 [a]2 Tim. 3:14; Titus 1:9 [b]Rom. 2:20; 6:17 [c]1 Tim. 1:10 [d]2 Tim. 2:2 [e]1 Tim. 1:14 [f]2 Tim. 1:1

13 [a]Retain the [b]standard of
[c]sound words [d]which you have
heard from me, in the [e]faith and
love which are in [f]Christ Jesus.

★14 [a]Rom. 8:9 [b]1 Tim. 6:20; 2 Tim. 1:12

14 Guard, through the Holy
Spirit who [a]dwells in us, the
[b]treasure which has been entrusted to *you.*

★15 [a]Acts 2:9 [b]2 Tim. 4:10, 11, 16

15 You are aware of the fact
that all who are in [a]Asia [b]turned
away from me, among whom are
Phygelus and Hermogenes.

★16-18
16 [a]2 Tim. 4:19 [b]2 Tim. 1:8 [c]Eph. 6:20

16 The Lord grant mercy to
[a]the house of Onesiphorus for he
often refreshed me, and [b]was not
ashamed of my [c]chains;

17 but when he was in Rome,
he eagerly searched for me, and
found me—

18 [a]1 Cor. 1:8; 3:13; 2 Tim. 1:12; 4:8 [b]Acts 18:19; 1 Tim. 1:3

18 the Lord grant to him to
find mercy from the Lord on [a]that
day—and you know very well
what services he rendered at
[b]Ephesus.

1:5 *Lois* is mentioned nowhere else. *your mother Eunice.* See Acts 16:1. Apparently both women had been converted under Paul's ministry.

1:7 *timidity.* cf. John 14:27 and Rev. 21:8. The believer is to have fear in the sense of awe (1 Pet. 1:17; 2:17) but not cowardice.

1:8 *the testimony of our Lord.* I.e., testifying, including by suffering, to our Lord.

1:10 *immortality* = deathlessness, imperishability.

1:12 *whom I have believed.* I.e., on whose trustworthiness I have staked my faith. *what I have entrusted.* Lit., the deposit. Paul's trust is well-founded, for God will preserve this deposit of faith in Christ until the day of judgment, when all dangers will be past. Some understand this to refer to God's deposit of gifts in Paul's life (as in v. 14 and 1 Tim. 6:20).

1:14 *the treasure.* Lit., the good deposit. I.e., the gospel.

1:15 *all who are in Asia.* I.e., all who are now in Asia who had formerly been with Paul in Rome. Asia was the Roman province embracing the western part of what is now called Asia Minor (Turkey). *Phygelus and Hermogenes* were a special disappointment to Paul and were known to Timothy.

1:16-18 *Onesiphorus,* who had ministered to Paul in Ephesus, sought him out in the dungeon where Paul was confined in Rome and ministered to him.

IV THE CHARACTER OF A SOLDIER OF CHRIST, 2:1–26

A He Is Strong, 2:1–2

★ 1 [a]2 Tim. 1:2 [b]Eph. 6:10 [c]2 Tim. 1:1

★ 2 [a]2 Tim. 1:13 [b]1 Tim. 6:12 [c]1 Tim. 1:18 [d]1 Tim. 1:12 [e][in Gr.] 2 Cor. 2:16; 3:5

2 You therefore, my [a]son, [b]be strong in the grace that is in [c]Christ Jesus.

2 And the things [a]which you have heard from me in the presence of [b]many witnesses, these [c]entrust to [d]faithful men, who will be [e]able to teach others also.

B He Is Single-minded, 2:3–4

3 [a]2 Tim. 1:8 [b]1 Cor. 9:7; 1 Tim. 1:18 [c]2 Tim. 1:1

★ 4 [a]2 Pet. 2:20

3 [a]Suffer hardship with *me,* as a good [b]soldier of [c]Christ Jesus.

4 No soldier in active service [a]entangles himself in the affairs of everyday life, so that he may please the one who enlisted him as a soldier.

C He Is Strict, 2:5–10

★ 5 [a]1 Cor. 9:25

5 And also if any one [a]competes as an athlete, he does not win the prize unless he competes according to the rules.

6 [a]1 Cor. 9:10

6 [a]The hard-working farmer ought to be the first to receive his share of the crops.

★7

7 Consider what I say, for the Lord will give you understanding in everything.

8 [a]Acts 2:24 [b]Matt. 1:1 [c]Rom. 2:16

8 Remember Jesus Christ, [a]risen from the dead, [b]descendant of David, [c]according to my gospel,

9 [a]2 Tim. 1:8; 2:3 [b]Phil. 1:7 [c]Luke 23:32 [d]1 Thess. 1:8 [e]Acts 28:31; 2 Tim. 4:17

★10 [a]Col. 1:24 [b]Luke 18:7; Titus 1:1 [c]2 Cor. 1:6; 1 Thess. 5:9 [d]1 Cor. 1:21 [e]2 Tim. 1:1; 2:1, 3 [f]2 Cor. 4:17; 1 Pet. 5:10

9 for which I [a]suffer hardship even to [b]imprisonment as a [c]criminal; but [d]the word of God [e]is not imprisoned.

10 For this reason [a]I endure all things for [b]the sake of those who are chosen, [c]that they also may obtain the [d]salvation which is in [e]Christ Jesus *and* with *it* [f]eternal glory.

D He Is Secure, 2:11–13

★11 [a]1 Tim. 1:15 [b]Rom. 6:8; 1 Thess. 5:10

11 [a]It is a trustworthy statement:

For [b]if we died with Him,
we shall also live with Him;
12 If we endure, [a]we shall also reign with Him;
If we [b]deny Him, He also will deny us;
13 If we are faithless, [a]He remains faithful; for [b]He cannot deny Himself.

12 [a]Matt. 19:28; Luke 22:29; Rom. 5:17; 8:17 [b]Matt. 10:33; 1 Tim. 5:8

★13 [a]Rom. 3:3; 1 Cor. 1:9 [b]Num. 23:19; Titus 1:2

E He Is Sound of Faith, 2:14–19

★14 [a]1 Tim. 5:21; 2 Tim. 4:1 [b]1 Tim. 6:4; 2 Tim. 2:23; Titus 3:9

14 Remind *them* of these things, and solemnly [a]charge *them* in the presence of God not to [b]wrangle about words, which is useless, *and leads* to the ruin of the hearers.

2:1 This verse seems to sum up the teaching of chapter 1: Timothy, you have the gift of power from God through Christ (1:7); now find your strength in this gift of grace.

2:2 *heard from me.* The content of Paul's teaching is not stated but was clearly understood by Timothy. *many witnesses.* Perhaps the elders at Timothy's ordination, or more likely the many who had at different times heard Paul's preaching.

2:4 *entangles.* A minister must put priority on his calling and be completely dedicated to his task and his Commander.

2:5 The picture in this verse is of an athlete who must play *according to the rules.* A minister must adhere to the requirements of his calling, making the Word and will of God his standard in all things.

2:7 *Consider.* If they would reflect on his teachings (in the previous verses), Christ would open up for them depths of meaning.

2:10 *For this reason.* I.e., because the Word of God remains unimprisoned (v. 9).

2:11 *died.* Perhaps a reference to the crucifixion of the sin nature, as in Gal. 2:20, but more likely a reference to physical death. I.e., if we die physically, we shall be raised physically.

2:13 *If we are faithless, He remains faithful.* A statement of the consistency of God's character, a strong promise to the believer of the security of his salvation even though he may lose all rewards (see 1 Cor. 3:15).

2:14 *wrangle about words.* I.e., indulge in word battles, wordy controversies, and quibbling about words. These are not only profitless but harmful to those who hear them.

★15 [a]Rom. 6:13; James 1:12 [b]Eph. 1:13; James 1:18

15 Be diligent to [a]present yourself approved to God as a workman who does not need to be ashamed, handling accurately [b]the word of truth.

16 [a]Titus 3:9 [b]1 Tim. 1:9; 6:20

16 But [a]avoid [b]worldly *and* empty chatter, for it will lead to further ungodliness,

★17 [a]1 Tim. 1:20

17 and their talk will spread like gangrene. Among them are [a]Hymenaeus and Philetus,

18 [a]1 Cor. 15:12 [b]1 Tim. 1:19; Titus 1:11

18 *men* who have gone astray from the truth saying that [a]the resurrection has already taken place, and thus they upset [b]the faith of some.

★19 [a]Is. 28:16f.; 1 Tim. 3:15 [b]John 3:33 [c]John 10:14; 1 Cor. 8:3 [d]Luke 13:27; 1 Cor. 1:2

19 Nevertheless, the [a]firm foundation of God stands, having this [b]seal, "[c]The Lord knows those who are His," and, "[d]Let every one who names the name of the Lord abstain from wickedness."

F He Is Sanctified, 2:20-23

★20-21
20 [a]Rom. 9:21

20 Now in a large house there are not only gold and silver vessels, but also vessels of wood and of earthenware, and [a]some to honor and some to dishonor.

21 [a]1 Tim. 6:11; 2 Tim. 2:16-18 [b]2 Cor. 9:8; Eph. 2:10; 2 Tim. 3:17

21 Therefore, if a man cleanses himself from [a]these *things,* he will be a vessel for honor, sanctified, useful to the Master, [b]prepared for every good work.

★22 [a]1 Tim. 6:11 [b]1 Tim. 1:14 [c]Acts 7:59 [d]1 Tim. 1:5

22 Now [a]flee from youthful lusts, and [a]pursue righteousness, [b]faith, love *and* peace, with those who [c]call on the Lord [d]from a pure heart.

23 [a]1 Tim. 6:4; 2 Tim. 2:14; Titus 3:9 [b]Titus 3:9; James 4:1

23 But refuse foolish and ignorant [a]speculations, knowing that they [b]produce quarrels.

G He Is a Servant, 2:24-26

24 [a]1 Tim. 3:3; Titus 1:7 [b]1 Tim. 3:2

24 And [a]the Lord's bond-servant must not be quarrelsome, but be kind to all, [b]able to teach, patient when wronged,

25 [a]Gal. 6:1; Titus 3:2; 1 Pet. 3:15 [b]Acts 8:22 [c]1 Tim. 2:4

25 [a]with gentleness correcting those who are in opposition, [b]if perhaps God may grant them repentance leading to [c]the knowledge of the truth,

★26 [a]1 Tim. 3:7 [b]Luke 5:10

26 and they may come to their senses *and escape* from [a]the snare of the devil, having been [b]held captive by him to do his will.

V THE CAUTION FOR A SOLDIER OF CHRIST, 3:1-17

A The Peril of Apostasy, 3:1-9

★ 1 [a]1 Tim. 4:1
2 [a]Phil. 2:21 [b]Luke 16:14; 1 Tim. 3:3; 6:10 [c]Rom. 1:30 [d]2 Pet. 2:10-12 [e]Luke 6:35 [f]1 Tim. 1:9
3 [a]Rom. 1:31 [b]1 Tim. 3:11 [c]Titus 1:8
4 [a]Acts 7:52 [Gr.] [b]Acts 19:36 [Gr.] [c]1 Tim. 3:6 [d]Phil. 3:19

3 But realize this, that [a]in the last days difficult times will come.

2 For men will be [a]lovers of self, [b]lovers of money, [c]boastful, [c]arrogant, [d]revilers, [c]disobedient to parents, [e]ungrateful, [f]unholy,

3 [a]unloving, irreconcilable, [b]malicious gossips, without self-control, brutal, [c]haters of good,

4 [a]treacherous, [b]reckless, [c]conceited, [d]lovers of pleasure rather than lovers of God;

2:15 *handling accurately.* I.e., correctly handling the Word of God, in both analysis and presentation—in contrast to the inane interpretations of false teachers.

2:17 *Hymenaeus and Philetus.* These troublemakers (Hymenaeus is also mentioned in 1 Tim. 1:20) were probably teaching that the doctrine of resurrection had only an allegorical or spiritual meaning. Gnostic teaching conceived of resurrection allegorically, as referring to acquaintance with truth and as occurring at baptism.

2:19 *seal.* A mark of authentication and ownership.

2:20-21 There will be some wicked persons (wood and earthenware) in every church, but (v. 21) no one need remain wicked.

2:22 *lusts.* Not only for immoral but also foolish things. Temptation is to be avoided by fleeing what hinders, by following what helps, and by seeking the company of spiritual people.

2:26 *held captive.* I.e., by Satan at Satan's will (see Eph. 2:3).

3:1 *in the last days.* The whole period between the writing of this letter and the Lord's return. As His return draws near, these characteristics will intensify (see 1 Tim. 4:1-5). The description that follows (vv. 2-9) is of mass corruption, of a breakdown of law and tradition.

★ 5 [a]Rom. 2:20 [b]1 Tim. 4:7 [c]1 Tim. 5:8 [d]Matt. 7:15; 2 Thess. 3:6
★ 6 [a]Jude 4 [b]1 Tim. 5:6; Titus 3:3 [c]Titus 3:3
7 [a]2 Tim. 2:25
★ 8 [a]Ex. 7:11 [b]Acts 13:8 [c]1 Tim. 6:5
9 [a]Luke 6:11 [Gr.] [b]Ex. 7:12; 8:18; 9:11

5 holding to a [a]form of [b]god-
liness, although they have [c]de-
nied its power; and [d]avoid such
men as these.
6 For among them are those
who [a]enter into households and
captivate [b]weak women weighed
down with sins, led on by [c]vari-
ous impulses,
7 always learning and never
able to [a]come to the knowledge of
the truth.
8 And just as [a]Jannes and
Jambres [b]opposed Moses, so these
men also oppose the truth, [c]men
of depraved mind, rejected as regards the faith.
9 But they will not make
further progress; for their [a]folly
will be obvious to all, [b]as also that
of those *two* came to be.

B The Protection from Apostasy, 3:10–17

10 [a]Luke 1:3 [Gr.]; Phil. 2:20, 22; 1 Tim. 4:6 [b]1 Tim 6:11
★11 [a]2 Cor. 12:10 [b]2 Cor. 1:5, 7 [c]Acts 13:14, 45, 50 [d]Acts 14:5 [e]Acts 14:19 [f]2 Cor. 11:23-27 [g]Rom. 15:31
★12 [a]John 15:20; Acts 14:22; 2 Cor. 4:9f.

10 But you [a]followed my
teaching, conduct, purpose, faith,
patience, [b]love, perseverance,
11 [a]persecutions, [b]sufferings,
such as happened to me at [c]Anti-
och, at [d]Iconium *and* at [e]Lystra;
what [f]persecutions I endured, and
out of them all [g]the Lord delivered me!
12 And indeed, all who desire
to live godly in Christ Jesus [a]will
be persecuted.
13 But evil men and impos-
tors [a]will proceed *from bad* to
worse, [b]deceiving and being deceived.
14 You, however, [a]continue
in the things you have learned
and become convinced of, knowing from whom you have learned
them;
15 and that [a]from childhood
you have known [b]the sacred writings which are able to [c]give you
the wisdom that leads to [d]salva-
tion through faith which is in
[e]Christ Jesus.
16 [a]All Scripture is inspired
by God and profitable for teaching, for reproof, for correction, for
training in righteousness;
17 that [a]the man of God may
be adequate, [b]equipped for every
good work.

13 [a]2 Tim. 2:16 [b]Titus 3:3
14 [a]2 Tim. 1:13; Titus 1:9
15 [a]2 Tim. 1:5 [b]John 5:47; Rom. 2:27 [c]Ps. 119:98f. [d]1 Cor. 1:21 [e]2 Tim. 1:1
★16 [a]Rom. 4:23f.; 15:4; 2 Pet. 1:20f.
17 [a]1 Tim. 6:11 [b]2 Tim. 2:21; Heb. 13:21

VI THE CHARGE TO A SOLDIER OF CHRIST, 4:1–5

4 [a]I solemnly charge *you* in the
presence of God and of
Christ Jesus, who is to [b]judge the
living and the dead, and by His
[c]appearing and His kingdom:
2 preach [a]the word; be ready
in season *and* out of season; [b]re-
prove, rebuke, exhort, with great
[c]patience and instruction.

★ 1 [a]1 Tim. 5:21; 2 Tim. 2:14 [b]Acts 10:42 [c]2 Thess. 2:8
★ 2 [a]Gal. 6:6; Col. 4:3; 1 Thess. 1:6 [b]1 Tim. 5:20; Titus 1:13; 2:15 [c]2 Tim. 3:10

3:5 *holding to a form of godliness.* Having the outer semblance of it without its spiritual dynamic.

3:6 *weak women.* These women, apparently because of sin, were changeable of mind, prone to accept new ideas and swayed by impulses.

3:8 *Jannes and Jambres.* Though these names do not appear in the O.T., in late Jewish, pagan, and certain early Christian writings they are applied to the Egyptian magicians who performed counterfeit miracles in opposition to Moses (Ex. 7:11, 22). They are symbols of the folly of opposing the truth.

3:11 *persecutions.* See Acts 13–14.

3:12 *to live godly.* Apparently involves an aggressive witness such as that Paul gave at the places listed in v. 11.

3:16 *All Scripture is inspired.* Lit., God-breathed; i.e., the Bible came from God through the men who wrote it (see 2 Pet. 1:21). God superintended these human authors so that, using their individual personalities, they composed and recorded without error God's Word to man. Christ attested to the fact that inspiration extends to the very words (Matt. 5:18; John 10:35). In the same verse, Paul quoted Deuteronomy and Luke as Scripture (1 Tim. 5:18), and Peter declared Paul's epistles to be Scripture (2 Pet. 3:16). Inspiration does not involve mechanical dictation but the accurate recording of God's words. Inspiration does not extend beyond the original manuscripts, though the texts we possess today have been transmitted with high accuracy.

4:1 *by His appearing and His kingdom.* When Christ appears, He will inaugurate the judgment and His faithful will be gathered into His kingdom.

4:2 *be ready in season.* I.e., always be ready, whether the time is opportune for preaching the gospel or not.

★ 3-4 3 a2 Tim. 3:1 b1 Tim. 1:10; 2 Tim. 1:13

3 For athe time will come
when they will not endure bsound
doctrine; but *wanting* to have
their ears tickled, they will accu-
mulate for themselves teachers in
accordance to their own desires;

4 a2 Thess. 2:11; Titus 1:14 b1 Tim. 1:4

4 and awill turn away their
ears from the truth, and bwill turn
aside to myths.

5 a1 Pet. 1:13 b2 Tim. 1:8 cActs 21:8 dLuke 1:1 eEph. 4:12; Col. 4:17

5 But you, abe sober in all
things, bendure hardship, do the
work of an cevangelist, dfulfill
your eministry.

VII THE COMFORT OF A SOLDIER OF CHRIST, 4:6-18

A A Good Finish to Life, 4:6-7

★ 6 aPhil. 2:17 bPhil. 1:23; 2 Pet. 1:14

6 For I am already being
apoured out as a drink offering,
and the time of bmy departure
has come.

★ 7 a1 Cor. 9:25f.; Phil. 1:30; 1 Tim. 1:18; 6:12 bActs 20:24; 1 Cor. 9:24 c2 Tim. 3:10

7 aI have fought the good
fight, I have finished bthe course, I
have kept cthe faith;

B A Good Future after Life, 4:8

★ 8 aCol. 1:5; 1 Pet. 1:4 b1 Cor. 9:25; 2 Tim. 2:5 c2 Tim. 1:12 dPhil. 3:11 e2 Tim. 4:1

8 in the future there ais laid
up for me bthe crown of righteousness, which the Lord, the
righteous Judge, will award to me
on cthat day; and not only to me,
but also to dall who have loved
His eappearing.

C Good Friends in Life, 4:9-18

9 aMake every effort to ★ 9-22 9 a2 Tim.
come to me soon; 1:4; 4:21; Ti-
10 for aDemas, having loved tus 3:12
bthis present world, has deserted ★10 aCol.
me and gone to cThessalonica; 4:14 b1 Tim.
Crescens *has gone* to dGalatia, 6:17 cActs
eTitus to Dalmatia. 17:1 dActs 16:6 e2 Cor. 2:13
11 aOnly bLuke is with me. ★11 a2 Tim.
Pick up cMark and bring him 1:15 bCol.
with you, dfor he is useful to me 4:14 cActs
for service. 12:12 dCol. 4:10; 2 Tim. 2:21
12 But aTychicus I have sent 12 aActs
to bEphesus. 20:4 bActs 18:19
13 When you come bring the ★13 aActs
cloak which I left at aTroas with 16:8
Carpus, and the books, especially
the parchments.
14 aAlexander the copper- ★14 aActs
smith did me much harm; bthe 19:33; 1 Tim.
Lord will repay him according to 1:20 bRom.
his deeds. 2:6; 12:19
15 Be on guard against him ★16 aActs 7:60; 1 Cor. 13:5
yourself, for he vigorously op-
posed our teaching. ★17 a1 Tim. 1:12; 2 Tim.
16 At my first defense no one 2:1 bTitus
supported me, but all deserted 1:3 c2 Tim.
me; amay it not be counted 4:5 dActs 9:15; Phil. 1:12ff.
against them. eRom. 15:31; 2 Tim.
17 But the Lord stood with 3:11 f1 Sam.
me, and astrengthened me, in or- 17:37; Ps.
der that through me bthe procla- 22:21
mation might be cfully accom- 18 a1 Cor.
plished, and that all dthe Gentiles 1:21 b1 Cor.
might hear; and I was edelivered 15:50; 2 Tim. 4:1; Heb.
out of fthe lion's mouth. 11:16; 12:22 cRom. 11:36; 2 Pet. 3:18
18 The Lord will deliver me

4:3-4 A description of people who were no longer content to hear the sound teaching of Paul, but who were impelled to turn to many different teachers of novelty and untruth.

4:6 *departure* = release. I.e., his death.

4:7 *the faith.* I.e., the recognized body of Christian doctrine (cf. Jude 3). Paul *kept* the faith in two senses: he was obedient to it, and he passed it on as he received it.

4:8 *laid up.* I.e., safely kept. *crown of righteousness.* One of the rewards (prizes) offered Christians, in this case for loving the coming of Christ. See note on 1 Cor. 3:14.

4:9-22 After a climactic testimony (vv. 6-8), Paul returns to treat worrisome, immediate personnel affairs.

4:10 Why *Demas* deserted Paul is not known.

4:11 *Mark* and Paul had overcome the differences that caused their earlier separation (Acts 15:36-41).

4:13 *the books.* Papyrus rolls. *the parchments.* Skins of vellum, used for more precious documents, in this case probably Paul's personal copies of portions of the O.T. This missionary-prisoner still wanted to study!

4:14 *Alexander.* Probably not the same as the one mentioned in 1 Tim. 1:20, since he is here identified as the coppersmith or metalworker. We may infer from v. 15 that he may have caused the arrest of Paul in some city, that he was still active, and that he was hostile to Paul's teachings.

4:16 *my first defense.* I.e., the preliminary hearing with which Paul's final trial opened (though some take this to mean Paul's first trial in Rome three years before).

4:17 *delivered out of the lion's mouth.* Paul was not immediately condemned and was spared from execution.

from every evil deed, and will
[a]bring me safely to His [b]heavenly
kingdom; [c]to Him *be* the glory
forever and ever. Amen.

VIII CONCLUDING GREETINGS, 4:19–22

★19 [a]Acts 18:2 [b]2 Tim. 1:16
19 Greet Prisca and [a]Aquila,
and [b]the household of Onesiphorus.
20 [a]Erastus remained at [b]Cor- ★20 [a]Acts 19:22 [b]Acts 18:1 [c]Acts 20:15
inth, but Trophimus I left sick at
[c]Miletus.
21 [a]Make every effort to ★21 [a]2 Tim. 4:9 [b]Titus 3:12
come before [b]winter. Eubulus
greets you, also Pudens and Linus
and Claudia and all the brethren.
22 [a]The Lord be with your 22 [a]Gal. 6:18; Phil. 4:23; Philem. 25 [b]Col. 4:18
spirit. [b]Grace be with you.

4:19 *Prisca and Aquila.* Devoted friends of Paul (Acts 18:2, 26; Rom. 16:3; 1 Cor. 16:19). *Onesiphorus.* See note on 1:16–18.

4:20 *Trophimus I left sick.* This happening cannot be fitted into Acts and thus indicates two imprisonments in Rome for Paul. Trophimus was an Ephesian (Acts 20:4; 21:29).

4:21 At least the four persons named here had not deserted Paul (v. 16). Nothing more is known of them.

INTRODUCTION TO THE LETTER OF PAUL TO TITUS

AUTHOR: Paul DATE: 65

Authorship *See the Introduction to 1 Timothy.*

Historical Background *The probable order of significant events is: (1) Paul was released from his house arrest in Rome (where we find him at the end of Acts), probably because his accusers did not choose to press their charges against him before Caesar (Acts 24:1; 28:30). Their case, therefore, was lost by default, and Paul was freed. (2) Paul visited Ephesus, left Timothy there to supervise the churches, and went on to Macedonia (northern Greece). (3) From there he wrote 1 Timothy (1 Tim. 1:3). (4) He visited Crete, left Titus there to supervise those churches, and went to Nicopolis in Achaia (southern Greece, Tit. 3:12). (5) Either from Macedonia or Nicopolis, he wrote this letter to encourage Titus. (6) He visited Troas (2 Tim. 4:13), where he was suddenly arrested, taken to Rome, imprisoned, and finally beheaded. (7) From Rome, during this second imprisonment, he wrote 2 Timothy.*

Titus *A Gentile by birth (Gal. 2:3), Titus was converted through the ministry of Paul (Tit. 1:4). He accompanied Paul to Jerusalem at the time of the apostolic council (Acts 15:2; Gal. 2:1-3). He was Paul's emissary to the church at Corinth during the third missionary journey (2 Cor. 7:6-7; 8:6, 16). Titus and two others took the letter we call 2 Corinthians to Corinth and urged the Corinthians to make good their promise to give to the poor in Jerusalem. Paul left Titus in Crete to use his administrative gifts to consolidate the work there. Artemas or Tychicus probably relieved Titus in Crete so he could join Paul in Nicopolis (Tit. 3:12), from where Paul sent him to Dalmatia (Yugoslavia) (2 Tim. 4:10). Tradition says he returned to Crete and died there.*

Contents *Important topics discussed in the letter include: qualifications for elders (1:5-9), instructions to various age groups (2:1-8), relationship to government (3:1-2), and the relation of regeneration to human works and to the Spirit (3:5).*

OUTLINE OF TITUS

I. Opening Greetings, 1:1-4
II. Elders in the Church, 1:5-9
- A. Their Desirability, 1:5
- B. Their Qualifications, 1:6-9

III. Offenders in the Church, 1:10-16
IV. Operation of the Church, 2:1-3:11
- A. Duties of the Minister, 2:1-10
- B. Living in Response to God's Grace, 2:11-15
- C. Demonstration of Good Works, 3:1-11
  1. In relation to governments, 3:1
  2. In relation to all people, 3:2-7
  3. In relation to false teachers, 3:8-11

V. Personal Messages and Greetings, 3:12-15

THE LETTER OF PAUL TO TITUS

I OPENING GREETINGS, 1:1–4

★ 1 [a]Rom. 1:1; James 1:1; Rev. 1:1 [b]2 Cor. 1:1 [c]Luke 18:7 [d]1 Tim. 2:4 [e]1 Tim. 6:3

1 Paul, [a]a bond-servant of God,
and an [b]apostle of Jesus
Christ, for the faith of those
[c]chosen of God and [d]the knowledge of the truth which is [e]ac-
cording to godliness,

2 [a]2 Tim. 1:1; Titus 3:7 [b]2 Tim. 2:13 [c]Rom. 1:2 [d]2 Tim. 1:9
3 [a]1 Tim. 2:6 [b]Rom. 16:25; 2 Tim. 4:17 [c]1 Tim. 1:11 [d]1 Tim. 1:1 [e]Luke 1:47; 1 Tim. 1:1; Titus 2:10; 3:4
★ 4 [a]2 Cor. 2:13 [b]2 Tim. 1:2 [c]2 Pet. 1:1 [d]Rom. 1:7 [e]1 Tim. 1:12; 2 Tim. 1:1

2 in [a]the hope of eternal life,
which God, [b]who cannot lie,
[c]promised [d]long ages ago,
3 but [a]at the proper time
manifested, *even* His word, in
[b]the proclamation [c]with which I
was entrusted [d]according to the
commandment of [e]God our Savior;
4 to [a]Titus, [b]my true child in
a [c]common faith: [d]Grace and
peace from God the Father and
[e]Christ Jesus our Savior.

II ELDERS IN THE CHURCH, 1:5–9

A Their Desirability, 1:5

★ 5 [a]Acts 27:7; Titus 1:12 [b]Acts 14:23 [c]Acts 11:30

5 For this reason I left you in
[a]Crete, that you might set in order what remains, and [b]appoint
[c]elders in every city as I directed
you,

B Their Qualifications, 1:6–9

★ 6 [a]1 Tim. 3:2-4; Titus 1:6-8 [b]1 Tim. 3:2 [c]Eph. 5:18 [d]Titus 1:10

6 namely, [a]if any man be
above reproach, the [b]husband of
one wife, having children who believe, not accused of [c]dissipation
or [d]rebellion.
7 For the [a]overseer must be
above reproach as [b]God's steward, not [c]self-willed, not quick-
tempered, not [d]addicted to wine,
not pugnacious, [e]not fond of sordid gain,
8 but [a]hospitable, [b]loving
what is good, sensible, just, devout, self-controlled,
9 [a]holding fast the faithful
word which is in accordance with
the teaching, that he may be able
both to exhort in [b]sound doctrine
and to refute those who contradict.

★ 7 [a]1 Tim. 3:2 [b]1 Cor. 4:1 [c]2 Pet. 2:10 [d]1 Tim. 3:3 [e]1 Tim. 3:3, 8
8 [a]1 Tim. 3:2 [b]2 Tim. 3:3
9 [a]2 Thess. 2:15; 1 Tim. 1:19; 2 Tim. 1:13 [b]1 Tim. 1:10; Titus 2:1

III OFFENDERS IN THE CHURCH, 1:10–16

10 [a]For there are many [b]re-
bellious men, [c]empty talkers and
deceivers, especially [d]those of the
circumcision,
11 who must be silenced because they are upsetting [a]whole
families, teaching [b]things they
should not *teach,* [c]for the sake of
sordid gain.
12 [a]One of themselves, a
prophet of their own, said, "[b]Cre-
tans are always liars, evil beasts,
lazy gluttons."
13 This testimony is true. For
this cause [a]reprove them [b]severe-
ly that they may be [c]sound in the
faith,
14 not paying attention to
Jewish [a]myths and [b]command-

10 [a]2 Cor. 11:13 [b]Titus 1:6 [c]1 Tim. 1:6 [d]Acts 11:2
11 [a]1 Tim. 5:4 [in Gr.]; 2 Tim. 3:6 [b]1 Tim. 5:13 [c]1 Tim. 6:5
★12 [a]Acts 17:28 [b]Acts 2:11; 27:7
13 [a]1 Tim. 5:20; 2 Tim. 4:2; Titus 2:15 [b]2 Cor. 13:10 [c]Titus 2:2
★14 [a]1 Tim. 1:4 [b]Col. 2:22 [c]2 Tim. 4:4

1:1 *for the faith . . . according to godliness.* Paul was commissioned to further the faith of God's elect so that they might acquire full knowledge of Christian truth.

1:4 *Titus.* He is not mentioned in Acts, but N.T. references to Titus' activities are found in 2 Cor. 2:13; 7:5–7, 13–14; 8:6, 16–17, 23; 12:18; Gal. 2:1, 3; 2 Tim. 4:10. *child.* A term of affection used also by Paul of Timothy and Onesimus.

1:5 *what remains.* A church is defective unless it has constituted leaders. In Crete these were appointed (= ordained) by Titus. See note on the elders at 1 Tim. 3:1.

1:6 *husband of one wife.* Wherever mentioned in the N.T., elders are seen as being married and as having children. This phrase may mean having only one wife at a time or it may mean being married only once (see 1 Tim. 5:9, where the similar phrase can only mean the latter). See also 1 Cor. 7:39 and 1 Tim. 5:14, where remarriage of a widow is permitted.

1:7 In Greek cities of the first century A.D. the vices described here were common.

1:12 Quoted from the Cretan poet Epimenides, who exaggerated for effect. To Cretanize was to lie.

1:14 *Jewish myths.* Speculations, of a Gnostic sort, supposedly based on O.T. scripture. For Gnosticism, see the Introduction to 1 John.

ments of men who [c]turn away
from the truth.

★15 [a]Luke 11:41; Rom. 14:20 [b]Rom. 14:14, 23 [c]1 Tim. 6:5

15 [a]To the pure, all things are
pure; but [b]to those who are defiled and unbelieving, nothing is
pure, but both their [c]mind and
their conscience are defiled.

16 [a]1 John 2:4 [b]1 Tim. 5:8 [c]Rev. 21:8 [d]Titus 3:3 [e]2 Tim. 3:8 [f]2 Tim. 3:17; Titus 3:1

16 [a]They profess to know
God, but by *their* deeds they [b]de-
ny *Him,* being [c]detestable and
[d]disobedient, and [e]worthless [f]for
any good deed.

IV OPERATION OF THE CHURCH, 2:1–3:11

A Duties of the Minister, 2:1–10

★ 1 [a]Titus 1:9

2 But as for you, speak the
things which are fitting for
[a]sound doctrine.

2 [a]Philem. 9 [b]1 Tim. 3:2 [c]Titus 1:13 [d]1 Tim. 1:2, 14

2 [a]Older men are to be
[b]temperate, dignified, [b]sensible,
[c]sound [d]in faith, in love, in perseverance.

★ 3 [a]1 Tim. 3:11 [b]1 Tim. 3:8

3 Older women likewise are
to be reverent in their behavior,
[a]not malicious gossips, nor [b]en-
slaved to much wine, teaching
what is good,
4 that they may encourage
the young women to love their
husbands, to love their children,

★ 5 [a]1 Tim. 5:14 [b]Eph. 5:22 [c]1 Tim. 6:1

5 *to be* sensible, pure,
[a]workers at home, kind, being
[b]subject to their own husbands,
[c]that the word of God may not be
dishonored.

6 [a]1 Tim. 5:1 [b]1 Tim. 3:2

6 Likewise urge [a]the young
men to be [b]sensible;

7 [a]1 Tim. 4:12

7 in all things show yourself
to be [a]an example of good deeds,
with purity in doctrine, dignified,

8 [a]2 Thess. 3:14; 1 Pet. 2:12

8 sound *in* speech which is
beyond reproach, in order [a]that
the opponent may be put to
shame, having nothing bad to say
about us.

9 [a]Eph. 6:5; 1 Tim. 6:1

9 Urge [a]bondslaves to be
subject to their own masters in
everything, to be well-pleasing,
not argumentative,

10 [a]Titus 1:3

10 not pilfering, but showing
all good faith that they may adorn
the doctrine of [a]God our Savior in
every respect.

B Living in Response to God's Grace, 2:11–15

★11 [a]2 Tim. 1:10; Titus 3:4 [b]1 Tim. 2:4

11 For the grace of God has
[a]appeared, [b]bringing salvation to
all men,

★12 [a]1 Tim. 6:9; Titus 3:3 [b]2 Tim. 3:12 [c]1 Tim. 6:17

12 instructing us to deny ungodliness and [a]worldly desires
and [b]to live sensibly, righteously
and godly [c]in the present age,

13 [a]2 Thess. 2:8 [b]1 Tim. 1:1; 2 Tim. 1:2; Titus 1:4; 2 Pet. 1:1

13 looking for the blessed
hope and the [a]appearing of the
glory of [b]our great God and Savior, Christ Jesus;

★14 [a]1 Tim. 2:6 [b]Ps. 130:8; 1 Pet. 1:18f. [c]Ezek. 37:23; Heb. 1:3; 9:14; 1 John 1:7 [d]Ex. 19:5; Deut. 14:2; Eph. 1:11; 1 Pet. 2:9 [e]Eph. 2:10; Titus 3:8; 1 Pet. 3:13

14 who [a]gave Himself for us,
[b]that HE MIGHT REDEEM US FROM EV-
ERY LAWLESS DEED and [c]PURIFY FOR
HIMSELF A [d]PEOPLE FOR HIS OWN POS-
SESSION, [e]zealous for good deeds.

15 [a]1 Tim. 4:13; 5:20; 2 Tim. 4:2 [b]1 Tim. 4:12

15 These things speak and
[a]exhort and [a]reprove with all authority. [b]Let no one disregard
you.

C Demonstration of Good Works, 3:1–11

1 In relation to governments, 3:1

★ 1 [a]2 Tim. 2:14 [b]Rom. 13:1 [c]2 Tim. 2:21

3 [a]Remind them [b]to be subject
to rulers, to authorities, to be
obedient, to be [c]ready for every
good deed,

1:15 Purity is an interior matter, of the mind and conscience, not external. See Luke 11:41.

2:1 *But.* I.e., in contrast to false teachers. *sound doctrine.* Lit., healthy teaching (as in 1:9, 13; 2:2). That which causes behavior to be in accord with belief.

2:3 *malicious gossips.* Apparently some of the older women were given to gossiping and drinking.

2:5 *that the word of God may not be dishonored.* Failure to observe the matters mentioned in this verse would expose the Word of God to contempt by the world.

2:11 *appeared.* The tense of the verb indicates a reference to the incarnation, Christ's first appearing.

2:12 *ungodliness* = irreverence. *worldly desires* = passions, overpowering attractions for the secular world.

2:14 *redeem us from every lawless deed.* I.e., release us from the bondage of sin. See note on redemption at Eph. 1:7.

3:1 *be subject* = to submit or subject oneself. The same Greek word is used in Rom. 13:1

2 *In relation to all people,* 3:2–7

2 to malign no one, [a]to be
uncontentious, [a]gentle, [b]showing
every consideration for all men.
3 [a]For we also once were
foolish ourselves, [b]disobedient,
[c]deceived, [d]enslaved to [e]various
lusts and pleasures, spending our
life in [f]malice and [f]envy, hateful,
hating one another.
4 But when the [a]kindness of
[b]God our Savior and *His* love for
mankind [c]appeared,
5 [a]He saved us, [b]not on the
basis of deeds which we have
done in righteousness, but [c]ac-
cording to His mercy, by the
[d]washing of regeneration and [e]re-
newing by the Holy Spirit,
6 [a]whom He poured out
upon us [b]richly through Jesus
Christ our Savior,
7 that being justified by His
grace we might be made [a]heirs
according to *the* hope of eternal
life.

★ 2 [a]1 Tim. 3:3; 1 Pet. 2:18 [b]2 Tim. 2:25
3 [a]Rom. 11:30; 1 Cor. 6:11; Col. 3:7 [b]Titus 1:16 [c]2 Tim. 3:13 [d]Rom. 6:6, 12 [e]2 Tim. 3:6; Titus 2:12 [f]Rom. 1:29
4 [a]Rom. 2:4; Eph. 2:7; 1 Pet. 2:3 [b]Titus 2:10 [c]Titus 2:11
★ 5 [a]Rom. 11:14; 2 Tim. 1:9 [b]Eph. 2:9 [c]Eph. 2:4; 1 Pet. 1:3 [d]John 3:5; Eph. 5:26; 1 Pet. 3:21 [e]Rom. 12:2
6 [a]Rom. 5:5 [b]Rom. 2:4; 1 Tim. 6:17
7 [a]Matt. 25:34; Mark 10:17; Rom. 8:17, 24; Titus 1:2

3 *In relation to false teachers,* 3:8–11

8 [a]This is a trustworthy
statement; and concerning these
things I [b]want you to speak confidently, so that those who have
[c]believed God may be careful to
[d]engage in good deeds. These
things are good and profitable for
men.
9 But [a]shun [b]foolish controversies and [c]genealogies and strife
and [d]disputes about the Law; for
they are [e]unprofitable and worthless.
10 [a]Reject a [b]factious man
[c]after a first and second warning,
11 knowing that such a man
is [a]perverted and is sinning, being
self-condemned.

★ 8 [a]1 Tim. 1:15 [b]1 Tim. 2:8 [c]2 Tim. 1:12 [d]Titus 2:7, 14; 3:14
9 [a]2 Tim. 2:16 [b]1 Tim. 1:4; 2 Tim. 2:23 [c]1 Tim. 1:4 [d]James 4:1 [e]2 Tim. 2:14
★10 [a]2 John 10 [b]Rom. 16:17 [c]Matt. 18:15f.
★11 [a]Titus 1:14

V PERSONAL MESSAGES AND GREETINGS, 3:12–15

12 When I send Artemas or
[a]Tychicus to you, [b]make every effort to come to me at [c]Nicopolis,
for I have decided to [d]spend the
winter there.
13 [a]Diligently help Zenas the
[b]lawyer and [c]Apollos on their
way so that nothing is lacking for
them.
14 And let [a]our *people* also
learn to [b]engage in good deeds to
meet [c]pressing needs, that they
may not be [d]unfruitful.
15 [a]All who are with me greet
you. Greet those who love us [b]in
the faith.
[c]Grace be with you all.

★12 [a]Acts 20:4; 2 Tim. 4:12 [b]2 Tim. 4:9 [c]2 Tim. 4:10 [d]2 Tim. 4:21
★13 [a]Acts 15:3 [b]Matt. 22:35 [c]Acts 18:24
14 [a]Titus 2:8 [b]Titus 3:8 [c]Rom. 12:13; Phil. 4:16 [d]Matt. 7:19; Phil. 1:11; Col. 1:10
15 [a]Acts 20:34 [b]1 Tim. 1:2 [c]Col. 4:18

---

and 1 Pet 2:13. *rulers . . . authorities* usually refer to angels (good angels as in Eph. 3:10 or evil angels as in Eph. 6:12), but here the reference is to human, governmental rulers. Though Christians are a "special" people elected by God, redeemed from the world and no longer dependent upon it, they are not above the necessity of getting along with the civil authorities who govern them.

3:2 *uncontentious.* Quarreling only arouses the hostility of non-Christians. Christian virtues are of an opposite sort.

3:5 *not on the basis of deeds . . . by the washing of regeneration.* Personal salvation is not achieved through good deeds but through the cleansing of the new birth. *renewing by the Holy Spirit* means either the initial act of conversion or, more probably, continual renewing by the Spirit throughout the life of the believer. In any case, salvation is God's gracious work, not a reward for man's worthwhile acts.

3:8 *these things.* I.e., the counsels of vv. 1–7. *engage in good deeds* probably has the general meaning of "apply oneself to good deeds," though the phrase may have the technical meaning of "enter honorable occupations."

3:10 *factious* —one who willfully chooses for himself and sets up a faction (see 1 Cor. 11:19; Gal. 5:20). Our responsibility is to reprimand such a person twice, then avoid him if he does not change.

3:11 *perverted.* Turned aside, and hence, self-condemned.

3:12 *Artemas.* Nothing more is known of him. *Tychicus.* See Acts 20:4; Eph. 6:21; Col. 4:7; 2 Tim. 4:12.

3:13 *Zenas.* Nothing more is known of him. *Apollos.* The well-known associate of Paul.

INTRODUCTION TO THE LETTER OF PAUL TO PHILEMON

AUTHOR: Paul DATE: 61

Background *Like Ephesians, Philippians, and Colossians, Philemon is one of the Prison Epistles, written during Paul's first confinement in Rome. Onesimus, one of the millions of slaves in the Roman Empire, had stolen from his master, Philemon, and had run away. Eventually, he made his way to Rome, where he crossed the path of the apostle Paul, who led him to faith in Christ (v. 10). Now Onesimus was faced with doing his Christian duty toward his master by returning to him. Since death would normally have been his punishment, Paul wrote this wonderful letter of intercession on Onesimus' behalf.*

Philemon was not the only slaveholder in the Colossian church (see Col. 4:1), so this letter gave guidelines for other Christian masters in their relationships to their slave-brothers. Paul did not deny the rights of Philemon over his slave, but he asked Philemon to relate the principle of Christian brotherhood to the situation with Onesimus (v. 16). At the same time, Paul offered to pay personally whatever Onesimus owed. This letter is not an attack against slavery as such, but a suggestion as to how Christian masters and slaves could live their faith within that evil system. It is possible that Philemon did free Onesimus and send him back to Paul (v. 14). It has also been suggested that Onesimus became a minister and later bishop of the church at Ephesus (Ignatius, To the Ephesians, *1).*

This is the most personal of all Paul's letters.

OUTLINE OF PHILEMON

I. Greetings, 1-3
II. Praise of Philemon, 4-7
III. Plea to Philemon, 8-17
IV. Pledge to Philemon, 18-21
V. Personal Matters, 22-25

THE LETTER OF PAUL TO PHILEMON

I GREETINGS, 1-3

★ 1 [a]Phil. 1:1 [b]Eph. 3:1; Philem. 9, 23 [c]Gal. 3:26; 1 Tim. 1:12; Philem. 9, 23 [d]2 Cor. 1:1 [e]Phil. 2:25 ★ 2 [a]Rom. 16:1 [b]Col. 4:17 [c]Phil. 2:25; 2 Tim. 2:3 [d]Rom. 16:5 3 [a]Rom. 1:7

1 [a]Paul, [b]a prisoner of [c]Christ
Jesus, and [d]Timothy our
brother, to Philemon our beloved
brother and [e]fellow-worker,
2 and to Apphia [a]our sister,
and to [b]Archippus our [c]fellow-
soldier, and to [d]the church in
your house:
3 [a]Grace to you and peace
from God our Father and the Lord
Jesus Christ.

II PRAISE OF PHILEMON, 4-7

4 [a]I thank my God always,
[b]making mention of you in my
prayers,
5 because I [a]hear of your
love, and of the faith which you
have toward the Lord Jesus, and
toward all the saints;
6 *and I pray* that the fellowship of your faith may become effective through the [a]knowledge of
every good thing which is in you
for Christ's sake.

4 [a]Rom. 1:8 [b]Rom. 1:9 5 [a]Eph. 1:15; Col. 1:4; 1 Thess. 3:6 ★ 6 [a]Phil. 1:9; Col. 1:9; 3:10

---

1 *a prisoner of Christ Jesus.* Better, for Jesus Christ; i.e., for His sake, in His service.
2 *Apphia* was likely Philemon's wife; and *Archippus,* his son.
6 *fellowship* = sharing.

7 [a]2 Cor. 7:4, 13 [b]1 Cor. 16:18; 2 Cor. 7:13; Philem. 20

7 For I have come to have
much [a]joy and comfort in your
love, because the hearts of the
saints have been [b]refreshed
through you, brother.

III PLEA TO PHILEMON, 8–17

★ 8–10
8 [a]2 Cor. 3:12; 1 Thess. 2:6 [b]Eph. 5:4
9 [a]Rom. 12:1 [b]Titus 2:2 [c]Philem. 1 [d]Gal. 3:26; 1 Tim. 1:12; Philem. 9, 23
10 [a]Rom. 12:1 [b]1 Cor. 4:14f. [c]Col. 4:9
13 [a]Phil. 1:7; Philem. 10
★14 [a]2 Cor. 9:7; 1 Pet. 5:2
★15 [a]Gen. 45:5, 8
★16 [a]1 Cor. 7:22 [b]Matt. 23:8; 1 Tim. 6:2 [c]Eph. 6:5; Col. 3:22

8 Therefore, [a]though I have
enough confidence in Christ to
order you *to do* that which is
[b]proper,
9 yet for love's sake I rather
[a]appeal *to you*—since I am such a
person as Paul, the [b]aged, and
now also [c]a prisoner of [d]Christ
Jesus—
10 I [a]appeal to you for my
[b]child, whom I have begotten in
my imprisonment, [c]Onesimus,
11 who formerly was useless
to you, but now is useful both to
you and to me.
12 And I have sent him back
to you in person, that is, *sending*
my very heart,
13 whom I wished to keep
with me, that in your behalf he
might minister to me in my [a]im-
prisonment for the gospel;
14 but without your consent I
did not want to do anything, that
your goodness should [a]not be as
it were by compulsion, but of
your own free will.
15 For perhaps [a]he was for
this reason parted *from you* for a
while, that you should have him
back forever,
16 [a]no longer as a slave, but
more than a slave, [b]a beloved
brother, especially to me, but how
much more to you, both [c]in the
flesh and in the Lord.
17 If then you regard me a
[a]partner, accept him as *you would*
me.

17 [a]2 Cor. 8:23; Philem. 6

IV PLEDGE TO PHILEMON, 18–21

★18
★19 [a]1 Cor. 16:21; 2 Cor. 10:1; Gal. 5:2 [b]2 Cor. 9:4
20 [a]Philem. 7
21 [a]2 Cor. 2:3

18 But if he has wronged you
in any way, or owes you anything, charge that to my account;
19 [a]I, Paul, am writing this
with my own hand, I will repay it
([b]lest I should mention to you
that you owe to me even your
own self as well).
20 Yes, brother, let me benefit from you in the Lord; [a]refresh
my heart in Christ.
21 [a]Having confidence in
your obedience, I write to you,
since I know that you will do even
more than what I say.

V PERSONAL MATTERS, 22–25

★22 [a]Acts 28:23 [b]Phil. 1:25; 2:24 [c]2 Cor. 1:11 [d]Acts 27:24; Heb. 13:19
23 [a]Col. 1:7 [b]Rom. 16:7 [c]Philem. 1
24 [a]Acts 12:12 [b]Acts 19:29; Col. 4:10 [c]Col. 4:14 [d]Philem. 1
25 [a]Gal. 6:18 [b]2 Tim. 4:22

22 And at the same time also
prepare me a [a]lodging; for [b]I hope
that through [c]your prayers [d]I
shall be given to you.
23 [a]Epaphras, my [b]fellow
prisoner in [c]Christ Jesus, greets
you,
24 *as do* [a]Mark, [b]Aristarchus,
[c]Demas, [c]Luke, my [d]fellow-work-
ers.
25 [a]The grace of the Lord
Jesus Christ be [b]with your spirit.

8–10 Paul could use his authority as an apostle to *order* Philemon. Instead Paul used the persuasions of love, age, and his imprisoned state, and simply appealed to Philemon (v. 10). The name *Onesimus* means useful, beneficial.

14 *your goodness.* I.e., Philemon's goodness, if he decided to send Onesimus back to serve Paul.

15 *perhaps.* A suggestion of a deeper purpose of God's providence in Onesimus' running away.

16 *a beloved brother.* Not legal emancipation for Onesimus, but a practical emancipation because of Philemon's changed attitude toward his slave, who was now also his brother in Christ.

18 *charge that to my account.* This Greek phrase is translated "imputed" in Rom. 5:13. It seems that Onesimus' offense included monetary loss to Philemon in addition to loss caused by the slave's running away. Paul asked Philemon to impute or reckon Onesimus' debt against Paul's account and to *accept him as you would me* (v. 17), a beautiful illustration of our sin imputed to Christ, wherein God receives us in the merit of His Son (2 Cor. 5:21).

19 *you owe to me even your own self.* Philemon was apparently converted under Paul's ministry.

22 *I shall be given to you.* Paul expected to be released from prison soon (see Phil. 1:25–26).

INTRODUCTION TO THE LETTER TO THE HEBREWS

AUTHOR: Uncertain DATE: 64-68

Authorship *Many suggestions have been made for the author of this anonymous book—Paul, Barnabas, Apollos, Silas, Aquila and Priscilla, and Clement of Rome. There are both resemblances and dissimilarities to the theology and style of Paul, but Paul frequently appeals to his own apostolic authority in his letters, while this writer appeals to others who were eyewitnesses of Jesus' ministry (2:3). It is safest to say, as did the theologian Origen in the third century, that only God knows who wrote Hebrews.*

Readership *Three questions are involved in determining the readership of this letter. (1) What was the racial background of these readers? Although some have held that they were Gentiles, all evidence points to their Jewish background—the title of the book, "to the Hebrews," the references to the prophets and angels ministering to Israel, and the citations concerning the Levitical worship. (2) Where did they live? Palestine or Italy have been the answers most often given. The preference seems to be Italy, for these readers were not poor (and the saints in Palestine were, 6:10; 10:34; Rom. 15:26); the Septuagint is used exclusively for quotations from the Old Testament (one would not expect this if the readers were Palestinian); and "those from Italy greet you" (13:24) sounds as though Italians outside of Italy are sending greetings back home. (3) What was their spiritual condition? Most were believers (3:1), though, as in every church group, there were doubtless some who merely professed Christianity. The author calls this letter a "word of exhortation" (13:22) necessitated by the fact that some were in danger of abandoning their faith in Christ and reverting to Judaism. The readers were being persecuted, though not to the point of being martyrs (10:32-34; 12:4), and in the face of this, some were running the risk of becoming apostate. The letter is a stirring apologetic for the superiority of Christ and Christianity over Judaism in terms of priesthood and sacrifice.*

Date *Various dates have been suggested for the writing of Hebrews, from the 60's to the 90's. However, its use in the book of 1 Clement, which was written in 95, requires a date some time before that. The lack in the book of any reference to the destruction of the temple in Jerusalem as the divine proof that the Old Testament sacrificial system was finished argues strongly for a date before 70. In addition, the mention of Timothy's recent release (13:23), if it was in connection with his ministry to Paul in Rome, requires a date in the late 60's.*

Style *The author displays outstanding literary and rhetorical skill. His style is a model of Hellenistic prose. Both the author and his readers are very familiar with the Old Testament in the Greek translation (the Septuagint). There are 29 direct quotations from the Old Testament plus 53 clear allusions to various other passages. These are used to demonstrate both the finality of the Christian revelation and its superiority to the old covenant.*

Contents *The theme of the book is the superiority of Christ and thus of Christianity. The words "better," "perfection," and "heavenly" appear frequently. The outline shows how the theme is developed by proving that Christ is superior both in His person and His priesthood. Favorite passages include 2:3 (so great a salvation), 4:12 (the living Word of God), 4:16 (the throne of grace), 7:25 (the intercession of Christ), 11:1 (the description of faith), 11:4-40 (the heroes of faith), 12:1-2 (the Christian race), and 13:20-21 (a great benediction).*

OUTLINE OF HEBREWS

I. The Superiority of the Person of Christ, 1:1-4:16
- A. Christ Is Superior to the Prophets, 1:1-4
- B. Christ Is Superior to the Angels, 1:5-2:18
  1. In His divine person, 1:5-14
  2. In His saving proclamation, 2:1-4
  3. In His delivering purpose, 2:5-18
- C. Christ Is Superior to Moses, 3:1-6
- D. Christ Is the Supreme Object of Faith, 3:7-4:16
  1. The catastrophe of unbelief, 3:7-19
  2. The consequences of unbelief, 4:1-10
  3. The cure for unbelief, 4:11-16

II. The Superiority of the Priesthood of Christ, 5:1-10:39
- A. Christ Is Superior in His Qualifications, 5:1-10
- B. Parenthetical Warning: Don't Degenerate from Christ, 5:11-6:20

THE LETTER TO THE HEBREWS

I THE SUPERIORITY OF THE PERSON OF CHRIST, 1:1–4:16

A Christ Is Superior to the Prophets, 1:1–4

★ 1-4
★1 [a]John 9:29; 16:13 [b]Acts 2:30; 3:21 [c]Num. 12:6, 8
1 God, after He [a]spoke long
ago to the fathers in [b]the
prophets in many portions and
[c]in many ways,
★ 2 [a]Matt. 13:39 [b]John 9:29; 12:25 [c]John 5:26 [d]Ps. 2:8 [e]John 1:3 [f]1 Cor. 2:7
2 [a]in these last days [b]has
spoken to us in [c]*His* Son, whom
He appointed [d]heir of all things,
[e]through whom also He made the
[f]world.
3 And He is the radiance of
His glory and the exact [a]represen-
tation of His nature, and [b]upholds ★ 3 [a]2 Cor. 4:4 [b]Col. 1:17 [c]Titus 2:14; Heb. 9:14 [d]Mark 16:19 [e]2 Pet. 1:17
all things by the word of His
power. When He had made [c]puri-
fication of sins, He [d]sat down at
the right hand of the [e]Majesty on
high;
4 having become as much 4 [a]Eph. 1:21; Phil. 2:9
better than the angels, as He has
inherited a more excellent [a]name
than they.

B Christ Is Superior to the Angels, 1:5–2:18

1 *In His divine person,* 1:5–14

★ 5 [a]Ps. 2:7; Acts 13:33; Heb. 5:5 [b]2 Sam. 7:14
5 For to which of the angels
did He ever say,

1:1-4 These verses comprise one majestic sentence in the Greek text and read like the opening of a formal Greek oration rather than the customary "greetings" of a letter.

1:1 *fathers.* I.e., forefathers. *in many portions and in many ways.* I.e., through laws, institutions, ceremonies, kings, judges, prophets.

1:2 *in these last days.* The *last days* here means the entire gospel dispensation extending from the first to the second advent of Christ. *the world.* Lit., the ages, including time, space, and the material world.

1:3 *radiance* = effulgence or flood of resplendent light. The word means an outshining, not a reflection. *the exact representation* of God's essence or *nature.* These expressions in v. 3 are strong assertions of the deity of Christ. *sat down at the right hand of the Majesty on high.* The picture of Christ being seated indicates the finished character of His once-for-all sacrifice for sin (10:10, 12), and the right hand indicates the place of honor which He occupies.

1:5 *the angels.* The word "angel" means messenger. It usually refers to an order of spirit beings, rarely to human beings (as in Luke 7:24; Jas. 2:25). All angels were originally created in a holy state but some followed Satan in his revolt against God and became the demons. Some demons are loose and some are confined (see notes on Matt. 7:22; 2 Pet. 2:4; Jude 6). Angels are created beings who must ultimately answer to their Creator (Col. 1:16). Since they are spirit beings, they are not bound by some of the restrictions that limit human beings (cf. Heb. 1:14; Acts 12:5-10). They are organized and ranked (Isa. 6:1-3; Dan. 10:13; Eph. 3:10; Jude 9). Angels ministered to Christ often during His first advent and will accompany Him at His return (Matt. 2:13; 4:11; 26:53; 28:2, 5; Luke 22:43; 2 Thess. 1:7-8). They serve believers (Heb. 1:14) and observe them (1 Cor. 4:9; 11:10). Michael is the only one designated an archangel (Dan. 10:13, 21; Jude 9), though Gabriel also has an important position (Luke 1:19, 26). *did He . . . say.* Quoting 2 Sam. 7:14 and Ps. 2:7. Never to an angel did God say that he was a son, only to and of Christ. 2 Sam. 7:14 was addressed to Solomon and Ps. 2:7 may have been sung to a monarch on the day of his coronation. Christ, explains the writer of Hebrews, is the ultimate fulfillment of these words.

"[a]THOU ART MY SON,
TODAY I HAVE BEGOTTEN THEE"?

And again,

"[b]I WILL BE A FATHER TO HIM,
AND HE SHALL BE A SON TO ME"?

★ 6 [a]Heb. 10:5 [b]Matt. 24:14 [c]Deut. 32:43 [Septuagint]; Ps. 97:7

6 And when He again [a]brings the first-born into [b]the world, He says,

"[c]AND LET ALL THE ANGELS OF GOD WORSHIP HIM."

★ 7 [a]Ps. 104:4

7 And of the angels He says,

"[a]WHO MAKES HIS ANGELS WINDS,
AND HIS MINISTERS A FLAME OF FIRE."

★ 8-9
8 [a]Ps. 45:6 [b]Deut. 33:27; Ps. 71:3; 90:1; 91:2, 9

8 But of the Son *He says,*

"[a]THY [b]THRONE, O GOD, IS FOREVER AND EVER,
AND THE RIGHTEOUS SCEPTER IS THE SCEPTER OF HIS KINGDOM.

9 [a]Ps. 45:7 [b]John 10:17; Phil. 2:9; Heb. 2:9 [c]Is. 61:1, 3

9 "[a]THOU HAST LOVED RIGHTEOUSNESS AND HATED LAWLESSNESS;
[b]THEREFORE GOD, THY GOD, HATH [c]ANOINTED THEE
WITH THE OIL OF GLADNESS ABOVE THY COMPANIONS."

★10-12
10 [a]Ps. 102:25

10 And,

"[a]THOU, LORD, IN THE BEGINNING DIDST LAY THE FOUNDATION OF THE EARTH,
AND THE HEAVENS ARE THE WORKS OF THY HANDS;

11 [a]Ps. 102:26 [b]Is. 51:6; Heb. 8:13

11 [a]THEY WILL PERISH, BUT THOU REMAINEST;
[b]AND THEY ALL WILL BECOME OLD AS A GARMENT,

12 [a]Ps. 102:26, 27 [b]Heb. 13:8

12 [a]AND AS A MANTLE THOU WILT ROLL THEM UP;
AS A GARMENT THEY WILL ALSO BE CHANGED.
BUT THOU ART [b]THE SAME,
AND THY YEARS WILL NOT COME TO AN END."

13 [a]Ps. 110:1; Matt. 22:44; Heb. 1:3 [b]Josh 10:24; Heb. 10:13

13 But to which of the angels has He ever said,

"[a]SIT AT MY RIGHT HAND,
[b]UNTIL I MAKE THINE ENEMIES
A FOOTSTOOL FOR THY FEET"?

★14 [a]Ps. 103:20f.; Dan. 7:10 [b]Matt. 25:34; Mark 10:17; Titus 3:7; Heb. 6:12 [c]Rom. 11:14; 1 Cor. 1:21; Heb. 2:3; 5:9; 9:28

14 Are they not all [a]ministering spirits, sent out to render service for the sake of those who will [b]inherit [c]salvation?

2 *In His saving proclamation,* 2:1-4

1 [a]Prov. 3:21 [Septuagint]

2 For this reason we must pay much closer attention to what we have heard, lest [a]we drift away *from it.*

★ 2 [a]Heb. 1:1 [b]Acts 7:53 [c]Heb. 10:28 [d]Heb. 10:35; 11:26

2 For if the word [a]spoken
through [b]angels proved unalterable, and [c]every transgression and disobedience received a just [d]recompense,

3 [a]Heb. 10:29; 12:25 [b]Rom. 11:14; 1 Cor. 1:21; Heb. 1:14; 5:9; 9:28 [c]Heb. 1:1 [d]Mark 16:20; Luke 1:2; 1 John 1:1

3 [a]how shall we escape if we
neglect so great a [b]salvation? After it was at the first [c]spoken through the Lord, it was [d]confirmed to us by those who heard,

4 [a]John 4:48 [b]Mark 6:14 [c]1 Cor. 12:4, 11; Eph. 4:7 [d]Eph. 1:5

4 God also bearing witness
with them, both by [a]signs and [a]wonders and by [b]various miracles and by [c]gifts of the Holy Spirit [d]according to His own will.

3 *In His delivering purpose,* 2:5-18

★ 5 [a]Matt. 24:14; Heb. 1:6; 6:5

5 For He did not subject to angels [a]the world to come, concerning which we are speaking.

1:6 A combination of Ps. 97:7 with Deut. 32:43 (Septuagint version, the Greek translation of the O.T.).

1:7 *winds.* Quoting Ps. 104:4. Angels are servants (as wind and fire are) and therefore subordinate to the Son.

1:8-9 Historically the psalm quoted (45:6-7) was probably sung at a Hebrew monarch's wedding. What was true of the ancient king by virtue of his office, the writer to the Hebrews sees to be wholly true of Christ by virtue of His nature. *Thy companions.* I.e., beyond all others.

1:10-12 Quoting Ps. 102:25-27. Christ is the Creator of all things and the One who, in the midst of change, is unchanging.

1:14 *ministering spirits.* The ministry of angels on behalf of believers continues today. The mention of *salvation* leads the writer into a discussion of this topic (2:1-18).

2:2 *the word spoken through angels.* Refers to the Mosaic law (Ps. 68:17; Acts 7:53). In later Judaism it was held that angels had delivered the law.

2:5 *the world to come.* Lit., the coming inhabited earth (as in Luke 2:1). A reference to the

6 [a]1 Thess. 4:6 [b]Heb. 4:4 [c]Ps. 8:4

6 But one has [a]testified
[b]somewhere, saying,

"[c]WHAT IS MAN, THAT THOU
REMEMBEREST HIM?
OR THE SON OF MAN, THAT
THOU ART CONCERNED
ABOUT HIM?

★ 7 [a]Ps. 8:5, 6

7 "[a]THOU HAST MADE HIM FOR
A LITTLE WHILE LOWER
THAN THE ANGELS;
THOU HAST CROWNED HIM
WITH GLORY AND HONOR,
AND HAST APPOINTED HIM
OVER THE WORKS OF THY
HANDS;

★ 8 [a]Ps. 8:6; 1 Cor. 15:27 [b]1 Cor. 15:25

8 [a]THOU HAST PUT ALL THINGS
IN SUBJECTION UNDER HIS
FEET."

For in subjecting all things to him,
He left nothing that is not subject
to him. But now [b]we do not yet
see all things subjected to him.

9 [a]Heb. 2:7 [b]Phil. 2:9; Heb. 1:9 [c]Acts 2:33; 3:13; 1 Pet. 1:21 [d]John 3:16 [e]Matt. 16:28; John 8:52 [f]Heb. 6:20; 7:25

9 But we do see Him who
has been [a]made for a little while
lower than the angels, *namely,*
Jesus, [b]because of the suffering of
death [c]crowned with glory and
honor, that [d]by the grace of God
He might [e]taste death [f]for every
one.

★10 [a]Luke 24:26 [b]Rom. 11:36 [c]Luke 13:32; Heb. 5:9; 7:28 [d]Acts 3:15; 5:31

10 For [a]it was fitting for Him,
[b]for whom are all things, and
[b]through whom are all things, in
bringing many sons to glory, to
[c]perfect the [d]author of their salvation through sufferings.

11 [a]Heb. 13:12 [b]Heb. 10:10 [c]Acts 17:28 [d]Matt. 25:40; Mark 3:34f.; John 20:17

11 For both He who [a]sancti-
fies and those who [b]are sanctified
are all [c]from one *Father;* for
which reason He is not ashamed
to call them [d]brethren,

12 [a]Ps. 22:22

12 saying,

"[a]I WILL PROCLAIM THY NAME
TO MY BRETHREN,
IN THE MIDST OF THE CONGRE-
GATION I WILL SING THY
PRAISE."

13 [a]Is. 8:17 [b]Is. 8:18

13 And again,

"[a]I WILL PUT MY TRUST IN
HIM."

And again,

"[b]BEHOLD, I AND THE CHILDREN
WHOM GOD HAS GIVEN
ME."

★14 [a]Matt. 16:17 [b]John 1:14 [c]1 Cor. 15:54-57; 2 Tim. 1:10 [d]John 12:31; 1 John 3:8

14 Since then the children
share in [a]flesh and blood, [b]He
Himself likewise also partook of
the same, that [c]through death He
might render powerless [d]him who
had the power of death, that is,
the devil;

15 [a]Rom. 8:15

15 and might deliver those
who through [a]fear of death were
subject to slavery all their lives.

★16

16 For assuredly He does not
give help to angels, but He gives
help to the descendant of Abraham.

★17 [a]Phil. 2:7; Heb. 2:14 [b]Heb. 4:15f.; 5:2 [c]Heb. 3:1; 4:14f; 5:5, 10; 6:20; 7:26, 28; 8:1, 3; 9:11; 10:21 [d]Rom. 15:17; Heb. 5:1 [e]Dan. 9:24; 1 John 2:2; 4:10

17 Therefore, He had [a]to be
made like His brethren in all
things, that He might [b]become a
merciful and faithful [c]high priest
in [d]things pertaining to God, to
[e]make propitiation for the sins of
the people.

18 [a]Heb. 4:15

18 For since He Himself was
[a]tempted in that which He has

---

millennial kingdom on earth, which will not be ruled by angels but by Christ and the redeemed.

2:7 *for a little while.* This may mean (1) for a short time, or (2) more likely, as some versions render it, a little lower in rank. In the order of creation, man is lower than angels, and in the incarnation, Christ took this lower place.

2:8 *his feet . . . him . . . him.* This refers to man (not Christ) who was given dominion over the creation (Gen. 1:28) but who lost it when he sinned (Rom. 8:20) and who will regain it in the future millennial kingdom because of Christ's death for sin (Heb. 2:10).

2:10 *to perfect.* I.e., the sufferings of Jesus made Him qualified to be the leader of man's salvation.

2:14 *flesh and blood was* an O.T. figure for human nature. *partook of the same.* I.e., the same human nature. *render powerless.* Lit., bring to nought or make inoperative or useless, but not annihilate, for the devil will exist in torment in the lake of fire forever (Rev. 20:10). This verse states the overriding purpose of Christ's accepting "a lower state."

2:16 Christ did not come to save fallen angels, but to save fallen men.

2:17 *to make propitiation.* Or, expiation. Propitiation refers to God's wrath being satisfied by the death of Christ (Rom. 3:25; 1 John 2:2). Expiation emphasizes the removal of sin by the sacrifice which satisfied God. Sin interrupts normal relations with God; expiation removes sin and restores the relationship.

suffered, He is able to come to the
aid of those who are tempted.

C Christ Is Superior to Moses, 3:1–6

3 Therefore, [a]holy brethren,
partakers of a [b]heavenly calling, consider Jesus, [c]the Apostle
and [d]High Priest of our [e]confes-
sion.
2 He was faithful to Him
who appointed Him, as [a]Moses
also was in all His house.
3 [a]For He has been counted
worthy of more glory than Moses,
by just so much as the builder of
the house has more honor than
the house.
4 For every house is built by
someone, but the builder of all
things is God.
5 Now [a]Moses was faithful
in all His house as [b]a servant, [c]for
a testimony of those things
[d]which were to be spoken later;
6 but Christ *was faithful* as
[a]a Son over His house [b]whose
house we are, [c]if we hold fast our
[d]confidence and the boast of our
[e]hope firm until the end.

1 [a]Acts 1:15; Heb. 2:11; 3:12; 10:19; 13:22 [b]Phil. 3:14 [c]John 17:3 [d]Heb. 2:17; 4:14f.; 5:5, 10; 6:20; 7:26, 28; 8:1, 3; 9:11; 10:21 [e]2 Cor. 9:13; Heb. 4:14; 10:23
2 [a]Ex. 40:16; Num. 12:7; Heb. 3:5
★ 3 [a]2 Cor. 3:7-11
5 [a]Ex. 40:16; Num. 12:7; Heb. 3:2 [b]Ex. 14:31; Num. 12:7 [c]Deut. 18:18f. [d]Heb. 1:1
6 [a]Heb. 1:2 [b]1 Cor. 3:16; 1 Tim. 3:15 [c]Rom. 11:22; Heb. 3:14; 4:14 [d]Eph. 3:12; Heb. 4:16; 10:19, 35 [e]Heb. 6:11; 7:19; 10:23; 11:1; 1 Pet. 1:3

D Christ Is the Supreme Object of Faith, 3:7–4:16

1 *The catastrophe of unbelief,* 3:7–19

7 Therefore, just as [a]the
Holy Spirit says,

"[b]TODAY IF YOU HEAR HIS
VOICE,
8 [a]DO NOT HARDEN YOUR
HEARTS AS WHEN THEY PRO-
VOKED ME,
AS IN THE DAY OF TRIAL IN
THE WILDERNESS,
9 [a]WHERE YOUR FATHERS
TRIED *Me* BY TESTING *Me,*
AND SAW MY WORKS FOR
[b]FORTY YEARS.
10 "[a]THEREFORE I WAS ANGRY
WITH THIS GENERATION,
AND SAID, 'THEY ALWAYS GO
ASTRAY IN THEIR HEART;
AND THEY DID NOT KNOW MY
WAYS';
11 [a]AS I SWORE IN MY WRATH,
'THEY SHALL NOT ENTER MY
REST.' "

12 [a]Take care, brethren, lest
there should be in any one of you
an evil, unbelieving heart, in falling away from [b]the living God.
13 But [a]encourage one another day after day, as long as it is
still called "Today," lest any one
of you be hardened by the [b]de-
ceitfulness of sin.
14 For we have become partakers of Christ, [a]if we hold fast
the beginning of our [b]assurance
firm until the end;
15 while it is said,

"[a]TODAY IF YOU HEAR HIS
VOICE,
DO NOT HARDEN YOUR
HEARTS, AS WHEN THEY
PROVOKED ME."

16 For who [a]provoked *Him*
when they had heard? Indeed,
[b]did not all those who came out
of Egypt *led* by Moses?
17 And with whom was He
angry for forty years? Was it not
with those who sinned, [a]whose
bodies fell in the wilderness?
18 And to whom did He
swear [a]that they should not enter
His rest, but to those who were
[b]disobedient?
19 And *so* we see that they
were not able to enter because of
[a]unbelief.

★ 7-11
7 [a]Acts 28:25; Heb. 9:8; 10:15 [b]Ps. 95:7; Heb. 3:15; 4:7
8 [a]Ps. 95:8
9 [a]Ps. 95:9, 10 [b]Acts 7:36
10 [a]Ps. 95:10
11 [a]Ps. 95:11; Heb. 4:3, 5
12 [a]Col. 2:8; Heb. 12:25 [b]Matt. 16:16; Heb. 9:14; 10:31; 12:22
13 [a]Heb. 10:24f. [b]Eph. 4:22
14 [a]Heb. 3:6 [b]Heb. 11:1 [Gr.]
15 [a]Ps. 95:7f.
16 [a]Jer. 32:29; 44:3, 8 [b]Num. 14:2, 11, 30; Deut. 1:35, 36, 38
17 [a]Num. 14:29; 1 Cor. 10:5
18 [a]Num. 14:23; Deut. 1:34f.; Heb. 4:2 [b]Rom. 11:30-32; Heb. 4:6, 11
★19 [a]John 3:36

3:3 Christ is better than Moses because Christ is the builder of God's house while Moses was but a servant in the house.

3:7-11 See Ps. 95:7-11. The children of Israel challenged God's authority over them by their rebellion in the wilderness (Num. 14–21). Because of this, they failed to enter into the rest of dwelling in Canaan and they perished in the wilderness.

3:19 *because of unbelief.* See Num. 14; 1 Cor. 10:10-11.

2 *The consequences of unbelief,* 4:1–10

★ 1 [a]Heb. 12:15

4 Therefore, let us fear lest, while a promise remains of entering His rest, any one of you should seem to have [a]come short of it.

2 [a]1 Thess. 2:13

2 For indeed we have had good news preached to us, just as they also; but [a]the word they heard did not profit them, because it was not united by faith in those who heard.

3 [a]Ps. 95:11; Heb. 3:11 [b]Matt. 25:34

3 For we who have believed enter that rest, just as He has said,

"[a]AS I SWORE IN MY WRATH,
THEY SHALL NOT ENTER MY REST,"

although His works were finished [b]from the foundation of the world.

★ 4 [a]Heb. 2:6 [b]Gen. 2:2 [c]Ex. 20:11; 31:17

4 For He has thus said [a]somewhere concerning the seventh *day,* "[b]AND GOD [c]RESTED ON THE SEVENTH DAY FROM ALL HIS WORKS";

★ 5-9
5 [a]Ps. 95:11; Heb. 3:11
6 [a]Heb. 3:18; 4:11

5 and again in this *passage,* "[a]THEY SHALL NOT ENTER MY REST."

6 Since therefore it remains for some to enter it, and those who formerly had good news preached to them failed to enter because of [a]disobedience,

7 [a]Heb. 3:7f. [b]Ps. 95:7f.

7 He again fixes a certain day, "Today," saying through David after so long a time just [a]as has been said before,

"[b]TODAY IF YOU HEAR HIS VOICE,
DO NOT HARDEN YOUR HEARTS."

8 For [a]if Joshua had given them rest, He would not have [b]spoken of another day after that. ★ 8 [a]Josh. 22:4 [b]Heb. 1:1

9 There remains therefore a Sabbath rest for the people of God.

10 For the one who has entered His rest has himself also [a]rested from his works, as [b]God did from His. 10 [a]Rev. 14:13 [b]Heb. 4:4

3 *The cure for unbelief,* 4:11–16

11 Let us therefore be diligent to enter that rest, lest anyone fall through *following* the same [a]example of [b]disobedience. ★11 [a]2 Pet. 2:6 [b]Heb. 3:18; 4:6

12 For [a]the word of God is [b]living and [c]active and sharper than any two-edged [d]sword, and piercing as far as the division of [e]soul and [e]spirit, of both joints and marrow, and [f]able to judge the thoughts and intentions of the heart. ★12 [a]Jer. 23:29; Eph. 5:26; Heb. 6:5; 1 Pet. 1:23 [b]Acts 7:38 [c]1 Thess. 2:13 [d]Eph. 6:17 [e]1 Thess. 5:23 [f]John 12:48; 1 Cor. 14:24f.

13 And [a]there is no creature hidden from His sight, but all things are [b]open and laid bare to the eyes of Him with whom we have to do. ★13 [a]2 Chr. 16:9; Ps. 33:13-15 [b]Job 26:6

14 Since then we have a great [a]high priest who has [b]passed through the heavens, Jesus [c]the Son of God, let us hold fast our [d]confession. 14 [a]Heb. 2:17 [b]Eph. 4:10; Heb. 6:20; 8:1; 9:24 [c]Matt. 4:3; Heb. 1:2; 6:6; 7:3; 10:29 [d]Heb. 3:1

4:1 Although God has promised believers today that they may enter His rest, some may fail to experience it because of unbelief.

4:4 See Gen. 2:2. After the work of creation was finished, God rested; i.e., He enjoyed the sense of satisfaction and repose that comes with the completion of a task. It is in this sense that *rest* is used in vv. 1 and 3.

4:5–9 The divine promise still holds good: the believer may enter into God's rest through faith. This is true both of salvation and sanctification. Rest in the Christian life comes through complete reliance on God's promises and full surrender to His will (2 Cor. 5:7; Col. 2:6).

4:8 *Joshua* (Moses' successor) could not lead all the people into the rest of dwelling in their promised land because of their unbelief. Likewise the believer today cannot enjoy a fully satisfying Christian life unless he believes all the promises of God, and even then he looks forward to that perfect future rest.

4:11 *Let us . . . be diligent.* The same Greek word is used in Eph. 4:3; 2 Tim. 2:15; 2 Pet. 1:10; 3:14.

4:12 *the word of God.* Here meaning His inspired Word, the Scriptures. *living and active.* It has the power to reach to the inmost parts of one's personality and to judge the innermost thoughts.

4:13 *with whom we have to do.* Better, to whom we must give an account—lit.,to whom is our word. A play on the Greek term for "word"; i.e., if our lives conform to the *word of God* (v. 12), then our word (account) in the day of judgment will be acceptable to God.

★15 [a]Heb. 2:17 [b]Heb. 2:18 [c]2 Cor. 5:21; Heb. 7:26
16 [a]Heb. 7:19 [b]Heb. 3:6

15 For we do not have [a]a high
priest who cannot sympathize
with our weaknesses, but one
who has been [b]tempted in all
things as *we are, yet* [c]without sin.
16 Let us therefore [a]draw
near with [b]confidence to the
throne of grace, that we may receive mercy and may find grace to
help in time of need.

II THE SUPERIORITY OF THE PRIESTHOOD OF CHRIST, 5:1–10:39

A Christ Is Superior in His Qualifications, 5:1–10

★ 1-10
1 [a]Ex. 28:1 [b]Heb. 2:17 [c]Heb. 7:27; 8:3f.; 9:9; 10:11 [d]1 Cor. 15:3; Heb. 7:27; 10:12
2 [a]Heb. 2:18; 4:15 [b]Eph. 4:18; Heb. 9:7 marg. [c]James 5:19; 1 Pet. 2:25 [d]Heb. 7:28
3 [a]1 Cor. 15:3; Heb. 7:27; 10:12 [b]Lev. 9:7; 16:6; Heb. 7:27; 9:7
★ 4 [a]Num. 16:40; 18:7; 2 Chr. 26:18 [b]Ex. 28:1; 1 Chr. 23:13
5 [a]John 8:54 [b]Heb. 2:17; 5:10 [c]Heb. 1:1, 5 [d]Ps. 2:7

5 For every high priest [a]taken
from among men is ap-
pointed on behalf of men in
[b]things pertaining to God, in order to [c]offer both gifts and sacrifices [d]for sins;
2 [a]he can deal gently with
the [b]ignorant and [c]misguided,
since he himself also is [d]beset
with weakness;
3 and because of it he is obligated to offer *sacrifices* [a]for sins,
[b]as for the people, so also for
himself.
4 And [a]no one takes the
honor to himself, but *receives it*
when he is called by God, even
[b]as Aaron was.
5 So also Christ [a]did not glorify Himself so as to become a
[b]high priest, but He who [c]said to
Him,

"[d]THOU ART MY SON,
TODAY I HAVE BEGOTTEN
THEE";

6 just as He says also in an- 6 [a]Ps. 110:4; Heb. 7:17 [b]Heb. 5:10; 6:20; 7:11, 17
other *passage,*

"[a]THOU ART A PRIEST FOREVER
ACCORDING TO [b]THE ORDER OF
MELCHIZEDEK."

7 In the days of His flesh, ★ 7 [a]Matt. 26:39, 42, 44; Mark 14:36, 39; Luke 22:41, 44 [b]Matt. 27:46, 50; Mark 15:34, 37; Luke 23:46 [c]Mark 14:36 [d]Heb. 11:7; 12:28
[a]He offered up both prayers and
supplications with [b]loud crying
and tears to the One [c]able to save
Him from death, and He was
heard because of His [d]piety.
8 Although He was [a]a Son, 8 [a]Heb. 1:2 [b]Phil. 2:8
He learned [b]obedience from the
things which He suffered.
9 And having been made 9 [a]Heb. 2:10
[a]perfect, He became to all those
who obey Him the source of eternal salvation,
10 being designated by God ★10 [a]Heb. 2:17; 5:5 [b]Heb. 5:6
as [a]a high priest according to [b]the
order of Melchizedek.

B Parenthetical Warning: Don't Degenerate from Christ, 5:11–6:20

11 Concerning him we have
much to say, and *it is* hard to explain, since you have become dull
of hearing.

4:15 *but one who has been tempted in all things as we are, yet without sin.* Not that Christ experienced every temptation man does, but rather that He was tempted in all areas in which man is tempted (the lust of the flesh, the lust of the eyes, and the pride of life, 1 John 2:16), and with particular temptations specially suited to Him. This testing was possible only because He took the likeness of sinful flesh (Rom. 8:3), for had there not been an incarnation, Jesus could not have been tempted (cf. Jas. 1:13). Yet our Lord was distinct from all other men in that He was *without sin*; i.e., He possessed no sin nature as we do. Because He endured and successfully passed His tests, He can now offer us mercy and grace to help in time of need, for He knows what we are going through.

5:1–10 The qualifications for high priest are stated in these verses, Aaron serving as the model.

5:4 See Ex. 28:1.

5:7 *offered up both prayers and supplications with loud crying and tears.* Refers to occasions like those of John 12:27 and the experience in Gethsemane (Matt. 26:39–44).

5:10 *according to the order of Melchizedek.* Our Lord could never have been a Levitical priest because He was born of the tribe of Judah (7:14) and not the tribe of Levi. Thus He must be associated with another order of priests, that of Melchizedek. Both Christ and Melchizedek were men (Heb. 7:4; 1 Tim. 2:5); both were king-priests (Gen. 14:18; Zech. 6:12–13); both were appointed directly by God (Heb. 7:21); both were called "King of righteousness" and "King of peace" (Isa. 11:5–9; Heb. 7:2).

★12 aGal. 4:3 bHeb. 6:1 cActs 7:38 d1 Cor. 3:2; 1 Pet. 2:2

12 For though by this time
you ought to be teachers, you
have need again for some one to
teach you [a]the [b]elementary principles of the [c]oracles of God, and
you have come to need [d]milk and
not solid food.

13 a1 Cor. 3:1; 14:20; 1 Pet. 2:2

13 For every one who par-
takes *only* of milk is not accustomed to the word of righteousness, for he is a [a]babe.

★14 a1 Cor. 2:6; Eph. 4:13; Heb. 6:1 b1 Tim. 4:7 cRom. 14:1

14 But solid food is for [a]the
mature, who because of practice
have their senses [b]trained to [c]dis-
cern good and evil.

★ 1 aPhil. 3:13f. bHeb. 5:12 cHeb. 5:14 dJohn 8:21; Heb. 9:14

6 Therefore [a]leaving [b]the elementary teaching about the
Christ, let us press on to [c]maturi-
ty, not laying again a foundation
of repentance from [d]dead works
and of faith toward God,

★ 2 aJohn 3:25; Acts 19:3f. bActs 6:6 cActs 17:31f.

2 of [a]instruction about
washings, and [b]laying on of
hands, and the [c]resurrection of
the dead, and [c]eternal judgment.

3 aActs 18:21

3 And this we shall do, [a]if
God permits.

★ 4-6
4 a2 Cor. 4:4, 6; Heb. 10:32 bJohn 4:10; Eph. 2:8 cGal. 3:2; Heb. 2:4

4 For in the case of those
who have once been [a]enlightened
and have tasted of [b]the heavenly
gift and have been made [c]partak-
ers of the Holy Spirit,

5 a1 Pet. 2:3 bEph. 6:17 cHeb. 2:5

5 and [a]have tasted the good
[b]word of God and the powers of
[c]the age to come,

6 aMatt. 19:26; Heb. 10:26f.; 2 Pet. 2:21; 1 John 5:16 bHeb. 10:29

6 and *then* have fallen away,
it is [a]impossible to renew them
again to repentance, [b]since they
again crucify to themselves the
Son of God, and put Him to open
shame.

7 a2 Tim. 2:6

7 For ground that drinks the
rain which often falls upon it and
brings forth vegetation useful to
those [a]for whose sake it is also
tilled, receives a blessing from
God;

8 aDeut. 29:22ff.

8 but if it yields thorns and
thistles, it is worthless and [a]close
to being cursed, and it ends up
being burned.

★ 9 a1 Cor. 10:14; 2 Cor. 7:1; 12:19; 1 Pet. 2:11; 2 Pet. 3:1; 1 John 2:7; Jude 3

9 But, [a]beloved, we are convinced of better things concerning
you, and things that accompany
salvation, though we are speaking
in this way.

10 aProv. 19:17; Matt. 10:42; 25:40; Acts 10:4 b1 Thess. 1:3 cRom. 15:25; Heb. 10:32-34

10 For [a]God is not unjust so
as to forget [b]your work and the
love which you have shown
toward His name, in having [c]min-
istered and in still ministering to
the saints.

11 aLuke 1:1; Heb. 10:22 bHeb. 3:6

11 And we desire that each
one of you show the same dili-

5:12 *though by this time.* Better, although by now. I.e., in consideration of the time they had been believers. *milk.* I.e., elementary truth (see 1 Cor. 3:1–3).

5:14 *the mature.* Christian maturity involves (1) time (v. 12); (2) growth in the knowledge of the Word of God (v. 13); and (3) experience in the use of the Word in discerning between good and evil (vv. 13–14).

6:1 *elementary teaching.* I.e., the basic teachings about Christ and the Christian religion. *maturity.* The exhortation to these people is for them to go on to Christian maturity and to stop wasting time and opportunities. They knew the first principles, or basics, of Christianity and are being exhorted to go on from there. *dead works.* I.e., sins.

6:2 *instruction about washings.* Or, as in some versions, baptisms. The distinction between various baptisms is a necessary part of basic Christian doctrine (e.g., the baptism of Jewish proselytes, baptism by John the Baptist, Christian baptism).

6:4–6 This much-debated passage has been understood in several ways. (1) Arminians hold that the people described in these verses are Christians who actually lose their salvation. If this be so, notice that the passage also teaches that it is impossible to be saved a second time. (2) Some hold that the passage refers not to genuine believers but to those who only profess to be believers. Thus the phrases in vv. 4–5 are understood to refer to experiences short of salvation (cf. v. 9). The "falling away" is from the knowledge of the truth, not personal possession of it. (3) Others understand the passage to be a warning to genuine believers to urge them on in Christian growth and maturity. To "fall away" is impossible (since, according to this view, true believers are eternally secure), but the phrase is placed in the sentence to strengthen the warning. It is similar to saying something like this to a class of students: "It is impossible for a student, once enrolled in this course, if he turns the clock back [which cannot be done], to start the course over. Therefore, let all students go on to deeper knowledge." In this view the phrases in vv. 4–5 are understood to refer to the conversion experience. Notice how the words "enlightened" (10:32), "taste" (2:9), and "partakers" (12:8) are used elsewhere in Hebrews.

6:9 An expression of confidence, though the writer speaks severely. *things that accompany salvation.* I.e., fruit in the Christian life.

gence so as to realize the [a]full assurance of [b]hope until the end,

12 [a]Heb. 13:7 [b]2 Thess. 1:4; James 1:3; Rev. 13:10 [c]Heb. 1:14

12 that you may not be slug-
gish, but [a]imitators of those who
through [b]faith and patience [c]in-
herit the promises.

13 [a]Gal. 3:15, 18 [b]Gen. 22:16; Luke 1:73

13 For [a]when God made the
promise to Abraham, since He
could swear by no one greater, He
[b]swore by Himself,

★14 [a]Gen. 22:16f.

14 saying, "[a]I WILL SURELY BLESS
YOU, AND I WILL SURELY MULTIPLY
YOU."

15 [a]Gen. 12:4; 21:5

15 And thus, [a]having pa-
tiently waited, he obtained the
promise.

16 [a]Gal. 3:15 [b]Ex. 22:11

16 [a]For men swear by one
greater *than themselves,* and with
them [b]an oath *given* as confirmation is an end of every dispute.

17 [a]Heb. 11:9 [b]Ps. 110:4; Prov. 19:21; Heb. 6:18

17 In the same way God, desiring even more to show to [a]the
heirs of the promise [b]the un-
changeableness of His purpose,
interposed with an oath,

★18 [a]Num. 23:19; Titus 1:2 [b]Heb. 3:6; 7:19

18 in order that by two unchangeable things, in which [a]it is
impossible for God to lie, we may
have strong encouragement, we
who have fled for refuge in laying
hold of [b]the hope set before us.

★19 [a]Lev. 16:2; Heb. 9:2f.

19 This hope we have as an
anchor of the soul, a *hope* both
sure and steadfast and one which
[a]enters within the veil,

★20 [a]John 14:2; Heb. 4:14 [b]Heb. 2:17; 5:6

20 [a]where Jesus has entered
as a forerunner for us, having become a [b]high priest forever according to the order of Melchizedek.

C Christ Is Superior in the Order of His Priesthood, 7:1–8:13

1 *The portrait of Melchizedek,* 7:1–3

7 For this [a]Melchizedek, king ★ 1 [a]Gen. 14:18-20; Heb. 7:6 [b]Mark 5:7
of Salem, priest of the [b]Most
High God, who met Abraham as
he was returning from the slaughter of the kings and blessed him,
2 to whom also Abraham
apportioned a tenth part of all *the
spoils,* was first of all, by the
translation *of his name,* king of
righteousness, and then also king
of Salem, which is king of peace.
3 Without father, without ★ 3 [a]Heb. 7:6 [b]Matt. 4:3; Heb. 7:1, 28
mother, [a]without genealogy, hav-
ing neither beginning of days nor
end of life, but made like [b]the
Son of God, he abides a priest
perpetually.

2 *The preeminence of the Melchizedek priesthood,* 7:4–8:13

4 Now observe how great ★ 4 [a]Acts 2:29
this man was to whom Abraham,
the [a]patriarch, gave a tenth of the
choicest spoils.
5 And those indeed of [a]the 5 [a]Num. 18:21, 26; 2 Chr. 31:4f.
sons of Levi who receive the
priest's office have commandment
in the Law to collect a tenth from
the people, that is, from their
brethren, although these are de-
scended from Abraham. ★ 6 [a]Heb. 7:3 [b]Heb. 7:1f. [c]Rom. 4:13
6 But the one [a]whose gene-
alogy is not traced from them

6:14 See Gen. 22:16–17.

6:18 *two unchangeable things.* The promise made to Abraham and the oath which rests on the very being of God.

6:19 *within the veil.* I.e., in the presence of God. Believers have as strong encouragement as Abraham had in his time, because Jesus has already entered into the presence of God and assures us of our entrance into heaven as well.

6:20 *forerunner.* A word used of a scout reconnoitering, or of a herald announcing the coming of a king; both concepts imply that others are to follow.

7:1 *Melchizedek* is clearly a type of Christ. Everything known about him from the O.T. is found in Gen. 14:17-20 and Ps. 110:4. He was a great king-priest, and it is to his order of priesthood that Christ belongs. See note on 5:10.

7:3 *Without father . . .* This does not mean that Melchizedek had no parents or that he was not born or did not die, but only that the Scriptures contain no record of these events so that he might be more perfectly likened to Christ.

7:4 *gave a tenth.* By taking the role of the one who tithed and the one who received the blessing (v. 1), Abraham, to whom God gave the promises, doubly acknowledged his inferiority to Melchizedek.

7:6 The proof that the Melchizedek priesthood (and Christ's) is superior to the Aaronic, or Levitical, priesthood is that Levi's great-grandfather Abraham paid tithes to Melchizedek, and that Levi, though unborn, was involved (v. 9).

[b]collected a tenth from Abraham, and [b]blessed the one who [c]had the promises.

7 But without any dispute the lesser is blessed by the greater.

★ 8 [a]Heb. 5:6; 6:20

8 And in this case mortal men receive tithes, but in that case one *receives them,* [a]of whom it is witnessed that he lives on.

9 And, so to speak, through Abraham even Levi, who received tithes, paid tithes,

10 for he was still in the loins of his father when Melchizedek met him.

★11 [a]Heb. 7:18f.; 8:7 [b]Heb. 9:6; 10:1 [c]Heb. 5:6; 7:17

11 [a]Now if perfection was through the Levitical priesthood (for on the basis of it [b]the people received the Law), what further need *was there* for another priest to arise [c]according to the order of Melchizedek, and not be designated according to the order of Aaron?

★12

12 For when the priesthood is changed, of necessity there takes place a change of law also.

13 [a]Heb. 7:14 [b]Heb. 7:11

13 For [a]the one concerning whom [b]these things are spoken belongs to another tribe, from which no one has officiated at the altar.

14 [a]Num. 24:17; Is. 11:1; Matt. 2:6 [Mic. 5:2]; Rev. 5:5

14 For it is evident that our Lord was [a]descended from Judah, a tribe with reference to which Moses spoke nothing concerning priests.

15 And this is clearer still, if another priest arises according to the likeness of Melchizedek,

16 [a]Heb. 9:10 [b]Heb. 9:14

16 who has become *such* not on the basis of a law of [a]physical requirement, but according to the power of [b]an indestructible life.

17 [a]Ps. 110:4; Heb. 5:6; 7:21

17 For it is witnessed *of Him,*

> "[a]THOU ART A PRIEST FOREVER
> ACCORDING TO THE ORDER OF MELCHIZEDEK."

18 For, on the one hand, there is a setting aside of a former commandment [a]because of its weakness and uselessness

18 [a]Rom. 8:3; Gal. 3:21; Heb. 7:11

19 (for [a]the Law made nothing perfect), and on the other hand there is a bringing in of a better [b]hope, through which we [c]draw near to God.

★19 [a]Acts 13:39; Rom. 3:20; 7:7f.; Gal. 2:16; 3:21; Heb. 9:9; 10:1 [b]Heb. 3:6 [c]Lam. 3:57; Heb. 4:16; 7:25; 10:1, 22; James 4:8

20 And inasmuch as *it was* not without an oath

21 (for they indeed became priests without an oath, but He with an oath through the One who said to Him,

> "[a]THE LORD HAS SWORN
> AND [b]WILL NOT CHANGE HIS MIND,
> 'THOU ART A PRIEST [c]FOREVER' ");

21 [a]Ps. 110:4; Heb. 5:6; 7:17 [b]Num. 23:19; 1 Sam. 15:29; Rom. 11:29 [c]Heb. 7:23f., 28

22 so much the more also Jesus has become the [a]guarantee of [b]a better covenant.

22 [a]Ps. 119:122; Is. 38:14 [b]Heb. 8:6

23 And the *former* priests, on the one hand, existed in greater numbers, because they were prevented by death from continuing,

24 but He, on the other hand, because He abides [a]forever, holds His priesthood permanently.

24 [a]Heb. 7:23f.

25 Hence, also, He is able to [a]save forever those who [b]draw near to God through Him, since He always lives to [c]make intercession for them.

★25 [a]1 Cor. 1:21 [b]Heb. 7:19 [c]Rom. 8:34; Heb. 9:24

26 For it was fitting that we should have such a [a]high priest, [b]holy, [c]innocent, undefiled, separated from sinners and [d]exalted above the heavens;

26 [a]Heb. 2:17 [b]2 Cor. 5:21; Heb. 4:15 [c]1 Pet. 2:22 [d]Heb. 4:14

27 who does not need daily, like those high priests, to [a]offer up sacrifices, [b]first for His own sins, and then for the *sins* of the people, because this He did [c]once for all when He [d]offered up Himself.

27 [a]Heb. 5:1 [b]Heb. 5:3 [c]Heb. 9:12, 28; 10:10 [d]Eph. 5:2; Heb. 9:14, 28; 10:10, 12

7:8 *in this case.* Refers to the Levitical priests. *in that case.* Refers to Melchizedek and his priesthood.

7:11 Another proof that Christ is superior to the law and its priesthood is that the law could not give the people *perfection,* i.e., complete communion with God. The sacrificial Levitical system never achieved its aim.

7:12 For Paul's different, but nonconflicting, argument on the abrogation of the Mosaic law, see Rom. 7:1-6; 2 Cor. 3:7-11; Gal. 3:19-25.

7:19 A *better hope* for effecting full and final removal of sin has been introduced, along with a new way of access to God.

7:25 *forever.* Christ's priesthood has authority (vv. 20-22) and permanence.

28 [a]Heb. 5:2 [b]Heb. 1:2 [c]Heb. 2:10

28 For the Law appoints men as high priests [a]who are weak, but the word of the oath, which came after the Law, *appoints* [b]a Son, [c]made perfect forever.

★ 1 [a]Heb. 2:17 [b]Heb. 1:3

8 Now the main point in what has been said *is this:* we have such a [a]high priest, who has taken His seat at [b]the right hand of the throne of the [b]Majesty in the heavens,

2 [a]Heb. 10:11 [b]Heb. 9:11, 24 [c]Ex. 33:7

2 a [a]minister in the sanctuary, and in the [b]true tabernacle, which the Lord [c]pitched, not man.

3 [a]Heb. 2:17 [b]Heb. 5:1; 8:4

3 For every [a]high priest is appointed [b]to offer both gifts and sacrifices; hence it is necessary that this *high priest* also have something to offer.

4 [a]Heb. 5:1; 8:3

4 Now if He were on earth, He would not be a priest at all, since there are those who [a]offer the gifts according to the Law;

★ 5 [a]Heb. 9:23 [b]Col. 2:17; Heb. 10:1 [c]Matt. 2:12; Heb. 11:7; 12:25 [d]Ex. 25:40

5 who serve [a]a copy and [b]shadow of the heavenly things, just as Moses was [c]warned *by God* when he was about to erect the tabernacle; for, "[d]SEE," He says, "THAT YOU MAKE ALL THINGS ACCORDING TO THE PATTERN WHICH WAS SHOWN YOU ON THE MOUNTAIN."

★ 6 [a]1 Tim. 2:5 [b]Luke 22:20; Heb. 7:22; 8:8; 9:15; 12:24

6 But now He has obtained a more excellent ministry, by as much as He is also the [a]mediator of [b]a better covenant, which has been enacted on better promises.

7 [a]Heb. 7:11

7 For [a]if that first *covenant* had been faultless, there would have been no occasion sought for a second.

8 [a]Jer. 31:31 [b]Luke 22:20; 2 Cor. 3:6; Heb. 7:22; 8:6, 13; 9:15; 12:24

8 For finding fault with them, He says,

"[a]BEHOLD, DAYS ARE COMING, SAYS THE LORD,
WHEN I WILL EFFECT [b]A NEW COVENANT
WITH THE HOUSE OF ISRAEL AND WITH THE HOUSE OF JUDAH;

9 [a]Jer. 31:32 [b]Ex. 19:5f.; Heb. 2:16 marg.

9 [a]NOT LIKE THE COVENANT WHICH I MADE WITH THEIR FATHERS
ON THE DAY WHEN I [b]TOOK THEM BY THE HAND
TO LEAD THEM OUT OF THE LAND OF EGYPT;
FOR THEY DID NOT CONTINUE IN MY COVENANT,
AND I DID NOT CARE FOR THEM, SAYS THE LORD.

10 [a]Jer. 31:33 [b]Rom. 11:27; Heb. 10:16 [c]2 Cor. 3:3

10 "[a]FOR [b]THIS IS THE COVENANT THAT I WILL MAKE WITH THE HOUSE OF ISRAEL
AFTER THOSE DAYS, SAYS THE LORD:
I WILL PUT MY LAWS INTO THEIR MINDS,
AND I WILL WRITE THEM [c]UPON THEIR HEARTS.
AND I WILL BE THEIR GOD,
AND THEY SHALL BE MY PEOPLE.

11 [a]Jer. 31:34 [b]Is. 54:13; John 6:45; 1 John 2:27

11 "[a]AND THEY SHALL NOT TEACH EVERY ONE HIS FELLOW-CITIZEN,
AND EVERY ONE HIS BROTHER, SAYING, 'KNOW THE LORD,'
FOR [b]ALL SHALL KNOW ME,
FROM THE LEAST TO THE GREATEST OF THEM.

12 [a]Jer. 31:34 [b]Heb. 10:17

12 "[a]FOR I WILL BE MERCIFUL TO THEIR INIQUITIES,
[b]AND I WILL REMEMBER THEIR SINS NO MORE."

13 [a]Luke 22:20; 2 Cor. 3:6; Heb. 7:22; 8:6, 8; 9:15; 12:24 [b]2 Cor. 5:17; Heb. 1:11

13 When He said, "[a]A new *covenant,*" He has made the first obsolete. [b]But whatever is becoming obsolete and growing old is ready to disappear.

D Christ Is Superior in His Priestly Ministry, 9:1–10:18

1 *The earthly priesthood,* 9:1–10

1 [a]Heb. 9:10 [b]Ex. 25:8; Heb. 8:2; 9:11, 24

9 Now even the first *covenant* had [a]regulations of divine

8:1 *the main point.* A priest must have something to offer (v. 3) and a sanctuary in which to do it. Christ was disqualified from using the earthly sanctuary because of His descent from the tribe of Judah; therefore, His sphere of service must be heaven.

8:5 *the pattern.* See Ex. 25:40.

8:6 The covenant Christ mediates is a better covenant, since it is enacted on better promises. In vv. 6-13, the new covenant is contrasted with *that first covenant* (v. 7); i.e., the Mosaic law (Ex. 19:5). Christ's blood is the basis of the new covenant (Matt. 26:28); Christians are ministers of it (2 Cor. 3:6); and it will yet have an aspect of its fulfillment in relation to Israel and Judah in the millennium (as predicted in Jer. 31:31-34).

worship and [b]the earthly sanctuary.

2 For there was [a]a tabernacle prepared, the outer one, in which *were* [b]the lampstand and [c]the table and [d]the sacred bread; this is called the holy place.

3 And behind [a]the second veil, there was a tabernacle which is called the [b]Holy of Holies,

4 having a golden [a]altar of incense and [b]the ark of the covenant covered on all sides with gold, in which *was* [c]a golden jar holding the manna, and [d]Aaron's rod which budded, and [e]the tables of the covenant.

5 And above it *were* the [a]cherubim of glory [b]overshadowing the mercy seat; but of these things we cannot now speak in detail.

6 Now when these things have been thus prepared, the priests [a]are continually entering [b]the outer tabernacle, performing the divine worship,

7 but into [a]the second only [b]the high priest *enters,* [c]once a year, [d]not without *taking* blood, which he [e]offers for himself and for the [f]sins of the people committed in ignorance.

8 [a]The Holy Spirit *is* signifying this, [b]that the way into the holy place has not yet been disclosed, while the outer tabernacle is still standing,

9 which *is* [a]a symbol for the present time. Accordingly both gifts and sacrifices are [b]offered which cannot [c]make the worshiper perfect in conscience,

10 since they *relate* only to [a]food and [b]drink and various [c]washings, [d]regulations for the body imposed until [e]a time of reformation.

2 [a]Ex. 25:8, 9 [b]Ex. 25:31-39 [c]Ex. 25:23-29 [d]Ex. 25:30; Lev. 24:5ff.; Matt. 12:4
3 [a]Ex. 26:31-33 [b]Ex. 26:33
★ 4 [a]Ex. 30:1-5; 37:25f. [b]Ex. 25:10ff.; 37:1ff. [c]Ex. 16:32f. [d]Num. 17:10 [e]Ex. 31:18; 32:15; Deut. 9:9, 11, 15
5 [a]Ex. 25:18ff. [b]Ex. 25:17, 20
6 [a]Num. 28:3 [b]Ex. 25:8, 9
★ 7-10
7 [a]Heb. 9:3 [b]Lev. 16:12ff. [c]Ex. 30:10; Lev. 16:34; Heb. 10:3 [d]Lev. 16:11, 14 [e]Heb. 5:3 [f]Num. 15:25; Heb. 5:2
8 [a]Heb. 3:7 [b]John 14:6; Heb. 10:20
9 [a]Heb. 10:1; 11:19 [b]Heb. 5:1 [c]Heb. 7:19
10 [a]Lev. 11:2ff.; Col. 2:16 [b]Num. 6:3 [c]Lev. 11:25; Num. 19:13; Mark 7:4 [d]Heb. 7:16 [e]Heb. 7:12

2 *Christ's priesthood,* 9:11-14

11 But when Christ appeared *as* a [a]high priest of the [b]good things to come, *He entered* through [c]the greater and more perfect tabernacle, [d]not made with hands, that is to say, [e]not of this creation;

12 and not through [a]the blood of goats and calves, but [b]through His own blood, He [c]entered the holy place [d]once for all, having obtained [e]eternal redemption.

13 For if [a]the blood of goats and bulls and [b]the ashes of a heifer sprinkling those who have been defiled, sanctify for the cleansing of the flesh,

14 how much more will [a]the blood of Christ, who through [b]the eternal Spirit [c]offered Himself without blemish to God, [d]cleanse your conscience from [e]dead works to serve [f]the living God?

3 *Christ's fulfillment of the promise,* 9:15-10:18

15 And for this reason [a]He is the [b]mediator of a [c]new covenant, in order that since a death has taken place for the redemption of the transgressions that were *committed* under the first covenant, those who have been [d]called may [e]receive the promise of [f]the eternal inheritance.

16 For where a covenant is, there must of necessity be the death of the one who made it.

17 For a covenant is valid *only* when men are dead, for it is never

11 [a]Heb. 2:17 [b]Heb. 10:1 [c]Heb. 8:2; 9:24 [d]Mark 14:58; 2 Cor. 5:1 [e]2 Cor. 4:18; Heb. 12:27; 13:14
12 [a]Lev. 4:3; 16:6, 15; Heb. 9:19 [b]Heb. 9:14; 13:12 [c]Heb. 9:24 [d]Heb. 7:27 [e]Heb. 5:9; 9:15
13 [a]Heb. 9:19; 10:4 [b]Num. 19:9, 17f.
14 [a]Heb. 9:12; 13:12 [b]1 Cor. 15:45; 1 Pet. 3:18 [c]Eph. 5:2; Heb. 7:27; 10:10, 12 [d]Acts 15:9; Titus 2:14; Heb. 1:3; 10:2, 22 [e]Heb. 6:1 [f]Matt. 16:16; Heb. 3:12
15 [a]Rom. 3:24 [b]1 Tim. 2:5; Heb. 8:6; 12:24 [c]Heb. 8:8 [d]Matt. 22:3ff.; Rom. 8:28f.; Heb. 3:1 [e]Heb. 6:15; 10:36; 11:39 [f]Acts 20:32
★16

9:4 *a golden altar.* Though the altar stood before the veil in the Holy Place, its ritual use was connected with the *Holy of Holies* (v. 3), especially on the Day of Atonement which is being described in these verses (see Lev. 16:12-13).

9:7-10 The fact that only the high priest could go into the Holy of Holies and that he had to go each year signified that no final offering for sin was made in O.T. times and that the offerings that were made could not cleanse the conscience. *reformation.* I.e., the change brought about by the completed sacrifice of Christ and His entering into heaven (vv. 11-12).

9:16 *the one who made it,* I.e., who made the covenant or will. This is strong proof that it is the death of Christ, not His life, which put into effect the new covenant with all its blessings. His sinless life qualified Him to be the suitable sacrifice for sin, but it was His death that made the payment for sin.

in force while the one who made
it lives.

18 Therefore even the first
covenant was not inaugurated
without blood.

19 [a]Heb. 1:1 [b]Ex. 24:6ff. [c]Heb. 9:12 [d]Lev. 14:4, 7; Num. 19:6, 18 [e]Ex. 24:7

19 For when every commandment had been [a]spoken by Moses
to all the people according to the
Law, [b]he took the [c]blood of the
calves and the goats, with [d]water
and scarlet wool and hyssop, and
sprinkled both [e]the book itself
and all the people,

20 [a]Ex. 24:8; Matt. 26:28

20 saying, "[a]THIS IS THE BLOOD
OF THE COVENANT WHICH GOD COM-
MANDED YOU."

21 [a]Ex. 24:6; 40:9; Lev. 8:15, 19; 16:14-16

21 And in the same way he
sprinkled both the [a]tabernacle
and all the vessels of the ministry
with the blood.

★22 [a]Lev. 5:11f. [b]Lev. 17:11

22 And according to the Law,
one may [a]almost *say,* all things
are cleansed with blood, and
[b]without shedding of blood there
is no forgiveness.

23 [a]Heb. 8:5

23 Therefore it was necessary
for the [a]copies of the things in the
heavens to be cleansed with
these, but [a]the heavenly things
themselves with better sacrifices
than these.

24 [a]Heb. 4:14; 9:12 [b]Heb. 8:2 [c]Heb. 9:12 [d]Matt. 18:10; Heb. 7:25

24 For Christ [a]did not enter a
holy place made with hands, a
mere copy of [b]the true one, but
into [c]heaven itself, now [d]to appear in the presence of God for
us;

25 [a]Heb. 9:7 [b]Heb. 9:2; 10:19

25 nor was it that He should
offer Himself often, as [a]the high
priest enters [b]the holy place [a]year
by year with blood not his own.

★26 [a]Matt. 25:34; Heb. 4:3 [b]Heb. 7:27; 9:12 [c]Matt. 13:39; Heb. 1:2 [d]1 John 3:5, 8 [e]Heb. 9:12, 14

26 Otherwise, He would have
needed to suffer often since [a]the
foundation of the world; but now
[b]once at [c]the consummation of
the ages He has been [d]manifested
to put away sin [e]by the sacrifice
of Himself.

27 And inasmuch as [a]it is appointed for men to die once and
after this [b]*comes* judgment,

27 [a]Gen. 3:19 [b]2 Cor. 5:10; 1 John 4:17

28 so Christ also, having been
[a]offered once to [b]bear the sins of
many, shall appear [c]a second time
for [f]salvation [d]without *reference*
to sin, to those who [e]eagerly await
Him.

★28 [a]Heb. 7:27 [b]1 Pet. 2:24 [c]Acts 1:11 [d]Heb. 4:15 [e]1 Cor. 1:7; Titus 2:13 [f]Heb. 5:9

10 For the Law, since it has
only [a]a shadow of [b]the
good things to come *and* not the
very form of things, can [c]never by
the same sacrifices year by year,
which they offer continually,
[d]make perfect those who draw
near.

★ 1-39
1 [a]Heb. 8:5 [b]Heb. 9:11 [c]Rom. 8:3; Heb. 9:9; 10:4, 11 [d]Heb. 7:19

2 Otherwise, would they not
have ceased to be offered, because
the worshipers, having once been
cleansed, would no longer have
had [a]consciousness of sins?

2 [a]1 Pet. 2:19

3 But [a]in those *sacrifices*
there is a reminder of sins year by
year.

3 [a]Heb. 9:7

4 For it is [a]impossible for the
[b]blood of bulls and goats to take
away sins.

4 [a]Heb. 10:1, 11 [b]Heb. 9:12f.

5 Therefore, [a]when He
comes into the world, He says,

"[b]SACRIFICE AND OFFERING
THOU HAST NOT DESIRED,
BUT [c]A BODY THOU HAST PRE-
PARED FOR ME;

★ 5 [a]Heb. 1:6 [b]Ps. 40:6 [c]Heb. 2:14; 5:7; 1 Pet. 2:24

6 [a]IN WHOLE BURNT OFFERINGS
AND *sacrifices* FOR SIN
THOU HAST TAKEN NO
PLEASURE.

6 [a]Ps. 40:6

7 "[a]THEN I SAID, 'BEHOLD, I
HAVE COME
(IN [b]THE ROLL OF THE BOOK IT
IS WRITTEN OF ME)
TO DO THY WILL, O GOD.' "

7 [a]Ps. 40:7, 8 [b]Ezra 6:2 4septuagint]; Jer. 36:2; Ezek. 2:9; 3:1f.

9:22 *almost.* For exceptions to the requirement of blood for cleansing permitted by the law see Lev. 5:11-13; Num. 16:46; 31:50.

9:26 *once* = once for all. *at the consummation of the ages.* The first coming of Christ. (cf. 1 Pet. 1:20).

9:28 *to bear the sins of many.* Quoted from Isa. 53:12. Isaiah was a significant source of early Christian interpretation of Christ. *without reference to sin.* I.e., apart from the sin question. In His first coming Christ dealt with sin once for all; in His second coming He will take redeemed sinners to Himself in the consummation of their salvation.

10:1-39 In this chapter the author emphasizes the finality of Christ's sacrifice by contrasting it with the lack of finality of the O.T. system of law and sacrifices. Christ's redemption needs no repetition and no supplementation. Therefore, a rejection of His sacrifice is final and unforgivable.

10:5 *He comes* . I.e., Christ.

8 After saying above, "[a]SAC-
RIFICES AND OFFERINGS AND [b]WHOLE
BURNT OFFERINGS AND *sacrifices* [c]FOR
SIN THOU HAST NOT DESIRED, NOR
HAST THOU TAKEN PLEASURE *in*
them" (which are offered according to the Law),
9 then He said, "[a]BEHOLD, I
HAVE COME TO DO THY WILL." He
takes away the first in order to establish the second.
10 By this will we have been
[a]sanctified through [b]the offering
of [c]the body of Jesus Christ [d]once
for all.
11 And every priest stands
daily ministering and [a]offering
time after time the same sacrifices, which [b]can never take away
sins;
12 but He, having offered one
sacrifice [a]for sins [b]for all time,
[c]sat down at the right hand of
God,
13 waiting from that time on-
ward [a]UNTIL HIS ENEMIES BE MADE A
FOOTSTOOL FOR HIS FEET.
14 For by one offering He has
[a]perfected [b]for all time those who
are sanctified.
15 And [a]the Holy Spirit also
bears witness to us; for after saying,

16 "[a]THIS IS THE COVENANT THAT
I WILL MAKE WITH THEM
AFTER THOSE DAYS, SAYS THE
LORD:
I WILL PUT MY LAWS UPON
THEIR HEART,
AND UPON THEIR MIND I WILL
WRITE THEM,"

He then says,

17 "[a]AND THEIR SINS AND THEIR
LAWLESS DEEDS
I WILL REMEMBER NO MORE."

8 [a]Ps. 40:6; Heb. 10:5f. [b]Mark 12:33 [c]Rom. 8:3
9 [a]Ps. 40:7, 8; Heb. 10:7
★10 [a]John 17:19; Eph. 5:26; Heb. 2:11; 10:14, 29; 13:12 [b]John 6:51; Eph. 5:2; Heb. 7:27; 9:14, 28; 10:12 [c]Heb. 2:14; 5:7; 1 Pet. 2:24 [d]Heb. 7:27
11 [a]Heb. 5:1 [b]Mic. 6:6-8; Heb. 10:1, 4
12 [a]Heb. 5:1 [b]Heb. 10:14 [c]Heb. 1:3
13 [a]Ps. 110:1; Heb. 1:13
14 [a]Heb. 10:1 [b]Heb. 10:12
15 [a]Heb. 3:7
★16-17
16 [a]Jer. 31:33; Heb. 8:10
17 [a]Jer. 31:34; Heb. 8:12

18 Now where there is forgiveness of these things, there is
no longer *any* offering for sin.

E **Parenthetical Warning: Don't Despise Christ,** 10:19-39

19 Since therefore, brethren,
we [a]have confidence to [b]enter the
holy place by the blood of Jesus,
20 by [a]a new and living way
which He inaugurated for us
through [b]the veil, that is, His
flesh,
21 and since *we have* [a]a great
priest [b]over the house of God,
22 let us [a]draw near with a
sincere heart in [b]full assurance of
faith, having our hearts
[c]sprinkled *clean* from an evil conscience and our bodies [d]washed
with pure water.
23 Let us hold fast the [a]con-
fession of our [b]hope without wa-
vering, for [c]He who promised is
faithful;
24 and let us consider how [a]to
stimulate one another to love and
[b]good deeds,
25 not forsaking our own [a]as-
sembling together, as is the habit
of some, but [b]encouraging *one*
another; and all the more, as you
see [c]the day drawing near.
26 For if we go on [a]sinning
willfully after receiving [b]the
knowledge of the truth, there no
longer remains a sacrifice for sins,
27 but a certain terrifying expectation of [a]judgment, and THE
[b]FURY OF A FIRE WHICH WILL CONSUME
THE ADVERSARIES.
28 [a]Anyone who has set aside
the Law of Moses dies without

19 [a]Heb. 3:6; 10:35 [b]Heb. 9:25
★20 [a]Heb. 9:8 [b]Heb. 6:19; 9:3
21 [a]Heb. 2:17 [b]1 Tim. 3:15; Heb. 3:6
22 [a]Heb. 7:19; 10:1 [b]Heb. 6:11 [c]Ezek. 36:25; Heb. 9:19; 12:24; 1 Pet. 1:2 [d]Acts 22:16; 1 Cor. 6:11; Eph. 5:26; Titus 3:5; 1 Pet. 3:21
23 [a]Heb. 3:1 [b]Heb. 3:6 [c]1 Cor. 1:9; 10:13; Heb. 11:11
★24 [a]Heb. 13:1 [b]Titus 3:8
★25 [a]Acts 2:42 [b]Heb. 3:13 [c]1 Cor. 3:13
★26 [a]Num. 15:30; Heb. 5:2; 6:4-8; 2 Pet. 2:20f. [b]1 Tim. 2:4
27 [a]John 5:29; Heb. 9:27 [b]Is. 26:11; 2 Thess. 1:7
28 [a]Deut. 17:2-6; Matt. 18:16; Heb. 2:2

10:10 *By this will.* I.e., by Christ's doing the will of God in becoming the sacrifice for sin.
10:16-17 See Jer. 31:33-34, quoted earlier in Heb. 8:10-12.
10:20 *a new and living way.* Christ is that way (cf. John 14:6; Heb. 4:14; 6:20; 7:24-25).
10:24 *to stimulate.* I.e., to stir up to an incitement or paroxysm of love and good works. To understand how strong this Greek word is, see its use in Acts 15:39 (sharp disagreement); 17:16 (being provoked); 1 Cor. 13:5 (provoked); Eph. 6:4 (provoke).
10:25 *our own assembling together.* I.e., the gathering of Christians for worship and edification. *the day.* I.e., of Christ's coming (also v. 37; 1 Cor. 3:13; Phil. 1:10).
10:26 *there no longer remains a sacrifice for sins.* If a person rejects the truth of Christ's death for sin, there is no other sacrifice for sin available and no other way to come to God. Only judgment remains (v. 27).

mercy on *the testimony of* two or
three witnesses.

★29 [a]Heb. 2:3 [b]Heb. 6:6 [c]Matt. 26:28; Heb. 13:20 [d]Eph. 5:26; Heb. 9:13f.; Rev. 1:5 [e]1 Cor. 6:11; Eph. 4:30; Heb. 6:4

29 [a]How much severer punishment do you think he will deserve [b]who has trampled under
foot the Son of God, and has regarded as unclean [c]the blood of
the covenant [d]by which he was
sanctified, and has [e]insulted the
Spirit of grace?

30 [a]Deut. 32:35; Rom. 12:19 [b]Deut. 32:36

30 For we know Him who
said, "[a]VENGEANCE IS MINE, I WILL
REPAY." And again, "[b]THE LORD
WILL JUDGE HIS PEOPLE."

31 [a]2 Cor. 5:11 [b]Matt. 16:16; Heb. 3:12

31 It is a [a]terrifying thing to
fall into the hands of the [b]living
God.

★32 [a]Heb. 5:12 [b]Heb. 6:4 [c]Phil. 1:30

32 But remember [a]the former
days, when, after being [b]enlight-
ened, you endured a great [c]con-
flict of sufferings,

33 [a]1 Cor. 4:9; Heb. 12:4 [b]Phil. 4:14 [Gr.]; 1 Thess. 2:14

33 partly, by being [a]made a
public spectacle through reproaches and tribulations, and
partly by becoming [b]sharers with
those who were so treated.

★34 [a]Heb. 13:3 [b]Matt. 5:12 [c]Heb. 9:15; 11:16; 13:14; 1 Pet. 1:4f.

34 For you [a]showed sympa-
thy to the prisoners, and accepted
[b]joyfully the seizure of your property, knowing that you have for
yourselves [c]a better possession
and an abiding one.

35 [a]Heb. 10:19 [b]Heb. 2:2

35 Therefore, do not throw
away your [a]confidence, which has
a great [b]reward.

★36 [a]Luke 21:19; Heb. 12:1 [b]Heb. 9:15

36 For you have need of [a]en-
durance, so that when you have
done the will of God, you may
[b]receive what was promised.

★37 [a]Hab. 2:3; Heb. 10:25; Rev. 22:20 [b]Matt. 11:3

37 [a]FOR YET IN A VERY LITTLE
WHILE,
[b]HE WHO IS COMING WILL
COME, AND WILL NOT DE-
LAY.

★38 [a]Hab. 2:4; Rom. 1:17; Gal. 3:11

38 [a]BUT MY RIGHTEOUS ONE
SHALL LIVE BY FAITH;
AND IF HE SHRINKS BACK, MY
SOUL HAS NO PLEASURE IN
HIM.

39 But we are not of those
who shrink back to destruction,
but of those who have faith to the
preserving of the soul.

III THE SUPERIORITY OF THE POWER OF CHRIST, 11:1–13:19

A The Power of Faith in Christ, 11:1–40

1 *The description of faith,* 11:1

★ 1 [a]Heb. 3:14 [Gr.] [b]Heb. 3:6 [c]Rom. 8:24; 2 Cor. 4:18; 5:7; Heb. 11:7, 27

11 Now faith is the [a]assur-
ance of *things* [b]hoped for,
the conviction of [c]things not seen.

2 *The examples of faith,* 11:2–40

★ 2 [a]Heb. 1:1 [b]Heb. 11:4, 39
★ 3 [a]Heb. 1:2 [b]Gen. 1; Heb. 1:2 [c]Heb. 6:5; 2 Pet. 3:5 [d]Rom. 4:17
★ 4 [a]Gen. 4:4; Matt. 23:35; 1 John 3:12 [b]Heb. 11:2 [c]Heb. 5:1 [d]Gen. 4:8-10; Heb. 12:24

2 For by it the [a]men of old
[b]gained approval.
3 By faith we understand
that the [a]worlds were prepared
[b]by the [c]word of God, so that
what is seen [d]was not made out of
things which are visible.
4 By faith [a]Abel offered to
God a better sacrifice than Cain,

10:29 The three indictments specified in this verse describe the enormity of the sin of unbelief.

10:32 *conflict of sufferings* = struggle with sufferings.

10:34 *to the prisoners.* Some Christians apparently had been imprisoned for their faith while others had experienced the *seizure* of their possessions.

10:36 *endurance* = patience.

10:37 See Hab. 2:3.

10:38 This quotation from Hab. 2:4 is used here to teach that the person who has been made righteous by God lives (and survives the coming ordeal) by faith. The believer trusts God in everything. Hab. 2:4 is also quoted in Rom. 1:17 and Gal. 3:11, where Paul uses it to teach that the one who is righteous by faith (rather than by works) shall live. Paul's emphasis is on salvation by faith; this writer's is on living by faith.

11:1 Faith is described in this great verse as the *assurance* (or reality, the same word translated "nature" in 1:3) *of things hoped for, the conviction* (as in John 16:8) *of things not seen.* Faith gives reality and proof of things unseen, treating them as if they were already objects of sight rather than of hope.

11:2 *men of old.* I.e., the O.T. patriarchs and heroes.

11:3 *the worlds were prepared.* Lit., the ages have been prepared (cf. 1:2). This means the preparation of all that the successive periods of time would contain.

11:4 *Abel.* Actually nothing is said here or in Gen. 4:3-5 as to why Abel's sacrifice was more acceptable, though the fact that it involved blood sacrifice is significant (see Heb. 12:24).

through which he [b]obtained the
testimony that he was righteous,
God testifying about his [c]gifts,
and through faith, though [d]he is
dead, he still speaks.
5 By faith [a]Enoch was taken
up so that he should not [b]see
death; and he was not found because God took him up; for he
obtained the witness that before
his being taken up he was pleasing to God.
6 And without faith it is impossible to please *Him,* for he
who [a]comes to God must believe
that He is, and *that* He is a re-
warder of those who seek Him.
7 By faith [a]Noah, being
[b]warned *by God* about [c]things
not yet seen, [d]in reverence [e]pre-
pared an ark for the salvation of
his household, by which he condemned the world, and became
an heir of [f]the righteousness
which is according to faith.
8 By faith [a]Abraham, when
he was called, obeyed by going
out to a place which he was to
[b]receive for an inheritance; and
he went out, not knowing where
he was going.
9 By faith he lived as an
alien in [a]the land of promise, as in
a foreign *land,* [b]dwelling in tents
with Isaac and Jacob, [c]fellow-
heirs of the same promise;
10 for he was looking for [a]the
city which has [b]foundations,
[c]whose architect and builder is
God.
11 By faith even [a]Sarah herself received ability to conceive,
even beyond the proper time of
life, since she considered Him
[b]faithful who had promised;
12 therefore, also, there was
born of one man, and [a]him as
good as dead at that, *as many de-*

★ 5 [a]Gen. 5:21-24 [b]Luke 2:26; John 8:51; Heb. 2:9
6 [a]Heb. 7:19
★ 7 [a]Gen. 6:13-22 [b]Heb. 8:5 [c]Heb. 11:1 [d]Heb. 5:7 [e]1 Pet. 3:20 [f]Gen. 6:9; Ezek. 14:14, 20; Rom. 4:13; 9:30
★ 8 [a]Gen. 12:1-4; Acts 7:2-4 [b]Gen. 12:7
9 [a]Acts 7:5 [b]Gen. 12:8; 13:3, 18; 18:1, 9 [c]Heb. 6:17
10 [a]Heb. 12:22; 13:14 [b]Rev. 21:14ff. [c]Heb. 11:16
★11 [a]Gen. 17:19; 18:11-14; 21:2 [b]Heb. 10:23
12 [a]Rom. 4:19 [b]Gen. 15:5; 22:17; 32:12

scendants [b]AS THE STARS OF HEAVEN
IN NUMBER, AND INNUMERABLE AS THE
SAND WHICH IS BY THE SEASHORE.
13 [a]All these died in faith,
[b]without receiving the promises,
but [c]having seen them and having welcomed them from a distance, and [d]having confessed that
they were strangers and exiles on
the earth.
14 For those who say such
things make it clear that they are
seeking a country of their own.
15 And indeed if they had
been thinking of that *country*
from which they went out, [a]they
would have had opportunity to
return.
16 But as it is, they desire a
better *country,* that is a [a]heavenly
one. Therefore [b]God is not
ashamed to be [c]called their God;
for [d]He has prepared a city for
them.
17 By faith [a]Abraham, when
he was tested, offered up Isaac;
and he who had [b]received the
promises was offering up his only
begotten *son;*
18 *it was he* to whom it was
said, "[a]IN ISAAC YOUR DESCENDANTS
SHALL BE CALLED."
19 He considered that [a]God is
able to raise *men* even from the
dead; from which he also received
him back as a [b]type.
20 By faith [a]Isaac blessed Jacob and Esau, even regarding
things to come.
21 By faith [a]Jacob, as he was
dying, blessed each of the sons of
Joseph, and [b]worshiped, *leaning*
on the top of his staff.
22 By faith [a]Joseph, when he
was dying, made mention of the
exodus of the sons of Israel, and
gave orders concerning his bones.

13 [a]Matt. 13:17 [b]Heb. 11:39 [c]John 8:56; Heb. 11:27 [d]Gen. 23:4; 47:9; Ps. 39:12; Eph. 2:19; 1 Pet. 1:1; 2:11
15 [a]Gen. 24:6-8
16 [a]2 Tim. 4:18 [b]Mark 8:38; Heb. 2:11 [c]Gen. 26:24; 28:13; Ex. 3:6, 15; 4:5 [d]Heb. 11:10; Rev. 21:2
★17 [a]Gen. 22:1-10; James 2:21 [b]Heb. 11:13
18 [a]Gen. 21:12; Rom. 9:7
19 [a]Rom. 4:21 [b]Heb. 9:9
★20 [a]Gen. 27:27-29, 39f.
★21 [a]Gen. 48:1, 5, 16, 20 [b]Gen. 47:31 [Septuagint]; 1 Kin. 1:47
★22 [a]Gen. 50:24f.; Ex. 13:19

11:5 *Enoch.* Enoch was saved from death by being *taken up* (Gen. 5:22–24).

11:7 *Noah.* His *reverence* was fear of God, or piety (Gen. 6:13–22).

11:8 *Abraham.* See Gen. 12:1–4.

11:11 *Sarah.* See Gen. 21:1–5.

11:17 *offered up Isaac.* See Gen. 22:1; Jas. 2:21. This was a severe test, for only through Isaac could Abraham have received the promises of the Lord.

11:20 *Isaac blessed Jacob and Esau.* See Gen. 27:26–40.

11:21 *Jacob . . . blessed each of the sons of Joseph.* See Gen. 48:1–22.

11:22 *Joseph.* See Gen. 50:24–25. Joseph showed his faith in God's promise to Abraham by requesting that his bones be buried in the Land of Promise.

23 By faith [a]Moses, when he was born, was hidden for three months by his parents, because they saw he was a beautiful child; and they were not afraid of the [b]king's edict.

24 By faith Moses, [a]when he had grown up, refused to be called the son of Pharaoh's daughter;

25 choosing rather to [a]endure ill-treatment with the people of God, than to enjoy the passing pleasures of sin;

26 [a]considering the reproach of Christ greater riches than the treasures of Egypt; for he was looking to the [b]reward.

27 By faith he [a]left Egypt, not [b]fearing the wrath of the king; for he endured, as [c]seeing Him who is unseen.

28 By faith he [a]kept the Passover and the sprinkling of the blood, so that [b]he who destroyed the first-born might not touch them.

29 By faith they [a]passed through the Red Sea as though *they were passing* through dry land; and the Egyptians, when they attempted it, were drowned.

30 By faith [a]the walls of Jericho fell down, [b]after they had been encircled for seven days.

31 By faith [a]Rahab the harlot did not perish along with those who were disobedient, after she had welcomed the spies in peace.

32 And what more shall I say? For time will fail me if I tell of [a]Gideon, [b]Barak, [c]Samson, [d]Jephthah, of [e]David and [f]Samuel and the prophets,

33 who by faith [a]conquered kingdoms, [b]performed *acts of* righteousness, [c]obtained promises, [d]shut the mouths of lions,

34 [a]quenched the power of fire, [b]escaped the edge of the sword, from weakness were made strong, [c]became mighty in war, [c]put foreign armies to flight.

35 [a]Women received *back* their dead by resurrection; and others were tortured, not accepting their release, in order that they might obtain a better resurrection;

36 and others experienced mockings and scourgings, yes, also [a]chains and imprisonment.

37 They were [a]stoned, they were [b]sawn in two, they were tempted, they were [c]put to death with the sword; they went about [d]in sheepskins, in goatskins, being destitute, afflicted, [e]ill-treated

38 (*men* of whom the world was not worthy), [a]wandering in deserts and mountains and caves and holes in the ground.

39 And all these, having [a]gained approval through their faith, [b]did not receive what was promised,

40 because God had provided [a]something better for us, so that [b]apart from us they should not be made perfect.

B The Power of Hope in Christ, 12:1-29

1 The debatable things of life, 12:1-2

12 Therefore, since we have so great a cloud of wit-

★23 aEx. 2:2 [Septuagint] bEx. 1:16, 22
24 aEx. 2:10, 11ff.
25 aHeb. 11:37
26 aLuke 14:33; Phil. 3:7f. bHeb. 2:2
27 aEx. 2:15; 12:50f.; 13:17f. bEx. 2:14; 10:28f. cCol. 1:15; Heb. 11:1, 13
★28 aEx. 12:21ff. bEx. 12:23, 29f.; 1 Cor. 10:10
★29 aEx. 14:22-29
★30 aJosh. 6:20 bJosh. 6:15f.
★31 aJosh. 2:9ff.; 6:23; James 2:25
★32 aJudg. 6-8 bJudg. 4-5 cJudg. 13-16 dJudg. 11-12 e1 Sam. 16:1, 13 f1 Sam. 1:20
★33 aJudg. 4, 7, 11, 14; 2 Sam. 5:17; 8:2; 10:12 b1 Sam. 12:4; 2 Sam. 8:15 c2 Sam. 7:11f. dJudg. 14:6; 1 Sam. 17:34; Dan. 6:22
★34 aDan. 3:23ff. bEx. 18:4; 1 Sam. 18:11; 19:10; 1 Kin. 19; 2 Kin. 6; Ps. 144:10 cJudg. 7:21; 15:8, 15f.; 1 Sam. 17:51f.; 2 Sam. 8:1-6; 10:15ff.
★35-38
35 a1 Kin. 17:23; 2 Kin. 4:36f.
36 aGen. 39:20; Jer. 20:2; 37:15
37 a1 Kin. 21:13; 2 Chr. 24:21 b2 Sam. 12:31; 1 Chr. 20:3 c1 Kin. 19:10; Jer. 26:23 d1 Kin. 19:13, 19; 2 Kin. 2:8, 13f.; Zech. 13:4 eHeb. 11:25; 13:3
38 a1 Kin. 18:4, 13; 19:9
★39 aHeb. 11:2 bHeb. 10:36; 11:13
40 aHeb. 11:16 bRev. 6:11
★ 1 aHeb. 10:39 bRom. 13:12; Eph. 4:22 [Gr.] c1 Cor. 9:24; Gal. 2:2 dHeb. 10:36

11:23 *Moses.* See Ex. 2:1-15.
11:28 *the Passover.* See Ex. 12:1-28.
11:29 *they passed through the Red Sea.* See Ex. 14:13-31.
11:30 *the walls of Jericho fell down.* See Josh. 6.
11:31 *Rahab.* See Josh. 2:1-21; 6:22-25; Jas. 2:25.
11:32 *Gideon* (Judg. 6:11; 8:32); *Barak* (Judg. 4:6-5:31); *Samson* (Judg. 13:24-16:31); *Jephthah* (Judg. 11:1-12:7); *David* (1 Sam. 16-17); *Samuel* (1 Sam. 7-10).
11:33 *shut the mouths of lions.* See Dan. 6 (Daniel); Judg. 14:5 (Samson); 1 Sam. 17:34 (David).
11:34 *quenched the power of fire.* See Dan. 3:23-28.
11:35-38 The background for much of what is in these verses is likely from the apocryphal book of 2 Maccabees (6:18-7:42).
11:35 *Women received back their dead by resurrection.* See 1 Kings 17:22-23 (the widow of Zarephath's son); 2 Kings 4:35-36 (the Shunammite's son).
11:39 *what was promised.* I.e., all that was included in the actual coming of the Messiah.
12:1 *a cloud of witnesses.* I.e., the heroes of

nesses surrounding us, let [a]us also
[b]lay aside every encumbrance,
and the sin which so easily entangles us, and let us [c]run with [d]en-
durance the race that is set before
us,

2 [a]Heb. 2:10 [b]Phil. 2:8f.; Heb. 2:9 [c]1 Cor. 1:18, 23; Heb. 13:13 [d]Heb. 1:3

2 fixing our eyes on Jesus,
the [a]author and perfecter of faith,
who for the joy set before Him
[b]endured the cross, [c]despising the
shame, and has [d]sat down at the
right hand of the throne of God.

2 The disciplines of life,
12:3–11

★ 3 [a]Matt. 10:24; Rev. 2:3 [b]Gal. 6:9; Heb. 12:5

3 For [a]consider Him who has
endured such hostility by sinners
against Himself, so that you may
not grow weary [b]and lose heart.

★ 4 [a]Heb. 10:32ff.; 13:13 [b]Phil. 2:8

4 [a]You have not yet resisted
[b]to the point of shedding blood in
your striving against sin;

★ 5-11
5 [a]Prov. 3:11 [b]Heb. 12:3

5 and you have forgotten the
exhortation which is addressed to
you as sons,

"[a]My son, do not regard
lightly the discipline of
the Lord,
Nor [b]faint when you are
reproved by Him;

6 [a]Prov. 3:12 [b]Ps. 119:75; Rev. 3:19

6 [a]For those [b]whom the
Lord loves He disci-
plines,
And He scourges every son
whom He receives."

7 [a]Deut. 8:5; 2 Sam. 7:14; Prov. 13:24; 19:18; 23:13f.

7 It is for discipline that you
endure; [a]God deals with you as
with sons; for what son is there
whom *his* father does not discipline?

8 [a]1 Pet. 5:9

8 But if you are without discipline, [a]of which all have become
partakers, then you are illegit-
imate children and not sons.

9 Furthermore, we had
earthly fathers to discipline us,
and we [a]respected them; shall we
not much rather be subject to
[b]the Father of spirits, and [c]live?

9 [a]Luke 18:2 [b]Num. 16:22; 27:16; Rev. 22:6 [c]Is. 38:16

10 For they disciplined us for
a short time as seemed best to
them, but He disciplines us for
our good, [a]that we may share His
holiness.

10 [a]2 Pet. 1:4

11 All discipline [a]for the moment seems not to be joyful, but
sorrowful; yet to those who have
been trained by it, afterwards it
yields the [b]peaceful fruit of righteousness.

11 [a]1 Pet. 1:6 [b]Is. 32:17; 2 Tim. 4:8; James 3:17f.

3 The direction of life,
12:12–17

12 Therefore, [a]strengthen the
hands that are weak and the
knees that are feeble,

12 [a]Is. 35:3

13 and [a]make straight paths
for your feet, so that *the limb*
which is lame may not be put out
of joint, but rather [b]be healed.

13 [a]Prov. 4:26; Gal. 2:14 [b]Gal. 6:1; James 5:16

14 [a]Pursue peace with all
men, and the [b]sanctification without which no one will [c]see the
Lord.

14 [a]Rom. 14:19 [b]Rom. 6:22; Heb. 12:10 [c]Matt. 5:8; Heb. 9:28

15 See to it that no one
[a]comes short of the grace of God;
that no [b]root of bitterness springing up causes trouble, and by it
many be [c]defiled;

15 [a]2 Cor. 6:1; Gal. 5:4; Heb. 4:1 [b]Deut. 29:18 [c]Titus 1:15

16 that *there be* no [a]immoral
or [b]godless person like Esau,
[c]who sold his own birthright for a
single meal.

★16 [a]Heb. 13:4 [b]1 Tim. 1:9 [c]Gen. 25:33f.

17 For you know that even afterwards, [a]when he desired to inherit the blessing, he was rejected, for he found no place for

17 [a]Gen. 27:30-40

---

faith mentioned in chapter 11 and others. *every encumbrance.* That which hinders the believer from being a winner. *the sin which so easily entangles us.* I.e., unbelief.

12:3 *Him.* Jesus.

12:4 *You have not yet resisted to the point of shedding blood.* None of the readers of this book had yet been martyred.

12:5–11 In these verses the writer discusses why Christians are disciplined. (1) It is part of the educational process by which a believer is fitted to share God's holiness (v. 10). (2) It is proof of a genuine love relationship between the heavenly Father and His children (vv. 6, 8). (3) It helps train them to be obedient (v. 9). (4) It produces the fruit of righteousness in their lives (v. 11). For additional teaching on this subject see the book of Job; Rom. 8:18; 2 Cor. 1:3–4; 4:16–17; 12:7–9; Phil. 1:29; 2 Tim. 3:12.

12:16 *Esau.* See Gen. 25:33. Though he may not have been *immoral* in the physical sense, Esau was immoral in the spiritual sense, being worldly and materialistic.

repentance, though he sought for
it with tears.

4 *The drive of life,* 12:18–24

★18–24 18 [a]2 Cor. 3:7-13; Heb. 12:18ff. [b]Ex. 19:12, 16ff.; 20:18; Deut. 4:11; 5:22 19 [a]Ex. 19:16, 19; 20:18; Matt. 24:31 [b]Ex. 19:19; Deut. 4:12 [c]Ex. 20:19; Deut. 5:25; 18:16 20 [a]Ex. 19:12f. 21 [a]Deut. 9:19 22 [a]Rev. 14:1 [b]Eph. 2:19; Phil. 3:20; Heb. 11:10; Rev. 21:2 [c]Heb. 3:12 [d]Gal. 4:26; Heb. 11:16 [e]Rev. 5:11 ★23 [a]Ex. 4:22; Heb. 2:12 marg. [b]Luke 10:20 [c]Gen. 18:25; Ps. 50:6; 94:2 [d]Heb. 11:40; Rev. 6:9, 11 24 [a]1 Tim. 2:5; Heb. 8:6; 9:15 [b]Heb. 9:19; 10:22; 1 Pet. 1:2 [c]Heb. 11:4

18 [a]For you have not come to
[b]*a mountain* that may be touched
and to a blazing fire, and to darkness and gloom and whirlwind,
19 and to the [a]blast of a trumpet and the [b]sound of words
which *sound was such that* those
who heard [c]begged that no further word should be spoken to
them.
20 For they could not bear the
command, "[a]IF EVEN A BEAST
TOUCHES THE MOUNTAIN, IT WILL BE
STONED."
21 And so terrible was the
sight, *that* Moses said, "[a]I AM FULL
OF FEAR AND TREMBLING."
22 But [a]you have come to
Mount Zion and to [b]the city of
[c]the living God, [d]the heavenly Jerusalem, and to [e]myriads of angels,
23 to the general assembly
and [a]church of the first-born who
[b]are enrolled in heaven, and to
God, [c]the Judge of all, and to the
[d]spirits of righteous men made
perfect,
24 and to Jesus, the [a]mediator
of a new covenant, and to the
[b]sprinkled blood, which speaks
better than [c]*the blood* of Abel.

5 *The duty of life,* 12:25–29

25 [a]Heb. 3:12 [b]Heb. 1:1 [c]Heb. 2:2f.; 10:28f. [d]Heb. 12:19 [Gr.] [e]Heb. 8:5; 11:7 26 [a]Ex. 19:18; Judg. 5:4f. [b]Hag. 2:6 ★27 [a]Is. 34:4; 54:10; 65:17; Rom. 8:19, 21; 1 Cor. 7:31; Heb. 1:10ff. 28 [a]Dan. 2:44 [b]Heb. 13:15, 21 29 [a]Deut. 4:24; 9:3; Is. 33:14; 2 Thess. 1:7; Heb. 10:27, 31

25 [a]See to it that you do not
refuse Him who is [b]speaking. For
[c]if those did not escape when
they [d]refused him who [e]warned
them on earth, much less *shall* we
escape who turn away from Him
who [e]*warns* from heaven.
26 And [a]His voice shook the
earth then, but now He has promised, saying, "[b]YET ONCE MORE I
WILL SHAKE NOT ONLY THE EARTH, BUT
ALSO THE HEAVEN."
27 And this *expression,* "Yet
once more," denotes [a]the removing of those things which can be
shaken, as of created things, in
order that those things which cannot be shaken may remain.
28 Therefore, since we receive
a [a]kingdom which cannot be
shaken, let us show gratitude, by
which we may [b]offer to God an
acceptable service with reverence
and awe;
29 for [a]our God is a consum-
ing fire.

C The Power of the Love of Christ, 13:1–19

1 *In relation to social duties,* 13:1–6

1 [a]Rom. 12:10; 1 Thess. 4:9; 1 Pet. 1:22 ★ 2 [a]Matt. 25:35; Rom. 12:13; 1 Pet. 4:9 [b]Gen. 18:3; 19:2 3 [a]Col. 4:18 [b]Matt. 25:36; Heb. 10:34 4 [a]1 Cor. 7:38; 1 Tim. 4:3 [b]1 Cor. 6:9; Gal. 5:19, 21; 1 Thess. 4:6 ★ 5 [a]Eph. 5:3; Col. 3:5; 1 Tim. 3:3 [b]Phil. 4:11 [c]Deut. 31:6; Josh. 1:5

13 Let [a]love of the brethren
continue.
2 Do not neglect to [a]show
hospitality to strangers, for by
this some have [b]entertained angels without knowing it.
3 [a]Remember [b]the prisoners,
as though in prison with them,
and those who are ill-treated,
since you yourselves also are in
the body.
4 [a]*Let* marriage *be held* in
honor among all, and let the *marriage* bed *be* undefiled; [b]for fornicators and adulterers God will
judge.
5 Let your character be [a]free
from the love of money, [b]being

12:18–24 The old covenant (the law) and the new covenant (the gospel) are contrasted by comparing Mt. Sinai, where the law was given, with Mt. Zion, the spiritual city, eternal in the heavens and symbolic of the gospel of grace.

12:23 *church of the first-born.* Lit., church of first-born ones. N.T. believers who belong to the church, the body of Christ. *spirits of righteous men made perfect.* Believers of O.T. times.

12:27 *those things which cannot be shaken.* I.e., the eternal kingdom to which Christians belong (v. 28).

13:2 *some have entertained angels without knowing it.* The word "angel" may refer to superhuman beings (see Gen. 18:1–8 for an example of such entertaining) or it may refer to a human being who is a messenger from God (see Jas. 2:25 for an example of such entertaining).

13:5 *He Himself has said.* See Deut. 31:6. The idea is: Christians need not be anxious (cf. Matt. 6:24–34).

content with what you have; for
He Himself has said, "[c]I WILL NEV-
ER DESERT YOU, NOR WILL I EVER FOR-
SAKE YOU,"
6 so that we confidently say,

> "[a]THE LORD IS MY HELPER, I
> WILL NOT BE AFRAID.
> WHAT SHALL MAN DO TO
> ME?"

2 *In relation to spiritual duties,* 13:7–19

7 Remember [a]those who led
you, who spoke [b]the word of God
to you; and considering the result
of their conduct, [c]imitate their
faith.
8 [a]Jesus Christ *is* the same
yesterday and today, *yes* and forever.
9 [a]Do not be carried away
by varied and strange teachings;
for it is good for the heart to [b]be
strengthened by grace, not by
[c]foods, [d]through which those who
were thus occupied were not
benefited.
10 We have an altar, [a]from
which those [b]who serve the tabernacle have no right to eat.
11 For [a]the bodies of those
animals whose blood is brought
into the holy place by the high
priest *as an offering* for sin, are
burned outside the camp.
12 Therefore Jesus also, [a]that
He might sanctify the people
[b]through His own blood, suffered
[c]outside the gate.
13 Hence, let us go out to
Him outside the camp, [a]bearing
His reproach.
14 For here [a]we do not have a
lasting city, but we are seeking
[b]*the city* which is to come.
15 [a]Through Him then, let us

6 [a]Ps. 118:6
7 [a]Heb. 13:17, 24 [b]Luke 5:1 [c]Heb. 6:12
8 [a]2 Cor. 1:19; Heb. 1:12
9 [a]Eph. 4:14; Jude 12 [b]2 Cor. 1:21; Col. 2:7 [c]Col. 2:16 [d]Heb. 9:10
10 [a]1 Cor. 10:18 [b]Heb. 8:5
★**11** [a]Ex. 29:14; Lev. 4:12, 21; 9:11; 16:27; Num. 19:3, 7
★**12** [a]Eph. 5:26; Heb. 2:11 [b]Heb. 9:12 [c]John 19:17
13 [a]Luke 9:23; Heb. 11:26; 12:2
14 [a]Heb. 10:34; 12:27 [b]Eph. 2:19; Heb. 2:5; 11:10, 16; 12:22
15 [a]1 Pet. 2:5 [b]Lev. 7:12 [c]Is. 57:19; Hos. 14:2

continually offer up a [b]sacrifice of
praise to God, that is, [c]the fruit of
lips that give thanks to His name.
16 And do not neglect doing
good and [a]sharing; for [b]with such
sacrifices God is pleased.
17 [a]Obey your leaders, and
submit *to them;* for [b]they keep
watch over your souls, as those
who will give an account. Let
them do this with joy and not
with grief, for this would be unprofitable for you.
18 [a]Pray for us, for we are
sure that we have a [b]good conscience, desiring to conduct ourselves honorably in all things.
19 And I urge *you* all the
more to do this, [a]that I may be
restored to you the sooner.

★**16** [a]Rom. 12:13 [b]Phil. 4:18
★**17** [a]1 Cor. 16:16; Heb. 13:7, 24 [b]Is. 62:6; Ezek. 3:17; Acts 20:28
18 [a]1 Thess. 5:25 [b]Acts 24:16; 1 Tim. 1:5
19 [a]Philem. 22

IV CONCLUDING BENEDICTIONS, 13:20–25

20 Now [a]the God of peace,
who [b]brought up from the dead
the [c]great Shepherd of the sheep
through [d]the blood of the [e]eternal
covenant, *even* Jesus our Lord,
21 [a]equip you in every good
thing to do His will, [b]working in
us that [c]which is pleasing in His
sight, through Jesus Christ, [d]to
whom *be* the glory forever and
ever. Amen.
22 But [a]I urge you, [b]brethren,
bear with this [b]word of exhortation, for [c]I have written to you
briefly.
23 Take notice that [a]our
brother Timothy has been released, with whom, if he comes
soon, I shall see you.
24 Greet [a]all of your leaders
and all the [b]saints. Those from
[c]Italy greet you.
25 [a]Grace be with you all.

20 [a]Rom. 15:33 [b]Acts 2:24; Rom. 10:7 [c]Is. 63:11; John 10:11; 1 Pet. 2:25 [d]Zech. 9:11; Heb. 10:29 [e]Is. 55:3; Jer. 32:40; Ezek. 37:26
★**21** [a]1 Pet. 5:10 [b]Phil. 2:13 [c]Heb. 12:28; 1 John 3:22 [d]Rom. 11:36
★**22** [a]Acts 13:15; Heb. 3:13; 10:25; 12:5; 13:19 [b]Heb. 3:1 [c]1 Pet. 5:12
★**23** [a]Acts 16:1; Col. 1:1
★**24** [a]1 Cor. 16:16; Heb. 13:7, 17 [b]Acts 9:13 [c]Acts 18:2
25 [a]Col. 4:18

13:11 *outside the camp.* See Lev. 4:21; 16:27.
13:12 *Jesus . . . suffered outside the gate.* See John 19:17–20.
13:16 *sharing* what you have (Phil. 4:18).
13:17 *your leaders.* Church leaders, as also in v. 7. *unprofitable for you* = not to your advantage.
13:21 *equip.* Or, fully provide, adjust, make ready. Some other occurrences of the Greek word are in Matt. 4:21; Gal. 6:1; 1 Thess. 3:10.
13:22 *bear* = be patient with. *briefly.* Perhaps also outspokenly.
13:23 *Timothy.* Apparently he had been imprisoned (see Acts 16:1; Rom. 16:21).
13:24 *saints* = believers.

INTRODUCTION TO THE LETTER OF JAMES

AUTHOR: James DATE: 45–50

The General Epistles *James, 1 and 2 Peter, 1, 2, and 3 John, and Jude were called by the early church the "General," "Universal," or "Catholic" epistles because their addresses (with the exceptions of 2 and 3 John) were not limited to a single locality. James, for example, is addressed "to the twelve tribes who are dispersed abroad" (1:1)—a designation for believers everywhere (likely all Jewish Christians at that early date).*

Authorship *Of the four men bearing the name James in the New Testament, only two have been proposed as the author of this letter—James the son of Zebedee (and brother of John) and James the half brother of Jesus. It is unlikely that the son of Zebedee was the author, for he was martyred in A.D. 44 (Acts 12:2). The authoritative tone of the letter not only rules out the two lesser known Jameses of the New Testament ("James the less" and the James of Luke 6:16) but points to the half brother of Jesus who became the recognized leader of the Jerusalem church (Acts 12:17; 15:13; 21:18). This conclusion is supported by the resemblances in the Greek between this epistle and the speech of James at the Council of Jerusalem (1:1 and Acts 15:23; 1:27 and Acts 15:14; 2:5 and Acts 15:13).*

Date *Some, denying the authorship by James because of the excellent Greek used, place the writing of the book at the very end of the first century. However, Galileans knew and used Greek well, along with Aramaic and Hebrew. Further, an early date is indicated by the lack of reference to the Jerusalem Council (A.D. 49), by the use of the word "synagogue" (assembly) for the church in 2:2, and by the strong expectation of the Lord's soon return (5:7–9).*

Canonicity *The canonical status of this letter was questioned until the church realized that its author was almost surely the half brother of Jesus. Luther did not question the genuineness of James, only its usefulness in comparison with Paul's epistles, because it says little about justification by faith, while elevating works.*

Contents *The book is concerned with the practical aspects of Christian conduct; it tells how faith works in everyday life. James's purpose was to provide concrete ethical instruction. Compared to Paul, James shows much less interest in formal theology, though the letter is not without theological statements (1:12; 2:1, 10–12, 19; 3:9; 5:7–9, 12, 14). Many subjects are discussed in this book, making it like a series of brief sayings arranged in the form of a letter. While there is little formal structure to the book, its many instructions explain how to be doers of the Word (1:22). In the 108 verses of the epistle there are references or allusions from 22 books of the Old Testament and at least 15 allusions to the teachings of Christ as embodied in the Sermon on the Mount. Among the key subjects discussed are faith and works (2:14–26), the use of the tongue (3:1–12), and prayer for the sick (5:13–16).*

OUTLINE OF JAMES

I. Greeting, 1:1
II. Trials, 1:2–18
- A. The Purpose of Trials, 1:2–12
- B. The Pedigree of Trials, 1:13–16
- C. The Purpose of God, 1:17–18

III. The Word, 1:19–27
IV. Partiality, 2:1–13
- A. The Command, 2:1
- B. The Conduct, 2:2–3
- C. The Consequences, 2:4–13

V. Faith and Works, 2:14–26
- A. The Inquiry, 2:14
- B. The Illustration, 2:15–17
- C. The Indoctrination, 2:18–26

VI. Sins of the Tongue, 3:1–12
- A. Its Bridling, 3:1–4
- B. Its Boasting, 3:5–12

VII. True Wisdom, 3:13–18
VIII. Worldliness, 4:1–17
- A. Its Cause, 4:1–2
- B. Its Consequences, 4:3–6
- C. Its Cure, 4:7–10
- D. Its Characteristics, 4:11–17

IX. Riches, Patience, and Swearing, 5:1–12
X. Prayer, 5:13–18
XI. The Conversion of the Erring, 5:19–20

THE LETTER OF JAMES

I GREETING, 1:1

★ 1 [a]Acts 12:2, 17 [b]Titus 1:1 [c]Rom. 1:1 [d]Luke 22:30 [e]John 7:35 [f]Acts 15:23

1 [a]James, a [b]bond-servant of
God and [c]of the Lord Jesus
Christ, to [d]the twelve tribes who
are [e]dispersed abroad, [f]greetings.

II TRIALS, 1:2–18

A The Purpose of Trials, 1:2–12

2 [a]Matt. 5:12; James 1:12; 5:11 [b]1 Pet. 1:6
3 [a]1 Pet. 1:7 [b]Heb. 6:12 [c]Luke 21:19
4 [a]Luke 21:19 [b]Matt. 5:48; Col. 4:12; 1 Thess. 5:23; James 3:2
5 [a]1 Kin. 3:9ff.; Prov. 2:3-6; James 3:17 [b]Matt. 7:7
★ 6 [a]Matt. 21:21 [b]Mark 11:23; Acts 10:20 [c]Eph. 4:14 Matt. 14:28-31
★ 8 [a]James 4:8 [b]2 Pet. 2:14
9 [a]Luke 14:11

2 [a]Consider it all joy, my
brethren, when you encounter
[b]various trials,
3 knowing that [a]the testing
of your [b]faith produces [c]endur-
ance.
4 And let [a]endurance have
its perfect result, that you may be
[b]perfect and complete, lacking in
nothing.
5 But if any of you [a]lacks
wisdom, let him ask of God, who
gives to all men generously and
without reproach, and [b]it will be
given to him.
6 But let him [a]ask in faith
[b]without any doubting, for the
one who doubts is like the surf of
the sea [c]driven and tossed by the
wind.
7 For let not that man expect
that he will receive anything from
the Lord,
8 *being* a [a]double-minded
man, [b]unstable in all his ways.
9 [a]But let the brother of
humble circumstances glory in his
high position;
10 and *let* the rich man *glory*
in his humiliation, because [a]like
flowering grass he will pass away.
11 For the sun rises with [a]a
scorching wind, and [b]withers the
grass; and its flower falls off, and
the beauty of its appearance is destroyed; so too the rich man in the
midst of his pursuits will fade
away.
12 [a]Blessed is a man who per-
severes under trial; for once he
has been approved, he will receive [b]the crown of life, which *the*
Lord [c]has promised to those who
[d]love Him.

★10 [a]1 Cor. 7:31; 1 Pet. 1:24
11 [a]Matt. 20:12 [b]Ps. 102:4, 11; Is. 40:7f.
★12 [a]Luke 6:22; James 5:11; 1 Pet. 3:14; 4:14 [b]1 Cor. 9:25 [c]Ex. 20:6; James 2:5 [d]1 Cor. 2:9; 8:3

B The Pedigree of Trials, 1:13–16

13 Let no one say when he is
tempted, "[a]I am being tempted by
God"; for God cannot be tempted
by evil, and He Himself does not
tempt any one.
14 But each one is tempted
when he is carried away and enticed by his own lust.
15 Then [a]when lust has conceived, it gives birth to sin; and
when [b]sin is accomplished, it
brings forth death.
16 [a]Do not be deceived, [b]my
beloved brethren.

★13 [a]Gen. 22:1
★14
15 [a]Job 15:35; Ps. 7:14; Is. 59:4 [b]Rom. 5:12; 6:23
★16 [a]1 Cor. 6:9 [b]Acts 1:15; James 1:2, 19; 2:1, 5, 14; 3:1, 10; 4:11; 5:12, 19

1:1 *to the twelve tribes who are dispersed abroad.* The letter is addressed to Jewish Christians (cf. 2:1; 5:7) scattered throughout the world.

1:6 *doubting.* I.e., going back and forth between belief and unbelief (cf. Rom. 4:20).

1:8 *a double-minded man.* I.e., a man of divided allegiance.

1:10 *his humiliation.* Either by losing his money or by being brought through some circumstance in order to realize that money means little and is at best transitory.

1:12 *once he has been approved.* After having stood the test. *crown of life.* One of the rewards or prizes for the Christian, kingly glory and life. See note on 1 Cor. 3:14.

1:13 *tempted.* To tempt is to test, try, prove, or solicit to evil. In vv. 2 and 12, the same Greek word is used to mean those trials which are designed to prove the quality of one's character. In this verse the word means "a solicitation to evil," and this, James says, is not from God but from man's own inner lust (v. 14). Any attempt at self-excuse is based on ignorance both of God and of the nature of temptation.

1:14 *carried away . . . enticed.* The picture behind these words is that of the hunter or fisherman luring his prey from its safe retreat.

1:16 *Do not be deceived.* Used also in 1 Cor. 6:9; 15:33; and Gal. 6:7.

C The Purpose of God, 1:17–18

17 Every good thing bestowed and every perfect gift is [a]from above, coming down from [b]the Father of lights, [c]with whom there is no variation, or shifting shadow.

★17 [a]John 3:3; James 3:15, 17 [b]Ps. 136:7; 1 John 1:5 [c]Mal. 3:6

18 In the exercise of [a]His will He [b]brought us forth by [c]the word of truth, so that we might be, as it were, the [d]first fruits among His creatures.

★18 [a]John 1:13 [b]James 1:15; 1 Pet. 1:3, 23 [c]2 Cor. 6:7; Eph. 1:13; 2 Tim. 2:15 [d]Jer. 2:3; Rev. 14:4

III THE WORD, 1:19–27

19 *This* [a]you know, [b]my beloved brethren. But let every one be quick to hear, [c]slow to speak *and* [d]slow to anger;

20 for [a]the anger of man does not achieve the righteousness of God.

21 Therefore [a]putting aside all filthiness and *all* that remains of wickedness, in humility receive [b]the word implanted, which is able to save your souls.

22 [a]But prove yourselves doers of the word, and not merely hearers who delude themselves.

23 For if any one is a hearer of the word and not a doer, he is like a man who looks at his natural face [a]in a mirror;

24 for *once* he has looked at himself and gone away, he has immediately forgotten what kind of person he was.

19 [a]1 John 2:21 [b]Acts 1:15; James 1:2, 16; 2:1, 5, 14; 3:1, 10; 4:11; 5:12, 19 [c]Prov. 10:19; 17:27 [d]Prov. 16:32; Eccles. 7:9
20 [a]Matt. 5:22; Eph. 4:26
★21 [a]Eph. 4:22; 1 Pet. 2:1 [b]Eph. 1:13; 1 Pet. 1:22f.
22 [a]Matt. 7:24-27; Luke 6:46-49; Rom. 2:13; James 1:22-25; 2:14-20
★23 [a]1 Cor. 13:12

25 But one who looks intently at the perfect law, [a]the *law* of liberty, and abides by it, not having become a forgetful hearer but an effectual doer, this man shall be [b]blessed in what he does.

★25 [a]John 8:32; Rom. 8:2; Gal. 2:4; 6:2; James 2:12; 1 Pet. 2:16 [b]John 13:17

26 If any one thinks himself to be religious, and yet does not [a]bridle his tongue but deceives his *own* heart, this man's religion is worthless.

26 [a]Ps. 39:1; 141:3; James 3:2-12

27 This is pure and undefiled religion [a]in the sight of *our* God and Father, to [b]visit [c]orphans and widows in their distress, *and* to keep oneself unstained by [d]the world.

27 [a]Rom. 2:13; Gal. 3:11 [b]Matt. 25:36 [c]Deut. 14:29; Job 31:16, 17, 21; Ps. 146:9; Is. 1:17, 23 [d]Matt. 12:32; Eph. 2:2; Titus 2:12; James 4:4; 2 Pet. 1:4; 2:20; 1 John 2:15-17

IV PARTIALITY, 2:1–13

A The Command, 2:1

2 [a]My brethren, [b]do not hold your faith in our [c]glorious Lord Jesus Christ with *an attitude of* [d]personal favoritism.

★ 1 [a]James 1:16 [b]Heb. 12:2 [c]Acts 7:2; 1 Cor. 2:8 [d]Acts 10:34; James 2:9

B The Conduct, 2:2–3

2 For if a man comes into your assembly with a gold ring and dressed in [a]fine clothes, and there also comes in a poor man in [b]dirty clothes,

★ 2 [a]Luke 23:11; James 2:3 [b]Zech. 3:3f.

3 and you pay special attention to the one who is wearing the

★ 3 [a]Luke 23:11; James 2:3

1:17 *Every good thing bestowed.* Both the gift and the act of giving. The point is that all these good things come from above. This statement may have come from an early Christian hymn. *Father of lights.* God is the source of all light—physical, intellectual, moral, and spiritual—and He does not change.

1:18 *His will.* God's will or purpose is the cause of our regeneration *(He brought us forth)* by means of the gospel message. *first fruits.* These first believers, largely Jewish in background, were the guarantee of a fuller harvest of believers to come.

1:21 *word implanted.* I.e., the gospel received as it was given (v. 18), as the word of truth.

1:23 *his natural face.* Lit., the face of his birth, his physical features. The contrast in vv. 23–25 is a simple one: the careless man looks in a mirror and forgets what he sees. The earnest man looks into the Word of God and acts upon what he sees there. *like a man.* The word for *man* is "male" and indicates that men, in contrast to women, who are more sensitive by nature, need this exhortation to careful observance of what they see in the Word.

1:25 *the perfect law, the law of liberty.* The Bible itself, though at the time this letter was written, only the O.T. and the teachings of Christ had scriptural authority. The Word of God is the means of regeneration (1:18), a mirror reflecting man's defects (1:23), the ethical guide for Christian living (1:25; 2:8), and the standard for judgment (2:12).

2:1 *personal favoritism.* I.e., show no partiality, especially in regard to people of position or wealth in the congregation.

2:2 *gold ring.* It was not uncommon for several to be worn as a mark of wealth and social distinction (Luke 15:22).

2:3 *by my footstool.* I.e., in a lowly place, on the floor.

[a]fine clothes, and say, "You sit here in a good place," and you say to the poor man, "You stand over there, or sit down by my footstool,"

C The Consequences, 2:4–13

★ 4 [a]Luke 18:6; John 7:24

4 have you not made distinctions among yourselves, and become judges [a]with evil motives?

5 [a]James 1:16 [b]Job 34:19; 1 Cor. 1:27f. [c]Luke 12:21; Rev. 2:9 [d]Matt. 5:3; 25:34 [e]James 1:12

5 Listen, [a]my beloved brethren: did not [b]God choose the poor of this world *to be* [c]rich in faith and [d]heirs of the kingdom which He [e]promised to those who love Him?

6 [a]Acts 8:3; 16:19

6 But you have dishonored the poor man. Is it not the rich who oppress you and personally [a]drag you into court?

7 [a]Acts 11:26; 1 Pet. 4:16

7 [a]Do they not blaspheme the fair name by which you have been called?

8 [a]Matt. 7:12 [b]Lev. 19:18

8 If, however, you [a]are fulfilling the royal law, according to the Scripture, "[b]YOU SHALL LOVE YOUR NEIGHBOR AS YOURSELF," you are doing well.

9 [a]Acts 10:34; James 2:1 [b]Deut. 1:17

9 But if you [a]show partiality, you are committing sin *and* are [b]convicted by the law as transgressors.

★10 [a]James 3:2; 2 Pet. 1:10; Jude 24 [b]Matt. 5:19; Gal. 5:3

10 For whoever keeps the whole law and yet [a]stumbles in one *point,* he has become [b]guilty of all.

11 [a]Ex. 20:14; Deut. 5:18 [b]Ex. 20:13; Deut. 5:17

11 For He who said, "[a]DO NOT COMMIT ADULTERY," also said, "[b]DO NOT COMMIT MURDER." Now if you do not commit adultery, but do commit murder, you have become a transgressor of the law.

12 So speak and so act, as those who are to be judged by [a]*the* law of liberty.

12 [a]James 1:25

13 For [a]judgment *will be* merciless to one who has shown no mercy; mercy triumphs over judgment.

13 [a]Prov. 21:13; Matt. 5:7; 18:32-35; Luke 6:37f.

V FAITH AND WORKS, 2:14–26

A The Inquiry, 2:14

14 [a]What use is it, [b]my brethren, if a man says he has faith, but he has no works? Can that faith save him?

★14 [a]James 1:22ff. [b]James 1:16

B The Illustration, 2:15–17

15 [a]If a brother or sister is without clothing and in need of daily food,

15 [a]Matt. 25:35f.; Luke 3:11

16 and one of you says to them, "[a]Go in peace, be warmed and be filled," and yet you do not give them what is necessary for *their* body, what use is that?

16 [a]1 John 3:17f.

17 Even so [a]faith, if it has no works, is dead, *being* by itself.

17 [a]Gal. 5:6; James 2:20, 26

C The Indoctrination, 2:18–26

18 [a]But someone may *well* say, "You have faith, and I have works; show me your [b]faith without the works, and I will [c]show you my faith [d]by my works."

18 [a]Rom. 9:19 [b]Rom. 3:28; 4:6; Heb. 11:33 [c]James 3:13 [d]Matt. 7:16f.; Gal. 5:6

19 You believe that [a]God is one. [b]You do well; [c]the demons also believe, and shudder.

★19 [a]Deut. 6:4; Mark 12:29 [b]James 2:8 [c]Matt. 8:29; Mark 1:24; 5:7; Luke 4:34; Acts 19:15

20 But are you willing to recognize, [a]you foolish fellow, that [b]faith without works is useless?

20 [a]Rom. 9:20; 1 Cor. 15:36 [b]Gal. 5:6; James 2:17, 26

2:4 *judges with evil motives.* To show favoritism to the rich is wrong in a number of ways. It shows one's value system to be false (v.3); it fails to honor the poor whom God honors (v. 5); it favors those who oppress you (v. 6); it is sin (v. 9).

2:10 *has become guilty of all.* One sin, small or great, makes a man a sinner and brings him under condemnation.

2:14 *Can that faith save him?* I.e., can a nonworking, dead, spurious faith save a person? James is not saying that we are saved by works, but that a faith that does not produce good works is a dead faith. James was not refuting the Pauline doctrine of justification by true faith, but a perversion of it. Both Paul and James define faith as a living, productive trust in Christ. Genuine faith cannot be "dead" to morality or barren to works. An illustration of spurious faith is given in vv. 15–16.

2:19 *God is one.* The unity of God was a fundamental belief in Judaism, but if that belief did not produce good deeds it was no better than the "monotheism" of the demons.

★21 [a]Gen. 22:9, 10, 12, 16-18

21 [a]Was not Abraham our father justified by works, when he offered up Isaac his son on the altar?

22 [a]John 6:29; Heb. 11:17 [b]1 Thess. 1:3

22 You see that [a]faith was working with his works, and as a result of the [b]works, faith was perfected;

★23 [a]Gen. 15:6; Rom. 4:3 [b]2 Chr. 20:7; Is. 41:8

23 and the Scripture was fulfilled which says, "[a]AND ABRAHAM BELIEVED GOD, AND IT WAS RECKONED TO HIM AS RIGHTEOUSNESS," and he was called [b]the friend of God.

★24

24 You see that a man is justified by works, and not by faith alone.

★25 [a]Heb. 11:31 [b]Josh. 2:4, 6, 15

25 And in the same way was not [a]Rahab the harlot also justified by works, [b]when she received the messengers and sent them out by another way?

26 [a]Gal. 5:6; James 2:17, 20

26 For just as the body without *the* spirit is dead, so also [a]faith without works is dead.

VI SINS OF THE TONGUE, 3:1-12

A Its Bridling, 3:1-4

★ 1 [a]Matt. 23:8; Rom. 2:20f.; 1 Tim. 1:7 [b]James 1:16; 3:10

3 [a]Let not many *of you* become teachers, [b]my brethren, knowing that as such we shall incur a stricter judgment.

★ 2 [a]James 2:10 [b]Matt. 12:34-37; James 3:2-12 [c]James 1:4 [d]James 1:26

2 For we all [a]stumble in many *ways.* [b]If any one does not stumble in what he says, he is a [c]perfect man, able to [d]bridle the whole body as well.

3 [a]Ps. 32:9

3 Now [a]if we put the bits into the horses' mouths so that they may obey us, we direct their entire body as well.

4 Behold, the ships also, though they are so great and are driven by strong winds, are still directed by a very small rudder, wherever the inclination of the pilot desires.

B Its Boasting, 3:5-12

5 [a]Ps. 12:3f.; 73:8f. [b]Prov. 26:20f.

5 So also the tongue is a small part of the body, and *yet* it [a]boasts of great things. [b]Behold, how great a forest is set aflame by such a small fire!

★ 6 [a]Ps. 120:3, 4; Prov. 16:27 [b]Matt. 12:36f.; 15:11, 18f. [c]Matt. 5:22

6 And [a]the tongue is a fire, the *very* world of iniquity; the tongue is set among our members as that which [b]defiles the entire body, and sets on fire the course of *our* life, and is set on fire by [c]hell.

7 For every species of beasts and birds, of reptiles and creatures of the sea, is tamed, and has been tamed by the human race.

8 [a]Ps. 140:3; Eccles. 10:11; Rom. 3:13

8 But no one can tame the tongue; *it is* a restless evil *and* full of [a]deadly poison.

★ 9 [a]James 1:27 [b]1 Cor. 11:7

9 With it we bless [a]*our* Lord and Father; and with it we curse men, [b]who have been made in the likeness of God;

10 from the same mouth come *both* blessing and cursing. My brethren, these things ought not to be this way.

11 Does a fountain send out from the same opening *both* fresh and bitter *water?*

2:21 *justified by works.* In Paul's writings, "justification" means to declare a sinner righteous in the sight of God; here in James it means "to vindicate" or "show to be righteous" before God and men. Abraham's justification in Paul's sense is recorded in Gen. 15:6; Abraham's justification in James's sense took place 30 or more years later in the patriarch's crowning act of obedience in offering Isaac (Gen. 22). By this act he proved the reality of his Gen. 15 faith.

2:23 *friend of God.* This title comes from 2 Chron. 20:7 and Isa. 41:8.

2:24 This verse is the reply to the question of v. 14. Unproductive faith cannot save, because it is not genuine faith. Faith and works are like a two-coupon ticket to heaven. The coupon of works is not good for passage, and the coupon of faith is not valid if detached from works.

2:25 *Rahab.* Her story is told in Josh. 2:1-21.

3:1 *teachers.* Since teachers use their tongues (to instruct others) more, they will be judged more strictly.

3:2 The theme of vv. 1-12 is found in the second clause, *If any one . . . he is a perfect man.* "Perfect" means mature, of full moral and spiritual growth.

3:6 *the course of our life.* I.e., the whole course of human existence. The tremendous destructive power of the tongue comes from *hell* (lit., Gehenna; see note on Matt. 5:22).

3:9 *in the likeness of God.* The divine image has been marred by sin, but not totally obliterated. Man's being made in the image of God is the basis for not cursing our fellow man.

12 [a]Matt. 7:16

12 [a]Can a fig tree, my brethren, produce olives, or a vine produce figs? Neither *can* salt water
produce fresh.

VII TRUE WISDOM, 3:13–18

★13 [a]James 2:18 [b]1 Pet. 2:12
14 [a]Rom. 2:8; 2 Cor. 12:20; James 3:16 [b]1 Tim. 2:4; James 1:18; 5:19
15 [a]James 1:17 [b]1 Cor. 2:6; 3:19 [c]2 Cor. 1:12 [d]2 Thess. 2:9f.; 1 Tim. 4:1; Rev. 2:24
16 [a]Rom. 2:8; 2 Cor. 12:20; James 3:14
17 [a]James 1:17 [b]2 Cor. 7:11; James 4:8 [c]Matt. 5:9; Heb. 12:11 [d]Phil. 4:5; Titus 3:2 [e]Luke 6:36 [f]James 2:4 [Gr.] [g]Rom. 12:9; 2 Cor. 6:6
★18 [a]Prov. 11:18; Is. 32:17

13 Who among you is wise
and understanding? [a]Let him
show by his [b]good behavior his
deeds in the gentleness of wisdom.
14 But if you have bitter [a]jeal-
ousy and selfish ambition in your
heart, do not be arrogant and *so*
lie against [b]the truth.
15 This wisdom is not that
which comes down [a]from above,
but is [b]earthly, [c]natural, [d]demon-
ic.
16 For where [a]jealousy and
selfish ambition exist, there is disorder and every evil thing.
17 But the wisdom [a]from
above is first [b]pure, then [c]peace-
able, [d]gentle, reasonable, [e]full of
mercy and good fruits, [f]unwaver-
ing, without [g]hypocrisy.
18 And the [a]seed whose fruit
is righteousness is sown in peace
by those who make peace.

VIII WORLDLINESS, 4:1–17

A Its Cause, 4:1–2

1 [a]Titus 3:9 [b]Rom. 7:23
★ 2 [a]James 5:6; 1 John 3:15

4 What is the source of quarrels and [a]conflicts among
you? Is not the source your pleasures that wage [b]war in your
members?
2 You lust and do not have;
so you [a]commit murder. And you
are envious and cannot obtain; *so*
you fight and quarrel. You do not
have because you do not ask.

B Its Consequences, 4:3–6

3 You ask and [a]do not receive, because you ask with
wrong motives, so that you may
spend *it* on your pleasures.
4 You [a]adulteresses, do you
not know that friendship with
[b]the world is [c]hostility toward
God? [d]Therefore whoever wishes
to be a friend of the world makes
himself an enemy of God.
5 Or do you think that the
Scripture [a]speaks to no purpose:
"He jealously desires [b]the Spirit
which He has made to dwell in
us"?
6 But [a]He gives a greater
grace. Therefore *it* says, "[b]GOD IS
OPPOSED TO THE PROUD, BUT GIVES
GRACE TO THE HUMBLE."

3 [a]1 John 3:22; 5:14
★ 4 [a]Is. 54:5; Jer. 2:2; Ezek. 16:32; Matt. 12:39 [b]James 1:27 [c]Rom. 8:7; 1 John 2:15 [d]Matt. 6:24; John 15:19
★ 5 [a]Num. 23:19 [b]1 Cor. 6:19; 2 Cor. 6:16
6 [a]Is. 54:7f.; Matt. 13:12 [b]Ps. 138:6; Prov. 3:34; Matt. 23:12; 1 Pet. 5:5

C Its Cure, 4:7–10

7 [a]Submit therefore to God.
[b]Resist the devil and he will flee
from you.
8 [a]Draw near to God and He
will draw near to you. [b]Cleanse
your hands, you sinners; and [c]pu-
rify your hearts, you [d]double-
minded.
9 [a]Be miserable and mourn
and weep; let your laughter be
turned into mourning, and your
joy to gloom.
10 [a]Humble yourselves in the
presence of the Lord, and He will
exalt you.

★ 7–10
7 [a]1 Pet. 5:6 [b]Eph. 4:27; 6:11f.; 1 Pet. 5:8f.
★ 8 [a]2 Chr. 15:2; Zech. 1:3; Mal. 3:7; Heb. 7:19 [b]Job 17:9; Is. 1:16; 1 Tim. 2:8 [c]Jer. 4:14; James 3:17; 1 Pet. 1:22; 1 John 3:3 [d]James 1:8
★ 9 [a]Neh. 8:9; Prov. 14:13; Luke 6:25
10 [a]Job 5:11; Ezek. 21:26; Luke 1:52; James 4:6

3:13 The question which opens this verse sets the theme for vv. 13–18. The answer is: The person who remembers his moral responsibilities.

3:18 *whose fruit is righteousness.* In contrast to 1:20.

4:2 *commit murder.* The logical, but not necessarily usual, outcome of lust. See Matt. 5:21–22.

4:4 *adulteresses.* Symbolic language for unfaithful creatures, as often in the O.T.

4:5 The thought may also be expressed as, Do you imagine there is no meaning to the Scripture that says, "The Spirit that dwells in us longs jealously over us"?

4:7–10 There are 10 verbs, all commands, in these verses, in a tense which indicates the need for a decisive and urgent break with the old life.

4:8 *double-minded.* See note on 1:8. Worldliness is basically divided allegiance.

4:9 *laughter.* Laughter is sometimes desirable (cf. Ps. 126:2), but not when it reflects worldly frivolity.

D Its Characteristics, 4:11–17

11 [a]Do not speak against one
another, [b]brethren. He who
speaks against a brother, or
[c]judges his brother, speaks
against [d]the law, and judges the
law; but if you judge the law, you
are not [e]a doer of the law, but a
judge *of it.*
12 There is *only* one [a]Lawgiv-
er and Judge, the One who is
[b]able to save and to destroy; but
[c]who are you who judge your
neighbor?
13 [a]Come now, you who say,
"[b]Today or tomorrow, we shall go
to such and such a city, and spend
a year there and engage in business and make a profit."
14 Yet you do not know what
your life will be like tomorrow.
[a]You are *just* a vapor that appears
for a little while and then van-
ishes away.
15 Instead, *you ought* to say,
"[a]If the Lord wills, we shall live
and also do this or that."
16 But as it is, you boast in
your arrogance; [a]all such boasting
is evil.
17 Therefore, [a]to one who
knows *the* right thing to do, and
does not do it, to him it is sin.

★11-12 **11** [a]2 Cor. 12:20; James 5:9; 1 Pet. 2:1 [b]James 1:16; 5:7, 9, 10 [c]Matt. 7:1; Rom. 14:4 [d]James 2:8 [e]James 1:22
12 [a]Is. 33:22; James 5:9 [b]Matt. 10:28 [c]Rom. 14:4
★13-17 **13** [a]James 5:1 [b]Prov. 27:1; Luke 12:18-20
14 [a]Job 7:7; Ps. 39:5; 102:3; 144:4
15 [a]Acts 18:21
16 [a]1 Cor. 5:6
17 [a]Luke 12:47; John 9:41; 2 Pet. 2:21

IX RICHES, PATIENCE, AND SWEARING, 5:1–12

5 [a]Come now, [b]you rich, [c]weep
and howl for your miseries
which are coming upon you.
2 [a]Your riches have rotted
and your garments have become
moth-eaten.
3 Your gold and your silver
have rusted; and their rust will be
a witness against you and will
consume your flesh like fire. It is
[a]in the last days that you have
stored up your treasure!
4 Behold, [a]the pay of the laborers who mowed your fields,
and which has been withheld by
you, cries out *against you;* and
[b]the outcry of those who did the
harvesting has reached the ears of
[c]the Lord of Sabaoth.
5 You have [a]lived luxurious-
ly on the earth and led a life of
wanton pleasure; you have fattened your hearts in [b]a day of
slaughter.
6 You have condemned and
[a]put to death [b]the righteous *man;*
he does not resist you.
7 Be patient, therefore,
[a]brethren, [b]until the coming of
the Lord. [c]Behold, the farmer
waits for the precious produce of
the soil, being patient about it,
until it gets [d]the early and late
rains.
8 [a]You too be patient;
[b]strengthen your hearts, for [c]the
coming of the Lord is [d]at hand.
9 [a]Do not complain, [b]breth-
ren, against one another, that you
yourselves may not be judged;
behold, [c]the Judge is standing
[d]right at the door.
10 As an example, [a]brethren,
of suffering and patience, take
[b]the prophets who spoke in the
name of the Lord.
11 Behold, we count those
[a]blessed who endured. You have
heard of [b]the endurance of Job
and have seen [c]the outcome of
the Lord's dealings, that [d]the Lord

1 [a]James 4:13 [b]Luke 6:24; 1 Tim. 6:9 [c]Is. 13:6; 15:3; Ezek. 30:2
2 [a]Job 13:28; Is. 50:9; Matt. 6:19f.
★ **3** [a]James 5:7, 8
★ **4** [a]Lev. 19:13; Job 24:10f.; Jer. 22:13; Mal. 3:5 [b]Ex. 2:23; Deut. 24:15; Job 31:38f. [c]Rom. 9:29
5 [a]Ezek. 16:49; Luke 16:19; 1 Tim. 5:6; 2 Pet. 2:13 [b]Jer. 12:3; 25:34
★ **6** [a]James 4:2 [b]Heb. 10:38; 1 Pet. 4:18
★ **7** [a]James 4:11; 5:9, 10 [b]John 21:22; 1 Thess. 2:19 [c]Gal. 6:9 [d]Deut. 11:14; Jer. 5:24; Joel 2:23
8 [a]Luke 21:19 [b]1 Thess. 3:13 [c]John 21:22; 1 Thess. 2:19 [d]Rom. 13:11, 12; 1 Pet. 4:7
9 [a]James 4:11 [b]James 4:11; 5:7, 10 [c]1 Cor. 4:5; Heb. 10:25; James 4:12; 1 Pet. 4:5 [d]Matt. 24:33; Mark 13:29
10 [a]James 4:11; 5:7, 9 [b]Matt. 5:12
★**11** [a]Matt. 5:10; 1 Pet. 3:14 [b]Job 1:21f.; 2:10 [c]Job 42:10, 12 [d]Ex. 34:6; Ps. 103:8

4:11–12 The person who judges his brother disobeys the law, thus putting himself above it and treating it with contempt.

4:13–17 The folly of forgetting God in business is another manifestation of worldliness. The itinerant merchants addressed here were Jews who carried on a lucrative trade throughout the world.

5:3 *have rusted.* The rich did not realize that *the last days* were already present (cf. 2 Tim. 3:1).

5:4 *Lord of Sabaoth* = Lord of Hosts (a familiar O.T. title). The Lord Almighty, the omnipotent sovereign, who is not oblivious to injustice.

5:6 *put to death the righteous.* This probably refers to the practice of the rich taking the poor ("the righteous") to court to take away what little they might have, thus "murdering" them.

5:7 *the early* (Oct.-Nov.) *and late* (Apr.-May) *rains.* Palestine has two rainy seasons annually.

5:11 *the endurance of Job.* Job was steadfast in

is full of compassion and *is* merciful.
12 But above all, [a]my brethren, [b]do not swear, either by
heaven or by earth or with any
other oath; but let your yes be
yes, and your no, no; so that you
may not fall under judgment.

★12 [a]James 1:16 [b]Matt. 5:34-37

X PRAYER, 5:13-18

13 Is anyone among you [a]suf-
fering? [b]Let him pray. Is anyone
cheerful? Let him [c]sing praises.
14 Is anyone among you sick?
Let him call for [a]the elders of the
church, and let them pray over
him, [b]anointing him with oil in
the name of the Lord;
15 and the [a]prayer offered in
faith will [b]restore the one who is
sick, and the Lord will [c]raise him
up, and if he has committed sins,
they will be forgiven him.
16 Therefore, [a]confess your
sins to one another, and pray for
one another, so that you may be
[b]healed. [c]The effective prayer of a
righteous man can accomplish
much.
17 Elijah was [a]a man with a
nature like ours, and [b]he prayed
earnestly that it might not rain;
and it did not rain on the earth for
[c]three years and six months.
18 And he [a]prayed again, and
[b]the sky poured rain, and the
earth produced its fruit.

13 [a]James 5:10 [b]Ps. 50:15 [c]1 Cor. 14:15
★14-15
14 [a]Acts 11:30 [b]Mark 6:13; 16:18
15 [a]James 1:6 [b]1 Cor. 1:21; James 5:20 [c]John 6:39; 2 Cor. 4:14
16 [a]Matt. 3:6; Mark 1:5; Acts 19:18 [b]Heb. 12:13; 1 Pet. 2:24 [c]Gen. 18:23-32
17 [a]Acts 14:15 [b]1 Kin. 17:1; 18:1 [c]Luke 4:25
18 [a]1 Kin. 18:42 [b]1 Kin. 18:45

XI THE CONVERSION OF THE ERRING, 5:19-20

19 My brethren, [a]if any
among you strays from [b]the truth,
and one turns him back,
20 let him know that he who
turns a sinner from the error of
his way will [a]save his soul from
death, and will [b]cover a multitude
of sins.

★19-20
19 [a]Matt. 18:15; Gal. 6:1 [b]James 3:14
20 [a]Rom. 11:14; 1 Cor. 1:21; James 1:21 [b]1 Pet. 4:8

---

his moral integrity. See Job. 1:21; 2:10; 13:15; 16:19; 19:25.

5:12 *do not swear.* Not all oaths are forbidden by this verse, only flippant, profane, or blasphemous ones. Oaths in the sense of solemn affirmations were enjoined in the law (Ex. 22:11) and were practiced by Christ (Matt. 26:63-64) and Paul (Rom. 1:9).

5:14-15 God may heal directly, through medicine, or in answer to prayer, as here. The oil is a symbol of the presence of God (cf. Ps. 23:5); it may also have been considered medicinal in James's day (cf. Luke 10:34), though hardly as being effective for all diseases. Prayers of faith are answered not simply because they are prayed in faith but only if they are prayed in the will of God (1 John 5:14). God does not always think it best to heal (cf. 2 Cor. 12:8). Here the healing is dependent on confession of sin. Historically, the Roman Catholic sacrament of extreme unction developed out of this practice, but the significance is entirely changed, for the Roman Catholic rite has death in view, not recovery.

5:14 *the elders of the church.* Elders are first mentioned in Acts 11:30 as recognized leaders of the churches. Their mention here and in Acts 14:23 relates to about the same period in the early church, in which they were the first leaders, before deacons, and long before bishops.

5:19-20 *any among you.* The reference is evidently to Christians, and the *death* is physical death which sin may cause (1 Cor. 11:30).

INTRODUCTION TO THE FIRST LETTER OF PETER

AUTHOR: Peter DATE: 63

Readership *This letter is addressed to "aliens, scattered" or, literally, the "sojourners of the disperson" (1:1). These were Christians who, like Israel of old, were scattered throughout the world, though the readers of this epistle were predominantly of Gentile rather than Jewish background (1:14; 2:9-10; 4:3-4). Their situation was one of suffering and trial (4:12), but not because of the empire-wide ban on Christianity, since that came later. The sufferings referred to are those which often come to Christians as they live faithfully in a pagan and hostile society. Persecution took the forms of slander, riots, local police action, and social ostracism. The readers are encouraged to rejoice and live above such reproach.*

Circumstances of Writing *That the apostle Peter was the writer (as stated in 1:1) is confirmed by the many similarities between this letter and Peter's sermons recorded in Acts (1:20 and Acts 2:23; 4:5 and Acts 10:42). The same Silvanus (also called Silas) who accompanied Paul on the second missionary journey was his amanuensis, or secretary (5:12; Acts 15:40).*

The place of writing was "Babylon" (5:13), a symbolic name for Rome much used by writers who wished to avoid trouble with the Roman authorities. Peter was in Rome during the last decade of his life and wrote this epistle about A.D. 63, just before the outbreak of Nero's persecution in 64. Peter was martyred about 67.

Contents *Peter himself states the theme of the letter in 5:12, "the true grace of God" in the life of a believer.*

OUTLINE OF 1 PETER

I. Salutation, 1:1-2
II. Grace Means Security, 1:3-12
  A. Doxology, 1:3-9
  B. The Prophets and the Gospel, 1:10-12
III. Grace Means Sobriety, 1:13-2:10
  A. In Holiness, 1:13-16
  B. In Fear, 1:17-21
  C. In Love, 1:22-25
  D. In Growth, 2:1-10
IV. Grace Means Submission, 2:11-3:12
  A. To Governments, 2:11-17
  B. To Masters, 2:18-25
  C. To Husbands, 3:1-7
  D. Recapitulation, 3:8-12
V. Grace Means Suffering, 3:13-4:19
  A. Reasons for Suffering, 3:13-4:6
  B. Reactions in Suffering, 4:7-19
VI. Grace Means Service, 5:1-11
VII. Concluding Remarks, 5:12-14

THE FIRST LETTER OF PETER

I SALUTATION, 1:1-2

★ 1 [a]2 Pet. 1:1 [b]1 Pet. 2:11 [c]James 1:1 [d]Acts 2:9 [e]Acts 16:6 [f]Acts 16:7 [g]Matt. 24:22
★ 2 [a]Rom. 8:29 [b]2 Thess. 2:13 [c]Rom. 1:5; 6:16; 16:19; 1 Pet. 1:14, 22 [d]Heb. 10:22; 12:24 [e]2 Pet. 1:2

1 [a]Peter, an apostle of Jesus
Christ, to those who reside as
[b]aliens, [c]scattered throughout
[d]Pontus, [e]Galatia, [d]Cappadocia,
[d]Asia, and [f]Bithynia, [g]who are
chosen
2 according to the [a]fore-
knowledge of God the Father, [b]by
the sanctifying work of the Spirit,
that you may [c]obey Jesus Christ
and be [d]sprinkled with His blood:
[e]May grace and peace be yours in
fullest measure.

II GRACE MEANS SECURITY, 1:3-12

A Doxology, 1:3-9

★ 3 [a]2 Cor. 1:3 [b]Gal. 6:16; Titus 3:5 [c]James 1:18 [d]2 Thess. 2:16 [e]1 Cor. 15:20
★ 4 [a]Acts 20:32; Rom. 8:17; Col. 3:24 [b]1 Pet. 5:4 [c]2 Tim. 4:8
5 [a]John 10:28; Phil 4:7 [b]Eph. 2:8 [c]1 Cor. 1:21 [d]Rom. 8:18
6 [a]Rom. 5:2 [b]1 Pet. 5:10 [c]1 Pet. 3:17 [d]James 1:2

3 [a]Blessed be the God and
Father of our Lord Jesus Christ,
who [b]according to His great mercy [c]has caused us to be born
again to [d]a living hope through
the [e]resurrection of Jesus Christ
from the dead,
4 to *obtain* an [a]inheritance
which is imperishable and undefiled and [b]will not fade away, [c]re-
served in heaven for you,
5 who are [a]protected by the
power of God [b]through faith for
[c]a salvation ready [d]to be revealed
in the last time.
6 [a]In this you greatly rejoice,
even though now [b]for a little
while, [c]if necessary, you have
been distressed by [d]various trials,
7 that the [a]proof of your
faith, *being* more precious than
gold which is perishable, [b]even
though tested by fire, [c]may be
found to result in praise and glory
and honor at [d]the revelation of
Jesus Christ;
8 and [a]though you have not
seen Him, you [b]love Him, and
though you do not see Him now,
but believe in Him, you greatly
rejoice with joy inexpressible and
full of glory,
9 obtaining as [a]the outcome
of your faith the salvation of your
souls.

7 [a]James 1:3 [b]Job 23:10; Ps. 66:10; Prov. 17:3; Is. 48:10; Zech. 13:9; Mal. 3:3; 1 Cor. 3:13 [c]Rom. 2:7, 10; 2 Cor. 4:17; Heb. 12:11 [d]Luke 17:30; 1 Pet. 1:13; 4:13
8 [a]John 20:29 [b]Eph. 3:19
9 [a]Rom. 6:22

B The Prophets and the Gospel, 1:10-12

10 [a]As to this salvation, the
prophets who [b]prophesied of the
[c]grace that *would come* to you
made careful search and inquiry,
11 seeking to know what person or time [a]the Spirit of Christ
within them was indicating as He
[b]predicted the sufferings of Christ
and the glories to follow.
12 It was revealed to them
that they were not serving themselves, but you, in these things
which now have been announced
to you through those who

★10-12
10 [a]Matt. 13:17; Luke 10:24; 1 Pet. 1:10-12 [b]Matt. 26:24; Luke 24:27, 44 [c]Col. 3:4; 1 Pet. 1:13
11 [a]Rom. 8:9; 2 Pet. 1:21 [b]Matt. 26:24; Luke 24:27, 44
★12 [a]1 Pet. 1:25; 4:6 [b]Acts 2:2-4 [c]Luke 2:13; Eph. 3:10; 1 Tim. 3:16

1:1 *aliens* = sojourners, exiles, foreign residents. The word is applied to those who settled in a town or region without making it their permanent place of residence. The readers, whose true citizenship was in heaven, are viewed as temporary residents of the provinces of Asia Minor named in this verse.

1:2 The idea expressed in this verse is that God in His wisdom has chosen us to salvation through the work of the Holy Spirit, applying in us the worth of the death of Christ so that we might be obedient to Him. *foreknowledge.* God's prior knowledge of all things, based on His causative relation to them, is the basis of our election. Foreknowledge involves God's active consciousness of all that it to come to pass (see 1:20; Rom. 8:29; 11:2 for the same word and concept; and see note on Eph. 1:5). *Father . . . Spirit . . . Christ.* An early formulation of the doctrine of the Trinity. *sprinkled with His blood* signifies the personal application of the sacrifice of Christ.

1:3 Here begins Peter's recital of the blessings of God's redeemed children, concluding at 2:10.

1:4 *undefiled* = unstained by evil. *will not fade away.* I.e., unimpaired by time.

1:10-12 Though the O.T. prophets spoke of grace being given to Gentiles, they did not understand all that was involved in God's saving Gentiles through a suffering Messiah (see Col. 1:26-27). The O.T. prophets did predict both the suffering (Isa. 53) and glory (Isa. 11) of the Messiah, without distinguishing that the former would be fulfilled at His first coming and the latter at His second.

1:12 *angels.* See note on Eph. 3:10.

[a]preached the gospel to you by [b]the Holy Spirit sent from heaven—things into which [c]angels long to look.

III GRACE MEANS SOBRIETY, 1:13–2:10

A In Holiness, 1:13–16

13 Therefore, [a]gird your minds for action, [b]keep sober *in spirit,* fix your [c]hope completely on the [d]grace to be brought to you at [e]the revelation of Jesus Christ.

14 As [a]obedient children, do not [b]be conformed to the former lusts *which were yours* in your [c]ignorance,

15 but [a]like the Holy One who called you, [b]be holy yourselves also [c]in all *your* behavior;

16 because it is written, "[a]YOU SHALL BE HOLY, FOR I AM HOLY."

★13 [a]Eph. 6:14 [b]Rom. 12:3; 1 Thess. 5:6, 8; 2 Tim. 4:5; Titus 2:6; 1 Pet. 4:7; 5:8 [c]1 Pet. 1:3 [d]Col. 3:4; 1 Pet. 1:10 [e]Luke 17:30; 1 Pet. 1:7; 4:13
★14 [a]1 Pet. 1:2 [b]Rom. 12:2; 1 Pet. 4:2f. [c]Eph. 4:18
15 [a]1 Thess. 4:7; 1 John 3:3 [b]2 Cor. 7:1 [c]James 3:13
★16 [a]Lev. 11:44f.; 19:2; 20:7

B In Fear, 1:17–21

17 And if you [a]address as Father the One who [b]impartially [c]judges according to each man's work, conduct yourselves [d]in fear during the time of your [e]stay *upon earth;*

18 knowing that you were not [a]redeemed with perishable things like silver or gold from your [b]futile way of life inherited from your forefathers,

19 but with precious [a]blood, as of a [b]lamb unblemished and spotless, *the blood* of Christ.

20 For He was [a]foreknown before [b]the foundation of the world, but has [c]appeared in these last times [d]for the sake of you

21 who through Him are [a]believers in God, who raised Him from the dead and [b]gave Him glory, so that your faith and [c]hope are in God.

★17 [a]Ps. 89:26; Jer. 3:19; Mal. 1:6; Matt. 6:9 [b]Acts 10:34 [c]Matt. 16:27 [d]2 Cor. 7:1; Heb. 12:28; 1 Pet. 3:15 [e]Eph. 2:19; 1 Pet. 2:11
18 [a]Is. 52:3; Matt. 20:28; 1 Cor. 6:20; Titus 2:14; Heb. 9:12; 2 Pet. 2:1 [b]Eph. 4:17
★19 [a]Acts 20:28; 1 Pet. 1:2 [b]John 1:29; Heb. 9:14
20 [a]Acts 2:23; Eph. 1:4; 1 Pet. 1:2; Rev. 13:8 [b]Matt. 25:34 [c]Heb. 9:26 [d]Heb. 2:14
21 [a]Rom. 4:24; 10:9 [b]John 17:5, 24; 1 Tim. 3:16; Heb. 2:9 [c]1 Pet. 1:3

C In Love, 1:22–25

22 Since you have [a]in obedience to the truth [b]purified your souls for a [c]sincere love of the brethren, fervently love one another from the heart,

23 for you have been [a]born again [b]not of seed which is perishable but imperishable, *that is,* through the living and abiding [c]word of God.

24 For,

"[a]ALL FLESH IS LIKE GRASS,
AND ALL ITS GLORY LIKE THE FLOWER OF GRASS.
THE GRASS WITHERS,
AND THE FLOWER FALLS OFF,

25 [a]BUT THE WORD OF THE LORD ABIDES FOREVER."

And this is [b]the word which was preached to you.

★22 [a]1 Pet. 1:2 [b]James 4:8 [c]John 13:34; Rom. 12:10; Heb. 13:1; 1 Pet. 2:17; 3:8
23 [a]John 3:3; 1 Pet. 1:3 [b]John 1:13 [c]Heb. 4:12
★24–25
24 [a]Is. 40:6ff.; James 1:10f.
25 [a]Is. 40:8 [b]Heb. 6:5
25 [a]Is. 40:8 [b]Heb. 6:5

D In Growth, 2:1–10

2 Therefore, [a]putting aside all malice and all guile and hypocrisy and envy and all [b]slander,

2 [a]like newborn babes, long for the [b]pure milk of the word, that by it you may [c]grow in respect to salvation,

3 if you have [a]tasted [b]the kindness of the Lord.

4 And coming to Him as to a living stone, [a]rejected by men, but choice and precious in the sight of God,

5 [a]you also, as living stones, are being built up as a [b]spiritual

1 [a]Eph. 4:22, 25, 31; James 1:21 [b]James 4:11
2 [a]Matt. 18:3; 19:14; Mark 10:15; Luke 18:17; 1 Cor. 14:20 [b]1 Cor. 3:2 [c]Eph. 4:15f.
3 [a]Heb. 6:5 [b]Ps. 34:8; Titus 3:4
★4–8
4 [a]1 Pet. 2:7
5 [a]1 Cor. 3:9 [b]Gal. 6:10; 1 Tim. 3:15 [c]Is. 61:6; 66:21; 1 Pet. 2:9; Rev. 1:6 [d]Rom. 15:16; Heb. 13:15

1:13 *gird your minds for action.* = be disciplined in your thinking. A figure of speech (lit., gird up the loins of your mind) based on the gathering and fastening up of the long Eastern garments so that they would not interfere with the individual's activity.
1:14 *do not be conformed.* The only other occurrence of this term is in Rom. 12:2.
1:16 *You shall be holy.* See Lev. 11:44–45.
1:17 *in fear.* I.e., reverently.
1:19 *unblemished and spotless.* Refers to the sinlessness of Christ (see Lev. 22:19–25).
1:22 *fervently* = earnestly.
1:24–25 See Isa. 40:6–8.
2:4–8 Christ is the living stone (v. 4), the cornerstone (v. 6), the rejected stone (v. 7), and the stumbling-stone (v. 8).

house for a holy [c]priesthood, to
[d]offer up spiritual sacrifices acceptable to God through Jesus
Christ.
6 For *this* is contained in
Scripture:

> "[a]BEHOLD I LAY IN ZION A
> CHOICE STONE, A [b]PRECIOUS
> CORNER *stone*,
> AND HE WHO BELIEVES IN HIM
> SHALL NOT BE DISAP-
> POINTED."

6 [a]Is. 28:16; Rom. 9:32, 33; 10:11; 1 Pet. 2:6, 8 [b]Eph. 2:20

7 [a]This precious value, then,
is for you who believe, but for
those who disbelieve,

> "[b]THE STONE WHICH THE
> BUILDERS [c]REJECTED,
> THIS BECAME THE VERY COR-
> NER *stone*,"

7 [a]2 Cor. 2:16; 1 Pet. 2:7, 8 [b]Ps. 118:22; Matt. 21:42; Luke 2:34 [c]1 Pet. 2:4

8 and,

> "[a]A STONE OF STUMBLING AND
> A ROCK OF OFFENSE";

[b]for they stumble because they
are disobedient to the word, [c]and
to this *doom* they were also appointed.

★ 8 [a]Is. 8:14 [b]1 Cor. 1:23; Gal. 5:11 [c]Rom. 9:22

9 But you are [a]A CHOSEN RACE,
A ROYAL [b]PRIESTHOOD, A [c]HOLY NA-
TION, [d]A PEOPLE FOR *God's* OWN POS-
SESSION, that you may proclaim
the excellencies of Him who has
called you [e]out of darkness into
His marvelous light;
10 [a]for you once were NOT A
PEOPLE, but now you are THE PEOPLE
OF GOD; you had NOT RECEIVED MER-
CY, but now you have RECEIVED
MERCY.

★ 9 [a]Deut. 10:15; Is. 43:20f. [b]Is. 61:6; 66:21; 1 Pet. 2:5; Rev. 1:6 [c]Ex. 19:6; Deut. 7:6 [d]Titus 2:14 [e]Is. 42:16; Acts 26:18; 2 Cor. 4:6

10 [a]Hos. 1:10; 2:23; Rom. 9:25; 10:19

IV GRACE MEANS SUBMISSION, 2:11–3:12

A To Governments, 2:11–17

11 [a]Beloved, [b]I urge you as
[c]aliens and strangers to abstain
from [d]fleshly lusts, which wage
[e]war against the soul.
12 [a]Keep your behavior excellent among the Gentiles, so
that in the thing in which they
[b]slander you as evildoers, they
may on account of your good
deeds, as they observe *them*, [c]glo-
rify God [d]in the day of visitation.
13 [a]Submit yourselves for the
Lord's sake to every human institution, whether to a king as the
one in authority,
14 or to governors as sent by
him [a]for the punishment of evildoers and the [b]praise of those
who do right.
15 For [a]such is the will of God
that by doing right you may [b]si-
lence the ignorance of foolish
men.
16 *Act* as [a]free men, and do
not use your freedom as a covering for evil, but *use it* as [b]bond-
slaves of God.
17 [a]Honor all men; [b]love the
brotherhood, [c]fear God, [d]honor
the king.

★11 [a]Heb. 6:9; 1 Pet. 4:12 [b]Rom. 12:1 [c]Lev. 25:23 [d]Rom. 13:14; [e]James 4:1

12 [a]2 Cor. 8:21; Phil. 2:15; Titus 2:8; 1 Pet. 2:15; 3:16 [b]Acts 28:22 [c]Matt. 5:16; 9:8; John 13:31; 1 Pet. 4:11, 16 [d]Is. 10:3; Luke 19:44

★13–17

13 [a]Rom. 13:1

14 [a]Rom. 13:4 [b]Rom. 13:3

★15 [a]1 Pet. 3:17 [b]1 Pet. 2:12

16 [a]John 8:32; James 1:25 [b]Rom. 6:22; 1 Cor. 7:22

17 [a]Rom. 12:10; 13:7 [b]1 Pet. 1:22 [c]Prov. 24:21 [d]Prov. 24:21; Matt. 22:21; 1 Pet. 2:13

B To Masters, 2:18–25

18 [a]Servants, be submissive
to your masters with all respect,
not only to those who are good
and [b]gentle, but also to those who
are unreasonable.
19 For this *finds* favor, if for
the sake of [a]conscience toward
God a man bears up under sor-
rows when suffering unjustly.
20 For what credit is there if,
when you sin and are harshly
treated, you endure it with patience? But if [a]when you do what
is right and suffer *for it* you pa-
tiently endure it, this *finds* favor
with God.
21 For [a]you have been called

18 [a]Eph. 6:5 [b]James 3:17

19 [a]Rom. 13:5; 1 Pet. 3:14, 17

20 [a]1 Pet. 3:17

21 [a]Acts 14:22; 1 Pet. 3:9 [b]1 Pet. 3:18; 4:1, 13 [c]Matt. 11:29; 16:24

2:8 *appointed.* The same divine purpose which has chosen some has ordained others (those who are disobedient) to the only alternative.

2:9 *a people for God's own possession.* I.e., God's own people.

2:11 Beginning here, and ending at 4:11, Peter sets forth the duties of Christians in the world.

2:13–17 Christians are to be law-abiding citizens. If the law of one's government violates the revealed will of God, then, of course, the believer must obey God, though he may have to suffer the penalties of that government's laws. See Rom. 13:1–7 and Titus 3:1–2.

2:15 *foolish men.* I.e., the slanderers mentioned in v. 12.

for this purpose, [b]since Christ also
suffered for you, leaving you [c]an
example for you to follow in His
steps,
22 WHO [a]COMMITTED NO SIN, NOR
WAS ANY DECEIT FOUND IN HIS
MOUTH;
23 and while being [a]reviled,
He did not revile in return; while
suffering, He uttered no threats,
but kept entrusting *Himself* to
Him who judges righteously;
24 and He Himself [a]bore our
sins in His body on the [b]cross,
that we [c]might die to sin and live
to righteousness; for [d]by His
wounds you were [e]healed.
25 For you were [a]continually
straying like sheep, but now you
have returned to the [b]Shepherd
and Guardian of your souls.

★22-24
22 [a]Is. 53:9; 2 Cor. 5:21
23 [a]Is. 53:7; Heb. 12:3; 1 Pet. 3:9
24 [a]Is. 53:4, 11; 1 Cor. 15:3; Heb. 9:28 [b]Acts 5:30 [c]Rom. 6:2, 13 [d]Is. 53:5 [e]Heb. 12:13; James 5:16
25 [a]Is. 53:6 [b]John 10:11; 1 Pet. 5:4

C To Husbands, 3:1-7

3 [a]In the same way, you wives,
[b]be submissive to your own
husbands so that even if any *of
them* are disobedient to the word,
they may be [c]won without a word
by the behavior of their wives,
2 as they observe your
chaste and respectful behavior.
3 [a]And let not your adorn-
ment be *merely* external—braid-
ing the hair, and wearing gold
jewelry, and putting on dresses;
4 but *let it be* [a]the hidden
person of the heart, with the imperishable quality of a gentle and
quiet spirit, which is precious in
the sight of God.
5 For in this way in former
times the holy women also, [a]who
hoped in God, used to adorn
themselves, being submissive to
their own husbands.
6 Thus Sarah obeyed Abraham, [a]calling him lord, and you
have become her children if you
do what is right [b]without being
frightened by any fear.
7 [a]You husbands likewise,
live with your wives in an understanding way, as with a weaker
[b]vessel, since she is a woman; and
grant her honor as a fellow-heir
of the grace of life, so that your
prayers may not be hindered.

★ 1 [a]1 Pet. 2:18; 3:7 [b]Eph. 5:22 [c]1 Cor. 9:19
★ 3 [a]Is. 3:18ff.; 1 Tim. 2:9
★ 4 [a]Rom. 7:22
5 [a]1 Tim. 5:5; 1 Pet. 1:3
6 [a]Gen. 18:12 [b]1 Pet. 3:14
★ 7 [a]Eph. 5:25; Col. 3:19 [b]1 Thess. 4:4

D Recapitulation, 3:8-12

8 To sum up, [a]let all be har-
monious, sympathetic, [b]brotherly,
[c]kindhearted, and [d]humble in
spirit;
9 [a]not returning evil for evil,
or [b]insult for insult, but giving a
[c]blessing instead; for [d]you were
called for the very purpose that
you might [e]inherit a blessing.
10 For

"[a]LET HIM WHO MEANS TO LOVE
LIFE AND SEE GOOD DAYS
REFRAIN HIS TONGUE FROM
EVIL AND HIS LIPS FROM
SPEAKING GUILE.
11 "[a]AND LET HIM TURN AWAY
FROM EVIL AND DO GOOD;
LET HIM SEEK PEACE AND PUR-
SUE IT.
12 "[a]FOR THE EYES OF THE LORD
ARE UPON THE RIGHTEOUS,
AND HIS EARS ATTEND TO
THEIR PRAYER,
BUT THE FACE OF THE LORD IS
AGAINST THOSE WHO DO
EVIL."

8 [a]Rom. 12:16 [b]1 Pet. 1:22 [c]Eph. 4:32 [d]Eph. 4:2; Phil. 2:3; 1 Pet. 5:5
★ 9 [a]Rom. 12:17; 1 Thess. 5:15 [b]1 Cor. 4:12; 1 Pet. 2:23 [c]Luke 6:28; Rom. 12:14; 1 Cor. 4:12 [d]1 Pet. 2:21 [e]Gal. 3:14; Heb. 6:14; 12:17
10 [a]Ps. 34:12, 13
11 [a]Ps. 34:14
12 [a]Ps. 34:15, 16

V GRACE MEANS SUFFERING, 3:13-4:19

A Reasons for Suffering, 3:13-4:6

13 And [a]who is there to harm
you if you prove zealous for what
is good?

13 [a]Prov. 16:7

2:22-24 *who committed no sin . . . bore our sins.* The sinless Jesus was the perfect substitute, in His death, for the sins of mankind.

3:1 *without a word.* I.e., an unsaved husband can better be won to Christianity by seeing it work in his wife's godly life than by always hearing about it from her lips.

3:3 This verse does not prohibit all jewelry; if it did, it would also prohibit all clothing! It condemns ostentation and enjoins modesty and meekness.

3:4 *hidden person* See Eph. 3:16.

3:7 *that your prayers may not be hindered.* The man who fails to give his wife due consideration can hardly pray with her.

3:9 This verse is an echo of Christ's words (Luke 6:27-28).

14 But even if you should [a]suffer for the sake of righteousness, [b]*you are* blessed. [c]AND DO NOT FEAR THEIR INTIMIDATION, AND DO NOT BE TROUBLED,

15 but sanctify [a]Christ as Lord in your hearts, always *being* ready [b]to make a defense to every one who asks you to give an account for the [c]hope that is in you, yet [d]with gentleness and [e]reverence;

16 and keep a [a]good conscience so that in the thing in which [b]you are slandered, those who revile your good behavior in Christ may be put to shame.

17 For [a]it is better, [b]if God should will it so, that you suffer for doing what is right rather than for doing what is wrong.

18 For [a]Christ also died for sins [b]once for all, *the* just for *the* unjust, in order that He might [c]bring us to God, having been put to death [d]in the flesh, but made alive [e]in the spirit;

19 in which also He went and [a]made proclamation to the spirits *now* in prison,

20 who once were disobedient, when the [a]patience of God [b]kept waiting in the days of Noah, during the construction of [c]the ark, in which a few, that is, [d]eight [e]persons, were brought safely through *the* water.

21 [a]And corresponding to that, baptism now saves you—[b]not the removal of dirt from the flesh, but an appeal to God for a [c]good conscience—through [d]the resurrection of Jesus Christ,

22 [a]who is at the right hand of God, [b]having gone into heaven, [c]after angels and authorities and powers had been subjected to Him.

14 [a]1 Pet. 2:19ff.; 4:15f. [b]James 5:11 [c]Is. 8:12f.; 1 Pet. 3:6
★15 [a]1 Pet. 1:3 [b]Col. 4:6 [c]1 Pet. 1:3 [d]2 Tim. 2:25 [e]1 Pet. 1:17
16 [a]1 Tim. 1:5; Heb. 13:18; 1 Pet. 3:21 [b]1 Pet. 2:12, 15
17 [a]1 Pet. 2:20; 4:15f. [b]Acts 18:21; 1 Pet. 1:6; 2:15; 4:19
18 [a]1 Pet. 2:21 [b]Heb. 9:26, 28; 10:10 [c]Rom. 5:2; Eph. 3:12 [d]Col. 1:22; 1 Pet. 4:1 [e]1 Pet. 4:6
★19 [a]1 Pet. 4:6
20 [a]Rom. 2:4 [b]Gen. 6:3, 5, 13f. [c]Heb. 11:7 [d]Gen. 8:18; 2 Pet. 2:5 [e]Acts 2:41; 1 Pet. 1:9, 22; 2:25; 4:19
★21 [a]Acts 16:33; Titus 3:5 [b]Heb. 9:14; 10:22 [c]1 Tim. 1:5; Heb. 13:18; 1 Pet. 3:16 [d]1 Pet. 1:3
22 [a]Mark 16:19 [b]Heb. 4:14; 6:20 [c]Rom. 8:38f.; Heb. 1:6

4

Therefore, since [a]Christ has suffered in the flesh, [b]arm yourselves also with the same purpose, because [c]he who has suffered in the flesh has ceased from sin,

2 [a]so as to live [b]the rest of the time in the flesh no longer for the lusts of men, but for the will of God.

3 For [a]the time already past is sufficient *for you* to have carried out the desire of the Gentiles, [b]having pursued a course of sensuality, lusts, drunkenness, carousals, drinking parties and abominable idolatries.

4 And in *all* this, they are surprised that you do not run with *them* into the same excess of [a]dissipation, and they [b]malign *you;*

5 but they shall give account to Him who is ready to judge [a]the living and the dead.

6 For [a]the gospel has for this purpose been preached even to those who are dead, that though they are judged in the flesh as men, they may live in the spirit according to *the will of* God.

★ 1 [a]1 Pet. 2:21 [b]Eph. 6:13 [c]Rom. 6:7
2 [a]Rom. 6:2; Col. 3:3 [b]1 Pet. 1:14
3 [a]1 Cor. 12:2 [b]Rom. 13:13; Eph. 2:2; 4:17ff.
4 [a]Eph. 5:18 [b]1 Pet. 3:16
★ 5 [a]Acts 10:42; Rom. 14:9; 2 Tim. 4:1
★ 6 [a]1 Pet. 1:12; 3:19

3:15 *sanctify Christ* = reverence Christ.

3:19 *made proclamation to the spirits now in prison.* Some understand this to mean that Christ, between His death and resurrection, descended into Hades and offered to those who lived before Noah (v. 20) a second chance for salvation, a doctrine that is without scriptural support. Others say that it was simply an announcement of His victory over sin to those in Hades without offering a second chance. Most likely this is a reference to the preincarnate Christ preaching through Noah to those who, because they rejected that message, are now spirits in prison.

3:21 *baptism.* Though water itself cannot save, baptism with water is the vivid symbol of the changed life of one who has a conscience at peace with God through faith in Christ.

4:1 The thought is: Christ suffered in the flesh. He is your example. So, arm yourselves by taking the same view of suffering as Christ took, which is to accept it in the will of God. Thereby the dominion of sin is broken in practical experience.

4:5 *the living and the dead.* I.e., all generations.

4:6 *those who are dead.* I.e., deceased Christians. The gospel was preached to those martyrs now dead. They were judged in the flesh and condemned to martyrdom according to human standards, but they are alive in the spirit after death. Another interpretation relates this preaching to that of 3:19.

B Reactions in Suffering, 4:7-19

7 [a]The end of all things is at
hand; therefore, [b]be of sound
judgment and sober *spirit* for the
purpose of prayer.
8 Above all, [a]keep fervent in
your love for one another, because [b]love covers a multitude of
sins.
9 [a]Be hospitable to one another without [b]complaint.
10 [a]As each one has received
a *special* gift, employ it in serving
one another, as good [b]stewards of
the manifold grace of God.
11 [a]Whoever speaks, *let him*
speak, as it were, the [b]utterances
of God; whoever serves, *let him*
do so as [c]by the strength which
God supplies; so that [d]in all things
God may be glorified through
Jesus Christ, [e]to whom belongs
the glory and dominion forever
and ever. Amen.
12 [a]Beloved, do not be surprised at the [b]fiery ordeal among
you, which comes upon you for
your testing, as though some
strange thing were happening to
you;
13 but to the degree that you
[a]share the sufferings of Christ,
keep on rejoicing; so that also at
the [b]revelation of His glory, [c]you
may rejoice with exultation.
14 If you are reviled [a]for the
name of Christ, [b]you are blessed,
[c]because the Spirit of glory and of
God rests upon you.
15 By no means [a]let any of
you suffer as a murderer, or thief,
or evildoer, or a [b]troublesome
meddler;

7 [a]Rom. 13:11; Heb. 9:26; James 5:8; 1 John 2:18 [b]1 Pet. 1:13
8 [a]1 Pet. 1:22 [b]Prov. 10:12; 1 Cor. 13:4ff.; James 5:20
9 [a]1 Tim. 3:2; Heb. 13:2 [b]Phil. 2:14
★10 [a]Rom. 12:6f. [b]1 Cor. 4:1
★11 [a]1 Thess. 2:4; Titus 2:1, 15; Heb. 13:7 [b]Acts 7:38 [c]Eph. 1:19; 6:10 [d]1 Cor. 10:31; 1 Pet. 2:12 [e]Rom. 11:36; 1 Pet. 5:11; Rev. 1:6; 5:13
★12 [a]1 Pet. 2:11 [b]1 Pet. 1:6f.
13 [a]Rom. 8:17; 2 Cor. 1:5; 4:10; Phil. 3:10 [b]1 Pet. 1:7; 5:1 [c]2 Tim. 2:12
14 [a]John 15:21; Heb. 11:26; 1 Pet. 4:16 [b]Matt. 5:11; Luke 6:22; Acts 5:41 [c]2 Cor. 4:10f., 16
15 [a]1 Pet. 2:19f.; 3:17 [b]1 Thess. 4:11; 2 Thess. 3:11; 1 Tim. 5:13

16 but if *anyone suffers* as a
[a]Christian, let him not feel
ashamed, but in that name let
him [b]glorify God.
17 For *it is* time for judgment
[a]to begin with [b]the household of
God; and if *it* [c]*begins* with us
first, what *will be* the outcome for
those [d]who do not obey the [e]gos-
pel of God?
18 [a]AND IF IT IS WITH DIFFICULTY
THAT THE RIGHTEOUS IS SAVED, WHAT
WILL BECOME OF THE [b]GODLESS MAN
AND THE SINNER?
19 Therefore, let those also
who suffer according to [a]the will
of God entrust their souls to a
faithful Creator in doing what is
right.

★16 [a]Acts 5:41; 28:22; James 2:7 [b]1 Pet. 4:11
★17 [a]Jer. 25:29; Ezek. 9:6; Amos 3:2 [b]1 Tim. 3:15; Heb. 3:6; 1 Pet. 2:5 [c]Rom. 2:9 [d]2 Thess. 1:8 [e]Rom. 1:1
18 [a]Prov. 11:31; Luke 23:31 [b]1 Tim. 1:9
19 [a]1 Pet. 3:17

VI GRACE MEANS SERVICE, 5:1-11

5 [a]Therefore, I exhort the elders among you, as *your* [b]fel-
low-elder and [c]witness of the sufferings of Christ, and a [d]partaker
also of the glory that is to be revealed,
2 shepherd [a]the flock of God
among you, [b]not under compulsion, but voluntarily, according to
the will of God; and [c]not for sordid gain, but with eagerness;
3 nor yet as [a]lording it over
those allotted to your charge, but
proving to be [b]examples to the
flock.
4 And when the Chief
[a]Shepherd appears, you will receive the [b]unfading [c]crown of
glory.
5 [a]You younger men, likewise, [b]be subject to your elders;
and all of you, clothe yourselves

★ 1 [a]Acts 11:30 [b]2 John 1; 3 John 1 [c]Luke 24:48; Heb. 12:1 [d]1 Pet. 1:5, 7; 4:13; Rev. 1:9
2 [a]John 21:16; Acts 20:28 [Gr.] [b]Philem. 14 [c]1 Tim. 3:8
3 [a]Ezek. 34:4; Matt. 20:25f. [b]John 13:15; Phil. 3:17; 1 Thess. 1:7
★ 4 [a]1 Pet. 2:25 [b]1 Pet. 1:4 [c]1 Cor. 9:25
★ 5 [a]Luke 22:26; 1 Tim. 5:1 [b]Eph. 5:21 [c]1 Pet. 3:8 [d]Prov. 3:34; James 4:6

4:10 *a special gift.* I.e., a spiritual gift. See note on 1 Cor. 1:7. This is the only occurrence of the word in the N.T. outside the writings of Paul.

4:11 *utterances of God.* One who speaks should preach God's words.

4:12 *do not be surprised.* Peter now turns to the trials of Christians in the world, concluding at 5:11.

4:16 *Christian.* See note on Acts 11:26.

4:17 The idea is this: If even Christians must be judged (by purging), what fate must await unbelievers who will be punished for their sins?

5:1 *elders.* See note on 1 Tim. 3:1. Elders are to feed, lead (but not lord it over), and be an example to their people.

5:4 *crown of glory.* Faithful church leaders, who are often dishonored on earth, will receive glory in heaven from Christ, the chief Shepherd. Victorious athletes were awarded floral crowns, which quickly faded away. See note on 1 Cor. 3:14.

5:5 *humility.* Christianity made humility a major virtue. It is an attitude of mind that realizes that one is without any reason for distinction in God's sight.

with [c]humility toward one another, for [d]GOD IS OPPOSED TO THE
PROUD, BUT GIVES GRACE TO THE HUM-
BLE.
6 [a]Humble yourselves,
therefore, under the mighty hand
of God, that He may exalt you at
the proper time,
7 casting all your [a]anxiety
upon Him, because He cares for
you.
8 [a]Be of sober *spirit,* [b]be on
the alert. Your adversary, [c]the
devil, prowls about like a roaring
[d]lion, seeking someone to devour.
9 [a]But resist him, [b]firm in
your faith, knowing that [c]the
same experiences of suffering are
being accomplished by your
brethren who are in the world.
10 And after you have suffered [a]for a little while, the [b]God
of all grace, who [c]called you to
His [d]eternal glory in Christ, will
Himself [e]perfect, [f]confirm,
strengthen *and* establish you.
11 [a]To Him *be* dominion forever and ever. Amen.

6 [a]James 4:10
★ **7** [a]Matt. 6:25
8 [a]1 Pet. 1:13 [b]Matt. 24:42 [c]James 4:7 [d]2 Tim. 4:17
9 [a]James 4:7 [b]Col. 2:5 [c]Acts 14:22; Heb. 12:8
10 [a]1 Pet. 1:6 [b]1 Pet. 4:10 [c]1 Cor. 1:9; 1 Thess. 2:12 [d]2 Cor. 4:17; 2 Tim. 2:10 [e]1 Cor. 1:10; Heb. 13:21 [f]Rom. 16:25; 2 Thess. 2:17; 3:3
11 [a]Rom. 11:36; 1 Pet. 4:11

VII CONCLUDING REMARKS, 5:12–14

12 Through [a]Silvanus, our
faithful brother (for so I regard
him), [b]I have written to you
briefly, exhorting and testifying
that this is [c]the true grace of God.
[d]Stand firm in it!
13 She who is in Babylon,
chosen together with you, sends
you greetings, and *so does* my
son, [a]Mark.
14 [a]Greet one another with a
kiss of love.
[b]Peace be to you all who are in
Christ.

12 [a]2 Cor. 1:19 [b]Heb. 13:22 [c]Acts 11:23; 1 Pet. 1:13; 4:10 [d]1 Cor. 15:1
★**13** [a]Acts 12:12
★**14** [a]Rom. 16:16 [b]Eph. 6:23

5:7 *He cares for you.* Lit., it matters to Him concerning you.

5:13 *my son, Mark.* John Mark, the writer of the Gospel, who was not Peter's natural son but his son in the faith.

5:14 *kiss of love.* The "holy kiss" (Paul's term, Rom. 16:16) was an expression of Christian love and was apparently restricted to one's own sex.

INTRODUCTION TO THE SECOND LETTER OF PETER

AUTHOR: Peter DATE: 66

Authorship *Many have suggested that someone other than Peter wrote this letter after* A.D. *80 because of (1) differences in style, (2) its supposed dependence on Jude, and (3) the mention of Paul's letters having been collected (3:16). However, using a different scribe or no scribe would also have resulted in stylistic changes; there is no reason why Peter should not have borrowed from Jude, though it is more likely that Jude was written later than 2 Peter; and 3:16 does not necessarily refer to all of Paul's letters but only those written up to that time. Furthermore, similarities between 1 and 2 Peter point to the same author, and its acceptance in the canon demands apostolic authority behind it. Assuming Petrine authorship, the letter was written just before his martyrdom in 67 and most likely from Rome.*

Contents *The letter is a reminder (1:12; 3:1) of the truth of Christianity as opposed to the heresies of false teachers. Important passages include those concerning the transfiguration (1:16-18), the inspiration of Scripture (1:21), and the certainty of the second coming of Christ (3:4-10).*

OUTLINE OF 2 PETER

I. Greetings, 1:1-2
II. The Development of Faith, 1:3-21
A. The Growth of Faith, 1:3-11
B. The Ground of Faith, 1:12-21
III. The Denouncing of False Teachers, 2:1-22
A. Their Conduct, 2:1-3
B. Their Condemnation, 2:4-9
C. Their Characteristics, 2:10-22
IV. The Design of the Future, 3:1-18
A. Derision, 3:1-7
B. Delay, 3:8-9
C. Dissolution, 3:10-13
D. Diligence, 3:14-18

THE SECOND LETTER OF PETER

I GREETINGS, 1:1-2

1 Simon Peter, a [a]bond-servant
and [b]apostle of Jesus Christ, to
those who have received [c]a faith
of the same kind as ours, by [d]the
righteousness of [e]our God and
Savior, Jesus Christ:
2 [a]Grace and peace be multiplied to you in [b]the knowledge of
God and of Jesus our Lord;

★ 1 [a]Rom. 1:1; Phil. 1:1; James 1:1; Jude 1 [b]1 Pet. 1:1 [c]Rom. 1:12; 2 Cor. 4:13; Titus 1:4 [d]Rom. 3:21-26 [e]Titus 2:13
★ 2 [a]Rom. 1:7; 1 Pet. 1:2 [b]John 17:3; Phil. 3:8

II THE DEVELOPMENT OF FAITH, 1:3-21

A The Growth of Faith, 1:3-11

3 seeing that His [a]divine
power has granted to us everything pertaining to life and godliness, through the true [b]knowl-
edge of Him who [c]called us by
His own glory and excellence.
4 For by these He has
granted to us His precious and
magnificent [a]promises, in order
that by them you might become
[b]partakers of *the* divine nature,
having [c]escaped the [d]corruption
that is in [e]the world by lust.
5 Now for this very reason
also, applying all diligence, in
your faith [a]supply [b]moral excellence, and in *your* moral excellence, [c]knowledge;
6 and in *your* knowledge,
[a]self-control, and in *your* self-
control, [b]perseverance, and in
your perseverance, [c]godliness;
7 and in *your* godliness,
[a]brotherly kindness, and in *your*
brotherly kindness, *Christian*
love.
8 For if these *qualities* are
yours and are increasing, they
render you neither useless nor
[a]unfruitful in the true [b]knowl-
edge of our Lord Jesus Christ.
9 For he who lacks these
qualities is [a]blind *or* short-
sighted, having forgotten *his* [b]pu-
rification from his former sins.
10 Therefore, brethren, be all
the more diligent to make certain
about His [a]calling and [b]choosing
you; for as long as you practice
these things, you will never
[c]stumble;
11 for in this way the entrance into [a]the eternal kingdom
of our [b]Lord and Savior Jesus
Christ will be [c]abundantly [d]sup-
plied to you.

3 [a]1 Pet. 1:5 [b]John 17:3; Phil. 3:8; 2 Pet. 1:2, 8; 2:20; 3:18 [c]1 Thess. 2:12; 2 Thess. 2:14; 1 Pet. 5:10
★ 4 [a]2 Pet. 3:9, 13 [b]Eph. 4:13, 24; Heb. 12:10; 1 John 3:2 [c]2 Pet. 2:18, 20 [d]2 Pet. 2:19 [e]James 1:27
5 [a]2 Pet. 1:11 [b]2 Pet. 1:3 [c]Col. 2:3; 2 Pet. 1:2
★ 6 [a]Acts 24:25 [b]Luke 21:19 [c]2 Pet. 1:3
7 [a]Rom. 12:10; 1 Pet. 1:22
8 [a]Col. 1:10 [b]John 17:3; Phil. 3:8; 2 Pet. 1:2, 3; 2:20; 3:18
★ 9 [a]1 John 2:11 [b]Eph. 5:26; Titus 2:14
★10 [a]Matt. 22:14; Rom. 11:29; 2 Pet. 1:3 [b]1 Thess. 1:4 [c]James 2:10; 2 Pet. 3:17; Jude 24
★11 [a]2 Tim. 4:18 [b]2 Pet. 2:20; 3:18 [c]Rom. 2:4; 1 Tim. 6:17 [d]2 Pet. 1:5

B The Ground of Faith, 1:12-21

12 Therefore, [a]I shall always
be ready to remind you of these
things, even though you *already*
know *them*, and have been established in [b]the truth which is present with *you*.
13 And I consider it [a]right, as
long as I am in [b]this *earthly*
dwelling, to [c]stir you up by way
of reminder,
14 knowing that [a]the laying
aside of my *earthly* dwelling is
imminent, [b]as also our Lord Jesus
Christ has made clear to me.
15 And I will also be diligent
that at any time after my [a]depar-

12 [a]Phil. 3:1; 1 John 2:21; Jude 5 [b]Col. 1:5f.; 2 John 2
★13 [a]Phil. 1:7 [b]2 Cor. 5:1, 4; 2 Pet. 1:14 [c]2 Pet. 3:1
★14 [a]2 Cor. 5:1; 2 Tim. 4:6 [b]John 13:36; 21:19
15 [a]Luke 9:31

1:1 *to those who have received a faith of the same kind as ours.* The thought is this: I write to those who have obtained a faith of equal standing with ours (i.e., the apostles') by reason of the impartiality of Christ's blessings.
1:2 *knowledge.* Lit., full or true knowledge (also in v. 3).
1:4 *by these.* I.e., by the glory and excellence (v. 3). *partakers of the divine nature.* The believer shares in the life of God by means of Christ and the Spirit living in him (Rom. 8:9; Gal. 2:20).
1:6 *self-control.* As in Gal. 5:23. *godliness.* The attitude and conduct of a person who is God-fearing.
1:9 *former sins.* Sins committed prior to conversion.
1:10 *make certain about His calling.* I.e., confirm one's profession of faith by godly living.
1:11 *abundantly.* A Christian life that can be rewarded will provide that abundant entrance into heaven.
1:13 *earthly dwelling.* I.e., Peter's human body.
1:14 *the laying aside of my earthly dwelling.* Because of Christ's prediction (John 21:18), Peter knew that he would soon die.

ture you may be able to call these
things to mind.
16 For we did not follow clev-
erly devised [a]tales when we made
known to you the [b]power and
coming of our Lord Jesus Christ,
but we were [c]eyewitnesses of His
majesty.
17 For when He received hon-
or and glory from God the Father,
such an [a]utterance as this was
made to Him by the [b]Majestic
Glory, "This is My beloved Son
with whom I am well-pleased"—
18 and we ourselves heard
this utterance made from heaven
when we were with Him on the
[a]holy mountain.
19 And *so* we have [a]the prophetic word *made* more [b]sure, to
which you do well to pay attention as to [c]a lamp shining in a
dark place, until the [d]day dawns
and the [e]morning star arises [f]in
your hearts.
20 But [a]know this first of all,
that [b]no prophecy of Scripture is
a matter of one's own interpretation,
21 for [a]no prophecy was ever
made by an act of human will,
but men [b]moved by the Holy
Spirit spoke from God.

★16 [a]1 Tim. 1:4; 2 Pet. 2:3 [b]Mark 13:26; 14:62; 1 Thess. 2:19 [c]Matt. 17:1ff.; Mark 9:2ff.; Luke 9:28ff.
17 [a]Matt. 17:5; Mark 9:7; Luke 9:35 [b]Heb. 1:3
18 [a]Ex. 3:5; Josh. 5:15
★19 [a]1 Pet. 1:10f. [b]Heb. 2:2 [c]Ps. 119:105 [d]Luke 1:78 [e]Rev. 22:16 [f]2 Cor. 4:6
★20 [a]2 Pet. 3:3 [b]Rom. 12:6
★21 [a]Jer. 23:26; 2 Tim. 3:16 [b]2 Sam. 23:2; Luke 1:70; Acts 1:16; 3:18; 1 Pet. 1:11

III THE DENOUNCING OF FALSE TEACHERS, 2:1-22

A Their Conduct, 2:1-3

2 But [a]false prophets also arose
among the people, just as
there will also be [b]false teachers
[c]among you, who will [d]secretly
introduce [e]destructive heresies,
even [f]denying the [g]Master who
[h]bought them, bringing swift destruction upon themselves.
2 And many will follow their
[a]sensuality, and because of them
[b]the way of the truth will be [c]ma-
ligned;
3 and in *their* [a]greed they
will [b]exploit you with [c]false
words; [d]their judgment from long
ago is not idle, and their destruction is not asleep.

★ 1 [a]Deut. 13:1ff.; Jer. 6:13 [b]2 Cor. 11:13 [c]Matt. 7:15; 1 Tim. 4:1 [d]Gal. 2:4; Jude 4 [e]1 Cor. 11:19; Gal. 5:20 [f]Jude 4 [g]Rev. 6:10 [h]1 Cor. 6:20
2 [a]Gen. 19:5ff.; 2 Pet. 2:7, 18; Jude 4 [b]Acts 16:17; 22:4; 24:14 [c][Gr.] Rom. 2:24; 1 Tim. 6:1
3 [a]1 Tim. 6:5; 2 Pet. 2:14; Jude 16 [b]2 Cor. 2:17 marg.; 1 Thess. 2:5 [c]Rom. 16:18; 2 Pet. 1:16 [d]Deut. 32:35

B Their Condemnation, 2:4-9

4 For [a]if God did not spare
angels when they sinned, but cast
them into hell and [b]committed
them to pits of darkness, reserved
for judgment;
5 and did not spare [a]the ancient world, but preserved [b]Noah,
a preacher of righteousness, with
seven others, when He brought a
[c]flood upon the world of the ungodly;
6 and *if* He [a]condemned the
cities of Sodom and Gomorrah to
destruction by reducing *them* to
ashes, having made them an [b]ex-
ample to those who would [c]live
ungodly thereafter;
7 and if He [a]rescued righteous Lot, oppressed by the [b]sen-
sual conduct of [c]unprincipled
men

★ 4 [a]Gen. 6; Jude 6 [b]Rev. 20:1f.
★ 5 [a]Ezek. 26:20; 2 Pet. 3:6 [b]1 Pet. 3:20 [c]2 Pet. 3:6
★ 6 [a]Gen. 19:24; Jude 7 [b]Matt. 10:15; 11:23; Rom. 9:29 [Is. 1:9]; Jude 7 [c]Jude 15
★ 7 [a]Gen. 19:16, 29 [b]Gen. 19:5ff.; 2 Pet. 2:2, 18; Jude 4 [c]2 Pet. 3:17

1:16 *eyewitnesses of His majesty.* Peter is referring here to his witnessing the transfiguration of Christ (Matt. 17:1-8). This event confirmed the truth of the O.T. prophecies and made them even more sure from a human viewpoint (2 Pet. 1:19).

1:19 *until the day dawns.* Possibly a reference to the second coming of Christ.

1:20 *one's own interpretation.* Several meanings are possible: (1) Prophecies must be interpreted in the light of other Scriptures; (2) prophecies are often capable of several fulfillments; (3) prophecies must be interpreted only with God's help, since they were given only as the prophets were moved by God, and not by any impulse of man.

1:21 *moved.* Lit., borne along. This shows the dual authorship of God's Word—the Holy Spirit guiding and guarding the men involved in the actual writing. See note on 2 Tim. 3:16.

2:1 *denying the Master who bought them.* The price for the sins of all men (including these false teachers) was paid by the death of Christ, though no man can have benefit of this forgiveness except through faith in the Savior. See 1 Cor. 6:20; 1 Pet. 1:18-19.

2:4 *angels when they sinned.* These are the fallen angels who sinned grievously by cohabiting with women, as described in Gen. 6:1-4. See Jude 6. The logic is that if God so punishes angels, surely He will not spare these false teachers.

2:5 *with seven others.* Noah was the eighth, along with the seven other members of his family (his wife and his three sons and their wives).

2:6 *Sodom and Gomorrah.* See Gen. 19:15-29.

2:7 *righteous Lot.* He was a righteous man in

8 (for by what he saw and
heard *that* [a]righteous man, while
living among them, felt *his* righteous soul tormented day after day
with *their* lawless deeds),
9 [a]*then* the Lord knows how
to rescue the godly from temptation, and to keep the unrighteous
under punishment for the [b]day of
judgment,

8 [a]Heb. 11:4
9 [a]1 Cor. 10:13; Rev. 3:10 [b]Matt. 10:15; Jude 6

C Their Characteristics, 2:10–22

10 and especially those who
[a]indulge the flesh in *its* corrupt
desires and [b]despise authority.
Daring, [c]self-willed, they do not
tremble when they [b]revile angelic
majesties,
11 [a]whereas angels who are
greater in might and power do not
bring a reviling judgment against
them before the Lord.
12 But [a]these, like unreason-
ing animals, [b]born as creatures of
instinct to be captured and killed,
reviling where they have no
knowledge, will in the destruction
of those creatures also be destroyed,
13 suffering wrong as [a]the
wages of doing wrong. They
count it a pleasure to [b]revel in the
[c]daytime. They are stains and
blemishes, [b]reveling in their deceptions, as they [d]carouse with
you;
14 having eyes full of adultery and that never cease from
sin; [a]enticing [b]unstable souls,
having a heart trained in [c]greed,
[d]accursed children;
15 forsaking [a]the right way
they have gone astray, having followed [b]the way of Balaam, the
son of Beor, who loved [c]the wages
of unrighteousness,
16 but he received a rebuke
for his own transgression; [a]*for* a
dumb donkey, speaking with a
voice of a man, restrained the
madness of the prophet.
17 These are [a]springs without
water, and mists driven by a
storm, [b]for whom the black darkness has been reserved.
18 For speaking out [a]arrogant
words of [b]vanity they [c]entice by
fleshly desires, by [d]sensuality,
those who barely [e]escape from
the ones who live in error,
19 promising them freedom
while they themselves are slaves
of corruption; for [a]by what a man
is overcome, by this he is enslaved.
20 For if after they have [a]es-
caped the defilements of the
world by [b]the knowledge of the
[c]Lord and Savior Jesus Christ,
they are again [d]entangled in them
and are overcome, [e]the last state
has become worse for them than
the first.
21 [a]For it would be better for
them not to have known the way
of righteousness, than having

★10 [a]2 Pet. 3:3; Jude 16, 18 [b]Ex. 22:28; Jude 8 [c]Titus 1:7
★11 [a]Jude 9
12 [a]Jude 10 [b]Jer. 12:3; Col. 2:22
★13 [a]2 Pet. 2:15 [b]Rom. 13:13 [c]1 Thess. 5:7 [d]1 Cor. 11:21; Jude 12
★14 [a]2 Pet. 2:18 [b]James 1:8; 2 Pet. 3:16 [c]2 Pet. 2:3 [d]Eph. 2:3
★15 [a]Acts 13:10 [b]Num. 22:5, 7; Deut. 23:4; Neh. 13:2; Jude 11; Rev. 2:14 [c]2 Pet. 2:13
16 [a]Num. 22:21, 23, 28, 30f.
★17 [a]Jude 12 [b]Jude 13
★18 [a]Jude 16 [b]Eph. 4:17 [c]2 Pet. 2:14 [d]2 Pet. 2:2 [e]2 Pet. 1:4; 2:20
19 [a]John 8:34; Rom. 6:16
★20 [a]2 Pet. 2:18 [b]2 Pet. 1:2 [c]2 Pet. 1:11; 3:18 [d]2 Tim. 2:4 [e]Matt. 12:45; Luke 11:26
21 [a]Ezek. 18:24; Heb. 6:4ff.; 10:26f.; James 4:17 [b]Gal. 6:2; 1 Tim. 6:14; 2 Pet. 3:2 [c]Jude 3

---

that he believed God and was vexed at the licentiousness of the wicked people about him, though his life was lived for himself.

2:10 *despise authority.* I.e., especially God's. False teachers speak rashly in disbelief of the power and authority of angels.

2:11 *against them.* Probably a reference to the false teachers. In other words, even though the false teachers speak evil of angels, angels do not denounce them but leave all judgment to God.

2:13 *reveling in their deceptions.* The false teachers turned Christian fellowship meals into riotous drinking parties.

2:14 *accursed children.* A phrase which simply means that the false teachers themselves, not their children, are accursed.

2:15 *the way of Balaam.* The covetousness of one who hires himself to do religious work for personal gain (see Num. 22:7, 17 and note on Jude 11). This "way" is contrasted with "the right way" (2 Pet. 2:15).

2:17 *springs without water.* The barrenness of the false teachers mocks the thirsty soul who sincerely wants to learn God's way from them. *mists driven by a storm.* These mists, like the false teachers, seem to promise refreshment, but in reality do no good. *the black darkness.* I.e., eternal torment (cf. Matt. 8:12).

2:18 *sensuality* = sexual excesses.

2:20 *escaped the defilements of the world.* These teachers had apparently made some sort of profession of the truth without possessing the new life of Christ. They then rejected what they professed, becoming slaves of corruption (v. 19) and showing their true, natural, unchanged condition (v. 22).

known it, to turn away from [b]the
holy commandment [c]delivered to
them.
22 It has happened to them
according to the true proverb, "[a]A
DOG RETURNS TO ITS OWN VOMIT,"
and, "A sow, after washing, *re-*
turns to wallowing in the mire."

22 [a]Prov. 26:11

IV THE DESIGN OF THE FUTURE, 3:1–18

A Derision, 3:1–7

3 This is now, [a]beloved, the
second letter I am writing to
you in which I am [b]stirring up
your sincere mind by way of reminder,
2 that you should [a]remem-
ber the words spoken beforehand
by [b]the holy prophets and [c]the
commandment of the Lord and
Savior *spoken* by your apostles.
3 [a]Know this first of all, that
[b]in the last days [c]mockers will
come with *their* mocking, [d]fol-
lowing after their own lusts,
4 and saying, "[a]Where is the
promise of His [b]coming? For *ever*
since the fathers [c]fell asleep, all
continues just as it was [d]from the
beginning of creation."
5 For when they maintain
this, it escapes their notice that
[a]by the word of God *the* heavens
existed long ago and *the* earth
was [b]formed out of water and by
water,
6 through which [a]the world
at that time was [b]destroyed, being
flooded with water.
7 But [a]the present heavens
and earth by His word are being
reserved for [b]fire, kept for [c]the
day of judgment and destruction
of ungodly men.

1 [a]1 Pet. 2:11; 2 Pet. 3:8, 14, 17 [b]2 Pet. 1:13
2 [a]Jude 17 [b]Luke 1:70; Acts 3:21; Eph. 3:5 [c]Gal. 6:2; 1 Tim. 6:14; 2 Pet. 2:21
3 [a]2 Pet. 1:20 [b]1 Tim. 4:1; Heb. 1:2 [c]Jude 18 [d]2 Pet. 2:10
4 [a]Is. 5:19; Jer. 17:15; Ezek. 11:3; 12:22, 27; Mal. 2:17; Matt. 24:48 [b]1 Thess. 2:19; 2 Pet. 3:12 [c]Acts 7:60 [d]Mark 10:6
★ 5 [a]Gen. 1:6, 9; Heb. 11:3 [b]Ps. 24:2; 136:6; Col. 1:17 [Gr.]
★ 6 [a]2 Pet. 2:5 [b]Gen. 7:21f.
7 [a]2 Pet. 3:10, 12 [b]Is. 66:15; Dan. 7:9f.; 2 Thess. 1:7; Heb. 12:29 [c]Matt. 10:15; 1 Cor. 3:13; Jude 7

B Delay, 3:8–9

8 But do not let this one *fact*
escape your notice, [a]beloved, that
with the Lord one day is as a
thousand years, and [b]a thousand
years as one day.
9 [a]The Lord is not slow
about His promise, as some count
slowness, but [b]is patient toward
you, [c]not wishing for any to perish but for all to come to repentance.

★ 8-9
8 [a]2 Pet. 3:1 [b]Ps. 90:4
9 [a]Hab. 2:3; Rom. 13:11; Heb. 10:37 [b]Rom. 2:4; Rev. 2:21 [c]1 Tim. 2:4; Rev. 2:21

C Dissolution, 3:10–13

10 But [a]the day of the Lord
[b]will come like a thief, in which
[c]the heavens [d]will pass away with
a roar and the [e]elements will be
destroyed with intense heat, and
[f]the earth and its works will be
burned up.
11 Since all these things are to
be destroyed in this way, what
sort of people ought you to be in
holy conduct and godliness,
12 [a]looking for and hastening
the coming of the day of God, on
account of which [b]the heavens
will be destroyed by burning, and
the [c]elements will melt with intense heat!
13 But according to His
[a]promise we are looking for [b]new
heavens and a new earth, [c]in
which righteousness dwells.

★10 [a]1 Cor. 1:8 [b]Matt. 24:43; 1 Thess. 5:2; Rev. 3:3; 16:15 [c]2 Pet. 3:7, 12 [d]Matt. 24:35; Rev. 21:1 [e]Is. 24:19; 34:4; Mic. 1:4; Gal. 4:3 [f]2 Pet. 3:7
★12 [a]1 Cor. 1:7 [b]2 Pet. 3:7, 10 [c]Is. 24:19; 34:4; Mic. 1:4; Gal. 4:3
13 [a]Is. 65:17; 66:22 [b]Rom. 8:21; Rev. 21:1 [c]Is. 60:21; 65:25; Rev. 21:27

D Diligence, 3:14–18

14 [a]Therefore, [b]beloved,
since you look for these things, be
diligent to be [c]found by Him in
peace, [d]spotless and blameless,

14 [a]1 Cor. 15:58; 2 Pet. 1:10 [b]2 Pet. 3:1 [c]1 Pet. 1:7 [d]Phil. 2:15; 1 Thess. 5:23; 1 Tim. 6:14; James 1:27

3:5 *it escapes their notice.* Or, they willfully ignore. Peter begins his attack on those who doubt the truth of Christ's return by referring to the dependability of God's word as demonstrated in Creation.

3:6 *flooded with water.* The judgment of the flood in the days of Noah also demonstrates the truthfulness of God's word.

3:8–9 To believers, Peter now says that the seeming delay of Christ's return is for the purpose of allowing more people to repent.

3:10 *the day of the Lord.* See note on 1 Thess. 5:2.

3:12 *on account of which.* I.e., after the dissolution of the present heavens, the day of God, which is eternity (Rev. 21:1), will come. The certainty of this dissolution makes doubly urgent a life of godliness now.

★15 [a]2 Pet. 3:9 [b]Acts 9:17; 15:25; 2 Pet. 3:2 [c]1 Cor. 3:10; Eph. 3:3

15 and regard the [a]patience of
our Lord *to be* salvation; just as
also [b]our beloved brother Paul,
[c]according to the wisdom given
him, wrote to you,

★16 [a]2 Pet. 3:14 [b]Heb. 5:11 [c]2 Pet. 2:14 [d]Is. 28:13; 2 Pet. 3:2

16 as also in all *his* letters,
speaking in them of [a]these things,
[b]in which are some things hard to
understand, which the untaught
and [c]unstable distort, as *they do*
also [d]the rest of the Scriptures, to
their own destruction.

17 You therefore, [a]beloved,
knowing this beforehand, [b]be on
your guard lest, being carried
away by [c]the error of [d]unprinci-
pled men, you [e]fall from your
own steadfastness,

17 [a]2 Pet. 3:1 [b]1 Cor. 10:12 [c]2 Pet. 2:18 [d]2 Pet. 2:7 [e]Rev. 2:5

18 but grow in the grace and
[a]knowledge of our [b]Lord and Savior Jesus Christ. [c]To Him *be* the
glory, both now and to the day of
eternity. Amen.

18 [a]2 Pet. 1:2 [b]2 Pet. 1:11; 2:20 [c]Rom. 11:36; 2 Tim. 4:18; Rev. 1:6

3:15 *regard . . . to be salvation.* I.e., understand that the delay of the return of the Lord is intended as an opportunity for men to be saved (see v. 9).

3:16 Paul's epistles are here put on a par with *the rest of the Scriptures.*

INTRODUCTION TO THE FIRST LETTER OF JOHN

AUTHOR: John DATE: 90

Authorship *Though it is generally agreed that the same person wrote the Gospel of John and these three epistles, some feel that they were not written (as traditionally held) by John the apostle, the son of Zebedee, but by another John (the elder or presbyter, 2 John 1; 3 John 1). It is argued that (1) an uneducated man (Acts 4:13) could not have written something so profound as this Gospel; (2) a fisherman's son would not have known the high priest as did John the apostle; and (3) an apostle would not have called himself an elder. But "uneducated" did not mean illiterate, but only without formal training in the rabbinic schools; some fishermen were well-to-do (cf. Mark 1:20); and Peter, though an apostle, called himself an elder (1 Pet. 5:1). Further, if John the elder is the "beloved disciple" and the author of the Gospel, why did he not mention John the son of Zebedee, an important figure in the life of Christ, in that Gospel? Every evidence points to John the elder being the same as John the apostle and the author of this letter.*

Date and Place of Writing *Strong tradition says that John spent his old age in Ephesus. Lack of personal references in this letter indicates that it was written in sermonic style to Christians all over Asia Minor (much like Ephesians). It was probably written after the Gospel and before the persecution under Domitian in 95, which places its writing in the late 80's or early 90's.*

Gnosticism *The hersey of Gnosticism had begun to make inroads among churches in John's day. Among its teachings were: (1) knowledge is superior to virtue; (2) the nonliteral sense of Scripture is correct and can be understood only by a select few; (3) evil in the world precludes God's being the only Creator; (4) the incarnation is incredible because deity cannot unite itself with anything material such as a body (Docetism); and (5) there is no resurrection of the flesh. The ethical standards of many Gnostics were low, so John emphasized the reality of the incarnation and the high ethical standard of the earthly life of Christ.*

Contents *The letter shows John's obvious affection for his "little children" and concern for their spiritual welfare. The book is filled with contrasts—light and darkness (1:6-7; 2:8-11); love of world and love of God (2:15-17); children of God and children of the devil (3:4-10); the Spirit of God and the spirit of Antichrist (4:1-3); love and hate (4:7-12, 16-21).*

OUTLINE OF 1 JOHN

I. Introduction: The Purpose of the Epistle, 1:1-4

II. Conditions for Fellowship, 1:5-2:2
- A. Conformity to a Standard, 1:5-7
- B. Confession of Sin, 1:8-2:2

III. Conduct in Fellowship, 2:3-27
- A. The Character of our Conduct—Imitation, 2:3-11
- B. The Commandment for our Conduct—Separation, 2:12-17
- C. The Creed for our Conduct—Affirmation, 2:18-27

IV. Characteristics of Fellowship, 2:28-3:24
- A. In Relation to our Prospect: Purity, 2:28-3:3
- B. In Relation to our Position: Righteousness and Brotherly Love, 3:4-18
- C. In Relation to our Prayers: Answers, 3:19-24

V. Cautions of Fellowship, 4:1-21
- A. Concerning False, Lying Spirits, 4:1-6
- B. Concerning a True, Loving Spirit, 4:7-21
  1. The ground of brotherly love, 4:7-10
  2. The glories of love, 4:11-21

VI. Consequences of Fellowship, 5:1-21
- A. Love for the Brethren, 5:1-3
- B. Victory over the World, 5:4-5
- C. Verification of Christ's Credentials, 5:6-12
- D. Assurance of Eternal Life, 5:13
- E. Guidance in Prayer, 5:14-17
- F. Freedom from Habitual Sin, 5:18-21

THE FIRST LETTER OF JOHN

I INTRODUCTION: THE PURPOSE OF THE EPISTLE, 1:1-4

★ **1** [a]John 1:1f.; 1 John 2:13, 14 [b]Acts 4:20 [c]John 19:35; 2 Pet. 1:16; 1 John 1:2 [d]John 1:14; 1 John 4:14 [e]Luke 24:39; John 20:27 [f]John 1:1, 4
2 [a]John 1:4; Rom. 16:26 [b]John 19:35; 1 John 1:1 [c]John 15:27 [d]John 10:28 [e]John 1:1
3 [a]John 19:35; 2 Pet. 1:16; 1 John 1:1 [b]Acts 4:20; 1 John 1:1 [c]John 17:3, 21
4 [a]1 John 2:1 [b]John 3:29

1 What was [a]from the beginning, what we have [b]heard, what we have [c]seen with our eyes, what we [d]beheld and our hands [e]handled, concerning the [f]Word of Life—

2 and [a]the life was manifested, and we have [b]seen and [c]bear witness and proclaim to you [d]the eternal life, which was [e]with the Father and was [a]manifested to us—

3 what we have [a]seen and [b]heard we proclaim to you also, that you also may have fellowship with us; and indeed our [c]fellowship is with the Father, and with His Son Jesus Christ.

4 And [a]these things we write, so that our [b]joy may be made complete.

II CONDITIONS FOR FELLOWSHIP, 1:5-2:2

A Conformity to a Standard, 1:5-7

★ **5** [a]John 1:19; 1 John 3:11 [b]1 Tim. 6:16; James 1:17
6 [a]John 8:12; 2 Cor. 6:14; Eph. 5:8; 1 John 2:11 [b]John 8:55; 1 John 2:4; 4:20 [c]John 3:21
★ **7** [a]Is. 2:5 [b]1 Tim. 6:16 [c]Titus 2:14; Heb. 9:14; Rev. 7:14

5 And [a]this is the message we have heard from Him and announce to you, that [b]God is light, and in Him there is no darkness at all.

6 [a]If we say that we have fellowship with Him and *yet* walk in the darkness, we [b]lie and [c]do not practice the truth;

7 but if we [a]walk in the light as [b]He Himself is in the light, we have fellowship with one another, and [c]the blood of Jesus His Son cleanses us from all sin.

B Confession of Sin, 1:8-2:2

★ **8** [a]Job 15:14; Prov. 20:9; Rom. 3:10ff.; James 3:2 [b]John 8:44; 1 John 2:4
★ **9** [a]Ps. 32:5; Prov. 28:13 [b]Titus 2:14; Heb. 9:14; Rev. 7:14
★**10** [a]Job 15:14; Prov. 20:9; Rom. 3:10ff.; James 3:2 [b]John 3:33; 1 John 5:10 [c]1 John 2:14
★ **1** [a]John 13:33; Gal. 4:19; 1 John 2:12, 28; 3:7, 18; 4:4; 5:21 [b]1 John 1:4 [c]Rom. 8:34; 1 Tim. 2:5; Heb. 7:25; 9:24 [d]John 14:16
★ **2** [a]Rom. 3:25; Heb. 2:17; 1 John 4:10 [b]John 4:42; 11:51f.; 1 John 4:14

8 [a]If we say that we have no sin, we are deceiving ourselves, and the [b]truth is not in us.

9 [a]If we confess our sins, He is faithful and righteous to forgive us our sins and [b]to cleanse us from all unrighteousness.

10 [a]If we say that we have not sinned, we [b]make Him a liar, and [c]His word is not in us.

2 [a]My little children, I am writing [b]these things to you that you may not sin. And if anyone sins, [c]we have an [d]Advocate with the Father, Jesus Christ the righteous;

2 and He Himself is [a]the propitiation for our sins; and not for ours only, but also [b]for *those of* the whole world.

III CONDUCT IN FELLOWSHIP, 2:3-27

A The Character of our Conduct—Imitation, 2:3-11

★ **3-5**
3 [a]1 John 2:5; 3:24; 4:13; 5:2 [b]1 John 2:4; 3:6; 4:7f. [c]John 14:15; 1 John 3:22, 24; 5:3

3 And [a]by this we know that we have come to [b]know Him, if we [c]keep His commandments.

1:1 *was.* The verb means "was already in existence," not "came into existence." I.e., at creation, *the beginning. handled.* The same Greek word is used in one of Christ's postresurrection appearances ("touch," Luke 24:39).

1:5 *from Him.* I.e., from Christ. *God is light.* I.e., God is holy and pure. This symbol was much used by John (John 1:4; 3:19-21; 8:12). Notice also the other "God is . . ." phrases in John 4:24 and 1 John 4:8.

1:7 *but if we walk in the light.* To walk in the light is to live in obedience to God's commandments. The contrast of light and darkness characterizes the section 1:5-2:17.

1:8 *have no sin.* A reference to the indwelling principle of sin rather than to acts of sin.

1:9 *confess* means to say the same thing about sin that God does.

1:10 *we have not sinned.* I.e., have not committed sin. Even believers sin; if we deny past sin and present guilt, we are deceiving ourselves, mocking God, and not walking in the light.

2:1 *Advocate.* Lit., one summoned alongside, a helper or patron in a lawsuit. Used only by John in the N.T. and translated "Helper" in John 14:16, 26; 15:26; 16:7.

2:2 *propitiation* = satisfaction. Christ is the only offering that satisfied God concerning sin (cf. Rom. 3:25). See note on Heb. 2:17.

2:3-5 Obedience to Christ's commandments is the down-to-earth test of our faith.

4 The one who says, "[a]I have come to [b]know Him," and does not keep His commandments, is a [c]liar, and [d]the truth is not in him;

★ 4 [a]Titus 1:10 [b]1 John 3:6; 4:7f. [c]1 John 1:6 [d]1 John 1:8

5 but whoever [a]keeps His word, in him the [b]love of God has truly been perfected. [c]By this we know that we are in Him:

★ 5 [a]John 14:23 [b]1 John 4:12 [c]1 John 2:3; 3:24; 4:13; 5:2

6 the one who says he [a]abides in Him [b]ought himself to walk in the same manner as He walked.

6 [a]John 15:4 [b]John 13:15; 15:10; 1 Pet. 2:21

7 [a]Beloved, I am [b]not writing a new commandment to you, but an old commandment which you have had [c]from the beginning; the old commandment is the word which you have heard.

7 [a]Heb. 6:9; 1 John 3:2, 21; 4:1, 7, 11 [b]1 John 3:11, 23; 4:21; 2 John 5 [c]1 John 2:24; 3:11; 2 John 5, 6

8 On the other hand, I am writing [a]a new commandment to you, which is true in Him and in you, because [b]the darkness is passing away, and [c]the true light is already shining.

★ 8 [a]John 13:34 [b]Rom. 13:12; Eph. 5:8; 1 Thess. 5:4f. [c]John 1:9

9 The one who says he is in the light and *yet* [a]hates his [b]brother is in the darkness until now.

9 [a]1 John 2:11; 3:15; 4:20 [b]Acts 1:15; 1 John 3:10, 16; 4:20f.

10 [a]The one who loves his brother abides in the light and there is no cause for stumbling in him.

★10 [a]John 11:9; 1 John 2:10, 11

11 But the one who [a]hates his brother is in the darkness and [b]walks in the darkness, and does not know where he is going because the darkness has [c]blinded his eyes.

11 [a]1 John 2:9; 3:15; 4:20 [b]John 12:35; 1 John 1:6 [c]2 Cor. 4:4; 2 Pet. 1:9

B The Commandment for our Conduct—Separation, 2:12–17

12 I am writing to you, [a]little children, because [b]your sins are forgiven you for His name's sake.

12 [a]1 John 2:1 [b]Acts 13:38; 1 Cor. 6:11

13 I am writing to you, fathers, because you know Him [a]who has been from the beginning. I am writing to you, young men, because [b]you have overcome [c]the evil one. I have written to you, children, because [d]you know the Father.

★13 [a]1 John 1:1 [b]John 16:33; 1 John 2:14; 4:4; 5:4f.; Rev. 2:7 [c]Matt. 5:37; 1 John 2:14; 3:12; 5:18f. [d]John 14:7; 1 John 2:3

14 I have written to you, fathers, because you know Him [a]who has been from the beginning. I have written to you, young men, because you are [b]strong, and the [c]word of God abides in you, and [d]you have overcome the evil one.

14 [a]1 John 1:1 [b]Eph. 6:10 [c]John 5:38; 8:37; 1 John 1:10 [d]1 John 2:13

15 Do not love [a]the world, nor the things in the world. [b]If any one loves the world, the love of the Father is not in him.

★15 [a]Rom. 12:2; James 1:27 [b]James 4:4

16 For all that is in the world, [a]the lust of the flesh and [b]the lust of the eyes and [c]the boastful pride of life, is not from the Father, but is from the world.

★16 [a]Rom. 13:14; Eph. 2:3; 1 Pet. 2:11 [b]Prov. 27:20 [c]James 4:16

17 And [a]the world is passing away, and *also* its lusts; but the one who does the will of God abides forever.

17 [a]1 Cor. 7:31

C The Creed for our Conduct—Affirmation, 2:18–27

18 Children, [a]it is the last hour; and just as you heard that [b]antichrist is coming, [c]even now many antichrists have arisen; from this we know that it is the last hour.

★18-27
18 [a]Rom. 13:11; 1 Tim. 4:1; 1 Pet. 4:7 [b]Matt. 24:5, 24; 1 John 2:22; 4:3; 2 John 7 [c]Mark 13:22; 1 John 4:1, 3

19 [a]They went out from us, but they were not *really* of us; for if they had been of us, they would have remained with us; but *they*

19 [a]Acts 20:30 [b]1 Cor. 11:19

2:4 *truth.* Not merely correct knowledge, but the demonstration of the reality of God's love.
2:5 *perfected.* I.e., realized in practice.
2:8 *the true light.* I.e., the revelation of God in Christ.
2:10 *there is no cause for stumbling in him.* I.e., there is nothing in him that would cause others to stumble.
2:13 *the evil one.* I.e., the devil.
2:15 *the world.* The world (Greek, *cosmos*) is that organized system headed by Satan which leaves God out and is a rival to Him. Though God loves the world of men (John 3:16), believers are not to love at all that which organizes them against God. See 1 John 5:19; John 3:19; Jas. 1:27; 4:4.
2:16 *pride of life.* Vainglory, display, or boasting about one's possessions.
2:18–27 The author now contrasts truth and falsehood.
2:18 *antichrist.* John speaks about (1) the spirit of antichrist (4:3) which refers to demonic forces behind antichristian teaching and activity; (2) the great coming Antichrist (Rev.

went out, [b]in order that it might
be shown that they all are not of
us.
20 But you have an [a]anoint-
ing from [b]the Holy One, and [c]you
all know.
21 I have not written to you
because you do not know the
truth, but [a]because you do know
it, and because no lie is [b]of the
truth.
22 Who is the liar but [a]the
one who denies that Jesus is the
Christ? This is [b]the antichrist, the
one who denies the Father and
the Son.
23 [a]Whoever denies the Son
does not have the Father; the one
who confesses the Son has the Father also.
24 As for you, let that abide
in you which you heard [a]from the
beginning. If what you heard
from the beginning abides in you,
you also [b]will abide in the Son
and in the Father.
25 And [a]this is the promise
which He Himself made to us:
eternal life.
26 These things I have written
to you concerning those who are
trying to [a]deceive you.
27 And as for you, the [a]a-
nointing which you received from
Him abides in you, and you have
no need for anyone to teach you;
but as His anointing [b]teaches you
about all things, and is [c]true and
is not a lie, and just as it has
taught you, you abide in Him.

★20 [a]2 Cor. 1:21; 1 John 2:27 [b]Mark 1:24; Acts 10:38 [c]Prov. 28:5; Matt. 13:11; John 14:26; 1 Cor. 2:15f.; 1 John 2:27
21 [a]James 1:19; 2 Pet. 1:12; Jude 5 [b]John 8:44; 18:37; 1 John 3:19
★22 [a]1 John 4:3; 2 John 7 [b]Matt. 24:5, 24; 1 John 2:18; 4:3; 2 John 7
23 [a]John 8:19; 16:3; 17:3; 1 John 4:15; 5:1; 2 John 9
24 [a]1 John 2:7 [b]John 14:23; 1 John 1:3; 2 John 9
25 [a]John 3:15; 6:40; 1 John 1:2
26 [a]1 John 3:7; 2 John 7
★27 [a]John 14:16; 1 John 2:20 [b]John 14:26; 1 Cor. 2:12; 1 Thess. 4:9 [c]John 14:17

IV CHARACTERISTICS OF FELLOWSHIP, 2:28–3:24

A In Relation to our Prospect: Purity, 2:28–3:3

28 And now, [a]little children,
abide in Him, so that when He
[b]appears, we may have [c]confi-
dence and [d]not shrink away from
Him in shame at His [e]coming.
29 If you know that [a]He is
righteous, you know that every
one also who practices righteousness [b]is born of Him.
3 See [a]how great a love the Father has bestowed upon us,
that we should be called [b]children
of God; and *such* we are. For this
reason the world does not know
us, because [c]it did not know Him.
2 [a]Beloved, now we are
[b]children of God, and [c]it has not
appeared as yet what we shall be.
We know that, when He [d]ap-
pears, we shall be [e]like Him, because we shall [f]see Him just as He
is.
3 And every one who has
this [a]hope *fixed* on Him [b]purifies
himself, just as He is pure.

B In Relation to our Position: Righteousness and Brotherly Love, 3:4–18

4 Every one who practices
sin also practices lawlessness; and
[a]sin is lawlessness.

★2:28–3:24
28 [a]1 John 2:1 [b]Luke 17:30; Col. 3:4; 1 John 3:2 [c]Eph. 3:12; 1 John 3:21; 4:17; 5:14 [d]Mark 8:38 [e]1 Thess. 2:19
29 [a]John 7:18; 1 John 3:7 [b]John 1:13; 3:3; 1 John 3:9; 4:7; 5:1, 4, 18 [3 John 11]
★ 1 [a]John 3:16; 1 John 4:10 [b]John 1:12; 11:52; Rom. 8:16; 1 John 3:2, 10 [c]John 15:18, 21; 16:3
2 [a]1 John 2:7 [b]John 1:12; 11:52; Rom. 8:16; 1 John 3:1, 10 [c]Rom. 8:19, 23f. [d]Luke 17:30; Col. 3:4; 1 John 2:28 [e]Rom. 8:29; 2 Pet. 1:4 [f]John 17:24; 2 Cor. 3:18
3 [a]Rom. 15:12; 1 Pet. 1:3 [b]John 17:19; 2 Cor. 7:1; 2 Pet. 3:13f.; 1 John 2:6
★ 4 [a]Rom. 4:15; 1 John 5:17

13:1–10); and (3) many antichrists present and active in his time and throughout church history. The ones of whom John is here speaking belonged to the visible church but were not believers (v. 19). They denied the reality of the incarnation of Christ and His relationship to the Father (vv. 21–23; cf. 2 John 7).

2:20 *you have an anointing from the Holy One.* I.e., you have been anointed by the Holy Spirit, and thus can discern between truth and error. See also note on 2:27.

2:22 *the liar.* The supreme liar is the one who denies that Jesus Christ came in the flesh, i.e., that He was both man and God. The separation of the human and the divine was an early (Docetic) heresy.

2:27 *you have no need for anyone to teach you.* The Spirit whom they had received would teach them how to distinguish truth from error (John 16:13). The Spirit may use human teachers to accomplish this (Eph. 4:11–14).

2:28–3:24 John's third great contrast is between life and death. (Cf. notes on 1:7 and 2:18.)

3:1 *children of God.* Born ones of God, as in John 1:12. We can, even now, know Him as a child knows its father; the future relationship no words can describe.

3:4 *sin is lawlessness.* Lawlessness is used here in its broadest sense, defection from any of God's standards.

5 And you know that He
[a]appeared in order to [b]take away
sins; and [c]in Him there is no sin.
6 No one who abides in Him
[a]sins; no one who sins has seen
Him or [b]knows Him.
7 [a]Little children, let no one
[b]deceive you; [c]the one who practices righteousness is righteous,
just as He is righteous;
8 the one who practices sin
is [a]of the devil; for the devil has
sinned from the beginning. [b]The
Son of God [c]appeared for this
purpose, [d]that He might destroy
the works of the devil.
9 No one who is [a]born of
God [b]practices sin, because His
seed abides in him; and he cannot
sin, because he is born of God.
10 By this the [a]children of
God and the [b]children of the devil
are obvious: any one who does
not practice righteousness is not
of God, nor the one who [c]does
not love his [d]brother.
11 [a]For this is the message
[b]which you have heard from the
beginning, [c]that we should love
one another;
12 not as [a]Cain, *who* was of
[b]the evil one, and slew his
brother. And for what reason did
he slay him? Because [c]his deeds
were evil, and his brother's were
righteous.
13 Do not marvel, brethren, if
[a]the world hates you.
14 We know that we have
[a]passed out of death into life, [b]be-
cause we love the brethren. He
who does not love abides in
death.
15 Every one who [a]hates his
brother is a murderer; and you
know that [b]no murderer has eternal life abiding in him.
16 We know love by this, that
[a]He laid down His life for us; and
[b]we ought to lay down our lives
for the [c]brethren.
17 But [a]whoever has the
world's goods, and beholds his
brother in need and [b]closes his
heart against him, [c]how does the
love of God abide in him?
18 [a]Little children, let us not
love with word or with tongue,
but in deed and [b]truth.

C In Relation to our Prayers: Answers, 3:19–24

19 We shall know by this that
we are [a]of the truth, and shall assure our heart before Him,
20 in whatever our heart condemns us; for God is greater than
our heart, and knows all things.
21 [a]Beloved, if our heart does
not condemn us, we have [b]confi-
dence before God;
22 and [a]whatever we ask we
receive from Him, because we
[b]keep His commandments and do
[c]the things that are pleasing in
His sight.
23 And this is His commandment, that we [a]believe in [b]the
name of His Son Jesus Christ, and
love one another, just as [c]He
commanded us.
24 And the one who [a]keeps
His commandments [b]abides in
Him, and He in him. And [c]we
know by this that [d]He abides in
us, by the Spirit which He has
given us.

5 [a]1 John 1:2; 3:8 [b]John 1:29; 1 Pet. 1:18-20; 1 John 2:2 [c]2 Cor. 5:21; 1 John 2:29
6 [a]1 John 3:9 [b]1 John 2:3; 3 John 11
7 [a]1 John 2:1 [b]1 John 2:26 [c]1 John 2:29
★ **8** [a]Matt. 13:38; John 8:44; 1 John 3:10 [b]Matt. 4:3 [c]1 John 3:5 [d]John 12:31; 16:11
★ **9** [a]John 1:13; 3:3; 1 John 2:29; 4:7; 5:1, 4, 18 [3 John 11] [b]James 1:18
10 [a]John 1:12; 11:52; Rom. 8:16; 1 John 3:1, 2 [b]Matt. 13:38; John 8:44; 1 John 3:8 [c]Rom. 13:8ff.; Col. 3:14; 1 Tim. 1:5; 1 John 4:8 [d]1 John 2:9
11 [a]1 John 1:5 [b]1 John 2:7 [c]John 13:34f.
★**12** [a]Gen. 4:8 [b]Matt. 5:37; 1 John 2:13f. [c]Ps. 38:20; Prov. 29:10; John 8:40, 41
13 [a]John 15:18; 17:14
14 [a]John 5:24 [b]John 13:35; 1 John 2:10
★**15** [a]Matt. 5:21f.; John 8:44 [b]Gal. 5:20f.
★**16-17**
16 [a]John 10:11; 15:13 [b]Phil. 2:17; 1 Thess. 2:8 [c]1 John 2:9
17 [a]James 2:15f. [b]Deut. 15:7 [c]1 John 4:20
18 [a]1 John 2:1; 3:7 [b]2 John 1; 3 John 1
19 [a]1 John 2:21
★**20**
21 [a]1 John 2:7 [b]1 John 2:28; 5:14
22 [a]Job 22:26f.; Matt. 7:7; 21:22; John 9:31 [b]1 John 2:3 [c]John 8:29; Heb. 13:21
23 [a]John 6:29 [b]John 1:12; 2:23; 3:18 [c]John 13:34; 15:12; 1 John 2:8
★**24** [a]1 John 2:3 [b]John 6:56; 10:38; 1 John 2:6, 24; 4:15 [c]John 14:17; Rom. 8:9, 14, 16; 1 Thess. 4:8; 1 John 4:13 [d]1 John 2:5

3:8 *practices* = continually practices. I.e., sins as a regular way of life.

3:9 *No one . . . practices sin . . . he cannot sin.* I.e., habitually (see note on v. 8). Habitual actions indicate one's character. *seed.* I.e., the divine nature given the one born of God (cf. John 1:13; 2 Pet. 1:4). This nature prevents the Christian from habitually sinning.

3:12 *Cain.* See Gen. 4:8.

3:15 *a murderer.* The heart that is full of hate is potentially capable of murder (cf. Matt. 5:21–22).

3:16–17 Self-sacrificing love is required of the believer. Though not many are called on to sacrifice their lives, all can give sacrificially of their substance. *world's goods* = the material necessities of life.

3:20 *God is greater than our heart.* We may be either too strict or too lenient in examining our lives; therefore, John's word of comfort is: God the all-knowing is also the all-loving.

3:24 *abides.* The same word as in John 15:1–10. To abide in Christ requires keeping His commandments.

V CAUTIONS OF FELLOWSHIP, 4:1–21

A Concerning False, Lying Spirits, 4:1–6

4 [a]Beloved, do not believe every [b]spirit, but test the spirits
to see whether they are from God;
because [c]many false prophets
have gone out into the world.
2 By this you know the
Spirit of God: [a]every spirit that
[b]confesses that [c]Jesus Christ has
come in the flesh is from God;
3 and every spirit that [a]does
not confess Jesus is not from God;
and this is the *spirit* of the [b]anti-
christ, of which you have heard
that it is coming, and [c]now it is
already in the world.
4 You are from God, [a]little
children, and [b]have overcome
them; because [c]greater is He who
is in you than [d]he who is in the
world.
5 [a]They are from the world;
therefore they speak *as* from the
world, and the world listens to
them.
6 [a]We are from God; [b]he
who knows God listens to us; [c]he
who is not from God does not listen to us. By this we know [d]the
spirit of truth and [e]the spirit of
error.

★ 1 [a]1 John 2:7 [b]Jer. 29:8; 1 Cor. 12:10; 1 Thess. 5:20f.; 2 Thess. 2:2 [c]Jer. 14:14; 2 Pet. 2:1; 1 John 2:18
2 [a]1 Cor. 12:3 [b]1 John 2:23 [c]John 1:14; 1 John 1:2
★ 3 [a]1 John 2:22; 2 John 7 [b]1 John 2:18, 22 [c]2 Thess. 2:3-7; 1 John 2:18
★ 4 [a]1 John 2:1 [b]1 John 2:13 [c]2 Kin. 2:16; Rom. 8:31; 1 John 3:20 [d]John 12:31
5 [a]John 15:19; 17:14, 16
6 [a]John 8:23; 1 John 4:4 [b]John 8:47; 10:3ff.; 18:37 [c]1 Cor. 14:37 [d]John 14:17 [e]1 Tim. 4:1

B Concerning a True, Loving Spirit, 4:7–21

1 *The ground of brotherly love,* 4:7–10

7 [a]Beloved, let us [b]love one
another, for love is from God; and
[c]every one who loves is [d]born of
God and [e]knows God.
8 The one who does not love
does not know God, for [a]God is
love.
9 By this the love of God
was manifested [a]in us, that [b]God
has sent His only begotten Son
into the world so that we might
live through Him.
10 In this is love, [a]not that we
loved God, but that [b]He loved us
and sent His Son *to be* [c]the propitiation for our sins.

★ 7-12
7 [a]1 John 2:7 [b]1 John 3:11 [c]1 John 5:1 [d]1 John 2:29 [e]1 Cor. 8:3; 1 John 2:3
8 [a]1 John 4:7, 16
9 [a]John 9:3; 1 John 4:16 [b]John 3:16f.; 1 John 4:10; 5:11
10 [a]Rom. 5:8, 10; 1 John 4:19 [b]John 3:16f.; 1 John 4:9; 5:11 [c]1 John 2:2

2 *The glories of love,* 4:11–21

11 [a]Beloved, if God so loved
us, [b]we also ought to love one another.
12 [a]No one has beheld God at
any time; if we love one another,
God abides in us, and His [b]love is
perfected in us.
13 [a]By this we know that we
abide in Him and He in us, because He has given us of His
Spirit.
14 And we have beheld and
[a]bear witness that the Father has
[b]sent the Son *to be* the Savior of
the world.
15 [a]Whoever confesses that
[b]Jesus is the Son of God, God
[c]abides in him, and he in God.
16 And [a]we have come to
know and have believed the love
which God has [b]for us. [c]God is
love, and the one who [d]abides in
love abides in God, and God
abides in him.
17 By this, [a]love is perfected
with us, that we may have [b]confi-
dence in [c]the day of judgment;
because [d]as He is, so also are we
in this world.
18 There is no fear in love;
but [a]perfect love casts out fear,

11 [a]1 John 2:7 [b]1 John 4:7
12 [a]John 1:18; 1 Tim. 6:16; 1 John 4:20 [b]1 John 2:5; 4:17f.
13 [a]Rom. 8:9; 1 John 3:24
14 [a]John 15:27; 1 John 1:2 [b]John 3:17; 4:42; 1 John 2:2
15 [a]1 John 2:23 [b]Rom. 10:9; 1 John 3:23; 4:2; 5:1, 5 [c]1 John 2:24; 3:24
★16 [a]John 6:69 [b]John 9:3; 1 John 4:9 [c]1 John 4:7, 8 [d]1 John 4:12f.
★17 [a]1 John 2:5; 4:12 [b]1 John 2:28 [c]Matt. 10:15 [d]John 17:22; 1 John 2:6; 3:1, 7, 16
18 [a]Rom. 8:15; Gal. 4:30f. [b]1 John 4:12

4:1 *do not believe every spirit.* Apparently some of John's readers were being lead astray by Gnosticism (see Introduction to 1 John).

4:3 *spirit of the antichrist.* The false prophets were influenced by demonic spirits.

4:4 *He who is in you.* I.e., the Holy Spirit (cf. 3:24). *he who is in the world.* I.e., Satan (cf. John 12:31).

4:7–12 This is one of John's greatest passages. *God is love.* Love is His supreme quality. God can be known only by those who live in love. Yet we could not know how, nor be able, to love Him if He had not first loved us. If we love one another, God abides in us and His love is perfected or matured in us (v. 12).

4:16 To live a love-filled life is to be God-filled.

4:17 *confidence in the day of judgment.* The believer who has practiced love during his earthly life will be able to approach the judgment seat of Christ without any shame. Such assurance is not presumption, because *as He is, so also are we in this world;* i.e., we are like Him in love.

because fear involves punishment, and the one who fears is not [b]perfected in love.

19 [a]1 John 4:10

19 [a]We love, because He first loved us.

20 [a]1 John 1:6, 8, 10; 2:4 [b]1 John 2:9, 11 [c]1 John 1:6 [d]1 John 3:17 [e]1 Pet. 1:8; 1 John 4:12

20 [a]If some one says, "I love God," and [b]hates his brother, he is a [c]liar; for [d]the one who does not love his brother whom he has seen, [e]cannot love God whom he has not seen.

21 [a]Lev. 19:18; Matt. 5:43f.; 22:37ff.; John 13:34 [b]1 John 3:11

21 And [a]this commandment we have from Him, that the one who loves God [b]should love his brother also.

VI CONSEQUENCES OF FELLOWSHIP, 5:1-21

A Love for the Brethren, 5:1-3

1 [a]1 John 2:22f.; 4:2, 15 [b]John 1:3; 3:3 marg.; 1 John 2:29; 5:4, 18 [c]John 8:42

5 [a]Whoever believes that Jesus is the Christ is [b]born of God; and whoever loves the Father [c]loves the *child* born of Him.

2 [a]1 John 2:5 [b]1 John 3:14

2 [a]By this we know that [b]we love the children of God, when we love God and observe His commandments.

3 [a]John 14:15; 2 John 6 [b]1 John 2:3 [c]Matt. 11:30; 23:4

3 For [a]this is the love of God, that we [b]keep His commandments; and [c]His commandments are not burdensome.

B Victory over the World, 5:4-5

4 [a]John 1:13; 3:3 marg.; 1 John 2:29; 5:1, 18 [b]1 John 2:13; 4:4

4 For whatever is [a]born of God [b]overcomes the world; and this is the victory that has overcome the world—our faith.

5 [a]1 John 4:15; 5:1

5 And who is the one who overcomes the world, but he who [a]believes that Jesus is the Son of God?

C Verification of Christ's Credentials, 5:6-12

★ 6 [a]John 19:34

6 This is the one who came [a]by water and blood, Jesus Christ; not with the water only, but with the water and with the blood.

7 [a]John 15:26; 16:13-15 [Matt. 3:16f.]

7 And it is [a]the Spirit who bears witness, because the Spirit is the truth.

8 [a]Matt. 18:16

8 For there are [a]three that bear witness, the Spirit and the water and the blood; and the three are in agreement.

9 [a]John 5:34, 37; 8:18 [b]Matt. 3:17; John 5:32, 37

9 [a]If we receive the witness of men, the witness of God is greater; for the witness of God is this, that [b]He has borne witness concerning His Son.

10 [a]Rom. 8:16; Gal. 4:6; Rev. 12:17 [b]John 3:18, 33; 1 John 1:10

10 The one who believes in the Son of God [a]has the witness in himself; the one who does not believe God has [b]made Him a liar, because he has not believed in the witness that God has borne concerning His Son.

11 [a]1 John 1:2; 2:25; 4:9; 5:13, 20 [b]John 1:4

11 And the witness is this, that God has given us [a]eternal life, and [b]this life is in His Son.

12 [a]John 3:15f., 36

12 [a]He who has the Son has the life; he who does not have the Son of God does not have the life.

D Assurance of Eternal Life, 5:13

13 [a]John 20:31 [b]1 John 3:23 [c]1 John 1:2; 2:25; 4:9; 5:11, 20

13 [a]These things I have written to you who [b]believe in the name of the Son of God, in order that you may know that you have [c]eternal life.

E Guidance in Prayer, 5:14-17

★14 [a]1 John 2:28; 3:21f. [b]Matt. 7:7; John 14:13; 1 John 3:22

14 And this is [a]the confidence which we have before Him, that, [b]if we ask anything according to His will, He hears us.

15 [a]1 John 5:18, 19, 20

15 And if we know that He hears us *in* whatever we ask, [a]we know that we have the requests which we have asked from Him.

5:6 *by water and blood.* The water refers to the inauguration of Christ's earthly ministry at His baptism by John (Mark 1:9-11); the blood refers to the close of His earthly life at His crucifixion. Jesus proved Himself to be the Christ (Messiah) at His baptism and by pouring out His soul to death.

5:14 *according to His will.* A gracious limitation, because God's will is always best for His children.

★16 [a]James 5:15 [b]Num. 15:30; Heb. 6:4-6; 10:26 [c]Jer. 7:16; 14:11

16 If any one sees his brother
committing a sin not *leading* to
death, [a]he shall ask and *God* will
for him give life to those who
commit sin not *leading* to death.
[b]There is a sin *leading* to death; [c]I
do not say that he should make
request for this.

17 [a]1 John 3:4 [b]1 John 2:1f.; 5:16

17 [a]All unrighteousness is sin,
and [b]there is a sin not *leading* to
death.

18 [a]1 John 5:15, 19, 20 [b]1 John 3:9 [c]James 1:27; Jude 21 [d]1 John 2:13 [e]John 14:30

F Freedom from Habitual Sin, 5:18–21

18 [a]We know that [b]no one
who is born of God sins; but He
who was born of God [c]keeps him
and [d]the evil one does not [e]touch
him.

19 [a]1 John 5:15, 18, 20 [b]1 John 4:6 [c]John 12:31; 17:15; Gal. 1:4

19 [a]We know that [b]we are of
God, and [c]the whole world lies in
the power of the evil one.

20 [a]1 John 5:15, 18, 19 [b]John 8:42; 1 John 5:5 [c]Luke 24:45 [d]John 17:3; Rev. 3:7 [e]John 1:18; 14:9; 1 John 2:23; Rev. 3:7 [f]1 John 1:2 [g]1 John 5:11

20 And [a]we know that [b]the
Son of God has come, and has
[c]given us understanding, in order
that we might know [d]Him who is
true, and we [e]are in Him who is
true, in His Son Jesus Christ. [f]This
is the true God and [g]eternal life.

★21 [a]1 John 2:1 [b]1 Cor. 10:7, 14; 1 Thess. 1:9

21 [a]Little children, guard
yourselves from [b]idols.

5:16 *sin not leading to death.* Believers can sin to the point where physical death results as the judgment of God (cf. 1 Cor. 11:30). The Greek reads *sin,* not *a sin,* in vv. 16 and 17.

5:21 *idols.* An idol is anything that substitutes for God.

INTRODUCTION TO THE SECOND LETTER OF JOHN

AUTHOR: John DATE: 90

Destination *The destination of this second letter is enigmatic. Some believe that the "chosen lady" is a figurative way of designating a particular church ("chosen sister," v. 13, would then mean a different church). Others hold that the letter was addressed to an individual Christian and her family (in which case the "sister" would be her natural sister).*

Date *The circumstances and subjects of this letter indicate that it was written about the same time as the other letters of John and from the same place, Ephesus. See the Introduction to 1 John.*

Contents *The main teaching of 2 John is walking in Christ's commandments.*

OUTLINE OF 2 JOHN

I. Introduction and Greeting, 1-3
II. Commendation for Walking in Truth, 4
III. Commandment to Love One Another, 5-6
IV. Cautions Concerning False Teachers, 7-11
V. Concluding Remarks and Greetings, 12-13

THE SECOND LETTER OF JOHN

I INTRODUCTION AND GREETING, 1-3

★ 1 [a]Acts 11:30; 3 John 1; 1 Pet. 5:1 [b]Rom. 16:13 [Gr.]; 1 Pet. 5:13; 2 John 13 [c]2 John 5 [d]1 John 3:18; 2 John 3; 3 John 1 [e]John 8:32; 1 Tim. 2:4
2 [a]2 Pet. 1:12 [b]1 John 1:8 [c]John 14:16
3 [a]Rom. 1:7; 1 Tim. 1:2

1 [a]The elder to the [b]chosen
[c]lady and her children, whom
I [d]love in truth; and not only I,
but also all who [e]know the truth,
2 for [a]the sake of the truth
which abides [b]in us and will be
[c]with us forever:
3 [a]Grace, mercy *and* peace
will be with us, from God the Father and from Jesus Christ, the
Son of the Father, in truth and
love.

II COMMENDATION FOR WALKING IN TRUTH, 4

★ 4 [a]3 John 3f.

4 [a]I was very glad to find
some of your children walking in
truth, just as we have received
commandment *to do* from the Father.

III COMMANDMENT TO LOVE ONE ANOTHER, 5-6

5 And now I ask you, lady, 5 [a]1 John 2:7 [b]1 John 3:11
[a]not as writing to you a new com-
mandment, but the one which we
have had [a]from the beginning,
that we [b]love one another.
6 And [a]this is love, that we ★ 6 [a]1 John 2:5; 5:3 [b]1 John 2:24 [c]1 John 2:7
walk according to His command-
ments. This is the commandment,
[b]just as you have heard [c]from the
beginning, that you should walk
in it.

---

1 *her children.* Either the congregation (if the *chosen lady* was a local church) or her natural offspring (if she was an individual Christian). *the truth.* I.e., the gospel message; also in v. 2.

4 *walking in truth.* Ordering one's life by the Word of God.

6 *love* is defined as obeying His commandments.

IV CAUTIONS CONCERNING FALSE TEACHERS, 7-11

★ 7 [a]1 John 2:26 [b]1 John 2:19; 4:1 [c]1 John 4:2f. [d]1 John 2:18

7 For [a]many deceivers have
[b]gone out into the world, those
who [c]do not acknowledge Jesus
Christ *as* coming in the flesh. This
is [a]the deceiver and the [d]anti-
christ.

★ 8 [a]Mark 13:9 [b]1 Cor. 3:8; Heb. 10:35

8 [a]Watch yourselves, [b]that
you might not lose what we have
accomplished, but that you may
receive a full reward.

9 [a]John 7:16; 8:31; 1 John 2:23

9 Any one who goes too far
and [a]does not abide in the teaching of Christ, does not have God;
the one who abides in the teaching, he has both the Father and
the Son.

★10 [a]1 Kin. 13:16f.; Rom. 16:17

10 If any one comes to you
and does not bring this teaching,
[a]do not receive him into *your*
house, and do not give him a
greeting;

★11 [a]1 Tim. 5:22; Jude 23

11 for the one who gives him
a greeting [a]participates in his evil
deeds.

V CONCLUDING REMARKS AND GREETINGS, 12-13

★12 [a]3 John 13, 14 [b]John 3:29; 1 John 1:4

12 [a]Having many things to
write to you, I do not want to *do*
so with paper and ink; but I hope
to come to you and speak face to
face, that your [b]joy may be made
full.

13 [a]2 John 1

13 The children of your [a]cho-
sen sister greet you.

---

7 *coming.* This present tense participle seems to include the past coming of Christ in flesh at the incarnation, the present continuance of His risen humanity, as well as His future coming to earth. By contrast, the perfect tense participle in 1 John 4:2 emphasizes only His incarnation. *antichrist.* See note on 1 John 2:18.

8 *we.* Better manuscripts read "you" (plural).

10 *do not receive him into your house.* I.e., do not give a false teacher hospitality.

11 *participates.* Lit., fellowships. He who gives such a person a greeting actually fellowships in the work of Antichrist.

12 *paper and ink.* The pith from papyrus reeds was cut into strips, which were laid across each other at right angles, pressed, and pasted together to form sheets of writing material. The word *ink* simply means black, for ink in ancient times was compounded of charcoal, gum, and water.

INTRODUCTION TO THE THIRD LETTER OF JOHN

AUTHOR: John DATE: 90

Characteristics of the Letter *This is a very personal letter, addressed to Gaius, which focuses on an ecclesiastical problem regarding traveling teachers. Gaius had given them hospitality, while Diotrephes, a self-assertive leader in one of the churches, had refused to receive them. John exhibits his apostolic authority in his rebuke of Diotrephes (v. 10). Demetrius, who himself may have been a traveling teacher, probably delivered the letter to Gaius.*

OUTLINE OF 3 JOHN

I. Opening Greetings, 1
II. The Influence of Gaius, 2-8
A. His Godly Life, 2-4
B. His Generous Treatment of Traveling Ministers, 5-8
III. The Indictment of Diotrephes, 9-11
A. His Selfish Ambition, 9
B. His Selfish Activities, 10-11
IV. The Introduction of Demetrius, 12
V. Concluding Remarks and Benediction, 13-14

THE THIRD LETTER OF JOHN

I OPENING GREETINGS, 1

★ 1 [a]2 John 1 [b]1 John 3:18; 2 John 1

1 [a]The elder to the beloved
Gaius, whom I [b]love in truth.

II THE INFLUENCE OF GAIUS, 2-8

A His Godly Life, 2-4

★2
3 [a]2 John 4 [b]Acts 1:15; Gal. 6:10; 3 John 5, 10
★ 4 [a]1 Cor. 4:14f.; 2 Cor. 6:13; Gal. 4:19; 1 Thess. 2:11; 1 Tim. 1:2; 2 Tim. 1:2; Philem. 10; 1 John 2:1 [b]2 John 3

2 Beloved, I pray that in all
respects you may prosper and be
in good health, just as your soul
prospers.
3 For I [a]was very glad when
[b]brethren came and bore witness
to your truth, *that is,* how you
[a]are walking in truth.
4 I have no greater joy than
this, to hear of [a]my children
[b]walking in the truth.

B His Generous Treatment of Traveling Ministers, 5-8

5 Beloved, you are acting
faithfully in whatever you accomplish for the [a]brethren, and especially *when they are* [b]strangers;
6 and they bear witness to
your love before the church; and
you will do well to [a]send them on
their way in a manner [b]worthy of
God.
7 For they went out for the
sake of [a]the Name, [b]accepting
nothing from the Gentiles.

★ 5 [a]Acts 1:15; Gal. 6:10; 3 John 3, 10 [b]Rom. 12:13; Heb. 13:2
★ 6 [a]Acts 15:3; Titus 3:13 [b]Col. 1:10; 1 Thess. 2:12
★ 7 [a]John 15:21; Acts 5:41; Phil. 2:9 [b]Acts 20:33, 35

---

1 *elder.* See note on 1 Tim. 3:1.
2 *be in good health.* I.e., physical health. Perhaps Gaius had been ill.
4 *my children.* I.e., beneficiaries of John's ministry, whom he had probably led to Christ.
5 *for the brethren, and . . . strangers.* Gaius had aided both "brethren" and "strangers," the latter being the more difficult and therefore the more praiseworthy form of hospitality (cf. Heb. 13:2). Traveling evangelists and teachers were dependent on men like Gaius for shelter and sustenance.
6 *send them on their way.* I.e., to help them on their journey with food, money, arrangements for companions, means of travel, etc.
7 *accepting nothing from the Gentiles.* These traveling missionaries declined to receive help from those who were not converted, lest they should appear to be selling the gospel.

8 Therefore we ought to
support such men, that we may
be fellow-workers with the truth.

III THE INDICTMENT OF DIOTREPHES, 9-11

A His Selfish Ambition, 9

9 [a]2 John 9 marg. 9 I wrote something to the
church; but Diotrephes, who
loves to [a]be first among them,
does not accept what we say.

B His Selfish Activities, 10-11

★10 [a]2 John 12 [b]2 John 10; 3 John 5 [c]Acts 1:15; Gal. 6:10; 3 John 3, 5 [d]John 9:34 10 For this reason, [a]if I come,
I will call attention to his deeds
which he does, unjustly accusing
us with wicked words; and not
satisfied with this, neither does he
himself [b]receive the [c]brethren,
11 [a]Ps. 34:14; 37:27 [b]1 John 2:29; 3:10 [c]1 John 3:6 and he forbids those who desire
to do so, and [d]puts *them* out of
the church.
11 Beloved, [a]do not imitate
what is evil, but what is good.
[b]The one who does good is of
God; [c]the one who does evil has
not seen God.

IV THE INTRODUCTION OF DEMETRIUS, 12

12 Demetrius [a]has received a 12 [a]Acts 6:3; 1 Tim. 3:7 [b]John 19:35; 21:24
good testimony from everyone,
and from the truth itself; and we
also bear witness, and [b]you know
that our witness is true.

V CONCLUDING REMARKS AND BENEDICTION, 13-14

13 [a]I had many things to ★13 [a]2 John 12
write to you, but I am not willing
to write *them* to you with pen and
ink;
14 but I hope to see you ★14 [a]John 20:19, 21, 26; Eph. 6:23; 1 Pet. 5:14 [b]John 10:3
shortly, and we shall speak face to
face. [a]Peace *be* to you. The
friends greet you. Greet the
friends [b]by name.

---

10 *puts them out of the church.* Some sort of exclusion, whether formal excommunication or not.

13 *pen.* This pen was a reed pointed at the end.

14 *Peace be to you.* In some texts and translations this phrase begins a new verse (15).

INTRODUCTION TO THE LETTER OF JUDE

AUTHOR: Jude DATE: 70-80

Authorship *Jude identifies himself as the brother of James (v. 1), the leader of the Jerusalem church (Acts 15), and the half brother of the Lord Jesus. Jude is listed among Christ's half brothers in Matthew 13:55 and Mark 6:3. Although, by his own statement, he intended to write a treatise on salvation, pressing circumstances required him to deal instead with the false teachers (v. 3).*

Purpose *This letter was written to defend the apostolic faith against false teachings which were arising in the churches. Alarming advances were being made by an incipient form of Gnosticism—not ascetic, like that attacked by Paul in Colossians, but antinomian. The Gnostics viewed everything material as evil and everything spiritual as good. They therefore cultivated their "spiritual" lives and allowed their flesh to do anything it liked, with the result that they were guilty of all kinds of lawlessness. (See "Gnosticism" in the Introduction to 1 John.)*

Extrabiblical Quotations *In verses 14 and 15, Jude quotes the pseudepigraphal apocalypse of 1 Enoch and in verse 9 alludes to a reference in another pseudepigraphal book, The Assumption of Moses. This does not mean that he considered these books to be inspired as the canonical Scriptures were. Paul quoted from heathen poets without implying their inspiration (Acts 17:28; 1 Cor. 15:33; Titus 1:12).*

Readership *The readers are not identified, but we know that they were beset by false teachers who were immoral, covetous, proud, and divisive.*

Contents *Condemning the heretics in no uncertain terms, Jude exhorts his readers to "contend earnestly for the faith" (v. 3).*

OUTLINE OF JUDE

I. The Salutation and Purpose, 1-4
II. Exposure of the False Teachers, 5-16
A. Their Doom, 5-7
B. Their Denunciation, 8-10
C. Their Description, 11-16
III. Exhortations to Believers, 17-23
IV. The Benediction, 24-25

THE LETTER OF JUDE

I THE SALUTATION AND PURPOSE, 1-4

1 [a]Jude, a [b]bond-servant of
Jesus Christ, and brother of
James, to [c]those who are the
called, beloved in God the Father,
and [d]kept for Jesus Christ:
2 [a]May mercy and peace and
love [b]be multiplied to you.
3 [a]Beloved, while I was
making every effort to write you
about our [b]common salvation, I
felt the necessity to write to you
appealing that you [c]contend earnestly for [d]the faith which was
once for all [e]delivered to [f]the
saints.
4 For certain persons have
[a]crept in unnoticed, those who
were long beforehand [b]marked
out for this condemnation, ungodly persons who turn [c]the grace
of our God into [d]licentiousness
and [e]deny our only Master and
Lord, Jesus Christ.

★ **1** [a]Matt. 13:55; Mark 6:3; [Luke 6:16; John 14:22; Acts 1:13?] [b]Rom. 1:1 [c]Rom. 1:6f. [d]John 17:11f.; 1 Pet. 1:5; Jude 21
2 [a]Gal. 6:16; 1 Tim. 1:2 [b]1 Pet. 1:2; 2 Pet. 1:2
★ **3** [a]Heb. 6:9; Jude 1, 17, 20 [b]Titus 1:4 [c]1 Tim. 6:12 [d]Acts 6:7; Jude 20 [e]2 Pet. 2:21 [f]Acts 9:13
★ **4** [a]Gal. 2:4; 2 Tim. 3:6 [b]1 Pet. 2:8 [c]Acts 11:23 [d]2 Pet. 2:7 [e]2 Tim. 2:12; Titus 1:16; 2 Pet. 2:1; 1 John 2:22

II EXPOSURE OF THE FALSE TEACHERS, 5-16

A Their Doom, 5-7

5 Now I desire to [a]remind
you, though [b]you know all things
once for all, that the Lord, [c]after
saving a people out of the land of
Egypt, subsequently destroyed
those who did not believe.
6 And [a]angels who did not
keep their own domain, but abandoned their proper abode, He has
[b]kept in eternal bonds under
darkness for the judgment of the
great day.
7 Just as [a]Sodom and Gomorrah and the [b]cities around
them, since they in the same way
as these indulged in gross immorality and [c]went after strange
flesh, are exhibited as an [d]examp-
le, in undergoing the [e]punish-
ment of eternal fire.

★ **5** [a]2 Pet. 1:12f.; 3:1f. [b]1 John 2:20 [c]1 Cor. 10:5-10; Heb. 3:16f.
★ **6** [a]2 Pet. 2:4 [b]2 Pet. 2:9
7 [a]2 Pet. 2:6 [b]Deut. 29:23; Hos. 11:8 [c]2 Pet. 2:2 [d]2 Pet. 2:6 [e]Matt. 25:41; 2 Thess. 1:8f.; 2 Pet. 3:7

B Their Denunciation, 8-10

8 Yet in the same manner
these men, also by dreaming, [a]de-
file the flesh, and [a]reject authority, and [a]revile angelic majesties.
9 But [a]Michael [b]the archangel, when he disputed with the
devil and argued about [c]the body
of Moses, did not dare pronounce
against him a railing judgment,
but said, "[d]THE LORD REBUKE YOU."
10 But [a]these men revile the
things which they do not understand; and [b]the things which they
know by instinct, [a]like unreason-
ing animals, by these things they
are destroyed.

★ **8** [a]2 Pet. 2:10
9 [a]Dan. 10:13, 21; 12:1; Rev. 12:7 [b]1 Thess. 4:16; 2 Pet. 2:11 [c]Deut. 34:6 [d]Zech. 3:2
10 [a]2 Pet. 2:12 [b]Phil. 3:19

---

1 Jude addresses the *called;* i.e., all Christians who have been called to a knowledge of God through Christ. They are *beloved in God* and *kept for Jesus Christ* at His second coming.

3 *contend earnestly for the faith which was once for all delivered.* I.e., stand for the body of truth once for all given, not to be added to or subtracted from (cf. Gal. 1:23).

4 *deny our only Master and Lord, Jesus Christ.* The Greek word here for "Master" may be translated "despot" (cf. Acts 4:24, 1 Tim. 6:1), and is applied here to Jesus. To deny Jesus as Lord was to disbelieve the most basic Christian tenet.

5 *destroyed those who did not believe.* The possibility of lapsing is illustrated by the disbelieving Israelites who were saved out of Egypt but subsequently destroyed.

6 *angels who did not keep their own domain.* A reference to that group of fallen angels whom Satan persuaded to cohabit with women (Gen. 6:1-4) and who were confined immediately because of the gross nature of that sin. The apocryphal book of Enoch describes their dramatic end. See note on 2 Pet. 2:4.

8 *angelic majesties.* Refers to angels (cf. 2 Pet. 2:10), though it may include leaders of the church as well.

C Their Description, 11-16

11 Woe to them! For they have gone [a]the way of Cain, and for pay they have rushed headlong into [b]the error of Balaam, and [c]perished in the rebellion of Korah.

★11 [a]Gen. 4:3-8; Heb. 11:4; 1 John 3:12 [b]Num. 31:16; 2 Pet. 2:15; Rev. 2:14 [c]Num. 16:1-3, 31-35

12 These men are those who are hidden reefs [a]in your love-feasts when they feast with you [b]without fear, caring for themselves; [c]clouds without water, [d]carried along by winds; autumn trees without fruit, doubly dead, [e]uprooted;

★12 [a]1 Cor. 11:20ff.; 2 Pet. 2:13 and marg. [b]Ezek. 34:2, 8, 10 [c]Prov. 25:14; 2 Pet. 2:17 [d]Eph. 4:14 [e]Matt. 15:13

13 [a]wild waves of the sea, casting up [b]their own shame like foam; wandering stars, [c]for whom the black darkness has been reserved forever.

13 [a]Is. 57:20 [b]Phil. 3:19 [c]2 Pet. 2:17; Jude 6

14 And about these also [a]Enoch, *in* the seventh *generation* from Adam, prophesied, saying, "[b]Behold, the Lord came with many thousands of His holy ones,

★14 [a]Gen. 5:18, 21ff. [b]Deut. 33:2; Dan. 7:10; Matt. 16:27; Heb. 12:22

15 [a]to execute judgment upon all, and to convict all the ungodly of all their ungodly deeds which they have done in an ungodly way, and of all the harsh things which [b]ungodly sinners have spoken against Him."

15 [a]2 Pet. 2:6ff. [b]1 Tim. 1:9

16 These are [a]grumblers, finding fault, [b]following after their *own* lusts; they speak [c]arrogantly, flattering people [d]for the sake of *gaining an* advantage.

16 [a]Num. 16:11, 41; 1 Cor. 10:10 [b]2 Pet. 2:10; Jude 18 [c]2 Pet. 2:18 [d]2 Pet. 2:3

III EXHORTATIONS TO BELIEVERS, 17-23

17 But you, [a]beloved, [b]ought to remember the words that were spoken beforehand by [c]the apostles of our Lord Jesus Christ,

17 [a]Jude 3 [b]2 Pet. 3:2 [c]Heb. 2:3

18 that they were saying to you, "[a]In the last time there shall be mockers, [b]following after their own ungodly lusts."

18 [a]Acts 20:29; 1 Tim. 4:1; 2 Tim. 3:1f.; 4:3; 2 Pet. 3:3 [b]Jude 4, 16

19 These are the ones who cause divisions, [a]worldly-minded, devoid of the Spirit.

★19 [a]1 Cor. 2:14f.; James 3:15

20 But you, [a]beloved, [b]building yourselves up on your most holy [a]faith; [c]praying in the Holy Spirit;

20 [a]Jude 3 [b]Col. 2:7; 1 Thess. 5:11 [c]Eph. 6:18

21 keep yourselves in the love of God, [a]waiting anxiously for the mercy of our Lord Jesus Christ to eternal life.

21 [a]Titus 2:13; Heb. 9:28; 2 Pet. 3:12

22 And have mercy on some, who are doubting;

★22

23 save others, [a]snatching them out of the fire; and on some have mercy with fear, [b]hating even the garment polluted by the flesh.

23 [a]Amos 4:11; Zech. 3:2; 1 Cor. 3:15 [b]Zech. 3:3f.; Rev. 3:4

IV THE BENEDICTION, 24-25

24 [a]Now to Him who is able to keep you from stumbling, and to [b]make you stand in the presence of His glory blameless with [c]great joy,

★24-25
24 [a]Rom. 16:25 [b]2 Cor. 4:14 [c]1 Pet. 4:13

25 to the [a]only [b]God our Savior, through Jesus Christ our Lord, [c]*be* glory, majesty, dominion and authority, [d]before all time and now and forever. Amen.

25 [a]John 5:44; 1 Tim. 1:17 [b]Luke 1:47 [c]Rom. 11:36 [d]Heb. 13:8

---

11 *the way of Cain.* I.e., his rejection of God's provision for acceptance with Himself (Gen. 4:1-12). Today, it is the rejection of God's offer of forgiveness through Christ. *the error of Balaam.* Balaam hired himself out as a prophet and epitomizes deceit and covetousness (cf. Num. 22-24; 2 Pet. 2:15; Rev. 2:14). *the rebellion of Korah.* The sin of Korah was rebellion against duly constituted authority (Num. 16).

12 *love-feasts.* These fellowship meals were eaten in connection with the Lord's Supper (see note on 1 Cor. 11:20). Pride, greed, and rebellion summarize the iniquities of the ungodly men (v. 4) who corrupted these love-feasts.

14 *Enoch.* Though this prophecy is found in the noncanonical book of Enoch (1:9), the original prophecy was uttered by the Enoch of the Bible (Gen. 5:19-24; cf. Heb. 11:5-6) and was later expanded and incorporated in the book of Enoch.

19 *ones who cause divisions.* I.e., heretical groups, who are *worldly-minded* or, as they are called in 1 Cor. 2:14, "natural." Jude declares that these false teachers were not truly redeemed (cf. Rom. 8:9).

22 *have mercy on.* Some manuscripts read "convince." *who are doubting.* Thus the verse says, "Have mercy on, or convince, those who are doubting."

24-25 One of the great benedictions of the N.T. *Savior.* God is the Savior of the O.T. and in the N.T. that title survives, occurring seven times.

INTRODUCTION TO THE REVELATION TO JOHN

AUTHOR: John DATE: 90's

Authorship *According to the book itself the author's name was John (1:4, 9, 22:8), a prophet (22:9). Traditionally this John has been identified as John the apostle, the son of Zebedee (see the Introduction to 1 John). That the style of the Revelation is different from that of the Gospel and the three epistles of John does not prove that the Revelation was written by a different John. The nature of apocalyptic literature, the fact that this revelation was given in a vision, and the circumstances of John's being a prisoner could easily account for the differences in style.*

Date *Clearly the Revelation was written in a period when Christians were threatened by Rome, undoubtedly by pressure to make them recant their faith and accept the cult of emperor worship. Some maintain that the book was written during Nero's persecution of Christians after the burning of Rome in* A.D. *64. However, the more probable date is during the harsh reign of that warped personality Domitian (*A.D. *81-96). This later date for the book was held by the church father Irenaeus and other early Christian writers, and it agrees better with the picture of complacency and defection of the churches in chapters 2 and 3. This dating is widely accepted by modern scholars.*

Interpretation *There are four principal viewpoints concerning the interpretation of this book: (1) the* preterist, *which views the prophecies of the book as having been fulfilled in the early history of the Church; (2) the* historical, *which understands the book as portraying a panorama of the history of the Church from the days of John to the end of time; (3) the* idealist, *which considers the book a pictorial unfolding of great principles in constant conflict, without reference to actual events; and (4) the* futurist, *which views most of the book (chaps. 4-22) as prophecy yet to be fulfilled. The futurist is the viewpoint taken in these notes, based on the principle of interpreting the text plainly.*

The book is a revelation, or apocalypse (1:1), and as such is expected to be understood. Much of it is frighteningly clear. Some symbols are explained (1:20; 17:1, 15), others are not. It is always important to notice carefully the words "like," "as," and "as it were" (6:1; 9:7), for these words indicate a comparison, not an identification.

Contents *This is the revelation of Jesus Christ, and He is the center of the entire book (1:1). In His risen glory (chap. 1) He directs His churches on earth (chaps. 2-3). He is the slain and risen Lamb to whom all worship is directed (chaps. 4-5). The judgments of the coming seven-year period of tribulation on this earth are the display of the wrath of the Lamb (chaps. 6-19; see especially 6:16-17), and the return of Christ to this earth is described in 19:11-21. The millennial reign of Christ is described in chapter 20, and the new heavens and new earth in chapters 21 and 22.*

The outline of the book is indicated in 1:19. The things which John had seen include the vision of the risen Christ in chapter 1. The "things which are" comprise the letters to the seven churches of Asia Minor in chapters 2 and 3. The "things which shall take place after these things" are the prophecies of chapters 4-22.

OUTLINE OF REVELATION

I. The Prologue, 1:1-8
- A. The Superscription, 1:1-3
- B. The Salutation, 1:4-8

II. "The Things Which You Have Seen," 1:9-20
- A. Circumstances of the Vision, 1:9-11
- B. Content of the Vision, 1:12-16
- C. Consequences of the Vision, 1:17-20

III. "The Things Which Are," 2:1-3:22
- A. The Message to Ephesus, 2:1-7
- B. The Message to Smyrna, 2:8-11
- C. The Message to Pergamum, 2:12-17
- D. The Message to Thyatira, 2:18-29
- E. The Message to Sardis, 3:1-6
- F. The Message to Philadelphia, 3:7-13
- G. The Message to Laodicea, 3:14-22

IV. "The Things Which Shall Take Place After These Things," 4:1-22:5
- A. The Tribulation Period, 4:1-19:21
  - 1. The throne in heaven, 4:1-11
    - a. The throne, 4:1-3
    - b. The throng, 4:4-8
    - c. The theme, 4:9-11
  - 2. The scroll in heaven, 5:1-14
    - a. The scroll, 5:1
    - b. The search, 5:2-5

c. The Savior-Sovereign, 5:6-7
d. The song, 5:8-14
3. The seal judgments, 6:1-17
a. First seal: cold war, 6:1-2
b. Second seal: open war, 6:3-4
c. Third seal: famine, 6:5-6
d. Fourth seal: death, 6:7-8
e. Fifth seal: martyrdom, 6:9-11
f. Sixth seal: physical disturbances, 6:12-17
4. Interlude: the redeemed of the tribulation, 7:1-17
a. The 144,000 Jews, 7:1-8
b. The multitude of Gentiles, 7:9-17
5. The six trumpet judgments, 8:1-9:21
a. The seventh seal opened, 8:1-6
b. First trumpet: the earth smitten, 8:7
c. Second trumpet: the sea smitten, 8:8-9
d. Third trumpet: the waters smitten, 8:10-11
e. Fourth trumpet: the heavens smitten, 8:12-13
f. Fifth trumpet: men smitten, 9:1-12
g. Sixth trumpet: men killed, 9:13-21
6. The little scroll, 10:1-11
7. The two witnesses, 11:1-19
a. Temple, 11:1-2
b. Time, 11:3
c. Traits, 11:4-6
d. Termination, 11:7-10
e. Translation, 11:11-14
f. Seventh trumpet, 11:15-19
8. War, 12:1-17
a. War on earth: phase I, 12:1-6
b. War in heaven, 12:7-12
c. War on earth: phase II, 12:13-17
9. The beast and his prophet, 13:1-18
a. The beast, 13:1-10
b. The false prophet, 13:11-18
10. Various announcements, 14:1-20
a. Concerning the 144,000, 14:1-5
b. Concerning the everlasting gospel, 14:6-8
c. Concerning beast worshipers, 14:9-13
d. Concerning the harvesting of the earth, 14:14-20
11. Prelude to the bowl judgments, 15:1-8
12. The bowl judgments, 16:1-21
a. First bowl: grievous sores, 16:1-2
b. Second bowl: seas smitten, 16:3
c. Third bowl: rivers smitten, 16:4-7
d. Fourth bowl: scorching, 16:8-9
e. Fifth bowl: darkness, 16:10-11
f. Sixth bowl: Euphrates dried, 16:12-16
g. Seventh bowl: widespread destruction, 16:17-21
13. Religious Babylon, 17:1-18
a. The description, 17:1-7
b. The interpretation, 17:8-18
14. Commercial Babylon, 18:1-24
a. Announcement, 18:1-3
b. Appeal, 18:4-8
c. Anguish, 18:9-19
d. Acclaim, 18:20-24
15. The second coming of Christ, 19:1-21
a. Announcements, 19:1-10
b. Advent of Christ, 19:11-16
c. Armageddon, 19:17-21

B. The Millennium, 20:1-15
1. Satan bound, 20:1-3
2. Saints resurrected, 20:4-6
3. Sinners rebelling, 20:7-9
4. Satan doomed, 20:10
5. Sinners judged, 20:11-15

C. The Eternal State, 21:1-22:5
1. Descent of the New Jerusalem, 21:1-8
2. Description of the New Jerusalem, 21:9-27
3. Delights of the New Jerusalem, 22:1-5

V. Epilogue, 22:6-21

A. Words of Comfort, 22:6-17
B. Words of Warning, 22:18-19
C. Closing Benediction, 22:20-21

THE REVELATION TO JOHN

I THE PROLOGUE, 1:1–8

A The Superscription, 1:1–3

1 The Revelation of Jesus
Christ, which [a]God gave Him
to [b]show to His bond-servants,
[c]the things which must shortly
take place; and He sent and com-
municated *it* [d]by His angel to His
bond-servant [e]John,
2 who bore witness to [a]the
word of God and to [b]the testimony of Jesus Christ, *even* to all
that he saw.
3 [a]Blessed is he who reads
and those who hear the words of
the prophecy, and heed the things
which are written in it; [b]for the
time is near.

★ **1** [a]John 17:8; Rev. 5:7 [b]Rev. 22:6 [c]Dan. 2:28f.; Rev. 1:19 [d]Rev. 17:1; 19:9f.; 21:9; 22:16 [e]Rev. 1:4, 9; 22:8
2 [a]1 Cor. 1:6; Rev. 1:9; 6:9; 12:17; 20:4 [b]Rev. 12:17
★ **3** [a]Luke 11:28; Rev. 22:7 [b]Rom. 13:11; Rev. 3:11; 22:7, 10, 12

B The Salutation, 1:4–8

4 [a]John to [b]the seven
churches that are in [c]Asia: [d]Grace
to you and peace, from [e]Him who
is and who was and who is to
come; and from [f]the seven Spirits
who are before His throne;
5 and from Jesus Christ, [a]the
faithful witness, the [b]first-born of
the dead, and the [c]ruler of the
kings of the earth. To Him who
[d]loves us, and released us from
our sins by His blood,
6 and He has made us *to be*
a [a]kingdom, [a]priests to [b]His God
and Father; [c]to Him *be* the glory
and the dominion forever and
ever. Amen.
7 [a]BEHOLD, HE IS COMING WITH
THE CLOUDS, and [b]EVERY EYE WILL SEE
HIM, EVEN THOSE WHO PIERCED HIM;
AND ALL THE TRIBES OF THE EARTH
WILL [c]MOURN OVER HIM. Even so.
Amen.
8 "I am [a]the Alpha and the
Omega," says the [b]Lord God,
"[c]who is and who was and who is
to come, the Almighty."

★ **4** [a]Rev. 1:1, 9; 22:8 [b]Rev. 1:11, 20 [c]Acts 2:9 [d]Rom. 1:7 [e]Ex. 3:14; Is. 41:4; Heb. 13:8; Rev. 1:8, 17; 4:8; 16:5 [f]Is. 11:2; Rev. 3:1; 4:5; 5:6; 8:2
★ **5** [a]John 8:14; 18:37; 1 Tim. 6:13; Rev. 3:14; 19:11 [b]1 Cor. 15:20; Col. 1:18 [c]Dan. 2:47; 1 Tim. 6:15; Rev. 17:14; 19:16 [d]Rom. 8:37
6 [a]Ex. 19:6 [b]Rom. 15:6 [c]Rom. 11:36
★ **7** [a]Dan. 7:13; Matt. 16:27f. [b]Zech. 12:10; John 19:37 [c]Luke 23:28
★ **8** [a]Is. 41:4; Rev. 21:6; 22:13 [b]Rev. 4:8; 11:17; 15:3

II "THE THINGS WHICH YOU HAVE SEEN," 1:9–20

A Circumstances of the Vision, 1:9–11

9 [a]I, John, your [b]brother and
[c]fellow-partaker in the tribulation
and [d]kingdom and [e]perseverance
which are in Jesus, was on the island called Patmos, [f]because of
the word of God and the testimony of Jesus.
10 I was [a]in the Spirit on [b]the
Lord's day, and I heard behind me
a loud voice [c]like *the sound* of a
trumpet,
11 saying, "[a]Write in a book
what you see, and send *it* to the

★ **9** [a]Rev. 1:1 [b]Acts 1:15 [c]Matt. 20:23; Acts 14:22; 2 Cor. 1:7; Phil. 4:14 [d]2 Tim. 2:12 [e]2 Thess. 3:5 [f]Rev. 1:2
★**10** [a]Matt. 22:43 [b]Acts 20:7 [c]Rev. 4:1
11 [a]Rev. 1:2, 19 [b]Rev. 1:4, 20 [c]Rev. 2:1 [d]Rev. 2:8 [e]Rev. 2:12 [f]Acts 16:14 [g]Rev. 3:1, 4 [h]Rev. 3:7 [i]Col. 2:1; Rev. 3:14

1:1 *of Jesus Christ* = from Jesus Christ. Jesus Christ gave this revelation from God, by means of an angel, to John. *shortly.* This word does not indicate that the events described in this book will necessarily occur soon, but that when they do begin to happen they will come to pass swiftly (the same Greek word is translated "speedily" in Luke 18:8).

1:3 *Blessed.* There are 7 beatitudes in Revelation. This is the first; the others are found at 14:13; 16:15; 19:9; 20:6; 22:7, 14. John wanted the book read at once, and preferably aloud, in the churches.

1:4 *seven.* The number 7, occurring 54 times in the book, appears more frequently than any other number. In the Bible it is associated with completion, fulfillment, and perfection (cf. Gen. 2:2; Ex. 20:10; Lev. 14:7; Acts 6:3). In the Revelation there are 7 churches and 7 spirits (1:4), 7 lampstands (1:12), 7 stars (1:16), 7 seals on the scroll (5:1), 7 horns and 7 eyes of the Lamb (5:6), 7 angels and 7 trumpets (8:2), 7 thunders (10:3), 7 heads of the dragon (12:3), 7 heads of the beast (13:1), 7 golden bowls (15:7), and 7 kings (17:10). *the seven Spirits.* Many understand this to refer to the Holy Spirit in His perfect fullness (see Isa. 11:2; Rev. 4:5), though some take this as a reference to 7 angels who are before God's throne.

1:5 *first-born of the dead.* I.e., Christ was the first to receive a resurrection body which is immortal. See Col. 1:15 where He is designated the firstborn of every creature (cf. Ps. 89:27).

1:7 See Matt. 24:29–30.

1:8 *the Alpha and the Omega.* The first and last letters of the Greek alphabet, indicating that the Lord God is the beginning and end of all things.

1:9 *Patmos.* A small island in the Aegean Sea, SW. of Ephesus.

1:10 *in the Spirit.* I.e., in a state of spiritual ecstasy.

[b]seven churches: to [c]Ephesus and
to [d]Smyrna and to [e]Pergamum
and to [f]Thyatira and to [g]Sardis
and to [h]Philadelphia and to [i]Laod-
icea."

B Content of the Vision, 1:12-16

12 And I turned to see the
voice that was speaking with me.
And having turned I saw [a]seven
golden lampstands;
13 and [a]in the middle of the
lampstands one [b]like a son of
man, [c]clothed in a robe reaching
to the feet, and [d]girded across His
breast with a golden girdle.
14 And His head and His
[a]hair were white like white wool,
like snow; and [b]His eyes were like
a flame of fire;
15 and His [a]feet *were* like
burnished bronze, when it has
been caused to glow in a furnace,
and His [b]voice *was* like the sound
of many waters.
16 And in His right hand He
held [a]seven stars; and out of His
mouth came a [b]sharp two-edged
sword; and His [c]face was like [d]the
sun shining in its strength.

★12 [a]Ex. 25:37; 37:23; Zech. 4:2; Rev. 1:20; 2:1
★13 [a]Rev. 2:1 [b]Ezek. 1:26; Dan. 7:13; 10:16; Rev. 14:14 [c]Dan. 10:5 [d]Rev. 15:6
★14 [a]Dan. 7:9 [b]Dan. 7:9; 10:6; Rev. 2:18; 19:12
15 [a]Ezek. 1:7; Dan. 10:6; Rev. 2:18 [b]Ezek. 43:2; Rev. 14:2; 19:6
★16 [a]Rev. 1:20; 2:1; 3:1 [b]Is. 49:2; Heb. 4:12; Rev. 2:12, 16; 19:15 [c]Matt. 17:2; Rev. 10:1 [d]Judg. 5:31

C Consequences of the Vision, 1:17-20

17 And when I saw Him, I
[a]fell at His feet as a dead man.
And He [b]laid His right hand upon
me, saying, "[c]Do not be afraid; [d]I
am the first and the last,
18 and the [a]living One; and I
[b]was dead, and behold, I am alive
forevermore, and I have [c]the keys
of death and of Hades.
19 "[a]Write therefore [b]the
things which you have seen, and
the things which are, and the
things which shall take place [c]af-
ter these things.
20 "As for the [a]mystery of the
[b]seven stars which you saw in My
right hand, and the [c]seven golden
lampstands: the [b]seven stars are
the angels of [d]the seven churches,
and the seven [e]lampstands are the
seven churches.

★17 [a]Dan. 8:17; 10:9, 10, 15 [b]Dan. 8:18; 10:10, 12 [c]Matt. 14:27; 17:7 [d]Is. 41:4; 44:6; 48:12; Rev. 2:8; 22:13
★18 [a]Luke 24:5; Rev. 4:9f. [b]Rom. 6:9; Rev. 2:8; 10:6; 15:7 [c]Job 38:17; Matt. 11:23; 16:19; Rev. 9:1; 20:1
★19 [a]Rev. 1:11 [b]Rev. 1:12-16 [c]Rev. 4:1
20 [a]Rom. 11:25 [b]Rev. 1:16; 2:1; 3:1 [c]Ex. 25:37; 37:23; Zech. 4:2; Rev. 1:12; 2:1 [d]Rev. 1:4, 11 [e]Matt. 5:14f.

III "THE THINGS WHICH ARE," 2:1-3:22

A The Message to Ephesus, 2:1-7

2 "To the angel of the church
in [a]Ephesus write:

★ 1 [a]Rev. 1:11 [b]Rev. 1:16 [c]Rev. 1:12f.

1:12 *lampstands.* These represent the 7 churches mentioned in v. 11 (see also v. 20).

1:13 Christ's clothing designates Him as priest and judge. Notice the description of the Ancient of Days in Dan. 7:9.

1:14 *His eyes were like a flame of fire.* Compare the figure used in 1 Cor. 3:13 in relation to judgment.

1:16 *in His right hand He held seven stars.* The right hand is the place of honor (cf. Eph. 1:20). The stars are the "angels of the seven churches" (v. 20). The word "angel" may mean a superhuman being, implying that each church has a special guardian angel or, more likely here, it refers to the human leader of each local church (see Luke 9:52 and Jas. 2:25 where the word "angel," translated "messenger," is used of human beings). *sword.* A symbol both of the truth and of the severity of the Word of God (Heb. 4:12).

1:17 *I am the first and the last.* In v. 8 God is called the Alpha and Omega. Here Christ gives Himself a similar title.

1:18 *the keys of death and of Hades.* The keys denote the authority of Christ over physical death and Hades, the place which temporarily holds the immaterial part of the unbeliever between death and the ultimate casting into the lake of fire (see Rev. 20:14).

1:19 This verse gives the basic outline of the book: (1) *things which you* (John) *have seen,* as recorded in chapter 1; (2) *things which are;* i.e., the present state of the churches (chaps. 2–3); and (3) *things which shall take place after these things.* The third section clearly begins with 4:1, since the same phrase is used there.

2:1 The 7 churches addressed in chapters 2 and 3 were actual churches of John's day. But they also represent types of churches in all generations. This idea is supported by the fact that only seven were selected out of the many that existed and flourished in John's time, and by the statement at the close of each letter that the Spirit was speaking to the churches (vv. 7, 11, etc.). *Ephesus.* Under Caesar Augustus, Ephesus became the capital of the Roman province called Asia, which today is the western portion of Turkey (Pergamum had been the capital earlier). It was the residence of the apostle John before and after his exile on Patmos, and it was the site of the great temple of Artemis (Latin, Diana) (see the Introduction to Ephesians).

The One who holds [b]the seven
stars in His right hand, the One
who walks [c]among the seven
golden lampstands, says this:
2 '[a]I know your deeds and
your toil and perseverance, and
that you cannot endure evil men,
and you [b]put to the test those
who call themselves [c]apostles,
and they are not, and you found
them *to be* false;

2 [a]Rev. 2:19; 3:1, 8, 15 [b]John 6:6; 1 John 4:1 [c]2 Cor. 11:13

3 and you have perseverance
and have endured [a]for My name's
sake, and have not grown weary.

★ 3 [a]John 15:21

4 'But I have *this* against you,
that you have [a]left your first love.

★ 4 [a]Jer. 2:2; Matt. 24:12

5 'Remember therefore from
where you have fallen, and [a]re-
pent and [b]do the deeds you did at
first; or else I am coming to you,
and will remove your [c]lampstand
out of its place — unless you repent.

★ 5 [a]Rev. 2:16, 22; 3:3, 19 [b]Heb. 10:32; Rev. 2:2 [c]Matt. 5:14ff.; Phil. 2:15; Rev. 1:20

6 'Yet this you do have, that
you hate the deeds of the [a]Nicola-
itans, which I also hate.

★ 6 [a]Rev. 2:15

7 '[a]He who has an ear, let him
hear what the Spirit says to the
churches. [b]To him who overcomes, I will grant to eat of [c]the
tree of life, which is in the [d]Para-
dise of God.'

★ 7 [a]Matt. 11:15; Rev. 2:17; 3:6, 13, 22; 13:9 [b]Rev. 2:11, 17, 26; 3:5, 12, 21; 21:7 [c]Gen. 2:9; 3:22; Prov. 3:18; 11:30; 13:12; 15:4; Rev. 22:2, 14 [d]Ezek. 31:8 [Septuagint]; Luke 23:43

B The Message to Smyrna, 2:8–11

8 "And to the angel of the
church in [a]Smyrna write:
[b]The first and the last, who
[c]was dead, and has come to life,
says this:

★ 8 [a]Rev. 1:11 [b]Rev. 1:17 [c]Rev. 1:18

9 'I know your [a]tribulation
and your [b]poverty (but you are
[b]rich), and the blasphemy by
those who [c]say they are Jews and
are not, but are a synagogue of
[d]Satan.

9 [a]Rev. 1:9 [b]2 Cor. 6:10; 8:9; James 2:5 [c]Rev. 3:9 [d]Matt. 4:10; Rev. 2:13, 24

10 'Do not fear what you are
about to suffer. Behold, the devil
is about to cast some of you into
prison, that you may be [a]tested,
and you will have tribulation [b]ten
days. Be [c]faithful until death, and
I will give you [d]the crown of life.

★10 [a]Rev. 3:10; 13:14ff. [b]Dan. 1:12, 14 [c]Rev. 2:13; 12:11; 17:14 [d]1 Cor. 9:25; Rev. 3:11

11 '[a]He who has an ear, let him
hear what the Spirit says to the
churches. [b]He who overcomes
shall not be hurt by the [c]second
death.'

★11 [a]Matt. 11:15; Rev. 2:7, 17, 29; 3:6, 13, 22; 13:9 [b]Rev. 2:7, 17, 26; 3:5, 12, 21; 21:7 [c]Rev. 20:6, 14; 21:8

C The Message to Pergamum, 2:12–17

12 "And to the angel of the
church in [a]Pergamum write:
The One who has [b]the sharp
two-edged sword says this:

★12 [a]Rev. 1:11 [b]Rev. 1:16; 2:16

13 'I know where you dwell,
where [a]Satan's throne is; and you
hold fast My name, and did not
deny [b]My faith, even in the days
of Antipas, My [c]witness, My
[d]faithful one, who was killed
among you, [e]where Satan dwells.

★13 [a]Matt. 4:10; Rev. 2:13, 24 [b]1 Tim. 5:8; Rev. 14:12 [c]Acts 22:20; Rev. 1:5; 11:3; 17:6 [d]Rev. 2:10; 12:11; 17:14 [e]Rev. 2:9

14 'But [a]I have a few things
against you, because you have

★14 [a]Rev. 2:20 [b]2 Pet. 2:15 [c]Acts 15:29; 1 Cor. 10:20; Rev. 2:20

2:3 *not grown weary.* I.e., have not given up.

2:4 *you have left your first love.* "Left" implies an intentional, not accidental, act. More than 30 years before, this church had been commended for its love (Eph. 1:15-16).

2:5 *remove your lampstand.* I.e., remove the usefulness of that local church.

2:6 *the Nicolaitans.* Followers of Nicolas (see Acts 6:5), according to early church fathers. These were apparently a sect which advocated license in matters of Christian conduct, including free love, though some understand from the meaning of the name ("conquering of the people") that they were a group which promoted a clerical hierarchy (see Rev. 2:15 also).

2:7 *To him who overcomes.* Not a reference to an especially spiritual group among the believers, but to all true Christians (cf. 1 John 5:5).

2:8 *Smyrna.* A seaport city about 35 miles N. of Ephesus (called Izmir today). It was a center of the imperial cult of Rome.

2:10 *you will have tribulation ten days.* This may refer to a ten-day period of intense persecution to come, or it may indicate ten periods of persecution from Nero to Diocletian. *crown of life.* The reward of one who is faithful under trial or unto death (see Jas. 1:12 and note on 1 Cor. 3:14).

2:11 *the second death.* I.e., eternal separation from God in the lake of fire (see 20:14; also note on Rom. 6:2).

2:12 *Pergamum.* About 45 miles N. of Smyrna, it boasted one of the finest libraries of antiquity and was the place where parchment was first used. It had once been the capital of the Roman province of Asia.

2:13 *where Satan dwells.* Lit., where Satan's throne is—a reference to Pergamum's worship either of the Roman emperor or of Zeus at his altar on the local acropolis (or both).

2:14 *the teaching of Balaam.* See notes on 2 Pet. 2:15 and Jude 11.

there some who hold the [b]teach-
ing of Balaam, who kept teaching
Balak to put a stumbling block
before the sons of Israel, [c]to eat
things sacrificed to idols, and to
commit *acts of* immorality.

15 [a]Rev. 2:6

15 'Thus you also have some
who in the same way hold the
teaching of the [a]Nicolaitans.

16 [a]Rev. 2:5 [b]Rev. 22:7, 20 [c]2 Thess. 2:8; Rev. 1:16

16 '[a]Repent therefore; or else [b]I
am coming to you quickly, and I
will make war against them with
[c]the sword of My mouth.

★17 [a]Rev. 2:7 [b]John 6:49f. [c]Is. 56:5; 62:2; 65:15 [d]Rev. 14:3; 19:12

17 '[a]He who has an ear, let him
hear what the Spirit says to the
churches. [a]To him who overcomes, to him I will give *some* of
the hidden [b]manna, and I will
give him a white stone, and a
[c]new name written on the stone
[d]which no one knows but he who
receives it.'

D The Message to Thyatira, 2:18–29

★18 [a]Rev. 1:11; 2:24 [b]Matt. 4:3 [c]Rev. 1:14f.

18 "And to the angel of the
church in [a]Thyatira write:
[b]The Son of God, [c]who has
eyes like a flame of fire, and His
feet are like burnished bronze,
says this:

19 [a]Rev. 2:2

19 '[a]I know your deeds, and
your love and faith and service
and perseverance, and that your
deeds of late are greater than at
first.

★20 [a]Rev. 2:14 [b]1 Kin. 16:31; 21:25; 2 Kin. 9:7 [c]Acts 15:29; 1 Cor. 10:20; Rev. 2:14

20 'But [a]I have *this* against you,
that you tolerate the woman [b]Jez-
ebel, who calls herself a prophetess, and she teaches and leads My
bond-servants astray, so that they
[c]commit *acts of* immorality and
eat things sacrificed to idols.

21 [a]Rom. 2:4; 2 Pet. 3:9 [b]Rom. 2:5; Rev. 9:20f.; 16:9, 11

21 'And [a]I gave her time to repent; and she [b]does not want to
repent of her immorality.

22 [a]Rev. 17:2; 18:9

22 'Behold, I will cast her upon
a bed *of sickness,* and those who
[a]commit adultery with her into
great tribulation, unless they repent of her deeds.

23 [a]Ps. 7:9; 26:2; 139:1; Jer. 11:20; 17:10; Matt. 16:27; Luke 16:15; Acts 1:24; Rom. 8:27

23 'And I will kill her children
with pestilence; and all the
churches will know that I am He
who [a]searches the minds and
hearts; and I will give to each one
of you according to your deeds.

★24 [a]Rev. 2:18 [b]1 Cor. 2:10 [c]Acts 15:28

24 'But I say to you, the rest
who are in [a]Thyatira, who do not
hold this teaching, who have not
known the [b]deep things of Satan,
as they call them — I [c]place no
other burden on you.

25 [a]Rev. 3:11 [b]John 21:22

25 'Nevertheless [a]what you
have, hold fast [b]until I come.

26 [a]Rev. 2:7 [b]Matt. 10:22; Heb. 3:6 [c]Ps. 2:8; Rev. 3:21; 20:4

26 'And [a]he who overcomes,
and he who keeps My deeds [b]un-
til the end, [c]TO HIM I WILL GIVE AU-
THORITY OVER THE NATIONS;

★27 [a]Rev. 12:5; 19:15 [b]Is. 30:14; Jer. 19:11

27 AND HE SHALL [a]RULE THEM
WITH A ROD OF IRON, [b]AS THE VESSELS
OF THE POTTER ARE BROKEN TO PIECES,
as I also have received *authority*
from My Father;

★28 [a]1 John 3:2; Rev. 22:16

28 and I will give him [a]the
morning star.

29 [a]Rev. 2:7

29 '[a]He who has an ear, let him
hear what the Spirit says to the
churches.'

2:17 *hidden manna.* Refers to the sufficiency of Christ for the believer's needs, as manna was for the Hebrews' during the wilderness wanderings. The *white stone* may refer to the custom of voting for the acquittal of an accused person by using a white stone (indicating that the believer can be assured of his acquittal before God, cf. Rom. 8:1); or it may refer to the sufficiency of Christ (from the custom of wearing amulets around the neck).

2:18 *Thyatira.* A city noted for its numerous trade guilds and for its wool and dyeing industry (see Acts 16:14). It was about 35 miles SE. of Pergamum.

2:20 *Jezebel.* This false prophetess may actually have been named Jezebel; more probably, however, she was a well-known woman whose actions made her a contemporary counterpart of the notorious Jezebel of 1 Kings 16 and 2 Kings 9.

2:24 *the deep things of Satan.* To those of you (John says) who have not been seduced by these false doctrines, these deep things of Satan, I say only . . .

2:27 *he shall rule them with a rod of iron.* A reference to Christ's reign on earth. See 12:5; 19:15; Ps. 2:9.

2:28 *the morning star.* Probably a reference to Christ Himself (cf. 22:16; 2 Pet. 1:19) or, perhaps, the immortal life that one will receive from Christ.

E The Message to Sardis, 3:1–6

3 "And to the angel of the
church in [a]Sardis write:
He who has [b]the seven Spirits
of God, and [c]the seven stars, says
this: [d]I know your deeds, that you
have a name that you are alive,
and you are [e]dead.
2 'Wake up, and strengthen
the things that remain, which
were about to die; for I have not
found your deeds completed in
the sight of My God.
3 '[a]Remember therefore what
you have received and heard; and
keep *it,* and [a]repent. If therefore
you will not wake up, [b]I will come
[c]like a thief, and you will not
know at [d]what hour I will come
upon you.
4 'But you have a few [a]people
in [b]Sardis who have not [c]soiled
their garments; and they will walk
with Me [d]in white; for they are
worthy.
5 '[a]He who overcomes shall
thus be clothed in [b]white garments; and I will not [c]erase his
name from the book of life, and [d]I
will confess his name before My
Father, and before His angels.
6 '[a]He who has an ear, let him
hear what the Spirit says to the
churches.'

★ 1 [a]Rev. 1:11 [b]Rev. 1:4 [c]Rev. 1:16 [d]Rev. 2:2; 3:8, 15 [e]1 Tim. 5:6
3 [a]Rev. 2:5 [b]Rev. 2:5 [c]1 Thess. 5:2; 2 Pet. 3:10; Rev. 16:15 [d]Matt. 24:43
★ 4 [a]Acts 1:15 marg.; Rev. 11:13 marg. [b]Rev. 1:11 [c]Jude 23 [d]Eccles. 9:8; Rev. 3:5, 18; 4:4; 6:11; 7:9, 13f.; 19:8, 14
5 [a]Rev. 2:7 [b]Rev. 3:4 [c]Luke 10:20; Rev. 13:8; 17:8; 20:12, 15; 21:27 [d]Matt. 10:32; Luke 12:8
6 [a]Rev. 2:7

F The Message to Philadelphia, 3:7–13

7 "And to the angel of the
church in [a]Philadelphia write:
[b]He who is holy, [c]who is true,
who has [d]the key of David, who
opens and no one will shut, and
who shuts and no one opens, says
this:
8 '[a]I know your deeds. Behold,
I have put before you [b]an open
door which no one can shut, because you have a little power, and
have kept My word, and [c]have
not denied My name.
9 'Behold, I will cause *those* of
[a]the synagogue of Satan, who say
that they are Jews, and are not,
but lie — behold, I will make
them to [b]come and bow down at
your feet, and to know that [c]I
have loved you.
10 'Because you have [a]kept the
word of [b]My perseverance, [c]I also
will keep you from the hour of
[d]testing, that *hour* which is about
to come upon the whole [e]world,
to test [f]those who dwell upon the
earth.
11 '[a]I am coming quickly; [b]hold
fast what you have, in order that
no one take your [c]crown.
12 '[a]He who overcomes, I will
make him a [b]pillar in the temple
of My God, and he will not go out
from it any more; and I will write
upon him the [c]name of My God,
and [d]the name of the city of My
God, [e]the new Jerusalem, which
comes down out of heaven from
My God, and My [f]new name.
13 '[a]He who has an ear, let him
hear what the Spirit says to the
churches.'

★ 7 [a]Rev. 1:11 [b]Rev. 6:10 [c]1 John 5:20; Rev. 3:14; 19:11 [d]Job 12:14; Is. 22:22; Matt. 16:19; Rev. 1:18
8 [a]Rev. 3:1 [b]Acts 14:27 [c]Rev. 2:13
9 [a]Rev. 2:9 [b]Is. 45:14; 49:23; 60:14 [c]Is. 43:4; John 17:23
★10 [a]John 17:6; Rev. 3:8 [b]Rev. 1:9 [c]2 Tim. 2:12; 2 Pet. 2:9 [d]Rev. 2:10 [e]Matt. 24:14; Rev. 16:14 [f]Rev. 6:10; 8:13; 11:10; 13:8, 14; 17:8
11 [a]Rev. 1:3; 22:7, 12, 20 [b]Rev. 2:25 [c]Rev. 2:10
★12 [a]Rev. 3:5 [b]1 Kin. 7:21; Jer. 1:18; Gal. 2:9 [c]Rev. 14:1; 22:4 [d]Ezek. 48:35; Rev. 21:2 [e]Gal. 4:26; Heb. 13:14; Rev. 21:2, 10 [f]Rev. 2:17
13 [a]Rev. 3:6

3:1 *Sardis.* The capital of ancient Lydia, situated about 30 miles S. of Thyatira. The imperial cult was strong there. *you are dead.* I.e., devoid of spiritual life and power.

3:4 *who have not soiled their garments.* I.e., persons who had remained faithful to Christ.

3:7 *Philadelphia.* The word means brotherly love. A lesser city than the others addressed, it was located about 38 miles SE. of Sardis. Its chief deity was Dionysus, the god of wine. *the key of David.* A quotation from Isa. 22:22, where it is a symbol of authority. Compare the "keys of death and of Hades" (1:18) and the "keys of the kingdom" (Matt. 16:19).

3:10 *I also will keep you from the hour of testing.* A promise that believers will be delivered from the tribulation period which will come upon the entire earth (Matt. 24:14–21; see note on 1 Thess. 4:17).

3:12 *a pillar in the temple of My God.* A promise that believers will be honored in the New Jerusalem, referring to the custom of honoring a magistrate by placing a pillar, in his name, in one of the temples in Philadelphia.

G The Message to Laodicea, 3:14-22

14 "And to the angel of the
church in [a]Laodicea write:
[b]The Amen, [c]the faithful and
true Witness, [d]the Beginning of
the creation of God, says this:
15 '[a]I know your deeds, that
you are neither cold nor hot; [b]I
would that you were cold or hot.
16 'So because you are luke-
warm, and neither hot nor cold, I
will spit you out of My mouth.
17 'Because you say, "[a]I am
rich, and have become wealthy,
and have need of nothing," and
you do not know that you are
wretched and miserable and poor
and blind and naked,
18 'I advise you to [a]buy from
Me [b]gold refined by fire, that you
may become rich, and [c]white garments, that you may clothe yourself, and *that* [d]the shame of your
nakedness may not be revealed;
and eyesalve to anoint your eyes,
that you may see.
19 '[a]Those whom I love, I reprove and discipline; be zealous
therefore, and [b]repent.
20 'Behold, I stand [a]at the door
and [b]knock; if any one hears My
voice and opens the door, [c]I will
come in to him, and will dine with
him, and he with Me.
21 '[a]He who overcomes, I will
grant to him [b]to sit down with Me
on My throne, as [c]I also overcame
and sat down with My Father on
His throne.
22 '[a]He who has an ear, let him
hear what the Spirit says to the
churches.' "

★**14** [a]Rev. 1:11 [b]2 Cor. 1:20 [c]Rev. 1:5; 3:7 [d]Gen. 49:3; Deut. 21:17; Prov. 8:22; John 1:3; Col. 1:18; Rev. 21:6; 22:13
15 [a]Rev. 3:1 [b]Rom. 12:11
★**16**
17 [a]Hos. 12:8; Zech. 11:5; Matt. 5:3; 1 Cor. 4:8
★**18** [a]Is. 55:1; Matt. 13:44 [b]1 Pet. 1:7 [c]Rev. 3:4 [d]Rev. 16:15
19 [a]1 Cor. 11:32; Heb. 12:6 [b]Rev. 2:5
★**20** [a]Matt. 24:33; James 5:9 [b]Luke 12:36; John 10:3 [c]John 14:23
21 [a]Rev. 2:7 [b]Matt. 19:28; 2 Tim. 2:12; Rev. 2:26; 20:4 [c]John 16:33; Rev. 5:5; 6:2; 17:14
22 [a]Rev. 2:7

IV "THE THINGS WHICH SHALL TAKE PLACE AFTER THESE THINGS," 4:1-22:5

A The Tribulation Period, 4:1-19:21

1 The throne in heaven, 4:1-11

a The throne, 4:1-3

4 After [a]these things I looked,
and behold, [b]a door *standing*
open in heaven, and the first voice
which I had heard, [c]like *the
sound* of a trumpet speaking with
me, said, "[d]Come up here, and I
will [e]show you what must take
place after these things."
2 Immediately I was [a]in the
Spirit; and behold, [b]a throne was
standing in heaven, and [c]One sitting on the throne.
3 And He who was sitting
was like a [a]jasper stone and a
[b]sardius in appearance; and *there
was* a [c]rainbow around the
throne, like an [d]emerald in appearance.

b The throng, 4:4-8

4 And [a]around the throne
were [b]twenty-four thrones; and
upon the thrones *I saw* [c]twenty-
four elders [d]sitting, clothed in
[e]white garments, and [f]golden
crowns on their heads.
5 And from the throne proceed [a]flashes of lightning and
sounds and peals of thunder. And

1 [a]Rev. 1:12ff., 19 [b]Ezek. 1:1; Rev. 19:11 [c]Rev. 1:10 [d]Rev. 11:12 [e]Rev. 1:19; 22:6
★ **2** [a]Rev. 1:10 [b]1 Kin. 22:19; Is. 6:1; Ezek. 1:26; Dan. 7:9; Rev. 4:9f. [c]Rev. 4:9
★ **3** [a]Rev. 21:11 [b]Rev. 21:20 [c]Ezek. 1:28; Rev. 10:1 [d]Rev. 21:19
★ **4** [a]Rev. 4:6; 5:11; 7:11 [b]Rev. 11:16 [c]Rev. 4:10; 5:6, 8, 14; 19:4 [d]Matt. 19:28; 2 Tim. 2:12; Rev. 2:26; 20:4 [e]Rev. 3:18 [f]Rev. 4:10
★ **5** [a]Ex. 19:16; Rev. 8:5; 11:19; 16:18 [b]Ex. 25:37; Zech. 4:2 [c]Rev. 1:4

3:14 *Laodicea.* A city about 90 miles due E. of Ephesus and 45 miles SE. of Philadelphia. Under Roman rule it was a wealthy city.
3:16 *I will spit you out of My mouth.* Lit., I will vomit. . . .
3:18 *gold . . . white garments . . . eyesalve.* These perhaps refer to the city's three main sources of wealth—banking, production of wool cloth, and medicines. Laodicea was a center for making medicines, including a tablet that was powdered, mixed with water, and smeared on the eyes.
3:20 *I stand at the door and knock.* How incredible that Christ should be kept outside His own church! How gracious that He should still seek entrance!
4:2 *I was in the Spirit.* As in 1:10.
4:3 *jasper.* Clear as crystal (cf. 21:11). *sardius.* Blood red. *emerald.* Light green.
4:4 *twenty-four elders.* Some understand these to be angelic beings, though it is likely that the 24 elders represent redeemed men who are glorified, crowned, and enthroned.
4:5 *seven Spirits of God.* See note on 1:4.

there were [b]seven lamps of fire
burning before the throne, which
are [c]the seven Spirits of God;

★ **6** [a]Ezek. 1:22; Rev. 15:2; 21:18, 21 [b]Rev. 4:4 [c]Ezek. 1:5; Rev. 4:8f.; 5:6; 6:1, 6; 7:11; 14:3; 15:7; 19:4 [d]Ezek. 1:18; 10:12

6 and before the throne
there was, as it were, a [a]sea of
glass like crystal; and in the center and [b]around the throne, [c]four
living creatures [d]full of eyes in
front and behind.

★ **7** [a]Ezek. 1:10; 10:14

7 [a]And the first creature *was*
like a lion, and the second creature like a calf, and the third creature had a face like that of a man,
and the fourth creature *was* like a
flying eagle.

8 [a]Ezek. 1:5; Rev. 4:6, 9; 5:6; 6:1, 6; 7:11; 14:3; 15:7; 19:4 [b]Is. 6:2 [c]Ezek. 1:18; 10:12 [d]Rev. 14:11 [e]Is. 6:3 [f]Rev. 1:8 [g]Rev. 1:4

8 And the [a]four living creatures, each one of them having
[b]six wings, are [c]full of eyes
around and within; and [d]day and
night they do not cease to say,

> "[e]HOLY, HOLY, HOLY, *is* THE
> [f]LORD GOD, THE ALMIGHTY,
> [g]who was and who is and
> who is to come."

c The theme, 4:9–11

9 [a]Ps. 47:8; Is. 6:1; Rev. 4:2 [b]Deut. 32:40; Dan. 4:34; 12:7; Rev. 10:6; 15:7

9 And when the living creatures give glory and honor and
thanks to Him who [a]sits on the
throne, to [b]Him who lives forever
and ever,

10 [a]Rev. 4:4 [b]Rev. 5:8, 14; 7:11; 11:16; 19:4 [c]Ps. 47:8; Is. 6:1; Rev. 4:2 [d]Deut. 32:40; Dan. 4:34; 12:7 [e]Rev. 4:4; 10:6; 15:7

10 the [a]twenty-four elders
will [b]fall down before Him who
[c]sits on the throne, and will worship [d]Him who lives forever and
ever, and will cast their [e]crowns
before the throne, saying,

11 [a]Rev. 1:6; 5:12 [b]Acts 14:15; Rev. 10:6; 14:7

> **11** "[a]Worthy art Thou, our
> Lord and our God, to re-
> ceive glory and honor and
> power; for Thou [b]didst
> create all things, and be-
> cause of Thy will they ex-
> isted, and were created."

*2 **The scroll in heaven,*** 5:1–14

a The scroll, 5:1

★ **1** [a]Rev. 4:9; 5:7, 13 [b]Ezek. 2:9, 10 [c]Is. 29:11; Dan. 12:4

5 And I saw in the right hand
of Him who [a]sat on the
throne a [b]book written inside and
on the back, [c]sealed up with
seven seals.

b The search, 5:2–5

2 [a]Rev. 10:1; 18:21

2 And I saw a [a]strong angel
proclaiming with a loud voice,
"Who is worthy to open the book
and to break its seals?"

3 [a]Phil. 2:10; Rev. 5:13

3 And no one [a]in heaven, or
on the earth, or under the earth,
was able to open the book, or to
look into it.

4 And I *began* to weep
greatly, because no one was
found worthy to open the book,
or to look into it;

★ **5** [a]Gen. 49:9 [b]Heb. 7:14 [c]Is. 11:1, 10; Rom. 15:12; Rev. 22:16

5 and one of the elders *said
to me, "Stop weeping; behold, the
[a]Lion that is [b]from the tribe of Judah, the [c]Root of David, has overcome so as to open the book and
its seven seals."

c The Savior-Sovereign, 5:6–7

★ **6** [a]Rev. 4:4; 5:8, 14 [b]John 1:29; Rev. 5:8, 12f.; 13:8 [c]Rev. 5:9, 12; 13:8 [d]Dan. 8:3f. [e]Zech. 3:9; 4:10 [f]Rev. 1:4

6 And I saw between the
throne (with the four living creatures) and [a]the elders a [b]Lamb
standing, as if [c]slain, having seven
[d]horns and [e]seven eyes, which are
[f]the seven Spirits of God, sent out
into all the earth.

4:6 *four living creatures.* Or, living ones. These may be angels, probably cherubim (cf. Ezek. 10:15–20), or they may be representations of the attributes of God Himself (since they are said to be in the center of the throne).

4:7 Many see a similarity between the four living ones and the fourfold manner in which Christ is portrayed in the Gospels. In Matthew He appears as the Lion of the tribe of Judah; in Mark, as the Servant who became the sacrifice for sin (the calf was a sacrificial animal, Heb. 9:12, 19); Luke's emphasis is on the Son of Man; and *a flying eagle* links Him with heaven, as does John's Gospel.

5:1 *a book.* Lit., a scroll. This may be called the "Book of Redemption," as it contains the story of man's fall through sin and rise through Christ (Heb. 2:5–9).

5:5 *the Lion that is from the tribe of Judah* (cf. Gen. 49:9), *the Root of David* (cf. Isa. 11:1, 10). The Messiah, John is assured, is competent and worthy to break the seven seals and open the scroll to release the plagues.

5:6 *as if slain.* Christ, the Lamb, bears the marks of His death (see Luke 24:40; John 20:20, 27) even in His glorified state. *horns* are a symbol of strength (cf. 1 Kings 22:11; Zech. 1:18).

7 [a]Rev. 5:1

7 And He came, and He took
[a]*it* out of the right hand of Him
who [a]sat on the throne.

d The song, 5:8–14

★ 8 [a]Rev. 4:6; 5:6, 11, 14 [b]Rev. 4:4; 5:6, 14 [c]Rev. 4:10 [d]John 1:29; Rev. 5:6, 12f.; 13:8 [e]Rev. 14:2; 15:2 [f]Rev. 15:7 [g]Ps. 141:2; Rev. 8:3f.

8 And when He had taken
the book, the [a]four living creatures and the [b]twenty-four elders
[c]fell down before the [d]Lamb, having each one a [e]harp, and [f]golden
bowls full of incense, which are
the [g]prayers of the saints.
9 And they *sang a [a]new
song, saying,

9 [a]Ps. 40:3; 98:1; 149:1; Is. 42:10; Rev. 14:3; 15:3 [b]Rev. 4:11 [c]Rev. 5:6, 12; 13:8 [d]1 Cor. 6:20; Rev. 14:3f. [e]Dan. 3:4; 5:19; Rev. 7:9; 10:11; 11:9; 13:7; 14:6; 17:15

"[b]Worthy art Thou to take
the book, and to break its
seals; for Thou wast [c]slain,
and didst [d]purchase for
God with Thy blood *men*
from [e]every tribe and
tongue and people and na-
tion.

10 [a]Rev. 1:6 [b]Rev. 3:21; 20:4

10 "And Thou hast made
them *to be* a [a]kingdom
and [a]priests to our God;
and they will [b]reign upon
the earth."

11 [a]Rev. 4:4 [b]Rev. 4:6; 5:6, 8, 14 [c]Rev. 4:4; 5:6, 14 [d]Dan. 7:10; Heb. 12:22; Jude 14; Rev. 9:16

11 And I looked, and I heard
the voice of many angels [a]around
the throne and the [b]living creatures and the [c]elders; and the
number of them was [d]myriads of
myriads, and thousands of thousands,

12 [a]Rev. 1:6; 4:11; 5:9 [b]John 1:29; Rev. 5:6, 13; 13:8

12 saying with a loud voice,
"[a]Worthy is the [b]Lamb that
was [b]slain to receive power
and riches and wisdom
and might and honor and
glory and blessing."

13 [a]Phil. 2:10; Rev. 5:3 [b]Rev. 5:1 [c]John 1:29; Rev. 5:6, 12f.; 13:8 [d]Rom. 11:36; Rev. 1:6

13 And [a]every created thing
which is in heaven and on the
earth and under the earth and on
the sea, and all things in them, I
heard saying,
"To Him who [b]sits on the
throne, and to the [c]Lamb,
[d]*be* blessing and honor
and glory and dominion
forever and ever."

14 [a]Rev. 4:6; 5:6, 8, 11 [b]1 Cor. 14:16; Rev. 7:12; 19:4 [c]Rev. 4:4; 5:6, 8 [d]Rev. 4:10

14 And the [a]four living creatures kept saying, "[b]Amen." And
the [c]elders [d]fell down and worshiped.

3 ***The seal judgments,*** 6:1–17
a First seal: cold war, 6:1–2

1 [a]John 1:29; Rev. 5:6, 12f.; 13:8 [b]Rev. 5:1 [c]Rev. 4:6; 5:6, 8, 11, 14 [d]Rev. 14:2; 19:6

6 And I saw when the [a]Lamb
broke one of the [b]seven seals,
and I heard one of the [c]four living
creatures saying as with a [d]voice
of thunder, "Come."

★ 2 [a]Zech. 1:8; 6:3f.; Rev. 19:11 [b]Zech. 6:11; Rev. 9:7; 14:14; 19:12 [c]Rev. 3:21

2 And I looked, and behold,
a [a]white horse, and he who sat on
it had a bow; and [b]a crown was
given to him; and he went out
[c]conquering, and to conquer.

b Second seal: open war, 6:3–4

3 [a]Rev. 4:7

3 And when He broke the
second seal, I heard the [a]second
living creature saying, "Come."

4 [a]Zech. 1:8; 6:2 [b]Matt. 10:34

4 And another, [a]a red horse,
went out; and to him who sat on
it, it was granted to [b]take peace
from the earth, and that *men*
should slay one another; and a
great sword was given to him.

c Third seal: famine, 6:5–6

5 [a]Rev. 4:7 [b]Zech. 6:2 [c]Ezek. 4:16

5 And when He broke the
third seal, I heard the [a]third living
creature saying, "Come." And I
looked, and behold, a [b]black
horse; and he who sat on it had a
[c]pair of scales in his hand.

★ 6 [a]Rev. 4:6f. [b]Rev. 7:3; 9:4

6 And I heard as it were a
voice in the center of the [a]four
living creatures saying, "A quart
of wheat for a denarius, and three
quarts of barley for a denarius;
and [b]do not harm the oil and the
wine."

d Fourth seal: death, 6:7–8

7 [a]Rev. 4:7

7 And when He broke the
fourth seal, I heard the voice of

5:8 *bowls.* Like saucers.

6:2 *he who sat on it.* Probably a reference to Antichrist (see note on 1 John 2:18). His method of conquest does not seem to include open warfare, since peace is not removed from the earth until the second seal is opened (v. 3). This corresponds to the description of delusion in 1 Thess. 5:3.

6:6 *denarius.* A Roman silver coin which had a normal purchasing power of 8 quarts of wheat or 24 of barley. A severe shortage of food is indicated. See note for Matt. 18:28.

the [a]fourth living creature saying, "Come."

8 And I looked, and behold, an [a]ashen horse; and he who sat on it had the name "[b]Death"; and [b]Hades was following with him. And authority was given to them over a fourth of the earth, [c]TO KILL WITH SWORD AND WITH FAMINE AND WITH PESTILENCE AND BY THE WILD BEASTS OF THE EARTH.

★ 8 [a]Zech. 6:3 [b]Prov. 5:5; Hos. 13:14; Matt. 11:23; Rev. 1:18; 20:13f. [c]Jer. 15:2f.; 24:10; 29:17f.; Ezek. 5:12, 17; 14:21

e Fifth seal: martyrdom, 6:9–11

9 And when He broke the fifth seal, I saw [a]underneath the [b]altar the [c]souls of those who had been slain [d]because of the word of God, and because of the [e]testimony which they had maintained;

10 and they cried out with a loud voice, saying, "[a]How long, O [b]Lord, [c]holy and true, wilt Thou refrain from [d]judging and avenging our blood on [e]those who dwell on the earth?"

11 And [a]there was given to each of them a white robe; and they were told that they should [b]rest for a little while longer, [c]until *the number of* their fellow servants and their brethren who were to be killed even as they had been, should be [d]completed also.

★ 9 [a]Ex. 29:12; Lev. 4:7; John 16:2 [b]Rev. 14:18; 16:7 [c]Rev. 20:4 [d]Rev. 1:2, 9 [e]Rev. 12:17

10 [a]Zech. 1:12 [b]Luke 2:29; 2 Pet. 2:1 [c]Rev. 3:7 [d]Deut. 32:43; Ps. 79:10; Luke 18:7; Rev. 19:2 [e]Rev. 3:10

★11 [a]Rev. 3:4, 5; 7:9 [b]2 Thess. 1:7; Heb. 4:10; Rev. 14:13 [c]Heb. 11:40 [d]Acts 20:24; 2 Tim. 4:7

f Sixth seal: physical disturbances, 6:12–17

12 And I looked when He broke the sixth seal, and there was a great [a]earthquake; and the [b]sun became black as [c]sackcloth *made* of hair, and the whole moon became like blood;

13 and [a]the stars of the sky fell to the earth, [b]as a fig tree casts its unripe figs when shaken by a great wind.

14 And [a]the sky was split apart like a scroll when it is rolled up; and [b]every mountain and island were moved out of their places.

15 And [a]the kings of the earth and the great men and the commanders and the rich and the strong and every slave and free man, hid themselves in the caves and among the rocks of the mountains;

16 and they *[a]said to the mountains and to the rocks, "Fall on us and hide us from the presence of Him [b]who sits on the throne, and from the [c]wrath of the Lamb;

17 for [a]the great day of their wrath has come; and [b]who is able to stand?"

★12 [a]Matt. 24:7; Rev. 8:5; 11:13; 16:18 [b]Matt. 24:29 [c]Is. 50:3; Matt. 11:21

13 [a]Matt. 24:29; Rev. 8:10; 9:1 [b]Is. 34:4

14 [a]Is. 34:4; 2 Pet. 3:10; Rev. 20:11; 21:1 [b]Is. 54:10; Jer. 4:24; Ezek. 38:20; Nah. 1:5; Rev. 16:20

15 [a]Is. 2:10f., 19, 21; 24:21; Rev. 19:18

★16 [a]Luke 23:30; Rev. 9:6 [b]Rev. 4:9; 5:1 [c]Mark 3:5

17 [a]Is. 63:4; Jer. 30:7; Joel 1:15; 2:1f., 11, 31; Zeph. 1:14f.; Rev. 16:14 [b]Ps. 76:7; Nah. 1:6; Mal. 3:2; Luke 21:36

4 Interlude: the redeemed of the tribulation, 7:1–17

a The 144,000 Jews, 7:1–8

7 After this I saw [a]four angels standing at the [b]four corners of the earth, holding back [c]the four winds of the earth, [d]so that no wind should blow on the earth or on the sea or on any tree.

2 And I saw another angel ascending [a]from the rising of the sun, having the [b]seal of [c]the living God; and he cried out with a loud voice to the [d]four angels to whom it was granted to harm the earth and the sea,

3 saying, "[a]Do not harm the earth or the sea or the trees, until we have [b]sealed the bond-servants of our God on their [c]foreheads."

1 [a]Rev. 9:14 [b]Is. 11:12; Ezek. 7:2; Rev. 20:8 [c]Jer. 49:36; Zech. 6:5; Matt. 24:31 [d]Rev. 7:3; 8:7; 9:4

2 [a]Is. 41:2; Rev. 16:12 [b]Rev. 7:3; 9:4 [c]Matt. 16:16 [d]Rev. 9:14

3 [a]Rev. 6:6 [b]John 3:33; Rev. 7:3-8 [c]Ezek. 9:4, 6; Rev. 13:16; 14:1, 9; 20:4; 22:4

6:8 *ashen* = a sickly, yellowish-green. *Death.* Probably representing the inevitable result of disease which accompanies war and famine.

6:9 *the souls of those who had been slain.* Evidently the martyrs of the first months of the tribulation period.

6:11 *rest for a little while longer.* I.e., wait a little while. It is difficult for these martyrs to understand why God would allow their murderers to live; yet God asks these saints to trust Him.

6:12 These cosmic disturbances are predicted elsewhere in Scripture (Isa. 34:4; Joel 2:30–31; Matt. 24:29).

6:16 When the tribulation comes, men will act as if they believe the end of the world is at hand.

★ 4 [a]Rev. 9:16 [b]Rev. 14:1, 3

4 And I heard the [a]number
of those who were sealed, [b]one
hundred and forty-four thousand
sealed from every tribe of the
sons of Israel:
5 from the tribe of Judah,
twelve thousand *were* sealed,
from the tribe of Reuben twelve
thousand, from the tribe of Gad
twelve thousand,
6 from the tribe of Asher
twelve thousand, from the tribe
of Naphtali twelve thousand,
from the tribe of Manasseh
twelve thousand,
7 from the tribe of Simeon
twelve thousand, from the tribe
of Levi twelve thousand, from the
tribe of Issachar twelve thousand,
8 from the tribe of Zebulun
twelve thousand, from the tribe
of Joseph twelve thousand, from
the tribe of Benjamin, twelve
thousand *were* sealed.

b The multitude of Gentiles,
7:9–17

★ 9 [a]Rev. 5:9 [b]Rev. 7:15 [c]Rev. 22:3 [d]Rev. 6:11; 7:14 [e]Lev. 23:40

9 After these things I
looked, and behold, a great multitude, which no one could count,
from [a]every nation and *all* tribes
and peoples and tongues, standing [b]before the throne and [c]be-
fore the Lamb, clothed in [d]white
robes, and [e]palm branches *were*
in their hands;

10 [a]Ps. 3:8; Rev. 12:10; 19:1 [b]Rev. 22:3

10 and they cry out with a
loud voice, saying,
"[a]Salvation to our God [b]who
sits on the throne, and to the
Lamb."

11 [a]Rev. 4:4 [b]Rev. 4:6 [c]Rev. 4:10

11 And all the angels were
standing [a]around the throne and
around [a]the elders and the [b]four
living creatures; and they [c]fell on
their faces before the throne and
worshiped God,

12 saying,
"[a]Amen, [b]blessing and glory
and wisdom and thanksgiving
and honor and power and might,
be to our God forever and ever.
[a]Amen."

12 [a]Rev. 5:14 [b]Rev. 5:12

13 And one of the elders [a]an-
swered, saying to me, "These who
are clothed in the [b]white robes,
who are they, and from where
have they come?"

13 [a]Acts 3:12 [b]Rev. 7:9

14 And I said to him, "My
lord, you know." And he said to
me, "These are the ones who
come out of the [a]great tribulation,
and they have [b]washed their
robes and made them [c]white in
the [d]blood of the Lamb.

14 [a]Matt. 24:21 [b]Zech. 3:3-5; Rev. 22:14 [c]Rev. 6:11; 7:9 [d]Heb. 9:14; 1 John 1:7

15 "For this reason, they are
[a]before the throne of God; and
they [b]serve Him day and night in
His [c]temple; and [d]He who sits on
the throne shall spread His [e]tab-
ernacle over them.

15 [a]Rev. 7:9 [b]Rev. 4:8; 22:3 [c]Rev. 11:19; 21:22 [d]Rev. 4:9 [e]Lev. 26:11; Ezek. 37:27; John 1:14; Rev. 21:3

16 "[a]They shall hunger no
more, neither thirst any more;
neither shall the sun beat down
on them, nor any heat;

16 [a]Ps. 121:5f.; Is. 49:10

17 for the Lamb in the center
of the throne shall be their [a]shep-
herd, and shall guide them to
springs of the [b]water of life; and
[c]God shall wipe every tear from
their eyes."

17 [a]Ps. 23:1f.; Matt. 2:6; John 10:11 [b]John 4:14; Rev. 21:6; 22:1 [c]Is. 25:8; Matt. 5:4; Rev. 21:4

5 The six trumpet judgments,
8:1–9:21

a The seventh seal opened,
8:1–6

8 And when He broke the
[a]seventh seal, there was [b]si-
lence in heaven for about half an
hour.
2 And I saw [a]the seven angels who stand before God; and
seven [b]trumpets were given to
them.

★ 1 [a]Rev. 5:1; 6:1, 3, 5, 7, 9, 12 [b]Rev. 5:9
2 [a]Matt. 18:10; Rev. 1:4; 8:6-13; 9:1, 13; 11:15 [b]1 Cor. 15:52; 1 Thess. 4:16

7:4 *one hundred and forty-four thousand sealed.* These are Jews from the 12 tribes (12,000 each) who are protected in order to perform some service for God during these days. Perhaps they are evangelists. The omission of the tribe of Dan may be because Dan was guilty of idolatry on many occasions (Lev. 24:11; Judg. 18; 1 Kings 12:28, 29).

7:9 *a great multitude.* This multitude is composed of many racial and geographic groups who will be redeemed during the tribulation period (v. 14). In these difficult days, many will find Christ as Savior.

8:1 *broke the seventh seal.* With the breaking of the seventh seal comes the second series of judgments—the seven trumpets. Apparently the judgments announced by the trumpets follow chronologically those of the other seals.

3 [a]Rev. 7:2 [b]Amos 9:1; Rev. 6:9 [c]Heb. 9:4 [d]Rev. 5:8 [e]Ex. 30:1, 3; Num. 4:11; Rev. 8:5; 9:13

3 And [a]another angel came and stood at the [b]altar, holding a [c]golden censer; and much [d]incense was given to him, that he might add it to the [d]prayers of all the saints upon the [e]golden altar which was before the throne.

4 [a]Ps. 141:2

4 And [a]the smoke of the incense, with the prayers of the saints, went up before God out of the angel's hand.

5 [a]Lev. 16:12 [b]Ezek. 10:2 [c]Rev. 4:5 [d]Rev. 6:12

5 And the angel took the censer; and he [a]filled it with the fire of the altar and [b]threw it to the earth; and there followed [c]peals of thunder and sounds and flashes of lightning and an [d]earthquake.

6 [a]Rev. 8:2

6 [a]And the seven angels who had the seven trumpets prepared themselves to sound them.

b *First trumpet: the earth smitten,* 8:7

★ 7 [a]Is. 28:2; Ezek. 38:22; Joel 2:30 [b]Zech. 13:8, 9; Rev. 8:7-12; 9:15, 18; 12:4 [c]Rev. 9:4

7 And the first sounded, and there came [a]hail and fire, mixed with blood, and they were thrown to the earth; and [b]a third of the earth was burnt up, and [b]a third of the [c]trees were burnt up, and all the green [c]grass was burnt up.

c *Second trumpet: the sea smitten,* 8:8–9

8 [a]Jer. 51:25 [b]Zech. 13:8, 9; Rev. 8:7-12; 9:15, 18; 12:4 [c]Ex. 7:17ff.; Rev. 11:6; 16:3

8 And the second angel sounded, and *something* like a great [a]mountain burning with fire was thrown into the sea; and [b]a third of the [c]sea became blood;

9 [a]Zech. 13:8, 9; Rev. 8:7-12; 9:15, 18; 12:4 [b]Is. 2:16

9 and [a]a third of the creatures, which were in the sea and had life, died; and a third of the [b]ships were destroyed.

d *Third trumpet: the waters smitten,* 8:10–11

10 And the third angel sounded, and a great star [a]fell from heaven, burning like a torch, and it fell on a [b]third of the rivers and on the [c]springs of waters;

10 [a]Is. 14:12; Rev. 6:13; 9:1 [b]Zech. 13:8, 9; Rev. 8:7-12; 9:15, 18; 12:4 [c]Rev. 14:7; 16:4

11 and the name of the star is called Wormwood; and a [a]third of the waters became [b]wormwood; and many men died from the waters, because they were made bitter.

★11 [a]Zech. 13:8, 9; Rev. 8:7-12; 9:15, 18; 12:4 [b]Jer. 9:15; 23:15

e *Fourth trumpet: the heavens smitten,* 8:12–13

12 And the fourth angel sounded, and a [a]third of the [b]sun and a third of the [b]moon and a [a]third of the [b]stars were smitten, so that a [a]third of them might be darkened and the day might not shine for a [a]third of it, and the night in the same way.

★12 [a]Zech. 13:8, 9; Rev. 8:7-12; 9:15, 18; 12:4 [b]Ex. 10:21ff.; Rev. 6:12f.

13 And I looked, and I heard an eagle flying in [a]midheaven, saying with a loud voice, "[b]Woe, woe, woe, to [c]those who dwell on the earth, because of the remaining blasts of the trumpet of the [d]three angels who are about to sound!"

13 [a]Rev. 14:6; 19:17 [b]Rev. 9:12; 11:14; 12:12 [c]Rev. 3:10 [d]Rev. 8:2

f *Fifth trumpet: men smitten,* 9:1–12

9 And the [a]fifth angel sounded, and I saw a [b]star from heaven which had fallen to the earth; and the [c]key of the [d]bottomless pit was given to him.

★ 1 [a]Rev. 8:2 [b]Rev. 8:10 [c]Rev. 1:18 [d]Luke 8:31; Rev. 9:2, 11

2 And he opened the bot-

2 [a]Gen. 19:28; Ex. 19:18 [b]Joel 2:2, 10

8:7 Though the implications are staggering, there is no reason not to understand this and the other judgments plainly.

8:11 *Wormwood.* Many species of wormwood grow in Palestine, and all have a strong, bitter (but not poisonous) taste, which causes the plant to be used as a symbol of bitterness, sorrow, and calamity. This plague will make a third part of the fresh water supply of the earth unfit for human consumption.

8:12 Compare Luke 21:25.

9:1 *a star.* Represents an intelligent creature, apparently the angel of the bottomless pit (v. 11). Note the "he" in v. 2. *the bottomless pit.* Lit., the shaft of the abyss (for other uses of this phrase see Luke 8:31; Rom. 10:7; Rev. 9:11; 11:7; 17:8; 20:1, 3). Luke 8:31 indicates that this is the abode of the demons.

tomless pit; and [a]smoke went up out of the pit, like the smoke of a great furnace; and [b]the sun and the air were darkened by the smoke of the pit.

★ 3 [a]Ex. 10:12-15; Rev. 9:7; Ex. [b]2 Chr. 10:11, 14; Ezek. 2:6; Rev. 9:5, 10

3 And out of the smoke came forth [a]locusts upon the earth; and power was given them, as the [b]scorpions of the earth have power.

★ 4-5
4 [a]Rev. 6:6 [b]Rev. 8:7 [c]Rev. 7:2, 3

4 And they were told that they should not [a]hurt the [b]grass of the earth, nor any green thing, nor any tree, but only the men who do not have the [c]seal of God on their foreheads.

5 [a]Rev. 9:10 [b]2 Chr. 10:11, 14; Ezek. 2:6; Rev. 9:3, 10

5 And they were not permitted to kill anyone, but to torment for [a]five months; and their torment was like the torment of a [b]scorpion when it stings a man.

6 [a]Job 3:21; 7:15; Jer. 8:3; Rev. 6:16

6 And in those days [a]men will seek death and will not find it; and they will long to die and death flees from them.

7 [a]Joel 2:4

7 And the [a]appearance of the locusts was like horses prepared for battle; and on their heads, as it were, crowns like gold, and their faces were like the faces of men.

8 [a]Joel 1:6

8 And they had hair like the hair of women, and their [a]teeth were like *the teeth* of lions.

9 [a]Jer. 47:3; Joel 2:5

9 And they had breastplates like breastplates of iron; and the [a]sound of their wings was like the sound of chariots, of many horses rushing to battle.

10 [a]2 Chr. 10:11, 14; Ezek. 2:6; Rev. 8:3, 5 [b]Rev. 9:19 [c]Rev. 9:5

10 And they have tails like [a]scorpions, and stings; and in their [b]tails is their power to hurt men for [c]five months.

★11 [a]Luke 8:31; Rev. 9:1, 2 [b]John 5:2; Rev. 16:16 [c]Job 26:6; 28:22; 31:12; Ps. 88:11 marg.; Prov. 15:11

11 They have as king over them, the angel of the [a]abyss; his name in [b]Hebrew is [c]Abaddon, and in the Greek he has the name Apollyon.

12 [a]Rev. 8:13; 11:14

12 [a]The first woe is past; behold, two woes are still coming after these things.

g *Sixth trumpet: men killed,* 9:13–21

13 [a]Ex. 30:2f., 10 [b]Rev. 8:3

13 And the sixth angel sounded, and I heard a voice from the four [a]horns of the [b]golden altar which is before God,

14 [a]Rev. 7:1 [b]Gen. 15:18; Deut. 1:7; Josh. 1:4; Rev. 16:12

14 one saying to the sixth angel who had the trumpet, "Release the [a]four angels who are bound at the [b]great river Euphrates."

★15 [a]Rev. 20:7 [b]Rev. 8:7; 9:18

15 And the four angels, who had been prepared for the hour and day and month and year, were [a]released, so that they might kill a [b]third of mankind.

★16 [a]Rev. 5:11 [b]Rev. 7:4

16 And the number of the armies of the horsemen was [a]two hundred million; [b]I heard the number of them.

17 [a]Dan. 8:2; 9:21 [b]Rev. 9:18; 14:10; 19:20; 20:10; 21:8 [c]Rev. 11:5

17 And this is how I saw [a]in the vision the horses and those who sat on them: *the riders* had breastplates *the color* of fire and of hyacinth and of [b]brimstone; and the heads of the horses are like the heads of lions; and [c]out of their mouths proceed fire and smoke and [b]brimstone.

★18 [a]Rev. 8:7; 9:15 [b]Rev. 9:17

18 A [a]third of mankind was killed by these three plagues, by the [b]fire and the smoke and the brimstone, which proceeded out of their mouths.

19 For the power of the horses is in their mouths and in their tails; for their tails are like serpents and have heads; and with them they do harm.

★20 [a]Rev. 2:21 [b]Deut. 4:28; Jer. 1:16; Mic. 5:13; Acts 7:41 [c]1 Cor. 10:20 [d]Ps. 115:4-7; 135:15-17; Dan. 5:23

20 And the rest of mankind, who were not killed by these plagues, [a]did not repent of [b]THE WORKS OF THEIR HANDS, so as not to

---

9:3 *locusts.* The facts that these creatures come from the abyss and their unusual description in vv. 7-11 indicate that they are demonic.

9:4-5 The limitations which God places upon the activities of these creatures show that He is still in full control of these events.

9:11 *Abaddon . . . Apollyon.* Both words mean destruction.

9:15 *the hour.* Lit., this particular hour.

9:16 *the armies.* The 200,000,000 creatures who compose this supernatural cavalry may be human beings or demons or demon-possessed humans. For other supernatural armies, see 2 Kings 2:11; 6:14–17; Rev. 19:14).

9:18 *by these three plagues.* I.e., by the fire, smoke, and brimstone.

9:20 The religion of many will involve demon and idol worship.

[c]worship DEMONS, AND [d]THE IDOLS
OF GOLD AND OF SILVER AND OF BRASS
AND OF STONE AND OF WOOD, WHICH
CAN NEITHER SEE NOR HEAR NOR WALK;

★21 [a]Rev. 9:20 [b]Is. 47:9, 12; Rev. 18:23 [c]Rev. 17:2, 5

21 and they [a]did not repent of
their murders nor of their [b]sorcer-
ies nor of their [c]immorality nor of
their thefts.

6 *The little scroll,* 10:1–11

1 [a]Rev. 5:2 [b]Rev. 18:1; 20:1 [c]Rev. 4:3 [d]Matt. 17:2; Rev. 1:16 [e]Rev. 1:15

10 And I saw another [a]strong
angel [b]coming down out
of heaven, clothed with a cloud;
and the [c]rainbow was upon his
head, and [d]his face was like the
sun, and his [e]feet like pillars of
fire;

2 [a]Rev. 5:1; 10:8-10 [b]Rev. 10:5, 8

2 and he had in his hand a
[a]little book which was open. And
he placed [b]his right foot on the
sea and his left on the land;

3 [a]Is. 31:4; Hos. 11:10 [b]Ps. 29:3-9; Rev. 4:5

3 and he cried out with a
loud voice, [a]as when a lion roars;
and when he had cried out, the
[b]seven peals of thunder uttered
their voices.

4 [a]Rev. 1:11, 19 [b]Rev. 10:8 [c]Dan. 8:26; 12:4, 9; Rev. 22:10

4 And when the seven peals
of thunder had spoken, [a]I was
about to write; and I [b]heard a
voice from heaven saying, "[c]Seal
up the things which the seven
peals of thunder have spoken,
and do not write them."

5 [a]Gen. 14:22; Ex. 6:8; Num. 14:30; Deut. 32:40; Ezek. 20:5; Dan 12:7

5 And the angel whom I saw
standing on the sea and on the
land [a]LIFTED UP HIS RIGHT HAND TO
HEAVEN,

★ 6 [a]Rev. 4:9 [b]Rev. 4:11 [c]Rev. 6:11; 12:12; 16:17; 21:6

6 AND SWORE BY [a]HIM WHO
LIVES FOREVER AND EVER, WHO
[b]CREATED HEAVEN AND THE THINGS IN
IT, AND THE EARTH AND THE THINGS IN
IT, AND THE SEA AND THE THINGS IN IT,
that [c]there shall be delay no
longer,

★ 7 [a]Rev. 11:15 [b]Amos 3:7; Rom. 16:25

7 but in the days of the voice
of the [a]seventh angel, when he is
about to sound, then [b]the mystery of God is finished, as He
preached to His servants the
prophets.

8 [a]Rev. 10:4 [b]Rev. 10:2

8 And [a]the voice which I
heard from heaven, *I heard* again
speaking with me, and saying,
"Go, take [b]the book which is
open in the hand of the angel
who [b]stands on the sea and on the
land."

★ 9 [a]Jer. 15:16; Ezek. 2:8; 3:1-3

9 And I went to the angel,
telling him to give me the little
book. And he *said to me, "[a]Take
it, and eat it; and it will make
your stomach bitter, but in your
mouth it will be sweet as honey."

10 And I took the little book
out of the angel's hand and ate it,
and it was in my mouth sweet as
honey; and when I had eaten it,
my stomach was made bitter.

11 [a]Rev. 11:1 [b]Ezek. 37:4, 9 [c]Rev. 5:9 [d]Rev. 17:10, 12

11 And [a]they *said to me,
"You must [b]prophesy again concerning [c]many peoples and nations and tongues and [d]kings."

7 *The two witnesses,* 11:1–19

a *Temple,* 11:1–2

★ 1 [a]Ezek. 40:3-42:20; Zech. 2:1; Rev. 21:15f. [b]Rev. 10:11

11 And there was given me a
[a]measuring rod like a staff;
and [b]someone said, "Rise and
measure the temple of God, and
the altar, and those who worship
in it.

★ 2 [a]Ezek. 40:17, 20 [b]Luke 21:24 [c]Is. 52:1; Matt. 4:5; 27:53; Rev. 21:2, 10; 22:19 [d]Dan. 7:25; 12:7; Rev. 12:6; 13:5

2 "And leave out the [a]court
which is outside the temple, and
do not measure it, for [b]it has been

9:21 *sorceries.* I.e., magical arts, potions, and poisons (see Gal. 5:20; Rev. 18:23; 21:8; 22:15). From the Greek word, we derive the English word "pharmacies."

10:6 *there shall be delay no longer.* I.e., when the seventh angel sounds his trumpet (11:15), the bowl judgments will be poured out (16:1–21) and the tribulation will come to an end with the return of Christ.

10:7 *the mystery of God.* Truth concerning God Himself which will not be revealed until His kingdom is established on earth.

10:9 The eating of the little scroll was to remind John that although these truths from God may be pleasant to his taste, they were bitter when digested, because they spoke of judgment. The revelation of God's judgment, on careful reflection, should always bring heaviness of heart to the child of God. Compare Ezek. 2:8–3:3.

11:1 *the temple of God.* Apparently the temple which will be built during the tribulation days, in which Jewish worship will be carried on during the first part of that period and in which, at the mid-point of the seven-year period, the man of sin will exalt himself to be worshiped (2 Thess. 2:4).

11:2 *forty-two months.* This equals three and one-half years and probably refers to the last half of the tribulation period.

given to the nations; and they will
[b]tread under foot [c]the holy city
for [d]forty-two months.

b Time, 11:3

3 "And I will grant *authority*
to my two [a]witnesses, and they
will prophesy for [b]twelve hundred and sixty days, clothed in
[c]sackcloth."

c Traits, 11:4-6

4 These are the [a]two olive
trees and the two lampstands that
stand before the Lord of the
earth.
5 And if any one desires to
harm them, [a]fire proceeds out of
their mouth and devours their enemies; and if any one would desire to harm them, [b]in this manner he must be killed.
6 These have the power to
[a]shut up the sky, in order that
rain may not fall during [b]the days
of their prophesying; and they
have power over the waters to
[c]turn them into blood, and to
smite the earth with every plague,
as often as they desire.

d Termination, 11:7-10

7 And when they have fin-
ished their testimony, [a]the beast
that comes up out of the [b]abyss
will [c]make war with them, and
overcome them and kill them.
8 And their dead bodies *will
lie* in the street of the [a]great city
which mystically is called [b]Sodom
and [c]Egypt, where also their Lord
was crucified.
9 And those from [a]the peo-

★ 3 [a]Rev. 1:5; 2:13 [b]Dan. 7:25; 12:7; Rev. 12:6; 13:5 [c]Gen. 37:34; 2 Sam. 3:31; 1 Kin. 21:27; 2 Kin. 19:1f.; Neh. 9:1; Esth. 4:1; Ps. 69:11; Joel 1:13; Jon. 3:5f., 8
★ 4 [a]Ps. 52:8; Jer. 11:16; Zech. 4:3, 11, 14
★ 5-6
5 [a]2 Kin. 1:10-12; Jer. 5:14; Rev. 9:17f. [b]Num. 16:29, 35
6 [a]Luke 4:25 [b]Rev. 11:3 [c]Rev. 8:8
★ 7 [a]Rev. 13:1ff. [b]Rev. 9:1 [c]Dan. 7:21; Rev. 13:7
★ 8 [a]Rev. 14:8; 16:19; 17:18; 18:2, 10, 16, 18, 19, 21 [b]Is. 1:9, 10; 3:9; Jer. 23:14; Ezek. 16:46, 49 [c]Ezek. 23:3, 8, 19, 27
9 [a]Rev. 5:9; 10:11 [b]1 Kin. 13:22; Ps. 79:2f.

ples and tribes and tongues and
nations *will* look at their dead
bodies for three and a half days,
and [b]will not permit their dead
bodies to be laid in a tomb.
10 And [a]those who dwell on
the earth *will* rejoice over them
and make merry; and they will
[b]send gifts to one another, because these two prophets tormented [a]those who dwell on the
earth.

e Translation, 11:11-14

11 And after the three and a
half days [a]the breath of life from
God came into them, and they
stood on their feet; and great fear
fell upon those who were beholding them.
12 And they heard a loud
voice from heaven saying to
them, "[a]Come up here." And
they [b]went up into heaven in the
cloud, and their enemies beheld
them.
13 And in that hour there was
a great [a]earthquake, and a tenth
of the city fell; and seven thousand people were killed in the
earthquake, and the rest were terrified and [b]gave glory to the [c]God
of heaven.
14 The second [a]woe is past;
behold, the third woe is coming
quickly.

f Seventh trumpet, 11:15-19

15 And the [a]seventh angel
sounded; and there arose [b]loud
voices in heaven, saying,
"[c]The kingdom of the world
has become *the kingdom* of our

10 [a]Rev. 3:10 [b]Neh. 8:10, 12; Esth. 9:19, 22
★11 [a]Ezek. 37:5, 9, 10, 14
12 [a]Rev. 4:1 [b]2 Kin. 2:11; Acts 1:9
★13 [a]Rev. 6:12; 8:5; 11:19; 16:18 [b]John 9:24; Rev. 14:7; 16:9; 19:7 [c]Rev. 16:11
14 [a]Rev. 8:13; 9:12
15 [a]Rev. 8:2; 10:7 [b]Rev. 16:17; 19:1 [c]Rev. 12:10 [d]Acts 4:26 [Ps. 2:2] [e]Dan. 2:44; 7:14, 27; Luke 1:33

11:3 *twelve hundred and sixty days.* This also equals three and one-half years and refers to the period of the ministry of the two witnesses.

11:4 *two olive trees.* For the symbolism see Zech. 4:3, 14. *two lampstands* that give out a witness (v. 3).

11:5-6 The miraculous powers of the two witnesses are reminiscent of those of Elijah and Moses (cf. Ex. 7:20; 8:1-12:29; 1 Kings 17:1; 18:41-45; 2 Kings 1:10-12).

11:7 *the beast.* The Antichrist (see note on 1 John 2:18), also called the man of lawlessness (2 Thess. 2:3). The same person is mentioned in Rev. 6:2; 13:1; 14:9, 11; 15:2; 16:2; 17:3, 13; 19:20; 20:10. He cannot kill these two witnesses until God allows him to.

11:8 *the great city.* I.e., Jerusalem.

11:11 *and they stood on their feet.* Imagine the effect the resurrection of these two men will have on those who, only the moment before, were viewing their corpses in the street!

11:13 *the rest.* Those who were not killed by the earthquake.

Lord, and of [d]His Christ; and [e]He
will reign forever and ever."

16 [a]Matt. 19:28; Rev. 4:4 [b]Rev. 4:10

16 And the twenty-four elders, who [a]sit on their thrones before God, [b]fell on their faces and
worshiped God,

17 [a]Rev. 1:8 [b]Rev. 19:6

17 saying,
"We give Thee thanks, [a]O Lord
God, the Almighty, who art and
who wast, because Thou hast
taken Thy great power and hast
begun to [b]reign.

18 [a]Ps. 2:1 [b]Dan. 7:10; Rev. 20:12 [c]Rev. 10:7; 16:6 [d]Ps. 115:13; Rev. 13:16; 19:5

18 "And [a]the nations were enraged, and Thy wrath came, and
[b]the time *came* for the dead to be
judged, and *the time* to give their
reward to Thy [c]bond-servants the
prophets and to the saints and to
those who fear Thy name, [d]the
small and the great, and to destroy those who destroy the
earth."

19 [a]Rev. 4:1; 15:5 [b]Heb. 9:4 [c]Rev. 4:5 [d]Rev. 16:21

19 And [a]the temple of God
which is in heaven was opened;
and [b]the ark of His covenant appeared in His temple, and there
were flashes of [c]lightning and
sounds and peals of thunder and
an earthquake and a [d]great hail-
storm.

*8 **War,*** 12:1–17

a War on earth: phase I, 12:1–6

★ 1 [a]Matt. 24:30; Rev. 12:3 [b]Rev. 11:19 [c]Gal. 4:26 [d]Ps. 104:2; Song of Sol. 6:10

12 And a great [a]sign appeared [b]in heaven: [c]a
woman [d]clothed with the sun,
and the moon under her feet, and
on her head a crown of twelve
stars;

2 [a]Is. 26:17; 66:6-9; Mic. 4:9, 10

2 and she was with child;
and she *[a]cried out, being in labor and in pain to give birth.

★ 3 [a]Rev. 12:1; 15:1 [b]Is. 27:1; Rev. 12:4, 7, 9, 13, 16f.; 13:2, 4, 11; 16:13; 20:2 [c]Rev. 13:1; 17:3, 7, 9ff. [d]Dan 7:7, 20, 24; Rev. 13:1; 17:12, 16 [e]Rev. 13:1; 19:12

3 And [a]another sign appeared in heaven: and behold, a
great red [b]dragon having [c]seven
heads and [d]ten horns, and on his
heads *were* [e]seven diadems.

★ 4 [a]Rev. 8:7, 12 [b]Dan. 8:10 [c]Is. 27:1; Rev. 12:3, 7, 9, 13, 16f.; 13:2, 4, 11; 16:13; 20:2 [d]Matt. 2:16

4 And his tail *swept away a
[a]third of the stars of heaven, and
[b]threw them to the earth. And the
[c]dragon stood before the woman
who was about to give birth, so
that when she gave birth [d]he
might devour her child.

★ 5 [a]Rev. 2:27 [b]2 Cor. 12:2

5 And she gave birth to a
son, a male *child,* who is to [a]rule
all the nations with a rod of iron;
and her child was [b]caught up to
God and to His throne.

★ 6 [a]Rev. 11:3; 13:5

6 And the woman fled into
the wilderness where she *had a
place prepared by God, so that
there she might be nourished for
[a]one thousand two hundred and
sixty days.

b War in heaven, 12:7–12

★ 7 [a]Jude 9 [b]Rev. 12:3 [c]Matt. 25:41

7 And there was war in
heaven, [a]Michael and his angels
waging war with the [b]dragon.
And the dragon and [c]his angels
waged war,

★ 9–11

8 and they were not strong
enough, and there was no longer
a place found for them in heaven.

9 [a]Rev. 12:3 [b]Gen. 3:1; 2 Cor. 11:3; Rev. 12:15; 20:2 [c]Matt. 4:10; 25:41 [d]Rev. 13:14; 20:3, 8, 10 [e]Luke 10:18; John 12:31

9 And the great [a]dragon was
thrown down, the [b]serpent of old
who is called the devil and [c]Satan,
who [d]deceives the whole world;
he was [e]thrown down to the
earth, and his angels were thrown
down with him.

10 [a]Rev. 11:15 [b]Rev. 7:10 [c]Job 1:11; 2:5; Zech. 3:1; Luke 22:31; 1 Pet. 5:8

10 And I heard [a]a loud voice
in heaven, saying,

12:1 *a woman.* She represents Israel, who gave Christ to the world (v. 5) and who will be persecuted severely during the tribulation (v. 13).

12:3 *a great red dragon.* Satan (v. 9).

12:4 *a third of the stars of heaven.* This may refer to Satan's past rebellion against God (Ezek. 28:15); if so, it suggests that a third of the angels joined Satan and were cast out of heaven with him. Or the reference may be to a meteor-shower judgment on the earth.

12:5 *her child was caught up to God.* A reference to the ascension of Christ.

12:6 *one thousand two hundred and sixty days.* The last three and one-half years of the tribulation period will see intense persecution of Israel. Details are given in vv. 13–17. No mention is made of the many hundreds of years between the ascension (v. 5) and the future tribulation (v. 6). See Dan. 9:27; Matt. 24:14, 21; 1 Thess. 4:17.

12:7 *Michael . . . the dragon.* This likely will occur at the mid-point of the tribulation. Michael is the only angel designated an archangel in the Bible (Jude 9).

12:9–11 Notice two of Satan's activities in these verses: to deceive the world and to accuse the brethren. The believer's defense against Satan is (1) to bank on the merits of the death of Christ, (2) to be active in witnessing, and (3) to be willing to make any sacrifice, including death (v. 11).

"Now the [b]salvation, and the power, and the [a]kingdom of our God and the authority of His Christ have come, for the [c]accuser of our brethren has been thrown down, who accuses them before our God day and night.

11 "And they [a]overcame him because of [b]the blood of the Lamb and because of [c]the word of their testimony, and they [d]did not love their life even to death.

11 [a]John 16:33; 1 John 2:13; Rev. 15:2 [b]Rev. 7:14 [c]Rev. 6:9 [d]Luke 14:26; Rev. 2:10

12 "For this reason, [a]rejoice, O heavens and [b]you who dwell in them. [c]Woe to the earth and the sea; because [d]the devil has come down to you, having great wrath, knowing that he has *only* [e]a short time."

12 [a]Ps. 96:11; Is. 44:23; Rev. 18:20 [b]Rev. 13:6 [c]Rev. 8:13 [d]Rev. 12:9 [e]Rev. 10:6

c War on earth: phase II, 12:13–17

13 And when the [a]dragon saw that he was thrown down to the earth, he persecuted [b]the woman who gave birth to the male *child.*

13 [a]Rev. 12:3 [b]Rev. 12:5

14 And the [a]two wings of the great eagle were given to the woman, in order that she might fly [b]into the wilderness to her place, where she *was nourished for [c]a time and times and half a time, from the presence of the serpent.

14 [a]Ex. 19:4; Deut. 32:11; Is. 40:31 [b]Rev. 12:6 [c]Dan. 7:25; 12:7

15 And the [a]serpent poured water [b]like a river out of his mouth after the woman, so that he might cause her to be swept away with the flood.

15 [a]Gen. 3:1; 2 Cor. 11:3; Rev. 12:9; 20:2 [b]Is. 59:19; Hos. 5:10

16 And the earth helped the woman, and the earth opened its mouth and drank up the river which the dragon poured out of his mouth.

17 And the dragon was enraged with the woman, and went off to [a]make war with the rest of her [b]offspring, who [c]keep the commandments of God and [d]hold to the testimony of Jesus.

17 [a]Rev. 11:7; 13:7 [b]Gen. 3:15 [c]1 John 2:3; Rev. 14:12 [d]Rev. 1:2; 6:9; [14:12]; 19:10

9 ***The beast and his prophet,*** 13:1–18

a The beast, 13:1–10

13 And he stood on the sand of the seashore.

And I saw a [a]beast coming up out of the sea, having [b]ten horns and [b]seven heads, and on his horns *were* [c]ten diadems, and on his heads *were* [d]blasphemous names.

★ 1 [a]Dan 7:3; Rev. 11:7; 13:14, 15; 15:2; 16:13; 17:8 [b]Rev. 12:3 [c]Rev. 12:3; 17:12 [d]Dan. 7:8; 11:36; Rev. 17:3

2 And the beast which I saw was [a]like a leopard, and his feet were *like those* of [b]a bear, and his mouth like the mouth of [c]a lion. And the [d]dragon gave him his power and his [e]throne and great authority.

★ 2 [a]Dan. 7:6; Hos. 13:7f. [b]Dan. 7:5 [c]Dan. 7:4 [d]Rev. 12:3; 13:4, 12 [e]Rev. 2:13; 16:10

3 And *I saw* one of his heads as if it had been slain, and his [a]fatal wound was healed. And the whole earth [b]was amazed *and followed* after the beast;

★ 3 [a]Rev. 13:12, 14 [b]Rev. 17:8

4 and they worshiped the [a]dragon, because he [a]gave his authority to the beast; and they worshiped the beast, saying, "[b]Who is like the beast, and who is able to wage war with him?"

4 [a]Rev. 12:3; 13:2, 12 [b]Ex. 15:11; Is. 46:5; Rev. 18:18

5 And there was given to him a mouth [a]speaking arrogant words and blasphemies; and authority to act for [b]forty-two months was given to him.

★ 5 [a]Dan. 7:8, 11, 20, 25; 11:36; 2 Thess. 2:3f. [b]Rev. 11:2

6 And he opened his mouth in blasphemies against God, to blaspheme His name and His tabernacle, *that is,* [a]those who dwell in heaven.

6 [a]Rev. 7:15; 12:12

7 And it was given to him to [a]make war with the saints and to

7 [a]Rev. 11:7 [b]Rev. 5:9

13:1 *And he stood.* I.e., the dragon. *a beast.* The Antichrist. See note on 11:7. Many emperors of Rome deified themselves but Antichrist will far outstrip all his predecessors in his blasphemous ways. *ten horns.* The ten kings that will give their power and authority to the Antichrist (17:12–13).

13:2 *the dragon gave him his power.* Satan gives Antichrist his power.

13:3 *his fatal wound was healed.* Apparently Satan will miraculously restore Antichrist to life in imitation of the resurrection of Christ. No wonder the world will acclaim Antichrist.

13:5 *forty-two months.* Apparently the last three and one-half years of the tribulation period during which Antichrist's power is practically unrestrained.

overcome them; and authority
over [b]every tribe and people and
tongue and nation was given to
him.
8 And all who [a]dwell on the
earth will worship him, *every one*
[b]whose name has not been written [c]from the foundation of the
world in the book of life of [d]the
Lamb who has been slain.
9 [a]If any one has an ear, let
him hear.
10 [a]If any one *is destined* for
captivity, to captivity he goes; [b]if
any one kills with the sword, with
the sword he must be killed. Here
is [c]the perseverance and the faith
of the saints.

8 [a]Rev. 3:10; 13:12, 14 [b]Rev. 3:5 [c]Matt. 25:34; Rev. 17:8 [d]Rev. 5:6
9 [a]Rev. 2:7
★10 [a]Is. 33:1; Jer. 15:2; 43:11 [b]Gen. 9:6; Matt. 26:52; Rev. 11:18 [c]Heb. 6:12; Rev. 14:12

b The false prophet, 13:11–18

11 And [a]I saw another beast
coming up out of the earth; and
he had [b]two horns like a lamb,
and he spoke as a [c]dragon.
12 And he [a]exercises all the
authority of the first beast [b]in his
presence. And he makes [c]the
earth and those who dwell in it to
[d]worship the first beast, whose
[e]fatal wound was healed.
13 And he [a]performs great
signs, so that he even makes [b]fire
come down out of heaven to the
earth in the presence of men.
14 And he [a]deceives [b]those
who dwell on the earth because of
[c]the signs which it was given him
to perform [d]in the presence of the
beast, telling those who dwell on
the earth to make an image to the
beast who *had the [e]wound of
the sword and has come to life.
15 And there was given to
him to give breath to the image of
the beast, that the image of the
beast might even speak and cause
[a]as many as do not [b]worship the
image of the beast to be killed.
16 And he causes all, [a]the
small and the great, and the rich
and the poor, and the free men
and the slaves, to be given a
[b]mark on their right hand, or on
their forehead,
17 and *he provides* that no
one should be able to buy or to
sell, except the one who has the
[a]mark, *either* [b]the name of the
beast or [c]the number of his name.
18 [a]Here is wisdom. Let him
who has understanding calculate
the number of the beast, for the
number is that [b]of a man; and his
number is six hundred and sixty-
six.

★11 [a]Rev. 13:1, 14; 16:13 [b]Dan. 8:3 [c]Rev. 13:4
12 [a]Rev. 13:4 [b]Rev. 13:14; 19:20 [c]Rev. 13:8 [d]Rev. 13:15; 14:9, 11; 16:2; 19:20; 20:4 [e]Rev. 13:3
13 [a]Matt. 24:24; Rev. 16:14; 19:20 [b]1 Kin. 18:38; Luke 9:54; Rev. 11:5; 20:9
14 [a]Rev. 12:9 [b]Rev. 13:8 [c]2 Thess. 2:9f. [d]Rev. 13:12; 19:20 [e]Rev. 13:3
15 [a]Dan. 3:3ff. [b]Rev. 13:12; 14:9, 11; 16:2; 19:20; 20:4
16 [a]Rev. 11:18; 19:5, 18 [b]Gal. 6:17; Rev. 7:3; 14:9; 20:4
17 [a]Gal. 6:17; Rev. 7:3; 14:9; 20:4 [b]Rev. 14:11 [c]Rev. 15:2
★18 [a]Rev. 17:9 [b]Rev. 21:17

10 Various announcements, 14:1–20

a Concerning the 144,000, 14:1–5

14 And I looked, and behold,
[a]the Lamb *was* standing
on [b]Mount Zion, and with Him
[c]one hundred and forty-four
thousand, having [d]His name and
the [d]name of His Father written
[e]on their foreheads.
2 And I heard a voice from
heaven, like [a]the sound of many
waters and like the [b]sound of
loud thunder, and the voice which
I heard *was* like *the sound* of
[c]harpists playing on their harps.
3 And they *sang [a]a new
song before the throne and before
the [b]four living creatures and the
[c]elders; and [d]no one could learn
the song except the [e]one hundred
and forty-four thousand who had
been [a]purchased from the earth.

★ 1 [a]Rev. 5:6 [b]Ps. 2:6; Heb. 12:22 [c]Rev. 7:4; 14:3 [d]Rev. 3:12 [e]Rev. 7:3
2 [a]Rev. 1:15 [b]Rev. 6:1 [c]Rev. 5:8
3 [a]Rev. 5:9 [b]Rev. 4:6 [c]Rev. 4:4 [d]Rev. 2:17 [e]Rev. 7:4; 14:1

13:10 Assurance that God will punish evildoers sustains the faith of those who are persecuted during these days. See also note on 14:12.

13:11 *another beast.* This man is Antichrist's lieutenant, who will enforce the worship of Antichrist by performing miracles (v. 13), by making and animating an image of Antichrist (vv. 14–15), by sentencing to death those who disobey (v. 15), and by requiring a mark on the hand or forehead in order that men may buy and sell (vv. 16–17).

13:18 *his number is six hundred and sixty-six.* Somehow, unknown to us, this number will play an important part in the identification of the Antichrist in a future day.

14:1 *the Lamb.* I.e., Christ. *one hundred and forty-four thousand.* Evidently the same group introduced in 7:4, though now their work on earth is finished and they are in heaven.

★ 4 [a]Matt. 19:12; 2 Cor. 11:2; Eph. 5:27; Rev. 3:4 [b]Rev. 3:4; 7:17; 17:14 [c]Rev. 5:9 [d]Heb. 12:23; James 1:18

4 [a]These are the ones who
have not been defiled with
women, for they have kept themselves chaste. These *are* the ones
who [b]follow the Lamb wherever
He goes. These have been [c]pur-
chased from among men [d]as first
fruits to God and to the Lamb.

5 [a]Ps. 32:2; Zeph. 3:13; Mal. 2:6; John 1:47; 1 Pet. 2:22 [b]Heb. 9:14; 1 Pet. 1:19; Jude 24

5 And no lie was found [a]in
their mouth; they are [b]blameless.

b Concerning the everlasting gospel, 14:6-8

★ 6 [a]Rev. 8:13 [b]1 Pet. 1:25; Rev. 10:7 [c]Rev. 3:10 [d]Rev. 5:9

6 And I saw another angel
flying in [a]midheaven, having [b]an
eternal gospel to preach to [c]those
who live on the earth, and to [d]ev-
ery nation and tribe and tongue
and people;

7 [a]Rev. 15:4 [b]Rev. 11:13 [c]Rev. 4:11 [d]Rev. 8:10

7 and he said with a loud
voice, "[a]Fear God, and [b]give Him
glory, because the hour of His
judgment has come; and worship
Him who [c]made the heaven and
the earth and sea and [d]springs of
waters."

★ 8 [a]Is. 21:9; Jer. 51:8; Rev. 18:2 [b]Dan. 4:30; Rev. 16:19; 17:5; 18:10 [c]Jer. 51:7 [d]Rev. 17:2, 4; 18:3

8 And another angel, a second one, followed, saying, "[a]Fall-
en, fallen is [b]Babylon the great,
she who has [c]made all the nations
drink of the [d]wine of the passion
of her immorality."

c Concerning beast worshipers, 14:9-13

9 [a]Rev. 13:12; 14:11 [b]Rev. 13:14f.; 14:11 [c]Rev. 13:16

9 And another angel, a third
one, followed them, saying with a
loud voice, "If any one [a]worships
the beast and his [b]image, and receives a [c]mark on his forehead or
upon his hand,

10 [a]Is. 51:17; Jer. 25:15f., 27; Rev. 16:19; 19:15 [b]Ps. 75:8; Rev. 18:6 [c]Ezek. 38:22; 2 Thess. 1:7; Rev. 19:20; 20:10, 14f.; 21:8 [d]Mark 8:38

10 he also will drink of the
[a]wine of the wrath of God, which
is mixed in full strength [b]in the
cup of His anger; and he will be
tormented with [c]fire and brimstone in the presence of the [d]holy
angels and in the presence of the
Lamb.

11 [a]Is. 34:8-10; Rev. 18:9, 18; 19:3 [b]Rev. 4:8 [c]Rev. 13:12; 14:9 [d]Rev. 13:17

11 "And the [a]smoke of their
torment goes up forever and ever;
and [b]they have no rest day and
night, those who [c]worship the
beast and his [c]image, and whoever receives the [d]mark of his
name."

★12 [a]Rev. 13:10 [b]Rev. 12:17 [c]Rev. 2:13

12 Here is [a]the perseverance
of the saints who [b]keep the commandments of God and [c]their
faith in Jesus.

13 [a]Rev. 20:6 [b]1 Cor. 15:18; 1 Thess. 4:16 [c]Rev. 11:18 [d]Rev. 2:7; 22:17 [e]Heb. 4:9f.; Rev. 6:11 [f]1 Tim. 5:25

13 And I heard a voice from
heaven, saying, "Write, '[a]Blessed
are the dead who [b]die in the Lord
[c]from now on!' " "Yes," [d]says the
Spirit, "that they may [e]rest from
their labors, for their [f]deeds follow with them."

d Concerning the harvesting of the earth, 14:14-20

14 [a]Matt. 17:5 [b]Rev. 1:13 [c]Ps. 21:3; Rev. 6:2

14 And I looked, and behold,
a [a]white cloud, and sitting on the
cloud *was* one [b]like a son of man,
having a golden [c]crown on His
head, and a sharp sickle in His
hand.

15 [a]Rev. 11:19; 14:17; 15:6; 16:17 [b]Joel 3:13; Mark 4:29; Rev. 14:18 [c]Jer. 51:33; Matt. 13:39-41

15 And another angel [a]came
out of the temple, crying out with
a loud voice to Him who sat on
the cloud, "[b]Put in your sickle
and reap, because the hour to
reap has come, because the [c]har-
vest of the earth is ripe."

16 And He who sat on the
cloud swung His sickle over the
earth; and the earth was reaped.

17 [a]Rev. 11:19; 14:15; 15:6; 16:17

17 And another angel [a]came
out of the temple which is in
heaven, and he also had a sharp
sickle.

18 [a]Rev. 16:8 [b]Rev. 6:9; 8:3 [c]Joel 3:13; Mark 4:29; Rev. 14:15 [d]Joel 3:13

18 And another angel, [a]the
one who has power over fire,
came out from [b]the altar; and he

14:4 *not . . . defiled with women.* This may simply mean that the 144,000 were unmarried, or it may indicate their purposeful celibate state of separation unto God (cf. 2 Cor. 11:2). *first fruits.* The salvation of the 144,000 will forerun the salvation of a larger group of Israelites, who will turn to the Lord at the end of the tribulation (cf. Isa. 2:3; Rom. 11:15).

14:6 *an eternal gospel to preach.* God's last call of grace to the world before the return of Christ in judgment.

14:8 *fallen is Babylon.* This fall is described in detail in chapters 17-18. For *Babylon,* see note on 17:5.

14:12 Saints will be able to endure, knowing that God will punish their enemies (vv. 9-11). See also note on 13:10.

called with a loud voice to him
who had the sharp sickle, saying,
"[c]Put in your sharp sickle, and
gather the clusters from the vine
of the earth, [d]because her grapes
are ripe."

19 [a]Is. 63:2f.; Rev. 19:15

19 And the angel swung his
sickle to the earth, and gathered
the clusters from the vine of the
earth, and threw them into [a]the
great wine press of the wrath of
God.

★20 [a]Heb. 13:12; Rev. 11:8 [b]Gen. 49:11; Deut. 32:14

20 And the wine press was
trodden [a]outside the city, and
[b]blood came out from the wine
press, up to the horses' bridles,
for a distance of two hundred
miles.

11 Prelude to the bowl judgments, 15:1–8

1 [a]Rev. 12:1, 3 [b]Rev. 15:6-8; 16:1; 17:1; 21:9 [c]Lev. 26:21 [d]Rev. 9:20

15 And I saw [a]another sign in
heaven, great and marvel-
ous, [b]seven angels who had [c]sev-
en plagues, *which are* [d]the last,
because in them the wrath of God
is finished.

2 [a]Rev. 4:6 [b]Rev. 12:11 [c]Rev. 13:1 [d]Rev. 13:14f. [e]Rev. 13:17 [f]Rev. 5:8

2 And I saw, as it were, a
[a]sea of glass mixed with fire, and
those who had [b]come off victorious from the [c]beast and from [d]his
image and from the [e]number of
his name, standing on the [a]sea of
glass, holding [f]harps of God.

3 [a]Ex. 15:1ff. [b]Josh. 22:5; Heb. 3:5 [c]Rev. 5:9f., 12f. [d]Deut. 32:3f.; Ps. 111:2; 139:14; Hos. 14:9 [e]Rev. 1:8 [f]1 Tim. 1:17 marg.

3 And they *sang the [a]song
of Moses [b]the bond-servant of
God and the [c]song of the Lamb,
saying,

"[d]GREAT AND MARVELOUS ARE
THY WORKS,
[e]O LORD GOD, THE AL-
MIGHTY;
RIGHTEOUS AND TRUE ARE
THY WAYS,
THOU [f]KING OF THE NATIONS.

4 [a]Jer. 10:7; Rev. 14:7 [b]Ps. 86:9; Is. 66:23 [c]Rev. 19:8

4 "[a]WHO WILL NOT FEAR, O
LORD, AND GLORIFY THY
NAME?
FOR THOU ALONE ART HOLY;
FOR [b]ALL THE NATIONS WILL
COME AND WORSHIP BEFORE
THEE,
For Thy [c]righteous acts
have been revealed."

★ 5 [a]Rev. 11:19 [b]Ex. 38:21; Num. 1:50; Heb. 8:5; Rev. 13:6

5 After these things I
looked, and [a]the temple of the
[b]tabernacle of testimony in
heaven was opened,

6 [a]Rev. 15:1 [b]Rev. 14:15 [c]Ezek. 28:13 [d]Rev. 1:13

6 and the [a]seven angels who
had the seven plagues [b]came out
of the temple, clothed [c]in linen,
clean *and* bright, and [d]girded
around their breasts with golden
girdles.

7 [a]Rev. 4:6 [b]Rev. 15:1 [c]Rev. 5:8 [d]Rev. 14:10; 15:1 [e]Rev. 4:9

7 And one of the [a]four living
creatures gave to the [b]seven angels seven [c]golden bowls full of
the [d]wrath of God, who [e]lives forever and ever.

8 [a]Ex. 19:18; 40:34f.; Lev. 16:2; 1 Kin. 8:10f.; 2 Chr. 5:13f.; Is. 6:4

8 And the temple was filled
with [a]smoke from the glory of
God and from His power; and no
one was able to enter the temple
until the seven plagues of the
seven angels were finished.

12 The bowl judgments, 16:1–21

a First bowl: grievous sores, 16:1–2

1 [a]Rev. 11:19 [b]Rev. 15:1 [c]Ps. 79:6; Jer. 10:25; Ezek. 22:31; Zeph. 3:8; Rev. 16:2ff. [d]Rev. 5:8

16 And I heard a loud voice
from [a]the temple, saying
to the [b]seven angels, "Go and
[c]pour out the [d]seven bowls of the
wrath of God into the earth."

★ 2 [a]Rev. 8:7 [b]Ex. 9:9-11; Deut. 28:35; Rev. 16:11 [c]Rev. 13:15-17; 14:9

2 And the first *angel* went
and poured out his bowl [a]into the
earth; and it became a loathsome
and malignant [b]sore upon the
men [c]who had the mark of the
beast and who worshiped his
image.

b Second bowl: seas smitten, 16:3

★ 3 [a]Ex. 7:17-21; Rev. 8:8f.; 11:6

3 And the second *angel*
poured out his bowl [a]into the sea,

14:20 Apparently a reference to Armageddon (16:16; cf. 19:17–19), when the blood from the slaughter will flow 200 miles, to the depth of about 4½ feet (14:20).

15:5 *the temple of the tabernacle of testimony.* I.e., the Holy of Holies.

16:2 *a loathsome and malignant sore.* Lit., foul and evil sore. Probably a plague of ulcers. The brief descriptions of these last seven judgments (vv. 2–12, 17–21) may suggest they occur in rapid succession.

16:3 *every living thing in the sea died.* See 8:9. Imagine the stench and disease that will accompany this.

and it became blood like *that* of a dead man; and every living thing in the sea died.

c Third bowl: rivers smitten, 16:4–7

4 [a]Rev. 8:10 [b]Ex. 7:17-20; Rev. 11:6

4 And the third *angel* poured out his bowl into the [a]rivers and the springs of waters; and they [b]became blood.

5 [a]John 17:25 [b]Rev. 11:17 [c]Rev. 15:4 [d]Rev. 6:10

5 And I heard the angel of the waters saying, "[a]Righteous art Thou, [b]who art and who wast, O [c]Holy One, because Thou didst [d]judge these things;

★ **6** [a]Rev. 17:6; 18:24 [b]Is. 49:26; Luke 11:49-51

6 for they poured out [a]the blood of saints and prophets, and Thou hast given them [b]blood to drink. They deserve it."

7 [a]Rev. 6:9; 14:18 [b]Rev. 1:8 [c]Rev. 15:3; 19:2

7 And I heard [a]the altar saying, "Yes, O [b]Lord God, the Almighty, [c]true and righteous are Thy judgments."

d Fourth bowl: scorching, 16:8–9

8 [a]Rev. 6:12 [b]Rev. 14:18

8 And the fourth *angel* poured out his bowl upon [a]the sun; [b]and it was given to it to scorch men with fire.

★ **9** [a]Rev. 16:11, 21 [b]Rev. 2:21 [c]Rev. 11:13

9 And men were scorched with fierce heat; and they [a]blasphemed the name of God who has the power over these plagues; and they [b]did not repent, so as to [c]give Him glory.

e Fifth bowl: darkness, 16:10–11

10 [a]Rev. 13:2 [b]Ex. 10:21f.; Is. 8:22; Rev. 8:12; 9:2

10 And the fifth *angel* poured out his bowl upon the [a]throne of the beast; and his kingdom became [b]darkened; and they gnawed their tongues because of pain,

★**11** [a]Rev. 16:9, 21 [b]Rev. 11:13 [c]Rev. 16:2 [d]Rev. 2:21

11 and they [a]blasphemed the [b]God of heaven because of their pains and their [c]sores; and they [d]did not repent of their deeds.

f Sixth bowl: Euphrates dried, 16:12–16

★**12** [a]Rev. 9:14 [b]Is. 11:15f.; 44:27; Jer. 51:32, 36 [c]Is. 41:2, 25; 46:11 [d]Rev. 7:2

12 And the sixth *angel* poured out his bowl upon the [a]great river, the Euphrates; and [b]its water was dried up, that [c]the way might be prepared for the kings [d]from the east.

★**13** [a]Rev. 12:3 [b]Rev. 13:1 [c]Rev. 13:11, 14; 19:20; 20:10 [d]Rev. 18:2 [e]Ex. 8:6

13 And I saw *coming* out of the mouth of the [a]dragon and out of the mouth of the [b]beast and out of the mouth of the [c]false prophet, three [d]unclean spirits like [e]frogs;

★**14** [a]1 Tim. 4:1 [b]Rev. 13:13 [c]Rev. 3:10 [d]1 Kin. 22:21-23; Rev. 17:14; 19:19; 20:8 [e]Rev. 6:17

14 for they are [a]spirits of demons, [b]performing signs, which go out to the kings of the [c]whole world, to [d]gather them together for the war of the [e]great day of God, the Almighty.

15 [a]Rev. 3:3, 11 [b]Luke 12:37 [c]Rev. 3:18

15 (Behold, [a]I am coming like a thief. [b]Blessed is the one who stays awake and keeps his garments, [c]lest he walk about naked and men see his shame.)

★**16** [a]Rev. 19:19 [b]Rev. 9:11 [c]Judg. 5:19; 2 Kin. 23:29f.; 2 Chr. 35:22; Zech. 12:11

16 And they [a]gathered them together to the place which [b]in Hebrew is called Har-[c]Magedon.

g Seventh bowl: widespread destruction, 16:17–21

17 [a]Eph. 2:2 [b]Rev. 11:15 [c]Rev. 14:15 [d]Rev. 10:6; 21:6

17 And the seventh *angel* poured out his bowl upon [a]the air; and a [b]loud voice came out of

---

16:6 *They deserve it.* I.e., they deserve to drink blood because they shed the blood of saints and prophets.

16:9 *they did not repent.* See v. 11 and 9:21.

16:11 *their sores.* I.e., those referred to in v. 2.

16:12 *the kings from the east.* Lit., the kings from the rising of the sun. The armies of the nations of the Orient will be aided in their march toward Armageddon by the supernatural drying up of the Euphrates River.

16:13 *the dragon.* Satan. *the beast.* Antichrist (13:1–10). *the false prophet.* The lieutenant (13:11–18).

16:14 *the war of the great day of God, the Almighty.* The war will consist of several battles, beginning with Antichrist's campaign into Egypt (Dan. 11:40–45) and including a siege of Jerusalem (Zech. 14:2) as well as the final battle at Armageddon (Rev. 16:16).

16:16 *Har-Magedon* (or *Armageddon).* Lit., Mount of Megiddo, near the city of Megiddo at the head of the plain of Esdraelon. This area was the scene of many O.T. battles, notably those of Barak with the Canaanites (Judg. 4) and of Gideon with the Midianites (Judg. 7).

the [c]temple from the throne, saying, "[d]It is done."
18 And there were flashes of
[a]lightning and sounds and peals
of thunder; and there was [b]a great
earthquake, [c]such as there had
not been since man came to be
upon the earth, so great an earthquake *was it, and* so mighty.
19 And [a]the great city was
split into three parts, and the
cities of the nations fell. And
[b]Babylon the great was [c]remem-
bered before God, to give her [d]the
cup of the wine of His fierce
wrath.
20 And [a]every island fled
away, and the mountains were
not found.
21 And [a]huge hailstones,
about one hundred pounds each,
*came down from heaven upon
men; and men [b]blasphemed God
because of the [c]plague of the hail,
because its plague *was extremely
severe.

18 [a]Rev. 4:5 [b]Rev. 6:12 [c]Dan. 12:1; Matt. 24:21
★19 [a]Rev. 11:8; 17:18; 18:10, 18f., 21 [b]Rev. 14:8 [c]Rev. 18:5 [d]Rev. 14:10
20 [a]Rev. 6:14; 20:11
21 [a]Rev. 8:7; 11:19 [b]Rev. 16:9, 11 [c]Ex. 9:18-25

13 *Religious Babylon,* 17:1-18
a *The description,* 17:1-7

17 [a]And one of the [b]seven
angels who had the [c]seven
bowls came and spoke with me,
saying, "Come here, I shall show
you [d]the judgment of the [e]great
harlot who [f]sits on many waters,
2 with whom [a]the kings of
the earth committed *acts of* immorality, and [b]those who dwell
on the earth were [c]made drunk
with the wine of her immorality."
3 And [a]he carried me away
[b]in the Spirit [c]into a wilderness;
and I saw a woman sitting on a
[d]scarlet beast, full of [e]blasphe-
mous names, having [f]seven heads
and ten horns.
4 And the woman [a]was
clothed in purple and scarlet, and
adorned with gold and precious
stones and pearls, having in her
hand [b]a gold cup full of abominations and of the unclean things of
her immorality,
5 and upon her forehead a
name *was* written, a [a]mystery,
"[b]BABYLON THE GREAT, THE
MOTHER OF HARLOTS AND
OF [c]THE ABOMINATIONS OF
THE EARTH."
6 And I saw the woman
drunk with the [a]blood of the
saints, and with the blood of the
witnesses of Jesus. And when I
saw her, I wondered greatly.
7 And the angel said to me,
"Why do you wonder? I shall tell
you the [a]mystery of the woman
and of the beast that carries her,
which has the [b]seven heads and
the ten horns.

1 [a]Rev. 1:1; 21:9 [b]Rev. 15:1 [c]Rev. 15:7 [d]Rev. 16:19 [e]Is. 1:21; Jer. 2:20; Nah. 3:4; Rev. 17:5, 15f.; 19:2 [f]Jer. 51:13; Rev. 17:15
2 [a]Rev. 2:22; 18:3, 9 [b]Rev. 3:10; 17:8 [c]Rev. 14:8
3 [a]Rev. 21:10 [b]Rev. 1:10 [c]Rev. 12:6, 14; 21:10 [d]Matt. 27:28; Rev. 18:12, 16 [e]Rev. 13:1 [f]Rev. 12:3; 17:7, 9, 12, 16
4 [a]Ezek. 28:13; Rev. 18:12, 16 [b]Jer. 51:7; Rev. 18:6
★5 [a]2 Thess. 2:7; Rev. 1:20; 17:7 [b]Rev. 14:8; 16:19 [c]Rev. 17:2
6 [a]Rev. 16:6
7 [a]2 Thess. 2:7; Rev. 1:20; 17:5 [b]Rev. 17:3

b *The interpretation,* 17:8-18

8 "The beast that you saw
[a]was and is not, and is about to
[b]come up out of the [c]abyss and to
[d]go to destruction. And [e]those
who dwell on the earth will [f]won-
der, [g]whose name has not been
written in the book of life [h]from
the foundation of the world,
when they see the beast, that [a]he
was and is not and will come.
9 "[a]Here is the mind which
has wisdom. The [b]seven heads are
seven mountains on which the
woman sits,
10 and they are seven [a]kings;
five have fallen, one is, the other

★8 [a]Rev. 13:3, 12, 14; 17:11 [b]Rev. 11:7; 13:1 [c]Rev. 9:1; 13:1 [d]Rev. 13:10; 17:11 [e]Rev. 3:10 [f]Rev. 13:3 [g]Rev. 3:5 [h]Matt. 25:34; Rev. 13:8
9 [a]Rev. 13:18 [b]Rev. 17:3
10 [a]Rev. 10:11

16:19 *the great city.* Either Jerusalem (11:8; cf. Zech. 14:4) or Babylon (Rev. 18:2).

17:5 *Babylon the Great.* Though the famous city of Babylon was on the Euphrates River, the name here seems to be a symbolic reference to Rome (see v. 9 and 1 Pet. 5:13). In chapter 17 Babylon represents the false religious system that will center in Rome during the tribulation period. In chapter 18 it represents more the political and commercial aspect of the revived Roman Empire headed by Antichrist. Thus the term stands both for a city and for a system (religious and commercial) related to the city (much like "Wall Street," which is both a place and a system). For other references to Babylon see Gen. 10:10; 11:9 ("Babel"); Isa. 13:19-20; Jer. 50-51. *mother of harlots.* The false religious system is unfaithful to the Lord and thus is described as a harlot (vv. 1, 15-16).

17:8 *is about to come up out of the abyss.* See 11:7. *and to go to destruction.* See 19:20.

has not yet come; and when he comes, he must remain a little while.

11 "And the beast which [a]was and is not, is himself also an eighth, and is *one* of the seven, and he [b]goes to destruction.

11 [a]Rev. 13:3, 12, 14; 17:8 [b]Rev. 13:10; 17:8

12 "And the [a]ten horns which you saw are ten kings, who have not yet received a kingdom, but they receive authority as kings with the beast [b]for one hour.

★12 [a]Rev. 12:3; 13:1; 17:16 [b]Rev. 18:10, 17, 19

13 "These have [a]one purpose and they give their power and authority to the beast.

13 [a]Rev. 17:17

14 "These will wage [a]war against the Lamb, and the Lamb will [b]overcome them, because He is [c]Lord of lords and [c]King of kings, and [d]those who are with Him *are the* [e]called and chosen and faithful."

14 [a]Rev. 16:14 [b]Rev. 3:21 [c]1 Tim. 6:15; Rev. 19:16 [d]Rev. 2:10f. [e]Matt. 22:14

15 And he *said to me, "The [a]waters which you saw where the harlot sits, are [b]peoples and multitudes and nations and tongues.

★15 [a]Is. 8:7; Jer. 47:2; Rev. 17:1 [b]Rev. 5:9

16 "And the [a]ten horns which you saw, and the beast, these will hate the harlot and will make her [b]desolate and [c]naked, and will [d]eat her flesh and will [e]burn her up with fire.

★16 [a]Rev. 17:12 [b]Rev. 18:17, 19 [c]Ezek. 16:37, 39 [d]Rev. 19:18 [e]Rev. 18:8

17 "For [a]God has put it in their hearts to execute His purpose by [b]having a common purpose, and by giving their kingdom to the beast, until the [c]words of God should be fulfilled.

17 [a]2 Cor. 8:16 [b]Rev. 17:13 [c]Rev. 10:7

18 "And the woman whom you saw is [a]the great city, which reigns over the kings of the earth."

18 [a]Rev. 11:8; 16:19

14 Commercial Babylon, 18:1–24

a Announcement, 18:1–3

18 After these things I saw [a]another angel [b]coming down from heaven, having great authority, and the earth was [c]illumined with his glory.

1 [a]Rev. 17:1, 7 [b]Rev. 10:1 [c]Ezek. 43:2

2 And he cried out with a mighty voice, saying, "[a]Fallen, fallen is Babylon the great! And she [b]has become a dwelling place of demons and a prison of every [c]unclean spirit, and a prison of every unclean and hateful bird.

2 [a]Rev. 14:8 [b]Is. 13:21f.; 34:11, 13-15; Jer. 50:39; 51:37; Zeph. 2:14f. [c]Rev. 16:13

3 "For all the nations have drunk of the [a]wine of the passion of her immorality, and [b]the kings of the earth have committed *acts of* immorality with her, and the [c]merchants of the earth have become rich by the wealth of her [d]sensuality."

3 [a]Rev. 14:8 [b]Rev. 17:2; 18:9 [c]Ezek. 27:9-25; Rev. 18:11, 15, 19, 23 [d]1 Tim. 5:11; Rev. 18:7, 9

b Appeal, 18:4–8

4 And I heard another voice from heaven, saying, "[a]Come out of her, my people, that you may not participate in her sins and that you may not receive of her plagues;

★ 4 [a]Is. 52:11; Jer 50:8; 51:6, 9, 45; 2 Cor. 6:17

5 for her sins have [a]piled up as high as heaven, and God has [b]remembered her iniquities.

5 [a]Jer. 51:9 [b]Rev. 16:19

6 "[a]Pay her back even as she has paid, and give back *to her* double according to her deeds; in the [b]cup which she has mixed, mix twice as much for her.

6 [a]Ps. 137:8; Jer. 50:15, 29 [b]Rev. 17:4

7 "[a]To the degree that she glorified herself and [b]lived sensuously, to the same degree give her torment and mourning; for she says in her heart, '[c]I sit *as* a queen and I am not a widow, and will never see mourning.'

7 [a]Ezek. 28:2-8 [b]1 Tim. 5:11; Rev. 18:3, 9 [c]Is. 47:7f.; Zeph. 2:15

8 "For this reason [a]in one day her plagues will come, pestilence and mourning and famine, and she will be [b]burned up with fire; for the Lord God who judges her [c]is strong.

★ 8 [a]Is. 47:9; Jer. 50:31f.; Rev. 18:10 [b]Rev. 17:16 [c]Jer. 50:34; Rev. 11:17f.

17:12 *ten kings.* The 10-nation federation which will form in the west and will be headed by Antichrist (see Dan. 7:23–24 and note on Rev. 13:1). *one hour.* I.e., for one purpose (as in Luke 22:53).

17:15 The apostate church will be ecumenical, or world-wide.

17:16 *these will hate the harlot.* The political power headed by Antichrist will overthrow the false church organization (probably at the mid-point of the tribulation).

18:4 *my people.* God's people are to separate themselves from the Babylonian system (cf. 2 Cor. 6:14–17; 1 John 2:15–17).

18:8 *in one day.* The judgment will be consummated in a single day, as happened once before to Babylon, when it was taken by Darius (Dan. 5:1, 3–5, 30).

c Anguish, 18:9-19

9 "And [a]the kings of the
earth, who committed *acts of* immorality and [b]lived sensuously
with her, will [c]weep and lament
over her when they [d]see the
smoke of her burning,
10 [a]standing at a distance because of the fear of her torment,
saying, '[b]Woe, woe, [c]the great
city, Babylon, the strong city! For
in [d]one hour your judgment has
come.'
11 "And the [a]merchants of the
earth [b]weep and mourn over her,
because no one buys their cargoes
any more;
12 cargoes of [a]gold and silver
and precious stones and pearls
and fine linen and purple and silk
and scarlet, and every *kind of* citron wood and every article of ivo-
ry and every article *made* from
very costly wood and bronze and
iron and marble,
13 and cinnamon and spice
and incense and perfume and
frankincense and wine and olive
oil and fine flour and wheat and
cattle and sheep, and *cargoes* of
horses and chariots and slaves
and [a]human lives.
14 "And the fruit you long for
has gone from you, and all things
that were luxurious and splendid
have passed away from you and
men will no longer find them.
15 "The [a]merchants of [b]these
things, who became rich from
her, will [c]stand at a distance because of the fear of her torment,
weeping and mourning,
16 saying, '[a]Woe, woe, [b]the
great city, she who [c]was clothed
in fine linen and purple and scarlet, and adorned with gold and
precious stones and pearls;
17 for in [a]one hour such great
wealth has been laid [b]waste!' And
[c]every shipmaster and every pas-
senger and sailor, and as many as
make their living by the sea,
[a]stood at a distance,
18 and were [a]crying out as
they [b]saw the smoke of her burning, saying, '[c]What *city* is like
[d]the great city?'
19 "And they threw [a]dust on
their heads and were crying out,
weeping and mourning, saying,
'[b]Woe, woe, the great city, in
which all who had ships at sea
[c]became rich by her wealth, for in
[b]one hour she has been laid
[d]waste!'

d Acclaim, 18:20-24

20 "[a]Rejoice over her, O
heaven, and you saints and [b]apos-
tles and prophets, because [c]God
has pronounced judgment for you
against her."
21 And a [a]strong angel [b]took
up a stone like a great millstone
and threw it into the sea, saying,
"Thus will Babylon, [c]the great
city, be thrown down with violence, and will not be found any
longer.
22 "And [a]the sound of harpists
and musicians and flute-players
and trumpeters will not be heard
in you any longer; and no crafts-
man of any craft will be found in
you any longer; and the [b]sound of
a mill will not be heard in you
any longer;
23 and the light of a lamp will
not shine in you any longer; and
the [a]voice of the bridegroom and
bride will not be heard in you any
longer; for your [b]merchants were
the great men of the earth, because all the nations were deceived [c]by your sorcery.
24 "And in her was found the
[a]blood of prophets and of saints
and of [b]all who have been slain
on the earth."

9 [a]Rev. 17:2; 18:3 [b]1 Tim. 5:11; Rev. 18:3, 7 [c]Ezek. 26:16f.; 27:35 [d]Rev. 14:11; 18:18; 19:3
10 [a]Rev. 18:15, 17 [b]Rev. 18:16, 19 [c]Rev. 11:8; 16:19; 18:16, 18, 19, 21 [d]Rev. 17:12; 18:8, 17, 19
11 [a]Ezek. 27:9-25; Rev. 18:3, 15, 19, 23 [b]Ezek. 27:27-34
★**12** [a]Ezek. 27:12-22; Rev. 17:4
13 [a]Ezek. 27:13; 1 Chr. 5:21 marg.; 1 Tim. 1:10
15 [a]Rev. 18:3 [b]Rev. 18:12, 13 [c]Rev. 18:10
16 [a]Rev. 18:10, 19 [b]Rev. 18:10, 18, 19, 21 [c]Rev. 17:4
17 [a]Rev. 18:10 [b]Rev. 17:16; 18:19 [c]Ezek. 27:28f.
18 [a]Ezek. 27:30 [b]Rev. 18:9 [c]Ezek. 27:32; Rev. 13:4 [d]Rev. 18:10
19 [a]Josh. 7:6; Job 2:12; Lam. 2:10 [b]Rev. 18:10 [c]Rev. 18:3, 15 [d]Rev. 17:16; 18:17
★**20** [a]Jer. 51:48; Rev. 12:12 [b]Luke 11:49f. [c]Rev. 6:10; 18:6ff.; 19:2
21 [a]Rev. 5:2; 10:1 [b]Jer. 51:63f. [c]Rev. 18:10
★**22-23**
22 [a]Is. 24:8; Ezek. 26:13; Matt. 9:23 [b]Eccles. 12:4; Jer. 25:10
23 [a]Jer. 7:34; 16:9 [b]Is. 23:8; Rev. 6:15; 18:3 [c]Nah. 3:4; Rev. 9:21
24 [a]Rev. 16:6; 17:6 [b]Matt. 23:35

18:12 *citron wood.* A dark, hard, and fragrant wood, valued by the Greeks and Romans for use in cabinet making.

18:20 *God has pronounced judgment for you against her.* I.e., God has judged her for her treatment of you. Heaven and the martyrs may now rejoice.

18:22-23 No music, no worker, no machinery, no light, no happiness shall be found in Babylon any more.

15 *The second coming of Christ,* 19:1-21

a *Announcements,* 19:1-10

★ 1 [a]Jer. 51:48; Rev. 11:15; 19:6 [b]Ps. 104:35 marg.; Rev. 19:3, 4, 6 [c]Rev. 7:10 [d]Rev. 4:11

19 After these things I heard, as it were, a [a]loud voice of a great multitude in heaven, saying,

"[b]Hallelujah! [c]Salvation and [d]glory and power belong to our God;

2 [a]Ps. 19:9 [b]Rev. 6:10 [c]Rev. 16:7 [d]Rev. 17:1 [e]Deut. 32:43; 2 Kin. 9:7; Rev. 16:6; 18:20

2 [a]BECAUSE HIS [b]JUDGMENTS ARE [c]TRUE AND RIGHTEOUS; for He has judged the [d]great harlot who was corrupting the earth with her immorality, and HE HAS [e]AVENGED THE BLOOD OF HIS BOND-SERVANTS ON HER."

3 [a]Ps. 104:35; Is. 34:10; Rev. 19:1, 4, 6 [b]Rev. 14:11

3 And a second time they said, "[a]HALLELUJAH! HER [b]SMOKE RISES UP FOREVER AND EVER."

4 [a]Rev. 4:4, 10 [b]Rev. 4:6 [c]Rev. 4:10 [d]Ps. 106:48; Rev. 5:14 [e]Ps. 104:35; Rev. 19:3, 6

4 And the [a]twenty-four elders and the [b]four living creatures [c]fell down and worshiped God who sits on the throne saying, "[d]Amen. [e]Hallelujah!"

5 [a]Ps. 115:13; 134:1; 135:1 [b]Rev. 11:18

5 And a voice came from the throne, saying,

"[a]GIVE PRAISE TO OUR GOD, ALL YOU HIS BOND-SERVANTS, [b]YOU WHO FEAR HIM, THE SMALL AND THE GREAT."

6 [a]Jer. 51:48; Rev. 11:15; 19:1 [b]Rev. 1:15 [c]Rev. 6:1 [d]Rev. 1:8

6 And I heard, as it were, [a]the voice of a great multitude and as [b]the sound of many waters and as the [c]sound of mighty peals of thunder, saying,

"[a]Hallelujah! For the [d]Lord our God, the Almighty, reigns.

7 [a]Rev. 11:13 [b]Matt. 22:2; 25:10; Luke 12:36; John 3:29; Eph. 5:23, 32; Rev. 19:9 [c]Matt. 1:20; Rev. 21:2, 9

7 "Let us rejoice and be glad and [a]give the glory to Him, for [b]the marriage of the Lamb has come and His [c]bride has made herself ready."

★ 8 [a]Rev. 15:6; 19:14 [b]Rev. 15:4

8 And it was given to her to clothe herself in [a]fine linen, bright *and* clean; for the fine linen is the [b]righteous acts of the saints.

9 [a]Rev. 17:1; 19:10 [b]Rev. 1:19 [c]Luke 14:15; 22:16 [d]Rev. 17:17; 21:5; 22:6

9 And [a]he *said to me, "[b]Write, '[c]Blessed are those who are invited to the marriage supper of the Lamb.'" And he *said to me, "[d]These are true words of God."

★10 [a]Rev. 22:8 [b]Acts 10:26; Rev. 22:9 [c]Rev. 1:1f. [d]Rev. 12:17

10 And [a]I fell at his feet to worship him. [b]And he *said to me, "Do not do that; I am a [c]fellow servant of yours and your brethren who [d]hold the testimony of Jesus; worship God. For the testimony of Jesus is the spirit of prophecy."

b *Advent of Christ,* 19:11-16

★11 [a]John 1:51; Rev. 4:1 [b]Rev. 6:2; 19:19, 21 [c]Rev. 3:14 [d]Is. 11:4

11 And I saw [a]heaven opened; and behold, a [b]white horse, and He who sat upon it *is* called [c]Faithful and True; and in [d]righteousness He judges and wages war.

★12 [a]Rev. 1:14 [b]Rev. 6:2; 12:3 [c]Rev. 2:17; 19:16

12 And His [a]eyes *are* a flame of fire, and upon His head *are* many [b]diadems; and He has a [c]name written *upon Him* which no one knows except Himself.

★13 [a]Is. 63:3 [b]John 1:1

13 And *He is* clothed with a [a]robe dipped in blood; and His name is called [b]The Word of God.

14 [a]Rev. 19:8 [b]Rev. 3:4; 19:8

14 And the armies which are in heaven, clothed in [a]fine linen, [b]white *and* clean, were following Him on white horses.

★15 [a]Rev. 1:16; 19:21 [b]Is. 11:4; 2 Thess. 2:8 [c]Rev. 2:27 [d]Rev. 14:19, 20

15 And [a]from His mouth comes a sharp sword, so that

19:1 *Hallelujah* = praise the Lord. The word occurs only in this chapter in the entire N.T. It does appear as a brief doxology in several Psalms, e.g., 150:1, 6.

19:8 *the righteous acts of the saints.* The good works of believers will constitute the wedding garment when the congregation of the faithful are joined to Him in marriage (cf. 2 Cor. 11:2; Eph. 5:26-27).

19:10 *Do not do that.* Men are not to worship angels, only God. *For the testimony of Jesus is the spirit of prophecy.* Prophecy is designed to unfold the loveliness of Jesus.

19:11 *heaven opened.* This is the second coming of Christ to the earth—during the war of Armageddon, in which He will be the Victor and in which all who oppose Him will be slain (vv. 19, 21). See notes on 14:20; 16:14, 16. *Faithful and True.* These terms have been used previously of Christ (1:5; 3:7).

19:12 *His eyes are a flame of fire.* See 1:14; 2:18. *a name written . . . which no one knows.* This is perhaps the same name He will write on the overcomer (2:17; 3:12).

19:13 *The Word.* This name, applied here to Christ, is found only in the writings of John (cf. John 1:1, 14; 1 John 1:1).

19:15 *wine press.* It consisted of two receptacles, or vats, placed at different levels, in the upper one of which the grapes were trodden, while the lower one received the juice (cf. 14:20).

[b]with it He may smite the nations;
and He will [c]rule them with a rod
of iron; and [d]He treads the wine
press of the fierce wrath of God,
the Almighty.

16 [a]Rev. 2:17; 19:12 [b]Rev. 17:14

16 And on His robe and on
His thigh He has [a]a name written,
"[b]KING OF KINGS, AND LORD
OF LORDS."

c *Armageddon,* 19:17-21

★17-18 17 [a]Rev. 19:21 [b]Rev. 8:13 [c]1 Sam. 17:44; Jer. 12:9; Ezek. 39:17 [d]Is. 34:6; Jer. 46:10

17 And I saw an angel standing in the sun; and he cried out
with a loud voice, saying to [a]all
the birds which fly in [b]midheav-
en, "[c]Come, assemble for the
[d]great supper of God;

18 [a]Ezek. 39:18-20 [b]Rev. 6:15 [c]Rev. 11:18; 13:16; 19:5

18 in order that you may [a]eat
the flesh of kings and the flesh
of commanders and the flesh of
mighty men and the flesh of
horses and of those who sit on
them and the flesh of all men,
[b]both free men and slaves, and
[c]small and great."

19 [a]Rev. 11:7; 13:1 [b]Rev. 16:14, 16 [c]Rev. 19:11, 21

19 And I saw [a]the beast and
[b]the kings of the earth and their
armies, assembled to make war
against Him who [c]sat upon the
horse, and against His army.

20 [a]Rev. 16:13 [b]Rev. 13:13 [c]Rev. 13:12 [d]Rev. 13:14 [e]Rev. 13:16f. [f]Rev. 13:15 [12] [g]Rev. 20:10, 14f.; 21:8 [h]Is. 30:33; Dan. 7:11; Rev. 14:10

20 And the beast was seized,
and with him the [a]false prophet
who [b]performed the signs [c]in his
presence, by which he [d]deceived
those who had received the [e]mark
of the beast and those who [f]wor-
shiped his image; these two were
thrown alive into the [g]lake of
[h]fire which burns with brimstone.

21 [a]Rev. 19:15 [b]Rev. 19:11, 19 [c]Rev. 19:17

21 And the rest were killed
with the sword which [a]came from
the mouth of Him who [b]sat upon
the horse, and [c]all the birds were
filled with their flesh.

B **The Millennium,** 20:1-15

1 ***Satan bound,*** 20:1-3

1 [a]Rev. 10:1 [b]Rev. 1:18; 9:1

20 And I saw [a]an angel coming down from heaven,
having the [b]key of the abyss and
a great chain in his hand.

★ 2 [a]Rev. 12:9 [b]Is. 24:22; 2 Pet. 2:4; Jude 6

2 And he laid hold of the
[a]dragon, the serpent of old, who
is the devil and Satan, and
[b]bound him for a thousand years,

3 [a]Rev. 20:1 [b]Dan. 6:17; Matt. 27:66 [c]Rev. 12:9; 20:8, 10

3 and threw him into the
[a]abyss, and shut *it* and [b]sealed *it*
over him, so that he should [c]not
deceive the nations any longer,
until the thousand years were
completed; after these things he
must be released for a short time.

2 ***Saints resurrected,*** 20:4-6

★ 4 [a]Dan. 7:9 [b]Matt. 19:28; Rev. 3:21 [c]Dan. 7:22; 1 Cor. 6:2 [d]Rev. 6:9 [e]Rev. 1:9 [f]Rev. 13:15 [12] [g]Rev. 13:16f. [h]Is. 26:14; John 14:19 [i]Rev. 3:21; 5:10; 20:6; 22:5

4 And I saw [a]thrones, and
[b]they sat upon them, and [c]judg-
ment was given to them. And I
saw [d]the souls of those who had
been [d]beheaded because of the
[e]testimony of Jesus and because
of the word of God, and those
who had not [f]worshiped the beast
or his image, and had not received
the [g]mark upon their forehead
and upon their hand; and they
[h]came to life and [i]reigned with
Christ for a thousand years.

★ 5 [a]Luke 14:14; Phil. 3:11; 1 Thess. 4:16

5 The rest of the dead did
not come to life until the thousand years were completed. [a]This
is the first resurrection.

6 [a]Rev. 14:13 [b]Rev. 2:11; 20:14 [c]Rev. 1:6 [d]Rev. 3:21; 5:10; 20:4; 22:5

6 [a]Blessed and holy is the
one who has a part in the first res-

19:17-18 So great will be the slaughter in the war of Armageddon that an angel will call together the fowls of heaven to eat the flesh of those who fall in battle.

20:2 *a thousand years.* Since the Latin equivalent for these words is "millennium," this period of time is called the millennium. It is the time when Christ shall reign on this earth (Isa. 2:3; Dan. 7:14; Zech. 14:9). Satan will not be free to work (Rev. 20:2), righteousness will flourish (Isa. 11:3-5), peace will be universal (Isa. 2:4), and the productivity of the earth will be greatly increased (Isa. 35:1-2). At the conclusion of the time Satan will be loosed to make one final attempt to overthrow Christ, but without success (Rev. 20:7-9).

20:4 *the souls of those who had been beheaded because of the testimony of Jesus.* These are the martyrs of the tribulation days who will share the joys of the millennial kingdom.

20:5 *The rest of the dead.* The wicked dead will be raised and judged after the millennium. *the first resurrection.* Refers back to the end of v. 4. This resurrection includes all the righteous (the resurrection of life, John 5:29, and the resurrection of the righteous, Luke 14:14), who will be raised before the millennium begins.

urrection; over these the [b]second
death has no power, but they will
be [c]priests of God and of Christ
and will [d]reign with Him for a
thousand years.

3 Sinners rebelling, 20:7-9

7 [a]Rev. 20:2

★ 8 [a]Rev. 12:9; 20:3, 10 [b]Rev. 7:1 [c]Ezek. 38:2; 39:1, 6 [d]Rev. 16:14 [e]Heb. 11:12

9 [a]Ezek. 38:9, 16; Hab. 1:6 [b]Deut. 23:14 [c]Ps. 87:2 [d]Ezek. 38:22; 39:6; Rev. 13:13

7 And when the thousand
years are completed, Satan will be
[a]released from his prison,
8 and will come out to [a]de-
ceive the nations which are in the
[b]four corners of the earth, [c]Gog
and Magog, to [d]gather them together for the war; the number of
them is like the [e]sand of the seashore.
9 And they [a]came up on the
broad plain of the earth and surrounded the [b]camp of the saints
and the [c]beloved city, and [d]fire
came down from heaven and devoured them.

4 Satan doomed, 20:10

10 [a]Rev. 20:2f. [b]Rev. 19:20; 20:14, 15 [c]Rev. 16:13 [d]Rev. 14:10f.

10 And [a]the devil who [a]de-
ceived them was thrown into the
[b]lake of fire and brimstone, where
the [c]beast and the [c]false prophet
are also; and they will be [d]tor-
mented day and night forever and
ever.

5 Sinners judged, 20:11-15

★11-15
11 [a]Rev. 4:2 [b]Rev. 6:14; 21:1 [c]Dan. 2:35; Rev. 12:8
★12 [a]Rev. 11:18 [b]Jer. 17:1, 10; Dan. 7:10 [c]Rev. 3:5; 20:15 [d]Rev. 11:18 [e]Matt. 16:27; Rev. 2:23; 20:13

11 And I saw a great white
[a]throne and Him who sat upon it,
from whose presence [b]earth and
heaven fled away, and [c]no place
was found for them.
12 And I saw the dead, the
[a]great and the small, standing before the throne, and [b]books were
opened; and another book was
opened, which is [c]*the book* of life;
and the dead [d]were judged from
the things which were written in
the books, [e]according to their
deeds.
13 And the sea gave up the
dead which were in it, and [a]death
and Hades [b]gave up the dead
which were in them; and they
were judged, every one *of them*
[c]according to their deeds.
14 And [a]death and Hades
were thrown into [b]the lake of fire.
This is the [c]second death, the lake
of fire.
15 And if anyone's name was
not found written in [a]the book of
life, he was thrown into the lake
of fire.

13 [a]1 Cor. 15:26; Rev. 1:18; 6:8; 21:4 [b]Is. 26:19 [c]Matt. 16:27; Rev. 2:23; 20:12

14 [a]1 Cor. 15:26; Rev. 1:18; 6:8; 21:4 [b]Rev. 19:20; 20:10, 15 [c]Rev. 20:6

15 [a]Rev. 20:12; 3:5

C The Eternal State, 21:1-22:5

1 Descent of New Jerusalem, 21:1-8

★ 1 [a]Is. 65:17; 66:22; 2 Pet. 3:13 [b]2 Pet. 3:10; Rev. 20:11

★ 2 [a]Rev. 11:2; 21:10; 22:19 [b]Rev. 3:12; 21:10 [c]Heb. 11:10, 16; Rev. 21:10 [d]Is. 61:10; Rev. 19:7; 21:9; 22:17

3 [a]Lev. 26:11f.; Ezek. 37:27; 48:35; Heb. 8:2; Rev. 7:15 [b]John 14:23; 2 Cor. 6:16

21 And I saw [a]a new heaven
and a new earth; for [b]the
first heaven and the first earth
passed away, and there is no
longer *any* sea.
2 And I saw [a]the holy city,
[b]new Jerusalem, [c]coming down
out of heaven from God, [d]made
ready as a bride adorned for her
husband.
3 And I heard a loud voice
from the throne, saying, "Behold,
[a]the tabernacle of God is among
men, and He shall [b]dwell among
them, and they shall be His people, and God Himself shall be
among them,

20:8 *Gog and Magog.* Symbolic names for the worldwide enemies of Christ.

20:11-15 Here is pictured the judgment of the unbelieving dead. It occurs at the close of the millennium; it is based on works, in order to show that the punishment is deserved (v. 12, though of course these unsaved people are first of all in this judgment because they rejected Christ as Savior during their lifetimes); and it results in everyone in this judgment being cast into the lake of fire. This is the resurrection of judgment (John 5:29).

20:12 *before the throne.* Upon which Christ sits as Judge (see v. 11; John 5:22, 27).

21:1 *a new heaven and a new earth.* The present creation will be destroyed so that it may be cleansed from all the effects of sin (2 Pet. 3:7, 10, 12).

21:2 *new Jerusalem.* This heavenly city will be the abode of all the saints (Heb. 12:22-24), the bride of Christ (Rev. 21:9-10), and the place Christ is preparing for His people (John 14:2). During the millennium the new Jerusalem (described in detail in Rev. 21:9-22:5) apparently will be suspended over the earth, and it will be the dwelling place of all believers during eternity (as is emphasized in 21:1-8).

4 [a]Rev. 7:17 [b]1 Cor. 15:26; Rev. 20:14 [c]Is. 25:8; 35:10; 51:11; 65:19 [d]2 Cor. 5:17; Heb. 12:27

4 and He shall [a]wipe away
every tear from their eyes; and
[b]there shall no longer be *any*
death; [c]there shall no longer be
any mourning, or crying, or pain;
[d]the first things have passed
away."

5 [a]Rev. 4:9; 20:11 [b]2 Cor. 5:17; Heb. 12:27 [c]Rev. 19:9; 22:6

5 And [a]He who sits on the
throne said, "Behold, I am [b]mak-
ing all things new." And He *said,
"Write, for [c]these words are
faithful and true."

6 [a]Rev. 10:6; 16:17 [b]Rev. 1:8; 22:13 [c]Is. 55:1; John 4:10; Rev. 7:17; 22:17 [d]Rev. 7:17

6 And He said to me, "[a]It is
done. I am the [b]Alpha and the
Omega, the beginning and the
end. [c]I will give to the one who
thirsts from the spring of the [d]wa-
ter of life without cost.

7 [a]Rev. 2:7 [b]2 Sam. 7:14; 2 Cor. 6:16, 18; Rev. 21:3

7 "[a]He who overcomes shall
inherit these things, and [b]I will be
his God and he will be My son.

★ 8 [a]1 Cor. 6:9; Gal. 5:19-21; Rev. 9:21; 21:27; 22:15 [b]Rev. 19:20 [c]Rev. 2:11

8 "[a]But for the cowardly and
unbelieving and abominable and
murderers and immoral persons
and sorcerers and idolaters and all
liars, their part *will be* in [b]the lake
that burns with fire and brimstone, which is the [c]second
death."

2 *Description of the New Jerusalem,* 21:9–27

9 [a]Rev. 17:1 [b]Rev. 15:7 [c]Rev. 15:1 [d]Rev. 17:1 [e]Rev. 19:7; 21:2

9 [a]And one of the seven angels who had the [b]seven bowls
full of the [c]seven last plagues,
came and spoke with me, saying,
"[d]Come here, I shall show you the
[e]bride, the wife of the Lamb."

10 [a]Ezek. 40:2; Rev. 17:3 [b]Rev. 1:10 [c]Rev. 21:2

10 And [a]he carried me away
[b]in the Spirit to a great and high
mountain, and showed me [c]the
holy city, Jerusalem, coming
down out of heaven from God,

★11 [a]Is. 60:1f.; Ezek. 43:2; Rev. 15:8; 21:23; 22:5 [b]Rev. 4:3; 21:18, 19 [c]Rev. 4:6

11 having [a]the glory of God.
Her brilliance was like a very
costly stone, as a [b]stone of [c]crys-
tal-clear jasper.

12 [a]Ezek. 48:31-34 [b]Rev. 21:15, 21, 25; 22:14

12 It had a great and high
wall, [a]with twelve [b]gates, and at
the gates twelve angels; and
names *were* written on them,
which are *those* of the twelve
tribes of the sons of Israel.
13 *There were* three gates on
the east and three gates on the
north and three gates on the
south and three gates on the west.
14 And the wall of the city
had [a]twelve foundation stones,
and on them *were* the twelve
names of the [b]twelve apostles of
the Lamb.

14 [a]Eph. 2:20; Heb. 11:10 [b]Acts 1:26

15 And the one who spoke
with me had a gold measuring
[a]rod to measure the city, and its
[b]gates and its wall.

15 [a]Rev. 11:1 [b]Rev. 21:12, 21, 25

16 And the city is laid out as a
square, and its length is as great
as the width; and he measured
the city with the rod, fifteen hundred miles; its length and width
and height are equal.
17 And he measured its wall,
seventy-two yards, *according to*
[a]human measurements, which are
also [b]angelic *measurements.*

17 [a]Deut. 3:11; Rev. 13:18 [b]Rev. 21:9

18 And the material of the
wall was [a]jasper; and the city was
[b]pure gold, like clear [c]glass.

18 [a]Rev. 21:11 [b]Rev. 21:21 [c]Rev. 4:6

19 [a]The foundation stones of
the city wall were adorned with
every kind of precious stone. The
first foundation stone was [b]jasper;
the second, sapphire; the third,
chalcedony; the fourth, [c]emerald;
20 the fifth, sardonyx; the
sixth, [a]sardius; the seventh, chrysolite; the eighth, beryl; the ninth,
topaz; the tenth, chrysoprase; the
eleventh, jacinth; the twelfth,
amethyst.

★19-20
19 [a]Ex. 28:17-20; Is. 54:11f.; Ezek. 28:13; Rev. 21:19, 20 [b]Rev. 21:11 [c]Rev. 4:3
20 [a]Rev. 4:3

21 And the twelve [a]gates
were twelve [b]pearls; each one of
the gates was a single pearl. And
the street of the city was [c]pure
gold, like transparent [d]glass.

21 [a]Rev. 21:12, 15, 25 [b]Is. 54:12; Rev. 17:4 [c]Rev. 21:18 [d]Rev. 4:6

22 And I saw [a]no temple in it,
for the [b]Lord God, the Almighty,
and the [c]Lamb, are its temple.

22 [a]Matt. 24:2; John 4:21 [b]Rev. 1:8 [c]Rev. 5:6; 7:17; 14:4

23 And the city [a]has no need
of the sun or of the moon to shine
upon it, for [b]the glory of God has

23 [a]Is. 24:23; 60:19, 20; Rev. 21:25; 22:5 [b]Rev. 21:11 [c]Rev. 5:6; 7:17; 14:4

21:8 *brimstone* = sulphur.
21:11 *jasper.* See note on 4:3.
21:19-20 *chalcedony.* Probably a greenish-blue agate stone. (The exact composition and color of all these precious stones is not known.) *sardonyx.* Red and white stone. *sardius.* Bright red. *chrysolite.* Golden in color. *beryl.* Sea green. *topaz.* Yellow-green. *chrysoprase.* Apple-green. *jacinth.* Blue. *amethyst.* Purple.

illumined it, and its lamp *is* the
[c]Lamb.
24 And [a]the nations shall
walk by its light, and the [b]kings
of the earth shall bring their glory
into it.
25 And in the daytime (for
[a]there shall be no night there) [b]its
gates [c]shall never be closed;
26 and [a]they shall bring the
glory and the honor of the nations
into it;
27 and nothing unclean and
no one who practices abomination and lying, [a]shall ever come
into it, but only those whose
names are [b]written in the Lamb's
book of life.

★24 [a]Is. 60:3, 5; Rev. 22:2 [b]Ps. 72:10f.; Is. 49:23; 60:16; Rev. 21:26
25 [a]Zech. 14:7; Rev. 21:23; 22:5 [b]Rev. 21:12, 15 [c]Is. 60:11
26 [a]Ps. 72:10f.; Is. 49:23; 60:16
27 [a]Is. 52:1; Ezek. 44:9; Zech. 14:21; Rev. 22:14f. [b]Rev. 3:5

3 Delights of the New Jerusalem, 22:1-5

22 And [a]he showed me a
[b]river of the [c]water of life,
clear [d]as crystal, coming from the
throne of God and of the Lamb,
2 in the middle of [a]its street.
And [b]on either side of the river
was [c]the tree of life, bearing
twelve *kinds of* fruit, yielding its
fruit every month; and the [b]leaves
of the tree were for the healing of
the nations.
3 And [a]there shall no longer
be any curse; and [b]the throne of
God and of the Lamb shall be in
it, and His bond-servants shall
[c]serve Him;
4 and they shall [a]see His
face, and His [b]name *shall be* on
their [c]foreheads.
5 And [a]there shall no longer
be *any* night; and they shall not
have need [b]of the light of a lamp
nor the light of the sun, because
the Lord God shall illumine them;
and they shall [c]reign forever and
ever.

★ 1-2
1 [a]Rev. 1:1; 21:9; 22:6 [b]Ps. 46:4; Ezek. 47:1 [c]Rev. 7:17; 22:17 [d]Rev. 4:6
2 [a]Rev. 21:21 [b]Ezek. 47:12 [c]Rev. 2:7; 22:14, 19
3 [a]Zech. 14:11 [b]Rev. 21:3, 23 [c]Rev. 7:15
4 [a]Ps. 17:15; 42:2; Matt. 5:8 [b]Rev. 14:1 [c]Rev. 7:3
5 [a]Zech. 14:7; Rev. 21:25 [b]Rev. 21:23 [c]Dan. 7:18, 27; Matt. 19:28; Rom. 5:17; Rev. 20:4

V EPILOGUE, 22:6-21
A Words of Comfort, 22:6-17

6 And [a]he said to me,
"[b]These words are faithful and
true"; and the Lord, the [c]God of
the spirits of the prophets, [d]sent
His angel to show to His bond-
servants the things which must
shortly take place.
7 "And behold, [a]I am coming
quickly. [b]Blessed is he who heeds
[c]the words of the prophecy of this
book."
8 And [a]I, John, am the one
who heard and saw these things.
And when I heard and saw, [b]I fell
down to worship at the feet of the
angel who showed me these
things.
9 And [a]he *said to me, "Do
not do that; I am a [b]fellow servant
of yours and of your brethren the
prophets and of those who heed
the words of [c]this book; worship
God."
10 And he *said to me, "[a]Do
not seal up [b]the words of the
prophecy of this book, [c]for the
time is near.
11 "[a]Let the one who does
wrong, still do wrong; and let the
one who is filthy, still be filthy;
and let the one who is righteous,
still practice righteousness; and
let the one who is holy, still keep
himself holy.
12 "Behold, [a]I am coming
quickly, and My [b]reward is with
Me, [c]to render to every man according to what he has done.
13 "I am the [a]Alpha and the
Omega, [b]the first and the last,
[c]the beginning and the end."
14 Blessed are those who
[a]wash their robes, that they may
have the right to [b]the tree of life,
and may [c]enter by the [d]gates into
the city.

6 [a]Rev. 1:1; 21:9 [b]Rev. 19:9; 21:5 [c]1 Cor. 14:32; Heb. 12:9 [d]Rev. 1:1; 22:16
7 [a]Rev. 1:3; 3:3, 11; 16:15; 22:12, 20 [b]Rev. 1:3; 16:15 [c]Rev. 1:11; 22:9, 10, 18f.
★ 8-9
8 [a]Rev. 1:1 [b]Rev. 19:10
9 [a]Rev. 19:10 [b]Rev. 1:1 [c]Rev. 1:11; 22:10, 18f.
10 [a]Dan. 8:26; Rev. 10:4 [b]Rev. 1:11; 22:9, 18f. [c]Rev. 1:3
★11 [a]Ezek. 3:27; Dan. 12:10
12 [a]Rev. 22:7 [b]Is. 40:10; 62:11 [c]Jer. 17:10; Matt. 16:27; Rev. 2:23
13 [a]Rev. 1:8 [b]Rev. 1:17 [c]Rev. 21:6
★14 [a]Rev. 7:14 [b]Rev. 22:2 [c]Rev. 21:27 [d]Rev. 21:12

21:24 *the nations.* The nations that exist on earth during the millennium.

22:1-2 These descriptive phrases indicate fullness of life and continuous blessing in the new Jerusalem.

22:8-9 Again John is commanded not to worship angels (see 19:10).

22:11 When Christ comes there will be no more opportunity for a man to change his destiny. What he is then he will be forever.

22:14 *Blessed are those who wash their robes.* I.e., believers.

★15 [a]Matt. 8:12; 1 Cor. 6:9f.; Gal. 5:19ff.; Rev. 21:8 [b]Deut. 23:18; Matt. 7:6; Phil. 3:2
16 [a]Rev. 1:1 [b]Rev. 1:1; 22:6 [c]Rev. 1:4, 11; 3:22 [d]Rev. 5:5 [e]Matt. 1:1 [f]Matt. 2:2; Rev. 2:28
17 [a]Rev. 2:7; 14:13 [b]Rev. 21:2, 9 [c]Rev. 21:6 [d]Rev. 7:17; 22:1

15 [a]Outside are the [b]dogs and
the sorcerers and the immoral
persons and the murderers and
the idolaters, and everyone who
loves and practices lying.
16 "[a]I, Jesus, have sent [b]My
angel to testify to you these
things [c]for the churches. I am
[d]the root and the [e]offspring of
David, the bright [f]morning star."
17 And the [a]Spirit and the
[b]bride say, "Come." And let the
one who hears say, "Come." And
[c]let the one who is thirsty come;
let the one who wishes take the
[d]water of life without cost.

★18 [a]Rev. 22:7 [b]Deut. 4:2; 12:32; Prov. 30:6 [c]Rev. 15:6-16, 21 [d]Rev. 22:7

B Words of Warning, 22:18–19

18 I testify to everyone who
hears [a]the words of the prophecy
of this book: if anyone [b]adds to
them, God shall add to him [c]the
plagues which are written in [d]this
book;
19 and if anyone [a]takes away
from the [b]words of the book of
this prophecy, God shall take
away his part from [c]the tree of
life and from the holy city,
[d]which are written in this book.

19 [a]Deut. 4:2; 12:32; Prov. 30:6 [b]Rev. 22:7 [c]Rev. 22:2 [d]Rev. 21:10-22:5

C Closing Benediction, 22:20–21

20 He who [a]testifies to these
things says, "Yes, [b]I am coming
quickly." Amen. [c]Come, Lord
Jesus.
21 [a]The grace of the Lord
Jesus be with all. Amen.

★20 [a]Rev. 1:2 [b]Rev. 22:7 [c]1 Cor. 16:22 marg.
21 [a]Rom. 16:20

22:15 *dogs.* Not animals, but people of low character (cf. Phil. 3:2).

22:18 For similar O.T. warnings against additions or omissions see Deut. 4:2; 12:32; Prov. 30:6.

22:20 *Yes, I am coming quickly.* The third occurrence of this promise (see vv. 7, 12). The believer's reaction is, "Do come, quickly, Lord Jesus!"

HARMONY OF THE GOSPELS*

Contents.	*Matt.*	*Mark*	*Luke*	*John*
Incidents of the Birth and Boyhood of Jesus Christ Till He was Twelve Years of Age.				
1. Introduction,.			1: 1–4	1: 1–14
2. The genealogies—Matthew the legal, Luke the natural descent, ...	1: 1–17		3: 23–38	
3. Birth of John announced to Zacharias, ...			1: 5–25	
4. Birth of Jesus announced to Mary at Nazareth six months later, ...			1: 26–38	
5. Mary's visit to Elizabeth, and her hymn,. . . .			1: 39–56	
6. John the Baptist's birth, and Zacharias' hymn,			1: 57–80	
7. The angel appears to Joseph, ...	1: 18–25			
8. Birth of Jesus at Bethlehem,.			2: 1–7	
9. Angelic announcement to the shepherds. (In spring flocks are watched by night.), ...			2: 8–20	
10. Circumcision of Jesus, and presentation in the temple, where He is welcomed by Simeon and Anna, 41 days after nativity (Lev. 12:3, 4)			2: 21–38	
11. Visit of the Magi, in the house—no longer in manger; epiphany to Gentiles,.	2: 1–12			
12. Flight into Egypt, ...	2: 13–15			
13. Herod's murder of the innocents,.	2: 16–18			
14. Return to Nazareth, fearing Archelaus' cruelty, shown from the first,.	2: 19–23		2: 39, 40	
15. Jesus, at the age of twelve, goes up to the Passover, and is found with the doctors in the temple; then follows His 18 silent years . . .			2: 41–52	
Inauguration of Christ's Public Ministry.				
16. Preparatory preaching of John the Baptist,. . .	3: 1–12	1: 1–8	3: 1–18	
17. Christ's baptism in river Jordan at Perean Bethany,.	3: 13–17	1: 9–11	3: 21–23	
18. The Spirit leads Him to desert of Judea, where Satan tempts Him, ...	4: 1–11	1: 12, 13	4: 1–13	
19. The Baptist's witness to Jesus,.				1: 15–34
20. Two of John's disciples follow Jesus; Andrew brings his brother Simon, ...				1: 35–42
21. Christ returns to Galilee; finds Philip, who in turn finds Nathanael,.				1: 43–51
22. First miracle at Cana, and visit to Capernaum,				2: 1–12
Public Ministry of Christ from the First Passover to the Second.				
23. Christ goes up to Jerusalem for the Passover, and, with a scourge, expels the sellers and money-changers from the temple; works miracles, convincing many, ...				2: 13–25
24. Nicodemus is convinced; has a night interview with Jesus, ...				3: 1–21
25. Christ leaves Jerusalem, stays eight months in N. E. Judea, and His disciples baptize.				3: 22, 4: 2
26. John, baptizing in Ænon, again witnesses to the Christ, ...				3: 23–36
27. Imprisonment of John, ...			3: 19, 20	

*Based on the harmony of A. R. Fausset.

	Contents.	*Matt.*	*Mark*	*Luke*	*John*
28.	John being cast into prison, Jesus leaves Judea for Galilee; John beheaded—not till A.D. 28 (Matt. 14:12-21), ...	4: 12	1: 14	4: 14, 15	4: 1-3
29.	Passing through Samaria, He converts a woman of Sychar, and through her many of the Samaritans, four months before harvest,				4: 4-42
30.	Commencement of His public ministry in Galilee, ...	4: 17	1: 14, 15	4: 14, 15	4: 43-45
31.	Visiting Cana again, He heals a nobleman's son sick at Capernaum, ...				4: 46-54
	From His Second to His Third Passover.				
32.	Returns to Jerusalem at the Passover, *"the* feast." His second Passover. From this to the third, His main Galilean ministry. Jesus cures an infirm man at Bethesda pool on the Sabbath. The Jews seek to kill Him for declaring Himself one with the Father in working,. . .				5: 1-47
33.	Returns to Galilee. A chasm between the earlier visit to Nazareth, while fresh from the Spirit's baptism, and this later visit to Galilee, and His sermon at Nazareth, as Luke 4:23 proves, ...			4: 14-30	
34.	He settles at Capernaum, and teaches in public,.	4: 13-17	1: 21, 22	4: 31-32	
35.	Miraculous catch of fishes; call of Simon, Andrew, James, and John, ...	4: 18-22	1: 16-20	5: 1-11	
36.	Jesus casts out a demon, ...		1: 23-28	4: 33-37	
37.	Cure of Simon's wife's mother, and other sick people, ...	8: 14-17	1: 29-34	4: 38-41	
38.	Circuit with the disciples through Galilee, . . .	4: 23-25	1: 35-39	4: 42-44	
39.	He heals a leper, and, shunning popularity, retires to the desert,.	8: 1-4	1: 40-45	5: 12-16	
40.	Returning to Capernaum, He heals a palsied man let down through the roof,.	9: 2-8	2: 1-12	5: 17-26	
41.	Call of Matthew, the feast, and discourse at his house—the new garment and new wine,. . .	9: 9-13	2: 13-17	5: 27-32	
42.	He answers objections as to the reason of His not fasting,.	9: 14-17	2: 18-22	5: 33-39	
43.	Returning towards Galilee, the disciples pluck grain on the Sabbath,.	12: 1-8	2: 23-28	6: 1-5	
44.	Healing a man's withered hand on the Sabbath, the Pharisees plot His death with the Herodians, ...	12: 9-14	3: 1-6	6: 6-11	
45.	He withdraws to the lake and heals many, . .	12: 15-21	3: 7-12		
46.	Ascending a hill west of the lake, after prayer all night, He chooses the Twelve; His charge,.	10: 1-42	3: 13-19	6: 12-19	
47.	Sermon on the mount, on the level below the hilltop, ...	5: 1-8:1		6: 20-49	
48.	Healing of the centurion's servant, ...	8: 5-13		7: 1-10	
49.	Raising of the widow's son at Nain, ...			7: 11-17	
50.	John Baptist's mission of inquiry from his dungeon at Machærus, ...	11: 2-19		7: 18-35	
51.	Jesus upbraids Chorazin, Bethsaida, and Capernaum, and invites the heavy-laden,.	11: 20-30			
52.	Anointing of His feet, in the Pharisee Simon's house, by the sinful but forgiven woman, . .			7: 36-50	
53.	Short circuit of two days' preaching through Galilee; women ministering,.			8: 1-3	
54.	Returning to Capernaum, He heals a blind and dumb demoniac, the Pharisees attributing the miracle to Beelzebub, ...	12: 22-37	3: 22-30	11: 14, 15, 17-23	

	Contents.	*Matt.*	*Mark*	*Luke*	*John*
55.	Seeking a sign, and the answer,	12: 38–45		[11:16, 24–36	
56.	His kinsfolk try to lay hold on Him as mad,	12: 46–50	3: 19–21, 31–35	8: 19–21	
57.	From a fishing vessel He speaks a series of seven parables, beginning with the parable of the sower,	13: 1–53	4: 1–34	8: 4–18	
58.	Jesus crosses the lake with His disciples, and calms a storm,	8: 18–27	4: 35–41	8: 22–25	
59.	He cures two demoniacs of Gadara, one being prominent,	8: 28–34	5: 1–20	8: 26–40	
60.	Returning to the west shore, He raises Jairus' daughter, and heals a woman with an issue of blood,	9:1,18–26	5: 21–43	8: 40–56	
61.	He heals two blind men and casts out a demon,	9: 27–34			
62.	Jesus visits Nazareth again, when His countrymen disbelieve in him,	13: 54–58	6: 1–6		
63.	Christ teaches throughout Galilee,	9: 35–38	6: 6		
64.	Sends forth the Twelve,	10:1–11:1	6: 7–13	9: 1–6	
65.	Herod, who has murdered John the Baptist, fears that Jesus is John risen from the dead,	14: 1–12	6: 14–29	9: 7–9	
66.	The Twelve return to Jesus, telling all they have done and taught. He withdraws with them to a desert on the other side of the Sea of Galilee, and feeds five thousand people,	14: 13–21	6: 30–44	9: 10–17	6: 1–14
67.	He sends the disciples across the lake westward to Bethsaida (close to Capernaum, distinct from Bethsaida Julias, northeast of the lake, Luke 9:10), and at night comes walking to them upon the water,	14: 22–33	6: 45–56		6: 15–21
68.	The miraculously-fed multitude seek and find Jesus at Capernaum. His discourse in the synagogue and Peter's confession,				6: 22–71
	From the Third Passover to the Beginning of the Last Passover Week.				
69.	Healings in the Gennesaret plain for a few days,	14: 34–36	6: 55, 56		
70.	Pharisees from Jerusalem object to His neglect of washing hands,	15: 1–20	7: 1–23		
71.	Jesus goes northward towards Tyre and Sidon. The Syrophenician woman's faith gains a cure for her daughter,	15: 21–28	7: 24–30		
72.	He returns through Decapolis, and, ascending a mount near the Sea of Galilee, heals many and feeds four thousand,	15: 29–38	7:31–8:9		
73.	He crosses the lake to Dalmanutha,	15: 39	8: 10		
74.	Pharisees and Sadducees require a sign,	16: 1–4	8: 11, 12		
75.	Embarking in the ship, He comes to Bethsaida (Julias). He warns against leaven of doctrine,	16: 4–12	8: 13–21		
76.	Healing of a blind man,		8: 22–26		
77.	Journey to the region of Cæsarea Philippi. Peter's confession,	16: 13–20	8: 27–30	9: 18–21	
78.	He foretells His death and resurrection. Reproof of Peter,	16: 21–28	8: 31–38, 9: 1	9: 22–27	
79.	The transfiguration on Mount Hermon six days later,	17: 1–13	9: 2–13	9: 28–36	
80.	Descending, the following day He casts out a demon which the disciples could not cast out,	17: 14–21	9: 14–29	9: 37–43	
81.	Jesus again foretells His death and resurrection,	17: 22, 23	9: 30–32	9: 44, 45	
82.	Temple-tribute money miraculously provided from a fish at Capernaum,	17: 24–27			

	Contents.	Matt.	Mark	Luke	John
83.	The disciples strive which shall be greatest. Jesus teaches a childlike, forgiving spirit. John tells of the disciples' forbidding one who cast out demons in Jesus' name,.	18: 1–35	9: 33–50	9: 46–50	
	Journey to the Feast of Tabernacle six months after the third Passover; this period ends with His arrival at Bethany before the last Passover, ...				7: 1–10
84.	He goes up from Galilee about the midst of the feast and teaches in the temple,.				7: 14
85.	The people are divided in opinion; the rulers try to seize Him; Nicodemus remonstrates, .				7: 11–53
86.	His charity, yet faithfulness, towards the adulteress,.				8: 1–11
87.	Jesus in the temple declares Himself the Light of the world, preexistent before Abraham. The Jews seek to stone Him, ...				8: 12–59
88.	Healing of the beggar, blind from his birth,. .				9
89.	Christ's discourse on Himself as the Good Shepherd and the Door, ...				10: 1–21
90.	Final departure for Jerusalem from Galilee through Samaria, ...			9: 51–56	
91.	Warnings to certain who would follow, ...			9: 57–62	
92.	Sending forth of the seventy, ...			10: 1–16	
93.	The seventy return, announcing their successful mission, ...			10: 17–24	
94.	In reply to a lawyer's general question about the whole law, Christ speaks the parable of the good Samaritan, ...			10: 25–37	
95.	Jesus in Bethany visits Mary and Martha, . . .			10: 38–42	
96.	He again teaches the disciples how to pray, . .			11: 1–13	
97.	Cure of the dumb demoniac; the Pharisees again attribute His miracles to Beelzebub; dines with one; woes to hypocritical lawyers; doom of the nation,.			11: 14–54	
98.	Exhortation to disciples, ...			12: 1–12	
99.	Appeal to Jesus to arbitrate about inheritance; parable of the rich fool, ...			12: 13–21	
100.	Discourses,.			12: 22–59	
101.	God's judgments; motive to repentance, ...			13: 1–5	
102.	Parable of the barren fig tree,.			13: 6–9	
103.	Cure of a woman with a spirit of infirmity, . .			13: 10–17	
104.	Jesus, at the Feast of Dedication in Jerusalem, proclaims His divine oneness with God. The Jews a third time seek to kill Him, when consequently He withdraws to Peræa, ...				10: 22–42
105.	His second journey toward Bethany on hearing of the sickness of Lazarus,.			13: 22	11: 1–16
106.	Pharisees urge Him to depart quickly from Peræa, on the plea that Herod will kill Him, and His answer,.			13: 31–35	
107.	Cure of man with the dropsy, ...			14: 1–6	
108.	Parable of the great supper, ...			14: 7–24	
109.	He warns the multitude to count the cost of discipleship, ...			14: 25–35	
110.	Many publicans crowd to Him, and on the Pharisees' murmuring, He utters the parables of the lost sheep, the lost coin, and the prodigal son,.			15: 1–32	
111.	To the disciples He speaks the parables of the unjust steward and the rich man and Lazarus,			16: 1–31	
112.	Sayings as to offenses; mutual forgiveness and profitableness never exceeding duty, ...			17: 1–10	

Contents.	*Matt.*	*Mark*	*Luke*	*John*
113. Arriving at Bethany, He raises Lazarus from the dead,				11: 17–46
114. Caiaphas and the Sanhedrin determine to put Jesus to death; unconscious prophecy,				11: 47–53
115. Jesus withdraws to Ephraim on the borders of Samaria,				11: 54
The Last Journey to Jerusalem through the midst of Samaria and Galilee.				
116. He heals ten lepers on the Samaritan frontier,			17: 11–19	
117. The Pharisees ask when the kingdom of God shall come; He foretells related events,			17: 20–37	
118. Parables of importunate widow and the Pharisee and publican,			18: 1–14	
119. Journey from Galilee through Peræa,	19: 1, 2	10: 1		
120. Pharisees question Him about divorce,	19: 3–12	10: 2–12		
121. Parents bring their children to Jesus to bless them,	19: 13–15	10: 13–16	18: 15–17	
122. The rich young ruler declines discipleship; Peter contrasts the disciples' self-sacrifice,	19: 16–30	10: 17–31	18: 18–30	
123. Parable of the laborers in the vineyard to warn against mercenary service,	20: 1–16			
124. Jesus goes before on His way to Jerusalem, and a third time foretells His death and resurrection,	20: 17–19	10: 32–34	18: 31–34	
125. James and John desire highest places next to Christ in the temporal kingdom,	20: 20–28	10: 35–45		
126. He heals two blind men near Jericho,	20: 29–34	10: 46–52	18:35–19:1	
127. Zaccheus climbs a sycamore tree, and is called down by Jesus; salvation comes to his house,			19: 2–10	
128. Near Jerusalem, when men think the kingdom of God shall immediately appear, Jesus corrects this thought by the parable of the pounds,			19: 11–27	
The Last Sabbath, Saturday, beginning at Friday sunset.				
129. The hostile Jews seek Him at Jerusalem; Pharisees command to take Him. Jesus reaches Bethany six days before the Passover. In the house of Simon the leper, Mary anoints His head and feet,	26: 6–13	14: 3–9		11: 55–57, 12: 1–8
130. Jews come to Bethany to see Jesus,				12: 9–11
The Last Passover Week, Ending with the Crucifixion.				
First Day of the Week.				
131. Jesus triumphantly enters Jerusalem. He weeps over the city as doomed. At eventide He returns to Bethany, having first entered the temple, and sternly looked round about upon all things (Zeph. 1: 12),	21: 1–11, 17	11: 1–11	19: 29–44	12: 12–19
Second Day.				
132. On His way from Bethany, Jesus curses the barren fig tree. He purges the temple at the close of the ministry as at the beginning, but without the scourge, and again returns to Bethany, after detecting at a glance the desecration in the court of the Gentiles,	21: 12–16, 18, 19	11: 12–19	19: 45, 46	
Third Day.				
133. On His way to Jerusalem, the fig tree being now withered up, Jesus teaches the lesson "that believing prayer can move mountains of hindrance,"	21: 20–22	11: 20–26		

Contents.	Matt.	Mark	Luke	John
134. Teaches in the temple. Deputation from the Sanhedrin challenges His authority. Parables of the two sons and the vineyard,.	21: 23–46	11: 27–33, 12: 1–12	20: 1–19	
135. Parable of the marriage feast, ...	22: 1–14			
136. The Pharisees, with the Herodians, try to entangle Him in His words. His reply from Cæsar's image on the coin, ...	22:15–22	12: 13–17	20: 20–26	
137. He battles the Sadducees' objections about the resurrection, ...	22: 23–33	12: 18–27	20: 27–40	
138. He replies to a lawyer on which one is the great commandment, ...	22: 35–40	12: 28–34		
139. Our Lord leaves them without answer to His question, If Christ be Son of David, how does David call him Lord?	22: 41–46	12: 35–37	20: 41–44	
140. Warns against scribes and Pharisees. Woe to Jerusalem, ...	23: 1–39	12: 38–40	20: 45–47	
141. He commends the widow's offering to God's treasury, ...		12: 41–44	21: 1–4	
142. Some Greeks desire to see Jesus. He accepts this as a pledge of His coming glory and the gathering in of the Gentiles. Jesus' prayer and the Father's answer heard by the disciples, .				12: 20–38
143. Leaving the temple, Jesus, sitting on Olivet with Peter, James, John, and Andrew, foretells the destruction of the temple and Jewish theocracy. The last days,.	24: 1–42	13: 1–37	21: 5–36	
144. Parables: The good man of the house, the wise and the evil servant, the ten virgins, the talents, the sheep and the goats,.	24: 43–51, 25: 1–46			
Fourth Day.				
145. *Beginning at sunset:* Jesus, two days before the Passover, announces His betrayal and crucifixion; the Sanhedrin consult to kill Jesus by subtlety. Judas, availing himself of his Master's retirement from them, covenants to betray Him. Most disbelieved; some rulers believed, but loving men's praise confessed Him not. Jesus' judgment, ...	26: 1–5, 14–16	14: 1, 2, 10, 11	22: 1–6	12: 36–50
Fifth Day.				
146. Jesus sends two disciples into the city to prepare for the Passover; follows with the rest in the afternoon, ...	26: 17–19	14: 12–16	22: 7–13	
Sixth Day.				
147. *At sunset:* Jesus celebrates the Passover in anticipation, ...	26:20	14: 17	22: 14	
148. Reproves the ambition of disciples, yet promises the kingdom,.			22: 24–30	
149. He teaches love and humility by washing disciples' feet,.				13: 1–20
150. He indicates His betrayer, who, however, did not leave till after the Lord's Supper (Luke 22: 21), ...	26: 21–25	14: 18–21	22: 21–23	13: 21–35
151. He foretells Peter's sifting by Satan, and restoration by His intercession; and scattering of the Twelve, ...	26: 31–35	14: 27–31	22: 31–38	13: 36–38
152. Ordains the Lord's Supper (1 Cor. 11: 23–25),.	26: 26–29	14: 22–25	22: 15–20	
153. Farewell address and intercessory prayer in the paschal chamber, all standing (John 14: 31), .				14–17: 26
154. His agony in Gethsemane,.	26: 30, 36–46	14: 26, 32–42	22: 39–46	18: 1, 4
155. His betrayal with a kiss, and apprehension. Peter cuts off, and Jesus heals, Malchus' ear,. .	26: 47–56	14: 43–52	22: 47–53	18: 2–12

Contents.	Matt.	Mark	Luke	John
156. He is brought before Annas first at night. Peter's three denials: (1) The *flesh* (Mark 14: 54); (2) the *world* (Matt. 26: 70—first cock-crowing, Mark 14: 68); (3) the *devil* (Mark 14:71, 72—the second cock-crowing; Ps. 1:1),.	26: 57, 58, 69–75	14: 53, 54, 66–72	22: 54–62	18: 13, 18, 25–27
157. Before Caiaphas, at first dawn, Jesus avows His Messiahship and Godhead. He is condemned for blasphemy and mocked, ...	26: 59–68	14: 55–65	22: 63–71	18: 19–24
158. Brought before Pilate for sentence of crucifixion, ...	27: 1, 2, 11–14	15: 1–5	23: 1–5	18: 28–38
159. Pilate sends Him to Herod; Herod sends Him back to Pilate, ...			23: 6–12	
160. Pilate seeks to release Him, but the Jews demand Barabbas. To appease them, Pilate scourges Him; the Jews clamor for His crucifixion as making Himself a king. Pilate, notwithstanding his wife's warning, sentences Jesus, ...	27: 15–26	15: 6–15	23: 13–25	18: 39; 19: 1–16
161. Jesus mocked by Roman soldiers with scarlet robe, crown of thorns, and reed, ...	27: 27–30	15: 16–19		
162. Judas' remorse; he presumptuously enters the temple, flings down the silver, and hangs himself (Acts 1: 18, 19), ...	27: 3–10			
163. Jesus bears His own cross to the city gate, where He is relieved by Simon of Cyrene; refuses stupefying myrrhed wine,.	27: 31–34	15: 20–23	23: 26–32	19: 16, 17
164. Crucified at Golgotha, probably outside the Damascus gate. Seven sayings on the cross, *three* relating to *others, four* to *himself:* (1) For his murderers—*"Father, forgive them,"* etc., ...	27: 35–44	15: 24–32	23: 33–38	19: 18–27
165. (2) The penitent thief promised paradise—*"Today,"* etc., ...			23: 39–43	
166. His garments divided and vesture cast lots for; (3) commends His mother to the care of John—*"Behold thy son,"* etc., ...				19: 23–27
167. Darkness over the land from sixth to ninth hour. Jesus' loud cry, (4) *"Eli, Eli,"* etc. Says, (5) *"I thirst,"* and receives the vinegar to fulfill Scripture; (6) *"It is finished"; (7) "Father, into thy hands I commend my spirit";* gives up the spirit; the veil of the temple rent. Centurion's testimony, ...	27: 45–54	15: 33–41	23: 44–49	19: 28–30
168. The side pierced by the soldier's spear and the blood and water attest His death and the truth of Scripture (Gen. 2: 21–23; Eph. 5: 30, 32; 1 John 5:6; Zech. 12:10). The body, taken down, is wrapped up with Nicodemus' aloes and myrrh, and buried in new tomb of Joseph of Arimathea, ...	27: 57–61	15: 42–47	23: 50–56	19: 31–42
Seventh Day.				
169. Pilate grants a guard, and they set a seal upon the sepulcher, ...	27: 62–66			
Christ's Resurrection, His Appearances during Forty Days, and Ascension.				
First Day—Easter Sunday.				
170. Resurrection at first dawn, ...	28: 2–4			
171. The women, coming with spices, find the sepulcher open and empty. Mary Magdalene returns to tell Peter and John, ...	28: 1	16: 1–4	24: 1–3	20: 1, 2
172. The other women, remaining, see two angels, who declare the Lord's resurrection, ...	28. 5–7	16: 5–7	24: 4–8	

Contents.	Matt.	Mark	Luke	John
173. Mary Magdalene returns to the sepulcher. Jesus reveals Himself to her. She reports to the disciples—*First* appearance, ...		16: 9–11		20: 11–18
174. Jesus meets the women (Mary mother of James, Salome, and Joanna) on their return to the city—*Second* appearance, ...	28: 8–10	16:8	24: 9–11	
175. Peter and John find the sepulcher empty, . . .			24:12	20: 3–10
176. Report of the guards to the chief priests, who bribe them, ...	28: 11–15			
177. Jesus seen by Peter (Cephas, 1 Cor. 15: 5)—*Third* appearance,.			24:34	
178. Seen by the two disciples on way to Emmaus—*Fourth* appearance, ...		16: 12, 13	24: 13–35	
179. Jesus appears to the ten, Thomas being absent—*Fifth* appearance,.		16: 14	24: 36–49	20: 19–23
Subsequent Appearances.				
180. Evening of Sunday after Easter day. Jesus appears to them again, Thomas being present—*Sixth* appearance, ...				20: 24–29
181. The eleven go into Galilee, to a mountain appointed. Jesus appears, and commands them to teach all nations—*Seventh* appearance, . .	28: 16–20	16: 15–18		
182. Jesus shows Himself at the Sea of Tiberias—*Eighth* appearance. Charges Simon to feed His lambs, sheep, and young sheep, ...				21: 1–24
183. Seen of above five hundred brethren at once (1 Cor. 15: 6), probably along with the eleven—*Ninth* appearance,.	28: 16			
184. He is seen by James, then by all the apostles (Acts 1: 3–8; 1 Cor. 15: 7)—*Tenth* appearance. In all, 538 (549 if the eleven, Matt. 28: 16, be distinct from the 500) persons are *specified* as having seen the risen Saviour; also, after His ascension, St. Paul (1 Cor. 15: 8),.				
185. The ascension, forty days after Easter (Acts 1: 9–12), ...		16: 19, 20	24: 50–53	
186. Purpose and conclusion, ...				20: 30, 31; 21: 25

INDEX TO PRINCIPAL SUBJECTS IN THE NOTES

"Send me where you want me to go"
Prayer Chapel - November 19, 1977
11:00 p.m.

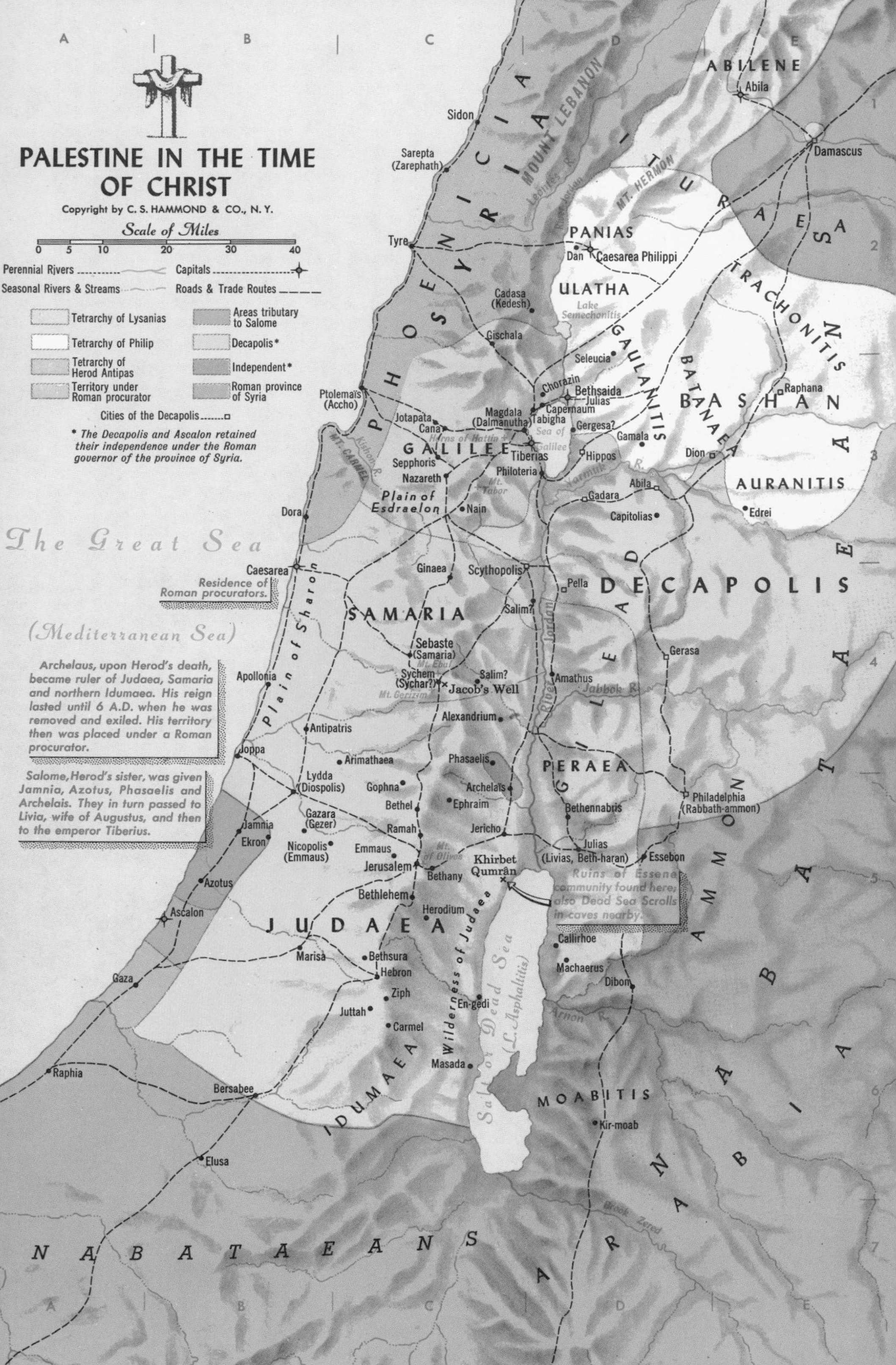

PALESTINE IN THE TIME OF CHRIST
Copyright by C. S. HAMMOND & CO., N. Y.
Scale of Miles
0 5 10 20 30 40
Perennial Rivers
Capitals
Seasonal Rivers & Streams
Roads & Trade Routes
Tetrarchy of Lysanias
Areas tributary to Salome
Tetrarchy of Philip
Decapolis*
Tetrarchy of Herod Antipas
Independent*
Territory under Roman procurator
Roman province of Syria
Cities of the Decapolis
* The Decapolis and Ascalon retained their independence under the Roman governor of the province of Syria.
The Great Sea
(Mediterranean Sea)
Residence of Roman procurators.
Archelaus, upon Herod's death, became ruler of Judaea, Samaria and northern Idumaea. His reign lasted until 6 A.D. when he was removed and exiled. His territory then was placed under a Roman procurator.
Salome, Herod's sister, was given Jamnia, Azotus, Phasaelis and Archelais. They in turn passed to Livia, wife of Augustus, and then to the emperor Tiberius.
Ruins of Essene community found here; also Dead Sea Scrolls in caves nearby.
PHOENICIA
SYRIA
ITURAEA
ABILENE
PANIAS
ULATHA
GAULANITIS
TRACHONITIS
BATANAEA
BASHAN
AURANITIS
GALILEE
SAMARIA
DECAPOLIS
GILEAD
PERAEA
JUDAEA
IDUMAEA
MOABITIS
AMMON
ARABIA
ARABIA NABATAEA
NABATAEANS
MOUNT LEBANON
MT. HERMON
MT. CARMEL
Sidon
Sarepta (Zarephath)
Tyre
Abila
Damascus
Dan
Caesarea Philippi
Cadasa (Kedesh)
Lake Semechonitis
Gischala
Seleucia
Chorazin
Bethsaida
Julias
Capernaum
Raphana
Ptolemaïs (Accho)
Jotapata
Cana
Magdala (Dalmanutha)
Tabigha
Horns of Hattin
Sea of Galilee
Gergesa?
Gamala
Tiberias
Hippos
Dion
Sepphoris
Nazareth
Philoteria
Yarmuk R.
Abila
Gadara
Mt. Tabor
Plain of Esdraelon
Nain
Edrei
Dora
Capitolias
Caesarea
Ginaea
Scythopolis
Pella
Plain of Sharon
Salim?
Sebaste (Samaria)
Mt. Ebal
Gerasa
Sychem (Sychar?)
Jacob's Well
Salim?
Amathus
Apollonia
Mt. Gerizim
Jabbok R.
River Jordan
Alexandrium
Antipatris
Joppa
Arimathaea
Phasaelis
Lydda (Diospolis)
Gophna
Archelais
Philadelphia (Rabbath-ammon)
Bethel
Ephraim
Bethennabris
Gazara (Gezer)
Jamnia
Ekron
Ramah
Jericho
Nicopolis (Emmaus)
Emmaus
Mt. of Olives
Khirbet Qumrân
Julias (Livias, Beth-haran)
Essebon
Jerusalem
Bethany
Azotus
Bethlehem
Herodium
Ascalon
Wilderness of Judaea
Callirhoe
Marisa
Bethsura
Machaerus
Hebron
Dead Sea (L. Asphaltitis)
Salt Sea
Gaza
Dibon
Ziph
En-gedi
Juttah
Arnon R.
Carmel
Masada
Raphia
Bersabee
Kir-moab
Elusa
Brook Zered

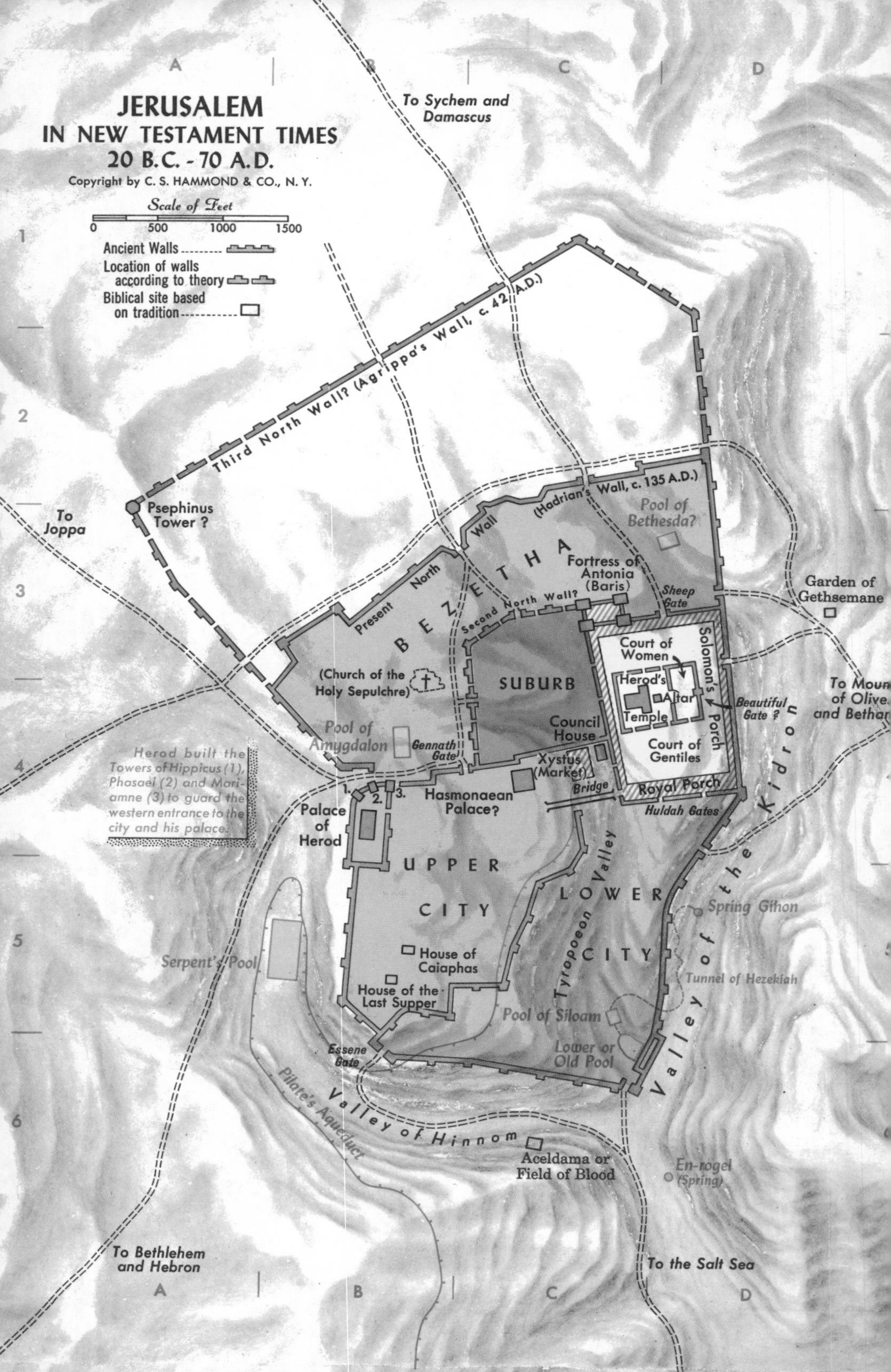

JERUSALEM
IN NEW TESTAMENT TIMES
20 B.C. - 70 A.D.
Copyright by C. S. HAMMOND & CO., N. Y.
Scale of Feet
0
500
1000
1500
Ancient Walls
Location of walls according to theory
Biblical site based on tradition
A
B
C
D
1
2
3
4
5
6
To Sychem and Damascus
Third North Wall? (Agrippa's Wall, c. 42 A.D.)
To Joppa
Psephinus Tower ?
Wall (Hadrian's Wall, c. 135 A.D.)
Pool of Bethesda?
Present North
B E Z E T H A
Fortress of Antonia (Baris)
Sheep Gate
Garden of Gethsemane
Second North Wall?
Court of Women
Solomon's Porch
(Church of the Holy Sepulchre)
SUBURB
Herod's Temple
Altar
Beautiful Gate ?
To Mount of Olives and Bethany
Council House
Court of Gentiles
Pool of Amygdalon
Gennath Gate
Herod built the Towers of Hippicus (1), Phasael (2) and Mariamne (3) to guard the western entrance to the city and his palace.
1.
2.
3.
Xystus (Market)
Bridge
Royal Porch
Hasmonaean Palace?
Huldah Gates
Palace of Herod
UPPER
CITY
Tyropoeon Valley
LOWER
CITY
Valley of the Kidron
Spring Gihon
Serpent's Pool
House of Caiaphas
House of the Last Supper
Tunnel of Hezekiah
Pool of Siloam
Essene Gate
Lower or Old Pool
Pilate's Aqueduct
Valley of Hinnom
Aceldama or Field of Blood
En-rogel (Spring)
To Bethlehem and Hebron
To the Salt Sea

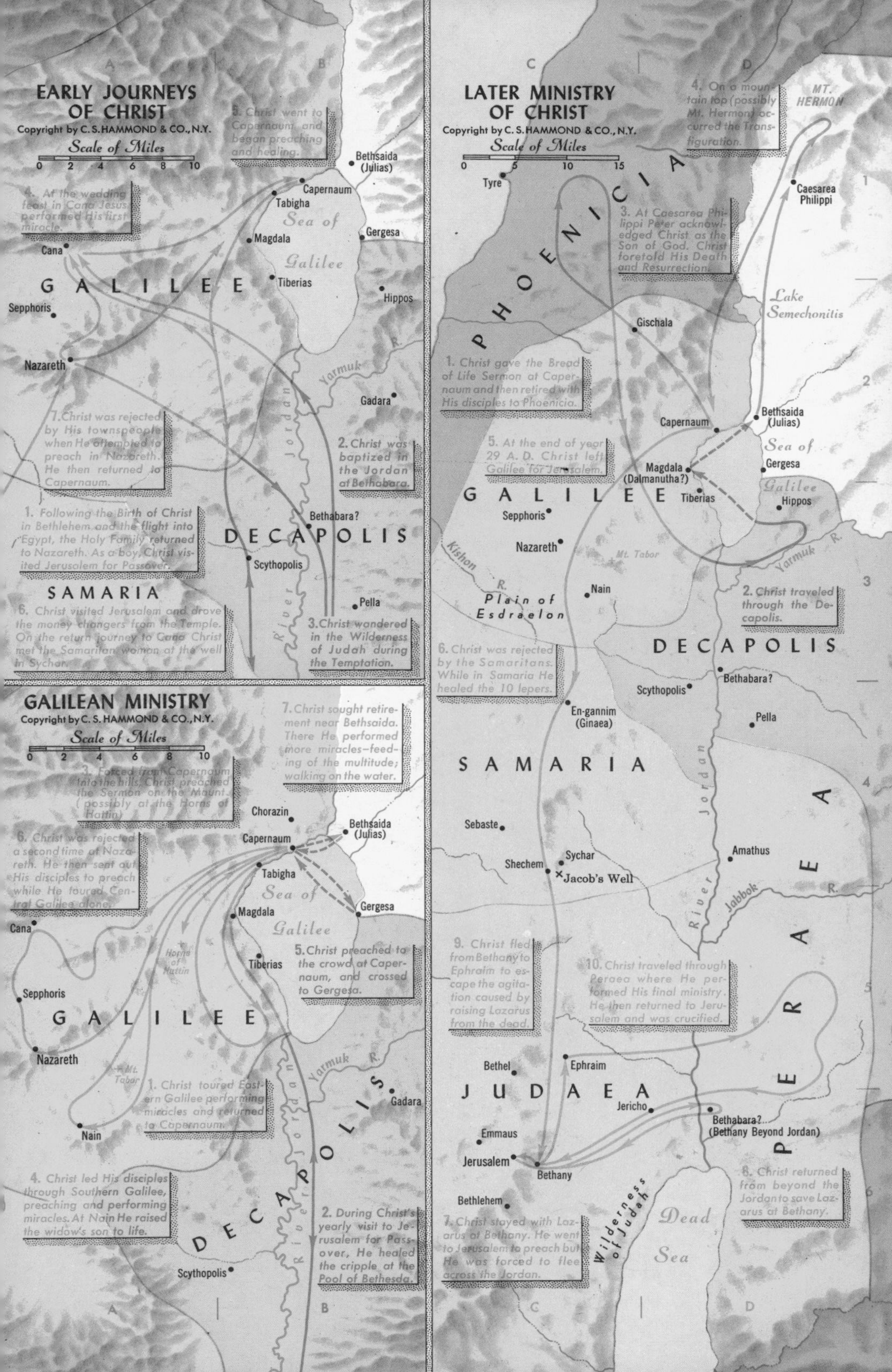
EARLY JOURNEYS OF CHRIST
Copyright by C. S. HAMMOND & CO., N.Y.
Scale of Miles
0 2 4 6 8 10
4. At the wedding feast in Cana Jesus performed His first miracle.
5. Christ went to Capernaum and began preaching and healing.
7. Christ was rejected by His townspeople when He attempted to preach in Nazareth. He then returned to Capernaum.
2. Christ was baptized in the Jordan at Bethabara.
1. Following the Birth of Christ in Bethlehem and the flight into Egypt, the Holy Family returned to Nazareth. As a boy, Christ visited Jerusalem for Passover.
6. Christ visited Jerusalem and drove the money changers from the Temple. On the return journey to Cana Christ met the Samaritan woman at the well in Sychar.
3. Christ wandered in the Wilderness of Judah during the Temptation.
Bethsaida (Julias)
Capernaum
Tabigha
Sea of Galilee
Magdala
Gergesa
Cana
GALILEE
Tiberias
Hippos
Sepphoris
Nazareth
Yarmuk R.
Gadara
River Jordan
Bethabara?
DECAPOLIS
Scythopolis
SAMARIA
Pella
GALILEAN MINISTRY
Copyright by C. S. HAMMOND & CO., N.Y.
Scale of Miles
0 2 4 6 8 10
3. Forced from Capernaum into the hills, Christ preached the Sermon on the Mount (possibly at the Horns of Hattin)
7. Christ sought retirement near Bethsaida. There He performed more miracles—feeding of the multitude; walking on the water.
6. Christ was rejected a second time at Nazareth. He then sent out His disciples to preach while He toured Central Galilee alone.
5. Christ preached to the crowd at Capernaum, and crossed to Gergesa.
1. Christ toured Eastern Galilee performing miracles and returned to Capernaum.
4. Christ led His disciples through Southern Galilee, preaching and performing miracles. At Nain He raised the widow's son to life.
2. During Christ's yearly visit to Jerusalem for Passover, He healed the cripple at the Pool of Bethesda.
Chorazin
Bethsaida (Julias)
Capernaum
Tabigha
Sea of Galilee
Gergesa
Magdala
Cana
Horns of Hattin
Tiberias
Sepphoris
GALILEE
Nazareth
Mt. Tabor
Yarmuk R.
Gadara
Nain
DECAPOLIS
River Jordan
Scythopolis
LATER MINISTRY OF CHRIST
Copyright by C. S. HAMMOND & CO., N.Y.
Scale of Miles
0 5 10 15
4. On a mountain top (possibly Mt. Hermon) occurred the Transfiguration.
MT. HERMON
Tyre
PHOENICIA
3. At Caesarea Philippi Peter acknowledged Christ as the Son of God. Christ foretold His Death and Resurrection.
Caesarea Philippi
Lake Semechonitis
Gischala
1. Christ gave the Bread of Life Sermon at Capernaum and then retired with His disciples to Phoenicia.
Capernaum
Bethsaida (Julias)
5. At the end of year 29 A.D. Christ left Galilee for Jerusalem.
Magdala (Dalmanutha?)
Sea of Galilee
Gergesa
GALILEE
Tiberias
Hippos
Sepphoris
Nazareth
Kishon R.
Mt. Tabor
Yarmuk R.
Nain
Plain of Esdraelon
2. Christ traveled through the Decapolis.
6. Christ was rejected by the Samaritans. While in Samaria He healed the 10 lepers.
DECAPOLIS
Bethabara?
Scythopolis
Pella
En-gannim (Ginaea)
SAMARIA
River Jordan
Sebaste
Amathus
Sychar
Shechem
Jacob's Well
Jabbok R.
PERAEA
9. Christ fled from Bethany to Ephraim to escape the agitation caused by raising Lazarus from the dead.
10. Christ traveled through Peraea where He performed His final ministry. He then returned to Jerusalem and was crucified.
Bethel
Ephraim
JUDAEA
Jericho
Bethabara? (Bethany Beyond Jordan)
Emmaus
Jerusalem
Bethany
Bethlehem
8. Christ returned from beyond the Jordan to save Lazarus at Bethany.
7. Christ stayed with Lazarus at Bethany. He went to Jerusalem to preach but He was forced to flee across the Jordan.
Wilderness of Judah
Dead Sea

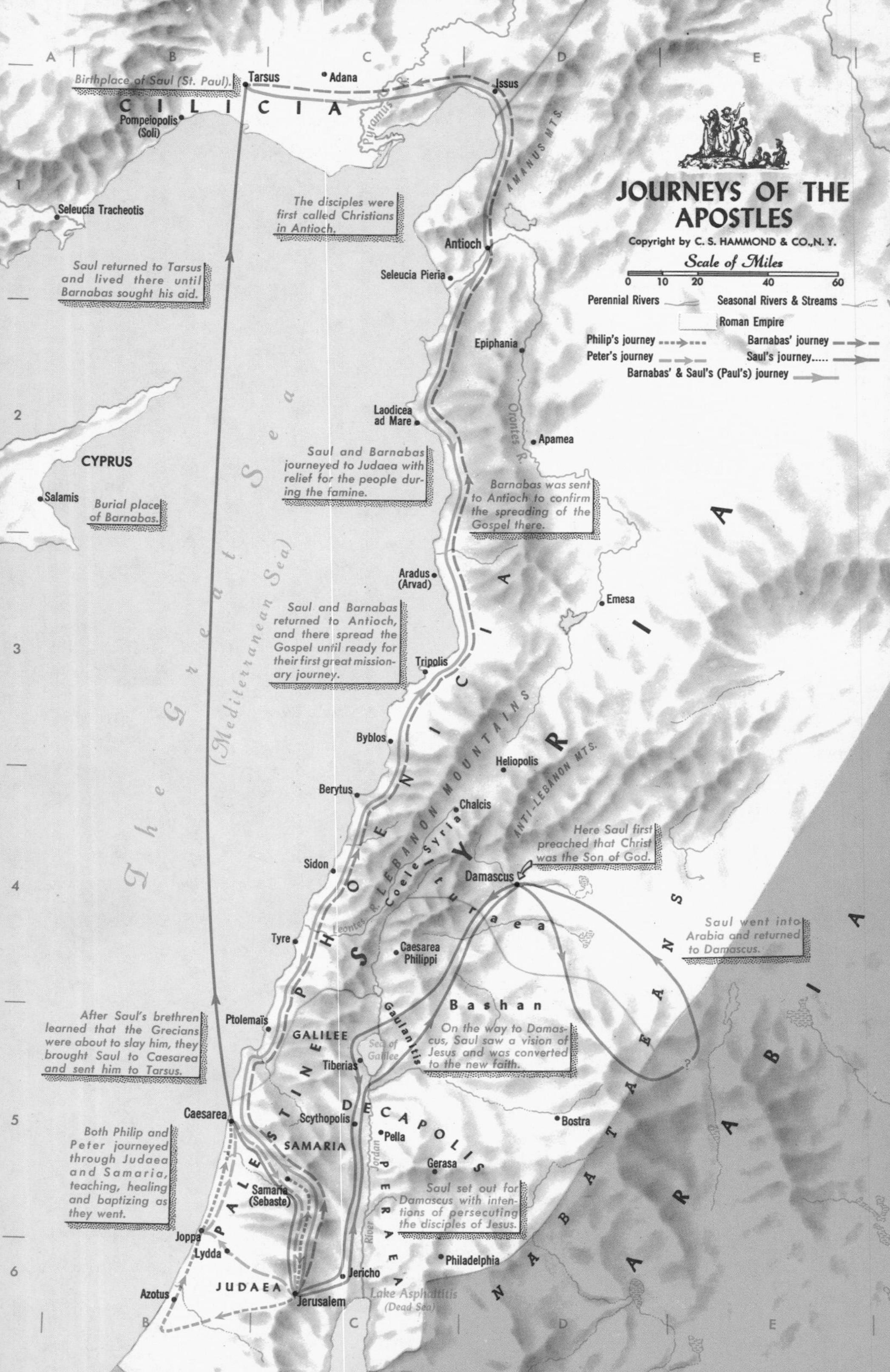

JOURNEYS OF THE APOSTLES
Copyright by C. S. HAMMOND & CO., N. Y.
Scale of Miles
0 10 20 40 60
Perennial Rivers
Seasonal Rivers & Streams
Roman Empire
Philip's journey
Barnabas' journey
Peter's journey
Saul's journey.....
Barnabas' & Saul's (Paul's) journey
Birthplace of Saul (St. Paul).
Tarsus
Adana
Issus
CILICIA
Pompeiopolis (Soli)
Pyramus R.
AMANUS MTS.
Seleucia Tracheotis
The disciples were first called Christians in Antioch.
Antioch
Seleucia Pieria
Saul returned to Tarsus and lived there until Barnabas sought his aid.
Epiphania
Laodicea ad Mare
Orontes R.
Apamea
CYPRUS
Salamis
Burial place of Barnabas.
Saul and Barnabas journeyed to Judaea with relief for the people during the famine.
Barnabas was sent to Antioch to confirm the spreading of the Gospel there.
The Great Sea
(Mediterranean Sea)
Aradus (Arvad)
Emesa
Saul and Barnabas returned to Antioch, and there spread the Gospel until ready for their first great missionary journey.
Tripolis
Byblos
Berytus
Heliopolis
LEBANON MOUNTAINS
ANTI-LEBANON MTS.
Chalcis
Coele Syria
PHOENICIA
SYRIA
Sidon
Here Saul first preached that Christ was the Son of God.
Damascus
Leontes R.
Ituraea
Tyre
Caesarea Philippi
Saul went into Arabia and returned to Damascus.
Bashan
Ptolemaïs
GALILEE
Gaulanitis
After Saul's brethren learned that the Grecians were about to slay him, they brought Saul to Caesarea and sent him to Tarsus.
Sea of Galilee
Tiberias
On the way to Damascus, Saul saw a vision of Jesus and was converted to the new faith.
NABATAEANS
ARABIA
Caesarea
DECAPOLIS
Scythopolis
Pella
Bostra
SAMARIA
Both Philip and Peter journeyed through Judaea and Samaria, teaching, healing and baptizing as they went.
PALESTINE
Gerasa
Samaria (Sebaste)
Jordan River
PERAEA
Saul set out for Damascus with intentions of persecuting the disciples of Jesus.
Joppa
Lydda
Philadelphia
Jericho
Azotus
JUDAEA
Jerusalem
Lake Asphaltitis (Dead Sea)
A B C D E
1 2 3 4 5 6

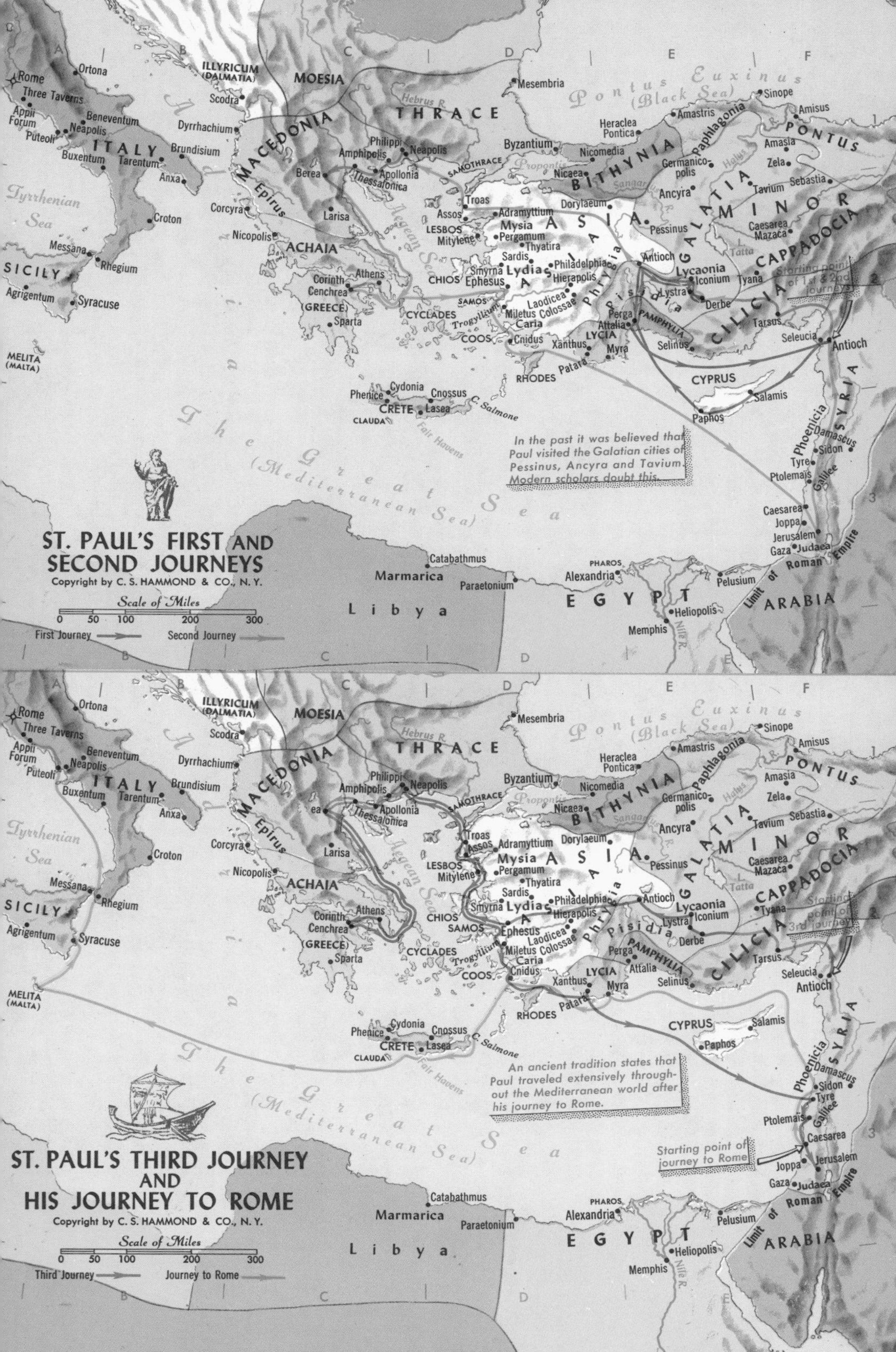

ST. PAUL'S FIRST AND SECOND JOURNEYS
Copyright by C. S. HAMMOND & CO., N. Y.
Scale of Miles
0 50 100 200 300
First Journey
Second Journey
In the past it was believed that Paul visited the Galatian cities of Pessinus, Ancyra and Tavium. Modern scholars doubt this.
Starting point of 1st & 2nd journeys
ITALY
Rome
Ortona
Three Taverns
Appii Forum
Beneventum
Neapolis
Puteoli
Buxentum
Tarentum
Brundisium
Anxa
Croton
Tyrrhenian Sea
Messana
Rhegium
SICILY
Agrigentum
Syracuse
MELITA (MALTA)
ILLYRICUM (DALMATIA)
Scodra
Dyrrhachium
MOESIA
MACEDONIA
THRACE
Hebrus R.
Mesembria
Philippi
Neapolis
Amphipolis
Apollonia
Thessalonica
Berea
SAMOTHRACE
Larisa
Epirus
Corcyra
Nicopolis
ACHAIA
Corinth
Athens
Cenchrea
(GREECE)
Sparta
Aegean Sea
CYCLADES
Pontus Euxinus (Black Sea)
Byzantium
Propontis
Heraclea Pontica
Amastris
Sinope
Amisus
Nicomedia
BITHYNIA
Paphlagonia
PONTUS
Germanicopolis
Amasia
Zela
Nicaea
Sangarius
Halys R.
Ancyra
Tavium
Sebastia
GALATIA
ASIA MINOR
Dorylaeum
Pessinus
Caesarea Mazaca
CAPPADOCIA
Tatta
Troas
Assos
Adramyttium
Mysia
LESBOS
Mitylene
Pergamum
Thyatira
Sardis
Smyrna
Lydia
Philadelphia
CHIOS
Ephesus
Hierapolis
ASIA
Phrygia
Antioch
Pisidia
Lycaonia
Iconium
Lystra
Derbe
Tyana
SAMOS
Trogyllium
Miletus
Laodicea
Colossae
Caria
COOS
Cnidus
Perga
Attalia
PAMPHYLIA
LYCIA
Xanthus
Myra
Patara
RHODES
CILICIA
Tarsus
Selinus
Seleucia
Antioch
CYPRUS
Salamis
Paphos
SYRIA
Phoenicia
Damascus
Sidon
Tyre
Ptolemais
Galilee
Caesarea
Joppa
Jerusalem
Gaza
Judaea
Limit of Roman Empire
ARABIA
Phenice
Cydonia
Cnossus
CRETE
Lasea
C. Salmone
CLAUDA
Fair Havens
The Great Sea (Mediterranean Sea)
Catabathmus
Marmarica
Paraetonium
Libya
PHAROS
Alexandria
EGYPT
Pelusium
Heliopolis
Memphis
Nile R.
ST. PAUL'S THIRD JOURNEY AND HIS JOURNEY TO ROME
Copyright by C. S. HAMMOND & CO., N. Y.
Scale of Miles
0 50 100 200 300
Third Journey
Journey to Rome
An ancient tradition states that Paul traveled extensively throughout the Mediterranean world after his journey to Rome.
Starting point of 3rd journey
Starting point of journey to Rome

THE SPREAD OF CHRISTIANITY
Copyright by C. S. HAMMOND & CO., N.Y.
Scale of Miles
0 100 200 400 600
INTRODUCTION OF CHRISTIANITY
Areas known to contain Christians at the time of Irenaeus, c. 185
185-325 (by the time of Constantine)
325-600 (by the time of Gregory I)
600-800 (by the time of Charlemagne)
800-1300
Northern limit of area permanently lost to Mohammedanism.
Christianity in Roman Britain was wiped out by the Anglo-Saxon invasion. The faith was reestablished in the 7th cent. by Irish missionaries.
The Christian Coptic Church was introduced on the Upper Nile and in Ethiopia in the 4th cent.
During the 7th cent. the Nestorian Christian Church introduced Christianity into Central Asia.
IRELAND
Clonard
BRITAIN
York
Lincoln
Caerleon
London
Canterbury
North Sea
Baltic Sea
Atlantic Ocean
Utrecht
Bremen
Saxons (785-805)
Thuringians (8th Cent.)
Alamanni (7th Cent.)
Magdeburg
Cologne
Fulda
Mainz
Trier
Rhine R.
Rouen
Reims
Paris
Nantes
Tours
Bourges
GAUL
Luxeuil
Augsburg
Regensburg
Czechs (c. 1000)
Pomeranians (1122-1130)
Marienburg
Prussians (13th Cent.)
Gnesen
Poles (962-1025)
Riga
Lithuanians (13th Cent.)
Russians (989-1015)
Kiev
Dnieper R.
Dniester R.
Don R.
Volga R.
Itil
Caspian Sea
Sea of Azov
Esztergom
Magyars (950-1050)
Bordeaux
Lyons
Vienne
Milan
Aquileia
Verona
Siscia
Toulouse
Astorga
Leon
Duero R.
Tagus R.
SPAIN
Saragossa
Tarragona
Merida
Toledo
Evora
Valencia
Faro
Cordova
Seville
Cadiz
Malaca
Cartagena
Tingis
Arles
Narbonne
Marseille
Genoa
Pisa
Florence
Ravenna
Ancona
CORSICA
SARDINIA
BALEARIC IS.
Rome
ITALY
Beneventum
Puteoli
Naples
Salona
Sirmium
Singidunum
Danube R.
Tomi
Chersonesus
Black Sea
Pityus
Preslav
Anchialus
Develtum
Sardica
Durazzo
Philippi
Thessalonica
Beroea
Larissa
Nicopolis
Corinth
Athens
Sparta
Constantinople
Chalcedon
Nicomedia
Amastris
Sinope
Nicaea
Ancyra
Troas
Pergamum
Thyatira
Smyrna
Sardis
Antioch
Iconium
Ephesus
Laodicea
Perga
Tarsus
Myra
RHODES
Cnossus
CRETE
Gortyna
CYPRUS
Salamis
Paphos
Vagarshapat
ARMENIA
Melitene
Edessa
Nisibis
Arbela
Antioch
Euphrates R.
Tigris R.
Ctesiphon
Seleucia
Palmyra
Tyre
Damascus
Caesarea
Jerusalem
Mediterranean Sea
Messina
SICILY
Syracuse
Hippo Regius
Cirta
Madaura
Carthage
Lambaesis
Hadrumetum
Caesarea
Leptis Magna
Cyrene
Berenice
Alexandria
Memphis
Oxyrrhynchus
EGYPT
Hermopolis
Nile R.
Ptolemais
Thebes
Red Sea
B
C
D
E
G
1
2
3
4

THE MINISTRY OF JESUS CHRIST

Year	Season	Feast	Events
26 A.D.	SPRING	Pentecost	**BEGINNING OF JOHN THE BAPTIST'S MINISTRY** MT 3:1-6; MK 1:2-6; LK 3:3-6
	SUMMER		
	AUTUMN	Tabernacles	**JESUS BAPTIZED**—MT 3:13-17; MK 1:9-11; LK 3:21-23
			40 DAYS IN WILDERNESS—THE THREE TEMPTATIONS MT 4:1-11; MK 1:12, 13; LK 4:1-13
		Dedication	**JESUS MEETS FIRST DISCIPLES**—JN 1:35-51
	WINTER		**FIRST MIRACLE—CANA**—JN 2:1-11
27 A.D.	SPRING	Passover	**FIRST CLEANSING OF TEMPLE**—JN 2:13-22
			NICODEMUS VISITS—JN 2:23—3:21
		Pentecost	**MEETS WOMAN AT WELL IN SAMARIA**—JN 4:5-42
			"THE GREAT GALILEAN MINISTRY"
	SUMMER		**HEALING AT CANA**—JN 4:46-54
			FIRST REJECTION AT NAZARETH—LK 4:16-31
	AUTUMN	Tabernacles	**JESUS HEADQUARTERED IN CAPERNAUM**-MT 4:13-16
			CALLS 4 FISHERS OF MEN—MT 4:18-22; MK 1:16-20; LK 5:1-11
		Dedication	**HEALS DEMONIAC ON SABBATH**—MK 1:21-28; LK 4:31-37
	WINTER		**CALLS MATTHEW**—MT 9:9-13; MK 2:13-17; LK 5:27-32
28 A.D.	SPRING	Passover	**HEALS LAME MAN ON SABBATH**—JN 5:1-47
		Pentecost	**SABBATH CONTROVERSIES**—MT 12:1-14; MK 2:23—3:6; LK 6:1-11
			CHOOSES TWELVE APOSTLES—MK 3:13-19; LK 6:12-16
			SERMON ON THE MOUNT—MT 5-7; LK 6:20-49
	SUMMER		**RAISES WIDOW'S SON AT NAIN**—LK 7:11-17
	AUTUMN	Tabernacles	
			"BUSY DAY"—MT 12:22—18:34; MK 3:19—5:20; LK 8:22-39
		Dedication	**SECOND REJECTION AT NAZARETH**—MT 13:54-58; MK 6:1-6
	WINTER		**THE 12 SENT FORTH**—MT 10:5-15; MK 6:7-13; LK 9:1-6
			JOHN THE BAPTIST BEHEADED—MT 14:1-12; MK 6:14-29; LK 9:7-9
			THE 12 RETURN—MK 6:30; LK 9:10
29 A.D.	SPRING	Passover	**FEEDS 5,000**—MT 14:13-21; MK 6:30-44; LK 9:10-17; JN 6:1-14
			REFUSES POPULAR DEMAND TO BE KING—JN 6:14-15, 34-59
		Pentecost	**WITHDRAWAL TO REGION OF TYRE AND SIDON**—MT 15:21; MK 7:24
			WITHDRAWAL TO NORTH AND EAST—MT 15:29; MK 7:31
	SUMMER		**FEEDING OF 4,000**—MT 15:30-38; MK 8:1-9
			WITHDRAWAL TO BETHSAIDA AND CAESAREA PHILIPPI
			THE TRANSFIGURATION—MT 17:1-8; MK 9:2-8; LK 9:28-36
	AUTUMN	Tabernacles	**PHARISEES ATTEMPT TO STONE JESUS**—JN 8:21-59
			JESUS HEALS A MAN BORN BLIND—JN 9:1-41
			THE MISSION OF THE SEVENTY—LK 10:1-24
		Dedication	**JESUS DENOUNCES THE PHARISEES**—LK 11:37-54
	WINTER		**MINISTRY IN PEREA**
30 A.D.	WINTER		**LAZARUS RAISED FROM THE DEAD**—JN 11:1-44
	SPRING	Passover	**LAST WEEK—TRIUMPHAL ENTRY—CRUCIFIXION—RESURRECTION** MT 21-28; MK 11-16; LK 19:29—24; JN 12:12—20:35
		Pentecost	**THE ASCENSION**—MK 16:19; LK 24:44-53; ACTS 1:3-12

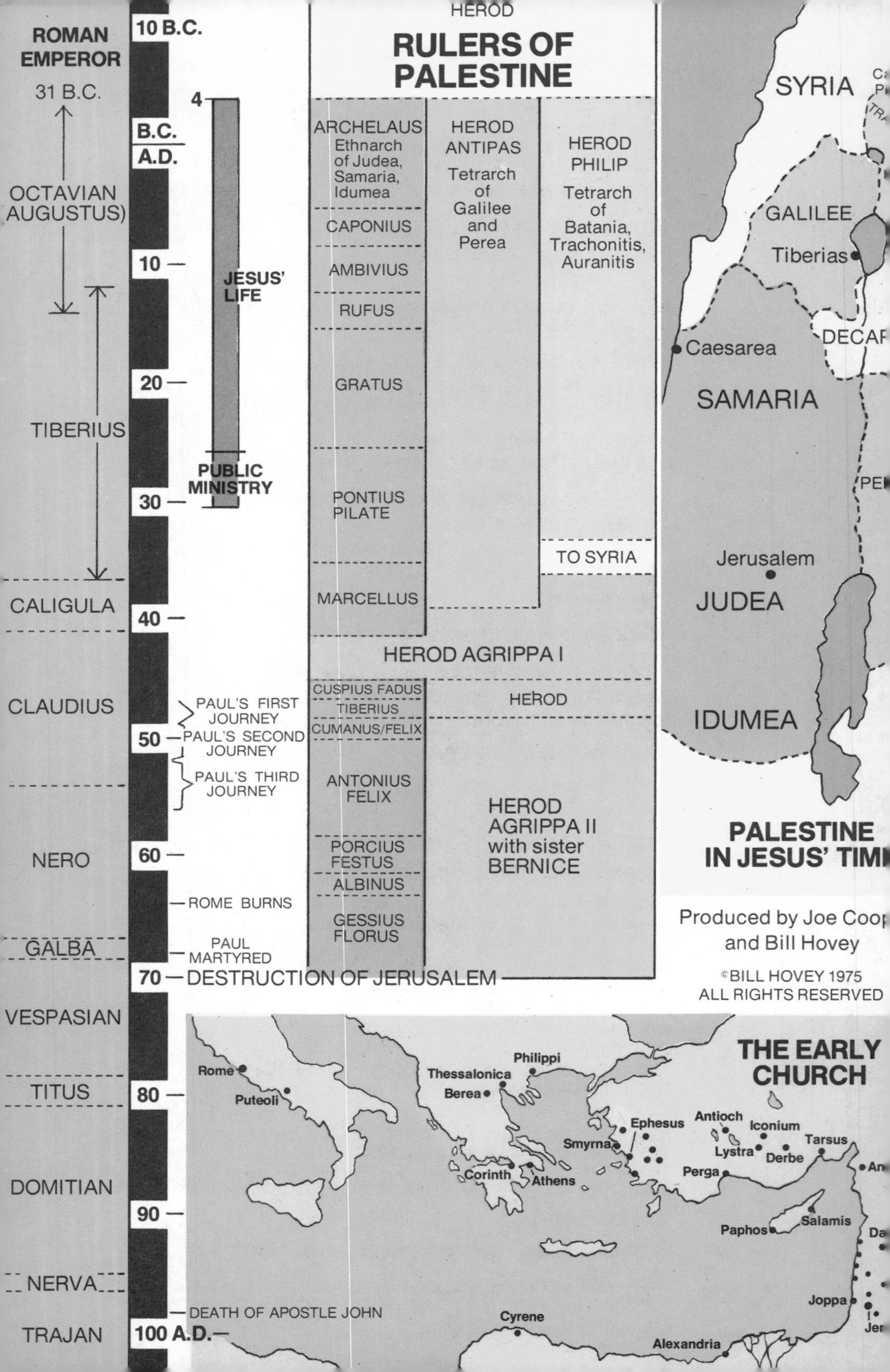

ROMAN EMPEROR
10 B.C.
HEROD
RULERS OF PALESTINE
31 B.C.
4 B.C.
A.D.
OCTAVIAN AUGUSTUS)
ARCHELAUS Ethnarch of Judea, Samaria, Idumea
HEROD ANTIPAS Tetrarch of Galilee and Perea
HEROD PHILIP Tetrarch of Batania, Trachonitis, Auranitis
CAPONIUS
10
AMBIVIUS
JESUS' LIFE
RUFUS
20
GRATUS
TIBERIUS
PUBLIC MINISTRY
30
PONTIUS PILATE
TO SYRIA
CALIGULA
MARCELLUS
40
HEROD AGRIPPA I
CUSPIUS FADUS
TIBERIUS
CUMANUS/FELIX
HEROD
CLAUDIUS
PAUL'S FIRST JOURNEY
50
PAUL'S SECOND JOURNEY
PAUL'S THIRD JOURNEY
ANTONIUS FELIX
HEROD AGRIPPA II with sister BERNICE
NERO
60
PORCIUS FESTUS
ALBINUS
ROME BURNS
GESSIUS FLORUS
GALBA
PAUL MARTYRED
70
DESTRUCTION OF JERUSALEM
VESPASIAN
TITUS
80
DOMITIAN
90
NERVA
DEATH OF APOSTLE JOHN
TRAJAN
100 A.D.
SYRIA
GALILEE
Tiberias
Caesarea
DECAP
SAMARIA
PE
Jerusalem
JUDEA
IDUMEA
PALESTINE IN JESUS' TIM
Produced by Joe Coop
and Bill Hovey
©BILL HOVEY 1975
ALL RIGHTS RESERVED
THE EARLY CHURCH
Rome
Puteoli
Philippi
Thessalonica
Berea
Ephesus
Antioch
Iconium
Smyrna
Lystra
Derbe
Tarsus
Perga
Corinth
Athens
Salamis
Paphos
Joppa
Cyrene
Alexandria